The

Best Baby Names

TREASURY

Your
Ultimate Naming Resource

Emily Larson
and the experts at mostbabynames.com

SOURCEBOOKS, INC.®
NAPERVILLE, ILLINOIS

Published by Sourcebooks, Inc.
P.O. Box 4410, Naperville, Illinois 60567–4410
(630) 961–3900
Fax: (630) 961–2168
www.sourcebooks.com

Library of Congress Cataloging-in-Publication Data

The deluxe baby name treasury / Sourcebooks.
    p. cm.
  1. Names, Personal.
  CS2377.D46 2008
  929.4'4—dc22

                                2008000867

                   Printed and bound in China.
                   OGP 10 9 8 7 6 5 4 3

✖ CONTENTS ✖

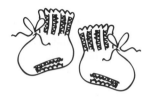

✖ *Introduction* ✖

Welcome to the *The Best Baby Names Treasury*.

For some lucky moms- and dads-to-be, finding the best name for Baby is easy. Maybe you had it all worked out by the time you were old enough to play house, or perhaps the perfect name came to you one night in a dream.

But if you're reading this, it means you still haven't decided on a moniker for your little miracle in the making. Well, you're in good company—plenty of parents struggle with the daunting task of choosing the right name, with the pressure only mounting as your due date approaches. How will you ever decide on a name that simultaneously suits your kid's as-yet unknown personality, charms everyone who hears it, plays up your personal preferences, and somehow fits into your family just right?

Satisfying all the elements that make up a marvelous name will be challenging, to say the least, but if you're ready to rise to the occasion, it's also a wonderful opportunity to let your creativity shine. For the moment, the name you choose will show off who you are and what's important to you. Will you try to have your child stand out from the pack with an unusual name, or would you prefer to honor a family tradition and stick to a tried-and-true classic? Do biblical names appeal to you, or are you drawn to flower names, virtue names, or even brand names? Are you the type to dream up a strange spelling, blend two names together, or use a name from a foreign language? That bun in your oven may have a few months to go, yet you're the ones who feel like you're living in a pressure cooker!

Fear not, baby-namers—we're here to put your minds at rest and help you handle the entire naming process with grace, ease, and style to spare. In the pages of this book you'll find everything you need to tackle the exciting task ahead of you. What makes *The Best Baby Names Treasury* so special is that we not only include the best baby names out there to inspire and delight you, but we've also clearly outlined everything you need to know, every step you need to take, and every mistake you need to avoid, in order to help you choose. We've also provided the perfect tools to make it even easier to organize and plan the entire process.

Beginning on page 70 is our collection of baby-name lists—30 pages total. The beauty of these lists is that names sharing something in common can often spark your imagination and provide that distinct touch you may be searching for. Of course, we've also listed every name in the proverbial book...more than one hundred thousand of them! Alternate spellings and variations are offered in case you want to spice things up, and the meanings will provide the knowledge you need to make the right choice. But before you get to all that, we'll break it all down for you in the opening chapters—from classic naming considerations such as sounding and spelling, to modern-day dilemmas such as popularity and trendiness. We'll also point out creative, even unexpected, sources for ideas, and new ways to put a spin on today's most popular names. We believe that once you understand exactly what it is that goes into every great name and learn how to personalize the naming process for your child, you're halfway there.

You'll also discover plenty of itemized steps to help you decide—everything from how to name like a pro (yes, there are professionals out there!), to what to do if you're expecting twins, triplets, or even more (there are lots of special considerations for expectant parents who will be naming in bulk!). And for those of you who've been to this dance before, we attack the questions surrounding naming siblings. We've also included something you may never have seen before—more than fifty quotes from real parents from across North America, discussing the hows and whys and what they'd do over if they could. This valuable advice from parents who've been there may speak to your own concerns, and open your eyes to post-naming problems you may not have considered.

The whole idea behind *The Best Baby Names Treasury* is to give you, the moms- and dads-to-be, the complete package, to assist you in your quest to find the perfect appellation during your gestation—a challenging enough time as it is without the added stress of baby-naming anxiety. To support your endless list-making and baby-name obsessions, at the back of the book you'll find plenty of labeled, removable stickers for marking favorites (there's a set for both mom and dad, so you'll be able to pass the book off to one another without confusion, plus some blank stickers for anyone from Big Sis to Great Grandma). Tear-out worksheets will make it even easier to keep track of your choices, and you can save them for posterity in Baby's book. And it's all tied up with a neat satin ribbon you can use as a bookmark—pretty and practical!

If you like what you see here, head over to our companion website at mostbabynames.com for more ideas on baby-naming.

But if ever the pressure gets to be too much, take a few days off and clear your head. (Turn to page 65 for a host of baby-naming games to lift your stress.) When you go back to the drawing board, do so with a lighter heart: Naming your baby isn't a chore, but rather a process best enjoyed with a healthy sense of humor. Giving your little one a name you adore, one that means something special, isn't only a gift, it's a blessing—the very first one you'll bestow upon your child. It's a big responsibility—no doubt about that!—but like parenthood itself, the small but sacred act of choosing a name for Baby is one paid back in dividends of joy, satisfaction, and love.

Chapter 1

❌ What's in a Name? ❌ More Than You May Realize!

Your baby's name is the first birthday present she'll be receiving, one that has the power to shape how she will be perceived and who she will become. That adorable little bun in your oven is counting on you to come up with a beautiful, strong name for her to grow up with and grow into—a perfect choice; the perfect name.

And it's all up to you!

Some parents take this responsibility more seriously than others. Indeed, the last few years have shown a dramatic rise in a sort of naming neurosis. Take, for example, the Chinese mom and dad who infamously tried to name their child "@" (yes, "at"—the ubiquitous symbol used in e-mail addresses). They claimed that, roughly translated, the sounds that make up "at" also mean "love him" in Chinese, but officials refused to allow it. Also in China, whose exploding population presumably makes it harder to stand out, another set of parents named their baby "Saddam SARS" in 2003, in honor of some of the more unpleasant global events that took place that year. A hemisphere away, a New Zealand couple recently tried to name their son "4real." After being shut down by the government, they settled on the far blander "Superman" instead, though they insist their little man of steel will go by "4real" anyway.

While these may be ludicrous examples, the sincerity and spirit of these parents is actually quite understandable, even laudable: In this world of billions, a name—the ultimate signature of personhood—may be the best way to make your child stand out from the get-go. We whole-heartedly agree that choosing Baby's handle should be a license to have fun (keeping certain respectful limits in mind, of course), whether you're trying for that one-in-a-million moniker or simply opting for a well-loved classic.

But remember: It is not Baby's name that will make her unique. Rather, it's who she will grow to become that sets her apart from the masses, no matter if you call her Jane or January, Mary or Marquise, Emily or Ember.

Now that it's your turn to choose, what will you do? How will you use this once-in-a-lifetime opportunity? There are so many things to consider that it might feel like it's almost impossible to begin. To help you along as you get ready to make your list, we've dissected some of the essential components, qualities, and characteristics that go into each and every name. So, without further ado, here are six things to think about for every twenty-first-century mom- and dad-to-be.

1. Impressions and Associations

You never get a second chance to make a first impression ... and the very first part of a first impression often comes in the form of a name. To understand what we mean, try the following exercise: Play a round of free-association with your significant other as a way to evaluate contenders on your list. Just shoot some names out at each other and see what happens—you may be surprised at the images and associations they bring to mind. It's not just the literal connections you may make with certain names—such as Saddam, Madonna, and Elvis—but more subtle assumptions that have simply entered the public consciousness in North America. For example, Bertha is a big woman; Dexter is a nerd; and Farrah is a babe with feathered hair.

This has to do with stereotypes, both good and bad. But the impressions we get from names also vary over time and space. The name Andrew, for example, dipped in popularity after the 1992 hurricane of the same name. This was especially true in Florida and Louisiana, where the storm hit hard, while in the Northwest, so very far away from all the devastation, the name actually retained its top-10 position. Predictably, Katrina dropped 136 places in a single year. Monica has suffered a similar fate since news of a certain scandal broke in 1998. The year after Princess Diana died, the name enjoyed a brief surge in popularity, as it did the year after she married Prince Charles in 1981.

It isn't always so cut and dried. There are plenty of names out there loaded with dubious associations—courtesy of popular culture, history, and current events—and yet some people choose them anyway. That's because, whether you realize it or not, your perception of a name is informed by many other factors, too: your personality, preferences, location, religion, economic status, and so on. If you teach a Modern Feminist Thought course at Berkeley, for example, you may not want to name your daughter Barbie, though a former pageant winner from Minnesota may actually have nothing but warm and fuzzy feelings for the name. But should you really worry about such things? Our feeling is that if a name works for you in your world, go for it!

2. Identity

Your name and your identity are inextricably linked. That's why so many parents feel anxious about the whole naming process—coming up with a name to suit somebody you haven't even met yet is a pretty tall order. But you needn't worry: As Baby grows up, he'll grow into his name, too. It will simply become a part of who he is, though in many ways—and this is the case with everyone—his name will say as much, if not more, about the people who named him!

A name often tells the story of its bearer. Think about it: What does your name say about you? When you're being introduced to someone else, what do you think it says about them? Whether you like it or not, a name can hold many hints and clues about its owner, including age, gender, social status, nationality, and religion, among others. As such, there are several ways that a name can reflect your child's unique identity. First, there's the family he's being born into. Endowing him with a name that has familial significance—whether it's the first name of a beloved great-grandparent who passed on, or your own maiden name—is an excellent way to tie together who your child is and where he came from with what he will be called. Religious, cultural, and geographic attributes of a family are also carried in a name, as are the expectations his parents may have of him. For example, calling your son Henry will perhaps make him feel a bit differently about himself than if you'd called him River. Consider these questions as you're making your list in order to infuse your choices with qualities that jive with your vision of him and his identity as a whole.

CAN YOU USE A NAME TO GIVE YOUR KID THE BEST POSSIBLE START?

In today's competitive world, where creativity and uniqueness are so highly valued, it can seem as if the Marys, Johns, Janes, and Marks of yesterday simply won't cut it. With nearly four million babies born in the United States every year, is it possible—or even advisable—for a name to give your little one an edge?

Many parents in the process of choosing have begun to look beyond the basics and are wondering if maybe a given name holds more power than we realize. Much has been made lately of not only which baby names are the most popular, what they mean, and where they come from, but also what impact the names may have on a child's life. Can a name actually set somebody on a particular path?

A popular book published in 2005 had everyone from sociologists to soccer moms talking about the impact a baby's name can have. In *Freakonomics: A Rogue Economist Explores the Hidden Side of Everything*, authors Steven Levitt and Stephen J. Dubner examined whether or not babies' names appeared to influence where they ended up and what they achieved. They compared naming data on kids living in higher-income communities born to well-educated parents with those living in poor neighborhoods among adverse social and educational opportunities. To do this, they examined how kids with racially distinct names fared in relation to their counterparts with more traditional names. They also looked at how baby-naming trends seem to trickle their way down the socioeconomic ladder, with the upper echelons abandoning their favorite monikers as soon as the lower levels adopt them.

For a while now, some nameologists have suggested that the reason that parents with low socioeconomic status or who live in depressed areas give their children offbeat, unusually spelled names is that the names reflect a desire for change. In breaking from the naming status quo, parents are trying to break from the past, endowing their offspring with the hope of a new tomorrow by giving them new sorts of names. In upper-class families, stability is valued above all else, so babies are consistently given more traditional monikers, often using family names and conservative names. (If it ain't broke, don't fix it!)

So, does this attempt to set babies on a particular path, either by naming them uniquely or by using the same names as the wealthy and elite, actually work?

Alas, it appears to be a classic case of wishful thinking—names are an indicator, not an influencer, of a person's life outcome, as is also suggested by the work of various sociologists and psychologists. Whether Baby is named Bill or Dakota, where Baby grows up, who his parents are, and how much education he receives will determine who he becomes, not the collection of letters on his birth certificate.

But don't give up and pick a name from these pages at random! Even though a name may be less influential than ornamental, choosing a pleasant name with positive associations might indeed lead others to have a favorable impression of your child. Odds are, if this is something you're wondering about, you don't have any reason to worry—for exactly that reason! You're already putting some serious thought into naming, which will carry you a long way toward giving Baby a leg up in life. To ensure that the name you choose will lend itself to success, make sure to carefully consider a name's impressions, associations, and meaning (discussed in this chapter) as you work your way toward the right moniker.

This Just In: A report published in *Psychological Science* indicates that a preference for our own names and initials—the so-called "name-letter" effect—can result in bad news for those whose initials match negative indicators. Psychologists in the marketing field discovered that students whose names began with A or B received higher grade point averages than those whose names began with C or D. In addition, major-league baseball players whose first or last names began with K (the symbol for strikeout) were actually more likely to strike out! This finding ties in with earlier studies showing that people make choices according to names that resemble their own—selecting careers and mates to match their names. Anna Anderson becomes an actuary, marries Abe Andrews, and settles in Albuquerque, for example. So what's a momma-to-be to do? Take it all with a grain of salt, and just consider it food for thought.

3. Meaning

A name is more than just the sum of its letters—virtually every moniker is imbued with a particular meaning. Whether it's an attribute, personality trait, season, person, quality, place, or even product, the names you're thinking about have an inherent connection to other concepts. Discovering the meaning behind the names on your list is all part of the fun of naming Baby. Our book spells out the meanings of more than one hundred thousand names (the alphabetical list begins on page 151). Since names can mean different things in different places and to different people, it's worth putting some time in to learn as much as you possibly can about the name you've chosen, both as a way to prevent negative associations and also as a source of inspiration.

Many parents-to-be cite meaning above all other attributes of a name as their primary inspiration for choosing it. In fact, deciding on a meaning first and then deciding on a name from the pool of contenders is a nice way to choose a firstborn's name, and possibly even other siblings' names down the road. There are two ways to approach this. You can start with an idea you love in a general way—say, for example, peace—and find out which names fit that concept, as Erin, Frieda, and Winifred do. Alternately, you can build from a more personal meaning that reflects your family specifically. If you're both army officers, for example, try Matilda, Louise, or Tyra, all of which mean "great in battle."

Of course, meanings needn't always be hidden or obscure. Virtue names are an excellent example of this idea—names like Faith, Grace, Hope, and Honor certainly do put meaning front and center. Place names, too—such as Brooklyn, Kenya, and India—might recall a favorite vacation spot, or even a point of conception! Wherever you find inspiration, try to choose a name for Baby that means something special to you and reflects positive attributes in general.

4. Popularity

There are people who like popular names, and there are people who don't. While one set of parents-to-be might choose the name Sophia because it ranked a solid sixth place on the list of names given out to baby girls, there are others who'd stay away from Sophia for precisely that reason. Choosing a popular name can mean lots of great things for your child: people will never be confused by her name, it will be easy to remember and spell (provided you don't get too creative on that front), and chances are it will never be a source of embarrassment. The downside? Expect your child to be known by Madison S. to distinguish her from the five others in her class, and possibly be fairly indifferent toward her name rather than loving it.

In general, popular baby names tend to be tried-and-true classics, though this is especially true for boys. Here's the most recent top-10 list compiled by the Social Security Administration 2008:

BOYS	GIRLS
1. Jacob	Emma
2. Michael	Isabella
3. Ethan	Emily
4. Joshua	Madison
5. Daniel	Ava
6. Alexander	Olivia
7. Anthony	Sophia
8. William	Abigail
9. Christopher	Elizabeth
10. Matthew	Chloe

50 years ago, this is what it looked like...

BOYS	GIRLS
1. Michael	Mary
2. David	Susan
3. James	Linda
4. Robert	Karen
5. John	Patricia
6. William	Debra
7. Mark	Deborah
8. Richard	Cynthia
9. Thomas	Barbara
10. Steven	Donna

And here's the list for a century ago, in 1908:

BOYS	GIRLS
1. John	Mary
2. William	Helen
3. James	Margaret
4. George	Ruth
5. Robert	Anna
6. Joseph	Dorothy
7. Charles	Elizabeth
8. Frank	Mildred
9. Edward	Alice
10. Thomas	Marie

As you may have noticed, the favorite boy names over the past century wouldn't sound out of place in a schoolyard today, while most of the girl names from decades past seem quite dated now. Perhaps this is because many of the favorite boy names are drawn from biblical sources. Girl names, on the other hand, often reflect current trends. As we all know, a name's popularity can rise and fall with the times, reflecting social preferences, values, and even pop culture. For example, while Mary was ranked number 1 for girls throughout the first half of the twentieth century, it has fallen by the wayside to some degree, perhaps because modern parents feel its religious association is a bit old-fashioned.

At the other end of the spectrum are names that skyrocket to popularity for one reason or another. Jacqueline, for example, reached its zenith in 1964, the year after John F. Kennedy was assassinated. More recently, the name Emma has made its mark, a rise that can be correlated to the fact that the character Rachel on the TV show *Friends* chose it for her daughter in 2002. In 2001, Emma was ranked at number 13 for girls, but by the end of 2003, it had climbed to number 2. In 2008, it reached number 1.

The Social Security Administration (SSA) keeps a tally of the most popular baby names each year, and lists the top 1000 on its website at www.ssa.gov/OACT/babynames. The rankings are interesting, but remember that some names may be more (or less) popular than they appear due to the fact that the SSA treats different spellings of the same name separately. If it didn't, Aiden (and its nine different spellings) would be number 1 for boys instead of Jacob.

THE TOP 10 BOTTOMS OUT!

In the twenty-first century, baby-naming has taken on virtually epic significance, although the desire for an original name is in fact a relatively recent trend. Several short decades ago, parents seemed content to name their kids Jennifer or Lisa, John or Bill. Ironically, the meteoric rise of many "unusual" and "unique" names has become so dramatic that these once-unheard-of monikers have in many cases usurped the staid and classic names previously perceived as too common! Names like Jasmine (ranked 43rd), Sydney (49th), and Destiny (48th) outrank Jane (310th) on the list of most popular names by hundreds of places! So if you're looking for something really unusual, try Jennifer (number 84), Lisa (number 605), or Linda, which dropped from number 1 to number 496 in just over fifty years.

The best evidence of this trend is in the market share accorded to popular monikers. So just how many kids are named from the list of the top-10 names? Not a whole lot, actually—and certainly not as many as used to be, which is what some interesting research recently conducted by the *Wall Street Journal* revealed. About 125 years ago, 43 percent of boys and 23 percent of girls born in the United States were named off the top-10 list, and that's how it went until the 1990s. But today, less than 10 percent of boys and girls are dubbed with these top-10 favorites. Sure, the names on these most-popular lists have changed dramatically, risen and fallen over time, but it has only been recently that parents have rejected the idea of using them altogether.

This is likely the result of two closely interrelated trends: unusual spellings and the quest for unique names. Remember that if there were only one way to spell Aiden, it would be number 1 on the list! Similarly, the deepening field of new and previously unknown names to choose from—inspired perhaps by our ever-increasing desire to stand out from the crowd in this world of billions—has allowed parents-to-be to spread the joy around, stealing from the pool of top-10 choices.

5. Branding

Only a few years ago, it would have seemed ridiculous to consider branding when choosing a name for your child. But in the twenty-first century, the act of naming children has begun to undergo the same sort of scrutiny that naming products does, with nameologists and naming consultants popping up to help with the process (more on them in Chapter 2). It's as if you're developing your child's own brand, following in the footsteps of folks like Martha Stewart, Estee Lauder, Miley Cyrus, and the Olsen Twins. On this end of the spectrum, personal branding can become complete identification with a product or service, while on the other end it can simply lead to an exceptionally thoughtful, well-researched name.

This may seem a little extreme to you, but it's no joke: Many parents-to-be ensure that the web domain is available for the name they've chosen. It's all part of modern mothers' and fathers' desire to have their kids stand out from the pack, to somehow ensure that they have the opportunity to excel in the public eye. Daunted? Don't be—consider it a call to creative arms! After all, avery.com and liam.com are already taken. If you're on the fence between Sarah Jane, Sarah Ann, and Sarah Lianne, for example, you can let your budget guide you: sarahjane.com is for sale for a cool $35,000, sarahann.com will set you back $2,500, and sarahlianne.com is available for only a few bucks a month. Whether you value branding as a notion or not, giving Baby a name she might one day be able to bank on certainly couldn't hurt.

6. Trends

Names, like fashion, go in and out of vogue. Each time period seems to have a certain naming style that defines it. Currently, the Courtneys, Chelseas, and Brittanys of the 1990s have been replaced with Emilys, Isabellas, and Madisons. So what exactly are the hottest trends in twenty-first-century baby-naming? We've identified seven current crazes that seem to be staying put for the foreseeable future.

🐦 **Old-Fashioned Favorites:** Sometimes, what's old is new again—a great way to describe one of today's hottest naming styles. Virtue names like Temperance and Prudence were very popular among America's Puritan settlers, and many parents continue to be drawn to this notion. The modern resurrection of this trend can be seen in the current popularity of names like Faith, Grace, Serenity, Miracle, and Destiny. Another example of the return to yesterday is names that, only a few decades ago, would have been eschewed by expectant couples as "grandparent" names—Mabel, Hazel, and Sadie for girls, and Henry, Nathan, and Abraham for boys.

🛒 **Last Names First:** There's something regal and important about last names that double as first names. Among the favorites: Mackenzie, Kennedy, Taylor, Jackson, Addison, Harper, Mason, Blake, Cooper, Carter, and Emerson. Interestingly, many of these names also appear to cross gender boundaries better than any others.

🛒 **Biblical Babies:** This trend has been going strong for a while now, especially among boys. Jacob, Joshua, Matthew, Daniel, David, Noah, and John are practically staples on the top 20. For girls, Abigail, Hannah, Sarah, Rachel, Leah, and Rebecca are never far from the top. As parents-to-be scour the Old and New Testaments for ideas, others, such as Jonah, Caleb, Naomi, and Miriam, are on the rise.

🛒 **United Kingdom Craze:** Names that seem, well, decidedly British have been climbing the charts. Choose from among the Scottish (Logan, McKinley, Blair), Celtic (Connor, Keegan, Evan), Welsh (Dylan, Evan, Meredith), Gaelic (Liam, Brendan, Ainsley), and Irish (Aidan, Brady, Fiona). English monikers are always in demand, from both the traditional names used by aristocracy (Victoria, Nigel, Charles, Gavin) to contemporary favorites (Portia, Pippa, Reece, Ian).

🛒 **Big-Screen Babies:** Modern moms- and dads-to-be have an affinity for movie monikers. Inspiration can come from the classics, such as *Gone with the Wind* (Scarlett is rising fast) or *Superman* (Nicolas Cage famously named his son Kal-El, Superman's real name). Contemporary favorites such as *The Matrix* inspired the surge in popularity of the name Trinity, which leapt from number 900 in 1993 to number 56 in 2003. *Lord of the Rings* lovers have spawned many an Arwen, and even the once-unusual name of the movie's main star—Elijah Wood—is clearly on the rise. Indeed, many actors themselves can take credit for jumps in a name's popularity, as with the names Ashton, Keira, and Reese. This even trickles down to celebrities' kids; names like Ava (Reese Witherspoon), Violet (Jennifer Garner), Shiloh (Angelina Jolie), and Kingston (Gwen Stefani) are all climbing the charts, perhaps thanks to their famous parents.

🛒 **Aiden and His Cousins:** Names that rhyme with Aiden are hot, especially for boys: Jayden, Caden, Braden, and Hayden. The Social Security Administration reports this as less of a trend for girls, with Jayden and Kayden as top choices.

🛒 **Special Spellings:** We could fill another book with all the creative ways parents have come up with to spell their babies' names. Think we're kidding? The Social Security Administration lists more than a dozen spellings of the name Caitlyn in the top 1000 names for girls. Love it or hate it, the creative-spelling trend is likely here to stay.

Chapter 2

✖ How to Choose: ✖ Finding the Right Name for Baby

Some parents-to-be have trouble finding even one name they like enough to use. Others, however, find the biggest challenge in narrowing down a long list of seemingly endless possibilities. Knowing exactly what to focus on is half the battle. If you keep your eyes on the prize, you'll see your list of favorites take shape.

But how can you even begin?

Start right here, with some of the most important facts and features you need to know right now. Consider us your baby-naming problem solver.

ADVICE FOR THE OVERWHELMED: THE SIX CARDINAL RULES OF BABY-NAMING

These are the most important points to consider, both in terms of the monikers themselves and the process of choosing them. It's what you need to know in order to let the best of the best shine through!

1. Say It Out Loud: A name might look great on paper, but the second it's said aloud it could very well lose its appeal. On the other hand, some names may seem like poor choices until they're actually spoken. Utter all the names you've chosen—first, middle(s), and last—in every possible combination in order to assess readability, pronunciation, and likeability.

2. Make It Personal: This is about more than just being creative. Often, the difference between a good name and a great name is that personal touch. Finding a name that means something special within your family context and/or to the two of you as a couple is key. Pick one from your family tree; salute your spiritual, cultural, or religious heritage; remember a beloved vacation spot—all are great angles for sourcing that perfect moniker.

3. Keep It Quiet: Unless you're ready to hear criticism and witness unpleasant reactions to your choices, keep your decision private until you introduce Baby to the world. At that point, people will be far less likely to run off at the mouth. Elderly family members in particular seem to have trouble being kind when hearing unusual names, and might also react poorly if you've decided to go against religious customs or carrying on a family naming tradition. The easiest way not to have these arguments or be forced into defending your favorites is to simply not open the door to discussing them at all.

4. Love It or Leave It: There are probably plenty of names you don't mind, but how many are there you absolutely adore? You must hold yourself to this highest possible standard and find one that satisfies all your needs, or else you may one day be prone to namer's remorse. The good news (if you're having a singleton) is that you need only settle on one. The bad news is that both you and your significant other need to agree on your child's name 100 percent, which makes it infinitely harder.

5. Be Kind to Your Kid: Beware of too-cute names, silly spellings, gender insensitivities, and even cruel associations. No matter what, you must always consider the fetal position first: Are you choosing a name Baby will grow to love, or could it conceivably be one she comes to hate? Keep this thought front and center at all times.

6. Do Your Research: Due diligence is not an option: You must research any and all names you decide upon, even if you could never imagine there being a problem. Get online and Google each name's back-story. Even the most seemingly benign associations can sour a name years down the road, when it's too late to change your mind. We know of one first-time mom who named her daughter Dora. It's a lovely name, to be sure, but veteran parents chuckled when they heard it, since virtually every preschooler under the sun knows *Dora the Explorer* is the most popular kids' show after *Sesame Street*. Worse, still, than naming Baby after a cartoon character would be unknowingly calling her Cindy if your last name is Margolis, or Jenna if your last name is Jameson—two of today's hottest "adult" entertainment stars!

SOUNDING IT OUT

The way a moniker sounds is probably the very first thing to either attract parents to a name or put them off of one. A quick glance at the aural similarities shared by today's most popular names suggests that certain sounds do boast a widespread appeal. Let's consider the top 50 names for babies. There are twenty-six letters in the alphabet, yet nearly 20 percent of all boys' names on the list begin with the letter "J"; for the girls, the letter "A" comes out ahead. That's not all—a full 50 percent of girls' names end with the "a" or "ah" sound, while a third of boys' names are two-syllable monikers that end with "n." There are plenty of other patterns, too, that suggest a global predilection for particular sounds.

Why? Lots of reasons explain these patterns—some sounds are easy to pronounce, whereas others are simply soft on the ear; many are familiar biblical intonations; and several have a natural rhythm and cadence that fit well within given names. Also, names with softer sounds can provide a way to balance out last names, which as a whole tend to be less melodic and more dissonant—sort of the unchosen naming wildcards of sound and style. Basically, you have to work with what you've got, and the way Baby's first name will sound in relation to your last name is a critical consideration.

The combination of first and last names must work well as a team; you can't trust a middle name to break up an unfavorable combo since most middles really aren't used on a daily basis. Firsts and lasts should flow nicely together, have rhythm, and their pronunciation should not be impeded by jarring sounds, ill-fitting letters, or abrupt syllabic blends. In general, lengthy and/or unusual surnames with complicated spellings and pronunciations warrant a simpler first name (e.g., Ike Wolfenstein), whereas short last names will hold up well under a longer, more elaborate introduction (e.g., Ichabod Wolf). Keeping an even keel within Baby's name as a whole is important. Say the names you've chosen aloud often, and trust your instincts. Does it sound "right" or does it sound "off"? Balancing syllables and sounds is all part of the fun, as long as you do it right.

Keep in mind that some sounds are easier to pronounce when adjacent to each other. Ending one name with a consonant and starting the next with a vowel (or vice versa) is usually a safe bet (e.g., Adam Alberts, Albert Adams; Davis Emory, Emory Davis). The opposite is true when the same vowel or consonant sounds are back to back (e.g., Mario Overton, Delia Adderley, Luke Kane, Cecily Easter). The same consonant sounds in a name adjacent to each other can create confusion when said aloud (e.g., Dylan Nate Taylor). Be conscious of the fact that some sound combos might make it difficult to determine where one name ends and the next begins (e.g., Joelle Lynn Dover, Eric Arsinoe, Steven Elson).

Of course, all possible combinations—first and middle name together, middle and last, first and last, and all three—must be considered for sound success. Sometimes, all that's required is a simple tweak here or there to achieve a name the ear loves. For example, Julie Levy would be improved by a change to Julia; Preston Bryce Cohen could be switched to Presley Bryce Cohen if you want to avoid somewhat rhyming first and last names. Again, saying it all out loud is crucial in deciding what works, so use each other as sounding boards and listen to your instincts when it comes to sounds.

SPELLING SPECIFICS

Spelling, like beauty, is in the eye of the beholder. Some people can't get enough of random "y"s and "h"s inserted into names, whereas purists object to even the slightest variation from the norm. As with most things, the sweet spot lies somewhere in between. If you use an unusual spelling for Baby's name, you may want to limit it to one (or at the very most two) changes maximum. Any more than that and you risk subjecting your family to certain unflattering stereotypes (extremely eccentric spellers are sometimes not considered to be well bred or well educated), plus your little one will surely bear the brunt of the confusion. (We've included a lot more on the lunacy of silly spelling in Chapter 3: Baby Namers Beware: The Top 10 Things NOT to Do, page 29).

We don't mean to suggest that putting your own creative touch on a name isn't a good idea; in fact, spelling is surely the easiest way to achieve this! Just try not to go too crazy. If you're not sure, ask yourself this: Would you be able to spell it or say it if you hadn't been the one who made it up? If the spelling belies the pronunciation you intended—Chelbea, Mah'k'henna, Burraydon—start over from scratch. Still not sure? Reduce it even further: Would a fifth grader be able to read it properly? Don't be stubborn on this point, no matter how much you may love the spelling you've concocted. Think of it from your unborn child's perspective—nobody wants to spend a lifetime introducing herself as "Qatherine with a Q" or "Anha, like Anna, not Anne-Ha."

Here are some ways to introduce more limited creative spelling into Baby's name:

🍼 Switch "i"s or "e"s for "y"s: Lysa, Angelyna, Aidyn, Alyx, Gavyn, Mychael, Elyzabeth.

🍼 Throw in a double consonant: Sammuel, Evvan, Lanndon, Marria, Addam.

🍼 Add a silent "h"or "e"on the end: Emmah, Faithe, Briannah, Lisah, Abigaile, Kendalle.

🍼 Choose "z" over "s": Jozephine, Jozeph, Izadore, Jezus, Izaac, Roze, Louiza.

🍼 Replace "x" with "ks": Aleks, Brackston, Aleksis, Mackswell, Lecksie.

NICKNAMING AND INITIALS

Nicknames can add an additional layer of fun to Baby's name. Not every parent-to-be chooses their child's name with a nickname in mind also, and yet most babies seem to find their parents calling them something completely different anyway! Little Abigail ended up as Abner for a few months; cutie-pie Yoanna somehow became Yo-yo; and Ariel Jacobson grew into A.J. for good. Big brothers and sisters often have adorable ways of changing the new addition's name, too, and the family will often follow suit. Before you know it, the girl you named Makayla is called Layla because her "big" sister pronounced it "My Layla" instead; Baby Dawn morphed into B.D.; and nobody knows Naomi by any name but Nome anymore. Most of these nicknames and terms of endearment fall by the wayside as your kid grows up, but from time to time, they stick. A person's name is like a living organism, and it changes, grows, and develops over time and place.

Some parents will deliberately choose to use a nickname as Baby's official legal name, putting Bob or Annie on the birth certificate instead of Robert or Anne. More common, though, are parents who intentionally adopt nicknames based on their child's full legal name. There are lots of reasons to name your daughter Margaret, for example, and yet choose to always call her Maggie. It's cuter-sounding and works better for a baby or young child, but it also allows little Maggie the option to go by her full name if she ever feels she's grown out of her nickname. This is especially true of boys' names. Billy, Jimmy, and Timmy may one day be glad to have William, James, and Timothy to fall back on when they're ready to be taken more seriously.

One common form of nicknaming is to go by a combination of one's initials instead. This method is often employed by parents whose sons have the same first and middle names as Dad does. Some letters seem to lend themselves particularly well to the practice—j, t, r, and m—though really the only requirement is that the letters sound good when standing on their own. Consider this if you're interested in keeping the possible use of initials open for Baby in the future. For example, J.R., L.C., B.D., and A.J. work much better than Z.X., Q.K., M.N., and R.R. It's also crucial, no matter what, to make sure the initials don't contain any accidental jokes or negative associations. So that means you can forget about P.U., F.K., B.S., and P.P.!

And then there are even those people whose initials become synonymous with their entire names, which seems to be especially common among presidents (F.D.R., J.F.K., and L.B.J.). Musicians, on the other hand, are prone to developing a combination of initials and nicknames, such as JLo (Jennifer Lopez) and rappers Eminem (Marshall Mathers), LL Cool J (Ladies Love Cool James) and P. Diddy (Sean Combs). Rarely, a sole letter can even take the place of a full name, like M from the James Bond movies, or even George "Dubya" Bush himself.

RELATIVE CHAOS:
DEALING WITH FRIENDS AND FAMILY

Names can elicit very passionate responses from everyone involved. Indeed, dealing with advice from others (especially family members) can stir up the many emotional aspects of this very personal process. Family fights, conflict with friends, criticisms left unsaid—it's all part of it. If possible, keep your names private. After all, too many cooks spoil the soup.

Sometimes, though, it can't be avoided. People find out, either through you or someone else. But even if you asked them for suggestions—not a bad idea, if you're having trouble finding names—remember that family and friends do not have the final say, though many seem to think they do. No matter what, as your unborn child's parents, you're allowed to stick to your guns. It's one of your absolutely sacred rights! Not only is a name the first gift you'll give your kid (apart from life itself, of course), but it's a joy and a privilege nobody should dare interfere with.

So what do you do when you don't get the response you'd hoped for? First of all, if not everyone loves the name you chose, try your hardest not to get too emotional. Simply explain that your mind is made up, that you love the name you picked out, and that nothing in the world is going to sway you. Even thank them kindly for their input, if you're the sort to worry about offending people, and tell them you hope they'll be respectful of your choice.

In some cases, compromise is in order, provided you can find a solution that works for both you as a couple and whoever happens to be stirring up a fuss. Situations in which you might feel bound to succumb to familial pressure could include religious or cultural reasons, if the name you've chosen for Baby could actually offend someone, or if not naming your child Fred means a five-generation tradition goes down the tubes.

But how to accommodate everyone? Creativity is the key to a successful compromise! Some parents-to-be who face enormous pressure—as is often the case when an expectation is there to name after a loved one—decide to use one name on the birth certificate and the other, the one they like better, as a sort of "unofficial" first name. An added benefit to this sort of plan is if you can somehow intertwine the two names. For example, instead of naming Baby Esther after her great-grandmother, choose Star—it sounds similar, means the same thing, and you'll still be able to tell everyone whom she was named for. Alternately, a much-preferred middle name can be used for all intents and purposes as a first name, though your kid's legal first name could be whatever it needs to be. Finding a solution that works can be difficult, but it might be preferred to months of discord or even a lifetime of hurt feelings.

WHERE TO GET IDEAS

If you've been poring over the names in this book and still haven't found that perfect moniker—or if you'd like to add to the list you already have before you narrow it down to a final few—inspiration is everywhere. You just have to know where to look! Yes, the world around us is filled with great ideas, and here are some of our favorite sources:

Your Family Tree: Tradition is good, especially when you dust off an old chestnut and put a modern spin on it. You needn't only look to parents and grandparents; sit down and sketch out your family tree as far back as you can go. Somewhere, in among the branches of distant cousins and great-greats, you may find a diamond in the rough.

Blending Favorites: Maybe you narrowed it down to two choices and can't decide, or perhaps you simply want Baby's name to reflect both her parents: Taylor and Lia become Talia, Chris and Ellen become Chriselle, Wilbert and Olivia become Willa, Andrew and Alexis become Andris. It's a super way to be original and give a moniker more meaning.

Variations on a Theme: Some groups of names go naturally together, and choosing from within a particular theme is a great way to narrow down the options or pick names for multiples or siblings. Try American cities (Lexington, Brooklyn, Austin), presidential surnames (McKinley, Carver, Lincoln), literary heroines (Moll, Jane, Catherine), or even names derived from baby animals (Colt, Joey, Fawn).

Art Attack: Scour your favorite movies, books, and music for ideas. Jazz fans may want to choose Ella or Miles; art-lovers, Jackson or Vincent; architecture buffs, Frank or Rennie; design enthusiasts, Andy or Keith.

Ask Around: Friends, family, and co-workers might have suggestions for names you never thought of. Canvass people for their favorites, and ask if they ever heard an interesting name that stands out. You're certainly not bound to anything—nor do you need to let them in on anything when you do decide—so play the field and have fun!

Sports Legends: It's an undeniable fact: Many famous athletes had really cool names! Sports fans might hit a home run by looking to the heroes of yesterday and today, from the pros (Venus, Brett, Lance, Mia) to Olympians (Mary Lou, Shannon, Bode, Apolo), to those heroes who tugged at our heartstrings (Terry, Kerri, Rudy).

Global Village: It may seem an unlikely approach, but maps, globes, and even road atlases are an amazing source of onomatological wealth. Look to street names, towns, rivers, mountains, and far-off places to yield a rich variety of meanings and sounds. If it's a place you happen to know and love, all the better.

Get a Library Card: Go to the library and just look stuff up! Pore through anything that piques your curiosity or inspires your imagination—Civil War heroes, French royalty, Roman history, ancient Incas, British genealogies, Japanese emperors, Native American warriors, and so on. Who knows? Out of the ruins of time, the perfect name might present itself. Even spending a few hours looking around on Wikipedia or some other online encyclopedia might lead you to some unlikely finalists.

TEN WAYS TO PUT A UNIQUE SPIN ON A POPULAR NAME

It's a classic naming conundrum: You love a name, but fear it's way too popular. But don't throw the baby name out with the bathwater! The reason these names are favored by all is because they satisfy so many of our top requirements, and that's certainly no reason to hold it against them. Instead, figure out a way to redeem the one you like. Here's how to get a few extra miles out of a moniker that's been adopted en-masse:

1. Play with Anagrams: If you can't do it yourself (or wordplay gives you a headache), visit an online anagram generator. Just plug in your favorites and see what comes out. Try Ami instead of Mia, Galon instead of Logan, or Nabira instead of Briana.

2. Change the Spelling: Provided you employ restraint, this may be the best way to change things up. Switching or adding even a single letter can have a big impact: Rion for Ryan, Isayah for Isaiah, Morgann for Morgan.

3. Use a Nickname: Choose to use a nickname up front, even on the birth certificate. If you're thinking Daniel, try Dan; Topher instead of Christopher; Liv instead of Olivia; Jackie instead of Jacqueline; Suki instead of Susan.

4. Two Middle Names: Deciding on two middle names will make a child with a common first name feel special. It's also a sneaky way to keep from having to decide on only one!

5. Hyphenate It: It's cute for kids, and the second or first part could always be dropped later on if they like. This generally works best if the second name is one syllable. Examples include Emma-Jean, Andrew-Tom, Chloe-Grace, Joshua-Dean, and Christopher-Lee.

6. Go to the Source: This book lists tons of variants for all the popular names. Choose Ellspeth for Elizabeth, Shaunden for Sean, Jessop for Joseph, Avalyn for Ava.

7. Switch Sides: Put a feminine spin on one of the most popular boys' names if you have a daughter, and vice versa if you have a son. Use Emory instead of Emma, Abe instead of Abigail, Jacoba instead of Jacob, Petra instead of Peter.

8. Play It Backwards: Nevaeh instead of Heaven is the most popular example of this trend, but there are others, too, such as Caasi, Alle, Nadia, Axela, and Nave. (Emma, Hannah, and Ava don't count!)

9. Remove a Letter or Two: It's easy, unusual, and the results are often wonderful: Annah for Hannah, Davi for David, Lillia for Lillian.

10. Found in Translation: You may be happier with the same name in a different language: Choose Marie over Mary, Wilhelm over William, Natalia over Natalie.

Also—see our "Alternatives to the Top 10" lists on page 97, where we give you ten options for each of the top-10 names.

BE YOUR OWN NAME CONSULTANT

The hottest thing in the world of baby-naming? Name consultants! As strange as it may sound to some, lots of parents-to-be are putting this crucial decision in the hands of a professional. Many modern moms and dads perhaps feel that pregnancy, childbirth, and impending parenthood is tough enough without having to go out on a creative limb, too. Though the consultants' suggestions obviously aren't binding, their well-researched advice is welcomed by harried moms and dads who need help honing their lists.

But maybe hiring a stranger to name the fruit of your loins feels too foolish. Or perhaps you're feeling more frugal and don't want to spend $50 on up to a few thousand for the personal touch of a pro. We want to help—we've broken down exactly what it is that these namers do so you can do it yourself:

1. *Document It*: Remember planning your wedding? Well, you're about to apply the same rigorous methodology to naming Baby. We've included tear-out worksheets in the back of the book for just this purpose. Use them to keep a record of everything, from gathering research and statistics to jotting down meanings and organizing lists of favorites.

2. *Discuss It*: The first thing a professional namer will do after she takes you on as a client is an exhaustive interview with both parents-to-be. Instead, do it on your own. Schedule a sit-down with your partner and lay it all out on the table. Ask each other the following questions: What sorts of names do you like? Are you hoping to name after a relative? Are there any spiritual or religious restrictions or traditions you'd like

to honor? Does your naming style swing toward the trendy or the traditional? Do you have any names in mind already? Do you like your own name? Why or why not? Discussing these things out loud will help crystallize your needs, likes, and dislikes.

3. *Prioritize It*: Clear out the clutter in your mind by identifying what's most important to you in choosing a name. Articulate this thought by writing it down, even if it's just a few sentences. Refer to it often in order to keep you focused and inspired. A few examples might be: "We want a feminine, lyrical name for Baby that reflects our African-American heritage," or "We want our twins' names to be easy to pronounce in English and Spanish, and to begin with the letter A or L."

4. *Formalize It*: Instead of keeping a running list in your head, adopt the more formal approach of professional namers. Keep a master list of names—one each for both first and middle, as well as possible combinations of the two. The names need not necessarily be in order of preference, though it may help. Update it regularly and be discriminating in which ones you add. Perhaps even keep dark-horse possibilities in a separate list. Beside the names, write down impressions, meanings, and points you like about each.

5. *Narrow It Down*: Whether you started with zero names or twenty, you're going to have to make a final decision. Very few parents leave that task to a professional, whose main job it is to provide clients with a short list that should meet all their needs. If choosing one by instinct works for you, go for it. Otherwise, the best way to come up with a winner is what earns consultants their exorbitant fees: research.

6. *Research It*: In most cases, the sources naming consultants use to do their research are accessible by the public. The Social Security Administration's name website (www.ssa.gov/OACT/babynames/) is the best site for finding out how popular or unpopular a name is—one of the most requested services asked of professional namers. The Internet is also the best place for learning about name meanings and associations. Admittedly, there's almost too much information out there—that's why a lot of people hire a namer in the first place—but if you're willing to do the legwork, everything you need to know is there for the Googling. Check and double check your findings, since different sources may list different meanings and/or origins for names. Once

parents hear the meanings behind the monikers they like, name consultants know that one or two will probably emerge as front-runners.

7. *Criticize It*: One advantage in having paid professional help is the impartiality he or she will provide. Sometimes, you may be too close or too attached to a name to see that it doesn't work. While a naming consultant will have no trouble telling you that calling your kid Mae West is ridiculous, you and your partner may be too wrapped up in your own little world to realize that this is not a good thing to name your daughter. So where should you look for truly impartial advice? Without a paid namer to put you in your place, turn to the cruel world of online baby-name message boards. Take the time to register so that you can post and ask the regulars what they think of your choices. The ensuing debates may help bring to light any issues you hadn't thought of, or even alternate suggestions you may prefer.

Chapter 3

✖ Baby Namers Beware: ✖ The Top 10 Things NOT to Do

If you're like most parents-in-waiting, you probably have a good list going by now. The problem is, with all those choices—and everything you've done to narrow it down already—you may still be looking at enough names to fill a baby name book of your own. The good news? We've got ten ways for you to pare it back even further.

Some names and naming styles are kinder and gentler than others. Remember, nobody thinks they're the ones burdening their kids with silly or extreme monikers, and yet, somehow, there are legions of children out there who may not be able to spell their own names until high school!

Yes, naming an innocent baby can go alarmingly wrong. To help hammer the point home, we've included plenty of real and ridiculous names spotted on those thriving online baby-naming message boards and, of course, trolled the best source of weird and wacky names anywhere—celebrity offspring!

So, without further ado, here's our list of the Top 10 Things NOT to Do When Naming Your Baby:

1. JUNIOR: JUST SAY NO
    The urge to name one's offspring after oneself runs deep. It's practically a biological imperative, a way to tell the world who your children are, where they come from, where they're going. But there's something that already takes all this into account: the surname. Most people in most places all over the world employ the device in one way or another to achieve a sense of historical and cultural continuity within their families.

    And yet so many parents choose to give Baby their given name as well. (The phenomenon is especially prevalent with naming sons, an equally perplexing custom since it's actually the daughters who often give up their surname when they get married down the road.) But think about it—naming your little one Something Junior can seem redundant. All of your kids are mini-yous in a sense; they're your offspring, for heaven's sake! There's no need to reiterate this fact by yoking your child with your own given name, to boot. Always remember that each child you have, while forever a part of you, is also an individual entity, both within your family and within the world. At least that's the goal, isn't it? Your child's given name is a wonderful way to celebrate this difference, this uniqueness of person and spirit, while her surname remains a way to connect her to her past and family history.

Case in point: George Foreman. The former heavyweight boxing champion of the world and master entrepreneur may have found success in the ring and with his Lean, Mean Grilling Machines, but he's a lightweight when it comes to naming his kids. Five of his sons are named George Junior, and he's even got a daughter named Georgetta. While this is obviously an extreme example, the reasoning behind his decision is actually quite sound: "One of the baddest feelings I had was that feeling of not knowing where I came from; what my roots were. I figured that with all of them having that name, they should know where they came from. It's never too late to get some roots."

Naming a child is an intense, emotionally loaded process to begin with, and when you add in something as personal as a parent's first name, the pressure can mount. You may feel like you have no choice, since family expectations can be particularly fierce in this regard. But remember one of the cardinal rules of naming: Parents need to agree on Baby's name 100 percent. As for the rest of the clan, hearts will be broken and tears will be shed if you decide against calling your son Frederick IV; but rest assured—the sun will continue to rise and set if you do not name your kid after pa, grandpa, and great-grandpa.

Or, consider this solution: Put Fred on the birth certificate so Baby will officially be Fred the Fourth, but choose a different middle name for your child to go by every day, one you'll use as if it were his given name from the get-go, provided you stick to it like glue. (There's no need to use a child's legal name anywhere except official documents such as birth certificates and passports, and schools can be instructed to use whatever name you tell them to for class lists and that sort of thing). It may be a pain later on when he's at the Department of Motor Vehicles applying for his license, and the first day of school will always require some name clarification, but overall it just might be worth it. Whatever you decide to do, please resist the temptation to simply call him Junior. What's cute on a three-year-old is often completely unadorable on a middle-age man, but more on that later.

2. CLEVER IS CRUEL

It's never kind to be cruel. You may think that choosing a witty name for your little one is a good way to have him or her stand out from the masses, but all it will do is mark your child's parents as a bit foolish themselves. We're not talking about naming your kid Einstein or Socrates here, but rather those names that employ wit, wisdom, or wordplay to make a point.

A few classic examples: Robin Banks, Adam Baum, Jay Walker, Amanda Lynn, Lisa Carr, Anita Lay, and who could forget good-old Seymour Butts and Phil McCracken? Actor Rob Morrow chose the name Tu for his daughter: Tu Morrow. Get it? Tu Morrow—as in, "The poor little girl will be teased again Tu Morrow, and then again the day after that..." No matter how drunk and in love you were when you conceived your son, calling him Jack Daniel won't be doing him any favors, either.

Keep in mind that your kid's first and last names will often be spoken aloud together—at school, in waiting rooms, at sporting events—and in addition how many times it will appear in print or online. Imagine that if every time someone heard your name, they giggled, snorted, groaned, or even outright laughed? Well, that's how little Abraham Burger will feel each time his teachers take attendance!

And it's not just kids that can be cruel. Very few adults have the self-control to ignore the obvious when being introduced to Bud Wiser. Okay, maybe most do, but you get the point—saddling a child with a name that might be the source of derision down the road can and will have an effect on the way she sees herself, and perhaps affect her socially as well. Consider nicknames, too (Harold Pitts's mom—this is for you).

3. NEGATIVE ASSOCIATIONS: MAYBE PARIS ISN'T SO PRETTY AFTER ALL

After the Bill Clinton scandal broke, the name Monica went from a respectable ranking of number 80 to pretty much dropping off the popularity chart. It now hovers at about 280, its lowest level in sixty years.

"But wait," you say. "It's a perfectly good name, and one my husband and I have always loved. That thing happened more than ten years ago. Why not use it? "

True, every day that passes makes it less and less likely that people will associate the moniker with the infamous White House intern.

The point is that negative associations are something you need to keep in mind.

Sometimes the descent is gradual: The name Britney peaked at number 137 in 2000, during the height of Britney Spears's popularity. By 2007 it had sunk like her record sales, dropping more than 300 percent, to number 564. The world into which your kid will be born is, alas, far from perfect, and while her little infant friends will have no clue who Britney is, their parents certainly will. Believe us—chuckles, groans, incredulous stares, and unkind things left unsaid are not the reactions you want when you introduce your new little bundle of joy to the world.

A few others to avoid these days might include Paris and Lindsay, lest you want your daughter's name to evoke images of drunk driving arrests, barefoot jaunts through public bathrooms, or failed attempts at rehab. Similarly, your son might not be off to a great start saddled with the Orenthal James (nickname: OJ), Osama, or Adolf.

"But those are silly examples," you scoff. Well, here's a true story to illustrate the point. Diana L. was pregnant with her first child. While not a large woman herself, heftiness ran in her family. She and her husband—who'd decided not to find out the sex of their baby—had chosen one girl name and one boy name. Despite all the begging and pleading of friends and loved ones, they were firm in their resolve to name their son Moby, being huge fans of the musician. Needless to say, everyone breathed a huge sigh of relief when Marlo was born.

Famous miscreants and great white whales aside, sometimes a name can itself be loaded with bad thoughts, as with this gem recently spotted online: Killian Daedalus. Think about it—Killian Daedalus. As if one death reference weren't enough, this poor kid bore two! Looks like little Killian can count out a career in medicine, undertaking, or public service.

Sometimes, though, the negative associations are less obvious. If Suri Cruise's famous parents knew that her name means "pick-pocket" in Japanese, and "pointy-nose" in parts of India, one wonders if they would have chosen it at all. And if only little Candida's mom knew that candida is a common form of yeast responsible for all those vaginal infections. The point? Research, research, research. We've said it before, and we'll say it again. Do your unborn child a favor and Google the heck out any name you choose—especially those unusual or made-up ones—before you commit to it on the birth certificate.

Similarly, choosing a name that reminds you of a certain someone you'd rather forget from your own past is not advised, either. Even if you've always loved, loved, loved the name Jackie, if that also happens to be the name of your husband's high school sweetheart, choose something else, for everyone's sake. The same goes for naming your baby boy after your recently deceased Great-Uncle Larry. While your parents may be pushing hard for Larry, if you remember him as a lecherous old coot with bad breath and a wandering eye, forget it. The good news here is that your baby's name needs to have positive connotations for the two of you and only you, so if your mom happens to hate the name Julie because it reminds her of a rotten little girl she taught in her kindergarten class thirty-five years ago, feel free to ignore her protests.

Of course, there is a little wiggle room. Some names—while certainly not evocative of sunshine or rainbows—may actually work despite their dubious associations. Babies named Oscar (the Grouch), Homer (Simpson), Delilah (evil hair-cutting temptress), and Cleo (conniving power-mad ancient vixen) are among a few that seem to have a loyal following, perhaps because some people like a name with a bit of an edge.

4. CONSIDER YOUR LAST NAME FIRST
    When choosing a name for Baby, your last name should be among the first things you think about. There are several factors you'll need to keep in mind: the way your surname sounds, the way it's spelled, and what it means. All too often, however, parents neglect one or all of these things, resulting in a life-long "oops"! Here, then, are four first-name/last-name issues to keep in mind:

    Melting in the Middle: Names like Pierce Sanderson, Jim Boelyn, Bob Loblaw (the butt of a famous sitcom joke), and Bill Lieber may roll off the tongue, but when said aloud, people will have no clue where the first name ends and the last name begins. Alternately, Ted Edison, Jack Ackerson, and Patricia Shand may be labeled stutterers when introducing themselves.
    Double Trouble: While some cultures around the world do employ the custom of using double names—same first and last names—using John if your surname is Johnson will make folks think that you lack creativity. Wally Wallace, Bob Roberts ... the list goes on and on. Remember, too, that if your last name can already stand as a first name or vice versa, you may not want to burden your kid with more of the same, as in Mason Plummer, Smith Jones, or Jake John.
    Negative Associations (Again!): Icky impressions can also result from the way a given name combines with a surname. If your last name is

Lester and you name your son Maurice, you might have a Moe Lester on your hands. So please pay attention—a little foresight is called for here. Write out all the possible nicknames, permutations, and combinations of the first/middle/last name you've chosen for your little one. Read them over and over. Say them aloud. Make sure nothing funny's going on. If only little Benjamin Dover's parents had done the same...

Famous or Infamous?: If you have a famous last name (or an infamous one), you'll need to be extra considerate. So you can forget about the name Charles, Mrs. Manson, and cross Lizzie off your list, Mr. Borden. Even harmless jokes like Lois Lane and William Tell send a message to your child: "Mom and Dad made a funny, but I'm the one who'll be paying the price for the rest of my life."

5. PET NAMES AND NOUN NONSENSE

When pop-star/philanthropist Bob Geldof famously named his daughter Fifi Trixibelle, the world wondered how a man could simultaneously be so kind to the impoverished masses and yet so cruel to his own child. John Cougar Mellencamp, apparently eager to continue the family tradition of animal naming, chose Speck Wildhorse for his son. While Tiger, Rover, Betsey, and Rex may be the perfect way to summon your cat, puppy, cow, or dinosaur, your kids are a little too high on the food chain to deserve being burdened with a moniker normally reserved for those without opposable thumbs.

The same goes for naming your kids after, well, things. In some cases, such as flower and gem names (like Iris and Ruby), or profession names (Hunter or Mason), noun naming can work very well. But in the quest for originality, the kindergarten rolls sometimes look as if parents simply threw a dart at a dictionary page. Cove, Frost, Launch, Tile, Valley, Arson, and Slide—all recently spotted on online baby-name message boards—will invariably be the objects of ridicule from day one. If you're going to name your kid after an inanimate object, better make sure it's one worthy of the honor.

Nowhere has this phenomenon come to fruition more than in the world of celebrity naming. From Jermaine Jackson's son Jermajesty, to Dweezil and Moon Unit Zappa, it doesn't take a degree in psychiatry to figure out that the rich and famous seem to cling to "unusual" names for their kids as a way to keep up the illusion that they are somehow different than the rest of us. Take the naming triad of the Demi Moore–Bruce Willis clan: three beautiful girls named Tallulah, Rumer, and Scout. With the arguable exception of Scout—nobly inspired by the name of fictional attorney Atticus Finch's daughter in the classic novel, *To Kill a Mockingbird*—these names are heavy stuff to handle for little girls. In fact, the now teenaged Tallulah is currently in the process of legally changing her name to Lula.

A few other outlandish celebrity noun and animal naming choices include: Erykah Badu's daughter Puma, Jason Lee's son Pilot Inspektor, David Duchovny's son Kyd, actress Shannyn Sossamon's son Audio Science, Penn Jillette's daughter Moxie CrimeFighter, Rachel Griffith's son Banjo, and tennis great Arthur Ashe's daughter Camera.

6. RHYMING: NO WAY, JOSE!

Some people seem to think it's cute and funny to give their child a name that rhymes with their last name. But Bones Jones and Sally Mullally aren't laughing, though their classmates surely are. Cases in point: Punk rocker Marc Bolan named his son Rolan, and most famously of all, David Bowie called his son Zowie. Zowie eventually went on to have his name changed to—wait for it—Joey. Hmmm...maybe the poor kid didn't mind playing the rhyming game after all.

In our real, non-rock-and-roll world, rhyming is still a problem, as speed skater/reality-show dancer Apolo Ohno and comedian Cheri Oteri can attest. (Ever hear Ohno's first name used without "Anton"? Rhyming could be why.) More often than not, these gaffes are a result of a lack of foresight—the Oteris probably thought Cheryl was a perfectly fine name for their little girl, and so the road to naming hell was paved with good intentions. So be careful, Mrs. Key: Victoria may be in your top three, but Vicky Key doesn't sound so hot. Other innocent examples might include Megan Reagan and Brandon Landon, or even subtler rhymes such as Blake Baker and Joel Foley.

Then again, all kinds of unavoidable combinations can occur in the real world. Girls named Jen fall in love with and marry boys named Penn, but there's not much you can do about that now. For the moment, just keep your wits about you—by keeping the deliberately cutesy rhyming names off your list from the get-go—and your kids will take it from there.

7. THE FUTURE IS NOW: TEMPTING FATE, GLOBE-TROTTING GAFFES, AND JUVENILE HIJINKS

We all want our kids to grow up to become good people. Our job as parents, after all, is not only to care for them, but also to help them achieve their full potential as adults. Because of this—and in spite of it—there are plenty of wishful thinkers out there who give their babies so-called virtue names. We're not talking about Faith, Hope, and Grace, names that seem to have been used enough to lose their super-pure overtones, but rather choices like Chastity, Destiny, Charisma, Temperance, and Prudence. Those little girls and little boys named Lucky, True, Peace, and Noble have tough names to live up to, to say the least.

In extreme cases, these kids might feel that the burden of their parents'—even the world's—expectations is simply too much to bear. They may become introverted, shy, embarrassed, or even rebel against exactly what it is they're expected to be. (A sixteen-year-old girl named Chastity will have no shortage of ideas about how not to live up to her name. Similarly, a little later down the road, when Lucky gets struck by lightning, or Justice gets six months in prison for tax evasion, we guarantee you the irony won't be lost on anyone.)

Since September 11, 2001, there has been a surge in patriotic virtue names such as America, Bravery, and Freedom. It's certainly a tribute, but one you should consider very carefully before signing that birth certificate. What if little America grows up and decides to join the Peace Corps, and is then stationed in a country where the mere mention of the United States might cause discomfort among the people she is trying to help? It may seem far-fetched, but it happens. You may want to choose something a little more subtle—perhaps a traditional name from the country you'd like to honor, or the name of a beloved president or civic leader.

Also keep in mind that a name that may sound so cute for a little kid right now is also one your child will have to live with she's all grown up. We're not just talking about Junior, here—there are dozens and dozens of cutie-pie choices out there that are ill-suited to adults. When it's time for Peaches, Dolly, Jo-Jo, Poppy, Daisy, Wendy-Sue, Jimmy-Jay, and Timmy to apply for their Social Security benefits or check into the retirement villa, their friends on the shuffleboard court may never let them live it down.

8. NOT SO SWEET: BAKERY BABIES AND KIDS FROM THE CLOUDS
We occasionally hear about a kid named Bean or Lovie, obvious prenatal nicknames that seemed to have stuck. Monikers like these are lamentably less rare than you might think; presumably the frustration of being unable to settle on a real name proved too much to bear for these parents. Equally saccharine is the barrage of names inspired by goodies from the bake shop or candy store. Names too sweet to bear—such as Skittle, Candy, Tootsie, Cookie, Toffee, and Flossie—make us want to run screaming for our toothbrushes.

Yes, babies are delicious (especially yours!), but while the bun in your oven may not mind being referred to as Jellybean or Figlet or Peanut, real children will not be so accommodating. A little girl saddled with the name Honey might go out of her way not to be sweet, and Sugar will surely tire of being told she's anything but. Kids with fruit names may fare marginally better—novelist Plum Sykes and Gwyneth Paltrow's little Apple quickly come to mind—but be forewarned: You may be serving up a lifetime of bad jokes for poor Clementine and Pumpkin.

For as long as parents have been trolling the aisles of the grocery store in search of pleasant-sounding fare for which to name their offspring, just as many have been looking to the heavens for inspiration, both literally and figuratively. The late great INXS frontman Michael Hutchence was guilty of this naming sin: Heavenly Hiraani Tiger Lily. Alas, he wasn't alone. Stormy, Angel, Rain, Zeus, Cloud, and Heaven are but a few examples of this trend, which only seems to be gathering steam. (Angel ranks in the thirties on the Social Security Administrations's list of the most popular names, and *The Matrix*–inspired name Trinity has skyrocketed since the movie's release!) Please remember, though, that these names also happen to be preferred by pole-dancers, drag queens, and "ladies of the evening." As in, "Little Moonbeam Rabinovitch never had a chance. She wanted to be a lawyer, but ended up a topless hostess..." And take note of the popular backwards spelling of Heaven—Nevaeh—currently ranked number 31 for girls. (Can Evol be far behind?) If you're looking for more originality in the divine, try something like Eden or Skye.

9. SILLY SPELLINGS: DON'T BE CRAYZEE!
The most common method modern parents seem to employ in order to assure themselves that their kids are extra-special is by spelling their names "uniquely." An informal survey of online baby-name forums reveals that there are two distinct camps in this matter: the parents who are all for it, and the ones who despise it with every fiber of their being. Check it out for yourself—you will surely come across more venom and vitriol in the discussion over whether onehotmama2232 should name her son Krystofurr or Christopher than on the circumcision, surrogacy, and breastfeeding debate boards combined.

It's a delicate discussion, one bound up with ideas of originality and creativity, but the fact remains: In a nutshell, creative spellings can be confusing, necessitate endless corrections, cause trouble with official documents, and maybe even engender negative stereotypes about your sweet little Muhrreyah or Kenna'deigh or Nyckolle. Giving your child such a uniquely spelled name may also give you the false impression that it's less popular than it is: The Social Security Administration notes that different spellings of the same name are counted separately in its popularity lists, significantly skewing the data. For example, if Madison, Maddison, Madisyn, Madisen, Madisson, Madysyn, and Madyson were counted as the same name, it would surely be number 1.

Real names spotted on the boards include the following: Asshleeigh, Dilyn, Uneeque, Suezynn, Braighdyn, Makinzye, Khassandra, Ce'Qwoia, Adecyn, Knoah, Knoraugh, Kryslyn, Zakeri...the list is endless.

This isn't to say that you should fear adding your own personal touch to a name. As we pointed out in Chapter 2, subtle changes, such as using a slightly different spelling of a popular moniker, can be a great way to make it your own. (Think Abbey instead of Abby, or Lia instead of Leah.) If you do decide to mix it up, you may want to respect the golden rule of alternative spelling: Stick to just one change and you'll be fine. So that's Desstiny or Destiney, but surely not both.

10. BREAK IT DOWN: INITIALS, LETTERS, AND ANAGRAMS
Poor little Arnold Scott Smith. The only girl who would date him was Tina Isabelle Truman. Yes, unanticipated trouble with initials, letters, and anagrams can be extremely difficult to deal with—just one more reason to put it all down on paper before you actually go ahead and fill out anyone's birth certificate. So break out that pencil, write down the name you've chosen in its entirety, and start reading between the lines: Are there any hidden messages in there you wouldn't want to be sending?

First of all, make sure the combination of the first letters of all the names do not spell anything funny. There are some combinations with obvious problems (Oliver Dustin Dennis, Helen Alice Gold, Danielle Uma Martin), and then there are subtler issues (Paul Arthur Preston, Mark Toby Vernon). Remember to also look for acronyms you may not want associated with your child, or even ones that might be annoying to deal with on the playground—CIA, DUI, KKK, SUV, DOA—basically, anything that could cause embarrassment or endless discussion down the road. Even some anagrams that subtly suggest other words should be considered off-limits (e.g., Finley Chad Kendall). Still not convinced it matters? Just ask David Isaac Klein.

Chapter 4

✖ Middle Names: ✖ Magic in the Middle

Ah, the middle name—the most neglected moniker of them all. Some parents, especially those who struggle with the naming process, bemoan middle names as yet another hurdle to overcome before Baby is born. Others recognize them for what they really are: a welcome opportunity to showcase creativity, solve naming conundrums, honor loved ones, and even have some fun!

Traditionally, most people don't really use their middle names on a daily basis, but that doesn't mean you shouldn't take them seriously. Lots of you employ your middle initial as an additional way to distinguish yourself, and you may even feel that your middle name is an important part of your identity and heritage. Those of you who already have children know that the middle name is also an excellent way to get your kid's attention, as in: "Sandra Carole Lipton, you come down here right now!" In fact, without hearing their middle names to drive mom or dad's point home, countless kids around the world might be confused as to how serious their parents actually are! Angry outbursts aside, choosing the right middle name for Baby is simply another chance to bestow the blessing of a beautiful, complete name.

The habit of giving a child more than one name became fairly commonplace in the Western world around the end of the eighteenth century, with the first recorded use of the term "middle name" occurring in 1835. Since then, people have embraced the tradition as a way to satisfy the multi constraints and responsibilities of naming their kids. Though it may se superfluous for any minimalists out there—especially if you don't hav middle name of your own—the middle name lends its bearer an additio layer of singularity, an aura of mystery even, in the sense that its nature a origins may be closely guarded, revealed only at will.

So when it comes to choosing a second moniker for your child, let creativity be your middle name. Give yourself bonus points for an inspired choice, since his middle name will surely become intricately connected with his sense of self as he ages. For example, have you ever wondered how many John Smiths there are in the United States? Roughly sixty thousand, at last count. But how many John Jupiter Smiths are there? Only one!

MINDING THE GAP: SOUNDS AND SYLLABLES

Although your child's middle name will probably not be used often, the way it sounds along with her first and last names is a crucial consideration. That word in the middle will act as a bridge between given name and surname, so when said aloud, it must flow well between the two. Parents with a good ear for names choose ones whose letter sounds complement each other. One way to do this is with gentle alliteration (Leilani Aliyah, Aurora Rianne, Benjamin Jacob). Slight rhyming or "off-rhymes" can also be effective in this way, as long as they're employed with subtle fluidity (Orlando Matteo and Anna Maria, as opposed to Jillian Lillian or Aiden Jayden).

Another factor is rhythm, as created by syllables and the emphasis placed upon them when spoken aloud. Often, people stick to one-syllable middle names, especially if they've chosen a longer first name or happen to have a complicated last name. This is especially true when naming girls. The one-syllable middle is very appealing because it can add a nice rhythm to a name, sort of a place to pause for impact before continuing on to the surname (Abigail Eve, Ilana Ruth, Tara Lynn). Two-syllable middle names also work very well with two- or three-syllable first names, especially if the accent in the middle name is on a different syllable than it is in the first name (Ellen Marie, Beatrice Nicole).

Parents of boys may find it more difficult to come up with a middle name that works. Of the twenty most popular boys' names, thirteen are effectively two-syllable names with the accent on the first syllable (Noah, Logan, Andrew). Since one-syllable middles for boys are fairly hard to come by, consider a three- or four-syllable middle name to achieve a nice rhythmical pat-rn (Brandon Gabriel, Tyler Anthony, Michael Alexander).

As always, you'll definitely need to say the entire name out loud in order etermine whether or not a middle name works. Ask yourself: Do the nes flow well together? Are they similar in style, or do they seem to be at s with one another? Be hypervigilant about identifying any potential blems that might arise when you add a certain middle into the mix. For mple, a middle name like Lee will make any first name sound like an adjective (Pearl Lee, Heaven Lee, Drew Lee), and could also alter the impression of what the first name is altogether (Emma Lee, Carl Lee, Elle Lee).

TRADITIONAL MIDDLE NAMES

The appeal of a classic middle name cannot be denied. Parents with very unusual middle names themselves may balk at putting their little ones through the same thing they went through, assuming they didn't enjoy the distinction of having a "weird" name, and may want to retreat to the comfort of time-tested favorites. Others who have traditional middle names themselves may want to pass along the practice. Parents unsure about even giving Baby a middle name may want to stay safe by choosing an oldie-but-goodie.

Unlike first names, middle names seem to be more immune to popular naming trends and flights of fancy. The classics endure as middle names because not only are these tried-and-true names loved by almost everyone, but also because they can be an effective way to ground a more unusual or trendy first name (Sequoia Rose, Rafferty Thomas, Elvira Katherine, Grayson James). Also interesting to note is that while there is an obvious cache of favorite middle names for girls, boys' middle monikers are drawn from pretty much the same pool as their first names. The list of the top 10 most popular boys' first and middle names are virtually the same, while the list for girls' firsts and seconds varies quite a bit.

Popular Middle Names for Girls

Anne
Lee
Rose
May
Grace
Mary
Hope
Joy
Kate/Katherine
Jane/Jean/Joan
Sue
Nicole
Faith
Beth
Elizabeth
Lynn
Claire

Another aspect of traditional naming is found in not only the choice of names, but the source of the monikers themselves. In the Western world, there is a custom of boys taking dad's first or middle name as their own middle name, and girls taking mom's first or middle name as theirs. Though it's not as popular a habit as it used to be, this is an excellent way to get around the "junior" or "II" designation, and yet still satisfy familial expectations without being deprived of the fun of choosing Baby's first name yourself.

Creative Middle Names

At the opposite end of the spectrum from traditional names are the unusual ones. Just as wild first names can benefit from less eccentric middle names, so too can traditional first names benefit from a slightly more inspired follow-up. Using a name that may not work well as a first name is actually an excellent starting point for choosing a middle name, and there are plenty of ways to add a creative touch to the process. Perhaps you've always loved the name Sage, but fear it may be too "out there" to use as a first name. Or maybe you want to commemorate the place where Baby was conceived, but can't quite bring yourself to choose London as a first name. The middle name is a chance to flex your naming muscles without having to be as cautious and sensitive as you need to be with a first name. So feel free to have fun, whether it's choosing a name you feel an unexplained affinity for, despite any rhyme or reason, or one you just don't have the guts to use up front.

Creativity can come into play in more subtle ways, too. If you actually like the idea of a traditional middle name but want to spice things up, use the classic middles as a starting point to create something more unique. This is a good path to take for those parents torn between the desire to use a traditional middle name that's been passed down through the generations, but who still want to add a personal touch. For example, choose Annette or Annika instead of Ann, Maya or Mayla instead of May, Johnson or Jay instead of John, Rain or Rye instead of Ryan.

Initial Here

As we've said, few people use their middle names on a daily basis. Sometimes, however, the first letter of one's middle name is adopted into more regular usage in order to further distinguish its bearer. Yes, employing the middle initial can add a certain panache to an otherwise plain-vanilla name. We're not suggesting you insist people refer to your three-day-old baby by her first name and middle initial, but rather that you consider how the middle initial works in conjunction with the rest of her name because one day she may actually use it! Mary Jones may become Mary P. Jones,

Jacob Johnson may choose Jacob J. Johnson, and Robert White may like Robert Q. White. Indeed, choosing a middle name that begins with a less-common letter—such as Q, V, or Z—is a great way to make using the middle initial a more enticing option.

It's not just a matter of choice. Often, people in the public eye, such as politicians and actors, will include their middle initial as a way to set themselves apart and make their names more memorable. So if you already have it planned out that your kid will become president, be the first to set foot on Mars, or win the Nobel Prize for literature, give the middle initial some careful consideration. There are actually lots of well-known people whose names we otherwise might not recognize without that middle initial to help them stand out:

George W. Bush
John F. Kennedy
George C. Scott
Hunter S. Thompson
Michael J. Fox
Samuel L. Jackson
Edward G. Robinson
William H. Macy
Vivica A. Fox

Maiden Name as Middle Name

Up until quite recently, there was a historical tradition of giving children their mother's maiden name as a middle name. While the habit has fallen away in recent decades, it remains a nice way to honor the maternal side of the family. After all, why should dad's surname be the only one to be passed down through the generations? Admittedly, the thought may be more appealing if you happened to have been a Carson or a Blair or something lyrical before you got married, though technically anything goes. If you really like the idea of embracing this custom but have decided against it because your maiden name is very difficult to pronounce or spell, consider a simpler stand-in with the same spirit. Choose Vaughn instead of Von Schlightenmeester, Milan instead of Milankovitch, or Rock instead of Rochefort.

Another point to think about if you do choose to use your maiden name as a middle name is whether to bestow it only upon your firstborn or to use it for all of your kids. If you do decide to use it across the board, this might be the perfect occasion to throw in an additional middle name for each child. This will allow every one of them to feel special and unique, while still remaining connected to the family tradition. This brings us to our next topic: multiple middle names.

Multiple Middles

An English couple recently made headlines all over the world when they gave their daughter twenty-five middle names. As if that weren't odd enough, the middle monikers in question were all derived from boxing greats. Yes, little Autumn Sullivan Corbett Fitzsimmons Jeffries Hart Burns Johnson Willard Dempsey Tunney Schmeling Sharkey Carnera Baer Braddock Louis Charles Walcott Marciano Patterson Johansson Liston Clay Frazier Foreman Brown's parents saw fit to saddle their precious infant with enough names to cause a technical knock-out! To be fair, it is a family tradition—Autumn's mom along with her two siblings have a total of 103 middle names between them, and she admits it took her until the age of ten to remember her own name.

Indeed, the British tradition—especially among royalty and aristocracy—is to give multiple middle names, usually three or four. The firstborn son often boasted the most impressive list of middle monikers, bearing great responsibility in case his parents weren't blessed with any more kids to carry on the family names. Their Royal Highnesses Prince William Arthur Philip Louis and Prince Henry Charles Albert David are a good example of the practice today, but less blue-blooded folk sometimes adopt the habit, too, as Kiefer Sutherland's parents did (his full name is Kiefer William Frederick Dempsey George Rufus Sutherland!).

What does this mean for you? If you're at an impasse between two middle names, or are arguing with your significant other about several names and can't seem to narrow your list down to just two, you may want to stick a few extras in there. Your child will probably appreciate the uniqueness of having more than just the usual one middle name, and it will also help her become a good speller! A word of warning, though: Try to keep it to two or three. Just because there's no legal limit on the number of middle names doesn't mean you should turn your child's birth certificate into a page from the phone book.

Missing Middles

At the opposite end of the spectrum, there are those among us who have no middle name at all. Only between 1 and 4 percent of babies born in the United States are not given middle names, a practice we'd urge you to carefully consider for two reasons: It's not practical and it could be annoying to your child. Think of it from her perspective: Imagine being left out of the fun when your friends are comparing middle names. Even if you grew up not liking your middle name, it's hard to deny that it was fun to share it occasionally, perhaps as a way to bond with pals, commiserate with others, or even as a way to take someone into your confidence.

Practically speaking, middle names have become so ubiquitous in the Western world that not having one can actually cause problems with paperwork. Before the dawn of the computer age, this may not have been an issue, but now that endless databases are an undeniable and necessary part of the way we organize information, collect data, and do business, appeasing the technological gods is the path of least resistance. Just ask one of the many baby boomers with the middle name NMI. Up until about twenty years ago, computers were programmed in such a way that they were designed to record exactly three names per person, often asking for a middle initial to enter into the middle field. If a person had no middle name at all, instead of leaving a blank space, these programs automatically inserted the acronym NMI—meaning No Middle Initial, a term used in military personnel documents—in its absence. And so it happened that countless people were actually running around the country with the middle name of NMI on all their official documents.

These days, that glitch has been resolved in most data processing programs, but why make things harder on your child than you have to?

Going by the Middle Name

If, for whatever reason, you must name Baby after a relative or use a traditional family name but you don't especially like the choice, why not promote your kid's middle name to first name for all intents and purposes? We like to think that Grandpa will always be smiling down on little Orville Jacob from heaven, despite the fact that all of his friends and loved ones know him as Jake. It's not just a matter of necessity or parental preference: Always consider the fact that one day, your child may decide to promote her middle name to first position. There are many reasons she may choose to do this. Perhaps she simply prefers it over the one you chose for her, or wants to use it as a way to guard her anonymity in certain professional or personal situations. Alternately, it may be a better way for her to stand out from the crowd. This added flexibility is just one more reason to give your kid a stupendous second name, especially if you're giving him a first name that's more common. (Parents of Rob Stephens and William Brown, we're talking to you!)

Indeed, many people in the public eye—including politicians, actors, and writers—will use their middle names as stage or pen names, keeping their real first names for private use only, and as a way to distinguish their private from professional lives. Here are a few famous folks who decided to go by their middle moniker instead:

Henry Warren Beatty
Troyal Garth Brooks

Stephen Grover Cleveland
John Calvin Coolidge
William Bradley Pitt
Adeline Virginia Woolf
Thomas Sean Connery
Francis Scott Fitzgerald
Ralph Dale Earnhardt
Hannah Dakota Fanning
William Clark Gable
Joseph Rudyard Kipling
Christopher Ashton Kutcher
Anna Eleanor Roosevelt
Matthew Ryan Phillippe
Laura Jean Reese Witherspoon
Lynn Nolan Ryan
Christa Brooke Camille Shields

Spiritual Middles

For countless parents-to-be around the world, the naming process involves more to consider than just personal preferences and family traditions—there's a religious element in there, too. In many cases, a child's first name can be dictated by a beloved custom or even a religious imperative. A middle name can be, well, a way around it!

The classic example of this is Canon 761—as decreed by Pope Benedict XV in 1917—which states that all Catholic children are to be given Christian names from a list of approved saints' names. (As an antidote to parents who were unwilling to do this, priests were instructed to choose and record a Christian name in the child's baptismal record anyway!). These days, parents wishing to respect the edict's spirit will sometimes give their kids the first or baptismal name of a saint, and then add a middle name of their choosing for the child to use as his first name. Similarly, in the Jewish tradition, babies are often expected to bear first names in honor of deceased relatives. While some modern parents wishing to fulfill the spirit of the obligation will choose a name with either the same first letter, the same Hebrew name, or the same meaning as that belonging to the relative being honored, others will simply adhere to the custom and give their kid a preferred middle name to go by on a daily basis.

Many Roman Catholic parents choose to give middle names out of respect for Mary, Joseph, and Jesus and to have their babies receive their protection. This is a common custom in France, Spain, Poland, and Italy, and defies traditional gender name boundaries. For example, Marie is used as the second half of several hyphenated boys' names in France, as with Jean-Marie. Hispanic parents often give their sons the middle name María, and their daughters the middle name José. Elsewhere, boys and girls born into the Sikh tradition are required to have the surname Singh and Kaur, respectively—names that symbolize gender equality and opposition to the caste system in India—but these days many parents will simply include these options as middle names instead.

Middle Name Mistakes

🛒 **Bad Jokes:** Whether the result of a poorly chosen middle initial or the combination of your child's first and middle names, problems can arise from names that Mom and Dad didn't think through. It may seem like a joke, but Isaac Paul Daily—a.k.a. I.P. Daily—isn't laughing, and neither is Kent C. Straight. The full-name no-no's are equally mortifying for your kids. It doesn't matter if they were named that way intentionally, or simply as a result of gaffes on their parents' part, but Pearl Lee Gates, A. Bruce Key, Liberty Belle, and Howard Hugh will most certainly not be laughing.

🛒 **Just a Letter:** Did you know that Harry S Truman's middle initial was just that—one lone letter? While his parents chose S as a way to pay respect to Harry's maternal and paternal grandfathers, both of whom had S names, the letter itself stands for absolutely nothing. Similarly, the Amish tradition-ally give their kids a middle name consisting of a single letter, taken from the first letter of the mother's maiden name and always used without a period after, as in Rachel S Smith or Samuel J King. Despite these examples, think hard about slipping in a solo letter. There's nothing fun about just having a G there to plug in on official forms.

🛒 **Too Much of a Good Thing:** Some people prefer not to give a middle name that has the same number of syllables or very similar sounds as the first name and last names, since it can result in either singsong silliness (Annemaria Ernestina Ingrassia) or jarring combinations (Fred Paul Lake, Tom Bart Bragg). Names like this can be tempting targets for playground taunts. Try to avoid overly obvious rhyming schemes, too: Tyler Skyler, Giselle Estelle, Brent Trent. While a name that is similar in style to the given name is always a good choice, anything too close can be a source of confusion, ridicule, or just plain boredom.

🛒 **No Middle Name at All:** Every kid wants a middle name, and, frankly, every grown-up does too—not only because it gives us something to put on all those government forms, but because it's yet another small way to distinguish ourselves from the billions of other human beings on the planet. Our middle names help ground our identities and carve out our sense of who we are within our families, communities, and the larger world around us.

Chapter 5

✖ Family Matters: ✖
Naming Siblings and Multiples

No doubt about it, naming your first child can be a difficult process. Still, there's at least one factor you don't have to deal with: considering your other kids' names! But if your family's growing—whether you're having your second or third child, or maybe even a few at once—that is no longer the case. Sure, in an ideal world you'd be naming each baby in a bubble, completely independent of any restricting outside issues or influences. But the truth is, you do have to consider other things, such as how Baby's name will sound in relation to her big brothers' names, or how Baby's name fits into your family's naming style. As always, you need to choose a moniker that suits your personal preferences—you like the way it sounds, what it means, the impression it gives—but the name also needs to be good in context, not only within the community and larger world Baby's being born into, but within your own family as well.

The suggestions and guidelines we've come up with to steer you through the process apply equally to singleton siblings and multiples. With twins and triplets, there are also some additional points to consider, so we've given some space to the issues—and errors—often associated with choosing many monikers at once. So welcome to the wild world of sibling naming. We hope you enjoy the ride!

SISTERS AND BROTHERS

If you've already named a kid or two, you bring valuable knowledge to the table. Perhaps you had a positive experience and, years later, remain delighted with the name you chose for your older child or children. If, on the other hand, you still have a twinge of regret or uncertainty—or even secretly wish you'd chosen differently the first time around—naming a new baby can be nerve-wracking. Fear not! This is your chance to put all that wisdom to good use and redeem yourself.

Indeed, the first step in naming the new baby should be to sit down and think about how you feel about your other kids' names. Discuss it in detail with your significant other, trying to identify both the things you love about the name(s) you've already chosen, as well as those characteristics you don't. Keep these points front and center in your mind as you begin the arduous task of choosing another.

The following factors (and faux-pas!) stand out among the key issues in naming siblings. Consider them carefully as both a source of inspiration and a way to put your mind at ease if you're feeling overwhelmed or unsure. Before you know it, you'll be well on your way to naming the next member of your family with confidence!

Consistency of Style

Names of a similar style are not only pleasing to the ear when said aloud together, but also work well on a more theoretical level. There's something subtly harmonious about a similar group of names for your similar group of kids. For example, if you call your first two children Hannah and Sarah, keep the style the same for your third kid: Hannah, Sarah, and Rachel works far better than Hannah, Sarah, and Kadence. For instance, what works better: Wyatt and Cody, or Wyatt and Fernando? Victoria and Elizabeth, or Victoria and Cheyenne?

Identifying and developing your family's naming style is perhaps the perfect starting point in your quest to name your children. Although you may not think you even have a distinguishing style, you'd be surprised to learn that you most likely do! Try the following simple exercise as a way to pinpoint exactly the sort of names you like. To begin with, write down all the names you can think of that appeal to you, just off the top of your head. They don't have to be ones you'd actually use, just names you like for one reason or another. Try to include as many as possible. Now look at the list. Do you see a pattern? Do you seem to like biblical names? The letter Z? Three-syllable names? French names? Trendy names? Now, apply this newfound knowledge.

All of these considerations bring us to our next point: themes.

Think about Themes

As with style, names of a certain theme share common traits, only more so. Themes are groups of names connected by a specific and unifying feature. Many parents like to stick to a certain theme when naming their kids, and as long as it's not too overt, this can be a great way to come up with a cohesive bunch of names. Themes are often inspired by a single meaning; for example, Abigail, Farrah, Hilary, and Joyce all mean "joy" in one way or another. Or, create a personal theme of your own—street names from the small town you and your partner grew up in, characters from your favorite author's works, the names of beloved patron saints, or ones inspired by your year-long honeymoon spent traveling the world. Basically, anything that's significant to you professionally, personally, or spiritually in a positive way can be a source of a good theme, whether it's names that mean "justice" for a family of lawyers, or names culled from the Chicago Bulls' dynasty from the 1990s for a family of basketball fans.

When choosing names that are somehow connected, the only caveat is to make sure your theme is subtle enough not to warrant chuckles from people upon hearing the names of all your kids at once. Combinations like Kirk, Spock, and McCoy, or Michael, Jermaine, and Tito, are not advised.

A few ideas to get you started:

Stupendous scientists: Louis, Jonas, Linus, Marie, Jane, Isaac

Beloved presidents: Madison, Jackson, Taylor, Grant, Wilson, Monroe

Romantic heroines: Jane, Elizabeth, Cathy, Josephine, Marian, Guinevere

Names that mean "pure": Caitlyn, Cathy, Glenda, Karen, Trina

Baseball legends: Lou, Babe, Ty, Nolan, Willie, Hank

Shakespeare's women: Juliet, Portia, Ophelia, Imogen, Beatrice

Names that mean "farmer": Bartholomew, George, Jerzey, Joren, Zory

African-American heroes: Rosa, Harriet, Sidney, Booker, Sojourner

Awesome aviators: Amelia, Howard, Wilbur, Chuck, Wiley, Bessie

Big Families: T for Two...or Three...or Four

If you're having trouble coming up with a name for your second or third child, consider this: Back in the old days, most families had way more than 2.1 kids—the national average in the United States today. In fact, just a few short decades ago in the late 1950s and early 1960s, the average number of children was 3.8! Coming up with enough names to manage such blossoming broods surely must have been a challenge in the past, which may have explained the popularity of such names as Octavia (Latin for "eighth-born child") during the Roman and Victorian times. Still, there are some number-name hold-outs that remain in modern usage, and despite the fact that they're rarely used literally anymore, they may be worth consideration if you have lots of kids or, say, nontuplets.

NUMBER NAMES

Third Child: Tryna (Greek), Ottah (Egyptian), Renzo (Japanese), San (Chinese), Tertia (Latin)

Fourth Child: Anana (African), Cuarto (Spanish), Delta and Tessa (Greek), Quartus (Latin), Rabah and Reba (Hebrew),

Fifth Child: Kinden (Latin), Penthia (Greek), Ponce (Spanish), Anum (African/Egyptian), Quincy and Quentin (English)

Sixth Child: Essien (African), Sixtus (Latin)

Seventh Child: Bathsheba (Hebrew), Saith (Welsh), Septima/Septimus (Latin)

Eighth: Octavia, Octavian, Octavius (Latin), Otto (German), Sheminith (Hebrew)

Ninth: Enea (Greek/Italian), Nona (Latin)

The big issue with naming in families with lots of kids is the first letter. You may have heard of the Dugger family, whose brood of seventeen kids has landed them national news spots and a few reality TV specials. What seems to fascinate people most about the Duggers, however, is that they've given all of their kids names beginning with the letter J: Joshua, Jana, John-David, Jill, Jessa, Jinger, Joseph, Josiah, Joy-Anna, Jedidiah, Jeremiah, Jason, James, Justin, Jackson, Johannah, and Jennifer. This is obviously an extreme example, but if you have more than two or three kids whose names begin with the same letter, it can become a bit too cute and repetitive. Try pairing them off with letters instead: Jonah, Jared, Max, and Mason, or Rebecca, Ryan, Harper, and Henry.

"But wait," you say. "I don't know that I'll have four kids. If I already have Jonah and Jared, won't poor Max feel left out?"

Actually, he probably won't. Odds are the only people who think about this one are the parents—it's doubtful that Max will even notice. It might even make him feel special—and isn't that how we want each kid to feel?

"Do They Sound Good Together?"

The way two or more names sound together is something every parent thinks about during the naming process. Saying them aloud to each other a few times and repeating them to yourself will give you an idea if the names jive together on an instinctual level. If you're not sure, try posting on an anonymous online baby-name discussion board. Sibling names are a favorite discussion topic on these sites, and you're sure to get lots of opinions on your choices. (Just remember to have a thick skin!) All in all, it's a better option than asking friends or relatives, whose suggestions and comments are more apt to be upsetting.

Of course, this is a very subjective approach to deciding whether or not the names you've chosen work well together. To make things easier, we next discuss a few empirical points to remember when it comes to naming siblings.

Sibling Names: What to Avoid

1. Too Much Rhyming: How many rhyming names you wish to include in your family is up to you, but any more than two and you will surely raise a few eyebrows. Subtle rhyming or names ending with or including similar sounds can definitely work well together—siblings named Jenny and Joey sound just fine, maybe because the hard "e" sound is arguably the most common sound for name endings. On the other hand, full-on rhyming pairs, like Chloe and Joey, or Paxon and Jackson, might be a little much for two kids, and definitely overwhelming for a set of three (Chloe, Joey, and Zoe!) As an alternative, mix things up by adding a name with three syllables instead—say, Jackson and Harrison—or alter the ending sound slightly with the second name, as in Jackson and Sheldon. Keep nicknames in mind as well, since Harold and Bartholomew will likely become Harry and Barry.

2. Nearly Identical Names: Sticking to a theme or style is one thing, but sometimes the names of siblings can be simply too similar, whether they rhyme or not. Reece and Royce, Jan and Jen, Don and Donna, Kristen and Kirsten—all are too close for comfort if you want each child to feel he or she was named as an individual. (This phenomenon is often found in twins, which we'll discuss in more detail shortly.)

3. Letting Big Brother and Sister Choose: It's a nice idea, but there are other ways to involve older siblings in the naming process. Asking for suggestions to be added to your list is fine, but don't promise anything unless you want to be stuck with a name like Elmo or Dora! All in all, having your other kids paint a name plate for the baby's door after you've decided on the winner is a much better idea.

4. Weird Combinations: Dorothy, Mildred, and Mackenzie sound like they were born in different centuries. It all goes back to style—identifying a style and being consistent is the only way to make sure you'll come up with a collection of names you love that also work well together as a group.

MULTIPLE MADNESS: TWINS, TRIPLETS, AND BEYOND

Coming up with a name for one kid is tough enough. What on earth do you do when you find out you're having two, three, or (gulp!) more? You're going to have to work hard—very hard—to find names that will be as unique and yet still so closely connected as your children themselves.

THE THREE CARDINAL RULES OF NAMING MULTIPLES

1. Don't Be Lazy: Just because you're having more than one kid at a time doesn't give you permission to pull names out of a hat. Give each child's naming process the focus and attention it deserves. Lazy naming takes many forms, from choosing monikers that are way too similar (if you planned to name the baby Maria before you knew you were having twins, think twice about naming her sister Mary) to the dreaded ABCDs of "alphabet naming," which we'll discuss in more detail on page 59. Avoid using common or boring names just because you feel overwhelmed. Instead, find ways to get inspired and enjoy this amazing opportunity to show your creative side!

2. Say Them Out Loud: Names of multiples will be said together more often than with regular siblings, so the factor of sound comes into play far more seriously now. Your twins' or triplets' names need to sound good not only standing up on their own, but with the word "and" stuck in between them, too. For example, pairings like "Pete and Tennant," "Kurt and Mark," or "Garrett, Rosalind, and Wade" don't exactly roll off the tongue. Think about any confusion that might arise. Might "Leanna and Dan" be confused for "Leanne and Anne"? Remember to invert the order of the names when you're saying them, too.

3. Honor Each Individual: Establishing a separate identity for each child is a very important priority for parents of twins and multiples, and this begins with their names. Your kids will be fighting their entire lives to prove to others that they are more than just a set of twins or triplets, and it is your responsibility to give them a leg up on that from day one. Each baby deserves a unique, thoughtful name to go through life with, and not some silly rhyme or source of embarrassment that will constantly draw attention to the fact that they once shared a womb for nine months.

Twin Trends

There are lots of ways to approach the task of naming your twins. A recent online poll revealed that 30 percent of parents of twins and other multiples chose their kids' names because they were "sound-alike, matching, or rhyming." Some 22 percent opted for names beginning with the same letter, while another 22 percent chose "completely unique and independent" names. About 8 percent based their decision on "similar meaning."

The most popular sets of names for twins will give you a clue as to what other parents in your situation were thinking when they named their kids:

BOYS
Jacob and Joshua
Matthew and Michael
Daniel and David
Isaac and Isaiah
Taylor and Tyler
Landon and Logan
Brandon and Bryan
Christian and Christopher
Andrew and Matthew
Joseph and Joshua

GIRLS
Ella and Emma
Madison and Morgan
Gabriella and Isabella
Faith and Hope
Mackenzie and Madison
Hailey and Hannah
Isabella and Sophia
Olivia and Sophia
Ava and Emma
Megan and Morgan

GIRL/BOY
Madison and Matthew
Emily and Ethan
Madison and Mason
Emma and Ethan
Natalie and Nathan

Zachery and Zoe
Samuel and Sophia
Emma and Jacob
Emma and William

What do these lists tell us? Mainly two things: That parents of twins like to name their kids using the same first or last letter (or even both), and that they generally use similar styles in naming their kids. Will you embrace the trends or go against the grain? The answer, as always, lies in your personal preferences.

Twins: What to Avoid

GENDER-BENDING BLUNDERS

Whether you're having identical or fraternal twins, their names will be among the primary ways people will come to distinguish them from one another, so gender-bending blunders must be averted at all costs. If you're having twin girls, give them names that are equally feminine. Think Isabella and Sarah, or Isabella and Sophia, instead of Isabella and Leslie, or Isabella and Blake. For boys, this is even more crucial: Choose Charles and David, instead of Charles and Sascha, or Charles and Riley. Imagine how you would feel if you were a boy named Vivian whose twin brother was named Mike, or a girl named Jesse Lee whose twin sister was named Arabelle Grace. With girl-boy twins, don't assume people will know that Morgan is your son and Dale is your daughter—stick to clearly masculine and feminine monikers for each. This isn't to say that unisex names aren't lovely; it's just that twins' names need to be not only well balanced in terms of their likeness to each other, but also able to avert any potential source of negative comparison later on in the schoolyard and further down the road.

RHYMING WITHOUT REASON

To rhyme or not to rhyme? That is the question! Once again, the rhyming debate is clearly a matter of personal preference. Simply put, some parents of twins hate it and some parents love it. In some ways, the habit of rhyming twins' names is in complete opposition to the third cardinal rule of naming multiples: honoring the individual. But names with similar sounds—say, Jenna and Barbara or Julian and Ryan—can work very well. These pairs, though ending with the same sound, are different enough from each other in terms of first letter, amount of syllables, and so forth, that they would never draw the chuckles or eye-rolling that twins named Milly and Tilly or Ryan and Bryan often do.

Too Similar, Too Separate

With twins, as with singleton siblings, one of the biggest pitfalls is choosing names that are either too similar or too separate. By naming your twins Joan and Joanne or Luke and Luca—especially if they're identical—you may be unintentionally hammering home the one point they will surely want to stress as they grow up: that they are separate and unique individuals despite the fact that they happen to have been born on the same day. On the opposite end of the spectrum, names that are too dissimilar may sound odd when said aloud together, as they most certainly will be countless times over the course of your kids' lives. A good example of this is ethnic names. When Mom and Dad come from different cultural, religious, and/or national backgrounds, it can be tempting for each to want to emphasize their distinct heritage through their kids' names. While the idea is nice, pairs like Christian and Yehuda, Svetlana and Juan, and Malik and Mary-Elizabeth are a bit jarring to most. Admittedly, some parents might feel the complete opposite—that diametrically opposed names reflect the blended beauty and diversity of their family.

Elizabeth V. and Michael A. found a harmonious solution to this issue when they had boy/girl twins recently. Elizabeth comes from a midwestern family, while Michael is of Nigerian descent. The couple chose Cecilia and Philip for first names, as they wanted traditional names that weren't overly popular, and also wanted to stay away from rhymes and identical first initials. The name Cecilia also honors a relative from Michael's family, while Philip bears his maternal grandfather's name. The twins' Nigerian heritage is expressed in their two middle names, both of which are in the language of Yoruba, Michael's ethnic group: Cecilia Abisola Taiwo (meaning, "we have birthed joy/blessing," and "first to taste the world") and Philip Oladele Kehinde (meaning, "joy/blessing has come home" and "second to taste the world"), showcasing their unique family blend.

Obvious Pairs

We urge you to think twice about naming your kids with obvious pairs that have strong associations, no matter how positive. Jack and Jill will be teased mercilessly whenever they fall down, Bob and Marley will surely grow to despise the reggae music you love so much, and Knight and Rider will never quite understand what it is their parents were trying to achieve by naming them after a fictional talking car. Sometimes, the connection between two names can be more subtle, but still worth avoiding. We suggest you do an Internet search for the names you've chosen, especially if you're not big into history, pop culture, or current events. How else would you ever have known that "Patty and Selma" are actually characters on The Simpsons, or that "Jack and Diane" is also the name of a famous rock-and-roll song? Obviously, the names you choose for your kids will not dictate their future—twins named Jack and Daniel or Tia and Maria won't necessarily grow up to be party animals, but they certainly will tire of hearing drinking jokes at the very least. Once again, it's about approaching the naming process in a considerate and thoughtful way.

PLAYING FAVORITES

Be fair and balanced when making your choices. Giving a traditional family name is fine for singletons, but think very carefully before doing this for twins. This is especially true if you plan to give your firstborn son his father's or grandfather's name, or the name of a beloved relative who has passed on. Imagine how the younger twin would feel, cheated out of the honor simply by virtue of having been born three minutes later. Nor should you give one twin a name that may have negative associations, for this will merely amplify the superiority of the other's name. As always, try to make sure you have chosen names that are well matched to each other in every regard—style, femininity or masculinity, meaning, and so on. Your kids will never know you went through the trouble of doing this, but if you don't, one or the other may resent you, and possibly even the sibling who got the "better" name.

Triplets, Quads, and Even Bigger Squads

Naming higher-order multiples is a daunting prospect, but it's also a pretty good way to prepare for the real deal when your supertwins come home! As with diaper changes and bottles, you're going to need a system. Putting some thought into how to approach naming your multiples won't be easy, but it will spare you some anxiety and hopefully allow you to come up with as many amazing names as you'll need for your amazing family.

Before you begin, keep these four points in mind:

1. *Be Patient*: Expect to be overwhelmed from time to time. With triplets, you've got at least six names to come up with (assuming you choose middle names, too), so there's a lot of work to be done. Because of this, don't worry about deciding on all the names in one sitting. This is going to take time! Plan regular "naming summits" to stay on top of things.

2. *Be Prolific*: The more darts you throw at a target, the more likely you are to hit it. Keep a list on the fridge, in the office, and in your purse so you can jot down any good ideas or names as they come to you (tear out our worksheets!). Think big and be creative. Come up with themes instead of just random names. This will not only help unify your brood, but will also act as a super source for names that work well

together. If you're having quads, for example, perhaps you could name one baby for each of his or her grandparents. Scour every source imaginable, from fiction and history to music and the natural world.

3. *Be Practical*: While you may have had your heart set on not finding out the genders, you'll probably have to give that dream up. With all the ultrasounds you'll be having between now and delivery day so your team of doctors can monitor the health of you and your babies and plan for their delivery, it's unlikely they'll be able to keep their genders a secret for long. Deciding their names in advance—instead of coming up with a slew of alternatives for every gender combination possible—makes the most sense.

4. *Be Prepared*: We don't want to cause any panic here, but you need to consider one very important fact: Higher-order multiples are almost always born prematurely, so you don't want to wait until the very last minute to decide on names.

Multiples: What to Avoid

With triplets and quads and beyond, avoid all the same things you would with twins (refer to the previous section), plus the following big no-no's:

OBVIOUS GROUPINGS. Twins named Matthew and Mark may be fine, but quads named Matthew, Mark, Luke, and John is a recipe for disaster. Apart from playground taunting, the kids will feel as if they were named as a group, and not the individuals they surely are. Themes are one thing, but employ a subtle approach. Instead of three month names—such as April, May, and June—try one month (April), a traditional flower (Lily for May), and a traditional birthstone (Pearl for June)

ALPHABET BABIES. In utero, your doctors will probably be referring to each of your babies by letter (A, B, C, D, and so on). It's the best way to keep them straight during the many ultrasound appointments and planning sessions your team of obstetricians and pediatricians will be having. Though it may seem natural, the alphabet-naming thing is pretty tired. Albert, Bob, Cameron, and David, or Alice, Betty, Cathy, and Dina, will wonder why their parents felt the need to remind them of their birth order on a daily basis, and you may unintentionally be setting up a power hierarchy among them.

SAME SOUNDS, DIFFERENT KIDS. Sean, Shand, Shea, and Shaw is overkill of the, um, highest order. Even the same sounds can cause confusion, no matter how they're spelled (Chris, Chloe, Kyle, and Kent). As a general rule, think about naming no more than two, or possibly three, of your children with the same beginning sound or ending sound. Giving your kids distinct-sounding monikers will also make it much easier for other people to learn their names.

RIDICULOUS RHYMING. While some twins may be able to pull it off, fully rhyming sets just sound silly on triplets and quads. Remember Donald Duck's nephews Huey, Dewey, and Louie? They may have been cute, but what works for ducklings is decidedly silly for human babies, which is why rhyming higher-order multiples is an absolute no-no. Tempted? Go for an off-rhyme instead of a full rhyme: If you love the "e" sound at the end of names, for example, triplets called Stacy, Wendy, and Lucy works much better than Stacy, Tracy, and Macy. Instead of Hayden, Jayden, and Brayden, think Hayden, Jay, and Brady.

Chapter 6

✖ Playing to Win: ✖ Name Games, Family Feuds, and Last-Minute Mayhem

For a lucky few, picking a name for Baby is a three-and-a-half-minute process. For most of us, though, this decision is among the most gut-wrenching experiences of our lives. The choices are endless, after all, and, as we've mentioned, there are so many factors to consider—spelling, meaning, family heritage, associations, syllables, siblings ... the list goes on and on. Hopefully, you've at least narrowed it down to a fabulous few by now. But what if you can't seem to make the final cut? What if you're mired in indecision, family squabbling, or denial? For those of you out there who've already spent countless hours poring over the pages of this book, picked the brains of friends and loved ones, and Googled every name from Aadi to Zygmunt and still haven't settled on anything, this chapter's for you!

A famous writer once said, "You can't wait for inspiration. You have to go after it with a club." That's why we've included plenty of games here, and even a few unconventional methods of naming your little one. Keep your sense of humor close—or at the very least, keep an open mind—because negotiating the minefield of eleventh-hour naming, bickering with your beloved, and crippling self-doubt require some creative maneuvering. But by the time we're done here, all your baby-naming stress will have melted away and you'll be well on your way to signing that birth certificate with bravado.

FAMILY FEUDS

We touched on family matters briefly in Chapter 2, but perhaps your relative conundrum just won't end. It's no wonder—the emotional aspects of naming your child are intense. Both you and your spouse are each bringing your individual preferences, personalities, and histories to the table—but always keep in mind that you're setting a precedent here. Handling the conflict in a mature and productive fashion is a great way to lay the groundwork for the much tougher parenting disputes that are sure to rear their ugly heads in years to come.

This isn't always easy. From how you feel about your own name to the long-standing family traditions you're expected to uphold, there's plenty of fodder for fighting. Add to that an opinionated in-law or two and things can get more than a little heated. Just remember that you love each other and you love the baby you've created together, so don't let all the baggage you're carrying get in the way of a civilized conversation.

Tough Love: Solving Spousal Squabbles

Settling any conflicts as early as possible is the key to enjoying your baby-naming experience, lest they drag out for forty long weeks and put a damper on your pregnancy. To this end, we've come up with eight rules to follow in order to keep things friendly while coming to a decision:

1. **Stay Cool**: Be sensitive and flexible from the start, or your discussions could degrade into full-blown arguments from Name One. When you feel the tension mounting, remember that everything's going to work out just fine. No kid ever went off to college without a name, and as far as we know, no pregnant woman ever divorced her husband citing "baby-naming" among their irreconcilable differences.

2. **Sleep on It**: Instead of instantly saying no to a name you don't like, agree to think about it if it's one your significant other is truly fond of. And don't just say you will, actually do it. Who knows? After conducting some research and rolling it around on your tongue for a few days, you may actually come to love Ramona, the name you so despised at first.

3. **No Name Calling**: Try not to insult the names on your spouse's list. A little humorous analysis here or there is fine, but you'll want to avoid such statements as "Amber is a whore's name," or "Chad is so snobby it makes me want to puke." Instead, use the old "stroke and slap" technique by prefacing your criticism with a compliment, as in: "Regina really is a beautiful name and I especially like that it means 'queen' in Latin, but it does sound like 'vagina,' and you know how cruel kids can be…"

4. **Remember That You Both Have a Say**: You may resent that while you've been putting your heart and soul into the process—poring over books, surfing the Internet for hours on end, researching your family tree, and

analyzing your own dreams—your significant other has been watching football. When he pulls stupid names out of the ether at halftime and shouts them out between mouthfuls of Doritos, it's tempting to go into constant veto mode. Unfortunately, you can't. You both have an equal say no matter what. Nor may you argue that you get extra points for carrying and/or delivering the child. It's not fair, but it's only fair.

5. **Don't Push Too Hard**: Don't get your maternity thong in a twist if your partner doesn't instantly love your top choice. Applying a bit of pressure is fine—parents often end up agreeing on a name one or the other wasn't crazy about at first—but you also need to know when to throw in the towel if you're simply not getting anywhere. If someone really, truly, deeply doesn't like a name, strike it off the list and then forget about it. Rehashing old choices is like crying over spilled breast milk.

6. **Offer Thoughtful Alternatives**: Not getting anywhere? Retreat to your separate corners and start over. Don't be random—search for new names you think your partner might like based on the ones he's already suggested. For example, alternatives to Regina might be similar-sounding three-syllable options that begin with the letter "r" (e.g., Rebecca, Riana, Ramona, Roberta), or names that share the same meaning (Darice, Candace, Raina, or even Queenie).

7. **Keep It Private**: Never enlist outsiders in your argument. Going behind his back and telling his mother that he seriously wants to name her unborn granddaughter Babe Ruth will not only cause a fight between him and her, but sends the following message loud and clear: "I'm willing to lie, cheat, and steal my way to victory, and I don't care if I undermine you in the process."

8. **Come Up with Creative Concessions**: Maybe the name you're only lukewarm about is the one your partner has his heart set on. Might it work as a middle name instead? Or maybe you get to pick this kid's name, but your spouse will have the honor for Baby Two. What may sound silly to some works perfectly well in other families. Figure out a way to make everyone happy.

"Nobody Asked You": Fighting with Friends and Family

In Chapter 2, How to Choose: Finding the Right Name for Baby, we suggested that you keep your names a surprise. This is admittedly easier said than done. In your enthusiasm for the great name you chose, you might have innocently shared it with friends and loved ones, hoping they'd be as delighted as the two of you are. Instead, one of them, some of them, or even all of them hate it. You're crushed and confused. Should you go back to the drawing board? Ignore them all? What's the right thing to do?

A combination of both is a prudent approach. To help you get past all this unpleasantness, here's a three-step process to evaluating the merits of outside opinions:

1. **Consider the Source:** If the person telling you you've made a bad choice was recently released from a mental institution, is too old to remember his or her own name, or generally likes to rain on your parade, ignore the opinion. If, however, it's coming from someone whose opinion you usually value, his or her arguments may be worth a second thought.

2. **Consider the Criticism:** It's hard not to be hurt by someone's criticism, and your knee-jerk reaction might be to simply ignore it completely. But don't throw the baby name out with the bath water—there may be some merit to the unwelcome comments, even if you take issue with their source. If, on the other hand, some blowhard is just trying to bully you due to his or her personal and/or baseless dislike of a name, forget about it and move on.

3. **Consider a Change:** There's no shame in changing your mind. If somebody has made a valid criticism of your chosen name, don't be stubborn just to make a point, because your kid will be the one who pays for any senseless pride on your part. For example, no amount of denial will change the fact that Lyle was the name of your grandmother's first husband—a convicted bigamist who took all her money and ran—even if it all happened before you were born and nobody ever bothered to tell you about him before now.

Phew! That was the hard part. Now, if you're sure you want to proceed with the name you've chosen, be firm in your resolve and stand together as one. The only way to do this is by deflecting any further criticism by completely refusing to discuss it. Ever. All you need from now on is one great line that firmly but politely gets your point across. Try something like: "I'm sorry you're disappointed, but we've found the right name for us," or "Please respect our wishes on this one; we're confident we've made the right choice." After hearing that twenty or thirty times, most naysayers will come to realize that ship has sailed and will eventually back off. It's not being rude; it's protecting yourselves, respecting your unborn child, and preventing senseless arguments.

Of course, some back-seat namers are more stubborn than others. When Shelby and Jon J. named their son Dakota instead of Dennis after Jon's late father, Jon's mother was heartbroken. She insisted that using the first initial simply wasn't good enough, and proclaimed she'd call her grandson Dennis no matter what. Shelby and Jon explained their feelings clearly and stuck to their guns, despite some serious manipulation, guilt, and threats from Grandma. She actually stayed true to her word for the first few weeks after little Dakota was born, prompting serious aggravation in his parents—and, thankfully, pressure from other family members who told her they were appalled by her childish behavior. Eventually, Grandma relented, even apologized, though to this day Shelby and Jon have a feeling she still calls their son Dennis when she comes over to baby-sit!

THE NAME GAMES

Deciding what to call your little bundle of joy should be enjoyable, not stressful, so we've compiled a few of our favorite ways to put the fun back in the naming process. Some of these diversions are perfect for baby showers—why struggle to come up with a name on your own when you can have others do the work for you?—while others are simply a good excuse for you and your partner to spend a few hours talking about the topic. Inspiration often comes from the unlikeliest sources, so even if you don't actually use any of the names these games will generate, it sure will be interesting to see where the fun takes you.

Broken Baby-Name Telephone

You've been toiling over this hot baby-name book for nine long months and all you've come up with is Altheodora Patrice. You like it, but you don't love it, and your significant other isn't convinced it's exactly quite right. Here's an idea: Invite a few couples over for a round of Baby-Name Broken Telephone. Whisper the name in your neighbor's ear and by the time it makes its way around the table and back to you, Altheodora Patrice will have blossomed into Elora Grace! Try it with all the names on your short list, and even with a few you don't like—you never know what a few tipsy pals with poor hearing can do to transform those less-than-stellar options into the right choice you've been searching for.

Flip a Coin, Save Your Marriage

Only for the very brave, this classic method of determining a winner can be used as a tiebreaker for those moms- and dads-to-be who have come to an absolute impasse over two names. While flipping a coin is always preferable to a duel or a divorce, be warned: It's not for the irresolute or the faint-of-heart. There's no point in playing if you're not going to live with the results—which also means that both choices must be a name you can live with.

Baby-Name Scrabble

Fix yourself a nice, fat milkshake and pour your significant other a big glass of wine. Dust off the old Scrabble board and get ready for some literary hi-jinks. The only rule in Baby Name Scrabble is to throw out the dictionary, because this is a proper-names-only affair. Start with plain old Jen, use the "J" to create Julie, add a "TTE" to the end and you've got Juliette! You can even keep score, if you like, though the real victor will be the one who comes up with the winning name for Baby, not the one who slaps "Quinzey" down on a triple-word-score square.

The Best Baby-Name Shower Games

Showers for first-time moms are practically a right of passage. Sure, you'll score lots of great gifts and have some good clean fun, but what if you could also take home the perfect name for Baby along with all the onesies and bibs? If you trust a bunch of elderly aunts to name your little one, by all means, organize a few rounds of naming nonsense. (You never know—one of them may actually come up with something you like!) Here are our four faves:

1. **Baby-Name Boggle**: See how many names the guests can come up with in five minutes by rearranging just the letters from the parents' first, middle, and last names.
2. **Baby-Name Geography**: The last letter in Mom's name becomes the first letter in a suggestion for Baby's name—so that's Jane, to Ellen, to Nancy, to Yvonne, to Elizabeth, to Hannah, and so on. Go around the room (no repeats!) until someone comes up with one you like. Oh, and bring a sleeping bag, because its going to take a while!
3. **Popularity Contest**: Everyone writes down their favorite girl and boy names, the mom-to-be narrows the list down to three semifinalists, and then shower guests vote on the winner.
4. **Pick a Letter**: If Mom has a letter (or two) in mind that she'd like Baby's name to start with, guests can write down as many names as they can think of beginning with that letter. She who comes up with the most names wins a prize, of course, but we challenge your group to come up with even a single name not included in our alphabetical name index beginning on page 152!

LAST-MINUTE MAYHEM

So much can happen in the wacky world of baby-naming. Mother Nature, in her infinite humor, sometimes throws expectant parents a surprise—say the name you picked suddenly seems ill-suited, or it turns out you should have been shopping for blue instead of pink. The antidote? As soon as that plus sign shows up on the home pregnancy test, you should make like a Boy Scout and be prepared. If, for example, you choose not to find out the sex of the baby, but have the perfect girl's name picked out, don't just cross your fingers and hope for the best. Murphy's Law dictates that you will have a son, so don't make the mistake of neglecting boys' names until the last minute. But what if you've done exactly that? Or what if Baby decides to make her grand entrance a month early? Maybe you didn't know you were pregnant until your water broke, and your frazzled spouse just bought this book in the hospital gift shop (yes, it happens!). Even if you're reading this in between contractions, fear not—we've got you covered.

"Is He a Jake or a John?"

There are a stalwart few who believe choosing a child's name in advance is an exercise in futility. "How can you name a kid without seeing her face?" they ask. Some parents-to-be come prepared with three or four names picked out and then decide once Baby's born. But no amount of planning can prevent a last-minute change of heart. What do you do when that perfect name you chose months ago flies right out the window? Mitch and Tammy S. knew from week twenty that they were expecting a baby boy, and promptly picked out a name they'd always loved—Noah. They referred to the little one as Noah throughout the pregnancy, even painting the letters of his name on the walls of the nursery. But right after "Noah" was born, Tammy and Mitch looked at him, then at each other, and shook their heads. "He's more of a Justin," they agreed in the delivery room, remembering the runner-up they'd thrown out so many weeks ago. A quick call to Grandpa took care of the "Noah" over the crib, and little Justin will never be the wiser. More important, Mom and Dad had the guts to trust their instincts and change their minds. The lesson here? Be flexible, listen to your hearts, and do what makes you both happy.

A Boy Named Sue

The studies prove it: A pregnant woman's instinct in guessing the gender of her child is absolutely ... useless. If you want to know for sure, you're going to have to get genetic testing. Most people who want to know Baby's gender—and that's roughly half of you—are content with the nearly-always-right results of the less invasive ultrasound technique. But "nearly always right" isn't quiet the same as "always right," and that's why you need to have a back-up plan.

Take the case of first-time parents-to-be Danna and Harold S. Although they were elated to learn that their "little man" looked great at their twenty-two-week ultrasound appointment, Danna and Harold were also understandably miffed, since they'd explicitly requested not to be told the sex of the baby. They'd read online somewhere that while it's fairly common to mistake girl parts for boy parts on ultrasounds, the reverse was practically unheard of. Months of frenzied shopping ensued—blue blankies, cowboy crib bedding, the whole nine yards—as well as plenty of naming discussions. When "Max" was born, everyone was quite amused by the fact that he was actually a bouncing baby girl. Good thing Molly looks precious in blue, but she spent the first three days of her life without a name because her unprepared parents had only chosen boy names, never imagining that modern technology occasionally gets it wrong!

Labor Pains

It's every nervous namer's worst nightmare: You're six centimeters dilated, your partner is hyperventilating, and you still haven't made a decision. While labor is obviously not the ideal time to be making important decisions, you're far beyond the luxury of a leisurely naming experience now. It's time to pull yourself up by the bootiestraps and choose!

Still not able to commit to one of your finalists? Looking for a great way to pass the time, release the tension, and take your mind off the contractions? Kill all those birds with one stone by playing a little game called Bedpan Baby-Namer. Tear out the worksheets in the back of this book, scribble down your finalists onto the lines, tear them into scraps, toss the papers into a bedpan, and have the doctor pick—it'll make a truly great dinner-party story for the rest of your lives.

If you don't even have a short list ... well, quite frankly, you should be ashamed of yourselves. But you also need some inspiration fast, so without further ado, here are some last-minute sources of inspiration.

OUR TOP 5 EXTREMELY LAST-MINUTE SOURCES OF BABY-NAME INSPIRATION

1. Join the Donors' List: Have your partner roam the wards, halls, and wings and mark down the names of various hospital benefactors commemorated by those ubiquitous bronze plaques.

2. Read Every Name Tag: The revolving door of interns, nurses, doctors, and labor support staff is bound to provide some inspiration, so check all IDs for ideas.

3. Meditate on It: Breathe in, breathe out. Breathe in, breathe out. Clear your mind, concentrate on nothing, and see what pops into your head.

4. Steal a Name: Mosey on down to the newborn nursery if you can (or send your partner on a reconnaissance mission) and see what the other cool parents named their kids. Interview the nurses, too—they'll be delighted to share their thoughts on naming, and nobody's seen more than they have.

5. Start a Contest: Publicly admit your folly and tell anyone and everyone who'll listen that you need a name for Baby ASAP! Post a sheet on the door of your room, attach a pen with a string, and offer a prize—dinner for two, an invitation to the bris, your eternal gratitude—whatever seems right.

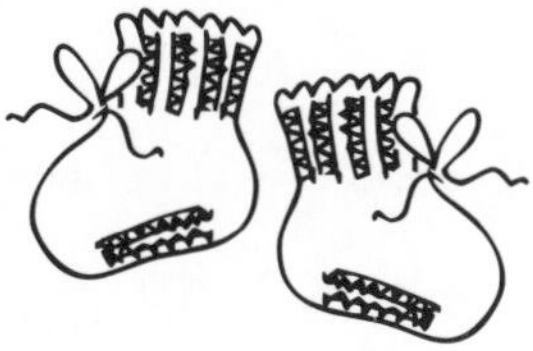

282 Fantastic Lists

African-American Names

GIRLS	BOYS
Cherise	Antwon
Imani	Denzel
Jada	Gervaise
Jayla	Imari
Kalinda	Jamar
Keisha	Juwan
Lateisha	Malik
Nakari	Nile
Raisha	Rashaun
Zeleka	Tariq

Muslim/Arabic Names

GIRLS	BOYS
Aisha	Akbar
Fatima	Aziz
Iamar	Farid
Jamila	Hanif
Nabila	Jafar
Oma	Kadar
Shadiya	Karim
Tamasha	Mehmet
Yamina	Sadik
Zahira	Tahir

Jewish Names

GIRLS	BOYS
Adaya	Amit
Dorit	Asael
Keturah	Chaim
Lilit	Itzak
Livya	Maluch
Mahalah	Noam
Miryam	Oran
Nissa	Raviv
Rivka	Talmai
Yafa	Yosha

Irish Names

GIRLS	BOYS
Caoimhe	Aidan
Ciara	Colin
Fiona	Conor
Moira	Kyan
Niamh	Murray
Shannon	Quinn
Siobhan	Teagan
Aisling	Sean
Aoife	Senan
Roisin	Tristan

Welsh Names

GIRLS	BOYS
Bryn	Alisdair
Carys	Calum
Catrin	Dafydd
Guinevere	Euam
Meredith	Gareth
Rhonwen	Hamish
Rhiannon	Lauchlan
Freya	Maddock
Phoebe	Quinn
Tam	Rhys

Native American Tribal Names

Cheyenne
Dakota
Apache
Navajo
Seminole
Comanche
Seneca
Shawnee
Shoshone
Cherokee

British Names

GIRLS	BOYS
Sienna	Ian
Nicola	Nigel
Poppy	Clive
Maisie	Winston
Pippa	Percy
Tamsin	Trevor
Gemma	Alastair
Portia	Hewitt
Saffron	Leland
Bridget	Cedric

Spanish Names

GIRLS	BOYS
Ana	Jesus
Isabela	Emilio
Bianca	Cristian
Maribel	Alonzo
Alessandra	Carlos
Diana	Felipe
Eva	Miguel
Valeria	Diego
Elena	Tomas
Camila	Alejandro

Scottish Names

GIRLS	BOYS
Amie	Jack
Abbie	Lewis
Isla	Callum
Eva	Ryan
Keira	Jamie
Freya	Liam
Charlotte	Kieran
Millie	Fraser
Ruby	Ewan
Iona	Finn

French Names

GIRLS	BOYS
Dominique	Marc
Josie	Yves
Helene	Michele
Amelie	Pierre
Lise	Jean
Genevieve	Luc
Simone	Tomas
Yvonne	Jacques
Colette	Gaston
Gabrielle	Didier

Scandinavian Names

GIRLS	BOYS
Marta	Anders
Annika	Roald
Else	Kristoffer
Elin	Johan
Malena	Sven
Amma	Henrik
Sonja	Mikkel
Linnea	Elias
Thea	Emil
Rakel	Jonas

German Names

GIRLS	BOYS
Käthe	Ranier
Minna	Dieter
Franka	Hans
Gertraud	Josef
Brigitte	Heinrich
Bianca	Georg
Heidi	Arno
Natja	Caspar
Katja	Stefan
Meike	Reinhold

Japanese Names

GIRLS	BOYS
Hina	Haruto
Nanami	Takahiro
Aoi	Daiki
Yui	Daisuke
Misaki	Kaito
Sakura	Ren
Miyu	Hayato
Kaeda	Shouta
Riko	Tatsuya
Ami	Yuuto

Italian Names

GIRLS	BOYS
Lucia	Rocco
Amalia	Raoul
Rosaria	Giorgio
Violetta	Giovanni
Flavia	Vito
Alessia	Giuseppe
Liliana	Lorenzo
Nicoletta	Carlo
Emiliana	Mario
Arianna	Matteo

Russian Names

GIRLS	BOYS
Nina	Ivan
Olga	Vladimir
Tatiana	Vadim
Alexandra	Yuri
Ekaterina	Nikita
Anastasia	Alexei
Nadia	Nikolai
Raisa	Mikhail
Natasha	Sergei
Daria	Fyodor

Greek Names

GIRLS	BOYS
Koren	Matthias
Anatola	Alexandros
Nerissa	Stavros
Delia	Constantine
Phoebe	Leander
Xanthe	Gregorios
Penelope	Loukas
Calista	Ionnes
Lydia	Andreas
Cassia	Claudios

Dutch Names

GIRLS	BOYS
Sofie	Caspar
Katryn	Pieter
Femke	Willem
Elisabeth	Anton
Beatrix	Klaas
Saskia	Joren
Gerda	Bram
Lotte	Otto
Romy	Hendrik
Marieke	Jacob

The Classics

GIRLS	BOYS
Elizabeth	Michael
Mary	James
Sarah	Matthew
Emily	Robert
Jane	David
Katherine	John
Margaret	Jacob
Eleanor	Nicholas
Anne	William
Grace	Andrew

Uniquely Unisex

Aidan	Alex
Ashton	August
Bailey	Blaine
Blake	Cameron
Christian	Dakota
Devin	Drew
Dylan	Evan
Harley	Hayden
Jaden	Jamie
Jordan	Kennedy
Lane	Logan
Mason	Morgan
Paris	Payton
Presley	Regan
Riley	Rory
Rowan	Sage
Sky	Skyler
Tyler	Peyton

Super Surnames

Sawyer	Taylor
Hunter	Hadley
Ashley	Bailey
Jefferson	Luther
Archer	Blaine
Bryce	Cole
Cortland	Dalton
Dexter	Drake
Everett	Fletcher
Gaige	Grant
Harley	Jarvis
Kelsey	Lynden
McKenzie	Otis
Reese	Tanner
Wade	Zaile

Most Popular Names: 1920s

GIRLS	BOYS
Mary	Robert
Dorothy	John
Helen	James
Betty	William
Margaret	Charles
Ruth	George
Virginia	Joseph
Doris	Richard
Mildred	Edward
Frances	Donald

Most Popular Names: 1930s

GIRLS	BOYS
Mary	Robert
Betty	James
Barbara	John
Shirley	William
Patricia	Richard
Dorothy	Charles
Joan	Donald

Margaret	George
Nancy	Thomas
Helen	Joseph

Most Popular Names: 1940s

GIRLS	BOYS
Mary	James
Linda	Robert
Barbara	John
Patricia	William
Carol	Richard
Sandra	David
Nancy	Charles
Sharon	Thomas
Judith	Michael
Susan	Ronald

Most Popular Names: 1950s

GIRLS	BOYS
Mary	James
Linda	Michael
Patricia	Robert
Susan	John
Deborah	David
Barbara	William
Debra	Richard
Karen	Thomas
Nancy	Mark
Donna	Charles

Most Popular Names: 1960s

GIRLS	BOYS
Lisa	Michael
Mary	David
Susan	John
Karen	James
Kimberly	Robert
Patricia	Mark
Linda	William
Donna	Richard
Michelle	Thomas
Cynthia	Jeffrey

Most Popular Names: 1970s

GIRLS	BOYS
Jennifer	Michael
Amy	Christopher
Melissa	Jason
Michelle	David
Kimberly	James
Lisa	John
Angela	Robert
Heather	Brian
Stephanie	William
Nicole	Matthew

Most Popular Names: 1980s

GIRLS	BOYS
Jessica	Michael
Jennifer	Christopher
Amanda	Matthew
Ashley	Joshua
Sarah	David
Stephanie	James
Melissa	Daniel
Nicole	Robert
Elizabeth	John
Heather	Joseph

Most Popular Names: 1990s

GIRLS	BOYS
Jessica	Michael
Ashley	Christopher
Emily	Matthew
Samantha	Joshua
Sarah	Jacob
Amanda	Nicholas
Brittany	Andrew
Elizabeth	Daniel
Taylor	Tyler
Megan	Joseph

Most Popular Names: 2000

GIRLS	BOYS
Emily	Jacob
Hannah	Michael
Madison	Matthew
Ashley	Joshua
Sarah	Christopher
Alexis	Nicholas
Samantha	Andrew
Jessica	Joseph
Taylor	Daniel
Elizabeth	Tyler

Most Popular Names: 2001

GIRLS	BOYS
Emily	Jacob
Madison	Michael
Hannah	Matthew
Ashley	Joshua
Alexis	Christopher
Sarah	Nicholas
Samantha	Andrew
Abigail	Joseph
Elizabeth	Daniel
Olivia	William

Most Popular Names: 2002

GIRLS	BOYS
Emily	Jacob
Madison	Michael
Hannah	Joshua
Emma	Matthew
Alexis	Ethan
Ashley	Andrew
Abigail	Joseph
Sarah	Christopher
Samantha	Nicholas
Olivia	Daniel

Most Popular Names: 2003

GIRLS	BOYS
Emily	Jacob
Emma	Michael
Madison	Joshua
Hannah	Matthew
Olivia	Andrew
Abigail	Ethan
Alexis	Joseph
Ashley	Daniel
Elizabeth	Christopher
Samantha	Anthony

Most Popular Names: 2004

GIRLS	BOYS
Emily	Jacob
Emma	Michael
Madison	Joshua
Olivia	Matthew
Hannah	Ethan
Abigail	Andrew
Isabella	Daniel
Ashley	William
Samantha	Joseph
Elizabeth	Christopher

Most Popular Names: 2005

GIRLS	BOYS
Emily	Jacob
Emma	Michael
Madison	Joshua
Abigail	Matthew
Olivia	Ethan
Isabella	Andrew
Hannah	Daniel
Samantha	Anthony
Ava	Christopher
Ashley	Joseph

Most Popular Names: 2006

GIRLS	BOYS
Emily	Jacob
Emma	Michael
Madison	Joshua
Isabella	Ethan
Ava	Matthew
Abigail	Daniel
Olivia	Christopher
Hannah	Andrew
Sophia	Anthony
Samantha	William

Most Popular Names: 2007

GIRLS	BOYS
Emily	Jacob
Isabella	Michael
Emma	Ethan
Ava	Joshua
Madison	Daniel
Sophia	Christopher
Olivia	Anthony
Abigail	William
Hannah	Matthew
Elizabeth	Andrew

Most Popular Names: 2008

GIRLS	BOYS
Emma	Jacob
Isabella	Michael
Emily	Ethan
Madison	Joshua
Ava	Daniel
Olivia	Alexander
Sophia	Anthony
Abigail	William
Elizabeth	Christopher
Chloe	Matthew

SEE WHAT'S HOT IN YOUR CORNER OF THE WORLD

Alabama

GIRLS	BOYS
Emma	William
Madison	James
Emily	Christopher
Hannah	John
Elizabeth	Jacob
Ava	Joshua
Addison	Jackson
Anna	Michael
Olivia	Ethan
Abigail	Noah
Chloe	Caleb
Ella	Cameron
Sarah	Jayden
Isabella	David
Mary	Samuel

Alaska

GIRLS	BOYS
Isabella	Aiden
Madison	Logan
Ava	Alexander
Abigail	Ethan
Emily	Jacob
Emma	William
Sophia	Michael
Alyssa	Tyler
Hannah	Noah
Natalie	James
Lillian	Daniel
Hailey	Joseph
Lily	Samuel
Elizabeth	Dylan
Grace	Elijah

Arizona

GIRLS	BOYS
Isabella	Angel
Emily	Jose
Mia	Daniel
Sophia	Anthony
Ashley	Jacob
Emma	David
Madison	Luis
Ava	Ethan
Samantha	Jesus
Elizabeth	Michael
Abigail	Joshua
Natalie	Christopher
Alyssa	Alexander
Olivia	Andrew
Alexis	Gabriel

Arkansas

GIRLS	BOYS
Madison	William
Emma	Jacob
Emily	Ethan
Addison	Jackson
Olivia	Christopher
Abigail	James
Hannah	Logan
Chloe	Caleb
Ava	Landon
Alexis	John
Isabella	Joshua
Alyssa	Michael
Anna	Hunter
Elizabeth	Hayden
Taylor	Aiden

California

GIRLS	BOYS
Emily	Daniel
Isabella	Anthony
Sophia	Angel

Ashley	Jacob
Samantha	David
Mia	Andrew
Natalie	Christopher
Emma	Joshua
Alyssa	Jose
Jocelyn	Diego
Elizabeth	Alexander
Ava	Michael
Abigail	Matthew
Kimberly	Ethan
Madison	Jonathan

Colorado

GIRLS	BOYS
Isabella	Jacob
Sophia	Daniel
Emma	Ethan
Olivia	Alexander
Abigail	Joshua
Addison	Noah
Emily	Joseph
Madison	Benjamin
Ava	Anthony
Hannah	Logan
Elizabeth	Andrew
Samantha	Gabriel
Ella	Michael
Ashley	William
Grace	Matthew

Connecticut

GIRLS	BOYS
Isabella	Michael
Olivia	Ryan
Ava	Andrew
Emma	Joseph
Emily	Anthony
Sophia	Alexander
Abigail	William
Madison	Nicholas
Julia	Christopher
Grace	Jacob

Samantha	Daniel
Hannah	Joshua
Elizabeth	Jayden
Sarah	Jack
Mia	John

Delaware

GIRLS	BOYS
Sophia	Michael
Ava	Ryan
Emily	Alexander
Madison	Christopher
Abigail	John
Isabella	Joshua
Emma	Anthony
Alyssa	Jacob
Olivia	Matthew
Hannah	William
Ashley	Nicholas
Addison	Ethan
Savannah	Jayden
Brianna	James
Ella	Joseph

District of Columbia

GIRLS	BOYS
Ashley	William
Sophia	John
Katherine	Christopher
Elizabeth	Michael
Caroline	Anthony
Kayla	Alexander
Madison	Daniel
Olivia	Kevin
Isabella	Andrew
Abigail	Noah
Zoe	Samuel
Anna	James
Emily	Jonathan
Jennifer	David
Hannah	Joshua

Florida

GIRLS	BOYS
Isabella	Anthony
Sophia	Michael
Emily	Christopher
Madison	Joshua
Ava	Daniel
Emma	Jayden
Mia	Jacob
Olivia	Alexander
Abigail	David
Ashley	Matthew
Brianna	Ethan
Samantha	Christian
Hannah	Gabriel
Alyssa	Nicholas
Elizabeth	Jonathan

Georgia

GIRLS	BOYS
Madison	William
Emily	Joshua
Emma	Christopher
Ava	Jacob
Abigail	Michael
Hannah	James
Elizabeth	Ethan
Isabella	Jayden
Olivia	John
Addison	Christian
Sophia	Andrew
Sarah	David
Anna	Daniel
Ashley	Jackson
Alyssa	Matthew

Hawaii

GIRLS	BOYS
Sophia	Noah
Ava	Ethan
Chloe	Joshua

Isabella	Isaiah
Emma	Elijah
Madison	Logan
Mia	Dylan
Maya	Jacob
Hailey	Jayden
Emily	Daniel
Olivia	Caleb
Sarah	Matthew
Kiana	Tyler
Alyssa	Ezekiel
Kayla	Mason

Idaho

GIRLS	BOYS
Emma	Jacob
Emily	Ethan
Olivia	Logan
Hannah	Isaac
Abigail	Michael
Addison	Joshua
Elizabeth	Daniel
Ava	Samuel
Hailey	Gabriel
Madison	Tyler
Taylor	Gavin
Brooklyn	William
Alexis	Noah
Grace	Aiden
Sophia	Jackson

Illinois

GIRLS	BOYS
Isabella	Daniel
Olivia	Anthony
Emily	Jacob
Ava	Alexander
Sophia	Michael
Emma	Joshua
Abigail	Matthew
Madison	William
Elizabeth	Andrew

Mia	Ethan
Addison	Christopher
Grace	Joseph
Hannah	David
Samantha	Ryan
Ashley	Nathan

Indiana

GIRLS	BOYS
Emma	Jacob
Ava	Ethan
Olivia	Noah
Madison	Logan
Addison	Andrew
Abigail	Elijah
Emily	Aiden
Isabella	Jackson
Hannah	Alexander
Elizabeth	Michael
Sophia	Gavin
Lillian	William
Chloe	Joseph
Alexis	Tyler
Grace	Joshua

Iowa

GIRLS	BOYS
Ava	Ethan
Emma	Jacob
Addison	Logan
Olivia	Noah
Grace	Jackson
Ella	Gavin
Abigail	Carter
Sophia	William
Madison	Alexander
Emily	Benjamin
Hannah	Owen
Elizabeth	Aiden
Isabella	Andrew
Chloe	Landon
Alexis	Mason

Kansas

GIRLS	BOYS
Addison	Ethan
Emma	Jacob
Ava	Jackson
Madison	Alexander
Emily	Noah
Abigail	Logan
Elizabeth	William
Olivia	Samuel
Isabella	Andrew
Sophia	Christopher
Hannah	Michael
Alexis	Tyler
Ella	Gavin
Samantha	Joshua
Grace	Daniel

Kentucky

GIRLS	BOYS
Madison	Jacob
Emma	William
Emily	Ethan
Addison	James
Olivia	Logan
Abigail	Noah
Hannah	Joshua
Ava	Michael
Isabella	Christopher
Alexis	Landon
Alyssa	Elijah
Chloe	Matthew
Elizabeth	Joseph
Kaylee	Brayden
Brooklyn	Jackson

Louisiana

GIRLS	BOYS
Madison	Jacob
Ava	Ethan
Emma	Joshua

Isabella	Michael
Olivia	Christopher
Emily	Noah
Addison	Landon
Abigail	Jayden
Alyssa	Joseph
Hannah	William
Chloe	John
Gabrielle	James
Sophia	Christian
Anna	Aiden
Elizabeth	Tyler

Maine

GIRLS	BOYS
Madison	Ethan
Abigail	Jacob
Olivia	Noah
Emma	William
Ava	Logan
Hannah	Benjamin
Emily	Alexander
Isabella	Connor
Ella	William
Grace	Joshua
Sophia	Samuel
Alexis	Zachary
Elizabeth	Owen
Lily	Gavin
Addison	Hunter

Maryland

GIRLS	BOYS
Madison	Michael
Emily	Christopher
Ava	Joshua
Olivia	Jacob
Abigail	William
Sophia	Ethan
Emma	Ryan
Isabella	Matthew
Hannah	Anthony

Grace	Alexander
Kayla	David
Elizabeth	James
Taylor	Daniel
Sarah	Andrew
Alyssa	Nicholas

Massachusetts

GIRLS	BOYS
Ava	Matthew
Isabella	Michael
Sophia	Ryan
Olivia	William
Emma	Jacob
Emily	Nicholas
Abigail	Anthony
Madison	Daniel
Ella	Alexander
Hannah	Andrew
Grace	John
Julia	Jack
Sarah	Joseph
Mia	Benjamin
Elizabeth	Joshua

Michigan

GIRLS	BOYS
Ava	Jacob
Madison	Ethan
Emma	Michael
Olivia	Logan
Isabella	Noah
Addison	Andrew
Sophia	Alexander
Emily	Tyler
Abigail	Joseph
Grace	Joshua
Hannah	Aiden
Alyssa	Matthew
Elizabeth	William
Ella	Nathan
Alexis	Jack

Minnesota

GIRLS	BOYS
Ava	Jacob
Olivia	Ethan
Emma	Logan
Addison	Jack
Sophia	Samuel
Grace	Alexander
Abigail	Benjamin
Ella	Gavin
Isabella	Noah
Emily	Andrew
Hannah	William
Elizabeth	Joseph
Madison	Mason
Anna	Jackson
Samantha	Isaac

Mississippi

GIRLS	BOYS
Madison	William
Emma	James
Chloe	Christopher
Hannah	John
Addison	Joshua
Anna	Ethan
Olivia	Jacob
Emily	Michael
Elizabeth	Jayden
Ava	Jordan
Alexis	Landon
Abigail	Tyler
Makayla	Cameron
Sarah	Caleb
Alyssa	Joseph

Missouri

GIRLS	BOYS
Emma	Jacob
Madison	Ethan
Ava	Logan

Addison	Andrew
Olivia	Noah
Sophia	William
Abigail	Michael
Emily	Jackson
Isabella	Mason
Hannah	Tyler
Alyssa	James
Elizabeth	Joseph
Chloe	Gavin
Ella	Landon
Alexis	Alexander

Montana

GIRLS	BOYS
Emma	Ethan
Madison	Logan
Olivia	Jacob
Addison	Noah
Emily	Mason
Ava	William
Isabella	Samuel
Abigail	Tyler
Alexis	Andrew
Chloe	Isaac
Sophia	Wyatt
Elizabeth	Austin
Hannah	Michael
Taylor	Ryan
Hailey	Aiden

Nebraska

GIRLS	BOYS
Addison	Jacob
Emma	Alexander
Ava	Jackson
Elizabeth	William
Emily	Ethan
Olivia	Noah
Grace	Andrew
Madison	Logan
Sophia	Gavin

Isabella	Michael
Ella	Owen
Hannah	Carter
Chloe	Samuel
Natalie	Joseph
Abigail	Landon

Nevada

GIRLS	BOYS
Emily	Anthony
Sophia	Angel
Isabella	Christopher
Madison	Daniel
Ava	Jacob
Emma	Alexander
Mia	David
Ashley	Michael
Samantha	Joshua
Abigail	Jose
Elizabeth	Andrew
Olivia	Ethan
Alyssa	Joseph
Alexis	Brandon
Hannah	Christian

New Hampshire

GIRLS	BOYS
Olivia	Jacob
Abigail	Logan
Ava	Ryan
Emma	Connor
Madison	Ethan
Sophia	Andrew
Isabella	Owen
Emily	Benjamin
Hannah	Alexander
Elizabeth	Matthew
Ella	William
Grace	Jack
Alexis	Noah
Chloe	Dylan
Hailey	Cameron

New Jersey

GIRLS	BOYS
Isabella	Michael
Emily	Matthew
Sophia	Daniel
Ava	Anthony
Olivia	Joseph
Samantha	Christopher
Ashley	Nicholas
Madison	Ryan
Emma	Joshua
Gianna	Alexander
Abigail	Andrew
Mia	Justin
Sarah	John
Julia	David
Gabriella	Jacob

New Mexico

GIRLS	BOYS
Isabella	Jacob
Sophia	Joshua
Emily	Michael
Nevaeh	Isaiah
Alyssa	Gabriel
Mia	Daniel
Abigail	Christopher
Madison	Angel
Ava	Ethan
Alexis	David
Samantha	Noah
Emma	Diego
Destiny	Elijah
Hailey	Isaac
Hannah	Jose

New York

GIRLS	BOYS
Isabella	Michael
Sophia	Matthew
Emily	Anthony
Olivia	Joseph
Ava	Daniel
Madison	Ryan
Emma	Christopher
Samantha	Jayden
Sarah	Joshua
Ashley	Nicholas
Abigail	Alexander
Kayla	David
Mia	Justin
Elizabeth	Jacob
Brianna	Ethan

North Carolina

GIRLS	BOYS
Madison	William
Emma	Jacob
Emily	Christopher
Ava	Joshua
Abigail	Ethan
Olivia	Michael
Hannah	James
Elizabeth	Noah
Isabella	Elijah
Addison	Daniel
Sarah	John
Alyssa	David
Sophia	Andrew
Ashley	Alexander
Chloe	Matthew

North Dakota

GIRLS	BOYS
Emma	Logan
Ava	Ethan
Olivia	Jacob
Madison	Jack
Abigail	Alexander
Emily	Gavin
Addison	Owen
Grace	Aiden
Hannah	Mason

Sophia	Brody
Taylor	Dylan
Ella	Andrew
Brooklyn	Isaac
Elizabeth	Landon
Hailey	Brayden

Ohio

GIRLS	BOYS
Ava	Jacob
Madison	Michael
Olivia	Ethan
Emma	Andrew
Isabella	Logan
Abigail	William
Addison	Alexander
Sophia	Tyler
Hannah	Joshua
Emily	Noah
Grace	Joseph
Elizabeth	Matthew
Alexis	James
Ella	Ryan
Chloe	Anthony

Oklahoma

GIRLS	BOYS
Emma	Ethan
Madison	Jacob
Emily	Joshua
Addison	Noah
Hannah	William
Elizabeth	James
Ava	Michael
Isabella	Logan
Abigail	Jackson
Chloe	David
Olivia	Christopher
Alexis	Mason
Brooklyn	Gabriel
Alyssa	Gavin
Avery	Alexander

Oregon

GIRLS	BOYS
Emma	Jacob
Sophia	Alexander
Isabella	Logan
Emily	Daniel
Olivia	Ethan
Elizabeth	Noah
Abigail	David
Hannah	Andrew
Ava	Anthony
Madison	William
Natalie	Benjamin
Addison	Joshua
Grace	Michael
Alexis	Aiden
Ella	Elijah

Pennsylvania

GIRLS	BOYS
Ava	Michael
Olivia	Jacob
Emma	Ryan
Madison	Logan
Isabella	Matthew
Abigail	Joseph
Emily	Ethan
Sophia	Nicholas
Hannah	Andrew
Sarah	Anthony
Grace	Joshua
Addison	Alexander
Elizabeth	Daniel
Ella	Noah
Alexis	William

Rhode Island

GIRLS	BOYS
Sophia	Michael
Ava	Anthony
Isabella	Jacob

Madison	Nicholas	Abigail	Jack
Olivia	Ethan	Elizabeth	Carson
Emily	Alexander	Sophia	Hunter
Emma	Matthew	Taylor	Alexander
Hannah	David	Alexis	Evan
Abigail	Christopher	Chloe	Aiden
Gianna	Jayden		
Grace	Joshua		
Mia	Nathan		

Tennessee

GIRLS	BOYS
Emma	William
Madison	Jacob
Emily	Ethan
Addison	James
Abigail	Joshua
Hannah	Christopher
Ava	Jackson
Chloe	Michael
Elizabeth	Noah
Olivia	Elijah
Isabella	Andrew
Anna	Matthew
Alyssa	John
Sarah	Samuel
Alexis	David

Julia and Ella and Lily appear under the first column as well:

Julia · Benjamin
Ella · Ryan
Lily · Joseph

South Carolina

GIRLS	BOYS
Madison	William
Emma	James
Emily	Christopher
Abigail	Michael
Ava	Joshua
Olivia	Jacob
Hannah	Jayden
Elizabeth	Ethan
Addison	John
Isabella	Noah
Alyssa	Andrew
Anna	Jackson
Sarah	Matthew
Chloe	Caleb
Taylor	Daniel

Texas

GIRLS	BOYS
Emily	Jose
Mia	Jacob
Isabella	Daniel
Madison	Christopher
Abigail	Angel
Ashley	Joshua
Sophia	David
Emma	Ethan
Alyssa	Juan
Ava	Anthony
Elizabeth	Michael
Natalie	Diego
Hannah	Jonathan
Samantha	Christian
Addison	Matthew

South Dakota

GIRLS	BOYS
Ava	Ethan
Emma	Mason
Olivia	Jacob
Addison	Gavin
Hannah	Noah
Grace	Jackson
Madison	Tyler
Emily	William
Ella	Carter

Utah

GIRLS	BOYS
Olivia	Ethan
Emma	Jacob
Abigail	Benjamin
Elizabeth	Joshua
Ava	Samuel
Addison	William
Brooklyn	Mason
Emily	Isaac
Sophia	James
Madison	Logan
Isabella	Andrew
Hannah	Gavin
Ella	Jackson
Samantha	Luke
Sarah	Jack

Vermont

GIRLS	BOYS
Ava	Logan
Emma	Jacob
Abigail	Alexander
Olivia	Mason
Ella	Noah
Madison	Caleb
Emily	Aiden
Sophia	Ethan
Hannah	Ryan
Grace	Owen
Lily	Samuel
Amelia	Evan
Alexis	Jackson
Taylor	William
Addison	Wyatt

Virginia

GIRLS	BOYS
Madison	William
Abigail	Jacob
Emily	Christopher

Olivia	Joshua
Emma	Michael
Isabella	Ethan
Hannah	James
Ava	Matthew
Elizabeth	Ryan
Sophia	John
Sarah	Daniel
Addison	Alexander
Samantha	Andrew
Ashley	Noah
Chloe	Chloe

Washington

GIRLS	BOYS
Olivia	Jacob
Emily	Ethan
Emma	Alexander
Sophia	Daniel
Isabella	Logan
Ava	Noah
Abigail	Benjamin
Madison	David
Elizabeth	Michael
Hannah	Samuel
Grace	Andrew
Hailey	William
Chloe	Anthony
Samantha	Joshua
Natalie	Gabriel

West Virginia

GIRLS	BOYS
Madison	Jacob
Emma	Ethan
Emily	Logan
Abigail	Austin
Hannah	Hunter
Isabella	Gavin
Alexis	Michael
Olivia	Noah
Ava	Tyler

Chloe	James
Addison	Matthew
Hailey	Joshua
Alyssa	Landon
Brooklyn	Christopher
Kaylee	William

Wisconsin

GIRLS	BOYS
Ava	Ethan
Emma	Jacob
Olivia	Logan
Sophia	Mason
Addison	Alexander
Isabella	Owen
Emily	Noah
Ella	Jack
Elizabeth	Benjamin
Abigail	Tyler
Grace	Michael
Hannah	Evan
Madison	Samuel
Hailey	William
Natalie	Andrew

Wyoming

GIRLS	BOYS
Madison	Ethan
Emma	James
Abigail	Gavin
Taylor	William
Alexis	Logan
Hannah	Michael
Addison	Wyatt
Elizabeth	Brayden
Brooklyn	Gabriel
Lily	Hunter
Emily	Jacob
Grace	Noah
Ava	Tyler
Samantha	Landon
Hailey	Aiden

DAD'S CORNER:
Get the Future Papa Involved with Some of These Father-Friendly Lists

Current MLB Ballpark Names

Camden	Jacob
Fenway	Wrigley
Chase	Shea
Miller	Rogers
Kauffman	Turner

Old MLB Ballpark Names

Crosley	Ebbets
Forbes	Griffith
Navin	Briggs
Fulton	Bennett
Jarry	Baker

Heisman Trophy Winners

Peyton	Nile
Paul	Roger
Archie	Herschel
Gino	Vinny
Carson	Troy

College Football Stadiums

Kyle	Kinnick
Neyland	Randall
Autzen	Kenan
Doak	Carter
Owen	Ryan
Bryant	Jordan
Williams	Brice
Michie	

Racecar Drivers
Helio	Arie
Ayrton	Juan Pablo
Denny	Kanaan
Nigel	Dario
Michael	Mario

Golfers
Padraig	Phil
Tiger	Vijay
Annika	Brandt
Ernie	Ben
Sam	Sergio

Horror Movie Monikers
Michael	Jason
Freddie	Carol Anne
Tangina	Jack
Christine	Carrie
King	Gage

A Sporting Chance
Espen	Olympic
Rodeo	Champ
Prize	

Rolling the Dice
Ace	Lucky
Nathan	Seven
Chance	Fortuna
Charm	Clover
Gamble	Serendipity

Refreshing Options
Miller	Sierra
Anchor	Adams
Pete	Yuengling
Stella	Beck
Guinness	Pauli
Corona	

City Kids
Austin	Memphis
Savannah	Phoenix
Brooklyn	Lexington
Alexandria	Boston
Houston	Dallas
Atlanta	Jackson
Chandler	Charlotte
Dayton	Carson
Helena	Branson
Trenton	Abilene

A Name Abroad
Ireland	Lourdes
Orly	Sydney
London	India
China	Kenya
Jordan	Cuba

Top State and Province Names
Montana	Rhodes
Alberta	Indiana
Alabama	Georgia
Dakota	Tenn
Virginia	Kansas

Biblical Beauties

Mary	Sarah
Rebecca	Rachel
Ruth	Naomi
Mara	Eden
Judith	Leah
Eve	Deborah
Anne	Dinah
Delilah	

Beyond Abraham

Jacob	Simon
Elijah	Malachi
Judah	Darius
Caleb	Tobias
Paul	Timothy
Jonah	Noah
Moses	Levi
Isaiah	

Mythological Monikers

Athena	Minerva
Apollo	Evander
Odysseus	Hector
Callista	Delia
Medea	Venus

Flavorful and Fun

Sage	Oregano
Cilantro	Cayenne
Thyme	Basil
Tarragon	Curry
Herb	Coriander
Cinnamon	Rosemary
Paprika	Parsley
Ginger	Marjoram
Saffron	Poppy
Vanilla	Pepper

Presidential Picks

McKinley	Jefferson
Lincoln	Adams
Harrison	Grant
Monroe	Taylor
Truman	Tyler
Carter	Kennedy
Reagan	Clinton
Madison	

Technology Lovers

Neo	Mac
Gates	Cipher
Ram	Chip
Bill	Della
Meg	Cody

Trendy Names Grandma Will Love

GIRLS	BOYS
Sophia	Albert
Matilda	Noah
Sadie	Samuel
Lily	Oscar
Sarah	Nathan
Natalie	Saul
Lauren	Benjamin
Hannah	Sidney
Jessica	Moe
Victoria	Christian

If You Love Fairy Tales

GIRLS	BOYS
Gretel	Hans
Belle	Jack
Goldie	Peter
Ariel	Andersen
Beatrix	Potter
Beauty	Aslan
Fiona	Kipling
Damsel	Orlando
Tabitha	Gulliver
Rose	Rowland

Holiday Names

GIRLS	BOYS
Noelle	Kris
Holly	Noel
Carol	Judah
Miriam	Nick
Eve	Valentine
Christmas	Elijah
Myrrha	Yuli
Esther	Balthazar
Merry	Garland
Bethlehem	Moses

Second Amendment Babies

Colt	Winchester
Flint	Sargent
Ruger	Steele
Smith	Charlton
Gunnar	Derringer

Baby Birds

Wren	Robin
Raven	Finch
Oriole	Falcon
Lark	Jay
Starling	Rhea

Green Thumbs

Ivy	Thorn
Fern	Flora
Aloe	Leaf
Blossom	Thistle
Acacia	Forrest

Vegetarian Options

Apple	Celery
Quince	Peaches
Plum	Kale
Cherry	Olive
Citron	Cress

Mineral Mites

Stone	Quartz
Jade	Rock
Clay	Stirling
Ora	Silver
Amethyst	Beryl

Ode to Nature

Lily	Summer
Clover	Fox
Juniper	Leaf
Mahogany	Rain
Sage	Sky

Aspiring Meteorologists

Raine	Gale
Duska	Misty
Flurry	Storm
Gustav	Aurora
Tempest	Zephyr

Born in Spring and Summer

GIRLS	BOYS
Season	Bud
Avril	Somerled
Posy	Leland
Lea	Kelby
Lilac	Sonny
June	Julian
Eartha	Mayer
Aviva	Ray
Sandy	Fielder
Meadow	Ridgely
Maia	

Born in Fall and Winter

GIRLS	BOYS
Autumn	Caldwell
Pumpkin	Rainier
Snow	North
Tahoma	Darcy
January	Winter
Crystal	Frost
Nevara	Rudy
Fria	Fallon
Lillith	Moore
Hailey	Gefen

Medieval Monikers

Guinevere	Arthur
Morgan	Igraine
Avalon	Tristan
Lance	Merlin
Galahad	Percival

In Line for the Throne

GIRLS	BOYS
Queenie	Prince
Malka	Royal
Reina	Barron
Victoria	Earl
Regina	Noble
Calipha	Kingston
Empress	Duke
Rajah	Sultan
Juno	Regent
Rhiannon	Knightley

For the Bright and Fiery

Asher	Astrid
Cole	Phoenix
Keegan	Ember
Bernie	Zohar
Seraphina	Aidan

Aquatots

GIRLS	BOYS
Lake	Lachlan
Pearl	Marshall
Brooke	River
Tallulah	Jordan
Nixie	Marland
Coral	Lincoln
Waverley	Thorpe
Oceana	Trent
Shannon	Sheldon
Lakisha	Dorian

Lil' Lovers

Apollo	Esmay
Romeo	Habib
Aimee	Torunn
Heart	Venus
Hartley	Amora

Lil' Fighters

Ali	George
Oscar	Rocky
Cassius	Jake
Laila	Jean-Claude
Evander	Frazier

Witches and Warlocks

GIRLS	BOYS
Glinda	Hagrid
Hecate	Harry
Endora	Salem
Sabrina	Severus
Wicca	Oz
Hester	LaVey
Zelda	Draco
Galadriel	Gandalf
Elvira	Albus
Wendy	Vincent

Cartoon Characters

GIRLS	BOYS
Jessica	Sylvester
Wilma	Bart
Daphne	Linus
Velma	Elmer
Maggie	Tom
Lucy	Garfield
Marge	Jerry
Patty	Charlie
Alice	Casper
Lilo	Nemo

Disney Delight

GIRLS	BOYS
Esmeralda	Timon
Bianca	Sebastian
Belle	Winston
Anastasia	Gaston
Dory	Philip
Minnie	Percy
Aurora	Oliver
Mulan	Fenton
Alice	Iago
Tiana	Angus

As Seen on (Kids') TV

GIRLS	BOYS
Dora	Thomas
Hannah	Kermit
Ruby	Hooper
Miley	Caillou
Gina	Oscar
Kim	Zack
Wendy	Cody
Rosita	Diego
Gabriella	Max
Lizzie	Finnegan

For Parents on Pointe

Anna	Mikhail
Karen	Rudolf
Swann	Margot
Twyla	Manon
Odette	Giselle

Crayola Choices

GIRLS	BOYS
Ruby	Slate
Violet	Albion
Magenta	Bruno
Kelly	Cobalt
Indigo	Grayer
Rose	Teal
Saffron	Navy
Tawny	Rusty
Greenlea	Ebon
Fuchsia	Tanner

Rock Band Wannabes

GIRLS	BOYS
Courtney	Slash
Joan	Bruce
Carly	Axl
Gwen	Eddie
Patti	Lars
Debbie	Jimmy
Apollonia	Jagger
Janis	Floyd
Alice	Ozzy
Avril	Ramone

Tree-Huggers-Turned-Kid-Huggers

Ash	Willow
Timber	Sitka
Oakley	Bircher
Sequoia	Cedric
Tilia	Linden

CHECK OUT THE
LATEST STARBABIES

Celebrity Singletons

Max Liron (Christina Aguilera and Jordan Bratman)

Nahla Ariela (Halle Berry and Gabriel Aubry)

Jagger Jonathan (Lindsay Davenport and Jonathan Leach)

Valentina Paloma (Salma Hayek and Francois-Henri Pinault)

Wilder Brooks (Oliver Hudson and Erinn Bartlett)

Story Elias (Jenna and Bodhi Elfman)

Orion Christopher (Chris Noth and Tara Wilson)

Alexander Pete (Naomi Watts and Liev Schreiber)

Barron William (Donald Trump and Melania Knauss)

Alabama Gypsy Rose (Drea De Matteo and Shooter Jennings)

Violet Anne (Jennifer Garner and Ben Affleck)

Coco (Courtney Cox and David Arquette)

Ramona (Maggie Gyllenhaal and Peter Sarsgaard)

Emerson Rose (Teri Hatcher and Jon Tenney)

Matilda Rose (Michelle Williams and Heath Ledger)

Makena'lei Gordon (Helen Hunt and Matthew Carnahan)

Olive (Isla Fisher and Sacha Baron Cohen)

Ruby Sweetheart (Tobey Maguire and Jennifer Meyer)

August Miklos (Mariska Hargitay and Peter Hermann)

Damian Charles (Liz Hurley)

Ptolemy John (Gretchen Mol and Kip Williams)

Stellan (Jennifer Connelly and Paul Bettany)

Kingston James (Gwen Stefani and Gavin Rossdale)

Roman Walker (Debra Messing and Daniel Zelman)

Sage Florence (Toni Collette and Dave Galafassi)

Milo William (Liv Tyler and Royston Langdon)

Beckett Robert Lee (Stella McCartney and Alasdhair Willis)

Harlow Winter Kate (Nicole Richie and Joel Madden)

Honor (Jessica Alba and Cash Warren)

Mason Walter (Melissa Joan Hart and Mark Wilkerson)

Sam Alexis (Tiger Woods and Elin Nordegren)

River Russell (Keri Russell and Shane Deary)

Celebrity Siblings

Grace, Stella, and August (Dave Matthews and Ashley Harper)

Eden and Savannah (Marcia Cross)

Laird, Quinn, and Roan (Sharon Stone)

Willow and Jaden (Will Smith and Jada Pinkett)

Jett and Ella Blue (John Travolta and Kelly Preston)

Tallulah, Darby, and Sullivan (Patrick Dempsey and Jillian Fink)

Brooklyn, Romeo, and Cruz (Victoria and David Beckham)

Rowan and Grier (Brooke Shields and Chris Henchy)

Presley and Kaya (Cindy Crawford and Rande Gerber)

Lily-Rose and Jack (Johnny Depp)

Reignbeau and Freedom (Ving Rhames)

Rocco, Lourdes and David (Madonna)

Rocket, Racer, Rebel, Rogue and Rhiannon (Robert Rodriguez)

Luca, Lola, and Fiona (Jennie Garth and Peter Facinelli)

Delilah and Amelia (Lisa Rinna and Harry Hamlin)

Deacon and Ava (Reese Witherspoon and Ryan Philippe)

Apple and Moses (Gwyneth Paltrow and Chris Martin)

Finley and Avery (Angie Harmon and Jason Sehorn)

Phinnaeus, Hazel, and Henry (Julia Roberts and Danny Moder)

Maddox, Zahara, Shiloh, and Pax (Angelina Jolie and Brad Pitt)

Brandon and Dylan (Pamela Anderson and Tommy Lee)

Dashiell John, Roman Robert and Ignatius Martin (Cate Blanchett and Andrew Upton)

Max and Emme (Jennifer Lopez and Marc Anthony)

Neriah, Sierra Sky, Heaven Rain, Shaya (Brooke Burke and David Charvet)

Stella and Liam (Tori Spelling)

African-American Literature Names

Langston	Walker
Maya	Zora
Marguerite	Celie
Toni	Booker
Wallace	Baldwin

Shakespearean Daughters, Sons, and Sonnets

GIRLS	BOYS
Ophelia	Duncan
Juliet	Horatio
Regan	Timon
Desdemona	Balthazar
Cymbeline	Macduff
Cordelia	Cassio
Miranda	Edmund
Titania	Lysander
Portia	Antonio
Rosalind	Lear

Young-Adult Novel Names

GIRLS	BOYS
Deenie	Phineas
Enid	Steven
Francie	Holden
Margaret	Tex
Scout	Bruce
Blair	Todd
Sally	Hardy
Nancy	Ned
Kristy	Peter
Ramona	Dan

Classical Classics

Ludwig	Wolfgang
Brahm	Ravel
Franz	Haydn
Felix	Cadence
Shubert	Johann

Jazz It Up

GIRLS	BOYS
Billie	Coltrane
Norah	Art
Ella	Max
Sarah	Dexter
Diana	Sonny
Nancy	Winton
Alice	Lester
Betty	Chet
Edith	Vaughn
Judy	Miles

Trekkie Tykes

Kirk	Gene
Majel	Scottie
Troi	McCoy
Jean-Luc	Riker
Diana	Wesley

Naturalists and Conservationists

Jane	Bindy
Darwin	Rachel
Gaia	Carson
Thoreau	Gifford
Parker	Walden

Pious Picks

Maria	Theresa
Dominica	Agnes
Clement	Jain
Gregory	John Paul
Pia	Benedict

Names that Hit the High Notes

Purcell	Aida
Kiri	Donna
Aria	Carmen
Isolde	Manon
Sullivan	Wagner

Romantic Poets

Keaton	Byron
Blake	Percy
Shelley	Hugo
Whitman	Poe
Emerson	Taylor

Beatlemania

Jude	Starr
Pepper	Rita
Sergeant	Eleanor
Lucy	Julia
Lennon	Ringo

Peaceniks

Shulamit	Dalai
Amity	Souleah
Concord	Shalom
Olive	Lawson
Solomon	Absalom

Lullaby Babies

GIRLS	BOYS
Serena	Galen
Luna	Placido
Naoko	Stillwell
Siesta	Tyrone
Aislinn	Callum
Docila	Angel
Imena	Melito
Stella	Brahm
Nalani	Mazal
Solange	Steadman

Alphabet Soup

Bea	CeCe
Didi	Gia
Gigi	Jay
Kay	Elle
Em	Zee

Four (or More!) Syllables

GIRLS	BOYS
Penelope	Alexander
Eliora	Maximilian
Ariadne	Jeremiah
Evangeline	Bartholomew
Orilia	Montgomery
Julianna	Zedekiah
Lorelani	Emilio
Valencia	Demetrius
Willamina	Emmanuel
Maricella	Ezekiel

One-Syllable Boys' Names

Blake	Dane
Cole	Luke
Drew	Hayes
Kai	Miles
Rhys	Grant

Kids Who Can Cook

GIRLS	BOYS
Nigella	Oliver
Julia	Jacques
Giada	Nobu
Rachael	Auguste
Ina	Emeril
Delia	Kennedy
Sara	Wolfgang
Mollie	James
Alice	Alain
Anne-Sophie	Ferran

Women in Power

Hillary	Condi
Golda	Margaret
Oprah	Eleanor
Josephine	Martha
Indira	Cleo

TOP ALTERNATIVES TO THE TOP 10

If you like an extremely popular name but wish it was more unique, here are some fresh alternatives you may find appealing.

Instead of Emily, Try...

Eliana	Elise
Emmaline	Emery
Ellery	Ellspeth
Amelia	Amalie
Eleanor	Briony

Instead of Jacob, Try...

Cale	Luke
Jameson	Jace
Jarrett	Jasper
Jeremy	Chase
Jacoby	Nathaniel

Instead of Emma, Try...

Emerson	Emlyn
Emi	Ada
Elodie	Emerald
Elyn	Estella
Elisa	Amaya

Instead of Michael, Try...

Mitchell	Eli
Miles	Maddux
Mathias	Micah
Ryder	Wyatt
Mason	Marcus

Instead of Madison, Try...

Mabel	Mya
Mae	Mallory
Melissa	Meadow
Matilda	Nadia
Roxana	Marin

Instead of Joshua, Try...

Josiah	Judd
Julian	Justice
Joaquin	Johan
Jonah	Rocco
Jesse	Joel

Instead of Isabella, Try...

Sable	Bel
Isla	Catalina
Imogen	Iris
Liliana	Willa
Lucinda	Jillian

Instead of Ethan, Try...

Emmett	Eliot
Ian	Cole
Evan	Dean
Heath	Eamon
Dunstan	Espen

Instead of Ava, Try...

Aimee	Avaline
Ada	Adeline
Adelaide	Ivy
Eve	Orly
Violet	Adalyn

Instead of Matthew, Try...

Maxwell	Matteo
Marius	Spencer
Cooper	Mark
Adam	Martin
Malcolm	Thaddeus

Instead of Abigail, Try...

Annabeth	Alice
Abilene	Anabella
Abby	Abbott
Amanda	Aislin
Delaney	Dahlia

Instead of Daniel, Try...

Dale	Darren
Darius	Davis
Landon	Gavin
Grant	Scott
Xavier	Derek

Instead of Olivia, Try...

Eveline	Eliot
Olive	Phoebe
Eloisa	Lydia
Cecilia	Dojna
Ruby	Lola

Instead of Christopher, Try...

Topher	Kip
Tristan	Simon
Clark	Clayton
Kendall	Beckett
Brent	Colton

Instead of Chloe, Try...

Penelope	Lela
Phoebe	Willa
Matilda	Karissa
Ivy	Poppy
Cora	Piper

Instead of Alexander, Try...

Alexei	Byron
Xander	Stuart
Zander	Malcolm
Marshall	Oliver
Philip	Oscar

Instead of Sophia, Try...

Sadie	Lila
Ellie	Faith
Grier	Sylvie
Lucy	Calista
Veronica	Rowan

Instead of Anthony, Try...

Adrian	Antony
Antonio	Anton
Eric	Charles
Campbell	Armstrong
Amos	Alton

Instead of Elizabeth, Try...

Elaina	Lisbet
Priscilla	Becca
Hazel	Arabella
Anastasia	Libby
Claire	Lyssa

Instead of William, Try...

Whitman	Wilder
Weston	Walker
Henry	Parker
Winston	Wesley
Wade	Brenner

Instead of Aiden, Try...

Aiden is the defacto Number One name for boys once alternate spellings are included.

Alden	Calder
Braden	Bryant
Holden	Sawyer
Owen	Oscar
Aaron	Fletcher

MEANINGFUL NAMES

Names that Mean Light

GIRLS	BOYS
Aileen	Uriel
Lucy	Lucien
Nora	Brendan
Jelena	Lux
Meira	Jairden
Nell	Barak
Elaine	Meir
Ora	Abner
Kira	Sinclair
Liora	Anwar

Names that Mean Wise

GIRLS	BOYS
Adhita	Shanahan
Kayah	Druce
Edelle	Witt
Monique	Raymond

Salvia	Sage
Ulima	Conroy
Sonya	Aldred
Cassidy	Hakim
Quinn	Altman
Saffi	Vivek

Names that Mean Blessing or Gift

GIRLS	BOYS
Trixie	Zeb
Grace	Theodore
Darona	Raleigh
Thea	Bennet
Mattea	Doren
Iva	Jonathan
Adora	Matthew
Dottie	Hans
Joanna	Boone
Ivana	Benicio

Note to Reader:

Find within the text the most popular names of 2008 for boys and girls designated by: ⊙

Find within the text the top twin names of 2008 for boys and girls designated by: ⊙

Girls Names

Aadi (Hindi) Child of the beginning
*Aadie, Aady, Aadey, Aadee, Aadea,
Aadeah, Aadye*

Aaralyn (American) Woman with song
*Aaralynn, Aaralyn, Aaralynn, Aaralin,
Aaralinn, Aaralinne, Aralyn, Aralynn,
Aralynne, Aralin, Aralinn, Aralinne,
Aralen, Aralenn, Aralenne*

Aase (Norse) From the tree-covered
mountain

Aba (African) Born on a Thursday
Abah, Abba, Abbah

Abarrane (Hebrew) Feminine form of
Abraham; mother of a multitude; mother
of nations
*Abarrayne, Abarraine, Abarane, Abarayne,
Abaraine, Abame, Abrahana*

Abdera (Greek) Woman of the city of
Abdera
*Abderah, Abderra, Abderrah, Abderia,
Abderiah*

Abeba (African) Woman who is delicate
and flowerlike
*Abedah, Abeeda, Abeida, Abyda,
Abeedah, Abeidah, Abydah, Abieda,
Abiedah, Abeada, Abeadah*

Abebe (African) Child who is asked for
*Abebi, Abebie, Abeby, Abebey, Abebye,
Abebee, Abebeah, Abebea*

Abedabun (Native American) Sight of
day; dawn's child

Abela (French) A breath or sigh; source
of life
*Abelah, Abella, Abelia, Abelya, Abellah,
Abeliah, Abelyah*

Abellone (Greek) Woman who is manly
*Abellona, Abellonia, Abellonea, Abelone,
Abelona*

Abena (African) Born on a Tuesday
*Abenah, Abeena, Abyna, Abina, Abeenah,
Abynah, Abinah*

Abeni (African) A girl child who was
prayed for
*Abenie, Abeny, Abeney, Abenye, Abenea,
Abeneah, Abenee*

Abeque (Native American) Woman who
stays at home

Aberdeen (Scottish) A woman from a city
in northeast Scotland
*Aberdeene, Aberdeena, Aberdeenah,
Aberdeenia, Aberdeane, Aberdean,
Aberdeana, Aberdyne, Aberdyn,
Aberdyna*

Aberfa (Welsh) From the mouth of the
river
Aberfah, Aberpha, Aberphah

Abertha (Welsh) One who is sacrificed
Aberthah

Abha (Indian) One who shines; a lustrous
beauty
Abhah

Abhilasha (Hindi) One who is desired
Abhilashah, Abhylasha, Abhylashah

Abia (Arabic) One who is great
Abiah

Abiba (African) First child born after the
grandmother has died
*Abibah, Abeeba, Abyba, Abeebah,
Abybah, Abeiba, Abeibah, Abieba,
Abiebah, Abeaba, Abeabah*

Abida (Arabic / Hebrew) She who wor-
ships or adores / having knowledge
*Abidah, Abeeda, Abyda, Abeedah,
Abydah, Abeida, Abeidah, Abieda,
Abiedah, Abeada, Abeadah*

Abiela (Hebrew) My father is Lord
*Abielah, Abiella, Abiellah, Abyela,
Abyelah, Abyella, Abyellah*

Abigail ✿ ❂ (Hebrew) The source of a
father's joy
*Abbigail, Abigael, Abigale, Abbygail,
Abygail, Abygayle, Abbygayle, Abbegale,
Abigayle, Abagail, Abaigael, Abaigeal,
Abbey, Abbie, Abbigail, Abie, Abby,
Abegayle, Abey, Abby, Abiageal, Abichail,
Avagail, Avigail, Avagale, Avigale,
Avagayle, Avichayil, Abbye*

Abijah (Hebrew) My father is Lord
Abija, Abisha, Abishah, Abiah, Abia,
Aviah, Avia

Abila (Spanish) One who is beautiful
Abilah, Abyla, Abylah

Abilene (American / Hebrew) From a town
in Texas / resembling grass
Abalene, Abalina, Abilena, Abiline,
Abileene, Abileen, Abileena, Abilyn,
Abilyne, Abilyna, Abilean, Abileane,
Abileana

Abiona (Yoruban) Born during a journey
Abionah, Abionia, Abioniah

Abir (Arabic) Having a fragrant scent
Abeer, Abyr, Abire, Abeere, Abbir, Abhir

Abira (Hebrew) A source of strength; one
who is strong
Abera, Abyra, Abyrah, Abirah, Abbira,
Abeerah, Abhira

Abital (Hebrew) My father is the dew; in
the Bible, the fifth wife of David
Avital, Abitall, Avitall

Ablah (Arabic) One who is perfectly
formed; full-figured woman
Abla

Abra (Hebrew / Arabic) Feminine form of
Abraham; mother of a multitude; mother
of nations / lesson; example
Abri, Abrah, Abree, Abria, Abbra, Abrah,
Abbrah

Abrianna (Italian) Feminine form of
Abraham; mother of a multitude; mother
of nations
Abriana, Abreana, Abryana, Abryann,
Abreanne, Abrielle, Abrienne, Abriell,
Abriele

Abrihet (African) Woman who emanates
light

Acacia (Greek) Thorny tree; one who is
naïve
Akacia, Acacya, Acaciah, Acatia, Acasha,
Acacyah, Asasia, Akaciah

Academia (Latin) From a community of
higher learning
Akademia, Academiah, Akademiah

Acadia (Canadian) From the land of plenty
Acadiah, Acadya, Akadia, Akadiah,
Akadya

Acantha (Greek) Thorny; in mythology, a
nymph who was loved by Apollo
Akantha, Ackantha, Acanthah, Akanthah,
Ackanthah

Acarnania (Latin) Woman from western
Greece

Accalia (Latin) In mythology, the foster
mother of Romulus and Remus
Accaliah, Acalia, Accalya, Acalya, Acca,
Ackaliah, Ackalia

Aceline (French) Born into nobility; highborn woman
Acelin, Asceline, Ascelin

Achaana (Navajo) One who is the
protector

Achall (Celtic) In mythology, a loving sister
who died of grief when her brother died
Achalle, Achal, Achale

Achlys (Greek) In mythology, the personification of sadness and misery

Achsah (Hebrew) Bracelet for the ankle
Achsa

Acima (Hebrew) Feminine form of Acim;
God will judge
Acimah, Achima, Achimah

Acrasia (Greek) One who overindulges
Acrasiah, Akrasia, Acrasy, Acrasey, Acrasi,
Acrasie, Acrasee, Acrasea, Acraseah, Acrasye

Adah (Hebrew) Ornament; beautiful
addition to the family
Adda, Adaya, Ada

Adair (Scottish) From the oak-tree ford
Adaire, Adaira, Adairia, Athdara, Athdare,
Athdaria, Athdair, Athdaire, Athdairia,
Athdaira

Adalgisa (Italian / German) One who is
noble / a highly valued promise
Adalgise, Adelgise, Adelvice, Adalgysa,
Adalgyse

Adalwolfa (German) A noble she-wolf

Adama (African) A beautiful child; regal and majestic
Adamah, Adamma, Adammah

Adamina (Hebrew) Feminine form of Adam; of the earth
Adamia, Adamiah, Adaminah, Adamynah, Adameena, Adamine, Adaminna, Addie, Adameenah, Adamiena, Adamienah, Adameina, Adameinah, Adameana, Adameanah

Adanna (African) Her father's daughter; a father's pride
Adana, Adanah, Adannah, Adanya, Adanyah

Adanne (African) Her mother's daughter; a mother's pride
Adane, Adayne, Adaine, Adayn, Adain, Adaen, Adaene

Adaoma (Ibo) A good woman

Adara (Greek / Arabic) Beautiful girl / chaste one; virgin
Adair, Adare, Adaire, Adayre, Adarah, Adarra, Adaora, Adar, Adra, Athdara

Addiena (Welsh) Woman of beauty
Addien, Addienne, Adiena, Adiene, Adien, Adienna, Addienna

Addin (Hebrew) One who is adorned; voluptuous
Addine, Addyn, Addyne

Addison ✪ (English) Daughter of Adam
Addeson, Addyson, Adison, Adisson, Adyson

Addula (Teutonic) One of noble cheer
Adula, Adulla, Addulla, Adulah, Addullah

Adeen (Irish) Little fire shining brightly
Adeene, Adean, Adeane, Adein, Adeine, Adeyn, Adeyne

Adela (German) Of the nobility; serene; of good humor
Adele, Adelia, Adella, Adelle, Adalene, Adelie, Adelina, Adali, Adalheida, Adilene, Adelaide, Adalaide, Adalaid, Adalayde, Adelaid, Adelayde, Adelade, Ada, Adelajda, Adelicia, Adelinda, Adeline, Adelheid, Adelheide, Adelisa, Adelise, Adelita, Adelynn, Adelyte, Adalicia, Ady, Adalina, Adaline, Adaliz, Adalyn, Addie

Adelpha (Greek) Beloved sister
Adelfa, Adelphe, Adelphie

Adeola (African) One who wears a crown of honor
Adeolah, Adeolla, Adeollah

Aderes (Hebrew) One who protects her loved ones

Aderyn (Welsh) Birdlike child
Aderyne, Aderin, Aderine

Adesina (Yoruban) The passage is open; acceptance
Adesinah, Adesine, Adeseena, Adesyna, Adeseenah, Adesynah, Adesiena, Adesienah, Adeseina, Adeseinah, Adeseana, Adeseanah

Adetoun (African) Princess; child of royalty
Adetouna

Adhama (Swahili) A child of glory
Adhamah, Adhamma, Adhammah

Adhara (Arabic) Maiden; the name of the second-brightest star in the constellation Canis Major
Adharah, Adharra, Adharrah

Adhelle (Teutonic) Lovely and happy woman
Adhella, Adhell, Adhele, Adhela

Adhiambo (African) Daughter born after sunset

Adhita (Hindi) A learned woman
Adhitta, Adhittah, Adhitah, Adhyta, Adhytah, Adhytta, Adhyttah

Adia (Swahili / English) Gift from God / wealthy; prosperous
Adea, Adiah, Addia, Adya, Adeah

Adiana (American) The night's falling reveals the angels' beauty
Adyana, Adianna, Adianah, Adyanna

Adianca (Native American) One who brings peace
Adianka, Adyanca, Adyanka

Adiba (Arabic) One who is polite, cultured, and refined
Adibah, Adeeba, Adyba, Adeebah, Adeaba, Adeabah, Adiebah, Adieba, Adeibah, Adeiba, Adeaba, Adeabah, Adybah

Adie (Hebrew / German) Jeweled ornament / noble and kind
Adi, Ady, Adey, Adye, Adee, Adea, Adeah

Adiella (Hebrew) An adornment of God
Adiela, Adielle, Adiell, Adiel, Adiele, Adyella, Adyela, Adyell, Adyel, Adyele

Adila (African / Arabic) One who is just and fair / equal
Adilah, Adeala, Adileh, Adilia, Adyla, Adeela, Adilla, Adillah

Adima (Teutonic) One who is renowned; noble
Adimah, Adimma, Adimmah, Adyma, Adymah, Adymma, Adymmah

Adina (Hebrew) One who is slender and delicate
Adinah, Adine, Adena, Adene, Adin, Adinam, Adyna, Adynah

Adira (Hebrew / Arabic) Powerful, noble woman / having great strength
Adirah, Adeera, Adyra, Adeerah, Adyrah, Adeira, Adeirah, Adiera, Adierah, Adeara, Adearah

Adishree (Hindi) One who is exalted
Adishrey, Adishry, Adishri, Adishrie, Adishrea, Adishreah, Adyshree, Adyshrea, Adyshreah, Adyshri, Adyshrie, Adyshry, Adyshrey

Aditi (Hindi) Unbound; limitless; in Hinduism, the goddess of consciousness, the sky, and fertility
Aditie, Adity, Aditee, Adithi, Adytee, Adytie, Adytey, Aditea, Aditeah, Aditye

Adiva (Arabic) One who is gentle and pleasant
Adivah, Addeva, Adeeva, Adyva, Adeevah, Adyvah, Adieva, Adievah, Adeiva, Adeivah, Adeava, Adeavah

Adjoa (African) Daughter born on a Monday; peaceful
Adwoa, Adjoah, Adwoah

Adlai (Hebrew) The Lord is just; an ornament
Adlay, Adlae, Adlaye

Admete (Greek) In mythology, a maiden who ordered one of Hercules's twelve labors
Admeta

Admina (Hebrew) Daughter of the red earth
Adminah, Admeena, Admyna, Admeenah, Admynah, Admeina, Admeinah, Admiena, Admienah, Admeana, Admeanah

Adoette (Native American) Of the large tree
Adoett, Adoet, Adoete, Adoetta, Adoeta

Adolpha (German) Feminine form of Adolph; noble she-wolf
Adolfa, Adolphina, Adolfina, Adolphine, Adolfine, Adoqhina

Adonia (Spanish / Greek) Beautiful / feminine form of Adonis; lady
Adonna, Adonya, Adoniah, Adonyah, Adonica, Adoncia

Adora (Latin) One who is beloved
Adore, Adorah, Adoria, Adoreh, Adorya, Adoriah, Adorlee, Adoree, Audora

Adorabella (Latin) Beautiful woman who is adored
Adorabelle, Adorabela, Adorabell, Adorabele, Adorabel

Adoración (Spanish) Having the adoration of all

Adowa (African) One who is noble

Adra (Arabic) One who is chaste; a virgin
Adrah

Adrasteia (Greek) One who will not run away; in mythology, another name for Nemesis, the goddess of vengeance

Adria (Greek) Feminine form of Adrian; from the Adriatic Sea region; woman with dark features
Adriah, Adrea, Adreana, Adreanna, Adreanah, Adrienna, Adriane, Adriene, Adrie, Adrienne, Adriana, Adrianna, Adrianne, Adriel, Adrielle

Adrina (Italian) Having great happiness
Adrinna, Adreena, Adrinah, Adryna, Adreenah, Adrynah

Adrita (Sanskrit) A respected woman
Adritah, Adryta, Adrytah, Adreeta, Adreetah, Adrieta, Adrietah, Adreita, Adreitah, Adreata, Adreatah

Aduna (Wolof) Woman of the world
Adunah, Adunna, Adunnah

Adya (Indian) Born on a Sunday

Aedon (Greek) In mythology, the queen of Thebes who killed her son and was turned into a nightingale

Aefentid (Anglo-Saxon) Born in the evening

Aegea (Latin / Greek) From the Aegean Sea / in mythology, a daughter of the sun who was known for her beauty

Aegina (Greek) In mythology, a sea nymph
Aeginae, Aegyna, Aegynah

Aelan (Hawaiian) Delicate and flowerlike

Aelfthryth (English) Having an elf's strength
Aelfthrith

Aelfwine (English) A friend of the elves
Aelfwyne, Aethelwine, Aethelwyne

Aello (Greek) In mythology, an Amazon woman, name meaning "whirlwind"; also in mythology, a Harpy, name meaning "swift storm"
Aelo

Aelwen (Welsh) Woman with a fair brow
Aelwenn, Aelwenne, Aelwin, Aelwinn, Aelwinne, Aelwyn, Aelwynn, Aelwynne

Aelwyd (Welsh) From the hearth

Aerona (Welsh) Berry; from the river
Aeronna, Aeronnah, Aeronah

Aerwyna (English) A friend of the ocean

Aethelreda (English) A maiden born into nobility

Aethra (Greek) In mythology, mother of Theseus

Aetna (Greek) In mythology, the goddess of volcanoes

Afaf (Arabic) A virtuous woman; pure; chaste
Afaaf, Afifah

Afafa (African) The firstborn daughter of a second husband
Afafah, Afaffa, Afaffah

Afia (African) Born on a Friday
Afi, Affi, Affia

Afkica (Gaelic) One who is pleasant and agreeable
Afkicah, Afkika, Afkikah

Afra (Hebrew / Arabic) Young doe / white; an earth color
Affra, Affrah, Afrah, Afrya, Afryah, Afria, Affery, Affrie, Affrey, Aphra, Affera, Affrye

Afraima (Arabic) Woman who is fertile
Afraimah, Afrayma, Afraymah, Afraema, Afraemah

Afreda (English / Arabic) Elf counselor / one who is created
Afredah, Afreeda, Aafreeda, Afrida, Afridah, Aelfraed, Afreedah, Afryda, Afrydah

Africa (English) One who is pleasant; from Africa
Afrika, Affreeca, Affrica, Africah, Afrycka, Afrycah, Afric, Affryka, Afrikah, Afryka, Afrykah

Afrodille (French) Daffodil; showy and vivid
Afrodill, Afrodil, Afrodile, Afrodilla, Afrodila

Afroze (Arabic) One who is enlightening and shines brightly

Afton (English) From the Afton river

Afua (African) Born on a Friday
Afuah, Afooa, Afooah

Afya (African) One in good health

Agapi (Greek) One who loves; affectionate
Agape, Agappe, Agapie, Agapy, Agapey, Agapee, Agapea, Agapeah

Agate (Greek) Refers to the translucent semiprecious stone
Agait, Agaite, Agayt, Agayte, Agaet, Agaete

Agatha (Greek) Good and kind; St. Agatha is the patron saint of bell-founders
Agathe, Agathie, Agathy, Agathi, Agata, Agotha, Agota, Agytha, Agathyah, Agatah, Agathia, Agacia, Agafia, Agaue, Aggie, Agi, Agoti, Agueda

Agave (Greek) In mythology, a queen of Thebes

Agbenyaga (African) Life is precious and dear

Aghamora (Irish) From the vast meadow
Aghamore, Aghamorra, Aghamoria, Aghamorea

Aghanashini (Indian) One who destroys sins

Aghaveagh (Irish) From the field of ancient trees
Aghavilla, Aghaville, Aghavila, Aghavile

Aglaia (Greek) Having splendor, beauty, and glory; in mythology, one of the three Graces
Aglaiah, Aglaye, Aglaya, Aglayah, Aglae, Agalaia, Agalia

Aglauros (Greek) In mythology, a woman who was turned into stone by Hermes

Agnes (Greek) One who is pure; chaste
Agneis, Agnese, Agness, Agnies, Agnus, Agna, Agne, Agnesa, Agnesca, Agnessa, Agneta, Agnete, Agneti, Agnetis, Agnetta, Aghna, Agnek, Agnella, Aigneis, Anezka, Anis, Annice, Annis

Agraciana (Spanish) One who forgives
Agracianna, Agracyanna, Agracyana, Agraciann, Agraciane, Agracyann, Agracyane, Agracianne, Agracyanne

Agrafina (Latin) Girl child born feetfirst
Agrafine, Agrafyna, Agrafynah, Agrafeena, Agrafeenah, Agrafiena, Agrafienah, Agrafeina, Agrafeinah, Agrafeana, Agrafeanah

Agrippa (Greek) One who is born feetfirst
Agripa, Agryppa, Agrypa

Agrippina (Latin) A colonist; the name of several highborn women of ancient Rome
Agrippinae, Agrippinna, Agripinna

Agrona (Celtic) In mythology, the goddess of war and death
Agronna, Agronia, Agrone

Agurtzane (Basque) Refers to the Virgin Mary; chaste; pure
Aitziber

Ahalya (Hindi) In Hinduism, a woman who was turned to stone by her husband

Ahana (Irish) From the little ford
Ahanah, Ahanna, Ahannah

Ahava (Hebrew) Dearly loved, cherished; the name of a river
Ahavah, Ahuva, Ahuvah, Ahivia, Ahuda, Ahave

Ahelia (Hebrew) Breath; a source of life
Ahelie, Ahelya, Aheli, Ahelee, Aheleigh, Ahelea, Aheleah, Ahely, Aheley, Ahelye

Ahellona (Greek) Woman who has masculine qualities
Ahelona, Ahellonna, Ahelonna

Ahimsa (Hindi) One who avoids inflicting harm; nonviolent
Ahisma, Ahymsa, Aheemsa, Aheimsa, Ahiemsa, Aheamsa

Ahinoam (Hebrew) In the Bible, one of David's wives

Ahladita (Indian) One who is in a cheerful mood
Ahladit, Ahladtya, Ahladida, Ahladyda

Ahlam (Arabic) Witty; imaginative; one who has pleasant dreams
Ahlaam, Ahlama, Ahlamah

Ahuva (Hebrew) One who is dearly loved
Ahuvah, Ahuda, Ahudah

Ai (Japanese) One who loves and is loved; indigo blue

Aiandama (Estonian) Woman who gardens

Aibhilin (Gaelic) Of the shining light
Aibhlin

Aida (English / French / Arabic) One who is wealthy; prosperous / one who is helpful / a returning visitor
Ayda, Aydah, Aidah, Aidee, Aidia, Aieeda, Aaida

Aidan (Gaelic) One who is fiery; little fire
Aiden, Adeen, Aden, Aideen, Adan, Aithne, Aithnea, Ajthne, Aedan, Aeden

Aife (Celtic) In mythology, a great warrior woman; also a woman who turned her stepchildren into swans
Aoife

Aifric (Irish) One who is pleasant and agreeable

Aiglentine (French) Resembling the sweet-brier rose
Aiglentina

Aikaterine (Greek) One who is pure

Aiken (English) Of the oak tree

Aiko (Japanese) Little one who is dearly loved

Aila (Finnish / Scottish) One who bears light / from a protected place
Ailia, Aili, Ailie

Ailani (Hawaiian) Woman who holds rank as high chief
Aelani, Aelaney, Ailana, Ailanah, Ailanie, Ailany, Ailaney, Ailanea, Ailaneah

Ailbhe (Irish) Of noble character; one who is bright

Aileen (Irish / Scottish) Light-bearer / from the green meadow
Ailean, Ailein, Ailene, Ailin, Aillen, Ailyn, Alean, Aleane, Ayleen, Aylean, Ayleyn, Aylin, Aylein, Aylyn, Aileana, Aileene, Ailey

Ailing (Mandarin) A clever love
Ailyng

Ailis (Irish) One who is noble and kind
Ailish, Ailyse, Ailesh, Ailisa, Ailise

Aille (Gaelic) One of great beauty

Ailna (German) One who is sweet and pleasant; of the nobility
Ailne

Ailsa (Gaelic / Hebrew) From the island of elves / consecrated to God
Ailsah, Ailse, Ailsie, Ailsia

Aim (American) To direct toward a target

Aimatia (Latin) From the garden of flowers
Aimatiah, Aimatea, Aimateah, Aymatia, Aymatiah, Aymatea, Aymateah

Aimiliana (Teutonic) A hardworking woman
Aimilianah, Aimilianna, Aimilionia

Ain (Irish / Arabic) In mythology, a woman who wrote laws to protect the rights of women / precious eye

Aina (African) Child born of a complicated delivery

Aine (Celtic) One who brings brightness and joy

Aingeal (Irish) Heaven's messenger; angel
Aingealag

Ainhoa (Basque) Refers to the Virgin Mary; chaste
Ainhoah, Aenhoa, Aenhoah

Aini (Arabic) Resembling a spring flower
Ainie, Ainy, Ainey, Ainee, Ainea, Aineah, Ainye

Ainia (Greek) One who is swift
Ainiah, Ainea, Aineah, Aynia, Ayniah, Aynea, Ayneah

Ainsley (Scottish) One's own meadow
Ainslie, Ainslea, Ainslee, Ainsleigh, Ainsly, Ainslei, Aynslie, Aynslea, Aynslee, Aynsleigh, Aynsley, Aynslie, Aynsly, Ainsleah, Aynsleah, Ainslye

Aintza (Basque) One who holds the glory
Aintzane

Aionia (Greek) Everlasting life
Aioniah, Aionea, Aioneah, Ayonia, Ayoniah, Ayonea, Ayoneah

Aira (American) Of the wind
Aera

Airic (Celtic) One who is pleasant and agreeable
Airick, Airik, Aeric, Aerick, Aerik

Airla (Greek) Of the celestial spheres; ethereal
Airlia, Aerla, Aerlia

Airleas (Irish) A promise; an oath

Airmed (Celtic) In mythology, the goddess of herbalism
Airmeda, Aermed, Aermeda

Aisha (Arabic) Lively; womanly; the name of the prophet Muhammad's favorite wife
Aiesha, Aishia, Aesha, Aeshia, Aaisha, Aieysha, Aheesha, Aischa, Aisa, Aiysha, Ayse, Aysa, Aysha, Aysia, Aeesha, Aeeshah, Aeshah, Aishah, Aisia, Aisiah, Asha, Ashah, Ashia, Ashiah, Ayeesa, Ayeesah, Ayeesha, Ayeeshah, Ayeisa, Ayeisah, Ayeishah, Ayisa, Ayisah, Ayisha, Ayishah, Ayesha, Ayska

Aisley (English) From the ash-tree meadow
Aisly, Aisli, Aislie, Aislee, Aisleigh, Aislye, Aysley, Aysli, Ayslie, Aysly, Ayslye, Ayslee, Aysleigh, Aislea, Ayslea, Aisleah, Aysleah

Aisling (Irish) A dream or vision; an inspiration
Aislin, Ayslin, Ayslinn, Ayslyn, Ayslynn, Aislyn, Aisylnn, Aislinn

Aissa (African) One who is thankful
Aisa

Aitama (Estonian) One who is helpful
Aitamah, Aytama, Aytamah

Aitana (Portuguese) The glorious one
Aitanah, Aitanna, Aitanne, Aitann, Aitannah

Aitheria (Greek) Of the wind
Aitheriah, Aitherea, Aithereah, Aytheria, Aytheriah, Aytherea, Aythereah

Aiya (Hebrew) One who is birdlike
Aiyah

Aiyana (Native American) An eternal bloom; forever beautiful
Aiyanna, Ayana, Ayanna, Aiyanah, Aiyonna, Aiyunna, Aianna, Ayiana, Ayianna

Aiza (Spanish) One who has honor
Aizza, Aizah, Aizzah

Aja (Yoruban) In mythology, a patroness of the forest, animals, and healers
Ajah, Ajaa, Ajae

Ajaya (Hindi) One who is invincible; having the power of a god
Ajay

Ajua (Ghanaian) Born on a Monday
Adwowa, Ajo, Aju, Ajuah

Aka (Maori / Turkish) Affectionate one / in mythology, a mother goddess
Akah, Akka, Akkah

Akakia (Greek) One who is naïve

Akako (Japanese) A red child

Akanke (African) She is loved by all who know her

Akasma (Turkish) A white climbing rose

Akela (Hawaiian) One who is noble
Akeyla, Akeylah, Akeelah, Akelah, Akelia, Akeliah, Akeya, Akella, Akellah

Akenehi (Maori) Woman who is pure; chaste
Akenehie, Akenehea, Akeneheah, Akenehy, Akenehey, Akenehee

Aki (Japanese) Born in autumn
Akey, Akie, Akee, Aky, Akea, Akeah, Akye

Akia (African) The firstborn child
Akiah, Akya, Akyah

Akiko (Japanese) Emanating a bright light

Akilah (Arabic) One who is intelligent, wise, and logical
Akila, Akeela, Akeila, Akiela, Akyla, Akillah, Akilia, Akeelah, Akeilah, Akielah, Akylah, Akeala, Akealah

Akili (Tanzanian) Having great wisdom
Akilea, Akilee, Akilie, Akylee, Akylie, Akyli, Akileah

Akilina (Latin) Resembling an eagle
Akilinah, Akileena, Akilyna, Akilinna, Ackilina, Acilina, Akylina, Akylyna

Akina (Japanese) Resembling a spring flower

Akira (Scottish) One who acts as an anchor
Akera, Akerra, Akiera, Akirah, Akiria, Akyra, Akirrah, Akeri, Akeira, Akeara

Akiva (Hebrew) One who protects and shelters
Akibe, Akiha

Akona (Maori) One who excites and enthuses
Akonah, Akonna, Akonnah

Akosua (African) Born on a Sunday

Akpenamawu (African) Thanks be to God
Akpena

Aksana (Russian) Form of Oksana, meaning "one who gives glory to God"
Aksanna, Aksanah, Aksannah

Akua (African) Born on a Wednesday

Akuti (Indian) A princess; born to royalty
Akutie, Akutea, Akuteah, Akuty, Akutey, Akutee, Akutye

Alabama (Native American) From a tribal town; from the state of Alabama

Alaia (Arabic / Basque) One who is majestic, of high worth / joy

Alaina (French) Beautiful and fair woman; dear child
Alayna, Alaine, Allaine, Alayne, Alainah, Aleine, Alenne, Allayne, Alleine, Alenne, Aleyne, Alaana, Alanae, Alanea, Alawna, Alane, Aleine, Alanah, Alanna, Alana, Alanis, Alannis, Allayna, Allena, Allene, Alonna, Alyn, Alyna, Alaena, Alaenah

Alair (French) One who has a cheerful disposition
Alaire, Allaire, Allair, Aulaire, Alayr, Alayre, Alaer, Alaere

Alake (Yoruban) One who is adored

Alala (Hawaiian) Resembling an endangered crow
Alalla, Alalah, Alallah

Alamea (Hawaiian) Precious as a child

Alameda (Native American / Spanish) From the cottonwood grove / from the poplar tree
Alamida, Alamyda, Alameeda, Alameida, Alamieda, Alameada

Alani (Hawaiian) From the orange tree
Alanee, Alanie, Alaney, Alannie, Alany, Alaini, Alanea

Alanza (Spanish) Feminine form of Alonzo; noble and ready for battle

Alaqua (Native American) Resembling the sweet gum tree

Alarice (German) Feminine form of Alaric; ruler of all
Alarise, Allaryce, Alarica, Alarisa, Alaricia, Alrica, Alryca, Alryque

Alaska (Native American) From the great land; from the state of Alaska

Alastrina (Scottish) Form of Alexandra, meaning "helper and defender of mankind"
Alastriane, Alastriana, Alastrinah, Alastryan, Alastrine, Alastryana, Alastryn, Alastryne, Alastrynia, Alastrynah, Alastriona

Alaula (Hawaiian) The light of dawn

Alaura (Latin) Form of Laura, meaning "crowned with laurel; from the laurel tree"
Alauri, Alaurie, Alauree, Alaurea, Alaureah, Alaury, Alaurey, Alaurye

Alavda (French) Resembling a lark

Alazne (Basque) A miracle child

Alba (Latin) From the highlands
Albia, Alby, Albina, Albah, Allba, Allbah

Albany (Latin) From the white hill; white-skinned
Albaney, Albani, Albanie, Albanee, Albanye, Albin, Alban, Albhda, Albinia, Albinka, Albiona, Aubine, Aubina, Albanea, Albaneah

Alberga (Latin / German) Of noble character / a white-skinned woman
Alberge, Albergah, Albergia, Albergiah, Albergea, Albergeah

Alberta (German) Feminine form of Albert; noble and bright
Alburta, Albyrta, Albirta, Albertina, Albertine, Albrette, Alberte, Alberteen, Albertyna, Alhertina, Alhertine, Auberta

Albina (Etruscan) In mythology, the goddess of the dawn
Albinah, Albyna, Albynah, Albeena, Albeenah, Albiena, Albienah, Albeina, Albeinah, Albeana, Albeanah

Albreda (English) One who receives counsel from the elves

Alcestis (Greek) In mythology, a woman who died in place of her husband and was later rescued from Hades by Hercules

Alcimede (Greek) Having great cunning; in mythology, the mother of Jason

Alcina (Greek) One who is strong-willed and opinionated
Alceena, Alcyna, Alsina, Alsyna, Alzina, Alcine, Alcinia, Alcyne, Alsine, Alsyn, Alzine, Alcinah, Alcee, Alceenah, Alcynah, Alcienah, Alciena, Alceina, Alceinah, Alceana, Alceanah

Alcippe (Greek) A mighty horse; in mythology, the daughter of Ares
Alkippe

Alcmene (Greek) In mythology, the mother of Hercules
Alcmena, Alcemyne, Alcamene, Alcumena

Alcyone (Greek) A kingfisher; the name of the brightest star in the constellation Taurus; in mythology, a sea nymph
Alcieone, Alcione

Alda (German / Spanish) Long-lived, old; wise; an elder
Aldah, Aldine, Aldina, Aldinah, Aldene, Aldona, Aldeana, Allda, Alldah

Aldea (Teutonic) One who is wealthy and prosperous
Aldeah, Aldya, Aldiya, Aldyah, Aldiyah

Aldercy (English) Woman who holds the rank of chief
Aldercey, Alderci, Aldercie, Aldercee, Aldercye, Aldercea, Alderceah

Aldis (English) From the ancient house
Aldys, Aldiss, Aldisse, Aldyss, Aldysse

Aldonsa (Spanish) One who is kind and gracious
Aldonza, Aldonsia, Aldonzia

Aldora (English) One who is noble and superior
Aldorah, Aldorra, Aldorrah

Aldreda (English) Feminine form of Aldred; one who provides wise counsel

Alecto (Greek) In mythology, one of the Furies
Alecta, Alekto, Alekto

Aleda (Latin) Small and winged
Aletta, Alida, Alita, Allete, Alleta, Alleda, Allida, Aluld, Alyda

Aledwen (Welsh) Feminine form of Aled; offspring
Aledwenn, Aledwenne, Aledwyn, Aledwynn, Aledwynne, Aledwena, Aledwyna, Aledwynna, Aledwenna, Aledwin, Aledwinn, Aledwinne, Aledwina, Aledwinna

Aleen (Celtic) Form of Helen, meaning "the shining light"
Aleena, Aleenia, Alene, Alyne, Alena, Alenka, Alynah, Aleine, Aleina, Aleine, Aleina, Aleane, Aleana

Aleeza (Hebrew) One who is joyful
Aleezah, Alieza, Aliezah, Aliza, Alizah, Alitza, Aliz, Aleeze, Alizia, Alize, Aleiza, Aleizah, Aleaza, Aleazah

Alegria (Spanish) One who is cheerful and brings happiness to others
Alegra, Aleggra, Allegra, Alleffra, Allecra

Alera (Latin) Resembling an eagle
Alerra, Aleria, Alerya, Alerah, Alerrah

Aleshanee (Native American) Girl who is always playful
Aleshanie, Aleshany, Aleshani, Aleshaney, Aleshanea, Aleshaneah, Aleshanye

Alesta (Scottish) Form of Alexandra, meaning "helper and defender of mankind"
Alestah

Alethea (Greek) One who is truthful
Aletheia, Alethia, Aletha, Aletea, Althaia, Alithea, Alathea, Aletia, Alithia, Althaea

Alexandra ✪ (Greek) Feminine form of Alexander; helper and defender of mankind
*Alexandria, Alexandrea, Alixandra, Alessandra, Alexis, Alondra, Aleksandra, Alejandra, Alexsandra, Alexandrina, Alandra, Alejandra, Alejandrina, Aleka, Alesandese, Alewndra, Alewndrina, **Alexa**, Alexandina, Alexandriana, Alexandrine, Alexandtea, Alexavia, Alexi, Alexia, Alexina, Alexine, Alexus, **Alexis**, Alexys, Alix, Alyssandra, Alyx, Axelia*

Alfonsa (Spanish) Feminine form of Alfonso; noble and ready for battle
Alfonsine, Alfonsia, Alonsa, Alonza, Alphonsa, Alphonza

Alfreda (German) Feminine form of Alfred; one who counsels the elves
Alfreeda, Alfrida, Alfrieda, Alfryda, Alfreida, Alfreada

Algoma (Native American) From the valley of flowers
Algomma, Algomia, Algomea, Algomiya, Algomya

Alhena (Arabic) A star in the constellation Gemini
Alhenah, Alhenna, Alhennah

Alice (German) Woman of the nobility; truthful; having high moral character
*Alyce, Alicia, Alecia, Alesia, Aleece, Aleecia, Aleesha, Alesha, Alessa, Ali, Alicea, Alisa, Alise, Alisanne, Aleasha, Aleashia, Aleasia, Aleassa, Alisea, Alishah, Alishay, Alissya, Alyssaya, Alishya, Aleeshya, Aleeshia, Alishia, Alisia, Alissa, Alisse, Alisz, Alli, Allie, Allisa, Allis, **Allison**, Alliss, Ally, Allyce, Allys, Allyse, Allyson, Allyssa, Alycia, Alys, Alysa, Alyse, Alysha, Alysia, Alyson, Alyss, **Alyssa**, Alysse, Alyssia*

Alika (Hawaiian) One who is honest
Alicka, Alicca, Alyka, Alycka, Alycca

Alike (Nigerian) Girl who drives away other women
Alyke

Alima (Arabic) Sea maiden; one who is learned in music and dance
Alimah, Alyma, Alymah, Aleema, Aleemah, Aliema, Aliemah, Aleima, Aleimah, Aleama, Aleamah

Alina (Arabic / Polish) One who is noble / one who is beautiful and bright
Aline

Alitash (African) May you always be found
Alytash, Alitasha, Alytasha, Alitashe, Alytashe

Alivette (English) Form of Olivetta, meaning "of the olive tree; one who is peaceful"
Alivet, Alivett, Alivetta, Alivete, Aliveta

Aliyah ✪ (Arabic) An ascender; one having the highest social standing
Aaliyah, *Aliya, Alliyah, Alieya, Aliyiah, Alliyia, Aleeya, Alee, Aleiya, Alea, Aleah, Alia, Aliah, Aliye, Aliyyah, Aleya, Aaleyah, Aleyah, Alya, Aaliya, Aaliyah*

Alka (Indian) Young girl with long curly hair
Alkah

Allona (Hebrew) Feminine form of Allon; one who is as strong as an oak
Allonia, Alona, Alonia, Atonia, Atona

Allsun (Irish) One who is honest

Allyriane (French) Resembling the lyre, a stringed instrument

Alma (Latin / Italian) One who is nurturing and kind / refers to the soul
Almah

Almarine (German) Refers to a work ruler
Almerin, Almerine, Almarin, Almaryne, Almaryn, Almeryn, Almeryne

Almas (Arabic) Resembling a diamond
Almaas

Almeta (Latin / Danish) One who is ambitious / resembling a pearl
Almeda

Almira (English) A princess; daughter born to royalty
Almeera, Almeira, Almiera, Almyra, Almirah, Almeerah, Almeirah, Almierah, Almyrah, Almeara, Almearah

Almodine (Latin) A highly prized stone
Almondyne, Almondeene, Almondeane, Almondeine, Almondiene

Almond (English) Resembling the almond nut
Almandina, Almandine

Almunda (Spanish) Refers to the Virgin Mary
Almundena, Almundina

Alodia (Spanish) Form of Elodia, meaning "a wealthy foreigner"
Alodiah, Alodya, Alodie, Alodi, Alody, Alodey, Alodee, Alodea, Alodeah, Alodye

Aloe (English) Resembling the aloe plant

Aloha (Hawaiian) One showing love, compassion, and affection

Alohilani (Hawaiian) From the bright sky
Alohilanie, Alohilany, Alohilaney, Alohilane, Alohilanea, Alohilaneah, Alohilanye

Aloise (Spanish) Feminine form of Aloysius; famous warrior
Aloisa, Aloisia, Aloysia

Aloma (Spanish) Form of Paloma, meaning "dovelike"
Alomah, Alomma, Alommah

Alonsa (French) Feminine form of Alonso; one who is ready for battle
Alonza

Alouette (French) Resembling a lark
Allouette, Alouetta, Alowette, Alouett, Alouet, Alouete, Aloueta

Alpa (Indian) A petite girl

Alpana (Indian) A beautiful decoration
Alpanah, Alpannah, Alpanna

Alpha (Greek) The firstborn child; the first letter of the Greek alphabet

Alphonsine (French) Feminine form of Alphonse; one who is ready for battle
Alphonsina, Alphonsyne, Alphonsyna, Alphonseene, Alphonseena, Alphonseane, Alphonseana, Alphonsiene, Alphonsiena, Alphonseine, Alphonseina

Alpina (Scottish) Feminine form of Alpin; blonde; white-skinned
Alpinah, Alpena, Alpeena, Alpyna, Alpeenah, Alpynah, Alpeina, Alpeinah, Alpiena, Alpienah, Alpeana, Alpeanah

Alsatia (English) Woman of the region Alsace

Alsoomse (Native American) One who is independent

Altagracia (Spanish) The high grace of the Virgin Mary
Alta

Altair (Arabic) Resembling the flying eagle; a bright star in the constellation Aquila
Altaire, Altaira, Altayr, Altayre, Altaer, Altaere, Altayra, Altaera

Althea (Greek) Possessing the power to heal; wholesome
Althia, Althaea, Altha, Altheda, Althya

Aludra (Arabic) A maiden; the name of a star in the constellation Canis Major
Aloodra

Alufa (Hebrew) One who is a leader
Alufah

Alula (Latin) As delicate and light as a feather

Aluma (Hebrew) A young maiden; chaste
Alumah, Alumit

Alumina (Latin) Surrounded by light
Allumina, Alumyna, Allumyna, Alumeena, Allumeena, Alumeana, Allumeana

Alura (English) A divine counselor
Allura, Alurea, Alhraed

Alva (Latin) One who has a fair complexion
Alvah

Alvar (German) Of the army of elves
Alvara, Alvaria, Alvarie, Alvare, Alvarr

Alvera (Spanish) Feminine form of Alvaro; guardian of all; speaker of the truth
Alveria, Alvara, Alverna, Alvernia, Alvira, Alvyra, Alvarita, Alverra

Alverdine (English) Feminine form of Alfred; one who counsels the elves
Alverdina, Alverdeene, Alverdeena, Alverdeane, Alverdeana, Alverdiene, Alverdiena, Alverdeine, Alverdeina

Alvina (English) Feminine form of Alvin; friend of the elves
Alvine, Alvinia, Alveena, Alvyna, Alvie, Alvy, Alvey, Alvee, Alvea, Alveah, Alvye

Alvita (Latin) One who has been anointed
Alvitah, Alveta, Alvyta, Alveeta, Alvytah, Alveetah, Alvieta, Alvietah, Alveita, Alveitah, Alveata, Alveatah

Alzena (Arabic) A lovely woman
Alzenah, Alzina, Alzan, Alzene

Ama (African) Born on a Saturday
Amah, Amma, Ammah

Amabel (Latin) One who is lovable
Amabell, Amabelle, Amabella, Amabela, Amabilis, Amable, Amabele

Amachi (African) The child is a gift of God
Amachie, Amachy, Amachey, Amachee, Amachye, Amachea, Amacheah

Amada (Spanish) One who is loved by all
Amadia, Amadea, Amadita, Amadah

Amadahy (Native American) Of the forest's water
Amadahey, Amadahi, Amadahie, Amadahee, Amadahea, Amadaheah, Amadahye

Amadea (Latin) Feminine form of Amedeo; loved by God
Amadya, Amadia, Amadine, Amadina, Amadika, Amadis

Amadi (African) One who rejoices
Amadie, Amady, Amadey, Amadye, Amadee, Amadea, Amadeah

Amadore (Italian) One who has the gift of love
Amadora, Amadorah, Amadorra, Amadorrah

Amal (Arabic) One with dreams and aspirations
A'mal, Amala, Aamaal

Amalfi (Italian) From an Italian town overlooking the Gulf of Salerno
Amalfey, Amalfy, Amalfie, Amalfee, Amalfea, Amalfeah

Amalia ✿ (German) One who is industrious and hardworking
*Amalea, Amalya, Amalie, Amalasanda, Amalasande, Amalasand, Amalasandia, Amalasandra, Amalija, Amaliji, **Amelia**, Amelie, Amalle, Amalda, Ameliya, Amilia, Amyleah, Amelita, Amylya, Amella, Amylia, Amely, Aimil, Amaline, Amalin, Amelinda, Amialiona*

Amalthea (Greek) One who soothes; in mythology, the foster mother of Zeus
Amaltheah, Amalthia, Amalthya

Amalur (Spanish) From the homeland
Amalure, Amalura, Amaluria

Aman (African) A trustworthy woman
Amana

Amanda (Latin) One who is much loved
Amandi, Amandah, Amandea, Amandee, Amandey, Amande, Amandie, Amandy, Amandya, Amandalee, Amandalyn, Amandia, Amandina, Amandine

Amandeep (Indian) Emanating the light of peace
Amanpreet, Amanjot

Amandla (African) A powerful woman

Amani (African / Arabic) One who is peaceful / one with wishes and dreams
Amanie, Amany, Amaney, Amanee, Amanye, Amanea, Amaneah

Amapola (Arabic) Resembling a poppy
Amapolah, Amapolla, Amapollah, Amapolia

Amara (Greek) One who will be forever beautiful
Amarah, Amarya, Amaira, Amaria, Amar, Amari, Amaree, Amarie, Amarri, Amarra

Amaranta (Latin) A flower that never fades
Amarante, Amarantha, Amantha, Amaranda, Amaranthe, Amaranth, Amare

Amariah (Hebrew) A gift of God

Amarina (Australian) Brought with the rain
Amarinah, Amarine, Amaryn, Amarin, Amarynah, Amaryne, Amareena, Amareenah, Amariena, Amarienah, Amareina, Amareinah, Amareana, Amareanah

Amaris (Hebrew) Fulfilling God's promise
Amariss, Amarys, Amaryss, Amarisa, Amarissa, Amarysa, Amaryssa, Amarise

Amaryllis (Greek) As fresh as a flower; sparkling
Amarilis, Amarillis, Amarylis, Amaryl, Amaryla, Amarylla

Amata (Latin / Spanish) In mythology, a queen who committed suicide / one who is dearly loved
Amatah

Amaya (Japanese) Of the night rain
Amayah, Amaia, Amaiah

Amber ☙ (French) Resembling the jewel; a warm honey color
Ambur, Ambar, Amberly, Amberlyn, Amberli, Amberlee, Ambyr, Ambyre, Ambra, Ambria, Ambrea, Ahmber, Amberia, Amberise, Amberjill, Amberlynn, Ambre

Ambika (Hindi) In Hinduism, one of the wives of Vichitravirya
Ambikah, Ambyka, Ambykah

Ambrosia (Greek) Immortal; in mythology, the food of the gods
Ambrosa, Ambrosiah, Ambrosyna, Ambrosina, Ambrosyn, Ambrosine, Ambrozin, Ambrozyn, Ambrozyna, Ambrozyne, Ambrozine, Ambrose, Ambrotosa, Ambruslne, Amhrosine

Amedee (French) One who loves God
Amedi, Amedie, Amedy, Amedey, Amedea, Amedeah, Amedye

America (Latin) A powerful ruler
Americus, Amerika, Amerikus

Amethyst (Greek) Resembling the purple gemstone; wine; in history, was used to prevent intoxication
Amathyste, Amethist, Amathist, Amethyste, Amathista, Amathysta, Amethista, Amethistia, Amethysta, Amethystia

Amhuinn (Gaelic) From the alder-tree river

Amica (Latin) One who is a beloved friend
Amicah, Amice, Amika, Amikah, Amyca, Amycah, Amyka, Amykah

Amina (Arabic) Honest; trustworthy; faithful; the mother of the prophet Muhammad
Aminah, Aamena, Aamina, Aminta, Aminda, Ameena, Ameenah, Amena, Amineh, Aminia, Amiena, Amienah, Ameina, Ameinah, Ameana, Ameanah

Amira (Arabic) A princess; one who commands
Amirah, Ameera, Amyra, Ameerah, Amyrah, Ameira, Ameirah, Amiera, Amierah, Ameara, Amearah

Amissa (Hebrew) One who is honest; a friend
Amisa, Amise, Amisia, Amiza, Amysa, Amysia, Amysya, Amyza

Amita (Indian) Feminine form of Amit; without limits; unmeasurable
Amitah, Ameeta, Amyta, Amitha, Ameetah, Amytah, Amieta, Amietah, Ameita, Ameitah, Ameata, Ameata

Amitola (Native American) Of the rainbow
Amitolah, Amytola, Amytolah, Amitolla, Amytolla, Amitollah, Amytollah

Amity (Latin) A dear friendship
Amitey, Amitee, Amiti, Amitie, Amytee, Amyti, Amytie, Amytey, Amyty, Amite, Amitee, Amitea, Amytea, Amiteah, Amyteah

Amlika (Indian) A nurturing woman; a mother
Amlikah, Amlyka, Amlykah

Amoke (Yoruban) One who is petted

Amoldina (Teutonic) Having the strength of an eagle
Amoldinah, Amoldeena, Amoldyna, Amoldena, Amoldine

Amorette (Latin) One who is beloved and loving
Amorete, Amorett, Amorit, Amoritt, Amoritte, Amoryt, Amortye, Amorytte, Amoreta, Amoretta, Amorita, Amoryta, Amor, Amora, Amorie, Amorina, Amory

Amorica (English) Woman of Britain
Amoricah, Amorika, Amoricka, Amoryca, Amoryka, Amorycka

Amparo (Spanish) One who offers shelter; a protector

Amphitrite (Greek) In mythology, a sea goddess and wife of Poseidon
Amfitrite

Amrita (Hindi) Having immortality; full of ambrosia
Amritah, Amritta, Amryta, Amrytta, Amrytte, Amritte, Amryte, Amreeta, Amreetah, Amrieta, Amrietah, Amreita, Amreitah, Amreata, Amreatah

Amritha (Indian) One who is precious
Amrytha

Amser (Welsh) A period of time

Amtullah (Arabic) A servant of Allah
Amtulla, Amtula, Amtulah

Amunet (Egyptian) In mythology, a fertility and mother goddess

Amy (Latin) Dearly loved
Aimee, Aimie, Aimi, Aimy, Aimya, Aimey, Amice, Amicia, Amie, Amye

Amymone (Greek) The blameless one; in mythology, a princess of Argos who bore a son to Poseidon

Amynta (Latin) Protector and defender of her loved ones
Amyntah, Amyntas, Aminta, Ameenta, Amenta

An (Chinese) One who is peaceful

Anaba (Native American) A woman returning from battle
Anabah, Annaba, Annabah

Anabal (Gaelic) One who is joyful
Anaball, Annabal, Annaball

Anafa (Hebrew) Resembling the heron
Anafah, Anapha, Anaphah

Anahid (Armenian) In mythology, the goddess of water and fertility

Anahita (Persian) The immaculate one; in mythology, a water goddess
Anahit, Anahyta, Anahyt

Anan (African) The fourth-born child
Anana

Ananda (Hindi) Feminine form of Anand; one who brings happiness
Anandah

Anani (Hawaiian) From the orange tree
Ananie, Ananee, Ananea, Ananeah, Anany, Ananey, Ananye

Anarosa (Spanish) A graceful rose
Annarosa, Anarose, Annarose

Anastasia (Greek) One who shall rise again
Anastase, Anastascia, Anastasha, Anastasie, Anastassia, Anastasya, Anastatia, Anestasia, Annastaysia, Anstace, Anstice, Anastazia, Anastazya, Anastacia, Anastashia, Anastazja, Anasztaizia, Annastasia, Anstey

Anasuya (Indian) One who is charitable
Anasuyah, Annasuya

Anat (Hebrew / Arabian) One who sings / in mythology, the goddess of fertility, war, and hunting
Anate, Anata, Anatie, Anati, Anaty, Anatey, Anatee, Anatea, Anateah

Anathema (Latin) One who is cursed and shunned
Anathemah, Annathema

Anatola (Greek) Woman from the East
Anatolah, Anatolya, Annatola, Anatolia, Annatolia, Annatolya, Anatole

Anaxarete (Greek) In mythology, an unfeeling woman who was turned to stone
Anawrete

Anaya (African) One who looks up to God
Anayah, Annaya

Anbar (Arabic) A fragrant or perfumed woman
Anbarre, Anbarr

Ancelin (French) A handmaiden
Anceline, Ancelina, Ancelyn, Ancelynn, Ancelynne

Ancelote (French) Feminine form of Lancelot; an attendant

Anchoret (Welsh / Latin) One who is loved / a hermit
Anachoret, Annchoret

Ancina (Latin) Form of Ann, meaning "a woman graced with God's favor"
Ancyna, Anncina, Anncyna, Anceina, Annceina, Anciena, Annciena, Anceena, Annceena, Anceana, Annceana

Andeana (Spanish) One who is leaving
Andeanna, Andeane, Andiana, Andianna, Andyana, Andyanna

Andes (Latin) Woman from the Andes

Andraste (Celtic) One who is invincible; in mythology, the goddess of victory
Andrasta, Andrastia

Andrea ✪ (Greek / Latin) Courageous and strong / feminine form of Andrew; womanly
Andria, Andrianna, Andreia, Andreina, Andreya, Andriana, Andreana, Andera, Andraia, Andreja, Andrya, Andris, Andrette, Aindrea, Anda, Andee, Andena, Andere, Andra, Andralyn, Andi, Andie, Andranetta, Andraya, Andreanna, Andree, Andras, Andrena, Andrienne, Andrianne, Andrina, Andren, Andrya, Anndrea, Anndria, Aundrea

Andromache (Greek) In mythology, a Trojan princess and the wife of Hector
Andromacha

Andromeda (Greek) A northern constellation; in mythology, the wife of Perseus
Andromyda, Andromida

Andsware (Anglo-Saxon) An answer; a gift
Andswaru, Andswara

Aneira (Welsh) The golden woman
Aneera, Anyra, Aneirah, Aneerah, Anyrah, Aniera, Anierah, Aneara, Anearah

Aneko (Japanese) An older sister
Aniko, Anyko

Anela (Hawaiian) A messenger of heaven; an angel
Anelah, Anella, Anellah, Anel, Anelle

Anemone (Greek) Resembling a wind-flower; breath

Anevay (Native American) One who is superior
Anevaye, Anavai, Anavae

Angela ✪ (Greek) A heavenly messenger; an angel
*Angelica, **Angelina**, Angelique, Anjela, Anjelika, Angella, Angelita, Angeline, Angelyn, Angelene, Angelin, Angelia, Ange, Anga, Angel, Angele, Angelee, Angelena, Angeles, Angeletta, Angelette, Angeli, Angelika, Angeliki, Angilia, Angelisa, Angelita, Angell, Angelle, Angelynn, Angie, Angyalka, Anielka, Anjelica, Anjelita*

Angeni (Native American) A spirit angel
Angeni, Angenie, Angenee, Angeny, Anjenee, Anjeney, Anjenie, Anjeny, Anjeenie, Anjeeny, Angenia, Angenea, Angeneah, Anjenea, Anjeneah

Angerona (Latin) In mythology, the goddess of winter, anguish, solstice, death, and silence
Angrona

Angevin (French) An angel of wine
Angevyn, Angeven

Angharad (Welsh) In mythology, the love of Peredur; one who is greatly loved
Anghard, Angharat

Angita (Latin) In mythology, goddess of healing and magic
Angyta, Angeeta, Angeta, Angeata, Angeita, Angieta

Anglides (English) In Arthurian legend, the mother of Alisander

Angrboda (Norse) In mythology, a giantess
Angerboda, Angerbotha

Angusina (Gaelic) Feminine form of Angus; of one choice
Angusinah, Angusyna, Angusynah, Angusiena, Angusienah, Anguseina, Anguseinah, Anguseena, Anguseenah, Anguseana, Anguseanah

Angwusnasomtaqa (Native American) A crow mother spirit

Anh (Vietnamese) One who offers safety and peace

Ani (Hawaiian) One who is very beautiful
Aneesa, Aney, Anie, Any, Aany, Aanye, Anea, Aneah, Anye

Aniceta (French) One who is unconquerable
Anicetta, Anniceta, Annicetta

Anila (Hindi) Child of the wind
Anilla, Anyla, Anylla, Anilah, Anylah, Anyllah

Anippe (Egyptian) A daughter of the Nile

Anisa (Arabic) One who is affectionate and friendly
Aneesa, Aneesah, Aneecia, Annisa, Annissa, Anyssa, Annyssa, Annysa, Anysa, Anysha, Anissa, Anisah, Aneisa, Aneisah, Aniesa, Aneisa, Aneasa, Aneasah

Anise (English) Resembling the herb
Aneese, Aneise, Anyse, Aniese, Anease

Anisha (Hindi) Born at the end of the night; form of Anna, meaning "a woman graced with God's favor"; form of Agnes, meaning "one who is pure; chaste"
Anicia, Aneisha, Annisha, Aanisha, Aeniesha, Aneasha, Anysha

Anjali (Indian) One who offers with both hands
Anjalie, Anjaley, Anjaly, Anjalee, Anjaleigh, Anjalea, Anjaleah, Anjalye

Anjanette (American) A gift of God's favor
Annjeanette, Anjeanette, Anjanique, Anjana

Ankareeda (Arabic) Resembling a night star; shining and graceful
Ankaryda, Ankareda, Ankarida, Ankareeta, Ankaryta, Ankareta, Ankarita

Ankine (Armenian) One who is valuable

Ankti (Native American) To repeat the dance
Anktie, Ankty, Anktey, Anktee, Anktea, Ankteah, Anktye

Anlicnes (Anglo-Saxon) One who has a good self-image
Anlienisse

Anna ✪ ✪ (Latin) A woman graced with God's favor
Annah, Ana, Ann, Anne, Anya, Ane, Annze, Anouche, Annchen, Anais, Anaise, Anaiss, Anays, Anayss, Ance, Anechka, Aneisha, Anessa, Aneta, Anetta, Anka, Anki, Anku, Anke, Ania, Anica, Anice, Anichka, Annaka, Anacka, Anikee, Anika, Aniki, Aniko, Anita, Anitchka, Anitia, Anitra, Aniya, Aniyah, Anja, Annette, Annora, Annorah, Anora, Antje, Asenka, Anyuta, Asenke, Anneke, Annas, Anni, Annick, Annie, Annika, Annike, Annikka, Annikke, Annikki, Anina, Annyna, Anyna, Anninah, Aninah, Annynah, Anynah, Annina, Annissa, Anny, Annys, Anouska, Ayn, Anyssa

Anna Christina (Latin) A graceful Christian
Anna Christina, Anna Kristina, Anna Chrystina, Anna Christeena, Anna Christyna, Anna Chrystyna, Ana Christina, Ana Kristina, Anna Christine, Anne Christine, Ana Christine, Anna Christie, Ana Christi

Anna Perenna (Latin) In mythology, a goddess who was the personification of the perennial year

Annabel (Italian) Graceful and beautiful woman
Annabelle, Annabell, Annabella, Annabele, Anabel, Anabell, Anabelle, Anabella, Anabela, Annabla, Anahella

Annabeth (English) Graced with God's bounty
Anabeth, Annabethe, Annebeth, Anebeth, Anabethe

Annakiya (African) Girl with a sweet face
Anakiya, Annakiyah, Anakiyah

Annalee (English) From the graceful meadow
Annali, Annalie, Annaleigh, Analee, Analeigh, Anali, Analie, Annalina, Anneli

Annalisa (Latin) Graced with God's bounty
Analisa, Analissa, Annelisa, Annelise, Analicia, Analiese, Analise, Analisia, Analyssa, Annalise, Annalissa, Annaliese, Anneliese

Annalynn (English) From the graceful lake
Analynn, Annalyn, Annaline, Annalin, Annalinn, Analyn, Analine, Analin, Analinn, Annalinda, Analinda, Annalynda, Analynda

Annapurna (Hindi) In Hinduism, the goddess of plenty

Annmarie (English) Filled with bitter grace
Annemarie, Annmaria, Annemaria, Annamarie, Annamaria, Anamarie, Anamaria, Anamari, Annemie

Annora (Latin) Having great honor
Anora, Annorah, Anorah, Anoria, Annore, Annorya, Anorya, Annoria

Annot (Hebrew) One who emanates light

Annunciata (Latin) Named for the Annunciation
Anunciata, Annuziata, Anuziata, Annunciatta, Annuziatta, Anunciacion

Annwn (Welsh) In mythology, the name of the Otherworld
Annwfn, Annwyn, Annwyfn, Annwfyn

Annwyl (Welsh) One who is loved

Anona (English) Resembling a pineapple
*Anonah, Annona, Annoniah, Annonya,
Annonia*

Anonna (Latin) In mythology, a goddess of
the harvest, food, and supplies
Annonna

Anouhea (Hawaiian) Having a soft, cool
fragrance

Anoush (Armenian) Having a sweet
disposition
Anousha, Anoushia

Anouska (French) One who is gracious
Annouska, Annushka, Anusha, Anyoushka

Ansa (Latin / Finnish) One who is constant
/ a virtuous woman
Anse

Anselma (German) Feminine form of
Anselm; having divine protection
Anselmah, Anzelma, Anzelmah

Ansley (English) From the noble's pasture-
land
*Ansly, Anslie, Ansli, Anslee, Ansleigh,
Anslea, Ansleah, Anslye*

Ansonia (German) Feminine form of
Anson; child of the divine
*Annesonia, Annsonia, Annsonya,
Ansonya, Ansonea, Annsonea, Annsoniya,
Ansoniya*

Antalya (Russian) Born with the morning's
first light
*Antaliya, Antalyah, Antaliyah, Antalia,
Antaliah*

Antandra (Latin) An Amazon warrior

Antea (Greek) In mythology, a woman who
was scorned and committed suicide
Anteia, Anteah

Anthea (Greek) Lady of the flowers
Anthia, Antheah, Anthya, Antha, Anthe

Anthemia (Greek) Resembling a flower in
bloom
*Antheemia, Anthemya, Anthymia,
Anthemea, Anthemeah*

Anticlea (Greek) In mythology, the mother
of Odysseus
Antiklea, Antiklia

Antigone (Greek) In mythology, the
daughter of Oedipus
*Antigoni, Antigonie, Antigony, Antigoney,
Antigonea, Antygone, Antygoni,
Antygonie, Antygonee*

Antiope (Greek) In mythology, a queen of
the Amazons

Antje (German) A graceful woman

Antonia (Latin) Feminine form of
Anthony; priceless and highly praisewor-
thy; a flourishing flower
*Antoinette, Antoneta, Antonella,
Antonette, Antonisha, Antonina,
Antoinetta, Antonetta, Antonie,
Antonietta, Antonique*

Anulika (African) One who recognizes
that happiness is best
*Anulicka, Anulica, Anulyka, Anuleka,
Anuleeka*

Anumati (Hindi) In Hinduism, moon god-
dess of prosperity, intellect, children, and
spirituality
*Anumatie, Anumatey, Anumatee,
Anumatia, Anumatea, Anumateah,
Anumatye*

Anuradha (Hindi) In Hinduism, goddess
of good fortune
Anurada

Anusree (Indian) A pretty woman
*Anusry, Anusrey, Anusri, Anusrie,
Anusrea, Anusreah, Anusrye*

Anwen (Welsh) A famed beauty
*Anwin, Anwenne, Anwinne, Anwyn,
Anwynn, Anwynne, Anwenn, Anwinn*

Anyango (African) One who is a good
friend

Aoibheann (Irish) Woman with a beautiful sheen; a name borne by several
princesses
Aoibheane, Aoibheanne

Aoife (Irish) A beautiful woman; in
mythology, a warrior princess
Aoiffe, Aoif, Aoiff

Aolani (Hawaiian) Cloud from heaven
*Aolaney, Aolanee, Aolaniah, Aolanie,
Aolany, Aolanya, Aolania, Aolanea,
Aolanea*

Apala (African) One who creates religious music
Apalla, Appalla, Appala, Apalah, Apallah, Appallah, Appalah

Apara (Yoruban) One who doesn't remain in one place
Aparra, Apparra, Appara, Aparah, Aparrah, Apparrah, Apparah

Aphrah (Hebrew) From the house of dust
Aphra

Aphria (Celtic) One who is pleasant and agreeable
Aphriah

Aphrodite (Greek) Love; in mythology, the goddess of love and beauty
Afrodite, Afrodita, Aphrodita, Aphrodyte, Aphhrodyta, Aphrodytah

Apirka (Gaelic) One who is pleasant and agreeable

Apollonia (Greek) A gift from the god Apollo
Apollina, Apolline, Apollonis, Apollinaris, Appolina, Appoline

Aponi (Native American) Resembling a butterfly
Aponni, Apponni, Apponi

Apphia (Hebrew) One who is productive
Apphiah

Apple (American) Sweet fruit; one who is cherished
Appel, Aple, Apel

Apria (Latin) Resembling an apricot
Aprea, Apriah, Aprya, Apreah, Apryah

April (English) Opening buds of spring; born in the month of April
Avril, Averel, Averill, Avrill, Apryl, Apryle, Aprylle, Aprel, Aprele, Aprila, Aprile, Aprili, Aprilla, Aprille, Aprielle, Aprial, Abril, Abrielle, Abrial, Aperira, Avrielle, Avrial, Abrienda, Avriel, Averyl, Averil, Avryl, Apryll

Apsaras (Indian) In mythology, nature spirits or water nymphs

Aqua (Greek) Of the water
Aquanetta, Aquanet, Aquaneta, Aquanett, Aquanette

Aquarius (Latin) The water-bearer; a constellation

Aquene (Native American) One who is peaceful
Aqueena, Aqueene, Aqueen

Aquila (Latin) Resembling an eagle; a constellation
Aquilla, Aquil, Aquileo, Aquill, Aquyl, Aquyll, Aquilas, Acquilla, Aquilino, Aquilina, Aquiline, Aquileene, Aquileena

Ar (Anglo-Saxon) A merciful woman

Ara (Arabic) An opinionated woman
Aira, Arah, Arae, Ahraya, Aaraa

Arabella (Latin) An answered prayer; beautiful altar
Arabel, Arabela, Arabelle, Arabele, Arabell

Araceli (Spanish) From the altar of heaven
Aricela, Arcilla, Aracelia, Arcelia, Aracely, Araseli, Arasely, Arceli, Aracelli, Aracele, Aracelea

Arachne (Greek) In mythology, a young woman who was changed into a spider by Athena
Arachnie, Arachni, Arachny, Arachney, Arackne, Aracknie, Arackni, Arackny, Arackney, Arachnee, Aracknee, Arakne, Araknie, Arakni, Arakny, Arakney, Araknee, Arachnea, Araknea, Arachneah, Arakneah

Aradia (Greek) In mythology, the goddess of witches; the daughter of Diana and Lucifer
Aradiah, Aradea, Aradeah

Arama (Spanish) Refers to the Virgin Mary
Aramah, Aramma, Arammah

Araminta (Hebrew) One who is lofty and exalted
Aramintah, Aramynta, Araminte

Aranka (Hungarian) The golden child

Aranrhod (Welsh) A large silver wheel; in mythology, the mother of a sea creature and a blob
Arianrhod, Arianrod

Arantxa (Basque) Resembling a thornbush

Ararinda (German) One who is tenacious
Ararindah, Ararynda, Araryndah

Arashel (Hebrew) From the strong and protected hill
Arashell, Arashelle, Arashele, Arashela, Arashella

Arava (Hebrew) Resembling a willow; of an arid land
Aravah, Aravva, Aravvah

Araxie (Armenian) From the river of inspiration
Araxi, Araxy, Araxey, Araxee, Araxea, Araxeah, Araxye

Arcadia (Greek / Spanish) Feminine form of Arkadios; woman from Arcadia / one who is adventurous
Arcadiah, Arkadia, Arcadya, Arkadya, Arckadia, Arckadya

Arcangela (Greek) Angel of high rank
Arcangel, Archangela, Archangelia, Archangelica

Arda (English) One who is warm and friendly
Ardi, Ardie, Ardy, Ardey, Ardee, Ardine, Ardea, Ardeah, Ardye

Ardala (Irish) Woman of high honor
Ardalla, Ardalle, Ardalia, Ardalah, Ardallah, Ardaliah

Ardara (Gaelic) From the stronghold on the hill
Ardarah, Ardarra, Ardaria, Ardarrah, Ardariah

Ardea (Greek) A fiery woman
Ardeah

Ardel (Latin) Feminine form of Ardos; industrious and eager
Ardelle, Ardella, Ardele, Ardelia, Ardelis, Ardela, Ardell

Arden (Latin / English) One who is passionate and enthusiastic / from the valley of the eagles
Ardin, Ardeen, Ardena, Ardene, Ardan, Ardean, Ardine, Ardun, Ardyn, Ardyne, Ardana, Ardeana, Ardenia, Ardeene

Ardith (Hebrew) From the field of flowers
Ardyth, Ardythe, Ardath, Ardice, Ardise, Ardisa, Ardyce, Ardyse, Ardyssa, Ardathe, Ardathia, Aridatha

Ardra (Celtic / Hindi) One who is noble / the goddess of bad luck and misfortune
Ardrah

Areebah (Arabic) One who is smart and witty
Areeba, Aribah, Ariba, Arybah, Aryba, Arieba, Ariebah, Areaba, Areabah, Areiba, Areibah

Arella (Hebrew) A messenger from heaven; an angel
Arela, Arelah, Arellah, Arelle, Areli, Arelie, Arely

Arete (Greek) In mythology, the queen of the Phaeacians

Aretha (Greek) One who is virtuous; excellent
Areta, Aretta, Arette, Areata, Areatha, Areathia, Areeta, Areetha, Arethea, Arethia, Aretina, Arita, Aritha, Arytha, Arythya, Aret

Arethusa (Greek) In mythology, a wood nymph

Argea (Greek) In mythology, the wife of Polynices
Argeia

Argel (Welsh) One who provides refuge
Argell, Argelle, Argele, Argella, Argela

Argenta (Latin) Resembling silver
Argentia, Argentina, Argene, Arjean

ArgIwyddes (Welsh) A distinguished lady

Argoel (Welsh) A prophetic sign
Argoell, Argoele, Argoelle, Argoela, Argoella

Argraff (Welsh) One who makes an impression
Argraffe, Argrafe

Aria (English) A beautiful melody
Ariah

Ariadne (Greek) Holy and chaste; in mythology, the woman who helped Theseus escape from the labyrinth
Ariadna, Aryadnah, Ariette, Aryadna, Ariadnah

Ariana ✿ (Welsh / Greek) Resembling silver / one who is holy
*Ariane, Arian, **Arianna**, Arianne, Aerian, Aerion, Arianie, Arieon, Aeriana, Ahriana, Ariena, Arianell, Arriana*

Arianwen (Welsh) Resembling silver; one who is holy or fair
Arianwyn, Arianwenn, Arianwenne, Arianwynn, Arianwynne, Arianwin, Arianwinn, Arianwinne

Aricia (Greek) In mythology, a niece of Aegeus rumored to be a black witch

Ariel (Hebrew) A lioness of God
Arielle, Ariele, Ariell, Arriel, Ahriel, Airial, Arieal, Ariela, Ariella, Aryela, Aryella, Arial, Areille, Ariellel, Ari

Aries (Latin) Resembling a ram; the first sign of the zodiac; a constellation

Arietta (Italian) A short but beautiful melody
Arieta, Ariete, Ariet, Ariett, Aryet, Aryeta, Aryetta, Aryette, Ariette

Arilda (Teutonic) A maiden of the hearth
Arilde, Arildha, Arildhe

Arin (English) Form of Erin, meaning "woman from Ireland"
Aryn

Arisje (Danish) Feminine form of Aris; one who is superior

Arissa (Greek) Feminine form of Aris; one who is superior
Arisa, Aris, Aryssa, Arysa, Arys

Arista (Latin) A harvester of corn
Aristana, Aristen

Arizona (Native American) From the little spring; from the state of Arizona

Arkansas (Native American) Of the down-river people; from the state of Arkansas

Arlais (Welsh) From the temple
Arlays, Arlaes, Arlaise, Arlayse, Arlaese

Arleigh (English) From the meadow of the hare
Arlee, Arlie, Arli, Arly, Arley, Arlea, Arleah, Arlye

Arlene (Irish) An oath; a pledge
Arleen, Arline, Arlena, Arlein, Arlen, Arleyne, Arlette, Arleta, Arlyne, Arlana, Arlenna, Arleene, Airleas, Arlane, Arleana, Arlet, Arletta, Arlina, Arlinda, Arly, Arlyn

Arliss (Irish) From the high fortress
Arlissa, Arlise, Arlyss, Arlyssa, Arlyse, Arlys, Arlis

Armanda (Spanish) Feminine form of Armando; battlemaiden

Armani (Persian) One who is desired; a goal
Armanee, Armanii, Armahni, Arman, Armanie, Armany, Armaney, Armanea, Armaneah

Armelle (French) A princess; born to royalty
Armell, Armele, Armel, Armella, Armela

Armenouhie (Armenian) A woman from Armenia

Armes (Welsh) One who foretells the future

Armide (Latin) An armed battlemaiden
Armid, Armidee, Armidea, Armydea, Armydee, Armydya, Armidia, Armydia, Armida, Armilda, Armilde

Armilla (Latin) A decorative bracelet
Armillah, Armila, Armilah, Armylla, Armyllah, Armyla, Armylah

Armine (Latin / German) Born into the nobility / a battlemaiden
Arminee, Arminey, Armini, Arminie, Armyn, Armyne, Armina, Arminel

Armona (Hebrew) A chestnut color of brown
Armonit, Armonah

Arnalda (German) One who is an eagle ruler
Arnolda, Arnaldia, Arnaldea, Arnoldia, Arnoldea

Arnelle (American) Feminine form of Arnold; the eagle rules
Arnel, Arnela, Arnessa, Arnisha, Arnell, Arnella

Arnette (English) A little eagle
Arnett, Arnetta, Arnete, Arneta, Arnet

Arnia (American) As strong as an eagle
Arniah, Arnea, Arnya, Arneah, Arnyah

Arnina (Hebrew) An enlightened one
Arninah, Arnyna, Arnynah, Aarnina, Arnine, Arnona

Arnon (Hebrew) From the river

Aroha (Maori) One who loves and is loved

Arona (Maori) One who is colorful and vivacious
Aronah, Aronnah, Aronna

Aronui (Maori) One who is greatly desired

Arrate (Basque) Refers to the Virgin Mary

Arrosa (Basque) Sprinkled with dew from heaven; resembling a rose
Arrose

Arseni (Russian) Feminine form of Arsenios; womanly
Arsenie, Arseny, Arsene, Arcene, Arceni, Arcenee, Arsenee, Arsenia, Arsenya, Arsenea, Arcenea, Arseneah, Arceneah

Artaith (Welsh) One who is tormented
Artaithe, Artayth, Artaythe, Artaeth, Artaethe

Artemis (Greek) Virgin huntress; in mythology, goddess of the hunt and the moon
Artemisa, Artemise, Artemys, Artema, Artemisia, Artemysia, Artemysya, Artemia, Artemus

Artha (Hindi) One who is prosperous; wealthy
Arthah, Arthi, Arthea

Arthurine (English) Feminine form of Arthur; as strong as a she-bear
Arthurina, Arthuretta, Arthuryne, Arthes, Arthene

Artis (Irish / English / Icelandic) Lofty hill; noble / rock / follower of Thor
Artisa, Artise, Artys, Artysa, Artyse, Artiss, Arti, Artina, Artine, Artice

Artois (French) Woman of the Netherlands

Arub (Arabic) A woman who loves her husband
Aruba, Arubah

Arundhati (Indian) One who is not restrained; the name of a star
Arundhatie, Arundhaty, Arundhatey, Arundhatee, Arundhatea, Arundhateah

Arusi (African) A girl born during the time of a wedding
Arusie, Arusy, Arusey, Arusee, Arusea, Aruseah, Arusye

Arva (Latin) From the sea; one who is fertile
Arvah, Arvia, Arvya

Arvida (English) Feminine form of Arvid; from the eagle tree
Arvidah, Arvidia, Arvada, Arvinda, Arvyda, Arvydah

Arwa (Arabic) A female mountain goat

Arwydd (Welsh) A prophetic sign

Arya (Indian) One who is noble and honored
Aryah, Aryana, Aryanna, Aryia

Arza (Hebrew) Cedar panels
Ariza, Arzice, Arzit

Arziki (African) One who is prosperous
Arzikie, Arzikee, Arzyki, Arzykie, Arzikea, Arzykea, Arziky, Arzikey, Arzyky, Arzykey

Asa (Japanese) Born in the morning
Asah

Asabi (African) Girl of select birth
Asabie, Asaby, Asabee, Asabey, Asabea, Asabeah, Asabye

Ascención (Spanish) Refers to the Ascension

Asdis (Scandinavian) A divine spirit; a goddess
Asdiss, Asdisse, Asdise, Asdys, Asdyss, Asdysse

Asela (Spanish) The foal of a donkey
Asella, Aselah, Asellah

Aselma (Gaelic) One who is fair-skinned
Aselmah

Asena (Turkish) In mythology, a she-wolf
Asenah, Asenna, Asennah

Asenath (Egyptian) A father's daughter; in the Bible, Joseph's Egyptian wife
Acenath, Asenathe, Acenathe

Asenka (Hebrew) Woman with grace
Asenkia, Asenke, Asenki, Asenkie, Asenkye

Asfoureh (Arabic) A birdlike woman

Asgre (Welsh) Having a noble heart

Asha (Sanskrit / African) Hope; in mythology, the wife of a Hindu demigod / one who is lively
Ashia, Ashah, Ashiah

Ashaki (African) A beautiful woman
Ashakie, Ashaky, Ashakey, Ashakee, Ashakea, Ashakeah, Ashakye

Ashanti (African) From a tribe in West Africa
Ashantee, Ashaunti, Ashaunte, Ashanta, Ashonti, Asante, Achante, Ashauntia, Ashaunty, Ashunti, Ashauntea, Ashantea, Ashanteah, Ashaunteah

Ashby (English) Home of the ash tree
Ashbea, Ashbie, Ashbeah, Ashbey, Ashbi, Ashbee

Asherat (Syrian) In mythology, goddess of the sea

Ashilde (Norse) One who fights for God
Ashilda, Ashild

Ashima (Hebrew) In the Bible, a deity worshipped at Hamath
Ashimah, Ashyma, Asheema, Ashimia, Ashymah, Asheemah, Asheima, Asheimah, Ashiema, Ashiemah, Asheama, Asheamah

Ashira (Hebrew) One who is wealthy; prosperous
Ashyra, Ashyrah, Ashirah, Asheera, Asheerah, Ashiera, Ashierah, Asheira, Asheirah, Asheara, Ashearah

Ashley ♀ ♂ (English) From the meadow of ash trees
Ashlie, Ashlee, Ashleigh, Ashly, Ashleye, Ashlya, Ashala, Ashleay, Ash, Ashby, Ashely, Ashla, Ashlan, Ashlea, Ashleah, Ashleen, Ashleena, Ashlen, Ashli, Ashlin, Ashling, Ashlinn, Ashlyn, Ashlynn, Ashleene, Ashlynne, Ashlyne, Ashlene, Ashtyn, Ashten, Ashtin, Ashtine, Ashtynne, Ashton

Ashra (Hebrew) One who is fortunate
Asheera, Ashirah, Ashrah, Ashira, Asheerah, Asheara, Ashearah, Ashyra, Ashyrah

Asia (Greek / English) Resurrection / the rising sun; a woman from the East; in the Koran, the woman who raised Moses
Aysia, Asya, Asyah, Azia, Asianne

Asima (Arabic) One who offers protection
Asimah, Aseema, Azima, Aseemah, Asyma, Asymah, Asiema, Asiemah, Aseima, Aseimah, Aseama, Aseamah

Asis (African) Of the sun
Asiss, Assis, Assiss

Asiya (Arabic) One who tends to the weak; healer
Asiyah

Aslaug (Norse) One who is devoted to God; in mythology, a queen

Asli (Turkish) One who is genuine and original
Aslie, Asly, Asley, Aslee, Asleigh, Aslea, Asleah, Alsye

Asma (Arabic) One having great prestige
Asmah

Asma (Arabic) One of high status

Aspasia (Greek) One who is welcomed; in mythology, a lover of Pericles
Aspasiah, Aspasya, Aspasea

Aspen (English) From the aspen tree
Aspin, Aspine, Aspina, Aspyn, Aspyna, Aspyne

Asphodel (Greek) Resembling a lily
Asfodel, Asfodelle, Asphodelle, Asphodela, Asphodella, Asfodela, Asfodella

Assaggi (African) A woman with strength
Assaggie, Assaggey, Assaggy, Assaggea, Assaggeah, Assaggee, Asagi, Asagie, Asagy, Asagey, Asagee, Asagea, Asageah

Assana (Irish) From the waterfall
Assane, Assania, Assanna, Asanna, Asana

Assunta (Latin) One who is raised up
Assuntah, Asunta, Asuntah

Astarte (Egyptian) In mythology, a goddess of war and love

Asthore (Irish) One who is dearly loved
Asthora, Asthoria, Asthorea, Asthoreah,
Asthor

Astra (Latin) Of the stars; as bright as
a star
Astera, Astrea, Asteria, Astrey, Astara,
Astraea, Astrah, Astree, Astria, Astrya,
Asta, Aasta, Aster, Astah, Astin

Astrid (Scandinavian) One with divine
strength
Astread, Astreed, Astrad, Astri, Astrod,
Astrud, Astryd, Astrida, Astrik, Astred,
Astlyr, Astlyrd

Asunción (Spanish) Refers to the Virgin
Mary's assumption into heaven

Asura (African) Daughter born during the
month of Ashur

Asvoria (Teutonic) One having divine
wisdom
Asvora, Asvorea, Asvorya, Asvore, Asvor,
Asvoriah, Asvoreah

Atalanta (Greek) Mighty huntress; in
mythology, a huntress who would only
marry a man who could beat her in a
footrace
Atalantah, Atlanta, Atlante, Atlantia,
Atlantya, Atalaya, Atlee, Atalante

Atalaya (Spanish) From the watchtower

Atalia (Hebrew) God is just; God is great
Atalie, Atali, Ataly, Ataley, Atalee,
Atalissa, Atalena, Atalina, Ataleena,
Atalyna, Atalea, Ataleah

Atara (Hebrew) Wearing a crown; one who
is blessed
Atarah, Atarya, Ataree, Ateara, Atera,
Aterah, Atarra, Ataret, Atarrah

Ate (Greek) In mythology, goddess of
irrationality and consequent punishment

Atgas (Welsh) One who is hateful

Athalia (Hebrew) The Lord is exalted
Athalie, Athalee, Athalea, Athaleah,
Athaliah, Athalei, Athaleigh, Athaley,
Athali, Athaly, Athalya, Athaleyah,
Athalyah, Athaleya

Athanasia (Greek) One having immortality

Athena (Greek) Wise; in mythology, the
goddess of war and wisdom
Athina, Atheena, Athene

Athilda (English) From the elder tree
Athilde, Athild, Atilda, Atilde, Atild,
Attheaeldre, Atheaeldre

Atia (Arabic) Of an ancient line

Atifa (Arabic) One who shows affection and
sympathy
Ateefa, Aatifa, Atipha, Ateepha, Aatipha,
Atufa, Atupha, Atufah, Atiefa, Ateifa,
Atyfa, Ateafa

Atira (Hebrew) One who bows in prayer
Atirah, Atyra, Atyrah, Ateera, Ateerah,
Atiera, Atierah, Ateira, Ateirah, Ateara,
Atearah

Atiya (Arabic) A gift from God
Atiyah, Atiyya, Atiyaa, Atiyyaa

Atmaja (Hindi) A precious daughter

Atropos (Greek) In mythology, one of the
three Fates
Atropes, Atropas, Antropas

Atsuko (Japanese) One of profound
emotions

Atsukpi (African) A female twin
Atsukpie, Atsukpy, Atsukpey, Atsukpee,
Atsukpea, Atsukpeah

Atthis (Greek) A woman from Attica; in
mythology, the daughter of Cranaus who
gave her name to Attica

Attracta (Irish) A virtuous woman; a saint
Athracht, Athrachta

Atun (Arabic) One who teaches; an
educator
Atunn, Aatoon, Aatun, Atunne, Atune

Aubrey ♀ (English) One who rules with
elf-wisdom
Aubree, Aubrie, Aubry, Aubri, Aubriana,
Aubrianne, Aubrianna, Aubrea, Aurbreah

Auburn (Latin) Having a reddish-brown
color
Aubirn, Auburne, Aubyrn, Abern, Abirn,
Aburn, Abyrn, Aubern

Audhilda (Norse) A wealthy woman warrior
Audhild, Audhilde

Audi (African) The last daughter born
Audie, Audy, Audey, Audee, Audlin,
Audney, Audlin, Audea, Audeah

Audrey ○ (English) Woman with noble
strength
Audree, Audry, Audra, Audrea, Adrey,
Audre, Audray, Audrin, Audriya, Audrie,
Audri, Audria, Audriana, Audrianna,
Audrielle, Audrina, Audreana, Audreanna,
Aude, Auda, Audelia, Audene, Aud,
Audreah

Audris (German) One who is fortunate
and wealthy; a form of Audrey, meaning
"woman with noble strength"
Audrys, Audrisa, Audrysa, Audrissa,
Audryssa, Audriz, Audriza, Audrisia,
Audrisya, Audfis

Aurelia (Latin) Feminine form of Aurelius;
golden-haired woman
Aurelie, Aurielle, Arela, Arell, Arelie,
Arella, Arely, Aurene, Aureli, Aurele,
Aurek, Aureliana, Aurelianna, Aureline,
Aurenne, Aurilia, Auriol, Aurlel, Aurnia,
Aurum, Aurelea

Aurkene (Basque) One who has a favorable
presence
Aurkena, Aurkenia, Aurkenne

Aurora (Latin) Morning's first light; in
mythology, the goddess of the dawn
Aurore, Aurea, Aurorette

Auryon (American) A great huntress

Auset (Egyptian) In mythology, another
name for Isis, the goddess of fertility
Ausett, Ausette, Auseta, Ausetta, Ausete

AVA

We had liked Ava for some time, but by the time I was pregnant, the name had skyrocketed in popularity. We searched for other options, thinking that she might want a unique name. But we couldn't find anything we thought was as beautiful and perfect for our baby, and it seemed silly not to choose Ava just because other people loved it too. —Shana, IL

Audumla (Norse) In mythology, a giant
cow from which Ymir nursed
Audhumla, Audhumbla

Auduna (Norse) One who has been deserted

Augusta (Latin) Feminine form of
Augustus; venerable; majestic
Augustina, Agustina, Augustine, Agostina,
Agostine, Augusteen, Augustyna, Agusta,
Augustia, Austina, Austen, Austin, Austine

Aulani (Hawaiian) The king's messenger
Aulaney, Aulanee, Aulanie, Aulany,
Aulania, Aulanya, Aulanea, Aulaneah,
Aulanye

Aulis (Greek) In mythology, a princess
of Attica
Auliss, Aulisse, Aulys, Aulyss, Aulysse

Aura (Greek) Gentle breeze; in mythology,
the goddess of breezes
Auria, Auriel, Auriana, Aurah, Aurea,
Auri, Aurya, Aure

Aurear (English) One who plays gentle
music
Aureare, Auriar, Auriare, Auryare

Austine (French) Feminine form of Austin;
one who is respected
Austina, Austyn, Austyna, Austeene,
Austeena, Austeine, Austeina, Austiene,
Austiena, Austeane, Austeana

Autonoe (Greek) In mythology, a woman
who was driven mad by Dionysus

Autumn ○ (English) Born in the fall
Autum

Ava ○ ○ (German / Iranian) A birdlike
woman / from the water
Avah, Avalee, Avaleigh, Avali, Avalie,
Avaley, Avelaine, Avelina, Aveline, Avelyn,
Avia, Avian, Aviana, Aviance, Avianna,
Avis, Aves, Avice, Avais, Aveis, Avise,
Avyce, Avyse, Avlynn

Avalbane (Gaelic) From the white orchard
Avalbayne, Availbaine, Avalbain,
Avalbanne

Avalon (Latin / English) From the island paradise/ in Arthurian legend, Arthur's burial place
Avallon, Avaloni, Avalona, Avalonia, Avalonie, Avalony, Avalonya, Avaron, Avarona, Avilon

Avani (Indian) From the earth
Avanie, Avany, Avaney, Avanee, Avanea, Avanye

Avari (American) From the heavens
Avarie, Avary, Avarey, Avaree, Avarea, Avarye

Avariella (American) A woman of great strength
Avarielle, Avariell, Avariel, Avariela

Avasa (Indian) One who is independent
Avasah, Avassa, Avasia, Avassah, Avasiah, Avasea, Avaseah

Avatara (Hindi) The incarnation of gods; descending
Avatarra, Avatarah, Avatari, Avatarie, Avatary, Avatarey, Avatarea, Avatareah, Avataree, Avatarrah

Ave (Latin) One to whom all bow

Avena (English) From the oat field
Avenah, Aviena, Avyna, Avina, Avinah, Avynah, Avienah, Aveinah, Aveina

Aveolela (Samoan) Resembling the rays of the sun

Avera (Hebrew) One who transgresses
Averah, Avyra, Avira

Averna (Latin) In mythology, the queen of the underworld
Avernah, Avirna

Avery ✪ (English) One who is a wise ruler; of the nobility
Avrie, Averey, Averie, Averi, Averee, Averea, Avereah

Aveta (Celtic) In mythology, the goddess of childbirth and midwives
Avetah, Avetta, Avettah

Avi (Hebrew) The Lord is my father
Avie, Avy, Avey, Avee, Aveah, Avea

Aviana (Latin) Blessed with a gracious life
Avianah, Avianna, Aviannah, Aviane, Avianne, Avyana, Avyanna, Avyane, Avyanne

Avichayil (Hebrew) Our Lord is strong
Abichall, Avigail, Avigayil

Aviva (Hebrew) One who is innocent and joyful; resembling springtime
Avivi, Avivah, Aviv, Avivie, Avivice, Avni, Avri, Avyva, Avivit

Avonaco (Native American) One who is lean and bearlike

Avonmora (Irish) From the great river
Avonmoria, Avonmore, Avonmorra, Avon, Avonmorea

Awel (Welsh) One who is as refreshing as a breeze
Awell, Awele, Awela, Awella

Awen (Welsh) A fluid essence; a muse; a flowing spirit
Awenn, Awenne, Awin, Awinn, Awinne, Awyn, Awynn, Awynne

Awena (Welsh) One who can foretell the future
Awenna, Awyna, Awynna, Awina, Awinna

Awenasa (Native American) One's home

Awendela (Native American) Of the morning
Awendele, Awendell, Awendel, Awendella

Awenita (Native American) Resembling a fawn
Awenyta, Awenieta, Awentia, Awinita, Awinyta, Awintia

Awhina (Maori) One who helps; a supporter
Awhyna, Awheina, Awhiena, Awheana, Awheena

Axelle (German / Latin / Hebrew) Source of life; small oak / axe / peace
Axella, Axell, Axele, Axl, Axela, Axelia, Axellia

Aya (Hebrew / Japanese) Birdlike woman; ability to fly swiftly / woven silk
Ayah, Aiya, Aia, Aiah, Aiyah

Ayala (Hebrew) Resembling a gazelle
Ayalah, Ayalla, Ayallah

Ayame (Japanese) Resembling an iris
Ayami, Ayamie, Ayamee, Ayamey, Ayamy, Ayamea, Ayameah

Ayan (African) One who is bright

Ayanna (Hindi / African) One who is innocent / resembling a beautiful flower
Ayana, Ayania, Ahyana, Ayna, Ayaniah, Ayannah

Ayasha (Native American) Dear little child
Ayashe

Ayita (Native American) First in the dance; hardworking
Aitah, Aiyta

Ayla (Hebrew) From the oak tree
Aylah, Aylana, Aylanna, Aylee, Aylea, Aylene, Ayleena, Aylena, Aylie, Aylin

Aylin (Turkish) Having a moonlit halo

Ayo (African) One who brings joy to others
Ayoka

Aysel (Turkish) Resembling the moonlight
Aysell, Aysele, Aysela, Aysella

Ayushmati (Hindi) A long-lived woman
Ayushi, Ayushie, Ayushy, Ayushee, Ayushea, Ayushea, Ayushey, Ayushmatie, Ayushmatey, Ayushmaty, Ayushmatea, Ayushmateah, Ayushmatee

Aza (Arabic / African) One who provides comfort / powerful
Azia, Aiza, Aizia, Aizha

Azadeh (Persian) Of the dry earth; free of material things

Azalea (Latin / Hebrew) Of the dry earth; resembling the flower / one who is spared by God
Azalia, Azaleah, Azaley, Azalee, Azaleigh, Azalie, Azalei, Azali, Azaly, Azelia, Azalya, Azelya, Azelea, Azelie, Aziel, Azhar, Azhara

Azana (African) One who is superior
Azanah, Azanna, Azannah

Azania (Hebrew) One who is heard by God
Azaniah, Azanea, Azaneah, Azaniya, Azaniyah

Azar (Persian) One who is fiery; scarlet
Azara, Azaria, Azarah, Azarra, Azarrah, Azarr

Azinza (African) A seamaiden; a mermaid
Azinzah, Azynzah, Azynza

Aziza (Arabic) One who is beloved and precious
Azizi, Azizah, Azize, Azzeza, Azeeza, Azeezah

Azmera (African) A great harvester
Azmerah, Azmerra, Azmerrah

Aznii (Chechen) A famed beauty
Azni, Aznie, Azny, Azney, Aznee, Aznea, Azneah

Azra (Hebrew) One who is pure; chaste
Azrah, Azraa

Azriel (Hebrew) God is my helper
Azrael, Azriell, Azrielle, Azriela, Azriella, Azraela

Azuba (Hebrew) One who assists others
Azubah

Azuka (African) One who celebrates past glory
Azuca, Azucka, Azukah

Azure (French / Persian) Sky blue / resembling a blue semiprecious stone
Azura, Azuree, Azurine, Azora, Azurah, Azurina, Azuryn, Azuryne

Azusena (Arabic) Resembling the lily
Azucena, Asucena, Azusa

Azzah (Arabic) A young female gazelle
Azza

Baako (African) The firstborn child
Bako, Bakko, Baakko

Baara (Hebrew) In the Bible, the wife of Shaharaim
Bara, Barah, Barra, Barrah

Bab (Arabic) From the gate

Baba (African) Born on a Thursday
Babah, Babba, Babbah, Baaba

Babette (French) Form of Barbara, meaning
"a traveler from a foreign land; a stranger";
form of Elizabeth, meaning "my God is
bountiful"
*Babett, Babete, Babet, Babbet, Babbett,
Babbette, Babbete, Babita, Babitta, Babbitta,
Babs*

Baby (English) A beloved child; a spoiled
daughter
*Babi, Babie, Babey, Babe, Bebe, Babea,
Babeah*

Baca (English) From the valley of tears
*Bacah, Bacca, Baka, Bakah, Backa,
Backah, Baccah*

Bach Yen (Vietnamese) A white-skinned
woman

Badia (Arabic) An elegant lady; one who is
unique
*Badiah, Badi'a, Badiya, Badea, Badya,
Badeah*

Badu (African) The tenth-born child
Badoo

Bahar (Arabic) Born during the spring
*Bahaar, Baharr, Baharre, Bahara, Baharah,
Baharra, Baharrah*

Bahati (African) One with good fortune
*Bahatie, Bahaty, Bahatii, Bahatee, Bahiti,
Bahyti, Bahyty, Bakht, Bahatea, Bahateah,
Bahatey*

Bahija (Arabic) A cheerful woman
*Bahijah, Bahiga, Bahigah, Bahyja, Bahyjah,
Bahyga, Bahygah*

Bahira (Arabic) One who is sparkling;
brilliant
*Bahirah, Baheera, Bahyra, Bahiera, Baheira,
Bahiya, Bahiyah, Baheerah, Bahyrah,
Baheirah, Bahierah, Baheara, Bahearah*

Balbina (Latin) A very strong woman
*Balbinah, Balbinna, Balbyna, Balbeena,
Balara, Balbine, Balbyne, Balera, Balere,
Balbeenah, Balbynah, Balbeina, Balbeinah,
Balbienah, Balbiena, Balbeana, Balbeanah*

Baila (Spanish) One who dances
Byla, Bayla, Baela

Bailey ✪ (English) From the courtyard
within castle walls; a public official
*Bailee, Bayley, Baylee, Baylie, Baili, Bailie,
Baileigh, Bayleigh, Baileah, Bailea, Baylea,
Bayleah, Baylee, Bayli*

Baina (African) A sparkling woman
Bayna, Baana, Baena, Bainah, Baenah

Baja (Spanish) From the lower region

Baka (Indian) Resembling a crane
Bakah, Bakka, Backa, Bacca

Bakarne (Basque) One who dwells in
solitude

Bakura (Hebrew) Resembling ripened fruit
Bakurah

Baldhart (German) A bold woman having
great strength
*Balhart, Baldhard, Balhard, Ballard,
Balard, Balarde*

Baligha (Arabic) One who is forever
eloquent
*Balighah, Baleegha, Balygha, Baliegha,
Baleagha, Baleigha*

Ballade (English) A poetic woman
Ballad, Ballaid, Ballaed, Ballayd

Ballari (Indian) One who walks softly
*Balari, Ballarie, Balarie, Ballary, Balary,
Ballarey, Balarey, Ballaree, Balaree,
Ballarea, Balarea, Ballareah, Balareah*

Bambina (Italian) A young daughter; a
baby girl
*Bambyna, Bambinna, Bambie, Bambi,
Bambey, Bambee, Bamhi, Bambea,
Bambeah*

Banan (Arabic) Having delicate fingertips

Banba (Irish) In mythology, a patron
goddess

Bandana (Spanish) A brightly colored
headwrap
Bandanah, Bandanna, Bandannah

Bandele (African) Child who is born away
from home
*Bandel, Bandelle, Bandell, Bandela,
Bandella*

B

Banji (African) The second-born of twins
Banjie, Banjey, Banjy, Banjee, Banjea, Banjeah

Banner (American) A decorative symbol
Baner, Bannyr, Banyr, Bannor, Bannar, Bannir

Bano (Arabic) A princess; a distinguished lady
Banow, Baano, Banoe, Banowe

Banon (Welsh) A woman sovereign

Bansuri (Indian) One who is musical
Bansurie, Bansari, Banseri, Bansurri, Bansury, Bansurey, Bansuree, Bansurea, Bansureah

Baptista (Greek) Feminine form of Baptiste; the baptizer
Baptistah, Baptistya, Baptistiya, Baptistia, Baptistina, Baptysta, Bapteesta, Baptiesta, Battista, Batista, Batysta, Bautista, Bautysta

Bara (Hebrew) One who is chosen
Barah, Barra, Barrah

Baraka (Arabic) A white-skinned woman; fair; having God's favor
Barakka, Baracka, Baracca, Barakah

Barbara (Latin) A traveler from a foreign land; a stranger
Barbra, Barbarella, Barbarita, Baibin, Baibre, Bairbre, Barbary, Barb, Barbi, Barbie, Barby, Barbey, Bobbie, Barbro, Barabal, Barabell, Basha, Basham, Baubie, Bobbi, Bobby, Bora, Borbala, Borhala, Borka, Boriska, Borsca, Borska, Borsala, Brosca, Broska

Barcelona (Spanish) Woman from the city in Spain

Barika (African) A flourishing woman; one who is successful
Barikah, Baryka, Barikka, Barykka, Baricka, Barycka, Baricca, Barycca

Barkarna (Basque) One who is lonely
Barkarne, Barkarnia, Barkarniah, Barkarnya, Barkarniya, Barkarn

Barr (English) A lawyer
Barre, Bar

Barran (Irish) From the little mountain's top
Barrane, Baran, Barane, Barrayne, Barayne, Baranne, Barann, Barrann

Barras (English) From among the trees

Barrett (German / English) Having the strength of a bear / an argumentative person
Barett, Barrette, Barette, Barrete, Barete, Barretta, Baretta, Barreta, Bareta

Barrie (Irish) A markswoman
Barea, Baree, Barey, Barri, Barria, Barriah, Barrya, Barryah, Barya, Baryah

Basanti (Indian) Born during the spring
Basantie, Basanty, Basantii, Basantey, Basantee, Basantea, Basanteah

Bashirah (Arabic) One who is joyful; a bringer of good tidings
Bashira, Basheera, Bashyra, Bashiera, Basheira, Basheyra, Bashiga, Bashyga, Bushra, Basheerah, Bashyrah, Bashierah, Basheirah, Basheyrah, Basheara, Bashearah

Basilia (Greek) Feminine form of Basil; of the royal line; queenly; one who is valiant
Basiliya, Basilya, Basilie, Basilea, Basylia, Basylya, Basili, Basylie, Basyli, Basileah

Basimah (Arabic) One who smiles a lot
Basima, Basimma, Basyma, Baseema, Basiema, Basmah, Basma, Basymah, Baseemah, Basiemah, Baseima, Baseimah, Baseama, Basemah

Bastet (Egyptian) A fiery woman; in mythology, goddess of fertility and the sun
Bastett, Bastette, Basteta, Bastetta

Bathild (German) Heroine of a bold battle
Bathilde, Bathilda

Bathsheba (Hebrew) The daughter of the oath, in the Bible, a wife of King David and mother of Solomon
Bathshebah, Bathsheeba, Bathshyba, Bathshieba, Bethsheba, Bethshebah

Bathshira (Arabic) The seventh daughter
Bathshirah, Bathsheera, Bathsheerah, Bathshiera, Bathshierah, Bathsheira, Bathsheirah, Bathsheara, Bathshearah, Bathshyra, Bathshyrah

Battseeyon (Hebrew) A daughter of Zion
Batseyon, Batseyonne, Battzion, Batzion

Batul (Arabic) Woman who is chaste; a virgin
Batulle, Batoole, Batool, Batula, Batulah, Betul, Betool, Betulle, Betula, Betoole

Batya (Hebrew) A daughter of God
Batyah, Batiya, Bitya, Bitiya, Bityah

Baucis (Greek) In mythology, the wife of
Philemon

Bay (French) Resembling a berry
Baye, Bai, Bae

Bayo (Nigerian) One who finds joy

Beadu (English) A warrior woman

Beagan (Gaelic) A petite woman

Beatha (Celtic) One who gives life
Betha, Beathah, Bethah

Beathag (Hebrew) One who serves God

Beathas (Scottish) Having great wisdom

Beatrice (Latin) One who blesses others
*Beatrix, Beatriz, Beatriss, Beatrisse, Bea,
Beatrize, Beatricia, Beatrisa, Beate, Beata,
Beat, Bee, Beitris, Betrys, Bettrys, Bice*

Bebba (Hebrew) One who is pledged to
God
Bebbah

Bebhinn (Irish) An accomplished singer
*Bebhin, Bebhynn, Bebhyn, Bevin, Bevinne,
Bevinn, Bevyn*

Bechira (Hebrew) One who is chosen
*Bechirah, Bechyra, Bechyrah, Becheara,
Bechearah, Becheera, Becheerah*

Beckett (English) From the small brook
Becket, Bekett, Beckette, Bekette, Beket

Becky (English) Form of Rebecca, meaning
"one who is bound to God"
*Beckey, Becki, Beckie, Becca, Becka, Bekka,
Beckee, Beckea, Beckeah*

Beda (German) A goddess; warrior woman
Bedah, Bedda, Beddah

Bedegrayne (English) From the castle
*Bedegraine, Bedegrain, Bedegrane,
Bedegraene, Bedegrayn, Bedegraen*

Bedelia (French) Woman of great strength
Bedelea, Bedeleah, Bedeliah

Befle (Latin) A beautiful and loving
woman
Beffle, Befel, Beffel

Begonia (English) Resembling the flower
*Begoniah, Begonea, Begoneah, Begoniya,
Begoniyah*

Begum (Arabic) A woman of rank
Bagum, Baegum, Baigum, Baygum

Behula (Indian) The perfect wife
*Behulah, Behulla, Behulia, Behoola,
Behullah, Behuliah, Behoolah, Behulea,
Behuleah*

Beige (French) Of the beige color

Bel (Indian) From the sacred wood

Belakane (English) An African queen
*Bellakane, Belakayne, Bellakayne,
Belakaine, Bellakaine, Belacane, Bellacane,
Belacayne, Bellacayne, Belacaine,
Bellacaine*

Belda (French) A fair maiden
Beldah, Bellda, Belldah

Belen (Spanish) Woman from Bethlehem

Belicia (Spanish) A woman dedicated
to God
*Beliciah, Beliciya, Belicya, Beleecia,
Belycia, Belishia, Belisha, Belyshia,
Beliecia, Belieciah, Beleicia, Beleiciah,
Beleacia, Beleaciah*

Belinda (English) A beautiful and tender
woman
*Belindah, Belynda, Balinda, Balynda,
Belienda, Beliendah, Balyndah, Belyndah,
Beleinda, Beleindah*

Belisama (Celtic) In mythology, a goddess
of rivers and lakes
*Belisamah, Belisamma, Belysama, Belisma,
Belysma, Belesama*

Bella (Italian) A woman famed for her
beauty
*Belle, Bela, Bell, Belita, Bellissa, Belva,
Belladonna, Belia, Bellanca, Bellance,
Bellini*

Bellona (Latin) In mythology, the goddess
of war
*Bellonah, Belona, Bellonna, Belonna,
Bellonia, Belonia*

Bem (African) A peaceful woman
Berne

Bena (Native American) Resembling a pheasant
Benah, Benna, Bennah

Benedicta (Latin) Feminine form of Benedict; one who is blessed
Benedikta, Benedetta, Benetta, Benecia, Benicia, Benita, Bennett, Bente

Benigna (Spanish) Feminine form of Benigno; one who is kind; friendly

Benjamina (Hebrew) Feminine form of Benjamin; child of my right hand
Benjameena, Benyamina, Benyameena, Benjameana, Benyameana, Benjamyna, Benyamyna

Bennu (Egyptian) Resembling an eagle

Bentlee (English) Feminine form of Bentley; from the clearing
Bentleigh, Bently, Bentli, Bentlie, Bentley, Bentlea, Bentleah

Beomia (Anglo-Saxon) Battlemaid
Beomiya, Bemia, Beorhthilde, Beorhthild, Beorhthilda, Beomea, Beomeah

Bera (Teutonic) Resembling a bear

Berangari (English) A warrior woman bearing a spear
Berangarie, Berangary, Berangarey, Berangarri, Berangaree, Berangaria, Berangariya, Berengari, Berengaria

Bergdis (Norse) Having divine protection
Bergdiss, Bergdisse, Bergdys, Bergdyss, Bergdysse

Berhane (African) My child is my light
Berhayne, Berhaine, Berhayn, Berhain, Berhaen, Berhaene

Berit (German) A glorious woman
Beret, Bereta, Berete, Berett, Beretta, Berette, Biret, Bireta, Birete, Birett, Biretta, Birette, Byret, Byreta, Byrete, Byrett, Byretta, Byrette

Bernadine (English) Feminine form of Bernard; one who has bearlike strength and courage
Bernadina, Bernadette, Bernadetta, Berdina, Berdine, Berdyne, Berdyna, Berangër, Bernadea, Bernarda, Bernetta, Bernette, Bernita, Bernelle, Berna, Berneen, Bernardina, Bernardine, Berne, Bern

Bernice (Greek) One who brings victory
Berenisa, Berenise, Berenice, Bernicia, Bernisha, Berniss, Bernyce, Bernys, Beryss

Beronica (English) Form of Veronica, meaning "displaying her true image"
Beronicah, Beronic, Beronicca, Beronicka, Beronika, Beronicha, Beronique, Beranique, Beroniqua, Beronnica, Beronice, Baronica, Baronika, Berhonica, Berinica, Berohnica, Bironica, Bironiqua, Bironika, Bironique, Beronka, Beronkia, Beronne, Byronica, Bronica, Bronika, Broniqua, Bronique, Byroniqua, Byronique, Byronika, Beruka, Beruszhka

Berry (English) Feminine form of Barry; fair-haired woman; resembling a berry fruit
Berrey, Berri, Berrie, Berree, Beri, Berie, Bery, Beree, Berey, Berrea, Berea, Berreah, Bereah

Bertha (German) One who is famously bright and beautiful
Berta, Berthe, Berth, Bertina, Bertyna, Bertine, Bertyne, Birte, Birtha, Birthe

Berthog (Welsh) A wealthy woman; one who is prosperous

Bertilda (English) A luminous battlemaiden
Bertilde, Bertild

Bertille (French) A heroine
Bertill, Bertile, Bertil, Bertylle, Bertyll, Bertyle, Bertyl

Bertrade (English) An intelligent advisor
Bertraide, Bertrayde, Bertraed, Beortbtraed, Bertraid, Bertrayd, Bertraede

Beruriah (Hebrew) Woman selected by God
Beruria, Beruriya, Berurea, Berurya, Berureah

Beryl (English) Resembling the pale-green precious stone
Beryll, Berylle, Beril, Berill, Berille

Bess (English) Form of Elizabeth, meaning "my God is bountiful"
Besse, Bessi, Bessie, Bessy, Bessey, Bessee, Bessea, Besseah

Bestla (Norse) In mythology, a frost giantess and mother of Odin

Beth (English) Form of Elizabeth, meaning "my God is bountiful"
Bethe

Bethabara (Hebrew) From the house of confidence
Bethebara, Bethabarra, Bethebarra, Bethbara, Bethbarra

Bethany (Hebrew) From the house of figs
Bethan, Bethani, Bethanie, Bethanee, Bethaney, Bethane, Bethann, Bethanne, Bethanea, Bethaneah

Bethea (Hebrew) A maidservant of God
Bethia, Betheah, Bethiya, Bethya, Betia, Betje, Bethiyah, Bethyah

Bethel (Hebrew) Of the house of God
Bethell, Bethele, Bethelle, Bethelia, Betheliya, Betheli, Bethelie, Bethely, Bethelee, Bethiar, Betheley, Betheleigh, Bethelea, Betheleah

Bethesda (Hebrew) From the house of mercy
Bethseda, Bethsaida

Betty (English) Form of Elizabeth, meaning "my God is bountiful"
Betti, Bettie, Bettey, Bettee, Bette, Betsy, Betsey, Betsi, Betsie, Betsee, Bettina, Bettine, Bettyne, Bettyna, Betje, Bettea, Betteah, Betsea, Betseah

Beulah (Hebrew) Woman who is claimed as a wife
Beula, Beulla, Bulah, Bula, Beullah

Beverly (English) From the beaver's stream
Beverlee, Beverley, Beverlie, Beverli, Beverlee, Beverleigh, Beverlea, Beverleah

Bevin (Welsh) Daughter of Evan
Bevan, Bevann, Bevanne, Bevina, Bevine, Bevinnah, Bevyn, Bevyna, Bevyne

Beyla (Norse) In mythology, an elf and minor goddess
Beylah, Bayla, Baylah

Beyonce (American) One who surpasses others
Beyoncay, Beyonsay, Beyonsai, Beyonsae, Beyonci, Beyoncie, Beyoncee, Beyoncea, Beyonceah

Bha (Indian) Having a starlike quality

Bharati (Hindi) In Hinduism, goddess of sacrifice
Bharatie, Bharaty, Bharatey, Bharatee, Bharatea, Bharateah, Barati, Baratie, Baraty, Baratey, Baratee, Baratea, Barateah

Bhavani (Indian) A giver of life
Bhavanie, Bhavany, Bhavaney, Bhavanee, Bhavanea, Bhavaneah, Bavani, Bavanie, Bavany, Bavaney, Bavanee, Bavanea, Bavaneah

Bhumidevi (Hindi) In Hinduism, goddess of the earth
Bhumi, Bhoomi, Bhu, Bhudevi

Bian (Vietnamese) A secretive woman

Bianca (Italian) A shining, fair-skinned woman
Bianka, Byanca, Blanca, Blanche, Biana, Bianna, Biankeh, Byanka, Blanch, Blanka

Bibi (African) A king's daughter; a lady
Bibsbebe, Beebee, Byby, Beabea

Bibiana (Italian) Form of Vivian, meaning "one who is full of life; vibrant"
Bibiane, Bibianna, Bibianne, Bibiann, Bibine

Bienvenida (Spanish) A welcome daughter
Bienvenidah, Bienvenyda, Bienvenita, Bienvenyta

Bifrost (Scandinavian) From the bridge
Bifroste, Byfrost, Byfroste

Bijou (French) As precious as a jewel

Bikita (African) Resembling an anteater
Bikitah, Bikyta, Bykita, Bykyta, Bikeyta, Bikeita, Bikieta, Bikeata

Bilhah (Hebrew) One who is bashful; in the Bible, a concubine of Jacob
Bilha, Baalah, Balah, Bala, Bilhan, Billha, Billhah

Billie (English) Feminine form of William; having a desire to protect
Billi, Billy, Billey, Billee, Billeigh, Billea, Billeah

Bilqis (Arabic) The queen of Sheba
Bilqys, Bilqees, Bilquis

Bimala (Indian) One who is pure
Bimalla, Bymala, Bimalah, Bemala, Bemalla, Bymala

Binah (Hebrew) Having intelligence and understanding
Bina, Bynah, Byna

Binga (German) From the hollow
Bingah, Bynga, Binge, Bynge, Bingeh, Byngeh

Binta (African) With God
Binte, Bint, Binti, Binty, Bintie, Bintee, Bintea, Binteah

Birdena (American) Resembling a little bird
Birdine, Byrdene, Byrdena, Birdina, Byrdina, Byrdine, Birdeena, Birdeene, Byrdeena, Byrdeene, Birdyna, Birdyne, Byrdyna, Byrdyne, Birdie, Birdi, Birdy, Birdey, Birdee, Burdette

Birkita (Celtic) Woman of great strength
Birkitah, Birkyta, Byrkita, Byrkyta, Birkeyta, Birkeita, Birkeata, Birkieta

Bisa (African) A daughter who is greatly loved
Bisah, Bissa, Bissah, Bysa, Bysah, Byssa, Byssah

Bisgu (Anglo-Saxon) A compassionate woman
Bisgue, Bysgu, Bysgue

Bithron (Hebrew) A child of song

Bixenta (Basque) A victorious woman

Bjork (Scandinavian) Of the birch tree
Bjorke, Björk

Blaine (Scottish/Irish) A saint's servant/a thin woman
Blayne, Blane, Blain, Blayn, Blaen, Blaene

Blair (Scottish) From the field of battle
Blaire, Blare, Blayre, Blaer, Blaere, Blayr

Blaise (French) One with a lisp or a stammer
Blayse, Blaze, Blaize, Blas, Blasa, Blase, Blasia, Blaese, Blaeze, Blayze

Blake (English) A dark beauty
Blayk, Blayke, Blaik, Blaike, Blaek, Blaeke

Blanchefleur (French) Resembling a white flower
Blancheflor, Blancheflour, Blancheflora

Blanda (Latin / Spanish) A mild-tempered woman / a flattering woman
Blandah, Blandina, Blandine, Blandyna, Blandyne

Blathnaid (Irish) As delicate as a flower
Blathnaide, Blathnade, Blathnayde, Blathnayd, Blathnaed, Blathnaede

Blenda (Latin) Dazzling
Blendah, Blinda, Blynda, Blindah, Blyndah

Bletsung (English) One who is blessed by God
Blerung, Blessing

Blimah (Hebrew) One resembling a blossom
Blima, Blime, Blyma, Blymah

Bliss (English) Filled with extreme joy
Blyss, Blysse, Blisse, Blix, Blyx

Blodwedd (Welsh) The face of a flower

Blodwen (Welsh) Resembling a white flower
Blodwenne, Blodwyn, Blodwynne, Blodwin, Blodwinne, Blodwenn, Blodwynn, Blodwinn

Blondell (French) A fair-haired woman
Blondelle, Blondele, Blondene, Blondel, Blondela, Blondella

Blossom (English) A woman who is lovely, fresh, and flowerlike
Blosom, Blossum, Blosum

Blue (American) A woman with bright-blue eyes
Blu

Bluebell (English) Resembling the blue flower
Bluebelle, Blubell, Blubelle, Bluebella, Blubella

Bluinse (Irish) A white-skinned woman
Bluince, Bluynse, Bluynce

Bluma (Hebrew) Resembling a flower's bloom
Blumah, Blumma, Blummah, Blooma, Bloomah

Bly (Native American) A tall child

Blyana (Irish) Woman of great strength
Blyanna, Bliana, Blianna, Blyann, Blyane, Blyanne, Bliane, Bliann, Blianne

Blythe (English) Filled with happiness
Blyth, Blithe, Blith

Bo (Chinese / Swedish) A precious daughter / a lively woman

Boadicea (English) A heroic queen

Bo-bae (Korean) A treasured child

Bodgana (Polish) A gift of God
Bodganah, Bodganna, Bodgane, Bodgann, Bodganne, Bogna, Bohdana, Bohdanna, Bohdane, Bohdann, Bohdanne, Bohgana, Bohganna, Bohgane, Bohgann, Bohganne

Bodil (Norse) A fighting woman
Bodile, Bodille, Bodila, Bodilla

Bolade (Nigerian) Honor comes

Bolanile (Nigerian) From the house of riches

Bolbe (Latin) From the town near the lake
Bolbi, Bolbie, Bolbee, Bolbea, Bolbeah, Bolby, Bolbey

Bona Dea (Latin) In mythology, an ancient fertility goddess

Bonamy (French) A very good friend
Bonamey, Bonami, Bonamie, Bonamee, Bonamei, Bonamea, Bonameah

Bonfilia (Italian) A good daughter
Bonfiliah, Bonfilea, Bonfileah, Bonfiliya, Bonfiliyah

Bonie (English) A well-behaved young woman
Boni, Bona, Bonea, Boneah, Bonee

Bonnie (Scottish) A pretty and charming girl
Bonny, Bonni, Bonita, Bonnibel, Bonnibelle, Bonnibele, Bonnibell, Bonney, Bonnee, Bonnea, Bonneah

Borbala (Hungarian) From a foreign land
Bora, Boriska, Borka, Borsala, Borsca, Borah, Borballa

Borghild (Norse) Strong in battle; in mythology, the wife of Sigmund
Borghilde, Borghilda

Borgny (Norwegian) One who offers help
Borgney, Borgni, Borgnie, Borgnee, Borgnea, Borgneah

Botan (Japanese) As fresh as a blossom
Botann, Botane, Botanne, Botana, Botanna

Botilda (Norse) A commanding heroine
Botild, Botilde

Boudicca (Celtic) A victorious queen
Boudicea, Bodiccea, Bodicea, Bodicia

Bozica (Slavic) Born at Christmastime
Bozicah, Bozicca, Bozika, Bozicka, Bozyca, Bozyka, Bozycka, Bozi

Bracha (Hebrew) One who is blessed
Brachah, Bracca, Braca, Bracka, Braka, Brakka

Bracken (English) Resembling a large, coarse fern
Braken, Braccan

Bradana (Scottish) Resembling the salmon
Bradanah, Bradanna, Bradan, Bradane, Bradann, Bradanne, Braydan, Braydana, Braydanne

Bradley (English) From the broad field
Bradlea, Bradleah, Bradlee, Bradlei, Bradleigh, Bradli, Bradlia, Bradliah, Bradlie, Bradly, Bradlya

Brady (Irish) A large-chested woman
Bradey, Bradee, Bradi, Bradie, Bradea, Bradeah

Braima (African) Mother of multitudes
Braimah, Brayma, Braema, Braymah, Braemah

Braith (Welsh) A freckled young woman
Braithe, Brayth, Braythe, Braeth, Braethe

Brandy (English) A woman wielding a sword; an alcoholic drink
Brandey, Brandi, Brandie, Brandee, Branda, Brande, Brandelyn, Brandilyn, Brandyn, Brandice, Brandyce, Brendy, Brendi, Brendi, Brendee, Brandea, Brandeah

Branice (English) God is gracious
Branyce, Branise, Branyse

Branka (Slowenian) Feminine form of Branislav; a glorious protector
Brankah, Brancka, Branckah, Brancca, Branccah

Brann (Welsh) A ravenlike woman
Branne, Bran

Branwen (Welsh) A dark beauty; in mythology, goddess of love and beauty
Branwenn, Branwenne, Branwyn, Branwynn, Branwynne, Brangwen, Brangwy, Bronwen, Bronwenn, Bronwenne, Bronwyn, Bronwynn, Bronwynne

Brasen (American) Woman filled with self-assurance
Brazen

Braulia (Spanish) One who is glowing
Brauliah, Braulea, Brauleah, Brauliya, Brauliyah

Brazil (Spanish) Of the ancient tree
Brasil, Brazile, Brazille, Brasille, Bresil, Brezil, Bresille, Brezille

Brett (English) Woman of Britain or Brittany
Bret, Bretta, Breta, Brette, Brit, Brita, Britta, Brite

Briallan (Welsh) Resembling a primrose
Briallen, Brialan, Brialen, Breeallan, Breeallen, Bryallan, Bryalan, Bryallen, Bryalen

Brianna ○ (Irish) Feminine form of Brian; from the high hill; one who ascends
Breanna, Breanne, Breana, Breann, Breeana, Breeanna, Breona, Breonna, Briana, Brianne, Briann, Briannah, Brienna, Brienne, Bryana, Bryann, Bryanna, Bryanne, Brina, Bryna, Briannon, Brianda, Bria, Bree, Brie, Brea, Brielle, Bryn, Bren, Brynn, Brenne, Brynne, Brynna, Brynnan, Brynelle

Briar (English) Resembling a thorny plant
Brier, Bryar, Bryer

BRENNA

We chose the name Brenna for my Irish heritage, and also because my husband and I and our two daughters all loved it. We have been surprised at how often she gets called Breanna though. It means "raven," but ironically she has very blonde hair! —Nancy, NC

Breck (Irish) A freckled girl
Brek, Brecken, Breckin, Breckan

Breena (Irish) From the fairy palace
Brina, Bryna, Breen, Brenee, Breene, Breina, Briena, Breyna

Breezy (English) An animated and light-hearted woman
Breezey, Breezi, Breezie, Breezee, Breezea, Breezeah

Bregus (Welsh) A frail woman

Brencis (Slavic) Crowned with laurel

Brenda (Irish) Feminine form of Brendan; a princess; wielding a sword
Brynda, Brinda, Breandan, Brendalynn, Brendolyn, Brend, Brienda

Brenna (Welsh) A ravenlike woman
Brinna, Brenn, Bren, Brennah, Brina, Brena, Brenah

Brennan (English) Resembling a little raven
Brennea, Brennen, Brennon, Brennyn

Brice (Welsh) One who is alert; ambitious
Bryce

Bridget (Irish) A strong and protective woman; in mythology, goddess of fire, wisdom, and poetry
Bridgett, Bridgette, Briget, Brigette, Bridgit, Bridgitte, Birgit, Birgitte, Birgitta, Berget, Bergitte, Bergit, Berit, Biddy, Bridie, Bride, Brid, Brigetta, Bridgetta, Brighid, Bidelia, Bidina, Breeda, Brigid, Brigida, Brigidia, Brigit, Brigitta, Brigitte, Brietta, Briette, Brigantia, Bryga, Brygida, Brygid

Brilliant (American) A dazzling and sparkling woman

Brimlad (Anglo-Saxon) From the seaway
Brymlad, Brimlod, Brymlod

Briseis (Greek) In mythology, the Trojan widow abducted by Achilles
Brisys, Brisa, Brisia, Brisha, Brissa, Briza, Bryssa, Brysa

Brisingamen (Norse) In mythology, Freya's charmed necklace

Brites (Portuguese) One who has power

Brittany (English) A woman from Great Britain
Britany, Brittanie, Brittaney, Brittani, Brittanee, Britney, Britnee, Britny, Britni, Britnie, Brittania, Brittnee, Brittni, Brittnie, Brittney, Brittny, Brettany, Brettani, Brettanie, Brettaney, Brettanee, Britaine, Britaina, Britani, Britania, Brittanya

Brona (Irish) A sorrowful woman
Bronah, Bronna, Bronnah

Brook ✪ (English) From the running stream
*Brooke, Brookie, **Brooklyn**, Brooklynn, Brooklynne*

Brucie (French) Feminine form of Bruce; from the brushwood thicket
Brucina, Brucine, Brucy, Brucey, Brucea, Bruceah, Brucee, Bruci

Bruna (German) A dark-haired woman
Brune, Brunella, Brunelle, Brunela, Brunele, Brunetta

Brunhild (German / Norse) A dark and noble battlemaiden / in mythology, queen of the Valkyries
Brunhilde, Brunhilda, Brunnehild, Brunnehilde, Brunnehilda, Brynhild, Brynhilde, Brynhilda

Bryony (English) Of the healing vine
Briony, Brione, Brioni, Brionna, Brionne, Brionee, Bryonee, Bryoni, Bryone, Bryonie, Brionie, Bryani, Bryanie, Bryanee, Brionea, Bryonea, Brioneah, Bryoneah

Buena (Spanish) A good woman
Buen, Buan

Buffy (English) Form of Elizabeth, meaning "my God is bountiful"
Buffi, Buffie, Buffey, Buffee, Buffea, Buffeah

Bulbul (Arabic) Resembling the nightingale

Bunny (American) Resembling a little rabbit
Bunni, Bunnie, Bunney, Bunnee, Bunnea, Bunneah

Bupe (African) A hospitable woman

Burgundy (French) Woman from a region of France known for its Burgundy wine
Burgandee, Burgandey, Burgandi, Burgandie, Burgandy, Burgunde, Burgundee, Burgundey, Burgundi, Burgundie, Burgandea, Burgundea

Burnett (French) Referring to the color of brown
Burnet, Burnette, Burnetta, Burneta, Burnete

Bushra (Arabic) A good omen
Bushrah

Butch (American) A manly woman

Buthaynah (Arabic) From the soft sand; having soft skin
Buthayna, Buthainah, Buthaina, Buthana, Buthanah

Butterfly (American) Resembling a beautiful and colorful winged insect

Bysen (Anglo-Saxon) A unique young lady
Bysan, Byson

Cable (American) Resembling a heavy rope; having great strength
Cabel

Cabot (French) A fresh-faced beauty

Cabrina (American) Form of Sabrina, meaning "a legendary princess"
Cabrinah, Cabrinna, Cabreena, Cabriena, Cabreina, Cabryna, Cabrine, Cabryne, Cabreene, Cabrynna

Cabriole (French) An adorable girl
Cabriolle, Cabrioll, Cabriol, Cabryole, Cabryolle, Cabryoll, Cabryol, Cabriola, Cabriolla, Cabryola, Cabryolla

Caca (Latin) In mythology, the sister of a giant and the original goddess of the hearth

Cacalia (Latin) Resembling the flowering plant
Cacaliah, Cacalea, Cacaleah

Cachet (French) Marked with distinction; a prestigious woman
Cachette, Cache, Cashlin, Cashet, Cachee, Cachey, Cachay, Cachai, Cachae

Cacia (Greek) Form of Acacia, meaning "thorny tree; one who is naïve"; form of Casey, meaning "a vigilant woman"
Caciah, Cacea, Caceah

Cactus (American) Resembling the spiny plant
Caktus

Caddy (American) An alluring woman
Caddi, Caddie, Caddey, Caddee, Caddea, Caddeah

Cade (American) A precocious young woman
Caid, Caide, Cayd, Cayde, Caed, Caede

Caden (English) A battlemaiden
Cadan, Cadin, Cadon

Cadence (Latin) Rhythmic and melodious; a musical woman
Cadena, Cadenza, Cadian, Cadienne, Cadianne, Cadiene, Caydence, Cadencia

Cadha (Scottish) From the steep mountain
Cadhah

Cadhla (Irish) A beautiful woman
Cadhlah

Cadis (Greek) A sparkling young girl
Cadiss, Cadisse, Cadys, Cadyss, Cadysse

Cadwyn (Welsh) A bright, strong chain
Cadwynn, Cadwynne, Cadwin, Cadwinne, Cadwinn, Cadwen, Cadwenn, Cadwenne

Cady (American) One who is pure; finding happiness in simplicity
Cade, Cadee, Cadey, Cadi, Cadie, Cadye, Caidie, Cadyna, Cadea, Cadeah

Cael (Celtic) Of the victorious people
Caele, Caell, Caelle

Caeneus (Greek) In mythology, a woman who became a man
Caenis, Caenius

Caesaria (Greek) Feminine form of Caesar; an empress
Caesariah, Caesarea, Caesareah, Caezaria, Caezariah, Caezarea, Caezareah, Cesaria, Cesariah, Cesarea, Cesareah, Cesarina, Cesariena, Cesaryna, Cesareina, Cesareana, Cesareena, Cesarie, Cesari, Cesary, Cesarey, Cesaree, Cesareah, Cesarea

Caethes (Welsh) A slave girl

Cafell (Welsh) A priestess who is an oracle
Cafelle, Cafele, Cafel, Caffel

Caffaria (Irish) One who is helmeted
Caffarea, Caffara, Caffariah, Caffarea, Caffareah

Cahira (Irish) Feminine form of Cahir; a woman warrior
Cahirah, Caheera, Cahyra, Caheira, Cahiera, Caheerah, Cahyrah, Caheirah, Cahierah, Caheara, Cahearah

Caia (Latin) One who rejoices
Cai, Cais

Caieta (Latin) In mythology, the woman who nursed Aeneas

Cailin (Gaelic) A young woman; a lass
Caelan, Caelyn, Caileen, Cailyn, Caylin, Cailean, Caolan, Caelin

Cailleach (Scottish) An old woman; in mythology, the mother of all
Caillic

Cain (Hebrew) A spear huntress; in the Bible, murdered his brother Abel
Caine, Cayn, Cayne, Caen, Caene

Cainell (Welsh) A beautiful young girl
Cainelle, Cainele, Cainel, Caynell, Caynelle, Caynele, Caynel, Caenell, Caenel

Cainwen (Welsh) A beautiful treasure
Cainwenn, Cainwenne, Cainwin, Cainwinn, Cainwinne, Cainwyn, Cainwynn, Cainwynne, Caynwen, Caynwenn, Caynwenne, Caynwin, Caynwinne, Caynwinn, Caynwyn, Caynwynn, Caywynne

Cairo (African) From the city in Egypt

Cakusola (African) One who has the heart of a lion
Cakusolah, Cakusolla, Cakusollah

Cala (Arabic) From the castle
Calah

Calais (French) From the city in France

Calandra (Greek) Resembling a songbird; a lark
Calendre, Calynda, Calinda, Calandria, Callyr, Calynda

Calantha (Greek) Resembling a lovely flower
Calanthe, Calanthia, Calanthiah, Calantheah, Calanthea

Calatea (Greek) A flowering woman
Calateah, Calatia, Calatiah, Calatee, Calati, Calatie, Calaty, Calatey

Caldwell (English) Of the cold well
Caldwelle, Caldwele, Caldwel

Cale (Latin) A respected woman
Cayl, Cayle, Cael, Caele, Cail, Caile

Caledonia (Latin) Woman of Scotland
Caledoniah, Caledoniya, Caledona, Caledonya, Calydona

Calia (American) A known beauty
Caliah, Calea, Caleah

Calida (Spanish) A woman who is warm and loving
Calidah, Calyda, Caleeda, Caleida, Calieda, Caleda, Calydah, Caleedah, Caleidah, Caliedah, Caledah, Caleada, Caleadah

California (Spanish) From paradise; from the state of California
Califia

Calise (Greek) A gorgeous woman
Calyse, Calice, Calyce

Calista (Greek) Form of Kallisto, meaning "the most beautiful"
Calissa, Calisto, Callista, Calyssa, Calysta, Calixte, Colista, Collista, Colisto, Caliesta, Caleista, Caleasta, Caleesta

Calla (Greek) Resembling a lily; a beautiful woman
Callah

Callan (Gaelic / German) One who is powerful in battle / a talkative woman
Callen, Callon, Callyn, Calynn, Calan

Callida (Latin) A fiery young girl
Callidah, Callyda, Calleeda, Calleida, Callieda, Calleda, Callydah, Calleedah, Calleidah, Calliedah, Calledah, Calleada, Calleadah

Callidora (Greek) A beautiful gift
Callidorah, Calidora, Callydora, Calydora, Callidorra

Calligenia (Greek) Daughter born with beauty
Caligenia, Calligeniah, Caligeniah, Callygenia, Calygenia, Calligenea, Caligenea

Calliope (Greek) Form of Kalliope, meaning "having a beautiful voice"; in mythology, the muse of epic poetry
Calliopee, Calliopy, Calliopi, Calliopie, Caliope, Caliopi, Caliopie, Caliopy, Calliopea, Calliopeah, Caliopea, Caliopeah, Caliopa

Callisto (Greek) Form of Kallisto, meaning "the most beautiful"; in mythology, a nymph who was changed into a she-bear
Callista, Calisto, Calista, Calysta, Calysto, Callysto, Callysta, Calliste, Calleesto, Calleisto, Calleisto, Calleasto

Calluna (Latin) Resembling heather
Callunah, Caluna, Calunna

Calpurnia (Latin) A woman of power
Calpurniah, Calpurnea, Capurneah, Calpernia, Calpernea, Calperniah, Calperneah

Caltha (Latin) Resembling a yellow flower
Calthah, Calthia, Calthiah, Caltheah, Calthea

Calumina (Scottish) A calm and peaceful woman
Caluminah, Calumeena, Calumeenah, Calumeina, Calumeinah, Calumiena, Calumienah, Calumyna, Calumynah, Calumeana, Calumeanah

Calvina (Spanish) Feminine form of Calvino; one who is bald
Calvinah, Calvyna, Calveena, Calviena, Calvena, Calvine, Calveene, Calvinna, Calveina, Calviena, Calveana, Calvean, Calvien, Calvein

Calybe (Greek) In mythology, a nymph who was the wife of Laomedon

Calypso (Greek) A woman with secrets; in mythology, a nymph who captivated Odysseus for seven years

Camassia (American) One who is aloof
Camassiah, Camasia, Camasiah, Camassea, Camasseah, Camasea, Camaseah

Cambay (English) From the town in India
Cambaye, Cambai, Cambae

Camber (American) Form of Amber, meaning "resembling the jewel"
Cambur, Cambar, Camberly, Camberlyn, Camberli, Camberlee, Cambyr, Cambyre, Cambra, Cahmber, Camberia, Camberise, Camberlynn, Cambre

Cambria (Latin) A woman of Wales
Cambriah, Cambrea, Cambree, Cambre, Cambry, Cambrey, Cambri, Cambrie, Cymreiges, Cambreah

Camdyn (English) Of the enclosed valley
Camden, Camdan, Camdon, Camdin

Cameka (American) Form of Tameka, meaning "a twin"
Camekah, Cameeka, Camieka, Cameika, Camecka, Cemeka, Cymeka, Comeka, Cameca, Cameeca, Camekia, Camecia

Camelot (English) Of the king's court; in Arthurian legend, King's Arthur's castle
Camalot, Camolot, Camylot

Cameo (English) A small, perfect child
Cammeo

Cameron (Scottish) Having a crooked nose
Cameryn, Camryn, Camerin, Camren, Camrin, Camron

Camilla ☙ (Italian) Feminine form of Camillus; a ceremonial attendant; a noble virgin
*Camile, Camille, **Camila**, Camillia, Caimile, Camillei, Cam, Camelai, Camelia, Camella, Camellia, Camela, Cammi*

Campbell (Scottish) Having a crooked mouth
Campbel, Campbelle, Campbele

Cana (Turkish) A beloved daughter
Canan

Canace (Greek) Born of the wind

Candace (Ethiopian / Greek) A queen / one who is white and glowing
Candice, Candiss, Candyce, Candance, Candys, Candyss

Candelara (Spanish) A spiritual woman
Candelora, Candelaria, Candelariah, Candelarea, Candelareah

Candida (Latin) A white-skinned woman
Candide

Candra (Latin) One who is glowing

Candy (English) A sweet girl; form of Candida, meaning "a white-skinned woman"; form of Candace, meaning "a queen / one who is white and glowing"
Candey, Candi, Candie, Candee, Candea, Candeah

Caneadea (Native American) From the horizon
Caneadeah, Caneadia, Caneadiah

Canei (Greek) One who is pure

Canens (Latin) The personification of song; in mythology, a nymph
Caniad, Cannia, Canta, Cantilena, Cantrix

Canika (American) A woman shining with grace
Canikah, Caneeka, Canicka, Canyka, Canycka, Caneekah, Canickah, Canykah, Canyckah, Caneika, Caneikah, Canieka, Caniekah, Caneaka, Caneakah

Canisa (Greek) One who is very much loved
Canisah, Canissa, Canysa, Caneesa, Canyssa

Cannelita (Italian) From the beautiful garden
Cannelitah, Canelita, Cannelyta, Canelyta, Canneleeta, Caneleeta, Canneleata, Caneleata, Canneleita, Caneleita, Cannelieta, Canelieta

Cannenta (Latin) A woman possessing healing powers

Cannes (French) A woman from Cannes

Cantabria (Latin) From the mountains
Cantabriah, Cantebria, Cantabrea, Cantebrea

Cantara (Arabic) From the small bridge
Cantarah, Cantarra, Cantera, Canterah, Canterra, Cantarrah, Canterrah

Caoilfhinn (Celtic) A slender and attractive woman

Caoimhe (Irish) One who is charming and beautiful

Capeka (Slavic) Resembling a young stork
Capekah, Capecca, Capeccah

Capelta (American) A fanciful woman

Capita (Latin) An intelligent and superior woman
Capitah, Capyta, Capeta, Capeeta, Capieta, Capeita, Capta, Capytah, Capetah, Capeetah, Capietah, Capeitah, Capeata, Capeatah

Caplice (American) One who is spontaneous
Caplise, Capleece, Capleese, Capliece, Capliese, Capleice, Capleise, Capleace, Caplease

Capote (Spanish) One who is protected; wearing a cloak

Caprice (Italian) One who is impulsive and unpredictable
Capri, Capricia, Capriana, Caprina, Capryce, Caprise, Capryse

Capricorn (Latin) The tenth sign of the zodiac; the goat

Caprina (Italian) Woman of the island Capri
Caprinah, Caprinna, Capryna, Capreena, Caprena, Capreenah, Carpynah, Capriena, Caprienah, Capreina, Capreinah, Capreana, Capreanah

Capucina (French) Resembling the watercress
Capucine, Capucinia, Capucinea

Cara (Italian / Gaelic) One who is dearly loved / a good friend
Carah, Caralee, Caralie, Caralyn, Caralynn, Carrah, Carra, Chara, Cahra, Caradoc, Caraf, Caraid, Carajean, Caralea, Caralisa, Carita, Carella, Carilla, Caraleigh, Caraleah

Cardea (Latin) In mythology, the goddess of thresholds
Cardeah, Cardia, Cardiah

Caresse (French) A woman with a tender touch
Caress, Caressa, Carressa

Carew (Latin) One who rides a chariot
Carewe, Crewe, Crew

Carina (Latin) Little darling
Carena, Carinna, Carrina, Cariana, Carin, Carine, Caren, Carinen, Caron, Carren, Carron, Carrin, Caryn, Caryna, Carynn, Careena, Cariena, Careina, Careana

Carinthia (English) From the city in Austria
Carinthiah, Carinthea, Carintheah, Carynthia, Carynthiah, Carynthea, Caryntheah

Carissa (Greek) A woman of grace
Carisa, Carrisa, Carrissa, Carissima

Carla (Latin) Feminine form of Carl; a free woman
Carlah, Carlana, Carlee, Carleen, Carleigh, Carlena, Carlene, Carletta, Carlette, Carley, Carli, Carlia, Carlie, Carlina, Carlisa, Carlita, Carlla, Carly, Carlyn, Carlen, Carlin, Carling, Carlea, Carleah

Carlanda (American) Our darling daughter
Carland, Carlande, Carlandia, Carlandiah, Carlandea, Carlandeah

Carlessa (American) One who is restless
Carlessah, Carlesa, Carlesah

Carlisa (Italian) A friendly woman
Carlisah, Carlissa, Carlissah, Carlysa, Carlysah, Carlyssa, Carlyssah

Carlisle (English) From the fort at Luguvalium
Carlysle, Carlyle, Carlile

Carmel (Hebrew) Of the fruitful orchard
Carmela, Carmella, Carmila, Carmilla, Carmel, Carmelle, Carmelita, Carmelina, Carmeline, Carmelia

Carmen (Latin) A beautiful song
Carma, Carmelita, Carmencita, Carmia, Carmie, Carmina, Carmine, Carmita, Carmyna, Carmyta, Carmea, Carman, Carmin, Carminda, Carmya

Carmensita (Spanish) One who is dear
Carmensyta, Carmensitah, Carmensytah, Carmens, Carmense

Carmenta (Latin) In mythology, the goddess of childbirth
Carminta, Carmynta

Carna (Latin) In mythology, a goddess who ruled the heart

Carnation (Latin) Resembling the flower; becoming flesh

Carnelian (Latin) Resembling the deep-red gem
Carnelyan, Carneliann, Carnelianne, Carnela, Carnelia

Carni (Latin) One who is vocal
Carnie, Carny, Carney, Carnee, Carnea, Carneah, Carnia, Carniah, Carnea, Carneah, Carniya, Carniyah, Carnielle, Carniele, Carniell, Carniella, Carniela

Carody (American) A humorous woman
Carodi, Carodey, Carodie, Carodee, Carodea, Carodeah

Carol (English) Form of Caroline, meaning "a joyous song; a small, strong woman"
Carola, Carole, Carolle, Carolla, Caroly, Caroli, Carolie, Carolee, Caroleigh, Carel, Caral, Caril, Carroll, Caryl

Carys (Welsh) One who loves and is loved
Caryss, Carysse, Caris, Cariss, Carisse, Cerys, Ceryss, Cerysse, Ceris, Ceriss, Cerisse

Cascadia (Latin) Woman of the waterfall
Cascadiya, Cascadea, Cascata

Casey (Irish) A vigilant woman
Casee, Casi, Casie, Casy, Cacey, Cacee, Cacy, Caci, Cacie, Caycee, Caycie, Caysie, Caysey, Casea, Caysea

Cashonya (American) A wealthy woman
Cashonyah, Cashona, Cashonah, Cashonia, Cashoniah, Cashonea, Cashoneah

Casilda (Latin / Spanish) Of the home / a warrior woman
Casildah, Cassilda, Casylda, Cassylda

CARSON

I liked Carson for a girl and Carter for a boy. My husband loved both names, but vice versa. After a challenging labor in which the epidural refused to commit, a peanut of a girl was born, and out of exasperation I said, "Now can I name this baby?!" My husband couldn't really say no. —Beth, IA

Caroline ♥ (Latin) Feminine form of Charles; a joyous song; a small, strong woman
Carolina, Carolan, Carolann, Carolanne, Carolena, Carolene, Carolena, Caroliana, Carolyn, Carolyne, Carolynn, Carrie, Carri, Carry, Caro, Carrey, Carree, Caree, Carrieann, Carilyn, Carilynne, Cary

Carrelle (American) A lively woman
Carrell, Carrel, Carrele, Carrella, Carrela

Carrington (English) A beautiful woman; a woman of Carrington
Carington, Carryngton, Caryngton

Carson (Scottish) From the swamp
Carsan, Carsen, Carsin

Carter (English) A transporter of merchandise
Cartar, Cartrell, Cartier

Cartimandua (Anglo-Saxon) A powerful queen

Caryatis (Greek) In mythology, goddess of the walnut tree
Carya, Cariatis, Caryatiss, Cariatiss, Caryatys, Cariatys, Caryatyss, Cariatyss

Casilda (Latin) Of the home
Casildah, Casild, Casilde, Casylda, Casyldah, Casyld, Casylde

Cason (Greek) A seer
Cayson, Caison, Caeson

Cassandra (Greek) An unheeded prophetess; in mythology, she foretold the fall of Troy
Casandra, Cassandrea, Cassaundra, Cassondra, Cass, Cassy, Cassey, Cassi, Cassie, Cassara

Cassia (Greek / Latin) Of the spice tree / feminine form of Cassius; one who is hollow; empty
Cassea, Cassiah, Casseah

Cassidy (Irish) Curly-haired girl
Cassady, Cassidey, Cassidi, Cassidie, Cassidee, Cassadi, Cassadie, Cassadee, Casidhe, Cassidea, Cassadea

Cassielle (Latin) Feminine form of Cassiel, an archangel
Cassiell, Cassiel, Cassiele, Cassiella, Cassiela

Cassiopeia (Greek) In mythology, the mother of Andromeda who was changed into a constellation after she died
Cassiopia, Cassiopiya, Cassiopea

Casta (Spanish) One who is pure; chaste
Castah, Castalina, Castaleena, Castaleina, Castaliena, Castaleana, Castalyna, Castara, Castarah, Castarra, Castarrah

Castalia (Greek) In mythology, a nymph transformed into a sacred spring
Castalea, Casta, Castaliann, Castalianne, Castaliana, Castaliah, Castaleah

Catava (Greek) One who is uncorrupted
Catavah

Catherine (English) One who is pure; virginal
Catharine, Cathrine, Cathryn, Catherin, Catheryn, Catheryna, Cathi, Cathia, Cathicen, Cathie, Cathlyn, Cathleen, Cathlin, Cathy, Catia, Catlee, Catlin, Catline, Catlyn, Cait, Caitie, Caitlin, Caitlan, Caitir, Cattee, Cat, Caitilin, Caitlyn, Caitlan, Caitland, Caitlinn, Caitlynn, Caitrin, Caitriona, Caitryn, Catalin, Catalina, Catalyn, Catalyna, Catarina, Catarine, Cate, Cateline, Catelyn, Catelyna, Caterina, Cath, Catharina, Catrin, Catrina, Catriona, Catylyn

Cathresha (American) One who is pure
Cathreshah, Cathreshia, Cathreshiah, Cathreshea, Cathresheah, Cathrisha, Cathrishah, Cathrysha, Cathryshah

Catima (Greek) One who is innocent
Catimah, Catyma, Catymah, Catiema, Catiemah, Cateima, Cateimah, Cateema, Cateemah, Cateama, Cateamah

Catrice (Greek) A wholesome woman
Catrise, Catryce, Catryse, Catreece, Catreese, Catriece, Catriese, Catreice, Catreise, Catreace, Catrease

Cavana (Irish) Feminine form of Cavan; from the hollow
Cavanna, Cavanah, Cavania, Cavaniya, Cavanea, Cavannah

Cavender (American) An emotional woman
Cavendar

Cayenne (French) Resembling the hot and spicy pepper

Caykee (American) A lively woman
Cayke, Cayki, Caykie, Caykey, Cayky, Caykea, Caikee, Caike, Caikey, Caiky, Caiki, Caikie, Caikea, Caekee, Caekey, Caeky, Caeki, Caekie, Caekea

Cayla (Hebrew / Gaelic) Crowned with laurel / one who is slender
Caela, Caila, Caileigh, Cailey, Cailie, Caleigh, Caley, Callie, Caylee, Cayleen, Cayleigh, Cayley, Caylia, Caylie, Cailley, Cali, Callee, Calli, Callia

Cayman (English) From the islands
Cayeman, Caman, Caiman, Caeman, Caymanne, Caimanne, Caemanne, Camanne

Ceallach (Gaelic) A bright-headed woman

Cecilia (Latin) Feminine form of Cecil; one who is blind; patron saint of music
Cecelia, Cecile, Cecilee, Cicely, Cecily, Cecille, Cecilie, Cicilia, Cicily, Cecia, Cece, Ceil, Cele, Celia, Celicia, Celie, Cili, Cilla, Ciss, Cissie, Cissi, Cissy

Cedrica (American) Feminine form of Cedric; one who is kind and loved
Cedricca, Cedrika, Cedricka, Cedra, Cedrina, Cedryna, Cedreena, Cedriana, Cedrianna, Cedrianne

Ceinwen (Welsh) A girl blessed with beauty
Ceinwenn, Ceinwenne, Ceinwin, Ceinwinn, Ceinwinne, Ceinwyn, Ceinwynn, Ceinwynne

Ceiteag (Scottish) A pure woman

Celaeno (Greek) In mythology, one of the Pleiades
Celeeno, Celeino, Celieno, Celeano, Celeyno

Celand (Latin) One who is meant for heaven
Celanda, Celande, Celandia, Celandea

Celandine (English) Resembling a swallow
Celandyne, Celandina, Celandyna, Celandeena, Celandena, Celandia, Celandea

Celery (American) Refers to the refreshing and healthy food
Celerey, Celeri, Celerie, Celerea, Celereah, Celeree

Celeste (Latin) A heavenly daughter
Celesta, Celestia, Celesse, Celestiel, Celisse, Celestina, Celestyna, Celestine, Celestyne, Celestielle, Celestyn, Ciel

Celina (Latin) In mythology, one of the daughters of Atlas who was turned into a star of the Pleiades constellation; feminine form of Celino; of the heavens; form of Selena, meaning "of the moon"
Celena, Celinna, Celene, Celenia, Celenne, Celicia, Celinda, Calina, Celine

Celisha (Greek) A passionate woman
Celishah, Celysha, Celyshah, Celiesha, Celieshah, Celeisha, Celeishah, Celeesha, Celeeshah, Celeasha, Celeashah

Celka (Latin) A celestial being
Celkah, Celki, Celkie, Celkee, Celkey, Celky, Celkea, Celkeah

Celosia (Greek) A fiery woman; burning; aflame
Celosiah, Celosea, Celoseah

Cenobia (Spanish) Form of Zenobia, meaning "sign or symbol"
Cenobiah, Cenobya, Cenobe, Cenobie, Cenobey, Cenovia, Cenobea, Cenobeah

Cera (French) A colorful woman
Cerah, Cerrah, Cerra

Cerea (Greek) A thriving woman
Cereah, Ceria, Ceriah

Ceres (Latin) Of the spring; in mythology, the goddess of agriculture and fertility
Ceress, Ceresse, Cerela, Cerelia, Cerealia

Ceridwen (Celtic) Beautiful poetry; in mythology, the goddess of poetry
Cerydwen, Ceridwyn, Ceridwin, Cerdwin, Ceridwenn, Ceridwenne, Ceridwynn, Ceridwynne, Ceridwinn, Ceridwinne

Cerina (Latin) Form of Serena, meaning "having a peaceful disposition"
Cerinah, Ceryna, Cerynah, Cerena, Cerenah, Ceriena, Cerienah, Cereina, Cereinah, Cereena, Cereenah, Cereana, Cereanah

Cerise (French) Resembling the cherry
Cerisa

Cesia (Spanish) A celestial being
Cesiah, Cesea, Ceseah

Chaba (Hebrew) Form of Hava, meaning "a lively woman; giver of life"
Chabah, Chaya, Chayka, Chaka, Chava, Chavah

Chablis (French) Resembling the dry white wine
Chabley, Chablie, Chabli, Chably, Chablea, Chableah, Chabliss, Chablisse, Chablys, Chablyss, Chablysse

Chadee (French) A divine woman; a goddess
Chadea, Chadeah, Chady, Chadey, Chadi, Chadie

Chaela (English) Form of Michaela, meaning "who is like God?"
Chaeli, Chaelie, Chaely, Chaeley, Chaelea, Chaeleah

Chahna (Hindi) One who brings light to the world
Chahnah

Chai (Hebrew) One who gives life
Chae, Chaili, Chailie, Chailee, Chaileigh, Chaily, Chailey, Chailea, Chaileah, Chaeli, Chaelie, Chaely, Chaeley, Chaelee, Chaelea, Chaeleah, Chaeleigh

Chailyn (American) Resembling a waterfall
Chailynn, Chailynne, Chaelyn, Chaelynn, Chaelynne, Chaylyn, Chaylynn, Chaylynne

Chaitali (Indian) Surrounded by light
Chaitalie, Chaitale, Chaitaly, Chaitaley, Chaitalee, Chaitalea, Chaitaleah, Chaitaleigh, Chaetali, Chaetalie, Chaetaly, Chaetaley, Chaetalee, Chaetalea, Chaetaleah, Chaetaleigh

Chaitra (Hindi) Born during the first month of the Hindi calendar
Chaetra, Chaitrah, Chaetrah, Chaytra, Chaytrah

Chakra (Arabic) A center of spiritual energy

Chala (American) An exuberant woman
Chalah, Challa, Challah

Chalciope (Greek) In mythology, a princess who was the sister of Medea

Chalette (American) Having good taste
Chalett, Chalet, Chalete, Chaletta, Chaleta

Chalice (French) Resembling a goblet
Chalyce, Chalise, Chalyse, Chalese

Chalina (Spanish) Form of Rosalina, meaning "resembling the beautiful and meaningful flower"
Chalinah, Chalyna, Chaleena, Chalena, Charo, Chaliena, Chaleina, Chaleana

Chalissa (American) One who is optimistic
Chalisa, Chalyssa, Chalysa

Challie (American) A charismatic woman
Challi, Challey, Chally, Challee, Challea, Challeah, Challeigh

Chalondra (African) An intelligent woman

Chalsey (American) Form of Chelsea, meaning "from the landing place for chalk"
Chalsy, Chalsi, Chalsie, Chalsee, Chalsea, Chalseah

Chamania (Hebrew) Resembling a sunflower
Chamaniah, Chamanea, Chamaneah, Chamaniya, Chamaniyah, Chamaran, Chamarann, Chamarana, Chamaranna

Chambray (French) Resembling the light-weight fabric
Chambraye, Chambrai, Chambrae, Chambree, Chambri, Chambrie, Chambry, Chambrey, Chambrea, Chambreah

Chameli (Hindi) Resembling jasmine
Chamelie, Chamely, Chameley, Chamelee, Chamelea, Chameleah, Chameleigh

Chamomile (American) Resembling the aromatic herb; one who is peaceful
Chamomyle, Camomile, Camomyle

Champagne (French) Resembling the sparkling wine

Chamunda (Hindi) In Hinduism, an aspect of the mother goddess
Camunda

Chan (Sanskrit) A shining woman

Chana (Hebrew) Form of Hannah, meaning "having favor and grace"
Chanah, Channa, Chaanach, Chaanah, Chanach, Channah

Chanal (American) A moonlike woman
Chanall, Chanalle

Chance (American) One who takes risks
Chanci, Chancie, Chancee, Chancea, Chanceah, Chancy, Chancey

Chanda (Sanskrit) An enemy of evil
Chandy, Chaand, Chand, Chandey, Chandee, Chandi, Chandie, Chandea, Chandeah

Chandani (Hindi) Born with the moon-beams
Chandanie, Chandany, Chandaney, Chandanee, Chandanea, Chandaneah

Chandelle (French) Resembling a candle
Chandel, Chantelle, Chantel, Chandell, Chantell

Chandler (English) A candlemaker
Chandlar, Chandlor

Chandra (Hindi) Of the moon; another name for the goddess Devi
Chandara, Chandria, Chaundra, Chandrea, Chandreah

Chanel (French) From the canal; a channel
Chanell, Chanelle, Channelle, Chenelle, Chenel, Chenell

Changla (Indian) An active woman

Chania (Hebrew) Blessed with grace from God
Chaniah, Chaneah, Chanea, Chaniya, Chaniyah

Chanicka (American) One who is dearly loved
Chanickah, Chanika, Chanikah, Chaniecka, Chaneicka, Chaneecka, Chanycka, Chaneacka, Chaneeka, Chaneika, Chanieka, Chanyka, Chaneaka

Chanina (Hebrew) The Lord is gracious
Chaninah, Chaneena, Chaneenah, Chanyna, Chanynah, Chaneana, Chaneanah, Chaniena, Chanienah, Chaneina, Chaneinah

Chanise (American) One who is adored
Chanyse, Chanice, Chanyce

Chanit (Hebrew) One who is ready for battle
Chanyt, Chanita, Chanyta

Channary (Cambodian) Of the full moon
Channarie, Channari, Channarey, Channaree, Chantrea, Chantria

Channing (English) An official of the church; resembling a young wolf
Channon, Channer, Channery, Channerie, Channerey, Channeree, Channeri, Channe

Chansanique (American) A singing girl
Chansaneek, Chansanik, Chansanike, Chansanyk, Chansani, Chansanie, Chansanee, Chansanea, Chansaneah, Chansany, Chansaney

Chantal (French) From a stony place; a beautiful singer
Chantalle, Chantel, Chantele, Chantell, Chantelle, Chantrell, Chauntel, Chantay, Chante, Chantae, Chaunte, Chanton, Chauntelle

Chantee (American) A talented singer
Chantey, Chanty, Chanti, Chantie, Chantea, Chanteah

Chanterelle (French) A prized singer
Chanterell, Chanterel, Chanterele, Chanterella, Chanterela

Chantilly (French) Resembling the beautiful lace
Chantilley, Chantilli, Chantillie, Chantillee, Chantilleigh, Chantillea, Chantilleah

Chantou (French) One who sings

Chantoya (American) A renowned singer

Chantrice (French) A singer
Chantryce, Chantrise, Chantryse

Chanya (Hebrew) Blessed with God's love
Chanyah

Chao (Chinese) One who surpasses others

Chapa (Native American) A superior woman
Chapah, Chappah, Chappa

Chapawee (Native American) Resembling a beaver
Chapawi, Chapawie, Chapawy, Chapawey, Chapawea, Chapaweah

Chaquanne (American) A sassy young woman
Chaquane, Chaquann, Chaquan, Chaquanna, Chaquana

Charbonnet (French) A giving and loving woman
Charbonay, Charbonaye, Charbonae, Charbonai, Charbonnay, Charbonnae, Charbonnai

Chardonnay (French) Resembling the wine
Chardonnaye, Chardonay, Chardonaye, Chardonnae, Chardonae, Chardonnai, Chardonai, Charde, Charday, Charday, Chardae, Chardai

Charille (French) A delightful woman; womanly
Charill, Charile, Charil, Charilla, Charila, Charylle, Charyll, Charyle, Charylla, Charyla

Charis (English) Having grace and kindness
Charisa, Charise, Charissa, Charisse, Chariss, Charys, Charyss, Charysse

Charish (American) A cherished woman
Charisha, Cherish, Cherysh, Charysh, Chareesh

Charisma (Greek) Blessed with charm
Charismah, Charizma, Charizmah, Charysma, Charyzma

Charity (Latin) A woman of generous love
Charitey, Chariti, Charitie, Charitee, Charyty, Charyti, Charytey, Charytie, Charytee, Charita, Charitea, Chariteah, Charytea, Charyteah

Charla ○ (English) Feminine form of Charles; a small, strong woman
*Charlee, Charlene, Charli, Charlie, Charly, Charlyn, Charlynn, Charlaine, Charlayne, Charleen, Charleena, Charleigh, Charlena, Charlette, Charline, Charlisa, Charlita, Charlize, Charlot, Charlotta, **Charlotte**, Carlita, Carlota, Carlotta, Chatlie, Cattie, Charlea*

Charlesetta (German) Feminine form of Charles; a small, strong woman
Charleseta, Charlesett, Charleset, Charlesette, Charlesete, Charlsetta, Charlseta

Charlesia (American) Feminine form of Charles; a small, strong woman
Charlesiah, Charlesea, Charleseah, Charlsie, Charlsi, Charlsy, Charlsey, Charlsee, Charlsea, Charlseah

Charlianne (American) A small, strong, and graceful woman
Charliann, Charliane, Charlianna, Charliana, Charliean, Charlieanne, Charlieann, Charlieana, Charlieanna

Charlshea (American) Filled with happiness
Charlsheah, Charlshia, Charlshiah

Charmaine (English) Charming and delightful woman
Charmain, Charmane, Charmayne, Charmian, Charmine, Charmion, Charmyan, Charmyn, Charmaen, Charmaen, Charm

Charminique (American) One who is dashing; charming
Charminik, Charminick, Charmynik, Charmynyk, Charmineek, Charmineyk, Charmonique, Charmonik, Charmonyk, Charmonick

Charnee (American) Filled with joy
Charny, Charney, Charnea, Charneah, Charni, Charnie

Charneeka (American) One who is obsessive
Charneekah, Charnykah, Charnieka, Charniekah, Charneika, Charneikah, Charneaka, Charneakah, Charnyka, Charnykah

Charnelle (American) One who sparkles
Charnell, Charnel, Charnele, Charnella, Charnela

Charnesa (American) One who gets attention
Charnesah, Charnessa, Charnessah

Charsetta (American) An emotional woman
Charsett, Charsette, Charset, Charsete, Charseta

Chartra (American) A classy lady
Chartrah

Chartres (French) One who plans
Chartrys

Charu (Hindi) One who is gorgeous
Charoo, Charou

Charumat (Hindi) An intelligent and beautiful woman
Charoomat, Charoumat

Chashmona (Hebrew) Born to royalty; a princess

Chasia (Hebrew) One who is protected; sheltered
Chasiah, Chasea, Chaseah, Chasya, Chasyah

Chasidah (Hebrew) A religious woman; pious
Chasida, Chasyda, Chasydah

Chasina (Aramaic) Having strength of character
Chasinah, Chasyna, Chasynah, Chasiena, Chasienah, Chaseina, Chaseinah, Chaseena, Chaseenah, Chaseana, Chaseanah, Chau

Chastity (Latin) Having purity; a woman of innocence
Chasity, Chasta, Chastina, Chastine, Chasida, Chassidy, Chastitey, Chastitie, Chastiti, Chastitee, Chastitea, Chastiteah

Chasya (Hebrew) One who offers shelter
Chasye

Chateria (Vietnamese) Born beneath the moonlight
Chateriah, Chaterea, Chatereah, Chateriya, Chateriyah

Chaucer (English) A demure woman
Chauser, Chawcer, Chawser

Chavela (Spanish) Form of Isabel, meaning "my God is bountiful"
Chavella, Chavelle, Chavele, Chavel, Chavell

Chavi (Egyptian) A precious daughter
Chavie, Chavy, Chavey, Chavee, Chavea, Chaveah

Chaviva (Hebrew) One who is dearly loved
Chavyva, Chavive, Chavyve, Chaveeva, Chaveevah, Chavieva, Chavievah, Chaveiva, Chaveivah, Chaveava, Chaveavah

Chavon (Hebrew) A giver of life
Chavonne, Chavonn, Chavona, Chavonna

Chazmin (American) Form of Jasmine, meaning "resembling the climbing plant with fragrant flowers"
Chaslyn, Chaslynn, Chasmeen, Chasmin, Chasmina, Chasminda, Chasmyn, Chasmyne, Chassamayn, Chazan, Chazmin, Chasmine, Chazmon, Chazmyn, Chazmyne, Chazzmin, Chazzmine, Chazzmon, Chazzmyn, Chazzmynn, Chasmyna, Chessamine, Chessamy, Chessamyn, Chasmeena, Chessimine, Chessimine

Chazona (Hebrew) A prophetess
Chazonah, Chazonna, Chazonnah

Chea (American) A witty woman
Cheah, Cheea, Cheeah

Cheche (African) A small woman

Chedra (Hebrew) Filled with happiness
Chedrah

Chedva (Hebrew) One who is joyous

Cheer (American) Filled with joy
Cheere

Cheifa (Hebrew) From a safe harbor
Cheifah, Cheiffa, Cheiffah

Chekia (American) A saucy woman
*Cheekie, Checki, Checkie, Checky,
Checkey, Checkee, Checkea, Checkeah*

Cheletha (American) One who smiles a lot
Chelethah, Chelethe, Cheleth

Chelone (English) Resembling a flowering
plant

Chelsea (English) From the landing place
for chalk
*Chelcie, Chelsa, Chelsee, Chelseigh,
Chelsey, Chelsi, Chelsie, Chelsy, Chelsia*

Chemarin (French) A dark beauty
*Chemarine, Chemaryn, Chemareen,
Chemarein, Chemarien*

Chemash (Hebrew) A servant of God
*Chemashe, Chemasha, Chemosh,
Chemoshe, Chemosha, Chemesh,
Chemeshe, Chemesha*

Chemda (Hebrew) A charismatic woman
Chemdah

Chemdia (Hebrew) One who loves God
*Chemdiah, Chemdea, Chemdeah,
Chemdiya, Chemdiyah*

Chen (Hebrew / Chinese) Having grace or
favor / of the dawn

Chenia (Hebrew) One who lives within the
grace of God
*Cheniah, Chenea, Cheneah, Cheniya,
Cheniyah*

Chenille (American) A soft-skinned
woman
Chenill, Chenil, Chenile, Chenilla, Chenila

Chenoa (Native American) Resembling a
white dove; peaceful

Chephzibah (Hebrew) Her father's delight

Chepi (Native American) In mythology, a
fairy spirit of the dead
*Cheppi, Chepie, Cheppie, Chepy, Cheppy,
Chepey, Cheppey, Chepea, Cheppea,
Chepeah, Cheppeah, Chepee, Cheppee*

Cher (French) One who is greatly loved; a
darling
*Chere, Cherée, Cherey, Cheri, Cherice,
Cherie, Cherise, Cherish, Cherina,
Cherisse, Chery, Cherye, Cherylee,
Cherylie, Chereen, Cherell, Cherelle,
Cherese, Cheresse, Charee, Cheree,
Cherisa, Cherita, Cherree, Cherea, Charea*

Cherika (French) One who is dear
*Chericka, Cheryka, Cherycka, Cherieka,
Cheriecka, Chereika, Chereicka, Cheryka,
Cherycka, Chereaka, Chereacka*

Cherlyn (American) One who is dearly
loved
*Cherlynn, Cherlynne, Cherlin, Cherlinn,
Cherlinne*

Chermona (Hebrew) From the sacred
mountain
Chermonah, Chermonnah, Chermonna

Cherokee (Native American) A tribal
name
*Cheroki, Cherokie, Cherokey, Cheroky,
Cherokeigh, Cherokea, Cherokeah*

Cherron (American) A graceful dancer
Cherronn, Cherronne

Cherry (English) Resembling a fruit-bear-
ing tree
*Cherrie, Cherri, Cherrey, Cherree, Cherrea,
Cherreah*

Cheryl (English) One who is greatly loved;
a darling
*Cheryll, Charil, Charyl, Cheriann,
Cherianne, Cherilyn, Cherilynn, Cherrell,
Cherrill, Cherryl, Cheryll, Cherylle, Chyril,
Chyrill, Cherlin, Cherrelle*

Chesley (English) From the meadow
*Chesli, Cheslie, Chesly, Chesleigh, Cheslea,
Chesleah, Cheslee*

Chesna (Slavic) One who is calm; bringer of peace
Chessa, Chessie, Chessy

Chesney (English) One who promotes peace
Chesny, Chesni, Chesnie, Chesnea, Chesneah, Chesnee

Chessteen (American) One who is needed
Chesstyn, Chessteene, Chesstyne, Chesstien, Chesstiene, Chesstein, Chessteine, Chesstean, Chessteane

Chestnut (American) Resembling the nut

Chet (American) A vivacious woman
Chett, Chette

Chevona (Irish) One who loves God
Chevonah, Chevonna, Chevonnah

Cheyenne (Native American) Unintelligible speaker
Cheyanna, Cheyenna, Cheyanne, Chiana, Chianna, Chayan, Chayanne

Cheyne (French) An oak-hearted woman
Cheney, Chane, Chayne, Chaney

Chhaya (Hebrew) One who loves life
Chhayah

Chi (African) Surrounded by light

Chiante (Italian) Resembling the wine
Chianti, Chiantie, Chiantee, Chianty, Chiantey, Chiantea

Chiara (Italian) Daughter of the light
Chiarah, Chiarra, Chiarrah

Chiba (Hebrew) One who loves and is loved
Chibah, Cheeba, Cheebah, Cheiba, Cheibah, Chieba, Chiebah, Cheaba, Cheabah, Chyba, Chybah

Chica (Spanish) A little girl
Chicah, Chicca, Chicka, Chika

Chick (American) A fun-loving girl
Chicki, Chickie, Chickee, Chicky, Chickey, Chickea

Chickoa (Native American) Born at daybreak
Chickoah, Chikoa, Chikoah

Chidi (Spanish) One who is cheerful
Chidie, Chidy, Chidey, Chidee, Chidea, Chideah

Chidori (Japanese) Resembling a shorebird
Chidorie, Chidory, Chidorey, Chidorea, Chidoreah, Chidoree

Chika (Japanese) A woman with great wisdom

Chikira (Spanish) A talented dancer
Chikirah, Chikiera, Chikierah, Chikeira, Chikeirah, Chikeera, Chikeerah, Chikyra, Chikyrah, Chikeara, Chikearah

Chiku (African) A talkative girl

Chilali (Native American) Resembling a snowbird
Chilalie, Chilalee, Chylali, Chylaly, Chilam, Chylam, Chilaleigh, Chilaly, Chilaley, Chilalea, Chilaleah

Childers (English) From a dignified family
Chylders, Chelders

Chimalis (Native American) Resembling a bluebird
Chymalis, Chimalys, Chymalys

Chimene (French) One who is ambitious
Chymene, Chimean, Chymean, Chimein, Chymein, Chimien, Chymien, Chimeen, Chymeen

China (Chinese) Woman from China
Chynna, Chyna, Chinah

Chinaka (African) God has chosen
Chinakah, Chynaka, Chinacka, Chinacca

Chinara (African) God receives
Chinarah, Chinarra, Chinarrah

Chinue (African) God's own blessing
Chinoo, Chynue, Chynoo

Chione (Egyptian) Daughter of the Nile

Chipo (African) A gift from God
Chippo, Chypo, Chyppo

Chiquita (Spanish) Little precious girl
Chyquita, Chiqueeta, Chiquyta, Chikita, Chykita, Chikeeta

Chiriga (African) One who is triumphant
Chyriga, Chyryga, Chiryga

Chirley (American) Form of Shirley, meaning "from the bright clearing"
Chirly, Chirli, Chirlie, Chirleigh, Chirlee, Chirlea, Chirleah

Chislaine (French) A faithful woman
Chislain, Chislayn, Chislayne, Chislaen,
Chislaene, Chyslaine, Chyslain, Chyslayn,
Chyslayne, Chyslaen, Chyslaene

Chitra (Hindi) In Hinduism, the goddess
of misfortune
Chitrah, Chytra, Chytrah

Chitsa (Native American) One who is fair
Chitsah, Chytsa, Chytsah

Chivonne (American) Filled with happiness
Chivonn, Chivone, Chivon, Chivonna,
Chivona, Chevonn, Chevonne, Chevon,
Chevone, Chivaughn, Chevaughn

Chiyena (Hebrew) Blessed with the Lord's
grace
Chiyenah

Chiyo (Japanese) Of a thousand years;
eternal

Chizoba (African) One who is
well-protected
Chizobah, Chyzoba, Chyzobah

Chizuko (Japanese) A bountiful woman
Chizu

Chosovi (Native American) Resembling a
bluebird
Chosovie, Chosovy, Chosovey, Chosovee,
Chosposi, Chosposie, Chosovea, Chosposy,
Chosposey, Chosposee, Chosposea

Christina (English) Follower of Christ
Christinah, Cairistiona, Christine,
Christin, Christian, Christiana,
Christiane, Christianna, Christi, Christie,
Christen, Christena, Christene, Christy,
Christyn, Christan, Christana,
Christanne, Christeen, Christeena,
Chrissa, Chrissie, Chrissy, Christa,
Chrysta, Crista, Crysta, Chryssa,
Christabel, Christabell, Christabella,
Cristabel, Cristabell, Christahel,
Christahella, Crissi, Crissa, Crissy,
Crissie, Cristen, Cristie, Cristin, Cristina,
Cristine, Cristiona, Cristy, Cristyn,
Chrystina, Chrystine, Chrystie, Chryssa,
Chrina, Chris, Cris, Carsten, Ciorstan

Christmas (English) Born during the
festival of Christ

Chrysantha (Greek) Defender of the
people
Chrisanna, Chrisanne, Chrysandra,
Crisanna, Chrysann, Crisanne, Crisann

CHRISTIANA

I was a television producer in New York, six months pregnant and fully entrenched in Fashion-Week hell. The phone rang (again) with a pitch from yet another desperate publicist who introduced herself as Christiana. I hated her story but loved her name. Out of a bad fashion pitch, Christiana was christened. —Yvette, NY

Chloe ✿ (Greek) A flourishing woman;
blooming
Chloë, Clo, Cloe, Cloey

Chloris (Greek) In mythology, goddess of
vegetation and spring
Chlorys, Chloriss, Chloryss

Cho (Japanese) Resembling a butterfly

Chofa (Polish) An able-bodied woman
Chofah, Choffa, Choffah

Cholena (Native American) A birdlike
woman
Cholenah, Cholyna, Choleena, Cholynah,
Choleenah

Chryseis (Latin) The golden daughter; in
mythology, a woman captured by
Agamemnon
Chrysilla

Chuki (African) Born during an unpleas-
ant time
Chukie, Chuky, Chukey, Chukee, Chukea,
Chukeah

Chula (Native American) Resembling a
colorful flower
Chulah, Chulla, Chullah

Chulda (Hebrew) One who can tell for-
tunes
Chuldah

Chulisa (American) A clever woman
Chulisah, Chulissa, Chulissah, Chulysa, Chulysah, Chulyssa, Chulyssah

Chuma (Hebrew) A warmhearted woman
Chumah, Chumma, Chummah, Chumi, Chumie, Chumee, Chumy, Chumey, Chumea, Chumeah, Chumina, Chumyna, Chumeena, Chumeina, Chumiena, Chumeana, Chumyna

Chumana (Native American) Covered with dew
Chumanah, Chumanna, Chumannah

Chumani (Native American) Resembling a dewdrop
Chumanie, Chumany, Chumaney, Chumanee, Chumanea, Chumaneah

Chun (Chinese) Born during spring

Chyou (Chinese) Born during autumn

Ciana (Italian) Feminine form of John; God is gracious
Cianna, Ciannait, Ceana, Ceanna, Cyana, Cyanna

Ciandra (Italian) Surrounded by light
Ciandrah, Cyandra, Cyandrah

Ciara (Irish) A dark beauty
Ceara, Ciaran, Ciarra, Ciera, Cierra, Ciere, Ciar, Ciarda, Cyara, Cyarra

Cicada (Latin) Resembling the high-pitched insect
Cicayda, Cicaida, Cicala, Cicaeda, Cikada, Cikayda, Cikaida, Cikaeda

Cidrah (American) One who is unlike others
Cidra, Cydrah, Cydra

Cierra (Irish) A clear-eyed woman
Cierrah, Cyerra, Cyerrah

Cinderella (French) Beautiful girl of the ashes
Cendrillon, Cenerentola, Cinderelle, Cinderela, Cinderele, Cinderell

Cinnamon (American) Resembling the reddish-brown spice
Cinnia, Cinnie

Cinta (Spanish) From the good mountain
Cintah, Cynta, Cyntah

Cinxia (Latin) In mythology, the goddess of marriage

Ciona (American) One who is steadfast
Cionah, Cyona, Cyonah

Cipporah (Hebrew) Form of Zipporah, meaning "a beauty; little bird"
Cippora, Ciporah, Cipora, Cypora, Cyppora, Ciproh, Cipporia, Cepora, Ceporrah, Ceppora, Cepporah

Ciqala (Native American) Our little one
Cyqala, Ciqalla, Cyqalla

Circe (Greek) In mythology, a sorceress who changed Odysseus's men into swine
Circee, Curce, Cyrce, Curcee, Cyrcee, Circie, Circi, Circea, Circy, Circey, Circeah

Citare (Greek) A musically talented woman
Citarr, Citar, Citara, Ciatarra, Cita

Citlali (Native American) A starlike child
Citlalli, Citlalie, Citlallie, Citlaly, Citlaley, Citlalee, Citlaleigh, Citlalea, Citlaleah

Claennis (Anglo-Saxon) One who is pure
Claenis, Claennys, Claenys, Claynnis, Claynnys, Claynys, Claynyss

Claiborne (Old English) Born of the earth's clay
Claiborn, Claibourn, Claibourne, Clayborn, Clayborne, Claybourn, Claybourne, Claeborn, Claeborne, Claebourn, Claebourne

Clancey (American) A lighthearted woman
Clancy, Clanci, Clancie, Clancee, Clancea, Clanceah

Clara ✿ (Latin) Famously bright
Claire, Clarinda, Clarine, Clarita, Claritza, Clarrie, Clarry, Clarabelle, Claretha, Claribel, Clarice, Clarahelle, Claral, Clare, Clair, Clarette, Clarinde, Claribelle, Claretta, Clareta, Clorinda, Chlorinda

Clarice (French) A famous woman; a form of Clara, meaning "famously bright"
Claressa, Claris, Clarisa, Clarise, Clarisse, Claryce, Clerissa, Clerisse, Cleryce, Clerysse, Claresta, Clariss, Clarissa, Clarrisa, Clariee, Claryssa, Clarysa

Clarimond (German) A shining protectress
*Clarimonda, Clarimonde, Clarimunde,
Clarimunda, Clarimund, Claramond,
Claramonda, Claramonde*

Clarity (American) One who is clear-minded
*Claritey, Claritee, Claritea, Clariteah,
Clariti, Claritie, Claryty, Clarytey,
Clarytee, Clarytea, Claryteah, Claryti,
Clarytie*

Clasina (Latin) An illuminated woman
*Clasinah, Clasyna, Clasiena, Claseina,
Claseena, Claseana, Clasynah, Clasienah,
Claseinah, Claseenah, Claseanah*

Claudia (Latin) Feminine form of Claud;
one who is lame
*Clauda, Claudella, Claudelle, Claudetta,
Claudette, Claudey, Claudie, Claudina,
Claudine, Claudy, Clodia, Clady, Clodagh*

Clava (Spanish) A sincere woman
Clavah, Clavva, Clavvah

Clelia (Latin) A glorious woman
*Cloelia, Cleliah, Clelea, Cleleah, Cloeliah,
Cloelea, Cloeleah*

Clematis (Greek) Resembling the flowering
vine
*Clematia, Clematice, Clematiss, Clematys,
Clematyss*

Clemence (Latin) An easygoing woman
Clemense

Clementine (French) Feminine form of
Clement; one who is merciful
*Clem, Clemence, Clemency, Clementia,
Clementina, Clementya, Clementyna,
Clementyn, Clemmie, Clemmy,
Clementyne*

Cleodal (Latin) A glorious woman
*Cleodall, Cleodale, Cleodel, Cleodell,
Cleodelle*

Cleopatra (Greek) A father's glory; of the
royal family
*Clea, Cleo, Cleona, Cleone, Cleonie,
Cleora, Cleta, Cleoni, Cleopetra, Cleonie,
Cleony, Cleoney, Cleonee, Cleonea,
Cleoneah*

Cleva (English) Feminine form of Clive;
woman of the cliffs

Clever (American) One who is quick-witted and smart

Cliantha (Greek) A flower of glory
*Clianthe, Cleantha, Cleanthe, Clyantha,
Clyanthe*

Clio (Greek) Glory; in mythology, the muse
of history

Cliodhna (Irish) A dark beauty

Cliona (Greek) One who has a good
memory
Clionah, Clionna, Clionnah

Clodovea (Spanish) Feminine form of
Clodoveo; a renowned warrior
Clodovia, Clodovya, Clodoviya

Cloreen (American) Filled with happiness
*Cloreene, Clorien, Cloriene, Clorein,
Cloreine, Clorean, Cloreane, Cloryn,
Cloryne, Cloreena, Cloriena, Cloreina,
Cloreana, Cloryna*

Cloris (Greek) A flourishing woman; in
mythology, the goddess of flowers
*Clores, Clorys, Cloriss, Clorisse, Cloryss,
Clorysse*

Clory (Spanish) One who smiles often
*Clorey, Clori, Clorie, Cloree, Clorea,
Cloreah*

Closetta (Spanish) A secretive woman
Closett, Closet, Closete, Closeta, Closette

Clotho (Greek) In mythology, one of the
three Fates

Clotilde (German) A woman famous in
battle
Clotild, Clotilda

Cloud (American) A lighthearted woman
*Cloude, Cloudy, Cloudey, Cloudee,
Cloudea, Cloudeah, Cloudi, Cloudie*

Clove (French) Resembling the spice; a nail

Clover (English) Resembling the meadow
flower
Claefer

Clydette (American) Feminine form of
Clyde; from the river
Clydett, Clydet, Clydete, Clydetta, Clydeta

Clymene (Greek) In mythology, the mother of Atlas and Prometheus
Clymena, Clymyne, Clymyn, Clymyna, Clymeena, Clymeina, Clymiena, Clymeana, Clymeene, Clymeine, Clymiene, Clymeane

Clytemnestra (Greek) In mythology, the wife and murderer of Agamemnon

Clytie (Greek) The lovely one; in mythology, a nymph who was changed into a sunflower
Clyti, Clytee, Clyty, Clytey, Clyte, Clytea, Clyteah

Co (American) A jovial woman
Coe

Coahoma (Native American) Resembling a panther

Coby (Hebrew) Feminine form of Jacob; the supplanter
Cobey, Cobi, Cobie, Cobee, Cobea, Cobeah

Cochava (Hebrew) Having a starlike quality
Cochavah, Cochavia, Cochavea, Cochaviah, Cochaveah

Cocheta (Italian) One who is pure
Cochetah, Cochetta, Cochettah

Cochiti (Spanish) The forgotten child
Cochitie, Cochyty, Cochitee, Cochitea, Cochiteah

Coco (Spanish) Form of Socorro, meaning "one who offers help and relief"

Cody (Irish / English) One who is helpful; a wealthy woman / acting as a cushion
Codi, Codie, Codey, Codee, Codia, Codea, Codier, Codyr, Codeah, Codiah

Coffey (American) A lovely woman
Coffy, Coffe, Coffee, Coffea, Coffeah, Coffi, Coffie

Coira (Scottish) Of the churning waters
Coirah, Coyra, Coyrah

Coiya (American) One who is coquettish

Cokey (American) An intelligent woman
Coky, Coki, Cokie, Cokee, Cokea, Cokeah

Colanda (American) Form of Yolanda, meaning "resembling the violet flower; modest"
Colande, Coland, Colana, Colain, Colaine, Colane, Colanna, Corlanda, Calanda, Calando, Calonda, Colantha, Colanthe, Culanda, Culonda, Coulanda, Colonda

Colby (English) From the coal town
Colbey, Colbi, Colbie, Colbee, Collby, Coalby, Colbea, Colbeah, Coalbee, Coalbie, Coalbi, Coalbey, Coalbea, Coalbeah

Cole (English) A swarthy woman; having coal-black hair
Col, Coal, Coale, Coli, Colie, Coly, Coley, Colee, Colea, Coleah, Coleigh

Colemand (American) An adventurer
Colmand, Colemyan, Colemyand, Colmyan, Colmyand

Colette (French) Of the victorious people
Collette, Coleta, Coletta, Colletta, Colet, Colete

Coligny (French) Woman from Cologne
Coligney, Colignie, Coligni, Colignee, Colignea, Coligneah

Colina (Scottish) Feminine form of Colin; of the victorious people
Coline, Colyna, Colyne, Colene, Colena

Colisa (English) A delightful young woman
Colisah, Colissa, Colissah, Colysa, Colysah, Colyssa, Colyssah

Colleen (Gaelic) A young peasant girl
Coleen, Colley, Collena, Collene, Collie, Colline, Colly, Collice, Collyne, Collyna

Colmcilla (Irish) Woman of the church; a dove
Colmcillah, Colmcila, Colmcylla, Colmcyla

Colola (American) A victorious woman
Colo, Cola

Coloma (Spanish) One who is calm and peaceful
Colom, Colomia, Colomiah, Colomea, Colomeah

Colorado (Spanish) From the red river; from the state of Colorado

Columba (Latin) Resembling a dove
*Columbia, Columbina, Columbine,
Colomba, Colombia, Colombina,
Colombe, Columbe*

Colwyn (Welsh) From the river
*Colwynne, Colwynn, Colwin, Colwinn,
Colwinne, Colwen, Colwenn, Colwenne*

Comfort (English) One who strengthens or
soothes others
*Comforte, Comfortyne, Comfortyna,
Comforteene, Comforteena, Comfortene,
Comfortena, Comfortiene, Comfortiena,
Comforteine, Comforteina, Comforteane,
Comforteana*

Comyna (Irish) A shrewd woman
*Comynah, Comina, Comeena, Comena,
Comeina, Comiena, Comeana*

Conary (Gaelic) A wise woman
*Conarey, Conarie, Conari, Conaree,
Conarea, Conareah*

Concepción (Spanish) Refers to the
Immaculate Conception
Concepta, Concetta, Conchetta, Conshita

Conchobarre (Irish) Feminine form of
Connor; a wolf-lover; one who is strong-
willed
Conchobarra, Conchobara, Conchobare

Concordia (Latin) Peace and harmony; in
mythology, goddess of peace
*Concordiah, Concordea, Concord,
Concorde, Concordeah*

Condoleezza (American) An intelligent
and sweet woman
*Condoleeza, Condoliza, Condolizza,
Condolyzza, Condolyza, Condoleesa,
Condoleessa, Condolyssa, Condolysa,
Condolisa, Condolissa*

Coneisha (American) A giving woman
*Coneishah, Coniesha, Conieshah,
Conysha, Conyshah, Coneesha,
Coneeshah, Coneasha, Coneashah*

Cong (Chinese) A clever girl

Connecticut (Native American) From the
place beside the long river; from the state
of Connecticut

Conradina (German) Feminine form of
Conrad; a bold counselor
*Conradine, Conradyna, Conradyne,
Conrada, Conradia, Conrade,
Conradeena, Conradiena, Conradeina,
Conradeana*

Conroe (American) From the town in
Texas
Conrow, Conro, Conrowe

Conroy (English) A stately woman
Conroi, Conroye

Conseja (Spanish) One who advises others

Constance (Latin) One who is steadfast;
constant
*Constantia, Constancia, Constanza,
Constantina, Congalie, Connal, Connie,
Constancy, Constanci, Constancie,
Constansie, Constansy, Constanze,
Constanzie*

Constanza (American) One who is constant; steadfast
Constanzia, Constanzea

Consuela (Spanish) One who provides
consolation
*Consuelia, Consolata, Consolacion, Chela,
Conswela, Conswelia, Conswelea,
Consuella, Conswella*

Content (American) One who is satisfied;
happy

Contessa (Italian) A titled woman; a
countess
*Countess, Contesse, Countessa, Countesa,
Contesa*

Cookie (American) One who is cute
Cooki, Cooky, Cookey, Cookee, Cookea

Cooper (English) One who makes barrels
Couper

Copeland (English) One who is good at
coping
Copelan, Copelyn, Copelynn

Copper (American) A red-headed woman
Coper, Coppar, Copar

Coppola (Italian) A theatrical woman
Copola, Copolla, Coppolla, Coppo, Copla

Cora (English) A young maiden; in mythology, another name for the goddess of the underworld
Corabel, Corabella, Corabelle, Corabellita, Coraima, Coralette, Coraletta, Coralete, Coralet, Corra, Corah

Coral (English) Resembling the semi-precious sea growth; from the reef
Coralee, Coralena, Coralie, Coraline, Corallina, Coralline, Coraly, Coralyn, Coralyne, Coralia, Coralin, Coralina, Coralea, Coraleah

Corazon (Spanish) Of the heart
Corazón, Corazana, Corazone, Corazona

Corbin (Latin) Resembling a crow; as dark as a raven
Corben, Corbet, Corbett, Corbie, Corbit, Corbitt, Corby, Corbyn, Corvin, Corbi

Corday (English) One who is well-prepared
Cordaye, Cordai, Cordae

Cordelia (Latin) A good-hearted woman; a woman of honesty
Cordella, Cordelea, Cordilia, Cordilea, Cordy, Cordie, Cordi, Cordee, Cordey, Cordelle

Cordula (Latin / German) From the heart / resembling a jewel
Cordulah, Cordulla, Cordullah, Cordoola, Cordoolah, Cordoolla, Cordoollah

Corey (Irish) From the hollow; of the churning waters
Cory, Cori, Coriann, Corianne, Corie, Corri, Corrianna, Corrie, Corry, Corre, Coree, Corella, Coretta, Corilla, Corisa, Corissa, Corita, Corlene, Corrella, Correlle, Corrissa, Coryssa, Corentine, Corette, Corrianne, Corea, Coreah, Correa, Correah

Corgie (American) A humorous woman
Corgy, Corgey, Corgi, Corgee, Corgea, Corgeah

Coriander (Greek) A romantic woman; resembling the spice
Coryander, Coriender, Coryender

Corina (Latin) A spear-wielding woman
Corinna, Coreen, Coreene, Coren, Corena, Corine, Correen, Correena, Corrin, Corrina, Corrine, Corenne, Corin, Corinda, Corinn, Corinne, Correna, Corrianne, Corrienne, Corrinda, Corrinn, Corrinna, Corryn, Coryn, Corynn, Corynne, Correnda, Corynna, Coreana, Correana

Corinthia (Greek) A woman of Corinth
Corinthiah, Corinthe, Corinthea, Corintheah, Corynthia, Corynthea, Corynthe

Coris (Greek) A beautiful singer
Corys, Corris, Corrys

Corky (American) An energetic young woman
Corki, Corkey, Corkie, Corkee, Corkea, Corkeah

Corliss (English) A carefree and cheerful woman
Corlisse, Corless, Corley, Corly, Corli, Corlie, Corlea, Corleah, Corlee, Corleigh

Cormella (Italian) A fiery woman
Cormellah, Cormela, Cormelah, Cormellia, Cormelia, Cormellea, Cormelea, Cormy, Cormey, Cormi, Cormie, Cormee, Cormea, Cormeah

Cornelia (Latin) Feminine form of Cornelius; referring to a horn
Cornalia, Corneelija, Cornela, Cornelija, Cornelya, Cornella, Cornelle, Cornie

Cornesha (American) A talkative woman
Corneshah, Corneisha, Corneishah, Corniesha, Cornieshah, Corneesha, Corneeshah, Corneasha, Corneashah, Cornysha, Corynshah

Corona (Spanish) A crowned woman
Coronna, Coronetta, Coronette, Carona, Coronete, Coronet, Coroneta

Coronis (Greek) In mythology, Apollo's lover who was killed by Artemis
Coronys, Coroniss, Coronisse, Coronyss, Coronysse

Corsen (Welsh) Resembling a reed

Cosette (French) Of the victorious people; little pet
Cosetta, Cozette, Cozetta, Coset, Cosete, Cozet, Cozete, Coseta, Cozeta

Cosima (Greek) Of the universe; a harmonious woman
Cosyma, Cosema, Coseema, Cosma, Cosimia, Cosimea, Cozma, Cozima, Cozimia, Coseama, Cosiema, Coseima, Cozeema, Coziema, Cozeima, Cozeama

Costner (American) One who is embraced by all
Cosner, Costnar, Cosnar, Costnor, Cosnor

Cota (Spanish) A lively woman
Cotah, Cotta, Cottah

Cotcha (American) A stylish woman
Cotchah, Catcha, Catchah

Cotia (Spanish) Full of life
Cotiah, Cotea, Coteah

Cotrena (American) One who is pure; chaste
Cotrina, Cotriena, Cotreina, Cotryna, Cotreena, Cotreana, Contrenah, Cotrinah, Cotrienah, Cotreinah, Cotrynah, Cotreenah, Cotreanah

Cotton (American) Resembling the comfortable fabric
Cotti, Cottie, Cotty, Cottey, Cottee, Cottea, Cotteah

Coty (French) From the riverbank
Cotey, Coti, Cotie, Cotee, Cotea, Coteah

Courtney (English) A courteous woman; courtly
Cordney, Cordni, Cortenay, Corteney, Cortland, Cortnee, Cortneigh, Cortney, Cortnie, Cortny, Courtenay, Courteneigh, Courteney, Courtland, Courtlyn, Courtnay, Courtnee, Courtnie, Courtny, Courtnea, Cortnea

Coventina (Anglo-Saxon) In mythology, the goddess of wells and springs
Coventinah, Coventyna, Coventeena, Coventena, Covintina, Covinteena, Covintyna, Covintena, Coventeana, Coventeina, Coventiena, Covinteana, Covintiena, Covinteina

Covin (American) An unpredictable woman
Covan, Coven, Covyn, Covon

Coy (English) From the woods, the quiet place
Coye, Coi

Cramer (American) Filled with joy
Cramir, Cramar, Cramor, Cramur

Crecia (Latin) Form of Lucretia, meaning "a bringer of light; a successful woman"
Crete, Crecea, Creciah, Creceah

Creda (English) A woman of faith
Credah, Cryda, Creida, Creyda, Crieda, Creada, Creeda, Crydah, Creidah, Creydah, Criedah, Creadah, Creedah

Cree (Native American) A tribal name
Crei, Crey, Crea, Creigh

Creiddylad (Welsh) Daughter of the sea; in mythology, the daughter of Llyr

Creirwy (Welsh) One who is lucky

Creola (American) Daughter of American birth but European heritage
Creole, Creolla, Criole, Criola, Criolla, Cryola, Cryolla

Crescent (French) One who creates; increasing; growing
Creissant, Crescence, Crescenta, Crescentia, Cressant, Cressent, Cressentia, Cressentya

Cressida (Greek) The golden girl; in mythology, a woman of Troy
Cressa, Criseyde, Cressyda, Crissyda

Creston (American) One who is worthy
Crestan, Cresten, Crestun, Crestin, Crest, Creste, Cresti, Crestie, Cresty, Crestey, Crestee, Crestea

Cresusa (English) One who is fickle
Cresusah, Cresussa, Cresussah

Creusa (Greek) In mythology, the wife of Aeneas

Cricket (American) Resembling a chirping insect of the night
Crycket, Criket, Cryket

Crimson (American) As rich and deep as the color
Crymson, Cremson, Crimsen, Crymsen, Crimsun, Crymsun

Criselda (American) Form of Griselda, meaning "a gray-haired battlemaid; one who fights the dark battle"
Cricelda, Cricely, Crisel, Criseldis, Crisella, Criselle, Criselly, Crishelda, Crishilde, Crissel, Crizel, Crizelda, Cryselde, Cryzelde, Criselde, Crizela, Crizzel, Cryselda

Crishona (American) A beautiful woman
Crishonah, Cryshona, Cryshonah, Crishonna, Crishonnah, Cryshonna, Cryshonnah

Crisiant (Welsh) As clear as a crystal
Crisiante, Crisianta, Crysiant, Crysyant, Crysianta, Crysiante, Crysyanta, Crysyante

Crispina (Latin) Feminine form of Crispin; a curly-haired girl
Crispyna, Crispeena, Crispena, Crispeina, Crispiena, Cripeana

Cristos (Greek) A dedicated and faithful woman
Crystos, Christos, Chrystos

Cruella (American) An evil, cruel woman
Cruelle, Cruell, Cruele, Cruel, Cruela

Crystal (Greek) Resembling clear, sparkling, brilliant glass
Cristal, Christal, Christel, Chrystal, Crystall, Crystell, Crystle, Crystalyn, Crystalynn, Crystalynne, Cristabelle, Crystabelle, Cristalena, Cristalyn, Chrystalline, Cristelle

Crystilis (Spanish) One who is focused
Crystilys, Crystylys, Cristylis, Cristilys

Csilla (Hungarian) One who provides defenses
Csillah, Csila, Csilah, Csylla, Csyllah, Csyla, Csylah

Cuba (Spanish) From the island
Cubah

Cullen (Irish) An attractive lady
Cullan, Cullun, Cullie, Cully, Culli, Culley, Cullea, Culleah, Cullee

Cullodina (Scottish) From the mossy ground
Cullodena, Culodina, Culodena, Cullodyna, Culodyna

Cumale (American) One with an open heart
Cumali, Cumalie, Cumaly, Cumaley, Cumalee, Cumaleigh, Cumahli, Cumahle, Cumahlee, Cumahleigh, Cumahlie, Cumahlea, Cumahleah, Cumahly, Cumahley

Cumthia (American) One with an open mind
Cumthiah, Cumthea, Cumtheah, Cumthiya, Cumthiyah

Cunina (Latin) In mythology, the protector of infants
Cuninah, Cunyna, Cuneena, Cuniena, Cuneina, Cuneana

Cupid (American) A romantic woman
Cupide, Cupyd, Cupyde

Curine (American) A good-looking woman
Curina, Curyna, Curyne, Curiena, Curiene, Cureina, Cureine, Cureena, Cureene, Cureana, Cureane, Curyna, Curyne

Curry (American) Resembling the spice
Currey, Curri, Currie, Curree, Currea, Curreah

Cursten (American) Form of Kirsten, meaning "follower of Christ"
Cirsten, Cerstin, Cirsten, Cirstie, Cirstin, Cirsty, Cirstyn, Cirstey, Cirstee, Cirsti, Cirstea

Cushaun (American) An elegant lady
Cushawn, Cusean, Cushauna, Cushawna, Cuseana, Cooshaun, Cooshauna, Cooshawn, Cooshawna, Coosean, Cooseana

Custelle (Latin) A majestic lady
Custele, Custell, Custella, Custela, Custel

Cwen (English) A royal woman; queenly
Cwene, Cwenn, Cwenne, Cwyn, Cwynn, Cwynne, Cwin, Cwinn, Cwinne

Cyan (English) Having blue-green eyes
Cyann, Cyanne, Cyana, Cyanna, Cyanea, Cyaneah, Cyania, Cyaniah

Cybele (Latin) A goddess of fertility and nature
Cybely, Cybeley, Cybelee, Cybeli, Cybelie, Cybelea, Cybeleah, Cybeleigh

Cybil (Greek) Form of Sybil, meaning "a prophetess; a seer"
Cibyla, Cybella, Cibil, Cibella, Cibilla, Cibley, Cibylla, Cybyla, Cybilla, Cybill, Cybille

Cydell (American) A girl from the country
Cydel, Cydelle, Cydele, Cydella, Cydela

Cydney (English) Form of Sydney, meaning "of the wide meadow"
Cydny, Cydni, Cydnie, Cydnee, Cidney, Cidnee, Cidnie, Cidni, Cidny, Cyd, Cydnea, Cydneah, Cidnea, Cidneah

Cylee (American) A darling daughter
Cyleigh, Cyli, Cylie, Cylea, Cyleah, Cyly, Cyley

Cylene (American) A melodious woman
Cyleen, Cylean, Cylein, Cylien, Cylyn, Cyleene, Cyleane, Cyleine, Cyliene, Cylyne

Cyllene (American) A sweetheart
Cylleen, Cyllean, Cyllein, Cyllien, Cyllyn, Cylleene, Cylleane, Cylleine, Cylliene, Cyllyne

Cyma (Greek) A flourishing woman
Cymah, Cymma, Cymmah

Cynara (Greek) Resembling a thistly plant
Cynarah, Cynarra, Cynaria, Cynarea, Cynarrah, Cynariah, Cynareah

Cyneburhleah (English) From the royal meadow
Cynburleigh, Cimburleigh, Cymberleigh, Cinberleigh, Cinburleigh, Cynberleigh, Cynburleigh, Cimberleigh, Cymburhleah, Cynberleah, Cymburleah, Cymberleah, Cymberly, Cymberley, Cymberlee, Cymberlie, Cymberli

Cynthia (Greek) Woman of Mount Kynthos; in mythology, another name for the moon goddess
Cinda, Cindee, Cindi, Cindie, Cindy, Cinnie, Cinny, Cinthia, Cintia, Cinzia, Cyn, Cynda, Cyndee, Cyndia, Cyndie, Cyndra, Cyndy, Cynnie, Cynthea, Cynthie, Cynthya, Cyntia, Cytia, Cynzia, Cindey, Cindia, Cindel, Cyndea, Cindea, Cinthea

Cyntrille (American) A gossipy woman
Cyntrill, Cyntril, Cyntrile, Cyntrilla, Cyntrila, Cyntrell, Cyntrelle, Cyntrella, Cyntrela, Cyntrele, Cyntrel

Cypris (Greek) From the island of Cyprus
Cyprien, Cyprienne, Cyprianne, Cipriana, Cypriane, Ciprienne, Cyprys, Cypryss, Cypriss

Cyrah (Persian) One who is enthroned; of the sun; feminine form of Cyrus; a lady
Cyra, Cira, Cirah

Cyrene (Greek) In mythology, a maiden-huntress loved by Apollo
Cyrina, Cyrena, Cyrine, Cyreane, Cyreana, Cyreene, Cyreena

Cyriece (American) One who is artistic
Cyreece, Cyreice, Cyreace, Cyryce

Cyrilla (Greek) Feminine form of Cyril; a noble lady
Ciri, Cerelia, Cerella, Cirilla, Cyrille, Cyrillia, Ciril, Cirila, Cirilia

Cytheria (Latin) In mythology, another name for the goddess of love and beauty
Cythera, Cytherea

Czarina (Russian) An empress; a female caesar
Czarinah, Czarinna, Czaryna, Czareena, Czarena, Cyzarine, Chezarina, Czarynah, Czareenah, Czarenah, Czareana, Czareanah, Czariena, Czarienah, Czareina, Czareinah

Czigany (Hungarian) A gypsy girl; one who moves from place to place
Cziganey, Czigani, Cziganie, Cziganee, Cziganea, Cziganeah

D

Dabney (French) One who is from Aubigny
Dabnie, Dabny, Dabni, Dabnee, Dabnea, Dabneah

Dabria (Latin) A heavenly messenger; an angel
Dabriah, Dabrea, Dabrya, Dabriya, Dabreah, Dabryah, Dabriyah

Dacey (Irish) Woman from the South
Daicey, Dacee, Dacia, Dacie, Dacy, Daicee, Daicy, Daci, Daici, Dacea, Daceah

Dada (African) A curly-haired young girl
Dadah, Dadda, Daddah

Daeshawna (American) The Lord is gracious
*Daeshan, Daeshaun, Daeshauna,
Daeshavon, Daeshawn, Daeshawntia,
Daeshon, Daeshona, Daiseana, Daiseanah,
Daishaughn, Daishaughna, Daishaughnah,
Daishaun, Daishauna, Daishaunah,
Daishawn, Daishawna, Daishawnah,
Daysean, Dayseana, Dayseanah,
Dayshaughna, Dayshaughnah, Dayshaun,
Dayshauna, Dayshaunah, Dayshawn,
Dayshawna*

Daisy (English) Of the day's eye;
resembling a flower
*Daisee, Daisey, Daisi, Daisie, Dasie, Daizy,
Daysi, Deysi, Deyzi, Daizie, Daizi, Daisha,
Daesgesage, Daisea, Daiseah, Daizee,
Dazea, Dazeah*

Dakini (Sanskrit) The sky dancer
*Dakinie, Dakyny, Dakyni, Dakynie,
Dakiny, Dakiney, Dakin, Dakiny, Dakinee,
Dakinea, Dakineah, Dakyney, Dakynee,
Dakynea, Dakyneah*

Dakota (Native American) A friend to all
Dakotah, Dakotta, Dakoda, Dakodah

DAHLIA
We named our daughter Dahlia because it means small branch in Hebrew—and she was the first branch for our new family tree. We still love it today, and she gets compliments almost every time someone asks her name. —Ruthie, Montreal

---

Daffodil (French) Resembling the yellow flower
*Daffodill, Daffodille, Dafodil, Dafodill,
Dafodille, Daff, Daffodyl, Dafodyl,
Dafodyll, Daffi, Daffie, Daffey, Daffee,
Daffea, Daffeah*

Daganya (Hebrew) Feminine form of Dagan; grain of the earth
*Daganyah, Dagania, Dagana, Daganna,
Daganiya, Dagian, Dagonya, Dagonia,
Dagoniya, Dagona*

Dagmar (Scandinavian) Born on a glorious day
*Dagmara, Dagmaria, Dagmarie, Dagomar,
Dagomara, Dagomar, Dagomaria,
Dagmarr, Dagomarr*

Dagny (Norse) Born on a bright new day
*Dagney, Dagni, Dagnie, Dagnee, Dagna,
Dagnia, Dagne, Dagnea, Dagneah*

Dahab (Arabic) The golden child
*Dhahab, Dahabe, Dahabia, Dahabea,
Dahabiah, Dahabeah*

Dahlia (Swedish) From the valley;
resembling the flower
Dahlea, Dahl, Dahiana, Dayha, Daleia

Dai (Japanese) The great one

Daira (Greek) One who is well-informed
Daeira, Danira, Dayeera

Dalal (Arabic) A flirtatious woman
Dalall, Dalale, Dalalle

Dale (English) From the small valley
*Dayle, Dael, Daelyn, Dail, Daile, Dalena,
Dalene, Dalenna, Dalina, Dalla, Dayla,
Daele, Dayl*

Dalia (Arabic / Hebrew) One who is gentle
/ resembling a slender tree branch
*Daliah, Dalit, Dalila, Daliya, Daliyah,
Dalya, Dalyah, Dalis, Daliyah, Dalea,
Daleah*

Dallas (Scottish) From the valley meadow
Dallis, Dalles, Dallin, Dallon, Dallys

Dalmace (Latin) Women from Dalmatia, a region of Italy
*Dalma, Dalmassa, Dalmatia, Dalmase,
Dalmatea*

Dalmar (African) A versatile woman
Dalmarr, Dalmare, Dalmarre

Daly (Irish) Of the assembly
*Daley, Dalee, Daleigh, Dali, Dalie, Dailey,
Daily, Dawley*

Damali (Arabic) A beautiful vision
*Damalie, Damaly, Damaley, Damalee,
Damaleigh, Damalea, Damaleah*

Damani (American) Of a bright tomorrow
*Damanie, Damany, Damaney, Damanee,
Damanea, Damaneah*

Damaris (Latin) A gentle woman
*Damara, Damaress, Damariss, Damariz,
Dameris, Damerys, Dameryss, Damiris,
Damris, Demaras, Demaris, Demarys,
Damalas, Damalis, Damalit, Damalla*

Damayanti (Indian) One who subdues
others; in Hinduism, the name of a
princess
*Damayantie, Damayanty, Damayantey,
Damayantee, Damayantea, Damayanteah*

Dame (English) A female knight
*Daim, Daime, Daym, Dayme, Daem,
Daeme*

Damhnait (Irish) Fawn
Devent, Downeti, Devnet, Downett

Damia (Greek) In mythology, a goddess of
nature
*Damea, Damiya, Dimaia, Damiah,
Dameah, Damiyah*

Damian (Greek) One who tames or
subdues others
*Damiane, Daimen, Daimon, Daman,
Damen, Dameon, Damiana, Damianna,
Damianus, Damien, Damion, Damon,
Damyan, Damyen, Damyon, Dayman,
Daymian, Daymon, Demyan, Damina*

Damisi (African) A cheerful daughter
*Damysi, Damisie, Damysie, Damisee,
Damysee, Damisea, Damysea, Damiseah,
Damyseah, Damisy, Damysy, Damisey,
Damysey*

Damita (Spanish) The little princess
*Damitah, Damyta, Dameeta, Damieta,
Damitta, Dameita, Dameata, Damytah,
Dameetah, Damietah, Damittah,
Dameitah, Dameatah*

Dana (English) Woman from Denmark
*Daena, Daina, Danaca, Danah, Dane,
Danet, Daney, Dania, Danica, Danna,
Danya, Dayna, Dayne*

Danae (Greek) In mythology, the mother
of Perseus
*Danay, Danaye, Danea, Danee, Dee,
Denae, Denay, Dene, Dinae, Dinay*

Dangelis (Italian) Form of Angela,
meaning "a heavenly messenger; an angel"
Dangela, Deangellis, Deangelis, Diangelis

Danica (Slavic) Of the morning star
*Danaca, Danika, Dannica, Dannika,
Donika, Donnica, Danyca, Danyka*

Danielle (Hebrew) Feminine form of
Daniel; God is my judge
*Daanelle, Danee, Danele, Danella,
Danelle, Danelley, Danette, Daney, Dani,
Dania, Danice, Danie, Daniela, Daniele,
Daniella, Danijela, Danila, Danit, Danita,
Danitza, Danna, Dannette, Danney,
Danni, Danniella, Dannielle, Danny,
Dannyce, Dany, Danya, Danyell,
Danyella, Danyelle, Dhanielle, Danise,
Dannah, Dannalee, Dannaleigh, Dannell,
Dannee, Dannelle, Dannia, Dannon,
Danuta, Danylynn*

Dante (Latin) An enduring woman;
everlasting
*Dantae, Dantay, Dantel, Daunte, Dontae,
Dontay, Donte, Dontae, Dawnte, Dauntay,
Dawntay, Dauntae, Dawntae*

Daphne (Greek) Of the laurel tree; in
mythology, a virtuous woman transformed
into a laurel tree to protect her from Apollo
*Daphna, Daphney, Daphni, Daphnie,
Daffi, Daffie, Daffy, Dafna, Dafne, Dafnee,
Dafneigh, Dafnie, Danfy, Daphnah, Daph,
Daveney, Davne, Daphnea, Daphneah,
Dafnea, Dafneah*

Dara (Hebrew / Gaelic) A wise woman /
from the oak tree
*Darah, Darda, Dareen, Daria, Darian,
Darissa, Darra, Darragh, Darrah, Darya,
Daracha, Daralis*

Darby (English) Of the deer park
*Darb, Darbee, Darbey, Darbie, Darrbey,
Darrbie, Darrby, Derby, Derbie, Derbey,
Derbee, Darbea, Darbeah*

Darcie (English) A dark beauty
*D'Arcy, Darcee, Darcel, Darcell, Darceigh,
Darcelle, Darcey, Darchelle, Darci, Darcia,
Darcy, Darice, Darsee, Darseigh, Darsey,
Darsie, Darcelle, Daray, Dorcey, Dorcy,
Dorci, Dorcie, Dorcee, Dorsey, Dorsy,
Dorsi, Dorsie, Dorsee, Darcea, Darceah,
Dorcea, Dorceah*

Daria (Greek) Feminine form of Darius; possessing good fortune; wealthy
Dari, Darian, Dariane, Darianna, Dariele, Darielle, Darien, Darienne, Darina, Darion, Darrelle, Darrian, Darya, Dhariana, Dorian, Dariana, Darinka, Darena, Dariya

Darice (Greek) Feminine form of Darius; possessing good fortune; wealthy
Dareece, Daryce, Dareese, Daryse, Darise

Daring (American) One who takes risks; a bold woman
Daryng, Derring, Dering, Deryng

Darlene (English) Our little darling
Dareen, Darla, Darleane, Darleen, Darleena, Darlena, Darlenny, Darlina, Darline, Darlinn, Darlyn, Darlyne, Darryleen, Darrylene, Darryline, Darlita, Darelene

Darnell (English) A secretive woman
Darnelle, Darnella, Darnae, Darnetta, Darnisha, Darnel, Darnele, Darnela, Darnette, Darnete, Darneta, Darnysha

Daron (Irish / English) The great one / from a small rocky hill
Darona, Daronah, Darron

Darva (Slavic) Resembling a honeybee
Darvah

Daryl (English) One who is greatly loved
Darel, Darille, Darolyn, Darrel, Darrell, Darrelle, Darrellyn, Darrill, Darrille, Darryl, Darrylene, Darrylin, Darryline, Darryll, Darrylyn, Darrylynn, Darylene, Darylin, Daryline, Daryll, Darylyn, Darylyne, Derrill, Darelle

Daryn (Greek) Feminine form of Darin; a gift of God
Darynn, Darynne, Darinne, Daren, Darenn, Darene

Datya (Hebrew) One who believes in God
Datia, Datiah, Datyah, Dateah, Datea

Davina (Scottish) Feminine form of David; the beloved one
Daveen, Davia, Daviana, Daviane, Davianna, Davida, Davidina, Davine, Davinia, Davita, Davy, Davynn, Davinah, Davite, Davyte, Davyna, Davyta, Davonna, Davi, Daveigh, Davan, Davin, Dava

Daw (Thai) Of the stars
Dawe

Dawn (English) Born at daybreak; of the day's first light
Dawna, Dawne, Dawnelle, Dawnetta, Dawnette, Dawnielle, Dawnika, Dawnita, Dawnyelle, Dawnysia, Dowan, Duwan, Dwan

Day (American) A father's hope for tomorrow
Daye, Dai, Dae

Daya (Hebrew) Resembling a bird of prey
Dayah, Dayana, Dayanara, Dayania, Dayaniah, Dayanea, Dayaneah

Dayo (African) Our joy has arrived

Dayton (English) From the sunny town
Dayten, Daytan

Dea (Greek) Resembling a goddess

Dea Roma (Latin) A goddess of Rome

Debonnaire (French) One who is suave; nonchalant
Debonair, Debonaire, Debonnayre, Debonayre, Debonaere, Debonnaere

Deborah (Hebrew) Resembling a bee; in the Bible, a prophetess
Debbera, Debbey, Debbi, Debbie, Debbra, Debby, Debee, Debera, Deberah, Debi, Debor, Debora, Debra, Debrah, Debralee, Debreanna, Debriana, Debs, Devora, Devorah, Deb, Debb, Debbee, Dobra, Devoria, Debira, Debiria, Devorit, Devra, Devri

December (American) Winter's child; born in December
Decimber, Decymber, Decembar, Decimbar, Decymbar

Dechtere (Celtic) In mythology, a virgin mother
Dechtire, Dechtyre

Decima (Latin) The tenth-born child
Decimah, Decema, Decyma, Decia, Decemah, Decymah

Deianira (Greek) In mythology, the wife of Heracles
Deianeira, Deianiera, Deianyra, Deianeera, Deianeara

Deidamea (Greek) In mythology, the mother of Achilles' only son
Deidameia, Deidamia, Deidameah, Deidameiah, Deidamiah

Deidre (Gaelic) A brokenhearted or raging woman
Deadra, Dede, Dedra, Deedra, Deedre, Deidra, Deirdre, Deidrie, Deirdra, Derdre, Didi, Diedra, Diedre, Diedrey, Dierdre, Deardriu, Dierdra

Deiene (Spanish) Born on a religious holiday
Deiena, Deine, Deina, Deikun

Deifilia (Latin) Daughter of God
Deifiliah, Deifilea, Deifileah

Deiondre (American) From the lush valley
Deiondra, Deiondria, Deiondrea, Deiondriya

Deja (French) One of remembrance
Daejah, Daejia, Daija, Daijah, Daijaah, Daijea, Daijha, Daijhah, Dayja, Dajah, Deija, Deijah, Dejah, Dejanae, Dejanee, Dejanique, Dejanira, Deyanira

Deka (African) A pleasing woman
Decca, Decka, Dekah, Deccah, Deckah

Dekla (Latvian) In mythology, a trinity goddess
Decla, Deckla, Deklah, Decklah, Declah

Delana (German) One who is a noble protector
Dalaina, Dalainah, Dalaine, Dalanah, Dalanna, Dalannah, Dalayna, Dalaynah, Delanah, Dalinah, Dalinda, Dalinna, Delania, Delanna, Delannah, Delanya, Deleina, Deleinah, Delena, Delenya, Deleyna, Deleynah, Dellaina

Delancey (French) Named for a street in New York City
Delancie, Delancy, Delanci, Delancea, Delanceah, Delancee

Delaney (Irish / French) The dark challenger / from the elder-tree grove
Delaina, Delaine, Delainey, Delainy, Delane, Delanie, Delany, Delayna, Delayne, Delani, Delainie, Delanea, Delainea, Delaeny, Delaeni, Delaenie, Delaenee, Delaenea

Delaware (English) From the state of Delaware
Delawair, Delaweir, Delwayr, Delawayre, Delawaire, Delawaer, Delawaere

Delbine (Greek) Resembling a flower
Delbina, Delbin, Delbyne, Delbyn, Delbyna, Delbeene, Delbeena, Delbeina, Delbeine, Delbiena, Delbiene, Delbeana, Delbeane

Delia (Latin) Woman from Delos; form of Cordelia, meaning "a good-hearted woman; a woman of honesty"
Delya, Deliya, Delea, Deelia, Deelea, Deelya, Deliah, Deleah, Deliyah, Delyah

Delicia (Latin) One who gives pleasure
Delice, Delisa, Delisha, Delissa, Deliza, Delyssa, Delicea, Deliciae, Delight, Delite, Delit, Deliz, Deliciah, Deliceah

Delilah (Hebrew) A seductive woman; in the Bible, the woman who discovered the source of Samson's strength
Dalila, Delila, Delyla, Dalyla, Dalilah, Delylah, Dalylah

Della (German) Born of the nobility
Delle, Dell, Dellene, Delline, Dellah, Dela, Delah

Delling (Scandinavian) One who is sparkling and witty
Dellyng, Delleng

Delma (German) A noble protector
Delmi, Delmy, Delmira, Delmah

Delmara (English) Feminine form of Delmar; woman of the sea
Delmaria, Delmare, Delma, Delmia, Delmarra, Dellmara, Dellmarra

Delphina (Greek) Woman from Delphi; resembling a dolphin
Delphine, Delphinea, Delphinia, Delfa, Delfin, Delfine, Delfyne, Delpha, Delfina, Delphia

Delta (Greek) From the mouth of the river; the fourth letter of the Greek alphabet
Dellta, Deltah, Delltah

Delu (African) The sole daughter
Delue, Deloo

Delyth (Welsh) A pretty young woman
Delythe, Delith, Delithe

Demelza (English) From the hill's fortress
Demelzah, Demelzia, Demelziah, Demelzea, Demelzeah

Demeter (Greek) In mythology, the goddess of the harvest
Demetra, Demitra, Demitras, Dimetria, Demetre, Demetria, Dimitra, Dimitre, Dimitria, Dimiter, Detria, Deetra, Deitra

Demi (Greek) A petite woman; half
Demie, Demee, Demy, Demey, Demye, Demia, Demiana, Demiane, Demianne, Demianna, Demiann, Demea, Demeah

Demos (Greek) Of the common people

Denali (Indian) A superior woman
Denalie, Denaly, Denally, Denalli, Denaley, Denalee, Denallee, Denallie, Denalley, Denalea, Denallea

Dendara (Egyptian) From the town on the river
Dendera, Dendaria, Denderia, Dendarra

Denim (American) Made of a strong cloth
Denym, Denem, Denam

Denise (French) Feminine form of Denis; follower of Dionysus
Deneigh, Denese, Dennet, Dennette, Deney, Deni, Denice, Deniece, Denisa, Denissa, Denisse, Denize, Denni, Dennie, Denisse, Dennise, Denny, Denyce, Denys, Denyse, Dinnie, Dinni, Dinny, Denisha

Denver (English) From the green valley

Deoch (Celtic) In mythology, a princess of Munster

Deolinda (Portuguese) God is beautiful
Deolynda, Deolenda

Deora (American) From a small town in Colorado

Dep (Vietnamese) A beautiful lady
Depp

Derica (American) Feminine form of Derek; a gifted ruler
Dereka, Dericka, Derrica, Derika, Derecka, Derecca, Deryca, Deryka, Derycca, Derycka

Dericia (American) An athletic and active woman
Dericiah, Derisea, Dericea, Derisia, Derycia, Derysia, Dericeah, Dericiyah, Dericiya

Derinda (English) Ruler of the people
Darinda, Derynda, Darynda, Derenda, Darenda

Derine (German) Feminine form of Derek; a gifted ruler
Deryne, Derina, Deryna, Deriena, Deriene, Dereina, Dereine, Dereena, Dereene, Dereana, Dereane

Derora (Hebrew) As free as a bird
Derorah, Derorra, Derorit, Drora, Drorah, Drorit, Drorlya, Derorice

Derry (Irish) From the oak grove
Derrey, Derri, Derrie, Derree, Derrea, Derreah

Derval (Irish) One's true desire; a poet's daughter
Dervala, Dervilia, Dervalia, Dervla, Dearbhail

Dervorgilla (Irish) A servant girl
Dervorgila, Derforgal, Derforgala

Deryn (Welsh) A birdlike woman
Derran, Deren, Derhyn, Deron, Derrin, Derrine, Derron, Derrynne, Derynne

Desdemona (Greek) An ill-fated woman
Dezdemona, Desmona, Dezmona

Desiree (French) One who is desired
Desaree, Desirae, Desarae, Desire, Desyre, Dezirae, Deziree, Desirat, Desideria, Desirata, Des, Desi, Dezi, Dezie, Dezy, Dezey, Dezee, Dezea, Desirai, Dezirai

Desma (Greek) Of the binding oath
Desme, Dezma, Dezme, Desmiah, Desmia, Desmea, Desmeah

Despina (Greek) The mistress; in mythology, the daughter of Demeter and Poseidon
Despoina, Despinna, Despyna, Despena, Despona, Despeina, Despiena, Despeena, Despeana

Dessa (Greek) Feminine form of Odysseus; one who wanders; an angry woman
Dessah

Desta (German) Hardworking woman
Destah

Destiny ✪ (English) Recognizing one's certain fortune; fate
Destanee, Destiney, Destiney, Destini, Destinie, Destine, Destina, Destyni, Destany, Destinea, Destanea, Destynea

Detta (Latin) Form of Benedetta, meaning "one who is blessed"
Dette, Dete, Deta, Dett

Deva (Hindi) A divine being
Devi, Daeva

Devamatar (Indian) Mother of the gods

Devana (Hindi) One who is in love
Devanah, Devanna, Devannah

Devany (Irish) A dark-haired beauty
Devaney, Devanie, Devinee, Devony, Devenny, Devani, Devanee, Devanea, Devaneah

Devera (Latin) In mythology, goddess of brooms
Deverah

Deverell (Welsh) Woman from the riverbank
Deverelle, Deverele, Deverel, Deverella, Deverela

Deverra (Latin) In mythology, goddess of midwives
Deverrah

Devika (Indian) The little goddess
Devicka, Devica, Devyka, Devycka, Devyca

Devon (English) From the beautiful farmland; of the divine
Devan, Deven, Devenne, Devin, Devona, Devondra, Devonna, Devonne, Devvon, Devyn, Devynn, Deheune, Devina, Devyna

Devota (Latin) A faithful woman

Dextra (Latin) Feminine form of Dexter; one who is skillful
Dex

Deyanira (Spanish) One who is capable of great destruction
Daianira, Dayanira, Dellanira, Diyanira

Dhana (Sanskrit) A wealthy woman; prosperous
Dhanna

Dharani (Hindi) A minor goddess
Dharanie, Darani, Daranie, Dharanee, Daranee, Dharany, Darany, Dharaney, Daraney, Dharanea, Daranea

Dharma (Hindi) The universal law of order
Darma

Dhisana (Hindi) In Hinduism, goddess of prosperity
Dhisanna, Disana, Disanna, Dhysana, Dhysanna

Dhyana (Hindi) One who meditates

Diamanta (French) Woman of high value; resembling a diamond
Diamanda, Diamonda, Diamantina, Diamantia, Diamantea, Diamante, Diamond, Diamonde, Diamonique, Diamontina

Diane (Latin) Of the divine; in mythology, goddess of the moon and the hunt
Danne, Dayann, Dayanna, Dayanne, Deana, Deane, Deandra, Deann, Deanna, Dede, Dee, DeeDee, Deeana, Deeane, Dianna, Di, Diahann, Diahanne, Diahna, Dian, Diandra, Diana, Diann, Deandria, Diannah, Dianne, Didi, Dyan, Dyana, Dyane, Dyann, Dyanna, Dyannah, Deon, Deona, Deondra, Deonna, Deonne, Deandrea, Deeandra, Deanda, Deanne, Deeanna, Deeanne, Deena, Dyanne

Dianthe (Greek) The flower of the gods
Diantha, Diandra, Diandre, Dyanthe, Dyantha, Dyandre, Dyandra

Diata (African) Resembling a lioness
Diatah, Dyata, Diatta, Dyatah, Dyatta, Diattah, Dyattah

Dice (American) One who likes to gamble
Dyce

Didina (French) One who is desired
Dideena, Dideina, Didiena, Dideana, Didyna

Dido (Latin) In mythology, the queen of Carthage who committed suicide
Dydo

Didrika (German) Feminine form of Dietrich; the ruler of the people
Diedericka, Diedricka, Diedrika, Dydrika, Didricka

Diega (Spanish) Feminine form of Diego; the supplanter

Dielle (Latin) One who worships God
Diele, Diell, Diella, Diela, Diel

Digna (Latin) She who is worthy
Digne, Deenya, Dinya, Dygna

Dike (Greek) In mythology, the goddess of justice

Dilys (Welsh) A perfect woman; one who is reliable
Dillys, Dylis, Dyllis, Dil, Dill, Dilly

Dimity (English) Resembling a sheer cotton fabric
Dimitee, Dimitey, Dimitie, Dimitea, Dimiteah, Dimiti

Dimona (Hebrew) Woman from the South
Dimonah, Dymona, Demona, Demonah, Dymonah

Dinah (Hebrew) One who is judged and vindicated; in the Bible, Jacob's only daughter
Dina, Dinora, Dinorah, Dyna, Dynah, Dena, Denna, Dene, Deneen, Denia, Denica

Dionne (English) Of the sacred spring
Dionna, Deiondra, Deon, Deonne, Dion, Diona, Diondra, Dione, Dionetta, Dionis, Deona, Deondra, Deonna

Dionysia (Greek) A gift from Dionysus, god of wine
Dionysea, Dionisa, Dionysa, Dionis, Dionysie, Dionyza, Dionyzia

Dior (French) The golden one
D'Or, Diorr, Diorre, Dyor, Deor, Dyorre, Deorre

Dipali (Indian) A row of lights
Deepali, Dypali, Dipalie, Deepalie, Dypalie, Dipaly, Deepaly, Dypaly, Dipalee, Deepalee, Dypalee, Dipalea, Deepalea, Dypalea, Dipaleigh, Deepaleigh, Dypaleigh

Dirce (Greek) In mythology, the wife of Lycus
Dyrce

Disa (English) Resembling an orchid

Discordia (Latin) In mythology, goddess of strife
Dyscordia, Diskordia, Dyskordia

Diti (Hindi) In Hinduism, an earth goddess
Dyti, Ditie, Dytie, Dity, Dyty, Ditey, Dytey, Ditee, Dytee, Ditea, Dytea

Ditza (Hebrew) One who brings joy
Ditzah, Diza, Dizah, Dytza, Dytzah, Dyza, Dyzah

Divina (Latin) One who is godlike
Devina, Divinah, Divone, Divya, Dyvina, Dyvyna

Divsha (Hebrew) As sweet as honey
Divshah, Dyvsha, Dyvshah

Dixie (English) Woman from the South; the tenth-born child
Dixi, Dixy, Dixey, Dixee, Dixea, Dixeah

Docilla (Latin) One who is calm and peaceful
Docila, Docylla, Docyla

Dohtor (Anglo-Saxon) Her father's daughter

Dojna (Eastern European) Song of Yearning
Doina

Dolores (Spanish) Woman of sorrow; refers to the Virgin Mary
Dalores, Delora, Delores, Deloria, Deloris, Dolorcita, Dolorcitas, Dolorita, Doloritas, Deloras, Delora, Deloros

Domela (Latin) The lady of the house
Domella, Domele, Domelle, Domell, Domhnulla, Domel

Domiduca (Latin) In mythology, a goddess who protects children on their way home

Domina (Latin) An elegant lady
Dominah, Domyna, Domynah

Dominique (French) Feminine form of Dominic; born on the Lord's day
Domaneke, Domanique, Domenica, Domeniga, Domenique, Dominee, Domineek, Domineke, Dominga, Domini, Dominica, Dominie, Dominika, Dominizia, Domino, Dominica, Domitia, Domorique, Dominy, Domonique

Domitiana (Latin) Feminine form of
Domitian; one who has been tamed
*Domitianna, Domitiane, Domitianne,
Domitiann, Domitilla*

Donna (Italian) A titled woman; feminine
form of Donald; ruler of the world
*Dahna, Dahnya, Dona, Donalie, Donella,
Donelle, Donetta, Donia, Donica,
Donielle, Donisha, Donita, Donnalee,
Donnalyn, Donna-Marie, Donnell,
Donnella, Donnelle, Donni, Donnica,
Donnie, Donnisse, Donny, Donya,
Donatella, Donalda, Donaldina, Donata,
Doneen*

Dorcas (Greek) Resembling a gazelle
Dorkas, Dorckas

Doreen (French / Gaelic) The golden one /
a brooding woman
*Dorene, Doreyn, Dorine, Dorreen, Doryne,
Doreena, Dore, Doirean, Doireann,
Doireanne, Doireana, Doireanna*

Doris (Greek) A gift from God; in mythol-
ogy, a daughter of Oceanus
*Doree, Dori, Doria, Dorian, Dorice, Dorie,
Dorisa, Dorita, Dorri, Dorrie, Dorris,
Dorry, Dorrys, Dory, Dorys, Doryse,
Dorianne, Dorianna, Doriana, Dorrian,
Dorelia, Dorea, Doralis, Doralie, Doralice,
Doralia*

Dorma (Latin) One who is sleeping
Dorrma, Dorrmah, Dormah

Dorona (Hebrew) A gift from God
Doran, Dorran

Dorothy (Greek) A gift of God
*Dasha, Dasya, Dodie, Dody, Doe, Doll,
Dolley, Dolli, Dollie, Dolly, Doortje, Dora,
Doretta, Dori, Dorika, Dorinda, Dorit,
Dorita, Doritha, Dorlisa, Doro, Doronit,
Dorota, Dorotea, Dorotha, Dorothea,
Dorothee, Dortha, Dorothée, Dorrit,
Dorthea, Dorthy, Dory, Dosha, Dosya, Dot,
Dottey, Dottie, Dotty, Dorottya, Dorri,
Doroata, Dorote, Doroteia, Doroteya,
Diorbhall, Doanna, Dorette, Dordei,
Dordie, Doda*

Douce (French) One who is sweet

Dove (American) Resembling a bird of
peace
Duv

Doveva (Hebrew) A graceful woman

Draupnir (Norse) In mythology, an arm
ring that was a source of endless wealth
Draupnyr, Draupneer

Drea (Greek) Form of Andrea, meaning
"courageous and strong / womanly"
Dria, Dreah, Driah, Driya, Driyah

Dreama (English) A beautiful dream; one
who produces joyous music
Dreema, Driema, Dreima, Dryma

Drew (English) Feminine form of Andrew;
brave and womanly
Dru, Drue, Droo

Drina (Spanish) Form of Alexandra, mean-
ing "helper and defender of mankind"
*Drinah, Dreena, Dreenah, Driena,
Drienah, Dryna, Drynah, Dreana,
Dreanah, Dreina, Dreinah*

Drisana (Indian) Daughter of the sun
*Dhrisana, Drisanna, Drysana, Drysanna,
Dhrysana, Dhrisanna, Dhrysanna*

Drury (French) One who is greatly loved
*Drurey, Druri, Drurie, Druree, Drurea,
Drureah*

Drusilla (Latin) Feminine form of Drusus;
a mighty woman
*Drewsila, Dru, Drucella, Drucie, Drucilla,
Drucy, Drue, Druesilla, Druscilla, Drusella,
Drisy, Drisi, Drusi, Drusie, Drusila*

Dryope (Greek) In mythology, a woman
who was turned into a black poplar tree
Driope

Duaa (Arabic) One who prays to God

Duana (Irish) Feminine form of Dwayne;
little, dark one
*Duane, Duayna, Duna, Dwana, Dwayna,
Dubhain, Dubheasa*

Duena (Spanish) One who acts as a chap-
erone

Duha (Arabic) Born in the morning
Dhuha, Duhr

Dulce (Latin) A very sweet woman
*Delcina, Delcine, Delsine, Dulcee, Dulcea,
Dulci, Dulcia, Dulciana, Dulcie,
Dulcibella, Dulcibelle, Dulcina, Dulcine,
Dulcinea, Dulcy, Dulsea, Dulsia, Dulsiana,
Dulsibell, Dulsibelle, Dulsine, Dulsee,
Dulcinia, Duka, Dukie, Dukine, Dukinea,
Dulda, Duldne, Duldnia*

Dumia (Hebrew) One who is silent
Dumiya, Dumiah, Dumiyah, Dumea,
Dumeah

Durdana (Arabic) Resembling a pearl
Durandana, Durindana, Durdaana,
Durriya

Durga (Hindi) One who is unattainable; in
Hinduism, a wife of Shiva
Doorga

Duscha (Russian) One who brings
happiness
Duschenka, Duschinka, Dusica, Dusa

Dusty (English) Feminine form of Dustin;
a brave fighter; from a dusty place
Dustey, Dustee, Dusti, Dustie, Dustye,
Dustine, Dustina, Dustyne, Dustyna,
Dustyn, Dustan, Dustea, Dusteah

Duvessa (Irish) A dark beauty
Duvessah, Duvesa, Dubheasa, Duvesah

Duyen (Vietnamese) A charming and
graceful woman

Dyani (Native American) Having the grace
of a deer
Dyanie, Dyany, Dyaney, Dyanee, Dyanye,
Dyanea, Dyaneah

Dylan (Welsh) Daughter of the waves
Dylana, Dylane, Dyllan, Dyllana, Dillon,
Dillan, Dillen, Dillian

Dympna (Irish) Form of Damhnait, meaning "fawn"; the patron saint of the insane
Dymphna, Dimpna, Dimphna

Dyre (Scandinavian) One who is dear to
the heart

Dysis (Greek) Born at sunset
Dysiss, Dysisse, Dysys, Dysyss, Dysysse

Eacnung (Anglo-Saxon) A fertile woman;
one who bears children

Eada (English) One who is prosperous;
wealthy
Eadah, Eadia, Eadea, Eadiah, Eadeah,
Eadda, Eaddah

Eadaion (German) A joyous friend

Eadburga (Anglo-Saxon) From the rich
fortress
Eadburgah, Edburga, Eadburgia,
Eadburgea, Edburgia, Edburgea

Eadignes (Anglo-Saxon) One who is blissful
Eadignys, Eadygnys, Edignes, Edygnes,
Edygnys

Eadlin (Anglo-Saxon) Born into royalty
Eadlinn, Eadlinne, Eadline, Eadlyn,
Eadlynn, Eadlynne, Eadlina, Eadlyna,
Eadlen, Eadlenn, Eadlenne

Eadrianne (American) One who stands out
Eadrian, Eadriann, Edriane, Edriana,
Edrianna

Ealasaid (Gaelic) One who is devoted to
God
Ealasayd, Ealasaida, Ealasayda

Ealga (Irish) Born into the nobility
Ealgah, Ealgia, Ealgea, Ealgiah, Ealgeah

Eara (Scottish) Woman from the East
Earah, Earra, Earrah, Earia, Earea, Earie,
Eari, Earee, Eary, Earey

Earla (English) A great leader
Earlah

Earline (English) Feminine form of Earl; a
noble woman; a great leader
Earlena, Earlene, Earlina, Earlyne, Earlyna,
Earleene, Earleena, Earleane, Earleana,
Earleine, Earleina, Earliene, Earliena

Early (American) Daughter born
prematurely
Earli, Earlie, Earley, Earlee, Earleigh,
Earlea, Earleah

Earna (English) Resembling an eagle
Earnah, Earnia, Earnea, Earniah, Earneah

Earric (English) A powerful young woman
Earrick, Earrik, Earrica, Earrika, Earricka

Eartha (German) Woman of the earth
Ertha, Earthe, Erthe

Easter (American) Born during the religious
holiday
Eastere, Eastre, Eastir, Eastar, Eastor,
Eastera, Easteria, Easterea

Easton (American) A wholesome woman
Eastan, Easten, Eastun, Eastyn

Eathelin (English) Noble woman of the waterfall
Eathelyn, Eathelinn, Eathelynn, Eathelina, Eathelyna, Ethelin, Ethelyn, Eathelen, Eathelena

Eathellreda (English) A noble young woman
Eathelreda, Eathellredia, Eathellredea, Eathelredia, Eathelredea, Ethelreda, Ethellreda

Ebba (English) Having the strength of the tide
Ebbah, Ebby, Ebbie, Ebbee, Ebbi, Ebbey, Ebbe, Ebb, Ebbea, Ebbeah

Ebban (American) A pretty woman
Ebann, Ebanne, Ebbann, Ebbanne

Ebed-melech (Hebrew) A servant in the king's house

Ebenezer (Hebrew) The stone of aid

Eber (Hebrew) One who moves beyond

Ebere (African) One who shows mercy
Eberre, Ebera, Eberia, Eberea, Eberria, Eberrea, Ebiere, Ebierre

Eberta (English) Feminine form of Ebert; wielding the shining sword
Ebertha, Ebertah, Ebyrta, Ebyrtha, Ebirta, Ebirtha

Ebony (Egyptian) A dark beauty
Eboni, Ebonee, Ebonie, Ebonique, Eboney, Ebonea, Eboneah

Ebrel (Cornish) Born during the month of April
Ebrell, Ebrele, Ebrelle, Ebriel, Ebriell, Ebriele, Ebrielle

Ebrill (Welsh) Born in April
Ebrille, Ebril, Evril, Evrill, Evrille

Ebronah (Hebrew) One who secures passage
Ebrona, Ebronna, Ebronnah, Ebronia, Ebronea, Ebroniah, Ebroneah

Ecaterina (Greek) Form of Catherine, meaning "one who is pure; virginal"
Ecaterinah, Ecateryna, Ecatereena, Ekaterina, Ekateryna, Ekatereena, Ecterine, Ecterina, Ecteryne, Ecteryna

Echidna (Greek) In mythology, a monster with the head of a nymph and the body of a serpent
Echidnia, Echidnea, Ekidna, Eckidna, Ekidnea, Eckidnea

Echo (Greek) Sound returned; in mythology, a nymph who pined away to nothing, leaving only the sound of her voice
Ekko, Ekho, Eko, Ecco, Ekow, Ecko

Ecstasy (American) Filled with extreme happiness
Ekstasy, Ecstacey, Ekstacey, Ecstacee, Ekstacee, Ecstacea, Ekstacea, Ecstaci, Ekstaci, Ecstacie, Ekstacie

Edalene (Gaelic) A queenly woman; one who is noble
Edaleen, Edaleene, Edalena, Edaleena, Edalyne, Edalyna, Edaline, Edalina, Ediline, Edilyne, Edilina, Edilyna, Edaleana, Edaleane

Edana (Irish) Feminine form of Aidan; one who is fiery; little fire
Edanah, Edanna, Ena, Ethna, Eithna, Etney, Eideann, Eidana, Eidanna, Eithne, Edaena, Edayna

Edda (German) Form of Hedwig, meaning "suffering strife during war"
Eddah, Edwige, Edwig, Edwiga

Edeen (Scottish) Woman from Edinburgh
Edeene, Edeena, Edeenia, Edeenea, Edine, Edina, Edean, Edeana, Edyne, Edyna

Edel (German) A clever woman
Edell, Edele, Edelle

Eden (Hebrew) Place of pleasure; in the Bible, the first home of Adam and Eve
Edenia, Edan, Edin, Edon

Edith (English) The spoils of war; one who is joyous; a treasure
Edythe, Edytha, Eda, Edee, Edie, Edita, Edelina, Eadgyth, Ede, Edeline, Edelyne, Edelyna, Edit, Editta, Edyt, Edytta, Edyta, Edyte, Edyth, Eydie

Edjo (Egyptian) In mythology, another name for Wadjet, a snake goddess

Edlyn (English) A woman of the nobility
Edlynn, Edlynne, Edlyne, Edlin, Edlinn, Edlen, Edlenne, Edla

Edmunda (English) Feminine form of Edmund; a wealthy protector
Edmonda, Eadmunda, Eadmonda, Edmundia, Edmundea, Edmundiya, Edmanda, Eadmanda, Edmee, Edmi, Edmie, Edmy, Edmey

Edna (Hebrew) One who brings pleasure; a delight
Ednah, Edena, Edenah

Edolia (Teutonic) A woman of good humor
Edoliah, Edolea, Edoleah, Edoli, Edolie, Edoly, Edoley, Edolee, Edoleigh

Edra (English) A powerful and mighty woman
Edrah, Edrea, Edreah, Edria, Edriah

Edreanna (American) A joyful woman
Edreana, Edreann, Edreanne, Edreane, Edrean

Edrei (Hebrew) A woman of great strength

Edrina (American) An old-fashioned woman
Edrinah, Edryna, Edrynah, Edreena, Edreenah

Edris (Anglo-Saxon) A prosperous ruler
Edriss, Edrisse, Edrys, Edryss, Edrysse

Edsel (American) One who is plain
Edsell, Edsele, Esdelle, Edzel, Edzell, Edzelle, Edzele

Edshone (American) A wealthy woman
Edshun

Eduarda (Portugese) Feminine form of Edward; a wealthy protector
Eduardia, Eduardea, Edwarda, Edwardia, Edwardea, Eduardina, Eduardyna, Edwardina, Edwardyna

Edurne (Basque) Feminine form of Edur; woman of the snow
Edurna, Edurnia, Edurnea, Edurniya

Edusa (Latin) In mythology, the protector goddess of children
Edussa, Educa, Edulica, Edulisa

Edwina (English) Feminine form of Edwin; one who is wealthy in friendship
Edwinna, Edwyna, Edwynna, Eadwina, Eadwyna, Edwena, Edwenna, Eddie, Eddy, Eddey, Eddee, Eddea, Eddi

Eferhild (English) A warrior who is as strong as a bear
Eferhilde, Eferhilda

Effemy (Greek) A talented songstress
Effemey, Effemi, Effemie, Effemee, Effemea

Efia (African) Born on a Friday
Efiah, Efea, Efeah, Effia, Effea

Efrat (Hebrew) My God is bountiful
Efrata, Efratia, Efratea

Efterpi (Greek) A maiden with a pretty face
Efterpie, Efterpy, Efterpey, Efterpee, Efterpea, Efterpeah

Egan (American) A wholesome woman
Egann, Egen, Egun, Egon

Egberta (English) Feminine form of Egbert; wielding the shining sword
Egbertha, Egbertina, Egbertyna, Egberteena, Egbertyne, Egberteene, Egbertine

Egeria (Latin) A wise counselor; in mythology, a water nymph
Egeriah, Egerea, Egereah, Egeriya, Egeriyah

Eglah (Hebrew) Resembling a heifer
Egla, Eglon, Eglona, Eglia, Egliah, Eglea, Egleah

Eglaim (Hebrew) Of the two ponds
Eglaima, Eglaimia, Eglaimea, Eglayma, Eglaymia, Eglaymea, Eglaem, Eglaema, Eglaemia, Eglaemea

Eglantine (English) Resembling the sweet-brier flower
Eglantyne, Eglanteene, Eglantina, Eglantyna, Eglanteena, Eglanteane, Eglanteana, Eglantiene, Eglantiena, Eglanteina, Eglanteine

Eguskine (Basque) Of the sunshine
Eguskyne, Eguskeene, Eguskina, Eguskyna, Eguskeena, Eguskeane, Eguskeana, Eguskiene, Eguskiena, Eguskeine, Eguskeina

Egypt (Hebrew) From the land of pyramids and the Nile
Egipt

Egzanth (American) A yellow-haired woman
Egzanthe, Egzantha, Egzanthia, Egzanthea, Egzanthiya, Egzanthya

Eibhlhin (Gaelic) Form of Evelyn, meaning "a birdlike woman"
Eibhlin, Eihhlin

Eidothea (Greek) In mythology, a sea nymph
Eidotheah, Eidothia, Eidothiah

Eileen (Gaelic) Form of Evelyn, meaning "a birdlike woman"
Eila, Eileene, Eilena, Eilene, Eilin, Eilleen, Eily, Eilean, Eileane, Eileine, Eilein, Eilien, Eiliene, Eilyn, Eilyne

Eileithyia (Greek) In mythology, goddess of childbirth
Eileithyea, Eilithia, Eileithia, Eileithiya

Eiluned (Welsh) Feminine form of Eluned; an idol worshipper
Elined, Eiluneda, Elineda, Eluned, Eluneda

Eilwen (Welsh) One with a fair brow
Eilwenne, Eilwin, Eilwinne, Eilwyn, Eilwynne

Eirene (Greek) Form of Irene, meaning "a peaceful woman"
Eireen, Eireene, Eiren, Eir, Eireine, Eirein, Eirien, Eiriene, Eirean, Eireane, Eiryn, Eiryne

Eires (Greek) A peaceful woman
Eiress, Eiris, Eiriss, Eirys, Eiryss

Eirian (Welsh) One who is bright and beautiful
Eiriann, Eiriane, Eiriana, Eirianne, Eirianna

Eirny (Scandinavian) Born of new healing
Eirney, Eirni, Eirnie, Eirnee, Eirnea, Eirneah

Ekanta (Indian) A devoted woman
Ekantah, Eckanta, Ecanta, Eckantah, Ecantah

Ekron (Hebrew) One who is firmly rooted
Eckron, Ecron

Elain (Welsh) Resembling a fawn
Elayn, Elaen

Elaine (French) Form of Helen, meaning "the shining light"
Ellaine, Ellayne, Elaina, Elayna, Elayne, Elaene, Elaena, Ellaina

Elama (Hebrew) Feminine form of Elam; a secretive woman
Elamah, Elamma, Elamia, Elamea, Elamiah, Elameah

Elana (Hebrew) From the oak tree
Elanna, Elanah, Elanie, Elani, Elany, Elaney, Elanee, Elan, Elanea, Elaneah

Elata (Latin) A high-spirited woman
Elatah, Elatta, Elattah, Elatia, Elatea, Elatiah, Elateah

Elath (Hebrew) From the grove of trees
Elathe, Elatha, Elathia, Elathea

Elberta (English) Form of Alberta, meaning "noble and bright"
Elburta, Elbyrta, Elbirta, Elbertina, Elbertine, Elbrette, Elberte, Elberteen, Elbertyna, Elbertyne

Elda (Italian) Form of Hilda, meaning "a battlemaiden; a protector"
Elde, Eldi, Eldie, Eldee, Eldy, Eldey, Eldea, Eldeah

Eldora (Greek) A gift of the sun
Eleadora, Eldorah, Eldorra, Eldoria, Eldorea

Eldoris (Greek) Woman of the sea
Eldorise, Eldoriss, Eldorisse, Eldorys, Eldoryss, Eldorysse

Eldreda (English) Feminine form of Eldred; one who provides wise counsel
Eldredah, Eldrida, Eldridah, Eldryda, Eldrydah, Eldride, Eldrede, Eldreada, Eldreadah

Eleacie (American) One who is forthright
Eleaci, Eleacy, Eleacey, Eleacee, Eleacea

Eleanor (Greek) Form of Helen, meaning "the shining light"
Eleanora, Eleni, Eleonora, Eleonore, Elinor, Elnora, Eleanore, Elinora, Elenora, Elenore, Eilidh, Eilinora, Eilinore, Eilionoir, Eilionoira, Elie, Elienor, Elienora, Eleinor, Eleinora, Elinore, Ellinor, Ellnora, Ellinora, Ellenor, Ellenora, Ellie, Elly, Elli, Ellee

Eleftheria (Greek) An independent woman; one who is free
Eleftheriah, Elefthera, Elefthereah, Elefteria, Elefteriah, Elefterea, Eleftereah, Elepheteria, Elephtheria

Elegy (American) A lasting beauty
Elegey, Elegi, Elegie, Elegee, Elegea

Elek (American) Resembling a star
Elec, Eleck

Elektra (Greek) Of the fiery sun; in
mythology, the daughter of Agamemnon
Electra, Elecktra

Elena (Spanish) Form of Helen, meaning
"the shining light"
*Elenah, Eleena, Eleenah, Elyna, Elynah,
Elina, Elinah, Eleni, Elenie, Elene, Eleene,
Elenitsa, Eleyn, Elenea, Eleneah*

Eleora (Hebrew) God is my light
*Eleorah, Eleoria, Eleorea, Eliora, Eliorea,
Eliorea, Elora, Eloria, Elorea*

Eleri (Welsh) Having smooth skin
Elerie, Elery, Elerey, Eleree, Elerea

Elethea (English) One who heals others
*Eletheah, Elethia, Elethiah, Elethiya,
Elethiyah, Eletheya, Eletheyah, Elthia,
Elthea*

Elettra (Latin) A shining woman
Elettrah, Eletra, Eletrah

Elexis (English) Form of Alexis, meaning
"helper and defender of mankind"
*Elexi, Elexia, Elexina, Elexine, Elexus,
Elexys, Elix, Elexa, Elexea, Elexeah, Elexie,
Elexy, Elexey, Elexee*

Elfin (American) A small girl; resembling
an elf
*Elfyn, Elfan, Elfun, Elfee, Elfy, Elfey, Elfea,
Elfie, Elfi, Elfe*

Elfrida (Greek) A peaceful ruler; a good
advisor
*Elfridah, Elfreda, Elfredah, Elfryda,
Elfrydah, Elfrieda, Elfriedah, Elfreida,
Elfreidah, Elfreada, Elfreadah*

Elga (Anglo-Saxon) Wielding an elf's spear
Elgan, Elgana, Elgania, Elganea

Eliana (Hebrew) The Lord answers our
prayers
*Eleana, Eli, Elia, Eliane, Elianna, Elianne,
Eliann, Elyana, Elyanna, Elyann, Elyan,
Elyanne, Elyane*

Elica (German) One who is noble
*Elicah, Elicka, Elika, Elyca, Elycka, Elyka,
Elsha, Elsje*

Elida (English) Resembling a winged
creature
*Elidah, Elyda, Eleeda, Eleda, Elieda,
Eleida, Eleada*

Elidad (Hebrew) Loved by God
Elidada, Elidade, Elydad, Elydada, Elydade

Elika (Hebrew) God will judge
Elikah, Elyka, Elicka, Elycka, Elica, Elyca

Eliphal (Hebrew) Delivered by God
*Eliphala, Eliphall, Eliphalla, Eliphelet,
Elipheleta*

Elisa (English) Form of Elizabeth, meaning
"my God is bountiful"
*Elicia, Elisamarie, Elise, Elisha, Elishia,
Elissa, Elisia, Elisse, Elysa, Elyse, Elysha,
Elysia, Elyssa, Elysse*

Elishaphat (Hebrew) God has judged
Elishafat, Elyshaphat, Elyshafat

Elisheba (Hebrew) God's promise; in the
Bible, the wife of Aaron
*Elishebah, Elishyba, Elisheeba, Elysheba,
Elysheeba, Elyshyba*

Eliska (Slavic) An honest woman; one who
is truthful
Elishka, Elyska, Elyshka

Elita (Latin) The chosen one
*Elitah, Elyta, Elytah, Eleta, Eletah, Elitia,
Elitea, Electa, Elekta*

Elite (Latin) A superior woman

Elizabeth ✪ (Hebrew) My God is bountiful
*Elisabet, Elisabeth, Elisabetta, Elissa,
Eliza, Elizabel, Elizabet, Elsa, Elspeth,
Elyza, Elsbeth, Else, Elsie, Elsy, Elza,
Elizabetta, Elizaveta, Elizavet, Elisamarie,
Elisavet, Elisaveta, Eilis, Elisheva, Elishia,
Ellisif, Els, Elzbieta, Erzebet, Erzsebet,
Elzira, Erihapeti, Erssike, Erzsi, Erzsok*

Elke (German) A noble and kind woman
*Elka, Elkie, Elki, Elkee, Elkey, Elkea,
Elkeah*

Ella ✪ ✿ (German) From a foreign land
*Elle, Ellee, Ellesse, Elli, Ellia, Ellie, Elly,
Ela, Ellea, Elleah*

Ellan (American) A coy woman
Ellane, Ellann

Ellema (African) A dairy farmer
Ellemah, Elema, Elemma, Ellemma, Elemah

Ellen (English) Form of Helen, meaning "the shining light"
Elin, Elleen, Ellena, Ellene, Ellyn, Elynn, Elen, Ellin

Ellender (American) One who is decisive
Elender, Ellandar, Elandar

Ellenweorc (Anglo-Saxon) A woman known for her courage

Ellery (English) Form of Hilary, meaning "a cheerful woman; bringer of joy"
Ellerey, Elleri, Ellerie, Elleree, Ellerea, Ellereah

Elletra (Greek) A shining woman
Elletrah, Eletra, Eletrah

Ellette (English) Resembling a little elf
Ellett, Ellete, Elette, Elete, Elletta, Elleta, Eleta, Ellet, Elet

Ellora (Indian) From the cave temples

Ellyanne (American) A shining and gracious woman
Ellianne, Ellyanna, Ellianna, Ellyann, Elliann, Ellyan, Ellian

Ellyce (English) Feminine form of Elijah; the Lord is my God
Ellecia, Ellice, Ellisha, Ellison, Elyce, Ellesse, Ellis

Elma (German) Having God's protection
Elmah

Elmas (Armenian) Resembling a diamond
Elmaz, Elmes, Elmis, Elmez, Elmiz

Elmina (Teutonic) One who is widelyknown
Elminah, Elmeena, Elmeenah, Elmyna, Elmynah, Elmine, Elmyne, Elmeene, Elmeina, Elmeinah, Elmiena, Elmienah, Elmeana, Elmeanah

Elmira (English) Form of Almira, meaning "a princess; daughter born to royalty"
Elmirah, Elmyra, Elmeera, Elmiera, Elmeira, Elmeara, Elmyrah, Elmeerah, Elmierah, Elmeirah, Elmearah

Elodia (Spanish) A wealthy foreigner
Elodiah, Elodea, Elodeah, Elodie, Elodi, Elodee, Elody, Elodey

Eloina (Latin) One who is trustworthy
Eloinia, Eloinea, Eloine, Eloyna, Eloyne, Eloynea

Eloisa (Latin) Form of Louise, meaning "a famous warrior"
Eloise, Eloiza, Eloisee, Eloize, Eloizee

Elon (African) Loved by God
Elona, Elonna, Elonia, Elonea, Eloniah, Eloneah

Elpida (Greek) Feminine form of Elpidius; filled with hope
Elpidah, Elpyda, Elpeeda, Elpieda, Elpeida, Elpeada, Espe, Elpydah, Elpeedah, Elpiedah, Elpeidah, Elpeadah

Elpidia (Spanish) A shining woman
Elpidiah, Elpidea, Elpideah, Elpie, Elpee, Elpea, Elpi, Elpy, Elpey, Elpidiya, Elpidiyah

Elrica (German) A great ruler
Elricah, Elrika, Elrikah, Elryca, Elrycah, Elryka, Elrykah, Elrick, Elryck

Elswyth (Anglo-Saxon) Of the willow tree
Elswith, Elswythe, Elswithe

Eltekeh (Hebrew) A God-fearing woman
Elteke, Elteckeh, Eltecke

Elton (American) A spontaneous woman
Elten, Eltan, Eltin, Eltyn, Eltun

Elu (Native American) A woman full of grace
Elue, Eloo

Elvia (Irish) A friend of the elves
Elva, Elvie, Elvina, Elvinia, Elviah, Elvea, Elveah, Elvyna, Elvyne, Elvin, Elveen, Elvine, Elfie, Elfi, Elvena, Elvene, Elvan, Elivina, Elwina, Elweena, Elwnya, Elwin, Elwinne, Elwyn, Elwynne

Elvira (Latin) A truthful woman; one who can be trusted
Elvera, Elvita, Elvyra, Elvirah, Elvyrah, Elwira

Elysia (Latin) One who is blissful; in mythology, refers to the land of the dead
Elysiah, Elysea, Elyseah

Ema (Polynesian / German) One who is greatly loved / a serious woman

Ember (English) A low-burning fire
Embar, Embir, Embyr

Emberatriz (Spanish) A respected lady
Emberatrise, Emberatreece, Emberatreese, Emberatryce, Emberatryse, Emberatrice

Emberli (American) A pretty young woman
Emberlie, Emberlee, Emberleigh, Emberly, Emberley, Emberlea

Emberlynn (American) As precious as a beautiful jewel
Emberlyn, Emberlyne, Emberlynne, Emberline, Emberlin, Emberlinn, Emberlinne, Emberlen, Emberlenn, Emberlenne

Embla (Norse) From the elm tree; in mythology, the first woman

Eme (German / Hawaiian) Having great strength / one who is dearly loved

Emelle (American) A kind and caring woman
Emell, Emel, Emele, Emella, Emela

Emma ✪ ✿ (German) One who is complete; a universal woman
Emmy, Emmajean, Emmalee, Emmi, Emmie, Emmaline, Emalee, Emalina, Emeline, Emaline, Emmalyn, Emmeline, Em, Emiline, Emelyn, Emelin, Emlyn

Emmanuela (Hebrew) Feminine form of Emmanuel; God is with us
Emmanuella, Emmanuele, Emmanuelle, Emunah, Emanuela, Emanuele, Emanuelle, Emanuella, Eman, Emman, Emmuna, Emann

Emmaus (Hebrew) From the place of hot baths
Emmaws, Emmas

Emme (German) One who is womanly

Emmylou (American) A universal ruler
Emmilou, Emmielou, Emylou, Emilou, Emielou

Emsley (English) A gift from God
Emsly, Emsli, Emslie, Emslee, Emsleigh, Emslea, Emsleah

EMELIA
We named our daughter Emelia Margaret after a great aunt and her grandmother (and we found out later that her paternal great-great grandmothers were named Emelia and Margaret). We wanted a traditional name yet something not found on any Top 100, list so there wouldn't be ten other girls with the same name in her class. —Meghan, WA

Emena (Latin) Born into a wealthy family
Emene, Emina, Emine, Emeena, Emeene

Emer (Irish) One who is swift; in mythology, the woman who possessed the six gifts of womanhood
Emyr, Emir

Emiko (Japanese) A child blessed with beauty
Emyko

Emily ✪ ✿ (Latin) An industrious and hardworking woman
Emilee, Emilie, Emilia, Emelia, Emileigh, Emeleigh, Emeli, Emelie, Emelee, Emiley, Emalei, Emilei, Emalee, Emalia, Emely, Emelye, Emele, Emere, Emera, Emmly, Emilea, Emileah

Emims (Hebrew) Of a terrifying people

Emylinda (American) One who is happy and beautiful
Emmylinda, Emylynda, Emmilinda, Emmilynda, Emilinda, Emilynda

Ena (Irish) A fiery and passionate woman
Enah, Enat, Eny, Enya

Encarnacion (Spanish) Refers to the Incarnation festival

Endah (Irish) A flighty woman
Endeh, Ende, Enda

Endia (American) A magical woman
Endiah, Endea, Endeah, Endie, Endi, Endee, Endy, Endey

Endora (Hebrew) From the fountain
Endorah, Endoria, Endorea, Endor, Endore, Endoriah, Endoreah, Endorra, Endorrah

Enedina (Spanish) One who is praised
Enedinah, Enedeena, Enedeenah, Enedeana, Enedeanah, Enedyna, Enedynah

En-eglaim (Hebrew) From the fountain of calves

En-gannim (Hebrew) From the fountain of gardens

Engedi (Hebrew) From the fountain of goats
Engedie, Engedy, Engedey, Engedea, Engedeah, Engedee

Engela (German) Feminine form of Engel; a heavenly messenger; an angel
Engelia, Engelea, Engelina, Engelyna, Engeleena, Engeleana, Engella

Engelbertha (German) A luminous angel
Engelberta, Engelberthe, Engelberte, Engelbertine, Engelbertina, Engelberteena, Engelberteen, Engelbertyna, Engelbertyne

Engracia (Spanish) A graceful woman
Engraciah, Engracea, Engraceah

En-hakkore (Hebrew) From the fountain of the crier

Enid (Welsh) One who gives life
Enide, Enit, Enite, Enyd, Enyde

Ennea (Greek) The ninth-born child
Enneah, Ennia, Enniah

Ennis (Irish) From the market town
Enniss, Ennisse, Ennys, Ennyss, Ennysse

Enore (English) One who is careful

Enrica (Spanish) Feminine form of Henry; ruler of the house
Enrika, Enricka, Enryca, Enryka, Enrichetta, Enrichette, Enriqua, Enriqueta, Enriquetta

Enslie (American) An emotional woman
Ensli, Ensley, Ensly, Enslee, Enslea, Ensleigh

Enye (Hebrew) Filled with grace

Enyo (Greek) In mythology, a war goddess

Eolande (Gaelic) Resembling the violet flower
Eoland, Eolanda, Eolandia, Eolandea

Eos (Greek) In mythology, goddess of the dawn
Eostre, Eosta, Eostia, Eostea, Eostria, Eostrea

Epaphras (Hebrew) A lovely and fair woman
Epaphroditus

Ephah (Hebrew) Woman of sorrow
Epha, Ephia, Ephea, Ephiah, Epheah

Ephes-dammim (Hebrew) Bound by blood

Ephesus (Hebrew) From the desired place

Ephphatha (Hebrew) An open-minded woman

Ephratah (Hebrew) One who is fruitful
Ephrata, Ephratia, Ephratea, Ephrath, Ephratha, Ephrathia, Ephrathea

Epicurean (Hebrew) Follower of Epicurus
Epicureana, Epicureane

Epifania (Spanish) Proof of our love
Epifaniah, Epifanea, Epifaneah, Epifaina, Epifainah, Epifayna, Epifaynah

Epione (Greek) In mythology, the wife of Asclepius
Epyone

Epona (Celtic) In mythology, goddess of horses
Eponah, Eponna, Eponia, Eponea, Eponnah, Eponiah, Eponeah

Eppy (Greek) One who is lively
Eppey, Eppi, Eppie, Eppee, Eppea

Equoia (American) The great equalizer
Equoiah, Ekoia, Ekoiah, Equowya, Equowyah, Ekowya, Ekowyah

Eramana (German) An honorable woman
Eramanna, Eramanah, Eramane, Eramann, Eramanne

Eranthe (Greek) As delicate as a spring flower
Erantha, Eranth, Eranthia, Eranthea

Erasema (Spanish) Filled with happiness
Eraseme, Erasyma, Erasyme, Erasima, Erasime

Erasma (Greek) A friendly young woman
Erasmah, Erasmia, Erasmea

Erasta (African) A peaceful woman

Erato (Greek) In mythology, the muse of lyric poetry

Ercilia (American) One who is frank
Erciliah, Ercilea, Ercileah, Ercilya, Ercilyah, Erciliya, Erciliyah

Erelah (Hebrew) A heavenly messenger; an angel
Erela, Erelia, Erelea, Ereliah, Ereleah

Erendira (Spanish) Daughter born into royalty
Erendirah, Erendiria, Erendirea, Erendyra, Erendyria, Erendyrea, Erendeera, Erendiera, Erendeira, Erendeara

Eres (Welsh) An admirable woman

Eriantha (Greek) A sweet and kind woman
Erianthe, Erianthia, Erianthea

Erica (Scandinavian / Latin) Feminine form of Eric; ever the ruler / resembling heather
Erika, Ericka, Erikka, Eryka, Erike, Ericca, Erics, Eiric, Eirica

Eriko (Japanese) A child with a collar
Eryko

Erimentha (Greek) A devoted protector
Erimenthe, Erimenthia, Erimenthea

Erin (Gaelic) Woman from Ireland
Erienne, Erina, Erinn, Erinna, Erinne, Eryn, Eryna, Erynn, Erea, Erie, Errin

Erinyes (Greek) In mythology, the Furies

Eriphyle (Greek) In mythology, the mother of Alcmaeon
Eriphile, Erifyle, Erifile

Eris (Greek) In mythology, goddess of discord
Eriss, Erisse, Erys, Eryss, Erysse

Erith (Hebrew) Resembling a flower
Erithe, Eritha, Erithia, Erithea

Erla (Irish) A playful young woman
Erlah

Erlina (Spanish) Form of Hermelinda, meaning "bearing a powerful shield"
Erline, Erleena, Erleene, Erlyne, Erlyna, Erlene, Erlena, Erleana, Erleane, Erleina, Erleine, Erliena, Erliene

Erlind (Hebrew) An angelic woman
Erlinde, Erlynd, Erlynde, Erlinda, Erlynda

Erma (German) One who is complete; universal
Ermah, Ermelinda, Ermalinda, Ermelinde, Ermalinde, Ermintrude, Ermyntrude

Ermine (Latin) A wealthy woman
Ermeen, Ermeena, Ermina, Ermyne, Ermyna, Ermeane, Ermeana, Ermie, Ermee, Ermi, Ermea, Ermy, Ermey

Ernestina (German) Feminine form of Ernest; one who is determined; serious
Ernesta, Ernestine, Ernesha, Erna, Ernestyne, Ernestyna, Ernesztina, Earnestyna, Earnestina, Earnesteena, Emesta, Emestina, Emestine, Emesteena, Emestyna, Emesteene, Emestyne, Enerstina, Enerstine, Enerstyne, Enerstyna, Enersteen, Enersteena, Earnesteana, Ernesteana, Enersteana

Erskina (Scottish) Feminine form of Erskine; from the highest point
Erskinah, Erskyna, Erskeena, Erskeana, Erskena, Erskeina, Erskiena

Erwina (English) Feminine form of Erwin; friend of the boar
Erwinna, Erwinah, Erwyne, Erwyna, Erwnynna, Earwina, Earwine, Earwyn, Earwyna, Earwinna, Earwynna, Erwena, Erwenna, Erwene

Erytheia (Greek) In mythology, one of the Hesperides
Erythia, Erythea, Eritheia, Erithia, Erithea

Esbelda (Spanish) A black-haired beauty
Esbellda, Ezbelda, Ezbellda, Esbilda, Ezbilda

Esdey (American) A warm and caring woman
Essdey, Esdee, Esdea, Esdy, Esdey, Esdi, Esdie, Esday, Esdai, Esdae, Esdaye

Esek (Hebrew) A quarrelsome woman
Eseka, Esekia, Esekea

Esen (Turkish) Of the wind

Eshah (African) An exuberant woman
Esha

Eshana (Indian) One who searches for the truth
Eshanah, Eshanna, Eshania, Eshanea, Eshannah, Eshaniah, Eshaneah

Eshcol (Hebrew) From the valley of grapes
Eshcole, Eshcola, Eshcoll, Eshcolle, Eshcolla

Eshe (African) Giver of life
Eshey, Eshay, Esh, Eshae, Eshai

Eshey (American) One who is full of life
Eshay, Eshaye, Eshae, Eshai, Eshe

Eshtaol (Hebrew) From the narrow pass
Eshtaole, Eshtaola

Eshtemoa (Hebrew) An obedient child
Eshtemoah, Eshtemo

Esi (African) Born on a Sunday
Esie, Esy, Esey, Esee, Esea, Eseah

Esiankiki (African) One who is pure; a maiden
Esiankikie, Esiankiky, Esiankyky, Esiankikey, Esiankykey, Esiankikee, Esiankikea, Esiankikeah

Esinam (African) God has heard
Esiname, Esynam, Esinama, Esynama, Esinamia, Esinamea

Eskama (Spanish) One who shows mercy
Eskamah, Eskamia, Eskamea, Eskame, Eskam

Esme (French) One who is esteemed
Esmai, Esmae, Esmay, Esmaye, Esmee

Esmeralda (Spanish) Resembling a prized emerald
Esmerald, Esmeralde, Ezmeralda, Ezmerald, Ezmeralde, Emerald, Esmeraude, Ezmeraude, Esmerelda, Ezmerelda, Emeralda, Emeraude, Emelda, Esma

Esne (English) Filled with happiness
Esnee, Esney, Esnea, Esni, Esnie, Esny

Esperanza (Spanish) Filled with hope
Esperanzah, Esperanzia, Esperanze, Esperanzea, Esperansa, Esperansah, Esperansia, Esperanse, Esperansea

Essence (American) A perfumed woman
Essince, Esense, Esince, Essynce, Esynce

Essien (African) A child of the people
Essienne, Esien, Esienne

Esta (Italian) Woman from the East
Estah, Easta, Estia, Estea, Eastia, Eastea

Estefana (Spanish) Feminine form of Stephen; crowned with laurel
Estefani, Estefania, Estefanie, Estefany, Estefaney, Estefanee, Estebana, Estebania, Estephanie, Estephani, Estephany, Estephaney, Estephanee, Esteva

Estella (Latin) Resembling a star
Estela, Estelle, Estelita, Estrella, Estrellita, Estee, Essie, Estralita, Estrela, Eustella

Estevina (Spanish) One who is adorned
Estevinah, Esteveena, Esteveenah, Estevyna, Estevynah, Esteveana, Esteveanah, Estevana, Estevanah

Esthelia (Spanish) A shining woman
Estheliah, Esthelea, Estheleah, Esthelya, Esthelyah, Estheliya, Estheliyah

Esther (Persian) Resembling the myrtle leaf
Ester, Eszter, Eistir, Eszti

Estherita (Spanish) A bright woman
Estherida, Estheryta, Estheryda

Estime (French) An esteemed woman

Estrid (Norse) Form of Astrid, meaning "one with divine strength"
Estread, Estreed, Estrad, Estri, Estrod, Estrud, Estryd, Estrida, Estrik, Estred

Esyllt (Welsh) Form of Isolda, meaning "a woman known for her beauty"
Eseult, Eseut, Esold, Esolda, Esolt, Esolte, Esota, Esotta, Esotte, Esoud, Esoude, Eyslk

Etain (Irish) In mythology, a sun goddess
Eteen, Eteyn, Etine, Etaina, Eteena, Eteyna, Etina, Etaine, Etayn, Etayne, Etaen, Etaene

Etana (Hebrew) A strong and dedicated woman
Etanah, Etanna, Etannah, Etania, Etanea, Ethana, Ethanah, Ethania, Ethanea, Ethanna

Etaney (Hebrew) One who is focused
Etany, Etanie, Etani, Etanee, Etanea

Etenia (Native American) One who is
wealthy; prosperous
*Eteniah, Etenea, Eteneah, Eteniya,
Eteniyah*

Eternity (American) Lasting forever
*Eternitie, Eterniti, Eternitey, Eternitee,
Eternyty, Eternyti, Eternytie, Eternytee,
Eternytea, Eternitea*

Etham (Hebrew) Of the fortress
Ethama, Ethame, Ethamia, Ethamea

Ethel (German) A noble woman
*Etel, Etilka, Eth, Ethelda, Ethelde, Etheld,
Ethelinde, Ethelind, Ethelinda*

Etheswitha (Anglo-Saxon) Daughter born
into royalty
*Etheswithe, Etheswith, Etheswytha,
Etheswyth, Etheswythe*

Ethna (Irish) A graceful woman
Ethnah, Eithne, Ethne, Eithna, Eithnah

Ethnea (Irish) A puzzle piece
Ethneah, Ethnia, Ethniah

Etoile (French) Resembling a star

Etsuko (Japanese) A delightful child

Etta (American) Ruler of the house
*Ettah, Etti, Ettie, Etty, Ettey, Ettee, Ettea,
Etteah*

Eudlina (Slavic) A generous woman
*Eudlinah, Eudleena, Eudleenah, Eudleana,
Eudleanah, Eudlyna, Eudlynah*

Eudocia (Greek) One who is esteemed
*Eudociah, Eudocea, Eudoceah, Eudokia,
Eudokea, Eudosia, Eudosea, Eudoxia,
Eudoxea*

Eudora (Greek) A good gift
*Eudorah, Eudoria, Eudorea, Eudoriah,
Eudoreah*

Eugenia (Greek) Feminine form of Eugene;
a wellborn woman
*Eugena, Eugenie, Eugina, Eugyna, Eugynia,
Eugynie, Eugeni, Evgenia, Eugenea,
Eugeny, Eugeney, Eugenee*

Eulalie (Greek) Well-spoken
*Eulalia, Eulia, Eula, Eulah, Eulallia,
Eulalea, Eulaleah, Eulalee, Eulaleigh,
Eulaly, Eulaley, Eulali*

Eulanda (American) A fair woman
Eulande, Euland, Eulandia, Eulandea

Eulee (Greek) The wolf ruler; ruler of all
Euleigh, Eule, Eulie, Euli, Euly, Euley

Eunice (Greek) One who conquers
*Eunise, Eunyce, Eunis, Euniss, Eunyss,
Eunysse*

Eunomia (Greek) In mythology, goddess
of order
*Eunomiah, Eunomea, Eunomeah, Eunoma,
Eunomah*

Euodias (Hebrew) A traveling woman
Euodia, Euodeas, Euodea

Euphemia (Greek) One who speaks well
*Euphemiah, Euphemea, Euphemeah,
Euphemie, Euphemi, Euphemy, Euphemey,
Euphemee, Effie, Effi, Effy, Effey, Effee,
Ephie, Ephi, Ephy, Ephey, Ephee, Eppie*

Euphrates (Hebrew) From the great river
Euphratees, Eufrates, Eufratees

Euphrosyne (Greek) Woman of good
cheer; in mythology, one of the three
Graces
*Euphrosyna, Euphrosine, Euphrosina,
Euphroseen, Euphroseena, Euphroseane,
Euphroseana*

Eurayle (Greek) In mythology, a Gorgon
Euryle, Euraile, Eurale, Eurael, Euraele

Europa (Greek) In mythology, the mother
of Minos

Eurybia (Greek) In mythology, a sea god-
dess and mother of Pallas, Perses, and
Astraios
*Eurybiah, Eurybea, Eurybeah, Euryba,
Eurybah*

Eurydice (Greek) In mythology, wife of
Orpheus
Euridice, Eurydyce, Euridyce

Eurynome (Greek) In mythology, the
mother of the Graces
*Eurynomie, Eurynomi, Eurynomey,
Eurynomee, Eurynomy, Eurynomea,
Eurynomeah*

Eustacia (Greek) Feminine form of
Eustace; having an abundance of grapes
*Eustaciah, Eustacea, Eustaceah, Eustatia,
Eustatiah*

Eustada (Latin) A calm and tranquil child

Euterpe (Greek) In mythology, muse of lyric poetry

Euvenia (American) A hardworking woman
Eveniah, Evenea, Eveneah, Eveniya, Eveniyah

Euzebia (Polish) One who is pious
Euzebiah, Euzebea, Euzebeah, Euzeba, Euzebiya, Euzebiyah

Eva (Hebrew) Giver of life; a lively woman
Eve, Evetta, Evette, Evia, Eviana, Evie, Evita, Eeva, Evika, Evike, Evacska, Ewa, Evacsa, Efa, Evelia, Evelien, Evea, Eveah

Eva Marie (American) A gracious giver of life
Eva Maria, Eva Mary, Eva Mariah

Evadne (Greek) In mythology, daughter of Poseidon and mother of Iamus
Evadine, Evadna, Euadne, Euadna, Euadine

Evalouise (American) A famous giver of life
Evaluise, Evalouisa, Eva Louise

Evana (English) Feminine form of Evan; God is gracious
Evanah, Evanna, Evannah, Evania, Evanea, Evaniya, Evanee, Evani, Evanie, Evany, Evaney, Evin, Evyn, Evina, Evyna, Evinna, Evynna, Eavan, Eavana, Eavani, Eavanie, Eavanee, Evaneah

Evangelina (Greek) A bringer of good news
Evangela, Evangeline, Evangelyn, Evangelia, Evangelyna, Evangelea, Evangeleena, Evangeleina, Evangeliena, Evangeleana

Evanth (Greek) Resembling a flower
Evanthe, Evantha, Evanthia, Evanthea, Evanthie, Evanthi, Evanthy, Evanthey, Evanthee

Evelyn ✿ (German) A birdlike woman
Evaleen, Evalina, Evaline, Evalyn, Evelin, Evelina, Eveline, Evelyne, Evelynn, Evelynne, Evie, Evlynn, Ewelina

Everilde (American) A great huntress
Everild, Everilda, Everhilde, Everhild, Everhilda

Evline (French) One who loves nature
Evleen, Evleene, Evlean, Evleane, Evlene, Evlyn, Evlyne

Evonne (French) Form of Yvonne, meaning "a young archer"
Evon, Evonna, Evony, Evonie, Evoney, Evonee, Evoni, Evonea, Evoneah

Exaltacion (Spanish) One who is lifted up

Exodus (Hebrew) Of the great deliverance
Exodis, Exodas, Exodos, Exodys

Eyota (Native American) A superior woman
Eyotah, Eyotta, Eyottah

Eyote (Native American) One who is great
Eyotee, Eyoti, Eyotie, Eyotea, Eyoty, Eyotey

Ezra (Hebrew) One who is helpful
Ezrah, Ezruh

Ezza (American) A healthy woman
Ezzah, Ezzia, Ezziah, Ezzea, Ezzeah

Fabia (Latin) Feminine form of Fabius; one who grows beans
Fabiah, Fabeea, Fabiya, Fabea, Fabeah, Fabiana, Fabianna, Fabiann, Fabianne, Fabienne, Fabiene, Fabiola, Fabra, Fabria, Fabrea, Favianna, Faviola, Faba, Fabah

Fabrizia (Italian) A laborer
Fabriziah, Fabrizea, Fabrizeah, Fabritzia, Fabritziah, Fabritzea, Fabritzeah

Fadhiler (Arabic) A virtuous woman
Fadhyler, Fadheler, Fadheeler, Fadilah, Fadila, Fadillah, Fadyla, Fadylla, Fadheela, Fadhila, Fadhealer, Fadheiler, Fadhieler

Fadwa (Arabic) A self-sacrificing woman
Fadwah

Faghira (Arabic) Resembling the jasmine flower
Faghirah, Fagira, Fagirah, Faghyra, Fagheera, Faaghira, Fagheara, Fagheira, Faghiera

Fahimah (Arabic) Form of Fatima, meaning "the perfect woman"
Fahima, Fahyma, Fahymah, Fahiema, Fahiemah, Faheima, Faheimah, Faheema, Faheemah, Faheama, Faheamah

Faida (Arabic) One who is bountiful
Faide, Fayda, Fayde, Faeda, Faede

Faiga (Germanic) A birdlike woman
Fayga, Faga, Faega

Faillace (French) A delicate and beautiful woman
Faillase, Faillaise, Falace, Falase, Fallase, Fallace

Faina (Anglo-Saxon) One who is joyful
Fainah, Fainia, Fayna, Faena, Fana, Faine, Faene, Fayne

Fainche (Irish) One who is free; independent

Fair (Latin) A beautiful woman; one who is light-skinned
Faire, Fayr, Fayre, Fare

Fairly (English) From the far meadow
Fairley, Fairlee, Fairleigh, Fairli, Fairlie, Faerly, Faerli, Faerlie, Faerley, Fayrly, Fayrley, Fayrleigh, Fayrlee, Fayrli, Fayrlie, Fayrlea

Fairoza (Arabic) Resembling turquoise; a precious stone
Fairozah, Faroza, Faeroza, Fairozia, Farozia, Faerozia, Fairuza, Fayroza, Fayrozia, Farozea, Fairozea, Faerozea, Fayrozea

Fairy (English) A tiny mystical being possessing magical powers
Fairie, Faerie, Faery, Fairi, Faeri, Fairee, Fairey, Faerey, Faeree, Fayry, Fayrey, Fayri, Fayrie, Fayree

Faith ○ ⊙ (English) Having a belief and trust in God
Faythe, Faithe, Faithful, Fayana, Fayanna, Fayanne, Fayane, Fayth, Fe, Fealty

Faizah (African) A victorious woman
Faiza, Fayza, Faza, Faeza, Feyza, Fathia, Fathea, Fathiya, Fauzia, Fawzia, Fawziya, Fawziyyah, Fee'iza

Fakhira (Arabic) A magnificent woman
Fakhirah, Fakhyra, Fakhyrah, Fakheera, Fakira, Fakirah, Fakeera, Fakyra, Faakhira, Fakhriyya, Fakheara, Fakeara

Fala (Native American) Resembling a crow
Falah, Falla, Fallah

Falak (Arabic) Resembling a star
Falack, Falac

Falesyia (Spanish) An exotic woman
Falesyiah, Falesiya, Falesiyah

Fall (American) Born during the autumn season
Falle

Fallon (Irish) A commanding woman
Fallyn, Faline, Falinne, Faleen, Faleene, Falynne, Falyn, Falina, Faleena, Falyna, Falon, Fallan, Falline

Falsette (American) A fanciful woman
Falsett, Falset, Falsete, Falsetta, Falseta

Fama (Latin) In mythology, the personification of fame
Famah, Famma, Fammah

Fana (African) One who provides light
Fanah, Fanna, Fannah

Fancy (English) A decorated and sparkling woman
Fancey, Fanci, Fancie, Fansy, Fansie, Fansi, Fancee, Fancea, Fansey, Fansee, Fansea

Fanetta (French) One who is crowned with laurels
Faneta, Fanette, Fanett, Fanete, Fanet

Fanfara (American) One who is excited
Fanfarah, Fanfarra, Fanfarrah

Fang (Chinese) Pleasantly fragrant

Fanta (African) Born on a beautiful day
Fantah, Fantia, Fantiah, Fantea, Fanteah

Fantasia (Latin) From the fantasy land
Fantasiah, Fantasea, Fantasiya, Fantazia, Fantazea, Fantaziya

Fantina (French) One who is playful and childlike
Fantinah, Fanteena, Fantyna, Fantine, Fanteen, Fanteene, Fantyn, Fantyne, Fanteana, Fanteina, Fantiena, Fanteane, Fanteine, Fantiene

Faoiltiama (Irish) A wolflike lady
Faoiltiarna

Faqueza (Spanish) A weakness

Fara (English) A traveling woman;
a wanderer

Farah (Arabic) One who is joyful; a
bringer of happiness
*Farhana, Farhanna, Farhane, Farhanne,
Farhayne, Farhaine, Farhayna, Farhaina,
Farihah, Fariha, Fareeha, Faryha, Farieha,
Farhaen, Farhaena*

Farfalla (Italian) Resembling a butterfly
*Farfallah, Farfala, Farfalle, Farfale,
Farfailini, Farfallone, Farfalah*

Farica (German) A peaceful sovereign
*Faricah, Farika, Faricka, Faryca, Faryka,
Farycka*

Faridah (Arabic) A unique woman
*Farida, Faryda, Farydah, Fareeda,
Fareedah, Farideh, Fareada, Fareadah,
Farieda, Fariedah, Fareida, Fareidah*

Faris (American) A forgiving woman
*Fariss, Farisse, Farys, Faryss, Farysse,
Farris, Farrys*

Farkhande (Arabic) One who is blessed
and happy
*Farkhand, Farkhanda, Farkhandia,
Farkhandea*

Farley (English) From the fern clearing
*Farly, Farli, Farlie, Farlee, Farleigh, Farlea,
Farleah*

Farrah (English / Arabic) Fair-haired
woman / one who bears the burden
Farra

Farren (English) One who is adventurous;
an explorer
*Faren, Farin, Faryn, Farran, Farrin, Farron,
Farryn, Ferran, Ferryn, Faran, Faron,
Farina, Farinna, Farena, Farana*

Farrow (American) A narrow-minded
woman
Farow, Farro, Faro

Farsiris (Persian) A princess; born to royalty
*Farsiriss, Farsirisse, Farsirys, Farsiryss,
Farsirysse, Farsyris, Farsyrys*

Faryl (American) One who inspires others
Farel, Farelle, Farylle, Faril, Farille

Farzana (Arabic) Having great wisdom
and intelligence
*Farzanah, Farzanna, Farzann, Farzanne,
Farzane, Farzaana, Farzania, Farzanea*

Fascienne (Latin) A dark beauty
Fuscienne, Fasciene, Fusciene

Fashion (American) A stylish woman
*Fashyun, Fashyn, Fashon, Fashi, Fashie,
Fashy, Fashea, Fasheah, Fashee*

Fasiha (Arabic) One who is eloquent and
literary
Fasihah, Fasyha, Faseeha, Fasieha, Faseaha

Fate (Greek) One's destiny
Fayte, Faite, Faete, Faet, Fait, Fayt

Fatima (Arabic) The perfect woman; in the
Koran, a daughter of Muhammad
*Fatimah, Fateema, Fatyma, Fateama,
Fatime, Fatyme, Fateem, Fateam, Fatuma,
Fatiema, Fateima*

Fatinah (Arabic) A captivating woman
*Fatina, Fateena, Fateenah, Fatyna, Fatynah,
Fatin, Fatine, Faatinah, Fateana, Fateanah,
Fatiena, Fatienah, Fateina, Fateinah*

Faulk (American) A respected woman
Falk, Fawlk, Faulke, Falke, Fawlke

Fauna (Greek) In mythology, a goddess of
nature and fertility
*Fawna, Faun, Fawn, Faunia, Fawnia,
Faunea, Fawnea, Fawne, Faune*

Faunee (Latin) One who loves nature
Fauny, Fauni, Faunie, Fauney

Fausta (Italian) A lucky lady; one who is
fortunate
*Fawsta, Faustina, Faustine, Faustyna,
Faustyne, Fausteena, Fausteene, Fawstina,
Fawstine, Fawstyna, Fawstyne, Fawsteena,
Fawsteene*

Fauve (French) An uninhibited and
untamed woman

Favor (English) One who grants her
approval
Faver, Favar, Favorre

Fay (English) From the fairy kingdom; a fairy or an elf
Faye, Fai, Faie, Fae, Fayette, Faylinn, Faylyn, Faylynn, Faylinne, Faylynne

Fayina (Russian) An independent woman
Fayinah, Fayena, Fayeena, Fayeana, Fayiena, Fayeina

Fayme (French) A renowned woman who is held in high esteem
Faime, Faym, Faim, Fame

Fayola (African) One who walks with honor
Fayolah, Fayolla, Fayollah

Fearchara (Scottish) One who is dearly loved
Fearcharah, Fearcharra, Fearcharia, Fearcharea

Feather (American) A lighthearted woman
Fether, Fhether, Feathyr

Febe (Polish) A bright woman
Febee, Febea, Febeah, Febi, Febie, Feby, Febey

February (American) Born in the month of February
Februari, Februarie, Februarey, Februaree, Februarea

Feechi (African) A woman who worships God
Feechie, Feechy, Feechey, Feechee, Fychi, Fychie, Fychey, Fychy, Feechea, Fychee, Fychea

Feeidha (Arabic) A generous woman

Feenat (Irish) Resembling a deer
Feynat, Finat, Fianait

Felder (English) One who is bright
Felde, Feldy, Feldea, Feldeah, Feldey, Feldee, Feldi, Feldie

Felicia (Latin) Feminine form of Felix; one who is lucky and successful
Falisha, Felisha, Felice, Felisa, Feliciona, Felecia, Feleta, Felcia, Fela, Felicienne, Filicia, Felicity, Feliciona, Felicita, Felicitas, Felicite, Felidtas, Felisberta, Felise, Felita, Felka, Felici, Felicie, Felicy, Felicey, Felicee, Felicea

Felina (Latin) A catlike woman
Felinah, Felyna, Feleena, Feline, Felynna, Feliena, Feleyna, Feleana, Feleina

Fellah (Arabic) An agricultural worker
Fella, Felah, Fela, Fellahin, Fellaheen, Fellahyn, Felahin, Felaheen, Felahyn

Femay (American) A classy lady
Femaye, Femae, Femai

Femi (African) God loves me
Femmi, Femie, Femy, Femey, Femee, Femea, Femeah

Femise (American) One who desires love
Femeese, Femease, Femice, Femeece, Femeace, Femmis, Femmys

Fenia (Scandinavian) A gold worker
Feniah, Fenea, Feneah, Feniya, Feniyah, Fenya, Fenyah, Fenja, Fenjah

Fenn (American) An intelligent woman
Fen

Feo (Greek) A gift from God
Feeo

Feodora (Russian) Form of Theodora, meaning "gift of God"
Feodorah, Feodorra, Feodore, Feodore, Fedorah, Fedora, Fedoria, Fedoriya, Fedorea, Fedosia, Fedorra

Fern (English) Resembling a green shade-loving plant
Ferne, Fyrn, Fyrne, Furn, Furne

Fernanda (Spanish) Feminine form of Fernando; an adventurous woman
Fernande, Fernand

Fernilia (American) A successful woman
Ferniliah, Fernilea, Fernileah, Fernilya, Fernilyah

Fernley (English) From the meadow of ferns
Fernly, Fernleigh, Fernlea, Fernleah, Fernlee, Fernli, Fernlie

Feronia (Latin) In mythology, a fertility goddess
Feroniah, Feronea, Feroniya, Feroneah, Feroniyah

Feryal (Arabic) Possessing the beauty of light
Feryall, Feryale, Feryalle

Feven (American) One who is shy
Fevun, Fevon, Fevan, Fevin

Ffion (Irish) Having a pale face

Fia (Portuguese / Italian / Scottish) A weaver / from the flickering fire / arising from the dark of peace
Fiah, Fea, Feah, Fya, Fiya, Fyah, Fiyah

Fiamma (Italian) A fiery lady
Fiammah, Fyamma, Fyammah, Fiama, Fiamah, Fyama, Fyamah

Fianna (Irish) A warrior huntress
Fiannah, Fiana, Fianne, Fiane, Fiann, Fian

Fiby (Spanish) A bright woman
Fibey, Fibee, Fibea, Fibeah, Fibi, Fibie

Fidelia (Latin) Feminine form of Fidel; a faithful woman
Fidelina, Fidessa, Fidelma, Fidella, Fidessa, Fedella, Fidelity, Fides, Fidelitey, Fidelitee, Fideliti, Fidelitie, Fidelitea

Fielda (English) From the field
Fieldah, Felda, Feldah

Fife (American) Having dancing eyes
Fyfe, Fifer, Fify, Fifey, Fifee, Fifea, Fifi, Fifie

Fifia (African) Born on a Friday
Fifiah, Fifea, Fifeah, Fifeea, Fifeeah

Filberta (English) Feminine form of Filibert; one who is dearly loved
Filiberta, Filbertha, Filibertha, Felabeorht, Felberta, Feliberta, Felbertha, Felibertha, Fulberta, Fulbertha, Fuliberta, Fulibertha

Filia (Greek) A beloved friend
Filiah, Fillia, Filiya, Filea, Fileah

Filipa (Spanish) Feminine form of Philip; a friend of horses
Filipah, Filipina, Filipeena, Filipyna, Filippa, Fillipa, Fillippa

Filma (Greek) One who is much loved
Fylma, Filmah, Fylmah

Filomena (Italian) Form of Philomena, meaning "a friend of strength"
Filomina, Filomeena, Filomyna, Filomenia, Filominia, Filomeenia, Filomynia, Filomeana, Filomeania, Filomenea

Fina (English) Feminine form of Joseph; God will add
Finah, Feena, Fyna, Fifine, Fifna, Fifne, Fini, Feana, Fiena, Feina

Finch (English) Resembling the bird
Fench, Finche, Fenche, Fynch, Fynche

Findabair (Celtic) Having fair eyebrows; in mythology, the daughter of Medb
Findabaire, Finnabair, Finnabaire, Findabhair, Findabhaire, Findabayr, Findabayre, Findabare, Findabaer, Findabaere

Fineen (Irish) A beautiful daughter
Fineena, Fineene, Fyneen, Fyneene, Fyneena, Finean, Fineane, Fineana, Fynean, Fyneane, Fyneana

Finesse (American) One who is smooth
Finese, Finess, Fines

Finn (Irish) One who is cool
Fin, Fyn, Fynn

Finnea (Gaelic) From the stream of the wood
Finneah, Finnia, Fynnea, Finniah, Fynnia

Fiona (Gaelic) One who is fair; a white-shouldered woman
Fionna, Fione, Fionn, Finna, Fionavar, Fionnghuala, Fionnuala, Fynballa, Fionnula, Finola, Fenella, Fennella, Finella, Finelle

Firdaus (Arabic) From the garden in paradise
Firdaws, Firdoos

Fire (American) A feisty and passionate woman
Fyre, Firey, Firy, Firi, Firie, Firee, Firea

Firmina (French) Feminine form of Firmin; a firm and strong woman
Firminah, Firmeena, Firmyna, Fermina, Ferminah, Fermeena, Fermyna, Firmeana, Fermeana

Firtha (Scottish) Woman of the sea
Fertha, Fyrtha, Firthe, Fyrthe, Ferthe

Fisseha (African) A bringer of happiness
Fissehah, Fiseha, Fisehah, Fysseha, Fyseha

Fjorgyn (Norse) In mythology, goddess of the earth and mother of Thor

Flair (English) An elegant woman of natural talent
Flaire, Flare, Flayr, Flayre, Flaer, Flaere

Flame (American) A passionate and fiery woman
Flaym, Flayme, Flaime, Flaim, Flaem, Flaeme

Flamina (Latin) A pious woman
Flaminah, Flamyna, Flamynah, Flamiena, Flamienah, Flameina, Flameinah, Flameena, Flameenah, Flameana, Flameanah

Flanders (English) Woman from Belgium
Flander, Flandars, Flandar, Flande, Fland

Flann (Irish) A red-haired woman
Flan, Flanna, Flana, Flynn, Flanne

Flannery (Gaelic) From the flatlands
Flanneri, Flannerie, Flannerey, Flannaree, Flannerea, Flannereah

Flash (American) Emanating bright light
Flashe, Flasha, Flashia, Flashea

Flavia (Latin) Feminine form of Flavius; a yellow-haired woman
Flaviah, Flavea, Flaviya, Fulvia, Fulvea, Fulviya, Flaveah, Flaviyah, Fulviah, Fulveah, Fulviyah, Fulvie, Fulvi, Fulvy, Fulvey, Fulvee

Flax (Latin) Resembling the plant with blue flowers
Flaxx, Flaxe, Flaxxe, Flacks, Flaks

Fleming (English) Woman from Belgium
Flemyng, Flemming, Flemmyng

Flemmi (Italian) A pretty young woman
Flemmie, Flemmy, Flemmey, Flemmea, Flemmeah, Flemmee

Fleta (English) One who is swift
Fletah, Flete, Fleda, Flita, Flyta

Flicky (American) A vivacious young woman
Flicki, Flickie, Flickea, Flickeah, Flickee, Flycki, Flyckie, Flyckee, Flyckea, Flyckeah, Flycky, Flyckey, Flicka

Flirt (American) A playfully romantic woman
Flyrt, Flirti, Flirtie, Flirty, Flirtey, Flirtea, Flirteah, Flirtee

Flis (Polish) A well-behaved girl
Fliss, Flisse, Flys, Flyss, Flysse

Flora (Latin) Resembling a flower; in mythology, the goddess of flowers
Fleur, Flor, Flori, Floria, Floressa, Floretta, Floriana, Florida, Florinda, Florita, Florrie, Florella, Floramaria, Flordelis, Flo, Florette, Florian, Floriane, Floriann, Florianna, Florice, Florka, Florinia, Flower, Fleurette, Fiorella, Fiorenza, Firenze, Floris, Flos, Floss, Flossie, Floy, Fjola, Forenza

Flordeperla (Spanish) A blooming pearl
Flordepearla, Flordeperle, Flordepearle, Flordeperl, Flordepearl

Florence (Latin) A flourishing woman; a blooming flower
Florencia, Florentina, Florenza, Florentine, Florentyna, Florenteena, Florenteene, Florentyne, Florenteane, Florenteana

Florizel (English) A young woman in bloom
Florizell, Florizelle, Florizele, Florizel, Florizella, Florizela, Florazel, Florazell, Florazelle, Florazele, Florazel, Florazella, Florazela

Fluffy (American) A fun-loving young woman
Fluffey, Fluffi, Fluffea, Fluffeah, Fluffee, Fluffie

Fog (American) A dreamer
Fogg, Foggy, Foggey, Foggi, Foggie, Foggea, Foggeah, Foggee

Fola (African) Woman of honor
Folah, Folla, Follah

Fonda (Spanish) Grounded to the earth
Fondah, Fondiah, Fondia, Fondea, Fondeah

Fondice (American) A friendly woman
Fondyce, Fondeece, Fondeace, Fondise, Fondyse, Fondeese, Fondease

Fontana (Italian) From the fountain
Fontanah, Fontanna, Fontane, Fontann, Fontanne, Fontaine, Fontayne, Fotina, Fountain, Fontaina, Fontaene, Fontayna, Fontaena

Fontenot (French) One who is special

Forba (Scottish) A headstrong young girl
Forbah, Forbia, Forbea, Forbiya, Forbiah, Forbeah, Forbiyah

Ford (English) From the water
Forde

Forest (English) A woodland dweller
Forrest

Forever (American) Everlasting

Forsythia (Latin) Resembling the flower
Forsythiah, Forsythea, Forsytheah, Forsithia, Forsithiah, Forsithea, Forsitheah

Fortney (Latin) Having great strength
Fortny, Fortni, Fortnie, Fortnea, Fortneah, Fortnee, Fourtney, Fourtny, Fourtni, Fourtnie, Fourtnea, Fourtneah, Fourtnee

Fortuna (Latin) A fortunate woman; in mythology, the goddess of fortune and chance
Fortunah, Fortuin, Fortuyn, Fortunata, Fortunatus

Fowler (English) One who traps birds
Fowlar, Fowlir, Fowla, Fowlia, Fowlea

Frances (Latin) Feminine form of Francis; woman from France; one who is free
Francesca, Francine, Francene, Francina, Francille, Francena, Franceska, Francisca, France, Francia, Fanceen, Fanchon, Franchesca, Francheska, Franci, Francie, Francique, Franciska, Franciszka, Franca, Fran, Francoise, Frangag, Franki, Frankie, Frannie, Franni, Franny, Frantiska, Franze, Franziska, Fanchone, Fani, Fania, Fannia, Fanny, Fannie, Fanni, Fanya, Fereng, Ferika, Ferike, French, Frenchie, Frenchi, Frenchy, Frenchey, Frenchee, Frenchea

Franchelle (French) A woman from France
Franchell, Franchel, Franchele, Franchella, Franchela

Frayda (Scandinavian) A fertile woman
Frayde, Freyda, Freyde, Fraida, Fraide, Fraeda, Fraede

Frea (Scandinavian) A noble woman

Fredella (American) Feminine form of Frederick; a peaceful ruler
Fredela, Fredelle, Fredell, Fredele, Fredel

Frederica (German) Feminine form of Frederick; a peaceful ruler
Frederika, Fredrika, Fredrica, Fredericka, Fredricka, Frederyca, Federikke, Freda, Frida, Fryda, Fredda, Fridda, Freddi, Freddie, Frieda, Freida, Frici, Frideborg, Friede, Friedegard, Friedegarde, Friederika, Friederike, Frikka, Fritzi, Fritzie

Freedom (American) An independent woman
Free

Freesia (Latin) Resembling the flower
Freesiah, Freasia, Freasiah, Freesea, Freeseah, Freasea, Freaseah, Freezia, Freazia, Freeziah, Freaziah

Freira (Spanish) A sister
Freirah, Freyira, Freyirah

Freya (Norse) A lady; in mythology, the goddess of love, beauty, and fertility
Freyah, Freyja, Freja

Freydis (Norse) Woman born into the nobility
Freydiss, Freydisse, Freydys, Fredyss, Fraidis, Fradis, Fraydis, Fraedis, Fraidys, Fradys, Fraedys

---

FRAN

We named our girl Fran Dandelion. We like the old-world simplicity of Fran, plus it makes me think of a rolling meadow. The Dandelion just belongs in that meadow, plus it touches a cute/hippie nerve in us. We now think all our kids' names will have some kind of plant or grain in them (Thistle, Rye ...).
—Ilana, TX

Franisbel (Spanish) A beautiful woman from France
Franisbell, Franisbelle, Franisbele, Franisbela, Franisbella, Fransabel, Fransabell, Fransabelle, Fransabele, Fransabela, Fransabella

Friedelinde (German) A gentle young woman
Friedelynde, Friedelind, Friedelynd, Friedelinda, Friedelynda

Frigg (Norse) In mythology, the mother goddess of the heavens, love, and the household
Frigga, Frig, Friga, Frygg, Frygga, Fryg, Fryga

Frodina (Teutonic) A wise and beloved friend
Frodinah, Frodyna, Frodeena, Frodine, Frodyne, Frodeen, Frodeene, Frodeana, Frodeane

Fronda (Latin) Resembling a leafy branch
Fronde, Frondah, Frondia, Frondiah, Frondea, Frondeah, Frondiya, Frondiyah, Frond

Fronia (Latin) A wise woman
Froniah, Fronea, Froniya, Froneah, Froniyah

Frosty (American) One who is cool and crisp
Frostey, Frostee, Frostea, Frosteah, Frosti, Frostie

Fructuose (Latin) One who is bountiful
Fructuosa, Fructuosia, Fructuosea, Fruta, Frue, Fru

Frula (German) A hardworking woman
Frulah, Frulla, Frullah

Fruma (Hebrew) One who is religious; pious
Frumma, Frumah, Frummah

Frythe (English) One who is calm and tranquil
Fryth, Frytha, Frith, Frithe, Fritha

Fuchsia (Latin) Resembling the flower
Fusha, Fushia, Fushea, Fewsha, Fewshia, Fewshea

Fudge (American) One who is stubborn; resembling the candy
Fudgi, Fudgey, Fudgy, Fudgie, Fudgea, Fudgeah

Fuensanta (Spanish) From the sacred fountain
Fuensantah, Fuensantia, Fuensantea, Fuensantiya, Fuenta

Fukayna (Egyptian) One who is intelligent
Fukaena, Fukaina, Fukana

Fulgencia (Latin) A glowing woman
Fulgenciah, Fulgencea, Fulgenceah

Fulla (Norse) In mythology, one of Frigga's handmaidens
Fullah, Fula, Fylla, Fyllah, Fyla

Furina (Latin) In mythology, the patroness of thieves
Furinah, Furyna, Fureena, Furrina, Furryna, Furreena, Fureana, Furreana

Fury (Greek) An enraged woman; in mythology, a winged goddess who punished wrongdoers
Furey, Furi, Furie, Furee, Furea, Fureah

Fushy (American) An animated woman
Fushey, Fushi, Fushee, Fushea, Fusheah, Fushie

Fyllis (Greek) Form of Phyllis, meaning "of the foliage"
Fylis, Fillis, Filis, Fylys, Fyllida, Fylida, Fillida, Filida, Fyllina, Fylina, Fyliss

Gaal (Hebrew) One who is filled with loathing
Gaale

Gaash (Hebrew) A trembling woman

Gabbatha (Hebrew) From the temple mound
Gabbathah, Gabbathe, Gabatha, Gabbathia, Gabbathea, Gabathia, Gabathea

Gabrielle ○ ♂ (Hebrew) Feminine form of Gabriel; heroine of God
*Gabriel, Gabriela, Gabriele, Gabriell, **Gabriella**, Gabriellen, Gabriellia, Gabrila, Gabryel, Gabryelle, Gabryella, Gaby, Gabysia, Gavi, Gavra, Gavraila, Gavriella, Gavrielle, Gavrila, Gavrilla, Gavrina, Gabbe, Gabbi, Gabbie, Gabi, Gabby*

Gada (Hebrew) One who is lucky; fortunate
Gadah

Gadara (Armenian) From the mountain's peak
Gadarah, Gadarra, Gadarine, Gadaryne, Gadarina, Gadaryna, Gadarrah, Gadareana, Gadariena, Gadareina

Gaea (Greek) Of the earth; in mythology, the mother of the Titans and the goddess of the earth
Gaia, Gaiana, Gaiea

Gael (Gaelic) Woman from Ireland
Gaela, Gaele

Gaelle (German) From a foreign land; a stranger

Gaetana (Italian) Woman from Gaeta
Gaetanah, Gaetanna, Gaetannah, Gaetane, Gaetanne

Gafna (Hebrew) Of the vine
Gafnah, Gaphna, Gaphnah, Gefen, Gephen

Gaho (Native American) A motherly woman

Gail (Hebrew) Form of Abigail, meaning "the source of a father's joy"
Gahl, Gaila, Gaile, Gaill, Gal, Gale, Galia, Gayel, Gayelle, Gayla, Gayle, Gayleen, Gaylene, Gayline, Gayll, Gaylla, Gaylle, Gaille

Gaira (Scottish) A petite woman
Gayra, Gara, Gairia, Gairea, Gaera

Gala (French / Scandinavian / Latin) A merrymaker; of the festive party / a singer / woman from Gaul
Galah, Galla, Gallah, Galia, Gallia, Gayla, Galea

Galatea (Greek) One with a milky-white complexion; in mythology, a statue brought to life
Galateah, Galatée, Galathea, Galatheah

Galeed (Hebrew) The mark of friendship
Galeeda, Galyde, Galyda, Galeid, Galeida, Galied, Galieda, Galead, Galeada

Galena (Greek) Feminine form of Galen; one who is calm and peaceful
Galene, Galenah, Galenia, Galenea

Gali (Hebrew) From the fountain
Galie, Galice, Galit, Galy, Galey, Galee, Galeigh, Galea, Galeah

Galiana (Arabic) The name of a Moorish princess
Galianah, Galianna, Galianne, Galiane, Galian, Galyana, Galyanna, Galyann, Galyane, Galyanne

Galiena (German) A haughty woman; one who is highborn
Galliena, Galiene, Galienne, Galyena, Galyene, Galyenne

Galila (Hebrew) From the rolling hills
Galilah, Gelila, Gelilah, Gelilia, Gelilya, Glila, Glilah, Galyla, Gelyla

Galilahi (Native American) An attractive young woman
Galilahie, Galilahy, Galilahey, Galilahee, Galilahea, Galilheah

Galilee (Hebrew) From the sacred sea
Galileigh, Galilea, Galiley, Galily, Galili, Galilie

Galina (Russian) Form of Helen, meaning "the shining light"
Galinah, Galyna, Galynah, Galeena, Galeenah, Galine, Galyne, Galeene, Galeane, Galeana

Galya (Hebrew) God has redeemed
Galyah, Galochka, Galenka, Geulah, Geula

Gamada (African) One who is pleased, pleasing
Gamadia, Gamadea, Gamadiya

Gambhira (Hindi) Born into the nobility; having great dignity
Gambhiri, Gambhirie, Gambhiria, Gambhirea, Gambheera, Gambheira, Gambhiera, Gambheara

Gamila (Arabic) Form of Jamilah, meaning "a beautiful and elegant lady"
Gameela, Gamela, Gamelia, Gamilah, Gameelah, Gamilia, Gamilla, Gamille, Gamelia, Gemila, Gemilla, Gemeela, Gemyla, Gameala, Gemeala

Gamma (Greek) The third letter of the Greek alphabet
Gammah

Gammadim (Hebrew) Of the daring and valorous people
Gammadym, Gammadeem, Gammadeam

Gana (Hebrew) Lady of the gardens
Ganah, Ganna, Gannah, Ganit, Ganet, Ganice, Ganya

Gandhari (Indian) In mythology, a princess who blindfolded herself when she married a blind man
Gandharie, Gandhary, Gandharey, Gandharee, Gandharea, Gandhareah

Ganieda (English) In Arthurian legend, Merlin's sister
Ganeida, Ganeyda, Ganeeda, Ganeada

Garaitz (Basque) A victorious woman
Garaytz, Garaetz, Garatz

Garan (Welsh) Resembling a stork

Garbi (Basque) One who is pure; clean
Garbie, Garby, Garbey, Garbee, Garbea, Garbeah

Garbina (Spanish) Refers to the ceremonial purification
Garbinah, Garbyna, Garbeena, Garbine, Garbyne, Garbeene, Garabina, Garabine

Gardenia (English) Resembling the sweet-smelling flower
Gardeniah, Gardenea, Gardeneah, Gardeniya, Gardynia, Gardynea, Gardena, Gardyna, Gardeena

Gardner (English) One who works the earth
Gardener, Gardie, Gardi, Gardiner, Gardea, Gardeah, Gardy, Gardey

Garima (Indian) A woman of importance
Garimah, Garyma, Gareema, Garymah, Gareemah, Gareama, Gareamah, Gariema, Gariemah, Gareima, Gareimah

Garland (French) Decorated with a wreath of flowers
Garlande, Garlanda, Garldina, Garldyna, Garldena

Garnet (English) Resembling the dark-red gem
Garnette, Granata, Grenata, Grenatta

Garron (French) One who protects others
Garan, Garen, Garin, Garion, Garon, Garran, Garren, Garrin, Geron

Gasha (Russian) One who is well-behaved
Gashah, Gashia, Gashea, Gashiah, Gasheah

Gaspara (Spanish) One who is treasured
Gasparah, Gasparra, Gasparrah

Gath-rimmon (Hebrew) Refers to the pomegranate press

Gauri (Indian) A fair-skinned woman
Gaurie, Gaury, Gaurey, Gauree, Gaura, Gaurea, Gaureah

Gavina (Latin) Feminine form of Gavin; resembling the white falcon; woman from Gabio
Gavinah, Gaveena, Gaveenah, Gavyna, Gavynah, Gavenia, Gavenea, Gaveana, Gaveanah, Gaviena, Gavienah, Gaveina, Gaveinah

Gay (French) A lighthearted and happy woman
Gaye, Gae, Gai

Gaynell (American) A bright woman full of joy
Gaynelle, Gaynel, Gaynele, Gaynella, Gaynela

Gaynor (Welsh) One with smooth and fair skin
Gaynora, Gaenor, Gaynoria, Gaenora, Gayner

Gayora (Hebrew) From the valley of sun
Gayoria, Gayorea

Gaza (Hebrew) Having great strength
Gazah, Gazza, Gazzah

Gazella (Latin) As graceful as a gazelle
Gazellah, Gazela, Gazelah, Gazelle, Gazele

Gazit (Hebrew) Of the cut stone
Giza, Gizah, Gisa, Gisah

Geba (Hebrew) From the hill
Gebah, Gebba, Gebbah

Gebal (Hebrew) Of the natural boundary
Gebale, Geball, Gebala, Geballa

Geder (Hebrew) From the fortress
Gederah, Gedera, Gederoth, Gederothee, Gederotha

Gefjun (Norse) In mythology, a goddess and prophetess
Gefjon, Gefyon, Gefn

Gehazi (Hebrew) From the valley of visions
Gehazie, Gehazy, Gehazey, Gehazee, Gehazea, Gehazeah

Geila (Hebrew) One who brings joy to others
Geela, Geelah, Geelan, Geilah, Geiliya, Geiliyah, Gelisa, Gellah, Gella

G

Gelasia (Greek) One who is always joking
and laughing
*Gelasiah, Gelasea, Gelaseah, Gelazia,
Gelaziah, Gelazea, Gelazeah*

Gelsomina (Italian) Resembling the
jasmine flower
*Gelsominah, Gelsomeena, Gelsomyna,
Gelsomeana, Gelsey, Gelsi, Gelsy, Gelsie,
Gelsee, Gelsea, Gelseah*

Gemini (Latin) The twins; the third sign of
the zodiac
*Gemineye, Gemyni, Gemella, Gemelle,
Gemina, Gemyna, Gemeena*

Gemma (Latin) As precious as a jewel
*Gemmalyn, Gemmalynn, Gem, Gema,
Gemmaline*

Gen (Japanese) Born during the spring

Gene (English) Form of Eugenia, meaning
"a wellborn woman"; form of Jean, meaning "God is gracious"
*Genia, Genie, Geni, Geny, Geney, Genee,
Genea, Geneah*

Generosa (Spanish) One who is giving,
generous
*Generosah, Generose, Generosia,
Generosea, Genera*

Genesis ✿ (Hebrew) Of the beginning; the
first book of the Bible
*Genesies, Genesiss, Genessa, Genisa,
Genisia, Genisis, Gennesis, Gennesiss*

Genet (African) From the garden of
paradise
Genete, Geneta, Genette, Genett, Genetta

Geneva (French) Of the juniper tree
*Genever, Genevia, Genevra, Genevre,
Genovefa, Genoveffa, Genoveva, Ginebra,
Gena, Ginevre*

Genevieve (French) Of the race of women;
the white wave
*Genavieve, Geneve, Geneveeve, Genevie,
Genivee, Genivieve, Gennie, Genny,
Genovera, Genoveva, Genica, Genna,
Genae, Genaya, Genowefa, Ginerva,
Ginebra, Ginessa, Ginevra*

Genista (Latin) Resembling the broom
plant
*Genistah, Geneesta, Ginista, Genysta,
Ginysta, Gynysta, Geneasta, Geneista,
Geniesta*

Genji (Japanese) Of the ruling clan
Genji, Genjy, Genjey, Genjee, Genjea

Gennesaret (Hebrew) From the garden of
riches

Gentry (English) Woman with a high
social standing
*Gentri, Gentrey, Gentrie, Gentree, Gentrea,
Gentreah*

Georgia (Greek) From the state of
Georgia; feminine form of George; one
who works the earth; a farmer
*Georgeann, Georgeanne, Georgina,
Georgena, Georgene, Georgetta, Georgette,
Georgiana, Georgianna, Georgianne,
Georgie, Georgienne, Georginah, Georgine,
Georgyann, Georgyanne, Georgyana,
Giorgia, Giorgina, Giorgyna, Georgitte,
Georgeina, Georgejean, Georjette, Gigi,
Geegee*

Geraldine (German) Feminine form of
Gerald; one who rules with the spear
*Geralda, Geraldeen, Geraldene,
Geraldina, Geralyn, Geralynn, Geralynne,
Gerdene, Gerdine, Geri, Gerianna,
Gerianne, Gerilynn, Gerri, Gerrilyn,
Gerroldine, Gerry, Giralda, Gerica,
Gericka, Gerika, Girelda, Geraldeane,
Geraldeana*

Geranium (Latin) Resembling the flower; a
crane
Geranyum, Geranum

Gerardine (English) Feminine form of
Gerard; one who is mighty with a spear
*Gerarda, Gerardina, Gerardyne, Gererdina,
Gerardyna, Gerrardene, Gerhardina,
Gerhardine, Gerhardyna, Gerhardyne,
Gerwalt, Gerwalta, Gerardeane,
Gerardeana*

Gerd (Scandinavian) One who is guarded;
protected
*Gerde, Gerda, Gerdie, Gerdi, Gerdy,
Gerdey, Gerdee, Garda, Geerda, Gjerta,
Gerdea, Gerdeah*

Gerizim (Hebrew) From the mountains
*Gerizima, Gerizime, Gerizimia, Gerizimea,
Gerizym, Gerizyme, Gerizyma, Gerizymea,
Gerizymia*

Germaine (Latin) Feminine form of Germain; one who is sisterly; woman from Germany
Germana, Germane, Germayn, Germayne, Germanna, Germaina, Germayna, Germaene, Germaena

Gersemi (Scandinavian) As precious as a jewel
Gersemie, Gersemy, Gersemey, Gersemee, Gersemea, Gersemeah

Gertrude (German) One who is strong with a spear
Geertruide, Geltruda, Geltrudis, Gert, Gerta, Gerte, Gertie, Gertina, Gertraud, Gertrud, Gertruda, Gertrudis, Gerty, Gertraude, Gertmda, Gertrudes, Gertrut, Gertea, Gerteah

Gerusha (Hebrew) Form of Jerusha, meaning "a faithful wife"
Gerushah, Geruscha, Garusha, Garuscha

Geshur (Hebrew) From the bridge
Geshura, Geshure, Geshuria, Geshurea, Geshuri, Geshurie, Geshuree, Geshurea, Geshureah, Geshury, Geshurey

Gessica (English) Form of Jessica, meaning "the Lord sees all"
Gess, Gessa, Gessaca, Gessaka, Gessalin, Gessalyn, Gesse, Gesseca, Gessey, Gessie, Gessika, Gesirae, Geslyn, Gessika, Gessicka, Geziree, Gessalynn, Gessamae, Gessana, Gessandra, Gesselyn, Gezeree, Gessi, Gessilyn, Gessina, Gesslyn, Gesslynn, Gessy, Gessye, Gesimae

Gethsemane (Hebrew) Worker of the oil press
Gethsemanie, Gethsemana, Gethsemani, Gethsemaney, Gethsemany, Gethsemanee, Gethsemanea

Geva (Hebrew) From the farm
Gevah, Gevia, Gevea, Geviah, Geveah

Gevira (Hebrew) A highborn daughter
Gevirah, Gevyra, Gevyrah, Geveera, Geveerah, Geviera, Gevierah, Geveira, Geveirah, Geveara, Gevearah

Gezana (Spanish) Refers to the doctrine of Incarnation
Gezanah, Gezanna, Gezania, Gezanea, Gezane, Gizana, Gizane, Gizania, Gizanea

Gezer (Hebrew) From the cliffs
Gezera, Gezeria, Gezerea, Gezerah, Gezere

Ghada (Arabic) A beautiful young girl
Ghadah, Ghadda, Ghaddah, Ghayda, Ghaydah

Ghaliya (Arabic) One who smells sweet
Ghaliyah, Ghaleeya, Ghaleeyah, Ghaleya, Ghaleyah, Ghaleaya, Ghaleayah

Ghalyela (African) One who is precious
Ghalyelah, Ghalyella, Ghalyele, Ghalyelle

Ghazala (Arabic) As graceful as a gazelle
Ghazalah, Ghazalla, Ghazaala, Ghazalia, Ghazalea, Ghazallah, Ghazaliah, Ghazaleah

Ghislaine (French) Born of the sweet oath
Ghislayne, Ghislane, Ghislaina, Ghislayna, Ghislana, Gislaine, Gislayne, Gislane, Guilaine, Guiliaine

Ghita (Italian) Resembling a pearl
Ghitah, Gheeta, Ghyta, Gheata, Gheita, Ghieta

Ghusun (Arabic) Of the trees' branches
Ghusune, Ghusoon, Ghusoone

Giacinta (Italian) Resembling the hyacinth
Giacynta, Giacenta, Gacenta, Gacynta, Gacinta, Giacintha, Giacyntha, Giancinta, Giancinte, Gyacinta, Gyacenta, Gyacynta

Gianna ❍ (Italian) Feminine form of John; God is gracious
Geonna, Gia, Giana, Ginara, Gianina, Gianella, Giannina, Gionna, Gianetta, Giannine, Ginetta, Ginette, Ginnette, Gianara, Geona, Geovana

Gibbethon (Hebrew) From the high house
Gibbethona, Gibbethonia, Gibbethonea, Gibbethone

Gibeah (Hebrew) From the hill town
Gibea, Gibia, Gibiah, Gibeon, Gibeona, Gibeonea, Gibeonia, Gibeoneah, Gibiya, Gibiyah

Gihon (Hebrew) Of the stream or river
Gihona, Gihonah, Gihonia, Gihonea, Gihoniah, Gihoneah

Gila (Hebrew) One who is forever joyous
Gilah, Gilia, Gili, Gilala, Gilal, Gilana, Gilat, Gilit, Geela, Geelah, Gilla, Gillah

Gilberta (German) Feminine form of Gilbert; of the bright pledge; a hostage
Gilbertha, Gilberthe, Gilbertina, Gilbertine, Gill, Gillie, Gilly, Gilberte, Gilbertyna, Gilbertyne, Gilberteena, Gilberteene, Gilbarta, Gilbarte, Gilen, Gijs

Gilboa (Hebrew) From the boiling springs
Gilboah, Gylboa, Gylboah

Gilda (English) The golden child
Gildah, Gilde, Gildie, Gildy, Gildi, Gildey, Gildee, Gildan, Gildana, Gildane, Gylda, Gyldan, Gildea, Gildeah

Gildas (Celtic) A woman in the service of the Lord
Gildes, Gildys

Gilead (Hebrew) From the mountain of testimony

Gillian (Latin) One who is youthful
Ghilian, Ghiliane, Ghillian, Gilian, Giliana, Gillan, Gillianna, Gillianne, Gillyanne, Gillien, Gillienne, Gillot

Gimbya (African) Daughter born to royalty; a princess
Gimbyah, Gimbiya, Gimbeya, Gimbaya, Gimbiyah, Gimbayah, Gimbeyah

Gimle (Norse) From the most beautiful place on earth
Gimli, Gimlie, Gimly, Gimley, Gimlee, Gimleigh, Gimlea, Gimleah, Gymle, Gymli, Gymlie, Gymleigh, Gymley, Gymly, Gymlee, Gymlea

Gimzo (Hebrew) From the valley of sycamores

Gina (Italian / English) A silvery woman / form of Eugenia, meaning "a wellborn woman"; form of Jean, meaning "God is gracious"
Geana, Geanndra, Geena, Geina, Gena, Genalyn, Geneene, Genelle, Genette, Ginamaria, Gineen, Ginelle, Ginette, Gin

Ginata (Italian) As delicate as a flower
Ginatah, Ginatta, Ginatia, Ginatea, Ginatiah, Ginateah

Ginger (English) A lively woman; resembling the spice
Gingee, Gingie, Ginjer, Gingea, Gingy, Gingey, Gingi

Ginnungagap (Norse) In mythology, the abyss that gave birth to all living things

Ginny (English) Form of Virginia, meaning "one who is chaste; virginal"
Ginnee, Ginnelle, Ginnette, Ginnie, Ginnilee, Ginna, Ginney, Ginni, Ginnea

Gioconda (Italian) A delightful daughter
Gyoconda, Geoconda

Gioia (Italian) One who brings joy
Gioya

Giona (Italian) Resembling the bird of peace
Gionah, Gionna, Gyona, Gyonna, Gionnah, Gyonah, Gyonnah

Giordana (Italian) Feminine form of Jordan; of the down-flowing river
Giordanah, Giordanna, Giordannah

Giovanna (Italian) Feminine form of John; God is gracious
Geovana, Geovanna, Giavanna, Giovana, Giovani, Giovanni, Giovanie, Giovanee, Giovaney, Giovany, Giovanea

Giselle (French) Of God's promise; a hostage
Ghisele, Ghisella, Gisela, Giselda, Gisele, Gisella, Giza, Gizela, Gizella, Gizelle, Gisel, Gisilberhta, Gisselle, Gisli, Gizi, Gizike, Gizus

Gita (Hindi / Hebrew) A beautiful song / a good woman
Gitah, Geeta, Geetah, Gitika, Gatha, Gayatri, Gitel, Gittel, Gutka

Gitana (Spanish) A gypsy woman
Gitanah, Gitanna, Gitannah, Gitane

Gitanjali (Indian) An offering of songs
Gitanjalie, Gytanjaly, Gitanjalee, Gytanjalee, Gitanjaly, Gytanjaly, Gitanjaley, Gytanjaley, Gitanjalea, Gytanjalea

Githa (Anglo-Saxon) A gift from God
Githah

Gitta (Gaelic) From of Bridgette, meaning "a strong and protective woman"
Gittah, Gitte, Gitteh

Gittaim (Hebrew) One who works the wine press
Gitaim, Gittaima, Gittaym, Gittayma, Gitaym, Gittaem, Gittaema, Gitaem

Giuditta (Italian) Form of Judith, meaning "woman from Judea"
Giudytta, Guidita, Guidyta, Guiditta

Giulia (Italian) Form of Julia, meaning "one who is youthful; daughter of the sky"
Giula, Giuliana, Giulietta, Giullia, Guilia, Guilie

Giustinia (Italian) Feminine form of Justin; one who is just and fair
Giustina, Giustyna, Giustinea, Giusteena, Giustiniah, Giustineah

Gizem (Turkish) A mysterious woman
Gizim, Gizam, Gizym, Gizema, Gizima, Gizyma, Gizama

Gjalp (Norse) In mythology, a frost giantess

Glade (English) From the meadow in the woods
Glayd, Glayde, Glaid, Glaide, Glaed, Glaede

Gladys (Welsh) Form of Claudia, meaning "one who is lame"
Gladdis, Gladdys, Gladi, Gladis, Gladyss, Gwladys, Gwyladyss, Gleda, Glad, Gladdie, Gladdy, Gladdi, Gladdey, Gladdea, Gladdee

Glain (Welsh) As precious as jewel
Glaine, Glaina, Glayne, Glayna, Glaen, Glayn, Glaene, Glaena

Glan (Welsh) From the seashore
Glann

Glauce (Greek) In mythology, a woman murdered by Medea

Glenda (Welsh) One who is good and fair
Glinda, Glynda, Glennda, Glynae

Glenna (Gaelic) From the valley between the hills
Gleana, Gleneen, Glenene, Glenine, Glen, Glenn, Glenne, Glennene, Glennette, Glennie, Glyn, Glynn, Glynna, Ghleanna

Glenys (Welsh) A holy woman
Glenice, Glenis, Glennice, Glennis, Glennys

Gloria (Latin) A renowned and highly praised woman
Glaura, Glaurea, Glora, Glorea, Gloree, Glorey, Gloreya, Glori, Gloriana, Gloriane, Glorianna, Glorianne, Gloribel, Gloribell, Glorie, Glorra, Glorria, Glory, Glorya, Gloryan, Gloryanna, Gloryanne, Gloriann, Gloriosa

Glynis (Welsh) From the narrow valley
Glennis, Glinnis, Glinyce, Glinys, Glinyss, Glynae, Glynice, Glynnis, Glynnes

Gna (Norse) In mythology, one of Frigg's handmaidens

Gobinet (Irish) Form of Abigail, meaning "the source of a father's joy"
Gobnait, Gobnat, Gubnat, Gobnayt, Gobnate, Gobynet, Gobinette, Gobynette

Godfreya (German) Feminine form of Godfrey; having the peace of God
Godfredya, Gotfreya, Godafrid, Godafryd

Godiva (English) Gift from God
Godivah, Godgifu, Godyva, Godyvah

Golan (Hebrew) One who has been exiled
Golana, Golanah, Golane, Golanne

Golda (English) Resembling the precious metal
Goldarina, Goldarine, Goldee, Goldi, Goldie, Goldina, Goldy, Goldia, Goldea, Golds

Goleuddydd (Welsh) Born on a bright day
Goleudydd, Goleu, Gwenddydd

Gorane (Slavic) Feminine form of Goran; woman from the mountain
Gorayne, Goraine, Gorain, Gorayn, Gorana, Goranna, Gorania, Goranea, Goraen, Goraene, Goraena

Gorawen (Welsh) One who brings joy to others
Gorawenne, Gorawin, Gorawyn, Gorawinne, Gorawynne, Gorawenn, Gorawinn, Gorawynn

Gordana (Serbian / Scottish) A proud woman / one who is heroic
Gordanah, Gordanna, Gordania, Gordaniya, Gordanea, Gordannah, Gordaniah, Gordaniyah, Gordaneah

Gormghlaith (Irish) Woman of sorrow
*Gormghlaithe, Gormley, Gormly, Gormlie,
Gormli, Gormlee, Gormleigh*

Gota (Swedish) Having great strength
Gotah, Gote, Goteh, Gotilda, Gotilde, Gotild

Gotzone (Basque) Feminine form of
Gotzon; a messenger of God; an angel
*Gotzonie, Gotzoni, Gotzona, Gotzonia,
Gotzonea, Gotzonee, Gotzony, Gotzoney*

Grace ✿ ✦ (Latin) Having God's favor; in
mythology, the Graces were the personifi-
cation of beauty, charm, and grace
*Gracee, Gracella, Gracelynn, Gracelynne,
Gracey, Gracia, Graciana, **Gracie**, Graciela,
Graciella, Gracielle, Gracija, Gracina,
Gracious, Grata, Gratia, Gratiana, Gratiela,
Gratiella, Grayce, Grazia, Graziella,
Grazina, Graziosa, Grazyna, Graca,
Graciene, Gracinha, Gradana, Gechina,
Gratiane, Grazinia, Gricie, Graci, Graece*

Graeae (Greek) In mythology, the personification of old age
Graiae

Grainne (Irish) One who loves and is loved
*Graine, Grainnia, Grania, Graynne,
Grayne, Graynia, Graenne, Graene,
Graenia*

Granada (Spanish) From the Moorish
kingdom
Granadda, Grenada, Grenadda

Greer (Scottish) Feminine form of
Gregory; one who is alert and watchful
Grear, Grier, Gryer

Gregoria (Latin) Feminine form of
Gregory; one who is alert and watchful
*Gregoriana, Gregorijana, Gregorina,
Gregorine, Gregorya, Gregoryna,
Gregorea, Gregoriya*

Greip (Norse) In mythology, a frost giantess

Greta (German) Resembling a pearl
*Greeta, Gretal, Grete, Gretel, Gretha,
Grethe, Grethel, Gretna, Gretta, Grette,
Grietje, Gryta, Gretchen, Gredel*

Grid (Norse) One who is peaceful; in
mythology, a frost giantess
Gryd

Grimhild (Norse) In mythology, a witch
*Grimhilde, Grimhilda, Grimild,
Grimilda, Grimilde*

Griselda (German) A gray-haired battle-
maid; one who fights the dark battle
*Gricelda, Gricely, Grisel, Griseldis, Grisella,
Griselle, Griselly, Grishelda, Grishilde,
Grissel, Grizel, Grizelda, Gryselde,
Gryzelde, Griselde, Grisjahilde, Giorsal,
Gnishilda, Grizela, Grizzel, Gryselda*

Griswalda (German) Woman from the
gray woodland
*Griswalde, Grizwalda, Grizwalde,
Griswald, Grizwald*

Gro (Norwegian) One who works the earth
Groa, Grow, Growe

Gryphon (Greek) In mythology, a beast rep-
resenting strength, protection, and
vigilance
Gryfon, Griffin, Griffon, Gryffin

Guadalupe (Spanish) From the valley of
wolves
Godalupe, Gwadalupe

Gudny (Swedish) One who is unspoiled
*Gudney, Gudni, Gudnie, Gudne, Gudnee,
Gudnea, Gudneah*

Gudrun (Scandinavian) A battlemaiden
*Gudren, Gudrid, Gudrin, Gudrinn,
Gudruna, Gudrunn, Gudrunne, Guthrun,
Guthrunn, Guthrunne*

Guida (Italian) One who acts as a guide
Geeda, Geida, Gieda, Geada, Gwyda, Gwida

Guinevak (English) In Arthurian legend,
Guinevere's sister
Gwenhwyfach, Gwenhwyvach

Guinevere (Welsh) One who is fair; of the
white wave; in mythology, King Arthur's
queen
*Guenever, Guenevere, Gueniver, Guenna,
Guennola, Guinever, Guinna, Gwen,
Gwenevere, Gweniver, Gwenn, Gwennie,
Gwennola, Gwennora, Gwennore,
Gwenny, Gwenora, Gwenore, Gwyn,
Gwynn, Gwynna, Gwynne, Guanhamara,
Guanhumora, Gvenour, Gwenhwyfar,
Gwenhwyvar, Gwenhyvar, Gwenifer,
Gwennor, Gwenyver*

Guiseppina (Italian) Feminine form of
Guiseppe; the Lord will add
*Giuseppyna, Giuseppa, Giuseppia,
Giuseppea, Giuseppie, Giuseppia,
Guiseppa, Giuseppina*

Gula (Babylonian) In mythology, a goddess
Gulah, Gulla, Gullah

Gulab (Arabic) Resembling the rose
Gulaab, Gul

Gulielma (German) Feminine form of
Wilhelm; determined protector
*Guglielma, Guillelmina, Guillielma,
Gulielmina, Guillermina*

Gulinar (Arabic) Resembling the
pomegranate
*Gulinare, Gulinear, Gulineir, Gulinara,
Gulinaria, Gulinarea*

Gullveig (Norse) In mythology, a dark
goddess
*Gullveiga, Gullveige, Gulveig, Gulveiga,
Gulveige*

Gulzar (Arabic) From the gardens
*Gulzare, Gulzaar, Gulzara, Gulzaria,
Gulzarea, Gulshan, Gulshana, Gulshania,
Gulshanea*

Gunhilda (Norse) A battlemaiden
*Gunhilde, Gunilda, Gunilla, Gunna,
Gunnel, Gunnhilda, Gunda, Gunnef,
Gunnhild, Gunnhildr*

Gunnlod (Norse) In mythology, the
daughter of Suttung

Guri (Hebrew) Resembling a young lioness
*Gurie, Guriele, Gurielle, Gurice, Gurit,
Gury, Gurey, Guree, Gureah, Gurea*

Gussie (English) Form of Augusta, meaning
"venerable; majestic"
*Gussi, Gussy, Gussey, Gussee, Gustela,
Gustella, Gustel, Gustele, Gustelle, Gusty,
Gussea, Gusseah*

Gustava (Swedish) Feminine form of
Gustave; from the staff of the gods
*Gustavah, Gustha, Guusa, Gustaafa,
Gusta, Gust*

Gwanwyn (Welsh) Born during the spring
*Gwanwynn, Gwanwynne, Gwanwin,
Gwanwinn, Gwanwinne, Gwanwen,
Gwanwenn, Gwanwenne*

Gwawr (Welsh) Born with the morning
light

Gwendolyn (Welsh) One who is fair; of
the white ring
*Guendolen, Guendolin, Guendolinn,
Guendolynn, Guenna, Gwen, Gwenda,
Gwendaline, Gwendalyn, Gwendolen,
Gwendolene, Gwendolin, Gwendoline,
Gwendolynn, Gwendolynne, Gwenna,
Gwenette, Gwenndolen, Gwenni, Gwennie,
Gwenny, Gwyn, Gwyndolyn, Gwynn,
Gwynna, Gwynne, Gwenn, Gwynda,
Gwendoloena, Gwendelyn, Gwendi,
Guennola, Gwener, Gwenllian, Gwylan,
Gwyndolen, Gwyndolin*

Gwyneth (Welsh) One who is blessed with
happiness
*Gweneth, Gwenith, Gwenyth, Gwineth,
Gwinneth, Gwinyth, Gwynith, Gwynna,
Gwynne, Gwynneth, Gwenneth,
Gwynedd, Gwennan*

Gypsy (English) A wanderer; a nomad
*Gipsee, Gipsey, Gipsy, Gypsi, Gypsie,
Gypsey, Gypsee, Gipsi, Gipsie, Gipsea,
Gypsea*

Gytha (English) One who is treasured
Gythah

Gzifa (African) One who is at peace
*Gzifah, Gzyfa, Gzyfah, Gziffa, Gziffah,
Gzyffa, Gzyffah*

Ha (Vietnamese) One who is kissed by the
sunshine

Haafizah (Arabic) One who loves literature
*Hafizah, Hafiza, Hafyzah, Hafeeza,
Hafeezah, Hafeazah, Hafeaza*

Haarisah (Hindi) Daughter of the sun
*Harisah, Haarysah, Harisa, Harysah,
Harysa, Haaresah, Haresah, Haresa*

Haarithah (Arabic) A heavenly messenger
Harithah, Haarithe, Haaritheh, Harithe

Habbai (Arabic) One who is much loved
Habbae, Habbay, Habbaye

Habiba (Arabic) Feminine form of Habib; one who is dearly loved; sweetheart
Habibah, Habeeba, Habyba, Habieba, Habeiba, Habika, Habyka, Habicka, Habycka, Habeabah, Habeaba, Habeebah, Habybah, Habiebah, Habeibah

Hachi (Native American / Japanese) From the river / having good fortune
Hachie, Hachee, Hachiko, Hachiyo, Hachy, Hachey, Hachikka

Hachilah (Hebrew) From the dark hill
Hachila, Hachyla, Hachylah, Hacheela, Hacheelah, Hachiela, Hachielah, Hacheilah, Hacheila, Hacheala, Hachealah

Hada (African) From the salty place
Hadah, Hadda, Haddah

Hadara (Hebrew) A spectacular ornament; adorned with beauty
Hadarah, Hadarit, Haduraq, Hadarra, Hadarrah

Hadassah (Hebrew) From the myrtle tree
Hadassa, Hadasah, Hadasa

Hadeel (Arabic) Resembling a dove
Hadil, Hadyl, Hadeil, Hadiel, Hadeal

Hadenna (English) From the meadow of flowers
Hadennah, Hadena, Hadynna, Hadinna, Hadyna, Hadina

Hadiya (Arabic) A gift from God; a righteous woman
Hadiyah, Hadiyyah, Haadiyah, Haadiya, Hadeeya, Hadeeyah, Hadieya, Hadieyah, Hadeiya, Hadeiyah, Hadeaya, Hadeayah

Hadlai (Hebrew) In a resting state; one who hinders
Hadlae, Hadlay, Hadlaye

Hadley (English) From the field of heather
Hadlea, Hadleigh, Hadly, Hedlea, Hedleigh, Hedley, Hedlie, Hadlee, Hadlie, Hadli, Hedly, Hedlee, Hedleah, Hedli

Hadria (Latin) From the town in northern Italy
Hadrea, Hadriana, Hadriane, Hadrianna, Hadrien, Hadrienne, Hadriah, Hadreah

Hady (Greek) One who is soulful
Hadey, Hadi, Hadie, Hadee, Hadea

Hadya (Arabic) Feminine form of Hadi; serving as a religious guide
Hadyah, Hadiya, Hadiyah

Hafsa (Arabic) Resembling a young lioness; a wife of Muhammad
Hafza, Hafsah, Hafzah, Haphsa, Haphza

Hafthah (Arabic) One who is protected by God
Haftha

Hafwen (Welsh) Possessing the beauty of summer
Hafwenne, Hafwin, Hafwyn, Hafwinne, Hafwynne, Hafwenn, Hafwinn, Hafwynn

Hagab (Hebrew) Resembling a grasshopper
Hagabah, Hagaba, Hagabe

Hagai (Hebrew) One who has been abandoned
Hagae, Hagay, Hagaye, Haggai, Haggae, Hagie, Haggie, Hagi, Haggi, Hagee, Haggee, Hagea, Haggea, Hagy, Haggy, Hagey, Haggey

Hagar (Hebrew) One who is forsaken; taking flight; a stranger
Haggar, Hagir, Hajar, Hagyr, Hagarr

Hagen (Irish) A youthful woman
Hagan, Haggen, Haggan

Haggith (Hebrew) One who rejoices; the dancer
Haggithe, Haggyth, Haggythe, Hagith, Hagithe, Hagyth, Hagythe

Hagne (Greek) One who is pure; chaste
Hagna, Hagni, Hagnie, Hagnee, Hagnea, Hagneah, Hagny, Hagney

Haiba (African) A charming woman
Hayba, Haibah, Haybah, Haeba, Haebah

Haidee (Greek) A modest woman; one who is well-behaved
Hadee, Haydee, Haydy, Haidi, Haidie, Haydi, Haydie, Haidy, Haedee, Haedi, Haedie, Haedy, Haedey, Haedea, Haidea, Haydea

Haimati (Indian) A queen of the snow-covered mountains
Haimatie, Haimaty, Haimatey, Haimatee, Haymati, Haymatie, Haymatee, Haimatea, Haymatea

Haimi (Hawaiian) One who searches for the truth
Haimie, Haimy, Haimey, Haimee, Haymi, Haymie, Haymee, Haimea, Haymea

Haiwee (Native American) Resembling the dove; bird of peace
Haiwea, Haiwie, Haiwi, Haiwy, Haiwey

Hajna (Hungarian) Form of Ann, meaning "a woman graced with God's favor"
Hajne

Hajnal (Hungarian) Born with the morning's first light
Hajnale, Hajnala, Hajnalla, Hajnalka

Hakana (Turkish) Feminine form of Hakan; ruler of the people; an empress
Hakanah, Hakanna, Hakane, Hakann, Hakanne

Hakidonmuya (Native American) Born during a period of expectation

Hakkoz (Hebrew) One who has the qualities of a thorn
Hakoz, Hakkoze, Hakoze, Hakkoza, Hakoza

Hala (Arabic) Possessing a lunar halo
Halah, Haala, Hila, Hilah

Halag (German) A religious woman; one who is pious

Halak (Hebrew) One who is bald; smooth

Halcyone (Greek) Resembling a kingfisher; born during a time of peace and calm
Halcyon, Halcyona, Halcyonia, Halcyonea

Halda (Scandinavian) One who is half Danish
Haldah, Haldane, Haldayn, Haldayne, Haldain, Haldaine, Haldaen, Haldaene, Haldana, Haldania, Haldanea, Halden, Haldin, Haldyn, Haldi, Haldie, Haldee, Haldea, Haldey, Haldy, Haldis

Haldana (Norse) One who is half Danish
Haldanah, Haldanna, Haldane, Haldayne, Haldaine, Haldaene

Haldis (Teutonic / Greek) A stone spirit / a reliable helper
Haldisa, Haldys, Haldiss, Haldisse, Haldyss, Haldysse, Halldis, Halldiss, Halldisse, Halldys, Halldyss, Halldysse

Haldora (Norse) Feminine form of Haldor; Thor's rock
Haldorah, Haldoria, Haldorea, Haldorra, Halldora, Halldorra, Halldoria, Halldorea

Hale (English) From the hall of light; a heroine
Hayle, Haile, Haylan, Haylen, Hael, Haele, Hayl

Haleigha (Hawaiian) Born with the rising sun
Haleea, Haleya, Halya

Halene (Russian) A steadfast woman
Haleen, Haleene, Halein, Haleine, Halien, Haliene

Haletta (Greek) A little girl from the meadow
Halett, Halet, Haleta, Halette, Halete

Haley ♀ ♂ (English) From the field of hay
Hailey, Hayle, Hailee, Haylee, Haylie, Haleigh, Hayley, Haeleigh, Haeli, Haili, Haily, Halea, Hayleigh, Hayli, Hailea, Haile, Hailie, Halie, Hali, Halee, Haelee

Halfrida (German) A peaceful woman
Halfryda, Halfrieda, Halfreida, Halfreeda, Halfreada

Halhul (Hebrew) One who is hollow inside; full of grief

Halia (Hawaiian) The remembrance of one who was loved

Halima (Arabic) A mild-mannered woman; one who is gentle
Halimah, Haleema, Haleemah, Haleima, Halyma, Helima, Helimah, Helyma, Heleema, Heleemah, Haleama, Haleamah, Heleama, Heleamah

Halimeda (Greek) Woman from the sea
Halameda, Halymeda, Halimyda, Halymyda, Halamyda, Halimida, Halamida

Halina (Greek / Polish) Born of the light / one who is calm
Halinah, Haleena, Haleenah, Halyna, Halynah, Haleina, Haleinah, Haleana, Haleanah, Haliena, Halienah, Halena, Halenah

Hall (American) One who is distinguished
Haul

Halla (African) An unexpected gift
Hallah

Hallam (English) From the valley
Hallem, Halam, Halem

Hallan (English) From the manor's hall
Hallen, Halan, Halen

Hallei (Hebrew) One who is much praised

Hallela (Hebrew) One who is praiseworthy
*Hallella, Halleli, Hallelie, Hallely, Halleley,
Hallelee, Hallelea*

Hallelujah (Hebrew) Praise the Lord our
God
Halleluja

Hamath (Hebrew) From the mighty fortress
*Hamathe, Hamoth, Hamothe, Hamatha,
Hamotha*

Hamida (Arabic) One who gives thanks
*Hamidah, Hamyda, Hameeda, Hameida,
Hamieda, Hameada, Hamydah, Hameedah,
Hameidah, Hamiedah, Hameadah*

Hamilton (American) A dreamer; one who
is wishful
*Hamylton, Hamilten, Hamylten,
Hamiltyn, Hamyltyn*

HANNAH

From the moment of conception I imagined having a daughter named Hannah. When I discussed it
with my husband, he responded, "like Hanna Barbera, the cartoon people?" Four hours after her
birth, Hannah Elizabeth received her name. When we announced it to the family, my father-in-law's
response was: "Like Hanna Barbera..." I responded, "different spelling." —Maureen, FL

Hallie (Scandinavian / Greek / English)
From the hall / woman of the sea / from
the field of hay
*Halley, Hallie, Halle, Hallee, Hally,
Halleigh, Hallea, Halleah*

Halo (Latin) Having a blessed aura
Haylo, Haelo, Hailo

Haloke (Native American) Resembling a
salmon
Haloka, Halokia, Halokea

Halona (Native American) Woman of
good fortune
Halonna, Halonah, Halonia, Halonea

Halsey (American) A playful woman
*Halsy, Halsee, Halsea, Halsi, Halsie,
Halcie, Halcy, Halcey, Halcea, Halcee,
Halci*

Halston (American) A stylish woman
*Halsten, Halstin, Halstun, Halstan,
Halstyn*

Halyn (American) A unique young woman
Halynn, Halynne, Halin, Halinn, Halinne

Halzey (American) A great leader
Halzy, Halzee, Halzea, Halzi, Halzie

Hama (Arabic) From the city on the river
Hamah, Hamma, Hammah

Hammon (Hebrew) Of the warm springs

Hamony (Latin) Form of Harmony, mean-
ing "unity; musically in tune"
*Hamoney, Hamoni, Hamonie, Hamonee,
Hamonea*

Hamula (Hebrew) Feminine form of
Hamul; spared by God
Hamulah, Hamulla, Hamullah

Hamutal (Hebrew) Of the morning dew
Hamutala, Hamutalle, Hamutalla

Hana (Japanese / Arabic) Resembling a
flower blossom / a blissful woman
Hanah, Hanako

Hanameel (Hebrew) A gift from God
*Hanameela, Hannameel, Hanamele,
Hanamelle, Hanamella, Hananeel,
Hananeela, Hanameal, Hanameala,
Hananeal, Hananeala*

Hanan (Arabic) One who shows mercy
and compassion

Hananna (Hebrew) Feminine form of
Hanan; one who is gracious
Hanannah, Hanana, Hananah

Hande (Turkish) A woman with an
infectious smile

Ha-neul (Korean) Of the sky

Hang (Vietnamese) Of the moon

Hanh (Vietnamese) From the apricot tree

Hanifa (Arabic) Feminine form of Hanif; a true believer; one who is upright
Hanifah, Haneefa, Haneefah, Hanyfa, Hanyfah, Haneifa, Haneifah, Haniefa, Haniefah, Haneafa, Haneafah

Hanika (Hebrew) A graceful woman
Hanikah, Haneeka, Haneekah, Hanyka, Hanykah, Haneika, Haneikah, Hanieka, Haniekah, Haneaka, Haneakah

Hanima (Indian) Of the waves
Hanimah, Hanyma, Haneema, Hanymah, Haneemah, Haneima, Haneimah, Haniema, Haniemah, Haneama, Haneamah

Hanita (Indian) Favored with divine grace
Hanitah, Hanyta, Haneeta, Hanytah, Haneetah, Haneita, Haneitah, Hanieta, Hanietah, Haneata, Haneatah

Haniyah (Arabic) One who is pleased; happy
Haniya, Haniyyah, Haniyya, Hani, Hanie, Hanee, Hany, Haney, Hanea, Haneah

Hannabel (German) Favored with grace and beauty
Hannabelle, Hannabell, Hannabele, Hannabela, Hannabella

Hannah ✪ ✿ (Hebrew) Having favor and grace; in the Bible, mother of Samuel
Hanalee, Hanalise, Hanna, Hanne, Hannele, Hannelore, Hannie, Hanny, Honna, Hannalee, Hendel, Hannaleigh, Honna, Hannea, Hanneka, Hannika, Hannela, Hannella, Hannalea

Hannette (American) One who is graceful
Hannett, Hannet, Hannete, Hannetta, Hanneta

Hansa (Indian) As graceful as a swan
Hansika, Hansini, Hansinie, Hansia, Hansea

Hansine (Hebrew) Feminine form of John; God is gracious
Hansyne, Hanseen, Hansinah, Hansina, Hansyna, Hannes, Hanseane, Hanseana, Hanseena

Hanya (Aboriginal) As solid as a stone

Hanzila (African) Traveling a road or path
Hanzilah, Hanzilla, Hanzillah, Hanzyla, Hanzylla, Hanzylah, Hanzyllah

Hao (Vietnamese) One who is perfectly behaved

Happy (American) A joyful woman
Happey, Happi, Happie, Happee, Happea

Haqikah (Egyptian) A truthful woman; one who is honest
Haqika, Haquikah, Haquika, Haqyka

Hara (Hebrew) From the mountainous land
Harah, Harra, Harrah

Haracha (African) Resembling a frog

Haradah (Hebrew) One who is filled with fear
Harada

Haralda (Norse) Feminine form of Harold; the ruler of an army
Haraldene, Haraldina, Harolda, Haroldene, Haroldina, Haraldia, Harelda, Hareldina, Hareldene, Harelde, Harolde, Haraldyna, Haroldyna, Hareldyna, Haraldyne, Haroldyne, Hareldyne

Harana (Hebrew) Feminine form of Haran; a great moutaineer; one who is parched
Haranah, Haranna, Haranne, Harane, Harann

Harhur (Hebrew) Possessing a burning heat
Harhure, Harhurr, Harhura, Harhurra

Harika (Turkish) A superior woman
Harikah, Haryka, Hareeka, Harykah, Hareekah, Hareaka, Hareakah

Harimanna (German) A warrior maiden
Harimanne, Harimana, Harimane

Harimanti (Indian) Born during the spring
Harimantie, Harymanti, Harimanty, Harymanty, Harymantie, Harimantea, Harymantea

Harinakshi (Indian) A doe-eyed young woman
Harinakshie, Harynakshi, Harinakshy, Harynakshy, Harinakshea, Harynakshea, Harynakshie

Harini (Indian) Resembling a deer
Harinie, Harinee, Hariny, Haryni,
Harynie, Haryny, Harinea, Harynea,
Harynee

Hariti (Indian) In mythology, the goddess
for the protection of children
Haritie, Haryti, Harytie, Haritee, Harytee,
Haritea, Harytea

Harla (English) From the fields
Harlah

Harlan (English) An athletic woman
Harlen, Harlon, Harlun, Harlyn

Harlequine (American) A romantic
woman
Harlequin, Harlequen, Harlequene,
Harlequinne, Harlequinn

Harley (English) From the meadow of the
hares
Harlea, Harlee, Harleen, Harleigh,
Harlene, Harlie, Harli, Harly

Harlow (American) An impetuous woman
Harlowe, Harlo, Harloe

Harmony (English / Latin) Unity; musically
in tune / in mythology, Harmonia was
the daughter of Ares and Aphrodite; a
beautiful blending
Harmonie, Harmoni, Harmonee,
Harmonia, Harmoney, Harmonea

Harper (English) One who plays or makes
harps
Harpur, Harpar, Harpir, Harpyr

Harrell (American) A great leader
Harel, Harell, Harrel, Harelle, Harrelle

Harriet (German) Feminine form of
Henry; ruler of the house
Harriett, Hanriette, Hanrietta, Harriette,
Harrietta, Harrette, Harriot, Harriotte,
Harriotte, Harriotta, Heirierte, Heirrierte

Harsha (Hebrew / Indian) An enchantress;
a hardworking woman / a bringer of
happiness
Harshada, Harshah, Harshini, Harshinie,
Harshyni, Harshynie, Harshita, Harshitah,
Harshinea

Hartley (American) A warmhearted woman
Hartly, Hartlee, Hartlea, Hartleigh,
Hartlie, Hartli

Haru (Japanese) Daughter born in the
spring
Haruko, Haruo, Haruki, Harue

Haruma (Hebrew) Feminine form of
Harum; one who is elevated

Haruphite (Hebrew) Born of autumn's
rain
Harupha, Haruphyte, Haruphita, Haruphitia

Harva (English) A warrior of the army

Hasibah (Arabic) Feminine form of Hasib;
one who is noble and respected
Hasiba, Hasyba, Hasybah, Haseeba,
Haseebah, Haseiba, Haseibah, Hasieba,
Hasiebah, Haseaba, Haseabah

Hasina (African) One who is good and
beautiful
Hasinah, Hasyna, Hasynah, Haseena,
Haseenah, Hasiena, Hasienah, Haseina,
Haseinah, Haseana, Haseanah

Hasita (Indian) A bringer of happiness
Hasumati

Hasna (Arabic) A beautiful woman
Hasnah, Hasnaa, Husinya, Husniyah,
Husna, Husn

Hassaanah (African) The first daughter
Hassanah, Hassana, Hassaana

Hasuna (Arabic) One who is well-behaved;
good
Hasunah

Hateya (Native American) Leaving foot-
prints in the sand

Hathor (Egyptian) In mythology, goddess
of love
Hathora, Hathoria, Hathorea, Hathore

Hatita (Hebrew) A traveling woman; an
explorer
Hatitah, Hatyta, Hatytah, Hateetah,
Hateeta, Hateata, Hateatah

Hatshepsut (Egyptian) A successful ruler;
a female pharoah
Hatchepsut

Hatsu (Japanese) The firstborn daughter

Haukea (Hawaiian) Of the white snow
Haukia, Haukeah, Haukiah, Haukiya,
Haukiyah

Haunani (Hawaiian) Of the heavenly dew
Haunanie, Haunany, Haunaney,
Haunanee, Haunanea

Haurana (Hebrew) Feminine form of
Hauran; woman from the caves
Hauranna, Hauranah, Haurann,
Hauranne, Haurane

Hausis (Native American) A wise old
woman
Hausisse, Hausiss, Hausys, Hausyss,
Hausysse

Haut (French) A stylish woman
Haute, Hauti, Hautie, Hautey, Hauty,
Hautee, Hautea

Hava (Hebrew) A lively woman; giver of life
Havah, Haya, Hayat, Havaa

Havana (Spanish) From the capital city of
Cuba
Havanah, Havanna, Havannah, Havane,
Havann, Havanne

Haven (English) One who provides a safe
place
Hayven, Havan, Hayvan, Havon, Hayvon,
Havin, Hayvin, Havyn, Hayvyn, Haeven,
Haevin, Haevan

Havilah (Hebrew) From the stretch of sand
Havila, Havillah, Havilla, Havily, Havili,
Havilli, Havilie, Havillie, Havilea,
Havillea

Haviland (American) A lively woman
Havyland, Havilande, Havylande,
Havilanda, Havylanda

Havva (Turkish) A giver of the breath of
life
Havvah, Havvia, Havviah

Hawa (African) One who is desired
Hawah

Hawadah (Arabic) A pleasant woman
Hawada

Hawaii (Hawaiian) From the homeland;
from the state of Hawaii

Hawazin (Arabic) A tribal name

Hawke (American) Resembling the bird
Hawki, Hawkie, Hawky, Hawkey,
Hawkee, Hawkea

Hawkins (American) A cunning woman
Haukins, Hawkens, Haukens, Hawkuns,
Haukuns

Hawlee (American) One who negotiates
Hawleigh, Hawli, Hawlie, Hawlea, Hawly,
Hawley

Hawwa (Arabic) A lively woman; a giver
of life
Hawaa, Hawwah, Hawwaa

Haya (Japanese / Hebrew) One who is
quick and light / form of Havva, meaning
"a giver of the breath of life"
Hayah

Hayam (Arabic) One who is madly in love
Hayaam

Haydee (American) A capable woman
Haydi, Haydea, Haydie, Haydie, Haydy,
Haydey

Hayden (English) From the hedged valley
Haden, Haydan, Haydn, Haydon, Hayes,
Haeden, Haedyn, Hadyn

Hayfa (Arabic) A slender and delicate
woman
Hayfah, Haifa, Haifah, Haefa, Haefah

Hayud (Arabic) From the mountain
Hayuda, Hayudah, Hayood, Hayooda

Hazan (Turkish) Born during autumn
Hazann, Hazanne, Hazana, Hazanna,
Hazane

Hazar (Arabic) Resembling a nightingale
Hazare, Hazara, Hazarra, Hazarre, Hazarr

Hazarenan (Hebrew) From the town of
fountains
Hazara, Hazarah, Hazarenanna, Hazarena,
Hazaryna

Hazargaddah (Hebrew) From the town of
fortune
Hazargadda, Hazargada, Hazargadah

Haze (American) One who is spontaneous
Haize, Haise, Hase, Hayze, Hayse, Haeze,
Haese, Hazi, Hazie, Hazy, Hazey, Hazee,
Hazea

Hazel (English) From the hazel tree
Hazell, Hazelle, Haesel, Hazle, Hazal,
Hayzel, Haezel, Haizel

Hazelelponi (Hebrew) A shadowed woman
Hazelelponie, Hazelelpony, Hazelelponey, Hazelelponee, Hazelelponea

Hazina (African) One who is treasured
Hazinah, Hazyna, Hazeena, Hazena, Hazeana, Hazynah, Hazeenah, Hazenah, Hazeanah

Hazor (Hebrew) From the stronghold
Hazora, Hazoria, Hazorea, Hazorya, Hazorra, Hazorah

Heart (American) One who is romantic
Hearte, Hart, Harte

Heartha (Teutonic) A gift from Mother Earth

Heather (English) Resembling the evergreen flowering plant
Hether, Heatha, Heath, Heathe

Heaven (American) From paradise; from the sky
Heavely, Heavenly, Hevean, Hevan, Heavynne, Heavenli, Heavenlie, Heavenleigh, Heavenlee, Heavenley, Heavenlea, Heavyn

Hebe (Greek) A youthful woman; in mythology, goddess of youth and spring and cupbearer to the gods
Heebee, Hebee, Heebe

Hebron (Hebrew) Born of the community; a good friend
Hebrona, Hebronah, Hebrone, Hebrun

Hecate (Greek) In mythology, a goddess of fertility and witchcraft
Hekate

Hecuba (Greek) In mythology, the mother of Paris, Hector, and Cassandra
Hekuba

Hedasaa (Hebrew) Resembling a star
Hedasa, Hedassa, Hedassaa

Hedia (Hebrew) Voice of the Lord
Hedya, Hediah, Hedyah, Hediya, Hediyah

Hedieh (Turkish) A gift from God

Hedva (Hebrew) A bringer of joy
Hedvah

Hedwig (German) Suffering strife during war
Hadvig, Hadwig, Hedvig, Hedviga, Hedvige, Hedwiga, Hedwige, Hedda, Heda, Heddi, Heddie, Hedi, Hedy, Haduwig, Hadu

Hedy (Greek) One who is pleasing; delightful; a sweetheart
Hedea, Hedeah, Hedyla, Hedylah

Heeni (Maori) Form of Jane, meaning "God is gracious"
Heenie, Heeny, Heeney, Heenee, Heenea, Heani, Heanie, Heany, Heaney, Heanee, Heanea

Heera (Indian) As precious as a diamond

Heget (Egyptian) In mythology, a frog goddess who symbolized fertility
Heqet, Heket, Hehet

Hehewuti (Native American) The warrior mother spirit
Hehewutie, Hehewute, Hehewuty, Hehewutey, Hehewutee, Hehewutea

Heidi (German) Form of Adelaide, meaning "of the nobility; serene; of good humor"
Heide, Heid, Heidie, Heidy, Heida, Haidee, Heidey, Hydi, Hydie, Hydey, Hydee, Hydy

Heidrun (Norse) In mythology, the goat who provided the gods with mead

Heilwig (German) Born of a safe war
Heilwyg

Heirnine (Greek) Form of Helen, meaning "the shining light"
Heirnyne, Heirneine, Heirniene, Heirneene, Heirneane

Hekaterine (Greek) Form of Catherine, meaning "one who is pure; virginal"
Hekateros, Hekateryn, Hekateryne, Hekaterina, Hekateryna, Hekaterin

Hel (Norse) In mythology, the goddess of the dead
Hela, Helah

Helam (Hebrew) From the wealthy village
Helama, Helamah, Helamma, Helame

Helbah (Hebrew) A healthy woman; one who is fertile
Helbon, Helba, Helbia, Helbona, Helbea

Held (Welsh) Surrounded by light

Heledd (Welsh) One who is highborn; a princess
Heled, Helede

Helen (Greek) The shining light; in mythology, Helen was the most beautiful woman in the world
Helene, Halina, Helaine, Helana, Heleena, Helena, Helenna, Hellen, Helaina, Helenka, Heleana, Heley, Helina, Heleanor, Helenore, Helenann, Hélène, Hellena, Hellene, Hellenor, Hellia, Heli, Helli, Helie, Hella, Helle

Helga (German) A holy woman; one who is successful

Helia (Greek) Daughter of the sun
Heliah, Helea, Heleah, Heliya, Heliyah, Heller, Hellar

Helice (Greek) Form of Helen, meaning "the shining light"
Helyce, Heleece, Heliece, Heleace

Helike (Greek) In mythology, a willow nymph who nurtured Zeus
Helica, Helyke, Helika, Helyka, Helyca

Helki (Native American) A sensuous woman
Helkie, Helky, Helkey, Helkee, Helkea

Helle (Greek) In mythology, the daughter of Athamas who escaped sacrifice on the back of a golden ram

Helma (German) Form of Wilhelmina, meaning "determined protector"
Helmah, Helmia, Helmea, Helmina, Helmyna, Helmeena, Helmine, Helmyne, Helmeen, Helmeene

Heloise (French) One who is famous in battle
Helois, Heloisa, Helewidis

Helsa (Danish) Form of Elizabeth, meaning "my God is bountiful"
Helsah, Helisa, Helise, Helissa, Helisse

Hemangini (Indian) The golden child; one who shines
Hemangi, Hemangie, Hema, Hemlata, Hem

Hemanti (Indian) Born during the early winter
Hemantie, Hemanty, Hemantey, Hemantee, Hemantea

Hemera (Greek) Born during daylight; in mythology, the goddess of the day
Hemerah, Hemerra, Hemyra, Hemira

Hen (English) Resembling the mothering bird

Hender (American) One who is embraced by all
Hendere

Heng (Chinese) An eternal beauty

Henley (American) A social butterfly
Henleigh, Henlee, Henly, Henlea, Henli, Henlie

Henrietta (German) Feminine form of Henry; ruler of the house
Henretta, Henrieta, Henriette, Henrika, Henryetta, Hetta, Hette, Hettie, Henrieeta, Hatsie, Hatsy, Hattie, Hatty, Hendrika, Henia, Henie, Henka, Hennie, Henrie, Henny, Henni, Henriqua, Henuite, Henuita, Hanrietta, Hanriette, Hanretta, Hanriet

Hensley (American) One who is ambitious
Hensly, Henslee, Hensleigh, Henslea, Hensli, Henslie

Hephzibah (Hebrew) She is my delight
Hepsiba, Hepzibeth, Hepsey, Hepsie, Hepsy, Hepzibah, Hepsee, Hepsea

Hera (Greek) The chosen heroine; in mythology, the wife of Zeus, and the goddess of marriage and childbirth
Here, Herah

Herdis (Scandinavian) A battlemaiden
Herdiss, Herdisse, Herdys, Herdyss, Herdysse

Herendira (American) A tender woman
Herendyra, Herendeera, Herendeara, Herendiera, Herendeira

Herise (American) A warmhearted woman
Heryse, Hereese, Heriese, Hereise, Herease

Herleen (American) A quiet and peaceful woman
Herleene, Herlean, Herleane, Herlein, Herleine, Herlien, Herliene, Herlyn, Herlyne

Hermandina (Greek) A wellborn woman
Hermandine, Hermandyna, Hermandeena, Hermandena, Hermandyne, Hermandeene, Hermandeane, Hermandeana

Hermelinda (Spanish) Bearing a powerful shield
Hermelynda, Hermalinda, Hermalynda, Hermelenda, Hermalenda

Hermia (Greek) Feminine form of Hermes; a messenger of the gods
Hermiah, Hermea, Hermila, Hermilla, Hermilda, Herminia, Hermenia, Herma, Hermina, Hermine, Hermione

Hermippe (Greek) In mythology, the mother of Orchomenus
Hermipe, Hermip, Hermipp

Hermona (Hebrew) From the mountain peak
Hermonah, Hermonna, Hermonnah

Hermosa (Spanish) A beautiful young woman
Hermossa, Hermosah, Hermoza, Hermosia, Hermozia, Hermosea, Hermozea

Hernanda (Spanish) One who is daring
Hernandia, Hernandea, Hernandiya

Hero (Greek) The brave defender; a heroine; in mythology, the lover of Leander who killed herself when she discovered his death
Heroe

Herodias (Greek) One who watches over others; in the Bible, the mother of Salome

Herra (Greek) Daughter of the earth
Herrah

Hersala (Spanish) A lovely woman
Hersalah, Hersalla, Hersallah, Hersalia, Hersaliah, Hersalea, Hersaleah

Herschelle (Hebrew) Feminine form of Hirsh; resembling a deer
Herschele, Herschell, Hershelle, Hershele, Hershell

Hersilia (Latin) In mythology, the wife of Romulus
Hersiliah, Hersilea, Hersileah, Hersylia, Hersylea, Hersyleah, Hersiliya, Hersiliyah

Hertha (English) Of the earth
Herthe, Herta, Herte

Hertnia (English) Of the earth
Hertniah, Hertnea, Hertneah, Hertniya, Hertniyah

Hervie (English) A battle-ready woman warrior
Hervi, Hervy, Hervey, Hervee, Hervea, Herveah

Heshbon (Hebrew) An industrious woman; one with great intelligence

Hesiena (African) The firstborn of twins
Hesienna, Hesienah, Heseina, Hasana, Hasanah, Hasanna, Hasane

Hesione (Greek) In mythology, a Trojan princess saved by Hercules from a sea monster

Hesper (Greek) Born under the evening star
Hespera, Hesperie, Hesperi, Hespery, Hesperey, Hesperee, Hesperea

Hesperia (Greek) In mythology, one of the Hesperides
Hesperiah, Hesperea, Hespereah

Hester (Greek) A starlike woman
Hestere, Hesther, Hesta, Hestar

Hestia (Greek) In mythology, goddess of the hearth
Hestiah, Hestea, Hesteah, Hestya, Hestyah

Hetal (Hindi) A friendly young girl
Hetall, Hetale, Hetalia, Hetalea, Hetala, Hetalla, Hetalle

Heulwen (Welsh) As bright as the light from the sun
Heulwenn, Heulwenne, Heulwin, Heulwinn, Heulwinne, Heulwyn, Heulwynn, Heulwynne

Heven (American) A pretty young woman
Hevin, Hevon, Hevun, Hevven, Hevvin, Hevvon, Hevvun

Heyzell (American) Form of Hazel, meaning "from the hazel tree"
Heyzel, Heyzelle, Heyzill, Heyzille, Heyzil

Hezer (Hebrew) A woman of great strength
Hezir, Hezyr, Hezire, Hezyre, Hezere

Hiah (Korean) A bright woman
Heija, Heijah, Hia

Hiawatha (Native American) She who makes rivers
Hiawathah, Hyawatha, Hiwatha, Hywatha

Hiba (Arabic) A gift from God
Hibah, Heba, Hebah

Hibernia (Latin) Woman from Ireland
*Hiberniah, Hibernea, Hybernia,
Hybernea, Hibernya, Hybernya*

Hibiscus (Latin) Resembling the showy flower
*Hibiskus, Hibyscus, Hibyskus, Hybiscus,
Hybiskus, Hybyscus, Hybyskus*

Hicks (American) A saucy woman
*Hiks, Hycks, Hyks, Hicksi, Hicksie,
Hicksee, Hicksy, Hicksey, Hicksea*

Hidayah (Arabic) One who provides
guidance for others
Hidaya, Hydayah, Hydaya

Hidde (German) An honorable woman
Hiddee, Hiddy, Hiddey, Hidda, Hiddea

Hide (Japanese) A superior woman
Hideyo

Hideko (Japanese) A superior woman
Hydeko

Hidi (African) One who is rooted to the earth
Hidie, Hidy, Hidey, Hidee, Hidea

Hien (Vietnamese) A meek and gentle
woman

Hierapolis (Hebrew) From the sacred city

Higgaion (Hebrew) One who meditates; a
pause for reflection

Hija (African) Her father's daughter

Hijrah (Arabic) Refers to the migration of
Muhammad
Hijra

Hikmah (Arabic) Having great wisdom
Hikmat, Hikma

Hilan (Greek) Filled with happines
*Hylan, Hilane, Hilann, Hilanne, Hylane,
Hylann, Hylanne*

Hilary (Greek) A cheerful woman; bringer
of joy
*Hillary, Hilaree, Hilarie, Hilarey, Hilari,
Hillari, Hillarie, Hillaree, Hillarey, Hillory,
Hilaire, Hilaria, Hilery, Hillery, Hiliary,
Hiliarie, Hylary, Hylarie, Hylari, Hylarey,
Hylaree, Hyllari, Hyllary, Hilaeira, Hiolair,
Hillarea, Hylarea, Hyllarea, Hilarea*

Hildar (Scandinavian) A feisty woman
*Hildarr, Hildare, Hildayr, Hildaer, Hyldar,
Hyldarr, Hyldare, Hyldayr, Hyldaer,
Hildair, Hyldair*

Hildebrand (German) Having great
strength
*Hildibrand, Hildebrande, Hildibrande,
Hyldebrand, Hyldibrand*

Hildegard (German) A battlemaiden; a
protector; in mythology, a Valkyrie
*Hildegarde, Hildagarde, Hildagard, Hilda,
Hilde, Hulda, Hylda, Hildred, Hildee,
Hildi, Hildie, Hildey, Hildy, Hildia,
Hildea, Hyldi, Hylda, Hylde, Hyldy,
Hyldegard, Hyldegarde, Hyldagard,
Hyldagarde, Hild, Hildegunn, Hildigunn,
Holda, Hyldea*

Hildemare (German) A glorious woman;
famous in battle
*Hildemara, Hildimar, Hildimara,
Hildemar, Hyldemare, Hyldemar,
Hyldemara*

Hildireth (German) An advisor during war
time
Hildreth

Hildur (Icelandic) A battlemaiden
Hildurr, Hyldur, Hyldurr, Hildura, Hyldura

Hilina (Hawaiian) Resembling a celestial
body
*Hilinah, Hileena, Hileenah, Hilyna,
Hilynah, Hileana, Hileanah, Hiliena,
Hilienah, Hileina, Hileinah*

Hilliard (English / German) From the hill /
a guardian during battle
Hiller, Hillierd, Hillyard, Hillyer, Hillyerd

Hilma (German) One who is protected
Hilmah, Hylma, Hylmah

Hilton (American) A wealthy woman
*Hylton, Hiltan, Hyltan, Hiltun, Hyltun,
Hillton, Hiltin, Hyltin*

Himalaya (American) Woman from the
mountains
Hymalaya

Hina (Polynesian) In mythology, a dual
goddess symbolizing day and night
*Hinna, Henna, Hinaa, Hinah, Heena,
Hena*

Hind (Arabic) Owning a group of camels;
a wife of Muhammad
Hynd, Hinde, Hynde

Hinda (Hebrew) Resembling a doe
*Hindah, Hindy, Hindey, Hindee, Hindi,
Hindie, Hynda, Hyndy, Hyndey, Hyndee,
Hyndi, Hyndie, Hindea, Hyndea, Hindal*

Hine (Polynesian) One who is chaste;
a maiden

Hinnom (Hebrew) From the deep ravine

Hinto (Native American) Having deep-blue
eyes

Hinton (American) A wealthy woman
Hynton, Hintan, Hyntan, Hintun, Hyntun

Hippodamia (Greek) A tamer of horses;
in mythology, a bride who was nearly
kidnapped by centaurs
*Hippodamea, Hippodameia, Hipodamia,
Hipodamea, Hipodameia*

Hippolyte (Greek) Feminine form of
Hippolytus; one who frees the horses; in
mythology, the queen of the Amazons
Hippolyta, Hippolite, Hippothoe

Hiral (Indian) A lustrous woman

Hiriwa (Polynesian) A silvery woman

Hirkani (Indian) Resembling a small
diamond
*Hirkanie, Hirkany, Hirkaney, Hirkanee,
Hirkanea*

Hiroko (Japanese) One who is noble and
generous
Hiriko, Hyroko, Hyriko, Hyryko

Hisa (Japanese) A long-lived woman
Hisah, Hysa, Hisako, Hisayo, Hisano

Hisaye (Japanese) An everlasting beauty
*Hisay, Hysaye, Hysay, Hisai, Hysai, Hisae,
Hysae*

Hisolda (Irish) Form of Isolda, meaning "a
woman known for her beauty"
*Hiseult, Hiseut, Hisold, Hisolde, Hisolt,
Hisolte, Hisota, Hisotta, Hisotte, Hisoud,
Hisoude*

Hitomi (Japanese) One who has beautiful
eyes
*Hitomie, Hitomee, Hitomea, Hitomy,
Hitomey*

Hiya (Indian) Of the heart

Hoa (Vietnamese) One who is peaceful;
resembling a flower
Hoah, Hoai

Hodaiah (Hebrew) One who praises God
Hodaviah, Hodiah, Hodijah, Hoda

Hodel (Hebrew) From the flowering myrtle
tree
Hodell, Hodele, Hodelle, Hodela, Hodella

Hodesh (Hebrew) Born during the new
moon
Hodesha, Hodeshah, Hodeshia, Hodeshea

Hodge (American) One who is confident
Hoge

Hoku (Polynesian) One who shines as
bright as a star
*Hokulani, Hokulanie, Hokulanee,
Hokulanea, Hokulany, Hokulaney*

Holbrook (English) From the brook on
the hillside
Holebrook, Holbrooke, Holebrooke

Holda (German) A secretive woman; one
who is hidden
Holde

Holden (English) One who is willing and
eager
Holdin, Holdyn, Holdan

Holder (English) One who has a beautiful
voice
Holdar, Holdir, Holdyr, Holdur

Holiday (American) Born on a festive day
*Holliday, Holidaye, Hollidaye, Holidai,
Hollidai, Holidae, Hollidae*

Holine (American) A special woman
*Holyne, Holeene, Holeane, Holeine,
Holene*

Holla (German) A secretive woman
Hollah

Hollander (Dutch) A woman from
Holland
*Hollynder, Hollender, Holander, Holynder,
Holender, Hollande, Hollanda*

Hollis (English) Near the valley of the holly bushes
Hollace, Holisa, Hollisa, Holise, Holyse, Hollice, Hollissa, Holyce, Hollyse, Hollisse, Holisse, Hollysa

Hollisha (English) A genius
Holleesha, Holleisha, Holliesha, Holleasha, Hollysha

Holly (English) Of the holly tree
Holli, Hollie, Hollee, Holley, Hollye, Hollyanne, Holle, Hollea, Hollei, Holleigh, Hollianne, Holleah, Hollyn, Holeena

Holsey (American) An easygoing woman
Holsy, Holsi, Holsie, Holsee, Holsea

Holton (American) One who is whimsical
Holten, Holtan, Holtin, Holtyn, Holtun

Holy (American) One who is pious or sacred
Holey, Holee, Holeigh, Holi, Holie, Holye, Holea, Holeah

Holyn (American) A fresh-faced woman
Holen, Holan, Holun, Holin

Homer (American) A tomboyish woman
Homar, Homir, Homyr, Homur, Homor

Honesty (American) One who is truthful and trustworthy
Honestey, Honesti, Honestie, Honestee, Honestea

Honey (American) A very sweet woman
Hony, Honie, Honi, Honee, Honye, Hunig, Honbria, Honbrie, Honbree, Honea

Hong (Vietnamese) A young girl with a rosy complexion

Honora (Latin) Having a good name and integrity; an honorable woman
Honour, Honoria, Honor, Honorata, Honoratas, Honnor, Honorina, Honorine, Honore, Honoree, Honori, Honorie, Honory, Honouri, Honourie, Honoury, Honoura, Honouria, Honoure, Honorea, Honourea

Honovi (Native American) As strong as a deer
Honovie, Honovee, Honovy, Honovey, Honovea

Hop (Vietnamese) One who is consistent

Hope ⚲ (English) One who has expectations through faith

Hopkins (American) One who is perky
Hopkens, Hopkans, Hopkin, Hopkyns

Hor (Hebrew) Woman from the mountains

Horatia (English) Feminine form of Horace; the keeper of time
Horacia, Horacya, Horatya, Horatiah, Hora, Horada, Horae

Horem (Hebrew) One who is dedicated to God
Horema, Horemah, Horym, Horyma

Horiya (Japanese) Woman of the gardens
Horiyah, Horya, Horyah

Horonaim (Hebrew) Of the two caverns
Horonaima, Horonama, Horonayma, Horonayme, Horonaem, Horonaema

Hortensia (Latin) Woman of the garden
Hartencia, Hartinsia, Hortencia, Hortense, Hortenspa, Hortenxia, Hortinzia, Hortendana, Hortendanna, Hortendane

Hosah (Hebrew) One who provides refuge
Hosa

Hosanna (Latin) Raising one's voice in praise of God
Hosannah, Hosann, Hosane, Hosanne, Hosana, Hosanah

Hoshi (Japanese) One who shines as brightly as a star
Hoshiko, Hoshie, Hoshee, Hoshy, Hoshey, Hoshiyo, Hoshea

Hotaru (Japanese) Resembling a firefly

Hourig (Slavic) A small, fiery woman

Houston (American) From the city in Texas
Hewston, Huston

Hova (African) Born into the middle class

Howardena (German) Feminine form of Howard; guardian of the home
Howardina, Howardyna, Howardeena, Howardiena, Howardeina, Howardeana

Hristina (Slavic) Form of Christina, meaning "follower of Christ"
Hristinah, Hristeena, Hristyna, Hristiena, Hristeina, Hristine, Hristyne, Hristeen, Hristeene

H

Hrothbeorhta (English) A famously bright woman
Hrothberta, Hrothbertina, Hrothnerta

Hua (Chinese) Resembling a flower

Huang (Chinese) Yellow

Hubab (Arabic) An ambitious and focused woman

Huda (Arabic) One who provides the right guidance
Hooda, Hudah, Hoodah, Houda, Houdah

Hudel (Scandinavian) One who is lovable
Hudell, Hudele, Hudelle, Hudela, Hudella

Hudes (Hebrew) Form of Judith, meaning "woman from Judea"

Hudi (Arabic) One who chooses the right path
Hudie, Hudy, Hudey, Hudee, Hudea

Hudson (English) One who is adventurous; an explorer
Hudsen, Hudsan, Hudsun, Hudsyn, Hudsin

Hudun (Arabic) One who is peaceful; quiet

Hue (Vietnamese) Resembling the lily flower

Hueline (German) An intelligent woman
Huelene, Huelyne, Hueleine, Hueliene, Hueleene, Huleane

Huette (German) Feminine form of Hugh; having a bright mind; an intelligent woman
Huguetta, Hugette, Huetts, Hughetta, Hughette, Hugiet, Huberta, Huberte, Hubertine, Hubertina, Huet, Hueta, Huetta, Huitta, Huitte, Hugetta, Hughette, Huyet, Huyete, Huyette, Huyett, Huyetta, Hughet, Hugiherahta, Huela, Huella

Huhana (Maori) Form of Susan, meaning "resembling a graceful white lily"
Huhanah, Huhanna, Huhanne, Huhann, Huhane

Huldah (Hebrew) Resembling a weasel; in the Bible, the name of a prophetess
Hulda

Hulde (German) One who is dearly loved

Huma (Arabic) A bird who brings good fortune
Humah, Humma, Humaa, Hummaa

Humairaa (Asian) A generous woman
Humaira, Humayraa, Humayra, Humaeraa, Humaera

Humita (Native American) One who shells corn
Humitah, Humyta, Humeeta, Humieta, Humeita, Humeata, Humytah, Humeetah, Humietah, Humeitah, Humeatah

Hunter (English) A great huntress and provider

Huong (Vietnamese) Having a delicate scent of a flower

Hur (Arabic) An untouched woman; a virgin

Huraira (Arabic) A red-haired woman
Hureaira, Hurairah, Hurayra, Hurayrah, Huraera, Huraerah

Huraiva (Arabic) A catlike woman
Huraivah, Hurayva, Hurava, Huraeva

Hurit (Native American) A beauty

Huriyah (Arabic) An independent woman; freedom
Huriya, Huriyyah, Hooriya, Huriyya, Hooriyah

Hurley (English) A healthy woman
Hurly, Hurli, Hurlie, Hurlee, Hurlea, Hurleigh

Hushai (Hebrew) A quick-witted woman
Hushae, Hushay, Husha, Hushaye

Hutena (Hurrian) In mythology, the goddess of fate
Hutenah, Hutenna, Hutyna, Hutina

Hutton (English) One who is knowledgeable
Huttan, Hutten, Huttun, Huttyn, Huttin

Huwaidah (Arabic) One who is gentle
Huwaydah, Huwaida, Huwayda, Huwaeda, Huwaedah

Huxlee (American) One who is creative
Huxleigh, Huxly, Huxley, Huxli, Huxlie, Huxlea

Huyana (Native American) Daughter of the rain
Huyanna, Huyane, Huyann, Huyanne

Huyen (Vietnamese) A woman with jet-black hair

Hvergelmir (Norse) In mythology, the wellspring of cold waters
Hvergelmire, Hvergelmira, Hvergelmeer, Hvergelmeera

Hyacinth (Greek) Resembling the colorful fragrant flower
Hyacintha, Hyacinthe, Hycinth, Hycynth, Hyacinthia, Hyacinthea, Hyacinthie, Hyacynth, Hyacyntha

Hyades (Greek) A cluster of stars in the constellation Taurus; in mythology, daughters of the ocean

Hyatt (English) From the high gate
Hyat, Hyate, Hyatte, Hiatt, Hiat, Hiate, Hiatte

Hydeira (Greek) Woman of the water
Hydira, Hydyra, Hydeyra, Hydeera, Hydeara, Hydiera

Hydra (Greek) A constellation; in mythology, a monster killed by Hercules

Hye (Korean) A graceful woman
Hea, Hei

Hygeia (Greek) In mythology, the goddess of health
Hygia, Hygeiah, Hygea

Hyndla (Norse) In mythology, a priestess

Hypatia (Greek) An intellectually superior woman
Hypasia, Hypacia, Hypate

Hypermnestra (Greek) In mythology, the mother of Amphiareos

Hypsipyle (Greek) In mythology, the queen of Lemnos
Hypsypyle, Hipsipyle, Hipsipile, Hypsipile, Hypsypile

Hyrrokkin (Norse) In mythology, a giantess
Hyrokin, Hyrrokin, Hyrokkin

Hyun (Korean) Having great wisdom

Iamar (Arabic) Of the moon
Iamarah, Iamaria, Iamarea, Iamarra, Iamariah, Iamareah, Iamarrah

Ianeke (Hawaiian) God is gracious
Ianeki, Ianekie, Ianeky, Ianekey, Ianekea, Ianekee

Ianna (Gaelic) Feminine form of Ian; God is gracious
Iannah, Iana, Ianah, Ionna, Iona

Ianthe (Greek) Resembling the violet flower; in mythology, a sea nymph and a daughter of Oceanus
Iantha, Ianthia, Ianthina, Ianthyna, Ianthea, Ianthiya, Ianthya

Iara (Brazilian) In mythology, a water queen
Iarah, Iarra, Iarrah

Ibernia (Irish) Woman of Ireland
Iberniah, Ibernea, Iberneah, Iberniya, Iberniyah, Ibernya, Ibernyah

Ibolya (Hungarian) Violet; resembling a flower
Ibollya, Ibolyah, Ibolia, Iboliya

Ibtesam (Arabic) One who smiles often
Ibtisam, Ibtysam

Ibtihaj (Arabic) A delight; bringer of joy
Ibtehaj, Ibtyhaj

Ida (Greek) One who is diligent; hardworking; in mythology, the nymph who cared for Zeus on Mount Ida
Idania, Idaea, Idalee, Idaia, Idania, Idalia, Idalie, Idana, Idaline, Idalina, Idette, Idetta, Idett, Idet, Ideta, Idete

Idaa (Hindi) Woman of the earth

Idahlia (Greek) One with a sweet disposition
Idahliah, Idahlea, Idahleah, Idahliya, Idahliyah, Idahlya, Idahlyah

Idalika (Arabic) A queen; born to royalty
Idalikah, Idalicca, Idalica, Idalicka, Idalyka, Idalykah

Idarah (American) A social butterfly
Idara, Idarra, Idarrah

Idasia (English) Filled with joy
Idasiah, Idasea, Idaseah

Ide (Irish) One who is thirsty; also the name of a saint
Ideh

Idelle (Welsh) One who is happy; bountiful
Idelisa, Idella, Idelissa, Idele, Idela

Idil (Latin) A pleasant woman
Idyl, Idill, Idyll

Idoia (Spanish) Refers to the Virgin Mary
Idoea, Idurre, Iratze, Izazkun

Idola (German) A hardworking woman
Idolah, Idolla, Idollah, Idolina, Idolyna, Idoleena, Idoleana, Idoleina, Idoliena

Idona (Scandinavian) A fresh-faced woman
Idonah, Idonna, Idonnah, Idonia, Idoniah, Idonea, Idoneah, Idonya, Idonyah

Idony (Scandinavian) One who has been reborn
Idoney, Idonee, Idonea, Idoni, Idonie

Idowu (African) Daughter born after twins

Idra (Aramaic) A flourishing woman
Idrah

Idriya (Hebrew) A wealthy woman
Idriyah, Idria, Idriah

Idun (Norse) In mythology, goddess of youth, fertility, and death
Iduna, Idunna, Idunn, Idunnor

Iduvina (Spanish) A dedicated woman
Iduvinah, Iduveena, Iduveenah, Iduviena, Iduvienah, Iduveina, Iduveinah, Iduveana, Iduveanah

Ierne (Irish) Woman from Ireland

Iesha (English) Form of Aisha, meaning "lively; womanly"
Ieshia, Ieshea, Ieesha, Ieasha, Ieashia, Ieashiah, Ieeshah, Ieeshia

Ifama (African) One's well-being
Ifamah, Ifamma, Ifammah

Ife (African) One who loves and is loved
Ifeh, Iffe

Ifeoma (African) A beautiful woman; a good thing
Ifeomah, Ifyoma, Ifyomah

Ignatia (Latin) A fiery woman; burning brightly
Igantiah, Ignacia, Ignazia, Iniga

Igone (Basque) Feminine form of Igon; ascension
Igona, Igoneh, Igonia, Igonea

Igraine (English) In Arthurian legend, Arthur's mother
Igrayne, Igrain, Igerne, Igrayn, Igraen, Igraene

Ihab (Arabic) A gift from God

Iheoma (Hawaiian) Lifted up by God

Ihsan (Arabic) Goodwill toward others
Ihsane, Ihsann, Ihsana, Ihsanna, Ihsanne

Ijada (Spanish) As beautiful as jade

Ikabela (Hawaiian) Form of Isabel, meaning "my God is bountiful"
Ikabell, Ikabelle, Ikabel, Ikabele, Ikabella

Ikea (Scandinavian) Having smooth skin
Ikeah, Ikiya, Ikiyah, Ikia, Ikiah

Ikeida (American) A spontaneous woman
Ikeidah, Ikeyda, Ikeydah, Ikeda, Ikedah, Ikieda, Ikiedah, Ikeeda, Ikeedah, Ikeada, Ikeadah

Iku (Japanese) A nurturing woman

Ila (Indian / French) Of the earth / from the island
Ilanis, Ilanys, Ilsa

Ilamay (French) From the island
Ilamaye, Ilamai, Ilamae

Ilana (Hebrew) Feminine form of Ilan; from the trees
Ilane, Ilania, Ilanit

Ilandere (American) Moon woman
Ilander, Ilanderre, Ilandera, Ilanderra

Ilaria (Italian) Form of Hilary, meaning "a cheerful woman; bringer of joy"
Illaire, Ilarea, Illaria, Ilaire, Ilariya, Illariya

Ildiko (Hungarian) Form of Hilda, meaning "a battlemaiden; a protector"
Ildyko, Ildicko, Ildycko, Ilda, Ildah

Ilena (English) Form of Aileen, meaning "the light-bearer; from the green meadow"
Ilene, Ilean, Ileen, Ileene, Ileena, Ilenna, Ileana

Ilepsie (Hebrew) Form of Hephzibah, meaning "she is my delight"
Ilepsi, Ilepsy, Ilepsey, Ilepsee, Ilepsea

Ilesha (Hindi) Of the earth
Ileshah, Ileesha, Ileeshah, Ileasha, Ileashah, Ilysha, Ilyshah

Ilham (Arabic) The heart's inspiration

Ilia (Greek) From the ancient city
Iliah, Ilea, Ileah, Iliya, Iliyah, Ilya, Ilyah

Iliana (Greek) Form of Helen, meaning "the shining light"
Ileana, Ileane, Ileanna, Ileanne, Illeanna, Illia, Illiana, Illianna, Illionya, Ilona, Ilonna, Iliona, Ilone, Ilonka, Illonna, Ilon

Ilima (Hebrew) The flower of Oahu
Ilimah, Illima, Ilyma, Ilymah, Iliema, Iliemah, Ileima, Ileimah, Ileema, Ileemah, Ileama, Ileamah

Ilisapesi (Tonga) The blessed child
Ilisapesie, Ilysapesi, Ilysapesy, Ilisapesy, Ilisapesea, Ilysapesie, Ilysapesea

Ilithyia (Greek) In mythology, goddess of childbirth
Ilithya, Ilithyia, Ilithyiah

Ilka (Slavic) A hardworking woman
Ilkah, Ilke, Ilkeh

Illinois (Native American) From the tribe of warriors; from the state of Illinois

Ilma (German) Form of Wilhelmina, meaning "determined protector"
Ilmah, Illma, Illmah

Ilori (African) A special child; one who is treasured
Illori, Ilorie, Illorie, Ilory, Illory, Ilorey, Illorey, Iloree, Illoree, Ilorea, Illorea

Ilse (German) Form of Elizabeth, meaning "my God is bountiful"
Ilseh, Ilsa, Ilsah, Ilisa, Illsa, Ilsae, Ilsaie, Ilyssa, Ilysa, Ilsea

Ilta (Finnish) Born at night
Iltah, Illta

Iluminada (Spanish) One who shines brightly
Iluminata, Ilumynada, Ilumynata, Iluska, Ilu

Ilyse (German / Greek) Born into the nobility / form of Elyse, meaning "my God is bountiful"
Ilysea, Ilysia, Ilysse, Ilysea

Ima (German) Form of Emma, meaning "one who is complete; a universal woman"
Imah, Imma, Immah

Imala (Native American) One who disciplines others
Imalah, Imalla, Imallah, Immala, Immalla

Iman (Arabic) Having great faith
Imani, Imanie, Imania, Imaan, Imany, Imaney, Imanee, Imanea, Imain, Imaine, Imaen, Imaene, Imayn, Imayne

Imanuela (Spanish) A faithful woman
Imanuella, Imanuel, Imanuele, Imanuell

Imara (Hungarian) A great ruler
Imarah, Imarra, Imarrah

Imari (Japanese) Daughter of today
Imarie, Imaree, Imarea, Imary, Imarey

Imelda (Italian) Warrior in the universal battle
Imeldah, Imalda, Imaldah

Imena (African) A dream
Imenah, Imenna, Imina, Imyna

Immaculata (Latin) Refers to the Immaculate Conception
Immaculatta, Immaculatah, Immaculada

Imogen (Gaelic / Latin) A maiden / one who is innocent and pure
Imogene, Imogenia, Imogine, Imojean, Imojeen, Imogenea, Immy, Immi, Immie

Imperia (Latin) A majestic woman
Imperiah, Imperea, Impereah, Imperial, Imperiel, Imperielle, Imperialle

Imtithal (Arabic) One who is polite and obedient
Imtithala, Imtithaal, Imtithalia, Imtithalea

Ina (Polynesian) In mythology, a moon goddess
Inah, Inna, Innah

Inaki (Asian) Having a generous nature
Inakie, Inaky, Inakey, Inakea, Inakee

In'am (Arabic) One who bestows kindness

Inanna (Sumerian) A lady of the sky; in mythology, goddess of love, fertility, war, and the earth
Inannah, Inana, Inanah, Inann, Inanne, Inane

Inara (Arabic) A heaven-sent daughter; one who shines with light
Inarah, Innara, Inarra, Innarra

Inari (Finnish / Japanese) Woman from the lake / one who is successful
Inarie, Inaree, Inary, Inarey, Inarea, Inareah

Inas (Arabic) One who is friendly and sociable
Inass, Inasse, Inasa, Inassa

Inaya (Arabic) One who cares for the well-being of others
Inayah, Inayat

Inca (Indian) An adventurer
Incah, Inka, Inkah, Incka, Inckah

Independence (American) One who has freedom
Independance, Indepindence, Indipindince, Indypyndynce

India (English) From the river; woman from India
Indea, Indiah, Indeah, Indya, Indiya, Indee, Inda, Indy, Indi

Indiana (English) From the land of the Indians; from the state of Indiana
Indianna, Indyana, Indyanna

Indiece (American) A capable woman
Indeice, Indeace, Indeece, Indiese, Indeise, Indeese, Indease

Indigo (English) Resembling the plant; a purplish-blue dye
Indygo, Indeego

Indira (Hindi) A beautiful woman; in Hinduism, another name for Lakshmi
Indirah, Indyra, Indiera, Indeera, Indeira, Indeara, Indyrah, Indierah, Indeerah, Indeirah, Indearah

Indra (Hindi) One who possesses the rain; in Hinduism, a deity of thunder and rain
Indrah, Indrani, Indranie, Indranee, Indrina

Indray (American) One who is outspoken
Indraye, Indrae, Indrai, Indree

Indre (Hindi) Woman of splendor

Indu (Hindi) Woman of the moon
Indukala, Induma

Indumati (Hindi) Born beneath the full moon
Indumatie, Indumaty, Indumatey, Indumatee, Indumatea

Ineesha (American) A sparkling woman
Ineeshah, Ineisha, Ineishah, Iniesha, Inieshah, Ineasha, Ineashah, Ineysha, Ineyshah

Ineke (Japanese) One who nurtures

Ines (Spanish) Form of Agnes, meaning "one who is pure; chaste"
Inez, Inesa, Inesita, Inessa, Inetta, Ineta

Infinity (American) A woman unbounded by space or time
Infinitey, Infiniti, Infinitie, Infinitee, Infinitye, Infinitea

Ingalill (Scandinavian) A fertile woman
Ingalyll, Ingalil, Ingalyl, Ingalille, Ingalylle

Ingalls (American) A peaceful woman

Ingeborg (Scandinavian) Protected by the god Ing
Ingaberg, Ingaborg, Inge, Ingegerg, Inngeborg, Ingibjorg, Inga, Ingunn, Ingunna, Injerd

Ingegard (Scandinavian) Of the god Ing's kingdom
Ingagard, Ingegerd, Ingagerd, Ingigard, Ingigerd

Ingelise (Danish) Having the grace of the god Ing
Ingelisse, Ingeliss, Ingelyse, Ingelisa, Ingelissa, Ingelysa, Ingelyssa

Inghean (Scottish) Her father's daughter
Ingheane, Inghinn, Ingheene, Ingheen, Inghynn

Ingrid (Scandinavian) Having the beauty of the god Ing
Ingred, Ingrad, Inga, Inge, Inger, Ingmar, Ingrida, Ingria, Ingrit, Inkeri

Iniguez (Spanish) A good woman

Iniko (African) Daughter born during hardship
Inicko, Inicco, Inico, Inyko, Inycko, Inycco, Inyco

Inis (Irish) Woman from Ennis
Iniss, Inisse, Innis, Inys, Innys, Inyss, Inysse

Ino (Greek) In mythology, the daughter of Cadmus

Inocencia (Spanish) One who is pure and innocent
Innocencia, Innocenta, Inocenta, Inocentia, Inoceneia, Innoceneia, Innocentia, Innocence

Inoke (Hawaiian) A faithful woman

Integra (Latin) A woman of importance

Integrity (American) One who is truthful; of good character
Integritey, Integritee, Integritea, Integriti, Integritie

Intisar (Arabic) One who is victorious; triumphant
Intisara, Intisarah, Intizar, Intizara, Intizarah, Intisarr, Intysarr, Intysar

Invidia (Latin) An envious woman
Invidiah, Invidea, Invideah, Invydia, Invydea, Invidiya, Invidiyah

Io (Greek) In mythology, a woman who was turned into a cow to elude Zeus

Iokina (Hawaiian) God will develop
Iokinah, Iokyna, Iokeena, Iokine, Iokyne, Iokeen, Iokeane, Iokeana

Iola (Greek) Of the violet-colored dawn
Iolah, Iolla, Iollah, Iole, Iolle, Inola, Inolah, Inolla, Inollah

Iolana (Hawaiian) Soaring like a hawk
Iolanah, Iolanna, Iolann, Iolanne, Iolane, Iolani, Iolanie, Iolanee, Iolany, Iolaney

Iolanthe (Greek) Resembling a violet flower
Iolanda, Iolanta, Iolantha, Iolante, Iolande, Iolanthia, Iolanthea

Iona (Greek) Woman from the island
Ionna, Ioane, Ioann, Ioanne

Ionanna (Hebrew) Filled with grace
Ionannah, Ionana, Ionann, Ionane, Ionanne

Ione (Greek) Resembling the violet flower
Ionie, Ioni, Ionee, Ioney, Iony

Ionia (Greek) Of the sea and islands
Ionya, Ionija, Ioniah, Ionea, Ionessa, Ioneah, Ioniya

Iora (Greek) A birdlike woman
Iorra, Ioria, Iorea, Iore, Iorie, Iori, Iory, Iorey, Ioree

Iorwen (Welsh) A beautiful woman
Iorwenn, Iorwenne, Iorwin, Iorwinn, Iorwinne, Iorwyn, Iorwynn, Iorwynne

Iosepine (Hawaiian) Form of Josephine, meaning "God will add"
Iosephine, Iosefa, Iosefena, Iosefene, Iosefina, Iosefine, Iosepha, Iosephe, Iosephene, Iosephina, Iosephyna, Iosephyna, Iosephyne, Iosepyne, Iosapine, Iosapyne, Iosepeen, Iosapeen

Iowa (Native American) Of the Iowa tribe; from the state of Iowa

Iphedeiah (Hebrew) One who is saved by the Lord
Iphedeia, Iphedia, Iphedea, Iphidea, Iphidia, Iphideia

Iphigenia (Greek) One who is born strong; in mythology, daughter of Agamemnon
Iphigeneia, Iphigenie, Iphagenia, Iphegenia, Iphegenie, Iphegeneia, Ifigenia, Ifegenia, Ifagenia

Iphimedeia (Greek) In mythology, the wife of Poseidon
Iphimedea, Iphimedea, Ifimedeia, Ifimedea, Ifimedia

Ipo (Hawaiian) A sweet woman; a darling

Ipsa (Indian) One who is desired
Ipsita, Ipsyta, Ipseeta, Ipseata, Ipsah

Ira (Hebrew / Indian) One who is watchful / of the earth
Irah, Irra, Irrah

Iratze (Basque) Refers to the Virgin Mary
Iratza, Iratzia, Iratzea, Iratzi, Iratzie, Iratzy, Iratzey, Iratzee

Irem (Turkish) From the heavenly gardens
Irema, Ireme, Iremia, Iremea

Irene (Greek) A peaceful woman; in
mythology, the goddess of peace
*Ira, Irayna, Ireen, Iren, Irena, Irenea,
Irenee, Irenka, Iriana, Irina, Irine, Iryna,
Irenke, Iryne, Irini, Irinia, Irynia*

Ireta (Greek) One who is serene
*Iretah, Iretta, Irettah, Irete, Iret, Irett,
Ireta*

Iris (Greek) Of the rainbow; a flower; in
mythology, a messenger goddess
*Irida, Iridiana, Iridianny, Irisa, Irisha, Irita,
Iria, Irea, Iridian, Iridiane, Iridianna, Iriss,
Irys, Iryss*

Irish (American) Woman from Ireland
Irysh, Irisha, Irysha

Irma (German) A universal woman
*Irmina, Irmine, Irmgard, Irmgarde,
Irmagard, Irmagarde, Irmeena, Irmyna,
Irmuska*

Irodell (American) A peaceful woman
Irodelle, Irodel, Irodele, Irodella, Irodela

Irta (Greek) Resembling a pearl
Irtah

Irune (Basque) Refers to the Holy Trinity
Iroon, Iroone, Iroun, Iroune

Irvette (English) Friend of the sea
*Irvetta, Irvett, Irvete, Irvet, Irveta, Irvina,
Irvinna, Irvena*

Isabel ✪ ◐ (Spanish) Form of Elizabeth,
meaning "my God is bountiful"
*Isabeau, Isabela, Isabele, Isabelita, Isabell,
Isabella, Isabelle, Ishbel, Isobel, Isobell,
Isobella, Isobelle, Issie, Issy, Izabel,
Izabella, Izabelle, Izzie, Izzy, Ibby, Ib, Ibbi,
Ibbie, Isa, Isibeal, Isibelle, Isibel, Isibell,
Isibella, Isibela, Isahel, Isahella, Isahelle,
Iseabal, Isobail, Isobael, Isohel*

Isabis (African) A beautiful child
Isabys, Isabiss, Isabisse, Isabyss, Isabysse

Isadore (Greek) A gift from the goddess Isis
*Isadora, Isador, Isadoria, Isidor, Isidoro,
Isidorus, Isidro, Isidora, Isidoria, Isidore,
Izidore, Izadore, Izidora, Izadora, Izidoria,
Izadoria*

Isairis (Spanish) A lively woman
Isairys, Isaeris, Isaerys, Isaire, Isaere, Isair

Isamu (Japanese) One who has a lot of
energy

Isana (German) A strong-willed woman
Isanah, Isanna, Isane, Isann, Isanne, Isan

Isaura (Greek) Of the soft breeze
Isaure, Isauria, Isaurea

ISABELLA
We decided to name our daughter Isabella because her name wasn't on any baby list at the time.
Ironically, others must have had the same thought because it's one of the more popular names of
that year! We also thought it would be difficult to abbreviate to anything but Bella. Instead everyone calls her Izzy (which makes us cringe). —Stefanie, IL

Isela (American) A giving woman
Iselah, Isella, Isellah

Isha (Indian / Hebrew) The protector / a
lively woman
Ishah

Ishana (Indian) A wealthy lady
*Ishanah, Ishanna, Ishannah, Ishann,
Ishanne, Ishane, Ishani, Ishanie, Ishany,
Ishaney, Ishanee, Ishara, Isharah, Isharra*

Ishi (Japanese) As solid as a rock
*Ishie, Ishy, Ishey, Ishee, Ishea, Isheah,
Ishiko*

Ishtar (Persian) In mythology, a mother
goddess of love and fertility
*Ishtarr, Ishtarre, Ishtara, Ishtarah, Ishtarra,
Ishtarrah*

Isi (Native American) Resembling a deer
Isie, Isee, Isey, Isy, Isea, Ise

Isis (Egyptian) In mythology, the most
powerful of all goddess

Isla (Gaelic) From the island
Islay, Islae, Islai, Isleta, Isletta, Islyta

Isleen (Gaelic) Form of Aislinn, meaning "a dream or vision; an inspiration"
Isleene, Islyne, Islyn, Isline, Isleine, Isliene, Islene, Isleyne, Isleane

Ismaela (Spanish) Feminine form of Ismael; God will listen
Ismaelah, Ismaila, Ismala, Ismalia, Ismalea, Ismayla

Ismat (Arabic) One who safeguards others
Ismate, Ismatte, Ismata, Ismatta, Ismatah

Ismay (French) Form of Esme, meaning "one who is esteemed"
Isme, Ismai, Ismae, Ismaa, Ismaye

Ismene (Greek) In mythology, the daughter of Oedipus and Jocasta
Ismeen, Ismeene, Ismyn, Ismyne, Ismine, Ismey, Ismenia, Ismenea, Ismi, Ismie, Ismini, Ismean, Ismeane, Ismea

Ismitta (African) Daughter of the mountains
Ismittah, Ismita, Ismytta, Ismyta

Isoke (African) A gift from God
Isoka, Isokah

Isolde (Celtic) A woman known for her beauty; in mythology, the lover of Tristan
Iseult, Iseut, Isold, Isolda, Isolt, Isolte, Isota, Isotta, Isotte, Isoud, Isoude, Izett

Isra (Arabic) One who travels in the evening
Israh, Isria, Isrea, Israt

Istas (Native American) A snow queen
Istass, Istasse, Istasa, Istassa, Isatas, Isatass

Ita (Irish) One who is thirsty
Itah, Itta, Ittah, Iti, Itie, Ity, Itey, Itee, Itea, Itka

Italia (Italian) Woman from Italy
Italiah, Italea, Italeah, Itala, Italla, Itali, Italie, Italy, Italey, Italee, Italeigh

Itiah (Hebrew) One who is comforted by God
Itia, Iteah, Itea, Itiyah, Itiya, Ityah, Itya

Itica (Spanish) One who is eloquent
Iticah, Itika, Itikah, Iticka, Itickah, Ityca, Itycah, Ityka, Itykah, Itycka, Ityckah

Itidal (Arabic) One who is cautious
Itidalle, Itidall, Itidale

Itinsa (Hawaiian) From the waterfall
Itinsah, Itynsa, Itynsah

Ito (Japanese) A delicate woman

Itsaso (Basque) Woman of the ocean
Itasasso, Itassaso, Itassasso

Ituha (Native American) As sturdy as an oak
Ituhah, Itooha, Itoohah, Itouha, Itouhah

Itxaro (Basque) One who has hope
Itxarro

Itzel (Spanish) Form of Isabel, meaning "my God is bountiful"
Itzell, Itzele, Itzelle, Itzela, Itzella

Itzy (American) A lively woman
Itzey, Itzi, Itzie, Itzea, Itzee

Iuana (Welsh) God is gracious
Iuanah, Iuanna, Iuannah, Iuanne, Iuan, Iuann, Iuane

Iudita (Hawaiian) An affectionate woman
Iuditah, Iudyta, Iudytah, Iudeta, Iudetah

Iuginia (Hawaiian) Form of Eugenia, meaning "a wellborn woman"
Iuginiah, Iuginea, Iugineah, Iugynia, Iugyniah, Iugynea, Iugyneah, Iugenia, Iugeniah, Iugenea, Iugeneah

Iulaua (Hawaiian) One who is eloquent

Iulia (Latin) Form of Julia, meaning "one who is youthful; daughter of the sky"
Iuliah, Iulea, Iulea, Iulie, Iuli, Iuly, Iuley, Iulee, Iuleigh, Iulius, Iuliet, Iuliette

Iusitina (Hawaiian) Form of Justine, meaning "one who is just and upright"
Iusitinah, Iusiteena, Iusiteenah, Iusityna, Iusitynah, Iusiteana, Iusiteanah

Ivana (Slavice) Feminine form of Ivan; God is gracious
Iva, Ivah, Ivania, Ivanka, Ivanna, Ivanya, Ivanea, Ivane, Ivanne

Iverem (African) One who is favored by God

Iviana (American) One who is adorned
Ivianah, Ivianna, Iviannah, Ivianne, Iviane, Ivian, Ivyana, Ivyanna, Ivyanne, Ivyane, Ivyann

Ivisse (American) A graceful woman
Iviss, Ivise, Iviese, Ivysse, Ivyss, Ivyse, Ivease, Iveese

Ivonne (French) Form of Yvonne, meaning "a young archer"
Ivonn, Ivon, Ivone, Ivona, Ivonna, Ivette, Ivett, Ivet, Ivete, Ivetta, Iveta

Ivory (English) Having a creamy-white complexion; as precious as elephant tusks
Ivorie, Ivorine, Ivoreen, Ivorey, Ivoree, Ivori, Ivoryne, Ivorea, Ivoreah, Ivoreane

Ivria (Hebrew) From the opposite side of the river
Ivriah, Ivrea, Ivreah, Ivriya, Ivriyah

Ivy (English) Resembling the evergreen vining plant
Ivee, Ivey, Ivie, Ivalyn, Ivyanne, Ivi, Ivyane, Ivea, Iveah

Iwa (Japanese) Of strong character
Iwah

Iwalani (Hawaiian) Resembling a seagull in the sky
Iwalanie, Iwalany, Iwalaney, Iwalanee, Iwalanea

Iwilla (American) She shall rise
Iwillah, Iwilah, Iwila, Iwylla, Iwyllah, Iwyla, Iwylah

Iwona (Polish) Form of Yvonne, meaning "a young archer"
Iwonah, Iwonne, Iwone, Iwonna, Iwonn, Iwon

Ixchel (Mayan) The rainbow lady; in mythology, the goddess of the earth, moon, and healing
Ixchell, Ixchelle, Ixchela, Ixchella, Ixchal, Ixchall, Ixchalle, Ixchala, Ixchalla

Iyabo (African) The mother is home

Iyana (Hebrew) A sincere woman
Iyanah, Iyanna, Iyannah, Iyanne, Iyane, Iyan

Izanne (American) One who calms others
Izann, Izane, Izana, Izan, Izanna

Izar (Spanish) A starlike woman
Izare, Izarre, Izarr, Izarra, Izara, Izaria, Izarea

Izdihar (Arabic) A flourishing woman; blooming
Izdihare, Izdihara, Izdiharia, Izdiharea, Izdiharra, Izdiharre

Izebe (African) One who supports others
Izeby, Izebey, Izebee, Izebea, Izebi, Izebie

Izefia (African) A childless woman
Izefiah, Izefya, Izefiya, Izephia, Izefa, Izepha, Izefea, Izephea

Izegbe (African) One who was asked for
Izegby, Izegbey, Izegbee, Izegbea, Izegbi, Izegbie

Izellah (American) A princess; a devoted woman
Izella, Izela, Izelah

Izolde (Greek) One who is philosophical
Izold, Izolda

Izso (Hebrew) One who is saved by God
Izsa, Izsah, Isso, Issa

Izusa (Native American) Resembling the white stone
Izusah, Izussa, Izuza, Izuzza

Izzy (American) A fun-loving woman
Izzey, Izzi, Izzie, Izzee, Izzea

Jaakkina (Finnish) Feminine form of Jukka; God is gracious
Jakkina, Jaakkinah, Jaakina, Jakina, Jakyna, Jakeena, Jadeana

Jaala (Hebrew) Resembling a she-goat of the wild
Jaalah

Jaantje (Hebrew) A gift from heaven
Jantje

Jaasau (Hebrew) One who makes goods; a fabricator

Jabmen (Arabic) Woman with a high forehead
Jabmin, Jabman, Jabmon, Jabmun

Jacaranda (Latin) Resembling the tree with purple flowers
Jacarannda, Jacarranda, Jacarandah, Jacarandia, Jacarandea, Jakaranda, Jackaranda

Jacey (American) Form of Jacinda, meaning "resembling the hyacinth"
Jacee, Jacelyn, Jaci, Jacine, Jacy, Jaicee, Jaycee, Jacie, Jaycey, Jaycie, Jayci, J.C., Jacea, Jaycea

Jachan (Hebrew) Woman of sorrow; one who mourns
Jachane, Jachana, Jachanne, Jachann, Jachanna

Jaden (Hebrew / English) One who is thankful to God / form of Jade, meaning "resembling the green gemstone"
Jadine, Jadyn, Jadon, Jayden, Jadyne, Jaydyn, Jaydon, Jaydine, Jadin, Jaydin, Jaidyn, Jaedan, Jaeden, Jaedin, Jaedon, Jaedyn, Jaidan, Jaidin, Jaidon, Jaidyn, Jaydan

---

JACQUELINE

We suspected we were having a boy, so we had settled on a boy's name but not a girl's. Of course, we wound up having a girl. We stared at her for a while trying to determine who she was. We decided she looked like a Jackie. Now she fits her name perfectly, although I don't know if she'll ever grow into Jacqueline. —Irene, CA

Jacinda (Spanish) Resembling the hyacinth
Jacenda, Jacenia, Jacenta, Jacindia, Jacinna, Jacinta, Jacinth, Jacintha, Jacinthe, Jacinthia, Jacynth, Jacyntha, Jacynthe, Jacynthia, Jakinda, Jakinta, Jaikinda, Jaekinda

Jacoba (Hebrew) Feminine form of Jacob; she who supplants
Jacobetta, Jacobette, Jacobine, Jacobyna, Jakobina, Jakoba, Jakobetta, Jakobette, Jakobine, Jakobyna, Jacobyne, Jackoba, Jackobine, Jackobina, Jackobyne, Jackobyna, Jakobe, Jakobie

Jacqueline (French) Feminine form of Jacques; the supplanter
Jacalin, Jacalyn, Jacalynn, Jackalin, Jackalinne, Jackelyn, Jacketta, Jackette, Jacki, Jackie, Jacklin, Jacklyn, Jacklynne, Jackqueline, Jacky, Jaclin, Jaclyn, Jacolyn, Jacqi, Jacqlyn, Jacqualine, Jacqualyn, Jacquel, Jacquelean, Jacqueleen, Jacquelin, Jacquelina, Jacquella, Jacquelle, Jacquelyn, Jacquelyne, Jacquelynn, Jacquelynne, Jacquenetta, Jacquenette, Jacquetta, Jacquette, Jacqui, Jacquine, Jaculine, Jakleen, Jaklyn, Jaquelin, Jaqueline, Jaquelyn, Jaquelynn, Jaquith, Jaquenetta, Jaquetta

Jaddua (Hebrew) One who is well-known
Jadduah, Jadua, Jaduah

Jade (Spanish) Resembling the green gemstone
Jada, Jadeana, Jadee, Jadine, Jadira, Jadrian, Jadrienne, Jady, Jaeda, Jaida, Jaide, Jayda, Jayde, Jaydee, Jadea, Jaydea

Jadwige (Polish) One who is protected in battle
Jadwyge, Jadwig, Jadwyg, Jadwiga, Jadwyga, Jadriga, Jadryga, Jadreega

Jadzia (Polish) A princess; born into royalty
Jadziah, Jadzea, Jadzeah, Jadziya, Jadziyah, Jadzya, Jadzyah

Jae (English) Feminine form of Jay; resembling a jaybird
Jai, Jaelana, Jaeleah, Jaeleen, Jaelyn, Jaenelle, Jaenette, Jaya, Jaylee, Jayleen, Jaylene, Jaylynn, Jaye, Jay, Jaylea

Jael (Hebrew) Resembling a mountain goat
Jaella, Jaelle, Jayel, Jaela, Jaele, Jayil

Jaen (Hebrew) Resembling an ostrich
Jaena, Jaenia, Jaenea, Jaenne

Jaffa (Hebrew) A beautiful woman
Jaffah, Jafit, Jafita

Jaganmatri (Indian) Mother of nations
Jaganmatrie, Jaganmatree, Jaganmata, Jaganmatria, Jaganmatrea

Jagrati (Indian) Of the awakening
Jagratie, Jagraty, Jagratey, Jagratee, Jagratea

Jaha (African) One who has dignity
Jahah

Jahana (Iranian) Feminine form of Jahan; a woman of the world
Jahane, Jahania, Jahanea, Jahanna, Jahanne

Jahath (Hebrew) Recognizing the importance of a union
Jahathe, Jahatha

Jahaziah (Hebrew) The Lord's vision
Jahaziel, Jahazia, Jahazea, Jahazeah, Jahaziell, Jahazielle

Jahia (African) One who is widely known
Jahiah, Jahea, Jaheah, Jahiya, Jahiyah

Jahnavi (Indian) Woman from the river
Jahnavie, Janavi, Janavie, Jahnavee, Janavee, Jahnavea, Janavea, Jahnavy, Janavy, Jahnavey, Janavey

Jahzara (African) One who is blessed with power and wealth
Jahzarah, Jazara, Jazarra, Jazarah

Jaione (Basque) Refers to the Nativity

Jaira (Hebrew) Feminine form of Jairus; she who shines
Jaera, Jayra, Jairia, Jairea

Jairdan (American) One who educates others
Jardan, Jayrdan, Jaerdan

Jakayla (Native American) One who is crowned with laurel
Jakaela, Jakaila

Jakim (Hebrew) One who brings others together; the establisher
Jakima, Jakimah, Jakime, Jakyma, Jakeema, Jakeima, Jakiema, Jakeama

Jala (Arabic) Woman of clarity
Jalah, Jalla, Jallah

Jaleh (Persian) Born of the rain

Jalen (American) One who is calm; a healer
Jaelan, Jaelin, Jaelon, Jailin, Jaillen, Jaillin, Jailon, Jalan, Jalin, Jalon, Jayelan, Jaylen, Jayelen, Jaylan, Jaylon, Jaylonn, Jalena, Jalina, Jalona, Jalana, Jailene, Jailyn, Jalene, Jalynn, Jalyn

Jalia (American) A noble woman
Jaliah, Jalea, Jaleah

Jalila (Arabic) An important woman; one who is exalted
Jalilah, Jalyla, Jalylah, Jaleela, Jaleelah, Jalil, Jaleala, Jalealah

Jaliyah (English) A gift of God
Jaliya, Jaleeya, Jaleeyah, Jalieya, Jaleyah, Jalieyah, Jaleya, Jaleaya

Jam (American) One who is sweet

Jamaica (American) From the island of springs
Jamaeca, Jamaika, Jemaica, Jamika, Jamieka, Jameika, Jamyka, Jemayka, Jamaeka, Jemaeka

Jamari (French) A woman warrior
Jamarie, Jamary, Jamarey, Jamaree, Jamarea

Jameelah (Arabic) A beautiful and elegant lady
Jameela, Jamela, Jamelia, Jamilah, Jamila, Jamilia, Jamilla, Jamille, Jamelia, Jemila, Jemilla, Jemeela, Jemyla, Jameala, Jemeala

Jamie (Hebrew) Feminine form of James; she who supplants
Jaima, Jaime, Jaimee, Jaimelynn, Jaimey, Jaimi, Jaimie, Jaimy, Jama, Jamee, Jamei, Jamese, Jamey, Jami, Jamia, Jamielee, Jamilyn, Jammie, Jayme, Jaymee, Jaymie, Jaymi, Jamesina, Jameson, Jamison, Jamese, Jaimica, Jame, Jamea, Jaimea

Jamuna (Indian) From the sacred river
Jamoona, Jamunah, Jamoonah, Jamouna, Jamounah

Janae (Hebrew) God has answered our prayers
Janai, Janais, Janay, Janaya, Janaye, Janea, Jannae, Jeanae, Jeanay, Jeanay, Jenae, Jenai, Jenay, Jenee, Jennae, Jennay, Jinae, Jinnea

Janan (Arabic) Of the heart and soul

Jane (Hebrew) Feminine form of John; God is gracious
Jaina, Jaine, Jainee, Janey, Jana, Janae, Janaye, Jandy, Janeczka, Janeen, Janel, Janela, Janelba, Janella, Janelle, Janean, Janeane, Janee, Janene, Janerita, Janessa, Jayney, Jania, Janica, Janie, Janina, Janine, Janique, Janka, Janna, Jannel, Jannelle, Janney, Janny, Jany, Jayna, Jayne, Jaynell, Jayni, Jaynie, Jenda, Jenella, Jenelle, Jenica, Jeniece, Jeni, Jenie, Jensina, Jensine, Jess, Jinna, Jonella, Jonelle, Joni, Jonie, Jeena, Jiana, Jianna, Janecska, Jenina, Jenine, Jensen, Jaen, Jaena

Janeeva (American) Resembling the juniper
Janeevah, Janyva, Janyvah, Janeava, Janeavah, Janeva, Janevah

Janet (Scottish) Feminine form of John; God is gracious
Janeta, Janeth, Janett, Janetta, Janette, Janit, Jannet, Janneth, Janetta, Jannette, Janot, Jenetta, Jenette, Jennet, Jennette, Jinnet, Jinnett

Janis (English) Feminine form of John; God is gracious
Janice, Janeece, Janess, Janessa, Janesse, Janessia, Janicia, Janiece, Janique, Janise, Janiss, Jannice, Jannis, Janyce, Jency, Jenice, Jeniece, Jenise, Jennice, Janisa, Janys, Jannys

Jannat (Arabic) From the garden of heaven
Jannate, Jannata, Jannatia, Jannatea, Jennet, Jenneta, Jennetia, Jennetea

Janoah (Hebrew) A quiet and calm child
Janoa, Jonoah, Jonoa, Janowa, Janowah

January (Latin) A winter child; born during the month of January
Januarie, Januari, Januarey, Januaree, Januarea

Janya (Indian) A lively woman; one who gives life
Janyah, Janiya, Janiyah

Japera (African) One who gives thanks to God
Japerah, Japerra, Japiera, Japeira, Japyra

Jara (Slavic) Daughter born in spring

Jarah (Hebrew) A sweet and kind woman

Jardena (Spanish / Hebrew) From the garden / form of Jordan; of the down-flowing river
Jardina, Jardenah, Jardinah, Jardeena, Jardyna, Jardeina, Jardiena, Jardeana, Jardeenah, Jardynah, Jardeinah, Jardienah, Jardeanah

Jarina (Greek) One who works the earth; a farmer
Jarine, Jarinah, Jarineh, Jaryne, Jaryna, Jaryn, Jareena, Jareene

Jarita (Indian) A birdlike woman
Jaritah, Jareeta, Jareetah, Jaryta, Jarytah, Jarieta, Jarietah, Jareita, Jareitah, Jareata, Jareatah

Jarnsaxa (Norse) In mythology, the mother of Magni by Thor
Jarnsax, Jarnsaxe, Jarnsaxia, Jarnsaxea

Jarvia (German) Having great intelligence
Jarvinia, Jarviah, Jarvea, Jarveah, Jarviya, Jarvinea, Jarvina

Jasher (Hebrew) One who is righteous; upright
Jashiere, Jasheria, Jasherea, Jashera, Jashiera

Jasmine ○ (Persian) Resembling the climbing plant with fragrant flowers
Jaslyn, Jaslynn, Jasmeen, Jasmin, Jasmina, Jasminda, Jasmyn, Jasmyne, Jassamayn, Jazan, Jazmin, Jazmine, Jazmon, Jazmyn, Jazmyne, Jazzmin, Jazzmine, Jazzmon, Jazzmyn, Jazzmynn, Jasmyna, Jessamine, Jessamy, Jessamyn, Jasmeena, Jessimine, Jessimine

Jauhera (Arabic) As precious as a jewel
Jauherah, Jawahar, Jawahara, Jawaahar, Jawahare, Johari, Johara, Joharra, Joharie, Joharee

Jaunie (American) A brave and courteous woman
Jauni, Jaunee, Jauny, Jauney, Jaunea

Javana (Hebrew) Feminine form of Javan; woman from Greece
Javane, Javanna, Javanne, Javann

Javiera (Spanish) Feminine form of Xavier; owner of a new house; one who is bright
Javierah, Javyera, Javyerah, Javeira, Javeirah

Jaxine (American) Form of Jacinda, meaning "resembling the hyacinth"
Jaxin, Jaxyne, Jaxeen, Jaxyn, Jaxeene, Jax, Jaxi, Jaxie, Jaxee, Jaxea

Jaya (Hindi) A victorious woman; in Hinduism, one of the names of the wife of Shiva
Jayah

Jayanti (Indian) Feminine form of Jayant; a victorious woman
Jayantie, Jayantee, Jayanty, Jayantey, Jayantea

Jaydra (Arabic) Filled with goodness
Jaydrah, Jadra, Jadrah, Jaidra, Jaedra

Jayla (Arabic) One who is charitable
Jaylah, Jaila, Jaela

Jazzelle (American) One who is promised; influenced by the style of music
Jazelle, Jazzele, Jazzell, Jazele, Jazell, Jazzlyn, Jazzette, Jazlyn, Jazlynn, Jazzalyn, Jazzy, Jazz, Jaslynn

Jean (Hebrew) Feminine form of John; God is gracious
Jeanae, Jeanay, Jeane, Jeanee, Jeanelle, Jeanetta, Jeanette, Jeanice, Jeanie, Jeanna, Jehane, Jeanne, Jeana, Jeanine, Jeannine, Jeanea

Jearim (Hebrew) Woman from the woodland
Jearym, Jeareem, Jeaream

Jearl (American) Form of Pearl, meaning "a precious gem of the sea"
Jearla, Jearle, Jearlie, Jearly, Jearline, Jearlina, Jearlea, Jearli, Jearley, Jearlee, Jearleigh

Jela (Swahili) Born of the suffering father
Jelah, Jella, Jellah

Jelena (Russian) Form of Helen, meaning "the shining light"
Jalaina, Jalaine, Jalayna, Jalena, Jelina, Jelka, Jelaena

Jemima (Hebrew) Our little dove; in the Bible, the eldest of Job's daughters
Jemimah, Jamina, Jeminah, Jemmimah, Jemmie, Jemmy, Jem, Jemmi, Jemmey, Jemmee, Jemmea

Jemina (Hebrew) One who is listened to
Jeminah, Jemyna, Jemynah, Jemeena, Jemeenah, Jemeina, Jemeinah, Jemiena, Jemienah, Jemeana, Jemeanah

Jemma (English) Form of Gemma, meaning "precious jewel"
Jemmah, Jema, Jemah, Jemmalyn, Jemalyn, Jemmalynn, Jemalynn

JENNIFER

"My oldest daughter was three when I was expecting our second child, and when we asked her if it was going to be a boy or a girl, she always said, 'It's going to be a girl and we are going to name her Jennifer.' After hearing that so often, we got worn down—Jennifer she is." —Diane, IA

Jecoliah (Hebrew) All things are possible through the Lord
Jecolia, Jecolea, Jecoleah, Jecholia, Jekolia, Jecoliya, Jekoliya, Jekolea

Jedida (Hebrew) One who is greatly loved
Jedidah, Jedyda, Jedydah, Jedeeda, Jedeedah, Jeddida, Jedieda, Jediedah, Jedeida, Jededah, Jedeada, Jedeadah

Jehaleleel (Hebrew) One who praises God
Jehalelel, Jahaleleil, Jehaleliel, Jehalelyl, Jehaleleal

Jehan (Arabic) Resembling a beautiful flower; woman of the world
Jihan, Jyhan

Jehonadab (Hebrew) The Lord gives liberally
Jonadab

Jehosheba (Hebrew) An oath of the Lord
Jehoshebah, Jehoshyba, Jehosheeba, Jehosheiba, Jehoshieba, Jehosheaba

Jehucal (Hebrew) An able-bodied woman
Jehucale, Jucal, Jehucala

Jena (Arabic) Our little bird
Jenah

Jenavieve (English) Form of Genevieve, meaning "of the race of women; the white wave"
Jenevieve, Jennavieve, Jeneva, Jenneva

Jendayi (Egyptian) One who is thankful
Jendayie, Jendayey, Jendayee, Jendaya, Jendayia, Jendayea

Jendyose (Ugandan) An accomplishment of the mother
Jendyosa, Jendyosia, Jendyosea, Jendyosi, Jendyosie

Jeneil (American) A champion
Jeneile, Jeneel, Jeneele, Jeneal, Jeneale

Jenis (Hebrew) Form of Genesis, meaning "of the beginning"
Jenesis, Jennis, Jenesys

Jennifer ✪ ⚥ (Welsh) One who is fair; a
beautiful girl
*Jenefer, Jeni, Jenifer, Jeniffer, Jenn, Jennee,
Jenni, Jennica, Jennie, Jenniver, Jenny, Jen,
Jenalee, Jenalynn, Jenarae, Jeneen, Jenene,
Jenetta, Jeni, Jenica, Jenice, Jeniece, Jenika,
Jenise, Jenita, Jenna, Jennessa, Jenni, Jennie,
Jennika, Jennilee, Jennilyn, Jennis, Jennita,
Jennyann, Jennylee, Jinni, Jinny, Jenai,
Jenae, Jenay, Jenalyn, Jenaya, Jenara,
Jenibelle, Jennelle*

Jenski (English) One who comes home
Jenskie, Jensky, Jenskey, Jenskee, Jenskea

Jeorjia (American) Form of Georgia,
meaning "one who works the earth; a farmer"
*Jeorgia, Jeorja, Jorja, Jorjette, Jorgette,
Jorjeta, Jorjetta, Jorgete, Jorjete, Jorgeta,
Jorgetta*

Jera (American) A religious woman
Jerah, Jerra, Jerrah

Jeraldine (English) Form of Geraldine,
meaning "one who rules with the spear"
*Jeraldeen, Jeraldene, Jeraldine, Jeralee, Jere,
Jeri, Jerilene, Jerrie, Jerrileen, Jerroldeen,
Jerry, Jeralyn, Jenralyn, Jerelyn, Jerilynn,
Jerilyn, Jerrilyn, Jerrica*

Jeremia (Hebrew) Feminine form of
Jeremiah; the Lord is exalted
*Jeremea, Jerimia, Jerimea, Jeree, Jeremee,
Jeremie, Jeremiya*

Jereni (Slavic) One who is peaceful
Jerenie, Jereny, Jereney, Jerenee

Jerica (American) One who is strong; a tal-
ented ruler
*Jerika, Jerrica, Jerrika, Jericka, Jericha,
Jerricka, Jerricha*

Jeriel (Hebrew) God has witnessed
Jeriele, Jeriela, Jerielle, Jeriell, Jeriella

Jermaine (French) Woman from Germany
*Jermainaa, Jermane, Jermayne, Jermina,
Jermana, Jermayna, Jermaen, Jermaena*

Jersey (English) From one of the Channel
Islands
*Jersy, Jersee, Jersi, Jersie, Jerzey, Jerzy,
Jerzee, Jerzi, Jerzie, Jersea, Jerzea*

Jerusha (Hebrew) A faithful wife
Jerushah, Jeruscha, Jarusha, Jaruscha

Jessenia (Arabic) As delicate as a flower
*Jesseniah, Jasenia, Jesenia, Jesenya,
Jessenya, Jassenia, Jasenya, Jassenya*

Jessica ✪ ⚥ (Hebrew) The Lord sees all
*Jess, Jessa, Jessaca, Jessaka, Jessalin,
Jessalyn, Jesse, Jesseca, Jessey, Jessie, Jessika,
Jesirae, Jeslyn, Jessika, Jessicka, Jeziree,
Jessalynn, Jessamae, Jessana, Jessandra,
Jesselyn, Jezeree, Jessi, Jessilyn, Jessina,
Jesslyn, Jesslynn, Jessy, Jessye, Jesimae*

Jestina (Welsh) Feminine form of Justin;
one who is just and upright
*Jesstina, Jestine, Jestyna, Jesstyna,
Jestyne, Jesstyne, Jesteena, Jessteena,
Jesteene, Jessteene*

Jesusa (Spanish) Refers to the Virgin Mary
Jesusah, Josune

Jethetha (Hebrew) Feminine form of
Jetheth; a princess
Jethethia, Jethethea, Jethethiya

Jethra (Hebrew) Feminine form of Jethro;
the Lord's excellence; one who has plenty;
abudance
*Jethrah, Jethria, Jethrea, Jethriya, Jeth,
Jethe*

Jetje (Teutonic) Ruler of the house

Jetta (Danish) Resembling the jet-black lus-
trous gemstone
*Jette, Jett, Jeta, Jete, Jettie, Jetty, Jetti,
Jettey, Jettee, Jettea*

Jewel (French) One who is playful; resem-
bling a precious gem
*Jewell, Jewelle, Jewelyn, Jewelene,
Jewelisa, Jule, Jewella, Juelline*

Jezebel (Hebrew) One who is not exalted;
in the Bible, the queen of Israel punished
by God
*Jessabell, Jetzabel, Jezabel, Jezabella,
Jezebelle, Jezibel, Jezibelle, Jezybell,
Jezabella*

Jezreel (Hebrew) The Lord provides
*Jesreel, Jezreele, Jesreele, Jezreal, Jezreale,
Jesreal, Jesreale*

Jia Li (Chinese) One who is beautiful and
kind

Jie (Chinese) One who is pure; chaste

Jiera (Lithuanian) A lively woman
Jierah, Jyera, Jyerah, Jierra, Jyerra

Jifunza (African) A self-learner
Jifunzah, Jifoonza, Jifoonzah, Jifounza, Jifounzah

Jigisha (Indian) One who wants to learn
Jigishah, Jigysha, Jigyshah

Jiles (American) Resembling a young goat
Jyles

Jill (English) Form of Jillian, meaning "one who is youthful"
Jillet, Jil, Jilli, Jillie, Jilly, Jillyan, Jyl, Jyll, Jyllina, Jylina

Jillian (English) Form of Gillian, meaning "one who is youthful"
Jilian, Jiliana, Jillaine, Jillan, Jillana, Jillane, Jillanne, Jillayne, Jillene, Jillesa, Jilliana, Jilliane, Jilliann, Jillianna, Jillianne, Jillyan, Jillyanna, Jillyanne, Jyllina

Jimena (Spanish) One who is heard
Jimenah, Jymena, Jimeena, Jimyna, Jymeena, Jymyna

Jimmi (English) Feminine form of Jimmy; she who supplants
Jimi, Jimmie, Jimie, Jimmy, Jimmey, Jimmee, Jimmea, Jimy, Jimey, Jimee, Jimea

Jin (Japanese / Chinese) A superior woman / a golden child; one who is elegant

Jina (Swahili) The named one
Jinah

Jinelle (Welsh) Form of Genevieve, meaning "of the race of women; the white wave"
Jinell, Jinele, Jinel, Jynelle, Jynell, Jynele, Jynel

Jinx (Latin) One who performs charms or spells
Jynx, Jinxx, Jynxx

Jiselle (American) Form of Giselle, meaning "of God's promise; a hostage"
Jisell, Jisele, Jisela, Jizelle, Joselle, Jisella, Jizella, Jozelle, Josella, Jozella

Jiva (Hindi) In Hinduism, one's immortal essence
Jivah, Jyva, Jyvah

Jivanta (Indian) One who gives life
Jivantah, Jevanta, Javanta, Jevantah, Javantah

Jo (English) Feminine form of Joseph; God will add
Jobelle, Jobeth, Jodean, Jodelle, Joetta, Joette, Jolinda, Jolisa, Jolise, Jolissa, Jo-Marie, Jonetia, Joniece, Jonique, Jonisa, Joquise, Jorene, Josanna, Josanne, Jovelle

Joakima (Hebrew) Feminine form of Joachim; God will judge
Joachima, Joaquina, Joaquine, Joaquima

Joan (Hebrew) Feminine form of John; God is gracious
Joane, Joanie, Joannue, Jone, Jonee, Joni, Jonie, Jo, Joann, Jo-Ann, Joanne, Jo-Anne, Joeanne, Joeann, Joeanna, Joeanne, Johanna, Joanna, Johannah

Jobey (Hebrew) One who is persecuted
Joby, Jobie, Jobi, Jobee, Jobina, Jobyna, Jobeena, Jobea

Jocasta (Greek) In mythology, the queen of Thebes who married her son
Jocastah, Jokasta, Jokastah, Jockasta, Joccasta

Jocelyn ☺ (German / Latin) From the tribe of Gauts / one who is cheerful, happy
Jocelin, Jocelina, Jocelinda, Joceline, Jocelyne, Jocelynn, Jocelynne, Josalind, Josaline, Josalyn, Josalynn, Joscelin, Josceline, Joscelyn, Joselina, Joseline, Joselyn, Joselyne, Josiline, Josilyn, Joslin, Josline, Joslyn, Jossline, Josselyn, Josslyn, Jozlyn, Joss

Jochebed (Hebrew) God is her glory
Jochebedaa, Jochebedia, Jochebedea

Jocosa (Latin) One who is gleeful and always joking
Jocose, Jocosia, Jocosea

Joda (Hebrew) An ancestor of Christ

Jody (English) Form of Judith, meaning "woman from Judea"
Jodey, Jodi, Jodie, Jodee, Jodea

Joelle (Hebrew) Feminine form of Joel; Jehovah is God; God is willing
Joela, Joelin, Joell, Joella, Joellen, Joelliane, Joellin, Joelly, Joellyn, Joely, Joelynn, Joetta, Jowella, Jowelle

Johnna (English) Feminine form of John; God is gracious
Johna, Johnelle, Johnetta, Johnette, Johnna, Johnnie, Johnda, Johyna, Jonalyn, Jonalynn, Jonay, Jonell, Jonetta, Jonette, Jonita, Jonna, Jonni, Jonnah, Jonnie, Jonnelle

Jokim (Hebrew) Blessed by God
Jokima, Jokym, Jokyme, Jokeem, Jokimia, Jokimea, Joka, Jokeam, Jokeame

Jokmeam (Hebrew) From the gathering of people
Jokmime, Jokmym, Jokmeem

Jolan (Greek) Resembling a violet flower
Jola, Jolaine, Jolande, Jolanne, Jolanta, Jolantha, Jolandi, Jolanka, Jolanna, Jolana

Jolene (English) Feminine form of Joseph; God will add
Joeline, Joeleen, Joeline, Jolaine, Jolean, Joleen, Jolena, Jolina, Joline, Jolleen, Jollene, Jolyn, Jolyna, Jolyne, Jolynn

Jolie (French) A pretty young woman
Joly, Joely, Jolee, Joleigh, Joley, Joli, Joliet, Jolietta, Joliette, Jolea

Jones (English) From the family of John
Jonesy, Jonesi, Jonesie, Jonesee, Jonesey, Jonesea

Jonina (Israeli) Resembling a little dove
Joninah, Jonyna, Jonynah, Joneena, Joneenah, Jonine, Jonyne, Joneene, Jonati, Jonatie, Jonatee, Jonatey, Jonaty, Joneana, Joneanah

Jonquil (English) Resembling the flower
Jonquill, Jonquille, Jonquile, Jonquila, Jonquilla

Joo-eun (Korean) Resembling a silver pearl

Jorah (Hebrew) Resembling an autumn rose
Jora

Jord (Norse) In mythology, goddess of the earth
Jorde

Jordan ♀ (Hebrew) Of the down-flowing river; in the Bible, the river where Jesus was baptized
Jardena, Johrdan, Jordain, Jordaine, Jordana, Jordane, Jordanka, Jordann, Jordanna, Jordanne, Jorden, Jordena, Jordenn, Jordie, Jordin, Jordyn, Jordynn, Jorey, Jori, Jorie, Jorrdan, Jorry, Jourdan, Jourdain

Jorgina (English) Form of Georgina, meaning "one who works the earth; a farmer"
Jorgeanne, Jorgelina, Jorjana, Jorjina, Jorjanna, Jorcina, Jorcyna, Jorceena, Jorciena, Jorceina, Jory

Jorryn (American) Loved by God
Jorran, Jorren, Jorron, Jorrun

Jorunn (Norse) One who loves horses

Josephine (Hebrew) Feminine form of Joseph; God will add
Josefa, Josefena, Josefene, Josefina, Josefine, Josepha, Josephe, Josephene, Josephina, Josephyna, Josephyna, Josephyne, Josette, Josetta, Joxepa, Josebe, Jose, Josie, Josee, Jozsa, Josina

Journey (American) One who likes to travel
Journy, Journi, Journie, Journee, Journye, Journea

Jovana (Spanish) Feminine form of Jovian; daughter of the sky
Jeovana, Jeovanna, Jovanna, Jovena, Jovianne, Jovina, Jovita, Joviana

Joy (Latin) A delight; one who brings pleasure to others
Jioia, Jioya, Joi, Joia, Joie, Joya, Joyann, Joyanna, Joyanne, Joye, Joyelle, Joyela, Joyella, Joyous, Joylyn

Joyce (English) One who brings joy to others
Joice, Joyceanne, Joycelyn, Joycelynn, Joyse, Joyceta

Jozachar (Hebrew) God has remembered
Jozachare, Jozachara, Jozacharia, Jozacharea

Juana (Spanish) Feminine form of Juan; God is gracious
Juanita, Janita, Juanetta, Juanisha, Juniata, Junita, Juwaneeta, Juwanita, Juandalynn

Juba (African) Born on a Monday
Jubah, Jubba, Jubia, Jubea

Jubilee (Hebrew) One who rejoices; a ram's horn
Jubileigh, Jubilie, Jubili, Jubily, Jubiley, Jubalee, Jubaleigh, Jubaley, Jubaly, Jubali, Jubalie, Jubalea, Jubilea

J

Juci (Hebrew) One who is praised
Jucika, Jucie, Jucee, Jucye, Jutka, Jucea, Jucey, Jucy

Juda (Arabic) Filled with goodness
Judah

Judith (Hebrew) Woman from Judea
Judithe, Juditha, Judeena, Judeana, Judyth, Judit, Judytha, Judita, Judite, Jutka, Jucika, Jutta, Judythe

Judy (Hebrew) Form of Judith, meaning "woman from Judea"
Judee, Judey, Judi, Judie, Judye, Judea

Juhi (Indian) Resembling a fragrant flower
Jui

Juin (French) Born during the month of June

Juji (African) One who is greatly loved
Jujie, Jujy, Jujey, Jujee, Jujea

Julia ☉ (Latin) One who is youthful; daughter of the sky
Jiulia, Joleta, Joletta, Jolette, Julaine, Julayna, Julee, Juleen, Julena, Juley, Juli, Juliaeta, Juliaetta, Juliana, Juliane, Juliann, Julianne, Julie, Julienne, Juliet, Julieta, Julietta, Juliette, Julina, Juline, Julinka, Juliska, Julissa, Julita, Julitta, Julyana, Julyanna, Julyet, Julyetta, Julyette, Julyne, Jooley, Joolie, Julisa, Julisha, Julyssa, Jolyon, Julcsa, Julene, Jules

July (Latin) Form of Julia, meaning "one who is youthful; daughter of the sky"; born during the month of July
Julye

Jumanah (Arabic) Resembling a silver pearl
Jumana, Jumanna, Jumannah

Jumoke (African) A child who is loved by all

June (Latin) One who is youthful; born during the month of June
Junae, Junel, Junelle, Junette, Junita, Junia

Juniper (Latin) Resembling the evergreen shrub with berries
Junyper, Junipyre, Junypyre

Juno (Latin) In mythology, queen of the heavens and goddess of marriage and women
Junot, Juneau, Juneaux

Justice (English) One who upholds moral rightness and fairness
Justyce, Justiss, Justyss, Justis, Justus, Justise

Justine (Latin) Feminine form of Justin; one who is just and upright
Justa, Justeen, Justeene, Justene, Justie, Justina, Justinn, Justy, Justyna, Justyne, Justeena, Justyna, Justea

Juturna (Latin) In mythology, goddess of fountains and springs
Jutorna, Jutourna

Juventas (Latin) In mythology, goddess of youth

Jwahir (African) The golden woman
Jwahyr, Jwaheer, Jwahear

Jyoti (Indian) Born of the light
Jyotika, Jyotis, Jyotie, Jyoty, Jyotey, Jyotee, Jyotea

Jyotsna (Indian) Woman of the moonlight

Kabibe (African) A petite woman
Kabybe

Kabira (African) One who is powerful
Kabirah, Kabyra, Kabyrah, Kabeera, Kabeerah, Kabeira, Kabeirah, Kabiera, Kabierah, Kabeara, Kabearah

Kacela (African) A great huntress
Kacelah, Kacella, Kacellah

Kachina (Native American) A spiritual dancer
Kachine, Kachinah, Kachineh, Kachyna, Kacheena, Kachynah, Kacheenah, Kacheana, Kacheanah

Kacondra (American) One who is bold
Kacondrah, Kacondria, Kacondriah, Kacondrea, Kacondreah, Kaecondra, Kaycondra, Kakondra, Kaekondra, Kaykondra

Kadence (American) Rhythmic and melodious; a musical woman
Kadian, Kadienne, Kadianne, Kadiene, Kaydence, Kaedence, Kadense, Kaydense, Kaedense

Kadin (Arabic) A beloved companion
Kadyn, Kadan, Kaden, Kadon, Kadun, Kaedin, Kaeden, Kaydin, Kayden

Kadisha (Hebrew) A holy woman; one who is religious
Kadishah, Kadysha, Kadeesha, Kadiesha, Kadeasha, Kadyshah, Kadeeshah, Kadieshah, Kadeashah

Kaede (Japanese) Resembling a maple leaf
Kaide, Kayde

Kaelyn (English) A beautiful girl from the meadow
Kaelynn, Kaelynne, Kaelin, Kailyn, Kaylyn, Kaelinn, Kaelinne

Kailasa (Indian) From the silver mountain
Kailasah, Kailassa, Kaylasa, Kaelasa, Kailas, Kailase

Kaimi (Polynesian) The seeker; one who searches
Kaimie, Kaimy, Kaimey, Kaimee, Kaimea

Kainda (African) The daughter of a great hunter
Kaindah, Kaynda, Kaenda, Kayndah, Kaendah

Kairos (Greek) Woman of opportunity
Kayros, Kaeros

Kaiya (Japanese) A forgiving woman
Kaiyo, Kaeya, Kaeyo

KAYLA

We named our daughter Kayla because the name Kay is so prominent in our family. Her paternal grandmother, maternal grandmother, and myself, her mother, all have the middle name of Kay. — Melissa, IA

K

Kafi (African) A quiet child; one who is well-behaved
Kaffi, Kafie, Kafy, Kafey, Kafee, Kaffy, Kaffie, Kaffey, Kaffee, Kafea, Kaffea

Kagami (Japanese) Displaying one's true image
Kagamie, Kagamy, Kagamey, Kagamee, Kagamea

Kai (Hawaiian) Woman of the sea
Kaia

Kaida (Japanese) Resembling a small dragon
Kaidah, Kaeda, Kayda, Kada, Kaedah, Kaydah, Kadah

Kaila ✿ (Hebrew) Crowned with laurel
*Kailah, **Kayla**, Kailan, Kaleigh, Kalen, Kaley, Kalie, Kalin, Kalyn, Kaela, Kaelee, Kaeleigh, Kaeley, Kaelene, Kaeli, Kaelie, Kaelah, Kaylah, Kayle, Kailene, Kailee, Kailey, Kaili, Kailyn, Kailynne, Kailin, Kalan, Kalea, Kalee, Kahli, Kalei, Kalia, Kaleah, Kalynn, Kaylan, Kaylana, Kaylin, Kaylen, Kayleah, Kaylea, **Kaylee**, Kayleigh, Kayley, Kayli, Kaylie, Kayleen, Kaylene, Kaylei, Kaylynn, Kaylyn, Keala*

Kailani (Hawaiian) Of the sky and sea
Kailanie, Kaylani, Kaylanie, Kaelani, Kaelanie, Kailany, Kaylany, Kailaney, Kaylaney, Kailanee, Kaylanee, Kailanea, Kaylanea, Kaelany, Kaelaney, Kaelanee, Kaelanea

Kajal (Indian) A woman with appealing eyes

Kakawangwa (Native American) A bitter woman

Kakra (Egyptian) The younger of twins
Kakrah

Kala (Arabic / Hawaiian) A moment in time / form of Sarah, meaning "princess; lady"
Kalah, Kalla, Kallah

Kalama (Hawaiian) Resembling a flaming torch
Kalamah, Kalamia, Kalamiah, Kalamea, Kalameah

Kalani (Hawaiian) From the heavens
Kalanie, Kalany, Kalaney, Kalanee, Kaloni, Kalonie, Kalonee, Kalony, Kaloney, Keilana, Keilani, Kalanea, Kalonea

Kalanit (Hebrew) Resembling a flower

Kaleen (Slavic) Resembling a delicate flower
Kaleena, Kaline, Kalynne, Kalyne, Kalina, Kalyna, Kaleene, Kalene, Kalena, Kaleane, Kaleana

Kalet (French) Having beautiful energy
Kalett, Kalete, Kalette, Kalay, Kalaye

Kali (Hindi) The dark one; in Hinduism, a destructive force

Kalidas (Greek) The most beautiful woman
Kalydas, Kaleedas, Kaleidas, Kaliedas, Kaleadas

Kalifa (Somali) A chaste and holy woman
Kalifah, Kalyfa, Kalyfah, Kaleefa, Kaleefah, Kalipha, Kalypha, Kaleepha, Kaleafa, Kaleafah, Kaleapha

Kalika (Greek / Arabic) Resembling a rosebud; one who is dearly loved
Kalikah, Kalyka, Kalykah, Kaleeka, Kaleekah, Kalica, Kalicca, Kalyca, Kaleeca, Kaleaka, Kaleakah

Kalilah (Arabic) A darling girl; sweetheart
Kalila, Kaleila, Kaleyla, Kaleela, Kaleilah, Kaleylah, Kaleelah, Kaliyah, Kaliya, Kaleala, Kalealah

Kalima (Arabic) An eloquent speaker
Kalimah, Kalyma, Kaleema, Kallima, Kalleema, Kallyma, Kaleama, Kalleama

Kalinda (Indian) Of the sun
Kalindah, Kalynda, Kalinde, Kalindeh, Kalindi, Kalindie, Kalyndi, Kalyndie, Kalindee, Kalyndee

Kalisha (American) A beautiful and caring woman
Kalishah, Kalysha, Kalyshah, Kaliesha, Kalieshah, Kaleisha, Kaleishah, Kaleesha, Kaleeshah, Kaleasha, Kaleashah

Kallan (Scandinavian / Gaelic) Of the flowing water / powerful in battle

Kallie (English) A beautiful girl
Kalli, Kallita, Kally, Kalley, Kallee, Kalleigh, Kallea, Kalleah

Kalliope (Greek) Having a beautiful voice; in mythology, the muse of epic poetry
Kalliopee, Kalliopy, Kalliopi, Kalliopie, Kaliope, Kaliopi, Kaliopie, Kaliopy, Kaliopee, Kalliopea, Kalipea

Kallisto (Greek) The most beautiful; in mythology, a nymph who was changed into a she-bear
Kallista, Kalisto, Kalista, Kalysta, Kalysto, Kallysto, Kallysta

Kalma (Finnish) In mythology, goddess of the dead

Kalonice (Greek) A victorious beauty
Kalonyce, Kaloneece, Kaloneace, Kaloniece, Kaloneice

Kalpana (Indian) Having a great imagination
Kalpanah, Kalpanna, Kalpannah

Kalwa (Finnish) A heroine

Kalyan (Indian) A beautiful and auspicious woman
Kalyane, Kalyanne, Kalyann, Kaylana, Kaylanna, Kalliyan, Kaliyan, Kaliyane, Kaliyanne, Kalliyane

Kama (Indian) One who loves and is loved
Kamah, Kamma, Kammah

Kamala (Arabic) A woman of perfection
Kamalah, Kammala, Kamalla

Kamali (Rhodesian) Having divine protection
Kamalie, Kamalli, Kamaly, Kamaley, Kamalee, Kamaleigh, Kamalea, Kamaleah

Kamana (Indian) One who is desired
Kamanah, Kammana, Kamanna, Kamna

Kamaria (African) Of the moon
Kamariah, Kamarea, Kamareah, Kamariya, Kamariyah

Kambiri (African) Newest addition to the family
Kambirie, Kambiry, Kambyry, Kambiree, Kambirea, Kambyree, Kambyrea, Kambyri

Kambo (African) A hardworking woman

Kambria (English) A woman of Wales
Kambriah, Kambreea, Kambrea, Kambriya

Kamea (Hawaiian) The one and only; precious one
Kameo

Kameko (Japanese) A turtle child; having a long life
Kamyko, Kamiko

Kameron (English) Form of Cameron, meaning "having a crooked nose"
Kamerin, Kameryn, Kamrin, Kamron, Kamryn, Kamren, Kameren, Kamran, Kameran

Kamilah (Arabic / Italian) The perfect one / form of Camilla, meaning "ceremonial attendant; a noble virgin"
Kamila, Kamilla, Kamillia, Kamille, Kamelia, Kamelea, Kamilia, Kamilea, Kami, Kamili, Kamlyn, Kammi, Kammie, Kamiila, Kamillra, Kamikla, Kamela, Kamella

Kamin (Indian) A joyful child
Kamen, Kamon, Kaman

Kamyra (American) Surrounded by light
Kamira, Kamera, Kamiera, Kameira, Kameera, Kameara

Kana (Japanese) A powerful woman

Kanan (Indian) From the garden

Kanani (Hawaiian) The beautiful girl
Kananie, Kanany, Kananey, Kananni, Kananee, Kananea, Kananeah

Kanara (Hebrew) Resembling a small bird
Kanarah, Kanarra, Kanarrah

Kanda (Native American) A magical woman
Kandah

Kandace (English) Form of Candace, meaning "a queen / one who is white and glowing"
Kandee, Kandi, Kandice, Kandis, Kandiss, Kandy, Kandyce, Kandys, Kandyss, Kandake, Kandie, Kandey, Kandea

Kande (African) The firstborn daughter

Kandra (American) A shining woman
Kandrah

Kane (Irish) A warrior woman ready for battle
Kaine, Kayne, Kaene, Kain, Kayn, Kaen

Kaneesha (American) A dark-skinned beauty
Kaneisha, Kaniesha, Kaneasha, Kanesha, Kanisha, Kanysha

Kanga (Native American) Resembling a raven

Kanika (African) A dark, beautiful woman
Kanikah, Kanyka, Kanicka, Kanycka, Kaneeka, Kaneecka, Kaneaka, Kaneacka

Kaniz (Arabic) A servant girl
Kaneez, Kanyz

Kannitha (Vietnamese) An angelic woman
Kannytha, Kanitha, Kanytha

Kanoni (African) Resembling a little bird
Kanonni, Kanonie, Kanony, Kanoney, Kanonee, Kanonea

Kansas (Native American) Of the south wind people; from the state of Kansas

Kantha (Indian) A delicate woman
Kanthah, Kanthe, Kantheh, Kanthia, Kanthia, Kanthea, Kantheah, Kanthiya, Kanthiyah, Kanthya, Kanthyah

Kanti (Native American) One who sings beautifully
Kantie, Kanty, Kantey, Kantee, Kantea

Kanya (Thai) A young girl; a virgin

Kaoru (Japanese) A fragrant girl
Kaori

Kaprice (English) Form of Caprice, meaning "one who is impulsive and unpredictable"
Kapricia, Kaprisha, Kapryce, Kaprycia, Kaprysha, Kapri, Kaprie, Kapry, Kaprey, Kapree, Kaprea, Kaprise, Kapryse, Kaprece, Kaprese, Kapreese, Kapreece, Kapreace, Kaprease

Kapuki (African) The firstborn daughter
Kapukie, Kapuky, Kapukey, Kapukee, Kapukea

Kara (Greek / Italian / Gaelic) One who is pure / dearly loved / a good friend
Karah, Karalee, Karalie, Karalyn, Karalynn, Karrah, Karra, Khara, Kahra

Karasi (African) Full of wisdom and life
Karasie, Karasy, Karasey, Karasee, Karasea

Karbie (American) An energetic woman
Karbi, Karby, Karbey, Karbee, Karbea

Karcsi (French) A joyful singer
Karcsie, Karcsy, Karcsey, Karcsee, Karcsea

Karen (Greek) Form of Katherine, meaning "one who is pure; virginal"
Karan, Karena, Kariana, Kariann, Karianna, Karianne, Karin, Karina, Karine, Karon, Karren, Karrin, Karyn, Karna, Keran, Keren, Keryn, Kerin, Kerryn, Kerrin

Karida (Arabic) A virgin; an untouched woman
Karidah, Karyda, Kareeda, Kareyda, Karieda, Kareada

Karima (Arabic) Feminine form of Karim; one who is generous and noble
Karimah, Kareema, Karyma, Kareama

K

Karina (Scandinavian, Russian) One who is dear and pure
Karinah, Kareena, Karyna, Kareana, Kariena, Kareina

Karisma (English) Form of Charisma, meaning "blessed with charm"
Kharisma, Karizma, Kharizma

Karissa (Greek) Filled with grace and kindess; very dear
Karisa, Karyssa, Karysa, Karessa, Karesa, Karis, Karise

Karla (German) Feminine form of Karl; a small, strong woman
Karly, Karli, Karlie, Karleigh, Karlee, Karley, Karlin, Karlyn, Karlina, Karline, Karleen, Karlen, Karlene, Karlesha, Karlysha, Karlea

Karma (Indian) One's actions determine one's destiny
Karmah

Karmel (Latin) Form of Carmel, meaning "of the fruitful orchard"
Karmelle, Karmell, Karmele, Karmela, Karmella

Karmelit (Hebrew) Of God's vineyard
Karmelita, Kannelite, Karmelitah, Karmelyte, Karmelyta, Karmelite, Karmit

Karmen (Latin) Form of Carmen, meaning "a beautiful song"
Karman, Karmin, Karmon, Karmine, Karmia, Karmina, Karmita, Karmyn

Karmiti (Native American) From the trees
Karmitie, Karmity, Karmitey, Karmitee, Karmyty, Karmyti, Karmytie, Karmytee, Karmitea, Karmytea

Karnesha (American) A feisty woman
Karneshah, Karnisha, Karnishah, Karnysha, Karnyshah

Karol (English) Form of Carol, meaning "a joyous song; a small, strong woman"
Karola, Karole, Karolle, Karolla, Karoly, Karoli, Karolie, Karolee, Karoleigh, Karel, Karal, Karil

Karoline (English) Form of Caroline, meaning "a joyous song; a small, strong woman"
Karolina, Karolinah, Karolyne, Karrie, Karie, Karri, Kari, Karry, Kary, Karlotta, Karee, Karielle

Karrington (English) One who is admired
Karington, Karryngton, Karyngton

Karsen (American) Feminine form of Carson; from the swamp
Karson, Karsin, Karsan, Karsyn

Karsten (Greek) The anointed one
Karstin, Karstine, Karstyn, Karston, Karstan, Kiersten, Keirsten

Karuna (Indian) A compassionate woman
Karunah, Karoona, Karoonah, Karouna, Karounah

Karyan (Armenian) The dark one

Kasen (Scandinavian) One who is pure; chaste
Kasin, Kasyn, Kasan, Kason, Kasienka

Kasey (Irish) Form of Casey, meaning "a vigilant woman"
Kacie, Kaci, Kacy, KC, Kacee, Kacey, Kasie, Kasi, Kasy, Kasee, Kacia, Kacea, Kayce, Kayci, Kaycie, Kaycee, Kaesha, Kasia, Kasea, Kaycea

Kashawna (American) One who enjoys debate
Kashawn, Kaseana, Kasean, Kashaun, Kashauna, Kashona, Kashonna

Kashmir (Sanskrit) From the state in India
Kashmira, Kasha, Kashmeer, Kazmir, Kazmira, Kazmeer, Kazhmir

Kashonda (American) A dramatic woman
Kashondah, Kashaunda, Kashaundah, Kashawnda, Kashawndah, Kashanda, Kashandah

Kashondra (American) A bright woman
Kashawndra, Kaseandra, Kashaundra, Kashandra, Kashondre, Kachaundra, Kachondra

Kasi (Indian) From the holy city; shining

Kasinda (African) Daughter born to a family with twins
Kasindah, Kasynda, Kasenda

Kasmira (Slavice) A peacemaker
Kasmirah, Kasmeera, Kasmeerah, Kasmyra, Kasmyrah, Kazmira, Kazmirah, Kazmyrah, Kazmyra, Kazmeera, Kazmeerah

Kassandra (English) Form of Cassandra, meaning "an unheeded prophetess"
Kassandrah, Kasandra, Kasaundra, Kassondra, Kassi, Kassia, Kassie, Kassy

Kassidy (English) Form of Cassidy, meaning "curly-haired girl"
Kassidey, Kassidi, Kassidie, Kassidee, Kasidy, Kasidey, Kasidi, Kasidie, Kasidee, Kassidea, Kasidea

Katriel (Hebrew) Crowned by God
Katriele, Katrielle, Katriell, Katriela, Katriella

Kauket (Egyptian) In mythology, an ancient goddess
Keket

KATIE

Our first daughter is Katie Jane. She is not Katherine or Kathleen, because I wanted her "official" first name to be what she was called on a regular basis. But I do end up explaining that it is not a nickname, which kind of defeats the purpose. She also gets called Kate quite often, which frustrates her and me. —Jane, IL

Kasumi (Japanese) From the mist
Kasumie, Kasume, Kasumy, Kasumey, Kasumee, Kasumea

Kataniya (Hebrew) A young girl
Kataniyah, Katanya, Katanyah

Katchi (American) A sassy woman
Katchie, Katchy, Katchey, Katchee, Katchea

Katera (American) One who celebrates
Katerah, Katerra, Katerrah, Katura, Katurah, Katurra, Katurrah

Katherine ♀ (Greek) Form of Catherine, meaning "one who is pure; virginal"
Katharine, Katharyn, Kathy, Kathleen, Katheryn, Kathie, Kathrine, Kathryn, Kathryne, Kaythrynn, Kady, Kadie, Kaethe, Kaira, Kaisa, Kaitlin, Kaitlan, Kaitleen, Kaitlyn, Kaitlynn, Kaska, Kat, Katherina, Kata, Katakin, Katalin, Katalina, Katalyn, Katanyna, Katarina, Katarin, Katarzyna, Katchen, Kate, Katelin, Kateline, Katelinn, Katelyn, Katelynn, Katen, Katerina, Kath, Kathe, Kathelyn, Kathleena, Kathlene, Kathlynn, Kathrina, Kati, Katia, Katica, Katie, Katilyn, Katine, Katinka, Katiya, Katja, Katle, Katlin, Katina, Katoka, Katri, Katria, Katriane, Katriana, Katrien, Katrikki, Katrin, Katrina, Katrine, Katrya, Katy, Katya, Katyenka, Katyuska, Kayiyn, Kaysa, Kolina, Koline, Kolena, Kolene, Koleyna, Kethryn, Kiska, Kitlyn

Kathlaya (American) A stylish woman

Katima (American) A daughter with power
Katimah, Kateema, Katyma, Katiema, Kateima, Kateama

Katrice (American) A graceful woman
Katryce, Katriece, Katreice, Katreace, Katrise, Katryse, Katriese, Katreise, Katrease

Kaula (Polynesian) Child of the heavens

Kaulana (Hawaiian) A well-known young woman
Kaulanah, Kaulanna, Kaulannah, Kaulanne, Kaulane

Kaveri (Indian) From the sacred river
Kaverie, Kauveri, Kauverie, Kavery, Kaverey, Kaveree, Kaverea, Kauvery, Kauverey, Kauveree, Kauverea

Kavi (Indian) A great poetess
Kavita, Kavindra, Kavie, Kavy, Kavey, Kavee, Kavea

Kavinli (American) One who is eager
Kavinlie, Kavinly, Kavinley, Kavinlee, Kavinlea, Kavinleigh

Kawthar (Arabic) From the river in paradise
Kawthare, Kawthara, Kawtharr

Kay (English / Greek) The keeper of the keys / form of Katherine, meaning "one who is pure; virginal"
Kaye, Kae, Kai, Kaie, Kaya, Kayana, Kayane, Kayanna, Kayann

Kayin (African) A long-awaited daughter
Kayen, Kayan, Kayon

Keahi (Hawaiian) A fiery woman
Keahie, Keahy, Keahey, Keahee, Keahea

Keana (Irish) Feminine form of Keane; of an ancient family
Keanna, Kiana, Kianna, Kyana, Kyanna, Keene, Keen, Kean, Keena, Keenat, Keiana, Keana, Kinnat

Keanu (Hawaiian) Resembling a cool mountain breeze

Kearney (Irish) The winner
Kearny, Kearni, Kearnie, Kearnee, Kearnea

Keaton (English) From a shed town
Keatan, Keatyn, Keatin, Keatun

Keavy (Irish) A lovely and graceful girl
Keavey, Keavi, Keavie, Keavee, Keavea

Kedma (Hebrew) Woman of the East

Keegan (Gaelic) Small and fiery woman
Keygan, Keigan, Kiegan, Kegan, Keagan

Keegsquaw (Native American) One who
is chaste; a virgin

Keelan (Irish) A slender and beautiful
woman
*Keylan, Keilan, Kielan, Kelan, Kealan,
Keelia*

Keisha (American) The favorite child; form
of Kezia, meaning "of the spice tree"
*Keishla, Keishah, Kecia, Kesha, Keysha,
Keesha, Kiesha, Keshia, Keishia, Keasha,
Keashia*

Keitha (Scottish) Feminine form of Keith;
woman of the wood
*Keetha, Keytha, Kietha, Keita, Kieta,
Keeltie, Keelti, Keeltey, Keeltee, Keelty,
Keeltea*

Kekona (Hawaiian) The second-born child

Kelby (Gaelic) From the waters
*Kelbey, Kelbi, Kelbie, Kelbee, Kelda,
Keldah, Kelbea*

Kelilah (Hebrew) A victorious woman
Kelila, Kelula, Kelulah, Kelyla, Kelylah

KEIRA

We wanted a name that was not too common, but not too absurd. Since I'm a teacher, it also had
to be a name that didn't conjure up any bad memories from past students. We love her name, but
lots of people pronounce it wrong, and if they aren't saying it wrong they are spelling it wrong! —
Jill, MD

Keenan (Irish) A small woman
Keanan, Keynan, Keinan, Kienan

Keeya (African) Resembling a flower
Keeyah, Kieya, Keiya, Keyya

Kefira (Hebrew) Resembling a young
lioness
*Kefirah, Kefiera, Kefeira, Kefeera, Kefyra,
Kephira, Kepheera, Kepheira, Kephiera,
Kephyra, Kepheara, Kefeara*

Kehinde (African) The second-born of twins
Kehindeh, Kehynde, Kehyndeh

Keidra (American) One who is alert; aware
*Keidrah, Kiedra, Kiedrah, Keadra, Keadrah,
Keydra, Keydrah, Keedra, Keedrah*

Keiki (Hawaiian) A precious baby;
resembling an orchid
*Kiki, Kyki, Keeki, Keki, Keyki, Kaki,
Kaeki, Kayki, Kaiki*

Keiko (Japanese) A respectful and
well-behaved child
*Kiko, Kyko, Keeko, Kako, Kayko, Kaeko,
Kaiko*

Kelis (American) A beautiful and talented
woman
Keliss, Kelisse, Kelys, Kelyss, Kelysse

Kellen (Gaelic) A slender, beautiful, and
powerful woman
Kellan, Kellyn, Kellin, Kellon, Kellun

Keller (Irish) One who is daring
Kellers, Kellar, Kellir, Kellyr

Kelly (Irish) A lively and bright-headed
woman
*Kelley, Kelli, Kellie, Kellee, Kelleigh, Kellye,
Keely, Keelie, Keeley, Keelyn, Keilah, Keila,
Keelia, Keelin, Keelyn, Kellyanne, Kella,
Keelea, Keeleigh, Keelee, Kellea*

Kelsey (English) From the island of ships;
of the ship's victory
*Kelsie, Kelcey, Kelcie, Kelcy, Kellsie, Kelsa,
Kelsea, Kelsee, Kelsi, Kelsy, Kellsey, Kelcea,
Kelcee*

Kember (American) A fun-loving woman

Kemella (American) One who is self-assured
Kemela, Kemell, Kemele, Kemel, Kemelle

Kemena (Spanish) Having great strength
Kemina, Kemeena, Kemyna

Kempley (English) From the meadow
Kemply, Kempli, Kemplie, Kemplee, Kempleigh, Kemplea, Kempleah

Kenae (Irish) A good-looking woman
Kenai, Kenay, Kenaye, Kennae, Kennai, Kennay, Kennaye

Kendall (Welsh) From the royal valley
Kendal, Kendyl, Kendahl, Kindall, Kyndal, Kyndall, Kenda

Kendi (African) One who is dearly loved
Kendie, Kendee, Kendy, Kendey, Kendea

Kendis (American) A pure woman; one who is chaste
Kendiss, Kendisse, Kendys, Kendyss, Kendysse

Kendra (English) Feminine form of Kendrick; having royal power; from the high hill
Kendrah, Kendria, Kendrea, Kindra, Kindria

Kenley (English) From the royal meadow
Kenlie, Kenli, Kenly, Kenlee, Kenleigh, Kenlea

Kenna (Celtic) Feminine form of Kenneth; a beauty; born of fire

Kennedy (Gaelic) A helmeted chief
Kennedi, Kennedie, Kennedey, Kennedee, Kenadia, Kenadie, Kenadi, Kenady, Kenadey, Kenadee, Kennedea, Kenadea

Kennice (English) A beautiful and gracious woman
Kennis, Kenice, Keniss, Kenys, Kennita, Kenita, Kenneece, Keneece, Kenyce, Kenneeta, Keneeta, Kennocha, Kenisha, Keniesha, Keneesha, Kenysha, Keneisha

Kensington (English) A brash lady
Kensyngton, Kensingtyn, Kinsington, Kinsyngton, Kinsingtyn

Kentucky (Native American) From the land of tomorrow; from the state of Kentucky
Kentucki, Kentuckie, Kentuckey, Kentuckee, Kentuckea

Kenwei (Arabic) Resembling a water lily

Kenya (African) An innocent; from the country of Kenya
Kenyatta, Kenia, Keniya, Kennya

Kenyangi (Ugandan) Resembling the white egret
Kenyangie, Kenyangy, Kenyangey, Kenyangee, Kenyangea

Kenzie (English) Form of Mackenzie, meaning "daughter of a wise leader; a fiery woman; one who is fair"
Kenzi, Kenzy, Kenzey, Kenzee, Kenzea

Keoshawn (American) One who is clever
Keoshawna, Keosean, Keoseana, Keoshaun, Keoshauna

Kepa (Basque) As solid as a stone
Kepah, Keppa, Keppah

Kerdonna (American) One who is loquacious
Kerdonnah, Kerdona, Kerdonah, Kerdonia, Kerdoniah, Kerdonea, Kerdoneah, Kirdonna, Kirdona, Kyrdonna, Kyrdona

Kerensa (Cornish) One who loves and is loved
Kerinsa, Keransa, Kerensia, Kerensea, Kerensya, Kerenz, Kerenza, Keranz, Keranza

Keres (Greek) In mythology, vengeful spirits of death and doom

Kermeilde (English) A gilded woman
Kermilda, Kermilla, Kermillie

Kerr (Scottish) From the marshland

Kerry (English) Form of Kiera, meaning "little dark-haired one"
Kerri, Kerrie, Kerrey, Kerree, Keri, Kerie, Kery, Keree, Keriana, Kerianna, Keriane, Kerianne, Kerilyn, Keriam, Kerilynne, Kern, Kerrianne, Kerrea, Kerea

Kerta (Teutonic) A brave woman warrior
Kertta, Kertu, Kerttu

Kerthia (American) A giving woman
Kerthiah, Kerthea, Kertheah, Kerthiya, Kerthiyah, Kerthie, Kerthi, Kerthee, Kerthea, Kerthy, Kerthey

Kesara (English) A girl with a beautiful head of hair
Kesare, Kesarah, Kesarra, Kesarre, Kesaria, Kesarea, Kesava, Kesave, Kesavia, Kesavea

K

Keshon (American) Filled with happiness
*Keyshon, Keshawn, Keyshawn, Kesean,
Keysean, Keshaun, Keyshaun, Keshonna,
Keyshonna, Keshawna, Keyshawna,
Keseana, Keyseana, Keshauna, Keyshauna*

Keshondra (American) Form of Keshon,
meaning "filled with happiness"
*Keshondrah, Keshawndra, Keshawndrah,
Keshaundra, Keshaundrah, Keshondriah,
Keshondria, Keshondrea, Keshondreah*

Ketaki (Indian) The golden daughter
Ketakie, Ketaky, Ketakey, Ketakee, Ketakea

Ketifa (Arabic) A flourishing woman; flowering
*Ketifah, Ketyfa, Keteefa, Ketipha,
Keteepha, Ketypha, Keteafa, Keteapha*

Ketura (Hebrew) Resembling incense
Keturah, Keturra

Kevina (Gaelic) Feminine form of Kevin; a
beautiful and beloved child
*Kevinah, Keva, Kevia, Kevinne, Kevyn,
Kevynn, Kevynne, Keveena, Keveene,
Kevinna, Kevine, Kevlyn, Kevlynne, Kevan,
Kevay, Keveana, Keveane*

Keydy (American) A knowledgeable woman
Keydey, Keydi, Keydie, Keydee, Keydea

Keyla (English) A wise daughter

Keyonna (American) An energetic woman
Keyonnah, Keyona, Keyonah

Kezia (Hebrew) Of the spice tree
Keziah, Kesia, Kesiah, Kesi, Kessie, Ketzia

Khadija (Arabic / African) The prophet
Muhammad's first wife; a perfect woman /
a child born prematurely
*Khadeeja, Khadijah, Khadyja, Kadija,
Kadijah, Kadeeja, Kadyja, Khadeaja, Kadeaja*

Khai (American) Unlike the others; unusual
Khae, Khay, Khaye

Khaki (American) Full of personality
Khakie, Khaky, Khakey, Khakee, Khakea

Khali (American) A lively woman
*Khalie, Khaly, Khaley, Khalee, Khaleigh,
Khalea*

Khalida (Arabic) Feminine form of Khalid;
an immortal woman
*Khalidah, Khaleeda, Khalyda, Khaalida,
Khulud, Khulood, Khaleada*

Khalilah (Arabic) Feminine form of Khalil;
a beloved friend
*Khalila, Khalyla, Khalylah, Kahlilia,
Khaleela, Khaleala*

Khaliqa (Arabic) Feminine form of Khaliq;
a creator; one who is well-behaved
*Khaliqah, Khalyqa, Khaleeqa, Kaliqua,
Kaleequa, Kalyqua, Khaleaqa, Kaleaqua*

Khanh (Vietnamese) Resembling
a precious stone
Khann, Khan

Khasa (Arabic) Of an ancient people
Khasah, Khassa, Kahsa, Kahsah

Khatiba (Arabic) Feminine form of Khatib;
one who leads the prayers; an orator
*Khateeba, Khatyba, Khateba, Khatibah,
Khateaba*

Khatiti (African) A petite woman
*Khatitie, Khatyty, Katiti, Katitie, Khatitee,
Khatitey, Khatitea, Katitee, Katitea, Katity,
Katitey*

Khatun (Arabic) A daughter born to nobility;
a lady
*Khatune, Khatoon, Khaatoon, Khanom,
Kanom, Khanam, Khaanam, Khatoun,
Khatoune*

Khawala (Arabic) A dancing servant girl
Khawalah, Khawalla, Kawala, Kawalah

Khayriyyah (Arabic) A charitable woman
Khayriyah, Khariyyah, Khariya, Khareeya

Khepri (Egyptian) Born of the morning sun
*Kheprie, Kepri, Keprie, Khepry, Kepry,
Khepree, Kepree, Kheprea, Keprea,
Kheprey, Keprey*

Khiana (American) One who is different
*Khianna, Khiane, Khianne, Khian, Khyana,
Khyanna, Kheana, Kheanna*

Khuyen (Vietnamese) An advisor

Ki (Korean) One who is reborn

Kiana (Hawaiian / Irish) Of the mountains /
feminine form of Kian; of an ancient family
*Kianna, Kiahna, Keanna, Keiana, Keona,
Keonna, Kia, Kiah, Kiahna, Kiani, Kianni,
Kiauna, Kiona, Kionah, Kioni, Kionna,
Kiandra, Keyanna, Keyah, Keya*

Kianga (African) Of the sunshine
Kyanga, Keanga

Kiaria (Japanese) Having great fortune

Kibibi (African) The little lady
Kibibe, Kibebe

Kichi (Japanese) The fortunate one
Kichie, Kichy, Kichey, Kichee, Kichea

Kiden (African) Daughter born after sons

Kidre (American) A loyal woman
*Kidrea, Kidreah, Kidria, Kidriah, Kidri,
Kidrie, Kidry, Kidrey, Kidree*

Kiele (Hawaiian) Resembling the gardenia
Kielle, Kiel, Kiell, Kiela, Kiella

Kienalle (American) Surrounded by light
Kienall, Kienale, Kienalla, Kienala, Kienal

Kienna (American) A brash woman
*Kiennah, Kiena, Kienah, Kyenna, Kyennah,
Kyena, Kyenah, Kienne, Kyenne*

Kiera (Irish) Feminine form of Kieran; little
dark-haired one
*Kierra, Kyera, Kyerra, Keaira, Keira,
Kieranne, Kierane, Kierana, Kiara, Keara,
Keeran, Keera, Keir, Kyra, Kyria, Kyrie,
Kyrene, Kira, Kiarra, Kera, Kerra, Kiora,
Kiri, Kirra, Kiriana, Kiran*

Kieu (Vietnamese) One who is beloved

Kiho (African) From the fog

Kijana (African) A youthful woman
Kijanna, Kijann, Kijan, Kijane, Kijanne

Kikka (German) The mistress of all
Kika, Kykka, Kyka

Kiku (Japanese) Resembling a mum

Kilenya (Native American) Resembling the
coughing fish
Kilenyah, Kileniya, Kileniyah

Killian (Irish) A warrior woman; of the
church
Kilian, Killiane, Killiana, Kiliane, Kiliana

Kimama (Native American) Resembling a
butterfly
Kimimela

Kimana (American) Girl from the meadow
*Kimanah, Kimanna, Kimannah, Kymana,
Kymanah, Kymanna, Kymannah*

Kimatra (Indian) A seductive woman

Kimball (English) Chief of the warriors;
possessing royal boldness
*Kimbal, Kimbell, Kimbel, Kymball,
Kymbal*

Kimberly ✪ (English) Of the royal fortress
*Kimberley, Kimberli, Kimberlee,
Kimberleigh, Kimberlin, Kimberlyn,
Kymberlie, Kymberly, Kymberlee, Kim,
Kimmy, Kimmie, Kimmi, Kym, Kimber,
Kymber, Kimberlie, Kimbra, Kimbro,
Kimbrough, Kinborough, Kimberlea,
Kimberleah, Kymberlea, Kymberleah*

Kimbrell (American) One who smiles a lot
*Kimbrelle, Kimbrel, Kimbrele, Kimbrella,
Kimbrela, Kymbrell, Kymbrelle, Kymbrel,
Kymbrele, Kymbrella, Kymbrela*

Kimeo (American) Filled with happiness
Kimeyo

Kimetha (American) Filled with joy
*Kimethah, Kymetha, Kymethah, Kimethia,
Kymethia, Kimethea, Kymethea*

Kimiko (Japanese) A noble child; without
equal

Kimone (American) A darling daughter
Kymone

Kin (Japanese) The golden child

Kina (Hawaiian) Woman of China

Kindle (American) To set fire; to arouse
Kindel, Kyndle, Kyndel

Kineks (Native American) Resembling a
rosebud

Kineta (Greek) One who is active; full of
energy
Kinetikos

Kinipela (Hawaiian) One who is fair;
white wave

Kinsey (English) The king's victory
*Kinnsee, Kinnsey, Kinnsie, Kinsee, Kinsie,
Kinzee, Kinzie, Kinzey, Kinnsea, Kinsea*

Kinsley (English) From the king's meadow
Kinsly, Kinslee, Kinsleigh, Kinslea, Kinsli, Kinslie, Kingsley, Kingsly, Kingslee, Kingsleigh, Kingslea, Kingsli, Kingslie

Kintra (American) A joyous woman
Kintrah, Kentra, Kentrah, Kintria, Kentria, Kintrea, Kentrea, Kintrey, Kintry, Kintri, Kintrie, Kintree, Kintrea

Kinza (American) A kinswoman
Kinzah, Kynza, Kynzah

Kioko (Japanese) A daughter born with happiness

Kipp (English) From the small pointed hill
Kip, Kipling, Kippling, Kypp, Kyp

Kirabo (African) A gift from God

Kirati (Indian) From the mountain
Kiratie, Kiraty, Kiratey, Kiratee, Kiratea

Kirby (English) From the church town
Kirbey, Kirbi, Kirbie, Kirbee, Kirbea, Kirbeah

Kiri (Indian) Resembling the amaranth flower
Kirie, Kiry, Kirey, Kiree, Kirea

Kirima (Eskimo) From the hill
Kirimah, Kiryma, Kirymah, Kirema, Kiremah, Kireema, Kireemah, Kireama, Kireamah

Kirit (Indian) One who is crowned
Kitra

Kisha (Russian) A genius
Kishah, Kysha, Kyshah

Kishi (African) From the hills
Kishie, Kishy, Kishey, Kishee, Kishea

Kismet (English) One's destiny; fate
Kizmet

Kiss (American) A caring and compassionate woman
Kyss, Kissi, Kyssi, Kissie, Kyssie, Kissy, Kyssy, Kissey, Kyssey, Kissee, Kyssee, Kissea, Kyssea

Kissa (African) Daughter born after twins
Kissah, Kyssa, Kyssah

Kit (American) Having great strength
Kitt, Kyt, Kytt

Kita (Japanese) Woman from the north

Kitoko (African) A beautiful woman

Kitty (English) Resembling a young cat; form of Katherine, meaning "one who is pure; virginal"
Kitti, Kittie, Kity, Kiti, Kitie, Kitee, Kittee, Kittea, Kitea

Kiva (Hebrew) Protected by God
Kivah, Kivi, Kiba

Kiwa (African) A lively woman
Kiwah, Kywa, Kywah, Kiewa, Kiewah, Keiwa, Keiwah, Keewa, Keewah, Keawa, Keawah

Kiwidinok (Native American) Woman of the wind

Kiya (Australian) Form of Kylie, meaning "from the narrow channel"
Kiyah, Kya, Kyah

Kiyoshi (Japanese) A quiet child; one who is pure
Kiyoshie, Kiyoshy, Kiyoshey, Kiyoshee, Kiyoshea

Kizzy (African) An energetic woman
Kizzey, Kizzi, Kizzie, Kizzee, Kizzea

Klara (Scandinavian) Form of Clara, meaning "famously bright"
Klarah, Klaire, Klariss, Klarissa, Klari, Klarika, Kalara, Kalate, Klarisza, Klarysa

Klaribel (Polish) A beautiful woman
Klarybel, Klaribell, Klarybell, Klaribelle, Klarybelle, Klaribela, Klarybela, Klaribella, Klarybella

Klaudia (English) Form of Claudia, meaning "one who is lame"
Klaudiah, Klaudine, Klaudeene, Klaudyne, Klaudette, Klaudett, Klaudete, Klaudeta, Klaudina, Klaudeena, Klaudyna, Klaudelle, Klaudele, Klaudell, Klauda, Klavdia

Klementine (Polish) Form of Clementine, meaning "one who is merciful"
Klem, Klemence, Klemency, Klementia, Klementina, Klementya, Klementyna, Klementyn, Klemmie, Klemmy, Klementyne

Kleopatra (English) Form of Cleopatra, meaning "a father's glory; of the royal family"
Klea, Kleo, Kleona, Kleone, Kleonie, Kleora, Kleta, Kleoni, Kleopetra, Kleonie, Kleony, Kleoney, Kleonee, Kleonea, Kleoneah

Klotild (Hungarian) A well-known lady
Klotilde, Klotilda, Klothild, Klothilde, Klothilda

Kobi (American) Woman from California
Kobie, Koby, Kobee, Kobey, Kobea

Kochava (Hebrew) Resembling a star

Kodi (English) Form of Cody, meaning "one who is helpful; a wealthy woman / acting as a cushion"
Kody, Kodie, Kodee, Kodey, Kodea, Kodia

Koemi (Japanese) Having a small smile
Koemie, Koemy, Koemey, Koemee, Koemea

Koffi (African) Born on a Friday
Koffie, Koffee, Koffea, Koffy, Koffey, Koffe

Kogan (English) A self-assured woman
Kogann, Kogen, Kogon, Kogin, Kogie, Kogi, Kogy, Kogey, Kogee, Kogea

Kohana (Japanese) Resembling a fragile flower
Kohanah, Kohanna, Kohannah

Koko (Japanese) The stork has come

Kolby (English) Form of Colby, meaning "from the coal town"
Kolbey, Kolbi, Kolbie, Kolbee, Kolbea

Koldobika (Teutonic) A renowned warrior
Koldobike

Kolette (English) Form of Colette, meaning "of the victorious people"
Kolete, Kolett, Koleta, Koletta, Kolet

Kolinka (Danish) Born to the victors
Kolinka, Koleenka, Kolynka, Kolenka

Komala (Indian) A delicate and tender woman
Komalah, Komalla, Komal, Komali, Komalie, Komalee, Komaleigh, Komalea

Kona (Hawaiian) A girly woman
Konah, Konia, Koniah, Konea, Koneah, Koni, Konie, Koney, Kony, Konee

Konane (Hawaiian) Daughter of the moonlight

Konstanza (English) Form of Constanza, meaning "one who is constant; steadfast"
Konstanze, Konstanzia, Konstanzea

Kora (Greek) A maiden; in mythology, another name for the goddess Persephone
Korah, Korra, Kore, Koren, Kori, Korie, Koree, Kory, Korey

Koral (American) Form of Coral, meaning "resembling the semiprecious sea growth"
Korale, Korall, Koralle

Kordell (English) Form of Cordelle, meaning "a good-hearted woman; a woman of honesty"
Kordel, Kordelle, Kordele, Kordela, Kordella

Korina (Latin) Form of Corina, meaning "a spear-wielding woman"
Korinna, Koreen, Koreene, Koren, Korena, Korine, Korreen, Korreena, Korrin, Korrina, Korrine, Korenne, Korin, Korinda, Korinn, Korinne, Korrena, Korrianne, Korrienne, Korrinda, Korrinn, Korrinna, Korryn, Koryn, Korynn, Korynne, Korrenda, Korynna, Koreana, Korreana

Kornelia (Polish) Form of Cornelia, meaning "referring to a horn"
Korneliah, Kornelie, Korneli, Kornela, Kornella, Kornelea, Korneliya, Korneleah

Koshatta (Native American) One who is diligent
Koshata, Koshatte, Koshate, Koshat, Koushatta, Koushata, Koushatte, Koushate, Koushat

Kosmo (Greek) A universal woman
Kosma, Kosmah, Kozmo, Kozma, Kasma, Kasmah, Kasmo, Kazma, Kazmo

Kosta (Latin) A steadfast woman
Kostia, Kostiah, Kostya, Kostya, Kostea, Kosteah, Kostusha

Kostya (Slavic) One who is faithful

Koto (Japanese) A harp player

Kourtney (American) Form of Courtney, meaning "a courteous woman; courtly"
Kourtny, Kordney, Kortney, Kortni, Kourtenay, Kourtneigh, Kourtni, Kourtnee, Kourtnie, Kortnie, Kortnea, Kourtnea

Kozue (Japanese) Of the trees
Kozu, Kozoo, Kozou

Krasna (Slavic) A beautiful daughter
Krasava

Kreeli (American) A charming and kind girl
*Kreelie, Krieli, Krielie, Kryli, Krylie,
Kreely, Kriely, Kryly, Kreelee, Krielee,
Krylee, Kreelea, Krielea, Krylea*

Krenie (American) A capable woman
Kreni, Kreny, Kreney, Krenee, Krenea

Kriemhild (Norse) In mythology, the wife
of Siegfried
Kriemhilda, Kriemhilde

Krishen (American) A talkative woman
*Kryshen, Krishon, Kryshon, Krishan,
Kryshan, Krishin, Kryshin*

Krissy (American) One who is friendly
Krissey, Krissi, Krissie, Krissee, Krissea

Kristina (English) Form of Christina,
meaning "follower of Christ"
*Kristena, Kristine, Kristyne, Kristyna,
Krystina, Krystine, Kristjana, Krisalyn,
Kris, Kristy, Kristi, Kristie, Kriszta,
Krisztina, Karasi, Kristin, Kristen,
Kristyn, Krysten, Krystin, Krystyn,
Kristian, Kristiana, Kristiane, Kristianna,
Kristianne, Kristel, Kristell, Kristeena,
Kristeene, Krista, Krysta, Krystka,
Kriska, Krystianna, Krystiana,
Krystynka, Krystyna, Krysia, Khristeen,
Khristen, Khristin, Khristina, Khristine,
Khristyana, Khristyna, Khrystina,
Khrystyn, Khrystyna, Khrystyne,
Khrustina, Kerstin, Kirsten, Kirstie,
Kirstin, Kirsty, Kirstyn, Kirsi*

Kriti (Indian) An exquisite work of art
*Kritie, Krity, Kritey, Kritee, Kryti, Kryty,
Krytie, Krytee, Kritea, Krytea*

Krupali (Indian) A forgiving woman
*Krupalie, Krupaly, Krupaley, Krupalee,
Krupaleigh, Krupalea, Krupaleah, Krupalia*

Krystal (English) Form of Crystal, meaning
"resembling clear, sparkling, brilliant glass"
*Kristal, Krystle, Krystalyn, Krystalynn,
Krystalynne, Kristabelle, Krystabelle,
Kristalena, Kristalyn, Khrystalline*

Ksana (Russian) Praise be to God
*Ksanochka, Ksena, Ksanna, Ksann, Ksane,
Ksanne*

Kubria (Arabic) A wise elder
Kubrea, Kubriah, Kubriya, Kubreah, Kubriyah

Kuma (Japanese) Resembling a bear
Kumah, Kooma, Koomah

Kumani (African) Fulfilling one's destiny
*Kumanie, Kumany, Kumaney, Kumanee,
Kumanea*

Kumari (Indian) Feminine form of Kumar;
a princess; another name for the goddess
Durga
*Kumarie, Kumaria, Kumara, Kumary,
Kumarey, Kumaree, Kumarea*

Kumi (Japanese) An everlasting beauty
Kumie, Kumy, Kumey, Kumee, Kumea

Kumiko (Japanese) A child who is forever
beautiful
Kumeeko, Kumyko

Kumuda (Indian) Resembling a flower
Kumud, Kumudia, Kumudea

Kumudavati (Indian) A woman among
lotuses

Kunigunde (German) Brave during time of
war
*Kundegunde, Kunigunda, Kundegunda,
Kunegunda, Kunegunde, Kunegundy,
Kunigundy, Kundegundy*

Kuniko (Japanese) From the country estate
Kuneeko, Kunyko

Kunti (Hindi) In Hinduism, the mother of
the Pandavas
*Kuntie, Kunty, Kuntey, Kuntea, Koonti,
Koontie, Koonty, Koontey, Koontee, Koontea*

Kuonrada (German) One who provides
bold counsel

Kura (Turkish) Of the river
Kurah

Kuron (African) One who gives thanks

Kurrsten (Scandinavian) Form of Kirsten,
meaning "follower of Christ"
*Kursten, Kurrstin, Kurstin, Kursti, Kurstie,
Kursty, Kurstee, Kurstea*

Kwanita (Native American) God is gracious
*Kwanitah, Kwaneeta, Kwanyta,
Kwaneata*

Kwesi (African) Born on a Saturday
Kwesie, Kwesy, Kwesey, Kwesee, Kwesea

Kyla ✪ (English) Feminine form of Kyle;
from the narrow channel
*Kylah, Kylar, Kyle, Kylee, Kyleigh, Kyley,
Kyli, Kylie, Kyleen, Kylene, Kyler, Kylia,
Kylianne, Kylin, Kya, Kiley, Kily, Kileigh,
Kilee, Kilie, Kili, Kilea, Kylea*

Kynthia (Greek) In mythology, another
name for the moon goddess
*Kynthiah, Kynthea, Kinthia, Kinthea,
Kynthiya, Kinthiya*

Kyoko (Japanese) One who sees her true
image

Kyrielle (French) A poetess
Kyriell, Kyriele, Kyriel, Kyriella, Kyriela

Laadan (Hebrew) A distinguished woman;
fair-skinned
Laden

Laasya (Indian) A graceful dancer
Laasyah, Lasya, Lasyah

Labana (Hebrew) Feminine form of
Labon; white; fair-skinned
*Labanah, Labanna, Labania, Labanea,
Labaniya, Labannah, Labaniah, Labaneah,
Labaniyah*

Labe (American) One who moves slowly
Labie, Labi, Laby, Labey, Labee, Labea

Labhaoise (Irish) A mighty battlemaiden;
crowned with laurel
Laoise, Laoiseach, Laobhaoise

Labiba (Arabic) Having great wisdom; one
who is intelligent
*Labibah, Labeeba, Labeebah, Labyba,
Labybah, Labieba, Labiebah, Labeiba,
Labeibah, Labeaba, Labeabah*

Labonita (Spanish) The beautiful one
*Labonitah, Laboneeta, Labonyta,
Labonieta, Laboneita, Laboneata*

Lacey (French) Woman from Normandy;
as delicate as lace
*Lace, Lacee, Lacene, Laci, Laciann, Lacie,
Lacina, Lacy, Lacyann, Laicee, Laicey,
Laisey, Laycie, Layci, Laycee, Lacea,
Laycea, Laicea*

Lachelle (American) A sweet woman
Lachell, Lachel, Lachele, Lachela, Lachella

Lachesis (Greek) In mythology, one of the
three Fates
Lachesiss, Lachesisse, Lachesys, Lacheses

Lachlan (Gaelic) From the land of the lochs
*Lochlan, Lachlana, Lochlana, Lachina,
Lachyna, Locke, Loche, Lacklan, Locklan*

Lacole (American) A sly woman
Lakole, Lucole, Lukole

Lacreta (Spanish) Form of Lucretia, meaning
"a bringer of light; a successful woman"
Lacrete, Lacrita, Lacrite, Lacryta, Lacryte

Lada (Slavic) In mythology, goddess of
love, harmony, and fertility
Ladah, Ladda, Laddah

LaDawn (American) As beautiful as the
sunrise
*Ladawn, LaDaun, Ladaun, LeDawn,
Ledawn, LeDaun, Ledaun*

Ladislava (Slavic) Feminine form of
Vladislav; a glorious ruler
*Ladislavah, Ladislavia, Ladislavea,
Ladyslava, Ladyslavia, Ladyslavea*

Ladonna (American) Form of Donna,
meaning "ruler of the world"
*Ladona, Ladonnah, Ladonah, Ledonna,
Ledona*

Ladrenda (American) One who is guarded
*Ladrendah, Ladrynda, Ladryndah,
Ladrinda, Ladrindah*

Lady (English) One who kneads bread; the
head of the house
*Lady, Ladee, Ladi, Ladie, Laidy, Laydy,
Laydi, Laydie, Laidi, Laidie, Laydee,
Laidee, Ladea, Laydea, Laidea*

Lael (Hebrew) One who belongs to God
Laele, Laelle

Laelia (Latin) Feminine form of Laelius; resembling the orchid
Laeliah, Laeliya, Laelea, Laeleah, Laeliyah, Laelya, Laelyah

Lafonde (American) One who is affectionate

Lage (Swedish) Woman from the ocean

Laguna (American) From the beach
Lagoona, Lagunah, Lagoonah, Lagouna, Lagounah

Lahela (Hawaiian) As innocent as a lamb
Lahelah, Lahella, Lahellah

Lahja (Finnish) Gift from God

Laila ✿ (Arabic) A beauty of the night; born at nightfall
*Laela, Laliah, Lailie, Laily, **Layla**, Laylah, Lailie, Laili, Laylie, Layli, Lailaa, Leila, Leela, Leelah, Leilah, Lela, Lelah, Lelia, Leyla, Loelia*

Laima (Latvian) One who is fortunate; in mythology, goddess of luck
Layma, Laema

Lainil (American) A softhearted woman
Lainill, Lainyl, Lainyll, Laenil, Laenill, Laenyl, Laenyll, Laynil, Laynill, Laynyl, Laynyll

Laire (Scottish) Resembling a mare
Lair, Laira, Lairia, Lairea, Layr, Layre, Laer, Laere

Lais (Greek) A legendary courtesan
Laise, Lays, Layse, Laisa, Laes, Laese

Laish (Hebrew) Resembling a lioness
Laisha, Lashia, Lashea, Laysh, Laishe, Layshe, Laysha, Laesh, Laeshe, Laesha

Lajean (French) A soothing woman
Lajeane, LaJean, LaJeane, Lajeanne, L'Jean

Lajila (Indian) One who is modest; shy
Lajyla, Lajeela, Lajeala

Lajita (Indian) A truthful woman
Lajyta, Lajeeta, Lajeata

Laka (Polynesian) In mythology, the patron goddess of dancers
Lakah

Lake (American) From the still waters
Laken, Laiken, Layken, Layk, Layke, Laik, Laike, Laeken, Laek, Laeke

Lakeisha (American / African) A lively and healthy woman / the favorite
Lakeesha, Lakecia, Lakesha, Lakeshia, Laketia, Lakeysha, Lakicia, Lakiesha, Lakisha, Lakitia, Laquisha, Lekeesha, Lekeisha, Lekisha, Laquiesha, Lakeasha, Lekeasha

Lakela (Hawaiian) A girly woman
Lakelah, Lakella, Lakellah

Lakia (Arabic) One who is treasured
Lakiah, Lakeea, Lakeah, Lakeya, Lakea, Lakiyah, Lakiya, Lakeyah

Laksha (Indian) As beautiful as a white rose
Lakshah, Lakshia, Lakshiya, Lakshea, Lakshya

Lakshmi (Hindi) A good omen; in Hinduism, the goddess of wealth, light, and beauty
Lakshmie, Lakshmy, Laxmi, Laxmie, Laxmy, Lakshmey, Laxmey, Lakshmee, Laxmee, Lakshmea, Laxmea

Lakya (Indian) Born on a Thursday

Lala (Slavic) Resembling a tulip
Lalah, Lalla, Lallah, Laleh

Lalage (Greek) One who often prattles
Lallie, Lally, Lalli, Lalley, Lallea, Lalleah

Lalaine (American) A hardworking woman
Lalain, Lalaina, Lalayn, Lalayne, Lalayna, Lalaen, Lalaene, Lalaena

Lalasa (Indian) Resembling a dove; one who is peaceful and promotes love
Lalasah, Lalassa, Lallassa, Lallasa

Laleema (Spanish) A devoted woman
Laleemah, Laleima, Laleimah, Laliema, Laliemah, Lalyma, Lalymah, Laleama, Laleamah

Lalia (Greek) One who is well-spoken
Lali, Lallia, Lalya, Lalea, Lalie, Lalee, Laly, Laley

Lalika (Indian) A lovely young woman
Lalica, Lalicka, Lalyka, Lalycka, Lalyca, Lalikah

Lalita (Indian) A playful and charming woman
Lalitah, Laleeta, Laleetah, Lalyta, Lalytah, Laleita, Laleitah, Lalieta, Lalietah, Laleata, Laleatah

Lamaara (Slavic) A girl from the mountains
Lamaarah, Lamara, Lamarah, Laamarra, Lamarra

Lamarian (American) One who is conflicted
Lamariane, Lamarean, Lamareane

Lamia (Greek) In mythology, a female vampire
Lamiah, Lamiya, Lamiyah, Lamea, Lameah

Lamika (American) One who is calm and peaceful
Lamikah, Lamyka, Lamykah, Lameeka, Lameekah, Lameika, Lameikah, Lamieka, Lamiekah, Lameaka, Lameakah

Lamis (Arabic) A soft-skinned woman
Lamiss, Lamisse, Lamys, Lamyss, Lamysse, Lamees, Lameese

L'Amour (French) One who loves and is loved
Lamour, Lamoure, L'Amoure, Lamore, Lamoura

Lamya (Arabic) Having lovely dark lips
Lamyah, Lamyia, Lama

Lan (Chinese) Resembling an orchid

Lana (German / Greek) Form of Alana, meaning "beautiful and fair woman; dear child" / form of Helen, meaning "the shining light"
Lanae, Lanette, Lanna, Lanny, Lannice, Lanice

Lanai (Hawaiian) A veranda; from the island
Lenai

Lanassa (Russian) A lighthearted woman; cheerful
Lanasa, Lanassia, Lanasia, Lanassiya, Lanasiya

Land (American) Of the earth
Lande, Landy, Landey, Landee, Landea, Landi, Landie

Landa (Spanish) Refers to the Virgin Mary

Landen (English) From the grassy meadow
Landin, Landyn

Landon (English) From the long hill
Landan, Lanton, Lantan

Landra (Latin) A wise counselor
Landrada, Landria, Landrea, Landradah

Landry (English) Of the rough terrain
Landrey, Landri, Landrie, Landree, Landrea, Landreah

Lane (English) One who takes the narrow path
Laine, Lainey, Laney, Lanie, Layne, Laina, Layna, Lainie, Laen, Laene, Laena, Laeni, Laenie, Lanee, Laynee, Laenee

Lanelle (American) One who takes the narrow path
Lanell, Lanele, Lanella, Lanela, Lanel

Lang (Scandinavian) Woman of great height

Langley (English) From the long meadow
Langly, Langli, Langlie, Langlee, Langleigh, Langlea

Lani (Hawaiian) From the sky; one who is heavenly
Lanikai

Lanka (Hindi) From the island fortress
Lankah, Lankia, Lankiah, Lankea, Lankeah

Lansing (English) Filled with hope
Lanseng, Lansyng

Lantana (English) Resembling the flower with orange or purple blossoms
Lantanah, Lantanna, Lantania, Lantanea, Lantaniya, Lantanya

Lanza (Italian) One who is noble and willing
Lanzah, Lanzia, Lanziah, Lanzea, Lanzeah

Laodamia (Greek) In mythology, daughter of Bellerophon
Laodamiah, Laodamea, Laodameah

Laoidheach (Gaelic) From the meadowland

Lapis (Egyptian) Resembling the dark-blue gemstone
Lapiss, Lapisse, Lapys, Lapyss, Lapysse

Laquanna (American) An outspoken woman
Laquana, Laquann, Laquane, Laquan

Laqueta (American) A quiet and well-behaved child
Laquetta, Laquita, Laquitta

Laquinta (American) The fifth-born child

Lara (Latin) One who is protected;
a cheerful woman
Larra, Laralaine, Laramae, Larina,
Larinda, Larita, Larya

Laramie (French) Shedding tears of love
Larami, Laramy, Laramey, Laramee,
Laramea

Larby (American) Form of Darby, meaning
"of the deer park"
Larbey, Larbi, Larbie, Larbee, Larbea

Larch (American) One who is full of life
Larche

Lareina (Spanish) The queen; one born to
royalty
Laraene, Larayne, Lareine, Larena, Larrayna,
Larreina, Laranya, Laraena, Larayna

Larenta (Latin) In mythology, an earth
goddess
Larentia, Larentea, Larynta

Larhonda (American) A flashy woman
Larhondah, Larhondia, Larhondiah,
Larhondea, Larhondeah, Laranda

Larissa (Latin) A lighthearted woman
Lari, Larisa, Laryssa, Lerissa, Lorissa,
Lyssa, Larisse, Laryssa, Larysse, Laurissa

Lark (English) Resembling the songbird
Larke

Larkin (American) A pretty young woman
Larkyn, Larkine, Larkyne, Larken,
Larkene, Larkun, Larkune

Larkspur (English) Resembling the blue
flower
Larkspurr, Larkspurre

Larrie (American) A tomboyish woman
Larri, Larry, Larrey, Larree, Larrea

Larsen (Scandinavian) Daughter of Lars
Larson, Larssen, Larsson

Larue (American) Form of Rue, meaning
"from the medicinal herb"
LaRue, Laroo, Larou

Lasha (Spanish) One who is forlorn
Lashah, Lashe

Lashanda (American) A brassy woman
Lashonda, Lashounda, Lashunda

Lashawna (American) Filled with happiness
Lashauna, Laseana, Lashona, Lashawn,
Lasean, Lashone, Lashaun

Lassie (Scottish) A young girl; one who is pure
Lassi, Lassey, Lassy, Lassee, Lass, Lassea

Lata (Indian) Of the lovely vine
Latah

Latanya (American) Daughter of the fairy
queen
Latanyah, Latonya, Latania, Latanja,
Latonia, Latanea

Latasha (American) Form of Natasha,
meaning "born on Christmas Day"
Latashah, Latascha, Latashia, Latasia,
Latashea, Latashiya

LaTeasa (Spanish) A flirtatious woman
Lateasa, Lateaza

Lathenia (American) A talkative woman
Latheniah, Lathena, Lathenah, Lathenea,
Latheneah

Latifah (Arabic) One who is gentle and kind
Latifa, Lateefa, Lateefah, Lateifa, Lateiffa,
Latiffa, Latyfa, Latiefa, Lateifah, Latiefah,
Lateafa, Lateafah, Latyfah

Latika (Indian) An elegant and majestic
lady
Latikah, Laticka, Latica, Lateeka, Latieka,
Lateaka, Latyka, Lateika

Latisehsha (American) A happy woman

Latona (Latin) In mythology, the Roman
equivalent of Leto, the mother of Artemis
and Apollo
Latonah, Latonia, Latonea, Lantoniah,
Latoneah

Latosha (American) Filled with happiness
Latoshia, Latoshah, Latoshiah, Latoshea,
Latosheah

Latoya (Spanish) One who is victorious
Letoya, Latoia, Latoria, Latorya, Latoyah,
Latoyla, Latoiya

Latrelle (American) One who laughs a lot
Latrell, Latrel, Latrele, Latrella, Latrela

Latrice (English) Born into the nobility
Latrecia, Latreece, Latreese, Latreshia,
Latricia, Leetriss, Letrice, Leatrice, Letreece

Latrisha (American) One who is high
maintenance
*Latrishah, Latrysha, Latryshah, Latriesha,
Latrieshah, Latreisha, Latreishah,
Latreesha, Latreeshah, Latreasha,
Latreashah*

Lavanya (Indian) One who is filled with
grace
*Lavania, Lavani, Lavanie, Lavany, Lavaney,
Lavanee, Lavanea, Lavaneah, Lavaniya*

Lave (Latin) One who is washed clean

LAUREN

Lauren was named in the hospital room after her delivery. I had picked out a boy's name, expecting
a boy. On my side table in the hospital was a bottle of Lauren perfume, and that was the name that
was chosen. —Lisa, VA

Lauda (Latin) One who is praised

Laudine (English) Lady of the fountain; in
Arthurian legend, the wife of Yvain
*Laudene, Laudyne, Laudina, Laudena,
Laudyna, Laudeen, Laudean, Laudeena,
Laudeana*

Laudonia (Italian) Praises the house
*Laudonea, Laudoniya, Laudomia,
Laudomea, Laudomiya*

Laufeia (Norse) From the wooded island
Laufia, Laufea, Laufeiya, Laufeya

Laura (Latin) Crowned with laurel; from the
laurel tree
*Lauraine, Lauralee, Laralyn, Laranca,
Larea, Lari, Lauralee, Laurana, Laure,
Laurel, Laurella, Laurence, Laurentia,
Laurentine, Laurestine, Lauretha, Lauretta,
Laurette, Lauri, Lauriane, Laurianne,
Laurice, Lauricia, Laurie, Laurina,
Laurinda, Laurine, Laurita, Laurnea,
Lavra, Lawra, Lollie, Lolly, Laural,
Lauralle, Laurell, Laurelle, Lauriel,
Lauralyn, Lauene, Lauica, Laurencia,
Lawrencia, Lonyn, Loura, Larunda,
Lawena, Laria*

Lauren ✿ (French) Form of Laura, meaning
"crowned with laurel; from the laurel tree"
*Laren, Larentia, Larentina, Larenzina,
Larren, Laryn, Larryn, Larrynn, Larsina,
Larsine, Laurenne, Laurin, Lauryn, Laurynn,
Laurena, Laurene, Laureen, Lareen*

Laurent (French) A graceful woman
Laurente, Lorent, Lorente

Lavada (American) One who is creative;
musically talented
Lavadah, Lavadia, Lavadea, Lavadiya

Laveda (Latin) One who is innocent;
cleansed
*Lavedah, Lavella, Lavelle, Laveta, Lavetta,
Lavette*

Lavender (English) Resembling the purple
flowering plant
*Lavinder, Lavandar, Lavander, Lavindar,
Lavynder, Lavyndar*

Laverne (Latin) Born in the spring; in
mythology, Laverna was the goddess of thieves
*Laverine, Lavern, Laverna, Laverrne,
Leverne, Loverna, Lavyrne, Lavyrna,
Lavernia, La Verne, La Vergne, Lativerna,
Levema*

Lavinia (Latin) In mythology, the daughter
of Latinus and wife of Aeneas
*Lavena, Lavenia, Lavina, Lavinie, Levenia,
Levinia, Livinia, Louvenia, Louvinia, Lovina,
Lovinia, Luvena, Luvenia, Luvina, Luvinia*

Lavita (American) A charming woman
*Lavitah, Laveeta, Laveetah, Laveata,
Laveatah, Lavieta, Lavietah, Laveita,
Laveitah, Lavyta, Lavytah*

Lavonne (French) Form of Yvonne, meaning
"a young archer"
*Lavonda, Lavonna, Lahvonne, Levonne,
Levonda, Lavonn*

Lawanda (American) Form of Wanda,
meaning "a wanderer"
*Lawandah, Lawannda, Lawahnda,
Lawonda, Lawonnda, Lawohnda,
Lawande, Lawandis*

Le (Chinese) One who brings joy to others

Lea (English) From the meadow
Lee, Leigh, Ley

Leaf (American) Woman of the forest
Leafi, Leafie, Leafy, Leafey, Leafee, Leafea

Leah ○ (Hebrew) One who is weary; in the Bible, Jacob's first wife
Leia, Leigha, Lia, Liah, Leeya

Leala (French) One who is faithful; loyal
Leola, Lealia, Lealie, Leal, Liealia

Leandra (Greek) Feminine form of Leander; resembling a lioness
Leandre, Leandria, Leanza, Leanda, Leiandra, Leodora, Leoine, Leoline, Leonelle

Leanna (Gaelic) Form of Helen, meaning "the shining light"
Leana, Leann, Leanne, Lee-Ann, Leeann, Leeanne, Leianne, Leyanne, Leigh-Anne, Leighanna, Leeahnne, Leane, Leianna, Leighanne, Leighna, Leena, Leauna

Leatrice (American) Form of Beatrix, meaning "one who blesses others"
Leatrix, Leatriz, Leatriss, Leatrisse, Leatrize, Leatricia, Leatrisa, Leate, Leata, Leat, Leitris, Letrys, Lettrys

Leba (Hebrew) One who is dearly loved
Lebah, Lebba, Lebbah

Lebonah (Hebrew) Refers to frankincense
Lebona, Lebonna, Lebonia, Lebonea, Leboniya, Levona, Levonia, Levonah, Levonea, Levonna

Lechsinska (Polish) A beautiful maiden of the forest

Lecia (English) Form of Alice, meaning "woman of the nobility; truthful; having high moral character"
Licia, Lecea, Licea, Lisha, Lysha, Lesha

Ledell (Greek) One who is queenly
Ledelle, Ledele, Ledella, Ledela, Ledel

Leela (Indian) An accomplished actress

Legarre (Spanish) Refers to the Virgin Mary
Legare, Legarra, Legara, Lera, Leira

Legend (American) One who is memorable
Legende, Legund, Legunde

Legia (Spanish) A bright woman
Legiah, Legea, Legeah, Legiya, Legiyah, Legya, Legyah

Lehava (Hebrew) A fiery woman; the little flame
Lehavah, Lehavia, Lehavea, Lehavit, Lehaviya

Lei (Hawaiian) Adorned with flowers

Leiko (Hawaiian) Resembling a small flower
Leeko, Lyko, Liko, Lieko

Leilani (Hawaiian) Child of heaven; adorned with heavenly flowers
Leia, Lalani, Leilanie, Leilanee, Leilaney, Leilany, Lalanie, Lalaney, Lalanee, Lalany, Leilanea, Lalanea

Leitha (Greek) One who is forgetful; in mythology, Lethe was the river of forgetfulness
Leith, Leithe, Lethe, Letha, Lethia, Lethea

Lejoi (French) Filled with happiness
Lejoy, Lejoye

Lemuela (Hebrew) Feminine form of Lemuel; devoted to God
Lemuelah, Lemuella, Lemuellah, Lemuel, Lemuele, Lemuelle

Lena (German) Form of Helen, meaning "the shining light"
Lina, Leena, Leyna, Leina, Lyna, Lenci, Lencie, Lency, Lencey, Lencee, Lenka, Lencea

Lenesha (American) One who smiles a lot
Lenesha, Leneesha, Leneeshah, Leniesha, Lenieshah, Leneisha, Leneishah, Leneasha, Leneashah, Lenysha, Lenyshah

Lenis (Latin) One who has soft and silky skin
Lene, Leneta, Lenice, Lenita, Lennice, Lenos, Lenys, Lenisse, Lenysse, Lenyce, Lenet

Lenmana (Native American) Talented with the flute
Lenmanna, Linmana, Linmanna, Lynmana, Lynmanna

Lennon (English) Daughter of love
Lennan, Lennin, Lenon, Lenan, Lenin

Lenore (Greek) Form of Eleanor, meaning "the shining light"
Lenor, Lenora, Lenorah, Lenorr, Lenorra, Lenorre, Leonora, Leonore, Lanora, Leanor, Leanora, Leanore, Leora, Leorah, Leeora, Liora, Leeor, Lior, Liorit, Leonor, Linore, Linor, Linora, Lenoa

Lenusy (Russian) As delicate as a flower
Lenusey, Lenusi, Lenusie, Lenusee, Lenusea

Leoda (German) Daughter of the people
Leota, Leodah, Leotah, Luete, Lueta

Leona (Latin) Feminine form of Leon; having the strength of a lion
Leeona, Leeowna, Leoine, Leola, Leone, Leonelle, Leonia, Leonie, Leontine, Leontina, Leontyne, Leontyna, Leowna, Leoma, Leonda, Leondra, Leondrea, Leonline, Leonela, Leoni, Leonine, Leonita, Leonlina, Leontin, Liona, Lione, Lyonene, Lyonet, Lyonette, Lyoneta, Lyonetta, Leonee, Leonea

Leonarda (French) Feminine form of Leonard; having the strength of a lion
Lenarda, Leonda, Lennarda, Leonarde, Lenna, Leondra, Leodora, Leoarrie

Leonsio (Spanish) One who is fierce
Leonsa, Leonsia, Leonsea, Leonsi, Leonsie, Leonsy, Leonsey, Leonsee

Leopolda (German) Feminine form of Leopold; a bold ruler of the people
Leopoldia, Leopoldea, Leopoldina, Leopoldyna, Leopoldeena, Leopoldeana, Leopoldena, Leopoldine, Leopoldyne, Leopoldeen

Leotie (Native American) Resembling a wildflower
Leoti, Leotee, Leoty, Leotey, Leotea

Lequoia (Native American) Form of Sequoia, meaning "of the giant redwood tree"
Lequoya, Lequoiya, Lekoya, Lekoia

Lerola (Latin) Resembling a blackbird
Lerolla, Lerolah, Lerolia, Lerolea

Lesham (Hebrew) Our precious child
Leshama, Leshamah, Leshamia, Leshamea, Leshamiya, Leshmya

Leslie (Gaelic) From the holly garden; of the gray fortress
Leslea, Leslee, Lesleigh, Lesley, Lesli, Lesly, Lezlee, Lezley, Lezlie, Lezleigh, Lezli, Lioslaith, Lezlea

Leta (Latin) One who is glad; joyful; loved by all
Leeta, Lita, Lida, Leeda, Leita, Leida, Leyta, Lyta, Leyda, Lyda, Loida, Loyda, Leda, Luda, Ledaea, Ledah

Letichel (American) Filled with happiness
Letichell, Letichele, Letichelle, Letichela, Letichella, Letishel, Letishell, Letishele, Letishelle, Letishela, Letishella

Letitia (Latin) One who brings joy to others
Laetitia, Laetizia, Latashia, Latia, Latisha, Letice, Leticia, Leticja, Letisha, Letizia, Letta, Lettice, Lettie, Lettitia, Letty, Letycja, Lateisha, Latesha, Laticia, Latitia

Leto (Greek) In mythology, mother of Apollo and Artemis

Letsey (American) Form of Letitia, meaning "one who brings joy to others"
Letsy, Letsee, Letsea, Letsi, Letsie

Leucippe (Greek) In mythology, a nymph
Lucippe, Leucipe, Lucipe

Leucothea (Greek) In mythology, a sea nymph
Leucothia, Leucothiah, Leucotheah

Levana (Latin) One who is raised up; in mythology, goddess and protector of newborns
Livana, Livaun, Levanah, Levanna, Levania, Levanea, Livanna, Livania, Livanea

Levane (Irish) Of the great elm
Levayne, Levaine, Levayn, Levain, Levaen, Levaene

Levia (Hebrew) One who joins forces with others
Leviah, Leviya, Leviyah, Levya, Levyah, Levea, Leveah

Levina (Latin) Resembling a lightning bolt
Levyna, Levena, Leveena, Leviena, Leveina, Leveana

Levitt (American) One who is straightforward
Levit, Levitte, Levytt, Levyt, Levytte

Levity (American) A lighthearted woman
Leviti, Levitie, Levitee, Levitea, Levitey

Levora (American) A homebody
Levorah, Levorra, Levorrah, Levoria, Levoriah, Levorea, Levoreah, Levorya, Levoryah

Lewa (African) A very beautiful woman
Lewah

Lewana (Hebrew) Of the white moon
Lewanah, Lewanna, Lewannah

Lexie (Greek) Form of Alexandra, meaning "helper and defender of mankind"
Lexa, Lexandra, Lexann, Lexi, Lexia, Lexina, Lexine, Lexus, Lexya, Lexea, Lex, Lexis, Lexiss, Lexy, Lexy, Lexee

Leya (Spanish) One who upholds the law
Leyah

Lezena (American) One who smiles often
Lezenah, Lezina, Lezinah, Lezyna, Lezynah, Lezene, Lyzena

Lhasa (Indian) From the sacred city
Lhasah, Lasa, Lassa, Laasa

Li (Chinese) Having great strength; one who is sharp

Liadan (Irish) An older woman; the gray lady
Leadan, Lyadan

Liana (French / English) Of the jungle vine; bound / form of Eliana, meaning "the Lord answers our prayers"
Liann, Lianna, Lianne, Liahna, Liahne, Liane, Liani, Lianie, Lianee, Liany, Lianey, Lyanne, Lyane, Lyana, Lyanna, Lianea

Libby (English) Form of Elizabeth, meaning "my God is bountiful"
Libba, Libbee, Libbey, Libbie, Libet, Liby, Lilibet, Lilibeth, Lilibet, Lillibet, Lilybet, Lilybeth, Lilybell, Lib, Libbea, Libea

Liberty (English) An independent woman; having freedom
Libertey, Libertee, Libertea, Liberti, Libertie, Libertas, Libera, Liber, Libyr

Libitina (Latin) In mythology, goddess of death
Lybitina, Lybytyna, Libitena, Libityna, Libiteena, Libiteana, Libitiena, Libiteina

Libni (Hebrew) A distinguished woman; fair-skinned
Libnie, Libney, Libny, Libnee, Libnea

Libra (Latin) One who is balanced; the seventh sign of the zodiac
Leebra, Leibra, Liebra, Leabra, Leighbra, Lybra

Librada (Spanish) One who is free
Libradah, Lybrada, Lybradah

Licia (Latin / English) Woman from Lycia / form of Alicia, meaning "woman of the nobility; truthful; having high moral character"
Liciah, Leecea, Leecia, Leesha, Lesia, Lisia, Lycia

Lidwina (Scandinavian) A friend to all
Lidwyna, Lidweena, Lidwiena, Lidweina, Lidweana

Lien (Vietnamese) Resembling the lotus
Lian

Lieselette (American) Form of Liesl, meaning "my God is bountiful"
Lieselet, Lieselete, Lieselett, Lieseleta, Lieseletta

Liesl (German) Form of Elizabeth, meaning "my God is bountiful"
Liezl, Liesa, Liese, Liesel, Liezel, Liesei, Liesheth, Liesi, Liesie

Lieu (Vietnamese) Of the willow tree

Light (American) A lighthearted woman
Lite, Lyte

Ligia (Greek) One who is musically talented
Ligiah, Ligya, Ligiya, Lygia, Ligea, Lygea, Lygya, Lygiya

Liguria (Greek) One who loves music
Liguriah, Lyguria, Lyguriah, Ligurea, Ligureah, Lygurea, Lygureah

Lila (Arabic / Greek) Born at night / resembling a lily
Lilah, Lyla, Lylah

Lilac (Latin) Resembling the bluish-purple flower
Lilack, Lilak, Lylac, Lylack, Lylak, Lilach

Lileah (Latin) Resembling a lily
Lilea, Lyleah, Lylea, Lilya, Lilyah, Lylya, Lylyah

Lilette (Latin) Resembling a budding lily
Lilett, Lilete, Lilet, Lileta, Liletta, Lylette, Lylett, Lylete, Lylet, Lyletta, Lyleta

Liliash (Spanish) Resembling a lily
Liliashe, Lilyash, Lilyashe

Liliha (Hawaiian) One who holds rank as chief

Lilith (Babylonian) Woman of the night
Lilyth, Lillith, Lillyth, Lylith, Lyllith, Lylyth, Lyllyth, Lilithe, Lylithe, Lilythe

Lillian ✿ (Latin) Resembling the lily
Lilian, Liliana, Liliane, Lilianne, Lilias, Lilas, Lillas, Lillias, Lilianna, Lillianna, Lilliane, Lilliann, Lillianna, Lillianne, Lillyan, Lillyanne, Lilyan, Lilyann, Lillis, Lilis

Lilo (Hawaiian) One who is generous
Lylo, Leelo, Lealo, Leylo, Lielo, Leilo

Liluye (Native American) Resembling the soaring hawk

Lily ✿ (English) Resembling the flower; one who is innocent and beautiful
Leelee, Lil, Lili, Lilie, Lilla, Lilley, Lilli, Lillie, Lillika, Lillita, Lilly, Lilybel, Lilybell, Lilybella, Lilybelle, Lillah, Lilia, Lilch, Lilika, Lilike

Lindley (English) From the pastureland
Lindly, Lindlee, Lindleigh, Lindli, Lindlie, Leland, Lindlea

Lindsay (English) From the island of linden trees; from Lincoln's wetland
Lind, Lindsea, Lindsee, Lindseigh, Lindsey, Lindsy, Linsay, Linsey, Linsie, Linzi, Linzee, Linzy, Lyndsay, Lyndsey, Lyndsie, Lynnsey, Lynnzey, Lynsey, Lynzey, Lynzi, Lynzy, Lynzee, Lynzie, Lindse

Ling (Chinese) As sweet as the tinkling of a bell
Lyng

Linn (Scottish) Resembling the cascade of a waterfall
Linne

LILY

When I was pregnant, I loved the name Lily—and the fact that my daughter would be Lily of Ali, sort of like my favorite flower, lily of the valley. It may sound corny, but I felt so physically connected to her that I loved the idea that our names would also be intertwined and connect us long after my pregnancy. —Ali, Montreal

---

Limber (African) One who is joyful
Lymber, Lember

Limor (Hebrew) Refers to myrrh
Limora, Limoria, Limorea, Leemor, Leemora, Leemoria, Leemorea

Lin (Chinese) Resembling jade; from the woodland

Lina (Arabic) Of the palm tree
Leena, Leina, Leyna, Lena, Lyna, Leana

Linda (Spanish) One who is soft and beautiful
Lindalee, Lindee, Lindey, Lindi, Lindie, Lindira, Lindka, Lindy, Lynda, Lynde, Lyndy, Lyndi, Lyndall, Lyndee, Lynnda, Lynndie, Lueinda, Lindea, Lyndea

Linden (English) From the hill of lime trees
Lindenn, Lindon, Lindynn, Lynden, Lyndon, Lyndyn, Lyndin, Lindin

Lindiwe (African) The daughter we have waited for

Linnea (Scandinavian) Resembling a small mountain flower; of the lime tree
Lenae, Linea, Linna, Linnae, Linnaea, Lynae, Lynea, Lynnae, Lynnea

Liriene (French) One who enjoys reading aloud
Lirienne, Liriena, Lirienna, Lirien, Lirienn

Liriope (Greek) In mythology, a nymph and the mother of Narcissus
Leiriope, Leirioessa

Lirit (Hebrew) One who is musically talented
Lirita, Liritia, Liritea, Leerit

Lisa (English) Form of Elizabeth, meaning "my God is bountiful"
Leesa, Liesa, Lisebet, Lise, Liseta, Lisette, Liszka, Lisebeth, Lisabet, Lisabeth, Lisabette, Lisbet, Lisbeth, Lisavet, Lissa, Lissette, Lyssa, Lysa, Lesa, Liesbet, Liisa, Lis, Leysa, Leisa, Leasa

Lishan (African) One who is awarded a medal
Lishana, Lishanna, Lyshan, Lyshana, Lyshanna

Lissie (American) Resembling a flower
Lissi, Lissy, Lissey, Lissee, Lissea

Liv (Scandinavian / Latin) One who protects others / from the olive tree
Livia, Livea, Liviya, Livija, Livvy, Livy, Livya, Lyvia, Livi, Livie, Livee

Livonah (Hebrew) A vibrant woman; full of life
Livona, Lyvonah, Lyvona, Levona, Levonah

Liya (Hebrew) The Lord's daughter
Liyah, Leeya, Leeyah, Leaya, Leayah

Liza (English) Form of Elizabeth, meaning "my God is bountiful"
Lyza, Leeza, Litsea, Litzea, Liz, Lizzie, Lizabeth, Lizandra, Lizann, Lizbet, Lizbeth, Lizeth, Lizette, Lizina, Lizzy, Lyzbeth, Lyzbet, Lyzabeth, Lyzz, Lizz, Lyz, Leyza, Liiza, Leza

Llamrei (English) In Arthurian legend, Arthur's steed

Llesenia (Spanish) Form of Yesenia, meaning "resembling a flower"
Lleseniah, Llesinia, Llesenya, Llecenia, Llasenya, Llesnia, Llessenia, Llessena, Llessenya, Llissenia, Llesenea, Lleseneah, Llesinea

Lleucu (Welsh) The treasured light
Lleyke

Lo (American) A feisty woman
Loe, Low, Lowe

Loanna (American) A gracious and loving woman
Loana, Loann, Loane, Loanne

Lodema (English) One who provides guidance
Lodemah, Lodima, Lodimah, Lodyma, Lodymah, Lodeema, Lodeemah

Lofn (Norse) In mythology, one of the principal goddesses

Logan (Gaelic) From the hollow
Logann, Logane, Loganne

Logestilla (French) Daughter of a legend
Logistilla, Logestila, Logistila, Logestylla, Logistylla, Logestile, Logestille, Logistile, Logistille

Loicy (American) A delightful woman
Loicey, Loicee, Loicea, Loici, Loicie, Loyce, Loice, Loyci, Loycie, Loycee, Loycea, Loycy, Loycey

Loire (French) From the river in France
Loir

Lois (Greek) A superior woman
Loes

Lojean (American) A bravehearted woman
Lojeane, Lojeanne

Lokelani (Hawaiian) Resembling a small red rose
Lokelanie, Lokelany, Lokelaney, Lokelanee, Lokelanea

Loki (Norse) In mythology, a trickster god
Lokie, Lokee, Lokey, Loky, Lokea, Lokeah, Lokia, Lokiah

Lola (Spanish) Form of Dolores, meaning "woman of sorrow"
Lolah, Lolla, Loela, Lolita, Lolitta, Loleta, Loletta, Lo, Loe

Loleen (American) Filled with joy
Loleena, Lolene, Lolena, Loliene, Loliena, Loleine, Loleina, Loleana, Loleane, Lolyne, Lolyna

Lomahongva (Native American) Of the pretty clouds

Lomasi (Native American) Resembling a beautiful flower
Lomasie, Lomasee, Lomasy, Lomasey, Lomasea

Lomita (Spanish) A good woman
Lomitah, Lomeeta, Lomeetah, Lomieta, Lomietah, Lomeita, Lomeitah, Lomeata, Lomeatah, Lomyta, Lomytah

Londa (American) One who is shy
Londah, Londe, Londeh, Londy, Londey, Londee, Londea, Londi, Londie

London (English) From the captial of England

Loni (English) Form of Leona, meaning "having the strength of a lion"
Lona, Lonee, Lonie, Lonna, Lonni, Lonnie, Lonee, Lony, Loney, Lonea, Lonnea, Lonnee, Lonny, Lonney

Lora (Latin) Form of Laura, meaning
"crowned with laurel; from the laurel tree"
*Lorabelle, Lorah, Loranna, Loreanna,
Loree, Lorenna, Lorey, Lori, Loribelle,
Lorinda, Lorita, Lorra, Lorrae, Lorree,
Lorrie, Lory, Lowra, Lorna, Loria, Lorian,
Loriane, Loriana, Loriann, Lorianne,
Lorianna, Lorie, Lorilla, Loriel, Lorilynn,
Lorrella, Loralle, Lorel, Lorelle, Lowrelle,
Lorand, Lorant, Loris, Lowri, Lowrie*

Loranden (American) A genius
*Lorandena, Lorandyn, Lorandyna, Luranden,
Lurandena, Lurandyna, Lurandyne*

Lordyn (American) An enchanting woman
*Lordynn, Lordynne, Lordin, Lordinn,
Lordinne, Lordyne, Lordine*

Lore (Basque / English) Resembling a
flower / form of Lora, meaning "crowned
with laurel; from the laurel tree"
Lorea

Lorelei (German) From the rocky cliff; in
mythology, a siren who lured sailors to
their deaths
*Laurelei, Laurelie, Loralee, Loralei, Loralie,
Loralyn, Lorilee, Lorilyn, Lura, Lurette,
Lurleen, Lurlene, Lurline, Lurlyne, Lorali,
Loreli, Laureli*

Loren (English) Form of Laura, meaning
"crowned with laurel; from the laurel tree"
*Lorin, Lorren, Lorrin, Lorryn, Loryn,
Lorena, Loreen, Loreene, Lorene, Lorenia,
Lorenna, Lorine, Larena, Lorrina, Lourana*

Loretta (Italian) Form of Laura, meaning
"crowned with laurel; from the laurel tree"
*Laretta, Larretta, Lauretta, Laurette,
Leretta, Loreta, Lorette, Lorretta,
Lowretta, Larette, Larrette*

Lorraine (French) From the kingdom of
Lothair
*Laraine, Larayne, Laurraine, Leraine,
Lerayne, Lorain, Loraina, Loraine,
Lorayne, Lorraina, Lorrayne, Laraene,
Larayne, Lareine, Larina, Larine, Larraine,
Lorenza, Lourine*

Lo-ruhamah (Hebrew) One who does not
receive mercy

Lottie (French) Form of Charlotte,
meaning "a small, strong woman"
*Lotti, Lotty, Lotte, Lottey, Lottee, Lotta,
Loti, Lotie, Lotye, Letya, Letje, Lottea, Lotea*

Lotus (Greek) Resembling the water lily
Lotas, Lotuss, Lotis, Lotiss, Lotass

Louise (German) Feminine form of Louis;
a famous warrior
*Loise, Louella, Louisa, Louisetta, Louisette,
Louisina, Louisiana, Louisiane, Louisine,
Louiza, Lovisa, Lowise, Loyise, Lu,
Ludovica, Ludovika, Ludwiga, Luella,
Luisa, Luise, Lujza, Lujzika, Luiza, Loyce,
Ludkhannah, Luijzika, Likla, Ludka, Lilka,
Luell, Luelle, Luigina, Loring, Lodoiska*

Lourdes (French) From the place of healing
and miracles
*Lurdes, Lourdecita, Lourdetta, Lourdette,
Louredes, Loordes, Lorda*

Louvain (English) From the city in
Belgium
Leuven, Loovain

Love (English) One who is full of affection
*Lovey, Loveday, Lovette, Lovi, Lovie, Lov,
Luv, Luvey, Luvee, Luvi, Luvie, Lovee,
Lovea, Luvea, Luvy*

Loveada (Spanish) A loving woman
*Loveadah, Loviada, Loviadah, Lovyada,
Lovyadah, Lovada*

Loveanna (American) A gracious and
loving woman
*Loveann, Lovean, Loveane, Loveanne,
Lovanna, Lovana, Lovann, Lovane, Lovanne*

Lovejoy (American) Filled with love and joy
*Lovjoy, Lovejoye, Lovjoi, Lovejoi, Luvjoi,
Luvjoy, Luvjoye*

Lovella (Native American) Having a soft spirit
Lovell, Lovela, Lovele, Lovelle, Lovel

Lovely (American) An attractive and
pleasant woman
*Loveli, Loveley, Lovelie, Lovelee, Loveleigh,
Lovelea*

Lowena (American) Form of Louise,
meaning "a famous warrior"
*Lowenna, Lowenah, Lowennah, Loweniah,
Lowenia, Lowenea, Loweneah*

Loyal (English) One who is faithful and true
*Loyalty, Loyalti, Loyaltie, Loyaltee,
Loyaltea, Loyaltey*

L

Luana (Hawaiian) One who is content and enjoys life
Lewanna, Lou-Ann, Louann, Louanna, Louanne, Luanda, Luane, Luann, Luanna, Luannah, Luanne, Luannie, Luwanna, Luwana, Lujuana

Luba (Hebrew) One who is dearly loved
Liba, Lubah, Libena, Lyuba, Lyubah

Lubaba (Arabic) A soulful woman
Lubabah, Lubabia, Lubaby, Lubabie, Lubabey, Lubabee, Lubabea, Lubabi

Luberda (Spanish) Surrounded by light
Luberdah, Luberdia, Luberdiah, Luberdea, Luberdeah, Luberdiya, Luberdiyah

Lubomira (Slavic) One who yearns for peace
Lubomirah, Lubomiria, Lubomirea, Lubomyra, Lubomyrah, Lubomeera, Lubomeira, Lubomiera

Lucasta (English) Feminine form of Lucas; woman from Lucanus
Luca, Lucania, Lucanea, Lukasta, Luka, Lukina

Lucerne (Latin) One who is surrounded by light
Lucerna, Luceria, Lucena, Lucenia, Lucenea, Lucernia, Lucernea, Lucero

Lucille (French) Form of Lucy, meaning "one who is illuminated"
Lusile, Loucille, Luciela, Lucila, Lucile, Lucilia, Lucilla, Lucyle, Luseele, Lucja, Lucyna, Lucylle, Luceil

Lucja (Polish) Lady of the light
Luscia

Lucky (American) One who is fortunate
Lucki, Luckie, Luckey, Luckee, Luckea, Luckette, Lucket, Lucketta, Luckete, Lucketa

Lucretia (Latin) A bringer of light; a successful woman; in mythology, a maiden who was raped by the prince of Rome
Lacretia, Loucrecia, Loucresha, Loucretia, Loucrezia, Lucrece, Lucrecia, Lucreecia, Lucreesha, Lucreisha, Lucresha, Lucrezia, Luighseach

Lucy (Latin) Feminine form of Lucius; one who is illuminated
Luce, Lucetta, Lucette, Luci, Lucia, Luciana, Lucianna, Lucida, Lucie, Lucienne, Lucina, Lucinda, Lucine, Lucita, Lucyna, Lucyja, Lucza, Lusita, Luz, Luzija, Lucinna, Liusaidh, Lucee, Lucea

Lucylynn (American) A lighthearted woman
Lucylyn, Lucylynne, Lucilynn, Lucilyn, Lucilynne

Ludivina (Slavic) One who is greatly loved
Ludivinah, Ludivyna, Ludivynah, Ludiveena, Ludiveenah, Ludiviena, Ludivienah, Ludiveina, Ludiveinah, Ludiveana, Ludiveanah

Ludmila (Slavic) Having the favor of the people
Ludmilah, Ludmilla, Ludmillah, Ludmyla, Ludmylla, Lyubochka, Lyudmila, Lyuha, Lubmilla, Lubmila, Ljudmila, Ljudumilu

Luenetter (American) A self-centered woman
Luenette, Luenett, Luenete, Luenet, Luenetta, Lueneta

Lulani (Polynesian) Sent from heaven
Lulanie, Lulaney, Lulany, Lulanee, Lulanea

Lully (American) One who soothes others
Lulli, Lullie, Lullee, Lulleigh, Lullea

Lulu (Hawaiian / African) A calm, peaceful woman / as precious as a pearl
Lu'lu, Luloah, Lula, Lo'loo, Looloo

Lulubell (American) A well-known beauty
Lulubelle, Lulubele, Lulubel, Lulubela, Lulubella

Lumina (Latin) Surrounded by a brilliant light
Luminah, Lumeena, Lumeenah, Lumyna, Lumynah, Luminosa

Luna (Latin) Of the moon; in mythology, the goddess of the moon
Lunah, Luneth, Lunetta, Lunette, Lunneta, Lunethe, Lunetha

Lundy (French / Gaelic) Born on a Monday / from the marshland
Lundey, Lundi, Lundie, Lundee, Lundea, Lunde, Lund

Lundyn (American) One who is unlike others
Lundynn, Lundynne, Lundan, Lundann, Lunden, Lundon

Luned (Welsh) Form of Eiluned, meaning "an idol worshipper"
Luneda, Lunedia, Lunedea

Lunet (English) Of the crescent moon
Lunett, Lunette, Luneta, Lunete, Lunetta

Lupita (Spanish) Form of Guadalupe, meaning "from the valley of wolves"
Lupe, Lupyta, Lupelina, Lupeeta, Lupieta, Lupeita, Lupeata

Luquitha (American) An affectionate woman
Luquithah, Luquithia, Luquithiah, Luquithea, Luquitheah, Luquithe, Luquetha

Lur (Spanish) Of the earth

Lurissa (American) A beguiling woman
Lurisa, Luryssa, Lurysa, Luressa, Luresa

Luvelle (American) Surrounded by light
Luvell, Luvel, Luvele, Luvela, Luvella

Luvina (English) Little one who is dearly loved
Luvinah, Luvena, Luvyna, Luveena, Luveina, Luviena, Luveana

Lux (Latin) Lady of the light
Luxe, Luxi, Luxie, Luxee, Luxea, Luxy, Luxey

Luyu (Native American) Resembling the dove

Luz (Spanish / Armenian) Refers to the Virgin Mary, Our Lady of Light / of the moon
Luzelena, Luzette, Luziana, Luzetta, Luzianna, Luzianne, Luzian, Luziane

Luzille (Spanish) A shining woman
Luzill, Luzil, Luzile, Luzila, Luzilla

Lyawonda (American) A beloved friend
Lyawanda, Lyawunda, Lywonda, Lywanda, Lywunda

Lycoris (Greek) Born at twilight
Lycoriss, Lycorisse, Lycorys, Lycorysse, Lycoryss

Lydia (Greek) A beautiful woman from Lydia
Lidia, Lidie, Lidija, Lyda, Lydie, Lydea, Liddy, Lidiy, Lidochka

Lykaios (Greek) Resembling a she-wolf

Lyle (English) From the island
Lisle, Lysle, Lile

Lymekia (Greek) Woman of royalty
Lymekiah, Lymekea, Lymekeah, Lymekiya, Lymekiyah, Lymekya, Lymekyah

Lynette (Welsh) A beautiful maiden; resembling a songbird
Lanette, Linett, Linette, Linnet, Lynet, Lynessa, Lynett, Lynetta, Lynnet, Lynnette, Lenette, Linet, Linetta, Linnette, Linnetta, Lonette, Linytte, Lynete, Lynley, Lyneth

Lynn (English) Woman of the lake; form of Linda, meaning "one who is soft and beautiful"
Linell, Linnell, Lyn, Lynae, Lyndel, Lyndell, Lynell, Lynelle, Lynlee, Lynley, Lynna, Lynne, Lynnelle, Lynnea

Lynton (English) From the town of lime trees
Lynten, Lyntan, Linton, Linten, Lintan

Lyonesse (English) From the lost land
Lyoness, Lyonness, Lyonnesse, Lyones

Lyra (Greek) One who plays the lyre
Lyria, Lyris, Lyrea, Lyre

Lyric (French) Of the lyre; the words of a song
Lyrica, Lyricia, Lyrik, Lyrick, Lyrika, Lyricka

Lysandra (Greek) Form of Alexandra, meaning "helper and defender of mankind"
Lisandra, Lissandra, Lizandra, Lisandrina, Lisandrine, Lissandrina, Lissandrine, Lyssandra, Lyssa, Lyaksandra

Lysett (American) A pretty young girl
Lysette, Lyset, Lysete, Lysetta, Lyseta

Lysimache (Greek) Feminine form of Lysimachus; released from battle
Lysimachie, Lysimachi, Lysimachee, Lysimacha, Lysimachia, Lysimachea

Lyssan (Greek) Form of Alexandra, meaning "helper and defender of mankind"
Lyssana, Lyssann, Lyssane, Lyssanne, Lysan, Lysann, Lysane, Lysanne, Lysana, Lysanna

Lytanisha (American) A scintillating woman
Lytanesha, Lytaniesha, Lytaneisha, Lytanysha, Lytaneesha, Lytaneasha

Maachah (Hebrew) One who has been oppressed; in the Bible, one of David's wives
Maacha

Maarath (Hebrew) From the desolate land
Maaratha, Marath, Marathe, Maratha, Maarathe

Maarii (German) Resembling a dragonfly

Maasiai (Hebrew) One who does God's work
Masiai, Maasai, Masai

Maat (Egyptian) In mythology, the goddess of truth, order, and justice

Maata (Australian) A highborn lady

Maath (Hebrew) A petite woman; small
Maathe, Maatha

Mab (Gaelic) One who is filled with joy

Mabel (English) One who is lovable
Mabelle, Mable, Maible, Maybel, Maybell, Maybelle, Mayble, Mablean, Mabelean, Mabeleen, Moibeal

Mabina (Celtic) One who is nimble
Mabbina, Mabene, Mabine, Mabena, Mabyna, Mabinah, Maeveen, Maevina, Maeveena, Maevine, Mabeana, Mabeena

Mabli (Welsh) The beautiful one
Mablie, Mably, Mabley, Mablee, Mableigh, Mablea

Mabyn (Welsh) One who is forever young
Mabyne, Mabin, Maben, Maban, Mabon

Macanta (Gaelic) A kind and gentle woman
Macan, Macantia, Macantea, Macantah

Macaria (Spanish) One who is blessed
Macarisa, Macarria, Maccaria, Makaria, Makarria, Macarea, Macareah

Macha (Native American / Irish / Scottish) Aurora / goddess of war / woman from the plains
Machara, Macharia, Macharea

Machi (Taiwanese) A good friend
Machie, Machy, Machey, Machee, Machea

Machiko (Japanese) A beautiful child; one who is taught the truth
Machika, Machyko, Machyka

Machpelah (Hebrew) From the double caves
Machpela, Machpellah, Machpella

Mackenna (Gaelic) Daughter of the handsome man
Mackendra, Mackennah, McKenna, McKendra, Makenna, Makennah

Mackenzie ○ ❂ (Gaelic) Daughter of a wise leader; a fiery woman; one who is fair
Mackenzey, Makensie, Makenzie, M'Kenzie, McKenzie, Meckenzie, Mackenzee, Mackenzy, Mackenzi, Mackenzea

Macy (French) One who wields a weapon
Macee, Macey, Maci, Macie, Maicey, Maicy, Macea, Maicea, Maecy, Maecey, Maeci, Maecie, Maecee, Maecea, Maici, Maicie, Maicee

Mada (Arabic) One who has reached the end of the path
Madah

Madana (Ethiopian) One who heals others
Madayna, Madaina, Madania, Madaynia, Madainia

Maddox (English) Born into wealth and prosperity
Madox, Madoxx, Maddoxx

Madeira (Spanish) From the place of sweet wine
Madiera, Madera, Madira, Madyra, Madeera, Madeara

Madelhari (German) A counselor to the troops
Madelharie, Madelhary, Madelharey, Madelharee, Madelharea

Madeline ✪ (Hebrew) Woman from Magdala
*Mada, Madalaina, Madaleine, Madalena, Madalene, Madalyn, Madalynn, Maddelena, Maddie, Maddy, Madel, Madelaine, Madelayne, Madeleine, Madelena, Madelene, Madelina, Madella, Madelle, Madelon, **Madelyn**, Madelyne, Madelynn, Madelynne, Madena, Madilyn, Madina, Madlen, Madlin, Madlyn, Mady, Madzia, Magda, Magdala, Magdalen, Magdalena, Magdalene, Magdalina, Magdaline, Magdalini, Magdeleine, Magdelina, Magdolna, Maidel, Maighdlin, Madalen, Madelia, Magdiel, Maialen, Makda, Malena, Malene, Malin, Matxalen, Modlen*

Madge (English) Form of Margaret, meaning "resembling a pearl / the child of light"

Madhavi (Indian) Feminine form of Madhav; born in the springtime
Madhavie, Madhavee, Madhavey, Madhavy, Madhavea

Madhu (Indian) As sweet as honey
Madhul, Madhula, Madhulika, Madhulia, Madhulea

Madhur (Indian) One who is gentle and kind
Madhuri, Madhurie, Madhura, Madhuria, Madhurea

Madihah (Arabic) One who is praiseworthy
Madeeha, Madiha, Madyha, Madyhah, Madeehah, Madeaha, Madieha, Madeiha

Madini (Swahili) As precious as a gemstone
Madinie, Madiny, Madiney, Madinee, Madyny, Madyni, Madinea, Madynie, Madyney, Madynee, Madynea

Madison ✪ ✪ (English) Daughter of a mighty warrior
Maddison, Madisen, Madisson, Madisyn, Madyson

Madoline (English) One who is accomplished with the stringed instrument
Mandalin, Mandalyn, Mandalynn, Mandelin, Mandellin, Mandellyn, Mandolin, Mandolyn, Mandolynne

Madonna (Italian) My lady; refers to the Virgin Mary
Madonnah, Madona, Madonah

Madora (Greek) A great ruler
Madorah, Madorra, Madorrah

Madra (Spanish) One who is motherly
Madre, Madrina, Madrena, Madrona, Madryna

Madri (Indian) In mythology, the second wife of Pandu
Madrie, Madry, Madrey, Madree, Madrea

Maeko (Japanese) A truthful child
Maekiko, Maekiyo, Masako, Maseko

Maemi (Japanese) Having a truthful smile
Maemie, Maemee, Maemy, Maemey, Maemea

Maera (Greek) In mythology, the daughter of Atlas

Maertisa (English) One who is well-known

Maeve (Irish) An intoxicating woman
Mave, Meave, Medb, Meabh

Mafuane (Egyptian) Daughter of the earth
Mafuann, Mafuanne, Mafuana, Mafuanna

Magali (English) Form of Margaret, meaning "resembling a pearl / the child of light"
Magaley, Magalie, Maggali, Magaly, Magalee, Magaleigh, Maggalie, Maggalee, Magalea, Maggalea

Magara (Rhodesian) A child who cries often
Magarah, Magarra, Magaria

Magena (Native American, Hebrew) One who is protected

Magic (American) One who is full of wonder and surprise
Majic, Magyc, Magik, Magick, Majik, Majick

Magna (Latin) Having great strength

Magnhilda (German) A strong battlemaiden
Magnild, Magnilda, Magnilde, Magnhild, Magnhilde, Maganhildi, Maganhildie, Maganhilde, Maganhilda

Magnolia (French) Resembling the flowering tree
Magnoliya, Magnoliah, Magnolea, Magnoleah, Magnoliyah, Magnolya, Magnolyah

Maha (African) A woman with beautiful eyes
Mahah

M

Mahadevi (Hindi) In Hinduism, a mother goddess
Mahadevie, Mahadevy, Mahadevey, Mahadevee, Mahadevea

Mahal (Native American) A tender and loving woman
Mahall, Mahale, Mahalle

Mahala (Arabic) One who is powerful yet gentle
Mahalia, Mahalah, Mahlah, Mahla, Mahalea, Mahaliah, Mahaleah

Mahalaleel (Hebrew) One who praises God
Maleleel, Malaleel, Mahaleel, Maheleel

Mahalia (Hebrew) One who is tender
Mahala, Mahalah, Mahalath, Mahali, Mahalee, Mahaliah, Mahalla, Mahelia, Mahaleigh, Mahalie, Mehalia, Mahalea

Mahanaim (Hebrew) Of the place of two camps
Mahanaime, Mahanaima, Mahanayme, Mahanaym, Mahanayma, Mahanaem, Mahanaema

Mahari (African) One who offers forgiveness
Maharie, Mahary, Maharey, Maharee, Maharai, Maharae, Maharea

Mahath (Hebrew) The act of grasping
Mahathe, Mahatha, Mahathia

Mahbubi (Arabic) One who is dearly loved; a sweetheart
Mabubi, Mahbubee, Mahbubie, Mabubie, Mabubee, Mahbubey, Mabubey

Mahdi (African) The expected daughter
Mahdie, Mahdy, Mahdey, Mahdee, Mahdea

Mahdis (Persian) A moonlike woman
Mahdiss, Mahdise, Mahdisse, Mahdys, Mahdyss, Mahdysse

Mahendra (Sanskrit) From the mountains
Mahindra, Mahendria, Mahindria, Mahendrea, Mahindrea, Mahyndra, Mahyndria, Mahyndrea

Maheona (Native American) A medicine woman
Maheo, Maheonia, Maheonea

Mahesa (Indian) A powerful and great lady
Maheshvari

Mahina (Hawaiian) Daughter of the moonlight
Maheena, Mahyna, Maheana, Maheyna, Mahiena, Maheina

Mahira (Arabic) A clever and adroit woman
Mahirah, Mahir, Mahire, Mahiria, Mahirea, Maheera, Mahyra, Mahiera, Maheira, Maheara

Mahjabin (Arabic) Having a high forehead
Maahjahbeen, Mahjabeen, Mahjabine, Mahjabyne, Maahjabyne

Mahlah (Hebrew) A diseased woman; one to be pitied
Mahli, Mahlon

Mahmoode (Arabic) One who is given praise
Mahmude, Mahmudee, Mahmoude, Mamoudee

Mahogany (English) Resembling the rich, dark wood
Mahogani, Mahoganey, Mahoganie, Mahogane, Mahogonee, Mahogonea

Mahola (Hebrew) One who enjoys dancing
Maholah, Maholla, Mahollah

Mahsa (Persian) Resembling the moon
Mahsah

Mahteab (Arabic) Born beneath the moon

Mahtowa (Sioux) A sacred she-bear
Mahtowah, Matowa

Maia (Latin / Maori) The great one; in mythology, the goddess of spring / a brave warrior
Maaja, Maiah, Maya, Maja, Mayah, Moia, Moja, Mya, Moya

Maibe (Egyptian) A dignified and serious lady

Maida (English) A maiden; a virgin
Maidel, Maidie, Mayda, Maydena, Maydey, Mady, Maegth, Magd, Maidel, Maeda

Maiki (Japanese) Resembling the dancing flower
Maikie, Maikei, Maikki, Maikee

Maile (Hawaian) From the sweet-smelling vine

Maille (Gaelic) Form of Molly, meaning "star of the sea / from the sea of bitterness" *Mailsi, Mailsea, Mailsie, Mailsy, Mailsey, Mailsee*

Maimun (Arabic) One who is lucky; fortunate *Maimoon, Maimoun*

Maimuna (Arabic) One who is trustworthy *Maimoona, Maimouna*

Maina (Indian) Resembling a bird

Maine (French) From the mainland; from the state of Maine

Maiolaine (French) As delicate as a flower *Maiolainie, Maiolani, Maiolaney, Maiolany, Maiolanee, Maiolayne, Maiolanea*

Mairwen (Welsh) One who is fair; form of Mary, meaning "star of the sea / from the sea of bitterness" *Mairwenn, Mairwenne, Mairwyn, Mairwynn, Mairwynne, Mairwin, Mairwinn, Mairwinne*

Maisara (Arabic) One who lives an effortless life *Maisarah, Maisarra, Maisarrah*

Maise (Gaelic) An adorned beauty *Mayse, Maisa, Maysa, Maese, Maesa*

Maisha (African) Giver of life *Maysha, Maishah, Mayshah, Maesha, Maeshah*

Maisie (Scottish) Form of Margaret, meaning "resembling a pearl / the child of light" *Maisee, Maisey, Maisy, Maizie, Mazey, Mazie, Maisi, Maizi, Maizee, Maizea, Maisea*

Maitane (English) One who is dearly loved *Maite, Maitena, Maitayne, Maitaine, Maitana, Maita, Maitea, Maitaene*

Maitland (English) From the meadow *Maitlanda, Maytland, Maetland, Maytlanda, Maetlanda, Maitlande, Maytlande, Maetlande*

Maitra (Sanskrit) A beloved friend *Maitri, Maitrie, Maitry, Maitrey, Maitree, Maitria, Maitrea*

Maitraka (Sanskrit) The little loving one *Maitrakah, Maitracka, Maytraka, Maytracka, Maetraka, Maetracka*

Maitreya (Sanskrit) One who offers love to all *Maitreyah, Maetreya, Maitraya, Maetraya*

Maitrya (Sanskrit) A benevolent woman *Matriya, Mitravan, Maitryi, Maitryie*

Maiya (Japanese) Of the rice valley *Maiyah*

Maizah (African) One who has good judgment and keen insight *Maiza, Mayzah, Mayzah, Maeza, Maezah*

Majaliwa (Swahili) Filled with God's grace *Majaliwah, Majalewa, Majalywa, Majalewah, Majalywah*

Majaya (Indian) A victorious woman *Majayah*

Majda (Arabic) A glorious woman *Majdah*

Majesta (Latin) One who has a royal bearing *Majestas, Majesty, Majesti, Majestie, Majestee, Majestey, Majestea, Majestic*

Majida (Arabic) Feminine form of Majid; noble glory *Majeeda, Majeedah, Majidah, Maji, Maajida*

Majime (Japanese) An earnest woman

Makaio (Hawaiian) A gift from God

Makala (Hawaiian) Resembling myrtle *Makalah, Makalla, Makallah*

Makani (Hawaiian) Of the wind *Makanie, Makaney, Makany, Makanee, Makanea*

Makara (Australian) The seven stars that make up the Pleiades *Makarah, Makarra, Makarrah*

Makareta (Maori) Form of Margaret, meaning "resembling a pearl / the child of light" *Makaretah, Makarita, Makaryta*

Makarim (Arabic) An honorable woman *Makarime, Makarym, Makaryme, Makarima, Makaryma*

M

Makato (Native American) Of the blue earth
Maka, Makata

Makea (Finnish) One who is sweet
Makeah, Makia, Makiah

Makeda (African) A queenly woman; greatness
Makedah

Makelina (Hawaiian) Form of Madeline, meaning "woman from Magdala"
Makelinah, Makeleena, Makelyna, Makeleana, Makeline, Makelyne, Makeleane, Makeleene

Makena (African) One who is filled with happiness
Makenah, Makeena, Makeenah, Makeana, Makeanah, Makyna, Makynah, Mackena, Mackenah

Makheloth (Hebrew) Woman of the congregation
Makhelothe, Makhelotha, Makhelothia

Makin (Arabic) An able-bodied woman
Makina, Makine, Makinya

Makiyo (Japanese) From the tree of truth
Makiko

Makkedah (Hebrew) From the herdsman's camp
Makkeda, Makedah, Makeda

Makoto (Japanese) A thankful woman

Makya (Native American) A huntress of eagles
Makyah, Makiya, Makiyah

Malak (Arabic) A heavenly messenger; an angel
Malaka, Malaika, Malayka, Malaeka, Malake, Malayk, Malaek, Malakia

Malana (Hawaiian) A lighthearted woman
Malanah, Malanna, Malannah

Malann (Hebrew) A great ruler
Malanne, Mallann, Mallanne

Malati (Indian) Resembling a fragrant flower
Malatie, Malaty, Malatey, Malatee, Malatea

Malaya (Spanish) An independent woman; one who is free
Malayah

Malcomina (Scottish) Feminine form of Malcolm; devotee of St. Columba
Malcomeena, Malcomyna, Malcominia, Malcominea, Malcomena, Malcomeina, Malcomiena, Malcomeana

Malcsi (Hungarian) An industrious woman
Malcsie, Malcsee, Malcsey, Malcsy, Malksi, Malksie, Malksy, Malksee, Malksey, Malcsea, Malksea

Maleda (Ethiopian) Born with the rising sun
Maledah

Mali (Thai / Welsh) Resembling a flower / form of Molly, meaning "star of the sea / from the sea of bitterness"
Malie, Malee, Maleigh, Maly, Maley

Malia (Hawaiian) Form of Mary, meaning "star of the sea / from the sea of bitterness"
Maliah, Malea, Maleah, Maleia, Maliyah, Maliya, Malya, Malyah

Maliha (Indian) A beautiful woman of great strength
Malihah, Malyha, Maleeha, Maleiha, Maleaha

Malika (Arabic) Destined to be queen
Malikah, Malyka, Maleeka, Maleika, Malieka, Maliika, Maleaka

Malila (Native American) Resembling the salmon
Malilah, Maleela, Maleila, Maliela, Malyla, Maleala

Malina (Hawaiian) A peaceful woman
Malinah, Maleena, Maleenah, Malyna, Malynah, Maleina, Maliena, Maleana

Malini (Indian) A gardener
Malinie, Maliny, Malinee, Maliney, Malinea

Malinka (Russian) As sweet as a little berry
Malinkah, Malynka, Maleenka, Malienka, Maleinka, Maleanka

Malise (Gaelic) A dark beauty
Malyse, Malese, Melusina

Maliza (Swahili) An accomplished woman
Malizah, Maleeza, Malyza, Malieza, Maleaza

Malka (Hebrew) A queenly woman
Malcah, Malkah, Malke, Malkia, Malkie, Milcah, Milka, Milke, Milca, Malha, Malhah

Mallika (Indian) Resembling jasmine
Mallikah, Malleeka, Malleika, Mallieka, Mallyka, Malleaka

Mallory (French) An unlucky young woman; ill-fated
Mallary, Mallerey, Mallery, Malloreigh, Mallorey, Mallori, Mallorie, Malorey, Malori, Malorie, Malory, Malloren, Mallorea, Malorea, Maloree

Mallow (Gaelic) Woman from the river; resembling the flowering plant
Mallowe, Mallo, Malloe, Malow, Malowe, Maloe

Malmuira (Scottish) A dark-skinned beauty
Malmurie, Malmuria, Malmura, Malmuri

Malone (Lithuanian) By the grace of God
Malona, Malonne, Maloni, Malonie, Malonia, Malony, Maloney, Malonee, Malonea

Malu (Hawaiian) A peaceful woman

Maluna (Hawaiian) One who rises above
Maloona, Malunia, Malunai, Maloonia, Maloonai, Malouna, Malounia, Malounai

Malva (Greek) One who is soft and slender
Malvah, Malvia, Malvea

Malvina (English) Having a smooth brow
Malvinah, Malveena, Malveenah, Malviena, Malveina, Malveana, Malvyna, Malvine, Malvyne

Malvinia (Latin) A beloved friend
Malvenia, Malvinea, Malvenea, Malvynia, Malvynea, Malviniya

Mamaki (Sanskrit) Darling little mother
Mamakie, Mamaky, Mamakey, Mamakee, Mamakea

Mamani (Incan) Resembling a falcon
Mamanie, Mamanee, Mamaney, Mamany, Mamanea

Mamie (English) Form of Mary, meaning "star of the sea / from the sea of bitterness"; form of Margaret, meaning "resembling a pearl / the child of light"
Maime, Mame, Maymie, Mayme, Maimie, Mamia, Mamee, Mamea, Mami

Mamiko (Japanese) Daughter of the sea
Mameeko, Mamyko

Mana (Polynesian) A charismatic and prestigious woman
Manah

Manal (Arabic) An accomplished woman
Manala, Manall, Manalle, Manalla, Manali

Manami (Japanese) Having a love of the ocean
Manamie, Manamy, Manamey, Manamee, Manamea

Manar (Arabic) Woman of the light
Manara, Manaria, Manarr, Manarre, Manarra, Manari, Manarri, Mannara, Mannarra

Manasa (Indian) Having great strength of mind
Maanasa, Manassa, Manasah

Mandana (Persian) Beauty everlasting
Mandanah, Mandanna, Mandannah

Mandeep (Indian) Having a bright mind
Mandeepe, Mandyp, Mandype, Mandeepa, Mandypa

Mandisa (African) A sweet woman
Mandisah, Mandysa, Mandysah

Mandraya (Sanskrit) An honorable woman
Mandray, Mandrayia, Mandraye

Mandy (English) Form of Amanda, meaning "one who is much loved"
Mandi, Mandie, Mandee, Mandey, Manda, Mandalyn, Mandalynn, Mandelina, Mandeline, Mandalyna, Mandea

Mangena (Hebrew) As sweet as a melody
Mangenah, Mangenna, Mangennah

Manhattan (English) From the whiskey town
Manhatton, Manhatan, Manhaton

M

Mania (Greek) In mythology,
the personification of insanity
Maniah, Mainia, Maynia, Maniya

Manika (Sanskrit) Her mind is a jewel
*Maanika, Manicka, Manyka, Manycka,
Manicca, Manica, Maniya, Manikya,
Maneka*

Manina (Polish) A warring woman
*Maninah, Maneena, Maneina, Manyna,
Maneana, Maniena*

Manisa (Native American) One who travels
on foot
Manisah, Manysa, Manysah

Manisha (Indian) Having great intelligence;
a genius
*Maneesha, Manishah, Manysha,
Maniesha, Maneisha, Maneasha*

Manjari (Indian) Of the sacred blossom
*Manjarie, Manjary, Manjarey, Manjaree,
Manjarea*

Manjula (Indian) A sweet young woman
*Manjulah, Manjulia, Manjulie, Manjule,
Manjuli*

Manjusha (Sanskrit) As treasured as a box
of gems
*Manjushah, Manjushia, Manjousha,
Manjoushia*

Manning (English) Daughter of Man
Maning, Mannyng, Manyng

Manoush (Persian) Born under the
sweet sun
*Manoushe, Manousha, Manoushai,
Manoushia, Manoushea*

Mansa (African) The third-born child
Mansah, Mansia

Mansi (Native American) Resembling a
picked flower
*Mansie, Mansy, Mansey, Mansee, Mansea,
Mausi, Mausie, Mausee, Mausy, Mausey,
Mausea*

Manto (Greek) A prophetess; in
mythology, mother of Mopsus
*Mantia, Mantika, Manteia, Mantea,
Mantai, Mantae*

Mantrana (Sanskrit) One who counsels
others
*Mantrini, Mantrania, Mantranna,
Mantrani, Mantrinie, Mantranie*

Mantreh (Persian) One who is pure; chaste
Mantre

Manuela (Spanish) Feminine form of
Emmanuel; God is with us
*Manuella, Manuelita, Manuelyta,
Manueleeta, Manoela, Manuel, Manuelle,
Manuele*

Manulani (Hawaiian) Resembling a bird
in the heavens
*Manulanie, Manulane, Manulaney,
Manulanee, Manulanea*

Manyara (African) A humble woman
Manyarah

Maola (Irish) A handmaiden
*Maoli, Maole, Maolie, Maolia, Maoly,
Maoley, Maolee, Maolea*

Maolmin (Gaelic) A woman holding rank
as chief
*Maolmine, Maolmina, Maolminia,
Maolmyn, Maolmyna, Maolmyne*

Maon (Hebrew) Woman of the home

Mapenzi (African) One who is dearly
loved
*Mpenzi, Mapenzie, Mapenze, Mapenzy,
Mapenzee, Mapenzea*

Mara (Hebrew) A grieving woman; one
who is sorrowful
*Marra, Mahra, Marah, Maralina,
Maralinda, Maraline*

Maralah (Hebrew) Born during the earth's
trembling
Marala, Marallah, Maralla

Maram (Arabic) One who is wished for
*Marame, Marama, Marami, Maramie,
Maramee, Maramy, Maramey, Maramea*

Maravilla (Spanish) One who is marveled
at; a miracle child
*Marivella, Marivilla, Marevilla, Marevella,
Maravella, Maraville, Marivel, Marivelle*

Marcail (Scottish) Form of Margaret, meaning "resembling a pearl / the child of light"
Marcaila, Marcaile, Marcayl, Marcayle, Marcayla, Marcael, Marcaele, Marcaela

Marcella (Latin) Feminine form of Marcellus; dedicated to Mars, the god of war
Marcela, Marcele, Marcelina, Marcelinda, Marceline, Marcelle, Marcellina, Marcelline, Marcelyn, Marchella, Marchelle, Marcile, Marcilee, Marcille, Marquita, Marsalina, Marsella, Marselle, Marsellonia, Marshella, Marsiella, Marcila, Marsil, Marsille, Marsilla, Marsila, Marsali

March (Latin) Born during the month of March
Marche

Marcia (Latin) Feminine form of Marcus; dedicated to Mars, the god of war
Marcena, Marcene, Marchita, Marciana, Marciane, Marcianne, Marcilyn, Marcilynn, Marcina, Marcine, Marcita, Marseea, Marsia, Martia, Marsha, Marek, Marcsa

Marcy (Latin) Form of Marcella or Marcia, meaning "dedicated to Mars, the god of war"
Marcey, Marci, Marcie, Marcee, Marsee, Marsey, Marsy, Marsie, Marsi, Marcea, Marsea

Marde (Latin) A woman warrior
Mardane, Mardayne

Mardea (African) The last-born child
Mardeah

Mardi (French) Born on a Tuesday
Mardie, Mardy, Mardey, Mardee, Mardea

Marelda (German) A famous woman warrior
Marelde, Mareldah, Marrelda, Marilda, Marilde, Mareld, Marild

Marenda (Latin) An admirable woman
Marendah

Margana (Sanskrit) One who seeks the truth
Marganah, Marganna, Margannah

Margaret (Greek / Persian) Resembling a pearl / the child of light
Maighread, Mairead, Mag, Maggi, Maggie, Maggy, Maiga, Malgorzata, Marcheta, Marchieta, Marga, Margalit, Margalo, Margareta, Margarete, Margarethe, Margaretta, Margarette, Margarida, Margarit, Margarita, Margarite, Margaruite, Marge, Marged, Margeen, Margeret, Margeretta, Margerie, Margerita, Marget, Margette, Margey, Marghanita, Margharita, Margherita, Marghretta, Margies, Margisia, Margit, Margita, Margize, Margred, Margret, Margrete, Margreth, Margrett, Margrit, Margrid, Marguarette, Marguarita, Marguerita, Marguerite, Marguita, Maarit, Marjeta, Margosha, Marjeta, Marared, Margaid, Marenka, Maret, Mererid

Marged (Welsh) Form of Margaret, meaning "resembling a pearl / the child of light"
Margred, Margeda, Margreda

Margo (French) Form of Margaret, meaning "resembling a pearl / the child of light"
Margeaux, Margaux, Margolo, Margot

Marhilda (German) A famous battlemaiden
Marhildi, Marhilde, Marhild, Marhildie, Marhildy, Marhildey, Marhildee, Marildi, Marildie

Mari (Hebrew) A wished-for daughter

Maria ○ (Spanish) Form of Mary, meaning "star of the sea / from the sea of bitterness"
Mariah, Marialena, Marialinda, Marialisa, Maaria, Mayria, Maeria, Mariabella, Mariabelle, Mariabell, Mariasha, Marea

Mariama (African) A gift from God
Mariamah, Mariamma, Mariame

Mariamne (Hebrew) A rebellious woman
Mamre, Meria

Mariane (French) A combination of Mary and Ann, meaning "star of the sea / from the sea of bitterness" and "a woman graced with God's favor"
Mariam, Mariana, Marian, Marion, Maryann, Maryanne, Maryanna, Maryane, Maryana, Marianne, Marianna, Mariann, Maryam, Marianda, Marien

Mariatu (African) One who is pure; innocent

Maribel (Spanish) Form of Mary, meaning "star of the sea / from the sea of bitterness"; the beautiful Mary
Maribell, Maribelle, Maribella, Maribele, Maribela, Marabel, Marabelle, Marabela, Marabella, Marybel, Marybell, Marybella, Marybelle, Marybele, Marybela

Marica (Latin) In mythology, a nymph and mother of Latinus

Maricela (Spanish) Form of Marcella, meaning "dedicated to Mars, the god of war"
Maricel, Maricella, Marisela, Maresella, Marisella, Maryzela, Marecela, Marecella

Maridhia (Swahili) One who is content
Maridha, Maridhea, Maridhe, Marydhia, Marydhiya

Marie (French) Form of Mary, meaning "star of the sea / from the sea of bitterness"
Maree, Marea

Mariel (Danish) Form of Mary, meaning "star of the sea / from the sea of bitterness"
Mariela, Mariele, Mariella, Marielle, Mariell, Mariola

Marietta (French) Form of Mary, meaning "star of the sea / from the sea of bitterness"
Mariette, Maretta, Mariet, Maryetta, Maryette, Marieta

Marifa (Arabic) Having great knowledge
Marifah, Maryfa, Maryfah, Maripha, Marypha

Marigold (English) Resembling the golden flower
Marrigold, Maragold, Maregold, Marygold, Marigolde

Marika (Danish) Form of Mary, meaning "star of the sea / from the sea of bitterness"
Marieke, Marijke, Marike, Maryk, Maryka

Mariko (Japanese) Daughter of Mari; a ball or sphere
Maryko, Mareeko, Marieko, Mareiko

Marilla (English) Of the shining sea
Marillah, Marila, Marillis, Marilis, Marella, Marela, Marelle

Marilyn (English) Form of Mary, meaning "star of the sea / from the sea of bitterness"
Maralin, Maralyn, Maralynn, Marelyn, Marilee, Marilin, Marillyn, Marilynn, Marilynne, Marlyn, Marralynn, Marrilin, Marrilyn, Marylin, Marylyn, Marylynn, Marilena, Mariline

Marina (Latin) Woman of the sea
Mareen, Mareena, Mareina, Marena, Marine, Marinda, Marinell, Marinella, Marinelle, Marinna, Maryn, Marin, Marinochka

Mariposa (Spanish) Resembling a butterfly
Maryposa, Marriposa, Marryposa, Mareposa, Maraposa

Mariska (Slavic) Form of Mary, meaning "star of the sea / from the sea of bitterness"
Maryska, Mariske, Maryske, Maruska, Maruske, Martuska

Marissa (Latin) Woman of the sea
Maressa, Maricia, Marisabel, Marisha, Marisse, Maritza, Mariza, Marrissa, Maryssa, Meris, Merissa, Meryssa, Marisa, Mareesa, Mareisa, Marysa, Marysia, Maris, Marris, Marys, Maryse, Marisol, Merise

Marjah (Sanskrit) One who is hopeful

Marjam (Slavic) One who is merry
Marjama, Marjamah, Marjami, Marjamie, Marjamy, Marjamey, Marjamee, Marjamea

Marjan (Polish) Form of Mary, meaning "star of the sea / from the sea of bitterness"
Marjann, Marjanne, Marjana, Marjanna, Marjon, Marjonn, Marjonne

Marjani (African) Of the coral reef
Marjanie, Marjany, Marjaney, Marjanee, Marjean, Marjeani, Marjeanie, Marijani, Marijanie

Marjolaina (French) Resembling the sweet flower
Marjolaine, Marjolayn, Marjolayne, Marjolayna, Marjolaene, Marjolaen, Marjolaena

Marjorie (English) Form of Margaret, meaning "resembling a pearl / the child of light"
Marcharie, Marge, Margeree, Margery, Margerie, Margery, Margey, Margi, Margie, Margy, Marja, Marje, Marjerie, Marjery, Marji, Marjie, Marjorey, Marjory, Marjy, Majori, Majorie, Majory, Majorey, Majoree, Marjo

Marka (African) Born during a steady rain
Markah

Markeisha (American) Form of Keisha, meaning "the favorite child"
Markeishla, Markeishah, Markecia, Markesha, Markeysha, Markeesha, Markiesha, Markeshia, Markeishia, Markeasha

Marketa (Slavic) Form of Margaret, meaning "resembling a pearl / the child of light"
Markeda, Markee, Markeeta, Markia, Markie, Markita, Marqueta, Marquetta

Markku (Scandinavian) A rebellious woman

Marlee (English) Of the marshy meadow
Marley, Marleigh, Marli, Marlie, Marly, Marlea

Marlene (German) A combination of Mary and Magdalene, meaning "star of the sea / from the sea of bitterness" and "woman from Magdala"
Marlaina, Marlana, Marlane, Marlayna, Marlayne, Marleen, Marleena, Marleene, Marleina, Marlen, Marlena, Marleni, Marna, Marlin, Marlina, Marline, Marlyn, Marlynne, Marla, Marlette

Marlis (German) Form of Mary, meaning "star of the sea / from the sea of bitterness"
Marlisa, Marliss, Marlise, Marlisse, Marlissa, Marlys, Marlyss, Marlysa, Marlyssa, Marlysse

Marlo (English) One who resembles driftwood
Marloe, Marlow, Marlowe, Marlon

Marmara (Greek) From the sparkling sea
Marmarra, Marmarah, Marmarrah

Marmarin (Arabic) Resembling marble
Marmareen, Marmarine, Marmareene, Marmarina, Marmareena

Marni (American) Form of Marina, meaning "woman of the sea"
Marna, Marne, Marnee, Marnell, Marney, Marnie, Marnina, Marnisha, Marnja, Marnya, Marnette, Marnetta, Marnia, Marnea

Maroth (Hebrew) Woman of sorrow; perfect grief
Marothe, Marotha, Marothia, Marothea, Marothiya

Marpessa (Greek) In mythology, the granddaughter of Ares
Marpesa, Marpessah, Marpesah, Marpe, Marpes

Marquise (French) Feminine form of the title marquis; born to royalty
Marchesa, Marchessa, Markaisa, Markessa, Marquesa, Marquessa, Marqui, Marquisa, Marquisha

Marsala (Italian) From the place of sweet wine
Marsalah, Marsalla, Marsallah

Martha (Aramaic) Mistress of the house; in the Bible, the sister of Lazarus and Mary
Maarva, Marfa, Marhta, Mariet, Marit, Mart, Marta, Marte, Martella, Martelle, Marth, Marthe, Marthena, Marthine, Marthini, Marthy, Marti, Martie, Martita, Martje, Martta, Marty, Mata, Matha, Matti, Mattie, Mirtha, Marva

Martina (English) Feminine form of Martin; dedicated to Mars, the god of war
Martynne, Martyne, Marteene, Marteena, Martyna, Martine, Martinne, Martynna, Marteen, Marteane, Martean, Marteana

Marvell (Latin) An extraordinary woman
Marve, Marvel, Marvela, Marvele, Marvella, Marvelle, Marvelyn, Marveille

Marvina (English) Feminine form of Marvin; friend of the sea
Marvinah, Marveena, Marveene, Marvyna, Marvyne, Marvadene, Marvene, Marvena, Marva

Marwarid (Arabic) Form of Margaret, meaning "resembling a pearl / the child of light"
Marwaareed, Marwareed, Marwaryd, Marwaryde, Marwaride

M

Mary ✪ (Latin / Hebrew) Star of the sea / from the sea of bitterness
Mair, Mal, Mallie, Manette, Manon, Manya, Mare, Maren, Maretta, Marette, Marice, Maridel, Mariquilla, Mariquita, Marita, Maritsa, Marya, Maribeth, Marybeth, Maryjo, Marylee, Marylou, Marylu, Masha, Mayra, Meiriona, Maryon, Maeron, Maeryn, Maija, Maiju, Maili, Maira, Maire, Mairi, Mairia, Mairona, Mallaidh, Marusya, Masia, Marynia, Marira, Marquilla, Maricruz, Marilu, Miren, Murron, Mura, Mearr, Mere, Mele

Maryland (English) Honoring Queen Mary; from the state of Maryland
Mariland, Maralynd, Marylind, Marilind

Maryweld (English) Mary of the woods
Marywelde, Marywelda, Mariweld, Mariwelde, Mariwelda

Marzhan (Slavic) From the coral reef
Marzhane, Marzhann, Marzhanne, Marzhana, Marzhanna

Masako (Japanese) Child of justice

Masalda (Hebrew) One who offers support; a good foundation
Masada, Masalde, Masaldia, Masaldea

Masami (African / Japanese) A commanding woman / one who is truthful
Masamie, Masamee, Masamy, Masamey, Masamea

Masara (African) A magical woman; a sorceress
Masaramusi, Masarra

Mashaka (African) A troublemaker; a mischievous woman
Mashakah, Mashakia, Mashake, Mashaki, Mashakie, Mashaky, Mashakey, Mashakee, Mashakea

Masika (Egyptian) Born during a rainstorm
Masikah, Masyka, Maseeka, Masieka, Maseika, Maseaka

Ma'sma (Arabic) One who is innocent
Maa'sma

Mason (English) A stoneworker
Maison, Mayson, Maisen, Masen, Maysen, Maeson, Maesen

Mas'ouda (Arabic) One who is fortunate; lucky
Maas'ouda

Masrekah (Hebrew) From the vineyard
Masreka, Masrecka, Masrekia, Masrekiah

Massachusetts (Native American) From the big hill; from the state of Massachusetts
Massachusets, Massachusette, Massachusetta, Massa, Massachute, Massachusta

Massah (Hebrew) One who tempts others
Massa

Massarra (Arabic) Filled with happiness

Massassi (African) In mythology, the first woman of earth
Massassie, Masasi, Masasie, Massasi, Masassi, Massassy, Masasy, Massassee, Masasee

Massima (Italian) A superior woman; the greatest

Mastura (Arabic) One who is pure; chaste
Mastoora, Masturah, Masturia, Masturiya, Mastooria, Mastoura, Mastrouria

Matana (Hebrew) A gift from God
Matanah, Matanna, Matannah, Matai

Matangi (Hindi) In Hinduism, the patron of inner thought
Matangy, Matangie, Matangee, Matangey, Matangea

Matea (Hebrew) Feminine form of Matthew; a gift from God
Mattea, Matthea, Matthia, Mathea, Mathia, Mateja, Matia, Mathia, Matthan, Matthanias

Matilda (German) One who is mighty in battle
Maitilde, Maltilda, Maltilde, Mat, Matelda, Mathilda, Mathilde, Matilde, Matti, Mattie, Matty, Mahault, Maitilda, Maiti, Matia, Mathild, Matyidy

Matisoon (Native American) Giver of life
Mati, Matisun, Matisune, Matisoone, Matisoun, Matisoune

Matriona (Latin) Lady of the house; a matron
Matrena, Matresha, Matrina, Matryna, Motreina

Matsuko (Japanese) Child of the pine tree

Mattox (English) A gift from God
*Matox, Mattoxx, Matoxx, Matoxa,
Mattoxi, Mattoxia*

Matuta (Latin) In mythology, goddess of
childbirth
Matutah

Maud (German) Form of Matilda, meaning
"one who is mighty in battle"
*Maude, Maudie, Maudi, Maudy, Maudee,
Maudey, Maudea*

Maureen (Irish) Form of Mary, meaning
"star of the sea / from the sea of bitterness"
*Maura, Maurene, Maurianne, Maurine,
Maurya, Mavra, Maure, Mo, Maurean,
Maureane*

Maurissa (Latin) Feminine form of
Maurice; a dark-skinned beauty
*Maurisa, Maurelle, Maurell, Maurella,
Maurita, Mauryta, Maurizia, Mauriza,
Maurise, Maurisse*

Mauve (French) Of the mallow plant
Mawve

Mave (Gaelic) One who brings joy to others
Mava

Mavelle (Celtic) Resembling a songbird
*Mavell, Mavele, Mavella, Mavela, Mavel,
Mavie*

Maven (English) Having great knowledge
Mavin, Mavyn

Mawiyah (Arabic) Possessing the essence
of life
Mawiya

Mawunyaga (African) God is great

Maxine (English) Feminine form of Max;
the greatest
*Maxeen, Maxena, Maxence, Maxene,
Maxi, Maxie, Maxime, Maximina,
Maxina, Maxy, Maxanda, Maxima,
Maxea*

May (Latin) Born during the month of
May; form of Mary, meaning "star of the
sea / from the sea of bitterness"
*Mae, Mai, Maelynn, Maelee, Maj, Mala,
Mayana, Maye, Mayleen, Maylene, Mei*

Maya ✿ (Indian / Hebrew) An illusion; a
dream / woman of the water

Mayes (English) From the meadow

Maylea (Hawaiian) Resembling a wild-
flower
*Maylee, Mayli, Maylie, Mayley, Mayly,
Mayleigh*

Maylin (American) Of the wondrous
waterfall
Maylen, Maylan

Maymunah (Arabic) One who is blessed
*Maymuna, Maymoona, Maymoonah,
Maymouna, Maymounah*

Maysa (Arabic) One who is graceful
Maysah

MAYA

My husband wanted to name our second child after Shea Stadium, the place where we met. I thought
it was a nice name for a dog, but not a child. When we chose Maya as her first name, we tried putting Shea behind it. I can't imagine a better combination now than Maya Shea. —Megan, TX

Maverick (American) One who is wild
and free
*Maverik, Maveryck, Maveryk, Mavarick,
Mavarik*

Mavis (French) Resembling a songbird
*Mavise, Maviss, Mavisse, Mavys, Mavyss,
Mavysse*

Mavonde (African) Of the abundant harvest
Mavonda, Mavondia, Mavondea

Maysun (Arabic) A woman with a beauti-
ful face
*Maysoon, Maysuna, Maysoona, Maysoun,
Maysouna*

Mayumi (Japanese) One who embodies
truth, wisdom, and beauty
*Mayumie, Mayumee, Mayumy, Mayumey,
Mayumea*

M

Mayuri (Indian) Resembling a peahen
Mayurie, Mayuree, Mayurey, Mayury, Mayurea

Mazarine (French) Having deep-blue eyes
Mazareen, Mazareene, Mazaryn, Mazaryne, Mazine, Mazyne, Mazeene

Mazel (Hebrew) One who is lucky
Mazell, Mazele, Mazelle, Mazela, Mazella

Mazhira (Hebrew) A shining woman
Mazhirah, Mazheera, Mazhyra, Mazheira, Mazhiera, Mazheara

Mazzaroth (Hebrew) A seer; refers to the twelve signs of the zodiac
Mazzarothe, Mazzarotha, Mazaroth, Mazarothe, Mazarotha

McKayla (Gaelic) A fiery woman
McKale, McKaylee, McKaleigh, McKay, McKaye, McKaela

Mead (English) From the meadow
Meade, Meed, Meede

Meadghbh (Celtic) One who is nimble

Meadow (American) From the beautiful field
Meadowe, Meado, Meadoe, Medow, Medowe, Medoe

Meahpaara (Arabic) Slice of the moon
Meahparah, Meahparra, Meapara

Meantuna (Arabic) One who is trustworthy
Meantoona, Meantouna

Meara (Gaelic) One who is filled with happiness
Mearah

Meciria (African) A kind and thoughtful woman
Meciriah, Mecyria, Mecyriah

Meda (Native American) A prophetess

Meddela (Swedish) A well-spoken woman
Medela, Meddella, Medella

Medea (Greek) A cunning ruler; in mythology, a sorceress
Madora, Medeia, Media, Medeah, Mediah, Mediya, Mediyah

Medeba (Hebrew) From the quiet waters
Medebah

Medina (Arabic) From the city of the prophet
Medinah, Medyna, Medynah, Medeena, Medeenah, Mediena, Medeina, Medeana, Mdina

Medini (Indian) Daughter of the earth
Medinie, Mediny, Mediney, Medinee, Medinea

Meditrina (Latin) The healer; in mythology, goddess of health and wine
Meditreena, Meditryna, Meditriena

Medora (Greek) A wise ruler
Medoria, Medorah, Medorra, Medorea

Medusa (Greek) In mythology, a Gorgon with snakes for hair
Medoosa, Medusah, Medoosah, Medousa, Medousah

Meena (Hindi) Resembling a fish; in Hinduism, the daughter of the goddess Usha
Meenah, Meana, Meanah

Meenakshi (Indian) Having beautiful eyes

Meera (Israeli) A saintly woman; woman of the light
Meerah, Meira, Meirah, Meir

Megaera (Greek) In mythology, a Fury
Magaere, Magaera, Megaere

Megan ○ ○ (Welsh) Form of Margaret, meaning "resembling a pearl / the child of light"
Maegan, Meg, Magan, Magen, Megin, Maygan, Meagan, Meaghan, Meagin, Meeghan, Meegan, Meghan, Megdn, Meggen, Megen, Meggan, Meggie, Meggy, Meganira, Meighan

Megha (Indian) Resembling a cloud
Meghana, Meghah

Megiddo (Hebrew) From the army's camp
Megiddon

Mehadi (Indian) Resembling a flower
Mehadie, Mehady, Mehadey, Mehadee, Mehadea

Mehalah (Hebrew) Filled with tenderness
Mehala, Mehalla, Mehallah

Mehalia (Hebrew) An affectionate woman
Mehaliah, Mehalea, Mehaleah, Mehaliya, Mehaliyah

Mehana (Hawaiian) A warm and friendly woman
Mehanah, Mehannah, Mehanna

Mehetabel (Hebrew) God makes one joyous
Mehitabelle, Mettabel, Meheytabel, Mehitabel, Mehitahelle

Mehuman (Hebrew) One who is faithful
Mehumann, Mehumane, Mehumana, Mehumanna

Mei (Latin / Hawaiian) The great one / May
Meiying

Meishan (Chinese) One who is virtuous and beautiful
Meishana, Meishawn, Meishaun, Meishon

Meiwei (Chinese) One who is forever enchanting

Mejarkon (Hebrew) From the clear waters
Mejarkona, Mejarkonia, Mejarkone

Meki (Croatian) A tender woman
Mekie, Mekee, Mekey, Meky, Mekea

Mekonah (Hebrew) A source of strength; a solid foundation
Mekona, Mekonia, Mekoniah, Mekonna

Melanctha (Greek) Resembling the black flower
Melancthia, Melancthea

Melangell (Welsh) A sweet messenger from heaven
Melangelle, Melangela, Melangella, Melangele, Melangel

Melanie ♥ (Greek) A dark-skinned beauty
Malaney, Malanie, Mel, Mela, Melaina, Melaine, Melainey, Melana, Melanee, Melaney, Melani, Melania, Melanney, Melannie, Melany, Mella, Mellanie, Melli, Mellie, Melloney, Melly, Meloni, Melonie, Melonnie, Melony, Melaena, Melanea, Malanea, Melonea

Melantha (Greek) Resembling a dark-violet flower
Melanthe, Melanthia, Melanthea, Malantha, Mallantha, Mellantha

Melba (Australian) From the city of Melbourne
Melbah, Mellba, Mellbah

Melcia (Teutonic) One who is ambitious and hardworking
Melciah

Melek (Arabic) A heavenly messenger; an angel
Melak

Melete (Greek) In mythology, the muse of medication
Meleet, Meelete, Meleat, Meleate

Meli (Native American) One who is bitter
Melie, Melee, Melea, Meleigh, Mely, Meley

Melia (Hawaiian / Greek) Resembling the plumeria / of the ash tree; in mythology, a nymph
Melidice, Melitine, Meliah, Meelia, Melya

Melika (Turkish) A great beauty
Melikah, Melicka, Melicca, Melyka, Melycka, Meleeka, Meleaka

Melina (Greek) As sweet as honey
Mellina, Meleana, Meleena, Melene, Melibella, Melibelle, Meline, Melyne, Melyna, Mellea, Melleta, Mellona, Meleda, Meleta

Melinda (Latin) One who is sweet and gentle
Melynda, Malinda, Malinde, Mallie, Mally, Malynda, Melinde, Mellinda, Mallee, Mallea

Meliora (Latin) One who is better than others
Melyora, Meliorah, Melyorah, Meleeora

Melisande (French) Having the strength of an animal
Malisande, Malissande, Malyssandre, Melesande, Melisandra, Melisandre, Melissande, Melissandre, Mellisande, Melysande, Melyssandre

Melisha (American) Form of Alisha, meaning "woman of the nobility; truthful; having high moral character"
Mellisha, Malicia, Malisha, Malitia, Melicia, Melitia, Mellicia, Melicia, Melysha

Melissa (Greek) Resembling a honeybee; in mythology, a nymph
Malissa, Mallissa, Mel, Melesa, Melessa, Melisa, Melise, Melisse, Melitta, Meliza, Mellie, Mellisa, Melly, Melosa, Milisa

Melita (Greek) As sweet as honey
Malita, Malitta, Melida, Melitta, Melyta,
Malyta, Meleeta, Meleata, Melieta,
Meleita

Melka (Polish) A dark-skinned beauty
Melkah

Melody (Greek) A beautiful song
Melodee, Melodey, Melodi, Melodia,
Melodie, Melodea

Melora (Greek) Resembling the golden
apple
Melorah, Melorra, Melorrah

Melpomene (Greek) In mythology, the
muse of tragedy

Melva (Celtic) One who holds the rank of
chief
Melvina, Mevah, Melvena, Melveena,
Melvyna

Menachema (Hebrew) One who offers
consolation
Menachemah

Menahem (Hebrew) One who comforts
others
Menahema, Menaheme, Menahemia,
Menahemai

Menaka (Indian) A heavenly maiden
Menacka, Menakah, Menakia

Mendi (Spanish) Refers to the Virgin Mary
Mendia, Mendie, Mendy, Mendey,
Mendee, Mendea

Mene (Hebrew) One whose deeds have
been weighed

Menefer (Egyptian) From the city of beauty
Meneferr, Meneferre, Menefere

Menora (Hebrew) Resembling the candelabra
Menorah

Menula (Lithuanian) Born beneath the
moon
Menulah, Menoola, Menoolah, Menoula,
Menoulah

Meonenim (Hebrew) A soothsayer; one
who foretells events
Meonenime, Meonenima, Meonenimia

Meoquanee (Native American) Lady in red
Meoquani, Meoquaney, Meoquanie,
Meoquany, Meoquanea

Mephaath (Hebrew) A lustrous woman
Mephath, Mephatha, Mephaatha

Meralda (Latin) Form of Esmeralda,
meaning "resembling a prized emerald"
Meraldah, Meraldia, Maralda, Maraldia

Merana (American) Woman of the waters
Meranah, Meranna, Merannah

Mercedes (Spanish) Lady of mercies;
refers to the Virgin Mary
Mercedez, Mersadize, Merced, Mercede,
Mercedeez

Mercer (English) A prosperous merchant

Mercurius (Hebrew) An orator; a messenger

Mercy (English) One who shows compassion
and pity
Mercey, Merci, Mercie, Mercilla, Mercina,
Mercena, Mersey, Mircea, Mercea, Mircy,
Mircie, Mersy, Mersie, Mersi

Merdeka (Indonesian) An independent
woman; one who is free
Merdekah, Merdecka, Merdecca

Meredith (Welsh) A great ruler; protector
of the sea
Maredud, Meridel, Meredithe, Meredyth,
Meridith, Merridie, Meradith, Meredydd

Meribah (Hebrew) A quarrelsome woman
Meriba

Mericia (Spanish) Woman of great merit
Mericiah, Mericea, Mericeah

Merle (French) Resembling a blackbird
Merl, Merla, Merlina, Merline, Merola,
Murle, Myrle, Myrleen, Myrlene, Myrline,
Maryl, Maryla

Merom (Hebrew) One who is elevated
Meroma, Meromia, Meromai, Merome,
Meromea

Merona (Hebrew) Resembling a sheep
Meronah, Merrona, Meroona, Meronna

Merope (Greek) In mythology, one of the
Pleiades
Meropi, Meropie, Meropy, Meropey,
Meropee, Meropea

Meroz (Hebrew) From the cursed plains
Meroza, Merozia, Meroze

Merrick (English) A great and powerful
ruler
*Merrik, Merryck, Merryk, Meryk,
Meryck*

Merry (English) One who is lighthearted
and joyful
*Merree, Merri, Merrie, Merrielle, Merrile,
Merrilee, Merrili, Merrily, Merryn,
Merrilie, Meri, Merrea, Merie*

Mert (Egyptian) One who loves silence
Mertekert

Mertice (English) A well-known lady
*Mertise, Mertyce, Mertyse, Mertysa,
Mertisa, Mertiece, Merteace*

Merton (English) From the village near the
pond
Mertan, Mertin, Mertun

Meryl (English) Form of Muriel, meaning
"of the shining sea"; form of Merle, mean-
ing "resembling a blackbird"
*Maryl, Meral, Merel, Merla, Merlyn,
Merryl, Meryle, Meryll, Mirla, Myrla,
Merula, Merolla*

Mesa (Spanish) From the flat-topped hill
Mesah, Messa, Messah

Mesi (Egyptian) Woman of the waters
Mesie, Mesy, Mesey, Mesee, Mesea

Meskhenet (Egyptian) A fated woman

Mesopotamia (Hebrew) From the land
between two rivers
Mesopotama, Mesopotamea

Messina (Arabic) The middle child
*Messinah, Massina, Mussina, Messena,
Messinia*

Meta (German / Latin) Form of Margaret,
meaning "resembling a pearl / the child of
light" / one who is ambitious
Metah, Metta, Mettah

Metea (Greek) A gentle woman
Meteah, Metia, Metiah

Metin (Greek) A wise counselor
Metine, Metyn, Metyne

Metis (Greek) One who is industrious
Metiss, Metisse, Metys, Metyss, Metysse

Metsa (Finnish) Woman of the forest
Metsah

Mettabel (Hebrew) Favored by God
*Mettabell, Mettabele, Mettabelle,
Mettabela, Mettabella*

Mettalise (Danish) As graceful as a pearl
*Metalise, Mettalisse, Mettalisa,
Mettalissa*

Meunim (Hebrew) Of the dwelling place
Mehunim

Mhina (African) A delightful lady
Mhinah, Mhinna, Mhena, Mhenah

Mia ✪ (Israeli / Latin) Feminine form of
Michael; who is like God? / form of Mary,
meaning "star of the sea / from the sea of
bitterness"
Miah, Mea, Meah, Meya

Miakoda (Native American) Possessing
the power of the moon
Myakoda, Miacoda, Myacoda

Mianda (Spanish) Of my journey
Miandah, Myanda, Miandia, Meanda

Mibzar (Hebrew) From the fortress
*Mibzarr, Mibzara, Mibzare, Mibzarre,
Mibzarra*

Micah (Hebrew) Feminine form of
Michael; who is like God?
*Micaiah, Mica, Meeca, Meica, Mika,
Myka, Mykah, Mikah*

Michaela ✪ ✪ (Celtic / Hebrew / English)
Feminine form of Michael; who is like
God?
*Macaela, MacKayla, **Makayla**, Mak,
Mechaela, Meeskaela, Mekea, Micaela,
Michal, Michael, Michaelina, Michaeline,
Michaila, Michalin, Mickee, Mickie, Miguela,
Miguelina, Miguelita, Mahalya, Mihaila,
Mihalia, Mihaliya, Mikaela, Mikayla, Mikella,
Mikelle, Mikhaila, Mikhayla, Miskaela,
Mychaela, Makaila, Micole, Mika, Mikkel,
Mekelle*

M

Michelle (French) Feminine form of Michael; who is like God?
Machelle, Mashelle, M'chelle, Mechelle, Meechelle, Me'Shell, Meshella, Michaella, Michela, Michele, Michelina, Micheline, Michell, Michella, Mishaila, Midge, Mischaela, Misha, Mishaelle, Mishelle, M'shell, Mychele, Mychelle, Myshell, Myshella, Michon, Miesha

Michewa (Tibetan) Sent from heaven
Michewah

Michigan (Native American) From the great waters; from the state of Michigan
Mishigan, Michegen, Mishegen

Michiko (Japanese) Child of beautiful wisdom
Michi, Michyko, Meecheeko, Mecheeko, Meechiko, Michee

Michima (Japanese) Possessing beautiful wisdom

Michmethah (Hebrew) A secretive woman; from the hiding place

Michri (Hebrew) Gift from God
Michrie, Michry, Michrey, Michree, Michrea

Michtam (Hebrew) One who has been given the gift of writing
Michtame, Michtaam, Michtami, Michtama

Mickey (American) Feminine form of Michael; who is like God?
Micki, Micky, Mickie, Mickee, Mickea

Middin (Hebrew) One who has been measured

Mide (Irish) One who is thirsty
Meeda, Mida

Midori (Japanese) Having green eyes
Midorie, Midory, Midorey, Midoree, Midorea

Mieko (Japanese) Born into wealth
Meeko, Meako

Mielikki (Finnish) A pleasant woman
Mieliki, Mielikkie, Mielikie

Miette (French) A petite, sweet young woman
Miett, Miet, Miete, Mieta, Mietta

Migdalia (Hebrew) Feminine form of Migdal; of the high tower
Migdala, Migdalla, Migdalea, Migdaliah, Migdaleah, Migdalgad, Migdaliya, Migdaliyah

Migdana (Hebrew) A gift from God
Migdanah, Migdanna, Migdania, Migdanea

Migina (Native American) Born beneath the returning moon
Migyna, Migena, Mygina, Mygyna

Migisi (Native American) Resembling an eagle
Migisie, Migysi, Mygisi, Migisy, Migisea

Mignon (French) One who is cute and petite
Mignonette, Mignonne, Mingnon, Minyonne, Minyonette

Migron (Hebrew) Woman of the cliffs
Migrona, Migrone, Migronai, Migronya

Mikaia (American) Of God's green earth

Mikaili (African) A godly woman
Mikailie, Mikayli, Mikali, Mikaylie, Mikalie

Miki (Japanese / Hawaiian) Of the beautiful tree / one who is nimble
Mikki, Mikko, Mika, Mikil

Mila (Slavic) One who is industrious and hardworking
Milaia, Milaka, Milla, Milia

Milada (Slavic) My daughter is my love
Miladah, Miladda, Millada

Milagros (Spanish) Lady of miracles; refers to the Virgin Mary
Milagritos, Milagrosa, Miligrosa, Miligritos

Milan (Latin) From the city in Italy; one who is gracious
Milaana

Milanka (Croatian) A sweet young woman
Milankaa, Milankai, Milanke, Milankia, Mylanka, Mylanke

Mildred (English) Woman of gentle strength
Mildri, Mildrid, Mildryd, Mildrie, Mildree, Mildraed, Millie, Milly, Milley, Milli, Millee, Millea, Mildrea

Milena (Slavic) The favored one
Mileena, Milana, Miladena, Milanka,
Mlada, Mladena

Miletum (Hebrew) From the seaport town

Mili (Hebrew) A virtuous woman
Milie, Mily, Miley, Milee, Milea, Mileigh

Miliana (Latin) Feminine form of
Emeliano; one who is eager and willing
Milianah, Milianna, Miliane, Miliann,
Milianne

Miliani (Hawaiian) Of the gentle caress
Milianie, Milianee, Miliany, Milianey,
Milianea

Milima (Swahili) Woman from the
mountains
Milimah, Mileema, Milyma

Miller (English) One who works at a mill
Millar, Millir, Mills

Millicent (French) A woman with great
strength and determination
Melicent, Mellicent, Mellie, Mellisent,
Melly, Milicent, Milisent, Millisent, Milzie,
Milicente

Millo (Hebrew) Defender of the sacred city
Milloh, Millowe, Milloe

Miloslava (Russian) Feminine form of
Miloslav; having the favor and glory of the
people
Miloslavah, Miloslavia, Miloslavea

Mima (Hebrew) Form of Jemima, meaning
"our little dove"
Mimah, Mymah, Myma

Mimala (Native American) A holy woman
Mimalah, Mimalla, Mimallah

Mina (Japanese / German) Woman from
the South / one who is greatly loved
Minah, Min, Minette, Minnette, Minna

Minako (Japanese) A beautiful child

Minal (Native American) As sweet as fruit
Minall, Minalle, Minala, Minalla

Minau (Persian) Child of heaven

Minda (Native American, Hindi) Having
great knowledge
Mindah, Mynda, Myndah, Menda, Mendah

Mindel (Hebrew) Form of Mary, meaning
"star of the sea / from the sea of bitterness"
Mindell, Mindelle, Mindele, Mindela,
Mindella

Mindy (English) Form of Melinda, meaning
"one who is sweet and gentle"
Minda, Mindee, Mindi, Mindie, Mindey,
Mindea

Minerva (Latin) Having strength of mind;
in mythology, the goddess of wisdom
Minervah, Menerva, Minirva, Menirva

Minetta (French) Form of Wilhelmina,
meaning "determined protector"
Minette, Mineta, Minete, Minett, Minet,
Mine

Ming Yue (Chinese) Born beneath the
bright moon

Mingmei (Chinese) A bright and
beautiful girl

Miniya (African) She is expected to do
great things
Miniyah

Minjonet (French) Resembling the small
blue flower
Minjonett, Minjonete, Minjonette,
Minjoneta, Minjonetta

Minka (Teutonic) One who is resolute;
having great strength
Minkah, Mynka, Mynkah, Minna, Minne

Minnesota (Native American) From the
sky-tinted waters
Minesota, Minnesoda, Minesoda,
Minisota, Minisoda

Minnie (English) Form of Wilhelmina,
meaning "determined protector"
Minny, Minni, Minney, Minnee, Minnea

Minor (American) A young woman; a lass

Minowa (Native American) One who has
a moving voice
Minowah, Mynowa, Mynowah

Minta (Greek) Form of Amynta, meaning
"protector and defender of her loved ones"
Mintha, Mintah, Minty, Minti, Mintie,
Mintee, Mintey, Mintea

Minuit (French) Born at midnight
Minueet

Minya (Native American) The older sister
Miniya, Minyah, Miniyah

Mio (Japanese) Having great strength

Mira (Indian / Slavic / Latin) One who is prosperous / a peaceful woman / one who is wonderful
Mirah, Mirana, Mireille, Mirella, Mirelle, Miri, Miriana, Mirielle, Mirilla, Mirka, Mirra, Myrella, MyrÈne, Myrilla, Mir, Mirko, Mirke

Mireya (Spanish) Form of Miranda, meaning "one who is worthy of admiration"
Miraya, Maraya, Mareya, Myrelle, Myrella

Miriam (Hebrew) Form of Mary, meaning "star of the sea / from the sea of bitterness"
Mariam, Maryam, Meriam, Meryam, Mirham, Mirjam, Mirjana, Mirriam, Miryam, Miyana, Miyanna, Myriam, Marrim, Mijam

Mirias (Greek) Woman of plenty
Miriass, Miriasse, Miriase, Miriasa, Miryas, Miryase, Miryasa

---

MIRANDA

The name Miranda means "worthy of admiration" and is a Shakespeare creation. It seems to fit, as Miranda has always been the one in the family who strives for admiration by singing, acting, and telling stories and jokes. Her middle name, Elisabeth, is after my mother, who survived a double aneurysm five months before Miranda was born. —Carla, IA

Mirabel (Latin / French) One who is wonderful / a rare beauty
Meribel, Meribelle, Mirabell, Mirabella, Mirabelle

Miracle (American) An act of God's hand
Mirakle, Mirakel, Myracle, Myrakle

Mirage (French) An illusion or fantasy

Mirai (Basque) A miracle child
Miraya, Mirari, Mirarie, Miraree, Mirae

Miranda (Latin) One who is worthy of admiration
Maranda, Meranda, Miran, Mirandah, Mirranda, Myranda

Mirani (Spanish) An attractive lady
Miranie, Mirany, Miraney, Miranee, Miranea

Mireille (French) One who is greatly admired
Mirella, Mireile, Mireilla, Mireila, Mireio, Mirei

Mirella (Hebrew) God has spoken
Mirela, Mirelah, Mirellah, Mirelle, Mirell, Mirele, Mirel

Miremba (Ugandan) A promoter of peace
Mirembe, Mirem, Mirembah, Mirembeh, Mirema

Mirinesse (English) Filled with joy
Miriness, Mirinese, Mirines, Mirinessa, Mirinesa

Mirit (Hebrew) One who is strong-willed

Miriuia (Latin) A marvelous lady

Miroslava (Slavic) Feminine form of Miroslav; one who basks in peaceful glory
Miroslavia, Miroslavea, Myroslava, Myroslavia, Myroslavea

Mirta (Spanish) Crowned with thorns
Mirtah, Meerta, Meertha, Mirtha

Misae (Native American) Born beneath the white sun
Mysae, Misay, Misaye, Mysay, Mysaye, Misai, Mysai

Mischa (Russian) Form of Michelle, meaning "who is like God?"
Misha

Misrak (African) Woman from the East
Misrake, Misraka, Misrakia

Mississippi (Native American) Of the great river; from the state of Mississippi
Misisipi, Mississippi, Mississipi, Mississippi, Misisippi

Missouri (Native American) From the town of large canoes
Missourie, Mizouri, Mizourie, Missoury, Mizoury, Missuri, Mizuri, Mizury, Missury

Missy (English) Form of Melissa, meaning "resembling a honeybee"
Missey, Misse, Missee, Missie, Missi, Missea

Mistico (Italian) A mystical woman
Mistica, Mystico, Mystica, Mistiko, Mystiko

Misty (American) Covered with dew; of the mists
Mistie, Misti, Mistey, Mistee, Mystee, Mysti, Mystie, Mysty, Mystey, Mystea, Mistea

Misu (Native American) Of the rippling waters
Misoo, Misou, Mysu, Mysoo, Mysou

Misumi (Japanese) A pure, beautiful woman
Misumie, Misumee, Misumy, Misumey, Misumea

Mitali (Indian) A friendly and sweet woman
Mitalie, Mitalee, Mitaleigh, Mitaly, Mitaley, Meeta, Mitalea

Mitena (Native American) Born beneath the new moon
Mitenah, Mytena, Mitenna, Mytenna

Mitexi (Native American) Born beneath the sacred moon
Mitexie, Mitexee, Mitexy, Mitexey, Mitexa, Mitexea

Mithcah (Hebrew) A sweet and pleasant woman
Mithca, Mithecah, Mitheca

Mitra (Persian) A heavenly messenger; an angel
Mitran, Mitrania, Mitrane, Mitrana

Mitsu (Japanese) Lady of light
Mitsuko

Mitylene (Hebrew) From the island city
Mityleen, Mitylean, Mityleene, Mityleane, Mitylen, Mitylein

Mitzi (German) Form of Mary, meaning "star of the sea / from the sea of bitterness"
Mitzie, Mitzy, Mitzey, Mitzee, Mitzea

Miya (Japenese) From the sacred temple
Miyah

Miyanda (African) One who is grounded
Miyandah, Myanda, Meyanda

Miyo (Japanese) A beautiful daughter
Miyoko

Mizar (Hebrew) A little woman; petite
Mizarr, Mizarre, Mizare, Mizara, Mizaria, Mizarra

Mizpah (Hebrew) From the watchtower
Mizpeh, Mizpa

Mliss (Cambodian) Resembling a flower
Mlissa, Mlisse, Mlyss, Mlysse, Mlyssa

Mnason (Hebrew) One who has a good memory

Mnemosyne (Greek) In mythology, goddess of memory

Moana (Hawaiian) Woman of the ocean
Moanna, Moanah, Moannah, Moane, Moaenne

Moani (Hawaiian) A fragrance on the gentle breeze
Moanie, Moany, Moaney, Moanee, Moanea

Mocha (Arabic) As sweet as chocolate
Mochah

Modesty (Latin) One who is without conceit
Modesti, Modestie, Modestee, Modestus, Modestey, Modesta, Modestia, Modestina, Modestine, Modestea

Modron (Welsh) In mythology, the divine mother

Moesha (American) Drawn from the water
Moisha, Moysha, Moeesha, Moeasha, Moeysha

Mohala (Hawaiian) Resembling the unfolding of a flower
Mohalah, Mohalla, Mohallah

Mohan (Indian) An attractive woman
Mohani, Mohana, Mohanie, Mohanee, Mohania, Mohanea

Mohini (Indian) The most beautiful
Mohinie, Mohinee, Mohiny, Mohiney, Mohinea

M

Moina (Celtic) A mild-mannered lady
Moyna, Moinah, Moynah

Moira (English) Form of Mary, meaning
"star of the sea / from the sea of bitterness"
*Moyra, Moire, Moyre, Moreen, Morene,
Morine*

Moirae (Greek) In mythology, the Fates
Moirai, Moerae, Moyrae, Moyrai

Moireach (Scottish) A respected lady

Moja (African) One who is content with life
Mojah

Moncha (Irish) A solitary woman
Monchah

Monet (French) Form of Monica, meaning
"a solitary woman / one who advises others"
Monay, Mone, Monai, Monae, Monee

Monica (Greek / Latin) A solitary woman
/ one who advises others
Monnica, Monca, Monicka, Monika, Monike

Monifa (Egyptian) One who is lucky
*Monifah, Monipha, Moniphah, Moneefa,
Moneifa, Moniefa, Moneafa*

MOLLY

It took months of debate before we realized nearly every Molly we had known had the attributes we
hoped our daughter would possess. The fact that it was my sister's name made it that much more
special. Now, to my sister's horror and our delight, we have Big Molly and Little Molly! —Mitzi, FL

Moke (Hawaiian) Feminine form of
Moses; savior
*Mokie, Mokei, Moky, Mokey, Mokee,
Mokea*

Moladah (Hebrew) A giver of life
Molada

Molara (Spanish) Refers to the Virgin
Mary
Molarah, Molarra, Molaria, Molarea

Molly (Irish) Form of Mary, meaning "star
of the sea / from the sea of bitterness"
*Moll, Mollee, Molley, Molli, Mollie,
Molle, Mollea*

Molpe (Greek) In mythology, a siren
*Molpie, Molpi, Molpa, Molpy, Molpey,
Molpee, Molpea*

Momo (Japanese) Resembling a peach
Momoko

Mona (Gaelic) One who is born into the
nobility
*Moina, Monah, Monalisa, Monalissa,
Monna, Moyna, Monalysa, Monalyssa*

Monahana (Gaelic) A religious woman
Monahanah, Monahanna, Monahannah

Monca (Irish) Having great wisdom
Moncah

Monique (French) One who provides wise
counsel
*Moniqua, Moneeque, Moneequa,
Moneeke, Moeneek, Moneaque,
Moneaqua, Moneake*

Monisha (Hindi) Having great intelligence
*Monishah, Monesha, Moneisha,
Moniesha, Moneysha, Moneasha*

Monita (Spanish) A noble woman
*Monitah, Moneeta, Monyta, Moneita,
Monieta, Moneata*

Monroe (Gaelic) Woman from the river
Monrow, Monrowe, Monro

Monserrat (Latin) From the jagged
mountain
Montserrat

Montague (French) Of the steep mountain
Montahue

Montana (Latin) Woman of the
mountains; from the state of Montana
Montanna, Montina, Monteene, Montese

Montsho (African) A dark-skinned beauty
Montshow, Montshowe, Montshoe

Mor (Celtic / Irish) An exceptional woman
More

Mora (Spanish) Resembling a blueberry
Morah, Morra, Morrah

Morag (Gaelic) One who embraces the sun

Moraika (Incan) A heavenly messenger; an angel
Moraikah, Morayka, Moraykah, Moraeka, Moraekah

Morcan (Welsh) Of the bright sea
Morcane, Morcana, Morcania, Morcanea

Moreh (Hebrew) A great archer; a teacher

Morela (Polish) Resembling an apricot
Morella, Morelah, Morellah, Morele, Morelle

Morena (Spanish) A brown-haired woman

Morgan ♂ ♀ (Welsh) Circling the bright sea; a sea dweller
Morgaine, Morgana, Morgance, Morgane, Morganica, Morgann, Morganne, Morgayne, Morgen, Morgin, Morgaen, Morgaene, Morgaena

Morguase (English) In Arthurian legend, the mother of Gawain
Marguase, Margawse, Morgawse, Morgause, Margause

Moriah (Hebrew) God is my teacher; of the hill country
Moraia, Moraiah, Moria, Morit, Moriel, Morice, Morise, Moriya

Morina (Japanese) From the woodland town
Morinah, Moreena, Moryna, Moriena, Moreina, Moreana

Morisa (Spanish) Feminine form of Maurice; a dark-skinned beauty
Morissa, Morrisa, Morrissa

Morley (English) Woman from the moor
Morly, Morli, Morlie, Morlee, Morleigh, Morlea

Morna (Irish) One who is affectionate; beloved
Mornah

Morrigan (Celtic) In mythology, a war goddess
Morrigane, Morigan, Morigane

Morrin (Irish) A long-haired woman
Morrina, Morrine, Morren, Morrene, Morrena

Morwenna (Welsh) Maiden of the white seas
Morwena, Morwina, Morwinna, Morwyn, Morwynna, Morwyna, Morwen, Morwenne

Moselle (Hebrew) Feminine form of Moses; savior
Mosell, Mosele, Mosel, Mosella, Mosela, Mosette, Moiselle, Moisella

Moserah (Hebrew) Disciplined in learning
Moseroth, Moserothe

Mosi (Egyptian) The firstborn child
Mosie, Mosee, Mosy, Mosey, Mosea

Mostyn (Welsh) Of the meadow's fortress
Mostynn, Mostynne, Mosteen, Mosteene, Mostine, Mostean, Mosteane

Motayma (Native American) A wise leader
Motaymah, Motaima, Motama, Motaema

Mouna (Arabic) One who is desired
Mounia, Muna, Munia

Mounira (Arabic) An illuminated woman
Mourneera, Mounyra, Mounera, Mouneara

Mridula (Indian) One who is soft to the touch
Mridulah, Mridulla, Mridullah

Mrinal (Hindi) Resembling a lotus blossom
Mrinalini, Mrinali, Mrinalie, Mrinalina, Mrinala

Muadhnait (Gaelic) A young noblewoman

Mu'azzama (Arabic) One who is respected

Mubarika (Arabic) One who is blessed
Mubaarika, Mubaricka, Mubaryka, Mubaricca, Mubarycca

Mubina (Arabic) One who displays her true image
Mubeena, Mubinah, Mubyna, Mubeana, Mubiena

Mudan (Mandarin) Daughter of a harmonious family
Mudane, Mudana, Mudayne, Mudaine, Mudann, Mudaen, Mudaena

Mudiwa (African) One who is greatly loved
Mudiwah, Mudywa, Mudywah

M

Mudraya (Russian) One with great wisdom and reason
Mudrayah, Mudraia

Mufidah (Arabic) One who is helpful to others
Mufeeda, Mufeyda, Mufyda, Mufeida, Mufieda, Mufeada

Mugain (Irish) In mythology, the wife of the king of Ulster
Mugayne, Mugaine, Mugane, Mugayn, Mugaen, Mugaene, Mugaina, Mugayna, Mugaena

Muhjah (Arabic) Our heart's blood
Muhja

Muhsana (Arabic) One who is well-protected
Muhsanah, Muhsanan, Muhsanna

Muiel (Irish) Woman of the sea
Muiell, Muielle, Muiele, Muireann, Murieall, Muirgheal

Muira (Scottish) Woman from the moor
Muire

Muirne (Irish) One who is dearly loved
Muirna

Mujahida (Arabic) A crusader
Mujaahida, Mujahyda, Mujaheeda, Mujaheada

Mujia (Chinese) A healer; medicine woman

Mujiba (Arabic) One who provides the answers
Mujeeba, Mujibah, Mujeebah, Mujeaba, Mujeabah

Mukantagara (Egyptian) Born during a time of war

Mukarramma (Egyptian) One who is honored and respected
Mukarama, Mukaramma, Mukkarama

Mulan (Chinese) Resembling a magnolia blossom
Mulana, Mulania, Mulane, Mulann, Mulanna, Mulanne

Muminah (Arabic) A pious woman
Mumina, Mumeena, Mumyna, Mumeina, Mumiena, Mumeana

Muna (Arabic) God is with me
Moona, Munah, Moonah

Munay (African) One who loves and is loved
Manay, Munaye, Munae, Munai

Munaya (African) The rainmaker
Munayah

Munazza (Arabic) An independent woman; one who is free
Munazzah, Munaza, Munazah

Muncel (American) A strong-willed woman
Muncele, Muncelle, Muncell, Muncela, Muncella

Munin (Scandinavian) One with a good memory
Munine, Munyn, Munyne, Munina, Munyna

Munira (Arabic) A lustrous and brilliant woman
Muneera, Munirah, Muneira, Muniera, Munyra, Munawwara, Munawara, Muneara

Muniya (Indian) Resembling a small bird
Muniyah

Muqaddasa (Arabic) One who is sacred

Murata (African) A beloved friend
Muraty, Muratia, Murati, Muratie, Muratee, Muratea

Muriel (Irish) Of the shining sea
Merial, Meriel, Merrill, Miureall, Murial, Muriella, Murielle, Merill, Merral, Merrall, Merril, Meriol, Murel

Murphy (Celtic) Daughter of a great sea warrior
Murphi, Murphie, Murphey, Murphee, Murfi, Murfy, Murfie, Murphea, Murfea

Musetta (French) Little muse; a joyful song
Musette, Musett, Muset, Musete, Museta

Mushana (African) Born with the morning's light
Mushanah, Mushania, Mushanna, Mushane

Musharrifa (Arabic) An exalted woman
Musharifa, Musharrifah, Musharifah, Musharyfa

Mushira (Arabic) A wise counselor
Mushirah, Musheera, Musheira, Mushiera, Musheara

Musidora (Greek) Gift of the Muses
Musadora, Musedora, Musidoria, Musadoria, Musedoria

Muslimah (Arabic) A devout believer
Muslima, Muslyma, Muslymah, Muslema, Muslemah

Musoke (African) Having the beauty of a rainbow

Mut (Egyptian) In mythology, the creator goddess

Myma (Irish) One who is greatly loved
Mymah

Myra (Greek) Form of Myrrh, meaning "resembling the fragrant oil"
Myrah, Myree, Myriah

Myrina (Latin) In mythology, an Amazon
Myrinah, Myreena, Myreina, Myriena, Myreana

Myrna (Gaelic) One who is much loved
Meirna, Merna, Mirna, Moina, Moyna, Muirna, Murna

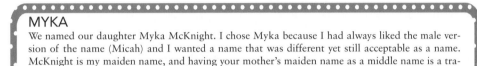

MYKA
We named our daughter Myka McKnight. I chose Myka because I had always liked the male version of the name (Micah) and I wanted a name that was different yet still acceptable as a name. McKnight is my maiden name, and having your mother's maiden name as a middle name is a tradition in Scotland. —Mandy, Edinburgh

Muta (Latin) In mythology, the personification of silence
Mute, Mutah, Muteh

Mutehhara (Arabic) One who is pure; chaste
Mutehara, Mutehharah, Muteharra, Muteharah

Mutia (African) An honored woman; respected
Mutiah, Mutiya, Mutiyah, Mutea, Muteah, Mutya, Mutyah

Mychau (Vietnamese) Known for her greatness

My-duyen (Vietnamese) A beautiful woman

Myfanawy (Welsh) A sweet and rare woman
Myfanawi, Myfanawie, Myfanawee, Myfanawea, Myfanawey

Myisha (Arabic) Form of Aisha, meaning "lively; womanly"
Myesha, Myeisha, Myeshia, Myiesha, Myeasha

Myka (Hebrew) Feminine of Micah, meaning, "Who is like God?"

Myla (English) Feminine form of Myles; one who is merciful
Mayla, Mylene, Myleen, Mylah, Myleene, Mylyne, Mylas, Mylean, Myleane

Myrrh (Egyptian) Resembling the fragrant oil

Myrta (Greek) Resembling the evergreen shrub myrtle
Myrtia, Myrtice, Mytra, Merta, Merte, Merteh

Myrtle (Latin) Of the sacred evergreen shrub
Myrtilla, Myrtisa, Myrtis, Mertice, Mertis, Mertle, Mirtie, Myrta, Myrtia, Myrtice, Myrtie, Myrtiece, Myrteace, Myrtee

Mystery (American) A lady of the unknown
Mysteri, Mysterie, Mysterey, Mysteree, Mistery, Misteri, Misterie, Misteree, Misterey, Mysterea, Misterea

Mystique (French) Woman with an air of mystery
Mystica, Mistique, Mysteek, Misteek, Mystiek, Mistiek, Mysteeque, Misteeque

Mythri (Indian) One who values friendship
Mythrie, Mithri, Mithrie, Mithree, Mythree, Mithry, Mithrey, Mythry, Mythrey, Mithrea, Mythrea

M

Naama (Hebrew) Feminine form of Noam; an attractive woman; good-looking
Naamah

Naarah (Hebrew) A young woman; a girl; in the Bible, one of Ashur's wives
Naarai, Naarae

Naava (Hebrew) A lovely and pleasant woman
Naavah, Nava, Navah, Navit

Nabiha (Arabic) One who is intelligent
Nabeeha, Nabyha, Nabihah, Nabeehah, Nabyhah, Nabeaha, Nabeahah

Nabila (Arabic) Daughter born into nobility; a highborn daughter
Nabilah, Nabeela, Nabyla, Nabeelah, Nabylah, Nabeala, Nabealah

Nabirye (Egyptian) One who gives birth to twins
Naberye

Nachine (Spanish) A fiery young woman
Nacheene, Nachyne, Nachina, Nachinah, Nachyna, Nacheena, Nacheane, Nacheana

Nadda (Arabic) A very generous woman
Naddah, Nada, Nadah

Nadetta (French) Form of Bernadette, meaning "one who has bearlike strength and courage"
Nadette, Nadett, Nadet, Nadete, Nadeta

Nadhira (Arabic) A flourishing woman; one who is precious
Nadhirah, Naadhira, Nadheera, Nadhyra, Nadhiera, Nadheira, Nadhera, Naadhirah, Nadheerah, Nadhyrah, Nadhierah, Nadheirah, Nadherah, Nadheara

Nadia (Slavic) One who is full of hope
Nadja, Nadya, Naadiya, Nadine, Nadie, Nadiyah, Nadea, Nadija, Nadka, Nadenka, Nadezhda, Nadusha, Nadiah, Nadeen, Nadeene, Nadean, Nadyne, Nadien, Nadin, Nadene, Nadina, Nadena, Nadyna, Nadyn, Nadeana, Nadeane, Nadeena, Naydene, Naydeen, Naydin, Naydyn, Naidene, Naidine, Naidyne, Naideen, Naydine, Nadezda, Nadiya, Nadjae, Nadjah, Nads, Nadyenka, Nadyuiska, Nadzia, Naiya, Naia, Naiyana, Naya, Nadege, Natia

Nadifa (African) One who is born between the seasons
Nadifah, Nadeefa, Nadyfa, Nadeefah, Nadyfah, Nadeafa, Nadeafah

Nadirah (Arabic) One who is precious; rare
Nadira, Nadyra, Nadyrah, Nadeera, Nadeerah, Nadra, Nadrah

Nadwah (Arabic) One who gives wise counsel
Nadwa

Naeemah (Egyptian) A kind and benevolent woman
Nayma, Nayima, Nayema

Naenia (Latin) In mythology, the goddess of funerals
Naenie, Naeni, Naeny, Naeney, Naenee, Naenea, Naeniah

Naeva (French) Born in the evening
Naevah, Naevia, Naevea, Nayva, Nayvah, Nayvia, Nayvea

Nafisa (Arabic) As precious as a gem
Nafeesa, Nafeeza, Nafisah, Nafeesah, Nafeezah, Nafysa, Nafysah, Nafeasa, Nafeasah

Nafuna (African) A child who is delivered feet first
Nafunah, Nafunna, Nafoona, Nafoonah, Naphuna, Naphunah, Naphoona, Naphoonah, Nafouna, Naphouna

Nagesa (African) Born during the time of harvest
Nagesah, Nagessa, Nagessah

Nagge (Hebrew) A radiant woman

Nagida (Hebrew) A wealthy woman
Nagidah, Nagyda, Nagydah, Negida, Negidah, Negyda, Negydah, Nageeda, Nageedah, Negeeda, Negeedah, Nageada, Nageadah

Nagina (Arabic) As precious as a pearl
*Nageena, Naginah, Nageenah, Nagyna,
Nagynah, Nageana, Nageanah*

Nahia (Basque) One who is greatly desired
Nahiah, Nahea, Naheah, Nahiya, Nahiyah

Nahid (Persian) One who is elevated; in
mythology, the goddess of love
*Naaheed, Naheed, Naheede, Nahyde,
Nahyd, Nahead, Naheade*

Naida (Greek) A water nymph
*Naiadia, Naidah, Nyad, Nayad, Naiad,
Nyada, Nayada, Niadah, Naeda, Naedah*

Nailah (Arabic) Feminine form of Nail; a
successful woman; the acquirer
*Na'ila, Na'ilah, Naa'ilah, Naila, Nayla,
Naylah, Naela, Naelah*

Naima (African / Arabic) A contented
woman / one who brings comfort and peace
*Na'ima, Na'imah, Naimah, Nayma, Naymah,
Naeema, Naeemah, Naema, Naemah*

Naira (Native American) A woman with
big eyes
Nairah, Nayra, Nayrah, Naera, Naerah

Nairi (Armenian) From the mountainous
land
Nairie, Nairy, Nairey, Nairee, Nairea

Nairna (Scottish) From the alder-tree river
Naime, Nairnia, Nairnea, Naerna, Nayrna

Nairobi (African) Woman from the capital
of Kenya
*Nairobie, Nairoby, Nairobey, Nairobee,
Nayrobi, Nayrobie, Nayroby, Nayrobey,
Nayrobee, Nairobea, Nayrobea*

Najam (Arabic) A starlike woman
Naja, Najah, Najama, Najma

Najia (Arabic) An independent woman;
one who is free
Naajia

Najiba (Arabic) An intellectually superior
woman; born into the nobility
*Najibah, Najeeba, Najeebah, Najyba,
Najybah, Najeaba, Najeabah*

Najila (Arabic) A woman with shining eyes
*Najilah, Najyla, Najylah, Najla, Najlah,
Nagla, Naglah, Najeela, Najeelah,
Najeala, Najealah*

Najja (African) The second-born child
Najjah

Najjiyya (Arabic) One who is beneficial to
others
Najjiyyah, Najiyah, Najiya

Najwa (Arabic) A secretve woman
Nagwa, Najwah, Nagwah

Najya (Arabic) A victorious woman
Najyah

Nakeisha (American) Form of Keisha,
meaning "the favorite child"
*Nakeesha, Nakysha, Nakeasha, Nakiesha,
Nakeysha, Narkeasha*

Naki (African) The firstborn daughter
Nakie, Naky, Nakey, Nakee, Nakye

Nakia (Arabic) One who is pure; chaste
*Nakiah, Nakea, Nakeah, Nakya, Nakyah,
Nakiya, Nakiyah, Nakeya, Nakeyah,
Nakiaya, Nakiea, Nakeyia*

Nala (African / Latin) A successful woman
/ of the olive tree
Nalah, Nalla, Nallah, Nalia, Nalea

Nalani (Hawaiian) A calmness of the
skies; heaven's calm
*Nalanie, Nalany, Nalaney, Nalany,
Nalanee, Nalaneigh, Nalanea, Nalania,
Nalanya, Nallely*

Naliaka (African) A future wife
*Naliakah, Nalyaka, Naliacca, Naliacka,
Nalyacka*

Nalin (Indian) Resembling the lotus flower
Naline, Naleen, Nalyne, Nalyn, Nalen

Nalini (Sanskrit) A beautiful and lovely
woman
*Nalinie, Naliny, Naliney, Nalinee, Nalyni,
Nalynie, Nalynee, Nalinea*

Nalo (African) A lovable daughter

Nami (Japanese) Woman of the waves
*Namie, Namee, Namy, Namey, Namika,
Namiko, Namea*

Namid (Native American) A star dancer
Namide, Namyd, Namyde

Namita (Papuan) In mythology, a mother goddess
Namitah, Nameeta, Namyta, Nameetah, Namytah, Nameata, Nameatah

Nana (Hawaiian / English) Born during the spring; a star / a grandmother or one who watches over children

Nancy (English) Form of Ann, meaning "a woman graced with God's favor"
Nainsey, Nainsi, Nance, Nancee, Nancey, Nanci, Nancie, Nancsi, Nanice, Nann, Nanncey, Nanncy, Nannie, Nanny, Nansee, Nansey, Ninacska, Nin, Ninockha, Nancea, Nansea

Nanda (Indian) One who is full of joy
Nandah, Nandia, Nandea

Nandalia (Australian) A fiery woman
Nandaliah, Nandalea, Nandaleah, Nandali, Nandalie, Nandalei, Nandalee, Nandaleigh, Nandaly, Nandaley, Nandalya

Nandini (Hindi) In Hinduism, a divine cow who can grant wishes
Nandinie, Nandiny, Nandiney, Nandinee, Nandinea

Nandita (Indian) A delightful daughter
Nanditah, Nanditia, Nanditea

Nanette (French) Form of Anna, meaning "a woman graced with God's favor"
Nanine, Nannette, Nettie, Netty, Nanetta, Nanete, Naneta, Nanelia, Nanna, Nette, Ninette, Nynette

Nangila (African) Born during travel
Nangilah, Nangyla, Nangeela, Nangylah, Nangeelah

Nani (Greek / Hawaiian) A charming woman / one who is beautiful
Nanie, Nanee, Naney, Nany, Nania, Nanya, Naniya, Nanea, Naniah, Naneah, Naniyah

Nanon (French) Form of Ann, meaning "a woman graced with God's favor"
Nanone, Nanona, Nanonia, Nanonea, Nanonya, Ninon, Ninone, Ninona, Ninonia, Ninonea, Ninonya, Ninan

Naoko (Japanese) An obediant daughter

Naomi (Hebrew / Japanese) One who is pleasant / a beauty above all others
Naoma, Naomia, Naomie, Nayomi, Naomee, Neoma, Neomi, Noami, Noémi, Noémie, Noemi, Noemie, Nohemi, Naomy, Naomey, Naomea

Napua (Hawaiian) Young woman of the flowers

Naqiba (Arabic) A strong leader
Naqeeba, Naqyba, Naqibah, Naqeebah, Naqybah

Nara (English) A contented woman
Narah, Narra, Narrah, Nareen, Nareene, Nareena, Nareane, Nareana

Narcissa (Greek) Resembling a daffodil; self-love; in mythology, a youth who fell in love with his reflection
Narcisa, Narcisse, Narkissa, Narcissah, Narcisah, Narcessa, Narcissus, Narcyssa, Narcysa, Nargis, Nargiss, Nargys, Naryss, Nargisse, Nargysse

Narda (Latin) One who is fragrantly anointed
Nardah, Nardia, Nardea, Nardiya, Nardya

Narella (Greek) A bright woman; intelligent
Narellah, Narela, Narelah, Narelle, Narell, Narele

Nariko (Japanese) A gentle child
Nari

Narmada (Indian) Woman of the river
Narmadah, Narmadia, Narmadea

Nascha (Native American) Resembling an owl

Nascio (Latin) In mythology, goddess of childbirth

Nasha (African) Born during the season of rain
Nashaly, Nashalee, Nashaley, Nashalia, Nashalea, Nashaleigh, Nashalie, Nashali

Nashita (Arabic) A lively woman; one who is energetic
Nashitah, Nashyta, Nasheeta, Nasheata, Nashieta, Nasheita

Nashota (Native American) The second-born of twins
Nashotah, Nashotta, Nashottah

Nashwa (Arabic) One who provides a feeling of ecstasy
Nashwah

Nasiba (Arabic) Feminine form of Nasib; one who is noble
Naseeba, Nasyba, Nasibah, Nasybah, Naseebah, Naseaba, Naseabah

Nasiha (Arabic) One who gives good advice
Naasiha, Nasihah, Naseeha, Naseehah, Nasyha, Nasyhah, Naseaha, Naseahah

Nasima (Arabic) As gentle as a breeze
Naasima, Nasimah, Naseema, Naseemah, Nasyma, Nasymah, Naseama, Naseamah

Nasira (Arabic) One who is victorious; a helper
Naasira, Nasirah, Naseera, Naseerah, Nasyra, Nasyrah, Naseara, Nasearah

Nasnan (Native American) Filled with music
Nasnane, Nasnana, Nasnann, Nasnanne, Nasnanna

Nastasia (Greek) Form of Anastasia, meaning "one who shall rise again"
Nastassia, Nastassija, Nastassja, Nastassiya, Nastassya, Nastasiya, Nastunye, Nastya

Nasya (Hebrew) A miracle child of God
Nasyah, Nasiya, Nasiyah, Nasia, Nasiah, Naysa

Nata (Latin) A strong swimmer

Natalie ○ ○ (Latin) Born on Christmas Day; refers to Christ's birthday
Natala, Natalee, Natalene, Natalia, Natalja, Natalina, Nataline, Nataly, Nataliya, Natalya, Natelie, Nately, Nathalee, Nathalia, Nathalie, Nathaliely, Nathalija, Nathaly, Natilie, Natividad, Nattilie, Nattie, Nettie, Nat, Natuche, Nadalia, Nadalie, Nasia, Natille, Natica, Natalea, Nathalea

Natana (Hebrew) Feminine form of Nathan; a gift from God
Natanah, Natania, Natanna, Nataniela, Nataniella, Natanielle, Nataniele, Nataniya, Natanya, Natanyah, Nathaniella, Nathanielle, Netanela, Netanella, Netania, Netanya, Nethania, Nathania

Natane (Native American) Her father's daughter
Natanne

Natasha (Russian) Form of Natalie, meaning "born on Christmas Day"
Nastaliya, Nastalya, Natacha, Natascha, Natashenka, Natashia, Natasia, Natosha, Natucha, Natyashenka, Natasa, Nathacha, Nitca

Nathifa (Arabic) One who is pure; clean
Nathifah, Nathipha, Nathiphah, Nathyfa, Nathyfah, Nathypha, Nathyphah, Nadhifa, Nadhyfa, Natifa, Natifah, Natyfa

Natividad (Spanish) Refers to the Nativity
Natividade, Natividada, Natyvydad, Nativydad, Natyvidad

Natsuko (Japanese) Child born during the summer
Natsu, Natsumi

Natura (Spanish) Woman of the outdoors
Naturah, Naturia, Naturea, Nature

Naunet (Egyptian) In mythology, goddess of the watery abyss
Nunet

Nausicaa (Greek) In mythology, a princess who is kind to Odysseus
Nausikaa, Nausica, Nausika

Nautica (English) Woman of the sea
Nautika, Nautia, Nautea, Nautyca, Nautyka

Naveen (Gaelic / Indian) A pleasant, lovely woman / one who is strong-willed
Naveena, Navine, Navyne, Navina, Navyna, Navean, Naveana

Navida (Iranian) Feminine form of Navid; bringer of good news
Navyda, Navidah, Navyda, Naveeda, Naveedah, Naveada, Naveadah

Navya (Indian) One who is youthful
Navyah, Naviya, Naviyah

Nawal (Arabic) A gift of God
Nawall, Nawalle, Nawala, Nawalla

Nawar (Arabic) Resembling a flower
Nawaar

Nayan (Indian) Having beautiful eyes
Nayana, Nayann, Nayane, Nayanne

Nayeli (Native American) One who loves and is loved
Nayelie, Nayely, Nayeley, Nayeli, Nayelee, Nayeleigh, Nayelea

Nazahah (Arabic) One who is pure and honest
Nazaha, Nazihah, Naziha

Nazakat (Arabic) A delicate woman
Nazaakat

Nazima (Arabic) One who is motherly
Naazima, Nazimah, Nazeema, Nazyma, Nazeama, Naziema, Nazeima

Nazira (Arabic) A spectator
Naazira, Nazirah, Nazyra, Nazeera, Nazeara

Nazneen (Farsi) A charming and beautiful woman
Nazneene, Naznine, Nazyne, Naazneen, Naznin, Naznean, Nazneane

Ndila (African) Resembling a goat
Ndyla, Ndilah, Ndylah

Nea (Swedish) Form of Linnea, meaning "resembling a small mountain flower; of the lime tree"
Neah

Neala (Gaelic) Feminine form of Neal; a champion
Neale, Nealla, Neila, Neile, Neilla, Neille, Neely, Neelie, Nealina, Neilina, Neelle, Neela, Nealie, Neali, Nelia, Nelea, Niall, Niala, Nialla, Niela, Nielsine

Nebraska (Native American) From the flat water land; from the state of Nebraska

Nebula (Latin) Woman of the mists
Nebulah, Nebulla, Nebulia, Nebulea

Nechama (Hebrew) One who provides comfort
Nehama, Nehamah, Nachmanit, Nachuma, Nechamah, Nechamit

Neci (Latin) A passionate woman; one who is fiery
Necia, Necie, Necee, Necy, Necey, Necea

Neda (Slavic) Born on a Sunday
Nedda, Nedah, Nedi, Nedie, Neddi, Neddie, Nedaa

Nediva (Hebrew) A giving and noble woman
Nedivah, Nedeeva, Nedyva, Nedeevah, Nedyvah, Nedeava, Nedeavah

Nedra (English) Woman of the underground
Nedrah, Neddra, Needra, Needrah

Neeharika (Indian) Of the morning dew
Neharika, Neeharyka, Neharyka

Neeja (Indian) Resembling a water lily
Neejah, Nyja, Neerja, Neerjah, Nyrja, Neaja, Neajah, Nearja

Neelam (Indian) As precious as a sapphire
Nelam, Nylam, Nealam, Neylam

Neema (African) Born into prosperity
Neemah, Neama, Neamah, Neyma, Neymah

Neena (Hindi) A woman who has beautiful eyes
Neenah, Neanah, Neana, Neyna, Neynah

Nefertiti (Egyptian) A queenly woman
Nefertari, Nefertyty, Nefertity, Nefertitie, Nefertitee, Nefertytie, Nefertitea

Negeen (Persian) As precious as a gem
Negeene, Negyne, Negyn, Negine, Negean, Negeane

Neginoth (Hebrew) An accomplished musician
Neginothe, Negynoth, Negynothe, Neginotha, Negynotha

Neha (Indian) One who loves and is loved
Nehah, Nyha, Nyhah

Nehama (Hebrew) One who provides comfort
Nehamah, Nehamma, Nehammah, Nehamia, Nehamea, Nehamiya

Nehanda (African) Our beautiful daughter has come to us
Nehandah, Nehandia, Nehandea, Nehandiya

Nehara (Hebrew) Born of the light
Neharah, Neharra, Nehira, Nehirah, Nehura, Nehurah, Nehora, Nehorah, Nahara, Naharah

Nehelamite (Hebrew) A dreamer
Nehelamitte, Nehelamit, Nehelamyte, Nehelamytte, Nehelamyt

Nehushta (Hebrew) Resembling copper
Nehushtah

Neith (Egyptian) In mythology, goddess of war and hunting
Neitha, Neytha, Neyth, Neit, Neita, Neitia, Neitea, Neithe, Neythe

Nekana (Spanish) Woman of sorrow
Nekane, Nekania, Nekanea

Nekhbet (Egyptian) In mythology, a goddess depicted as a vulture
Nechbet, Nekbet, Nekhebit

Nelly (English) Form of Helen, meaning "the shining light"
Nel, Nelida, Nell, Nella, Nellene, Nellie, Nellwen, Nellwin, Nelle, Nelley, Nelli, Nellee, Nellis, Nelma, Nellwinne, Nellwenne, Nellwyn, Nellwynne, Nelwina, Nelwena, Nellwina, Nellwena, Nelda, Nelleke

Nelsey (English) Form of Kelsey, meaning "from the island of ships; of the ship's victory"
Nellsea, Nellseigh, Nellsey, Nellsie, Nelsea, Nelseigh, Nelsie, Nelsy, Nelsee, Nellsee, Nellsy, Nellsi

Nemera (Hebrew) Resembling a leopard
Nemerah, Nemerra, Nemeria, Nemerea, Nemerya, Nemra

Nemesis (Greek) In mythology, goddess of vengeance
Nemisiss, Nemisys, Nemisyss, Nemysis, Nemysiss, Nemysys, Nemysyss

Neneca (Spanish) Form of Amelia, meaning "one who is industrious and hardworking"
Nenecah, Nenica, Nenneca, Nennica

Neo (African) A gift from God

Neola (Greek) One who is youthful
Neolla, Neolah, Neollah

Neoma (Greek) Born under the new moon
Neomea, Neomenia, Neomia, Neomenea, Neomah, Neona, Neonea, Neonia, Neonah

Nephele (Greek) In mythology, a nymph created from a cloud
Nephelle, Nephel, Nephell, Nephelia, Nephelea

Nephthys (Egyptian) In mythology, one of the nine most important deities; the lady of the house

Neptunine (Latin) Feminine form of Neptune, the god of the sea
Neptuna, Neptunia, Neptunea, Neptunina, Neptuninia, Neptuninea

Nera (Hebrew) Resembling a flickering candle; born during Hannukah
Nerah, Neriya, Nerit

Nerea (Basque) Daughter of mine
Nereah, Neria, Neriah

Nereida (Greek) A sea nymph; in mythology, the Nereids were mermaids
Nereyda, Nerida, Nireida, Nerine, Narine, Nerida, Nerina, Neried, Nerin, Ninfa

Nerio (Latin) In mythology, the wife of the god of war

Nerissa (Italian / Greek) A black-haired beauty / form of Nereida, meaning "a sea nymph"
Narissa, Naryssa, Nericcia, Neryssa, Narice, Nerice, Neris

Nerita (Greek) Woman from the sea
Neritah, Nereeta, Nereetah, Neryta, Nerytah, Nirita, Nireta, Nyrita, Nyreta, Nereata, Nereatah

Nerola (Italian) Resembling the orange flower
Nerolia, Nerolie, Nerolea, Neroli, Neroley, Neroly, Nerolee, Neroleigh

Nerthus (German) In mythology, goddess of fertility
Nerthos, Nerthous

Nerys (Welsh) A daughter born into nobility
Neris, Neriss, Neryss, Nerisse, Nerysse

Nessa (Hebrew / Greek) A miracle child / form of Agnes, meaning "one who is pure; chaste"
Nesha, Nessah, Nessia, Nessya, Nesta, Neta, Netia, Nessie, Nessy, Nessi, Nessey, Nessee, Nest, Nestia, Nesy, Netta, Netah, Nettah, Neysa, Niesha

Nethinim (Hebrew) Those who are set apart; given
Nethinima, Nethynima, Nethynym, Nethynyma, Nethinimia, Nethinimea

Netis (Native American) One who is trustworthy
Netiss, Netisse, Netys, Netyss, Netysse

Neva (Latin) From the place covered with snow
Nevah, Neve, Nevara, Nevarra, Nevaria, Nevarea, Nieve, Neiva, Nieva, Neive

Nevada (Latin) From the state of Nevada; form of Neva, meaning "from the place covered with snow"

Nevaeh (American) Child from heaven

Neveah ☼ (Slavic) Resembling a butterfly
Nevea, Neviah, Neviya, Nevia, Neviyah

Nevina (Scottish) Feminine form of Nevin; daughter of a saint
Nevinah, Neveena, Nevyna, Nevinne, Nevynne, Neveene, Neveana, Neveane

Newlyn (Gaelic) Born during the spring
Newlynn, Newlynne, Newlin, Newlinn, Newlinne, Newlen, Newlenn, Newlenne

Neylan (Turkish) The child of our desire
Neylana, Neylanna, Neylann, Neylanne, Neylane

Neziah (Hebrew) One who is pure; a victorious woman
Nezia, Nezea, Nezeah, Neza, Nezah, Neziya, Neziyah

Ngaio (Maori) From the trees; a clever woman

Ngaire (Maori) A yellow-haired woman
Ngare, Ngair, Ngayre, Ngaira, Ngara, Nyree, Nyri, Nyrie, Nyrea, Ngaer, Ngaera

Ngoc (Vietnamese) As precious as jade

Nguyet (Vietnamese) Woman of the moon

Nhi (Vietnamese) Our little one
Nhie, Nhee, Nhea, Nhy, Nhey

Nhung (Vietnamese) Resembling velvet

Nia (Welsh / African) A lustrous woman / one with a purpose
Niah, Nya, Nyah, Niya, Niyah

Niabi (Native American) Resembling a fawn
Niabie, Niabee, Niabey, Niaby, Nyabi, Nyabie, Niabea, Nyabea, Nyaby, Nyabey, Nyabee

Niagara (English) From the famous waterfall
Niagarah, Niagarra, Niagarrah, Nyagara, Nyagarra

Niamh (Irish) A bright woman; in mythology, daughter of the sea god

Nibelung (Norse) In mythology, a follower of Siegfried
Nabelung, Nebelung, Nybelung

Nicanor (Hebrew / Spanish) A conqueror / of the victorious army
Nicanora, Nicanorre, Nicanorra, Nicanore

Nichelle (American) A victorious young woman
Nachell, Nichele, Nishell, Nishelle, Nishele, Nychelle, Nychele, Nyshelle, Nyshele

Nicia (English) Form of Berenice, meaning "one who brings victory"
Niciah, Neecia, Nicija, Nicci, Nicea

Nicole (Greek) Feminine form of Nicholas; of the victorious people
Necole, Niccole, Nichol, Nichole, Nicholle, Nickol, Nickole, Nicol, Nicola, Nikita, Nikki, Nikkole, Nikky, Niko, Nikol, Nikola, Nikole, Nikoleta, Nikoletta, Nikole, Nikolia, Niquole, Niquolle, Nychole, Nycholl, Nykia, Nycole, Nykole, Nykolia, Nyquole, Nyquolle, Nicoletta, Nicolette, Nicoleta, Nicolete, Nickie, Nicki, Nicky, Nickey, Nickee, Nichola, Nicolleta, Nicollet, Nakeeta, Nakita, Nickita, Nikeeta, Niquita, Nikolaevna, Nijole

Nicosia (English) Woman from the capital of Cyprus
Nicosiah, Nicosea, Nicoseah, Nicotia, Nicotea

Nida (Native American / Arabic) An elflike woman
Needah, Nidah, Needa, Nyda, Nydah, Neada, Neadah

Nidia (Spanish) One who is gracious
Nydia, Nidiah, Nydiah, Nidea, Nideah, Nibia, Nibiah, Nibea, Nibeah, Nydia, Nydea, Nybia, Nybea

Nigelia (Arabic) Feminine form of Nigel; a champion
Nigeliah, Nigela, Nigella, Nigelea

Nigesa (African) Daughter of the harvest
Nigessa, Nigese, Nigesse, Nygesa, Nygessa

Nighean (Scottish) A young woman; a maiden
Nighinn, Nigheen

Night (American) Born in the evening; child of the darkness
Nite, Nyt, Nyte, Nyght

Nika (Russian) Form of Veronica, meaning "displaying her true image"
Nyka, Nicka, Nicca, Nica

Nike (Greek) One who brings victory; in mythology, goddess of victory
Nikee, Nikey, Nykee, Nyke

Nikhila (Indian) Feminine form of Nikhil; one who is complete
Nikhilah, Nikhilla, Nykhila, Nykhyla

Nilam (Arabic) Resembling a precious blue stone
Neelam, Nylam, Nilima, Nilyma, Nylyma, Nylima, Nealam, Nealama

Nilda (Italian) Form of Brunhilda, meaning "a dark and noble battlemaiden"
Nilda, Nild, Nilde, Nillda, Nillde, Nilld

Nile (Egyptian) From the Nile river
Nilea, Nilia, Nila, Nyla, Naila

Nilofar (Arabic) Resembling the water lily
Neelofar, Nylofar, Nealofar

Niloufer (Indian) Of the heavens

Nilsine (Scandinavian) Feminine form of Neil; a champion
Nilsina, Nilsyne, Nilsyna, Nylsine, Nylsyna, Nylsina, Nylsyne, Nilsa

Nimah (Arabic) Blessed by God
Ni'mah, Nima, Nymah, Nyma, Nimat, Nymat

Nimeesha (African) A princess; daughter born to royalty
Nimeeshah, Nimiesha, Nimisha, Nimysha, Nymeesha, Nymisha, Nymysha, Nimeasha, Nymeasha

Nina (Spanish / Native American) A little girl / a fiery woman
Ninah, Nyna, Neena, Neenah, Nena, Neneh, Neina, Nenna, Ninacska, Nineta, Ninete, Ninetta, Ninette, Ninnette, Ninon, Ninochka, Ninoska, Ninotchka

Nini (African) As solid as a stone
Ninie, Niny, Niney, Ninee, Ninea

Niobe (Greek) Resembling a fern; in mythology, a weeping queen who turned to stone
Niobee, Niobeh, Nyobe, Nyobee, Niobey, Nyobey, Niobea, Nyobea, Niobi, Nyobi, Niobie, Nyobie

Nipa (Indian) From the brook
Nipah, Nypa, Nypah

Nira (Hebrew) Of the plowed field
Niria, Nirea, Niran, Nirela, Nirit

Nirit (Hebrew) Resembling a flowering plant
Nurit, Nurita, Nureet, Nirita, Nureeta

Nirvana (English) In a state of ultimate bliss
Nirvanah, Nervana, Nirvanna, Nervanna, Nyrvana, Nyrvanna, Narvana, Narvanna

Nisa (Arabic) A lady
Neesaa, Nisaa, Neesa, Neasa

Nisha (Indian) Born at night
Neesha, Niesha, Neisha, Nysha, Neasha

Nishan (African) One who wins awards
Nishann, Nishanne, Nishana, Nishanna, Nyshan, Nyshana

Nishi (Japanese) Woman from the West
Nishie, Nishee, Nishey, Nishy, Nishea

Nishtha (Indian) A woman of faith
Nishthia, Nishthea

Nissa (Scandinavian / Hebrew) A friendly elf / one who tests others
Nisse, Nissah, Nissnana, Nissanit, Nyssa, Nysa, Nysse

Nita (Native American / Spanish / Hebrew) Resembling a bear / God is giving / having grace
Nitah, Neeta, Nyta, Neetah, Nytah, Neata, Neatah

Nitara (Indian) One who is deeply rooted
Nitarah, Nitarra, Nitarrah, Nytara, Nytarra

Nitika (Native American) As precious as a gem
Nitikah, Nityka, Nytika, Nytyka

Nitsa (German) Form of Irene, meaning "a peaceful woman"
Nitsah, Nytsa, Nytsah

N

Nituna (Native American) My daughter
Nitunah, Nytuna, Nytunah, Nitunna,
Nitoona, Nytoona, Nitouna, Nytouna

Nitya (Indian) An eternal beauty
Nithya, Nithyah, Nityah

Nitza (Hebrew) A budding young woman;
a blossom
Nitzah, Nitzana, Nitzanna, Nitzaniya,
Nytza, Nytzana, Nytzaniya, Nizana

Niu (Chinese) A young girl

Nivedita (Indian) One who is dedicated to
helping others
Niveditah, Nivedeeta, Nivedyta, Nyvedita,
Nyvedyta, Nivedeata, Nyvedeata

Nixie (German) A beautiful water sprite
Nixi, Nixy, Nixey, Nixee, Nixea

Niyati (Hindi) Realizing one's destiny; fate
Niyatie, Niyatee, Niyatey, Niyaty, Niyatea

Nizhoni (Native American) A beautiful
woman
Nizhonie, Nyzhoni, Nyzhonie, Nizhony,
Nizhoney, Nizhonea, Nyzhony, Nyzhoney,
Nyzhonea, Nizhonee, Nyzhonee

Njemile (African) An upstanding woman
Njemille, Njemyle, Njemylle

Nkechi (African) One who is loyal
Nkechie, Nkechy, Nkechey, Nkechee,
Nkechea

Noa (Hebrew) An active woman;
movement
Noah, Nowa, Nowah

Nobah (Hebrew) A howling woman
Noba, Nobia, Nobiah, Nobea, Nobeah

Noel (French) Born at Christmastime
Noelle, Noela, Noele, Noeleen, Noelene,
Noeline, Noeliz, Noell, Noella, Noelleen,
Noelynn, Nowel, Noweleen, Nowell, Noe,
Noelia, Nohely

Noelani (Hawaiian) Born of the mist of
heaven
Noelanie, Noelany, Noelaney, Noelanee,
Nohealani, Nohealanie, Nohealanee,
Noelanea, Nohealanea

Nogah (Hebrew) A bright woman; one
who is lustrous
Noga

Nokomis (Native American) A daughter
of the moon
Nokomiss, Nokomisse, Nokomys,
Nokomyss, Nokomysse

Nola (Irish) Form of Finola, meaning "one
who is fair; a white-shouldered woman"
Nolah, Nolla, Nollah, Nowla, Nuala,
Nualla, Nula, Nulla, Noola, Noolla, Nuallan

Nolan (Irish) A champion of the people
Nollan, Nolana, Noland, Nolanda, Nolen,
Nolene, Nolin, Nolynn

Nolcha (Native American) Of the sun
Nolchia, Nolchea

Noma (Hawaiian / African) One who sets
an example / a farmer
Nomah, Nomma, Nommah

Nomusa (African) One who is merciful
Nomusah, Nomusha, Nomusia, Nomusea,
Nomushia, Nomushea

Nona (Latin) The ninth-born child
Nonah, Noni, Nonie, Nonna, Nonnah,
Nonnie, Nonni, Nuna, Nunna

Nora (English) Form of Eleanor, meaning
"the shining light"; form of Honora, mean-
ing "having a good name and integrity; an
honorable woman"
Norah, Noora, Norella, Norelle, Norissa,
Norri, Norrie, Norry, Noreen, Noreena,
Norene, Norine, Norena, Norina, Norma,
Normina, Normie, Normee, Normi,
Neorah, Noirin, Norabel

Norberta (German) Femining form of
Norbert; a bright heroine from the North
Norberte, Norbertha, Norberaht, Norberthe

Nordica (German) Woman from the North
Nordika, Nordicka, Nordyca, Nordyka,
Nordycka, Norda, Norell, Norelle,
Norella, Norele, Norela

Noriko (Japanese) One who upholds the law
Nori

Normandie (French) Woman from
Normandy
Normandi, Normandee, Normandy,
Normandey, Normandea

Norna (Scandinavian) In mythology,
goddess of fate
Nornah, Norne, Norn

Nortia (Etruscan) In mythology, goddess of chance
Nortiah

Nosiwe (African) Mother of the homeland

Noura (Arabic) Having an inner light
Nureh, Nourah, Nure

Nourbese (Egyptian) A superior woman
Nurbese, Nourbeze, Nurbeze

Nousha (Iranian) A sweet woman; one who is pleasant
Noushah, Noushia, Noushiah, Noushea, Nousheah

Nova (Latin / Native American) New; a bright star / a butterfly chaser
Novah, Novia, Novea, Novelle, Novele, Novella, Novela, Novy, Novey, Novee, Novie, Novi

November (American) Born in the month of November
Novimber, Novymber

Novia (Spanish) A girlfriend
Noviah, Novea, Noveah

Nox (Latin) In mythology, the personification of night
Noxi, Noxia, Noxea, Noxy, Noxey, Noxie, Noxee

Noya (Arabic) One who is beautifully ornamented
Noyah, Noy, Noye

Nozomi (Japanese) One who brings hope to others
Nozomie, Nozomy, Nozomey, Nozomee, Nozomea

Nsia (African) The sixth-born child

Nsonowa (African) The seventh-born child

Nthanan (African) A starlike woman

Nubia (Egyptian) A woman from Nubia; resembling a cloud
Nubea, Nubiah, Nubeah, Nubiane, Nubiann, Nubianna, Nubiana, Nubianne

Nudar (Arabic) The golden daughter
Nudhar, Nudara, Nudaria, Nudarea

Nuha (Arabic) Having great wisdom
Nuhah

Nuka (Native American) The younger daughter
Nukah, Nucka, Nucca

Nunzia (Italian) One who makes announcements; a messenger
Nunziah, Nunzea, Nunzeah, Nunciata, Nuncia, Nuncea, Nunziata, Nunziatina, Nunziateena, Nunziatyna

Nuo (Chinese) A graceful woman

Nura (Arabic) Woman of the light
Noor, Nour, Noura, Nur, Nureen, Nurine, Nuru

Nuray (Turkish) Born under the bright moon
Nuraye, Nurai, Nurae

Nuria (Catalan) Refers to the Virgin Mary
Nuriah, Nurea, Nureah, Nuriya, Nuriyah

Nurin (Arabic) A luminous woman
Nurine, Nurina, Nuryne, Nureen, Nureene, Nuryna, Nureena

Nuru (African) Born during the daylight

Nusa (Hungarian) Woman of grace
Nusah, Nussa, Nussah, Nusi, Nusie, Nusia, Nusea

Nut (Egyptian) In mythology, a goddess of the sky

Nuttah (Native American) Child of my heart
Nutta

Nya (African) A tenacious woman
Nyah

Nyala (African) Resembling an antelope
Nyalah, Nyalla, Nyallah

Nyarai (African) One who is humble
Nyarae, Nyara, Nyaria, Nyarea

Nydia (English) Of the nest
Nydiah

Nyfain (Welsh) A pious woman
Nefyn, Nyfaine, Nyfayne, Nyfayn, Nefayn, Nefain, Nyfaen, Nefaen

Nympha (Greek) In mythology, a beautiful minor deity
Nymph, Nymphe

N

Nyneve (English) In Arthurian legend, another name for the lady of the lake
Nineve, Niniane, Ninyane, Nyniane, Ninieve, Niniveve

Nyoka (African) A snakelike woman
Nyokah, Nioka, Niokah

Nyura (Ukrainian) A graceful woman
Nyrurah, Nyrurra, Niura, Neura

Nyx (Greek) Born at night; in mythology, the goddess of night
Nyxi, Nyxie, Nyxee, Nyxe, Nyxea

—— ••• O ••— ——

Oadira (Arabic) A powerful woman
Oadirah, Oadyra, Oadyrah, Oadeera, Oadeerah, Oadeara, Oadearah

Oaisara (Arabic) A great ruler; an empress
Oaisarah, Oaisarra, Oaisarrah

Oakley (American) From the field of oak trees
Oakly, Oaklee, Oakleigh, Oakli, Oaklie, Oakes, Oake, Oaklea

Oamra (Arabic) Daughter of the moon
Oamrah, Oamira, Oamyra, Oameera

Oanez (Breton) Form of Agnes, meaning "one who is pure; chaste"
Ownah, Owna, Oaneza, Oanezia, Oanezea

Oba (African) In mythology, the goddess of rivers
Obah, Obba, Obbah

Obala (African) A river goddess
Obalah, Oballa, Oballah, Obalia, Obaliah, Obalea, Obaleah, Obla, Oblah

Obax (African) As delicate and beautiful as a flower
Obaxx, Obaxe, Obaxa, Obaxia, Obaxea

Obedience (American) A well-behaved and complying child
Obeedience, Obediance, Obedienne, Obedianne, Obey, Obeye, Obede, Obedi, Obedie, Obedy, Obedey, Obedee, Obedea

Obelia (Greek) One who acts as a pillar of strength
Obeliah, Obeliya, Obelea, Obelie, Obeli, Obeley, Obely, Obeleah

Obioma (African) A kind and caring woman
Obiomah, Obeoma, Obeomah, Obyoma, Obyomah

Oceana (Greek) Feminine form of Oceanus, father of the rivers; from the ocean
Oceania, Ocean, Oceanea, Oceane

Octavia (Latin) Feminine form of Octavius; the eighth-born child
Octaviana, Octavianne, Octavie, Octiana, Octoviana, Ottavia, Octavi, Octavy, Octavey, Octavee, Octavea

October (American) Born during autumn; born in the month of October
Oktober, Octobar, Oktobar

Ocypete (Greek) In mythology, a Harpy

Oda (German) Wielding a spear of the elves
Odah, Odiana, Odiane, Odianna, Odianne, Odiann, Ordalf, Ordalph

Odahingum (Native American) Of the rippling waters

Odanda (Spanish) From the well-known land
Odandah, Odandia, Odandea, Odande

Oddfrid (Norse) As sharp as the point of a sword
Oddfride, Oddfrida, Oddfreid, Oddfreide, Oddfreida, Odd, Oddfryd, Oddfryda

Oddnaug (Norse) A pointed woman
Oddnauge, Oddnauga, Oddvieg, Oddviege, Oddviega, Oddny, Oddni, Oddney, Oddnie, Oddnee, Oddnea

Oddrun (Scandinavian) Our secret love

Oddveig (Scandinavian) One who wields a spear

Ode (Egyptian / Greek) Traveler of the road / a lyric poem
Odea

Odeda (Hebrew) Having great strength
Odedia, Odedah, Odede

Odele (Greek / German) A sweet melody / one who is wealthy
Odela, Odelet, Odelette, Odelina, Odeline, Odell, Odella, Odelle, Odeletta, Odelyn, Odelyna

Odelia (Hebrew) One who praises God
Oda, Odeelia, Odelinda, Odellia, Odilia, Odelea, Odellea

Odelita (Spanish) One who sings
Odelitah, Odelyta, Odelytah, Odeleeta, Odeleetah, Odeleata, Odeleatah, Odeleta, Odeletah

Odera (Hebrew) One who plows the earth
Oderah, Oderra, Oderrah, Oderia, Oderria, Oderea, Oderrea

Odessa (Greek) Feminine form of Odysseus; one who wanders; an angry woman
Odissa, Odyssa, Odessia, Odissia, Odyssia, Odysseia

Odetta (French) A wealthy woman; one who is prosperous
Odette, Odeta, Odete, Odett

Odharnait (Gaelic) A pale-skinned woman
Omat

Odila (French) Form of Otthild, meaning "one who is prosperous in battle; the fortunate heroine"
Odile, Odilia, Odolia, Odilea, Odola, Odalis, Odalys

Odina (Latin / Scandinavian) From the mountain / feminine form of Odin, the highest of the gods
Odinah, Odeena, Odeene, Odeen, Odyna, Odyne, Odynn, Odeana, Odeane

Odiya (Hebrew) Song of the Lord
Odiyah, Odya, Odyah

Oenone (Greek) In mythology, a nymph who acted as a healer
Oenonie, Oenonee

Ofa (Polynesian) One who loves and is loved
Ofah, Offa, Offah, Opha, Ophah

Ogenya (Hebrew) God provides assistance
Ogenyah, Ogeniya, Ogeniyah

Ogin (Native American) Resembling the wild rose

Ohanna (Armenian) A gift from God
Ohannah, Ohana, Ohanah, Ohanny, Ohanney, Ohanni, Ohannie, Ohannea, Ohannee

Ohara (Japanese) One who meditates
Oharah, Oharra, Oharrah

Ohela (Hebrew) One who lives in a tent
Ohelah

Oheo (Native American) A beautiful woman

Ohio (Native American) Of the good river; from the state of Ohio

Oighrig (Gaelic) A freckled child

Oihane (Spanish) From the woodland
Oihanne, Oihana, Oihanna, Oihann, Oihaine, Oihain, Oihayn, Oihayne, Oihaen, Oihaene

Oilell (Celtic) In mythology, a queen
Oilelle, Oilel, Oilele, Oilella, Oilela

Oira (Latin) One who prays to God
Oyra, Oirah, Oyrah

Oisin (Irish) Resembling a young deer
Oisine, Oisina, Oisinia, Oisinea, Oisinn, Oisinne, Oisinna

Ojal (Indian) A dream or vision
Ojall, Ojale, Ojala, Ojalle, Ojalla

Ojufemi (Egyptian) Loved by the gods
Ojufemie, Ojufemy, Ojufemey, Ojufemee, Olufemi, Olufemie, Olufemee, Olufemy, Olufemey, Ojufemea, Olufemea

Okalani (Hawaiian) Form of Kalani, meaning "from the heavens"
Okalanie, Okalany, Okalaney, Okalanee, Okaloni, Okalonie, Okalonee, Okalony, Okaloney, Okeilana, Okelani, Okelani, Okelanie, Okelany, Okelaney, Okelanee, Okalanea, Okalonea, Okelanea

Okei (Japanese) Woman of the ocean

Oki (Japanese) From the center of the ocean
Okie, Oky, Okey, Okee, Okea

Oklahoma (Native American) Of the red people; from the state of Oklahoma

Okoth (African) Born during rainfall
Okothe, Okotha, Okothia, Okothea, Okothiya

Oksana (Russian) One who gives glory to God
Oksanah, Oksanna, Oksania, Oksanea, Oksaniya, Oksanochka

Ola (Nigerian / Hawaiian / Norse) One who is precious / giver of life; well-being / a relic of one's ancestors
Olah, Olla, Ollah

Olabisi (Egyptian) One who brings joy to others
Olabisie, Olabisy, Olabisey, Olabisee, Olabisea

Olaide (American) A thoughtful woman
Olaid, Olaida, Olayd, Olayde, Olayda, Olaed, Olaede, Olaeda

Olena (Russian) Form of Helen, meaning "the shining light"
Olenah, Olenia, Olenya, Olinija, Olinia

Olesia (Polish) Form of Alexandra, meaning "helper and defender of mankind"
Olesiah, Olexa, Olexia, Olexea, Olex

Olethea (Latin) Form of Alethea, meaning "one who is truthful"
Oletheia, Olethia, Oletha, Oletea, Olthaia, Olithea, Olathea, Oletia, Olithia, Olthaea, Oleta

Olga (Scandinavian) One who is blessed and successful
Olgah, Olenka, Olia, Oliah, Olya

OLIVIA

We chose the name Olivia because we thought it was a beautiful name. Little did we know it would later help her learn. In kindergarten, she was always so happy to have the name with the most syllables and the most vowels to count out in class. Bonus. —Amy, KS

Olathe (Native American) A lovely young woman

Olaug (Scandinavian) A loyal woman

Olayinka (Yoruban) Surrounded by wealth and honor
Olayenka, Olayanka

Oldriska (Czech) A noble ruler
Oldryska, Oldri, Oldrie, Oldry, Oldrey, Oldree, Oldrea

Oldwin (English) A special and beloved friend
Oldwinn, Oldwinne, Oldwina, Oldwinna, Oldwyn, Oldwynn, Oldwynne, Oldwyna, Oldwynna, Oldwen, Oldwenn, Oldwenne, Oldwenna

Oleda (English) Resembling a winged creature
Oldedah, Oleta, Olita, Olida, Oletah, Olitah, Olidah

Oleia (Greek) One who is smooth

Oleisa (Greek) Form of Elizabeth, meaning "my God is bountiful"
Oleisia, Oleisah, Oleisia, Oleesa, Oleasa, Oleysa

Oliana (Hawaiian) Resembling the oleander
Olianah, Olianna, Oleana, Oleanna, Oliane, Oliann, Oleane, Oleann, Oleanne

Olidie (Spanish) Surrounded by light
Olidi, Olidy, Olidey, Olidee, Olidea, Olydie, Olydi, Olydie, Olydy, Olydey, Olydee, Olydea

Olina (Hawaiian) One who is joyous
Oline, Oleen, Oleene, Olyne, Oleena, Olyna, Olin

Olinda (German) Resembling a wild fig; a protector of the land
Olindah, Olynda, Olynda, Olenda, Olendah

Olisa (Native American) Devoted to God
Olisah, Olissa, Olissah, Olysa, Olyssa

Olivia ✿ ⚦ (Latin) Feminine form of Oliver; of the olive tree; one who is peaceful
Oliviah, Oliva, Olive, Oliveea, Olivet, Olivetta, Olivette, Olivija, Olivine, Olivya, Ollie, Olva, Olia, Oliff, Oliffe, Olivie, Olivi, Olivey, Olivee, Olivy, Oliveria, Oleta, Olida, Oilbhe

Olubayo (African) A dazzling woman
Olubaya, Oloubayo, Oloubaya

Olvyen (Welsh) Form of Olwen, meaning "one who leaves a white footprint"
Olvyin

Olwen (Welsh) One who leaves a white footprint
Olwenn, Olwin, Olwyn, Olwynne, Olwynn, Olwenne, Olwinn, Olwinne, Olwena, Olwenna, Olwina, Olwinna, Olwyna, Olwynna

Olympia (Greek) From Mount Olympus; a goddess
Olympiah, Olimpe, Olimpia, Olimpiada, Olimpiana, Olypme, Olympie, Olympi, Olympy, Olympey, Olimpi, Olimpie, Olympas

Oma (Arabic) A great leader; one who is commanding
Omma

Omah (Hebrew) From the cedar tree
Omette, Omett, Omete, Ometta, Ometa, Ornetta, Ornette

Omana (Indian) A lovely woman
Omanah, Omanna, Omannah

Omanie (American) An exuberant woman
Omani, Omany, Omaney, Omanee, Omanea

Omayra (Latin / Spanish) Having a pleasant fragrance / one who is dearly loved
Omayrah, Omaira, Omairah, Omaera, Omaerah

Omega (Greek) The last great one; the last letter of the Greek alphabet
Omegah, Omegia, Omegiah

Omemee (Native American) Resembling a dove
Omemea, Omemi, Omemie, Omemey, Omemy

Omesha (American) A spendid woman
Omeshah, Omeesha, Omeeshah, Omeasha, Omeashah, Omeisha, Omeishah, Omiesha, Omieshah, Omysha, Omyshah

Omie (Italian) A homebody
Omi, Omee, Omea, Omy, Omey

Ominotago (Native American) Having a beautiful voice

Omolara (African) A welcomed daughter
Omolarah, Omolarra, Omolarrah

Omorose (Egyptian) One who is beautiful
Omorosa, Omorosia, Omorosie, Omorosi, Omorosee, Omorosea, Omorosey, Omorosy

Omphale (Greek) In mythology, a queen of Lydia
Omphaile, Omphayle, Omfale, Omfaile, Omfayle, Omphael, Omphaele, Omphaela

Omri (Arabic) A red-haired woman
Omrie, Omree, Omrea, Omry, Omrey

Omusa (African) One who is adored
Omusah, Omousa, Omousah

Omusupe (African) One who is precious
Omusuppe, Omusepe, Omuseppe

Omyra (English) Form of Myra, meaning "resembling the fragrant oil"
Omeira, Omira, Omeera, Omiera, Omeara, Omera

Ona (Hebrew) Filled with grace
Onit, Onat, Onah

Onaedo (African) The golden child
Onaydo, Onaido

Onaona (Hawaiian) Having a sweet fragrance
Onanonah

Onatah (Native American) Daughter of the earth
Onata, Onatia, Onatiah, Onatea, Onateah

Onawa (Native American) One who is wide-awake
Onawah

Ondine (Latin) Resembling a small wave
Ondina, Ondyne, Ondinia, Ondyna

Ondrea (Slavic) Form of Andrea, meaning "courageous and strong / womanly"
Ondria, Ondrianna, Ondreia, Ondreina, Ondreya, Ondriana, Ondreana, Ondera, Ondraia, Ondreja, Ondrya, Ondris, Ondrette, Oindrea, Onda, Ondee, Ondena, Ondere, Ondra, Ondralyn, Ondi, Ondie, Ondranetta, Ondraya, Ondreanna, Ondree, Ondreah, Ondras, Ondrena, Ondrienne, Ondrianne, Ondrina, Ondren, Ondrya, Onndrea, Onndria, Odra

Oneida (Native American) Our long-awaited daughter
Onieda, Oneyda, Onida, Onyda

Onella (Greek) Lady of light
Onela, Onellia, Onellea, Onelia, Onelea

Onesha (American) A patient woman
Oneshah, Oneisha, Oneishah, Oniesha, Onieshah, Oneesha, Oneeshah, Oneasha, Oneashah, Onysha, Onyshah, Oneshia, Oneshiah, Oneshea, Onesheah

Onesiphorus (Hebrew) One who brings in profit

Ongela (English) Form of Angela, meaning "a heavenly messenger; an angel"
Ongelica, Ongelina, Ongelique, Onjela, Onjelika, Ongella, Ongelita, Ongeline, Ongelyn, Ongelene, Ongelin, Ongelia, Onge, Onga, Ongel, Ongele, Ongelee, Ongelena, Ongeles, Ongeletta, Ongelette, Ongeli, Ongelika, Ongeliki, Ongilia, Ongelisa, Ongelita, Ongell, Ongelle, Ongelynn, Ongie, Ongyalka, Onielka, Onjelica, Onjelita, Onnjel, Onjella

Oni (Native American) Born on sacred ground
Onie, Ony, Oney, Onee, Onea

Onia (Latin) Our one and only
Oniah, Onya, Onyah, Oniya, Oniyah

Onida (Native American) The one who has been expected
Onidah, Onyda, Onydah

Onora (Irish) Form of Honora, meaning "having a good name and integrity; an honorable woman"
Onour, Onoria, Onor, Onorata, Onoratas, Onnor, Onorina, Onorine, Onore, Onoree, Onori, Onorie, Onory, Onouri, Onourie, Onoury, Onoura, Onouria, Onoure, Ohnicio, Omora, Omorra

Ontibile (African) Protected by God
Ontibyle, Ontybile, Ontybyle

Ontina (American) An open-minded woman
Ontinah, Onteena, Onteenah, Onteana, Onteanah, Ontiena, Ontienah, Onteina, Onteinah, Ontyna, Ontynah

Onyx (Latin) As precious as the stone
Onix, Onyks, Oniks, Onycks, Onicks

Oona (Gaelic) Form of Agnes, meaning "one who is pure; chaste"
Oonaugh, Oonagh, Oonah, Ouna, Ounah, Ounagh, Ounaugh

Oota dabun (Native American) Born beneath the daystar

Opa (Native American) As wise as an owl
Opah, Oppa, Oppah

Opal (Sanskrit) A treasured jewel; resembling the iridescent gemstone
Opall, Opalle, Opale, Opalla, Opala, Opalina, Opaline, Opaleena, Opaleene, Opalyna, Opalyne, Opel

Ophel (Hebrew) From the temple hill
Ophela, Ophie, Ophi, Ophy, Ophey, Ophee, Ophea

Ophelia (Greek) One who offers help to others
Ofelia, Ofilia, Ophélie, Ophelya, Ophilia, Ovalia, Ovelia, Opheliah, Ofeliah, Ophelie

Ophira (Hebrew) Feminine form of Ophir; from a place of wealth; golden
Ophirah, Opheera, Ophyra, Ophiera, Opheira, Ofira, Ofeera, Ofeira, Ofiera, Ofyra, Opheara, Ofeara

Ophrah (Hebrew) Resembling a fawn; from the place of dust
Ofra, Ofrit, Ophra, Oprah, Orpa, Orpah, Ofrat, Ofrah

Opportina (Latin) One who seizes opportunity
Oportina, Opportyna, Oportyna, Opporteena, Oporteena, Opporteana, Oporteana, Opportine, Opportyne, Opporteen, Opportean

Ops (Latin) In mythology, the goddess of harvests

Ora (Latin) One who prays to God
Orah, Orra, Orrah, Orit, Orya

Oralee (Hebrew) The Lord is my light
Oralie, Orali, Oraleigh, Oraly, Oraley, Oralit, Orlee, Orli, Orlie, Orly, Orley, Orleigh, Oralea, Orlea

Oraleyda (Spanish) Born with the light of dawn
Oraleydah, Oraleida, Oraleidah, Oralida, Oralidah, Oralyda, Oralydah, Oraleda, Oraledah, Oralieda, Oraliedah

Oralia (Latin) Form of Aurelia, meaning "golden-haired woman"
Orelia, Oraliah, Oriel, Orielle, Oriell, Oriele, Oriella, Oriela, Orlena, Orlene, Orielda, Orial, Oriall, Orialle, Oriala, Orialla

Orane (French) Born at sunrise
Oraine, Orayne, Oriane, Orania, Oraen,
Oraene

Orange (Latin) Resembling the sweet fruit
Orangetta, Orangia, Orangina, Orangea

Orbelina (American) One who brings
excitement
Orbelinah, Orbeleena, Orbeleenah,
Orbeleana, Orbeleanah, Orbelyna, Orbelynah,
Orbie, Orbi, Orby, Orbey, Orbee, Orbea

Orbona (Latin) In mythology, goddess
who provided children to those without
Orbonah, Orbonna, Orbonnah

Ordell (Latin) Of the beginning
Ordelle, Ordele, Ordel, Ordella, Ordela,
Orde

Orea (Greek) From the mountains
Oreah

Oreille (Latin) A golden woman
Oreile, Oreill, Oreilla, Oreila

Orela (Latin) Announcement from the gods
Orelah, Orella, Orellah, Orila, Orilla,
Orelda, Oracle, Oracula

Orenda (Iroquois) A woman with magical
powers

Orene (French) A nurturing woman
Oreene, Oreen, Oreane, Orean, Orena,
Oreena, Oreana

Orfea (Greek) Feminine form of Orpheus;
having a beautiful voice
Orfeah, Orfeya, Orfia, Orphea, Orpheya,
Orphia

Orfelinda (Spanish) Having the beauty of
the dawn
Orfelynda, Orphelinda, Orphelynda,
Orfelenda, Orphelenda

Orguelleuse (English) One who is arrogant

Oria (Latin) Woman from the Orient
Oriah, Orien, Orienne, Oriena, Orienna

Oriana (Latin) Born at sunrise
Oreana, Orianna, Oriane, Oriann, Orianne

Oribel (Latin) A beautiful golden child
Orabel, Orabelle, Orabell, Orabela,
Orabella, Oribell, Oribelle, Oribele,
Oribela, Oribella, Orinda, Orynda

Orin (Irish) A dark-haired beauty
Orine, Orina, Oryna, Oryn, Oryne

Orino (Japanese) One who works outside
the home
Oryno, Oreno

Orinthia (Hebrew / Gaelic) Of the pine
tree / a fair lady
Orrinthia, Orenthia, Orna, Ornina,
Orinthea, Orenthea, Orynthia, Orynthea

Oriole (Latin) Resembling the gold-speckled
bird
Oreolle, Oriolle, Oreole, Oriola, Oriolla,
Oriol, Oreola, Oreolla

Orion (Greek) The huntress; a constellation

Oritha (Greek) One who is motherly
Orithe, Orith, Orytha, Oryth, Orythe,
Orithia, Orithea, Orythia, Orythea

Orithna (Greek) One who is natural
Orithne, Orythna, Orythne, Orithnia,
Orythnia, Orithnea, Orythnea, Orithniya,
Orythniya

Orla (Gaelic) The golden queen
Orlah, Orrla, Orrlah, Orlagh, Orlaith,
Orlaithe, Orghlaith, Orghlaithe

Orlain (French) One who is famous
Orlaine, Orlaina, Orlaen, Orlaene,
Orlaena, Orlayn, Orlayne, Orlayna

Orlanda (Latin) Feminine form of
Orlando; from the renowned land
Orlandia, Orlandea, Orlantha, Orlande,
Orlanthe, Orlanthia, Orlanthea

Orlenda (Russian) Resembling an eagle
Orlinda, Orlynda

Orlina (French) The golden child
Orlinah, Orlyna, Orlynah, Orlean,
Orleane, Orleana, Orleans, Orleene,
Orleena

Orma (African) An independent woman;
one who is free
Ormah

Ormanda (German) Woman of the sea
Ormandy, Ormandey, Ormadee, Ormandi,
Ormandie, Ormandea

Orna (Irish / Hebrew) One who is
pale-skinned / of the cedar tree
Ornah, Ornette, Ornetta, Ornete, Orneta,
Obharnait, Ornat

Ornella (Italian) Of the flowering ash tree
Ornelle, Ornell, Ornela, Ornele, Ornel

Ornice (Irish) A pale-skinned woman
*Ornyce, Ornise, Orynse, Orneice, Orneise,
Orniece, Orniese, Orneece, Orneese,
Orneace, Ornease*

Orphne (Greek) In mythology, a nymph
and mother of Ascalaphus
*Orphnie, Orphny, Orphney, Orphnee,
Orphnea*

Orquidea (Spanish) Resembling the orchid
*Orquideah, Orquidia, Orquida,
Orquidana, Orquidiya*

Orsa (Latin) Form of Ursula, meaning
"resembling a little bear"
*Orsah, Orsalina, Orsaline, Orsel, Orselina,
Orseline, Orsola, Orssa*

Orszebet (Hungarian) Form of Elizabeth,
meaning "my God is bountiful"
*Orsebet, Orszebeth, Orsebeth, Orzebet,
Orzebeth, Orzsebet, Orzsebeth*

Ortensia (Latin) From the garden
*Ortensiah, Ortensea, Ortenseah, Ortense,
Ortenze, Ortenzia, Ortenzea, Ortensiana,
Ortensie, Ortensi, Ortensy, Ortensey,
Ortensee, Ortenzi, Ortenzie, Ortenzee*

Orthia (Greek) One who takes the straight
path
*Orthiah, Orthea, Ortheah, Orthiya,
Orthiyah*

Ortruda (Teutonic) Resembling a serpent
*Ortrud, Ortrude, Ortrouda, Ortroude,
Ortroud*

Ortygia (Greek) In mythology, an island
where Artemis and Apollo were born
Ortegia, Ortigia

Orva (Anglo-Saxon / French) A courageous
friend / as precious as gold
Orvah

Orynko (Ukrainian) A peaceful woman
Orinko, Orynka, Orinka

Orzora (Hebrew) Having the strength of
God
*Orzorah, Orzorra, Orzorrah, Orzoria,
Orzorea*

Osaka (Japanese) From the city of industry
*Osaki, Osakie, Osakee, Osaky, Osakey,
Osakea*

Osanna (English) Form of Hosanna,
meaning "raising one's voice in praise of
God"
*Osannah, Osann, Osane, Osanne, Osana,
Osanah*

Osarma (American) One who is sleek
Osarmah

Osberga (Anglo-Saxon) A queenly woman
Osburga, Ozberga, Ozburga

Oseye (Egyptian) One who is filled with
happiness

Osithe (Italian) Woman from Italy
Osith, Osyth, Osythe, Ositha, Osytha

Osma (English) Feminine form of
Osmond; protected by God
Osmah, Ozma, Ozmah

Ostia (Italian) From the ancient city
Ostiah, Ostea, Osteah, Ostiya, Ostiyah

Osyka (Native American) One who is
eagle-eyed
Osykah, Osika, Osikah, Oseka, Osekah

Otamisia (Greek) The perfect one
Otameesia, Ottamisia, Ottmeesia

Otha (Anglo-Saxon) The little rich child
*Othili, Othilie, Othily, Othiley, Othilee,
Othia, Othea, Othilea, Othileigh*

Otina (American) A fortunate woman
*Otinah, Otyna, Otynah, Oteena, Oteenah,
Oteana, Oteanah, Otiena, Otienah,
Oteina, Oteinah*

Otrera (Greek) In mythology, the mother
of the Amazons
Otreria, Otrerea, Otrere

Otthild (German) One who is prosperous
in battle; the fortunate heroine
*Otthilda, Ottila, Ottilia, Ottalia, Ottilie,
Ottolie, Ottiline, Ottoline, Otthilde,
Otylia, Ottillia, Otilie, Otka*

Otzara (Hebrew) Possessing great wealth
and treasure
Otzarah, Otzarra, Otzarrah, Ozara, Ozarra

Oudsiyya (Arabic) One who is pious
Oudsiya, Oudsiyyah, Oudsiyah

Ouida (English) Form of Louise, meaning "a famous warrior"

Ourania (Greek) A heavenly woman
Ouraniah, Ouranea, Ouraneah, Ouraniya, Ouraniyah

Ova (Latin) Giver of life; egg
Ovah, Ovia, Ovea, Ove

Overton (English) From the upper side of town
Overtown

Ovida (Hebrew) One who worships God
Ovidah, Ovyda, Ovydah, Oveda, Ovedah, Ovieda, Oviedah, Oveida, Oveidah, Oveeda, Oveedah, Oveada, Oveadah

Ovyena (Spanish) One who helps others
Ovyenah, Oviena, Ovienah, Oviyena, Oviyenah

Owena (Welsh) A highborn woman
Owenah, Owenna, Owennah, Owenia, Owenea

Oya (Native American) One who has been called for
Oyah

Oyama (African) One who has been called
Oyamah, Oyamma, Oyammah, Oyamia, Oyamea, Oyamiah, Oyameah

Oz (Hebrew) Having great strength
Oza, Ozia, Ozz, Ozzi, Ozzie, Ozzy, Ozzey, Ozzee, Ozzea

Ozera (Hebrew) Woman of merit
Ozerah, Ozerra, Ozerrah, Ozeria, Ozeriah, Ozerea, Ozereah

Ozioma (American) Having strength of character
Oziomah, Ozeoma, Ozeomah, Ozyoma, Ozyomah

Ozora (Hebrew) One who is wealthy
Ozorah, Ozorra, Ozorrah

p

Paavna (Hindi) One who is pure; chaste
Pavna, Paavnah, Pavnah, Paavani, Pavani, Pavany, Pavaney, Pavanie, Pavanee, Pavanea

Pabiola (Spanish) A little girl
Pabiolla, Pabiolah, Pabiollah, Pabyola, Pabeola, Pabeolla, Pabyolla

Paca (Spanish) One who is free

Pace (American) A charismatic young woman
Paice, Payce, Paece, Pase, Paise, Payse, Paese

Pacifica (Spanish) A peaceful woman
Pacifika, Pacyfyca, Pacyfyka, Pacifyca, Pacifyka, Pacyfica, Pacyfika

Packard (German) From the brook; a peddler's pack
Packarde, Pakard, Pakarde, Pacard, Pacarde

Pacquita (Latin) One who is unbounded; free; independent
Pacquitah, Pacquyta, Pacqueta, Paquita, Paqueta, Pakita, Packita

Padgett (French) One who strives to better herself
Padget, Padgette, Padgete, Padgeta, Padgetta, Padge

Padma (Hindi) Resembling the lotus flower; in Hinduism, another name for the goddess Lakshmi
Padmah, Padmia, Padmini, Padminia, Padmea, Padminea

Page ○ (English) A young assistant
Paige, Payge, Paege

Pageant (American) A dramatic woman
Pagent, Padgeant, Padgent

Pahana (Native American) A lost white-skinned sibling
Pahanah, Pahanna, Pahann, Pahanne, Pahane, Pahan

Paisley (English) Woman of the church
Paisly, Paisli, Paislie, Paislee, Paysley, Paysly, Paysli, Payslie, Payslee, Pasley, Pasly, Pasli, Paslie, Paslee, Paizley, Payzley, Pazley, Paislea, Paizlea, Paslea, Payslea

P

Paiva (Finnish) Born during daylight
Paeva, Payva

Paka (African) A catlike woman
Pakah, Pakka, Packa, Pacca

Paki (African) A witness of God
*Pakki, Packi, Pacci, Pakie, Pakkie, Paky,
Pakky, Pakey, Pakkey, Pakee, Pakkee, Pakea,
Pakkea*

Pakuna (Native American) Resembling a
deer running through the hills
*Pakunah, Pakoona, Packuna, Pacuna,
Pakouna, Pacouna*

Pakwa (Native American) Resembling
a frog
Pakwah

Pala (Native American) Woman of
the water
Palah

Palakika (Hawaiian) One who is dearly
loved
*Palakyka, Palakeka, Palakeeka, Palakieka,
Palakeika, Palakeaka*

Palani (Hawaiian) An independent woman
*Pallani, Palanie, Palany, Palaney, Palanee,
Pallanee, Palanea, Pallanea, Pallanie,
Pallany, Pallaney*

Palba (Spanish) A fair-haired woman

Palemon (Spanish) A kindhearted woman
Palemond, Palemona, Palemonda

Pales (Latin) In mythology, goddess of
shepherds and flocks
Paless, Palesse, Palus, Palles, Pallus

Palesa (African) Resembling a flower
Palessa, Palesah, Palysa, Palisa, Paleesa

Palila (Hawaiian) A birdlike woman
*Palilla, Palilah, Pallila, Pallilla, Palyla,
Palylla*

Paliuli (Polynesian) Woman from the
paradise garden
Paliulie, Paliuly, Paliuley, Paliulee, Paliulea

Pallas (Greek) Full of wisdom and
understanding; a maiden; in mythology, a
friend of Athena
Palla

Pallavi (Indian) Resembling new leaves
*Palavi, Pallavie, Palavie, Pallavy, Palavy,
Pallavey, Palavey, Pallavee, Palavee,
Pallavea, Palavea*

Palmira (Spanish / Latin) Feminine form of
Palmiro; a pilgrim / from the city of palm
trees
*Palmyra, Palmera, Palmeira, Palmiera,
Palmer, Palmyr, Palma, Pameera, Palmeara*

Paloma (Spanish) Dovelike
*Palomah, Palloma, Palomina, Palomyna,
Palomeena, Poloma, Palomeana, Palomeina,
Palomiena*

Palti (Hebrew) My escape; deliverance
Paltie, Palty, Paltee, Paltey, Paltea

Pamba (African) In mythology, the mother
of the people

Pamela (English) A woman who is as sweet
as honey
*Pamelah, Pamella, Pammeli, Pammelie,
Pameli, Pamelie, Pamelia, Pamelea, Pamelee,
Pameleigh, Pamelina, Pameleena, Pamelyna*

Pamuy (Native American) Born during the
water moon

Pana (Native American) Resembling a
partridge
Panah

Panagiota (Greek) Feminine form of
Panagiotis; a holy woman

Panchali (Indian) A princess; a highborn
woman
*Panchalie, Panchaly, Panchalli, Panchaley,
Panchalee, Panchalea, Panchaleigh*

Panda (English) Resembling the bamboo-
eating animal
Pandah

Pandara (Indian) A good wife
Pandarah, Pandarra, Pandaria, Pandarea

Pandia (Greek) In mythology, the
personification of brightness
*Pandiah, Pandea, Pandiya, Pandya,
Pandeah, Pandiyah, Pandyah*

Pandita (Indian) A studious woman
*Panditah, Pandyta, Pandeta, Pandeyta,
Pandeeta, Pandeata*

Pandora (Greek) A gifted, talented woman; in mythology, the first mortal woman, who unleashed evil upon the world
Pandorah, Pandorra, Pandoria, Pandorea, Pandoriya

Pang (Chinese) One who is innovative

Pangiota (Greek) One who is sacred
Pangyota, Pangeota

Pani (Polynesian) In mythology, goddess of plants and fertility
Panni, Panie, Pany, Paney, Pannie, Panee, Panea

Paniz (Persian) A girl who is as sweet as sugar
Panize, Panyz, Panez, Panizia, Panizea

Pankita (Indian) A young girl; one who is liberal
Pankitah, Pankyta, Panketa, Pankeeta, Pankieta, Pankeita, Pankeata

Panna (Hindi) Resembling an emerald
Pannah

Panola (Greek) One who is all-knowing
Panolah, Panolla, Panollah, Panolia, Panoliah, Panolea, Panoleah, Panoliya, Panoliyah

Panphila (Greek) Daughter who is loved by all
Panphilah, Panphilla, Panfila, Panfilah, Panfilla

Pansy (English) As delicate as a flower; a thoughtful girl
Pansey, Pansi, Pansie, Pansee, Panzi, Panzy, Panzie, Panzee, Pansea, Panzea

Panthea (Greek) Of the gods and goddesses
Pantheah, Panthia, Panthiya, Pantheia, Panthya

Panther (American) Resembling the wild animal
Panthar, Panthur, Panthir, Panthyr

Pantxike (Latin) A woman who is free
Pantxikey, Pantxikye, Pantxeke, Pantxyke

Panya (Slavic / Latin) An enthroned woman; crowned with laurel / a small child; mousy
Panyah, Panyin, Panyen

Papina (Native American) Resembling ivy
Papinah, Papyna, Papena, Papeena, Papiena, Papeina, Papeana

Papina (African) Of the vine
Papyna, Papeena, Papiena, Papeina, Papeana

Paprika (English) Resembling the spice; a lively woman
Paprikah, Papryka, Papreka, Papricka, Paprycka, Paprecka, Papreeka, Papreaka, Papreika, Paprieka

Para (Finnish) In mythology, household spirits

Paraaha (Russian) Born on Good Friday
Paraha, Parashy, Parashie, Parashi, Parashey, Parashee, Parashea

Paradise (English) From the perfect place
Paradice, Paradyse, Paradyce

Paras (Indian) A woman against whom others are measured

Parcae (Latin) In mythology, a name that refers to the Fates
Parca, Parcia, Parcee, Parsae, Parsee, Parsia, Parcea

Pari (Persian) A fairylike young girl
Parie, Pary, Parey, Paree, Parisa, Parihan, Parehan, Paryhan, Parea

Paris (English) Woman of the city in France
Pariss, Parisse, Parys, Paryss, Parysse

Park (Chinese) Of the cypress tree
Parke, Parka

Parker (English) The keeper of the park

Parley (English) One who negotiates
Parly, Parli, Parlie, Parlee, Parleigh, Parlea

Parmida (Persian) Daughter born to royalty
Parmidah, Parmyda, Parmeda, Parmeeda, Parmita, Parmyta, Parmeta, Parmeeta, Parmeada, Parmeata

Parminder (Hindi) An attractive lady
Parmender, Parmynder, Parmindar, Parmendar, Parmyndar

Parnika (Indian) A successful woman
Parnikah, Parnikka, Parnicka, Parnyka, Parneka, Parnita, Parneta, Parnyta

Parrish (Latin) Woman of the church
Parish, Parrishe, Parishe, Parrysh, Parysh, Paryshe

Parry (Welsh) Daughter of Harry
Parri, Parrie, Parrey, Parree, Parrea

Parsley (American) Resembling the garnish
Parslee, Parsleigh, Parsly, Parsli, Parslie, Parslea

Parson (English) A member of the clergy
Parsan, Parsun, Parsin, Parsyn

Parthenia (Greek) One who is chaste; a virgin
Parthenie, Parthenea, Partheniya, Partheniah, Partheni, Partheny, Partheney, Parthenee, Parthenea

Parthenope (Greek) In mythology, a siren

Parvaneh (Persian) Resembling a butterfly
Parveneh, Parvane, Parvene

Parvani (Indian) Born during a full moon
Parvanie, Parvany, Parvaney, Parvanee, Parvanea

Parvati (Hindi) Daughter of the mountain; in Hinduism, a name for the wife of Shiva
Parvatie, Parvaty, Parvatey, Parvatee, Pauravi, Parvatea, Pauravie, Pauravy, Pauravee, Pauravea

Parvin (Persian) Cluster of stars in the constellation Taurus
Parvine, Parveen, Parveene, Parvyn, Parvynne, Parvean, Parveane

Pascale (French) Feminine form of Pascal; born on Easter
Pascaleh, Pascala, Pascaline, Pasclina, Pascalla, Pascalia, Pascha

Pascasia (French) Born on Easter
Paschasia, Pasua

Paschel (African) A spiritual woman
Paschell, Paschele, Paschelle, Paschela, Paschella

Pash (French) A clever woman
Pashe, Pasch, Pasche

Pasha (Greek) Woman of the sea
Pashah, Passha, Passhah

Pasiphae (Greek) In mythology, the wife of Minos and mother of the Minotaur
Pasiphay, Pasiphai

Pasithea (Greek) In mythology, the oldest of the Graces
Pasitheah, Pasithia, Pasithiya, Pasithee, Pasithi, Pasithie

Passion (American) A sensual woman
Pashon, Pashun, Pasyun, Passyun

Pastora (Spanish) A shepherdess
Pastore, Pastoria, Pastorea, Pastoriya

Paterekia (Hawaiian) An upper-class woman
Paterekea, Pakelekia, Pakelekea

Pati (African) One who fishes
Patie, Paty, Patey, Patee, Patea

Patia (Latin) An open-minded woman

Patia (Greek) One who is intellectually superior

Patience (English) One who is patient; an enduring woman
Patiencia, Paciencia, Pacencia, Pacyncia, Pacincia, Pacienca

Patrice (French) Form of Patricia, meaning "of noble descent"
Patriece, Patreece, Patreace, Patreice, Patryce

Patricia (English) Feminine form of Patrick; of noble descent
Patrisha, Patrycia, Patrisia, Patsy, Patti, Patty, Patrizia, Pattie, Padraigin, Pat

Patrina (American) Born into the nobility
Patreena, Patriena, Patreina, Patryna, Patreana

Paula (English) Feminine form of Paul; a petite woman
Paulina, Pauline, Paulette, Paola, Pauleta, Pauletta, Pauli, Paulete, Pabla, Paulita, Pavlina, Pavleena, Pavlyna, Pavliena, Pavla

Pausha (Hindi) Resembling the moon
Paushah

Pavan (Indian / Latin) Resembling a fresh breeze / a dancer of the court
Pavane, Pavania, Pavana, Pavanea

Pavati (Native American) From the clear waters
Pavatie, Pavaty, Pavatey, Pavatee, Pavatea

Pax (Latin) One who is peaceful; in mythology, the goddess of peace
Paxi, Paxie, Paxton, Paxten, Paxtan, Paxy, Paxey, Paxee, Paxea

Payton ✿ (English) From the warrior's village
*Paton, Peyton, Paeton, Paiton, Payten,
Peyten, Paiten*

Paz (Arabic) The golden one
*Paza, Pazia, Pazice, Pazit, Pazz, Pazzy, Pazzi,
Pazzie, Pazzee, Pazzea, Pazzey*

Peace (American) A harmonious woman

Peaches (American) As sweet as the fruit
*Peeches, Peachy, Peachey, Peachee, Peachea,
Peachi, Peachie*

Peakalika (Hawaiian) Filled with happiness

Pearl (Latin) A precious gem of the sea
*Pearla, Pearle, Pearlie, Pearly, Pearline,
Pearlina, Pearli, Pearley, Pearlee, Pearlea,
Pearleigh, Pearleah*

Pebbles (American) Resembling a small rock

Pecola (American) A brazen woman
Pecolah, Pekola, Pekolah

Pedzi (American) A golden woman
Pedzie, Pedzy, Pedzey, Pedzee, Pedzea

Peggy (English) Form of Margaret, meaning
"resembling a pearl / the child of light"
*Peggi, Peggie, Pegeen, Peg, Peigi, Peggee,
Peggea, Peggey*

Pegma (Greek) Filled with happiness
Pegmah, Pegmia, Pegmiah, Pegmea, Pegmeah

Peke (Hawaiian) A giving woman

Pela (Polish) Woman of the sea
Pelah, Pella, Pellah

Pelagia (Greek) Feminine form of Pelagius;
woman of the sea
*Pelagiah, Pelagea, Pelagiya, Pelageah,
Pelagla, Pelaglah, Pelagie, Pelagy, Pelagi,
Pelagey, Pelagee, Pelagias, Pelaga*

Pele (Hawaiian) From the volcano

Peleka (Hawaiian) Having great strength
Pelekah, Pelika, Pelikah, Pelyka, Pelykah

Pelham (English) One who is thoughtful
Pellam, Pelhim, Pellham, Pelim

Pelia (Hebrew) A marvelous woman
Peliah, Peliya, Peliyah, Pelea, Peleah

Pelicia (Greek) A weaving woman
Peliciah, Pelicea, Peliciya, Pelycia, Pelycea

Pelipa (African) One who loves horses
Pelypa, Peliepa, Peleipa, Peleepa, Peleapa

Pellikita (Latin) A bringer of happiness
Pellikitah, Pelikita, Pellkita, Pelkita

Pellonia (Latin) A defender against enemies
Pelloniah, Pelonia, Pellonea, Pelonea

Pelopia (Greek) In mythology, the wife of
Thyestes and mother of Aegisthus
Pelopiah, Pelopea, Pelopeah, Pelopiya

Pelulio (Hawaiian) A treasure from the sea
Pelulia, Peluliyo, Peluliya

Pemba (African) A powerful woman
Pembah, Pembia, Pembiah, Pembea, Pembeah

Pembroke (English) From the broken hill
Pembrook, Pembrok, Pembrooke

Pemphredo (Greek) An alarm; in
mythology, one of the three Graces

Penarddun (Celtic) In mythology, the wife
of Llyr

Penda (African) One who loves and is
loved
Pendah, Penha, Penhah

Pendant (French) A decorated woman
Pendent, Pendante, Pendente

Penelope (Greek) Resembling a duck; in
mythology, the faithful wife of Odysseus
*Penelopy, Penelopy, Penelopey, Penelopi,
Penelopie, Penelopee, Penella, Penelia, Pen,
Penn, Penne, Penny, Pennie, Penni, Penney,
Peni, Pennea, Penelopea*

Penia (Greek) In mythology, the personification of poverty
Peniah, Penea, Peniya, Peneah, Peniyah

Penninah (Hebrew) Resembling a precious
stone
*Penina, Peninah, Peninna, Penyna, Pennyna,
Penine, Penyne*

Pennsylvania (English) The land of Penn;
from the state of Pennsylvania

Pensee (French) A thoughtful woman
Pense, Pensi, Pensie, Pensy, Pensey, Pensea

Penthea (Greek) The fifth-born child
*Penthia, Pentheah, Penthiah, Penthiya,
Penthiyah*

Penthesilea (Greek) In mythology, a queen of the Amazons

Peony (Greek) Resembling the flower
Peoney, Peoni, Peonie, Peonee, Peonea

Pepin (French) An awe-inspiring woman
Peppin, Pepine, Peppine, Pipin, Pippin, Pepen, Pepan, Peppen

Pepita (Spanish) Feminine form of Joseph; God will add
Pepitah, Pepitta, Pepitia, Pepitina

Pepper (American) Resembling the pepper plant; flavorful
Peper

Peppy (American) A cheerful woman
Peppey, Peppi, Peppie, Peppee, Peppea

Perach (Hebrew) A flourishing woman
Pericha, Percha, Pircha, Perchiya, Pirchiya

Perahta (German) A glorious woman
Perata, Perchta, Perchte

Perdita (Latin) A lost woman
Perditah, Perditta, Perdy, Perdie, Perdi, Perdee, Perdea, Perdeeta, Perdeata

Perdix (Latin) Resembling a partridge
Perdixx, Perdyx, Perdyxx

Peregrina (Latin) A traveler; a wanderer
Peregrine, Peregrinna, Peregrinia, Peregrinea, Perrin

Perel (Latin) One who has been tested
Perell, Perelle, Perela, Perele, Perella

Perfecta (Spanish) One who is flawless
Perfecte, Perfectia, Perfectea, Perfect, Perfection

Peri (Persian / English) In mythology, a fairy / from the pear tree
Perry, Perri, Perie, Perrie, Pery, Perrey, Perey, Peree, Perree, Perrea, Perea

Peridot (Arabic) One who is treasured

Periwinkle (English) Resembling the flower
Perriwinkle, Perywinkle, Perrywinkle

Perla (Latin) An important woman
Perlah

Perlace (Spanish) Resembling a small pearl
Perlase, Perlaice, Perlaise, Perlayce, Perlayse

Perlette (French) Resembling a small pearl
Perlett, Perlet, Perlete, Perleta, Perletta

Perlie (Latin) Resembling a pearl
Perli, Perly, Perley, Perlee, Perlea, Perleigh

Perlina (American) Resembling a small pearl
Perlinah, Perlyna, Perlynah, Perleena, Perleenah, Perleana, Perleanah, Perliena, Perlienah, Perleina, Perleinah

Pernella (Scandinavian) As solid as a rock
Pernell, Pernela, Pernele, Pernel, Pernelle

Peron (Latin) One who travels

Perouze (Armenian) Resembling the turquoise gem
Perooze, Perouse, Peroose, Perouza, Perousa

Perpetua (Latin) One who is constant; steadfast

Perse (Greek) From the water; in mythology, one of the Oceanids
Persa, Perseis

Persephone (Greek) In mythology, the daughter of Demeter and Zeus who was abducted to the underworld
Persephoni, Persephonie, Persephony, Persephoney, Persephonee, Persefone, Persefoni, Persefonie, Persefony, Persefoney, Persefonee

Pershella (American) A generous woman
Pershela, Pershel, Pershell, Pershele, Pershelle

Persis (Greek) Woman of Persia
Persiss, Persisse, Persys, Persyss, Persysse

Perzsi (Hebrew) A woman devoted to God
Perzsie, Perzsy, Perzsee, Perzsike, Perke, Perzsey, Perzsea

Pesha (Hebrew) A flourishing woman
Peshah, Peshia, Peshiah, Peshea, Pesheah, Peshe

Petronela (Latin) Feminine form of Peter; as solid and strong as a rock
Petronella, Petronelle, Petronia, Petronilla, Petronille, Petrona, Petronia, Petronel, Petronele, Pernila, Pernilla, Parnella, Pedra, Petra, Petrine, Pedrine, Perrine, Peirene, Peronel, Peronelle, Peta, Pier, Piera, Pierra, Pierce, Pierette, Pietra, Pita

Petula (Latin) An impatient woman
Petulah, Petulla, Petoola, Petoula

Petunia (English) Resembling the flower
Petuniah, Petuniya, Petunea, Petoonia, Petounia

Phaedra (Greek) A bright woman; in mythology, the wife of Theseus
Phadra, Phaidra, Phedra, Phaydra, Phedre, Phaedre

Phailin (Thai) Resembling a sapphire
Phaylin, Phaelin, Phalin

Phan (Asian) One who shares with others

Phashestha (American) One who is decorated
Phashesthea, Phashesthia, Phashesthiya

Pheakkley (Vietnamese) A faithful woman
Pheakkly, Pheakkli, Pheakklie, Pheakklee, Pheakkleigh, Pheakklea

Pheba (Greek) One who smiles a lot
Phebah, Phiba, Phibah

Pheme (Greek) In mythology, the personification of fame
Phemie, Phemia, Phemi, Phemy, Phemey, Phemee, Phemea

Phenice (American) One who enjoys life
Phenyce, Phenise, Phenyse, Phenicia, Phenicea

Phenyo (African) A victorious woman

Pheodora (Greek) A supreme gift
Pheodorah, Phedora, Phedorah

Phernita (American) A well-spoken woman
Pherneeta, Phernyta, Phernieta, Pherneita, Pherneata

Phia (Italian) A saintly woman
Phiah, Phea, Pheah

Philadelphia (Greek) One who offers sisterly love
Philly, Phillie, Philli, Philley, Phillee, Phillea

Philana (Greek) One who adores mankind
Philena, Philanna, Philanne, Philenne, Philenna, Philene, Phileane, Phileene

Philantha (Greek) A woman who loves flowers
Philanthia, Philanthea, Philanthiya

Philberta (English) Feminine form of Philibert; one who is dearly loved
Philiberta, Philbertha, Philibertha, Philberte, Philiberte, Philiberthe, Philberthe

Phile (Greek) Feminine form of Philo; one who loves and is loved
Phila

Philippa (English) Feminine form of Philip; a friend of horses
Phillippa, Philipa, Phillipa, Philipinna, Philippine, Phillipina, Phillipine, Pilis, Pippa

Philise (Greek) A loving woman
Phileese, Philease, Phileise, Philiese, Philyse, Philese

Philomel (Greek) Resembling a nightingale
Philomela, Philomele, Philomell, Philomelle, Philomella

Philomena (English) A friend of strength
Philomina, Philomeena, Philomyna, Philomenia, Philominia, Philomeenia, Philomynia, Phiomeana

Philyra (Greek) A woman who loves music
Philyre, Philyria, Philyrea

Phiona (Scottish) Form of Fiona, meaning "one who is fair; a white-shouldered woman"
Phionna, Phyona, Phyonna, Phione, Phionne, Phyone, Phyonne

Phira (Greek) One who loves music
Phirah, Pheera, Pheerah, Phiera, Phierah, Pheira, Pheirah, Pheara, Phearah

Phoebe (Greek) A bright, shining woman; in mythology, another name for the goddess of the moon
Phebe, Phoebi, Phebi, Phoebie, Phebie, Pheobe, Phoebee, Phoebea, Phebee, Phebea

Phoena (Greek) Resembling a mystical bird
Phoenah, Phoenna, Phena, Phenna

Phoenix (Greek) A dark-red color; in mythology, an immortal bird
Phuong, Phoenyx

Phonsa (American) Filled with joy
Phonsah, Phonsia, Phonsiah, Phonsea, Phonseah, Phonza, Phonzia, Phonzea

Photina (American) A stylish woman
Photeena, Photeana, Photiena, Photeina, Photyna

Phylicia (Greek) One who is fortunate
Phyliciah, Phylicea, Phyliceah, Phylecia, Phylecea, Phyleciah, Phyleceah

Phyllis (Greek) Of the foliage; in mythology, a girl who was turned into an almond tree
Phylis, Phillis, Philis, Phylys, Phyllida, Phylida, Phillida, Philida, Phyllina, Phylina, Phyliss

Phyre (Armenian) One who burns brightly
Phyra, Phyria, Phyrea

Pia (Italian / Polynesian) One who is pious / from the land of ice

Piedad (Spanish) A devout woman
Piedade, Piedadd, Pyedad

Pierina (Greek) One who is dependable
Pierinah, Piereena, Piereenah, Piereana, Piereanah, Pieryna, Pierynah

Pilar (Spanish) Resembling a pillar; having great strength
Pilarre, Pylar, Pylarre

Pili (Egyptian) The second-born child
Pilie, Pily, Piley, Pilee, Pilea, Pileigh

Pilialoha (Hawaiian) One who is dearly loved

Pililani (Hawaiian) Having great strength
Pililanie, Pililany, Pililaney, Pililanee, Pililanea

Pilisi (Hawaiian) Living the simple life
Pilisie, Pilisy, Pilisey, Pilisee, Pilisea

Piluki (Hawaiian) Resembling a small leaf
Pilukie, Piluky, Pilukey, Pilukee, Pilukea

Pilvi (Italian) A cheerful woman
Pilvie, Pilvee, Pilvea, Pilvy, Pilvey

Pineki (Hawaiian) Resembling a peanut
Pinekie, Pineky, Pinekey, Pinekee, Pinekea

Ping (Chinese) One who is peaceful
Pyng

Pinga (Inuit) In mythology, goddess of the hunt, fertility, and healing
Pingah, Pyngah, Pyngah

Pingjarje (Native American) Resembling a young doe
Pingjarji, Pingjarjie, Pingjarjy, Pingjarjey, Pingjarjee, Pingjarjea

Pink (American) One who is healthy
Pinke, Pinka, Pinki, Pinkie, Pinky, Pinkey, Pinkee, Pinkea

Pinquana (Native American) Having a pleasant fragrance
Pinquan, Pinquann, Pinquanne, Pinquanna, Pinquane

Piper (English) One who plays the flute
Pipere, Piperel, Piperell, Piperele, Piperelle, Piperela, Piperella, Pyper, Pypere, Pyperelle, Pyperella

Pippi (French / English) A friend of horses / a blushing young woman
Pippie, Pippy, Pippey, Pippee, Pippea

Pirene (Greek) Of the sacred well
Pireen, Pireene, Piryne, Pirynne, Pireane, Pireane, Pyrene, Pyreen, Pyrean

Pirouette (French) A ballet dancer
Piroette, Pirouett, Piroett, Piroueta, Piroeta, Pirouetta, Piroetta, Pirouet, Piroet

Pisces (Latin) The twelfth sign of the zodiac; the fishes
Pysces, Piscees, Pyscees, Piscez, Pisceez

Pitana (American) One who is adorned
Pitanna, Pytana, Pytanna, Pitania, Pytania, Pitanea, Pytanea

Pitarra (American) An intriguing woman
Pitarrah, Pitara, Pitarah

Pithasthana (Hindi) In Hinduism, a name for the wife of Shiva

Pity (American) A sorrowful woman
Piti, Pitie, Pitey, Pitee, Pitea

Pixie (Celtic) A playful sprite; a fairy or elfin creature
Pixi, Pixy, Pixey, Pixee, Pixea

Placida (Italian) Feminine form of Placido; one who is calm; tranquil
Placidah, Placyda, Placeda, Placeyda, Placidia, Placidea, Placeeda, Placeada

Platinum (English) As precious as the metal
Platynum, Platnum, Platie, Plati, Platee, Platy, Platey, Platea

Platona (Spanish) A beloved friend
Platonia, Platonea, Platonya, Platoniya

Platt (French) From the plains
Platte

Pleasance (French) One who is agreeable
Plaisance, Playsance, Plasance, Plesance

Pleshette (American) An extravagent woman
*Pleshett, Pleshet, Pleshete, Plesheta,
Pleshetta*

Pleun (American) One who is good with
words
Pleune

Plum (American) Resembling the fruit

Po (Italian) A lively woman

Pocahontas (Native American) Filled
with joy
*Pokahontas, Pocohontas, Pokohontas,
Pocahantas, Pakahantas*

Podarge (Greek) In mythology, one of the
Harpies

Poe (English) A mysterious woman

Poetry (American) A romantic woman
Poetrey, Poetri, Poetrie, Poetree, Poetrea

Polete (Hawaiian) A kind young woman
Polet, Polett, Polette, Poleta, Poletta

Polina (Russian) A small woman
*Polinah, Poleena, Poleenah, Poleana,
Poleanah, Poliena, Polienah, Poleina,
Poleinah, Polyna, Polynah*

Polly (English) Form of Mary, meaning
"star of the sea / from the sea of bitterness"
*Polley, Polli, Pollie, Pall, Paili, Paley, Paliki,
Poll, Pollyanna, Pollyana, Pollee, Pollea*

Polyhymnia (Greek) In mythology, the
muse of sacred songs and dance
Polyhymniah, Polymnia, Polymniah

Polyxena (Greek) In mythology, a daughter
of Priam who was loved by Achilles
*Polyxenah, Polyxenia, Polyxenna, Polyxene,
Polyxenea*

Pomona (Latin) In mythology, goddess of
fruit trees
*Pomonah, Pomonia, Pomonea, Pamona,
Pamonia, Pamonea*

Pompa (American) An arrogant woman
*Pompah, Pompy, Pompey, Pompee, Pompea,
Pompi, Pompie*

Pompeya (Latin) Feminine form of Pompey;
fifth-born child; woman from Pompeii
Pompaya, Pompaiya, Pompaeya

Poni (African) The second-born daughter
*Ponni, Ponie, Ponnie, Pony, Ponny, Poney,
Ponney, Ponee, Ponnee, Ponea, Ponnea*

Poodle (American) Resembling the dog;
one with curly hair
Poudle, Poodel, Poudel

Pooky (American) A cute and cuddly girl
Pookey, Pooki, Pookie, Pookee, Pookea

Poonam (Hindi) A kind and caring woman
Pounam

Poppy (English) Resembling the red flower
*Poppey, Poppi, Poppie, Poppee, Popi, Popie,
Popy, Poppea, Popee, Popey, Popea*

Pora (Hebrew) A fertile woman
*Porah, Porrah, Porra, Poria, Poriah, Porea,
Poreah*

Porter (Latin) The doorkeeper

Portia (Latin) Piglike woman; an offering
Portiah, Porsha, Porscha

Posala (Native American) Born at the end
of spring
Posalah, Posalla, Posallah

Posh (American) A fancy young woman
Poshe, Posha

Posy (English) Resembling a bouquet of
flowers; form of Josephine, meaning "God
will add"
*Posey, Posi, Posie, Posee, Pozy, Pozey, Pozi,
Pozie, Pozee, Posea, Pozea*

Potina (Latin) In mythology, goddess of
children's food and drink
*Potinah, Potyna, Potena, Poteena, Potiena,
Poteina, Poteana*

Pounamu (Maori) A treasured gift

Powder (American) A lighthearted woman
*Powdar, Powdir, Powdur, Powdor, Powdi,
Powdie, Powdy, Powdey, Powdee, Powdea*

Prabhu (Indian) A mighty woman

Pradeepta (Indian) Feminine form of
Pradeep; one who provides light
Pradypta, Pradeapta, Pradeypta

Pragyata (Hindi) One who is knowledgeable

Prairie (American) From the flatlands
Prairi, Prairy, Prairey, Prairee, Prairea

Praise (Latin) One who expresses admiration
Prayse, Praize, Prayze, Praze, Praese, Praeze

Pramada (Indian) One who is indifferent

Pramlocha (Hindi) In Hinduism,
a celestial nymph

Prarthana (Hindi) One who prays

Pratibha (Hindi) An understanding woman
Pratibhah, Pratybha, Pratybhah

Pratima (Indian) An image or icon
*Pratimah, Pratema, Pratyma, Prateema,
Prateima, Pratiema, Prateama*

Precia (Latin) An important lady
Preciah, Presha, Preshah, Pretia, Pretiah

Precious (American) One who is treasured
Preshis, Preshys

Preeti (Indian) One who loves and is loved
Priti, Preetie, Pritie, Pritika, Priya, Preati

Prema (Hindi) One who is dearly loved
Premah, Premma, Premmah

Premlata (Hindi) A loving woman
Premlatah, Premlatta, Premlatia, Premlatea

Prentice (English) A student; an apprentice
Prentyce, Prentise, Prentyse

Prescilian (Spanish) A fashionable woman
Presciliann, Prescilianne

Presencia (Spanish) One who presents
herself well
*Presenciah, Presencea, Presenceah,
Presenciya, Presenciyah*

Presley (English) Of the priest's town
*Presly, Presle, Presli, Preslie, Preslee,
Presleigh, Preslea, Prezley, Prezly, Prezli,
Prezlie, Prezlee, Prezleigh, Prezlea*

Pribislava (Polish) One who is glorified
*Pribislavia, Pribislavea, Pribislawa, Pribka,
Pribuska*

Prima (Latin) The firstborn child
*Primalia, Primma, Pryma, Primia, Primea,
Preema, Preama*

Primavera (Spanish) Born during spring

Primola (Latin) Resembling a primrose
*Primolah, Primolia, Primoliah, Primolea,
Primoleah*

Primrose (Latin) The first rose; resembling
the flower
*Prymrose, Primula, Primulia, Primrosa,
Prymrosa*

Princess (English) A highborn daughter;
born to royalty
*Princessa, Princesa, Princie, Princi, Princy,
Princee, Princey, Princea, Prinsess, Prinscella,
Prinscelle, Princella, Princelle, Prinscilla*

Prisca (Latin) From an ancient family
*Priscah, Priska, Priscca, Priscka, Piroska,
Pirosca, Piroscka, Piri*

Priscilla (Latin) Form of Prisca, meaning
"from an ancient family"
*Priscella, Precilla, Presilla, Prescilla,
Prisilla, Prisella, Prissy, Prissi, Prissie,
Prissey, Prissee, Prissea, Prisy, Pris, Priss*

Prisisima (Spanish) Having great wisdom
Prisima

Prisma (Hindi) One who is cherished
Prismah, Prizma, Prizmah

Pristina (Latin) One who is unspoiled
*Prystina, Pristeena, Prysteena, Pristeana,
Prysteana, Pristyna, Prystyna, Pristiena,
Prystiena, Pristeina, Prysteina*

Prochora (Latin) One who guides others
*Prochorah, Prochoria, Prochoriah,
Prochorea, Prochoreah*

Procne (Greek) In mythology, an Athenian
princess

Promise (American) A faithful woman
*Promice, Promyse, Promyce, Promis,
Promiss, Promys, Promyss*

Proserpina (Latin) In mythology, goddess
of the underworld
*Proserpinah, Proserpyna, Proserpeena,
Proserpiena, Proserpeana*

Prospera (Latin) One who is fortunate
Prosperia, Prosper, Prosperea, Prosperous

Protima (Hindi) One who dances
*Protimah, Proteema, Proteemah, Proteima,
Proteimah, Protiema, Protiemah,
Proteama, Proteamah, Protyma, Protymah*

Prova (French) Woman of the province
Provah, Provva, Provvah, Provia, Proviah, Provea, Proveah

Prudence (English) One who is cautious and exercises good judgment
Prudencia, Prudensa, Prudensia, Prudentia, Predencia, Predentia, Prue, Pru

Prunella (Latin) Resembling a little plum
Prunellah, Prunela, Prunellia, Prunelia, Prunelle, Prunele, Prunell, Prunel

Pryce (American / Welsh) One who is very dear / an enthusiastic child
Price, Prise, Pryse

Pryor (American) A wealthy woman; prosperous
Pryar, Pryer, Pryier

Psyche (Greek) Of the soul; in mythology, a maiden loved by Eros

Pua (Hawaiian) Resembling a flower

Puck (English) A mischievous fairy

Puja (Hindi) In Hinduism, a religious ritual
Pujah, Pooja, Pouja

Pulcheria (Italian) A chubby baby
Pulcheriah, Pulcherea, Pulchereah, Pulcherya, Pulcheryah, Pulcheriya, Pulcheriyah

Pules (Native American) Resembling a pigeon

Pulika (African) An obedient and well-behaved girl
Pulikah, Pulicca, Pulicka, Pulyka, Puleeka, Puleaka

Puma (Latin) Resembling the mountain lion
Pumah, Pumma, Pooma, Poomah, Pouma

Purity (English) One who is chaste; clean
Puritey, Puritee, Puriti, Puritie, Pura, Pureza, Purisima, Pure, Puritea

Purnima (Hindi) Born beneath the full moon
Purnyma, Purnema, Purneima, Purniema, Purneema, Purneama

Pyera (Italian) Formidable woman
Pyerah, Pyerra, Pyerrah, Pyira, Pyirra, Pyirah, Pyirrah

Pyllyon (English) An enthusiastic woman
Pylyon

Pyrena (Greek) A fiery woman
Pyrenah, Pyrina, Pyrinah, Pyryna, Pyrynah, Pyreena, Pyreenah, Pyriena, Pyrienah, Pyreina, Pyreinah, Pyreana, Pyreanah

Pyria (American) One who is cherished
Pyriah, Pyrea, Pyreah, Pyriya, Pyriyah, Pyra, Pyrah

Pyrrha (Greek) In mythology, Pandora's daughter

Pythia (Greek) A prophetess; in mythology, a priestess of Apollo
Pythiah, Pythea, Pytheah, Pythiya, Pythiyah

Qadesh (Syrian) In mythology, goddess of love and sensuality
Quedesh, Qadesha, Quedesha, Qadeshia, Quedeshia, Quedeshiya

Qadira (Arabic) Feminine form of Qadir; powerful; capable
Qadirah, Qadyra, Qadyrah, Qadiria, Qadirra, Quadira, Quadyra, Qadeera, Qadeira, Qadeara

Qamra (Arabic) Of the moon
Qamrah, Qamar, Qamara, Qamrra, Qamaria, Qamrea, Qamria

Qeturah (Hebrew) Form of Keturah, meaning "resembling incense"
Qetura, Qeturra, Qeturia, Qeturiya, Qeterea

Qi (Chinese) A life force

Qiana (American) One who is gracious
Qianah, Qiania, Qyana, Qianna, Qiannia, Qyanna, Qianne, Qiann, Qianiya

Qiao (Chinese) One who is beautiful; attractive

Qimat (Indian) A valuable woman
Qimate, Qimatte, Qimata, Qimatta

Qing Yuan (Chinese) From the clear spring

Qitarah (Arabic) Having a nice fragrance
Qitara, Qytarah, Qytara, Qitaria, Qitarra, Qitarria, Qytarra, Qytarria, Qitaria, Qytaria, Qitariya, Qitarriya

Qoqa (Chechen) Resembling a dove

Quan (Chinese) A compassionate woman

Quana (Native American) One who is
aromatic; sweet-smelling
*Quanah, Quanna, Quannah, Quania,
Quaniya, Quanniya, Quannia, Quanea*

Quanda (American) A beloved companion;
friend
*Quandah, Quannda, Quandia, Quandiah,
Quandea, Quandeah*

Quaneisha (American) A royal hawk
*Quanesha, Quanisha, Quaniesha,
Quaynisha, Quanishia, Quynisha,
Quynishia, Queenisha, Qynisha, Qynysha,
Quaneesha, Quaneasha, Quanecia,
Quaneasa, Qynisha, Qynecia, Qwanisha,
Quanessa, Quannezia, Queisha, Queshya,
Queshia, Qeysha*

Quanella (American) A sparkling woman
*Quanell, Quanel, Quanela, Quanelle,
Quanele*

Quanika (American) Form of Nika, meaning
"displaying her true image"
*Quanikah, Quanica, Quanicka, Quanyka,
Quanikka, Quaniqua, Quanykka,
Quanique, Queenika, Quaniki, Quanyki,
Quaneeka, Quaneaka*

Quantina (American) A courageous queen
*Quantinah, Quanteena, Quanteenah,
Quantyna, Quantynah, Quantiena,
Quantienah, Quanteina, Quanteinah,
Quanteana, Quanteanah*

Quartilla (Latin) The fourth-born child
*Quartillah, Quartila, Quartylla, Quartyla,
Quartille, Quartylle, Quartile, Quartyle*

Qubilah (Arabic) One who is agreeable;
pleasing
*Qubila, Quibilah, Quabila, Quabyla,
Qubyla, Qubilla, Qubylla*

Queen (English) A woman sovereign
*Queene, Queenie, Queeni, Queena,
Queeny, Quenna, Queenika, Queenique,
Queenya, Queenia, Queenette, Queeney,
Queeneta, Queaney, Queany, Queani,
Queanie, Queania, Queanya, Queanee,
Quean*

Quella (English) One who pacifies; quiet
*Quell, Quelle, Quellah, Quela, Quele,
Quelia, Quellia*

Quenby (Scandinavian) Womanly; feminine
*Quenbey, Quenbi, Quenbie, Quenbye,
Quenbee, Queenby, Queenbey, Queenbi,
Queenbie, Queenbee, Quenbea, Queenbee*

Quennell (French) From the small oak tree
*Quennel, Quenell, Quennelle, Quynnell,
Quynel, Quynele, Quynnel, Quynnelle*

Querida (Spanish) One who is dearly
loved; beloved
*Queridah, Queryda, Querydah, Querrida,
Queridda, Querridda, Quereeda, Quereada*

Questa (Latin) One who searches; a seeker
*Questah, Queste, Quest, Quysta, Quyste,
Quessta, Questia, Questea*

Queta (Spanish) Head of the household
Quetah, Quetta, Quettah

Quiana (American) Living with grace;
heavenly
*Quianah, Quianna, Quiane, Quian, Quianne,
Quianda, Quiani, Quianita, Quyanna,
Quyana, Quyann, Quyanne, Quionna*

Quies (Latin) A peaceful woman; bringer
of tranquility
Quiese, Queise, Queis, Quiesse, Quiess

Quilla (Incan / English) In mythology,
goddess of the moon / a quill
*Quillah, Quila, Quilah, Quille, Quyla,
Quylla, Quylle, Quyle*

Quinby (Scandinavian) From the queen's
estate
*Quinbey, Quinbi, Quinbie, Quinbee,
Quinbea, Quynby, Quynbey, Quynbi,
Quynbie, Quynbee, Quynbea*

Quincy (English) The fifth-born child
*Quincey, Quinci, Quincie, Quincee, Quincia,
Quinncy, Quinnci, Quyncy, Quyncey,
Quynci, Quyncie, Quyncee, Quynncy*

Quincylla (American) The fifth-born child
Quincilla, Quincyla, Quincila

Quinevere (English) Form of Guinevere,
meaning "one who is fair; of the white wave"
*Quineviere, Quineverre, Quynevere,
Quineveire*

Quinlan (Gaelic) One who is slender and
very strong
*Quinnlan, Quynlan, Qwinlan, Quinlane,
Quinlania, Quinlanna, Quinlann,
Quinlanne*

Quinn (German) Woman who is queenly
Quin, Quinne, Quina, Quynn, Qwin,
Quiyn, Quyn, Quinna, Qwinn, Qwinne

Quintana (Latin / English) The fifth girl /
queen's lawn
Quintanah, Quinella, Quinta, Quintina,
Quintanna, Quintann, Quintara,
Quintona, Quintonice, Quyntana,
Quyntanna, Quyntara, Quinela, Quynella,
Quynela, Quinetta, Quinita, Quintia,
Quyntina, Quyntilla, Quyntila

Quintessa (Latin) Of the essence
Quintessah, Quintesa, Quintesha,
Quintisha, Quintessia, Quyntessa,
Quintosha, Quinticia, Quintesse, Quintice,
Quyntesse

Quinyette (American) The fifth-born child
Quinyett, Quinyet, Quinyeta, Quinyette,
Quinyete

Quirina (Latin) One who is contentious
Quirinah, Quiryna, Quirynah, Quireena,
Quireenah, Quireina, Quireinah, Quiriena,
Quirienah, Quireana, Quireanah

Quirita (Latin) A loyal citizen
Quiritah, Quiritta, Quiryta, Quirytta,
Quyryta, Quyrytta, Quiritte, Quirytte,
Quyrytte

Quiritis (Latin) In mythology, goddess of
motherhood
Quiritiss, Quiritisse, Quirytis, Quirytys,
Quiritys, Quirityss

Quisha (American) Having a beautiful
mind
Quishah

Quiterie (French) One who is peaceful;
tranquil
Quiteri, Quitery, Quiterey, Quiteree,
Quiterye, Quyterie, Quyteri, Quyteree,
Quytery, Quyterey, Quyterye, Quiteria,
Quyteria, Quita

Quorra (Italian) From the heart
Quorrah, Quora, Quorah, Quoria,
Quorria, Quoriya, Quorriya

Ra (English) Resembling a doe

Raananah (Hebrew) An unspoiled child
Rananah, Ranana, Raanana, Rananna,
Raananna

Rabab (Arabic) Resembling a pale cloud
Raabab

Rabah (Hebrew) The fourth-born child
Raba, Rabba, Rabbah

Rabea (German) Resembling a raven
Rabeah

Rabiah (Egyptian / Arabic) Born in the
springtime / of the gentle wind
Rabia, Raabia, Rabi'ah, Rabi

Raca (Hebrew) A vain or empty woman
Racah, Racca, Raccah

Rachana (Hindi) Born of the creation
Rachanna, Rashana, Rashanda, Rachna

Rachel ✪ (Hebrew) The innocent lamb; in
the Bible, Jacob's wife
Rachael, Racheal, Rachelanne, Rachelce,
Rachele, Racheli, Rachell, Rachelle, Rachil,
Raechel, Raechell, Raychel, Raychelle,
Rashell, Rashelle, Raychel, Rechell, Rakel

Radcliffe (English) Of the red cliffs
Radcleff, Radclef, Radclif, Radclife,
Radclyffe, Radclyf, Radcliphe, Radclyphe

Radella (English) An elfin counselor
Radell, Radel, Radele, Radella, Radela,
Raedself, Radself, Raidself

Radeyah (Arabic) One who is content;
satisfied
Radeya, Radhiya, Radhiyah, Radhia,
Radhiah, Radhea, Radheah

Radha (Hindi) A successful woman; in
Hinduism, one of Krishna's consorts
Radhah, Radhika, Radhikah, Radheeka,
Radhyka, Radheaka

Radmilla (Slavic) Hardworking for the
people
Radilla, Radinka, Radmila, Redmilla, Radilu

Radwa (Arabic) From the mountain in Medina
Radwah, Radhwa, Radhwah

Rae (English) Form of Rachel, meaning "the innocent lamb"
Raedell, Raedine, Raelaine, Raelani, Raelee, Raeleen, Raelena, Raelene, Raelina, Raella, Raelyn, Raelynn, Raelynne, Raenisha, Ray, Raye, Rayette, Raylene, Raylina, Rayma, Raynelle, Rayona, Rayla, Raynesha, Raynisha, Raylyn, Raylynn, Raelin

Raeka (Spanish) A beautiful and unique woman
Raekah, Rayka, Raika, Raykah, Raikah

Rafa (Arabic) One who is happy and prosperous
Rafah, Raafa, Raffa, Raffah

Rafela (Hebrew) Form of Raphaela, meaning "the divine healer"
Rafelah, Rafellah, Rafella, Rafele, Rafelle

Rafferty (Gaelic) A prosperous lady; wealthy
Raffertey, Rafferti, Raffertie, Raffertee, Raffertea

Rafi'a (Arabic) An exalted woman
Rafia, Rafi'ah, Rafee'a, Rafeea, Rafeeah, Rafiya, Rafiyah

Rafiga (Arabic) A pleasant companion; a sweetheart
Rafigah, Rafeega, Rafeegah, Rafyga, Rafygah

Rafiki (African) A beloved friend
Rafikie, Rafiky, Rafikey, Rafikee, Rafikea, Raficki, Rafickie, Raficci

Raghd (Arabic) A pleasant young woman

Ragnall (English) In Arthurian legend, Gawain's wife
Ragnal, Ragnalle, Ragnalla, Ragnale, Ragnala, Ragnallia, Ragnallea

Ragnara (Swedish) Feminine form of Ragnar; one who provides counsel to the army
Ragnarah, Ragnarra, Ragnaria, Ragnarea, Ragnari, Ragnarie, Ragnary, Ragnarey, Ragnaree

Ragnfrid (Norse) One who gives beautiful advice
Ragnfride, Ragnfrida, Ragna, Ragnfryd, Ragnfryde, Ragnfryda, Ragni, Ragnie, Ragny, Ragney, Ragnee, Ragnea

Ragnhild (Norse / Teutonic) One who provides counsel in battle / an all-knowing being
Ragnild, Ragnhilda, Ragnhilde, Ragnilda, Ranillda, Renild, Renilda, Renilde, Reynilda, Reynilde, Ragnilde

Rahab (Hebrew) A trustworthy and helpful woman
Rahabe, Rahabb, Rahaba, Rahabah

Rahi (Arabic) Born during the springtime
Rahii, Rahy, Rahey, Rahee, Rahea, Rahie

Rahil (Hebrew) Form of Rachel, meaning "the innocent lamb"
Rahill, Raaheel, Rahille, Rahila, Rahilla, Raheela, Rahel, Rahelle

Rahimah (Arabic) A compassionate woman; one who is merciful
Rahima, Raheema, Raheemah, Raheima, Rahiema, Rahyma, Rahymah, Raheama, Raheamah

Rahimateh (Arabic) Filled with grace
Rahimate, Rahimata, Rahimatia, Rahymateh, Rahymata

Rai (Japanese) One who is trustworthy

Ra'idah (Arabic) A great leader
Raidah, Raida, Ra'ida, Raa'idah

Raina (Polish) Form of Regina, meaning "a queenly woman"
Raenah, Raene, Rainah, Raine, Rainee, Rainey, Rainelle, Rainy, Reina, Reinella, Reinelle, Reinette, Reyna, Reynalda, Reynelle, Reyney, Reine, Ranee, Reia

Rainbow (American) As colorful as the rainbow; symbolizing promise
Rainbowe, Raynbow, Raynebow, Raynebowe, Reinbow, Reinbowe

Raisa (Hebrew / Greek) As beautiful as the rose / one who is carefree
Raisabel, Raisse, Raiza, Raizel, Rayzel, Ra'isa, Raisie, Raizie, Raisi, Raizi, Rayzi, Rayzie, Ra'eesa

Raissa (French) A great thinker
Raisa, Raissah, Rayssa, Raysa, Raison, Rayson, Raeson, Raessa

Raja (Arabic) One who is filled with hope
Rajah

Rajani (Hindi) Born at night; in Hinduism, another name for the goddess Kali
Rajanie, Rajany, Rajaney, Rajanee, Rajanae, Rajni, Rajnie, Rajny, Rajney, Rajnee, Rajnea, Rajanea

Rakhshanda (Arabic) A lustrous woman
Rakshanda, Rakhshonda, Rakshonda, Rakshona, Rakhsha, Raksha

Rakkath (Hebrew) From the shore town
Rakkathe, Rakkatha, Rakath, Rakathe, Rakatha, Rakkon, Rakon, Rakkona, Rakona

Raleigh (English) From the clearing of roe deer
Raileigh, Railey, Raley, Rawleigh, Rawley, Raly, Rali, Ralie, Ralee, Rawli, Rawlie, Rawlee, Rawly

Ralphina (English) Feminine form of Ralph; wolf counsel
Raphine, Ralpheene, Ralpheyne, Ralfina, Ralfeene, Ralfine

Rama (Hebrew) One who is exalted
Ramah, Ramath, Ramatha, Ramathe

Ramira (Spanish) A sensible and thoughtful woman
Ramirah, Rameera, Rameerah, Rameira, Ramiera, Ramyrah, Ramyra, Rameirah, Ramierah, Rameara, Ramearah

Ramla (African) A prophetess
Ramlah, Ramli, Ramlie, Ramly, Ramley, Ramleigh, Ramlee, Ramlea

Ramona (Spanish) Feminine form of Ramon; one who offers wise protection
Ramee, Ramie, Ramoena, Ramohna, Ramonda, Ramonde, Ramonita, Ramonna, Ramowna, Remona, Remonna, Romona, Romonda, Romonde, Romonia, Raimunda, Raimonda, Raimona

Ramsey (English) From the raven island; from the island of wild garlic
Ramsay, Ramsie, Ramsi, Ramsee, Ramsy, Ramsea

Ramya (Hindi) An elegant and beautiful woman
Ramyah, Ramiya, Ramiyah, Ramia, Ramiah

Rana (Arabic) An eye-catching woman; to gaze upon
Ranah, Ra'naa, Rand, Raniyah, Ranarauna, Ranaraunaa, Raunaa

Ranait (Irish) A charming woman; one who is prosperous
Ranalt, Rathnait, Ranaite, Rathnaite, Ranalta

Randi (English) Feminine form of Randall; shielded by wolves; form of Miranda, meaning "one who is worthy of admiration"
Randa, Randee, Randelle, Randene, Randie, Randy, Randey, Randilyn, Randilynn, Randilynne

Rani (Hebrew) A lovely singer; a queenly woman
Rania, Ranice, Ranique, Ranit, Ranica, Ranita, Ranite, Ranith, Ranitta, Raanee, Rane, Ranie

Ranielle (American) Form of Danielle, meaning "God is my judge"
Ranele, Ranelle, Raniele, Raniela, Raniella, Raniel

Ranjita (Indian) Feminine form of Ranjit; a charming and delightful woman
Ranjitah, Ranjyta, Ranjytah, Ranjeeta, Ranjeetah

Ranveig (Norse) A house woman
Rannveig, Ranveiga, Ranveige, Ronnaug, Ronaug

Raonaid (Gaelic) Form of Rachel, meaning "the innocent lamb"
Raonaide, Raonaida, Raonayd, Raonayde, Raonaild, Raonailde, Raonailda, Raoghnailt

Raoule (French) Feminine form of Raoul; wolf counsel
Raoula, Raula

Raphaela (Hebrew) Feminine form of Raphael; the divine healer
Rafaela, Rafaelia, Raffaella, Raffaela, Raffaele, Raffaella, Rafella, Rafelle, Raphaella, Raphaelle, Raphayella, Raphella, Refaella, Refella, Rephaela, Rephayelle

Raphah (Hebrew) A tall, looming woman
Rapha, Raphae, Raphia, Raphiah, Raphea, Rapheah

Raphu (Hebrew) One who has been healed by God
Raphoo, Raphou

Raquel (Spanish) Form of Rachel, meaning "the innocent lamb"
Racquel, Racquell, Raquela, Raquelle, Roquel, Roquela, Rakel, Rakell

R

Rasha (Arabic) Resembling a young gazelle
Rashah, Raisha, Raysha, Rashia, Raesha

Rashida (Arabic) Feminine form of
Rashid; a righteous woman; one who is
guided in the right direction
*Rasheda, Rasheeda, Rasheedah, Rasheida,
Rashidah, Rashyda, Rachida, Raashida,
Raashidah*

Rashmika (Indian) A sweet woman
*Rashmikah, Rashmyka, Rashmeeka,
Rashmeika*

Ratana (Thai) Resembling a crystal
*Ratanah, Ratanna, Ratannah, Rathana,
Rathanna*

Rati (Hindi) In Hinduism, goddess of passion and lust
Ratie, Ratea, Ratee, Raty, Ratey

Ratna (Indian) As precious as a jewel
Ratnah, Ratnia, Ratnea

Ratri (Indian) Born in the evening
Ratrie, Ratry, Ratrey, Ratree, Ratrea

Raven (English) Resembling the black bird;
a dark and mysterious beauty
*Ravina, Rayvenne, Rayven, Rayvinn,
Ravyn, Raevin, Raeven, Ravenne*

Rawdah (Arabic) One who works the
earth; a gardener
Rawda, Rawdha, Rawdhah

Rawiyah (Arabic) One who recites ancient
poetry
Rawiya, Rawiyya, Rawiyyah

Rawnie (English) An elegant lady
Rawni, Rawny, Rawney, Rawnee, Rawnea

Raya (Israeli) A beloved friend
Rayah

Rayann (English) An innocent woman full
of grace
*Raeann, Raeanna, Raeanne, Rayana,
Rayanna, Rayanne, Rayane, Raeane,
Raeana, Raiann, Raiane, Raianne,
Raianna, Raiana*

Raymonde (German) Feminine form of
Raymond; one who offers wise protection
*Raymondi, Raymondie, Raymondee,
Raymondea, Raymonda, Raymunde,
Raymunda*

Rayna (Hebrew / Scandinavian) One who
is pure / one who provides wise counsel
*Raynah, Raynee, Rayni, Rayne, Raynea,
Raynie*

Rayya (Arabic) One who's thirst has been
quenched
Rayyah

Raziah (Hebrew) God's secret; a mysterious
woman
*Razia, Razi, Raziela, Raziella, Razili,
Raziella, Raziel, Raziele, Razie, Razee*

Raziya (Swahili) A good-natured woman;
one who is agreeable
Raziyah

Reanna (Irish) Form of Rhiannon, meaning
"the great and sacred queen"
*Reannah, Reanne, Reannon, Reanon,
Reann, Reana, Reeanne, Reanan, Reannan*

Reba (Hebrew) Form of Rebecca, meaning
"one who is bound to God"
*Rebah, Reeba, Rheba, Rebba, Ree, Reyba,
Reaba*

Rebecca (Hebrew) One who is bound to
God; in the Bible, the wife of Isaac
*Rebakah, Rebbeca, Rebbecca, Rebbecka,
Rebbie, Rebeca, Rebeccah, Rebeccea,
Rebeccka, Rebecha, Rebecka, Rebeckah,
Rebeckia, Rebecky, Rebeha, Rebeka,
Rebekah, Rebekha, Rebekka, Rebekkah,
Rebekke, Rebeque, Reveka, Revekah,
Revekka, Ribecca, Rebi, Rimca*

Redell (English) From the red meadow
Redel, Redelle, Redele, Redella, Redela

Redmonde (American) Feminine form of
Redmond; one who offers wise protection
*Redmondi, Redmondie, Redmondee,
Redmondea, Redmonda, Redmunde,
Redmunda*

Reed (English) A red-haired lady
Read, Reade, Reid, Reida

Refugia (Spanish) Feminine form of
Refugio; one who is sheltered; protected
*Refugiah, Refugiya, Refugiyah, Refugea,
Refugeah*

Regan (Gaelic) Born into royalty; the little
ruler
*Raegan, Ragan, Raygan, Reganne, Regann,
Regane, Reghan, Reagan, Reaghan, Reegan*

Regina (Latin) A queenly woman
Regeena, Regena, Reggi, Reggie, Régine, Regine, Reginette, Reginia, Reginna, Rejine, Reginy

Rehan (Armenian) Resembling a flower
Rehane, Rehann, Rehanne, Rehana, Rehanna, Rehanan, Rehannan, Rehania, Rehanea, Rehaniya

Rehema (African) A compassionate woman
Rehemah, Rehemma, Rehemia, Rehemiya, Rehemea

Rehoboth (Hebrew) From the city by the river
Rehobothe, Rehobotha, Rehobothia

Reiko (Japanese) One who is thankful
Rei

Reinheld (Teutonic) A wise and strong ruler
Reinhelde, Reinhelda, Reinhold, Reinholde, Reinholda

Rekha (Indian) One who walks a straight line
Rekhah, Reka, Rekah

Rella (English) Form of Ella, meaning "from a foreign land"
Rellah, Rela, Relah

Remedios (Spanish) Feminine form of Remedio; assisted by God
Remedy, Remedi, Remedie, Remedee, Remedey, Remedea

Remphan (Hebrew) Follower of the false god
Remphana, Remphane, Remphaine, Remphayn, Remphena, Remphaen, Remphaina, Remphayna, Remphaena

Remy (French) Woman from the town of Rheims
Remi, Remie, Remmy, Remmi, Remmie, Remy, Remmey, Remey, Rhemy, Rhemmy, Remee, Remmee

Ren (Japanese) Resembling a water lily

Rena (Hebrew) One who sings a joyous song
Reena, Reene, Rina, Rinah, Rinna, Rinnah, Renna, Rennah

Renée (French) One who has been reborn
Ranae, Ranay, Ranée, Renae, Renata, Renay, Renaye, René, Rene, Reneisha, Renell, Renelle, Renie, Renisha, Renne, Rennie, Renny, Rhianaye, Rrenae, Renee, Rennay, Renate

Renenet (Egyptian) In mythology, the personification of fortune

Reneta (Latin) A dignified woman
Renetah, Renetta, Renettah

Renita (Latin) One who stands firm; resistant
Reneeta, Renyta, Reneata, Renieta, Reneita

Renuka (Indian) Resembling fine grains of sand
Renukah, Renooka, Renookah, Renouka, Renoukah

Rephidim (Hebrew) One who offers support
Rephidima, Rephydim, Rephydima, Rephidem, Rephydem, Rephedem

Reseda (Latin) Resembling the mignonette flower
Resedah, Reselda, Resedia, Reseldia

Resen (Hebrew) From the head of the stream; refers to a bridle

Reshma (Arabic) Having silky skin
Reshmah, Reshman, Reshmane, Reshmann, Reshmanne, Reshmana, Reshmanna, Reshmaan, Reshmia, Reshmea

Reuela (Hebrew) A feminine form of Reuel; a friend of God
Reuelah, Reuella, Reuellah, Reuelia, Reuelea, Reueliah, Reueleah

Reumah (Hebrew) One who has been exalted
Reuma, Reumia, Ruemiah, Ruema, Ruemah

Reveka (Hebrew) A captivating woman
Revekah, Revecka, Reveckah

Rexanne (Latin) A queen full of grace
Rexalla, Rexana, Rexanna, Rexane, Rexella, Rexetta, Rexina, Rexine

Reya (Spanish) A queenly woman
Reyah, Reyeh, Reye, Reyia, Reyiah, Reyea, Reyeah

Reyhan (Arabic) One who is favored by
God
Reyhann, Reyhane, Reyhanne, Reyhana,
Reyhanna, Reyhanah, Reyhannah

Reza (Hungarian) Form of Theresa, meaning
"a harvester"
Rezah, Rezia, Reziah, Rezi, Rezie, Rezy,
Rezee, Resi, Resee, Resie, Resea, Resy,
Resey, Rezea, Resea

Rezeph (Hebrew) As solid as a stone
Rezepha, Rezephe, Rezephia, Rezephah,
Rezephiah

Rhan (Welsh) One's destiny
Rhane, Rhanne, Rhann, Rhanna, Rhana

Rhawn (Welsh) A woman with long and
coarse hair
Rhawne, Rhaun, Rhaune, Rhawna,
Rhauna

Rhaxma (African) A sweet-tempered
woman
Rhaxmah, Rhaxima, Rhaxmia,
Rhaxmana, Rhaxmae, Rhaxmai

Rhea (Greek) Of the flowing stream;
in mythology, the wife of Cronus and
mother of gods and goddesses
Rea, Rhae, Rhaya, Rhia, Rhiah, Rhiya,
Rheya

Rhea Silvia (Latin) In mythology, a Vestal
virgin and mother of Remus and Romulus
Rhea Silva, Rea Silvia, Rea Silva

Rheda (Anglo-Saxon) A divine woman;
a goddess
Rhedah

Rhedyn (Welsh) Resembling a fern
Rhedynn, Rhedyne, Rhedynne, Rhedin,
Rheden

Rhesa (Hebrew) An affectionate woman
Rhesah, Rhesia, Rhesiah, Rheza, Rhezah,
Rhezia, Rheziah

Rheta (Latin) Feminine form of Rhett;
a well-spoken woman
Rhetah, Retta, Rhetta

Rhiamon (Welsh) A magical woman;
a witch
Rhiamone, Rhiamona, Rhiamonia,
Rhiamonea, Rhyamon, Rhyamone,
Rhyamona, Rhyamonia, Rhyamonea

Rhiannon (Welsh) The great and sacred
queen
Rheanna, Rheanne, Rhiana, Rhiann,
Rhianna, Rhiannan, Rhianon, Rhyan,
Riannon, Rianon, Rheann, Rhian, Rhiain,
Rhyanon, Rhyannon

Rhianwen (Welsh) A comely young woman
Rhianwenn, Rhianwenne, Rhianwyn,
Rhianwynn, Rhianwynne, Rhianwin,
Rhianwinn, Rhianwinne, Rhyanwen,
Rhyanwin, Rhyanwyn

Rhoda (Greek) Resembling a rose;
a woman from Rhodes
Rhodeia, Rhodia, Rhodie, Rhody, Roda, Rodi,
Rodie, Rodina, Rodyna, Rodine, Rhodyna,
Rhodine, Rhodina, Rhodee, Rhodea

Rhodantha (Greek) From the rosebush
Rhodanthe, Rhodanta, Rhodante,
Rodantha, Rodanthe, Rodanta, Rodante

Rhode (Greek) In mythology, the oldest
daughter of Oceanus and wife of Helios
Rhodus

Rhodes (Greek) From the Greek island

Rhonda (Welsh) Wielding a good spear
Rhondelle, Rhondene, Rhondiesha,
Rhonette, Rhonnda, Ronda, Rondel,
Rondelle, Rondi, Ronnda, Rhondah,
Rhondia, Rhondea

Rhys (Welsh) Having great enthusiasm
for life
Rhyss, Rhysse, Reece, Reese, Reice, Reise,
Reace, Rease, Riece, Riese

Ria (Spanish) From the river's mouth
Riah

Riane (Gaelic) Feminine form of Ryan;
little ruler
Riana, Rianna, Rianne, Ryann, Ryanne,
Ryana, Ryanna, Riann, Riayn, Ryane, Rye,
Ryen, Ryenne, Ryette, Ryetta, Rynn

Riblah (Hebrew) A fruitful woman; giver
of life
Ribla, Ryblah, Rybla, Riblia, Rybliah,
Ribliah, Ribliya, Ribliyah

Rica (English) Form of Frederica, meaning
"peaceful ruler"; form of Erica, meaning
"ever the ruler / resembling heather"
Rhica, Ricca, Ricah, Rieca, Riecka, Rieka,
Riqua, Ryca, Rycca, Ryka, Rika, Rikka

R

Ricarda (German) Feminine form of Richard; a brave and strong ruler
Richanda, Richarda, Richardella, Richardene, Richardette, Richardina, Richardyne, Richenda, Richenza, Richette, Richia, Richilene, Richina, Richmal, Richmalle, Ricadonna, Ricadona

Richael (Irish) A saintly woman
Raichael

Richelle (American) Combination of Ricarda and Rachel, meaning "a brave and strong ruler" and "the innocent lamb"
Richel, Richela, Richele, Richella, Richell, Rychelle, Rychell, Rychele, Rychella, Rychela

Rickie (English) Form of Frederica, meaning "peaceful ruler"; form of Erica, meaning "ever the ruler / resembling heather"
Ricki, Ricky, Ricquie, Riki, Rikki, Rikky, Ryckie, Ricci, Rikie, Rickee, Rikee, Rickena, Rike

Rida (Arabic) One who is favored by God
Ridah, Reda, Reeda, Redah, Reedah, Ryda, Rydah

Riddhi (Indian) A prosperous woman
Riddhie, Riddhy, Riddhey, Riddhee, Riddhea

Ridhwana (Arabic) A pleasant woman
Ridhwanah, Ridhwanna, Ridwana, Ridwanna, Ridhwaana, Ridwaana, Ridhaa, Ridha, Ridhah

Rigg (English) Woman from the ridge
Rigge, Rigga, Riggi, Riggie, Riggee, Riggia, Riggea, Rygg, Rygge, Rygga

Rigmor (Swedish) A queenly woman
Rigmore, Rigmorr, Rigmorre, Rigmora, Rigmorra, Rigmoria, Rigmorea

Rihana (Arabic) Resembling sweet basil
Rihanah, Rihanna, Rihannah, Ryhana, Ryhanna, Raihana, Raihaana, Raihanna, Raihanah

Riley ⚪ (Gaelic) From the rye clearing; a courageous woman
Reilley, Reilly, Rilee, Rileigh, Ryley, Rylee, Ryleigh, Rylie, Rilie, Rili, Reileigh, Rilea, Rylea, Ryson, Rysen, Ryesen, Ryelana

Rilla (German) From the small brook
Rillah, Rilletta, Rillette, Rille, Rillia, Rillie, Rillea, Rilly, Rilley

Rima (Arabic) Resembling the white antelope
Rimah, Reema, Reemah, Ryma, Rymah, Rim, Reem, Reama, Reamah

Rimona (Arabic) Resembling the pomegranate
Rimonah, Rimonia, Rimonna, Rimonea, Rymona, Rymonia, Rymonea

Rin (Japanese) A pleasant companion
Rinako

Rind (Norse) In mythology, a giantess
Rinda, Rindia, Rindea, Rindi, Rindie, Rindee, Rindy, Rindey

Rini (Japanese) Resembling a young rabbit
Rinie, Rinee, Rinea, Riny, Riney

Rio (Spanish) Woman of the river
Rhio

Riona (Irish) A queenly woman
Rionah, Rionach, Rionagh, Rionna, Rionnagh, Rionnah, Rioghnach

Risa (Latin) One who laughs often
Risah, Reesa, Riesa, Rise, Rysa, Rysah, Riseh, Risako

Rishona (Hebrew) The firstborn child
Rishonah, Ryshona, Rishonna, Ryshonna

Rissah (Hebrew) Covered with dew
Rissa, Ryssa, Ryssah

Rita (Spanish) Form of Margarita, meaning "resembling a pearl / the child of light"
Ritta, Reeta, Reita, Rheeta, Riet, Rieta, Ritah, Reta, Reit, Reata

Rithmah (Hebrew) From the valley of broom bushes
Rithma, Rythmah, Rythma, Rithmia, Rithmiah

Ritsa (Greek) Form of Alexandra, meaning "helper and defender of mankind"
Ritsah, Ritza, Ritzah, Ritsia, Ritsea, Ritzia, Ritzea

Riva (Hebrew / French) Form of Rebecca, meaning "one who is bound to God" / from the shore
Reeva, Reevabel, Reva, Rifka, Rivalee, Rivi, Rivka, Rivke, Rivkah, Rivy, Rivie, Rivah, Rivekka, Rive, Reava

Rizpah (Greek) One who is filled with hope
Rizpa, Ritzpa, Ritzpah, Rhizpa, Rhizpah

Roana (Spanish) A woman with reddish-brown skin
Roane, Roann, Roanne, Roanna, Roan, Rhoan, Rhoane, Rhoana

Roberta (English) Feminine form of Robert; one who is bright with fame
Reberta, Roba, Robbee, Robbey, Robbi, Robbie, Robby, Robeena, Robella, Robelle, Robena, Robenia, Robertena, Robertene, Robertha, Robertina, Robetta, Robette, Robettina, Ruperta, Rupetta, Robertia, Rupette

Robin (English) Form of Roberta, meaning "one who is bright with fame"; resembling the red-breasted songbird
Robbin, Robee, Robena, Robene, Robenia, Robi, Robina, Robine, Robinet, Robinett, Robinette, Robinia, Robyn, Robyna, Robynette, Robynn, Robynne, Robinetta, Robynetta, Rohine, Rohina

Roch (German) A glorious woman
Roche, Rocha

Rochelle (French) From the little rock
Rochel, Rochele, Rochell, Rochella, Rochette, Roschella, Roschelle, Roshelle

Rocio (Spanish) Covered with dewdrops
Roceo, Rociyo

Roderica (German) Feminine form of Roderick; a famous ruler
Roddie, Rodericka, Roderiga, Roderika, Roderqua, Roderique, Roderiga, Roderyca, Roderyka

Rohana (Indian) Resembling sandalwood
Rohanah, Rohannah, Rohanna, Rohane, Rohann, Rohan, Rohanne

Rohini (Indian) A beautiful woman
Rohinie, Rohiny, Rohiney, Rohinee, Rohinea

Roja (Spanish) A red-haired lady
Rojah

Rolanda (German) Feminine form of Roland; well-known throughout the land
Rolandah, Rolandia, Roldandea, Rolande, Rolando, Rollanda, Rollande

Roline (English) Form of Caroline, meaning "a joyous song; a small, strong woman"
Roelene, Roeline, Rolene, Rollene, Rolleen, Rollina, Rolline, Rolyne, Roleine, Roliene

Roma (Italian) Woman from Rome
Romah, Romma, Romalda, Romana, Romelia, Romelle, Romilda, Romina, Romaana, Romaine, Romayne, Romaina, Romayna, Roman, Romane, Romania, Romeine, Romene, Romea, Romala, Romella, Romelle, Rommola, Romolla, Romola, Romula, Romy, Romi, Romie, Romia

Romhilda (German) A glorious battle-maiden
Romhilde, Romhild, Romeld, Romelde, Romelda, Romilda, Romild, Romilde, Ruomhildi, Ruomhild, Ruomhilde, Ruomhilda

Romney (Welsh) Of the winding river
Romny, Romni, Romnie, Romnee, Romnea

Rona (Scottish) From the rough island
Rhona, Ronah, Rhonah, Ronella, Ronelle, Ronna, Ronalee, Ronaleigh

Ronalda (English) Feminine form of Ronald; the ruler's counsel
Ronalde, Ronaldia, Ronaldiya, Ronaldea

Ronat (Gaelic) Resembling a seal
Ronan, Ronana, Ronann, Ronane, Ronana, Ronanna

Rong (Chinese) A glorious woman
Ronga, Rongia, Rongiya, Rongea

Ronli (Hebrew) My joy is the Lord
Ronlie, Ronlee, Ronleigh, Ronly, Ronley, Ronlea, Ronia, Roniya, Roniah

Ronni (English) Form of Veronica, meaning "displaying her true image"
Ronae, Ronay, Ronee, Ronelle, Ronette, Roni, Ronica, Ronika, Ronisha, Ronna, Ronnee, Ronnelle, Ronnella, Ronnette, Ronney, Ronnie, Ronny

Rory (Gaelic) The red queen
Rorie, Rorey, Roree, Rorea, Rori

Rosabel (English) Resembling the beautiful rose
Rosabell, Rosabele, Rosabelle, Rosabela, Rosabella, Rozabel, Rozabell, Rozabele, Rozabelle, Rozabela, Rozabella

Rosalba (Latin) Resembling the white rose
Rosalbah, Rosalbia, Rosalbea, Rhoswen, Rhoswenn, Rhoswyn, Rhoswynn

Rosalie (Italian) Of the rose garden
*Rosalee, Rosaley, Rosalia, Roselia, Rosella,
Roselle, Rozalia, Rozalie, Rozele, Rozelie,
Rozely, Rozella, Rozelle, Rozellia, Rosel,
Rozali, Rosali, Rosalea, Rosaleigh*

Rosalind (German / English) Resembling a
gentle horse / form of Rose, meaning
"resembling the beautiful and meaningful
flower"
*Ros, Rosaleen, Rosalen, Rosalin, Rosalina,
Rosalinda, Rosalinde, Rosaline, Rosalinn,
Rosalyn, Rosalynd, Rosalynda, Rosalynn,
Rosanie, Roselin, Roselina, Roselind,
Roselinda, Roselinde, Roseline, Roselinn,
Roselyn, Roselynda, Roselynde, Roslyn,
Roslynn, Roslynne, Roz, Rozalin, Rozalind,
Rozalinda, Rozalynn, Rozalynne, Rozelin,
Rozelind, Rozelinda, Rozelyn, Rozelynda,
Rhoslyn, Rhozlyn, Roslin, Rozlin*

Rosamond (German) Protector of horses;
the rose of the world
*Rosamonde, Rosamund, Rosamunda,
Rosemond, Rosemonda, Rosmund,
Rosmunda, Rozamond, Rozamund,
Rosamunde, Rozmonda, Rozmond,
Rozmund, Rozmunda*

Rosario (Spanish) Refers to the rosary and
Our Lady of the Rosary
*Rosaria, Rasario, Rasaria, Rosareo,
Rasareo*

Rose (Greek) Resembling the beautiful and
meaningful flower
*Rasia, Rasine, Rasja, Rasya, Rosa, Rosella,
Roselle, Rosena, Rosenah, Rosene, Rosetta,
Rosette, Rosey, Rosheen, Rosie, Rosina,
Rosine, Rosio, Rosita, Rosy, Roza, Roze,
Rozele, Rozella, Rozene, Rozina, Rozsa,
Rozsi, Rozsika, Rozy, Ruza, Ruzena,
Ruzenka, Ruzha, Ruzsa, Rosai, Rosay,
Rosee, Rosae, Roesia, Rohais, Rhosyn,
Rois, Roisin, Ros, Russu, Ruusu, Rozeena,
Rozyuka, Rhodia*

Roseanne (English) Resembling the
graceful rose
*Ranna, Rosana, Rosanagh, Rosanna,
Rosannah, Rosanne, Roseann, Roseanna,
Rosehannah, Rossana, Rossanna, Rozanna,
Rozanne, Rozeanna, Rosanie*

Roselani (Hawaiian) Resembling a
heavenly rose
*Roselanie, Roselany, Roselaney, Roselanee,
Rosalanea*

Rosemary (Latin / English) The dew of
the sea / resembling a bitter rose
*Rosemaree, Rosemarey, Rosemaria,
Rosemarie, Rosmarie, Rozmary,
Rosamaria, Rosamarie*

Roshan (Indian) The shining light
*Roshana, Roshandra, Roshaundra,
Roshawn, Roshawna, Roshni, Roshnie,
Roshny, Roshney, Roshnee, Roshnea*

Ross (Gaelic) Woman from the headland
Rosse, Rossa, Rosslyn, Rosslynn, Rosslynne

Roux (French) A red-haired woman

Rowa (Arabic) A lovely vision
Rowah

Rowan (Gaelic) Of the red-berry tree
*Rowann, Rowane, Rowanne, Rowana,
Rowanna*

Rowdy (American) A spirited woman
Rowdey, Rowdi, Rowdie, Rowdee, Rowdea

Rowena (Welsh / German) One who is fair
and slender / having much fame and happiness
*Rhowena, Roweena, Roweina, Rowenna,
Rowina, Rowinna, Rhonwen, Rhonwyn,
Rowyna*

Roxanne (Persian) Born with the morning's
first light
*Roksanne, Roxana, Roxandra, Roxana,
Roxane, Roxann, Roxanna, Roxeena,
Roxene, Roxey, Roxi, Roxiane, Roxianne,
Roxie, Roxine, Roxy, Roxyanna, Ruksana,
Ruksane, Ruksanna*

Roya (English) Feminine form of Roy; a
red-haired woman
Roiya, Royanna, Royleen, Roylene, Roia

Royale (French) A regal and elegant lady
*Royalla, Royalene, Royalina, Royall,
Royalle, Royalyn, Royalynne, Roial,
Roialle, Roiall, Roiale*

Ruana (Indian) One who is musically
inclined
*Ruanah, Ruanna, Ruannah, Ruane,
Ruann, Ruanne*

Rubaina (Indian) A bright woman
*Rubaine, Rubain, Rubayne, Rubayn,
Rubayna, Rubana, Rubane, Rubaena,
Rubaen, Rubaene*

Rubena (Hebrew) Feminine form of
Reuben; behold, a daughter!
Reubena, Reubina, Rubenia

Ruby (English) As precious as the red
gemstone
*Rubee, Rubetta, Rubey, Rubi, Rubia,
Rubianne, Rubie, Rubina, Rubinia,
Rubyna, Rubyne, Roobee, Rubea*

Rudella (German) A well-known woman
*Rudela, Rudelah, Rudell, Rudelle, Rudel,
Rudele, Rudy, Rudie, Rudey, Rudea,
Rudee, Rudi*

Rudrani (Indian) Feminine form of Rudra,
the god of death
*Rudranie, Rudranee, Rudrany, Rudraney,
Rudranea*

Rue (Greek) From the medicinal herb
Ruta, Rou

Rufina (Latin) A red-haired woman
*Rufeena, Rufeine, Ruffina, Rufine, Ruffine,
Rufyna, Ruffyna, Rufyne, Ruffyne,
Rufeina, Ruphina, Ruphyna, Rufa, Rufah,
Ruffa, Ruffah, Rufeana*

Ruhamah (Hebrew) One who has been
given mercy
*Ruhama, Ruhamma, Ruhammah,
Ruhamia, Ruhamea, Ruhamiah,
Ruhameah*

Ruhette (Latin) As precious as a small
jewel
Ruhete, Ruhett, Ruhet, Ruhetta, Ruheta

Ruhi (Arabic) A spiritual woman
*Roohee, Ruhee, Ruhie, Ruhy, Ruhey,
Roohi, Roohie, Ruhea, Roohea*

Rui (Japanese) An affectionate woman

Ruihi (Maori) Form of Lucy, meaning "one
who is illuminated"
Ruihie, Ruihee, Ruihea, Ruihey, Ruihy

Rukan (Arabic) A confident and steadfast
woman
*Rukann, Rukane, Rukanne, Rukanna,
Rukana, Rukanah*

Rukmini (Hindi) Adorned with gold;
in Hinduism, the first wife of Krishna
*Rukminie, Rukminy, Rukminey,
Rukminee, Rukminea, Rukminni,
Rukminii*

Rumah (Hebrew) One who has been
exalted
*Ruma, Rumia, Rumea, Rumiah, Rumeah,
Rumma, Rummah*

Rumer (English) A gypsy

Rumina (Latin) In mythology, a protector
goddess of mothers and babies
*Ruminah, Rumeena, Rumeenah, Rumeina,
Rumiena, Rumyna, Rumeinah, Rumienah,
Rumynah, Rumeana, Rumeanah*

Rumor (American) A falsity spread by
word of mouth
Rumer, Rumora, Rumera, Rumoria, Rumeria

Runa (Scandinavian) Feminine form of
Rune; of the secret lore
Runah, Roona, Roone

Runcina (Latin) In mythology, goddess of
agriculture
*Rucinah, Ruceena, Ruceina, Ruciena,
Rucyna, Ruceana*

Rupali (Indian) A beautiful woman
*Rupalli, Rupalie, Rupalee, Rupallee,
Rupal, Rupa, Rupaly, Rupaley, Rupalea*

Ruqayyah (Arabic) A gentle woman; a
daughter of Muhammad
Ruqayya, Ruqayah, Ruqaya

Rusalka (Slavic) A woodland sprite
Rusalke, Rusalk, Rusalkia, Rusalkea

Rusty (American) A red-haired woman;
a fiery woman
Rusti, Rustie, Rustee, Rustey, Rustea

Ruth (Hebrew) A beloved companion
*Ruthe, Ruthelle, Ruthellen, Ruthetta,
Ruthi, Ruthie, Ruthina, Ruthine, Ruthy,
Ruthey, Ruta, Rute, Rut, Ruthann,
Ruthanne, Ruthane, Ruthana, Ruthanna*

Ruwaydah (Arabic) One who walks softly
*Ruwayda, Ruwaidah, Ruwaida, Ruwaeda,
Ruwaedah*

Ryba (Slavic) Resembling a fish
Rybah, Rybba, Rybbah

Ryder (American) An accomplished
horsewoman
Rider

Ryo (Japanese) An excellent woman
Ryoko

Saada (African) One who aids others;
a helper
Saadaa, Saadah

Saadiya (Arabic) One who brings good
fortune
*Sadiya, Sadiyah, Sa'diah, Sadia, Sadiah,
Saadiyah*

Saba (Greek / Arabic) Woman from Sheba /
born in the morning
Sabah, Sabaa, Sabba, Sabbah, Sabaah

Sabana (Spanish) From the open plain
*Sabanah, Sabanna, Sabann, Sabanne,
Sabane, Saban*

Sabi (Arabic) A lovely young lady
*Sabie, Saby, Sabey, Sabee, Sabbi, Sabbee,
Sabea*

Sabiha (Arabic) One who is beautiful;
attractive
*Sabihah, Sabyha, Sabeeha, Sabeiha,
Sabieha, Sabeyha, Sabeaha*

Sabina (Italian) Of an ancient culture
*Sabinah, Sabeena, Sabiena, Sabeina,
Sabyna, Saveena, Savina, Sabenah, Sabiny,
Saby, Sebina, Sebinah, Sebyna, Sebynah,
Sabena, Sabeana*

Sabine (Latin) Of a tribe in ancient Italy
*Sabeen, Sabene, Sabienne, Sabyne, Sebine,
Sebyn, Sebyne, Sabin, Sabyn, Sabeene,
Sabean, Sabeane*

Sabirah (Arabic) Having great patience
*Sabira, Saabira, Sabeera, Sabiera, Sabeira,
Sabyra, Sabirra, Sabyrra, Sabeerra, Sabeara*

Sabiya (Arabic) Born in the morning / of
an easterly wind
*Sabaya, Sabayah, Sabea, Sabia, Sabiah,
Sabiyah, Sabya, Sabyah*

Sable (English) One who is sleek
*Sabel, Sabela, Sabelah, Sabele, Sabella,
Sabelle*

Sabra (Hebrew) Resembling the cactus
fruit; to rest
*Sabrah, Sebra, Sebrah, Sabrette, Sabbra,
Sabraa, Sabarah, Sabarra, Sabarrah,
Sabera, Sabira, Sabre, Sabara*

Sabria (Latin) Woman from Cyprus
*Sabriah, Sabreea, Sabrea, Sabreah, Sabrya,
Sabriya, Sabri, Sabree, Sabrie, Sabrea,
Sabry, Sabrey*

Sabriel (American) A hero of God
*Sabrielle, Sabriell, Sabryel, Sabryelle,
Sabriele, Sabryele, Sabryell, Sabriela,
Sabriella, Sabryela, Sabryella*

Sabrina (English) A legendary princess
*Sabrinah, Sabrinna, Sabreena, Sabriena,
Sabreina, Sabryna, Sabrine, Sabryne,
Sabreene, Sabrynna, Sabreanah,
Sabreenah, Sabreen, Sabreane, Sabrene,
Sabrena, Sabrin, Sabrinas, Sabrinia,
Sabriniah, Sebree, Subrina, Sabrynah,
Sabreana*

Sacha (Greek) Form of Alexandra, meaning
"helper and defender of mankind"
*Sachenka, Sachka, Sache, Sachia, Sachah,
Sachea*

Sachet (Hindi) Having consciousness
Sachett, Sachette

Sachi (Japanese) Child of bliss; one who is
blessed
*Sachie, Sachy, Sachey, Sachee, Sachiko,
Saatchi, Sachea*

Sada (Japanese) The pure one
Sadda, Sadaa, Sadako, Saddaa

Sadaf (Indian / Iranian) Resembling a pearl
/ resembling a seashell
*Sadafa, Sadafah, Sadafia, Sadafea,
Sadafiya, Sadafe*

Sadah (Arabic) Form of Zada, meaning
"fortunate one; lucky; prosperous"
Sada, Sayda, Saida, Sayeda, Saeda

Sadbh (Irish) One who is well-behaved
Sadb

Sade (Yoruban) One who is honorable
*Sadea, Saedea, Shadae, Shadai, Shaday,
Sharde*

Sadella (American) A beautiful fairylike
princess
*Sadel, Sadela, Sadelah, Sadele, Sadell,
Sadellah, Sadelle, Sydel, Sydell, Sydella,
Sydelle*

Sadhana (Hindi) A devoted woman
*Sadhanah, Sadhanna, Sadhannah,
Sadhane, Sadhanne, Sadhann, Sadhan*

S

Sadhbba (Irish) A wise woman
Sadhbh, Sadhba

Sadie (English) Form of Sarah, meaning "princess; lady"
Sadi, Sady, Sadey, Sadee, Saddi, Saddee, Sadiey, Sadye, Saedee, Saedi, Saedie, Saedy, Saide, Saidea, Saidee, Saidey, Saidi, Saidia, Saidie, Saidy, Seidy, Saddie, Sadia, Sadea, Saedea

Sadiqa (Arabic) One who is sincere; truthful
Sadiqaa, Saadiqa, Sadyqa, Sadiqua, Sadiquah

Sadira (Persian) Of the lotus tree
Sadirah, Sadiera, Sadeira, Sadyra, Sadirra, Sadeera, Sadyrra, Sadra, Sadrah, Sadyrah, Sadyre, Sadire, Sadeara

Sadiya (Arabic) One who is fortunate; lucky
Sadiyah, Sadiyyah, Sadya, Sadyah

Sadzi (American) Having a sunny disposition
Sadzee, Sadzey, Sadzia, Sadziah, Sadzie, Sadzya, Sadzyah, Sadzy, Sadzea

Safa (Arabic) One who is innocent and pure
Safah, Saffa, Sapha, Saffah, Saphah

Safara (African) Her place in this world
Safarra, Safaria, Safarah, Safariya

Saffi (Danish) Having great wisdom
Saffie, Saffy, Saffee, Saffey, Saffye, Safee, Safey, Safie, Safy, Safi, Saffea, Safea

Saffron (English) Resembling the yellow flower
Saffrone, Saffronn, Saffronne, Safron, Safronn, Safronne, Saffronah, Safrona, Safronah, Safrone, Safronna, Safronnah, Saffrona

Safia (Arabic / African) One who is pure / having the lion's share
Safiah, Saffia, Safya, Safyah, Safiya, Safiyeh, Safiyyah, Saffiya, Safeia, Safeya, Safiyah

Safiwah (Arabic) One who is tranquil; peaceful
Safiwa, Safywah, Safywa, Saphiwa, Saphiwah

Saga (Norse) Seeing one; in mythology, goddess of poetry and history
Sagah, Sagga

Sagara (Hindi) From the ocean
Sagarra, Sagarah, Saggara, Saggarra, Sagaria, Sagarea

Sage (English) Wise one; type of spice
Saige, Sayge, Saege, Sagia, Saig, Sayg, Saeg

Sagira (Egyptian) The little one
Sagirah, Sageera, Sagyra, Sagiera, Sageira, Saqhira, Sagirra, Sagyrra

Sagittarius (Latin) The ninth sign of the zodiac; the archer
Sagitarius, Saggitarius, Sagitarios, Sagittarios

Sahar (Arabic) Of the dawn; awakening
Saharr, Sahare, Saharre, Saheer, Saher

Sahara (Arabic) Of the desert
Saharah, Saharra, Sahra, Saharia, Sahariya, Saharrah, Sahira, Sahrah, Sahari

Saheli (Indian) A beloved friend
Sahelie, Sahely, Saheley, Sahelee, Saheleigh, Sahyli, Sahelea

Sahiba (Indian) A young lady; a maiden
Sahibah, Saheeba, Sahyba, Saheiba, Sahieba, Saheyba, Saheaba

Sahila (Indian) One who provides guidance
Sahilah, Saheela, Sahyla, Sahiela, Saheila, Sahela, Sahilla, Sahylla, Saheella, Saheala

Sahirah (Egyptian) One who is pristine; clean
Sahira, Saheera, Sahiera, Saheira, Sahyra, Sahera, Sahirra, Saheerra, Sahyrra, Saheara

Sahkyo (Native American) Resembling the mink
Sakyo

Sai (Egyptian / Japanese) In mythology, the personification of destiny / one who is talented
Sae, Say, Saye, Saiko

Saida (Arabic) Fortunate one; one who is happy
Saidah, Sa'ida, Sayida, Saeida, Saedah, Said, Sayide, Sayidea, Sayda, Saydah, Saeda

Saihah (Arabic) One who is useful; good
Saiha, Sayiha

Sailor (American) One who sails the seas
Sailer, Sailar, Saylor, Sayler, Saylar, Saelor, Saeler, Saelar, Saler, Salor, Salar, Salore

Saima (Arabic) A fasting woman
Saimah, Saimma, Sayima

Saira (Arabic) A woman who travels; a wanderer
Sairah, Sairra, Sayra, Sairi, Sairie, Sairy, Sairey, Sairee, Sairea

Sajili (Indian) One who is decorated; adorned
Sajilie, Sajily, Sajyly, Sajiley, Sajyley

Sajni (Indian) One who is dearly loved
Sajnie, Sajny, Sajney, Sajnee, Sajnea

Sakae (Japanese) One who is prosperous
Sakai, Sakaie, Sakay, Sakaye

Sakari (Native American) A sweet girl
Sakarie, Sakary, Sakarri, Sakarey, Sakaree, Sakarree, Sakarah, Sakarrie, Sakaria, Sakariah, Sakarya, Sakaryah, Sakkara, Sakkarah, Sakara, Sakarea, Sakarrea

Saki (Japanese) One who wears a cloak
Sakiko, Sakia, Sakiah, Sakie, Saky, Sakya, Sakyah, Sakee, Sakea

Sakina (Indian / Arabic) A beloved friend / having God-inspired peace of mind
Sakinah, Sakeena, Sakiena, Sakeina, Sakyna, Sakeyna, Sakinna, Sakeana

Sakti (Hindi) In Hinduism, the divine energy
Saktie, Sakty, Sakkti, Sackti, Saktee, Saktey, Saktia, Saktiah, Saktya, Saktyah, Saktea

Saku (Japanese) Remembrance of the Lord
Sakuko

Sakujna (Indian) A birdlike woman
Sakujnah, Sakoujna, Sakoujnah

Sakuna (Native American) Resembling a bird
Sakunah, Sakoona, Sakoonah, Sakouna, Sakounah

Sakura (Japanese) Resembling a cherry blossom
Sakurah, Sakurako, Sakurra

Sala (Hindi) From the sacred sala tree
Salah, Salla, Sallah

Salacia (Latin) In mythology, a sea goddess
Salaciah, Salacea, Salasea, Salaciya, Salasia, Salasiya

Salal (English) An evergreen shrub with flowers and berries
Sallal, Salall, Sallall, Salalle, Salale, Sallale

Salali (Native American) Resembling a squirrel
Salalie, Salaly, Salaley, Salalee, Salaleigh, Salalli, Salallie, Salllali, Salaleah, Salalei, Salalia, Salaliah, Salalya, Salalyah, Salalea

Salama (Egyptian) One who is peaceful and safe
Salamah, Salma, Salamma, Sallama

Salamanca (Spanish) A woman from a city in western Spain

Salamasina (Samoan) A princess; born to royalty
Salamaseena, Salamasyna, Salamaseana, Salamaseina, Salamasiena

Salem (Arabic) One who is at peace
Saleme, Saleem

Salette (English) Form of Sally, meaning "princess; lady"
Salet, Saleta, Saletah, Salete, Salett, Saletta, Salettah, Sallet, Salletta, Sallettah, Sallette

Salihah (Arabic) One who is agreeable; correct
Saliha, Saaleha, Salyha, Saleeha, Saleaha

Salima (Arabic) One who is healthy and safe
Salimah, Saleema, Salyma, Saliema, Selima, Saleyma, Sileema, Salema, Salim, Salymah, Salma, Salmah, Saleama

Salina (French) One of a solemn, dignified character
Salin, Salinah, Salinda, Salinee, Sallin, Sallina, Sallinah, Salline, Sallyn, Sallyna, Sallynah, Sallyne, Sallynee, Salyn, Salyna, Salynah, Salyne, Salana, Salanah, Salane, Salean, Saleana, Saleanah, Saleane, Salen, Salenah, Salenna, Sallene, Salena

Salliann (English) A gracious princess
Saleann, Saleanna, Saleannah, Saleanne, Saleean, Saleeana, Saleeanah, Saleeane, Saleeann, Saleeanna, Saleeannah, Saleeanne, Salian, Saliana, Salianah, Saliane, Saliann, Salianna, Saliannah, Salianne, Salleeann, Salleeanna, Salleeannah, Salleeanne, Sallian, Salliana, Sallianah, Salliane, Sallianna, Salliannah, Sallianne, Sally-Ann, Sally-Anne, Sallyann, Sallyanna, Sallyannah, Sallyanne

Sally (English) Form of Sarah, meaning "princess; lady"
Salley, Salli, Sallie, Sallee, Salleigh, Salia, Saliah, Salie, Saliee, Sallia, Salliah, Sailee, Saileigh, Sailey, Saili, Sailia, Sailie, Saily, Sal, Salaid, Salea, Saleah, Salee, Salei, Saleigh, Saley, Sallea, Salleah, Sallei, Sallya, Sallyah, Sallye, Saly, Salya, Salyah, Salye, Sali

Saloma (Hebrew) One who offers peace and tranquility
Salomah, Salome, Salomia, Salomiah, Schlomit, Shulamit, Salomeaexl, Salomma, Salaome, Salomea, Salomee, Salomei, Salomey, Salomi, Salomya, Salomyah

Saloni (Hindi) A beautiful dear one
Salonie, Salony, Saloney, Salonee, Salonni, Salloni, Sallonee, Salonea

Salus (Latin) In mythology, goddess of health and prosperity; salvation
Saluus, Salusse, Saluss

Salva (Latin) A wise woman
Salvah, Salvia, Salvina, Salvinia, Salviya, Sallviah, Salviah, Salviana, Salvianah, Salviane, Salvianna, Salviannah, Salvianne, Salvinah, Salvine, Salvyna, Salvynah, Salvyne, Sallvia

Salvadora (Spanish) Feminine form of Salvador; savior
Salvadorah, Salvadoria, Salbatora, Salbatoria, Salvatora, Salvatoria

Salwa (Arabic) One who provides comfort; solace
Salwah

Samah (Arabic) A generous, forgiving woman
Sama, Samma, Sammah

Samala (Hebrew) One who is requested by God
Samalah, Samale, Sammala, Sammalah, Samalla, Samallah

Samanfa (Hebrew) Form of Samantha, meaning "one who listens well"
Samanffa, Sammanfa, Sammanffa, Semenfa, Semenfah, Samenffa, Semenffah

Samantha ☉ (Aramaic) One who listens well
Samanthah, Samanthia, Samanthea, Samantheya, Samanath, Samanatha, Samana, Samanitha, Samanithia, Samanth, Samanthe, Samanthi, Samanthiah, Sementha, Sementha, Simanta, Smantha, Samantah, Smanta, Samanta, Sammatha, Samatha, Samea, Samee, Samey, Samie, Samy, Samye, Sami, Sammanth, Sammanthia, Sammanthiah, Sammanthya, Sammanthyah, Sammantha, Sammi, Sammie, Sammy, Samm, Samma, Sammah, Sammee, Sammey, Sammijo, Sammyjo

Samar (Arabic) One who provides evening conversation
Samarr, Samare, Samarre

Samara (Hebrew) Protected by God
Samarah, Samaria, Shemariah, Samarra, Samarie, Samariya, Samaira, Samar, Samary, Sammar, Sammara, Samora, Samarah, Samari, Samariah, Samarrea, Sameria, Saimara

Sameh (Arabic) One who forgives
Sammeh, Samaya, Samaiya

Samihah (Arabic) One who is generous; magnanimous
Samiha, Sameeha, Samyha, Sameaha, Sameyha, Samieha, Sameiha

Samina (Arabic) A healthy woman
Saminah, Samine, Sameena, Samyna, Sameana, Sameina, Samynah

Samira (Arabic) Feminine form of Samir; companion for evening conversation
Samirah, Samire, Sameera, Samyra, Sameira, Samera, Samiria, Samirra, Samyrah, Samyre, Samiriah, Sameara

Samone (Hebrew) Form of Simone, meaning "one who listens well"
Samoan, Samoane, Samon, Samona, Samonia

Sampada (Indian) A blessing from God
Sampadah, Sampadda, Sampadia, Sampadiya, Sampadea, Sampadya

Sampriti (Indian) An attachment
Sampritie, Samprity, Sampritey, Sampritee, Sampryti, Sampryty, Sampritti, Sampritea

Samuela (Hebrew) Feminine form of Samuel; asked of God
Samuelah, Samuella, Samuell, Samuelle, Sammila, Sammile, Samella, Samielle, Samilla, Samille, Samiella, Samelia

Samularia (Hebrew) Sweet one forever
Samulariah, Samulara, Samularra,
Samulariya, Samularea, Samulareah

Samya (Arabic) One who is exalted
Samiyah, Samia, Samiha, Sammia,
Sammiah, Sammya, Sammyah, Samyah,
Samiah, Samiya

Sana (Persian / Arabic) One who emanates
light / brilliance; splendor
Sanah, Sanna, Sanako, Sanaah, Sane,
Saneh

Sanaa (Swahili) Beautiful work of art
Sanae, Sannaa

Sancha (Spanish) Feminine form of
Sancho; saintly; holy
Sanchah, Sanchia, Sancia, Sancta, Sanchiya,
Sanchiah, Sanchie, Sanchya, Sanchyah,
Sanciah, Sancie, Sanctia, Sancya, Sancyah,
Santsia, Sanzia, Sanziah, Sanzya, Sanzyah,
Sancharia, Sanche, Sancheska, Sanceska

Sandeep (Punjabi) One who is enlightened
Sandeepe, Sandip, Sandipp, Sandippe,
Sandeyp, Sandeype

Sandhya (Hindi) Born at twilight; name of
the daughter of the god Brahma
Sandhiya, Sandhyah, Sandya, Sandyah

Sandia (Spanish) Resembling a watermelon
Sandiah, Sandea, Sandya, Sandeea, Sandiya

Sandra (Greek) Form of Alexandra, meaning
"helper and defender of mankind"
Sandrah, Sandrine, Sandy, Sandi, Sandie,
Sandey, Sandee, Sanda, Sondra, Shandra,
Sandira, Sandah, Sandirah, Sandrica,
Sanndra, Sahndra, Sandia, Sandiah,
Sandiey, Sandine, Sanndie, Sandea, Sandye

Sandrea (Greek) Form of Sandra, meaning
"helper and defender of mankind"
Sandreah, Sandreea, Sandreia, Sandreiah,
Sandrell, Sandrella, Sandrellah, Sandrelle,
Sandria, Sandriah, Sanndria

Sandrica (Greek) Form of Sandra, meaning
"helper and defender of mankind"
Sandricca, Sandricah, Sandricka,
Sandrickah, Sandrika, Sandrikah,
Sandryca, Sandrycah, Sandrycka,
Sandryckah, Sandryka, Sandrykah

Sandrine (Greek) Form of Alexandra,
meaning "helper and defender of mankind"
Sandrin, Sandreana, Sandreanah,
Sandreane, Sandreen, Sandreena,
Sandreenah, Sandreene, Sandrene,
Sandrenna, Sandrennah, Sandrenne,
Sandrianna, Sandrina, Sandrinah,
Sandryna, Sandrynah, Sandryne

Sangita (Indian) One who is musical
Sangitah, Sangeeta, Sangeita, Sangyta,
Sangieta, Sangeata

Sangrida (Norse) In mythology, a Valkyrie
Sangridah, Sangridda, Sangryda, Sangrydah

Saniya (Indian) A moment in time preserved
Saniyah, Sanya, Sanea, Sania

Sanjeet (Indian) One who is invincible
Sanjit, Sanjitte, Sanjeete, Sanjeat, Sanjeate

Sanjna (Indian) A conscientious woman

Sanjula (Indian) One who is beautiful;
attractive
Sanjulah, Sanjulla, Sanjoula, Sanjoulah

Sanne (American) Form of Susanna,
meaning "resembling a graceful white lily"

Santana (Spanish) A saintly woman
Santa, Santah, Santania, Santaniah,
Santaniata, Santena, Santenah, Santenna,
Shantana, Shantanna

Santuzza (Italian) One who is holy
Santuzzah, Santuza, Santuzah, Santuzzia,
Santuzia, Santouza, Santouzza

Sanura (African) One who is kittenlike
Sanurah, Sanuria, Sanurea, Sanurra

Sany (Indian) Born on a Sunday
Saney, Sanie, Sani, Sanee, Sanni, Sannee,
Sanea

Sanyu (Japanese) One who brings happiness

Saoirse (Gaelic) An independent woman;
having freedom
Saoyrse

Sapna (Hindi) A dream come true
Sapnah, Sapnia, Sapniah, Sapnea,
Sapneah, Sapniya, Sapniyah

Sapphire (Arabic / English) One who is
beautiful / a precious gem
Sapphira, Sapphirah, Saffir, Saffira, Saffire,
Safire, Safira, Sapphyre, Saffyre

S

Sarah ✪ ☉ (Hebrew) Princess; lady; in the Bible, wife of Abraham
Sara, Sari, Sariah, Sarika, Saaraa, Sarita, Sarina, Sarra, Saara, Saarah, Saaraah, Saarrah, Sharita, Sharie, Sharri, Sharrie, Sharry, Shary, Shari, Soraya

Sarai (Hebrew) One who is contentious and argumentative
Sarae, Saray, Saraye

Saraid (Irish) One who is excellent; superior
Saraide, Saraed, Saraede, Sarayd, Sarayde

Sarama (African / Hindi) A kind woman / in Hinduism, Indra's dog
Saramah, Saramma, Sarrama, Sarramma

Saran (African) One who brings joy to others
Sarane, Sarran, Saranne, Saranna, Sarana, Sarann

Sarasvati (Hindi) In Hinduism, goddess of learning and the arts
Sarasvatti, Sarasvatie, Sarasvaty, Sarasvatey, Sarasvatee, Sarasvatea

Saraswati (Hindi) Owning water; in Hinduism, a river goddess
Saraswatti, Saraswatie, Saraswaty, Saraswatey, Saraswatee, Saraswatea

Sarda (African) One who is hurried; quick
Sardah, Sardda, Sardia, Sardiya, Sardea

Sardinia (Italian) Woman from a mountainous island
Sardiniah, Sardinea, Sardineah, Sardynia, Sardyniah, Sardynea, Sardyneah

Saree (Arabic) Most noble woman
Sarri, Sarie, Sarey, Sary, Sarea

Sarff (Welsh) Resembling a snake; serpentine
Sarf, Sarffe, Sarph, Sarphe

Sarika (Indian / Hungarian) Resembling a parrot / form of Sarah, meaning "princess; lady"
Sarikah, Sareeka, Saryka, Saricka, Saricca, Saryca, Sarica, Sareaka

Sarisha (Hindi) One who is charming; pleasing
Sarysha, Sareesha, Sariesha, Sareysha, Sareasha

Sarki (African) Woman who has the rank of chief
Sarkie, Sarky, Sarkey, Sarkee, Sarkeigh, Sarkki, Sarcki, Sarckie, Sarkea

Sarohildi (German) An armored battlemaiden
Sarohildie, Sarohildy, Sarohildey, Sarohyldi, Sarohyldy, Sarohilde, Sarohilda, Serhild, Serhilda, Serihilde, Serilda, Serilde, Serohilda, Serohilde, Serohild, Serohildi

Sarsoureh (Arabic) A buglike woman
Sarsoure, Sasureh, Sasure

Saryu (Indian) From the river
Saryyu, Saryue

Sasa (Japanese) One who is helpful; gives aid
Sasah

Sasha (Russian) Form of Alexandra, meaning "helper and defender of mankind"
Sascha, Sashenka, Saskia

Sason (Hebrew) One who brings joy
Sasson, Sasone

Sati (Hindi) One who speaks the truth; in Hinduism, a goddess
Satti, Satie, Satty, Saty, Satey, Sattey, Satee, Sattee, Satea, Sattea

Satin (French) A glossy, smooth fabric
Satine, Sattin, Sattine, Satyn, Satyne, Satynne, Sateen, Sateene, Satean, Sateane

Satinka (Native American) A magical dancer
Satinkah, Satincka, Satynka, Satynka

Sato (Japanese) Of a sweet nature

Satu (Finnish) From a fairy tale
Sattu, Satue

Saturday (American) Born on a Saturday
Saturdaye, Saterday, Satarday, Satirday, Saturdai, Saturdae, Saterdai, Saterdae

Saturnina (Spanish) Gift of Saturn, the god of agriculture
Saturneena, Saturnyna, Saturninia, Saturniniya, Saturneana

Satya (Indian) The unchangeable truth
Satiya, Satyana

Satyavati (Hindi) In Hinduism, the mother of Vyasa
Satyavatti, Satyavatie, Satyavaty, Satyavatey, Satyavatee, Satyavatea

Sauda (Swahili) A dark beauty
Saudaa, Sawda, Saudda

Saura (Hindi) Of the heavens
Sawra

Savannah ✿ (English) From the open, grassy plain
Savanna, Savana, Savanne, Savann, Savane, Savanneh

Savarna (Hindi) Daughter of the ocean
Savarnia, Savarnea, Savarniya, Savarneia

Saveage (English) In Arthurian legend, the sister of Lyones
Saveyage, Saviage, Savage

Saveria (Italian) Feminine form of Xavier; owner of a new house; one who is bright
Saveriah, Saverea, Saverya, Savereea, Saveriya

Savitri (Hindi) In Hinduism, the daughter of the god of the sun
Savitari, Savitrie, Savitry, Savitarri, Savitarie, Savitree, Savitrea, Savitrey

Savvy (American) Smart and perceptive woman
Savy, Savvi, Savvie, Savvey, Savee, Savvee, Savvea, Savea

Sawsan (Arabic) Form of Susannah, meaning "resembling the graceful white lily"
Sausan, Sawsann, Sawsanna, Sawsanne, Sausanne, Sausanna

Sawyer (English) A woodcutter
Sauyer

Saxona (English) Of the sword people
Saxonah, Saxonia, Saxen, Saxon, Saxons, Saxton, Saxonna, Saxonea, Saxoniya, Saxone

Sayo (Japanese) Born at night
Sayoko, Sayomi, Sayori, Sayyo

Sayyam (Arabic) A fasting woman
Sayyawm, Saaim, Sayam, Sayiam, Sayame

Sayyida (Arabic) A mistress
Sayyidah, Sayida, Sayyda, Seyyada, Seyyida, Seyada, Seyida

Scarlet (English) Vibrant red color; a vivacious woman
Scarlett, Scarlette, Skarlet, Skarlette, Skarlett

Scelflesh (English) From the meadow

Schaaph (Hebrew) One who is thoughtful
Schaph, Schaphe

Scholastica (Latin) Having knowledge; learned; a student
Scholastic, Scholastika, Skolastica, Skolastika, Scholastyca, Skolastyka

Scirocco (Arabic) Of a warm wind

Scorpio (Latin) The eighth sign of the zodiac; a scorpion
Scorpia, Scorpius, Scorpiya, Skorpio, Skorpia, Skorpya, Scorpya

Scota (Irish) Woman of Scotland
Scotta, Scotah, Skota, Skotta, Skotah

Scotia (Latin) A woman from Scotland
Skotia, Scosha, Skosha

Scout (American) An explorer
Scoutt, Scoutte, Skout

Scylla (Greek) In mythology, a sea monster
Scyla, Skylla, Skyla

Sea'iqa (Arabic) Thunder and lightning
Seaqa, Seaqua

Searlait (French) Petite and womanly
Searlaite

Season (Latin) A fertile woman; one who embraces change
Seazon, Seeson, Seezon, Seizon, Seasen, Seasan, Seizen, Seizan

Sebastiana (Italian) Feminine form of Sebastian; one who commands respect
Sebastianna, Sebastiane, Sebastienne, Sebastiene, Sebastene, Sebastina, Sebasteene, Sebastyne, Sebastyna

Sebille (English) In Arthurian legend, a fairy
Sebylle, Sebill, Sebile, Sebyle, Sebyl

Sebiya (Arabic) A lovely young girl
Sebiyah, Sebeeya, Sebeia, Sebeea, Sebeya, Sebeaya

Secunda (Latin) The second-born child
Secundah, Secuba, Secundus, Segunda, Sekunda

S

Seda (Armenian) Voices of the forest
Sedda, Sedah, Seddah

Sedona (American) Woman from a city in Arizona
Sedonah, Sedonna, Sedonnah, Sedonia, Sedonea

Seema (Greek) A symbol; a sign
Seyma, Syma, Seama, Seima, Siema

Sefarina (Greek) Of a gentle wind
Sefarinah, Sefareena, Sefareenah, Sefaryna, Sefarynah, Sefareana, Sefareanah

Seghen (African) An ostrichlike woman

Segovia (Spanish) From a city in central Spain
Segoviah, Segovea, Segoveah, Segoviya, Segoviyah, Segovya, Segovyah

Segulah (Hebrew) One who is precious
Segula, Segulla, Segullah, Segoula, Segoulla

Seiko (Japanese) The force of truth

Seina (Spanish) Innocent one; pure

Sekai (African) One who brings laughter and great joy

Sekhmet (Egyptian) The powerful one; in mythology, a goddess of war and vengeance
Sakhmet, Sekhmeta, Sakhmeta, Sekhmette, Sakhmette, Sekhmetta, Sakhmetta

Sela (Hebrew / African) As strong as a rock / a savior
Sella, Sele, Seleta, Selata, Selah

Selam (African) She is peaceful
Selamawit, Sellam

Selas (African) Refers to the Trinity
Sellas, Selass, Selasse, Selasa, Selassa

Selby (English) Of the manor of the farm
Selbey, Selbi, Selbie, Selbee, Selbye, Selbea

Selene (Greek) Of the moon; in mythology, the goddess of the moon
Selena, Seline, Salena, Saline, Saleen, Salina, Salena, Salena, Salene, Selina, Saleena, Saleenah, Saleene, Salleen, Salleena, Salleenah, Salleene, Seleane, Seleana, Saleane, Saleana

Selima (Hebrew) One who brings comfort and peace
Selimah, Seleema, Seliema, Seleima, Selyma, Selimma, Seleyma, Seleama

Selma (German) Form of Anselma, meaning "having divine protection"
Selmah

Sema (Arabic) A divine omen; a known symbol
Semah

Semadar (Hebrew) Resembling a berry
Semadarr, Semadarre, Semadara, Semadaria, Semadarea

Semele (Greek) In mythology, one of Zeus's lovers and the mother of Dionysus
Semelle, Semyle

Semine (Danish) In mythology, the goddess of the sun, moon, and stars
Semyne, Semeene, Semeane, Semeine, Semiene

Semira (African / Hebrew) One who is fulfilled / from heaven
Semirah, Semeera, Semyra, Semeira, Semeyra, Semeara

Semiramis (Hebrew) From the highest heaven
Semyramis, Semiramys, Semyramys

Sen (Vietnamese) Resembling the lotus flower

Sena (Latin) One who is blessed
Senna, Senah, Sennah

Senalda (Spanish) A sign; a symbol
Senaldah, Senaldia, Senaldiya, Senaldea, Senaldya

Seneca (Native American) A tribal name
Senecka, Senecca, Seneka

Senga (Greek) Form of Agnes, meaning "one who is pure; chaste"
Sengah, Sengya, Sengyah, Sengia, Sengiah, Sengea, Sengeah, Sengiya, Sengiyah

Sennett (French) One who is wise
Senett, Sennette, Senette, Senet, Senete, Sennetta, Senetta, Senneta, Seneta

Senona (Spanish) A lively woman
Senonah, Senonna, Senonia, Senoniya, Senonea

Senta (German) Acting as an assistant
Sentah, Sente

Sentia (Latin) In mythology, goddess of children's development
Sentiah, Sensia, Senzia

Seonaid (Gaelic) A gift from God
Seonaide, Seonayde, Seonayd, Seonaede,
Seonaed, Seonade

Seosaimhin (Irish) A fertile woman
Seosaimhthin

Sephora (Hebrew) A beautiful bird
Sephorah, Sefora, Sephorra, Seforra,
Sephoria

September (American) Born in the month
of September
Septimber, Septymber, Septemberia,
Septemberea

Septima (Latin) The seventh-born child
Septimah, Septeema, Septyma, Septeama

Sequoia (Native American) Of the giant
redwood tree
Sequoya, Sequoiya, Sekoia, Sekoya

Serafina (Latin) A seraph; a heavenly
winged angel
Serafinah, Serafine, Seraphina, Serefina,
Seraphine, Sera

Seren (Welsh) From the starlight
Serin, Seran, Seron, Serun

Serena (Latin) Having a peaceful
disposition
Serenah, Serene, Sereena, Seryna, Serenity,
Serenitie, Serenitee, Serepta, Serina,
Sereana

Serendipity (American) A fateful meeting;
having good fortune
Serendipitey, Serendipitee, Serendipiti,
Serendipitie, Serendypyty

Serilda (Greek) An armed woman of war
Serild, Serilde, Sarilda, Sarildah, Serildah,
Serylda, Seryldah

Serpuhi (Armenian) One who is pious
Serpuhie, Serpuhy, Serpuhey, Serpuhee,
Serpuhea

Serwa (African) As precious as a jewel
Serwah, Serwi, Serwy, Serwia, Serwiya,
Serwie

Sesame (English) Resembling the flavorful
seed
Sesami, Sesamie, Sesamy, Sesamey,
Sesamee, Sesamea

Sesen (African) One who longs for more
Sesenn, Sesenne, Sesena, Sesenna

Sesha (Hindi) In Hinduism, a serpent who
represents time
Seshia, Seshea, Seshiya

Sesheta (Egyptian) In mythology, goddess
of the stars

Sevati (Indian) Resembling the white rose
Sevatie, Sevatti, Sevate, Sevatee, Sevatea,
Sevaty, Sevatey, Sevti, Sevtie, Sevtee, Sevtea,
Sevty, Sevtey

Sevda (Turkish) A parent's great love
Sevdah

Seven (American) The seventh-born child
Sevene, Seveen, Seveene, Sevyn, Sevyne,
Sevin

Severa (Italian) Feminine form of Severo;
one who is stern
Severra, Severah, Severia, Severea, Severiya,
Severya, Severana, Severanna, Severeen,
Severeene, Severine, Severyne

Sevilen (Turkish) One who loves and is
loved
Sevilene, Sevilyn, Sevilynn, Sevilynne,
Sevileen, Sevileene, Seviline, Sevilyne

Sevilla (Spanish) A woman from Seville
Sevil, Sevila, Sevilah, Sevile, Sevill,
Sevillah, Seville, Sevyl, Sevyla, Sevylah,
Sevyle, Sevyll, Sevylla, Sevyllah, Sevylle

Sevita (Indian) One who is cherished
Sevitta, Sevitah, Seveta, Seveeta, Sevyta,
Sevieta, Seveita, Seveata

Sezja (Russian) A protector of mankind

Shabana (Arabic) A maiden belonging to
the night
Shabanah, Shabanna, Shabaana,
Shabanne, Shabane

Shabiba (Arabic) A godmother
Shabibah, Shabeebah, Shabeeba,
Shabyba, Shabibba, Shabeba, Shabeaba,
Shabeabah

Shabnam (Arabic) Of the morning's dew
Shabname, Shabnamn

Shabnan (Persian) A falling raindrop
Shabnane, Shabnann, Shabnanne

Shada (Native American) Resembling a pelican
Shadah, Shadda, Shaddah

Shadha (Arabic) An aromatic fragrance
Shadhah

Shadi (Persian) One who brings happiness and joy
Shadie, Shady, Shadey, Shadee, Shadea

Shadiyah (Arabic) A singer; one who is musical
Shadiya, Shadiyya, Shadiyaa, Shadeeya, Shadeya

Shadow (English) Shade from the sun
Shadowe, Shadoe

Shafiqa (Arabic) A compassionate woman
Shafiqah, Shafiqua, Shafeeqa, Shafeequa

Shagufa (Arabic) A flourishing woman; budding
Shagufah, Shagupha, Shagoofa, Shagoopha, Shagufta, Shagoufa, Shagoupha

Shahdi (Persian) One who is happy
Shahdie, Shahdy, Shahdey, Shahdee, Shahdea

Shahida (Arabic) A witness
Shahidah, Shahyda, Shaahida, Shaahyda

Shahina (Arabic) Resembling a falcon
Shahinah, Shaheenah, Shaheena, Shahyna, Shahinna, Shaheana, Shahynah, Shaheanah

Shahla (Arabic) Having bluish-black eyes
Shahlah, Shahlaa

Shahnaz (Arabic) A king's pride
Shanaz, Shahnaaz, Shahnazze, Shanazz, Shanazze

Shahzadi (Arabic) A princess; born into royalty
Shahzadie, Shahzaadee, Shahzadee, Shahzady, Shahzadey, Shahzadea

Shai (Gaelic) A gift of God
Shay, Shae, Shayla, Shea, Shaye

Shaibya (Indian) A faithful wife
Shaibyah, Shaybya, Shabya, Shaibia, Shaibiya, Shaebya

Shaila (Indian) Of the mountain stone
Shailah, Shayla, Shaylah, Shaela, Shailla

Sha'ira (Arabic) Poetess or singer
Shairah, Shaira, Shaa'ira, Shira, Sheera, Shiri

Sha'ista (Arabic) One who is polite and well-behaved
Shaistah, Shaista, Shaa'ista, Shayista, Shaysta

Shakila (Arabic) Feminine form of Shakil; beautiful one
Shakilah, Shakela, Shakeela, Shakeyla, Shakyla, Shakeila, Shakiela, Shakina, Shakilla, Shakeala

Shakira (Arabic) Feminine form of Shakir; grateful; thankful
Shakirah, Shakiera, Shaakira, Shakeira, Shakyra, Shakeyra, Shakura, Shakirra, Shakeara

Shakti (Indian) A divine woman; having power
Shaktie, Shakty, Shaktey, Shaktee, Shaktye, Shaktea

Shalimar (Indian) A Guerlain perfume; a famous garden in Pakistan
Shalimarr, Shalimare, Shalimarre, Shalimara, Shalimarra

Shalini (Indian) One who is modest
Shalinie, Shaliny, Shalyni, Shalinee, Shalyny, Shalinea, Shalynee

Shaliqa (Arabic) One who is sisterly
Shaliqah, Shaliqua, Shaleeqa, Shaleequa, Shalyqa, Shalyqua

Shalishah (Hebrew) Place name from the Bible
Shalesa, Shalesah, Shalese, Shalessa, Shalice, Shalicia, Shaliece, Shalisa, Shalisah, Shalise, Shalisha, Shalishea, Shalisia, Shalisiah, Shalissa, Shalissah, Shalisse, Shalyce, Shalys, Shalysa, Shalysah, Shalyse, Shalyss, Shalyssa, Shalyssah, Shalysse, Shaleashah, Shaleesha, Shaleashah, Shaleeshah

Shalom (Hebrew) One who is peaceful

Shama (Arabic) The lighted mark
Shamah, Shamma, Shammah

Shamara (Arabic) Woman who is ready for battle
Shamarah, Shamarra, Shamarrah, Shamaria, Shamarie

Shamima (Arabic) A woman full of flavor
Shamimah, Shameema, Shamiema, Shameima, Shamyma, Shameama

Shamira (Hebrew) A guardian; protector
*Shamirah, Shameera, Shamiera, Shameira,
Shamyra, Shameara*

Shamita (Indian) A peacemaker
*Shamitah, Shamyta, Shameeta, Shamitta,
Shameata*

Shana (Hebrew) God is gracious
*Shanah, Shanna, Shania, Shanae, Shanaia,
Shane, Shanessa, Shanelle, Shanell, Shandi,
Shanice, Shaniece, Seana, Shaana,
Shaanah, Shan, Shanda, Shandae,
Shandah, Shannda*

Shandy (English) One who is rambunctious;
boisterous
*Shandey, Shandee, Shandi, Shandie,
Shandye, Shandea*

Shani (African) A marvelous woman
*Shanie, Shany, Shaney, Shanee, Shanni,
Shanea, Shannie, Shanny, Shanney,
Shannee, Shannea*

Shanice (American) Form of Janice, meaning
"God is gracious"
*Shaneace, Shanease, Shaneece, Shaneese,
Shaneise, Shanicea, Shannice, Sheneice,
Shenyce*

Shanika (American) A woman from a
settlement in Africa
*Shanica, Shanicah, Shanicca, Shanicka,
Shanickah, Shanieka, Shanikah, Shanike,
Shanikia, Shanikka, Shanikqua, Shanikwa,
Shanyca, Shanycah, Shanycka, Shanyckah,
Shanyka, Shanykah, Shineeca, Shonnika,
Shaneeka, Shaneaka*

Shanley (Gaelic) Small and ancient woman
*Shanleigh, Shanlee, Shanly, Shanli, Shanlie,
Shanlea*

Shannelle (English) Form of Chanel,
meaning "from the canal; a channel"
*Shanele, Shanel, Shanell, Shanelle,
Shannele, Shannelle, Shannell*

Shannon (Gaelic) Having ancient wisdom;
river name
*Shanon, Shannen, Shannan, Shannin,
Shanna, Shannae, Shannun, Shannyn*

Shanta (Hindi) One who is calm
Shantah, Shantta, Shantia, Shantea, Shantiya

Shantelle (American) Form of Chantal,
meaning "from a stony place; a beautiful
singer"
*Shantell, Shantel, Shantele, Shanton,
Shantal, Shantale*

Shanti (Indian) One who is peaceful; tranquil
*Shantie, Shanty, Shantey, Shantee, Shantea,
Shanata, Shante*

Shaquana (American) Truth in life
*Shaqana, Shaquanah, Shaquanna,
Shaqanna, Shaqania*

Sharara (Arabic) Born of lightning; a spark
Shararah, Sharaara, Shararra

Sharifah (Arabic) Feminine form of Sharif;
noble; respected; virtuous
*Sharifa, Shareefa, Sharufa, Sharufah,
Sharyfa, Sharefa, Shareafa, Shariefa, Shareifa*

Sharik (African) One who is a child of God
*Shareek, Shareake, Sharicke, Sharick,
Sharike, Shareak, Sharique, Sharyk,
Sharyke, Sharyque*

Sharikah (Arabic) One who is a good
companion
*Sharika, Shareeka, Sharyka, Shareka,
Shariqua, Shareaka*

Sharise (English) Form of Charis, meaning
"having grace and kindness"
*Shareace, Sharease, Shereece, Shareese,
Sharese, Sharesse, Shariece, Sharis, Sharise,
Sharish, Shariss, Sharisse, Sharyce, Sharyse*

Sharlene (French) Feminine form of
Charles; a small, strong woman
*Sharleene, Sharleen, Sharla, Sharlyne,
Sharline, Sharlyn, Sharlean, Sharleane*

Sharmane (English) Form of Charmaine,
meaning "charming and delightful woman"
*Sharman, Sharmaine, Sharmain,
Sharmayne, Sharmayn, Sharmaen,
Sharmaene*

Sharmila (Indian) One who provides
comfort, joy, and protection
*Sharmilah, Sharmyla, Sharmeela,
Sharmilla, Sharmylla*

Sharon (Hebrew) From the plains;
a flowering shrub
*Sharron, Sharone, Sharona, Shari, Sharis,
Sharne, Sherine, Sharun, Sharin, Sharan,
Sharen*

S

Shashi (Hindi) Of the moonlight;
a moonbeam
Shashie, Shashy, Shashey, Shashee, Shashea

Shasmecka (African) A princess;
highborn girl
*Shasmecca, Shasmeka, Shasmeckia,
Shasmeckiya*

Shasta (Native American) From the triple-peaked mountain
*Shastah, Shastia, Shastiya, Shastea,
Shasteya*

Shasti (Hindi) In Hinduism, a protective
goddess of children
Shastie, Shasty, Shastee, Shastey, Shastea

Shauna (Irish) Feminine form of Shaun;
God is gracious
*Shawna, Shaunna, Shawnna, Seana,
Seanna, Shawnessa, Shawnnessy, Shona*

Shavon (American) Variant of Siobhan,
meaning "God is gracious"
*Shavonne, Schavon, Schevon, Shavan,
Shavaun, Shavone, Shavonia, Shavonn,
Shavonni, Shavonnia, Shavonnie,
Shavontae, Shavonte, Shavoun, Sheavon,
Shivaun, Shivawn, Shivon, Shivonne,
Shyvon, Shyvonne*

Shawnee (Native American) A tribal name
*Shawni, Shawnie, Shawnea, Shawny,
Shawney, Shawnea*

Shayla (Irish) Of the fairy palace
*Shaylah, Shaylagh, Shaylain, Shaylan,
Shaylea, Shayleah, Shaylla, Sheyla*

Shaylee (Gaelic) From the fairy palace;
a fairy princess
*Shalee, Shayleigh, Shailee, Shaileigh,
Shaelee, Shaeleigh, Shayli, Shaylie, Shayly,
Shayley, Shaeli, Shaelie, Shaely, Shaeley,
Shaili, Shailie, Shaily, Shailey*

Shayna (Hebrew) A beautiful woman
*Shaynah, Shaine, Shaina, Shaena,
Shayndel, Shana, Shaynae, Shaynee,
Shayney, Shayni, Shaynia, Shaynie,
Shaynna, Shaynne, Shayny, Shayne*

Shea (Gaelic / Irish) Of admirable character
/ from the fairy palace
Shearra, Sheah

Sheba (Hebrew) An oath; a biblical place
Shebah, Sheeba, Shyba, Sheyba, Sheaba

Sheehan (Celtic) Little peaceful one;
peacemaker
*Shehan, Sheyhan, Shihan, Shiehan, Shyhan,
Sheahan*

Sheela (Indian) One of cool conduct and
character
Sheelah, Sheetal

Sheena (Gaelic) God's gracious gift
*Sheenah, Shena, Shiena, Sheyna, Shyna,
Sheana, Sheina*

Sheherezade (Arabic) One who is a city
dweller

Sheila (Irish) Form of Cecilia, meaning
"one who is blind"
*Sheilah, Sheelagh, Shelagh, Shiela, Shyla,
Selia, Sighle, Sheiletta, Sheilette, Sheilett,
Sheileta, Sheyla, Sheala*

Sheiramoth (Hebrew) Musician of the
temple
*Sheiramothe, Sheramoth, Shyramoth,
Shiramoth, Sheeramoth*

Shelby (English) From the willow farm
*Shelbi, Shelbey, Shelbie, Shelbee, Shelbye,
Shelbea*

Shelley (English) From the bank's meadow
*Shelly, Shelli, Shellie, Shellee, Shelleigh,
Shella, Shellaine, Shellana, Shellany, Shellea,
Shelleah, Shellei, Shellene, Shellian,
Shelliann, Shellina, Shell*

Shepry (American) A mediator who is
honest and friendly
*Sheprey, Shepri, Sheprie, Shepree, Sheprye,
Sheprea*

Shera (Aramaic) A very bright light
*Sheara, Shearah, Sheera, Sheerah, Sherae,
Sherah, Sheralla, Sheralle, Sheray, Sheraya*

Sheridan (Gaelic) One who is wild and
untamed; a searcher
*Sheridann, Sheridanne, Sherydan,
Sherridan, Sheriden, Sheridon, Sherrerd,
Sherida, Sheridane, Sherideen, Sheridian,
Sheridin, Sheridyn, Sherridana, Sherridane,
Sherridanne, Sherridon, Sherrydan,
Sherrydana, Sherrydane, Sherrydin,
Sherrydon, Sherrydyn, Sherydana,
Sherydane*

S

Sherise (Greek) Form of Charis, meaning "having grace and kindness"
Sherisse, Sherissa, Sheris, Sheriss, Sherys, Sheryse, Sherysse, Sherysa, Sherisa, Scherise, Sherece, Shereece, Sherees, Shereese, Sherese, Shericia, Sherrish, Sherryse, Sheryce

Sherry (English) Form of Cherie, meaning "one who is greatly loved; a darling"
Sherrey, Sherri, Sherrie, Sherie, Sheri, Sherree, Sherea, Sherrea

Sheryl (English) Form of Cheryl, meaning "one who is greatly loved; a darling"
Sheryll, Sherylle, Sherylyn, Sheryle, Sherile, Sherill, Sherille, Sharilyn, Sherilin, Sherilina, Sherilinah, Sheriline, Sherilyna, Sherilynah, Sherilyne, Sherilynn, Sherilynna, Sherilynnah, Sherilynne, Sherilyn

Sheshebens (Native American) Resembling a small duck

Shields (English) A loyal protector
Sheelds, Sheylds, Shylds, Shilds, Shealds

Shifra (Hebrew) A beautiful midwife
Shifrah, Shiphrah, Shiphra, Shifria, Shifriya, Shifrea

Shika (Japanese) A little, gentle deer
Shicka, Shicca, Sheka, Shecka, Shyka, Shycka, Sheeka

Shikha (Indian) Flame burning brightly
Shikhah, Shikkha, Shekha, Shykha

Shiloh (Hebrew) One who is peaceful; abundant
Shilo, Shyloh, Shylo

Shilpa (Indian) Strong as a rock
Shilpah, Shilpha, Shylpa, Shylpha

Shima (Native American) Little mother
Shimah, Shimma, Shyma, Shymah

Shin (Korean) One having faith and trust
Shinn, Shyn, Shynn

Shina (Japanese) A virtuous woman; having goodness
Shinah, Shinna, Shyna, Shynna

Shira (Hebrew) My joyous song
Shirah, Shiray, Shire, Shiree, Shiri, Shirit

Shirin (Persian) One who is sweet and pleasant
Sheerin, Sheereen, Shirina, Shirinia, Shiriniya, Shiryn, Shirynn, Shirynne

Shirley (English) From the bright clearing
Shirly, Shirlie, Shirli, Shirleigh, Shirlee, Shirl, Shirlyn, Shirlea, Sherle, Sherley, Sherly, Sherli, Sherlie, Sherlee, Sherlea, Sherleigh

Shobha (Indian) An attractive woman
Shobhah, Shobbha, Shoba, Shobhan, Shobhane

Shobhna (Indian) A shiny ornament
Shobhnah, Shobbhna, Shobna, Shobhnan, Shobhnane

Shona (Irish) Form of Joan, meaning "God is gracious"
Shiona, Shonagh, Shonah, Shonalee, Shone, Shonette

Shoney (Celtic) In mythology, a sea goddess
Shony, Shoni, Shonie, Shonee, Shonni, Shonea, Shonnie

Shoshana (Arabic) Form of Susan, meaning "resembling a graceful white lily"
Shosha, Shoshan, Shoshanah, Shoshane, Shoshanha, Shoshann, Shoshanna, Shoshannah, Shoshauna, Shoshaunah, Shoshaunah, Shoshawna, Shoshona, Shoushan, Shushana, Sosha, Soshana

Shoshone (Native American) A tribal name
Shoshoni, Shoshonie, Shoshonee, Shoshonea, Shoshony, Shoshoney

Shradhdha (Indian) One who is faithful; trusting
Shraddha, Shradha, Shradhan, Shradhane

Shreya (Indian) A lucky woman
Shreyah

Shriya (Indian) One who is wealthy; prosperous
Shriyah, Shreeya, Shreeyah

Shruti (Indian) Having good hearing
Shrutie, Shruty, Shrutey, Shrutee, Shrutye, Shrutea

Shu Fang (Chinese) One who is gentle and kind

Shulamit (Hebrew) One who is peaceful; tranquil
Shulamite, Schulamit, Scholamit, Shulamitte, Shulamith, Shulamithe, Shulamitha

S

Shuman (Native American) One who charms rattlesnakes
Shumane, Shumaine, Shumayne, Shumanne, Shumanna, Shumaene

Shunnareh (Arabic) Pleasing in manner and behavior
Shunnaraya, Shunareh, Shunarreh

Shura (Russian) Form of Alexandra, meaning "helper and defender of mankind"
Shurah, Shurra, Shurrah

Shyann (English) Form of Cheyenne, meaning "unintelligible speaker"
Shyanne, Shyane, Sheyann, Sheyanne, Sheyenne, Sheyene

Shyla (English) Form of Sheila, meaning "one who is blind"
Shya, Shyah, Shylah, Shylan, Shylana, Shylane, Shylayah, Shyle, Shyleah, Shylee, Shyley, Shyli, Shylia, Shylie, Shylyn

Shysie (Native American) A quiet child
Shysi, Shysy, Shysey, Shysee, Shycie, Shyci, Shysea, Shycy, Shycey, Shycee, Shycea

Sian (Welsh) Form of Jane, meaning "God is gracious"
Sianne, Siann, Siane, Sione, Siana, Siania, Sianya, Sianna

Siany (Irish) Having good health
Sianie, Sianey, Sianee, Siani, Sianea

Siara (Arabic) One who is holy and pure
Siaraa, Siarah, Syara, Siarra, Syarra

Sibeal (Irish) Form of Isabel, meaning "my God is bountiful"
Sibeall, Sibealle, Sibeale, Sybeal, Sybeale, Sybeall

Sibyl (English) A prophetess; a seer
Sybil, Sibyla, Sybella, Sibil, Sibella, Sibilla, Sibley, Sibylla, Sibly, Sibli, Siblie, Siblee, Siblea, Sibleigh

Sicily (Italian) A woman from the large island off Italy
Sicilie, Sicili, Siciley, Sicilee, Sicilea, Sicileigh

Siddhi (Hindi) Having spiritual power
Sidhi, Syddhi, Sydhi

Siddiqa (Arabic) A righteous friend
Siddiqua, Sidiqa, Siddeeqa, Siddyqa, Siddeequa, Siddyqua

Side (Anatolian) Resembling a pomegranate, symbolizing abundance

Sidera (Latin) A luminous woman
Siderra, Sydera, Syderra, Sideria, Sideriya, Siderea

Sidero (Greek) In mythology, stepmother of Pelias and Neleus
Siderro, Sydero, Sideriyo

Sidonie (French) Feminine form of Sidonius; woman of Sidon
Sidonia, Sidone, Sidoniya, Sidonea, Sidony, Sidoni, Sidoney, Sidonee

Sidra (Latin) Resembling a star
Sidrah, Sydra, Sidriya, Sydriya

Sieglinde (German) Winning a gentle victory

Sienna (Italian) Woman with reddish-brown hair
Siena, Siennya, Sienya, Syenna, Syinna, Syenya

Sierra (Spanish) From the jagged mountain range
Siera, Syerra, Syera, Seyera, Seeara

Sigfreda (German) A woman who is victorious
Sigfreeda, Sigfrida, Sigfryda, Sigfreyda, Sigfrieda, Sigfriede, Sigfrede

Sigismonda (Teutonic) A victorious defender
Sigismunda

Signia (Latin) A distinguishing sign
Signiya, Signea, Signeia, Signeya, Signa

Signy (Scandinavian) A newly victorious woman
Signe, Signi, Signie, Signey, Signee, Signild, Signilde, Signilda, Signea

Sigourney (Scandinavian / French) A woman who conquers / a daring queen
Sigourny, Sigourni, Sigournie, Sigournee, Sigournye, Sigournea, Sigurney, Sigurny, Sigurni, Sigurnie, Sigurnea, Sigurnee

Sigrid (Scandinavian) A victorious advisor
Sigryd, Sigryde, Sigrith, Sigrath, Sigrathe, Siri

Sigrun (Scandinavian) Having won a secret victory

Sigyn (Norse) In mythology, the wife of Loki

Siham (Arabic) Resembling an arrow

Sihar (Arabic) An enchanting woman
*Syhar, Sihara, Syhara, Sihari, Siharie,
Sihary, Siharey, Siharee, Siharea, Siharia*

Sihu (Native American) As delicate as a
flower

Sika (African) A woman with money
Sikah, Sikka, Sicka, Syka, Sykka, Sicca

Sikina (Arabic) A devout and peaceful
woman
*Sikinah, Sikyna, Sickina, Sickyna, Sikeena,
Sikena, Sikeyna, Sikeana*

Sila (Indian) A well-behaved, chaste woman
Silah, Silla, Syla, Sylah, Sylla

Silana (French) One who is dignified; a lady
*Silanah, Silanna, Sylana, Sylanna, Silane,
Silann, Silan, Silanne*

Sileas (Scottish) A woman who remains
youthful
Silis, Silys, Syleas, Silias, Sile, Silyas

Silence (American) A quiet and well-
behaved child
*Silince, Silense, Silinse, Sylence, Sylense,
Sylince, Sylinse*

Silka (Latin) Form of Cecelia, meaning
"one who is blind"
*Silke, Silkia, Silkea, Silkie, Silky, Silkee,
Sylka, Sylke, Silja, Silken, Silkan*

Silvana (Latin) Feminine form of Silvanus;
a woodland dweller
*Silvanna, Silvane, Silvanne, Silva, Silvia,
Silviya, Sylvia, Sylvya, Sylva, Sylvana,
Sylvanna, Sylvane, Sylvanne, Silvestra*

Silver (English) A precious metal; white-
skinned
Sylver, Silvera, Sylvera, Silvere, Sylvere

Silwa (Arabic) Resembling a quail
Silwah, Sylwa, Sylwah

Sima (Arabic) One who is treasured; a prize
Simma, Syma, Simah, Simia, Simiya

Simcha (Hebrew) One who is joyous
*Simchia, Simchea, Symcha, Symchia,
Symchea*

Simin (Iranian) A silvery woman
Simeen, Seemeen, Symeen, Symyn, Simyn

Simona (Italian) Feminine form of Simon;
one who listens well
*Simonah, Simonna, Symona, Simone,
Symone, Simoni, Simony, Simonee,
Simoney, Simonie*

Simran (Indian) One who meditates
*Simrana, Simrania, Simrann, Simranne,
Simrane, Simranna*

Sina (Samoan) In mythology, goddess of
the moon

Sine (Scottish) Form of Jane, meaning
"God is gracious"
*Sinead, Sineidin, Sioned, Sionet, Sion,
Siubhan, Siwan, Sineh*

Sinmore (Norse) In mythology, the wife of
Surt
*Sinmorre, Sinmora, Sinmorra, Synmore,
Synmora*

Sinobia (Greek) Form of Zenobia, meaning
"sign or symbol"
*Sinobiah, Sinobya, Sinobe, Sinobie,
Sinovia, Senobia, Senobya, Senobe,
Senobie, Senobey, Senovia*

Sinopa (Native American) Resembling a
fox

Sinope (Greek) In mythology, one of the
daughters of Asopus

Sintra (Spanish) A woman from the town
in Portugal

Siobhan (Irish) Form of Joan, meaning
"God is gracious"
*Shibahn, Shibani, Shibhan, Shioban,
Shobana, Shobhana, Siobahn, Siobhana,
Siobhann, Siobhon, Siovaun, Siovhan*

Sippora (Hebrew) A birdlike woman
*Sipporah, Sipora, Syppora, Sypora, Siporra,
Syporra*

Siran (Armenian) An alluring and lovely
woman

Siren (Greek) A seductive and beautiful
woman; in mythology, a sea nymph whose
beautiful singing lured sailors to their deaths
*Sirene, Sirena, Siryne, Siryn, Syren, Syrena,
Sirine, Sirina, Sirinia, Sirenia*

S

Siria (Spanish / Persian) Bright like the sun / a glowing woman
Siriah, Sirea, Sireah, Siriya, Siriyah, Sirya, Siryah

Siroun (Armenian) A lovely woman
Sirune

Sive (Irish) A good and sweet girl
Sivney, Sivny, Sivni, Sivnie, Sivnee, Sivnea

Siyanda (African) The village is expanding

Skaoi (Norse) In mythology, a mountain giantess and goddess of skiers

---

SLOANE

My husband and I named our girls Cameron and Sloane … because we're obsessed with the movie *Ferris Bueller's Day Off*! —Brenda, MD

Sirpuhi (Armenian) One who is holy; pious
Sirpuhie, Sirpuhy, Sirpuhey, Sirpuhea, Sirpuhee

Sirvat (Armenian) Resembling a beautiful rose

Sisay (African) A blessing from God; an omen of good things to come
Sisaye, Sissay, Sissaye

Sisi (African) Born on a Sunday
Sisie, Sisea, Sisee, Sisy, Sisey

Sisika (Native American) Resembling a bird

Sissy (English) Form of Cecilia, meaning "one who is blind"
Sissey, Sissie, Sisley, Sisli, Sislee, Sissel, Sissle, Syssy, Syssi

Sita (Hindi) In Hinduism, goddess of the harvest and wife of Rama

Sitara (Indian) Of the morning star
Sitarah, Sitarra, Sitaara, Siteare

Sitembile (African) A woman worthy of trust
Sitembyle

Siti (African) A distinguished woman; a lady
Sitie, Sity, Sitey, Sitee, Sitea

Sitka (English) A woman from a city in western Alaska
Sytka

Siv (Norse) A beautiful bride; in mythology, the wife of Thor
Sif

Sky (American) From the heavens

Skye (Gaelic) Woman from the Isle of Skye

Skylar (English) One who is learned; a scholar
Skylare, Skylarr, Skyler, Skylor, Skylir, Skylur

Slaine (Irish) A woman of good health
Slain, Slayne, Slane, Slany, Slanee, Slania, Slainie, Slanie, Slaney, Siany, Slaen, Slaene

Sloane (Irish) A strong protector; a woman warrior
Sloan, Slone

Smita (Indian) One who smiles a lot

Snana (Native American) Having a sound like bells
Snanah, Snanna, Snannah

Snow (American) Frozen rain
Snowy, Snowie, Snowi, Snowey, Snowee, Snowea, Sno

Snowdrop (English) Resembling a small white flower

Socorro (Spanish) One who offers help and relief
Socoro, Sokorro, Sokoro, Sockorro, Sockoro

Sohalia (Indian) Of the moon's glow
Sohaliah, Sohalea, Sohaliya, Sohaleah, Sohalya

Sokanon (Native American) Born of the rain

Solace (Latin) One who gives comfort
Solase

Solada (Thai) One who listens well

S

Solaina (French) A dignified and respected woman
Solaine, Solayna, Solanya, Solaynya, Solainia, Solaena

Solana (Latin / Spanish) Wind from the East / of the sunshine
Solanah, Solanna, Solann, Solanne

Solange (French) One who is religious and dignified

Solaris (Greek) Of the sun
Solarise, Solariss, Solarisse, Solarys, Solaryss, Solarysse, Sol, Soleil, Solstice

Solita (Latin) One who is solitary
Solitah, Solida, Soledad, Soledada, Soledade

Solona (Greek) Feminine form of Solon; wisdom
Solonah, Solone, Solonie, Soloni, Solony, Soloney, Solonee, Solonea

Solveig (Norse) The strength of the house
Solvig, Solveige, Solvige

Soma (Indian) An exalted woman; one who gives praise

Somatra (Indian) Of the excellent moon

Sona (Arabic) The golden one
Sonika, Sonna

Sonora (Spanish) A pleasant-sounding woman
Sonorah, Sonoria, Sonorya, Sonoriya

Soo (Korean) Having an excellent, long life

Sooleawa (Native American) Resembling silver

Sophie ♀ ♂ (Greek) Having great wisdom and foresight
Sophia, *Sofiya, Sofie,* **Sofia**, *Sofi, Sofiyko, Sofronia, Sophronia, Sophy, Sonia, Sonya, Sonja*

Sora (Native American) Resembling a chirping songbird
Sorah, Sorra, Sorrah

Sorano (Japanese) Of the heavens

Sorcha (Gaelic) One who is bright; intelligent; form of Sarah, meaning "princess; lady"
Sorchah, Sorchia, Sorchiah, Sorchea, Sorcheah, Sorchiya, Sorchiyah, Sorchya, Sorchyah

Sorina (Romanian) Feminine form of Sorin; of the sun
Sorinah, Sorinna, Sorinia, Soriniya, Sorinya, Soryna, Sorynia, Sorine, Soreena, Soreana

Soroushi (Persian) A bringer of happiness
Soroushie, Soroushy, Soroushey, Soroushee, Soroushea, Sorushi, Sorushie, Sorushy, Sorushey, Sorushea, Sorushee

Sorrel (French) From the surele plant
Sorrell, Sorrelle, Sorrele, Sorrela, Sorrella

Soubrette (French) One who is coquettish
Soubrett, Soubret, Soubrete, Soubretta, Soubreta

Southern (American) Woman of the South

Sovann (Cambodian) The golden one
Sovane, Sovanne, Sovana, Sovanna, Sovania, Sovaniya

Soyala (Native American) Born during the winter solstice
Soyalah, Soyalla, Soyalia, Soyaliya, Soyalya

Sparrow (English) Resembling a small songbird
Sparro, Sparroe, Sparo, Sparow, Sparowe, Sparoe

Spencer (English) An administrator; dispenser of provisions
Spenser, Spincer, Spinser

Speranza (Italian) Form of Esperanza, meaning "filled with hope"
Speranzia, Speranzea, Speranziya, Speranzya

Spes (Latin) In mythology, goddess of hope

Spica (Latin) One of the brightest stars
Spicah, Spicka, Spika, Spicca, Spyca, Spycka, Spyka

Spring (English) Refers to the season; born in spring
Spryng

Sraddha (Hindi) One having faith and trust
Sraddhah, Sradha, Sradhah

Sroda (African) A respected woman
Srodah, Srodda, Sroddah

Sslama (Egyptian) One who is peaceful

S

Stacey (English) Form of Anastasia, meaning "one who shall rise again"
Stacy, Staci, Stacie, Stacee, Stacia, Stasia, Stasy, Stasey, Stasi, Stasie, Stasee, Steise, Stacea, Stasea

Stanislava (Slovene) Feminine form of Stanislav; government's glory
Stanislavah, Stanyslava, Stanislavia, Stanislaviya, Stanislavya, Stanyslavia

Stansie (Italian) One who is constant; steadfast
Stansi, Stansey, Stansy, Stansee, Stansea, Stanzie, Stanzi, Stanzy, Stanzey, Stanzee, Stanzea

Star (American) A celestial body
Starr, Starre, Starry, Starrie, Starri, Starling, Starla

Starbuck (American) An astronaut

Stella (English) Star of the sea
Stela, Stelle, Stele, Stellah, Stelah

Stephanie (Greek) Feminine form of Stephen; crowned in victory
Stephani, Stephany, Stephaney, Stephanee, Stephene, Stephana, Stefanie, Stefani, Stefany, Stefaney, Stefanee, Steffani, Steffanie, Stephania, Stefania, Steffine, Stephenie, Stesha, Stephie, Stephi, Stephy, Stephia, Stefia

Stockard (English) From the yard of tree stumps
Stockhard, Stockhard, Stokkard

Storm (American) Of the tempest; stormy weather; having an impetuous nature
Storme, Stormy, Stormi, Stormie, Stormey, Stormee, Stormia, Stormea

Strephon (Greek) One who turns
Strephone, Strephonn, Strephonne, Strep

Struana (Scottish) From the stream
Struanna, Struanah, Struanne, Struan, Struann, Struane

Styx (Greek) In mythology, the river of the underworld
Stixx, Styxx, Stix

Suadela (Latin) In mythology, goddess of persuasion
Suadelah, Suadell, Suadelle, Suadele, Suada

Suave (American) A smooth and courteous woman
Swave

Subha (Indian) One who is beautiful; attractive

Subhadra (Hindi) In Hinduism, the sister of Krishna

STELLA

We chose Stella because it is classic and there aren't many Stellas out there. And it's a beautiful-sounding name. Unfortunately, every time we tell it to people, inevitably someone does their best Marlon Brando impression: "Stella!!! Pick up those toys!" But I don't care; it's still a great name. —Sarah, IL

S

Stetson (English) Child of one who is crowned
Stetsun, Stetsan, Stetsin, Stetsyn, Stetsen

Stevonna (Greek) A crowned lady
Stevonnah, Stevona, Stevonah, Stevonia, Stevonea, Stevoniya

Stheno (Greek) A mighty woman; in mythology, one of the Gorgons

Stina (Danish) Form of Christina, meaning "follower of Christ"
Stinna, Stinne, Stine, Styna, Stynna, Styne, Stynne, Steena, Steana

Subhaga (Indian) A fortunate person

Subhuja (Hindi) An auspicious Apsara (heavenly nymph)

Subira (African) One who is patient
Subirah, Subirra, Subyra, Subyrra, Subeera, Subeara, Subeira, Subiera

Suchin (Thai) A beautiful thought

Suchitra (Indian) A beautiful picture
Suchitrah, Suchytra, Suchitran, Suchitrane

Sugar (American) A sweetheart

Sughra (Arabic) A pure young woman
Sughraa, Sughrah

Suha (Arabic) The name of a star

Suhaila (Arabic) Feminine form of Suhail;
a gentle woman; bright star
*Suhayla, Suhaela, Suhala, Suhailah,
Suhaylah, Suhaelah, Suhalah*

Suhaymah (Arabic) The little arrow
*Suhayma, Suhaimah, Suhaima, Suhaemah,
Suhaema*

Sujata (Indian) From a good social class
*Sujatah, Sujatta, Sujatia, Sujatea, Sujatiya,
Sujatya*

Sukanya (Indian) A well-behaved young
woman
Sukanyah, Sukania, Sukaniah, Sukaniya

Suki (Japanese) One who is dearly loved
*Sukki, Sooki, Sookie, Suky, Sooky, Sukie,
Sukey, Sukee, Sukea, Sookey, Sookee, Sookea*

Suksma (Indian) A fine young lady
Suksmah

Sully (Gaelic / English) A dark-eyed
woman / from the south meadow
*Sulley, Sulli, Sullie, Sullee, Sullye, Sulleigh,
Sullea*

Sultana (Arabic) An empress; queen; ruler
Sultanah, Sultaana, Sultanna

Sulwyn (Welsh) One who shines as bright
as the sun
*Sulwynne, Sulwynn, Sulwinne, Sulwin,
Sulwen, Sulwenn, Sulwenne*

Suma (English / Egyptian) Born during the
summer / to ask
Sumah, Summa, Summah

Sumana (Indian) A good-natured woman
*Sumanah, Sumanna, Sumane, Sumanne,
Sumann*

Sumayah (Arabic) One with pride
*Sumaya, Sumayyah, Sumayya, Sumaiya,
Sumaiyah, Sumaiyya, Sumaeya, Sumaeyah*

Sumehra (Arabic) Having a beautiful face
Sumehrah, Sumehraa, Sumehrae, Sumehrai

Sumey (Asian) Resembling a delicate
flower
Sumy, Sumee, Sumea

Sumi (Japanese) One who is elegant and
refined
Sumie

Sumiko (Japanese) Child of goodness

Sumitra (Indian) A beloved friend
*Sumitrah, Sumita, Sumytra, Sumyta,
Sumeetra, Sumeitra, Sumietra, Sumeatra*

Summer (American) Refers to the season;
born in summer
Sommer, Sumer, Somer, Somers

Sun (Korean) An obedient child

Suna (Turkish) A swanlike woman

Sunanda (Indian) Having a sweet character
*Sunandah, Sunandia, Sunandiya,
Sunandea, Sunandya*

Sunbul (Arabic) Resembling an ear of
grain
*Sunbool, Sunbulle, Sunbull, Sunbule,
Sunboole, Sunboul, Sunboule*

Sunday (American) Born on a Sunday
Sundae, Sundai, Sundaye

Sundown (American) Born at dusk

Sunee (Thai) A good thing

Sunhilda (Teutonic) A sun battlemaiden
*Sunhild, Sunhilde, Sonnehilde, Sonnehilda,
Sonnehild*

Sunila (Indian) Feminine form of Sunil;
very blue
Sunilah, Sunilla, Sunilya, Suniliya

Sunita (Indian) One who is well-behaved;
having good morals
*Sunitah, Sunitra, Sunitrah, Sunitha, Suniti,
Suneeta, Suneata*

Sunki (Native American) To catch up with
*Sunkie, Sunky, Sunkey, Sunkye, Sunkee,
Sunkea*

Sunniva (English) Gift of the sun
Synnove, Synne, Synnove, Sunn

Sunny (American) Of the sun; one who is
brilliant and cheerful
*Sunni, Sunney, Sunnie, Sunnea, Sunnye,
Sonnenschein*

S

Suparna (Indian) Resembling a beautiful leaf
Suparnah, Suparniya, Suparnia, Suparnya, Suparnea

Suprabha (Indian) A radiant woman; brilliant

Supriti (Indian) One's true love
Supritie, Supritye, Supryty, Supryti, Supritee, Suprytee, Supritea, Suprytea

Supriya (Indian) One who is dearly loved; beloved
Supriyya, Supriyaa, Supriyah

Surabhi (Indian) Having a lovely fragrance
Surbhii, Surabhie, Surabhy, Surabhey, Surabhee, Surabhea

Suravinda (Indian) A beautiful attendant
Suravindah, Suravynda, Suravindia, Suravindiya

Surotama (Indian) An auspicious Apsara (heavenly nymph)
Surotamma, Surotamah

Suri (Armenian / Sanskrit / Hebrew) Wealthy / mother of the sun / go away

Suruchi (Indian) Having good taste
Suruchie, Suruchy, Suruchey, Suruchee, Suruchea

Surupa (Indian) One who is beautiful

Susannah (Hebrew) Resembling a graceful white lily
Susanna, Susanne, Susana, Susane, Susan, Suzanna, Suzannah, Suzanne, Suzane, Suzan, Susette, Suzette, Sueanne, Suelita, Suellen, Sukey, Susie, Suzie, Sue, Susy, Susey, Susi, Suzy, Suzi, Suzey, Susa, Suza, Suzetta, Shoshana, Shoshanah, Shoshanna, Shoushan, Shousnan, Shushana, Shushanna, Sonel, Sosanna, Sousan, Siusan, Souzan, Soki

Sushanti (Indian) A peaceful woman; tranquil
Sushantie, Sushanty, Sushantey, Sushantee, Sushantea

Sushila (Indian) One who is well-behaved; good conduct
Sushilah, Sushilla, Sushyla, Sushiela, Susheila, Susheela, Susheala

Sushma (Indian) A beautiful woman
Sushmah

Sushmita (Indian) Having a beautiful smile
Sushmitah, Sushmeeta, Sushmeata, Sushmyta

Suvarna (Indian) The golden one; having good color
Suvarnah, Suvarniya, Suvarnya

Suzu (Japanese) One who is long-lived
Suzue, Suzuko

Suzuki (Japanese) Of the bell tree
Suzukie, Suzukey, Suzuky, Suzukee, Suzukye, Suzukea

Svaha (Hindi) In Hinduism, a minor goddess

Svea (Swedish) From the motherland

Sveta (Slavic) A brilliant star's light
Svetta, Svetlana, Svetlanna, Svetlania, Svetlaniya

Swagata (Indian) One who is welcome
Swagatah, Swagatta

Swanhilda (Norse) A woman warrior; in mythology, the daughter of Sigurd
Swanhild, Swanhilde, Svanhilde, Svanhild, Svenhilde, Svenhilda

Swann (Scandinavian) A swanlike woman
Swan, Swawn, Swaantje, Swantje, Swana, Swanna

Swapnali (Indian) A dreamlike child
Swapnalie, Swapnalee, Swapna, Swapnaly, Swapnaley, Swapnalea

Swarna (Indian) The golden one

Swarupa (Indian) One who is devoted to the truth

Swati (Indian) The name of a star
Swatie, Swaty, Swatey, Swatee, Swatea

Sweta (Indian) A light-skinned woman; fair

Sydelle (Hebrew) A princess; born to royalty
Sydell, Sydele, Sydel, Sidelle, Sidell, Sidele, Sidel

Sydney ✪ (English) Of the wide meadow
Sydny, Sydni, Sydnie, Sydnea, Sydnee, Sidney, Sidne, Sidnee, Sidnei, Sidneya, Sidni, Sidnie, Sidny, Sidnye

Syna (Greek) Two together
Synah

Syrinx (Greek) In mythology, a nymph transformed into reeds
Syrinks

Taariq (Swahili) Resembling the morning star
Tariq, Taarique, Tarique

Taban (Gaelic) A genius; one of immeasurable intelligence
Tabban, Tabann, Tabanne, Tabana, Tabanna

Tabia (African / Egyptian) One who makes incantations / a talented woman
Tabiah, Tabya, Tabea, Tabeah, Tabiya

Tabina (Arabic) A follower of Muhammad
Tabinah, Tabyna, Tabeena, Tabeana

Tabita (African) A graceful woman
Tabitah, Tabyta, Tabytah, Tabeeta, Tabeata, Tabieta, Tabeita

Tabitha (Greek) Resembling a gazelle; known for beauty and grace
Tabithah, Tabbitha, Tabetha, Tabbetha, Tabatha, Tabbatha, Tabotha, Tabbotha, Tabytha, Tabbytha, Tabiatha, Tabithia, Tabtha, Tabathia, Tabathe, Tabby, Tabbey, Tabbie, Tabbi, Tabbee

Tablita (Native American) A woman wearing a tiara
Tablitah, Tableta, Tableeta, Tablyta, Tableyta, Tableata

Tabora (Spanish) One who plays a small drum
Taborah, Taborra, Taboria, Taborya

Taborri (Native American) Having a voice that carries
Taborrie, Taborry, Taborrey, Taborree, Tabori, Taborie, Tabory, Taborey, Taboree, Taborea

Tacincala (Native American) Resembling a deer
Tacincalah, Tacyncala, Tacyncalah, Tacincalla, Tacyncalla

Tacita (Latin) Feminine form of Tacitus; mute; silenced
Tacitah, Taceta, Tacyta, Taycita, Taycyta, Tasita, Tacey, Taci, Tacie, Tacy, Tacee, Tacea, Taicey, Taici, Taicie, Taicee, Taicy, Taicea, Taycey, Taycy, Tayci, Taycie, Taycee, Taycea

Tadita (Native American) Having great ability as a runner
Taditah, Tadeta, Tadyta, Taditta, Tadetta, Tadytta, Tadeeta, Tadeata

Taffy (Welsh) One who is much loved
Taffey, Taffi, Taffie, Taffee, Taffye, Tafy, Tafey, Taffia, Tafia, Taffea, Tafea, Taffine

Tafui (African) One who gives glory to God

Tahapenes (Hebrew) A secret temptation
Tahpenes

Tahirah (Arabic) One who is chaste; pure
Tahira, Taheera, Taheira, Tahyra, Tahera, Taahira, Tahiria, Tahiara, Taherri, Tahirra, Taheara

Tahiyya (Arabic) A greeting of cheer
Tahiyyah, Tahiya, Taheeyya, Taheeya

Tahki (Native American) From the cold
Tahkie, Tahky, Tahkey, Tahkee, Tahkye, Taki, Tahkea

Tahsin (Arabic) Beautification; one who is praised
Tahseen, Tahsene, Tahsyne, Tasine, Tahseene, Tahsean, Tahseane

Tahupotiki (Maori) A beloved child
Tahupotikie, Tahupotikki, Tahupotyki

Tahzib (Arabic) One who is educated and cultured
Tahzeeb, Tahzebe, Tahzybe, Tazib, Tazyb, Tazeeb, Tahzeab, Tazeab

Tai (Chinese / Vietnamese) A very big woman / one who is talented and prosperous

Taima (Native American) A loud crash of thunder
Taimah, Tayma, Taimi, Taimie, Taimy, Taimey, Taimee, Taimma, Taymi, Taymie, Taymmi, Taymmie, Taymy, Taymmy, Taimia, Taema, Taemi, Taemie, Taemy, Taemey

Taini (Native American) Born during the returning moon
Tainie, Tainy, Tainey, Tainee, Tainni, Tayni, Taynie, Tayney, Tayny, Taynee, Tainia, Tainn, Tainea, Taynea, Taeni, Taenie, Taeny, Taeney, Taenea, Taenee

Taipa (Native American) One who spreads her wings
Taipah, Taypa, Taypah, Taippa, Taepa, Taepah

Taisa (Greek) One who is bound; the bond
Taisah, Tais, Taysa, Tays, Thais, Thays, Thaisa, Thaysa, Taiza

Taite (English) One who is cheerful; pleasant and bright
Tait, Tayt, Tayte, Taita, Tayta, Tayten, Taet, Taete, Taeta, Tate

Taithleach (Gaelic) A quiet and calm young lady

Taja (African / Hindi) One who is mentioned / wearing a crown
Tajah, Tajae, Teja, Tejah

Tajsa (Polish) A princess; born into royalty
Tajsah, Tajsia, Tajsi, Tajsie, Tajsy, Tajsey, Tajsee, Tajsea

Taka (Japanese) Tall and honorable woman
Takah, Takka, Tacka

Takako (Japanese) A lofty child

Takala (Native American) Resembling a corn tassel
Takalah, Takalla, Takalya

Takara (Japanese) A treasured child; precious possession
Takarah, Takarra, Takarya, Takaria, Takra

Takoda (Native American) Friend to everyone
Takodah, Takodia, Takodya, Takota

Takouhi (Armenian) A queen
Takouhie, Takouhy, Takouhey, Takouhee, Takouhea

Tala (Native American) A stalking wolf
Talah, Talla

Talaith (Welsh) One who wears a royal crown
Talaithe, Talayth, Talaythe, Talaeth, Talaethe

Talasi (Native American) Resembling a cornflower
Talasie, Talasee, Talasea, Talasy, Talasey, Talasya, Talasia

Talia (Hebrew / Greek) Morning dew from heaven / blooming
Taliah, Talea, Taleah, Taleya, Tallia, Talieya, Taleea, Taleia, Taleiya, Tylea, Tyleah, Taleana, Tylia, Tahlia, Tahleah, Tahleea, Tahleia, Talaya, Talayia, Taliya, Taliyah, Taliatha, Talley, Taley, Tally, Taly, Talli, Tali, Tallie, Talie, Tallee, Talee, Talya

Talihah (Arabic) One who seeks knowledge
Taliha, Talibah, Taliba, Talyha, Taleehah, Taleahah

Taline (Armenian) Of the monastery
Talene, Taleen, Taleene, Talyne, Talinia, Talinya, Taliniya

Talisa (American) Consecrated to God
Talisah, Talysa, Taleesa, Talissa, Talise, Taleese, Talisia, Talisya, Talease, Taleasa

Talisha (American) A damsel; an innocent
Talesha, Taleisha, Talysha, Taleesha, Tylesha, Taleysha, Taleshia, Talishia, Tylesia, Talesia, Taliesha, Taleasha

Talitha (Arabic) A maiden; young girl
Talithah, Taletha, Taleetha, Talytha, Talithia, Talethia, Tiletha, Talith, Talethe, Talythe, Talita, Taleatha

Tallis (French) Of the forest; woodland dweller
Talliss, Tallisse, Tallys, Tallyse, Taliss, Talis, Talise, Talyss, Talyse, Taleese, Taleyse, Taleise, Taliese, Talease, Taleece, Taleace, Taliece, Taleice, Talice, Taleyce, Talissa, Talisa, Tallysa, Talysa, Talisia, Talissa, Talysia

Tallulah (Native American) Running water; leaping water
Tallula, Talula, Talulah, Tallulla

Talon (French) Resembling a claw
Talen, Talan, Tallon, Talin, Tallin, Talyn, Taelyn, Taelon, Tallen

Talor (Hebrew) Touched by the morning's dew
Talore, Talora, Talori, Talorie, Talorey, Talory, Talorye, Taloria, Talorya, Talorra, Talorea

Tam (Vietnamese) Close to the heart

Tama (Japanese / Native American) As precious as a jewel / a thunderbolt
Tamah, Tamaa, Tamala, Tamaiah, Tamalia, Tamalya

Tamanna (Indian) One who is desired
Tamannah, Tamana, Tamanah, Tammana, Tammanna

Tamara (Hebrew / Sanskrit) From the palm tree / a spice
Tamarah, Tamarra, Tamarya, Tamaria, Tamaira, Tammara, Tamora, Temara, Tamari, Tamarie, Tamura, Tymara, Tomara, Tamary, Tamarey, Tamera, Tamerra, Timera, Tamarae, Tamaree, Tamar, Tamor, Tamour, Tamer, Tameria, Tammera, Tamerai, Tamoya, Tameran, Tamyra, Tamyria, Tamra, Tammra, Tamira, Tamirra, Tamiria, Tamarla, Tamarsha, Tamijo, Tammy, Tamy, Tami, Tamie, Tamee, Tamey, Tammey, Tammee, Tamlyn, Tamya, Tamia, Tameia, Tamiya, Tamilyn, Tamryn

Tamasha (African) Pageant winner
Tamasha, Tomosha, Tomasha, Tamashia, Tamashya

Tambre (English) One who brings great joy; music
Tamber, Tambreh, Tambrey, Tambry, Tambrie, Tambri, Tambree, Tambrea

Tameka (Aramaic) A twin
Tamekah, Tameeka, Tamieka, Tameika, Tamecka, Temeka, Tymeka, Tomeka, Tameca, Tameeca, Tamekia, Tamecia, Tameaka

Tamesis (Celtic) In mythology, the goddess of water; also the source of the name for the river Thames
Tamesiss, Tamesys, Tamesyss

Tamiko (Japanese) Child of the people; sweet
Tameko, Tamicko, Tammiko, Tamyko, Tameeko, Tamiyo, Tamika, Tamicka, Tamica, Tameeka, Tameiko, Tamieko, Tamikia, Tamycko, Tamyka, Tamycka, Timiko, Timika, Tomiko, Tomika, Tymiko, Tymika, Tamike, Tamiqua, Tameako, Tameaka

Tamma (Hebrew) One who is perfect; without flaw
Tammah, Teme, Temima

Tanaquil (Latin) Worshipped in the home
Tanaquille, Tanaquile, Tannaquil

Tanaya (Indian) Daughter of mine
Tanayah, Tannaya, Tanayya

Tandice (American) A team player
Tandyce, Tandise, Tandyse, Tandy, Tandey, Tandi, Tandie, Tandee, Tandea, Tandis, Tandia, Tandye, Tandya, Tanda, Tandalaya

Tandra (African) Having a beauty mark; a mole
Tandrah, Tandrea, Tandria, Tandrya, Tandriya

Tanesha (African) Born on a Monday
Taneshah, Taneesha, Tanisha, Taniesha, Tanishia, Tanitia, Tannicia, Tanniece, Tannisha, Tenicia, Teneesha, Tinecia, Tiniesha, Tynisha, Tainesha, Taneshya, Taneasha, Taneisha, Tahniesha, Tanashia, Tanashea, Tanishea, Taneshea, Tanysha, Tanicha, Tanasha, Tanesia, Tanessa

Tangerina (English) From the city of Tangiers
Tangerinah, Tangereena, Tangeryna, Tangereana, Tangerine, Tangeryne

Tangia (American) The angel
Tangiah, Tangya, Tangiya, Tangeah

Tanginika (American) A lake goddess
Tanginikah, Tanginica, Tanginicka, Tangynika, Tanginyka

Tangwystl (Welsh) A pledge of peace

Tani (Japanese / Melanesian / Tonkinese) From the valley / a sweetheart / a young woman
Tanie, Tany, Taney, Tanee, Tanni, Tanye, Tannie, Tanny, Tanney, Tannee, Tanea, Tannea

Taniel (American) Feminine form of Daniel; God is my judge
Tanielle, Tanial, Tanialle, Taniele, Taniell, Taniela, Taniella

Tanika (American) Queen of the fairies
Tanikah, Taneeka, Tanyka, Tanica, Tanicka, Taniqua, Tanikka, Tannika, Tianika, Tannica, Tianeka, Taneka, Tanikqua, Taneaka

Tanith (Phoenician) In mythology, the goddess of love, fertility, moon, and stars
Tanithe, Tanyth, Tanythe, Tanitha, Tanytha, Tanithia

Tanner (English) One who tans hides
Taner, Tannar, Tannor, Tannis

Tansy (English / Greek) An aromatic yellow flower / having immortality
Tansey, Tansi, Tansie, Tansee, Tansye, Tansea, Tancy, Tanzy, Tansia, Tansya

Tanuja (Indian) My daughter
Tanujah, Tanujia, Tanujya, Tanujiya

Tanushri (Indian) One who is beautiful; attractive
Tanushrie, Tanushry, Tanushrey, Tanushree, Tanushrea

Tanvi (Indian) Slender and beautiful woman
Tanvie, Tanvy, Tanvey, Tanvee, Tanvye, Tannvi, Tanvea

Tao (Chinese) Resembling a peach; symbol of long life

Tapanga (African) One who is sweet and unpredictable
Tapangah

Tapati (Indian) In mythology, the daughter of the sun god
Tapatie, Tapaty, Tapatey, Tapatee, Tapatye, Tapatea

Taphath (Hebrew) In the Bible, Solomon's daughter
Tafath, Taphathe, Tafathe

Tapi (Indian) From the river
Tapie, Tapy, Tapey, Tapee, Tapti, Tapea, Taptie, Tapty, Taptey, Taptee, Taptea

Tappen (Welsh) Top of the rock
Tappan, Tappin, Tappon, Tapen, Tappene

Tara (Gaelic / Indian) Of the tower; rocky hill / star; in mythology, an astral goddess
Tarah, Tarra, Tayra, Taraea, Tarai, Taralee, Tarali, Taraya, Tarha, Tarasa, Tarasha, Taralynn, Tarrah

Tarachand (Indian) Silver star
Tarachande, Tarachanda, Tarachandia, Tarachandea, Tarachandiya, Tarachandya

Taraka (Indian) In mythology, a woman who was turned into a demon
Tarakah, Tarakia, Taracka, Tarackia, Tarakya, Tarakiya

Tarala (Indian) Resembling a honeybee
Taralah, Taralia, Taralla, Taralea, Taralya, Taraliya

Tarana (African) Born during daylight
Taranah, Tarania, Taranna

Taraneh (Persian) A beautiful melody; a song
Tarane, Taranne, Taranneh, Tarannum, Taranum

Taree (Japanese) A bending branch
Tarea, Tareya

Taregan (Native American) Resembling a crane
Tareganne, Taregann

Tareva-chine(shanay) (Native American) One with beautiful eyes

Tarian (Welsh) One acting as a shield; offering refuge
Tariane, Tarianne, Taryan, Taryanne

Tariana (American) From the holy hillside
Tariana, Tarianna, Taryana, Taryanna

Tarika (Indian) A starlet
Tarikah, Taryka, Tarykah, Taricka, Tarickah

Tarin (Irish) From the high, rocky hill
Tarine, Taryn, Tarynn, Tarryn, Taren, Tarene, Tareen, Tarrin, Tarren, Tarron, Tarryne, Taryne, Tarina, Tareena, Taryna, Tarrina, Tarrena, Tarryna

Tarisai (African) One to behold; to look at
Tarysai

Tarpeia (Latin) In mythology, a woman killed for an act of treason
Tarpeiah, Tarpia, Tarpya, Tarpiea

Tarub (Arabic) One who is merry; bringer of happiness
Tarube, Taroob, Tarrub, Taruh, Taroub, Taroube

Tasanee (Thai) A beautiful view
Tasane, Tasani, Tasanie, Tasany, Tasaney, Tasanye, Tasanea

Taskin (Arabic) One who provides peace; satisfaction
Taskine, Taskeen, Taskeene, Taskyne, Takseen, Taksin, Taksyn

Taslim (Arabic) One who offers salutation and submission
Taslime, Tasleem, Tasleeme, Taslyme, Taslym

Tasmine (American) A twin
Tasmin, Tazmine, Tasmeen, Tasmyne,
Tasmynne, Tasmeene, Tazmeen, Tazmyne,
Tasmina, Tazmina, Tasmyna, Tazmyna

Tasnim (Arabic) From the fountain of
paradise
Tasnime, Tasneem, Tasneeme, Tasnyme,
Tasnym, Tasneam, Tasneame

Tasya (Slavic) Form of Anastasia, meaning
"one who shall rise again"
Tasia, Tasyah, Tazia, Tazya, Tasiya,
Taziya

Tatiana (Slavic) Queen of the fairies
Tatianah, Tatianna, Tatyana, Tatyanna,
Tiahna, Tiane, Tianna, Tiauna

Tatum (English) Bringer of joy; spirited
Tatom, Tatim, Tatem, Tatam, Tatym

Taura (English) Feminine form of Taurus;
an astrological sign; the bull
Taurah, Tauras, Taurae, Tauria, Taurina,
Taurinia, Taurya, Tauryna

Tava (Swedish) Form of Gustava, meaning
"from the staff of the gods"
Tavah, Tave, Taveh

Tavi (Aramaic) One who is well-behaved
Tavie, Tavee, Tavy, Tavey, Tavea

Tavia (Latin) Form of Octavia, meaning
"the eighth-born child"
Taviah, Tavya, Tavea, Taveah, Tavita,
Tavitah, Taviya

Tawana (American) Form of Wanda,
meaning "a wanderer"
Tawanah, Tawanna, Taiwana, Tawanda

Taweret (Egyptian) In mythology, the god-
dess of pregnant women and childbirth
Tawerett, Tawerette, Tawerete, Tauret,
Taurett, Taurette, Taurete

Tawia (African) First child born after twins
Tawiah, Tawya, Tawyah, Tawiya,
Tawiyah, Tawea, Taweah

Tawny (Irish / English) From the green
field / light brown; a warm sandy color
Tawney, Tawni, Tawnie, Tawnee, Tawnia,
Tawnya, Tawniya, Tawnea

Tayanita (Native American) Resembling a
young beaver
Tayanitah, Tayanitia, Tayanyta,
Tayanytah, Tayaneeta, Tayanieta,
Tayaneita, Tayaneata

Tayce (French) Silence; peace
Taice, Tace, Taece, Taeyce, Taycia, Tayse,
Taise, Taese, Tase

Tayen (Native American) Born during the
new moon
Tayin, Tayon, Tayan, Tayene, Tayenne,
Tayine

Taylor ☉ (English) Cutter of cloth; one
who alters garments
Tailor, Taylore, Taylar, Tayler, Talour,
Taylre, Tailore, Tailar, Tailour, Taylour

Tayten (American) Beautiful happiness
Taytan, Tayton, Taytin, Taytene

Tazanna (Native American) A princess;
born into royalty
Tazannah, Tazana, Tazanah, Tazanne,
Tazane, Tazann

Tazara (African) A railway line
Tazarah, Tazarra, Tazarrah

Teagan (Gaelic) One who is attractive;
good-looking
Tegan, Tegau, Teegan, Teygan

Teal (American) Resembling a bright-
colored duck; a greenish-blue color
Teale, Teala, Teela, Tealia, Tealiya

Teamhair (Irish) In mythology, a place
where kings met
Teamhaire, Teamhare, Teamharre

Teca (Hungarian) Form of Theresa,
meaning "a harvester"

Tedra (Greek) A supreme gift
Tedrah, Tedre, Tedreh

Teenie (American) The small one
Tynie, Teynie, Teeny, Teeney, Teenee,
Teenye, Teeni, Teenea

Tefnut (Egyptian) In mythology, the goddess of water and fertility
Tefnutte, Tephnut, Tephnutte

Tehya (Native American) One who is precious
Tehyah, Tehiya, Tehiyah

Teige (American) A poet; one who is good-
looking

Teigra (Greek) Resembling a tiger
Teigre

T

Tekla (Greek) Glory of God
Teklah, Tekli, Teckla, Tecla, Thecla, Theckla, Thekla, Theclah, Theccla

Telephassa (Latin) In mythology, the queen of Tyre
Telephasa, Telefassa, Telefasa

Teleri (English) In Tolkien's works, those who came last; an elf clan
Telerie, Telery, Telerey, Teleree, Telleri, Telerea, Tellerie

Tellus (Latin) In mythology, the mother earth
Telus

Telyn (Welsh) Resembling a harp
Telynn, Telin, Telynne, Telinn, Telinne

Tema (Hebrew) One who is righteous; palm tree
Temah, Temma, Temmah

Temira (Hebrew) A tall woman
Temirah, Temeera, Temyra, Temiera, Temeira, Temeara

Temperance (English) Having self-restraint
Temperence, Temperince, Temperancia, Temperanse, Temperense, Temperinse

Tempest (French) One who is stormy; turbulent
Tempeste, Tempist, Tempiste, Tempesta, Tempress, Tempestt, Tempestta, Tempany, Tempani, Tempanie, Tempaney, Tempanee, Tempanea

Templa (Latin) Of the temple; sanctuary
Templah, Temple, Tempa, Tempy, Tempey, Tempi, Tempie, Tempee, Tempea

Tendai (African) Thankful to God
Tenday, Tendae, Tendaa, Tendaye

Tender (American) One who is sensitive; young and vulnerable
Tendere, Tendera, Tenderia, Tenderre, Tenderiya

Tenesea (American) Gathering place near water
Teneseah, Tenesia, Tennesea, Teness, Tenesse

Tenshi (Japanese) A messenger of God; an angel
Tenshie, Tenshy, Tenshey, Tenshee, Tenshea

Teranika (Gaelic) Victory of the earth
Teranikah, Teranieka, Teraneika, Teraneeka, Teranica, Teranicka, Teranicca, Teraneaka

Terehasa (African) The blessed one
Terehasah, Terehasia, Terehasea, Terehasiya, Terehasya

Terentia (Latin / Greek) One who is tender / a guardian
Terentiah

Terpsichore (Greek) In mythology, the muse of dancing and singing
Terpsichora, Terpsichoria, Terpsichoriya

Terra (Latin) From the earth; in mythology, an earth goddess
Terrah, Terah, Teralyn, Terran, Terena, Terenah, Terenna, Terrena, Terrenna, Terrene, Taran

Terrian (Greek) One who is innocent
Terriane, Terrianne, Terriana, Terianna, Terian, Terianne

Terrwyn (Welsh) A brave girl
Terrwyne, Terrwin, Terrwinne, Terwyn, Terwynne, Terrwynne, Terrwen, Terrwenn, Terrwenne

Tertia (Latin) The third-born child
Tertiah, Tertius, Tertullus, Terza, Terceira, Terceirah

Teryl (English) One who is vivacious and bright
Terryl, Teryll, Terylle, Terryll

Tesia (Polish) Loved by God
Tesiah, Tezia, Teziah

Tethys (Greek) In mythology, a sea goddess
Tethyss, Tethysse, Tethis, Tethiss, Tethisse

Tetsu (Japanese) A strong woman
Tetsue

Tetty (English) Form of Elizabeth, meaning "my God is bountiful"
Tettey, Tetti, Tettie, Tettee, Tettea

Teva (Hebrew / Scottish) Child of nature / a twin
Tevah, Tevva, Tevvah

Tevy (Cambodian) An angel
Tevey, Tevi, Tevie, Tevee, Tevea

Texas (Native American / English) A beloved friend / from the state of Texas
Texis, Texasia, Texus, Texa, Tex, Texcean, Texan, Texana, Texanna

Thaddea (Greek) Feminine form of Thaddeus; of the heart; courageous
Thaddeah, Thadea, Thaddia, Thadia, Thadina, Thadine, Thaddina, Thaddine, Thadyna, Thada, Thadda, Thadie, Thadya, Thadyne, Taddea, Thady

Thalassa (Greek) From the sea
Thalassah, Thalasa, Thalasse

Thalia (Greek) In mythology, the muse of comedy; joyful
Thaliah, Thaleia, Thalya, Thalie, Thali, Thaly, Thaley, Thalee, Thalea, Thaleigh

Thana (Arabic) One showing gratitude; thankfulness
Thanah, Thayna, Thaina, Thanna, Thane

Thandiwe (African) The loving one
Thandywe, Thandiewe, Thandeewe, Thandie, Thandi, Thandee, Thandy, Thandey

Thao (Vietnamese) One who is respectful of her parents

Thara (Arabic) One who is wealthy; prosperous
Tharah, Tharra, Tharrah, Tharwat

Theia (Greek) A goddess; in mythology, the mother of the sun, moon, and dawn
Thea, Thia, Thya

Thelma (Greek) One who is ambitious and willful
Thelmah, Telma, Thelmai, Thelmia, Thelmalina

Thelred (English) One who is well-advised
Thelrede, Thelread, Thelredia, Thelredina, Thelreid, Thelreed, Thelryd

Thelxepeia (Latin) In mythology, a siren
Thelxepia, Thelxiepeia

Thema (African) A queen
Themah, Theema, Thyma, Theyma, Theama

Themba (African) One who is trusted
Thembah, Thembia, Thembiya, Thembya

Themis (Greek) In mythology, the goddess of law and order
Themiss, Themisse, Themys, Themyss, Themysse

Thena (Greek) Form of Athena, meaning "wise"
Thina, Theena, Thyna, Theana

Thenoma (Greek) The name of God
Thenomah, Thenomia, Thenomea, Thenomiya, Thenomya

Theodora (Greek) Feminine form of Theodore; gift of God
Theodorah, Theodorra, Theadora, Teodora, Teodory, Teodozji, Theda, Thedya, Theodosia, Teddy, Teddey, Teddi, Teddie, Teddee, Teddea

Theola (Greek) One who is divine; godly
Theolah, Theona, Theone, Theolla, Theollah

Theophania (Greek) Manifestation of God
Theophaniah, Theophanie, Theophaneia, Theophane, Theofania, Theofaniya

Theophilia (Greek) Feminine form of Theophilus; loved by God
Theophiliah, Theophila, Theofilia, Theofiliya, Theofila

Theora (Greek) A watcher
Theorra, Theoria, Theoriya, Theorya

Theoris (Egyptian) One who is superior
Theoriss, Theorisse, Theorisa, Theorys, Theoryss, Theoyrsse, Theorysa

Thera (Greek) One who is untamed; wild
Thira, Therra

Theresa (Greek) A harvester
Teresa, Theresah, Theresia, Therese, Thera, Tresa, Tressa, Tressam, Treszka, Toireasa

Therona (Greek) Feminine form of Theron; huntress
Theronah, Theronia, Theroniya, Theronea, Theronya

Theta (Greek) Eighth letter of the Greek alphabet
Thetta

Thetis (Greek) In mythology, a sea nymph
Thetiss, Thetisse, Thetys, Thetyss, Thetysse

T

Thi (Vietnamese) One who inspires poetry

Thirza (Hebrew) A delightful lady
Thirsa, Therza, Thersa

Thisbe (Greek) In mythology, the lover of
Pyramus who committed suicide
*Thisby, Thisbey, Thisbi, Thisbie, Thisbee,
Thizbe, Thizbie, Thisbea, Thizbi, Thizby,
Thizbey, Thizbee, Thizbea*

Thistle (English) Resembling the prickly,
flowered plant
Thistel, Thissle, Thissel

Thomasina (Hebrew) Feminine form of
Thomas; a twin
*Thomasine, Thomsina, Thomasin,
Tomasina, Tomasine, Thomasa,
Thomaseena, Thomaseana, Thomaseina,
Thomasiena, Thomasyna, Tomaseena,
Tomaseana, Tomaseina, Tomasiena,
Tomasyna*

Thoosa (Greek) In mythology, a sea
nymph
*Thoosah, Thoosia, Thoosiah, Thusa,
Thusah, Thusia, Thusiah, Thousa,
Thousah, Thousia, Thousiah*

Thorberta (Norse) Brilliance of Thor
Thorbiartr, Thorbertha

Thorbjorg (Norse) Protected by Thor
Thorborg, Thorgerd

Thordia (Norse) Spirit of Thor
*Thordiah, Thordis, Tordis, Thordissa,
Tordissa, Thoridyss*

Thorgunna (Norse) Warrior for Thor
*Thorgunn, Thorgun, Thorgunnah,
Torgunna, Torgunn, Torguna*

Thorhilda (Norse) Thor's maiden
Thorhilde, Thorhildah, Thorhild, Torhilda

Thu (Vietnamese) Born in autumn

Thuong (Vietnamese) One who is loved
tenderly

Thurayya (Arabic) The seven stars in the
constellation Taurus
Thuraya, Thurayaa, Thurayyaa

Thuy (Vietnamese) One who is gentle and
pure
Thuye, Thuyy, Thuyye

Thwayya (Arabic) A starlet
Thwaya, Thwayaa, Thwayyaa

Thy (Vietnamese / Greek) A poet / one who
is untamed
Thye

Thyra (Greek) The shield-bearer
Thyrah, Thira, Thirah

Tia (Spanish / Greek) An aunt / daughter
born to royalty
*Tiah, Tea, Teah, Tiana, Teea, Tya, Teeya,
Tiia, Tiye, Tyah, Tyja, Tianda, Tiandria,
Tiante, Tialeigh, Tiamarie*

Tiara (Latin) One who is crowned
*Tiarah, Tiarea, Tiari, Tiaria, Tyara, Teearia,
Tiarra, Tiarie, Tiaree, Tiary, Tiarey*

Tiaret (African) Resembling a lioness
Tiarett, Tiarette, Tiarret

Tiassale (African) It is forgotten
Tiasale

Tibelda (German) The boldest one
*Tibeldah, Tybelda, Tibeldia, Tibeldina,
Tibelde, Tibeldie, Tibeldi, Tibeldy,
Tibeldey, Tibeldee, Tibeldea*

Tiberia (Italian) Of the Tiber river
*Tiberiah, Tiberiya, Tiberya, Tibeeria,
Tibearia, Tibieria, Tibeiria*

Tiegan (Aztec) A little princess in a big
valley
Tiegann, Tieganne

Tien (Vietnamese) A fairy child; a spirit
Tienne, Tienn

Tienette (Greek) Crowned with laurel in
victory
Tienett, Tienet, Tienete, Tieneta, Tienetta

Tierney (Gaelic) One who is regal; lordly
Tiernie, Tierni, Tiernee, Tierny, Tiernea

Tierra (Spanish) Of the earth
Tierrah, Tiera, Tierah

Tieve (Celtic) From the hillside

Tiffany (Greek) Form of Theophania,
meaning "manifestation of God"
*Tiffaney, Tiffani, Tiffanie, Tiffanee, Tifany,
Tifaney, Tifanee, Tifani, Tifanie, Tiffeny,
Tiffney, Tyfany, Tyffany, Tyfani, Tyfanni,
Tyffani, Tifanny, Tiffanny, Tiphany,
Tiphanie, Tiffanea, Tifanea*

Tiger (American) A powerful cat; resembling a tiger
Tigyr, Tyger, Tygyr

Tigerlily (English) An orange flower with black spots
Tigerlilly, Tigerlili, Tigerlilli, Tigerlilie, Tigerlillie, Tygerlily, Tiger Lily

Tigris (Persian) The fast one; tiger
Tigrisa, Tigrisia, Tigriss, Tigrisse, Tigrys, Tigryss, Tigrysse

Tikva (Hebrew) One who has hope
Tikvah, Tickva, Ticva

Tilda (German) Form of Matilda, meaning "one who is mighty in battle"
Tildah, Tilde, Tildea

Timber (English) From the wood
Timbar, Tymber, Tymbar

Timberly (American) A tall ruling woman
Timberley, Timberli, Timberlie, Timberlee, Timberleigh, Timberlea

Timothea (English) Feminine form of Timothy; honoring God
Timotheah, Timothia, Timothya, Timothiya

Tina (English) From the river; also shortened form of names ending in -tina
Tinah, Teena, Tena, Teyna, Tyna, Tinna, Teana

Ting (Chinese) Graceful and slim woman

Tiombe (African) One who is shy
Tiombey, Tiomby, Tiombi, Tiombie, Tiombee, Tiombea

Tiponi (Native American) A child of importance
Tiponni, Tipponi, Tiponie, Tipony, Tiponey, Tiponee, Tiponea

Tiponya (Native American) Resembling the great horned owl
Tiponiya, Tiponia

Tipper (Irish) One who pours water; a well
Tippar, Tippor, Tippur, Tippyr

Tira (Indian) Resembling an arrow

Tirza (Hebrew) One who is pleasant; a delight
Tirzah

Tisa (African) The ninth-born child
Tisah, Tiza

Tisha (English) Form of Letitia, meaning "one who brings joy to others"
Tishah, Tysha, Teisha, Tishia, Tyshia, Tishal, Tish, Tiesha

Tisiphone (Greek) In mythology, a Fury
Tisiphona, Tisiphonia, Tisiphonea, Tisiphonya, Tisiphoniya

Tita (Latin) Holding a title of honor
Titah, Teeta, Tyta, Teata

Titania (Latin / English) Of the giants / queen of the fairies
Titaniya, Titanea, Titaniah, Titaneah, Titaniyah, Titanya, Titanyah

Tiva (Native American) One who loves to dance
Tivah, Tivva, Tivvah

Tivona (Hebrew) Lover of nature
Tivonna, Tivone, Tivonia, Tivoniya

Toakase (Tonga) A woman of the sea
Toakasse, Toakasia, Toakasiya, Toakaseh

Toan (Vietnamese) Form of An-toan, meaning "safe and secure"
Toane, Toanne

Tobi (Hebrew) Feminine form of Tobias; God is good
Tobie, Toby, Tobey, Tobee, Toba, Tobit, Toibe, Tobea

Toinette (French) Form of Antoinette, meaning "priceless and highly praiseworthy; a flourishing flower"
Toinett, Toinete, Toinet, Toineta, Toinetta

Toki (Japanese / Korean) One who grasps opportunity; hopeful / resembling a rabbit
Tokie, Toky, Tokey, Tokye, Tokiko, Tokee, Tokea

Tola (Polish / Cambodian) Form of Toinette, meaning "priceless and highly praiseworthy; a flourishing flower" / born during October
Tolah, Tolla, Tollah

Tolinka (Native American) Having a coyote's hearing
Tolinkah, Tolynka, Tolinca, Tolincka, Toleenka, Toleanka

Tomiko (Japanese) Child of wealth
Tomyko

Tomoko (Japanese) One who is intelligent
Tomoyo

Toni (English) Form of Antoinette, meaning "priceless and highly praiseworthy; a flourishing flower"
Tonie, Tony, Toney, Tonee, Tonya, Tonia, Tonisha, Tonea, Tonny, Tonni, Tonnie, Tonnee, Tonney, Tonnea

Topanga (Native American) Where the mountain meets the sea
Topangah

Topaz (Latin) Resembling a yellow gemstone
Topazz, Topaza, Topazia, Topaziya, Topazya, Topazea

Topper (English) The most outstanding; excellent
Topsy, Toper, Topsi, Topsie, Topsee, Topsea, Topsey

Tora (Scandinavian) Feminine form of Thor; thunder
Thora, Thorah, Torah

Tordis (Norse) A goddess
Tordiss, Tordisse, Tordys, Tordyss, Tordysse

Toril (Scandinavian) Female warrior inspired by Thor
Torill, Torille, Torila, Torilla

Torny (Norse) New; just discovered
Torney, Tornie, Torni, Torne, Torn, Tornee, Tornea

Torra (Irish / Scottish) From the rocky top / from the castle

Torrin (Gaelic) From the craggy hills
Torin, Torrine, Torran, Toran, Torren, Toren, Torean, Torion, Torrian

Torunn (Norse) Thor's love
Torun, Torrun, Torrunn

Tory (American) Form of Victoria, meaning "victorious woman; winner; conqueror"
Torry, Torey, Tori, Torie, Torree, Tauri, Torye, Toya, Toyah, Torrey, Torri, Torrie, Toriana

Tosca (Latin) From the Tuscany region
Toscah, Toscka, Toska, Tosckah, Toskah

Tosha (English) Form of Natasha, meaning "born on Christmas Day"
Toshah, Toshiana, Tasha, Tashia, Tashi, Tassa

Toshi (Japanese) Mirror image
Toshie, Toshy, Toshey, Toshee, Toshea

Tosia (Latin) One who is inestimable
Tosiah, Tosya, Tosyah, Tosiya, Tozia, Tozea, Toziya

Totie (English) Form of Dorothy, meaning "a gift of God"
Toti, Tottie, Toty, Totey, Totee, Totea

Totsi (Native American) Wearing moccasins
Totsie, Totsy, Totsey, Totsee, Totsye, Totsea

Tourmaline (Singhalese) A stone of mixed colors
Tourmalyne, Tourmalina, Tourmalinia

Tova (Hebrew) One who is well-behaved
Tovah, Tove, Tovi, Toba, Toibe, Tovva

Toviel (Hebrew) God is good
Toviya, Tuviya, Tovielle, Toviell, Toviele, Toviela, Toviella

Tracey (Latin / English) A woman warrior / one who is brave
Tracy, Traci, Tracie, Tracee, Trace, Tracen, Tracea, Tracia, Traicey, Traicee, Traicy, Traisey, Traisee, Traisy, Tracie, Trasie, Traycie, Trayci, Traysie, Traysi, Tracilee, Tracilyn, Tracina, Tracell

Tranquilla (Spanish) One who is calm; tranquil
Tranquillah, Tranquila, Tranquille, Tranquile

Trapper (American) One who sets traps
Trappor, Trappur, Trappar, Trappir, Trappyr

Treasa (Irish) Having great strength
Treasah, Treesa, Treisa, Triesa, Treise, Treese, Toirease

Trella (Spanish) Form of Estelle, meaning "resembling a star"
Trellah, Trela, Trelah

Tress (English) A long lock of hair
Tresse, Trese, Tressa, Tressia, Tressiya, Tressya, Tressea

Treva (English / Celtic) From the homestead near the sea / one who is prudent
Trevah, Trevina, Trevva, Trevia, Treviya, Trevea, Trevya

Trilby (English / Italian) A soft felt hat / one who sings trills
Trillby, Trilbey, Trilbi, Trilbie, Trilbie, Trillare, Trillaire, Trilbee, Trilbea

Trina (Greek) Form of Catherina, meaning "one who is pure; virginal"
Trinah, Treena, Triena, Treina, Tryna, Triana, Trind, Trine, Trinh, Trinda, Treana

Trinetta (French) A little innocent
Trinettah, Trineta, Trinitta, Trenette, Trinette, Trinet, Trinete

Trinity ✪ (Latin) The holy three
Trinitey, Triniti, Trinitie, Trinitee, Trynity, Trynitey, Tryniti, Trynitie, Trynitee, Trinyty, Trinytey, Trinyti, Trinytie, Trinytee, Trynyty, Trini

Trisha (Latin) Form of Patricia, meaning "of noble descent"
Trishah, Trishia, Tricia, Trish, Trissa, Trisa

Trishna (Polish) In mythology, the goddess of the deceased, and protector of graves
Trishnah, Trishnia, Trishniah, Trishnea, Trishneah, Trishniya, Trishniyah, Trishnya, Trishnyah

Trisna (Indian) The one desired
Trisnah, Trisnia, Trisniah, Trisnea, Trisneah, Trisniya, Trisniyah, Trisnya, Trisnyah

Trissie (Latin) Form of Beatrice, meaning "one who blesses others"
Trissi, Trissy, Trissey, Trissee, Trissia, Trissiya, Trissea

Trista (English) Feminine form of Tristan; one who is sorrowful
Tristah, Trysta, Tristia, Trystia, Tristana, Triste, Tristen, Tristessa, Tristina, Tristyn, Tristyne

Triveni (Hindi) Confluence of three sacred rivers
Trivenie, Triveney, Triveny, Trivenee, Tryveni, Tryvenie, Tryveney, Tryveny, Tryvenee, Tryvyny, Tryvyni, Trivyny, Trivyni, Trivenea

Trivia (Latin) Of the three ways; in mythology, the goddess of the crossroads
Triviah, Trivya, Tryvia, Tryvya

Trixie (English) Form of Beatrice, meaning "one who blesses others"
Trixi, Trixy, Trixey, Trixee, Trixye, Trix, Tryx, Tryxie, Tryxy, Trixea, Tryxea

Trudy (German) Form of Gertrude, meaning "one who is strong with a spear"
Trudey, Trudi, Trudie, Trude, Trudye, Trudee, Truda, Trudia, Trudel, Trudchen, Trudessa, Trudea

Truly (English) One who is genuine; sincere
Truleigh, Truley, Truli, Trulie, Trulee, Trulea, Trula, Trulah

Trupti (Indian) State of being satisfied
Truptie, Trupty, Truptey, Truptee, Trupte, Truptea

Trusha (Indian) Having great thirst
Trushah, Trushya, Trushia, Trushiya, Trushea

Tryamon (English) In Arthurian legend, a fairy princess
Tryamonn, Tryamonne, Tryamona, Tryamonna

Tryna (Greek) The third-born child
Trynah

Tryne (Greek) An innocent woman

Tryphena (Greek) One who is dainty; delicate
Tryphenah, Trypheena, Typhiena, Tryphana, Tryphaena, Tryphyna, Tryfena, Tryfeena, Tryfenna, Trifena, Trifeena, Trifeyna, Trifiena, Trifyna, Tryfyna, Tryphaina, Trifine, Tryfeana, Trifeana

Tryphosa (Hebrew) Thrice shining; soft
Tryphosah, Tryphosia, Triphosa, Trifosa, Tryfosa

Tsifira (Hebrew) One who is crowned
Tsifirah, Tsifyra, Tsiphyra, Tsiphira, Tsipheera, Tsifeera

Tuccia (Latin) A vestal virgin

Tuesday (English) Born on Tuesday
Tuesdaye, Tewsday, Tuesdai, Tuesdae, Tewsdai, Tewsdaye, Tewsdae

Tugenda (German) One who is virtuous
Tugendah, Tugendia, Tugendiya, Tugendea, Tugendya

Tula (Hindi) Balance; a sign of the zodiac
Tulah, Tulla, Tullah

Tulasi (Indian) A sacred plant; basil plant
Tulasie, Tulasy, Tulasey, Tulasee, Tulsi,
Tulasea, Tulsie, Tulsy, Tulsey, Tulsee, Tulsea

Tullia (Irish) One who is peaceful
Tulliah, Tullea, Tulleah, Tullya, Tulia,
Tulea, Tuleah, Tulya, Tulliola, Tully,
Tullie, Tulley, Tullye, Tulliya

Tusti (Hindi) One who brings happiness
and peace
Tustie, Tusty, Tustey, Tustee, Tuste, Tustea

Tutilina (Latin) In mythology, the protec-
tor goddess of stored grain
Tutilinah, Tutileena, Tutileana, Tutilyna,
Tutileina, Tutiliena, Tutilena, Tutylina,
Tutylyna

Tuuli (Finnish) Of the wind
Tuulie, Tuulee, Tuula, Tuuly, Tuuley, Tuulea

Tuwa (Native American) Of the earth
Tuwah, Tuwia, Tuwiya, Tuwea, Tuwya,
Tuwiah, Tuwiyah, Tuweah, Tuwyah

Tuyen (Vietnamese) An angel
Tuyenn, Tuyenne, Tuyena, Tuyenna

Tuyet (Vietnamese) Snow-white woman
Tuyett, Tuyete, Tuyette, Tuyeta, Tuyetta

Tvishi (Hindi) A ray of bright light; energy
Tvishie, Tvishee, Tvishye, Tvishey, Tvishy,
Tvishea

Twyla (English) Woven with double thread
Twylah, Twila, Twilah, Twylla, Twilla

Tyler (English) Tiler of roofs

Tyme (English) The aromatic herb thyme
Time, Thyme, Thime

Tyne (English) Of the river
Tyna

Tyra (Scandinavian) Feminine form of Tyr,
the god of war and justice
Tyrah, Tyrra, Tyrrah

Tyro (Greek) In mythology, a woman who
bore twin sons to Poseidon

Tyronica (American) Goddess of battle
Tyronicah, Tyronyca, Tyronicka,
Tyronika, Tyronycka, Tyronyka

Tzefanya (Hebrew) Protected by God
Tzefanyah, Tzephanya, Tzefaniya, Tzephaniya

Tzidkiya (Hebrew) Righteousness of the
Lord
Tzidkiyah, Tzidkiyahu

Tzigane (Hungarian) A gypsy
Tzigan, Tzigain, Tzigaine, Tzigayne

Tzilla (Hebrew) A defender of her loved
ones
Tzillah, Tzila, Tzilah, Tzilia, Tzillia

Tzivia (Hebrew) Resembling a doe
Tziviah, Tzivea, Tziveah, Tziveea, Tziviya

Tziyona (Hebrew) Woman of Zion
Tziyonah, Tziyonna, Tziyone, Tziyyona,
Tziyyonah

Tzzipporah (Hebrew) Form of Zipporah,
meaning "a beauty; little bird"
Tzzippora, Tzipporah, Tzippora, Tzzipora,
Tzziporah, Tsipporah, Tsippora, Tsipora,
Tzippa, Tzippah

U (Korean) One who is gentle and
considerate

Uadjit (Egyptian) In mythology, a snake
goddess
Ujadet, Uajit, Udjit, Ujadit

Ualani (Hawaiian) Of the heavenly rain
Ualanie, Ualany, Ualaney, Ualanee,
Ualanea, Ualania, Ualana

Uald (Teutonic) A brave ruler
Ualda, Ualdah, Ualdia, Ualdaa, Ualdae,
Ualdai

Uberta (Italian) A bright woman
Ubertah, Ubertha, Ubert, Uberte, Uberthe

Uchechi (African) Of God's will
Uchechie, Uchechy, Uchechey, Uchechee,
Uchechea, Uchecheah

Uchenna (African) God's will
Uchennah, Uchena, Uchenah

Udavine (American) A thriving woman
Udavyne, Udavina, Udavyna, Udevine,
Udevyne, Udevina, Udevyna

Udele (English) One who is wealthy; prosperous
Udelle, Udela, Udella, Udelah, Udellah, Uda, Udah

Uela (American) One who is devoted to God
Uelah, Uella, Uellah

Uganda (African) From the country in Africa
Ugandah, Ugaunda, Ugaundah, Ugawnda, Ugawndah, Ugonda, Ugondah

Ugolina (German) Having a bright spirit; bright mind
Ugolinah, Ugoleena, Ugoliana, Ugolyna, Ugoline, Ugolyn, Ugolyne

Ujana (African) A young woman
Ujanah, Uyana, Uyanah, Ujanna

Ula (Irish) Jewel of the sea
Ulah, Ulaa, Ulai, Ulae

Ulalia (Greek) Form of Eulalia, meaning "well-spoken"
Ulaliah, Ulalya, Ulalyah

Ulan (African) Firstborn of twins
Ulann, Ulanne

Ulanda (American) One who is confident
Ulandah, Ulandia, Ulandiah, Ulandea, Ulandeah, Ulandiya, Ulandiyah

Ulani (Hawaiian) One who is cheerful
Ulanie, Ulany, Ulaney, Ulanee, Ulana, Ulanya, Ulania, Ulane

Ulda (American) One who can foretell the future
Uldah, Uldia, Uldiah, Uldea, Uldeah, Uldiya, Uldiyah

Uldwyna (English) A special and beloved friend
Uldwynah, Uldwina, Uldwaina, Uldweena

Ule (English) One who shoulders burdens
Ulle

Ulicia (Irish) Feminine form of Ulik; playful heart
Uliciah, Uliscia, Uleacia, Ulecea, Uleicia, Uleisia, Uleisya, Uleighcia, Uleighsya, Uleighsia, Ulicea, Ulicha, Ulichia, Ulician, Ulicija, Uliecia, Ullicea, Ulisha, Ulishia, Ulishya, Ulishaya, Ulishea, Uleesha

Ulielmi (Polynesian) An intelligent lady
Ulielmie, Ulielmee, Ulielmy, Ulielmey, Ulielmea, Uleilmeah

Ulima (Arabic) One who is wise and astute
Ulimah, Ullima, Ulimma, Uleema, Uleama, Ulyma, Uleima, Uliema

Ulla (German) A willful woman
Ullah, Ullaa, Ullai, Ullae

Ulphi (American) A lovely woman
Ulphie, Ulphy, Ulphey, Ulphee, Ulphea, Ulpheah, Ulphia, Ulphiah, Ulphiya, Ulphiyah

Ulrica (German) Feminine form of Ulric; wolf ruler; ruler of all
Ulricah, Ulrika, Ulrikah, Ulrique, Ulrike, Ulryca, Ulryka, Ulricka, Ulrycka, Ulryqua, Ullrica, Ullrika, Ullricka, Ulka, Uli, Ulie, Uly, Uley, Ulee, Uleigh, Ulli

Ultima (Latin) One who is aloof; endmost
Ultimah, Ultyma, Ultymah

Ulu (African) Second-born child
Ullu

Ululani (Hawaiian) Born of heavenly inspiration
Ululanie, Ululany, Ululaney, Ululanee, Ululanya, Ululania

Ulva (German) Resembling the wolf
Ulvah, Ulvia, Ulvya

Ulyssia (American) Feminine form of Ulysses; one who wanders; an angry woman
Ulyssiah, Ulyssea, Ulysseah, Ulissia, Ulissiah, Ulissea, Ulisseah, Ulissya, Ulyssya, Ulyssi, Ulissi, Ulyssie, Ulissie, Ulyssy, Ulissy, Ulyssey, Ulissey, Ulyssee, Ulissee

Uma (Hindi) Mother; in mythology, the goddess of beauty and sunlight
Umah, Umma

Umay (Turkish) One who is hopeful
Umaa, Umai, Umae

Umayma (Arabic) Little mother
Umaymah, Umaema, Umaima

Umberla (French) Feminine form of Umber; providing shade; of an earth color
Umberlah, Umberly, Umberley, Umberlee, Umberleigh, Umberli, Umberlea, Umberlie, Umberleah, Umberlina, Umberlyna, Umberleina, Umberliena, Umberleena, Umberleana

Umeko (Japanese) One who is patient; a plum-blossom child
Umeeko, Umeiko, Umeyo, Ume

Ummi (African) Born of my mother
Ummie, Ummy, Ummey, Ummee, Umi

Umnia (Arabic) One who is desired
Umniah, Umnea, Umneah, Umniya, Umniyah

Una (Irish / Latin / Native American) Form of Agnes, meaning "one who is pure; chaste" / unity; one / a fond memory
Unah, Unna, Unagh, Uny, Unnah

Undine (Latin) From the waves; in mythology, a female water spirit
Undene, Undeen, Undyn, Undyne, Undina, Undinah, Undyna, Undinia, Undynia, Undinya

Undra (American) A long-suffering woman
Undrah, Undria, Undriah, Undreah, Undrea, Undriya, Undriyah

Unelina (Latin) Woman who is bearlike
Unelinah, Uneleena, Unelena, Unelyna, Uneleana, Unelinia

Unice (Greek) Form of Eunice, meaning "one who conquers"
Unise, Unyce, Unyse

Unique (American) Unlike others; the only one
Unikue, Unik, Uniquia, Uniqia, Uniqua, Unikqua, Unika, Unicka, Unica

Unity (American) Woman who upholds oneness; togetherness
Unitey, Unitie, Uniti, Unitee, Unitea, Unyty, Unytey, Unytie, Unyti, Unytee, Unytea, Unite, Unita, Unyta

Unn (Norwegian) She is loved

Unni (Norse / Hebrew) One who is modest / a musician of the temple
Unnie, Unny, Unney, Unnee

Ura (Indian) Loved from the heart
Urah, Urra

Ural (Slavic) From the mountains
Urall, Urale, Uralle

Urania (Greek) From the heavens; in mythology, the muse of astronomy
Uraniah, Uraniya, Urainia, Urainiah, Uraina, Uranya, Uranie

Urbai (American) One who is gentle
Urbae, Urbay, Urbaye

Urbana (Latin) From the city; city dweller
Urbanah, Urbanna, Urbane, Urbania, Urbanya, Urbanne

Urbi (Egyptian) Born to royalty; a princess
Urbie, Urby, Urbey, Urbea, Urbeah, Urbee

Urenna (African) A father's pride
Urennah, Urena, Urenah, Urennia, Urennya, Urenya

Uri (Hebrew) My light; light of the Lord
Urie, Ury, Urey, Uree, Uria, Uriah

Uriana (Greek) From the unknown; heavenly
Urianah, Urianna, Uryana, Uryanna, Uriane, Uriann, Urianne, Uryan, Uryane, Uryann, Uryanne

Uriela (Hebrew) The angel of light
Uriella, Urielle, Uriel, Uriele, Uriell

Urika (Native American) One who is useful to all
Urikah, Urica, Uricka, Uryka, Uryca, Urycka, Uriqua, Uryqua, Uricca, Urycca

Urit (Hebrew) Emanating a bright light
Uryt, Urita, Uritah, Uryta, Urytah, Urice, Urith

Ursula (Greek) Resembling a little bear
Ursulla, Ursela, Ursella, Ursala, Ursalla, Ursola, Ursolla, Ursila, Ursilla, Urzula, Urzulla, Ursel, Ursule, Ursulina, Ursillane, Ursulyna, Ursylyn, Urzuli, Ursule, Ursanne, Ursa, Ursey, Ursy, Ursi, Ursie, Ursee, Ursea, Uschi

Urta (Latin) Resembling the spiny plant
Urtah

Urvasi (Hindi) In Hinduism, the most beautiful of the celestial maidens
Urvasie, Urvasy, Urvasey, Urvasee

Usagi (Japanese) Resembling a rabbit
Usagie, Usagy, Usagey, Usagee

Usha (Indian) Born at dawn; in mythology, the daughter of heaven, and the name of a demon princess
Ushah, Ushas, Ushai

Usher (Latin) From the mouth of the river
Ushar, Ushir, Ussher, Usshar, Usshir, Ushur, Usshur

Ushi (Chinese) Resembling an ox
Ushie, Ushy, Ushey, Ushee

Usoa (Basque) Woman who is dovelike
Usoah

Uta (German / Japanese) Fortunate maid
of battle / poem
Utako, Ute

Utah (Native American) People of the
mountains; from the state of Utah

Utas (Latin) A glorious woman

Utica (African) From the ancient city
*Uticah, Utika, Utikah, Uticka, Utickah,
Utyca, Utycah, Utyka, Utykah, Utycka,
Utyckah, Uttica, Uttika, Uttyca, Uttyka,
Utticka, Uttycka*

Utopia (American) From the ideally
perfect place
Utopiah, Utopea, Utopeah

Uttara (Indian) A royal daughter
*Uttarae, Uttarai, Uttaray, Utara, Utarae,
Utarai, Utaray*

Uttasta (Arabic) From the homeland
Uttastah, Utasta, Utastah

Uzbek (Turkish) From Uzbekistan
Uzbeck, Uzbec, Uzbeka, Uzbecka, Uzbeca

Uzetta (American) One who is serious
Uzeta, Uzett, Uzet, Uzette, Uzete

Uzma (Spanish) A capable woman
Uzmah, Usma, Usmah

Uzoma (African) One who takes the right
path
Uzomah, Uzomma, Uzommah

Uzuri (African) A known beauty
Uzurie, Uzury, Uzurey, Uzuree

Uzzi (Hebrew / Arabic) God is my strength
/ a strong woman
*Uzzie, Uzzy, Uzzey, Uzzee, Uzi, Uzie, Uzy,
Uzey, Uzee, Uzza, Uza, Uzzia, Uzia, Uzzya,
Uzya, Uzziye*

V

Vachya (Indian) One who is well-spoken
Vachyah, Vachia, Vach, Vac

Vacuna (Latin) A victorious woman
Vacunah, Vacunia, Vacunea

Vaetilda (Norse) Mother of the Skraeling
children
Vaetild, Vaetilde, Vaetildha, Vaetildhe

Vafara (French) One who is brave
*Vafarah, Vafarra, Vaphara, Vapharra,
Vafaria, Vafarya*

Vail (English) From the valley
Vaile, Vale, Vayl, Vayle, Valle

Vailea (Polynesian) From the talking
waters
*Vaileah, Vaileigh, Vailee, Vailey, Vaily,
Vailie, Vailei, Vaili, Vailya, Vaylea, Vayleah,
Vayleigh, Vaylee, Vayley, Vayly, Vaylie,
Vaylei, Vayli, Vaylya*

Vaisakhi (Indian) The beginning of spring

Vala (German) The chosen one; singled out
Valah, Valla

Valborga (Swedish / German) A powerful
mountain / protecting ruler
Valborgah, Valborg

Valda (Teutonic / German) Spirited in
battle / famous ruler
*Valdah, Valida, Velda, Vada, Vaida, Vayda,
Vaeda*

Valdis (Norse) In mythology, the goddess
of the dead
Valdiss, Valdys, Valdyss

Valeda (Latin) A brave and strong woman
*Valedah, Valida, Valeeda, Valyda, Valeida,
Valieda*

Valencia (Spanish) One who is powerful;
strong; from the city of Valencia
*Valenciah, Valyncia, Valencya, Valenzia,
Valancia, Valenica, Valanca, Valecia,
Valence*

V

Valene (Latin) Form of Valentina, meaning "one who is vigorous and healthy"
Valeen, Valeene, Valean, Valeane, Valine, Valien, Valyn, Valynn, Valain, Valaine, Valena, Valeena, Valeana, Valina, Valaina

Valentina (Latin) One who is vigorous and healthy
Valentinah, Valentine, Valenteena, Valenteana, Valentena, Valentyna, Valantina, Valentyne, Valentia, Valentya, Valtina, Valentijn, Valyn, Val, Valle

Valerie ☉ (Latin) Feminine form of Valerius; strong and valiant
*Valeri, Valeree, Valerey, Valery, Valarie, Valari, **Valeria**, Vallery, Valeraine, Valere, Valara, Valerye, Valera, Valaria, Valeriana, Veleria, Valaree, Vallerie, Valleri, Valka, Vairy, Valry, Vallirie, Valora, Valorie, Val, Valle*

Valeska (Slavic) A glorious ruler
Valeskah, Valezka, Valesca, Valeshka, Valisha, Valeshia, Valdislava

Valiant (English) One who is brave
Valiante, Valeant, Valeante

Valkyrie (Scandinavian) In mythology, the handmaidens who led slain heroes to Valhalla
Valkry, Valkri, Valkrie, Valkree, Valkrea, Valkreah, Valki, Valkie, Valkee, Valkea, Valkey, Valky, Valkeah, Valkrey

Valley (American) Between the mountains
Valey, Valy, Vali, Valie, Valee, Vally, Valli, Vallie, Vallee, Valeigh, Valleigh, Valei, Vallei

Valma (Finnish) A dedicated protector
Valmah

Valmai (Welsh) Resembling a spring flower
Valmae, Valmay

Valonia (Latin) From the valley
Valoniah, Vallonia, Vallonya, Valonya, Vallonea, Valonea, Valione, Valionia, Valona, Valyona, Valyonia, Valyonya, Vallon

Valterra (American) Of the strong earth
Valterrah, Valtera, Valteira

Vamia (Spanish) An energetic woman
Vamiah, Vamea, Vameah, Vamie, Vami, Vamee, Vamea, Vameah, Vamey, Vamy

Vanda (German) Form of Wanda, meaning "a wanderer"
Vandah, Vande, Vandana, Vandi, Vandetta, Vandella, Vannda, Vanditta

Vandani (Hindi) One who is honorable and worthy
Vandany, Vandaney, Vandanie, Vandanee, Vandania, Vandanya

Vanessa ☉ (Greek) Resembling a butterfly
Vanessah, Vanesa, Vannesa, Vannessa, Vanassa, Vanasa, Vanessia, Vanysa, Vanyssa, Varnessa, Vanessica, Vanesha, Vaniessa, Vanissa, Vanneza, Vaneza, Vannysa, Vanika, Vaneshia, Vanesia, Vanisa, Venessa

Vanetta (Greek) Form of Vanessa, meaning "resembling a butterfly"
Vanettah, Vaneta, Vanette, Vanete, Vanett, Vanita, Vanitta, Vanneta, Vannita, Venetta

Vangie (Greek) Form of Evangelina, meaning "a bringer of good news"
Vangi, Vangy, Vangey, Vangee

Vania (Russian) Form of Anna, meaning "a woman graced with God's favor"
Vaniah, Vanea, Vanya, Vannya, Vanna, Vanija, Vanja, Vaniya, Vanka, Vannia, Vanina, Vannea

Vanity (English) Having excessive pride
Vanitey, Vanitee, Vaniti, Vanitie, Vanitty, Vanyti, Vanyty, Vanytie

Vanmra (Russian) A stranger; from a foreign place
Vanmrah

Vanna (Cambodian) Golden-haired woman
Vannah, Vana, Vanae, Vannie, Vanny, Vannalee, Vannaleigh, Vanelly, Vanelley

Vanora (Scottish) From the white wave
Vanorah, Vannora, Vanorey, Vanory, Vanorie, Vanori, Vanoree, Vanorea, Vanoria, Vanorya

Vanthe (Greek) Form of Xanthe, meaning "yellow-haired woman; blonde"
Vanth, Vantha, Vanthia

Var (Scandinavian) In mythology, a goddess who punishes those who break promises
Varr, Varre

Vara (Greek) The stranger; one who is careful
Varah, Varia, Varra

Varana (Hindi) Of the river
Varanah, Varanna, Varanne, Varann

Varda (Hebrew) Resembling a rose
Vardah, Vardia, Vardina, Vardissa, Vardita, Vardysa, Vardyta, Vardit, Vardis, Vardisse, Vardice, Vardyce, Vardys, Vardyse, Vardina, Varyna, Vardinia, Vardin, Vardine, Vardyn, Vardyne, Vadit, Vared

Varina (Slavic / English) Yet to be discovered / thorn
Varinah, Varyna, Vareena

Varouna (Hindi) Infinite
Varounah

Varsha (Hindi) Of the rain
Varshah

Vartouhi (Armenian) As beautiful as a rose
Vartoughi, Vartoughie, Vartouhie

Varuna (Hindi) Wife of the sea
Varunah, Varuna, Varun, Varunani, Varuni

Varvara (Slavic) Form of Barbara, meaning "a traveler from a foreign land; a stranger"
Varvarah, Varenka, Varinka, Varyusha, Varushka, Vavka, Vava, Varya, Vavara, Vavarah

Vasanti (Hindi) Refers to the spring season
Vasantie, Vasanta, Vasantah, Vasant, Vasante

Vashti (Persian) A lovely woman
Vashtie, Vashty, Vashtey, Vashtee

Vasiliki (Greek) Feminine form of Basil; royalty
Vasilikie, Vasiliky, Vasilikey, Vasilikee, Vasilisa, Vasilisia, Vasilissa, Vassillissa

Vassy (Persian) A beautiful young woman
Vassey, Vassie, Vassi, Vassee, Vasy, Vasey, Vasie, Vasi, Vasee

Vasta (Persian) One who is pretty
Vastah

Vasteen (American) A capable woman
Vasteene, Vastiene, Vastien, Vastein, Vasteine, Vastean, Vasteane

Vasuda (Hindi) Of the earth
Vasudah, Vasudhara, Vasundhara, Vasudhra, Vasundhra

Vasumati (Hindi) Of unequaled splendor
Vasumatie, Vasumatey, Vasumaty, Vasumatee

Vatusia (African) She leaves us behind
Vatusiah, Vatutia, Vatushia, Vatuseah, Vatuzia, Vatusya, Vatuzya

Vaughn (English) The little beloved one
Vaughan, Vaun, Vawn, Vaunne

Vayu (Hindi) A vital life force; the air
Vayyu

Veata (Cambodian) Of the wind
Veatah

Veda (Sanskrit) Having sacred knowledge
Vedah, Veida, Vedad, Veleda

Vedas (Hindi) Eternal laws of Hinduism

Vedette (French) From the guard tower
Vedete, Vedett, Vedet, Vedetta, Vedeta

Vedi (Sanskrit) Filled with wisdom
Vedie, Vedy, Vedey, Vedee, Vedea, Vedeah

Vedis (German) Holy spirit of the forest
Vediss, Vedisse, Vedys, Vedyse, Vedyss, Vedysse, Vedissa, Vedyssa, Vidis, Vidisse, Vidys, Vidyss, Vidyse, Videssa

Vega (Latin) A falling star
Vegah

Velanie (American) Form of Melanie, meaning "a dark-skinned beauty"
Valaney, Valanie, Vel, Vela, Velaina, Velaine, Velainey, Velana, Velanee, Velaney, Velani, Velania, Velanney, Velannie, Velany, Vella, Vellanie, Velli, Vellie, Velloney, Velly, Veloni, Velonie, Velonnie, Velony, Velaena

Veleda (Teutonic) Of inspired wisdom
Veledah

Velika (Slavic) A wondrous woman
Velikah, Velyka, Velicka, Velicca, Velycka, Velycca

Velinda (American) Form of Melinda, meaning "one who is sweet and gentle"
Valynda, Velinde, Vellinda, Velynda, Valinda, Valinde

V

Vellamo (Finnish) In mythology, the goddess of the sea
Velamo, Vellammo

Velma (German) Form of Wilhelmina, meaning "determined protector"
Velmah, Vellma, Valma, Vilma, Vylma, Vylna

Velvet (English) Wearing a soft fabric; velvety
Velvete, Velvette, Velvett, Velvit, Velvyt, Velveta, Velvetta, Velouette

Venda (African) Of the Bantu people
Vendah, Vendaa, Vendae, Vendai

Venecia (Latin) Woman of Venice
Veneciah, Venicia, Vanecia, Vanetia, Venesha, Venisha, Veniesa, Venishia, Veneece, Venise, Veniece, Veneise, Venyce, Vonysia, Vonizia, Vonizya, Vonysya, Venetia, Venitia, Vinetia, Vinita, Venita, Venetya, Veneta, Venetta, Vynita, Vynyta, Vonitia, Vonita, Venezia, Veniza, Venice, Venke

Veneranda (Spanish) One who is honored
Venerandah, Veneradah, Venerada

Ventana (Spanish) As transparent as a window
Ventanah, Ventanna, Ventane, Ventanne

Ventura (Spanish) Having good fortune
Venturah, Venturra

Venus (Greek) In mythology, the goddess of love and beauty
Venis, Venys, Vynys, Venusa, Venusina, Venusia

Venya (Hindi) One who is lovable
Venyah, Venyaa

Vera (Latin / Slavic) The truth / one with faith
Verah, Veera, Verra, Viera, Vira, Veira, Vyra, Vere, Vara, Verla, Verka, Verasha, Vjera

Veradis (Latin) One who is genuine; truthful
Veradise, Veradys, Veradisa, Verdissa, Veradysa, Veradyssa, Veradisia, Veraditia

Verbena (Latin) Sacred limb; sacred plants
Verbenae, Verbane, Verbenia, Verbeen, Verbeene, Verbeena, Verbene, Verbina, Verbine, Verbyna, Verbyne, Verbyn, Verben, Verbin

Verda (Latin) Springlike; one who is young and fresh
Verdah, Verdea, Virida, Verdy, Verdey, Verde, Verdi, Verdie, Verdee

Verdad (Spanish) An honest woman
Verdada, Verdadah

Verena (German) Protector and defender
Verenah, Verina, Vereena, Veryna, Vereana, Vereene, Verine, Verene, Veryn, Veryne, Vereane, Verean, Verin, Varyn, Varyna, Varyne, Verinka, Verunka, Verusya, Veroshka, Virna

Verenase (Swedish) One who is flourishing
Verenese, Verennase, Vyrenase, Vyrennase, Vyrenese, Verenace, Vyrenace

Verity (Latin) One who is truthful
Veritey, Veriti, Veritie, Veritee, Veritea, Verita, Veryty, Veryti, Verytie, Verytey, Verytee, Verytea, Veryta, Verochka

Verlee (American) Form of Verity, meaning "one who is truthful"
Verley, Verly, Verli, Verlie, Verlee, Verleigh, Verlea, Verlia

Verlene (Latin) A vivacious woman
Verleen, Verleene, Verlean, Verleane, Verlein, Verleine, Verlyn, Verlyne, Verlena, Verleena, Verleana, Verleina, Verlyna

Verlita (Spanish) One who is growing
Verlitah, Verlida, Verlidah, Verlyta, Verlytah, Verlyda, Verlydah

Vermekia (American) A natural beauty
Vermekiah, Vermekea, Vermekeah, Vermy, Vermey, Vermee, Vermea, Vermeah, Vermi, Vermie

Vermont (French) From the green mountain; from the state of Vermont
Vermonte

Verna (Latin / English) Born in the springtime / feminine form of Vernon; alder tree
Vernah, Vyrna, Virna, Verne, Verla, Vernia, Verasha, Verneta, Vernette, Vernetta, Vernita, Virida, Virnell, Vernetia

Verona (Italian) Woman from Verona
Veronah, Veronaa, Veronae, Veronia

Veronica (Latin) Displaying her true image
*Veronicah, Veronic, Veronicca, Veronicka,
Veronika, Veronicha, Veronique, Veranique,
Veroniqua, Veronnica, Veronice, Varonica,
Varonika, Verhonica, Verinica, Verohnica,
Vironica, Vironiqua, Vironika, Vironique,
Veronka, Veronkia, Veronne, Vyronica,
Vronica, Vronika, Vroniqua, Vronique,
Vyroniqua, Vyronique, Vyronika, Veruka,
Veruszhka*

Vertrelle (American) One who is organized
Vertrell, Vertrel, Vertrele, Vertrela, Vertrella

Veruca (Latin) A type of wart
Verucah, Verucka, Verucia, Verutia, Verusia

Vesna (Slavic) Messenger; in mythology,
the goddess of spring
Vesnah, Vezna, Vesnia, Vesnaa

Vespera (Latin) Evening star; born in the
evening
Vesperah, Vespira, Vespeera, Vesperia, Vesper

Vesta (Latin) In mythology, goddess of the
hearth, home, and family
*Vestah, Vestee, Vestea, Vesty, Vestey, Vestie,
Vesti, Vessy, Vesteria, Vest*

Vetaria (Slavic) A regal woman
Vetariah, Vetarea, Vetareah

Vevay (Welsh) Of the white wave
Vevae, Vevai

Vevila (Gaelic) Woman with a
melodious voice
*Vevilah, Veveela, Vevyla, Vevilla, Vevylla,
Vevylle, Vevyle, Vevillia*

Vevina (Irish) A sweet lady; pleasant
*Vevinah, Vevyna, Veveena, Veveana,
Vevine, Vevyne, Veveene, Vevean*

Vian (English) One who is full of life;
vivacious
Veean, Vean, Veane, Vyan, Vyanne, Vyane

Vianca (American) Form of Bianca,
meaning "a shining, fair-skinned woman"
*Viancah, Vianka, Viancka, Vyanca,
Vyanka, Vyancka, Vianica, Vianeca,
Vyaneca, Vyanica*

Vibeke (Danish) A small woman
Vibekeh, Vibeek, Vibeeke, Vybeke, Viheke

Vibhuti (Hindi) Of the sacred ash;
a symbol
Vibuti, Vibhutie, Vibhutee

Victoria ☺ (Latin) Victorious woman;
winner; conqueror
*Victoriah, Victorea, Victoreah, Victorya,
Victorria, Victoriya, Vyctoria, Victorine,
Victoreana, Victoriana, Victorina,
Victoryna, Victoreena, Viktoria, Vicktoria,
Viktorina, Vyctoria, Vyktoria, Vyctorina,
Vyktorina, Vyctoryna, Vyktoryna,
Victoryn, Vyctorine, Vyctoryn, Vyktorine,
Vyktoryn, Vyktoryne, Vitoria, Vicki, Vickie,
Vicky, Vickey, Vikki, Vicka, Vika, Victriv,
Victriva*

Vida (Latin / Hebrew) Life / one who is
dearly loved
*Vidah, Veeda, Vieda, Vyda, Vidett, Vidette,
Videtta, Videte, Videta, Videlle, Vidella,
Videll, Videle, Videla*

Vidonia (Latin) Of the vine branch
*Vidoniah, Vidonya, Vydonia, Vydonya,
Vedonia*

Vidya (Indian) Having great wisdom
Vidyah

Vienna (Latin) From the wine country;
from Vienna
*Vienne, Vienette, Vienetta, Venia, Venna,
Vena, Vennia*

Viera (Spanish) A lively woman
*Vierah, Vierra, Vierrah, Vyera, Vyerah,
Vyerra, Vyerrah*

Viet (Vietnamese) A woman from Vietnam
Vyet, Viett, Vyett, Viette, Vyette

Vigdis (Scandinavian) A goddess of war
Vigdiss, Vigdisse, Vigdys, Vigdyss

Vigilia (Latin) Wakefulness; watchfulness
Vigiliah, Vygilia, Vygylia, Vijilia, Vyjilia

Vignette (French) From the little vine
*Vignete, Vignet, Vignetta, Vignett, Vigneta,
Vygnette, Vygnete, Vygnet, Vygnett,
Vygneta, Vygnetta*

Vika (Scottish) From the creek
Vikah, Veeka, Veecka, Vicka, Vicca

Vilhelmina (Swedish) Form of Wilhemina,
meaning "determined protector"
*Vilhelminah, Vylhelmina, Vylhelmyna,
Vilhelmine, Villemina, Vilhelmine, Vilhemine,
Vilhemina, Villamena, Villene, Villette, Villa,
Vimene, Vimine, Vilhelmeena, Villiamina,
Vilma, Vilmetta, Vilmanie, Vilmayra, Vylma,
Villiemae, Vilmet, Vilna*

V

Vilina (Hindi) One who is dedicated
Vilinah, Vileena, Vileana, Vylina, Vyleena,
Vyleana, Vylyna, Vilinia, Vilinya

Villetta (French) From the country estate
Villettah, Vileta, Villeta, Viletta, Vyleta,
Vylletta, Vylleta, Vyletta, Vileta

Villette (French) From the small village
Vilette, Villete, Vilete, Vilet, Vilett, Villet,
Villett, Vylet, Vylete, Vylett, Vylette, Vyllet,
Vyllete, Vyllette

Vilmaris (Greek) Protector from the sea
Vilmarise, Vilmarice, Vilmarisa, Vilmarissa,
Vilmarisia, Vilmariss, Vilmarys, Vilmaryss

Vimala (Indian) Feminine form of Vamal;
clean and pure
Vimalah, Vimalia, Vimalla

Vina (Spanish / Hindi) From the vineyard /
in mythology, the musical instrument of
the goddess of wisdom
Vinah, Veena, Vinna, Vyna, Vynna,
Vinesha, Vinisha, Vinita, Viniece, Vinora,
Vinique

Vinata (Hindi) In Hinduism, the daughter
of Daksha, wife of Kasyapa, and mother
of Garuda
Vinatah

Vinaya (Hindi) One with discipline; good
behavior
Vinayah

Vincentia (Latin) Feminine form of
Vincent; conquerer; triumphant
Vincentiah, Vincenta, Vincensia, Vincenzia,
Vyncentia, Vyncyntia, Vyncenzia,
Vycenzya, Vincenza, Vicenta, Vincensa,
Vincentina, Vincentena, Vicentah, Vicynta,
Viecinta, Vycenta, Viecynta, Visenta,
Visynta, Vysenta

Vincia (Spanish) One who is forthright
Vinciah, Vyncia, Vynciah, Vincea, Vinceah,
Vyncea, Vynceah

Vinia (Latin) Wine
Viniah, Vynia, Vynya

Viola (Italian) A stringed instrument; a
form of Violet, meaning "resembling the
purplish-blue flower"
Violah, Viole, Vyola, Violanie, Violani,
Violaney, Violany, Violaine, Violaina,
Violanta, Violante, Violeine, Vyoila,
Vyolani, Vyolanie, Vyolania, Vyolanya,
Violanth, Violanthe, Violantha

Violet (French) Resembling the purplish-
blue flower
Violett, Violette, Violete, Vyolet, Vyolett,
Vyolette, Vyolete, Violeta, Violetta,
Vyoleta, Vyoletta, Violatta

Virendra (Indian) One who is brave and
noble
Virendrah, Vyrendrah, Virindra, Virendria

Virgilia (Latin) A staff-bearer
Virgiliah, Virgillia, Virgilya, Virgilea,
Virgileah, Virjilia, Virjillia, Virjilya,
Virjilea, Virjileah, Vyrgilia, Vyrgylya,
Virgily, Virgiley, Virgilie, Virgili, Virgilee,
Virgileigh

Virginia (Latin) One who is chaste;
virginal; from the state of Virginia
Virginiah, Virginnia, Virgenya, Virgenia,
Virgeenia, Virgeena, Virgene, Virgena,
Virgine, Verginia, Verginya, Virjeana,
Virjinea, Virjinia, Vyrjinia, Vyrginia,
Vyrgynia, Vyrgynya, Virgenie

Virgo (Latin) The virgin; a constellation;
the sixth sign of the zodiac

Viridis (Latin) Youthful and blooming;
green; innocent
Viridiss, Viridys, Viridyss, Vyridis, Vyridys,
Vyrydys, Virdis, Viridissa, Viridia,
Viridianai, Viridiani, Viridiana

Virika (Hindi) One who is brave
Virikah, Viricka, Virica, Vyrika, Vyricka,
Vyrica, Vyryka, Viricca

Virtue (Latin) Having moral excellence,
chastity, and goodness
Virtu, Vyrtue, Vyrtu, Vertue, Vertu

Visola (African) Longings are as waterfalls
Visolah, Visolaa, Visolae, Visolai, Visolia,
Visolla

Vita (Latin) Feminine form of Vitus; life
Vitah, Vitta, Veeta, Veetta, Vyta, Vytta,
Vitia, Vitella, Vitka, Vitalina, Vitaliana

Viveka (German) Little woman of the
strong fortress
Vivekah, Vivecka, Vyveka, Viveca, Vyveca,
Vivecca, Vivika, Vivieka, Vivyka

Vivian (Latin) One who is full of life; vibrant
Viviane, Vivianne, Viviann, Vivien, Viviene, Vivienne, Vivienn, Vivyan, Vivyann, Vivyanne, Vyvian, Vyviann, Vyvianne, Vyviane, Vyvyan, Vyvyann, Vyvyanne, Vyvyane, Viviana, Vivianna, Vivyana, Vyvyana, Vivina, Vivia, Viveca, Vivion, Viva, Vivan, Vyva, Vive, Vyv, Viv, Vivi, Vevey, Vevay, Vivie, Vivee

Vixen (American) A flirtatious woman
Vixin, Vixi, Vixie, Vixee, Vixea, Vixeah, Vixy, Vixey

Vlasta (Slavic) A friendly and likeable woman
Vlastah, Vlastia, Vlastea, Vlastiah, Vlasteah

Volante (Italian) One who is veiled
Volanta, Volantia, Volantea

Voleta (Greek) The veiled one
Voletah, Voletta, Volita, Volitta, Volyta, Volytta, Volet, Volett, Volette, Volit, Volitt, Volitte, Volyt, Volytt, Volytte

Volupia (Latin) Sensual pleasure; in mythology, the goddess of pleasure
Volupiah, Volupeah, Volupya, Volupyah

Volva (Scandinavian) In mythology, a female shaman
Volvah, Volvya, Volvaa, Volvae, Volvai, Volvay, Volvia

Vonda (Russian) Form of Wanda, meaning "a wanderer"
Vondah, Vonde, Vondana, Vondi, Vondetta, Vondella, Vonnda, Vonditta, Vondia

Vondila (African) Woman who lost a child
Vondilah, Vondilla, Vondilya, Vondilia, Vondyla, Vondylya

Vondra (Slavic) A woman's love; a loving woman
Vondrah, Vondria, Vondrea, Vondreah, Vondrya

Voni (Slavic) An affectionate woman
Vonie, Vony, Voney, Vonee, Vonea, Voneah

Vonna (French) Form of Yvonne, meaning "a young archer"
Vonnah, Vona, Vonah, Vonnia, Vonnya, Vonia, Vonya, Vonny, Vonney, Vonnie, Vonni

Vonnala (American) A sweetheart
Vonnalah, Vonnalla, Vonnallah, Vonala, Vonalah, Vonalla, Vonallah

Vonshae (American) One who is confident
Vonshay, Vonshaye, Vonshai

Vor (Norse) In mythology, an omniscient goddess
Vore, Vorr, Vorre

Voshkie (Armenian) The golden one
Voshki, Voshkey, Voshky, Voshkee, Voshckie, Voshcki, Voshckey, Voshcky, Voshcky, Voshckee

Voyage (American) One who enjoys travel

Vui (Vietnamese) One who is cheerful

Vulpine (English) A cunning woman; like a fox
Vulpyne, Vulpina, Vulpyna

Vyomini (Indian) A gift of the divine
Vyominie, Vyominy, Vyominey, Vyominee, Vyomyni, Vyomyny, Viomini, Viomyni, Viomyny, Vyomine

Wade (English) To cross the river ford
Wayde, Waid, Waide, Waddell, Wadell, Waydell, Waidell, Waed, Waede

Wafa (Arabic) One who is faithful; devoted
Wafah, Wafaa, Waffa, Wapha, Waffah, Waphah

Wafiqah (Arabic) A successful woman
Wafiqa, Wafiqaa, Wafeeqah, Wafeeqa, Wafyqa, Wafyqah, Wafieqa, Wafieqah, Wafeiqa, Wafeiqah

Wagaye (African) My sense of value; my price
Wagay, Wagai, Wagae

Wahibah (Arabic) The generous one; a giver
Wahiba, Waheeba, Wahyba, Waheebah, Wahybah, Wahieba, Wahiebah, Waheiba, Waheibah, Waheaba, Waheabah, Wabibah, Wabibah, Wabyba, Wabybah, Wabeeba, Wabeebah, Wabeiba, Wabeibah, Wabieba, Wabiebah, Wabeaba, Wabeabah

Wahidah (Arabic) Feminine form of Wahid; unique; one and only
Wahida, Waheeda, Wahyda, Waheedah, Waydah, Wahieda, Wahiedah, Waheida, Waheidah, Waheada, Waheadah

Wahifah (Arabic) Lady-in-waiting; servant
Wahifa, Waheefa, Wahyfa, Waheefah, Wahyfah, Waheifa, Waheifah, Wahiefa, Wahiefah, Waheafa, Waheafah

Wainani (Hawaiian) Of the beautiful waters
Wainanie, Wainany, Wainaney, Wainanee, Wainanea, Wainaneah

Wajihah (Arabic) One who is distinguished; eminent
Wajiha, Wajeeha, Wajyha, Wajeehah, Wajyhah, Wajieha, Wajiehah, Wajeiha, Wajeihah, Wajeaha, Wajeahah

Wakana (Japanese) A thriving woman
Wakanah, Wakanna, Wakannah

Wakanda (Native American) One who possesses magical powers
Wakandah, Wakenda, Wakinda, Wakynda

Wakeen (American) A feisty woman
Wakeene, Wakien, Wakiene, Wakein, Wakein, Wakean, Wakeane

Wakeishah (American) Filled with happiness
Wakeisha, Wakieshah, Wakiesha, Wakesha, Wakeshah, Wakeesha, Wakeeshah, Wakysha, Wakyshah, Wakeasha, Wakeashah

Waki (Native American) A place of protection
Wakie, Waky, Wakey, Wakee, Wakeah, Wakea

Walburga (German) Ruler of the fortress; protection
Walburgah, Walburgha, Walborgd, Waldhurga, Walba, Walda, Welda

Walda (German) One who has fame and power
Waldah, Wallda, Walida, Waldine, Waldina, Waldyne, Waldyna, Welda, Wellda, Waldeana

Waleria (Polish) A sweet woman
Waleriah, Walerea, Walereah, Waleriya, Waleriyah

Walidah (Arabic) Newly born child
Walida, Walyda, Waleeda, Walada, Walad, Waleedah, Walydah, Waleida, Waleidah, Walieda, Waliedah, Waleada, Waleadah

Waliyya (Arabic) A holy lady; saint
Waliyyah, Waliya, Waliyah, Waliyyaa, Waliyaa

Walker (English) Walker of the forests
Wallker, Walkher

Wallis (English) Feminine form of Wallace; from Wales
Walis, Wallise, Walise, Wallys, Wallyse, Walliss, Walice, Wallisa, Wallysa, Waleis

Walta (African) One who acts as a shield
Waltah

Waltraud (Teutonic) Strong foreign ruler
Waltraude, Waltrawd, Waltrawde

Wambui (African) One who delivers a song; singer
Wamboi

Wan (Chinese) One who is gentle and gracious

Wanda (German) A wanderer
Wandah, Wannda, Wahnda, Wonda, Wonnda, Wohnda, Wande, Wandis, Wandy, Wandie, Wandey, Wandee, Wandely, Wandja, Wandzia, Wandea

Wandella (American) From the little tree
Wandellah, Wandela, Wandelah

Waneta (Native American) One who changes; a shapeshifter
Wanetah, Waneeta, Wanita, Wanneeta, Waneata, Waneita, Wanite, Wanete, Wanneta, Wannete, Waunita, Wonita, Wonyta, Wonnita, Wynita

Wanetta (English) A paleskinned woman
Wanettah, Wanette, Wannette, Wannetta, Wonetta, Wonette, Wonitta, Wonitte, Wonnyta, Wonnyte, Wann

Wangari (African) Resembling the leopard
Wangarie, Wangarri, Wangary, Wangarey, Wangaria, Wangaree

Wanyika (African) Of the bush
Wanyikka, Wanyicka, Wanyicca, Wanyica

Wapeka (Native American) One who is skillful; adroit
Wapekah

W

Waqi (Arabic) Falling; swooping
Waqqi

Warda (German / Arabic) A guardian / resembling a rose
Wardah, Wardia, Wardeh, Wardine, Wardena, Wardenia, Wordah

Warma (American) A caring woman
Warm, Warme, Warmia, Warmiah, Warmea, Warmeah

Warna (German) One who defends her loved ones
Warnah

Warner (German) Of the defending army
Werner, Wernher, Warnher, Worner, Wornher

Waseemah (Arabic) Feminine form of Waseem; beautiful
Waseema, Waseeme, Wasime, Waseme, Wasimah, Wasima, Wasyma

Washi (Japanese) Resembling an eagle
Washie, Washy, Washey, Washee, Washea, Washeah

Weeko (Native American) A beautiful girl
Weyko, Wieko, Weiko

Wehilani (Hawaiian) A heavenly adornment
Wehilanie, Wehilany, Wehilaney, Wehilanee, Wehilanea, Wehilaneah

Wei (Chinese) One who is valuable and brilliant

Welcome (English) A welcome guest
Welcom, Welcomme

Welsie (English) From the West
Welsy, Welsi, Welsey, Welsee, Welss, Welssa, Welsia, Welsea, Welseah

Wende (Teutonic) A wanderer
Wendelin, Wendelina, Wendeline, Wendelle, Wendalla, Wendalle, Wendalina, Wendaline, Wendall, Wendella, Wendelly

Wendy (Welsh) Form of Gwendolyn, meaning "one who is fair; of the white ring"
Wendi, Wendie, Wendee, Wendey, Wenda, Wendia, Wendea, Wendya, Wendye, Wendaine, Wendayne, Wuendy

---

Wattan (Japanese) From the homeland
Watan, Wattane

Wauna (Native American) A snow goose singing
Waunah, Waunakee

Wava (Slavic) Form of Barbara, meaning "a traveler from a foreign land; a stranger"
Wavah, Wavya, Wavia

Waverly (English) Of the trembling aspen
Waverley, Waverlie, Waverli, Waverlee, Waverleigh, Waverlea, Waverleah

Waynette (English) One who makes wagons
Waynett, Waynet, Waynete, Wayneta, Waynetta

Wednesday (American) Born on a Wednesday
Wensday, Winsday, Windnesday, Wednesdae, Wensdae, Winsdae, Windnesdae, Wednesdai, Wendsai, Winsdai, Wednesdaie

Weronikia (Polish) Form of Veronica, meaning "displaying her true image"
Weronicka, Weronykia, Weronikya, Weronika, Weronikka, Weronyka, Weronica, Weronicia

Wesley (English) From the western meadow
Wesly, Weslie, Wesli, Weslee, Weslia, Wesleigh, Weslea, Weslei, Weslene, Wesla, Weslya, Weslyn, Wesleah

Whisper (English) One who is soft-spoken
Whysper, Wisper, Wysper

Whitley (English) From the white meadow
Whitly, Whitlie, Whitli, Whitlee, Whitleigh, Whitlea, Whitlia, Whitlya, Whytley, Whytlie, Whytlea, Whytlee, Whytli, Whytly, Whytlya, Whitlei, Whittley, Whitlei

Whitney (English) From the white island
Whitny, Whitnie, Whitni, Whitnee, Whittney, Whitneigh, Whytny, Whytney, Whytnie, Whytni, Whytnee, Whytne, Witney, Whitne, Whiteney, Whitnei, Whitteny, Whitnye

W

Whitson (English) A white-haired lady
Whitsone, Whitsonne, Whytson, Whytsone, Whytsonne, Whitsona, Whytsona

Whoopi (English) One who is excited and happy
Whoopey, Whoopy, Whoopie, Whoopee, Whoopea, Whoopeah

Whynesha (American) A kindhearted woman
Whyneisha, Whyniesha, Whyneasha, Whynysha, Wynesha, Wyneisha, Wyniesha, Wyneasha, Whyneesha, Wyneesha, Whynesa, Whynessa, Wynesa, Wynessa

Wibeke (Scandinavian) A vibrant woman

Wicapi Wakan (Native American) A holy star

Widad (Arabic) One offering love and friendship
Widadd, Wydad, Wydadd

Wido (German) A warrior maiden
Wydo

Wijdan (Arabic) A sentiment
Widjan

Wijida (Arabic) An excited seeker
Wijidah, Weejida, Weejidah, Wijeeda, Wijeedah, Wijyda, Wijydah, Wijieda, Wijiedah, Wijeida, Wijeidah, Wijeada, Wijeadah

Wiktoria (Polish) Form of Victoria, meaning "victorious woman; winner; conqueror"
Wiktoriah, Wicktoria, Wyktoria, Wycktoria, Wikitoria, Wiktorja, Wicktorja, Wyktorja, Wycktorja, Wikta

Wilda (German) One who is untamed; wild; forest dweller
Wildah, Wylda, Willda, Wilde, Wylde, Whilda

Wileen (Teutonic) A firm defender
Wiline, Wilean, Wileane, Wilyn, Wileene, Wilene, Wyleen, Wyline, Wylean, Wyleane, Wylyn, Wylyne, Wyleen, Wyleene, Wylene, Wileena

Wiley (English) Of the willows
Wily, Wilie, Wili, Wilee, Wileigh, Wilea, Wileah

Wilfreda (English) Feminine form of Wilfred; determined peacemaker
Wilfredah, Wilfreeda, Wilfrida, Wilfreada, Wilfryda

Wilhelmina (German) Feminine form of Wilhelm; determined protector
Wilhelminah, Wylhelmina, Wylhelmyna, Wilhelmine, Willemina, Wilhelmine, Wilhemine, Wilhemina, Willamena, Willene, Willette, Willa, Wimene, Wimine, Vilhelmina, Williamina, Wilma, Wilmetta, Wilmanie, Wilmayra, Wylma, Williemae, Wilmet, Wilna, Wilmot

Willow (English) From the willow tree; symbol of healing and grace
Willo, Willough, Wyllow, Wylow, Wyllo

Wilona (English) One who is hoped for; desired
Wilonah, Willona, Wilone, Willone, Wylona, Wylone

Wilva (Teutonic) A determined woman; persistent
Wilvah, Wylva, Wylvah

Wind (American) Moving air; windy
Wynd, Windy, Windie, Windi, Windee, Windea, Windia, Wyndy, Wyndie, Wyndee, Wyndi, Wyndey, Wyndea, Wyndia

Winda (Swahili) A great huntress
Windah

Winema (Native American) A female chief
Winemah, Wynema, Wynemah

Winetta (American) One who is peaceful
Wineta, Wynetta, Wyneta, Winet, Winett, Winette, Wynet, Wynett, Wynette

Wing (Chinese) Woman of glory
Winge, Wyng

Winifred (German / Gaelic) Peaceful friend / fair; white-skinned
Winafred, Winifrid, Winefred, Winefrid, Winifride, Winifreda, Winfrieda, Winfreda, Winefride, Winifryd, Winnafred, Winifryda, Winnefred, Winnafred, Winniefred, Winnifrid, Wynifred, Wynafred, Wynifrid, Wynafrid, Wynefryd, Wynefred, Winnie, Wynnie

Winna (African) A beloved friend
Winnah, Wina, Wyna, Wynna, Winah, Wynah, Wynnah

Winnielle (African) A victorious woman
*Winniell, Winniele, Winniel, Winniella,
Winniela*

Winola (German) Gracious and charming
friend
*Winolah, Wynola, Winolla, Wynolla,
Wynolah, Winollah, Wynollah*

Winona (Native American) Firstborn
daughter
*Winonah, Wynona, Wanona, Wenona,
Wynonna, Winonna, Wynnona, Winnona*

Winsome (English) A kind and beautiful
lady
Wynsome, Winsom, Wynsom

Winta (African) One who is desired
*Wintah, Whinta, Wynta, Whynta, Whintah,
Wyntah, Whyntah*

Winter (English) Born during the winter
season
Wintr, Wynter, Winteria, Wynteria

Wira (Polish) Form of Elvira, meaning "a
truthful woman; one who can be trusted"
Wirah, Wyra, Wiria, Wirke

Wisal (Arabic) Communion in love
Wisalle, Wisall

Wisconsin (French) Gathering of waters;
from the state of Wisconsin
*Wisconsyn, Wisconsen, Wisconson,
Wysconsin, Wysconsen, Wysconson*

Wisia (Polish) Form of Victoria, meaning
"victorious woman; winner; conqueror"
*Wisiah, Wysia, Wysya, Wicia, Wikta,
Wiktoria, Wykta, Wyktoria*

Wistar (German) One who is respected
*Whistar, Wystar, Whystar, Wistarr, Wister,
Wystarr, Wyster*

Wisteria (English) Resembling the flowering
vine
*Whisteria, Wysteria, Whysteria, Wisterea,
Whisterea, Wysterea, Whysterea*

Woody (American) A woman of the forest
*Woodey, Woodi, Woodie, Woodee,
Woodea, Woodeah, Woods*

Wova (American) A brassy woman
Wovah, Whova, Whovah

Wren (English) Resembling a small songbird
*Wrenn, Wrene, Wrena, Wrenie, Wrenee,
Wreney, Wrenny, Wrenna*

Wub (African) One who is gorgeous
Wubb, Wubbe

Wyanet (Native American) A famously
beautiful woman
*Wyanete, Wyanette, Wyanett, Wyanetta,
Wyaneta, Wynette, Wianet, Wianette,
Wianete, Wianett, Wianetta, Wianeta*

Wyetta (French) A feisty woman
Wyett, Wyeta, Wyette, Wyete

Wylie (American) A clever and coy
woman
*Wyli, Wylee, Wylea, Wyleah, Wyly, Wyley,
Wiley, Wily, Wilee, Wileigh, Wilea, Wileah,
Wili, Wilie, Wyleigh*

Wyn (Welsh) Form of Guinevere, meaning
"one who is fair; of the white wave"
*Wynn, Wynne, Wyne, Wynnie, Wynie,
Wynee, Wyny, Wyney, Wynea, Wyneah*

Wynda (Scottish) From the narrow passage
Wyndah, Winda, Windah

Wynstelle (Latin) One who is chaste; pure
*Wynstell, Wynstele, Wynstella, Wynstela,
Winstelle, Winstell, Winstele, Winstel,
Wynstel, Winstella, Winstela*

Wyoming (Native American) Of the
mountains and valleys; from the state of
Wyoming
*Wyoma, Wyomin, Wyomine, Wyomia,
Wyomya, Wyome, Wyoh, Wyomie, Wyomi,
Wyomee, Wyomey, Wyomy, Wyomea,
Wyomeah*

Wyss (Welsh) One who is fair
Wysse, Whyss, Whysse, Wyse, Whyse

W

Xabrina (Latin) Form of Sabrina, meaning "a legendary princess"
Xabrinah, Xabreena, Xabryna, Xabriena, Xabreina

Xadrian (American) From the Adriatic
Xadrianne, Xadriane, Xadrien, Xadrienne, Xadriene, Xadrean, Xadreane

Xalvadora (Spanish) Form of Salvadora, meaning "savior"
Xalvadorah, Xalbadora, Xalbadorah, Xalvadoria, Xalbadoria

Xanadu (African) From the exotic paradise

Xandra (Greek) Form of Alexandra, meaning "helper and defender of mankind"
Xandrah, Xander, Xandria, Xandrea, Xandreia, Xandrya, Xandy, Xandie, Xandi, Xandey, Xandy, Xandee

Xannon (American) Ancient goddess
Xanon, Xannan, Xanan, Xannen, Xanen, Xannin, Xanin

Xantara (American) Protector of the Earth
Xantarah, Xanterra, Xantera, Xantarra, Xantarrah, Xanterah, Xanterrah

Xanthe (Greek) Yellow-haired woman; blonde
Xantha, Xanthia, Xana, Xanna, Xanne, Xanthippe, Xantippie

Xaquelina (Galician) Form of Jacqueline, meaning "the supplanter"
Xaqueline, Xaqueleena, Xaquelyna, Xaquelayna, Xaqueleana

Xara (Hebrew) Form of Sarah, meaning "princess; lady"
Xarah, Xarra, Xarya, Xarie, Xarri, Xarrie, Xarry, Xari, Xary, Xaria, Xarria

Xaviera (Basque / Arabic) Feminine form of Xavier; owner of a new house; one who is bright
Xaviere, Xavierra, Xavierre, Xavyera, Xavyere, Xiveria, Xavia, Xavaeir, Xaviar, Xaviara, Xavior, Xaviero, Xavian, Xavyer, Xavery, Xaver, Xavon, Xabier, Xzavier, Xxavier, Xizavier, Xevera, Xeveria

Xenia (Greek) One who is hospitable; welcoming
Xena, Xenea, Xenya, Xinia, Xeniah, Xeenia, Xenah, Xina, Xyna, Xene, Xeena, Xia

Xenobia (Greek) Form of Zenobia, meaning "sign or symbol"
Xenobiah, Xenobya, Xenobe, Xenobie, Xenobey, Xenovia, Xenobee, Xenoby, Xenobea, Xenobeah

Xerena (Latin) Form of Serena, meaning "sign or symbol"
Xerenah, Xerene, Xeren, Xereena, Xeryna, Xereene, Xerenna

Xetsa (African) A female twin
Xetsah, Xetse, Xetseh

Xexilia (American) Form of Celia, meaning "one who is blind"
Xexila, Xexilea, Xexileah, Xexilya

Xhosa (African) Leader of a nation
Xosa, Xhose, Xhosia, Xhosah, Xosah

Xiang (Chinese) Having a nice fragrance
Xyang, Xeang, Xhiang, Xhyang, Xheang

Xiao Hong (Chinese) Of the morning rainbow

Ximena (Spanish) Form of Simone, meaning "one who listens well"
Ximenah, Xymena, Ximono, Xymona

Xin Qian (Chinese) Happy and beautiful woman

Xinavane (African) A mother; to propagate
Xinavana, Xinavania, Xinavain, Xinavaine, Xinavaen, Xinavaene

Xing (Chinese) A star
Xhing

Xing Xing (Chinese) Twin stars
Xhing Xhing

Xiomara (Spanish / Teutonic) Famous in battle / from the glorious forest
Xiomarah, Xiomayra, Xiomaris, Xiomaria, Xiomarra, Xiomarrah

Xirena (Greek) Form of Sirena, meaning "a seductive and beautiful woman"
Xirenah, Xireena, Xirina, Xirene, Xyrena, Xyreena, Xyrina, Xyryna, Xyrine, Xyrene, Xyren

Xiu (Chinese) One who is elegant

Xiu Juan (Chinese) One who is elegant and graceful

Xiu Mei (Chinese) A beautiful plum

Xi-Wang (Chinese) One with hope

Xochiquetzal (Aztec) Resembling a flowery feather; in mythology, the goddess of love, flowers, and the earth

Xochitl (Native American) From the place of many flowers
Xochilt, Xochilth, Xochil, Xochiti

Xola (African) Stay in peace
Xolah, Xolia, Xolla, Xollah

Xolani (African) One who asks forgiveness
Xolanie, Xolaney, Xolany, Xolanee, Xolanea, Xolneah

Xuan (Vietnamese) Born in the spring
Xuana, Xuania, Xuanne, Xuane

Xue (Chinese) Woman of snow

Xue Fang (Chinese) Woman of fragrant snow

Xuxa (Portuguese) Form of Susanna, meaning "resembling a graceful white lily"
Xuxah, Xuxxa, Xuxia

Xyleena (Greek) One who lives in the forest
Xylina, Xyliana, Xylinia, Xylona, Xileana, Xileena, Xilina, Xilyna, Xyleana, Xylyna, Xilona, Xilonia, Xylonia, Xylonya, Xyleen, Xyleene, Xylin, Xyline, Xyleana, Xylyn, Xylyne, Xilean, Xileane, Xileen, Xileene, Xilin, Xiline, Xilyne, Xylean, Xilon, Xylone, Xilone, Xylon

Xylia (Greek) Form of Sylvia, meaning "a woodland dweller"
Xiliah, Xilya, Xilia

Xylophia (Greek) One who loves the forest
Xylophiah, Xylophila, Xilophia, Xilophila

Xyza (Gothic) Of the sea
Xyzah

Y

Ya akove (Hebrew) One who replaces another (can also be hyphenated: Ya-akove)

Yabel (Latin) One who is lovable
Yabell, Yabele, Yabelle, Yabela, Yabella

Yachi (Japanese) Eight thousand
Yachie, Yachee, Yachey, Yachy, Yachea, Yacheah

Yachne (Hebrew) One who is gracious and hospitable
Yachnee, Yachney, Yachnie, Yachni, Yachnea, Yachneah

Yacquelin (Spanish) Form of Jacquelin, meaning "the supplanter"
Yacalin, Yacalyn, Yacalynn, Yackalin, Yackalinne, Yackelyn, Yacketta, Yackette, Yacki, Yackie, Yacklin, Yacklyn, Yacklynne, Yackqueline, Yacky, Yaclin, Yaclyn, Yacolyn, Yacqi, Yacqlyn, Yacqualine, Yacqualyn, Yacquel, Yacquelean, Yacqueleen, Yacquelin, Yacquelina, Yacquella, Yacquelle, Yacquelyn, Yacquelyne, Yacquelynn, Yacquelynne, Yacquenetta, Yacquenette, Yacquetta, Yacquette, Yacqui, Yacquine, Yaculine, Yakleen, Yaklyn, Yaquelin, Yaqueline, Yaquelyn, Yaquelynn, Yaquith, Yaquenetta, Yaquetta

Yadira (Hebrew) A beloved friend
Yadirah, Yadyra, Yadirha, Yadeera, Yadeerah, Yadyrah, Yadeira, Yadeirah, Yadiera, Yadiera, Yadeara, Yadearah

Yadra (Spanish) Form of Madra, meaning "one who is motherly"
Yadre, Yadrah

Yael (Hebrew) Having the strength of God
Yaell, Yaelle, Yaella, Yaele, Yaela, Yaeli

Yaffa (Hebrew) A beautiful woman
Yaffah, Yaffit, Yafit, Yafeal

Yafiah (Arabic) Having a high standing
Yafia

Yair (Hebrew) God will teach
Yaire, Yayr, Yayre, Yaer, Yaere

Yaki (Japanese) A tenacious young woman
Yakie, Yaky, Yakey, Yakea, Yakeah, Yakee

Yakini (African) An honest woman
Yakinie, Yakiney, Yakiny, Yackini, Yackinie, Yackiney, Yackiny, Yakinee, Yakinea, Yakineah

Yakira (Hebrew) One who is precious; dear to the heart
Yakirah, Yakyra, Yakeera, Yakiera, Yakeira, Yahaira, Yahara, Yahira, Yahayra, Yajaira, Yajara, Yajira, Yajayra

Yakootah (Arabic) Resembling an emerald; precious stone
Yakoota, Yakuta, Yakutah

Yalena (Greek) Form of Helen, meaning "the shining light"
Yalenah, Yalina, Yaleena, Yalyna, Yalana, Yaleana, Yalane, Yaleene, Yaline, Yalyne, Yaleane, Yalenchka, Yalene, Yalens

Yaletha (American) Form of Oletha, meaning "one who is truthful"
Yalethia, Yalethea

Yalgonata (Polish) Form of Margaret, meaning "resembling a pearl / the child of light"
Yalgonatta

Yama (Japanese) From the mountain
Yamma, Yamah, Yammah

Yamha (Arabic) Resembling a dove
Yamhah

Yamileth (Spanish) A graceful young girl
Yamilethe, Yamyleth, Yamylethe

Yamilla (Arabic) A beautiful woman
Yamillah, Yamila, Yamilah, Yamylla, Yamyllah, Yamyla, Yamylah, Yamille, Yamill, Yamyl, Yamyll, Yamylle

Yamin (Hebrew) Right hand
Yamine, Yamyn, Yamyne, Yameen, Yameene, Yamein, Yameine, Yamien, Yamiene

Yaminah (Arabic) One who is right and proper
Yamina, Yameena, Yameenah, Yamyna, Yamini, Yemina, Yemini, Yesmina

Yamka (Native American) A budding flower; blossom
Yamkah, Yamcka, Yamckah

Yamuna (Indian) From the sacred Yamuna river
Yamunah, Yamoona, Yamoonah

Yana (Hebrew) He answers
Yanna, Yaan, Yanah, Yannah

Yanaba (Native American) One who is brave
Yanabah

Yanamai (Basque) Having bitter grace; refers to the Virgin Mary
Yanamaria, Yanamarie, Yanamay, Yanamaye, Yanamae

Yancy (Native American) A sassy woman; a Yankee
Yancey, Yanci, Yancie, Yancee, Yancea, Yanceah

Yanessa (American) Form of Vanessa, meaning "resembling a butterfly"
Yanessah, Yanesa, Yannesa, Yannessa, Yanassa, Yanasa, Yanessia, Yanysa, Yanyssa, Yarnessa, Yanessica, Yanesha, Yaniessa, Yanissa, Yanneza, Yaneza, Yannysa, Yanika, Yaneshia, Yanesia, Yanisa, Yenessa

Yang (Chinese) Of the sun

Yanisha (American) One with high hopes
Yanishah, Yaneesha, Yaneeshah, Yaniesha, Yanieshah, Yaneisha, Yaneishah, Yanysha, Yanyshah, Yaneasha, Yaneashah

Yanka (Slavic) God is good
Yancka, Yancca, Yankka

Yannis (Hebrew) A gift of God
Yanis, Yanys, Yannys, Yanni, Yani, Yanee, Yaney, Yanie, Yany, Yannee, Yanney, Yanny, Yannie

Yaqu' (Arabic) Resembling a hyacinth; a sapphire
Yaaqu', Yaaqoo'

Yara (Brazilian) In mythology, the goddess of the river; a mermaid
Yarah, Yarrah, Yarra

Yardenah (Hebrew) From the river Jordan
Yardena, Yardina, Yardeena, Yardyna, Yardenna, Yardennah

Yardley (English) From the fenced-in meadow
Yardly, Yardleigh, Yardli, Yardlie, Yardlee, Yardlea, Yarley, Yarly, Yeardly, Yeardley, Yeardleigh, Yeardlee, Yeardli, Yeardlie

Yareli (American) The Lord is my light
Yarelie, Yareley, Yarelee, Yarely, Yaresly, Yarelea, Yareleah

Yarina (Russian) Form of Irene, meaning "a peaceful woman"
Yarinah, Yaryna, Yarine, Yaryne, Yerina, Yerine, Yeryna, Yeryne

Yarkona (Hebrew) Having green eyes; innocent
Yarkonah, Yarkonna, Yarkonnah

Yarmilla (Slavic) A merchant; trader
Yarmillah, Yarmila, Yarmyla, Yarmylla, Yarmille, Yarmylle

Yaser (Arabic) One who is wealthy and prosperous
Yasera, Yaseria

Yashira (Japanese) Blessed with God's grace
Yashirah, Yasheera, Yashyra, Yashara, Yashiera, Yashierah, Yasheira, Yasheirah, Yasheara, Yashearah

Yashona (Hindi) A wealthy woman
Yashonah, Yashawna, Yashauna, Yaseana, Yashawnah, Yashaunah, Yaseanah

Yasirah (Arabic) One who is lenient
Yasira, Yaseera, Yasyra, Yasiera, Yaseira, Yaseerah, Yasyrah, Yasierah, Yaseirah

Yasmine (Persian) Resembling the jasmine flower
Yasmin, Yasmene, Yasmeen, Yasmeene, Yasmen, Yasemin, Yasemeen, Yasmyn, Yasmyne, Yasiman, Yassmen, Yasmia, Yasmenne, Yassmeen, Yasmina, Yasmeena, Yasmyna, Yesmina, Yasminda, Yashmine, Yasmain, Yasmaine, Yasma, Yaasmeen, Yaasmin, Yasmon, Yasmeni, Yasiman, Yasimine, Yazmin, Yazmine, Yazmeen, Yazmyn, Yazmyne, Yazmen, Yazmene, Yazmina, Yazmyna, Yazzmine, Yazzmyne, Yazzmeen, Yesmine, Yesmin, Yesmeen, Yesmean, Yesmyn, Yesmyne

Yasu (Japanese) One who is calm; tranquil
Yazoo, Yasuko, Yasuyo

Yatima (African) An orphan
Yatimah, Yateema, Yatyma, Yateemah, Yatymah, Yatiema, Yatiemah, Yateima, Yateimah

Yaura (American) One who is desired
Yara, Yaure, Yaur

Yauvani (Hindi) Full of youth
Yauvanie, Yauvaney, Yauvany, Yauvanee, Yauvanea, Yauvaneah

Yaxha (Spanish) Green-colored water; from the city of Yaxha
Yaxhah

Ydel (Hebrew) One who praises God
Ydele, Ydell, Ydelle

Yebenette (American) A small woman
Yebenett, Yebenet, Yebenete, Yebeneta, Yebenetta, Yebe, Yebey, Yeby, Yebee, Yebi, Yebie, Yebea, Yebeah

Yedda (English) Having a beautiful voice; a singer
Yeddah, Yeda, Yedah

Yedidah (Hebrew) A beloved friend
Yedida, Yedyda, Yedydah, Yedeeda, Yedeedah

Yehudit (Hebrew) Form of Judith, meaning "woman from Judea"
Yuta, Yuhudit

Yei (Japanese) A flourishing woman

Yeira (Hebrew) One who is illuminated
Yeirah, Yaira, Yeyra, Yairah, Yeyrah

Yejide (African) Image of her mother
Yejid

Yelena (Russian) Form of Helen, meaning "the shining light"
Yelenah, Yelina, Yeleena, Yelyna, Yelaina, Yelana, Yeleana, Yelenna, Yellayna, Yellena, Yilena, Yilina, Yileena, Yilyna, Yilaina, Yilana, Yileana, Yilenna, Yelane, Yelene, Yelenne, Yelain, Yeleane, Yelen, Yeline

Yelisabeta (Russian) Form of Elizabeth, meaning "my God is bountiful"
Yelizabeta, Yelizabeth, Yelizabeth, Yelisabet, Yelizabet

Yelizavetam (Hebrew) Form of Elizabeth, meaning "my God is bountiful"
Yelizaveta, Yelysaveta

Yemaya (African) An intelligent woman
Yemay, Yemaye, Yemai, Yemae, Yemye

Yen (Chinese) One who is desired
Yenie, Yeny, Yenny, Yeni

Yenene (Native American) A medicine man; wizard poisoning a person who is sleeping
Yenyne, Yenine, Yenena, Yenina, Yenyna

Yenge (African) A hardworking woman
Yenga, Yengeh, Yengah

Yggsdrasil (Norse) The tree that binds Earth, heaven, and hell

Ygraine (English) Form of Igraine, the mother of Arthur in Arthurian legend
Ygrane, Ygrayne, Ygrain, Ygrayn, Ygraen, Ygraene

Yi (Chinese) One who brings happiness

Yi Min (Chinese) An intelligent woman

Yi Ze (Chinese) Happy and shiny as a pearl

YOHANNA

An old priest wrote Joanne on my mother's birth certificate instead of the Dutch Johanna (pronounced with a Y), which was actually my mother's intended name. She always complained about not having an interesting name and being called Jo. I gave my daughter the Hebrew name Yohanna in honor of my mother. Everybody calls her Yo! —Rachelle, NY

Yepa (Native American) A winter princess; snow woman
Yepah, Yeppa, Yeppah

Yera (Basque) Having bitter grace; refers to the Virgin Mary
Yerah, Yerra, Yerrah

Yeriel (Hebrew) Founded by God
Yerial, Yeriele, Yerielle, Yerialle, Yeriale

Yesenia (Arabic) Resembling a flower
Yeseniah, Yesinia, Yesenya, Yecenia, Yasenya, Yesnia, Yessenia, Yessena, Yessenya, Yissenia

Yeshi (African) For a thousand
Yeshie, Yeshey, Yeshy, Yeshee, Yeshea, Yesheah

Yessica (Hebrew) Form of Jessica, meaning "the Lord sees all"
Yesica, Yessika, Yesika, Yesicka, Yessicka, Yesyka, Yesiko

Yestin (Welsh) One who is just
Yestine, Yestyn, Yestyne

Yetta (English) Form of Henrietta, meaning "ruler of the house"
Yettah, Yeta, Yette, Yitta, Yettie, Yetty

Yeva (Slavic) Form of Eve, meaning "giver of life; a lively woman"
Yevah, Yevunye, Yevon, Yetsye, Yevtsye

Yihana (African) One deserving congratulations
Yihanah, Yhana, Yihanna, Yihannah, Yhanah, Yhanna, Yhannah

Yin (Chinese) A silvery woman

Yinah (Spanish) A victorious woman
Yina, Yinna, Yinnah

Yitta (Hebrew) One who emanates light
Yittah, Yita, Yitah

Ylwa (Scandinavian) Resembling a she-wolf
Ylwha

Ynes (French) Form of Agnes, meaning "one who is pure; chaste"
Ynez, Ynesita

Yoana (Hebrew) Form of Joana, meaning "God is gracious"
Yoanah, Yoanna, Yoannah, Yohana, Yohanna, Yohanka

Yobachi (African) One who prays to God
Yobachie, Yobachey, Yobachee, Yobachea, Yobacheah, Yobachy

Yocheved (Hebrew) Of God's glory

Y

Yodelle (American) An old-fashioned woman
Yodell, Yodel, Yodele, Yodella, Yodela, Yodette, Yodete, Yodet, Yodetta, Yodeta, Yode, Yodey, Yody, Yodie, Yodi, Yodee, Yodea, Yodeah

Yoella (Hebrew) One who loves God
Yoellah, Yoelah, Yoela

Yogi (Hindi) One who practices yoga
Yogini, Yoginie, Yogie, Yogy, Yogey, Yogee, Yogea, Yogeah

Yohance (African) A gift from God
Yohanse

Yoki (Native American) Of the rain
Yokie, Yokee, Yoky, Yokey, Yokea, Yokeah

Yoko (Japanese) A positive child; good girl
Yo

Yolanda (Greek) Resembling the violet flower; modest
Yolande, Yoland, Yolana, Yolain, Yolaine, Yolane, Yolanna, Yorlanda, Yalanda, Yalando, Yalonda, Yolantha, Yolanthe, Yolette, Yulanda, Yulonda, Youlanda, Yolonda

Yolie (Greek) Resembling the violet flower
Yoli, Yolee, Yoley, Yoly, Yolea, Yoleah

Yomaris (Spanish) I am the sun
Yomariss, Yomarise, Yomarris

Yon (Korean) Resembling a lotus blossom

Yona (Hebrew) Feminine form of Jonah; dove
Yonah, Yonina, Yonita, Yonee, Yony, Yoney, Yonie, Yoni, Yoneena, Yonine, Yonyna, Yoneene, Yonati, Yonat, Yonit, Yonita, Yonyta

Yordana (Hebrew) Feminine form of Jordan; of the down-flowing river
Yordanah, Yordanna, Yordannah, Yordane, Yordain, Yordaine, Yordayn, Yordayne, Yordaen, Yordaene, Yordan

Yori (Japanese) One who is trustworthy; reliable
Yoriyo, Yoriko

York (English) From the yew settlement
Yorck, Yorc, Yorke, Yorki, Yorkie, Yorky, Yorkey, Yorkee, Yorkea, Yorkeah

Yoruba (African) Woman from Nigeria
Yorubah, Yorubba, Yorubbah

Yoseba (Hebrew) Form of Josephine, meaning "God will add"
Yosebah, Yosebe, Yosepha, Yosephina, Yosefa, Yosifa, Yosyfa, Yuseffa, Yosefina, Yosifina, Yosyfina, Yuseffina

Yoshe (Japanese) A beautiful girl

Yoshi (Japanese) One who is respectful and good
Yoshie, Yoshy, Yoshey, Yoshee, Yoshiyo, Yoshiko, Yoshino, Yoshea, Yosheah

Yovana (American) Form of Yvonne, meaning "a young archer"
Yovanah, Yovanna, Yovannah, Yovann, Yovane, Yovanne, Yoviana, Yovianna, Yovian, Yovianne, Yoviane, Yovhanna, Yovhannah, Yovhana, Yovhanah

Yovela (Hebrew) One who is full of joy; rejoicing
Yovelah, Yovella, Yovelle, Yovele

Ysabel (Spanish) Form of Isabel, meaning "my God is bountiful"
Ysabelle, Ysabela, Ysabele, Ysabell, Ysabella, Ysbel, Ysibel, Ysibela, Ysibele, Ysibell, Ysibelle, Ysibella, Ysobel, Ysobela, Ysobella, Ysobele, Ysobelle, Ysybel, Ysybelle, Ysybell, Ysybele, Ysybela, Ysybella

Ysane (English) A graceful woman
Ysanne, Ysann, Ysana, Ysanna, Ysanah, Ysannah

Ysbail (Welsh) A spoiled girl
Ysbale, Ysbayle, Ysbaile, Ysbayl, Ysbael, Ysbaele

Yseult (Celtic / German / English) One who is fair / ruler of ice / in Arthurian legend, an Irish princess who married the king of Cornwall
Yseulte, Ysolt, Ysolte, Ysold, Ysolde

Yu (Asian) Resembling jade

Yu Jie (Chinese) Resembling a pure, beautiful jade

Yue (Chinese) Of the moonlight

Yue Yan (Chinese) One who is happy and beautiful

Yuette (American) A capable woman
Yuett, Yuete, Yuet, Yueta, Yuetta

Yuki (Japanese) Woman of the snow
Yukie, Yuky, Yukey, Yukee, Yukiko, Yukiyo, Yukea, Yukeah

Yulan (Spanish) A splendid woman
Yulann

Yule (English) Daughter of Christmastime
Yulle

Yulia (Russian) Form of Julia, meaning "one who is youthful; daughter of the sky"
Yulie, Yula, Yulka, Yulya, Yulene, Yuleen, Yuleene, Yuleena, Yulena, Yulean, Yuleane, Yuleana, Yulenia, Yulilya, Yulenke, Yulenka, Yulinke, Yulinka, Yuliana, Yuliani

Yumi (Japanese) A beautiful bow
Yumie, Yumy, Yumey, Yumee, Yumiko, Yumiyo, Yumako, Yumea, Yumeah

Yumn (Arabic) One with good fortune and success

Yuna (African) A gorgeous woman
Yunah, Yunna, Yunnah

Yuri (Japanese) Resembling a lily
Yurie, Yury, Yurey, Yuree, Yuriko, Yuriyo, Yurea, Yureah

Yuriana (American) A graceful lily
Yurianna, Yuriane, Yurianne, Yuriann

Yusra (Arabic) One who is most prosperous
Yusraa, Yusriyah

Yuta (Hebrew / Japanese) One who is awarded praise / one who is superior
Yutah, Yoota, Yootah

Yvana (Slavic) Form of Ivana, meaning "God is gracious"
Yvanna, Yvanya, Yvannya, Yvan, Yvania, Yvannia, Yvanah, Yvannah

Yvonne (French) A young archer; possibly a combination of Anna and Eve, meaning "a woman graced with God's favor" and "a giver of life; a lively woman"
Yvonna, Yvone, Yvon, Yvonnie, Yvonny, Yvonnia, Yavonne, Yavonna, Yavonda, Yavanda, Yavanna, Yavanne, Yveline, Yvette, Yvett, Yvet, Yvetta, Yveta, Yevette, Yevett, Yevetta, Yavette

Zabel (Armenian) Form of Isabel, meaning "my God is bountiful"
Zabela, Zabelah, Zabella, Zabele, Zabelle, Zabele, Zabelia, Zabeliah, Zabelea, Zabeleah

Zabrina (American) Form of Sabrina, meaning "a legendary princess"
Zabreena, Zabrinah, Zabrinna, Zabryna, Zabryne, Zabrynya, Zabreana, Zabreane, Zabreenia, Zabrinia, Zabrinnia, Zabrynia, Zabrine

Zaccai (Hebrew) One who is pure and just
Zaccae, Zacae, Zacii, Zaccii, Zacai, Zackai, Zackae, Zakai, Zakae

Zachah (Hebrew) Form of Zacharie, meaning "God is remembered"
Zacha, Zachie, Zachi, Zachee, Zachea, Zacheah

Zacharie (Hebrew) God is remembered
Zacharee, Zacharey, Zacaree, Zaccaree, Zacari, Zaccari, Zecharie, Zecharee, Zecharey, Zacara, Zacceaus, Zacaria, Zachoia, Zackaria, Zakaria, Zakira, Zackeisha, Zackeria, Zacharea, Zachareah, Zakarea, Zakareah, Zacarea, Zacareah

Zada (Arabic) Fortunate one; lucky; prosperous
Zayda, Zaida, Zayeda, Zayedah, Zadda, Zaddah, Zadah, Zaeda, Zaedah

Zafara (Hebrew) One who sings
Zaphara, Zafarra, Zapharra, Zafarah, Zafarrah, Zapharah, Zapharrah

Zafirah (Arabic) She who is victorious; successful
Zafira, Zafyra, Zafyre, Zafire, Zafinah, Zafina, Zayfina, Zayfinah, Zafyna, Zafynah, Zafiera, Zafierah, Zafeira, Zafeirah, Zafiena, Zafienah, Zafeina, Zafeinah

Zagir (Armenian) Resembling a flower
Zagiri, Zagirie, Zagiree, Zagirea, Zagireah, Zagiry, Zagirey, Zagira, Zagirah

Zahar (Hebrew) Of the morning light; dawn
Zahir, Zahyr, Zaher

Zahavah (Hebrew) The golden one
Zahava, Zachava, Zahavya, Zechava, Zehavia, Zehava, Zehuva, Zehavit, Zehavi, Zehave, Zeheva

Zahia (Arabic) Feminine form of Zahi; brilliant and beautiful
Zahiah, Zaheea, Zaheeah

Zahida (Arabic) Feminine form of Zahid; one who is pious
Zaahida, Zahidah, Zaheeda, Zaheedah, Zaheida, Zaheidah, Zahieda, Zahiedah, Zahyda, Zahydah

Zahirah (Arabic) One who is shining, luminous; dazzling
Zahira, Zaheera, Zaheerah, Zahiera, Zahierah, Zaheira, Zaheirah, Zahyra, Zahyrah

Zahiya (Arabic) A brilliant woman; radiant
Zahiyah, Zehiya, Zehiyah, Zeheeya, Zaheeya, Zeheeyah, Zaheeyah, Zaheiya, Zaheiyah, Zahieya, Zahieyah

Zahra (Arabic / Swahili) White-skinned / flowerlike
Zahrah, Zahraa, Zahre, Zahreh, Zahara, Zaharra, Zahera, Zahira, Zahyra, Zeehera, Zahria, Zahirra, Zaherra

Zahvala (Serbo-Croatian) One who is grateful
Zahvalla, Zahvallah, Zahvalah, Zavala, Zavalah, Zavalla, Zavallah

Zaiba (Arabic) One who is beautiful and adorned
Zaibaa, Zaib, Zaibah, Zayba, Zaybah, Zaeba, Zaebah

Zaidee (Arabic) One who is rich; prosperous
Zaidie, Zaidi, Zaidey, Zaidy, Zaydee, Zaydie, Zaydi, Zaydey, Zaydy, Zaidea, Zaydea, Zayda, Zaedi, Zaedie, Zaedy, Zaedey, Zaedee, Zaedea, Zaedeah

Zaina (Arabic) A beautiful woman
Zainah, Zainna, Zeina, Zeinna, Zeinnah, Zainnah, Zinaida, Zinaidah, Zeinah, Zaynah, Zayna, Zaena, Zaenah

Zainab (Arabic) A fragrant flowering plant
Zaynab, Zaenab

Zainabu (Swahili) One who is known for her beauty
Zaynabu, Zaenabu

Zaira (Arabic / Irish) Resembling a rose / form of Sara, meaning "princess; lady"
Zairah, Zayra, Zayrah, Zaera, Zaerah

Zaire (African) A woman from Zaire; form of Zara, meaning "princess; lady / day's awakening; dawn"
Zair, Zaeire, Zaeir

Zaka (Swahili) One who is pure; chaste
Zaaka, Zacka, Zakka, Zacca, Zakah, Zackah, Zaccah

Zakelina (Russian) Form of Jacqueline, meaning "the supplanter"
Zakelinah, Zakelyna, Zakeleena, Zacelina, Zacelyna, Zackelina, Zackelyna, Zakeleana, Zakeline, Zakelyn, Zakelyne, Zaceline, Zacelyn, Zackelin, Zackelyn, Zakeleen, Zakelin

Zakia (Arabic / Swahili) One who is chaste; pure / an intelligent woman
Zakiah, Zakea, Zakeia, Zakiya, Zakiyah, Zakeya, Zakaya, Zakeyia, Zakiyyah, Zakiyya, Zakkiyya, Zakiyaa, Zakya, Zakeah

Zala (Slovene) One who is beautiful; from the river
Zalah, Zalla, Zallah

Zale (Greek) One who has the strength of the sea
Zail, Zaile, Zayle, Zayl, Zael, Zaele

Zalika (Swahili) Born into royalty; well-born
Zalikah, Zalyka, Zalik, Zulika, Zuleika, Zaliki, Zalike, Zaleeka, Zaleekah, Zaleika, Zaleikah, Zalieka, Zaliekah

Zalina (French) Form of Selene, meaning "of the moon"
Zalinah, Zaleana, Zaleena, Zalena, Zalyna, Zaleen, Zaleene, Zalene, Zaline, Zalyne, Zaleane, Zaleina, Zaleinah, Zaliena, Zalienah

Zalisha (Swahili) To enrich; one who cultivates the land
Zalishah, Zaleesha, Zaleeshah, Zalysha, Zalyshah, Zaleisha, Zaleishah, Zaliesha, Zalieshah, Zaleasha, Zaleashah

Zaltana (Native American) From the high mountain
Zalantah, Zaltanah, Zalanta, Zaltanna, Zaltannah

Zama (Latin) One from the town of Zama
Zamah, Zamma, Zammah

Zamara (Hebrew) A songstress
Zemarah, Zamarah, Zamarra, Zamarrah, Zemara, Zemarra, Zemarrah, Zema, Zamirra, Zamirrah, Zamirah, Zamira

Zambda (Hebrew) One who meditates
Zambdah

Zambee (African) Woman from Zambia
Zambe, Zambi, Zambie, Zamby, Zambey, Zambea, Zambeah

Zamella (Zulu) One who strives to succeed
Zamellah, Zamy, Zamie, Zami, Zamey, Zamee, Zamea, Zameah

Zamilla (Greek) Having the strength of the sea
Zamillah, Zamila, Zamilah, Zamylla, Zamyllah, Zamyla, Zamylah

Zamir (Hebrew) An intelligent ruler
Zamire, Zameer, Zameere, Zamyr, Zamyre

Zamora (Spanish) From the city of Zamora
Zamorah, Zamorrah, Zamorra

Zamurrad (Arabic) Resembling an emerald; a precious stone
Zamurad, Zamurrada, Zamurada

Zamzummim (Hebrew) Of the race of giants
Zamzumim, Zumim

Zan (Chinese) One who offers support and praise

Zana (Romanian / Hebrew) In mythology, the three Graces / form of Susanna, meaning "resembling a graceful white lily"
Zanna, Zanah, Zannah

Zandra (Greek) Form of Alexandra, meaning "helper and defender of mankind"
Zandrah, Zanndra, Zahndra, Zandria, Zandrea, Zandrya, Zandry, Zandrie, Zondra, Zondria, Zondrya, Zohndra, Zohndria, Zohndrya, Zandree, Zandreah

Zane (Scandinavian) One who is bold
Zain, Zaine, Zayn, Zayne, Zaen, Zaene

Zaneta (Hebrew) A gracious gift from God
Zanetah, Zanita, Zaneeta, Zanetta, Zanyta, Zanete, Zanett, Zanette, Zanitra

Zannika (Native American) One who is healthy
Zannicka, Zanika, Zanicka, Zannyka, Zanyka

Zanoah (Hebrew) One who is prone to forgetfulness
Zanoa

Zanta (Swahili) A beautiful young woman
Zantah

Zanthe (Greek) Form of Xanthe, meaning "yellow-haired woman; blonde"
Zantha, Zanthia, Zanth, Zanthiya, Zanthea, Zantheah

Zara (Hebrew / Arabic) Form of Sarah, meaning "princess; lady" / day's awakening; dawn
Zarah, Zarra, Zareh, Zari, Zarie, Zaree, Zarri, Zarrie, Zarry, Zary, Zaria, Zareya, Zarea, Zariya, Zarya, Zarria, Zayra, Zareah, Zarreah, Zarree

Zarahlinda (Hebrew) Of the beautiful dawn
Zaralinda, Zaralynda, Zarahlindah, Zaralyndah, Zarahlynda, Zarahlyndah, Zaralenda, Zarahlenda

Zaria (Russian / Slavic) Born at sunrise / in mythology, the goddess of beauty; the heavenly bride
Zarya, Zariah, Zaryah

Zariel (American) The lion princess
Zariell, Zariele, Zarielle, Zariela, Zariella

Zarifa (Arabic) One who is successful; moves with grace
Zarifah, Zaryfa, Zaryfah, Zareefa, Zareefah, Zariefa, Zariefah, Zareifa, Zareifah, Zareafa, Zareafah

Zarina (African) The golden one; made of gold
Zarinah, Zareena, Zareenah, Zarena, Zarinna, Zaryna, Zarynna, Zareana, Zareane, Zarene, Zareene, Zarinne, Zaryne, Zarienah, Zariena, Zareina, Zareinah

Zarita (Spanish) Form of Sarah, meaning "princess; lady"
Zaritah, Zareeta, Zaritta, Zaryta, Zareata, Zarite, Zareete, Zaryte, Zareate, Zarieta, Zarietah, Zareita, Zareitah

Zarmina (Arabic) A bright woman
Zarminah, Zarmeena, Zarmeenah, Zarmiena, Zarmienah, Zarmeinah, Zarmeina, Zarmyna, Zarmynah, Zarmeana, Zarmeanah

Zarna (Hindi) Resembling a spring of water
Zarnah, Zarnia, Zarniah

Zarola (Arabic) A great huntress
Zarolla, Zarolia, Zarolya, Zarolea, Zarolah, Zarollah, Zaroleah, Zaroliah, Zarolyah

Zarqa (Arabic) Having bluish-green eyes; from the city of Zarqa
Zarqaa

Zasha (Russian) Form of Sasha, meaning "helper and defender of mankind"
Zascha, Zashka, Zasho, Zashenka, Zosha, Zoscha, Zoshka

Zashawna (American) A spontaneous young woman
Zashawne, Zashauna, Zashaune, Zashane, Zashayne, Zashaine, Zashaene, Zaseana, Zaseane, Zashona, Zashone

Zauditu (African) She is the crown
Zawditu, Zewditu, Zaudytu, Zawdytu, Zewdytu

Zaviera (Spanish) Form of Xaviera, meaning "owner of a new house; one who is bright "
Zavierah, Zavira, Zavera, Zavyera, Zavirah, Zaverah, Zavyerah

Zavrina (English) Form of Sabrina, meaning "a legendary princess"
Zavrinah, Zavreena, Zavreenah, Zavriena, Zavrienah, Zavryna, Zavrynah, Zavreina, Zavreinah, Zavreana, Zavreanah

Zawadi (Swahili) A gift; a present
Zawati, Zawadia, Zawatia, Zawady, Zawaty, Zawadie, Zawadee, Zawadea, Zawadeah, Zawadey, Zawatie, Zawatey, Zawatee, Zawatea, Zawateah

Zaya (Tibetan) A victorious woman
Zayah

Zayit (Hebrew) From the olive tree
Zayita, Zayitah

Zaylee (English) A heavenly woman
Zayleigh, Zayli, Zaylie, Zaylea, Zayleah, Zayley, Zayly, Zalee, Zaleigh, Zalie, Zali, Zaley, Zaly, Zalea, Zaleah

Zaypana (Tibetan) A beautiful woman
Zaypanah, Zaypo, Zaypanna, Zaypannah

Zaza (Hebrew / Arabic) Belonging to all / one who is flowery
Zazah, Zazu, Zazza, Zazzah, Zazzu

Zazula (Polish) An outstanding woman
Zazulah, Zazulla, Zazullah

Zdenka (Slovene) Feminine form of Zdenek; from Sidon
Zdena, Zdenuska, Zdenicka, Zdenika, Zdenyka, Zdeninka, Zdenynka

Zdeslava (Czech) Glory of the moment
Zdevsa, Zdysa, Zdisa, Zdyska, Zdiska, Zdislava, Zdyslava

Zea (Latin) Of the wheat field; grain
Zeah, Zia, Ziah

Zeahire (Arabic) One who is distinguished; outstanding

Zeal (American) One with passion; enthusiastic devotion
Zeale, Zeel, Zeele, Zeyl, Zeyle, Ziel, Ziele

Zebba (Persian) A known beauty
Zebbah, Zebara, Zebarah, Zebarra, Zebarrah

Zebina (Greek) One who is gifted
Zebinah, Zebeena, Zebeenah, Zebeana, Zebeanah, Zebyna, Zebynah, Zebiena, Zebienah, Zebeina, Zebeinah

Zehara (Hebrew) Surrounded by light
Zeharah, Zeharra, Zeharrah

Zehave (Hebrew) A golden child
Zehava, Zehavi, Zehavit, Zehuva, Zehavie, Zehavee, Zehavea, Zehaveah, Zehavy, Zehavey

Zehira (Hebrew) One who is protected
Zehirah, Zeheera, Zehyra, Zehiera, Zeheerah, Zehyrah, Zehierah, Zeheira, Zeheirah, Zeheara, Zehearah

Z

Zeinab (Somali) One who is good and well-behaved

Zela (Greek) One who is blessed with happiness
Zelah

Zelda (German) Gray-haired battlemaiden
Zeldah, Zelde, Zellda

Zeleia (Greek) In mythology, a city that was home to Padarus
Zeleiah

Zelene (English) Of the sunshine
Zeline, Zeleen, Zeleene, Zelyn, Zelyne, Zelean, Zeleane, Zelen, Zelein, Zeleine

Zelfa (American) One who stays in control
Zelfah, Zelpha, Zelphah

Zelia (Greek / Spanish) Having great zeal / of the sunshine
Zeliah, Zelya, Zelie, Zele, Zelina, Zelinia

Zelinda (German) Shield of victory
Zelindah, Zelynda, Zalinda, Zalynda, Zelyndah, Zalindah, Zalyndah

Zella (German) One who resists
Zellah

Zelma (German) Form of Selma, meaning "having divine protection"
Zelmah, Zalma, Zalmah

Zemirah (Hebrew) A joyous melody
Zemira, Zemyra, Zimira, Zymira, Zymyra, Zemila, Zemilah, Zemeela, Zemyla, Zimyla, Zymyla

Zena (African) One having great fame
Zenah, Zina, Zeena, Zenna, Zana, Zeana, Zeina

Zenaida (Greek) White-winged dove; in mythology, a daughter of Zeus
Zenaidah, Zenayda, Zenaide, Zenayde, Zinaida, Zenina, Zenna, Zenaydah, Zenaeda, Zenaedah

Zenas (Greek) One who is generous

Zenda (Persian) A sacred woman
Zendah, Zinda, Zindah, Zynda, Zyndah

Zenechka (Russian) Form of Eugenia, meaning "a wellborn woman"

Zenevieva (Russian) Form of Genevieve, meaning "of the race of women; the white wave"
Zenavieve, Zeneve, Zeneveeve, Zenevie, Zenivee, Zenivieve, Zennie, Zenny, Zenovera, Zenoveva, Zenica, Zenna, Zenae, Zenaya, Zenowefa, Zinerva, Zinebra, Zinessa, Zinevra

Zenia (Greek) Form of Xenia, meaning "one who is hospitable; welcoming"
Zeniah, Zeenia, Zenya, Zennia, Zenea, Zeenya

Zenobia (Greek) Sign or symbol; in mythology, a child of Zeus
Zenobiah, Zenobya, Zenobe, Zenobie, Zenobey, Zenovia, Zenobee, Zenoby, Zenobea, Zenobeah

Zenochka (Russian) One who is born of Zeus

Zephyr (Greek) Of the West wind
Zephyra, Zephira, Zephria, Zephra, Zephyer, Zefiryn, Zefiryna, Zefyrin, Zefyrina, Zefyryn, Zefyryna, Zafirin, Zafirina, Zyphire, Zefuyn

Zeppelina (English) Born during a beautiful storm
Zepelina, Zeppeleana, Zepeleana, Zeppelyna, Zepelyna, Zeppeleina, Zepeleina, Zeppeliena, Zepeliena, Zeppeleena, Zepeleena

Zera (Hebrew) A sower of seeds
Zerah, Zeria, Zeriah, Zera'im, Zerra, Zerrah

Zeraldina (Polish) Form of Geraldina, meaning "one who rules with the spear"
Zeraldinah, Zeraldeena, Zeraldeenah, Zeraldiena, Zeraldienah, Zeraldeina, Zeraldeinah, Zeraldyna, Zeraldynah, Zeraldeana, Zeraldeanah

Zerdali (Turkish) Resembling the wild apricot
Zerdalie, Zerdaly, Zerdaley, Zerdalya, Zerdalia, Zerdalee, Zerdalea, Zerdalea

Zerelda (Teutonic) An armored battlemaiden
Zerelde, Zereld

Zerena (Turkish) The golden woman
Zerenah, Zereena, Zereenah, Zeriena, Zerienah, Zereina, Zereinah, Zeryna, Zerynah, Zereana, Zereanah

Zerlina (Latin) Of the beautiful dawn
Zerlinah, Zerleena, Zerlyna, Zerleen,
Zerline, Zerlyn, Zerlyne, Zerlean,
Zerleane, Zerleana, Zerlee, Zerla,
Zerlinda, Zaralinda

Zerrin (Turkish) A golden woman
Zerren, Zerran, Zerryn, Zerron

Zesiro (African) The firstborn of twins
Zesyro, Zeseero, Zesiero, Zeseiro, Zesearo

Zesta (American) One with energy and
gusto
Zestah, Zestie, Zestee, Zesti, Zesty, Zestey,
Zestea, Zesteah

Zeta (Greek) Born last; the sixth letter of
the Greek alphabet
Zetah

Zetta (Portuguese) Resembling the rose
Zettah

Zeuxippe (Greek) In mythology, the
daughter of the river Eridanos

Zhen (Chinese) One who is precious and
chaste
Zen, Zhena, Zenn, Zhenni

Zhenga (African) An African queen
Zhengah, Zenga, Zengah

Zhi (Chinese) A woman of high moral
character

Zhong (Chinese) An honorable woman

Zhuo (Chinese) Having great intelligence

Zi (Chinese) A flourishing young woman

Zia (Arabic) One who emanates light;
splendor
Ziah, Zea, Zeah, Zya, Zyah

Ziarre (American) Goddess of the sky
Ziarr, Zyarre, Zyarr

Ziazan (Armenian) Resembling a rainbow
Ziazann, Zyazan, Zyazann

Zigana (Hungarian) A Gypsy girl
Ziganah, Zygana, Zigane, Ziganna,
Zigannah, Zyganna, Zygannah, Zyganah

Zihna (Native American) One who spins
Zihnah, Zyhna, Zyhnah

Zilias (Hebrew) A shady woman; a shadow
Zilyas, Zylias, Zylyas

Zillah (Hebrew) The shadowed one
Zilla, Zila, Zyla, Zylla, Zilah, Zylah,
Zyllah

Zilpah (Hebrew) One who is frail but dig-
nified; in the Bible, a concubine of Jacob
Zilpa, Zylpa, Zilpha, Zylpha, Zylpah,
Zilphah, Zylphah

Zilya (Russian) Form of Theresa, meaning
"a harvester"
Zilyah, Zylya, Zylyah

Zimbab (African) Woman from Zimbabwe
Zymbab, Zimbob, Zymbob

Zimra (Hebrew) Song of praise
Zimrah, Zimria, Zemira, Zemora,
Zamora, Zamira, Zymria, Zamyra

Zimzi (Hebrew) My field, my vine
Zimzie, Zimzee, Zimzea, Zimzeah,
Zimzey, Zimzy

Zina (African / English) A secret spirit /
welcoming
Zinah, Zyna, Zynah, Zine, Zineh

Zinat (Arabic) A decoration; graceful beauty
Zeenat, Zynat, Zienat, Zeinat, Zeanat

Zinchita (Incan) One who is dearly loved
Zinchitah, Zinchyta, Zinchytah,
Zincheeta, Zincheetah, Zinchieta,
Zinchietah, Zincheita, Zincheitah,
Zincheata, Zincheatah

Zinerva (Celtic / Russian) One who is fair;
pale / one who is wise
Zinervah, Zynerva, Zynervah

Zinnia (Latin) A brilliant, showy, rayed
flower
Zinia, Zinna, Zinya, Zeenia, Zynia,
Zynya, Zinniah, Ziniah

Zintka Mani (Native American)
Resembling a bird that walks

Zintkala (Native American) Resembling a
bird
Zintkalah, Zintkalla, Zintkallah,
Zyntkala, Zyntkalah, Zyntkallah,
Zyntkalla

Zintkala Kinyan (Native American)
Resembling a flying bird
*Zintkalah Kinyan, Zintkalla Kinyan,
Zintkallah Kinyan, Zyntkala Kinyan,
Zyntkalah Kinyan, Zyntkallah Kinyan,
Zyntkalla Kinyan*

Zintkala Lowansa (Native American)
Resembling a songbird
*Zintkalah Lowansa, Zintkalla Lowansa,
Zintkallah Lowansa, Zyntkala Lowansa,
Zyntkalah Lowansa, Zyntkallah
Lowansa, Zyntkalla Lowansa*

Zintkato (Native American) Resembling a
bluebird

Zinyeza (African) One who is aware
Zinyezah, Zynyeza, Zynyezah

Ziona (Hebrew) One who symbolizes
goodness
Zionah, Zyona, Zyonah

Zipporah (Hebrew) A beauty; little bird;
in the Bible, the wife of Moses
*Zippora, Ziporah, Zipora, Zypora,
Zyppora, Ziproh, Zipporia*

Zira (African) The pathway
*Zirah, Zirra, Zirrah, Zyra, Zyrah, Zyrra,
Zyrrah*

Ziracuny (Native American) From the
water
*Ziracuni, Ziracunie, Ziracuney, Ziracunee,
Ziracunea, Ziracuneah, Zyracuny,
Zyracuni, Zyracuni, Zyracunee,
Zyracuney, Zyracunea, Zyracuneah*

Zisel (Hebrew) One who is sweet
*Zissel, Zisal, Zysel, Zysal, Zyssel, Zissal,
Zyssal*

Zita (Latin / Spanish) Patron of housewives
and servants / little rose
*Zitah, Zeeta, Zyta, Zeetah, Zytah, Zieta,
Zietah, Zeita, Zeitah, Zeata, Zeatah*

Zitomira (Slavic) To live famously
*Zitomirah, Zytomira, Zitomeera,
Zitomyra, Zytomyra, Zytomirah,
Zitomeerah, Zytomeera, Zytomeerah*

Ziva (Hebrew) One who is bright, radiant;
splendor
*Zivah, Zivia, Ziv, Zeeva, Zivi, Zyva,
Zivanka*

Ziwa (Swahili) Woman of the lake
Ziwah, Zywa, Zywah

Zizi (Hungarian) Dedicated to God
Zeezee, Zyzy, Ziezie, Zeazea, Zeyzey

Zizilia (Slavic) In mythology, the goddess
of love and sexuality
Zezilia, Zizila, Zezila, Zyzilia, Zyzila

Zlata (Slavic) Feminine form of Zlatan;
golden
Zlatta, Zlatah, Zlattah

Zlhna (Native American) To be spinning

Zoa (Greek) One who is full of life; vibrant

Zocha (Polish) Form of Sophie, meaning
"having great wisdom and foresight"
Zochah, Zosia, Zotia, Zosiah, Zotiah

Zoe ✪ ♀ (Greek) A life-giving woman; alive
*Zoë, Zoee, Zowey, Zowie, Zowe, Zoelie,
Zoeline, Zoelle, **Zoey**, Zoelie, Zoel, Zooey,
Zoie, Zoi, Zoye, Zoia, Zoya, Zoyara,
Zoyya, Zoy, Zoyenka, Zoyechka*

Zofia (Slavic) Form of Sophia, meaning
"having great wisdom and foresight"
*Zofiah, Zophia, Zophiah, Zophya, Zofie,
Zofee, Zofey, Zofi, Zofy, Zophee, Zophy,
Zophie, Zophi, Zophey*

Zohar (Hebrew) Emanating a brilliant
light; sparkle
*Zohara, Zohera, Zoheret, Zohra, Zoharra,
Zoharah, Zoharrah, Zoharr*

Zohreh (Persian) One who brings happiness
Zohrah, Zahrah, Zehrah

Zola (Italian / African) A piece of earth /
one who is quiet and tranquil
Zolah, Zoela, Zoila, Zolla, Zollah

Zona (Latin) A decorative sash; belt
Zonah, Zonia, Zonna, Zonnah

Zonta (Native American) An honest
woman

Zoom (American) An energetic woman
*Zoomi, Zoomie, Zoomy, Zoomey,
Zoomee, Zoomea, Zoomeah*

Zora (Slavic) Born at dawn; aurora
*Zorah, Zorna, Zorra, Zorya, Zorane,
Zory, Zorrah, Zorey, Zoree, Zorea,
Zoreah, Zori, Zorie*

Zoralle (Slavic) A heavenly and delicate
woman
Zorale, Zorall, Zoral

Zorana (Sanskrit) A woman of power
*Zordena, Zoranah, Zordenah, Zorrana,
Zorranna*

Zore (Slavic) Form of Zora, meaning
"born at dawn; aurora"
Zorka, Zorcka, Zorkah, Zorckah, Zorke

Zoria (Basque) One who is lucky
Zoriah

Zorina (Slavic) Golden-haired woman
*Zorinah, Zoryna, Zoreena, Zoreane,
Zoreana, Zorean, Zoree, Zoreen, Zoreene,
Zorie, Zori, Zorin, Zorine, Zoryne*

Zoriona (Basque) One who is happy

Zosa (Greek) A lively and energetic woman
Zosah

Zsa Zsa (Hungarian) Form of Susan,
meaning "resembling a graceful white lily"
*Zhazha, Zsuka, Zsuzsa, Zsuzsanna,
Zsuzsi, Zsuzsie, Zsuzsee*

Zsofia (Greek) Form of Sophia, meaning
"having great wisdom and foresight"
*Zsofie, Zsofi, Zsofiah, Zsophia, Zsophie,
Zsophi, Zsofika*

Zuba (English) One who is musically talented
Zubah, Zubba, Zubbah

Zubaida (Arabic) A laborer; a hardwork-
ing woman
*Zubaidah, Zubayda, Zubaydah, Zubaeda,
Zubaedah*

Zubeda (Swahili) The best one
Zubedah

Zudora (Arabic) A laborer; a hardworking
woman
Zudorah, Zudorra, Zudorrah

Zula (African) One who is brilliant; from
the town of Zula
*Zul, Zulay, Zulae, Zulai, Zulah, Zulla,
Zullah*

Zuleika (Arabic) One who is brilliant and
lovely; fair
*Zuleikah, Zulaykha, Zeleeka, Zulekha,
Zuleyka*

Zulema (Arabic) Form of Salama, mean-
ing "one who is peaceful and safe"
*Zulima, Zuleima, Zulemah, Zulimah,
Zalama, Zulyma, Zuleyma, Zuleyka*

Zulma (Arabic) A vibrant woman
Zulmah

Zuni (Native American) One who is creative
*Zunie, Zuny, Zuney, Zunee, Zunea,
Zuneah*

Zurafa (Arabic) A lovely woman
*Zurafah, Zirafa, Zirafah, Ziraf, Zurufa,
Zurufah, Zuruf, Zuraffa, Zuraffah*

Zuri (Swahili / French) A beauty / lovely
and white
*Zurie, Zurey, Zuria, Zuriaa, Zury, Zuree,
Zurya, Zurisha, Zurea, Zureah*

Zuriel (Hebrew) The Lord is my rock
*Zurielle, Zurial, Zuriella, Zuriela, Zuriele,
Zuriale, Zurialle*

Zurina (Spanish) One who is fair-skinned
*Zurinah, Zurine, Zurinia, Zurinna,
Zureena, Zureenah, Zurienah, Zuriena,
Zureina, Zureinah, Zurynah, Zuryna*

Zuwena (African) One who is pleasant
and good
*Zuwenah, Zwena, Zwenah, Zuwenna,
Zuwennah, Zuwyna, Zuwynah*

Zuyana (Sioux) One who has a brave heart
Zuyanah, Zuyanna, Zuyannah

Zuza (Polish) Form of Susan, meaning
"resembling a graceful white lily"
*Zuzah, Zusa, Zuzia, Zuzu, Zuzana,
Zuzka, Zuzanka, Zuzanny*

Zuzena (Basque) One who is correct
Zuzenah, Zuzenna, Zuzennah

Zweena (Arabic) A beautiful woman
*Zweenah, Zwina, Zwinah, Zwyna,
Zwynah, Zwiena, Zwienah, Zweina,
Zweinah, Zweana, Zweanah*

Zwi (Scandinavian) Resembling a gazelle
Zui, Zwie, Zwee, Zwey, Zwy, Zwea, Zweah

Zylia (Greek) Form of Xylia, meaning
"a woodland dweller"
*Zyliah, Zylea, Zyleah, Zilia, Zylina, Zyline,
Zylin, Zylyn, Zylyna, Zilina, Ziline, Zilyna,
Zilin*

Zyta (Polish) Form of Theresa, meaning "a harvester"
Zytta, Zytah, Zyttah

Zytka (Polish) Resembling a rose; form of Zoe, meaning "a life-giving woman; alive"
Zytkah, Zytcka, Zytckah

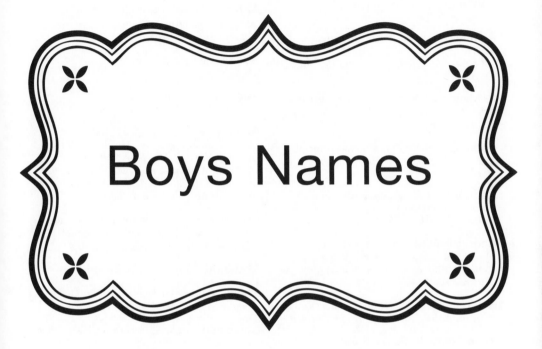

Boys Names

Aabha (Indian) One who shines
Abha, Abbha

Aabharan (Hindu) One who is treasured; jewel
Abharan, Abharen, Aabharen, Aabharon, Abharon

Aabheer (Indian) One who herds cattle
Abheer, Aabher, Abher, Abhear, Aabhear, Abhyr, Aabhyr

Aadarsh (Indian) One who has principles
Adarsh, Aadersh, Adersh, Addarsh, Addersh

Aadesh (Indian) A message or command; to make a statement
Adesh, Adhesh, Addesh

Aadi (Hindi) Child of the beginning
Aadie, Aady, Aadey, Aadee, Aadea, Aadeah, Aadye, Aadhi, Aadhie, Aadhy, Aadhey, Aadhee

Aafreen (Indian) One who encourages others
Afreen, Aafrene, Aafrean, Afrene, Afrean

Aage (Norse) Representative of ancestors
Age, Ake, Aake

Aarif (Arabic) A learned man
Arif, Aareef, Areef, Aareaf, Areaf, Aareif, Areif, Aarief, Arief, Aaryf, Aryf

Aaron ✿ (Hebrew) One who is exalted; from the mountain of strength
Aaran, Aaren, Aarin, Aaro, Aaronas, Aaronn, Aarron, Aaryn, Aeron, Aeryn, Aharon, Ahran, Ahren, Ahron, Airen, Airyn, Aran, Arand, Arek, Aren, Arend, Arin, Arnie, Aron, Aronne, Arran, Arron, Arun, Auron, Ayren, Ayron

Abasi (Swahili) One who is stern
Abasie, Abasy, Abasey, Abasee, Abasea

Abayomi (African) A bringer of joy
Abayomie, Abayomy, Abayomey, Abayomee, Abayomea

Abba (Arabic) A father
Abbah, Aba, Abah

Abbas (Arabic) One who is stern; in Islam, Muhammad's uncle
Ab, Abba, Abas

Abbey (Hebrew) A father's joy
Abby, Abbi, Abbie, Abbee, Abbea, Abbye

Abbott (English) The leader of a monastery; a fatherly man
Abbot, Abot, Abott

Abda (Arabic) A servant
Abdah

Abdi (Hebrew) My servant
Abdie, Abdy, Abdey, Abdee, Abdea

Abdul (Arabic) A servant of God
Abdal, Abdall, Abdalla, Abdallah, Abdel, Abdell, Abdella, Abdellah, Abdoul, Abdoull, Abdoulla, Abdoullah, Abdull, Abdalah, Abdulla, Abdualla, Abdulah, Abdulla, Abedellah, Abdullah

Abe (Hebrew) Form of Abraham, meaning "father of a multitude; father of nations"
Ab, Abi, Abey, Abie, Abee, Abea, Aby

Abebe (African) One who is flourishing

Abedi (African) One who worships God
Abedie, Abedy, Abedey, Abedee, Abedea

Abednago (Aramaic) Servant of Nabu, the god of wisdom
Abednego

Abejundio (Spanish) Resembling a bee
Abejundo, Abejundeo, Abedjundiyo, Abedjundeyo

Abel (Hebrew) The life force; breath
Abele, Abell, Abelson, Able, Avel, Avele

Abelard (German) Of noble strength
Abelardo, Abelarde

Abena (African) Born on a Tuesday
Abenah, Abina, Abinah, Abyna, Abynah

Abida (Arabic / Hebrew) He who worships or adores / having knowledge
Abidah, Abeeda, Abyda, Abeedah, Abydah, Abeida, Abeidah, Abieda, Abiedah, Abeada, Abeadah, Abidan, Abiden, Abidin, Abidyn, Abidon, Abidun

Abiel (Hebrew) God is the father
Abiell, Ahbiell, Ahbiel, Abyel, Aybell, Abyell, Aybel

Abijah (Hebrew) The Lord is my father
*Abia, Abbia, Abbiah, Abiam, Abija,
Abbija, Abbijah*

Abimelech (Hebrew) The Father is king
*Abymelech, Abimeleck, Abimelek,
Abymeleck, Abymelek, Abimelec, Abymelec*

Abir (Arabic / Hebrew) Having a pleasant
fragrance / one who is strong
*Abeer, Abear, Abyr, Abier, Abeir, Abhir,
Abhyr, Abheer, Abhear, Abheir, Abhier,
Abeeri, Abeerie, Abiri, Abirie, Abirey, Abiry*

Abisha (Hebrew) A gift from God
Abidja, Abidjah, Abijah, Abishai

Abner (Hebrew) Father of the light
Abnor, Abnar, Abnur, Abnir, Abnyr

Abraham (Hebrew) Father of a multitude;
father of nations
*Abarran, Avraham, Aberham, Abrahamo,
Abrahan, Abrahim, Abram, Abrami,
Abramo, Abrams, Abran, Abramio,
Abrian, Abriel*

Absalom (Hebrew) The father of peace
*Absalon, Abshalom, Absolem, Absolom,
Absolon, Avshalom, Avsholom*

Abu (African) A father
Abue, Aboo, Abou

Abundio (Spanish) A man of plenty
*Abbondio, Abondio, Aboundio, Abundo,
Abundeo, Aboundeo, Abondeo*

Acacio (Greek) Of the thorny tree
Achazio, Accacio, Achacio, Acazio

Ace (English) One who excels; number one;
the best
*Acee, Acer, Acey, Acie, Ayce, Aci, Acy,
Acea*

Acelin (French) Born into nobility
Aceline, Acelene, Acelyn, Acelyne, Acel

Achav (Hebrew) An uncle
Achiav

Achidan (Hebrew) My brother judged
Abidan, Amidan, Avidan

Achilles (Greek) In mythology, a hero
whose only vulnerability was his heel
*Achill, Achille, Achillea, Achilleo,
Achilleus, Achillios, Achillius, Akil,
Akilles, Akillios, Akillius, Aquil, Aquiles,
Aquilles*

Achim (Hebrew) God will judge
Acim, Ahim, Achym, Acym, Ahym

Achiram (Hebrew) My brother has been
exalted
Achyram, Achirem, Achyrem

Achishar (Hebrew) My brother lifts his
voice in song
*Achyshar, Amishar, Amyshar, Avishar,
Avyshar*

Aciano (Spanish) Resembling the blue-
bottle flower
Acyano

Acilino (Spanish) Form of Aquila, mean-
ing "resembling an eagle"
*Acileeno, Acilyno, Acileino, Acilieno,
Acileano*

Ackerley (Old English) From the meadow
of oak trees
*Accerly, Acklea, Ackleigh, Ackley, Acklie,
Ackerlea, Ackerleigh, Ackerly, Ackerleah*

Acton (English) From the town of oak
trees
Actun, Akton, Aktun

Adael (Hebrew) God witnesses
Adaele, Adayel, Adayele

Adahy (Native American) One who lives in
the forest
Adahey, Adahi, Adahie, Adahee, Adahea

Adair (German) A wealthy spearman
*Adaire, Adare, Adayre, Adayr, Adaer,
Adaere*

Adal (German) Possessing qualities of high
moral character

Adalfieri (German) Of the noble oath
*Adalfierie, Adalfiery, Adalfierey,
Adalfieree, Adelfieri, Adelfierie, Adelfiery,
Adelfierey, Adelfieree*

Adalgiso (German) One who is noble
Adelgiso, Adalgyso, Adelgyso

Adalhard (German) Of noble strength
*Adalard, Adelard, Adellard, Adelhard,
Adallard*

Adalrich (German) A noble ruler
*Adalric, Adalrick, Adelric, Adelrich,
Adelrick, Adalrik, Adalric*

Adam ✪ (Hebrew) Of the earth
Ad, Adamo, Adams, Adan, Adao, Addam, Addams, Addem, Addis, Ade, Adem, Adim, Adnet, Adnon, Adnot, Adom, Atim, Atkins

Adamson (English) The son of Adam
Adamsson, Addamson, Adamsun, Adamssun, Addamsun

Adar (Hebrew) A noble man
Adarr, Adaar

Addison (English) The son of Adam
Adison, Addisen, Addeson, Adisson, Adisen, Adeson

Addy (Teutonic) One who is awe-inspiring
Addey, Addi, Addie, Addee, Addea, Adi, Ady, Adie, Adey, Adee, Adea

Adel (Hebrew / German) God is eternal / a highborn man

Adelpho (Greek) A brotherly man
Aldelfo, Adelfus, Adelfio, Adelphe

Aden (Hebrew) One who is handsome and adorned
Adan, Adin, Adon, Adun, Adyn

Adham (Arabic) Having dark features; a black-haired man
Adhem, Adhom, Adhum, Adhim, Adhym

Adil (Arabic) A righteous man; one who is fair and just
Adyl, Adiel, Adeil, Adeel, Adeal, Adyeel

Adir (Hebrew) A majestic and noble man
Adeer, Adear, Adier, Adeir, Adyr

Aditya (Hindi) Of the sun
Adithya, Adithyan, Adityah, Aditeya, Aditeyah

Adiv (Hebrew) One who is considerate and polite
Adeev, Adeeve, Adeave, Adeav, Adiev, Adieve, Adeiv, Adeive, Adyv, Adyve

Adjatay (African) A prince; born to royalty
Adjataye, Adjatae, Adjatai

Adlai (Hebrew) My ornament
Adlay, Adlaye, Adlae, Adley, Adly, Adlee, Adleigh, Adlea, Adlie, Adli, Atley, Atly, Atlee, Atlea, Atleigh, Atli, Atlie

Adler (German) Resembling a soaring eagle
Adlar, Adlor, Adlir, Adlyr, Adlur

Admon (Hebrew) Of the red earth
Admen, Adman, Admun, Admin, Admyn

Adnah (Hebrew) An ornamented man
Adna

Adnan (Arabic) One who settles in a new region
Adnen, Adnon, Adnun, Adnin, Adnyn

Adney (English) From the nobleman's island
Adny, Adni, Adnie, Adnee, Adnea, Addney, Addny, Addni, Addnie, Addnee, Addnea

Adolph (German) A noble, majestic wolf
Adolf, Adolphe, Adolphus, Adolfus, Adolpho, Adolfo, Adaulfo, Addolf, Addolph, Adulfus, Adollf, Adalwolf

Adonia (Greek) God is my lord
Adon, Adonias, Adonijah, Adoniya

Adonis (Greek) In mythology, a handsome young man loved by Aphrodite
Addonia, Adohnes, Adonys, Adones

Adrian ✪ (Latin) A man from Hadria
Ade, Adiran, Adrain, Adrean, Adreean, Adreyan, Adreeyan, Adriaan, Adriano, Adrien, Adrin, Adrino, Adrion, Adron, Adryan, Adya, Arjen, Aydrean, Aydreean, Aydrian, Aydrien

Adriel (Hebrew) From God's flock
Adriell, Adriele, Adryel, Adryell, Adryele

Adwin (African) A great thinker; one who is creative
Adwinn, Adwinne, Adwen, Adwenne, Adwenn, Adwyn, Adwynn, Adwynne

Aegeus (Greek) Resembling a young goat; in mythology, a king and father of Theseus
Aigeos, Aigeus

Aekley (English) From the oak-tree meadow
Aekly, Aekleigh, Aeklee, Aeklea, Aekleah, Aekli, Aeklie

Aelfhere (English) An elf or divine warrior
Aelfhare, Aelvhere, Aelvhar, Aelvhare

Aelfric (English) An elf ruler
Aelfryc, Aelfrick, Aelfryck, Aelfrik, Aelfryk

Aelfwine (English) A friend of the elves
Aelfwynne, Aelfwin, Aelfwinn, Aelfwyn, Aelfwynn, Aelfwen, Aelfwenn, Aelfwenne

Aeneas (Greek) To be worthy of praise
Aenneas, Aineas, Aineias, Aineis, Ainneas

Aeolus (Greek) One who changes quickly; in mythology, god of the winds
Aeolos, Aiolos, Aiolus

Aeson (Greek) In mythology, the father of Jason
Aesun, Aison, Aisun, Ayson, Aysun

Afi (Norse) One who is grandfatherly
Afie, Afee, Afea, Afey, Afy

Afif (Arabic) One who is chaste; pure
Afeef, Afief, Afeif, Affeef, Affif, Afyf, Afeaf

Africa (English) One who is pleasant; from Africa
Afrika, Affreeca, Affrica, Africah, Afrycka, Afrycah, Afric, Affryka, Afrikah, Afryka, Afrykah, Africano, Afrikano, Afrycano, Afrykano, Afro

Agamemnon (Greek) One who works slowly; in mythology, the leader of the Greeks at Troy
Agamemno, Agamenon

Agapito (Spanish) A kind and loving person
Agapeto, Agapetus, Agapios, Agapitus

Agathias (Greek) One who is good and honorable
Agathios, Agathius, Agatha, Agathos

Aghy (Irish) A friend of the horse
Aghey, Aghi, Aghie, Aghee, Aghea, Aghe

Agnolo (Italian) A heavenly messenger; an angel
Agnolio, Agnoleo

Ahab (Hebrew) An uncle

Ahearn (Celtic) Lord of the horses
Ahern, Ahearne, Aherne, Aherin

Ahiga (Native American) One who fights
Ahyga

Ahmed (Arabic) One who always thanks God; a name of Muhammad
Achmad, Achmed, Ahmaad, Ahmad, Ahmet, Ahmod, Amad, Amadi, Amahd, Amed

Ahsan (Arabic) One who is merciful
Ahson, Ahsun, Ahsen, Ahsin, Ahsyn

Aidan ✪ (Irish) A fiery young man
Aiden, Aedan, Aeden, Aidano, Aidyn, Ayden, Aydin, Aydan, Aidin, Aedin, Aedyn, Aideyn, Aidenn, Aedenn, Aidann, Aedann, Aydann, Aydenn, Aideynn

Aiken (English) Constructed of oak; sturdy
Aikin, Aicken, Aickin, Ayken, Aykin, Aycken, Ayckin

Ailesh (Hindi) The lord of everything
Aylesh, Aileshe, Ayleshe

Aime (French) One who is loved

Aimery (Teutonic) Ruler of work
Aimory, Aimerey, Aimeric, Amerey, Aymeric, Aymery, Aymerey, Aimeri, Aimerie, Aimeree, Aimerea, Aimorey, Aimori, Aimorie, Aimoree, Amery, Ameri, Amerie, Ameree

Aimon (Teutonic) Ruler of the house; a protector
Aimond, Aymon, Aimund, Aimun, Aymun, Aymond, Aymund

Ainsley (Scottish) One's own meadow
Ainslie, Ainslea, Ainslee, Ainsleigh, Ainsly, Ainslei, Aynslie, Aynslea, Aynslee, Aynsleigh, Aynsley, Aynslie, Aynsly, Ainsleah, Aynsleah, Ainslye

Ainsworth (English) From Ann's estate
Answorth, Annsworth, Ainsworthe, Answorthe, Annsworthe

Aisley (English) From the ash-tree meadow
Aisly, Aisli, Aislie, Aislee, Aisleigh, Aislye, Aysley, Aysli, Ayslie, Aysly, Ayslye, Ayslee, Aysleigh, Aislea, Ayslea, Aisleah, Aysleah

Ajax (Greek) In mythology, a hero of the Trojan war
Aias, Aiastes, Ajaxx, Ajaxe

Ajayi (African) One who is born facedown
Ajayie, Ajaye, Ajayee, Ajayea, Ajayey

Ajit (Indian) One who is invincible
Ajeet, Ajeat, Ajeit, Ajiet, Ajyt

Akbar (Arabic) All-powerful and great
Acbar, Ackbar, Akbarr, Acbarr, Ackbarr

Akeno (Japanese) From the shining field
Akeeno, Akeano, Akyno, Akeyno, Akino

Akiko (Japanese) Surrounded by bright light
Akyko

Akili (Arabic) One who is wise
Akilie, Akily, Akiley, Akilee, Akilea, Akil, Akyl

Akim (Russian) God will judge
Akeem, Akeam, Akiem, Akeim, Akym, Akeym

Akin (African) A brave man; a hero
Akeen, Akean, Akein, Akien, Akyn

Akiva (Hebrew) One who protects or provides shelter
Akyva, Akeeva, Akeava, Akieva, Akeiva, Akeyva

Alard (German) Of noble strength
Aliard, Allard, Alliard

Alaric (German) A noble ruler
Alric, Alrick, Alarick, Alarico, Aleric, Alerick, Allaric, Allarick, Alleric, Allerick, Alrick

Alastair (Scottish) Form of Alexander, meaning "helper and defender of mankind"
Alasdair, Alasteir, Alaster, Alastor, Alaisdair, Alaistair, Alaister, Aleister, Alester, Alistair, Alistar, Alister, Allaistair, Allaster, Allastir, Allistair, Allister, Allistir, Allysdair, Allystair, Allyster, Alysdair, Alysdare, Alystair, Alyster, Alli, Allie, Ally, Alley, Allee, Allea

Alban (Latin) One who is white or fair; a man from Alba
Albain, Alban, Albano, Albany, Albie, Albin, Albinet, Albis, Alby, Albys, Albey, Auban, Auben, Aubin, Albi, Albee, Albaney, Albani, Albanie, Albanee

ALISTAIR

We named our son Alistair. We wanted something different so he wouldn't end up with ten classmates with the same name. Alistair was a name that always stuck with me from a TV show called *You Can't Do That on Television.* —Kelly, WA

Akmal (Arabic) A perfect man
Aqmal, Akmall, Aqmall, Acmal, Acmall, Ackmal, Ackmall

Akram (Arabic) A generous man
Akrem, Akrim, Akrym, Akrom, Akrum

Aladdin (Arabic) One who is noble in his faith
Aladin, Aladdyn, Aladyn

Alaire (French) Filled with joy
Alair, Alaer, Alaere, Alare, Alayr, Alayre

Alake (African) One who is honored
Alaik, Alaike, Alayk, Alayke, Alaek, Alaeke

Alamar (Arabic) Covered with gold
Alamarr, Alemar, Alemarr, Alomar, Alomarr

Alan (German / Gaelic) One who is precious / resembling a little rock
Ailean, Ailin, Al, Alain, Alun, Aland, Alann, Alano, Alanson, Alen, Alin, Allain, Allan, Allayne, Allen, Alley, Alleyn, Alleyne, Allie, Allin, Allon, Allyn, Alaen, Allaen

Albany (Latin) From the white hill; white-skinned
Albaney, Albani, Albanie, Albanee, Albanye, Albin, Alban, Albhda, Aubine, Albanea, Albaneah

Albaric (French) A blonde-haired ruler
Albarik, Albarick, Albaryc, Albaryk, Albaryck

Alberich (Teutonic) A skillful ruler
Alberic, Alberik, Alberick, Alberyk, Alberyck, Alberyc

Albert (German) One who is noble and bright
Alberto, Albertus, Alburt, Albirt, Aubert, Albyrt, Albertos, Albertino

Albion (Latin / Celtic) One who is white or fair / from the rocks or crag
Albyon, Albeon

Alcander (Greek) Having strength and power
Alcindor, Alcandor, Alcinder, Alkander, Alkender, Alcender, Alkindor, Alkandor, Alkendor

Alcott (English) From the old cottage
*Alcot, Allcot, Allcott, Alkott, Alkot,
Allkot, Allkott*

Alden (English) An old friend
Aldan, Aldin, Aldyn, Aldon, Aldun

Aldo (German) Old or wise one; elder
Aldous, Aldis, Aldus, Alldo, Aldys

Aldred (English) An old advisor
Alldred, Aldraed, Alldraed, Aldread, Alldread

Aldrich (English) An old king
*Aldric, Aldridge, Aldrige, Aldrin, Aldritch,
Alldrich, Alldridge, Aldrick, Aldrik,
Aldryc, Aldryck, Aldryk, Aldrych, Audric,
Audrick, Audrik*

Aldwin (English) A wise old friend
*Aldwinn, Aldwinne, Aldwyn, Aldwynne,
Aldwine, Aldwynn, Aldwen, Aldwenn,
Aldwenne*

Alec (Greek) Form of Alexander, meaning
"helper and defender of mankind"
*Alek, Aleck, Alic, Alik, Alick, Alyc, Alyck,
Alyk, Aleco, Alecko, Aleko, Alecos, Alekos,
Aleckos*

Aled (Welsh) A child; offspring

Alejandro (Spanish) Form of Alexander,
meaning "helper and defender of
mankind"
Alejandrino, Alejo

Alem (Arabic) A wise man
Alerio

Aleron (Latin) A winged one
Aileron, Alerun, Ailerun

Alex ☻ (English) Form of Alexander,
meaning "helper and defender of mankind"
*Aleks, Alecks, Alecs, Allex, Alleks, Allecks,
Allecs*

Alexander ☻ ☻ (Greek) Helper and
defender of mankind
*Alaxander, Aleksandar, Aleksander,
Aleksandr, Aleksanteri, Alesandro,
Alessandre, Alessandri, Alessandro, Alexan,
Alexandre, Alexandro, Alexandros,
Alisander, Alissander, Alissandre, Alixandre,
Alsandare, Alyksandr*

Alexis (Greek) Form of Alexander, mean-
ing "helper and defender of mankind"
*Aleksei, Aleksi, Aleksio, Aleksios, Aleksius,
Alexei, Alexey, Alexi, Alexio, Alexios,
Alexius, Alexus, Alexy, Alexie, Alexee*

Alfio (Italian) A white-skinned man
Alfeo, Alfiyo, Alfeyo

Alfonso (Italian) Prepared for battle; eager
and ready
*Alphonse, Affonso, Alfons, Alfonse,
Alfonsin, Alfonsino, Alfonz, Alfonzo,
Alphons, Alphonse, Alphonso, Alphonsus,
Alphonz*

Alfred (English) One who counsels the elves
*Ahlfred, Ailfred, Ailfrid, Ailfryd, Alf,
Alfey, Alfie, Alfre, Alfredas, Alfrey,
Alfredo, Alfredos, Alfy, Alfee, Alfea,
Alford, Alferd*

Alger (English) One who is noble; an elf
spear
*Alga, Algar, Allgar, Allger, Algor, Allgor,
Algur, Allgur, Algir, Allgir, Algyr, Allgyr*

Algernon (French) One who has a
mustache
*Algernone, Algey, Algie, Algy, Aljernon,
Allgernon, Algi, Algee, Algea*

Algis (German) One who wields a spear
Algiss, Algisse, Algys, Algyss, Algysse

Ali (Arabic) The great one; one who is exalted
Aliyy, Alie, Aly, Aley, Alee, Aleigh, Alea

Alison (English) The son of a noble
*Alisson, Allcen, Allison, Allisoun, Allson,
Allyson*

Almanzo (German) One who is highly
esteemed; precious
*Alma, Alman, Allmanzo, Almenzo,
Allmenzo*

Almarine (German) A work ruler
*Almarin, Almarino, Almareen, Almereen,
Almerene, Almerine, Almarene*

Aloiki (Hawaiian) Form of Aloysius,
meaning "a famous warrior"
*Aloikie, Aloiky, Aloikey, Aloikee, Aloikea,
Aloyki, Aloykie, Aloykey, Aloyky, Aloykee,
Aloykea*

Alon (Hebrew) Of the oak tree
Allona, Allon, Alonn

Alonzo (Spanish) Form of Alfonso, mean-
ing "prepared for battle; eager and ready"
*Alonso, Alanso, Alanzo, Allonso, Allonzo,
Allohnso, Allohnzo, Alohnso, Alohnzo*

Aloysius (German) A famous warrior
*Ahlois, Aloess, Alois, Aloisio, Aloisius,
Aloisio, Aloj, Alojzy, Aloys*

Alpha (Greek) The firstborn child; the first
letter of the Greek alphabet
Alphah, Alfa, Alfah

Alpheus (Hebrew) One who succeeds
another
*Alfaeus, Alfeos, Alfeus, Alpheaus,
Alphoeus, Alphius, Alphyus*

Alpin (Scottish) One who is fair-skinned
*Alpine, Ailpein, Ailpin, Alpyn, Ailpyn,
Alpyne*

Alston (English) Of the elf stone
*Alsdon, Alsten, Alstin, Allston, Allstonn,
Alstun, Alstyn, Alstan*

Alta (Latin) To be elevated
Alto, Altus, Allta, Alltus, Altos, Alltos

Altair (Greek) Resembling a bird
*Alltair, Altaer, Altayr, Alltayr, Alltaer,
Altare, Alltare, Alltayre*

Alter (Hebrew) One who is old
Allter, Altar, Alltar

Altman (German) One who is prudent; an
old man
Altmann, Alterman, Altermann, Altmann

Alton (English) From the old town
*Aldon, Aldun, Altun, Alten, Allton, Alltun,
Allten*

Alucio (Spanish) One who is bright and
shining
Allucio, Alucido, Aluxio, Aluzio

Aluf (Hebrew) One who is in charge
Alouf, Aluph, Alouph

Alured (Latin) Form of Alfred, meaning
"one who counsels the elves"
Ailured

Alva (Hebrew) A bright man
Alvah

Alvar (English) Of the army of elves
Allvar, Allvarso, Alvarso, Allvaro

Alvaro (Spanish) Guardian of all
*Alavaro, Alavero, Alvero, Alverio, Alvareo,
Alvario*

Alvern (Latin) Of the spring's growth
*Alverne, Alvarn, Alvarne, Alvurn, Alvurne,
Alvirn, Alvirne*

Alvin (English) Friend of the elves
*Alven, Alvan, Alvon, Alvyn, Alvun, Alvi,
Alvie, Alvy, Alvey, Alvee, Alvea*

Alvis (Norse) In mythology, a dwarf who
fell in love with Thor's daughter
Alvise, Alvisse, Alviss, Alvys, Alvyss, Alvysse

Amadeus (Latin) Loved by God
*Amadee, Amadei, Amadeo, Amado,
Amadeusz, Amadi, Amadieu, Amadis,
Amado, Amando, Amati, Amato, Amatus,
Amedeo, Amyot*

Amadour (French) A lovable man
Amador, Amadore, Amadoure

Amal (Hebrew / Hindi / Arabic) A hardwork-
ing man / one who is pure / filled with hope
*Amahl, Amali, Amel, Amalie, Amaly,
Amaley, Amalee, Amalea, Amaleigh*

Amalio (Spanish) An industrious man
Amelio, Amallio, Amellio, Ameleo, Amaleo

Amani (African / Arabic) One who is
peaceful / one with wishes and dreams
*Amanie, Amany, Amaney, Amanee,
Amanye, Amanea, Amaneah*

Amari (African) Having great strength; a
builder
Amarie, Amaree, Amarea, Amary, Amarey

Amarillo (Spanish) The color yellow
Amarilo, Amaryllo, Amarylo

Amasa (Hebrew) A burden
Amasah, Ammasa, Amahsa, Ammahsa

Amaury (French) A ruler
*Amauri, Amaurie, Amaurey, Amauree,
Amaurea*

Ambrose (Greek) Immortal; in mythology,
ambrosia was the food of the gods
*Ambrosia, Ambrosius, Ambrosios,
Ambroeus, Ambroise, Ambros, Ambrosi,
Ambrosio, Ambrossij, Ambroz, Ambrus,
Ambe, Ambroggio, Ambrogio, Ambi,
Ambie, Amby, Ambey*

Amerigo (Italian) Ruler of the home
America, Americo, Americus, Amerika, Ameriko, Amerikus, Arrigo

Ames (French) A beloved friend
Amos, Aimes, Aymes

Amid (Arabic) A general
Ameed, Amead, Amied, Ameid, Amyd

Amiel (Hebrew) The God of my people
Amyel, Amiell, Amyell

Amil (Hindi) One who is invaluable
Ameel, Ameal, Ameil, Amiel, Amyl

Amin (Arabic) One who faithful and trustworthy
Ameen, Amean, Amein, Amien, Amyn

Amir (Arabic /Hebrew) A prince / from the treetop
Ameer, Ameir, Amer, Amiran, Amiri, Amear, Amyr, Amier

Amit (Hindi) Without limit; endless
Ameet, Ameat, Ameit, Amiet, Amyt

Amitai (Hebrew) One who is truthful
Amiti, Amitay, Amitaye, Amitae, Amitie, Amity, Amitey, Amitee, Amitea

Amjad (Arabic) Having glory and honor
Amjaad, Amjed

Ammar (Arabic) A long and prosperous life
Ammer, Amr

Ammon (Hebrew) One who teaches or builds
Amon, Amnon, Ammnon

Amor (French) One who is loves and is loved
Amore

Amory (German) Ruler and lover of one's home
Aimory, Amery, Amorey, Amry, Amori, Amorie, Amoree, Amorea

Amos (Hebrew) To carry; hardworking
Amoss, Aymoss, Aymos

Amram (Hebrew) Of the mighty nation

Amyas (Latin) One who is loved
Amias, Amyes, Amyees

Anael (Hebrew) The name of an archangel
Anaele

Analu (Hawaiian) Form of Andrew, meaning "manly; a warrior"
Analue, Analoo, Analou

Anastasios (Greek) One who is resurrected
Anastas, Anastase, Anastagio, Anastasio, Anastasius, Anastatius, Anastice, Anastius, Anasto, Anstas, Anstasios, Anstasius, Anstice, Anstis, Anstiss

Anatole (Greek) Born with the break of day
Anatolius, Anatol, Anatolio, Antal, Antol, Antole, Antolle, Anatoli, Anatolie, Anatolee, Anatolea, Anatoly, Anatoley

Anchor (English) One who is reliable and stable
Ancher, Anker, Ankor

Anderson (English) The son of Andrew
Andersun, Andersson, Anderssun, Anders

Andino (Italian) Form of Andrew, meaning "manly; a warrior"
Andyno, Andeeno, Andeano, Andieno, Andeino

André (French) Form of Andrew, meaning "manly; a warrior"
Andrae, Andras, Andreas, Andrei, Andrej, Andres, Andreus, Andrey, Andris, Andrius, Aundray

Andrew ✪ ✪ (Greek) Manly; a warrior
Adem, Aindrea, Aindreas, Andie, Andonia, Andor, Andresj, Andrewes, Andrews, Andrey, Andrezj, Andrian, Andriel, Andries, Andrij, Andrija, Andrius, Andro, Andros, Andru, Andruw, Andrzej, Andy, Antero

Andrik (Slavic) Form of Andrew, meaning "manly; a warrior"
Andric, Andrick, Andryk, Andryck, Andryc

Androcles (Greek) A glorious man
Androclus, Androclos, Androclas

Aneirin (Welsh) One who is noble
Aneiryn, Anierin, Anieryn, Aneurin, Aneuryn

Aneislis (Gaelic) A careful and thoughtful person
Anieslis, Aneislys, Anieslys

Angel ✪ (Greek) A messenger of God
Andjelko, Ange, Angelino, Angell, Angelmo, Angelo, Angie, Angy, Aniol, Anjel, Anjelo, Anyoli

Angus (Scottish) One force; one strength; one choice
Aengus, Anngus, Aonghus

Anicho (German) An ancestor
Anico, Anecho, Aneco, Anycho, Anyco

Aniketos (Greek) One who remains unconquered
Anicetus, Aniceto, Anisio, Aniseto, Anicetos, Anisetos, Anicio

Ankur (Indian) One who is blossoming; a sapling

Annan (Celtic) From the brook
Anan

Anscom (English) From the valley of the majestic one
Anscomb, Anscombe, Anscoomb, Anscoombe

Ansel (French) One who follows nobility; protection from God
Ancell, Ansell, Anselm, Anselme, Anselmi, Anselmo, Anselmie, Anselmy, Anselmey

Ansley (English) From the noble's pastureland
Ansly, Anslie, Ansli, Anslee, Ansleigh, Anslea, Ansleah, Anslye

Anson (English) The son of Ann or Agnes
Annson, Annsen, Annsonia, Ansson, Ansen, Ansonia

Antaeus (Greek) Son of the Earth; in mythology, an invincible giant wrestler
Antaios, Antaius, Antaeos, Anteo, Anteus

Antares (Greek) A giant red star; the brightest star in the constellation Scorpio

Antenor (Spanish) One who antagonizes
Antener, Antenar, Antenir, Antenyr, Antenur

Anthony ✪ ✪ (Latin) A flourishing man; from an ancient Roman family
Antal, Anthone, Anthoney, Anntoin, Antin, Anton, Antone, Antonello, Antoney, Antoni, Antonije, Antonin, Antonino, Antonio, Antonius, Antons, Antony, Antun, Anthany

Antioco (Italian) A stubborn man
Antioch, Antio, Antiochos, Antiochus, Antioko, Antiocko, Antiocho

Antoine (French) Form of Anthony, meaning "a flourishing man; from an ancient Roman family"
Antione, Antjuan, Antuan, Antuwain, Antuwaine, Antuwayne, Antuwon, Antwahn, Antwain, Antwaine, Antwan, Antwaun, Antwohn, Antwoin, Antwoine, Antwon, Antwone

Anwar (Arabic) Surrounded by light
Anwarr, Annwar, Annwarr

Anwell (Welsh) One who is loved dearly
Anwel, Anwil, Anwill, Anwyl, Anwyll

Aodh (Celtic) A fiery man; in mythology, the sun god
Aed, Aodhagan, Aoden, Aodhan, Aodan

Apache (Native American) A tribal name
Apachi, Apachie, Apachee, Apachea, Apachy, Apachey

Apollo (Greek) In mythology, the god of archery, music, and poetry
Apollon, Apollos, Apolo

Apollonio (Greek) A follower of Apollo
Apolonio, Apollonios, Apolonios, Apollonius, Apolonius, Apolloneo, Apoloneo

Apostolos (Greek) An apostle; a messenger of God
Apostolo, Apostolio, Apostolios, Apostoleo, Apostoleos

Aquarius (Latin) The water bearer; a constellation

Aquila (Latin) Resembling an eagle; also the name of a constellation
Acquila, Acquilino, Acquilla, Akila, Akilino, Akilla, Aquilina, Aquilino, Aquilla

Aquilo (Latin) Of the north wind
Aquillo, Aquilino, Aquillino

Ara (Armenian / Latin) A legendary king / of the altar; the name of a constellation
Araa, Aira, Arah, Arae, Ahraya

Aram (Assyrian) One who is exalted
Arram

Aramis (French) A swordsman
Arramis, Aramys, Aramiss, Aramyss, Arramys

Arcadio (Greek) From an ideal country paradise
Alcadio, Alcado, Alcedio, Arcadios, Arcadius, Arkadi, Arkadios, Arkadius, Arkady, Arkadie, Arkadey, Arkadee, Arkadea

Arcelio (Spanish) From the altar of heaven
Arcelios, Arcelius, Aricelio, Aricelios, Aricelius

Archard (German) A powerful holy man
Archerd, Archird, Archyrd

Archelaus (Greek) The ruler of the people
Archelaios, Arkelaos, Arkelaus, Arkelaios, Archelaos

Archer (Latin) A skilled bowman
Archar, Archor, Archur, Archir, Archyr, Archere

Archibald (French) One who is bold, brave, and genuine
Archaimbaud, Archambault, Archibaldo, Archibold, Archimbald, Archimbaldo, Arquibaldo, Arquimbaldo, Archi, Archie, Archy, Archey, Archee

Archimedes (Greek) A master of thought
Arkimedes, Arquimedes, Archimeedes, Arkimeedes, Arquimeedes

Ardal (Gaelic) Having the valor of a bear
Ardghal

Ardell (Latin) One who is eager
Ardel, Ardelle, Ardele

Arden (Latin / English) One who is passionate and enthusiastic / from the valley of the eagles
Ardan, Arrden, Arrdan, Ardin, Arrdin, Ard, Ardyn, Arrdyn, Ardy, Ardi, Ardie, Ardee, Ardey

Ardley (English) Of the home-lover's meadow
Ardly, Ardleigh, Ardlee, Ardli, Ardlie, Ardlea, Ardleah, Ardsleigh, Ardslee, Ardslea, Ardsleah, Ardsli, Ardslie, Ardsly, Ardsley

Ardmore (Latin) One who is zealous
Ardmorre, Ardmorr, Ardmor

Ardon (Hebrew) The color bronze
Arrdon, Ardun, Arrdun

Arduino (German) A valued friend
Ardwino, Arrduino, Ardueno

Ares (Greek) In mythology, god of war
Areis, Areys, Arees, Areas

Argento (Latin) Resembling silver
Argentio, Argentino

Argus (Greek) One who is vigilant and watchful
Argos

Argyle (Scottish) A diamond pattern
Argyll, Argile

Ari (Hebrew) Resembling a lion or an eagle
Aree, Arie, Aristide, Aristides, Arri, Ary, Arye, Arrie, Arry, Arrye

Aric (Scandinavian) Form of Eric, meaning "ever the ruler"
Aaric, Arick, Aarick, Arik, Aarik, Arric, Arrick, Arrik, Arrict, Arict

Ariel (Hebrew) A lion of God
Arielle, Ariele, Ariell, Arriel, Ahriel, Airial, Arieal, Arial, Areille, Ariellel

Aries (Latin) Resembling a ram; the first sign of the zodiac; a constellation
Arese, Ariese

Arion (Greek) A poet or musician
Arian, Arien, Aryon

Aris (American) Form of Aristeo, meaning "the best"
Arris, Arys, Aryss

Aristeo (Spanish) The best
Aristio, Aristo, Aristeyo, Aristos, Aristiyo, Aristeides, Aristides, Aristide

Aristotle (Greek) Of high quality
Aristotelis, Aristotellis

Arius (Greek) Enduring life; everlasting; immortal
Areos, Areus, Arios

Arizona (Native American) From the little spring; from the state of Arizona

Arjuna (Hindi) The white one
Arjun, Arjune

Arkansas (Native American) Of the down-river people; from the state of Arkansas

Arledge (English) From the hare's lake
Arlidge, Arlledge, Arllidge, Arrledge, Arrlidge

Arlen (Gaelic) A solemn, binding promise
Arlan, Arland, Arlend, Arlando, Arlendo, Arlenn, Arlann, Arles, Arlas, Arlin, Arlind, Arlindo, Arlinn, Arlyn, Arllen, Arlleno, Arllend

Arley (English) From the hare's meadow
Arlea, Arleigh, Arlie, Arly, Arleah, Arli, Arlee

Arliss (Hebrew) Of the pledge
Arlyss, Aryls, Arlis, Arlisse, Arlysse

Arlo (Spanish) From the barberry tree
Arlow, Arlowe, Arrlo, Arrlow, Arrlowe

Armand (French) Of the army; a soldier
Arman, Armande, Armando, Armani, Armond, Armonde, Armondo, Armanie, Armany, Armaney, Armanee, Armante, Armaan, Armanno, Arminlo, Arminius, Armin

Armon (Hebrew) Resembling a chestnut
Armoni, Armonie, Armonno, Armony, Armoney, Armonee

Armstrong (Scottish) A strong warrior
Armstrang

Arnan (Hebrew) One who is quick; filled with joy

Arne (Norse) Resembling an eagle
Arni, Arnie, Arney, Arny, Arnee, Arnea, Arn

Arnett (French) Resembling a little eagle
Arnat, Arnet, Arnot, Arnott, Arnatt

Arno (German) An eagle-wolf
Arnoe, Arnou, Arnoux, Arnow, Arnowe

Arnold (German) The eagle ruler
Arnaldo, Arnaud, Arnauld, Arnault, Arnd, Arndt, Arnel, Arnell, Arnoldo, Arnoud, Arnout

Arnon (Hebrew) From the torrent river

Arrio (Spanish) A belligerent man
Aryo, Ario, Arryo

Arsenio (Greek) A manly man
Arcenio, Arcinio, Arsanio, Arseenio, Arseinio, Arsemio, Arsen, Arsene, Arseni, Arsenios, Arsenius, Arseno, Arsenyo, Arsinio, Arsino

Artemas (Greek) A follower of the goddess Artemis
Artemio, Artemis, Artemus, Artimas, Artimis, Artimus

Arthur (Celtic) As strong as a bear; a hero
Aart, Arrt, Art, Artair, Arte, Arther, Arthor, Arthuro, Artie, Arto, Artor, Artro, Artturi, Artur, Arturo, Artus, Arty, Arthel, Arthus

Arundel (English) From the eagle's valley
Arundell, Arundele, Arondel, Arondell, Arundale, Arundayl, Arundayle, Arundael, Arundaele, Arundail, Arundaile

Arvad (Hebrew) A wanderer; voyager
Arpad

Arvid (Norse) From the eagle's tree
Arvyd, Arved, Arvod, Arvud

Arvin (English) A friend to everyone
Arvinn, Arvinne, Arven, Arvenn, Arvenne, Arvyn, Arvynn, Arvynne, Arvis, Arviss, Arvys, Arvyss, Arwen, Arwenn, Arwenne, Arwyn, Arwynn, Arwynne, Arwin, Arwine, Arwinn, Arwinne

Arvind (Indian) Resembling a lotus
Arvynd, Arvinde, Aryvnde

Asa (Hebrew) One who heals others
Asah, Ase, Aseh

Asad (Arabic) A fortunate man
Assad, Asaad

Asael (Hebrew) God has created
Asaya, Asayel, Asahel, Asiel, Asiell, Asaell

Asaph (Hebrew) One who gathers or collects
Asaf, Asaphe, Asafe, Asiph, Asiphe, Asif, Asife

Ascanius (Latin) In mythology, the son of Aeneas
Ascanios, Ascanious

Ascott (English) One who lives in the eastern cottage
Ascot

Asgard (Norse) From the courtyard of the gods; in mythology, the dwelling place of the gods
Asgarde

Ash (English) From the ash tree
Ashe

Ashby (English) From the ash-tree farm
Ashbi, Ashbie, Ashbee, Ashbea, Ashbey

Asher (Hebrew) Filled with happiness
Ashar, Ashor, Ashir, Ashyr, Ashur

Ashford (English) From the ash-tree ford
Asheford, Ashenford

Ashley (English) From the meadow of
ash trees
*Ashely, Asheley, Ashelie, Ashlan, Ashleigh,
Ashlen, Ashli, Ashlie, Ashlin, Ashling,
Ashlinn, Ashly, Ashlyn, Ashlynn*

Ashraf (Arabic) A distinguished man
Asheraf, Ashraph, Asheraph

Ashton (English) From the ash-tree town
*Asheton, Ashtun, Ashetun, Ashtin,
Ashetin, Ashtyn, Ashetyn, Aston, Astun*

Athol (Gaelic) From the new Ireland
Atholl

Atif (Arabic) A kind man
*Ateef, Ateaf, Atief, Ateif, Atyf, Atiph,
Ateeph, Ateaph, Atieph, Ateiph, Atyph*

Atlas (Greek) In mythology, a Titan who
carried the world on his shoulders
Attlas, Atlass, Attlass

Atley (English) From the meadow
*Atlea, Atlee, Atleigh, Attlee, Attleigh,
Atleah, Atly, Atli, Atlie, Attlea, Attleah,
Attli, Attlie, Attly, Attley*

ASHER

We named our son Asher because my grandmother's maiden name is Assh and we wanted to honor
that branch of our family, many of whom are quite elderly. Also, my husband's name is Dan (not
Daniel), which is one of the twelve tribes of Israel, and we liked the fact that Asher is one of the
twelve tribes, too. —Jackie, Montreal

Asim (Arabic) A protector or guardian
*Aseem, Aseam, Aseim, Asiem, Asym, Azim,
Azeem, Azeam, Azeim, Aziem, Azym*

Aslan (Turkish) Resembling a lion
Aslen, Azlan, Azlen

Aspen (American) From the aspen tree
Aspin, Aspyn, Aspon, Aspun, Aspan

Astraeus (Greek) In mythology, one of the
Titans
Astraios

Aswin (English) A spear friend
*Aswinn, Aswinne, Aswyn, Aswynn,
Aswynne, Aswen, Aswenn, Aswenne,
Aswine*

Athanasois (Greek) Having eternal life
*Atanasio, Atanasios, Atanasius, Athan,
Athanasius*

Athelstan (English) Of the noble stone
*Athelston, Athelsten, Athelstin, Athelstyn,
Athelstun*

Athens (Greek) From the capital of Greece
Athenios, Athenius, Atheneos, Atheneus

Atherton (English) From the town near the
spring
Athertun

Atsushi (Japanese) A compassionate warrior
*Atsushie, Atsushy, Atsushey, Atsushee,
Atsushea*

Atticus (Latin) A man from Athens
Attikus, Attickus, Aticus, Atickus, Atikus

Attila (Hungarian) One who is fatherly
*Atila, Atilano, Atilo, Attilia, Attilio,
Attileo*

Atwater (English) One who lives at the
water
Attwater

Atwell (English) One who lives at the spring
Attwell, Atwel, Attwel

Atwood (English) One who lives at the forest
Attwood, Atwode, Attwode

Atworth (English) One who lives at the
farmstead
Attworth, Atworthe, Attworthe

Auberon (French) A royal bear
Auberron, Auberun, Auberrun

Aubrey (English) One who rules with elf-
wisdom
*Aubary, Aube, Aubery, Aubry, Aubury,
Aubrian, Aubrien, Aubrion, Aubri, Aubrie,
Aubree, Aubrea*

Auburn (Latin) Having a reddish-brown color
Aubirn, Auburne, Aubyrn, Abern, Abirn, Aburn, Abyrn, Aubern

Auden (English) An old friend
Audin, Audyn, Audan, Audon, Audun

Audey (English) Of noble strength
Audi, Audie, Audee, Audea, Audy

Audley (English) From the old meadow
Audly, Audleigh, Audlee, Audlea, Audleah, Audli, Audlie

Audrey (English) Of noble strength
Audry, Audree, Audri, Audrie, Audrea

August (Latin) One who is venerable; majestic
Auguste, Agosto, Augusto, Augi, Augie, Augy, Augey, Augee, Augea

Augustine (Irish) Form of August, meaning "one who is venerable; majestic"
Agoston, Aguistin, Agustin, Augustin, Augustyn, Avgustin, Augusteen, Agosteen, Agostino, Agustino

Augustus (Latin) Form of August, meaning "one who is venerable; majestic"
Augustos, Augostus, Augostos, Agostos, Agostus

Aurelio (Latin) The golden one
Aurelius, Aurilius, Aurilio, Aurelian, Aureliano, Aureli, Aurelie, Aurely, Aureley, Aurelee, Aureleigh, Aurelo

Austin ☉ (English) Form of August, meaning "one who is venerable; majestic"
Austen, Austyn, Austan, Auston, Austun

Autrey (English) Form of Audrey, meaning "of noble strength"
Autry, Autri, Autrie, Autree, Autrea

Avenall (French) From the oat field
Avenal, Aveneil, Aveneill, Avenel, Avenell, Avenil, Avenill, Avenelle

Avery (English) One who is a wise ruler; of the nobility
Avrie, Averey, Averie, Averi, Averee, Averea, Avereah, Avri, Avry, Avrey, Avree, Avrea

Aviel (Hebrew) My father is Lord
Aviell, Avyel, Avyell

Aviram (Hebrew) My Father is mighty
Avyram, Avirem, Avyrem

Avishae (Hebrew) The gift of my Father
Avyshae, Avishay, Avyshay, Avishaye, Avyshaye, Avishai, Avyshai

Avital (Hebrew) The father of the morning's dew
Avitall, Avytal, Avytall

Avner (Hebrew) My Father is the light
Avnar, Avnor, Avnur, Avnir, Avnyr

Avon (Celtic) Of the river
Avun, Aven, Avan, Avin, Avyn

Avram (Hebrew) My Father is exalted
Avrem, Avrim, Avrym, Avrom, Avrum

Avshalom (Hebrew) My Father is peace
Avsalom

Axel (German / Latin / Hebrew) Source of life; small oak / axe / peace
Aksel, Ax, Axe, Axell, Axil, Axill, Axl

Aya (Hebrew) Resembling a bird
Ayah

Ayawamat (Native American) An obedient man

Ayers (English) The heir to a fortune
Ayer, Aires, Aire

Aylmer (English) A renowned and noble man
Aillmer, Ailmer, Allmer, Ayllmer

Aylward (English) A noble guardian
Ailward, Aylwerd, Ailwerd

Aylwen (English) A noble friend
Aylwenn, Aylwenne, Aylwin, Aylwine, Aylwinn, Aylwinne, Aylwyn, Aylwynn, Aylwynne

Ayman (Arabic) One who is fortunate; lucky
Aymen, Aymeen, Aymean, Aymin, Aymein, Aymien, Aymyn

Ayo (African) Filled with happiness
Ayoe, Ayow, Ayowe

Ayubu (African) One who perseveres

Az (Hebrew) Having great strength

Aza (Arabic) One who provides comfort

Azad (Arabic) One who is free

Azamat (Arabic) A proud man; one who is majestic

Azariah (Hebrew) One who is helped by God
Azaria, Azarya, Azria, Azriah, Azuria, Azuriah, Azarious, Azaryah, Azaryahu

Azarni (Japanese) Resembling the thistle flower
Azarnie, Azarny, Azarney, Azarnee, Azarnea

Azekel (African) One who praises the lord
Azekell, Azekil, Azekill, Azekyl, Azekyll

Azhar (Arabic) A famous and shining man
Azhare, Azhair, Azhaire, Azhayr, Azhayre, Azhaer, Azhaere

Azi (African) One who is youthful
Azie, Azy, Azey, Azee, Azea

Azibo (African) Of the earth
Azybo

Azikiwe (African) One who is full of life
Azikiwi, Azikiwie, Azikiwy, Azikiwey, Azikiwee, Azikiwea

Aziz (Arabic) The all-powerful
Azeez, Aziez, Azeiz, Azeaz, Azyz, Azize

Azizi (African) The precious one
Azizie, Azizy, Azizey, Azizee, Azizea

Azmer (Islamic) Resembling a lion
Azmar, Azmir, Azmyr, Azmor, Azmur

Azmera (African) The harvester

Azra (Hebrew) One who is pure; chaste
Azrah, Azraa

Azrael (Hebrew) One who is helped by God
Azraeil, Azrial, Azriel, Azreel, Azreil, Azreal, Azryl, Azril

Azraff (Arabian) An elegant man
Azraf

Azure (French / Persian) Sky blue / resembling a blue semiprecious stone
Azzure, Azuree, Azurine, Azore, Azurah, Azureen, Azuryn, Azuryne, Azuri, Azurie, Azury, Azurey

Azzam (Arabic) One who is determined
Azam

B

Baahi (Arabic) One who is magnificent
Baahie, Baahy, Baahey, Baahee, Baahea

Baakir (African) The eldest child
Baakeer, Baakyr, Baakear, Baakier, Baakeir

Baback (Persian) A loving father
Babak, Babac

Babar (Turkish) Resembling a tiger
Baber, Babir, Babyr, Babor, Babur, Babr

Babatunde (African) One who resembles his grandfather
Babatund, Babatundi, Babatundie, Babatundy, Babatundey, Babatundee

Babson (English) The son of Barbara
Babsun, Babsen, Babsan, Babsin, Babsyn

Babu (African / Hindi) One who is grandfatherly / a fierce man
Babue, Baboo, Babou

Baby (English) A beloved child; a spoiled son
Babi, Babie, Babey, Babe, Bebe, Babea, Babe

Bacchus (Latin) In mythology, the god of wine
Baccus, Baakus, Baackus, Backus, Bach, Bache

Bachelor (French) An unmarried man
Bachellor, Batcheler, Batcheller, Batchelor, Batchellor, Bachelar, Bachellar, Batchelar, Batchellar, Bachelur, Bachellur, Batchelur, Batchelur, Bachelir, Bachellir, Batchelir, Batchelir, Bachelyr, Bachellyr, Batchelyr, Batchelyr, Bacheler, Bacheller, Batch

Bachir (Hebrew) The oldest son
Bacheer, Bachear, Bachier, Bacheir, Bachyr

Bacon (American) One who is outspoken
Bakon, Bacun, Bakun

Badar (Arabic) Born beneath the full moon
Badarr, Bade, Bader, Badr, Badrani, Badranie, Badrany, Badraney, Badranee, Badranea

B

Badawi (Arabian) A nomad
Badawie, Badawy, Badawee,
Badawea

Baden (German) One who bathes
Badin, Badyn, Badan, Badon, Badun

Badger (American) A difficult man
Badgar, Badgyr, Badgir, Badgor, Badgur,
Badgent, Badgeant, Bagent, Bageant

Badi (Arabic) A wonderful man
Badie, Bady, Badey, Badee, Badea

Badru (African) Born beneath the full
moon
Badrue, Badrou, Badroo

Badu (African) The tenth-born child
Badue, Badoo, Badou

Baethan (Irish) The foolish one
Bathan, Baethen, Baythan, Baythen,
Bathen, Baithan, Baithen

Baghel (Arabic) Resembling an ox
Baghell, Baghele, Baghelle

Baha (Arabic) A glorious and splendid
man
Bahah

Bahadur (Arabic) A courageous man

Bahari (African) A man of the sea
Baharie, Bahary, Baharey, Baharee, Baharea

Bahij (Arabic) A delightful man
Baheej, Baheaj, Baheij, Bahiej, Bahyj

Bahir (Arabic) A shining man
Baheer, Bahear, Bahier, Baheir, Bahyr

Bahjat (Arabic) One who brings joy to
others
Bahgat

Bailey (English) From the courtyard within
castle walls; a public official
Bailee, Bayley, Baylee, Baylie, Baili, Bailie,
Baileigh, Bayleigh, Baileah, Bailea, Baylea,
Bayleah, Baylee, Bayli

Bailintin (Irish) A valiant man
Bailinten, Bailentin, Bailenten, Bailintyn,
Bailentyn

Bain (Irish) A fair-haired man
Baine, Bayn, Bayne, Baen, Baene, Bane,
Baines, Baynes, Baenes, Banes

Bainbridge (English) From the bridge over
the pale water
Baynbridge, Baenbridge, Banebridge,
Bainbrige, Baynbrige, Baenbrige, Banebrige

Baird (Gaelic) A minstrel; a poet
Bairde, Bayrd, Bayrde, Bayerd, Baerd, Baerde

Bairn (Gaelic) A child
Bairne, Bayrn, Bayrne, Baern, Baerne

Bajnok (Hungarian) A victorious man
Bajnock, Bajnoc

Bakari (Swahili) One who is promised
Bakarie, Bakary, Bakarey, Bakaree, Bakarea

Baker (English) One who bakes
Bakar, Bakor, Bakur, Bakir, Bakyr

Bakhit (Arabic) A lucky man
Bakheet, Bakheat, Bakheit, Bakhiet,
Bakhyt, Bakht

Bal (Hindi) Having great strength

Bala (Hindi) One who is youthful
Balu, Balue, Balou

Balamani (Indian) A young jewel
Balamanie, Balamany, Balamaney,
Balamanee, Balamanea

Balark (Hindi) Born with the rising sun

Balasi (Basque) One who is flat-footed
Balasie, Balasy, Balasey, Balasee, Balasea

Balbir (Indian) A strong man
Balbeer, Balbear, Balbier, Balbeir, Balbyr

Balbo (Latin) One who mutters
Balboe, Balbow, Balbowe, Ballbo, Balbino,
Balbi, Balbie, Balby, Balbey, Balbee, Balbea

Baldemar (German) A famous and bold
man
Baldemarr, Baldomar, Baldomero, Baumar,
Baldomarr, Baldemero, Baumer, Baumor,
Baumir, Baumur, Baumyr

Balder (English / Norse) Of the brave army
/ in mythology, the god of light
Baldar, Baldur, Baldor, Baldir, Baldyr

Baldev (Indian) Having great strength

B

Baldric (German) A brave ruler
Baldrik, Baldrick, Baldryc, Baldryk,
Baldryck, Balderic, Balderik, Balderick,
Balderyc, Balderyk, Balderyck, Baudric,
Baudrik, Baudrick, Baudryc, Baudryk,
Baudryck

Baldwin (German) A brave friend
Baldwine, Baldwinn, Baldwinne, Baldwen,
Baldwenn, Baldwenne, Baldwyn,
Baldwynn, Baldwynne, Baldewin,
Baldovino, Balduin, Balduino, Balldwin,
Balldwyn, Balldwen, Baudoin, Baldi,
Baldie, Baldy, Baldey, Baldee

Balendin (Basque) A strong and brave man
Balendyn, Balendon, Balendun, Balendan,
Balenden

Balfour (Gaelic) From the grazing land
Balfer, Balfor, Balfore, Ballfour, Ballfer,
Ballfor, Ballfore

Balfre (Spanish) A courageous man
Balfri, Balfrie, Balfrey, Balfry, Balfree,
Balfrea

Balgair (Scottish) Resembling a fox
Balgaire, Balgayr, Balgayre, Balgaer,
Balgaere, Balgare

Baliff (French) A steward
Balyff, Balif, Balyf

Balint (Latin) A healthy and strong man
Balent, Balin, Balen, Balynt, Balyn

Ballard (German) A strong and brave man
Balard, Ballhard, Balhard, Ballardt,
Balardt, Ballhardt, Balhardt

Balloch (Scottish) From the grazing land

Balraj (Hindi) A strong ruler

Balthasar (Babylonian) Baal protect the
king; in the Bible, Baltazar was one of the
three wise men
Baldassare, Baltasar, Baltazar, Balthasaar,
Balthazaar, Balthazar, Balto, Belshazzar,
Baldasarre, Baldassario, Baltsaros

Balwin (English) Form of Baldwin, mean-
ing "a brave friend"
Balwinn, Balwinne, Balwine, Balwen,
Balwenn, Balwenne, Balwyn, Balwynn,
Balwynne

Banan (Irish) A white-skinned man
Banen, Banon, Banin, Banyn, Banun

Bancroft (English) From the bean field
Bancrofte, Banfield, Banfeld, Bankroft,
Bankrofte

Bandana (Spanish) A brightly colored
headwrap
Bandanah, Bandanna, Bandannah

Bandele (African) One who is born away
from home
Bandel, Bandelle, Bandell

Bandy (American) A feisty man
Bandey, Bandi, Bandie, Bandee, Bandea

Banji (African) The second born of twins
Banjie, Banjy, Banjey, Banjee, Banjea

Banjo (English) One who plays the musical
instrument
Banjoe, Banjow, Banjowe

Banner (French) One who holds the flag;
an ensign bearer
Baner, Bannor, Bannur, Bannir, Bannyr,
Bannar, Bannerman, Banerman,
Bannermann, Banermann

Banning (Gaelic) A blonde-haired child
Bannyng, Baning, Banyng

Bannock (Gaelic) Oat bread that is
unleavened
Bannok, Bannoc, Bannoch

Bansi (Indian) One who plays the flute
Bansie, Bansy, Bansey, Bansee, Bansea

Bao (Vietnamese / Chinese) To order / one
who is prized

Baptist (Latin) One who is baptized
Baptiste, Battista, Battiste, Bautiste,
Bautista

Baqir (Arabic) A learned man
Baqeer, Baqear, Baqier, Baqeir, Baqyr,
Baqer

Barak (Hebrew) Of the lightning flash
Barrak, Barac, Barrac, Barack, Barrack

Baram (Hebrew) The son of the nation
Barem, Barum, Barom, Barim, Barym

Barber (French) One who trims or shaves
beards
Barbour, Barbar, Barbor, Barbir, Barbyr,
Barbur

B

Barbod (Persian) A hero

Barclay (English) From the meadow of birch trees
Barcley, Barklay, Barkley, Barklie, Barrclay, Barrklay, Barklea, Barkleah, Barkli, Barkly

Bard (English) A minstrel; a poet
Barde, Bardo

Barden (English) From the barley valley; from the boar's valley
Bardon, Bardun, Bardin, Bardyn, Bardan, Bardene

Bardol (Basque) A farmer
Bardo, Bartol

Bardolf (English) An axe-wolf
Bardolph, Bardalf, Bardalph, Bardulf, Bardulph, Bardawulf, Bardawulph, Bardawolf, Bardawolph

Bardrick (Teutonic) An axe ruler
Bardric, Bardrik, Bardryck, Bardryk, Bardryc, Bardarick, Bardaric, Bardarik, Bardaryck, Bardaryk, Bardaryc, Bardarich, Bardrich

Barek (Arabic) One who is noble
Barec, Bareck

Barend (German) The hard bear
Barende, Barind, Barinde, Barynd, Barynde

Baris (Turkish) A peaceful man
Bariss, Barys, Baryss, Barris, Barrys, Barriss, Barryss

Barker (English) A shepherd
Barkar, Barkir, Barkyr, Barkor, Barkur, Bark, Barke

Barksdale (English) From the valley of birch trees
Barksdayl, Barksdayle, Barksdail, Barksdaile, Barksdael, Barksdaele, Barksdell, Barksdel

Barlaam (Hebrew) The name of a hermit
Barlam

Barlow (English) From the bare hill
Barlowe, Barlo, Barloe, Barrlow, Barrlowe, Barrlo, Barrloe

Barnabas (Hebrew) The son of the prophet; the son of encouragement
Barna, Barnaba, Barnabé, Barnabee, Barnabey, Barnabie, Barnabus, Barnaby, Barnebas, Barnebus, Barnebi, Barnabea

Barnes (English) One who lives near the barns
Barns, Barn, Barne

Barnett (English) Of honorable birth
Barnet, Baronet, Baronett

Barney (English) Form of Barnabas, meaning "the son of the prophet; the son of encouragement"
Barny, Barni, Barnie, Barnee, Barnea, Barner

Barnum (English) From the baron's estate
Barnam, Barnem, Barnom, Barnham, Barnhum, Barnhem

Baron (English) A title of nobility
Barron, Barun, Barrun, Barin, Barrin, Baren, Barren, Baryn, Barryn, Baran, Barran

Barr (English) A lawyer
Barre, Bar

Barra (Gaelic) A fair-haired man

Barram (Irish) A handsome man
Barrem, Barrim, Barrym, Barrom, Barrum

Barrett (German / English) Having the strength of a bear / one who argues
Baret, Barrat, Barratt, Barret, Barrette

Barric (English) From the grain farm
Barrick, Barrik, Barryc, Barryk, Barryck, Beric, Beryc, Berik, Beryk, Berick, Beryck

Barry (Gaelic) A fair-haired man
Barrey, Barri, Barrie, Barree, Barrea, Barrington, Barryngton, Barringtun, Barryngtun, Barringten, Barryngten

Bartholomew (Aramaic) The son of the farmer
Bart, Bartel, Barth, Barthelemy, Bartho, Barthold, Bartholoma, Bartholomaus, Bartholomé, Barthlomeo, Barthol, Barthold, Bartholomeus, Bartin, Bartle, Bartolome, Bartolomeo, Bartolommeo, Bartome, Bartow, Bartt, Bartholemew, Bartholomaios, Barto, Bartalan, Barta, Bates, Bartholemus

Bartlett (French) Form of Bartholomew, meaning "the son of the farmer"
Bartlet, Bartlitt, Bartlit, Bartlytt, Bartlyt

Bartley (English) From the meadow of
birch trees
*Bartly, Bartli, Bartlie, Bartlee, Bartlea,
Bartleah, Bartleigh*

Bartoli (Spanish) Form of Bartholomew,
meaning "the son of the farmer"
*Bartolie, Bartoly, Bartoley, Bartolee,
Bartoleigh, Bartolea, Bartolo, Bartolio*

Barton (English) From the barley town
Bartun, Barten, Bartan, Bartin, Bartyn

Bartram (Scandinavian) The glorious
raven
Bartrem, Barthram, Barthrem

Baruch (Hebrew) One who is blessed
*Boruch, Baruchi, Baruchie, Baruchey,
Baruchy, Baruchee, Baruchea, Baruj*

Baruti (African) One who teaches others
Barutie, Baruty, Barutey, Barutea, Barutee

Barwolf (English) The axe-wolf
Barrwolf, Barwulf, Barrwulf

Bary (Celtic) A marksman
Bari, Barie, Barey, Baree, Barea

Basant (Arabic) One who smiles often
Basante

Base (English) A short man

Bash (African / American) The forerunner /
one who likes to party
*Bashe, Bashi, Bashie, Bashy, Bashey,
Bashee, Bashea*

Bashir (Arabic) A bringer of good news
Basheer, Bashear, Bashier, Basheir, Bashyr

Bashiri (African) A prophet
*Bashirie, Bashiry, Bashirey, Bashiree,
Bashirea*

Basil (Greek) Of the royal family; a kingly
man
*Basile, Basilic, Basilides, Basileios, Basilie,
Basilio, Basilius, Bazeel, Bazeelius, Bazil,
Bazyli*

Basim (Arabic) A smiling man
*Baseem, Baseam, Basiem, Baseim, Basym,
Bahsim, Bahseem, Bahseam, Bahseim,
Bahsiem, Bahsym, Bassam*

Basir (Turkish) An intelligent man
Baseer, Basear, Basier, Baseir, Basyr

Bass (English) Resembling the fish
*Bassy, Bassey, Bassi, Bassie, Bassee,
Bassea*

Bassett (English) A little person
Baset, Basset, Basett

Bastian (French) Form of Sebastian,
meaning "the revered one"
Bastien, Bastiaan

Basy (American) A homebody
Basey, Basi, Basie, Basee, Basea, Basye

Batal (Arabic) A hero

Baul (English) Resembling a snail
Baule, Bawl, Bawle

Baurice (American) Form of Maurice,
meaning "a dark-skinned man; Moorish"
*Baurell, Baureo, Bauricio, Baurids, Baurie,
Baurin, Baurio, Baurise, Baurits, Bauritius,
Bauritz, Baurizio, Bauro, Baurus, Baury,
Baurycy*

Bavol (English) Of the wind
Bavoll, Bavole, Bavolle

Baxley (English) From the baker's meadow
*Baxly, Baxlea, Baxleah, Baxlee, Baxleigh,
Baxli, Baxlie*

Baxter (English) A baker
*Baxtor, Baxtar, Baxtir, Baxtyr, Baxtur, Bax,
Baxe*

Bay (Vietnamese / English) The seventh-
born child; born during the month of July
/ from the bay
Baye, Bae, Bai

Bayard (French) An auburn-haired man
*Baiardo, Bajardo, Bayhard, Baylen, Baylon,
Baylan, Baylun, Baylin, Baylyn*

Bayless (French) One who leases a bay
Bayles, Baylless, Baylles

Bayode (African) One who brings joy

Bayou (French) From the slow-moving
river
Bayu, Bayue

Bazi (Arabic) One who is generous
Bazie, Bazy, Bazey, Bazee, Bazea

Beacher (English) One who lives near the beech trees
Beache, Beech, Beeche, Beach, Beecher, Beachy, Beachey, Beachi, Beachie, Beachee, Beachea, Beechy, Beechey, Beechi, Beechie, Beechee, Beechea

Beacon (English) A signalling light
Beacan, Beacun, Beacen, Beackon, Beackan, Beacken, Beacken, Beecon, Beeckon, Beecun, Beeckun, Beecan, Beeckan, Beecen, Beecken, Beakon, Beakun, Beaken, Beakan, Beekon, Beekun, Beekan, Beeken

Beagan (Gaelic) The small one
Beagen, Beagun, Beagon, Beagin, Beagyn, Beegan, Beegen, Beegin, Beegyn, Beegon, Beegun

Beal (French) A handsome man
Beals, Beale, Beall, Bealle

Beaman (English) A beekeeper
Beeman, Beamon, Beemon, Beamen, Beemen, Beamun, Beemun, Beamin, Beemin, Beamyn, Beemyn

Beamer (English) One who plays the trumpet
Beamor, Beamir, Beamyr, Beamur, Beamar, Beemer, Beemar, Beemir, Beemyr, Beemor, Beemur

Bean (Scottish) One who is lively
Beann, Beane

Beanon (Irish) A well-behaved boy
Beanan, Beanin, Beanyn, Beanun, Beanen, Beinean, Beineon, Binean

Beasley (English) From the pea meadow
Beasly, Beasli, Beaslie, Beaslee, Beaslea, Beasleah, Beasleigh

Beate (German) One who is serious
Beatte, Beahta, Beahtae, Bayahtah

Beattie (Gaelic) One who brings joy
Beatty, Beattey, Beatti, Beattee, Beattea, Beaty, Beatey, Beati, Beatie, Beatee, Beatea

Beau (French) A handsome man; an admirer
Beaudan, Beaudine, Beauden, Beaudin, Beaudyn, Beauregard

Beauchamp (French) From the beautiful field
Beecham, Beachem, Beechem, Beachem

Beauford (French) From the beautiful ford
Beauforde, Beauferd, Beauferde, Beaufurd, Beaufurde

Beaufort (French) From the beautiful fortress

Beaumont (French) From the beautiful mountain
Beaumonte, Belmont, Bellmont, Belmonte, Bellmonte

Beaver (American) Resembling the animal
Beever, Beiver, Biever

Becher (Hebrew) The firstborn son

Beck (English) From the small stream; from the brook
Becker, Becke, Beckar, Beckor, Beckur, Beckir, Beckyr, Beckett, Becket

Bedar (Arabic) One who is attentive
Beder, Bedor, Bedur, Bedyr, Bedir

Bede (English) One who prays; the name of a saint
Beda

Bedell (French) A messenger
Bedel, Bedelle, Bedele, Bedall, Bedal, Bedalle, Bedale

Bedrich (Czech) A peaceful ruler
Bedrych, Bedrick, Bedryck, Bedrik, Bedryk, Bedric, Bedryc

Beebe (English) One who farms bees
Beeson, Beesun, Beesin, Beesyn, Beesen, Beesan

Behrouz (Persian) A lucky man
Behrooz, Behrouze, Behrooze, Behruze

Beige (American) One who is tranquil
Bayge, Baige, Beyge, Baege

Beircheart (Anglo-Saxon) Of the intelligent army

Bekele (African) He has grown
Bekel, Bekelle, Bekell, Bekeel, Bekeal, Bekeil, Bekiel

Bela (Slavic) A white-skinned man
Belah, Bella, Bellah

Belay (African) A superior man
Belaye, Belai, Belae

Beldane (English) From the beautiful glen
*Beldayn, Beldayne, Beldaen, Beldaene,
Beldain, Beldaine*

Belden (English) From the beautiful valley
*Beldan, Beldon, Beldun, Beldin, Beldyn,
Bellden, Belldan, Belldon, Belldun, Belldin,
Belldyn, Beldene, Belldene*

Belen (Greek) Of an arrow
Belin, Belyn, Belan, Belon, Belun

Belindo (English) A handsome and tender
man
*Belyndo, Belindio, Belyndio, Belindeo,
Belyndeo, Belindiyo, Belyndiyo, Belindeyo,
Belyndeyo*

Belisario (Spanish) One who wields a
sword
*Belisareo, Belisarios, Belisarius, Belisareos,
Belisareus*

Bellamy (French) A handsome friend
*Bellamey, Bellami, Bellamie, Bellamee,
Bellamea, Bell, Belamy, Belamey, Belami,
Belamie, Belamee, Belamea*

Bem (African) A peaceful man

Bemossed (Native American) A walker

Bemus (Greek) The foundation
*Beemus, Beamus, Bemis, Beemis, Beamis,
Bemys, Beemys, Beamys*

Ben (English) Form of Benjamin, meaning
"son of the south; son of the right hand"
*Benn, Benni, Bennie, Bennee, Benney,
Benny, Bennea, Benno, Benji, Benjie, Benjy,
Benjey, Benjee, Benjea*

Benaiah (Hebrew) God has established
Benaia, Benaya, Benayah, Benayahu, Beniah

Benci (Hungarian) One who is blessed
Bencie, Bency, Bencey, Bencee, Bencea

Benedict (Latin) One who is blessed
*Bendick, Bendict, Benedetto, Benedick,
Benedicto, Benedictos, Benedictus, Benedikt,
Benedikte, Bengt, Benicio, Benito, Bennedict,
Bennedikt, Bennett, Benet, Benett, Bennet,
Benoit, Bennito, Bennt, Bent, Bendek,
Bendyk, Benes, Benneit*

BENNETT

My husband Brent and I ran off and eloped in Florida. I jokingly told Brent's cousin, Jason Isaac, that I would name our first son after him if he came to our wedding. He and some other friends surprised us by attending! Our son is named Bennett Isaac. Bennett is my maiden name. —Cynthia, MI

Bellarmine (Italian) One who is
handsomely armed
*Bellarmin, Bellarmeen, Bellarmeene,
Bellarmean, Bellarmeane, Bellarmyn,
Bellarmyne*

Bello (African) One who helps others

Belton (English) From the beautiful town
Bellton, Beltun, Belltun, Belten, Bellten

Beluchi (African) God's approval
*Beluchie, Beluchy, Beluchey, Beluchee,
Beluchea*

Belvedere (Italian) One who is beautiful to
see
*Bellveder, Bellvedere, Bellvidere, Belveder,
Belvider, Belvidere*

Belvin (American) Form of Melvin, meaning "a friend who offers counsel"
Belven, Belvyn, Belvon, Belvun, Belvan

Benigno (Italian) One who is wellborn and
kind
*Benygno, Benignio, Benigneo, Benygnio,
Benygneo*

Benjamin ○ ⊙ (Hebrew) Son of the south;
son of the right hand
*Benejamen, Beniamino, Benjaman,
Benjamen, Benjamino, Benjamon,
Benjiman, Benjimen, Benyamin,
Benyamino, Binyamin, Binyamino*

Benjiro (Japanese) One who enjoys peace
Benjyro

Benoni (Hebrew) The son of my sorrow
*Benonie, Benony, Benoney, Benonee,
Benonea*

Benson (English) The son of Ben
*Bensen, Bensun, Bensan, Bensin, Bensyn,
Bensonand, Bense, Bence, Binse, Bince*

Bentley (English) From the meadow of
bent grass
*Bently, Bentleigh, Bentlea, Bentleah,
Bentlee, Bentli, Bentlie*

Benton (English) From the town in the
grassy place
Bentun, Benten, Bentan, Bentin, Bentyn

Benvenuto (Italian) One who is welcome

Beowulf (Anglo-Saxon) An intelligent
wolf
Beowolf, Beowulfe, Beowolfe

Berdy (German) Having a brilliant mind
Berdey, Berdee, Berdea, Berdi, Berdie

Berend (German) As brave as a bear
*Berand, Berind, Berynd, Berond, Berund,
Behrend, Behrind, Behrynd, Behrand,
Behrond, Behrund*

Beresford (English) From the barley ford
*Beresforde, Beresfurd, Beresfurde,
Beresferd, Beresferde, Berford, Berforde,
Berfurd, Berfurde, Berferd, Berferde*

Berg (German) From the mountain
Bergh, Burg, Burgh

Bergen (Scandinavian) One who lives on
the mountain; one who lives on the hill
*Bergan, Bergin, Bergyn, Bergon, Bergun,
Birgen, Birgan, Birgon, Birgun, Birgin, Birgyn*

Berger (French) A shepherd
*Bergar, Bergor, Bergur, Bergir, Bergyr,
Bergeron, Bergeren, Bergeran, Bergerun,
Bergerin, Bergeryn*

Berilo (Spanish) Resembling a pale-
green gem
Berillo, Berylo, Beryllo

Berkeley (English) From the meadow of
birch trees
*Berkely, Berkeli, Berkelie, Berkelea,
Berkeleah, Berkelee, Berkeleigh, Berkley,
Berkly, Berkleigh, Berklee, Berklea,
Berkleah, Berkli, Berklie, Berk, Berke*

Berlin (German) From the borderline

Berlyn (German) The son of Berl
Burlyn

Bern (Scandinavian) Resembling a bear
*Berne, Berni, Bernie, Berny, Berney,
Bernee, Bernea, Bernis, Bernys*

Bernal (German) Having the strength of
a bear
*Bernald, Bernhald, Bernhold, Bernold,
Bernol*

Bernard (German) As strong and brave as
a bear
*Barnard, Barnardo, Barnhard, Barnhardo,
Bearnard, Bernardo, Bernarr, Bernd,
Berndt, Bernhardo, Burnard, Bernadyn,
Bernadin, Bernaden, Benard, Benat*

Berry (English) Resembling a berry fruit
Berrey, Berri, Berrie, Berree, Berrea

Bert (English) One who is illustrious
Berte, Berti, Bertie, Bertee, Bertea, Berty, Bertey

Berthold (German) Having bright strength
*Berthoud, Bertol, Bertoll, Bertold,
Bertolde, Bertell, Bertel, Bertill, Bertil,
Bertyll, Bertyl, Bertolt*

Berton (English) From the bright town
Bertan, Berten, Bertin, Bertyn, Bertun

Bertram (German) The renowned bright
raven
*Beltran, Beltrano, Bertran, Bertrand,
Bertrando, Bertranno*

Berwin (English) A friend of the bear;
a bright friend
*Berwine, Berwinn, Berwinne, Berwen,
Berwenn, Berwenne, Berwyn, Berwynn,
Berwynne*

Bethel (Hebrew) The house of God
*Bethell, Bethele, Bethelle, Betuel, Betuell,
Betuele, Betuelle*

Bevan (Welsh) The son of Evan
*Beavan, Beaven, Bev, Beven, Bevin, Bevon,
Bevvan, Bevvin, Bevvon, Bevun, Beavon,
Beavun, Bevvun, Beavin*

Beverly (English) From the beaver's stream
*Beverlee, Beverley, Beverlie, Beverli,
Beverlee, Beverleigh, Beverlea, Beverleah*

Bevis (Teutonic) An archer
*Beviss, Bevys, Bevyss, Beavis, Beaviss,
Beavys, Beavyss*

Biagio (Italian) One who has a stutter
Biaggio

Bickford (English) From the axman's ford
*Bickforde, Bickfurd, Bickfurde, Bickferd,
Bickferde, Biecaford*

Bienvenido (Spanish) One who is welcome
Beinvenido

Biff (American) A bully
Biffe, Bif, Byff, Byffe, Byf

Bill (English) Form of William, meaning "the determined protector"
Byll, Billi, Billie, Billy, Billey, Billee, Billea, Billeigh

Birch (English) From the birch tree
Birche, Burche, Burch, Birk, Birke

Birchall (English) From the birch manor
Burchall, Birchell, Burchell

Birkett (English) From the birch headland
Birket, Birkit, Birkitt, Burket, Burkett, Burkit, Burkitt, Birkhead, Birkhed

Birkey (English) From the island of birch trees
Birky, Birkee, Birkea, Birki, Birkie

Birney (English) From the island with the brook
Birny, Birnee, Birnea, Birni, Birnie

Birtle (English) From the bird hill
Bertle, Byrtle, Byrtel, Birtel

Bishop (English) A religious overseer
Byshop, Bishopp, Byshopp

Bjorn (Scandinavian) Resembling a bear
Björn, Bjorne, Bjarn, Bjarne

Black (English) A dark-skinned man
Blak, Blac, Blacke

Blackburn (English) From the dark brook
Blackburne, Blackborn, Blackborne, Blackbourn, Blackbourne

Blackstone (English) Of the dark stone

Blackwell (English) From the dark spring
Blackwel, Blackwelle, Blackwele

Blade (English) One who wields a sword or knife
Blayd, Blayde, Blaid, Blaide, Blaed, Blaede

Bladen (English) A hero
Bladan, Bladon, Bladun, Bladin, Bladyn

Blagden (English) From the dark valley
Blagdon, Blagdan, Blagdun, Blagdin, Blagdyn

Blaine (Scottish / Irish) A saint's servant / a thin man
Blayne, Blane, Blain, Blayn, Blaen, Blaene, Blainy, Blainey, Blaini, Blainie, Blainee, Blayni, Blaynie, Blaynee, Blayney, Blayny, Blaeni, Blaenie, Blaeny, Blaeney, Blaenee

Blair (Scottish) From the field of battle
Blaire, Blare, Blayre, Blaer, Blaere, Blayr

Blaise (French) One with a lisp or a stammer
Blais, Blaisdell, Blaese, Blase, Blayse, Blaes, Blays, Blasien, Blasius

Blake ○ ○ (English) A dark, handsome man
Blayk, Blayke, Blaik, Blaike, Blaek, Blaeke

Blakely (English) From the dark meadow
Blakeley, Blakeli, Blakelie, Blakeleigh, Blakelea, Blakeleah, Blakelee

Blakeney (English) From the dark island
Blakeny, Blakeni, Blakenie, Blakenee, Blakenea

Blanco (Spanish) A blonde-haired man; a fair-skinned man
Bianco

Blandon (Latin) A gentle man; one who is mild-tempered
Blanden, Blandan, Blandin, Blandyn, Blandun, Blantun, Blanton, Blantin, Blantyn, Blanten, Blantan

Blanford (English) From the gray-haired man's ford
Blanforde, Blanferd, Blanferde, Blanfurd, Blanfurde, Blandford, Blandforde, Blandferd, Blandferde, Blandfurd, Blandfurde

Blaze (Latin / American) Form of Blaise, meaning "one with a lisp or a stammer" / a fiery man
Blaize, Blaiz, Blayze, Blayz, Blaez, Blaeze

Bliss (English) Filled with happiness
Blis, Blyss, Blys

Blondell (English) A fair-haired boy
Blondel, Blondele, Blondelle

Blythe (English) One who is cheerful and carefree
Blyth, Blith, Blithe, Bligh, Blighthe, Blighth, Bly

Bo (Chinese / Swedish) A precious son / a lively man
Boe

B

Boaz (Hebrew) One who is swift
Boaze, Boas, Boase

Bob (English) Form of Robert, meaning "one who is bright with fame"
Bobbi, Bobbie, Bobby, Bobbey, Bobbee, Bobbea

Boden (French / Scandinavian) One who brings news; a herald / one who provides shelter or is sheltered
Beaudean, Bodie, Bodin, Bodine, Bowden, Bowdin, Bowdyn, Bodyn, Bodi, Body, Bodey, Bodee, Bodea

Bogart (French) One who is strong with the bow
Bogaard, Bogaart, Bogaerd, Bogey, Bogie, Bogi, Bogy, Bogee, Bogea, Boghart, Boghard

Bolivar (Spanish) A mighty warrior
Bolevar, Bolivarr, Bolevarr, Bollivar, Bollivarr, Bollevar, Bollevarr

Bolton (English) From the town with many bends
Boltin, Boltyn, Boltun, Boltan, Bolten, Boulton, Boultan, Boulten, Boultun, Boultin, Boultyn, Boalton, Boaltun, Boalten, Boaltin, Boaltyn, Boaltan

Bonamy (French) A good friend
Bonamey, Bonami, Bonamie, Bonamee, Bonamea

Bonar (French) A gentleman; one who is mannerly
Bonnar, Bonor, Bonnor, Boner, Bonner, Bonur, Bonnur, Bonir, Bonnir, Bonyr, Bonnyr

Bonaventure (Latin) One who undertakes a blessed venture
Bonaventura, Buenaventure, Buenaventura, Bueaventure, Bueaventura

Bond (English) A peasant farmer
Bonde

Boniface (Latin) Having good fortune; one who is benevolent
Bonifacio, Bonifaceo, Bonifacius, Bonifacios, Bonifaco

Booker (English) One who binds books; a scribe
Bookar, Bookir, Bookyr, Bookur, Bookor

Boone (Latin) A good man
Boon

Booth (English) One who lives in a small hut
Boothe, Boot, Boote, Bothi, Bothe, Bothie, Bothy, Bothey, Bothee, Bothea

Borak (Arabic) Of the lightning
Borack, Borac

Bordan (English) From the boar's valley
Borden, Bordin, Bordyn, Bordon, Bordun

Borg (Scandinavian) From the castle
Borge, Borj, Borje

Boris (Slavic) A warrior; having battle glory
Boriss, Borys, Boryss, Borris, Borrys

Bosley (English) From the meadow near the forest
Bosly, Boslee, Boslea, Bosleah, Bosleigh, Bosli, Boslie, Bozley, Bozly, Bozlea, Bozleah, Bozleigh, Bozlee, Bozli, Bozlie

Boston (English) From the town near the forest; from the city of Boston
Bostun, Bostin, Bostyn, Bosten, Bostan

Boswell (English) From the spring near the forest
Boswel, Boswelle, Boswele

Bosworth (English) From the enclosure near the forest
Bosworthe

Botolf (English) The messenger wolf
Botolff, Botolph, Botulf, Botulff, Botulph

Bourbon (French) Resembling the liquor
Borbon, Bourban, Borban, Bourben, Borben, Bourbin, Borbin, Bourbyn, Borbyn, Bourbun, Borbun

Bourne (English) From the brook
Bourn, Born, Borne

Bouvier (Latin) Resembling an ox

Bowen (Welsh) The son of Owen
Bowon, Bowan, Bowun, Bowin, Bowyn

Bowie (Gaelic) A blonde-haired man
Bowi, Bowy, Bowey, Bowee, Bowea

Boyce (French) One who lives near the forest
Boice, Boyse, Boise

Boyd (Celtic) A blonde-haired man
Boyde, Boid, Boide, Boyden, Boydan, Boydin, Boydyn, Boydon, Boydun, Boiden, Boidan, Boidon, Boidun, Boidin, Boidyn

Boyne (Irish) Resembling a white cow
Boyn, Boin, Boine

Boynton (Irish) From the town near the river Boyne
Boyntun, Boynten, Boyntin, Boyntan, Boyntyn

Bracken (English) Resembling the large fern
Braken, Brackan, Brakan, Brackin, Brakin, Brackyn, Brakyn, Brackon, Brakon, Brackun, Brakun

Brad (English) One who has broad shoulders
Bradd

Bradburn (English) From the wide brook
Bradburne, Bradborn, Bradborne, Bradbourn, Bradbourne

Braddock (English) From the broadly spread oak
Bradock, Braddoc, Bradoc, Braddok, Bradok

Braden ✪ (Gaelic / English) Resembling salmon / from the wide valley
*Bradan, Bradon, Braden, Bradin, Bradyn, Braddon, Braddan, Braddin, Braddyn, Bradden, Braydon, Braydan, **Brayden**, Braydin, Braydyn, Braedon, Braeden, Braedan, Braedin, Braedyn, Braidon, Braiden, Braidan, Braidin, Braidyn, Bradene*

Bradford (English) From the wide ford
Bradforde, Bradferd, Bradferde, Bradfurd, Bradfurde

Bradley (English) From the wide meadow
Bradly, Bradlea, Bradleah, Bradlee, Bradleigh, Bradli, Bradlie

Brady ✪ (Irish) The son of a large-chested man
Bradey, Bradee, Bradea, Bradi, Bradie, Braidy, Braidey, Braidee, Braidea, Braidi, Braidie, Braydee, Braydea, Braydy, Braydey, Braydi, Braydie, Braedi, Braedie, Braedee, Braedea, Braedy, Braedey

Brainard (English) A brave raven
Braynard, Branard, Braenard, Brainerd, Braynerd, Braenerd, Branerd

Bram (Gaelic / Irish) Resembling a raven / a thicket of wild gorse
Brahm, Bramm, Brahmm, Brom, Brohm

Bramley (English) From the wild gorse meadow; from the raven's meadow
Bramly, Bramlee, Bramlea, Bramleah, Bramleigh, Bramli, Bramlie

Bramwell (English) From the bramble bush spring; from the raven's spring
Brammell, Bramwel, Bramwyll, Branwell, Branwill, Branwyll, Bramwill

Branch (Latin) An extension
Branche

Brand (English / Norse) A fiery torch / one who wields a sword
Brande, Brandell, Brander, Brando, Brant, Brandt, Brannt, Brantt, Brantli, Brantlie, Brantlea, Brantlee, Brantleigh, Brantly, Brantley

Brandon ✪ ✪ (English) From the broom or gorse hill
Brandun, Brandin, Brandyn, Brandan, Branden, Brannon, Brannun, Brannen, Brannan, Brannin, Brannyn

Branley (English) From the raven's meadow
Branly, Branli, Branlie, Branlee, Branleigh, Branlea, Branleah

Branson (English) The son of Brand or Brandon
Bransun, Bransen, Bransan, Bransin, Bransyn

Branton (English) From the broom or gorse town
Brantun, Brantin, Branten, Brantyn, Brantan, Branston, Branstun, Bransten, Branstin, Branstyn, Branstan

Braulio (Spanish) One who is glowing
Braulo, Brauleo, Brauliyo, Brauleyo, Bravilio, Braviliyo, Bravileo, Bravileyo, Bravlio, Bravleo

Braun (German) Having great strength
Braune, Brawn, Brawne, Brauni, Braunie, Brauny, Brauney, Braunee, Braunea, Brawni, Brawnie, Brawnee, Brawnea, Brawney, Brawny

Bravo (Italian) An excellent man
Brahvo, Bravoe, Bravow, Bravowe, Brahvoe, Bravvo

Brawley (English) From the meadow at the hillslope
Brawly, Brawli, Brawlie, Brawlea, Brawleah, Brawleigh, Brawlee, Brauly, Brauley, Brauli, Braulie, Braulea, Brauleah, Brauleigh, Braulee

Braxton (English) From Brock's town
Braxtun, Braxten, Braxtan, Braxtin,
Braxtyn

Bray (English) One who cries out
Braye, Brai, Brae

Brazier (English) One who works with
brass
Braiser, Braser, Brayser, Braizer, Brazer,
Braezer, Braeser, Brayzer

Brazil (English) From the country of Brazil
Brasil, Brazyl, Brasyl

Breck (Gaelic) One who has freckles
Brek, Brec, Brecken, Breckan, Breckin,
Breckyn, Breckon, Breckun, Brexton,
Brextun, Brextin, Brextyn, Brextan,
Brexten

Bredon (Celtic) One who wields a sword
Bredan, Bredin, Bredyn, Breden, Bredun

Breen (Irish) From the fairy place
Breene, Brean, Breane, Brein, Breine

Breezy (American) A lighthearted man
Breeze, Breezey, Breezi, Breezie, Breezee,
Breezea

Brendan (Irish) Born to royalty; a prince
Brendano, Brenden, Brendin, Brendon,
Brendyn, Brendun

Brennan (Gaelic) A sorrowful man; a
teardrop
Brenan, Brenn, Brennen, Brennin, Brennon,
Brennun, Brennyn, Brenin, Brenyn, Brenon,
Brenun, Brenen

Brent (English) From the hill
Brendt, Brennt, Brentan, Brenten, Brentin,
Brenton, Brentun, Brentyn, Brentt

Brentley (English) From the meadow near
the hill
Brently, Brentlea, Brentleah, Brentleigh,
Brentlee, Brentli, Brentlie

Brett (Latin) A man from Britain or Brittany
Bret, Breton, Brette, Bretton, Brit, Briton,
Britt, Brittain, Brittan, Britte, Britton

Brewster (English) One who brews
Brewer, Brewstere

Brian ♂ ♀ (Gaelic / Celtic) Of noble birth /
having great strength
Briano, Briant, Brien, Brion, **Bryan,**
Bryant, Bryen, Bryent, Bryon

Briar (English) Resembling a thorny plant
Brier, Bryar, Bryer

Brice (Scottish / Anglo-Saxon) One who is
speckled / the son of a nobleman
Bryce, Bricio, Brizio, Brycio, Bryzio

Brick (English) From the bridge
Bryck, Bric, Bryc, Brik, Bryk, Brickman,
Brikman, Bricman, Bryckman, Brykman,
Brycman, Bridger, Brydger, Briger, Bryger

Brigham (English) From the homestead
near the bridge
Brigg, Briggham, Briggs

Brighton (English) From the town near the
bridge
Brightun, Brighten, Brightin, Brightyn,
Brightan

Brinley (English) From the burnt meadow
Brinly, Brinli, Brinlie, Brinleigh, Brinlea,
Brinleah, Brinlee, Brindley, Brindly, Brindli,
Brindlie, Brindleigh, Brindlea, Brindleah,
Brindlee, Brynley, Brynly, Brynli, Brynlie,
Brynleigh, Brynlea, Brynleah, Brynlee,
Bryndley, Bryndly, Bryndli, Bryndlie,
Bryndleigh, Bryndlea, Bryndleah, Bryndlee

Bristol (English) From the city in England
Brystol, Bristow, Brystow

Brock (English) Resembling a badger
Broc, Brok, Brocke, Brockman, Brokman,
Brocman

Brockhoist (English) From the badger's
den
Brokhoist, Brochoist

Brockley (English) From the badger
meadow
Brockly, Brockli, Brocklie, Brocklea,
Brockleah, Brocklee, Brockleigh

Brockton (English) From the badger town
Brokton, Brocton, Brocktun, Broktun,
Broctun, Brockten, Brokten, Brocten,
Brocktin, Broktin, Broctin, Brocktyn,
Broktyn, Broctyn

Broderick (English) From the wide ridge
Broderik, Broderic, Brodrick, Brodryk,
Brodryc, Brodrik, Brodric, Broderyck,
Broderyc, Broderyk, Brodrig, Broderig

Brodie (Scottish) From the castle Brodie
Broden, Brodan, Brodin, Brodyn, Brodon,
Brodun

B

Brody ✪ (Gaelic) From the ditch
Brodey, Brodi, Brodie, Brodee, Brodea

Brogan (Gaelic) One who is sturdy;
reliable
*Broggan, Brogen, Broggen, Brogon,
Broggon, Brogun, Broggun, Brogin,
Broggin, Brogyn, Broggyn*

Broin (Celtic) Resembling a raven
Broine, Broyn, Broyne

Bromley (English) From the broom meadow
*Bromly, Bromli, Bromlie, Bromlee,
Bromlea, Bromleah, Bromleigh, Broomli,
Broomlie, Broomly, Broomley, Broomleigh,
Broomlea, Broomleah, Broomlee*

Bromwell (English) From the spring where
the broom grows
*Bromwel, Bromwill, Bromwil, Bromwyll,
Bromwyl*

Bronco (Spanish) Resembling an unbroken
horse
Bronko, Broncko

Bronson (English) The son of Brown
*Bronnson, Bronsen, Bronsin, Bronsonn,
Bronsson, Bronsun, Bronnsun, Bronssun,
Bronsenn, Bronssen, Bronsinn, Bronssin*

Brooks (English) From the running stream
Brookes, Brook, Brooke

Brookson (English) The son of Brooks
*Brooksen, Brooksun, Brooksone,
Brooksan, Brooksin, Brooksyn*

Broughton (English) From the fortress
town
*Broughtun, Broughten, Broughtin,
Broughtyn, Broughtan*

Brown (English) One who has a russet
complexion
*Browne, Broun, Broune, Brun, Bron,
Brune, Brone*

Bruce (Scottish) A man from Brieuse; one
who is wellborn; from an influential family
*Brouce, Brooce, Bruci, Brucie, Brucey,
Brucy, Brucee, Brucea*

Bruno (German) A brown-haired man
*Brunoh, Brunoe, Brunow, Brunowe, Bruin,
Bruine, Brunon, Brunun, Brunen, Brunan,
Brunin, Brunyn, Bruino*

Brunswick (German) From Bruno's village
*Brunswic, Brunswik, Brunswyck,
Brunswyc, Brunswyk*

Brutus (Latin) A dull-witted man
Bruto

Bryn (Welsh) From the hill
Brinn, Brin, Brynn

Brynmor (Welsh) From the large hill
*Brynmore, Brinmor, Brinmore, Brynnmor,
Brynnmore, Brinnmor, Brinnmore*

Bryson (Welsh) The son of Brice
*Brysen, Brysin, Brysun, Brysyn, Brycen,
Brycin, Brycyn, Brycun*

Buagh (Irish) A victorious man
Buach

Bubba (German) A boy
Buba, Bubbah, Bubah

Buck (English) Resembling a male deer
*Buk, Buc, Bucki, Buckie, Bucky, Buckey,
Buckee, Buckea*

Buckley (English) From the deer meadow
*Buckly, Buckli, Bucklie, Bucklea, Buckleah,
Bucklee, Buckleigh*

Buckminster (English) From the
monastery where deer live
Buckmynster

Bud (English) One who is brotherly
*Budd, Buddi, Buddie, Buddee, Buddea,
Buddey, Buddy*

Buddha (Sanskrit) One who has achieved
spiritual enlightenment

Budha (Hindi) Another name for the planet
Mercury
Budhan, Budhwar

Budhil (Indian) A learned man
*Budheel, Budheal, Budheil, Budhiel,
Budhyl*

Buell (German) One who lives on a hill
Buel, Bueller, Buhl, Buhler, Buehl, Buehler

Bulat (Russian) Having great strength
Bulatt

Bundar (Arabic) One who is smart and
wealthy
Bunder, Bundor, Bundur, Bundir, Bundyr

B

Bundy (English) A free man
Bundey, Bundi, Bundie, Bundee, Bundea

Bunmi (African) My gift
*Bunmie, Bunmy, Bunmey, Bunmee,
Bunmea*

Burbank (English) From the riverbank of
burrs
Burrbank, Burhbank

Burchard (English) As strong as a castle
*Bucardo, Burckhardt, Burgard, Burgaud,
Burkhart, Burckhart, Burkhardt*

Burdett (English) Resembling a bird
Burdet, Burdette, Burdete

Burdon (English) One who lives at the castle
*Burdun, Burdan, Burden, Burdin, Burdyn,
Burhdon, Burhdun, Burhden, Burhdan,
Burhdin, Burhdyn*

Burford (English) From the castle near the
ford
*Burforde, Burfurd, Burfurde, Burferd,
Burferde, Buford, Buforde, Bufurd, Bufurde,
Buferd, Buferde*

Burgess (German) A free citizen of the
town
*Burges, Burgiss, Burgis, Burgyss, Burgys,
Burgeis*

Burke (French) From the fortress on the hill
*Berk, Berke, Birk, Bourke, Burk, Birke,
Bourk, Byrk, Byrke*

Burl (English) From the knotted wood
Burle, Burrel, Burrell, Burell, Burel

Burleigh (English) From the meadow of
knotted wood
*Burlea, Burleah, Burlee, Burli, Burlie,
Burley, Burly, Byrleigh, Byrlea, Byrleah,
Byrli, Byrlie, Byrly, Byrley, Byrlee*

Burnaby (Norse) From the warrior's estate
*Burnabey, Burnabi, Burnabie, Burnabee,
Burnabea*

Burne (English) Resembling a bear; from
the brook; the brown-haired one
*Burn, Beirne, Burnis, Byrn, Byrne, Burns,
Byrnes*

Burnell (French) The small brown-
haired one
*Burnel, Burnelle, Burnele, Brunell, Brunel,
Brunele, Brunelle*

Burnet (French) Having brown hair
*Burnett, Burnete, Burnette, Bernet,
Bernett, Bernete, Bernette*

Burney (English) From the island with the
brook
*Burny, Burnee, Burnea, Burni, Burnie,
Beirney, Beirnie, Beirny, Beirni, Beirnee,
Beirnea, Burneig, Beirnig*

Burr (English) A bristle

Burt (English) From the fortress
Burte, Burtt

Burton (English) From the fortified town
Burtun, Burten, Burtin, Burtyn, Burtan

Busby (Scottish) From the village near the
thicket
*Busbey, Busbee, Busbea, Busbi, Busbie,
Bussby, Bussbey, Bussbi, Bussbie, Bussbee,
Bussbea*

Butch (American) A manly man
Butcher

Butler (English) The keeper of the bottles
(wine, liquor)
*Buttler, Butlar, Buttlar, Butlor, Buttlor,
Butlir, Buttlir, Butlyr, Buttlyr*

Buzz (Scottish) A popular young man
*Buzze, Buzzi, Buzzy, Buzzee, Buzzea, Buzzy,
Buzzey*

Bwana (Swahili) A gentleman
Bwanah

Byford (English) One who lives near
the ford
Byforde, Byferd, Byferde, Byfurd, Byfurde

Byrd (English) Resembling a bird
*Byrde, Bird, Birde, Byrdi, Byrdie, Byrdee,
Byrdea, Byrdy, Byrdey, Birdi, Birdie, Birdee,
Birdea, Birdey, Birdy*

Byron (English) One who lives near the
cow sheds
*Byrom, Beyren, Beyron, Biren, Biron,
Buiron, Byram, Byran, Byren, Byrem,
Byrun, Byrum*

C

Cabalero (Spanish) A horseman or a knight
Caballero, Cabaliero, Caballiero, Cabalerio, Caballerio, Cabalereo, Caballareo

Cable (French) One who makes rope
Cabel, Caibel, Caible, Caybel, Cayble, Caebel, Caeble, Cabe

Cabot (French) One who sails
Cabbot

Cabrera (Spanish) An able-bodied man
Cabrere, Cabrero, Cabrerio, Cabreriyo, Cabrereo, Cabrereyo

Cack (American) Full of laughter
Cak, Cac, Cackie, Cacki, Cacky, Cackey, Cackee, Cackea

Cactus (American) Resembling the prickly plant
Caktus, Cacktus

Cadarn (Welsh) Having great strength
Cadern, Cadorn, Cadurn, Cadirn, Cadyrn

Cadby (English) From the warrior's settlement
Cadbey, Cadbee, Cadbea, Cadbi, Cadbie

Cadda (English) A warring man
Cada, Caddah, Cadah

Caddarik (English) A leader during battle
Caddarick, Caddaric, Caddaryk, Caddaryck, Caddaryc, Cadarik, Cadarick, Cadaric, Cadaryk, Cadaryck, Cadaryc

Caddis (English) Resembling a worsted fabric
Caddys, Caddiss, Caddice, Caddyss

Caddock (Welsh) One who is eager for war
Caddoc, Caddok, Caddog

Cade (English / French) One who is round / of the cask
Caid, Caide, Cayd, Cayde, Caed, Caede, Caden, Cayden, Caiden, Caeden, Cadon, Caydon, Caedon, Caidon, Cadan, Caydan, Caedan, Caidan, Cadin, Caedin, Caydin, Caidin, Cadyn, Caedyn, Caydyn, Caidyn

Cadell (Welsh) Having the spirit of battle
Cadel, Caddell, Caddel

Caden ☼ (Welsh) Spirt of battle

Cadence (Latin) Rhythmic and melodious; a musical man
Cadenze, Cadense, Cadian, Cadienne, Cadince, Cadiene, Caydence, Cadinse, Caidence, Caidense, Caidenze, Caydense, Caydenze, Caedence, Caedense, Caedenze

Cadman (Welsh) A wise warrior
Cadmon, Cadmun, Cadmin, Cadmyn, Cadmen, Caedman, Caedmon, Caedmun, Caedmin, Caedmyn, Caedmen, Caydman, Caydmon, Caydmun, Caydmen, Caydmin, Caydmyn, Caidman, Caidmon, Caidmun, Caidmen, Caidmin, Caidmyn

Cadmus (Greek) A man from the East; in mythology, the man who founded Thebes
Cadmar, Cadmo, Cadmos, Cadmuss

Cadogan (Welsh) Having glory and honor during battle
Cadogawn, Cadwgan, Cadwgawn, Cadogaun, Cadwgaun

Caduceus (Greek) The symbol of the medical profession; in mythology, Hermes's insignia
Caduseus, Caducius, Cadusius, Caducios, Cadusios

Caelan (Gaelic) A slender warrior; one who is slender and fair
Cailan, Caylan, Calan, Caelen, Cailen, Caylen, Calen, Cailon, Caylon, Caelon, Calon, Cailin, Caylin, Caelin, Calin, Cailyn, Caelyn, Caylyn, Calyn

Caellum (Celtic) A brave warrior
Caellom, Caillum, Caillom, Cayllom, Cayllum

Caesar (Latin) An emperor; having a full head of hair
Caezar, Casar, César, Cesar, Cesare, Cesaro, Cesario, Cezar, Chezare, Caesarius, Ceasar, Ceazer, Ceasario

Caflice (Anglo-Saxon) A brave man
Caflyce, Caflise, Caflyse

Cahal (Celtic) One who is strong in battle
Cahall, Cahale, Cahalle

Cahil (Turkish) A young boy
Cahyl, Caheel, Caheal, Caheil, Cahiel

Cahir (Irish) A mighty warrior
Caheer, Cahear, Cahier, Caheir, Cahyr

Cain (Hebrew) One who wields a spear; something acquired; in the Bible, Adam and Eve's first son, who killed his brother Abel
Cayn, Caen, Cane, Caine, Cayne, Caene

Caindale (English) From the valley with the clear river
Caindail, Caindayl, Caindaile, Caindayle, Caindell, Cayndale, Cayndail, Cayndaile, Cayndayl, Cayndayle, Cayndell, Caendail, Caendaile, Caendale, Caendayl, Caendayle, Caendell, Canedell, Canedail, Canedaile, Canedayl, Canedayle, Canedale

Caird (Scottish) A traveling metal worker
Cairde, Cayrd, Cayrde, Caerd, Caerde

Cairn (Gaelic) From the mound of rocks
Cairne, Cairns, Caern, Caerne, Caernes

Cairo (Arabic) One who is victorious; from the capital of Egypt

Cais (Vietnamese) One who rejoices

Caith (Irish) Of the battlefield
Caithe, Cayth, Caythe, Cathe, Caeth, Caethe

Caius (Latin) One who rejoices
Cai, Caio

Cajetan (English) A man from Gaeta
Cajetano, Cajetanio, Cajetaneo

Calbert (English) A cowboy
Calberte, Calburt, Calburte, Calbirt, Calbirte, Calbyrt, Calbyrte

Calder (Scottish) Of the rough waters or stream
Caldar, Caldor, Caldur, Caldir, Caldyr, Caldre

Caldwell (English) From the cold spring
Cadwell, Caldwel, Cadwel

Cale (English) Form of Charles, meaning "one who is manly and strong / a free man"
Cail, Caile, Cayl, Cayle, Cael, Caele

Caleb ✪ ⚥ (Hebrew) Resembling a dog
Cayleb, Caileb, Caeleb, Calob, Cailob, Caylob, Caelob

Caley (Gaelic) One who is lean
Caly, Cali, Calie, Caleigh, Calee, Calea, Cailey, Caily, Cailee, Cailea, Caileigh, Caili, Cailie, Cayley, Cayly, Caylee, Cayleigh, Caylea, Cayli, Caylie, Caeley, Caely, Caelee, Caeleigh, Caelea, Caeli, Caelie

Calhoun (Gaelic) From the narrow forest
Callhoun, Colhoun, Colquhoun, Coillcumhann

Calian (Native American) A warrior of life
Calien, Calyan, Calyen

Calibur (English) Form of Excalibur, in mythology, King Arthur's sword
Calibor, Caliborn, Caliborne, Calibourn, Calibourne, Caliburn, Caliburne

Calix (Greek) A handsome man
Calyx, Calex, Calax, Calox, Calux

Callis (Latin) Resembling a chalice
Callys, Callice, Callyce, Callyx

Calogero (Italian) Of fair old age
Calogeros, Calogerus, Calogerio, Calogereo

Calum (Gaelic) Resembling a dove
Callum, Calom, Callom

Calumet (French) Resembling a reed
Callumet

Calvagh (Irish) One who is bald
Calvaugh, Callough

Calvert (English) One who herds cows; a cowboy
Calbert, Calvirt, Calbirt, Calvurt, Calburt, Calvex

Calvin (French) The little bald one
Calvyn, Calvon, Calven, Calvan, Calvun, Calvino, Calvinio, Calvineo, Cal

Camara (African) One who teaches others

Camden (Gaelic) From the winding valley
Camdene, Camdin, Camdyn, Camdan, Camdon, Camdun

Cameo (English) A small, perfect child
Cammeo

Cameron ✪ ✪ (Scottish) Having a crooked nose
Cameren, Cameran, Camerin, Cameryn, Camerun, Camron, Camren, Camran, Camrin, Camryn, Camrun, Cameroon, Camero, Camaeron, Camri, Camrie, Camry, Camrey, Camree, Camrea, Cam, Camy, Camey, Camee, Camea, Cami, Camie

Camilo (Latin) One who is born free; one who is noble
Camillo, Camylo, Camyllo, Camillus, Camyllus

Campbell (Scottish) Having a crooked mouth
Campbel, Cambell, Cambel, Camp, Campe, Cambeul, Cambeull, Campbeul, Campbeull

Campion (English) The champion
Campian, Campien, Campiun

Can (Turkish) One who is dearly loved

Canby (English) From the farm near the reeds
Canbey, Canbi, Canbie, Canbee, Canbea

Candan (Turkish) A sincere man
Canden, Candin, Candyn, Candon, Candun

Candelario (Spanish) Refers to the feast of Candlemas
Candelareo, Candelaro, Candelerio, Candelero, Candelariyo, Candelareyo

Candido (Latin) One who is white; pure; chaste
Candide, Candidio, Candideo, Candydo, Candyde, Candydio, Candydeo

Canfield (English) From the field of reeds
Canfeld, Cannfield, Cannfeld

Canh (Vietnamese) Of the endless environment

Canice (Irish) A handsome man
Canyce, Canis, Caniss, Canys, Canyss, Canicius, Cainneach

Cannon (French) An official of the church
Canon, Canning, Caning, Cannyng, Canyng, Cannan, Canan, Cannun, Canun

Canute (Scandinavian) A knot
Cnute, Cnut

Canyon (Spanish / English) From the foot-path / from the deep ravine
Caniyon, Canyun, Caniyun

Caolan (Irish) A lean man
Caolen, Caolin, Caolyn, Caolun, Caolon

Capek (Czech) Resembling a small stork
Capec, Capeck

Capp (French) A chaplain
Cap, Capps, Caps

Capricorn (Latin) The tenth sign of the zodiac; the goat

Car (Celtic) A warrior

Caradoc (Welsh) One who is much loved
Caradok, Caradock, Caradog, Caradawc, Caradawk, Caradawck, Caradawg

Carbry (Celtic) One who drives a chariot
Carbrey, Carbri, Carbrie, Carbree, Carbrea

Carden (English) One who cards wool
Cardan, Cardin, Cardyn, Cardon, Cardun, Card, Carde

Cardew (Celtic) From the dark fortress
Cardou, Cardu, Cardoo

Carew (Latin) Of the chariot
Carewe, Crew, Crewe

Cargan (Gaelic) From the small rock
Cargen, Cargon, Cargun, Cargin, Cargyn

Carl ✪ (German) Form of Karl, meaning "a free man"
*Carel, Carlan, Carle, Carlens, Carlitis, Carlin, Carlo, **Carlos**, Carrel, Carol, Caroly, Carlen, Caarl, Caarlo, Carlis, Carlys, Carroll, Carolus, Carrol, Caroll, Caryl, Caryll, Carolos*

Carley (English) From the farmer's meadow
Carly, Carli, Carlie, Carleigh, Carlea, Carleah

Carlomagno (Spanish) Charles the great
Carlmagno, Carlemagno

Carlow (Ireland) From a town in Ireland
Carlowe, Carloe

Carlsen (Scandinavian) The son of Carl
Carlssen, Carlson, Carlsson, Carlsun, Carllsun, Carlsin, Carllsin, Carlsyn, Carllsyn

Carlton (English) From the free man's town
Carltun, Carltown, Carston, Carstun, Carstown, Carleton, Carletun, Carlten, Carsten, Carleten

Carlyle (English) From the fort at Luguvalium
Carlile, Carlisle

Carmelo (Hebrew) From the fruitful orchard
Carmello, Carmel, Carmeli, Carmelie, Carmely, Carmeley, Carmelee, Carmelea, Carmeleigh, Carmi, Carmie, Carmee, Carmea, Carmy, Carmey

Carmichael (Scottish) A follower of Michael

Carmine (Latin / Aramaic) A beautiful song / the color crimson
Carman, Carmen, Carmin, Carmino, Carmyne, Carmon, Carmun, Carmyn

Carnell (English) The defender of the castle
Carnel, Carnele, Carnelle, Carne, Carn

Carney (Irish) The victor
Cearnach, Carny, Carni, Carnie, Carnee, Carnea

Carnig (Armenian) Resembling a lamb
Carnigg, Carnyg, Carnygg

Carollan (Irish) The little champion
Carolan, Carollen, Carolen, Carollin, Carolin, Carollyn, Carolyn

Carpenter (Latin) One who makes carriages
Carpentar, Carpentor, Carpentur, Carpentir, Carpentyr, Charpentier

Carr (Scandinavian) From the swampy place
Carre

Carrick (Irish) From the rocks
Carrik, Carric, Carryck, Carryk, Carryc, Carick, Carik, Caric, Caryc, Caryk, Caryck

Carrington (English) From the rocky town
Carryngton, Carringtun, Carryngtun, Carringten, Carryngten

Carson ⚫ (Scottish) The son of a marsh dweller
Carsen, Carsun, Carsan, Carsin, Carsyn

Carswell (English) From the watercress spring
Carswel, Caswell, Caswel, Cresswell, Creswell, Creswel, Cresswel

Carter ⚫ (English) One who transports goods; one who drives a cart
Cartar, Cartir, Cartyr, Cartor, Cartur, Cartere, Cartier, Cartrell, Cartrel

Cartland (English) From Carter's land
Carteland, Cartlan, Cartlend, Cartelend, Cartlen

Carvell (French) From the village near the swamp
Carvelle, Carvel, Carvele, Carvil, Carvile, Carville, Carvill

Carver (English) One who carves wood
Carvar, Carvor, Carvir, Carvyr, Carvur

Cary (Celtic / Welsh / Gaelic) From the river / from the fort on the hill / having dark features
Carey, Cari, Carie, Caree, Carea, Carry, Carrey, Carri, Carrie, Carree, Carrea

Case (French) Refers to a chest or box
Cace

Casey (Gaelic) One who is alert; watchful
Casy, Casi, Casie, Casee, Cacey, Cacy, Caci, Cacie, Cacee, Caycey, Caycy, Cayci, Caycie, Caycee, Caicey, Caicy, Caici, Caicie, Caicee, Caysey, Caysy, Caysi, Caysie, Caysee, Caisey, Caisy, Caisi, Caisie, Caisee

Casimir (Slavic) One who demands peace
Casimeer, Casmire, Casimiro, Casmir, Casimear, Casimyr, Casimeir, Casimier

Caspar (Persian) The keeper of the treasure
Casper, Caspur, Caspor, Caspir, Caspyr

Caspian (English) From the sea
Caspien, Caspion, Caspiun

Cassander (Spanish) A brother of heroes
Casander, Casandro, Cassandro, Casandero, Cassandero

Cassidy (Gaelic / Irish / Welsh) A clever man / a curly-haired man / one who is ingenious
Cassidey, Cassidi, Cassidie, Cassidee, Cassady, Cassadey, Cassadi, Cassadie, Cassadee, Cassedy, Cassedey, Cassedi, Cassedie, Cassedee, Cass

Cassiel (Hebrew) The name of an archangel
Cassiell, Casiel, Casiell

Cassius (Latin) One who is empty; hollow; vain
Cassios, Cassio, Cach, Cache, Cashus, Cashos, Cassian, Cassien, Cassianus

Castel (Spanish) From the castle
Castell, Castal, Castall, Castol, Castoll, Castul, Castull, Castil, Castill, Castyl, Castyll

Castor (Greek) Resembling a beaver; in mythology, one of the Dioscuri
Castur, Caster, Castar, Castir, Castyr, Castorio, Castoreo, Castoro, Castro

Cat (American) Resembling the animal
Catt, Chait, Chaite

Cathair (Celtic) A fighter
Cathaire, Cathayr, Cathayre, Cathaer, Cathaere, Cathare, Cathaoir

Cathal (Gaelic) The ruler of the battle
Cathel, Cathol, Cathul, Cathil, Cathyl

Cathan (American) Form of Nathan, meaning "a gift from God"
Caithan, Cathun, Cathon, Cathen, Caithun, Caithon, Caithen, Caethan, Caethun, Caethon, Caethen, Caythan, Caythun, Caython, Caythen

Cathmore (Irish) A renowned fighter
Cathmor, Cathemore, Cathemor

Catlin (Irish) One who is pure; chaste
Catlon, Catlyn, Catlun, Catalin, Catalyn, Catalen, Catalan, Catlen, Catlan, Catalon, Catalun

Cato (Latin) One who is all-knowing
Cayto, Caito, Caeto

Caton (Spanish) One who is knowledgable
Caten, Catun, Catan, Catin, Catyn

Catori (Native American) A spiritual man
Catorie, Catory, Catorey, Catoree, Catorea

Cauley (Scottish) A righteous man; a relic
Cauly, Caulee, Cauleigh, Caulea, Cauli, Caulie, Cawley, Cawly, Cawleigh, Cawlee, Cawlea, Cawli, Cawlie

Cavan (Gaelic) A handsome man
Caven, Cavin, Cavyn, Cavon, Cavun

Cavanagh (Irish) A follower of Kevin
Cavanaugh, Cavanaw, Cavanawe

Cavell (Teutonic) One who is bold
Cavel, Cavele, Cavelle

Caxton (English) From the lump settlement
Caxtun, Caxten

Ceallach (Irish) A bright-headed man
Ceallachan

Ceard (Scottish) A smith
Ceardach

Ceastun (English) From the army camp
Ceaston, Ceasten, Ceastan, Ceastin, Ceastyn, Ceaster, Ceastar, Ceastor, Ceastir, Ceastyr, Ceastur

Cecil (Latin / Welsh) One who is blind / the sixth-born child
Cecilio, Cecilius, Celio

Cedric (Welsh) One who is kind and loved; of the spectacular bounty
Caddaric, Ced, Cedrick, Cedrik, Cedryc, Cedryk, Cedryck

Cedro (Spanish) Form of Isadoro, meaning "a gift of Isis"
Cedroe, Cedrow, Cedrowe, Cidro, Cidroe, Cidrow, Cidrowe

Celesto (Latin) From heaven
Célestine, Celestino, Celindo, Celestyne, Celestyno

Celso (Italian) One who is lofty
Celsius, Celsus

Cendrick (English / Gaelic) A royal ruler / the champion
Cendric, Cendricks, Cendrik, Cendrix, Cendryck, Cenrick, Cenrik, Cenricks, Cendryk, Cendryc, Cenric, Cendriek, Cendryek, Cenrich, Cendrich, Cenriek, Cenryk, Cynric, Cynrick, Cynrik, Cynrich, Cyneric, Cynerik, Cynerick, Cynerich

Cenehard (English) A bold guardian
Cenhard, Cynhard, Cynehard

Cenewig (English) A bold warrior
Cenwig, Cenwyg, Cenewyg

Cephas (Hebrew) As solid as a rock

Cerdic (Anglo-Saxon) A king
Cerdick, Cerdik, Cerdyc, Cerdyc, Cerdyck

Cermak (Czech) Resembling a robin
Cermac, Cermack

Cerny (Czech) A black-haired man
Cerney, Cerni, Cernie, Cernee, Cernea

Cerys (Welsh) One who is dearly loved
Ceris, Ceryss, Ceriss

Cestmir (Slavic) From the fortress
Cestmeer, Cestmear, Cestmeir, Cestmier, Cestmyr

Chacha (African) Having great strength

Chad (English) One who is warlike
Chaddie, Chadd, Chadric, Chadrick, Chadrik, Chadryck, Chadryc, Chadryk

Chadburn (English) From the warrior's stream
Chadburne, Chadborn, Chadborne, Chadbourn, Chadbourne, Chadbyrn, Chadbyrne

Chadwick (English) From Chad's dairy farm
Chadwik, Chadwic, Chadwyck, Chadwyk, Chadwyc

Chael (Latin) A heavenly messenger; an angel
Chaele

Chagai (Hebrew) One who meditates

Chai (Hebrew) A giver of life
Chaika, Chaim, Cahyim, Cahyyam

Chairo (Spanish) Having a sacred name
Chiro

Chaka (African) A great king
Chakah

Chakra (Arabic) A center of spiritual energy

Chale (Spanish) A strong man
Chail, Chaile, Chael, Chaele, Chayl, Chayle

Chalkley (English) From the chalk meadow
Chalkly, Chalkleigh, Chalklee, Chalkleah, Chalkli, Chalklie, Chalklea

Chalmers (French) A chamber servant
Chalmer, Chamber, Chambers, Chalmar, Chalmars

Chamberlain (English) The chief officer of the noble's household
Chambellan, Chamberlin, Chamberlyn, Chamberlen

Champion (English) A warrior; the victor
Champeon, Champiun, Champeun, Champ

Chan (Spanish / Sanskrit) Form of John, meaning "God is gracious" / a shining man
Chayo, Chano, Chawn, Chaun

Chanan (Hebrew) God is compassionate
Chanen, Chanin, Chanyn, Chanun, Chanon

Chance (English) Having good fortune
Chanse, Chantz, Chanze, Chaunce, Chancey, Chancy, Chanci, Chancie, Chancee, Chancea

Chancellor (French) The office holder; the keeper of the records
Chancelor, Chansellor, Chanselor, Chauncellor, Chauncelor, Chaunsellor, Chaunselor, Chanceller, Chanceler, Chanseller, Chanseler, Chaunceller, Chaunceler, Chaunsellor, Chaunseler

Chand (Hindi) Born beneath the moon's light
Chande, Chandak, Chandan

Chandler (English) One who makes candles
Chandlar, Chandlor, Chandlur, Chandlir, Chandlyr

Chaney (French) From the oak tree
Chany, Chani, Chanie, Chanee, Chanea, Chalney, Chalny, Chalni, Chalnie, Chalnee, Cheney, Cheny, Cheni, Chenie, Chenee

Chang (Chinese) One who is unhindered

Chaniel (Hebrew) The grace of God
Chanyel, Chaniell, Chanyell

Chann (English) Resembling a young wolf
Channe, Channon, Channun, Channen, Channan, Channin, Channyn, Channer, Channar, Channir, Channor, Channur, Channyr

Channing (French / English) An official of the church / resembling a young wolf
Channyng, Canning, Cannyng

Chanoch (Hebrew) A dedicated man
Channoch, Chanok, Chanoc, Chanock, Channok, Channoc, Channock

Chansomps (Native American) Resembling a locust

Chantry (French) One who sings
Chantrey, Chantri, Chantrie, Chantree, Chantrea

Chao (Chinese) The great one

Chapal (Indian) One who is quick

Chaparral (Spanish) From the dwarf oak
Chaparrall, Chaparal, Chaparall

Chaplin (English) A secretary; a spiritual guide
Chaplain, Chaplinn, Chaplyn, Chappelin, Chappelyn

Chapman (English) A merchant; a peddler
Chapmann, Chap, Chappy, Chappi, Chappey, Chappie, Chappee

Chappel (English) One who works in the chapel
Capel, Capell, Capello, Cappel, Chappell

Charles ○ (English / German) One who is manly and strong / a free man
Charls, Chas, Charli, Charlie, Charley, Charly, Charlee, Charleigh, Charlea, Chaz, Chazz, Chars

Charleson (English) The son of Charles
Charlesen, Charlesin, Charlesyn, Charlesan, Charlesun

Chatwin (English) A warring friend
Chatwine, Chatwinn, Chatwinne, Chatwen, Chatwenn, Chatwenne, Chatwyn, Chatwynn, Chatwynne

Chauncey (French / English) An office holder; keeper of records / having good fortune
Chauncy, Chaunci, Chauncie, Chauncee, Chaunsey, Chaunsy, Chaunsie, Chaunsi, Chaunsee, Chawncey, Chawncy, Chawnci, Chawncie, Chawncee, Chawnsey, Chawnsy, Chawnsi, Chawnsie, Chawnsee

Chavez (Spanish) A dream maker
Chaves

Chaviv (Hebrew) One who is dearly loved
Chaveev, Chaveav, Chaviev, Chaveiv, Chavyv, Chavivi, Chavivie, Chavivy, Chavivey, Chavivee

Chay (Gaelic) From the fairy place
Chaye, Chae

Chayim (Hebrew) A giver of life
Chayem

Chayton (Native American) Resembling a falcon
Chaiton, Chaeton, Chaton, Chayten, Chaiten, Chaeten, Chaten

CHARLIE
We chose to name our son Charlie after his grandfather. But it seemed just right since we have a beagle—just like Charlie Brown and his beagle, Snoopy. —Maggie, IL

Charlot (French) The son of Charlemagne

Charlton (English) From the free man's town
Charleton, Charltun, Charletun, Charleston, Charlestun

Charro (Spanish) A cowboy
Charo

Chase ○ (English) A hunstman
Chace, Chasen, Chayce, Chayse, Chaise, Chaice, Chaece, Chaese, Chacen, Chaycen, Chaysen, Chaisen, Chaicen, Chaecen, Chaesen, Chaseyn, Chayson, Chaison, Chaeson, Chason

Che (Spanish) Form of José, meaning "God will add"
Chepe, Chepito

Cheikh (African) A learned man

Chelsey (English) From the landing place for chalk
Chelsee, Chelseigh, Chelsea, Chelsi, Chelsie, Chelsy, Chelcey, Chelcy, Chelci, Chelcie, Chelcee, Chelcea

Chen (Hebrew / Chinese) Having grace or favor / of the dawn

Cherokee (Native American) A tribal name
Cheroki, Cherokie, Cherokey, Cheroky, Cherokeigh, Cherokea, Cherokeah

Cherut (Hebrew) One who is free
Cheroot, Cherout, Cherute, Cheroote, Cheroute

Cheslav (Russian) From the fortified camp
Cheslaw

Chesley (English) From the meadow
Chesli, Cheslie, Chesly, Chesleigh, Cheslea, Chesleah, Cheslee

Chesmu (Native American) A gritty man
Chesmue, Chesmew, Chesmoo

Chesney (English) One who promotes peace
Chesny, Chesni, Chesnie, Chesnea, Chesneah, Chesnee

Chester (Latin) From the camp of the soldiers
Chet, Chess, Cheston, Chestar, Chestor, Chestur, Chestir, Chestyr

Chetwin (English) From the cottage on the winding lane
Chetwen, Chetwyn, Chetwynd, Chetwynn, Chetwenn, Chetwinn

Cheung (Chinese) Having good fortune

Chiamaka (African) The splendor of God

Chibale (African) A kinship
Chibail, Chibaile, Chibael, Chibaele, Chibayl, Chibayle, Chybale, Chybail, Chybaile, Chybael, Chybaele, Chybayl, Chybayle

Chicahua (Nahuatl) Having great strength

Chicha (African) One who is dearly loved
Chicah, Chyca, Chycah

Chick (English) Form of Charles, meaning "one who is manly and strong / a free man"
Chik, Chicki, Chickie, Chicky, Chickey, Chickee, Chickea, Chic

Chico (Spanish) A boy; a lad

Chidi (African) God exists
Chidie, Chidy, Chidey, Chidee, Chidea, Chydi, Chydie, Chydee, Chydea, Chydy, Chydey

Chieko (Japanese) One who has grace and wisdom

Chien (Vietnamese) A combative man

CHRISTIAN

I wanted to name my son Christopher but my husband didn't want a name that common. We compromised on Christian so that he could shorten it to Chris if he didn't like his full name. To be honest, it is still growing on me. I am not sure I like that his name is a common noun and is regularly mistyped as "Christina." —Laura, WA

Chevalier (French) A knight or horseman
Cheval, Chevall, Chevy, Chevi, Chevey, Chevie, Chevee, Chevea, Chevel, Chevell

Cheveyo (Native American) A spirit warrior

Cheyenne (Native American) Of the tribe of the Great Plains; of the unintelligible speakers
Cheyann, Cheyen, Cheyan, Chian, Chiann, Chayan, Chayann

Cheyne (French) An oak-hearted man
Chane, Cheyn, Chain, Chaine, Chayn, Chayne, Chaen, Chaene

Chi (Chinese) Life energy

Chike (African) God is powerful
Chyke

Chiko (Japanese) Of the pledge

Chilly (American) One who is cold
Chilley, Chilli, Chillie, Chillee, Chillea

Chilton (English) From the farm near the spring
Chiltun, Chylton, Chyltun, Chelton, Cheltun, Chilten, Chylten, Chill, Chyll

Chimalli (Nahuatl) One who is shielded
Chimallie, Chimalley, Chimally, Chimallee, Chimallea

Chimalsi (African) A proud man
Chimalsie, Chimalsy, Chimalsey, Chimalsee, Chimalsea

Chimelu (African) One who is made of God
Chimelue, Chimeloo, Chimelou

Chin (Korean) One who is precious
Chyn

Chinh (Vietnamese) A righteous man

Chinja (Indian) Our son
Chynja

Chino (Spanish) A man from China
Chyno

Chintak (Hindi) A great thinker
Chintac, Chintack, Chyntak, Chyntac, Chyntack

Chinua (African) One who is blessed by God

Chip (English) Form of Charles, meaning "one who is manly and strong / a free man"
Chyp, Chipp, Chypp, Chipper, Chypper

Chiram (Hebrew) One who is noble
Chirem, Chyram, Chyrem

Chiron (Greek) A wise tutor
Chyron, Chirun, Chyrun

Chochmo (Native American) From the mud mound

Chogan (Native American) Resembling a blackbird
Chogen, Chogon, Chogun, Chogin, Chogyn

Choni (Hebrew) A gracious man
Chonie, Chony, Choney, Chonee, Chonea

Choovio (Native American) Resembling an antelope
Chooveo

Choviohoya (Native American) Resembling a young deer

Christian ✪ ✿ (Greek) A follower of Christ
Chrestien, Chretien, Chris, Christan, Christer, Christiano, Christie, Christo, Christos, Christy, Cristian, Cristen, Crystian, Cristiano, Cristino, Criston, Cristos, Cristy, Christiaan, Chrystian, Cretien, Christien

Christiansen (Danish) The son of Christian
Christianson, Christiansun, Christiansan

Christmas (English) Born during the festival of Christ

Christopher ✪ ✿ (Greek) One who bears Christ inside
Christof, Christofer, Christoffer, Christoforo, Christoforus, Christoph, Christophe, Christophoros, Cristobal, Cristofer, Cristoforo, Cristovano, Cristoval, Christofor

Chuchip (Native American) A deer spirit

Chuck (English) Form of Charles, meaning "one who is manly and strong / a free man"
Chucke, Chucki, Chuckie, Chucky, Chuckey, Chuckee, Chuckea

Chul (Korean) One who stands firm

Chun (Chinese) Born during the spring

Churchill (English) From the hill near the church
Churchil, Churchyll, Churchyl

Cian (Irish) From an ancient family
Cein, Cianan, Ceinan

Ciaran (Gaelic) A black-haired man; having dark features
Ciaren, Ciaron, Ciarun, Ciarin, Ciaryn, Cerin, Ceran, Ceron, Cerun, Cerin, Ceryn

Cicero (Latin) Resembling a chickpea
Ciceron

Cid (Spanish) A lord
Cyd

Cillian (Gaelic) One who suffers strife

Cinco (Spanish) The fifth-born child
Cynco

Cipriano (Spanish) A man from Cyprus
Cypriano, Cyprian, Ciprian, Cyprianus, Ciprianus, Cyprianos, Ciprianos

Ciqala (Native American) The little one

Ciriaco (Greek) A lord

Cirilo (Spanish) One who is noble

Cirrus (Latin) A lock of hair; resembling the cloud
Cyrrus

Cisco (Spanish) Form of Francisco, meaning "a man from France; one who is free"
Cysco, Cisko, Cysko, Ciscko, Cyscko

Citlali (Nahuatl) Resembling a star
Citlalie, Citlaly, Citlaley, Citlalee, Citlalea

Claiborne (English) Born of the
earth's clay
*Claiborn, Claibourn, Claibourne,
Clayborn, Clayborne, Claybourn,
Claybourne, Claeborn, Claeborne,
Claebourn, Claebourne*

Clair (Latin) One who is bright
Clare, Clayr, Claer, Clairo, Claro, Claero

Clancy (Celtic) Son of the red-haired warrior
*Clancey, Clanci, Clancie, Clancee, Clancea,
Clansey, Clansy, Clansi, Clansie, Clansee,
Clansea*

Clarence (Irish) From the Clare river
*Claran, Clarance, Clarens, Claron,
Clarons, Claronz, Clarrance, Clarrence,
Clarri, Clarrie, Clarry, Clarrey, Clarree,
Clarrea, Clarendon*

Clark (English) A cleric; a clerk
Clarke, Clerk, Clerke, Clerc

Claude (English) One who is lame
*Claud, Claudan, Claudell, Claidianus,
Claudicio, Claudien, Claudino, Claudio,
Claudius, Claudon, Clodito, Clodo,
Clodomiro, Claudus, Claudios*

Clay (English) Of the earth's clay

Clayland (English) From the land of clay
Claland

Clayton (English) From the town settled
on clay
*Claytun, Clayten, Claytin, Claytyn,
Claytan, Cleyton, Cleytun, Cleytan,
Cleyten, Cleytin, Cleytyn*

Cleander (English) Form of Leander,
meaning "a lion of a man"
*Cliander, Cleandre, Cliandre, Cleandro,
Cliandro, Cleandrew, Cleandros,
Cleanther, Cleiandros, Cleand, Cleande*

Cleanth (Greek) A philosopher
*Cleanthes, Cleante, Cleanto, Cleneth,
Clianth, Clianthes, Cleanthe*

Cleary (Irish) A learned man; a scholar
Cleari, Clearie, Clearey, Clearee, Clearea

Cleavant (English) From the cliffs
*Cleavon, Cleevant, Cleeve, Cleevont,
Cleavont, Cleevon, Cleave*

Clement (Latin) A merciful man
*Clem, Clemencio, Clemens, Clemente,
Clementino, Clementius, Clemmie,
Clemmons, Clemmy, Clemmi, Clemmee,
Clemmey, Clementios*

Cleon (Greek) A well-known man
Cleone, Clion, Clione, Clyon, Clyone

Cleophas (Greek) Having a vision of glory
*Cleofas, Cleofaso, Cleophus, Cleophos,
Cleofus, Cleofos*

Cletus (Greek) One who has been
summoned
*Clete, Cletis, Cletos, Cleytus, Cleetus,
Cleatus, Cleetos, Cleatos*

Cleveland (English) From the land of cliffs
*Cleaveland, Cleavland, Cleeveland,
Cleevland*

Clever (American) One who is smart
Clevar, Clevor, Clevur, Clevir, Clevyr

Clevon (English) From the cliff
Clevun, Clevin, Clevyn, Cleven, Clevan

Cliff (English) Form of Cliffton, meaning
"from the town near the cliff"
Cliffe, Clyff, Clyffe, Clifft, Clift, Clyfft, Clyft

Clifford (English) From the ford near the
cliff
Clyfford, Cliford, Clyford

Cliffton (English) From the town near the
cliff
*Clifftun, Clyffton, Clyfftun, Cliffeton,
Clyffeton, Cliffetun, Clyffetun*

Clifland (English) From the land of the
cliffs
Cliffland, Clyfland, Clyffland

Clinton (English) From the town on the
hill
*Clynton, Clintun, Clyntun, Clint, Clynt,
Clinte, Clynte*

Cliry (English) A beloved friend
Clirey, Cliree, Clirea, Cliri, Clirie

Clive (English) One who lives near the cliff
Clyve, Cleve

Clove (French) Resembling the spice; a nail

Clovis (French) A renowned warrior
Clovys, Clodoveo, Clovisito, Clovio, Clovito

Cloy (French) One who works with nails
Cloye, Cloi, Cloyce, Cloyd, Cloice, Cloid

Clud (Welsh) One who is lame

Cluny (Irish) From the meadow
Cluney, Cluni, Clunie, Clunee, Clunea, Cluneah

Clyde (Scottish) From the river Clyde
Clide, Clywd, Clydel, Clydell

Coakley (English) From the charcoal
meadow
Coakly, Coakli, Coaklie, Coakleigh, Coaklee, Coaklea, Coakleah, Cokeley, Cokelie, Cokeli, Cokely, Cokeleigh, Cokelee, Cokelea, Cokeleah

Cobb (English) From the cottage
Cob, Cobbet, Cobbett, Cobett, Cobet

Cobden (English) From the cottage in the
valley
Cobdenn, Cobdale, Cobdail, Cobdaile, Cobdell, Cobdel, Cobdayl, Cobdayle, Cobdael, Cobdaele

Cobham (English) From the cottage in the
village
Cobbham, Cobam, Cobbam

Coby (English) Form of Jacob, meaning
"he who supplants"
Cobey, Cobee, Cobea, Cobi, Cobie

Cochise (Native American) A renowned
warrior
Cocheece, Cochiece, Cocheice, Cocheace, Cochyce

Cochlain (Irish) One who is hooded
Cochlaine, Cochlayn, Cochlayne, Cochlaen, Cochlaene, Cochlane

Cockburn (Scottish) From the rooster's
stream
Cockbern, Cockbirn, Coburn, Cobern, Cobirn, Cockburne, Cockberne, Cockbirne, Coburne, Coberne, Cobirne

Cockrell (French) Resembling a young rooster
Cockrel, Cokrell, Cokrel, Cockrill, Cockril, Cockerel, Cockerell

Cody (Irish / English) One who is helpful;
a wealthy man / acting as a cushion
Codi, Codie, Codey, Codee, Codeah, Codea, Codier, Codyr

Coffin (English) A container; one who
makes coffins
Coffyn, Coffen, Coffan, Coffon, Coffun

Colbert (French) A famous and bright man
Colvert, Culbert, Colburt, Colbirt, Colbyrt, Colbart, Culburt, Culbirt, Culbyrt, Culbart, Colvirt, Colvyrt, Colvart

Colby (English) From the coal town
Colbey, Colbi, Colbie, Colbee, Collby, Coalby, Colbea, Colbeah, Coalbee, Coalbie, Coalbi, Coalbey, Coalbea, Coalbeah

Colden (English) From the dark valley
Coldan, Coldon, Coldun, Coldin, Coldyn, Coldell, Coldale, Coldail, Coldael, Coldayl, Coldayle, Codaile, Coldaele

Cole ✿ (English) Having dark features;
having coal-black hair
Coley, Coli, Coly, Colie, Colee, Coleigh, Colea, Colson, Colsun, Colsen, Colsan, Colsin, Colsyn

Coleman (English) One who burns
charcoal; resembling a dove
Colemann, Colman, Colmann, Colm, Colme

Coleridge (English) From the dark ridge
Colerige, Colridge, Colrige

Colgate (English) From the dark gate
Colegate, Colgait, Colegait, Colgayt, Colegayt, Colgaet, Colegaet

Colin (Scottish) A young man; form of
Nicholas, meaning "of the victorious
people"
Cailean, Colan, Colyn, Colon, Colun, Colen, Collin, Collan, Collen, Collyn, Collun, Collon, Collins

Coll (Irish) Form of Nicholas, meaning "of
the victorious people"
Colla, Colle

Colley (English) A dark-haired man
Colly, Colli, Collie, Collee, Colleigh, Collea

Collier (English) A coal miner
Collyer, Colier, Colis, Collayer, Collis, Colyer

Colorado (Spanish) From the red river;
from the state of Colorado

Colt ○ (English) A young horse; from the coal town
*Colte, Colten, **Colton**, Coltun, Coltan, Coltin, Coltyn, Coltrain, Coltrane, Coleton, Collton, Colston*

Colter (English) A horse herdsman
Coltere, Coltar, Coltor, Coltir, Coltyr, Coulter, Coultar, Coultir, Coultyr, Coultor, Coultur

Columba (Latin) Resembling a dove; the name of a saint
Collumbano, Colombain, Colum, Columbano, Columbanus, Columcille, Colombe, Columbia, Colam, Columbine., Columbo, Columbus, Colombo, Colombus

Colwyn (Welsh) From the river in Wales
Colwynn, Colwynne, Colwin, Colwinn, Colwinne, Colwen, Colwenn, Colwenne

Coman (Arabic) One who is noble
Comen, Comin, Comyn, Comon, Comun

Comanche (Native American) A tribal name
Comanchi, Comanchie, Comanchee, Comanchea, Comanchy, Comanchey

Comhghall (Irish) A fellow hostage
Cowall, Cowal

Como (Latin) From the province

Comus (Latin) In mythology, the god of mirth and revelry
Comos, Comes, Comas, Comis, Comys

Conaire (Irish) One who is wise
Conair, Conaer, Conaere, Conayr, Conayre

Conall (Celtic) Resembling a wolf; having strength and wisdom
Conal

Conan (English / Gaelic) Resembling a wolf / one who is high and mighty
Conant

Concord (Latin) Of peace and harmony
Concorde

Condon (Celtic) A dark, wise man
Condun, Condan, Conden, Condin, Condyn

Coney (English) Resembling a rabbit
Cony, Coni, Conie, Conee, Conea

Cong (Chinese) A clever man

Conlan (Gaelic) A hero
Conlen, Conlon, Conlun, Conlin, Conlyn

Conleth (Irish) One who is wise
Conlethe

Conley (Gaelic) One who is pure; chaste
Conly, Conlie, Conli, Conleigh, Conlee, Conlea

Conn (Irish) The chief
Con

Connal (Celtic) One who is high and mighty
Connall, Connell, Connel

Connecticut (Native American) From the place beside the long river; from the state of Connecticut

Connery (Scottish) A daring man
Connary, Connerie, Conneri, Connerey, Connarie, Connari, Connarey, Conary, Conery, Conarie, Conari, Conarey, Coneri, Conerie, Conerey

Connie (Irish) Form of Constantine, meaning "one who is steadfast; firm"
Conni, Conny, Conney, Connee, Connea

Connor ○ (Gaelic) A wolf-lover
Conor, Conner, Coner, Connar, Conar, Connur, Conur, Connir, Conir, Connyr, Conyr

Conrad (German) A brave and bold ruler; a bold advisor
Conrade, Conrado, Corrado, Conradin

Conroy (Irish) A wise advisor
Conroye, Conroi

Constantine (Latin) One who is steadfast; firm
Constans, Constanz, Constant, Constantin, Constantino, Constantius, Costa, Constantio, Constanze, Constanty

Consuelo (Spanish) One who offers consolation
Consuel, Consuelio, Consueleo, Consueliyo, Consueleyo

Conway (Gaelic) The hound of the plain; from the sacred river
Conwaye, Conwai, Conwae, Conwy

Cook (English) One who prepares meals for others
Cooke

Cooney (Irish) A handsome man
Coony, Cooni, Coonie, Coonee, Coonea

Cooper ⊙ (English) One who makes barrels
*Coop, Coopar, Coopir, Coopyr, Coopor,
Coopur, Coopersmith, Cupere*

Corbett (French) Resembling a young
raven
*Corbet, Corbete, Corbette, Corbit,
Corbitt, Corbite, Corbitte*

Corbin (English) Resembling a raven
*Corben, Corban, Corbyn, Corbon, Corbun,
Corbe, Corbi, Corbie, Corby, Corbey,
Corbee, Corbea, Corbinian, Corvin,
Corvan, Corven, Corvon, Corvun, Corvyn*

Corcoran (Gaelic) Having a ruddy
complexion
Cochran

Cordell (English) One who makes cord
*Cord, Cordale, Cordas, Corday, Cordelle,
Cordel, Cordaye, Cordai, Cordae*

Cordero (Spanish) Resembling a lamb
Corderio, Corderiyo, Cordereo, Cordereyo

Corey (Irish) From the hollow; of the
churning waters
*Cory, Cori, Corie, Coree, Corea, Correy,
Corry, Corri, Corrie, Corree, Correa*

Coriander (Greek) A romantic man;
resembling the spice
Coryander, Coriender, Coryender

Cork (Gaelic) From the swampland
*Corki, Corkie, Corke, Corkee, Corkea,
Corkey, Corky*

Corlan (Irish) One who wields a spear
Corlen, Corlin, Corlyn, Corlon, Corlun

Corliss (English) A benevolent man
*Corlis, Corlyss, Corlys, Corless, Corles,
Corley, Corly, Corlee, Corleigh, Corli,
Corlea, Corlie*

Cormick (Irish) A charioteer
*Cormyck, Cormik, Cormyk, Cormic,
Cormyc, Cormac, Cormack, Cormak,
Cormag*

Cornelius (Latin) Refers to a horn
*Cornall, Cornel, Corneille, Cornelio,
Cornelious, Cornell, Cornelus, Corney,
Cornilius, Corny, Corni, Cornie, Cornee,
Cornea*

Cornwallis (English) A man from
Cornwall
Cornwalis, Cornwallace, Cornwalace

Corrado (German) A bold counselor
Corrade, Corradeo, Corradio

Corrick (English) A benevolent ruler
*Corryck, Corrik, Corryk, Corric, Corryc,
Corick, Coryck, Corik, Coryk, Coric, Coryc*

Corridon (Irish) One who wields a spear
*Corridan, Corridun, Corriden, Corridin,
Corridyn*

Corrin (Irish) One who wields a spear
*Corryn, Corran, Corren, Corron, Corrun,
Corin, Coryn, Coren, Coran, Coron,
Corun*

Cort (English) A court attendant; a
courtier
*Cortland, Corty, Court, Courtland,
Cortey, Corti, Cortie, Cortee, Courty,
Courtey, Courti, Courtie, Courtee*

Cortez (Spanish) A courteous man
Cortes

Corwin (English) A friend of the heart
*Corwinn, Corwinne, Corwyn, Corwynn,
Corwynne, Corwen, Corwenn, Corwenne,
Corwine*

Corydon (Greek) One who is ready for
battle
*Coridon, Corydun, Coridun, Corydan,
Coridan, Coryden, Coriden, Corydin,
Coridin, Corydyn, Coridyn*

Cosgrove (Gaelic) The champion
Cozgrove, Cosgrave, Cozgrave

Cosmo (Greek) The order of the universe
*Cosimo, Cosmé, Cosmos, Cosmas, Cozmo,
Cozmos, Cozmas*

Coster (English) A peddler
Costar, Costor, Costir, Costyr, Costur

Cotton (American) Resembling or farmer
of the plant
Cottin, Cotten, Cottyn, Cottun, Cottan

Coty (French) From the riverbank
Cotey, Coti, Cotie, Cotee, Cotea

Cougar (American) Resembling the wild
animal
Couger, Cougor, Cougir, Cougyr, Cougur

Coulson (French) Form of Nicholas,
meaning "of the victorious people"
Colson, Coulsun, Colsun

Courtney (English) A courteous man;
courtly
*Cordney, Cordni, Cortenay, Corteney,
Cortni, Cortnee, Cortneigh, Cortney,
Cortnie, Cortny, Courtenay, Courteneigh,
Courteney, Courtnay, Courtnee, Courtnie,
Courtny, Courtnea, Cortnea, Courtni,
Court, Courte*

Covell (English) From the cave on the
slope
Covel, Covyll, Covyl

Covert (English) One who provides shelter
Couvert

Covey (English) A brood of birds
*Covy, Covi, Covie, Covee, Covea, Covvey,
Covvy, Covvi, Covvie, Covvee, Covvea*

Covington (English) From the town near
the cave
Covyngton, Covingtun, Covyngtun

Cowan (Irish) From the hollow near the
hill; one of twins
Cowen, Cowin, Cowyn, Cowon, Cowun

Cowrie (African) Resembling the shell
*Cowry, Cowrey, Cowri, Cowree, Cowrea,
Courey, Coury, Couri, Courie, Couree,
Courea*

Cox (English) A coxswain
*Coxe, Coxi, Coxie, Coxey, Coxy, Coxee,
Coxea*

Coy (English) From the woods
Coye, Coi

Coyan (French) A modest man
*Coyen, Coyon, Coyun, Coyin, Coyne,
Coyn*

Coyle (Irish) A leader during battle
Coyl, Coil, Coile

Craddock (Welsh) One who is much loved
*Craddoc, Craddok, Cradock, Cradoc,
Cradok*

Craig (Gaelic) From the rocks; from the
crag
*Crayg, Craeg, Craige, Crayge, Craege,
Crage, Crag*

Cramer (German) A peddler
*Craymer, Craimer, Craemer, Cramar,
Craymar, Craimar, Craemar, Cramor,
Craimor, Craymor, Craemor, Cramir,
Craymir, Craimir, Craemir*

Crandell (English) From the valley of
cranes
*Crandel, Crandale, Crandail, Crandaile,
Crandayl, Crandayle, Crandael, Crandaele,
Crandal, Crandall*

Crane (English) Resembling the long-
legged bird
*Crain, Craine, Crayn, Crayne, Craen,
Craene*

Cranford (English) From the crane's ford
*Cranforde, Cranferd, Cranferde, Cranfurd,
Cranfurde*

Cranley (English) From the meadow of
cranes
*Cranly, Cranleigh, Cranli, Cranlie, Cranlee,
Cranlea, Cranleah*

Cranston (English) From the crane town
Cranstun, Cranton, Crantun

Craven (English) A cowardly man
Cravin, Cravyn, Cravan, Cravon, Cravun

Crawford (English) From the crow's ford
*Crawforde, Crawferd, Crawferde,
Crawfurd, Crawfurde*

Cree (Native American) A tribal name
Crei, Crey, Crea, Creigh

Creed (Latin) A guiding principle; a belief
*Creede, Cread, Creade, Creedon, Creadon,
Creedun, Creadun, Creedin, Creadin,
Creedyn, Creadyn, Creeden, Creaden,
Creedan, Creadan*

Creek (English) From the small stream
Creeke, Creak, Creake, Creik, Creike

Creighton (Scottish) From the border
town
*Creightun, Crayton, Craytun, Craiton,
Craitun, Craeton, Craetun, Crichton,
Crichtun*

Creketun (English) From the town near
the creek
*Creketon, Creketen, Creekton, Creektun,
Creekten*

Crescent (French) One who creates; increasing; growing
Creissant, Crescence, Cressant, Cressent, Crescant

Crevan (Gaelic) Resembling a fox
Creven, Crevin, Crevyn, Crevon, Crevun

Cricket (American) Resembling a chirping insect of the night
Crycket, Criket, Cryket, Crickit, Cryckit

Crisanto (Spanish) Resembling the gold flower
Cresento, Crisento, Crizant, Crizanto, Crisantio, Crizantio, Crisanteo, Crizanteo

Crispin (Latin) A curly-haired man
Crisspin, Crepin, Crespin, Crispian, Crispino, Crispo, Crispus, Crispos, Crispyn, Crespyn, Crispen, Crespen

Crockett (English) A crook; a shepherd
Crock, Crocket, Croquet, Croquett, Crooke, Crookes, Crooks

Crofton (English) From the town of cottages
Croftun, Croften, Croffton, Crofftun, Croff ten, Croft, Crofte

Crogher (Irish) One who loves hounds
Crohoore, Crohoor

Cromwell (English) One who lives near the winding stream
Cromwel, Cromwill, Cromwil, Cromwyll, Cromwyl, Crom

Cronan (Irish) The small, dark one
Cronen, Cronyn, Cronin, Cronon, Cronun

Cronus (Greek) In mythology, the youngest Titan
Cronos, Cronas, Crones, Cronis, Cronys

Crosby (English) From the farm near the cross
Crosbey, Crosbi, Crosbie, Crosbee, Crosbea

Crosley (English) From the meadow near the cross
Crosleigh, Croslee, Croslea, Crosleah, Crosly, Crosli, Croslie

Crowell (English) From the spring near the cross
Crowel

Crowther (English) A fiddler
Crowthir, Crowthyr, Crowthar, Crowthor, Crowthur, Crother, Crothir, Crothyr, Crothur, Crothor, Crothar

Cruz (Spanish) Of the cross
Cruzito, Cruze, Cruiz, Cruize

Cualli (Nahuatl) A good man
Cuallie, Cually, Cualley, Cuallee, Cualleigh, Cuallea

Cuarto (Spanish) The fourth-born child
Cuartio, Cuartiyo, Cuarteo, Cuarteyo

Cuetzpalli (Nahuatl) Resembling a lizard
Cuetzpallie, Cuetzpally, Cuetzpalley, Cuetzpallee, Cuetzpallea

Cuinn (Celtic) An intelligent man
Cuin, Cuinne, Cuine

Cullen (Gaelic) A good-looking young man
Cullin, Cullyn, Cullan, Cullon, Cullun

Culum (Gaelic) Resembling a dove

Culver (English) Resembling a dove
Culvar, Culvir, Culvyr, Culvor, Culvur, Colver, Colvar, Colvir, Colvyr, Colvor, Colvur

Cunningham (Gaelic) From the village of milk
Conyngham, Cuningham, Cunnyngham, Cunyngham

Cuong (Vietnamese) One who is healthy and prosperous

Curcio (French) One who is courteous
Curceo

Curley (English) Having great strength
Curly, Curlie, Curli, Curleigh, Curlee, Curlea

Curragh (Gaelic) From the moor

Curran (Gaelic) One who wields a dagger; a hero
Curry, Currey, Curri, Currie, Curree, Currea

Curro (Spanish) One who is free
Currito

Curt (English) A brave counselor
Curte

Curtis (English) One who is courteous; polite
Curtiss, Curtys, Curtyss, Curtice, Curcio, Curtell

Custodio (Spanish) A guardian
Custodeo, Custodiyo, Custodeyo

Cuthbert (English) One who is bright and famous
Cuthbeorht, Cuthburt, Cuthbirt, Cuthbyrt

Cutler (English) One who makes knives
Cutlar, Cutlor, Cutlir, Cutlyr, Cutlur

Cyan (English) Having blue-green eyes
Cyen, Cyin, Cyon, Cyun

Cydney (English) Form of Sydney, meaning "of the wide meadow"
Cydny, Cydni, Cydnie, Cydnee, Cidney, Cidnee, Cidnie, Cidni, Cidny, Cyd, Cydnea, Cydneah, Cidnea, Cidneah, Cid

Cynbel (Welsh) A warrior chief
Cynbal, Cynbell, Cynball, Cynbil, Cynbill

Cyneley (English) From the royal meadow
Cynely, Cyneli, Cynelie, Cynelee, Cynelea, Cyneleah, Cyneleigh

Cyrano (French) A man from Cyrene
Cyran, Cyranno, Cirano, Ciranno, Ciran

Cyril (Greek) A master or lord
Ciril, Cirilio, Cirillo, Cirilo, Cy, Cyrill, Cyrille, Cyrillus

Cyrus (Persian) A king
Cirus, Ciro, Cyro, Cyris, Ciris

Czar (Russian) An emperor

Dabeet (Indian) A warrior
Dabeat, Dabeit, Dabiet, Dabyt, Dabit

Dabi (Hebrew) One who is dearly loved
Dabie, Daby, Dabey, Dabee, Dabea

Dabir (Arabic) One who teaches others
Dabeer, Dabear, Dabeir, Dabier, Dabyr

Dabney (French) One who is from Aubigny
Dabnie, Dabny, Dabni, Dabnee, Dabnea, Dabneah

Dace (French) Born to the nobility
Daice, Dayce, Daece, Dacian, Dacien, Dacio, Dacius, Dacios, Dacias, Daceas

Dacey (Gaelic / Latin) A man from the south / a man from Dacia
Dacy, Dacee, Dacea, Daci, Dacie, Daicey, Daicy, Daicee, Daicea, Daici, Daicie, Daecey, Daecey, Daecee, Daecea, Daeci, Daecie, Daycey, Daycy, Daycee, Daycea, Dayci, Daycie

Dack (English) From the French town of Dax
Dacks

Dada (African) A curly-haired man
Dadah

Dadrian (English) Form of Adrian, meaning "a man from Hadria"
Dade, Dadiran, Dadrain, Dadrean, Dadreean, Dadreyan, Dadreeyan, Dadriaan, Dadriano, Dadrien, Dadrin, Dadrino, Dadrion, Dadron, Dadryan, Dadya, Darjen, Daydrean, Daydreean, Daydrian, Daydrien

Daedalus (Greek) A craftsman
Daldalos, Dedalus

Daelan (American) Form of Waylon, meaning "from the roadside land"
Daelin, Daelyn, Daelon, Daelen, Daylan, Daylin, Daylyn, Daylon, Daylen, Dailan, Dailen, Dailin, Dailyn, Dailon, Dalan, Dalen, Dalon, Dalin, Dalyn

Dag (Scandinavian) Born during the daylight
Dagney, Dagny, Dagnee, Dagnea, Dagni, Dagnie, Daeg, Dagget, Daggett, Daggan, Daggen, Daggon, Daggun, Daggin, Daggyn

Dagan (Hebrew) Of the grain; of the earth
Daigan, Daygan, Daegan

Dagen (Irish) A black-haired man
Dagon, Dagun, Dagin, Dagyn, Deegen, Deegon, Deegun, Deegin, Deegyn, Daegan, Daegon, Daegun, Daegin, Daegyn

Dagobert (German) Born on a bright and shining day
Dagoberto, Dagbert, Dagoburt, Dagoburto, Dagburt, Dagobirt, Dagobirto, Dagbirt

Dagwood (English) From the shining forest
Dagwode

Dahy (Irish) One who is quick
Dahey, Dahi, Dahie, Dahee, Dahea

Dai (Japanese / Welsh) One who is large / a shining man

Daijon (American) A gift of hope
Dayjon, Daejon, Dajon

Dailey (Gaelic) Of the assembly
Daily, Dailee, Dailea, Daileigh, Daili, Dailie, Daly, Daley, Dalee, Dalea, Daleigh, Dali, Dalie, Dawley, Dawly, Dawlee, Dawleigh, Dawlea, Dawli, Dawlie, Daeley, Daely, Daelee, Daelea, Daeleigh, Daeli, Daelie

Dainan (Australian) A kindhearted man
Dainen, Dainon, Dainun, Dainyn, Dainin, Daynan, Daynen, Daynon, Daynun, Daynin, Daynyn, Daenan, Daenen, Daenin, Daenyn, Daenon, Daenun

Dainard (English) A bold and courageous Dane
Danehard, Danehardt, Daneard, Daneardt, Dainehard, Dainhard, Daynard, Daynhard, Daynhardt, Dainhardt

Daire (Irish) A wealthy man
Dair, Daere, Daer, Dayr, Dayre, Dare, Dari, Darie, Dary, Darey, Daree, Darea

Daithi (Irish) The beloved; one who is quick
Daithie, Daithy, Daithey, Daithee, Daithea, Daythi, Daythie, Daythey, Daythy, Daythee, Daythea, Daethi, Daethie, Daethy, Daethey, Daethee, Daethea

Daivat (Hindi) A powerful man

Dakarai (African) Filled with happiness

Dakota (Native American) A friend to all
Daccota, Dakoda, Dakodah, Dakotah, Dakoeta, Dekota, Dekohta, Dekowta, Dakoeta, Dakoetah

Daksha (Indian) A brilliant man
Dakshah

Daktari (African) One who heals others
Daktarie, Daktary, Daktarey, Daktaree, Daktarea

Dalai (Indian) A peaceful man

Dalbert (English) The bright and shining one
Dalburt, Dalbirt, Dalbyrt

Dale (English) From the valley
Dail, Daile, Dael, Daele, Dayl, Dayle

Dalgus (American) An outdoorsy man
Dalgas, Dalgos, Dalges, Dalgis, Dalgys

Dalil (Arabic) One who acts as a guide
Daleel, Daleal, Daleil, Daliel, Dalyl

Dallan (Irish) One who is blind
Dalan, Dallen, Dalen, Dallon, Dalon, Dallun, Dalun

Dallas (Scottish) From the dales; from the city in Texas
Dalles, Dallis, Dallys, Dallos, Dallus

Dallin (English) From the valley
Dalin, Dallyn, Dalyn

Dalmar (African) One who is versatile

Dalston (English) An intelligent man
Dalsten, Dalstin, Dalstyn, Dalstun, Dalstan

Dalton (English) From the town in the valley
Daltun, Dalten, Daltan, Daltin, Daltyn, Daleton, Daletun, Daletin, Daletyn, Daleten, Daletan, Daulton, Daultun, Daulten, Daultan, Daultin, Daultyn, Dallton, Dalltun, Dallten, Dalltan, Dalltin, Dalltyn, Dalt, Dalte

Dalziel (Scottish) From the little field

Damacio (Spanish) One who is calm
Damasio, Damazio, Damaceo, Damaseo, Damazeo, Damaso, Damazo

Damario (Greek / Spanish) Resembling a calf / one who is gentle
Damarios, Damarius, Damaro, Damero, Damerio, Damereo, Damareo, Damerios, Damerius

Damaris (Greek) One who is gentle
Damariss, Damarys, Damaryss

Damary (Greek) One who is tamed
Damarey, Damari, Damarie, Damaree, Damarea

Damaskenos (Greek) A man from Damascus
Damaskinos, Damaskus, Damascus, Damaskeno, Damaskino, Damasco, Damasko

Damek (Slavic) Of the red earth
Damec, Dameck, Damik, Damic, Damick, Damyk, Damyc, Damyck

Damel (American) A strong-willed man
Damell, Damele, Damelle

Damerae (Jamaican) A joyous boy
Dameray, Dameraye, Damerai, Damarae, Damaray, Damaraye, Damarai

Damian (Greek) One who tames or subdues others
Daemon, Daimen, Daimon, Daman, Damen, Dameon, Damiano, Damianos, Damianus, Damien, Damion, Damon, Damyan, Damyen, Damyon, Dayman, Daymian, Daymon, Daeman, Daemen, Damean, Damyean, Damyun, Damyn, Damiean

Damir (Slavic) One who promotes peace
Dameer, Damear, Damier, Dameir, Damyr

Damis (Arabic) A dark-skinned man
Damiss, Damys, Damyss

Damisi (African) A cheerful man
Damisie, Damisy, Damisey, Damisee, Damisea

Dan (English) Form of Daniel, meaning "God is my judge"
Dann, Danny, Danni, Dannie, Dannee, Dannea, Dani, Danie, Dany, Daney, Danee, Danea

Danawi (Arabic) A worldly man
Danawie, Danawy, Danawey, Danawee, Danawea

Dandre (American) A lighthearted man
Dandray, Dandraye, Dandrae, Dandree

Dane (English) A man from Denmark
Dain, Daine, Dayn, Dayne, Daen, Daene, Dana, Danon, Danin, Danun, Danan, Danen, Danyn

Daneil (American) The champion
Daneile, Daneel, Daneele, Daneal, Daneale

Danely (Scandinavian) A man from Denmark
Daneley, Daneli, Danelie, Danelee, Daneleigh, Danelea, Daineley, Dainely, Dainelee, Daineleigh, Dainelea, Daineli, Dainelie, Daynely, Dayneley, Daynelee, Daynelea, Dayneli, Daynelie

Dang (Vietnamese) One who is praiseworthy

Danger (American) One who takes great risks
Dainger, Daynger, Daenger, Dangery, Dangerey, Dangeree, Dangerea, Dangeri, Dangerie

Danh (Vietnamese) A famous man

Daniachew (African) A mediator

Danick (American) One who is friendly and well-liked
Danyck, Danik, Danyk, Danic, Danyc, Dannick, Dannyck, Dannik, Dannyk, Dannic, Dannyc

Daniel ○ ⊙ (Hebrew) God is my judge
Danal, Daneal, Danek, Danell, Danial, Daniele, Danil, Danilo, Danko, Dannel, Dantrell, Danyal, Danyel

Danno (Japanese) From the gathering in the field

Dannon (Hebrew) Form of Daniel, meaning "God is my judge"
Dannun, Dannan, Dannen, Dannin, Dannyn

Danso (African) A reliable man
Dansoe, Dansow, Dansowe

Dante (Latin) An enduring man; everlasting
Dantae, Dantay, Dantel, Daunte, Dontae, Dontay, Donte, Dontae, Dawnte, Dauntay, Dawntay, Dauntae, Dawntae, Dontrell, Dohntay, Dohntaye, Dohntae, Dontell

Danton (English) From Dan's town
Danten, Dantin, Dantyn, Dantun, Dantan

Dantre (American) A faithful man
Dantray, Dantraye, Dantrae, Dantrey, Dantri, Dantrie, Dantry, Dantrey, Dantree, Dantrea, Dontre, Dontray, Dontraye, Dontrae, Dontrai, Dontrey, Dontri, Dontrie, Dontree, Dontry, Dontrea, Dontrey

Danuta (Polish) A gift from God

Daoud (Arabian) Form of David, meaning "the beloved one"
Daoude, Dawud, Doud, Daud, Da'ud

Daphnis (Greek) In mythology, the son of Hermes
Daphnys

Daquan (American) A high-spirited man
Dakwan, Daquann, Dakwann, Dequan, Dequann, Dekwan, Dekwann

Dar (Hebrew) Resembling a pearl
Darr

Daray (Gaelic) A dark-skinned man
Daraye, Darai, Darae

Darbrey (Irish) A lighthearted man; a free man
Darbry, Darbri, Darbrie, Darbree, Darbrea

Darby (English) Of the deer park
Darb, Darbee, Darbey, Darbie, Darrbey, Darrbie, Darrby, Derby, Derbie, Derbey, Derbee, Darbea, Darbeah

Darcel (French) Having dark features
Darcell, Darcele, Darcelle, Darcio, Darceo

Darcy (Gaelic) Having dark features
Darcey, Darcee, Darcea, Darci, Darcie, D'Arcy, Darsy, Darsey, Darsee, Darsea, Darsi, Darsie, Darce, Darse

Dardanus (Greek) In mythology, the founder of Troy
Dardanio, Dardanios, Dardanos, Dard, Darde

Dareh (Armenian) A wealthy man

Darek (English) Form of Derek, meaning "the ruler of the tribe"
Darrek, Darec, Darrec, Darreck, Dareck

Daren (African) One who is born at night

Darence (American) Form of Clarence, meaning "from the Clare river"
Darense, Darance, Darens, Daron, Darons, Daronz, Darrance, Darrence

Darion (Greek) A gift
Darian, Darien, Dariun, Darrion, Darrian, Darrien, Daryon, Daryan, Daryen, Darryon, Darryen, Darryan

Darius (Greek) A kingly man; one who is wealthy
Darias, Dariess, Dario, Darious, Darrius, Derrius, Derrious, Derrias

Darko (Slavic) A manly man
Darkoe, Darkow, Darkowe, Dark, Darke

Darlen (American) A sweet man; a darling
Darlon, Darlun, Darlan, Darlin, Darlyn

Darnell (English) From the hidden place
Darnall, Darneil, Darnel, Darnele, Darnelle

Darnley (English) From the grassy meadow
Darnly, Darnleigh, Darnlee, Darnlea, Darnleah, Darnli, Darnlie

Darold (English) Form of Harold, meaning "the ruler of an army"
Darrold, Derald, Derrald, Derold, Derrold

Darrah (Gaelic) From the dark oak tree
Darra, Darach, Darrach, Daragh, Darragh

Darrel (English) One who is dearly loved
Darel, Dariel, Dariell, Darral, Darrell, Darrill, Darrol, Darroll, Darry, Darryl, Darryll, Daryl, Derell, Derrall, Derrel, Derrell, Derril, Derrill, Deryl, Deryll, Dareau, Derryl, Derryll

Darren (Gaelic / English) A great man / a gift from God
Darran, Darrin, Darryn, Darron, Darrun, Daren, Darin, Daran, Daryn, Daron, Darun, Derron, Derrun, Derrin, Derryn, Derran, Derren, Deron, Derun, Derin, Deryn, Deran, Deren

Darrett (American) Form of Garrett, meaning "one who is mighty with a spear"
Darett, Darret, Darretson, Darritt, Darrot, Darrott, Derrit, Derritt, Derrity, Darrity, Daret

Darroch (Irish) An oak-hearted man; one who is strong
Darrick, Darryck, Darrik, Darryk, Darric, Darryc, Darick, Daryck, Darik, Daryk, Daric, Daryc, Darrock, Darock, Daroch, Darri, Darrie, Darry, Darrey, Darree

Darrow (English) One who wields a spear
Darrowe, Darro, Darow, Darowe, Daro, Darroe, Daroe, Darroh, Daroh

Darshan (Hindi) Of a vision
Darshon

Dart (English) From the river
Darte

Dart (American) One who is fast
Darte, Darrt, Darrte, Darti, Dartie, Dartee, Dartea, Darty, Dartey

Dartagnan (French) A leader
D'Artagnan

Darton (English) From the deer town
Dartun, Darten, Dartan, Dartin, Dartyn, Deortun

D

Darvell (French) From the eagle town
Darvel, Darvele, Darvelle

Darvin (English) Form of Darwin, meaning "a beloved friend"
Darvinn, Darvinne, Darvyn, Darvynn, Darvynne, Darven, Darvenn, Darvenne

Darwin (English) A beloved friend
Darwine, Darwinn, Darwinne, Darwen, Darwenn, Darwenne, Darwyn, Darwynn, Darwynne, Darwon

Das (Indian) A slave; a servant
Dasa

Dasan (Native American) A great ruler

Dash (American) A charming man; one who is fast
Dashe, Dashy, Dashey, Dashee, Dashea, Dashi, Dashie, Dashell, Dashel, Dashele, Dashelle, Dasher

Dasras (Indian) A handsome man

Dasya (Indian) A servant

Dat (Vietnamese) One who is accomplished

Dathan (Hebrew) From the spring
Dathen, Dathin, Dathyn, Dathon, Dathun

Daudi (African) One who is dearly loved
Daudie, Daudy, Daudey, Daudee, Daudea

Davian (English) Form of David, meaning "the beloved one"
Davien, Davion, Daviun, Davyen, Davyan, Davyon, Davyun, Daveon, Davean, Daveun

David ✪ ❶ (Hebrew) The beloved one
Dave, Davey, Davi, Davidde, Davide, Davie, Daviel, Davin, Daven, Davon, Davy, Davyd, Davydd, Davan

Davidson (English) The son of David
Davydson, Davidsun, Davydsun, Davidsen, Davydsen, Davidsin, Davydsin, Davidsyn, Davydsyn, Davidsone, Davison, Davisen, Davisun, Davysen, Davyson, Davysun

Davis (English) The son of David
Davies, Daviss, Davys, Davyss

Davonte (American) One who is energetic
Devontay, Devontaye, Devontae, Devontai, Devonte, Devontay, Devontaye, Devontae, Devontai

Davu (African) Of the beginning
Davue, Davoo, Davou, Davugh

Dawar (Arabian) A wanderer
Dawarr

Dawber (English) A humorous man
Dawbar, Dawbor, Dawbir, Dawbyr, Dawbur, Dawbi, Dawbie, Dawbee, Dawbea, Dawby, Dawbey

Dawk (American) A spirited man
Dawke, Dauk, Dauke, Dawkin, Daukin, Dawkins, Daukins

Dawson (English) The son of David
Dawsan, Dawsen, Dawsin, Dawsyn, Dawsun, Daw, Dawe, Dawes

Dax (French) From the French town Dax
Daxton, Daxtun, Daxten, Daxtan, Daxtin, Daxtyn, Daxi, Daxie, Daxee, Daxea, Daxy, Daxey

Day (American) Born during the daylight
Daye, Dai, Dae

Dayakar (Indian) A kind man

Dayanand (Hindi) A compassionate man
Dayanande, Dayan

Dayo (African) Our joy has arrived
Dayoe, Dayow, Dayowe

Dayton (English) From the sunny town
Dayten, Daytan, Daytin, Daytyn, Daytun, Daiton, Daitun, Daiten, Daitan, Daitin, Daityn, Daeton, Daetun, Daetin, Daetyn, Daeten, Daetan

De (Vietnamese) Born to royalty

Deacon (Greek) The dusty one; a servant
Deecon, Deakon, Deekon, Deacun, Deecun, Deakun, Deekun, Deacan, Deecan, Deakan, Deekan, Deacen, Deecen, Deaken, Deeken, Deacin, Deecin, Deakin, Deekin, Deak, Deek, Deke

Dean (English) From the valley; a church official
Deane, Deen, Deene, Dene, Deans, Deens, Deani, Deanie, Deany, Deaney, Deanee, Deanea

DeAndre (American) A manly man
D'André, DeAndrae, DeAndray, DeAndre, Diandray, Diondrae, Diondray

Deangelo (Italian) A messenger from God
Deangelo, De'Angelo, Diangelo, DiAngelo, D'Angelo, Deanjelo, De'Anjelo, D'Anjelo

Deanza (Spanish) A smooth man
Denza

Dearborn (English) From the deer brook
Dearborne, Dearbourn, Dearbourne, Dearburn, Dearburne, Deerborn, Deerborne, Deerbourn, Deerbourne, Deerburn, Deerburne, Derebourne, Derebourn, Dereborn, Dereborne, Dereburn, Dereburne

Dearon (American) One who is much loved
Dearan, Dearen, Dearin, Dearyn, Dearun

Debonair (French) One who is nonchalant
Debonnair, Debonnair, Debonaire, Debonnaire, Debonnaire

Debythis (American) An unusual man
Debiathes, Debithis, Debiathis, Debythys, Debithys, Debiathys

December (American) Winter's child; born in December
Decimber, Decymber, Decembar, Decimbar, Decymbar

Decimus (Latin) The tenth-born child
Decimos, Decimo, Decimu, Decio

Decker (German / Hebrew) One who prays / a piercing man
Deker, Decer, Dekker, Deccer, Deck, Decke

Declan (Irish) The name of a saint

Dedrick (English) Form of Dietrich, meaning "the ruler of the tribe"
Dedryck, Dedrik, Dedryk, Dedric, Dedryc

Deegan (Irish) A black-haired man
Deagan, Degan, Deegen, Deagen, Degen, Deegon, Deagon, Degon, Deegun, Deagun, Degun, Deegin, Deagin, Degin, Deegyn, Deagyn, Degyn

Deems (English) The son of the judge
Deams, Deims, Diems, Deyms

Deepak (Indian) One who carries the little lamp
Dipak, Deipak, Diepak, Deapak, Dypak

Deeter (American) A friendly woman
Deater, Deter, Deetar, Deatar, Detar, Deetor, Deator, Detor, Deetur, Deatur, Detur

DeForest (English) One who lives near the forest
Deforest, DeForrest, Deforrest

Deinorus (American) A lively man
Denorius, Denorus, Denorios, Deinorius, Deinorios

Deiondre (American) From the valley
Deiondray, Deiondraye, Deiondrae

Dejuan (American) A talkative man
Dejuane, Dewon, Dewonn, Dewan, Dewann, Dwon, Dwonn, Dajuan, Dajuane, Dawon, Dawonn, Dawan, Dawann

Dekel (Hebrew) From the palm tree
Dekell, Dekele, Dekelle, Dekle

Delancy (Irish) From the elder tree grove
Delancey, Delancee, Delancea, Delanci, Delancie

Delaney (Irish / French) The dark challenger / from the elder-tree grove
Delany, Delanee, Delanea, Delani, Delanie, Delainey, Delainy, Delaini, Delainie, Delainee, Delainea, Delaeney, Delaeny, Delaenee, Delaenea, Delaeni, Delaenie, Delayney, Delayny, Delaynee, Delaynea, Delayni, Delaynie, Delane, Delaine, Delaene, Delayne, Delano, Delayno, Delaeno, Delaino

Delaware (English) From the state of Delaware
Delawair, Delaweir, Delwayr, Delawayre, Delawaire, Delawaer, Delawaere

Delbert (English) One who is noble; a bright man
Delburt, Delbirt, Delbyrt, Dilbert, Dilburt, Dilbirt, Dilbyrt, Dealbeorht, Dealbert

Delgado (Spanish) A slim man
Delgadio, Delgadeo

Delius (Greek) A man from Delos
Delios, Delos, Delus, Delo

Dell (English) From the small valley
Delle, Del

Delling (Norse) A scintillating man
Dellyng, Deling, Delyng, Dellinger, Dellynger, Delinger, Delynger

Delman (English) A man from the valley
Dellman, Delmann, Dellmann

Delmar (French) A man of the sea
Delmarr, Delmor, Delmorr, Delmore,
Delmare, Delmer, Delmere, Delmoor

Delmis (Spanish) A beloved friend
Delmiss, Delmisse, Delmys, Delmyss,
Delmysse

Delmon (English) A man of the mountain
Delmun, Delmen, Delmin, Delmyn,
Delmont, Delmonte, Delmond, Delmonde

Delmy (American) Form of Delmar, meaning
"a man of the sea"
Delmey, Delmee, Delmea, Delmi, Delmie

Delphin (Greek) Resembling a dolphin
Delfin, Delfino, Delfinos, Delfinus,
Delphino, Delphinos, Delphinus

Delroy (French) The king
Delray, Delrick, Delrico, Delroi, Delron,
Delren, Delran, Delrin, Delryn, Delrun,
Delryck, Delrik, Delryk, Delric, Delryc

Delsi (American) An easygoing guy
Delsie, Delsy, Delsey, Delsee, Delsea,
Delci, Delcie, Delcee, Delcea, Delcy,
Delcey

Delton (English) From the town in the
valley
Deltun, Deltin, Deltyn, Deltan, Delten

Delvin (English) A godly friend
Delvinn, Delvinne, Delvyn, Delvynn,
Delvynne, Delven, Delvenn, Delvenne,
Delvon, Delvonn, Delvonne, Delevin,
Delevinn, Delevinne, Delevyn, Delevynn,
Delevynne

Delwin (English) A friend from the valley
Delwine, Delwinn, Delwinne, Delwen,
Delwenn, Delwenne, Delwyn, Delwynn,
Delwynne

Demarcus (American) The son of Marcus
DeMarcus, DaMarkiss, DeMarco,
Demarkess, DeMarko, Demarkus,
DeMarquess, DeMarquez, DeMarquiss,
Damarcus, Damarkus

Demario (American) The son of Mario
Demarrio, DeMario, D'Mario, Dimario,
DiMario

Dembe (African) A peaceful man
Dembi, Dembie, Dembee, Dembea,
Dembey, Demby

Demetrick (American) Of the earth
Demetryck, Demetric, Demetryc,
Demetrik, Demetryk

Demetrius (Greek) A follower of the
goddess Demeter
Dametrius, Demetri, Demetrice, Demetrio,
Demetris, Demitri, Demitrios, Demitrius,
Dhimitrios, Dimetre, Dimitri, Dimitrios,
Dimitrious, Dimitry, Dmitri, Dmitrios,
Dmitry, Dimas, Demas

Demissie (African) The destroyer
Demissi, Demissy, Demissey, Demissee,
Demissea

Demont (French) Man of the mountain
Demonte, Demond, Demonde, Demunt,
Demunte, Demund, Demunde

Demos (Greek) Of the people
Demus, Demmos, Demmus

Demothi (Native American) A talker
Demothie, Demothy, Demothey,
Demothee, Demothea

Dempsey (Irish) A proud man
Dempsy, Dempsi, Dempsie, Dempsee,
Dempsea

Dempster (English) One who judges
Dempstar, Dempstor, Dempstur, Dempstir,
Dempstyr

Denali (American) From the national park
Denalie, Denaly, Denaley, Denalee,
Denalea, Denaleigh

Denby (Scandinavian) From the Danes
village
Denbey, Denbi, Denbie, Denbee, Denbea,
Danbey, Danby, Danbee, Danbea, Danbi,
Danbie

Denham (English) From the village in the
valley

Denholm (Scandinavian) From the home
of the Danes

Denim (American) Made of a strong cloth
Denym, Denem, Denam

Denley (English) From the meadow near
the valley
Denly, Denlea, Denleah, Denlee, Denleigh,
Denli, Denlie

Denman (English) One who lives in the valley
Denmann, Denmin, Denmyn, Denmen, Denmon, Denmun

Denmark (Scandinavian) From the country of Denmark
Denmarck, Denmarc, Denmarq

Dennis (French) A follower of Dionysus
Den, Denies, Denis, Dennes, Dennet, Denney, Dennie, Denys, Denny, Dennys, Denni, Dennee, Dennea, Deni, Denie, Denee, Denea, Deny, Deney

Dennison (English) The son of Dennis
Denison, Dennisun, Denisun, Dennisen, Denisen, Dennisan, Denisan, Dennisin, Denisin, Dennisyn, Denisyn, Dennyson, Denyson

Denton (English) From the town in the valley
Dentun, Dentin, Dentyn, Dentan, Denten, Denti, Dentie, Denty, Dentey, Dentee, Dentea

Denver (English) From the green valley
Denvar, Denvor, Denvir, Denvyr, Denvur

Denzel (English) From a place in Cornwall
Denzell, Denziel, Denzil, Denzill, Denzyl, Denzyll

Deo (Greek) A godly man

Deodar (Sanskrit) From the divine wood
Deodarr

Deogol (Anglo-Saxon) A secretive man

Deonte (French) An outgoing man
Deontay, Deontaye, Deontae, Dionte, Diontay, Diontaye, Diontae

Deorsa (Gaelic) Form of George, meaning "one who works the earth; a farmer"

Deotis (American) A learned man; a scholar
Deotiss, Deotys, Deotyss, Deotus, Deotuss

Derek (English) The ruler of the tribe
Dereck, Deric, Derick, Derik, Deriq, Derk, Derreck, Derrek, Derrick, Derrik, Derryck, Derryk, Deryck, Deryk, Deryke, Dirk, Dirke, Dyrk, Dyrke, Dirck, Dierck, Dieric, Dierick

Derland (English) From the deer's land
Derlande, Durland, Durlande, Derlen, Derlin, Derlyn, Durlin, Durlyn, Durlen

Dermot (Irish) A free man
Dermott, Dermod, Dermud, Dermut, Dermutt

Derry (Gaelic) From the grove of oak trees
Derrey, Derree, Derrea, Derri, Derrie

Dervin (English) A gifted friend
Dervinn, Dervinne, Dervyn, Dervynn, Dervynne, Dervon, Dervan, Dervun, Derven, Dervenn, Dervenne

Derward (English) A guardian of the deer
Derwerd, Deerward, Deerwerd, Deorward, Deorwerd, Derwent

Derwin (English) A friend of the deer; a gifted friend
Derwine, Derwinn, Derwinne, Derwen, Derwenn, Derwenne, Derwyn, Derwynn, Derwynne, Deorwine

Deshae (American) A confident man
Deshay, Deshaye, Deshai, Deshi, Deshie, Deshy, Deshey, Deshee, Deshea

Deshan (Hindi) Of the nation
Deshal, Deshad

Deshawn (African American) God is gracious
Dashaun, Dashawn, Desean, Deshane, DeShaun, D'Shawn, Deshon, DeShawn

Desiderio (Latin) One who is desired; hoped for
Derito, Desi, Desideratus, Desiderios, Desiderius, Desiderus, Dezi, Diderot, Desie, Dezie, Desy, Dezy, Desey, Dezey, Desee, Dezee, Desea, Dezea, Didier, Dizier, Deseo, Des, Dez

Desmond (Gaelic) A man from South Munster
Desmonde, Desmund, Desmunde, Dezmond, Dezmonde, Dezmund, Dezmunde, Desmee, Dezmee, Desmea, Dezmea, Desmi, Dezmi, Desmie, Dezmie, Desmy, Dezmy, Desmey, Dezmey, Desmon, Dezmon, Desmun, Dezmun

Desperado (Spanish) A renegade

Destin (French) Recognizing one's certain fortune; fate
Destyn, Deston, Destun, Desten, Destan

Destrey (American) A cowboy
Destry, Destree, Destrea, Destri, Destrie

Detlef (German) One who is decisive
Detleff, Detlev

Deuce (American) A gambling man
Deuse, Dewce, Dewse

Deutsch (German) A German

Dev (Indian) A kingly man

Deval (Hindi) A divine man
Dev, Devak

Devanshi (Hindi) A divine messenger
*Devanshie, Devanshy, Devanshey,
Devanshee, Devanshea*

Devante (Spanish) One who fights wrong-
doing

Deverell (French) From the riverbank
*Deverel, Deveral, Deverall, Devereau,
Devereaux, Devere, Deverill, Deveril,
Deverick, Deveryck, Deverik, Deveryk,
Deveric, Deveryc, Devery, Deverey, Deveree,
Deverea, Deveri, Deverie, Devry, Devrey,
Devree, Devrea, Devri, Devrie*

Devine (Gaelic / French) Resembling an ox
/ of the divine

Devisser (Dutch) A fisherman
Deviser, Devysser, Devyser

Devland (Irish) A courageous man
*Devlande, Devlind, Devlinde, Devlend,
Devlende*

Devlin (Gaelic) Having fierce bravery; a
misfortunate man
Devlyn, Devlon, Devlen, Devlan, Devlun

Devon (English) From the beautiful farm-
land; of the divine
*Devan, Deven, Devenn, Devin, Devonn,
Devone, Deveon, Devonne, Devvon,
Devy, Devynn, Deheune, Devun, Devunn,
Devion, Deavon, Deavun, Deavin, Deavyn,
Devron, Devren, Devrin, Devryn*

Devoss (Dutch) Resembling a fox

Dewey (Welsh) A highly valued man
Dewy, Dewee, Dewea, Dewi, Dewie, Duey

Dewitt (Flemish) A blonde-haired man
*DeWitt, Dewytt, DeWytt, Dewit, DeWit,
Dewyt, DeWyt*

Dexter (Latin) A right-handed man; one
who is skillful
*Dextor, Dextar, Dextur, Dextir, Dextyr,
Dexton, Dextun, Dexten, Dextan, Dextin,
Dextyn, Dex, Dexe*

Dhyanesh (Indian) One who meditates
Dhianesh, Dhyaneshe, Dhianeshe

Dia (African) The champion

Diallo (African) One who is bold

Diamond (English) A highly valued man;
resembling the gem; a bright protector
*Diamont, Diamonde, Diamonte, Diamund,
Diamunde, Diamunt, Diamunte, Diamon*

Diarmid (Irish) A free man
*Diarmaid, Diarmait, Diarmi, Diarmie,
Diarmee, Diarmea, Diarmy, Diarmey*

Dice (American) A gambling man
Dyce

Dichali (Native American) One who talks
a lot
*Dichalie, Dichaly, Dichaley, Dichalee,
Dichalea, Dichaleigh*

Dick (English) Form of Richard, meaning
"a powerful ruler"
Dik, Dic, Dyck, Dyc, Dyk

Dickinson (English) The son of Dick
Dicken, Dickens, Dickson, Dickenson

Dickran (Armenian) The name of a king
Dikran, Dicran, Dyckran, Dykran, Dycran

Diego ✪ (Spanish) Form of James, meaning "he who supplants"
Dyego, Dago

Dien (Vietnamese) A farmer

Diesel (American) Having great strength
Deisel, Diezel, Deizel, Dezsel

Dietmar (German) One who is famous
Dietmarr, Deitmar, Deitmarr

Dietrich (German) The ruler of the tribe
*Dietrick, Dietryck, Dietrik, Dietryk, Dietric,
Dietryc, Dieter, Dietar, Dietor, Dietur, Dietir,
Dietyr, Deidrich, Deidrick, Deidryck,
Deidrik, Deidryk, Deidric, Deidryc*

Digby (Norse) From the town near the
ditch
Digbey, Digbee, Digbea, Digbi, Digbie

Diggory (English) From the dyke
*Diggorey, Diggori, Diggorie, Diggoree,
Diggorea, Digory, Digorey, Digoree,
Digorea, Digori, Digorie, Diggery,
Diggerey, Diggeree, Diggerea, Diggeri,
Diggerie, Digery, Digerey, Digeree, Digerea,
Digeri, Digerie*

Diji (African) A farmer
Dijie, Dijee, Dijea, Dijy, Dijey

Dilip (Indian) Of the royalty
Deleep, Dileap, Dilyp

Dillon (Gaelic) Resembling a lion;
a faithful man
*Dillun, Dillen, Dillan, Dillin, Dillyn,
Dilon, Dilan, Dilin, Dilyn, Dilen, Dilun,
Dillion, Dillian, Dillien, Dill*

Dima (Slavic) A mighty warrior
Dyma, Dimah, Dymah

Din (African) A great man
Dyn

Dinesh (Hindi) Of the sun
Dineshe, Dynesh, Dyneshe

Dingo (Australian) Resembling the wild dog
Dyngo

Dinh (Vietnamese) One who is peaceful; calm

Dino (Italian) One who wields a little sword
*Dyno, Dinoh, Dynoh, Deano, Deanoh,
Deeno, Deenoh, Deino, Deinoh*

Dinos (Greek) Form of Constantine,
meaning "one who is steadfast; firm"
*Dynos, Deanos, Deenos, Deinos, Dinose,
Dinoz, Dinoze*

Dins (American) One who climbs to the top
Dinz, Dyns, Dynz

Dinsmore (Celtic) From the fortress on
the hill
*Dinsmor, Dinnsmore, Dinnsmor,
Dynsmore, Dynsmor, Dynnsmore,
Dynnsmor, Dinny, Dinni, Dinney, Dinnie,
Dinnee, Dinnea*

Diogenes (Greek) An honest man
Dyogenes

Dion (Greek) Form of Dionysus, in mytholo-
gy, the god of wine and revelry
*Deion, Deon, Deonn, Deonys, Deyon,
Diandre, Diondre, Dionte, Dondre,
Diondray, Diandray, Diondrae, Diandrae*

Dionizy (Polish) Form of Dionysus, in
mythology, the god of wine and revelry
*Dionizey, Dionizi, Dionizie, Dionizee,
Dionizea*

Dionysus (Greek) In mythology, the god of
wine and revelry
*Dionio, Dionisio, Dioniso, Dionysios,
Dionysos, Dionysius, Dionysio, Dionyso,
Deonysis, Deonysus, Deonisis, Deonisus,
Dionis*

Dior (French) The golden one
*D'Or, Diorr, Diorre, Dyor, Deor, Dyorre,
Deorre*

Diron (American) Form of Darren, mean-
ing "a great man / a gift from God"
*Dirun, Diren, Diran, Dirin, Diryn, Dyron,
Dyren, Dyran, Dyrin, Dyryn, Dyrun*

Dix (English) The tenth-born child
*Dixe, Dixx, Dyx, Dyxe, Dyxx, Dixo,
Dyxo*

Dixon (English) The son of Dick
Dixen, Dixin, Dixyn, Dixan, Dixun

Doane (English) From the rolling hills
Doan

Dobber (American) An independent man
Dobbar, Dobbor, Dobbur, Dobbir, Dobbyr

Dobbs (English) A fiery man
Dobbes, Dobes, Dobs

Dobi (African) One who does laundry
Dobie, Doby, Dobey, Dobee, Dobea

Dobromir (Polish) A good man
*Dobromeer, Dobromear, Dobromier,
Dobromeir, Dobromere, Dobromyr,
Dobrey, Dobree, Dobrea, Dobri, Dobrie,
Dobry*

Doctor (American) A physician; one who
heals others
*Docter, Doctur, Doctar, Doktor, Doktur,
Dokter, Doktar, Dock, Doc, Dok*

Dodek (Polish) A hero
Dodeck, Dodec

Dodge (English) Form of Roger, meaning
"a famous spearman"
*Dodger, Doge, Dodgson, Dodds, Dodd,
Dod, Dods*

Dog (American) Resembling the animal; one who is loyal
Dawg, Daug, Dogg, Doggie, Doggi, Doggy, Doggey, Doggee, Doggea

Doherty (Irish) One who is harmful
Dohertey, Doherti, Dohertie, Dohertee, Dohertea, Dougherty, Doughertey, Dougherti, Doughertie, Doughertee, Doughertea, Douherty, Douhertey, Douherti, Douhertie, Douhertee, Douhertea

Dohosan (Native American) From the bluff
Dohosen, Dohoson, Dohosun, Dohosin, Dohosyn

Doire (Scottish) From the grove
Doyre, Dhoire, Dhoyre

Dolan (Gaelic) A dark-haired man; one who is bold
Dolen, Dolon, Dolun, Dolin, Dolyn

Dolgen (American) A tenacious man
Dolgan, Dolgin, Dolgyn, Dolgun, Dolgon, Dolge, Dolg

Domokos (Hungarian) One who belongs to God
Domokus, Domonkos, Domonkus, Domos

Don (Scottish) From of Donald, meaning "ruler of the world"
Donn, Donny, Donney, Donnie, Donni, Donnee, Donnea, Donne, Donnan, Donnen, Donnon, Donnun, Donnin, Donnyn

Donaciano (Spanish) Having dark features
Donace, Donase, Donasiano

Donagh (Celtic) A brown-haired warrior
Donaghie, Donaghy, Donaghey, Donaghi, Donaghee, Donaghea

Donahue (Irish) A dark warrior
Donahoe, Donohoe, Donohue, Donahugh, Donohugh

Donald (Scottish) Ruler of the world
Donold, Donuld, Doneld, Donild, Donyld

Donar (Teutonic) In mythology, the god of thunder
Doner, Donor, Donur, Donir, Donyr

DOMINICK

We decided to name our son Dominick after my husband's grandfather. We were unable to tell him before he unexpectedly passed away six weeks prior to my due date. We like to think that Papa knows and spends some time watching over our little boy. —Dawn, PA

Dolph (German) A noble wolf
Dolf, Dollfus, Dollfuss, Dollphus, Dolphus, Dolfus

Domani (Italian) Man of tomorrow
Domanie, Domany, Domaney, Domanee, Domanea

Domevlo (African) One who doesn't judge others
Domivlo, Domyvlo

Domingo (Spanish) Born on a Sunday
Domyngo, Demingo, Demyngo

Dominic ☼ (Latin) A lord
Demenico, Dom, Domenic, Domenico, Domenique, Domini, Dominick, Dominico, Dominie, Dominik, Dominique, Domenik, Domenick, Dominie, Dominy, Dominey, Dominee, Dominea, Domino

Domnall (Gaelic) A world ruler
Domhnall, Domnull, Domhnull

Donatello (Spanish) A gift from God
Donato, Donatien, Donatus, Donatelo, Donatio, Donateo, Donat, Donzel, Donzell, Donzele, Donzelle

Donder (Dutch) Resembling thunder
Dondar, Dondor, Dondur, Dondir, Dondyr

Dong (Vietnamese) Born during the winter

Donis (English) Form of Adonis, in mythology, a handsome young man loved by Aphrodite
Donys, Donnis, Donys, Dones, Donnes

Donkor (African) A humble man
Donkur, Donkir, Donkyr, Donker, Donkar

Donnan (Irish) A brown-haired man
Donnen, Donnon, Donnun, Donnin, Donnyn

Donnell (Scottish) Ruler of the world; a brown-haired warrior
Donnel, Donell, Donel, Donnall, Donal, Donnal, Donall, Donnelly, Donnelley, Donnelli, Donnellie, Donnellee, Donally, Donalley, Donalli, Donallie, Donallee, Donaly, Donaley, Donali, Donalie, Donalee, Donnally, Donnalley, Donnallee, Donnallea, Donnalli, Donnallie

Donovan (Irish) A brown-haired chief
Donavan, Donavon, Donevin, Donevon, Donoven, Donovon, Donovin, Donovyn, Donaven, Donavin, Donavyn, Donevyn, Donevan, Doneven

Dontavius (English) Form of Dante, meaning "an enduring man; everlasting"
Dantavius, Dawntavius, Dewontavius, Dontavious, Dontav, Dontave

Donton (American) One who is confident
Dontun, Daunton, Dauntun, Donti, Dontie, Donty, Dontey, Daunti, Dauntie, Dauntey, Daunty

Donyale (American) One who is regal
Donyail, Donyaile, Donyael, Donyaele, Donyayl, Donyayle

Donyell (American) A faithful man
Donyel, Donyele, Donyelle, Danyel, Danyell, Danyele, Danyelle

Doocey (American) A quick-witted man
Doocy, Doocee, Doocea, Dooci, Doocie

Dooley (Irish) A dark hero
Dooly, Doolee, Doolea, Dooleigh, Dooli, Doolie

Dor (Hebrew) Of this generation
Doram, Doriel, Dorli, Dorlie, Dorlee, Dorlea, Dorleigh, Dorly, Dorley

Doran (Irish) A stranger; one who has been exiled
Doren, Dorin, Doryn

Dorek (Polish) A gift from God
Dorec, Doreck

Dorian (Greek) Of the ancient Greek tribe, the Dorians
Dorrian, Dorien, Dorrien, Dorion, Dorrion, Doriun, Dorriun, Dori, Dorri, Dorie, Dorrie, Dorry, Dory, Dorey, Dorrey, Doree, Dorree, Dorrea, Dorea

Dorjan (Hungarian) A dark man
Dorjen, Dorjin, Dorjyn, Dorjon, Dorjun

Doron (Hebrew) A gift; the dweller
Dorron, Dorun, Dorrun, Doroni, Doronie, Doronee, Dorone, Doronea, Dorony, Doroney, Dorroni, Dorronie, Dorronee, Dorronea, Dorrone, Dorrony, Dorroney

Dorran (Irish) A dark-haired man
Dorren, Dorrin, Dorryn, Dorrell, Dorrel, Dorrance, Dorrence

Dorset (English) Of the people who live near the sea
Dorsett, Dorsete, Dorsette, Dorzet, Dorzete, Dorzett, Dorzette

Dorsey (Gaelic) From the fortress near the sea
Dorsy, Dorsee, Dorsea, Dorsi, Dorsie

Dosne (Celtic) From the sand hill
Dosni, Dosnie, Dosney, Dosny, Dosnee, Dosnea

Dost (Arabic) A beloved friend
Doste, Daust, Dauste, Dawst, Dawste

Dotan (African) A hardworking man
Doten, Dotin, Dotyn, Doton, Dotun

Dotson (English) The son of Dot
Dotsen, Dotsan, Dotsin, Dotsyn, Dotsun, Dottson, Dottsun, Dottsin, Dottsyn, Dottsan, Dottsen

Dougal (Celtic) A dark stranger
Dougall, Dugal, Dugald, Dugall, Dougald, Doughal, Doughald, Doughall, Dughall

Douglas (Scottish) From the black river
Douglass, Dugaid, Doug, Doughlas, Dougy, Dougey, Dougi, Dougie, Dougee, Dougea, Duglass, Dughlass, Duglas, Dughlas

Dour (Scottish) A man from the water
Doure

Dov (Hebrew) Resembling a bear
Dohv, Dahv

Dove (American) A peaceful man
Dovi, Dovie, Dovy, Dovey, Dovee, Dovea

Dover (Welsh) From the water
Dovor, Dovar, Dovur, Dovir, Dovyr

Dovev (Hebrew) One who speaks softly
Doviv, Dovyv

Dow (Irish) A dark-haired man
Dowe, Dowson, Dowsun, Dowsen,
Dowsan, Dowsin, Dowsyn, Dowan,
Dowen, Dowon, Dowyn, Dowin, Dowun

Dowd (American) A serious-minded man
Dowde, Dowed, Dowdi, Dowdie, Dowdy,
Dowdey, Dowdee, Dowdea

Doyle (Gaelic) A dark stranger
Doile, Doyl, Doil, Doy, Doye, Dowle,
Dowl, Doyal

Doylton (English) From Doyle's town
Doyltun, Doylten, Doyltan, Doyltin, Doyltyn

Drade (American) A serious-minded man
Draid, Draide, Drayd, Drayde, Draed,
Draede, Dradell, Dradel

Dragon (American) Resembling the fire-
breathing creature
Dragan, Dragen, Dragun, Dragin, Dragyn

Drake (English) Resembling a dragon
Draik, Draike, Draek, Draeke, Drayk,
Drayke, Draco, Dracko, Drako, Dracon,
Drackon, Drakon, Drago, Draico, Draicko,
Draiko, Drayco, Draycko, Drayko, Draeco,
Draecko, Draeko, Draicon, Draickon,
Draikon, Draycon, Drayckon, Draykon,
Draecon, Draeckon, Draekon, Draygo,
Draigo, Draego, Dracul, Drakul

Draper (English) One who sells cloth
Drapar, Drapor, Drapur, Drapir, Drapyr

Drayce (American) Form of Drake, mean-
ing "resembling a dragon"
Drayse, Draice, Draise, Draece, Draese,
Drace, Drase, Dracie, Draci, Dracey, Dracy,
Dracee, Dracea, Drasy, Drasey, Drasee,
Drasea, Drasi, Drasie

Drefan (Anglo-Saxon) A troublemaker
Drefon, Drefun, Drefen, Drefin, Drefyn

Dreng (Anglo-Saxon) A mighty warrior;
one who is brave
Drenge, Dring, Dringe, Dryng, Drynge

Dreogan (Anglo-Saxon) A suffering man
Dreogen, Dreogon, Dreogun, Dreogin,
Dreogyn

Drew (Welsh) One who is wise
Drue, Dru, Droo, Drou, Dryw, Druw

Drexel (American) A thoughtful man
Drexell, Drexele, Drexelle, Drex, Drexe

Driscoll (Celtic) A mediator; one who is
sorrowful; a messenger
Dryscoll, Driscol, Dryscol, Driskoll,
Dryskoll, Driskol, Dryskol, Driskell,
Dryskell, Driskel, Dryskel

Druce (Gaelic / English) A wise man; a
druid / the son of Drew
Drews, Drewce, Druece, Druse, Druson,
Drusen, Drusin, Drusyn, Drusan, Drusun,
Drywson, Drywsen, Drywsan, Drywsun,
Drywsin, Drywsyn, Drewson, Drewsun,
Drewsan, Drewsen, Drewsin, Drewsyn

Drugi (German) Having great strength
Drugie, Drugy, Drugey, Drugee, Drugea

Drummond (Scottish) One who lives on
the ridge
Drummon, Drumond, Drumon,
Drummund, Drumund, Drummun,
Drumun, Drummand, Drumand,
Drumman, Druman

Drury (French) One who is dearly loved
Drurey, Druri, Drurie, Druree, Drurea,
Drewry, Drewrey, Drewri, Drewrie,
Drewree, Drewrea

Dryden (English) From the dry valley
Driden, Drydan, Dridan, Drydon, Dridon,
Drydun, Dridun, Drydin, Dridin, Drydyn,
Dridyn, Drygedene

Drystan (Welsh) Form of Tristan, meaning
"a sorrowful man"
Drystan, Dris, Dristam, Dristen, Dristian,
Dristin, Driston, Dristram, Dristyn, Driste,
Drysten, Dryston, Drystyn

Duane (Gaelic) A dark or swarthy man
Dewain, Dewayne, Duante, Duayne,
Duwain, Duwaine, Duwayne, Dwain,
Dwaine, Dwayne, Dawayne, Dwane

Duarte (Spanish) A wealthy guardian
Duartay, Duartaye, Duartai, Duartae,
Duardo, Duard, Duarde, Dueart, Duearte,
Duart, Duartee, Duartea, Duarti, Duartie,
Duarty, Duartey

Dubh (Scottish) A black-haired man
Dub, Dubg, Dubb, Dubv

Dublin (Irish) From the capital of Ireland
Dublyn, Dublen, Dublan, Dublon, Dublun

Duc (Vietnamese) One who has upstanding
morals

Dude (American) A cowboy

Dudley (English) From the people's meadow
*Dudly, Dudlee, Dudlea, Dudleah,
Dudleigh, Dudli, Dudlie*

Due (Vietnamese) A virtuous man

Duer (Celtic) A heroic man

Duff (Gaelic) A swarthy man
Duffe, Duffi, Duffie, Duffee, Duffea

Dugan (Gaelic) A dark and swarthy man
Doogan, Dougan, Douggan, Duggan

Duke (English) A title of nobility; a leader
*Dooke, Dook, Duki, Dukie, Dukey, Duky,
Dukee, Dukea*

Dulal (Indian) One who is dearly loved
Dulall, Dullal, Dullall

Dume (African) Resembling a bull

Dumi (African) One who inspires others
Dumie, Dumy, Dumey, Dumee, Dumea

Dumisani (African) A great leader
*Dumisanie, Dumisany, Dumisaney,
Dumisanee, Dumisanea*

Dumont (French) Man of the mountain
Dumonte, Dumount, Dumounte

Dunbar (Gaelic) From the castle at the
headland
*Dunbarr, Dunbaron, Dunbaran, Dunbarin,
Dunbaryn, Dunbaren, Dunbarun*

Duncan (Scottish) A dark warrior
Dunkan, Dunckan, Dunc, Dunk, Dunck

Dundee (Scottish) From the town on the
Firth of Tay
Dundea, Dundi, Dundie, Dundy, Dundey

Dung (Vietnamese) A brave man; a heroic
man

Dunham (Celtic) A brown-haired man

Dunia (American) Having dark features
Duniah, Dunya, Dunyah, Duniya, Duniyah

Dunley (English) From the hilly meadow
*Dunly, Dunli, Dunlie, Dunleigh, Dunlea,
Dunleah, Dunnley, Dunnly, Dunnleigh,
Dunnlee, Dunnlea, Dunnleah, Dunnli,
Dunnlie*

Dunlop (Scottish) From the muddy hill

Dunmore (Scottish) From the fortress on
the hill
Dunmor

Dunn (Gaelic) A brown-haired man
Dun, Dunne, Dune

Dunphy (American) A dark and serious
man
*Dunphey, Dunphi, Dunphie, Dunphee,
Dunphea, Dunphe*

Dunstan (English) From the hill of brown
stones
*Dunsten, Dunstin, Dunstyn, Dunston,
Dunstun*

Dunton (English) From the town on the hill
Duntun, Dunten, Duntan, Duntin, Duntyn

Durand (Latin / French) An enduring man /
one who stands firm
*Duran, Durant, Durante, Durrant,
Durrand, Durande, Durrande, Durandt*

Durango (French) Having great strength
Durengo, Duringo, Duryngo

Durbin (Latin) One who lives in the city
Durbyn, Durban, Durben, Durbon, Durbun

Dureau (French) Having great strength
*Dureaux, Dureax, Durell, Durel, Durelle,
Durele*

Durga (Hindi) The unreachable

Durin (Norse) In mythology, one of the
fathers of the dwarves
Duryn, Duren, Duran, Duron, Durun

Durjaya (Hindi) One who is difficult to
defeat

Durrell (English) One who is strong and
protective
Durrel, Durell, Durel

Durward (English) A gatekeeper
*Durwerd, Durwald, Durwarden,
Durwerden, Derward, Derwerd,
Derwarden, Derwerden*

Durwin (English) A friend of the deer
*Durwinn, Durwinne, Durwine, Durwen,
Durwenn, Durwenne, Durwyn, Durwynn,
Durwynne*

Duryea (Gaelic) An enduring man

Dusan (Slavic) God is my judge
Dusen, Duson, Dusun, Dusin, Dusyn

Duscha (Slavic) Filled with the divine spirit

Dustin (English / German) From the dusty area / a courageous warrior
Dustyn, Dusten, Dustan, Duston, Dustun, Dusty, Dustey, Dusti, Dustie, Dustee, Dustea, Duster

Dutch (German) From the Netherlands

Duvall (French) From the valley
Duval, Duvale

Dwade (English) A dark traveler
Dwaid, Dwaide, Dwayd, Dwayde, Dwaed, Dwaede

Dwan (American) A fresh-faced man
Dwawn, Dwaun, Dewan, Dewawn, Dewaun

Dweezel (American) A creative man
Dweezell, Dweeze, Dweezil, Dweezill, Dweezyl, Dweezyll, Dweezi, Dweezie, Dweezy, Dweezey, Dweezee, Dweezea

Dwight (Flemish) A white- or blonde-haired man
Dwite, Dwhite, Dwyght, Dwighte

Dwyer (Gaelic) A dark and wise man
Dwire

Dyami (Native American) Resembling an eagle
Dyamie, Dyamy, Dyamey, Dyamee, Dyamea, Dyame

Dyer (English) A creative man
Dier, Dyar, Diar, Dy, Dye, Di, Die

Dylan ✪ (Welsh) Son of the sea
Dyllan, Dylon, Dyllon, Dylen, Dyllen, Dylun, Dyllun, Dylin, Dyllin, Dylyn, Dyllyn, Dillon

Dymas (Greek) In mythology, the father of Hecabe
Dimas

Dynell (American) A man of the sea
Dynel, Dynele, Dynelle, Dinell, Dinel, Dinele, Dinelle

Dyre (Scandinavian) A dear and precious man
Dyr, Dyri, Dyrie, Dyry, Dyrey, Dyree

Dyson (American) Form of Tyson, meaning "one who is high-spirited; fiery"
Dysen, Dysan, Dysun, Dysin, Dysyn, Dison, Disan, Disen, Disun, Disin, Disyn

Dyumani (Indian) Of the sun
Dyumanie, Dyumany, Dyumaney, Dyumanee, Dyumanea

Dzigbode (African) One who is patient

Eachan (Irish) A horseman
Eachann, Echan, Echann

Eadburt (English) A wealthy man
Eadbert, Eadbirt, Eadbyrt, Eadbeorht

Eagan (Irish) A fiery man
Eegan, Eagen, Eegen, Eagon, Eegon, Eagun, Eegun, Ea

Eagle (Native American) Resembling the bird
Eegle, Eagel, Eegel

Eamon (Irish) Form of Edmond, meaning "a wealthy protector"
Eaman, Eamen, Eamin, Eamyn, Eamun, Eamonn, Eames, Eemon, Eeman, Eemen, Eemin, Eemyn, Eemun, Eemes

Ean (Gaelic) Form of John, meaning "God is gracious"
Eion, Eyan, Eyon, Eian

Earl (English) A nobleman
Earle, Erle, Erl, Eorl

Earlham (English) From the earl's village
Erlham

Earlston (English) From the earl's town
Earlstun, Erlston, Erlstun, Earlton, Earltun, Erlton, Erltun

Early (American / English) One who is punctual / from Earl's meadow
Earley, Earli, Earlie, Earleigh, Earlee, Earlea, Earleah, Erly, Erley, Erleigh, Erlee, Erlea, Erleah, Erli, Erlie

Earm (Anglo-Saxon) A wretched man
Erm, Eerm, Eirm

Earnan (Irish) A knowing man
Earnen, Earnin, Earnyn, Earnon, Earnun, Ernan, Ernen, Ernon, Ernun, Ernin, Ernyn

Earvin (English) Friend of the sea
Earven, Earvan, Earvyn, Earvon, Earvun, Ervin, Ervyn, Erven, Ervan, Ervon, Ervun, Ervine

Easey (American) An easygoing man
Easy, Easi, Easie, Easee, Easea, Eazey, Eazy, Eazi, Eazie, Eazee, Eazea, Ezy, Ezey, Ezee, Ezea, Ezi, Ezie

Eastman (English) A man from the east
Eestman, East, Easte, Eest, Eeste

Easton (English) From the eastern town
Eeston, Eastun, Eestun

Eaton (English) From the island village
Eatton, Eton, Etton, Eyton, Eytton, Eatun, Etun, Eytun, Etawn, Etaun, Eatawn, Eataun

Eben (Hebrew) As solid as a rock
Eban, Ebon, Ebin, Ebyn, Ebun, Eb, Ebbe

Ebenezer (Hebrew) The rock of help
Ebbaneza, Ebeneezer, Ebeneser, Ebenezar, Eveneser, Evenezer, Ebenzer, Ebby, Ebbey, Ebbea, Ebbee, Ebbi, Ebbie

Eberhard (German) As strong as a boar; as brave as a boar
Eberado, Eberhardt, Eberdt, Ebert, Eberte, Eberhart, Eburhard, Eburhart, Eburhardt, Eburt, Eburdt

Eberlein (German) Resembling a small boar
Eberleen, Eberlean, Eberlien, Eberlin, Eberlyn, Eberle, Eberley, Eberly, Eberlee, Eberleigh, Eberlea, Eberli, Eberlie

Ebisu (Japanese) In mythology, the patron god of fishermen
Ebysu, Ebisue, Ebysue, Ebisoo, Ebysoo, Ebisou, Ebysou

Eblis (Arabic) A devilish man
Ebliss, Eblisse, Eblys, Eblyss, Eblysse

Ebo (African) Born on a Tuesday
Eboe, Ebow, Ebowe

Ebrahim (Arabic) Form of Abraham, meaning "father of a multitude; father of nations"
Ebraheem, Ebraheim, Ebrahiem, Ebraheam, Ebrahym

Echo (Greek) Sound returned
Ekko, Ekho, Eko, Ecco, Ekow, Ecko

Eckerd (German) One who is sacred
Ekerd, Ecerd, Eckherd, Eckhert, Ekherd

Eckhard (German) Of the brave sword point
Eckard, Eckardt, Eckhardt, Ekkehard, Ekkehardt, Ekhard, Ekhardt

Ed (English) Form of Edward, meaning "a wealthy protector"
Edd, Eddi, Eddie, Eddy, Eddey, Eddee, Eddea, Edi, Edie, Edy, Edey, Edee, Edea

Edan (Celtic) One who is full of fire
Edon, Edun

Edbert (English) One who is prosperous and bright
Edberte, Edburt, Edburte, Edbirt, Edbirte, Edbyrt, Edbyrte

Edel (German) One who is noble
Edelin, Edlin, Edell, Edlen, Edelen, Edelyn, Edlyn

Edelmar (English) One who is noble
Edelmarr

Eden (Hebrew) Place of pleasure; in the Bible, the first home of Adam and Eve
Eaden, Eadin, Edin, Ednan, Edyn

Edenson (English) Son of Eden
Eadenson, Edensun, Eadensun, Edinson, Edinsun, Edensen, Eadensen

Eder (Hebrew) Of the flock
Edar, Edir, Edyr, Edor, Edur

Edet (African) Born on the market day
Edett, Edete

Edgar (English) A powerful and wealthy spearman
Eadgar, Eadger, Edgard, Edgardo, Edghur, Edgur, Edger, Edgor, Eadgur, Eadgor, Eadgir, Edgir, Eadgyr, Edgyr, Eadgard

Edge (American) A trendsetter
Edgi, Edgie, Edgey, Edgy, Edgee, Edgea

Edilberto (Spanish) One who is noble
Edylberto, Edilbert, Edylbert, Edilburt, Edylburt, Edylbirt, Edilbirt, Edylberto, Edilburto, Edylburto, Edilbirto, Edylbirto

Edison (English) Son of Edward
Eddison, Edisun, Eddisun, Edisen, Eddisen, Edisyn, Eddisyn, Edyson, Eddyson, Edysun, Eddysun, Edysen, Eddysen, Edson, Edsun, Edsen, Eddis, Eddys, Eddiss, Eddyss

Edlin (Anglo-Saxon) A wealthy friend
*Edlinn, Edlinne, Edlyn, Edlynn, Edlynne,
Eadlyn, Eadlin, Edlen, Edlenn, Edlenne,
Eadlinn, Eadlinne, Eadlynne, Eadlynn*

Edmar (English) Of the wealthy sea
*Edmarr, Eddmar, Eddmarr, Eadmar,
Eadmarr*

Edmond (English) A wealthy protector
*Edmon, Edmund, Edmonde, Edmundo,
Edmondo, Edmun, Edmunde, Eadmund,
Eadmunde, Eadmond, Eadmonde, Ede*

Edom (Hebrew) A red-haired man
Edum, Edam, Edem, Edim, Edym

Edred (Anglo-Saxon) A king
Edread, Edrid, Edryd

Edrian (Latin) A man from Hadria
*Ede, Ediran, Edrain, Edrean, Edreean,
Edreyan, Edreeyan, Edriaan, Edriano,
Edrien, Edrin, Edrino, Edrion, Edron,
Edryan, Edya, Erjen, Eydrean, Eydreean,
Eydrian, Eydrien*

Edric (English) A prosperous and lucky ruler
*Edrik, Eddrick, Ederic, Ederick, Edrich,
Edrick, Edryc, Edryk, Edryck, Edri, Edrie,
Edry, Edrey, Edree, Eadric, Eadrick,
Eadrik, Eadryc, Eadryck, Eadryk*

Edrigu (Basque) A famous ruler
*Edrygu, Edrigue, Edrygue, Edrigou,
Edrygou, Edingu, Edyngu, Edingu,
Edingue, Edyngue, Edingou, Edyngou*

Edsel (German / English) One who is noble
and bright / from the wealthy man's house
*Edsil, Edsyl, Edsal, Edsol, Edsul, Edsell,
Edcell, Edcel, Edcil, Edcyl*

Edwald (English) A wealthy ruler
Edwaldo, Edwalde, Edwaldio, Edwaldeo

Edward (English) A wealthy protector
*Eadward, Edik, Edouard, Eduard,
Eduardo, Edvard, Edvardas, Edwardo,
Ewart, Edoardo, Edorta*

Edwardson (English) The son of Edward
Edwardsun, Eadwardsone, Eadwardsun

Edwin (English) A wealthy friend
*Edwinn, Edwinne, Edwine, Edwyn,
Edwynn, Edwynne, Edwen, Edwenn,
Edwenne, Eadwin, Eadwyn, Eadwen,
Easwine, Edwy, Edwey, Edwee, Edwea,
Edwi, Edwie*

Effiom (African) Resembling a crocodile
Efiom, Effyom, Efyom, Effeom, Efeom

Efigenio (Greek) Form of Eugene, mean-
ing "a wellborn man"
*Ephigenio, Ephigenios, Ephigenius,
Efigenios, Efigenius*

Efisio (Italian) A man from Ephesus

Efrain (Spanish) Form of Ephraim, mean-
ing "one who is fertile; productive"
*Efraine, Efrayn, Efrayne, Efraen, Efraene,
Efrane, Efren, Efran, Efrun, Efrin, Efryn*

Efrat (Hebrew) One who is honored
Efratt, Ephrat, Ephratt

Efron (Hebrew) Resembling a songbird
*Ephron, Efroni, Ephroni, Efronie,
Ephronie, Efrony, Ephrony, Efroney,
Ephroney, Efronee, Ephronee*

Efton (American) Form of Ephraim, meaning "one who is fertile; productive"
Eftun, Eften, Eftan, Eftin, Eftyn

Egan (Gaelic) A little flame; one who is fiery
Egen, Egin, Egyn, Egann, Eghan, Eghann

Egbert (English) One who wields a brilliant
sword
*Egberte, Egburt, Egburte, Egbirt, Egbirte,
Egbyrt, Egbyrte*

Egborn (English) One who is ready
*Egborne, Egbourn, Egbourne, Egbern,
Egberne, Egburn, Egburne*

Egerton (English) From the town on the
edge; from Edgar's town
*Egertun, Edgerton, Edgertun, Egarton,
Egartun, Edgarton, Edgartun*

Egesa (Anglo-Saxon) One who creates terror
Egessa, Egeslic, Egeslick, Egeslik

Egeus (American) A protective man
Egius, Eges, Egis

Eghert (German) An intelligent man
*Egherte, Eghurt, Eghurte, Eghirt, Eghirte,
Eghyrt, Eghyrte*

Egidio (Italian) Resembling a young goat
*Egydio, Egideo, Egydeo, Egidiyo, Egydiyo,
Egidius, Egydius, Egidios, Egydios*

Egil (Scandinavian) Of the sword's point or edge
Egyl, Eigil, Eigyl

Eginhard (German) One who is strong with a sword
Eginard, Eginhardt, Einhard, Einhardt, Einard

Egmont (French) A fierce defender
Egmonte, Egmunt, Egmunte, Egmond, Egmonde, Egmund, Egmunde, Egmon, Egmun

Egon (German) Of the sword's point
Egun

Egor (Russian) One who works the earth; a farmer
Eigor, Eygor

Egyed (Hungarian) A shield-bearer
Egied

Ehren (German) An honorable man
Ehran, Ehrin, Ehryn, Ehron, Ehrun

Ehud (Hebrew) One who loves and is loved

Eikki (Finnish) A powerful man
Eikkie, Eikky, Eikkey, Eikkee, Eikkea, Eiki, Eikie, Eiky, Eikey, Eikee, Eikea

Eilad (Hebrew) God is eternal

Eilam (Hebrew) One who is eternal
Elam, Eilem, Elem, Eilim, Elim, Eilym, Elym, Eilom, Elom, Eilum, Elum

Eilert (Scandinavian) Of the hard point
Elert, Eilart, Elart, Eilort, Elort, Eilurt, Elurt, Eilirt, Elirt, Eilyrt, Elyrt

Eilif (Norse) One who is immortal
Elif, Eilyf, Elyf

Eilon (Hebrew) From the oak tree
Eilan, Eilin, Eilyn, Eilen, Eilun

Eimhin (Irish) One who is swift
Eimhyn, Eimarr, Eimar

Einar (Scandinavian) A leading warrior
Einer, Ejnar, Einir, Einyr, Einor, Einur, Ejnir, Ejnyr, Ejnor, Ejnur, Ejner

Einion (Welsh) An anvil
Einyon, Enion, Enyon, Einian, Enian

Einri (Teutonic) An intelligent man
Einrie, Einry, Einrey, Einree, Einrea

Eisa (Arabic) Form of Jesus, meaning "God is my salvation"
Eisah, Eissa, Eissah

Eisig (Hebrew) One who laughs often
Eisyg

Ejnar (Danish) A warrior
Ejnarr

Eknath (Hindi) A poet
Ecknath, Ecnath, Eknathe, Ecknathe, Ecnathe

Ekon (African) Having great strength
Ekun, Ekan, Eken, Ekin, Ekyn

Ekram (Hindi) One who is honored
Eckram, Ecram

Eladio (Spanish) A man from Greece
Eladeo, Eladiyo, Eladeyo

Elbert (English / German) A wellborn man / a bright man
Elberte, Elburt, Elburte, Elbirt, Elbirte, Ethelbert, Ethelburt, Ethelbirt, Elber, Elbur, Elbir

Elbis (American) One who is exalted
Elbys, Elbiss, Elbyss, Elbase, Elbace, Elbus, Elbuss

Elbridge (English) From the old bridge
Ellbridge, Elbrige, Ellbrige, Elbrydge, Elbryge, Ellbrydge, Ellbryge

Elchanan (Hebrew) God is gracious
Elchana, Elhanan, Elhannan, Elchannan, Elhana

Eldan (English) From the valley of the elves

Elden (English) An old friend
Eldin, Eldyn, Eldwin, Eldwinn, Eldwinne, Eldwen, Eldwenn, Eldwenne, Eldwyn, Eldwynn, Eldwynne, Eldwine

Elder (English) From the elder tree
Eldir, Eldyr, Eldor, Eldur, Eldar

Eldon (English) From the sacred hill
Eldun

Eldorado (Spanish) The golden man

Eldred (English) An old, wise advisor
Eldrid, Eldryd, Eldrad, Eldrod, Edlrud, Ethelred, Ethelread, Eldread

Eldrian (English) An old, wise ruler
Eldryan, Eldriann, Eldryann, Eldrien,
Eldryen, Eldrienn, Eldryenn

Eldrick (English) An old, wise ruler
Eldrik, Eldric, Eldryck, Eldryk, Eldryc,
Eldrich, Eldrych

Eldridge (German) A wise ruler
Eldredge, Eldrege, Eldrige, Eldrydge,
Eldryge

Eleazar (Hebrew) God will help
Elazar, Eleasar, Eleazaro, Eliazar, Eliezer,
Elazaro, Eleazaro, Elazer

Elegy (Spanish) One who is memorable
Elegey, Elegi, Elegie, Elegee, Elegea

Elek (Hungarian) Form of Alexander,
meaning "helper and defender of mankind"
Elec, Eleck

Eleodoro (Spanish) A gift from the sun

Elford (English) From the old ford
Ellford, Elforde, Ellforde, Elfurd, Ellfurd

Elgan (Welsh) Of the bright circle
Elgen, Elgann, Elgenn

Elger (English) One who wields an elf spear
Ellger, Elgar, Ellgar, Elgir, Ellgir, Elgyr,
Ellgyr, Elgor, Ellgor, Elgur, Ellgur, Elga

Elgin (English) A noble man; one who is
white-skinned
Elgyn, Elgine, Elgyne, Eljin, Eljine, Eljyn,
Eljyne

Eli ✿ (Hebrew) One who has ascended; my
God on high
Ely, Elie, Eliy, Elye

Eliachim (Hebrew) God will establish
Eliakim, Elyachim, Elyakim, Eliachym,
Eliakym

Eliam (Hebrew) The God of my nation
Elami, Elamie, Elamy, Elamey, Elamee,
Elamea, Elyam

Elian (Spanish) A spirited man
Elyan, Elien, Elyen, Elion, Elyon, Eliun,
Elyun

Elias (Hebrew) Form of Elijah, meaning
"Jehovah is my God"
Elia, Elice, Ellice, Elyas, Ellyce

Elihu (Hebrew) My God is He
Elyhu, Elihue, Elyhue, Elihugh, Elyhugh

Elijah ✿ ✪ (Hebrew) Jehovah is my God
Elija, Eliyahu, Eljah, Elja, Elyjah, Elyja,
Elijuah, Elyjuah

Elim (Hebrew) From the oasis
Elym, Eleem, Eleam, Eleim, Eliem

Elimelech (Hebrew) God is kind
Elymelech, Elimelek, Elimeleck, Elymelek,
Elymeleck

Elimu (African) Having knowledge of
science
Elymu, Elimue, Elymue, Elimoo, Elymoo

Eliphalet (Hebrew) God is my deliverance
Elifalet, Elifelet, Eliphelet, Elyphalet,
Elyfalet, Elyfelet, Elyphelet

Eliron (Hebrew) My God is song
Elyron, Elirun, Elyrun, Eliran, Elyran,
Eliren, Elyren, Elirin, Elyrin, Eliryn, Elyryn

Elisha (Hebrew) God is my salvation
Elisee, Eliseo, Elisher, Eliso, Elisio, Elysha,
Elysee, Elyseo, Elysio, Elysher, Elyso, Elizeo,
Elishah, Elyshah, Elishua, Ellsha, Elsha

Elkanah (Hebrew) One who belongs to God
Elkana, Elkannah, Elkanna, Elkan, Elken,
Elkon, Elkun, Elkin, Elkyn, Ellkan,
Ellken, Ellkon, Ellkon, Ellkin, Ellkyn,
Ellkanna

Ellard (German) A noble and brave man
Ellerd, Ellird, Ellyrd, Ellord, Ellurd,
Eallard, Ealhhard

Ellery (English) From the alder tree
Ellerey, Elleri, Ellerie, Elleree, Ellerea,
Ellary, Ellarey, Ellari, Ellarie, Ellaree,
Ellarea, Ellar, Eller

Ellesmere (English) From Ellis's pond
Ellesmeer, Ellesmir, Ellesmyr, Elesmere,
Elesmeer, Elesmir, Elesmyr

Elliott (English) Form of Elijah, meaning
"Jehovah is my God"
Eliot, Eliott, Elliot, Elyot, Elyott, Ellyott,
Ellyot

Ellis (English) Form of Elias, meaning
"Jehovah is my God"
Elliss, Ellyss, Ellys, Elliston, Ellyston,
Ellice, Ellise

Ellison (English) The son of Elias
Elison, Ellyson, Elyson, Ellisun, Elisun,
Ellysun, Elysun, Eallison, Ealison

Ellory (Cornish) Resembling a swan
*Ellorey, Elloree, Ellorea, Ellori, Ellorie,
Elory, Elorey, Elorea, Eloree, Elori, Elorie*

Ellsworth (English) From the nobleman's
estate
*Elsworth, Ellswerth, Elswerth, Ellswirth,
Elswirth*

Ellwood (English) From the nobleman's
forest; from the old forest
*Elwood, Ellwode, Elwode, Ealdwode,
Ealdwood*

Elman (English) A nobleman
Elmann, Ellman, Ellmann

Elmer (English) A famous nobleman
*Ellmer, Elmar, Ellmar, Elmir, Ellmir, Elmyr,
Ellmyr, Ellmor, Elmor, Elmur, Ellmur*

Elmo (English / Latin) A protector / an
amiable man
Elmoe, Elmow, Elmowe

Elmore (English) From the moor of the
elm trees
Ellmore, Elmoor, Ellmoor

Elmot (American) A lovable man
Elmott, Ellmot, Ellmott

Elne (Anglo-Saxon) A courageous man
Elni, Elnie, Elny, Elney, Elnee, Elnea

Elof (Swedish) The only heir
Eluf, Eloff, Eluff, Elov, Ellov, Eluv, Elluv

Eloi (French) The chosen one
Eloy, Eligio, Eligius

Elois (German) A famous warrior
Eloys, Eloyis, Elouis

Elon (Hebrew) From the oak tree
Elan, Elin, Elen, Elyn, Elun

Elonzo (Spanish) Filled with happiness
Elonso

Elpidio (Spanish) A fearless man; having
heart
*Elpydio, Elpideo, Elpydeo, Elpidios,
Elpydios, Elpidius, Elpydius*

Elpidos (Greek) Filled with hope
Elpydos, Elpido, Elpydo

Elrad (English) One who provides noble
counsel
*Ellrad, Elred, Ellred, Elrod, Ellrod, Elrud,
Ellrud, Elrid, Ellrid, Elryd, Ellryd*

Elroy (Irish / English) A red-haired young
man / a king
*Elroi, Elroye, Elric, Elryc, Elrik, Elryk,
Elrick, Elryck*

Elsdon (English) From the nobleman's hill
Elsdun, Elsden, Elsdin, Elsdyn, Elsdan

Elston (English) From the nobleman's town
*Ellston, Elstun, Ellstun, Elson, Ellson,
Elsun, Ellsun*

Elsu (Native American) Resembling a flying
falcon
Elsue, Elsoo, Elsou

Elton (English) From the old town
*Ellton, Eltun, Elltun, Elten, Ellten, Eltin,
Elltin, Eltyn, Elltyn, Eltan, Elltan*

Elu (Native American) One who is full of grace
Elue, Eloo, Elou

Eluwilussit (Native American) A holy man

Elvey (English) An elf warrior
Elvy, Elvee, Elvea, Elvi, Elvie

Elvin (English) A friend of the elves
*Elvinn, Elvyn, Elvynn, Elvinne, Elvynne,
Elwin, Elwinn, Elwinne, Elwen, Elwenn,
Elwenne, Elwyn, Elwynn, Elwynne, Elwine,
Elven, Elvenn, Elvenne, Elvine, Elvern,
Elvirn, Elvyrn, Elvind, Elvynd, Elvend*

Elvio (Spanish) A blonde-haired man
Elviyo, Elveo, Elveyo, Elvo, Evoy

Elvis (Scandinavian) One who is wise
Elviss, Elvys, Elvyss

Elwell (English) From the old spring
*Elwel, Ellwell, Ellwel, Elwill, Ellwill, Elwil,
Elwill*

Elwold (English) An old Welshman
Elwald, Ellwold, Ellwald

Elzie (English) Form of Ellsworth, meaning
"from the nobleman's estate"
*Elzi, Elzy, Elzey, Elzee, Elzea, Ellzi, Ellzie,
Ellzee, Ellzea, Ellzy, Ellzey*

Emberto (Italian) One who is assertive
*Embert, Emburto, Emburt, Embirto,
Embirt, Embyrto, Embyrt*

Emeric (German) The work ruler
*Emerick, Emerik, Emric, Emrick, Emrik,
Emeryc, Emeryck, Emeryck, Emryc,
Emryk, Emryck, Emmerich*

Emerson (German) The son of Emery
Emersun

Emery (German) The work ruler; the
strength of home
*Emerey, Emeri, Emerie, Emeree, Emerea,
Emmery, Emmerey, Emmeri, Emmerie,
Emmeree, Emmerea, Emory, Emmory,
Emorey, Emmorey, Emori, Emmori,
Emorie, Emmorie, Emoree, Emmoree,
Emorea, Emmorea*

Emest (German) One who is serious
*Emeste, Emesto, Emestio, Emestiyo,
Emesteo, Emesteyo, Emo, Emst, Emste*

Emeth (Hebrew) A faithful man
Emethe

Emil (Latin) One who is eager; an
industrious man
*Emelen, Emelio, Emile, Emilian, Emiliano,
Emilianus, Emilio, Emilion, Emilyan, Emlen,
Emlin, Emlyn, Emlynn, Emyl, Emyle*

Emir (Arabic) A prince; a ruler
*Emeer, Emire, Emeere, Emear, Emeare,
Emyr, Emyre*

Emmanuel (Hebrew) God is with us
*Eman, Emanual, Emanuel, Emanuele,
Emmanual, Emmonual, Emmonuel,
Emonual, Emonuel, Emuel*

Emmett (German) A universal man
Emmet, Emmit, Emmitt, Emmot, Emmott

Emre (Turkish) One who is brotherly
Emreh, Emra, Emrah, Emreson, Emrason

Emrys (Welsh) An immortal man

Emsley (English) A gift from God
*Emsly, Emslee, Emslea, Emsleigh, Emsli,
Emslie*

Enando (German) A bold man
Enandio, Enandiyo, Enandeo, Enandeyo

Enapay (Native American) A brave man
Enapaye, Enapai, Enapae

Enar (Swedish) A great warrior
Ener, Enir, Enyr, Enor, Enur

Endicott (English) From the cottage at the
end of the lane
*Endicot, Endycott, Endycot, Endecott,
Endecot*

Endre (Hungarian) Form of Andre,
meaning "manly; a warrior"
Endray, Endraye, Endrai, Endrae, Endree

Endymion (Greek) In mythology, a handsome young man whose youth was preserved in eternal sleep
*Endymyon, Endimion, Endimyon,
Endymeon, Endimeon*

Enea (Italian) The ninth-born child

Eneas (Spanish) One who is praised
Enneas

Engel (German) A messenger from heaven;
an angel
*Engle, Engelo, Engjell, Enjell, Engell, Enjel,
Enjelo*

Engelbert (German) As bright as an angel
*Englebert, Englbert, Engelburt, Engleburt,
Englburt, Englebirt, Engelbirt, Englbirt,
Englebyrt, Engelbyrt, Englbyrt, Englbehrt*

Enkoodabooaoo (Native American) One
who lives alone
Enkoodabaoo

Enlai (Chinese) One who is thankful

Ennis (Gaelic) From the island; the only
choice
Ennys, Enniss, Ennyss, Enis, Enys

Enno (German) One who is strong with a
sword
Ennoh, Eno, Enoh, Ennoe, Enoe

Enoch (Hebrew) One who is dedicated to God
Enoc, Enok, Enock

Enos (Hebrew) A man
Enoes, Enows

Enrique (Spanish) The ruler of the estate
*Enrico, Enriko, Enricko, Enriquez, Enrikay,
Enreekay, Enrik, Enric, Enrick, Enrike,
Enryco, Enryko, Enrycko, Enryk, Enryc,
Enryck*

Ensign (Latin) A badge or symbol

Enver (Turkish) A bright child
Envar, Envir, Envyr, Envor, Envur

Enyeto (Native American) One who walks like a bear

Enzi (African) A strong young boy
Enzie, Enzee, Enzea, Enzy, Enzey

Enzo (Italian) The ruler of the estate
Enzio, Enzeo, Enziyo, Enzeyo

Eoin Baiste (Irish) Refers to John the Baptist

Ephah (Hebrew) Of the darkness
Epha

Ephraim (Hebrew) One who is fertile; productive
Efraim, Efrayim, Efrem, Efrim, Ephraem, Ephream, Ephrem, Ephrim, Ephrym, Ephram, Ephron

Epicurus (Greek) One who enjoys the pleasures of life
Epycurus, Epicuros, Epycuros, Epicurius, Epycurius, Epicurios, Epycurios

Epifanio (Spanish) One who brings light
Epefano, Epefanio, Epephanio, Epifan, Epifano, Epiphany, Epifany, Epiphani, Epifani, Epiphanie, Epifanie, Epiphaney, Epifaney, Epiphafanee, Epifanee, Epiphaneo, Epifaneo

Eran (Hebrew) One who has been awakened

Erasmus (Greek) One who is dearly loved
Erasme, Erasmios, Erasmo, Erazmo

Erasto (African) A peaceful man
Erastio, Erastiyo, Erasteo, Erasteyo

Erastus (Greek) A loving man
Eraste, Erastos

Erc (Irish) A red-haired young man
Erk, Earc, Eark, Earck, Erck

Ercole (Italian) A splendid gift
Ercolo, Ercolio, Ercoleo, Ercoliyo, Ercoleyo

Erhard (German) A man of strong resolve
Erhardt, Erhart

Erian (Anglo-Saxon) One who ploughs
Eriann, Eryan, Eryann

Eric ✪ (Scandinavian) Ever the ruler
Erek, Erich, Erick, Erik, Eriq, Erix, Errick, Eryk, Eryck, Eryc, Ericas, Erickas, Erikas, Erec, Ereck

Ericson (Scandinavian) The son of Eric
Ericsun, Erickson, Ericksun, Erikson, Eriksun, Erycson, Erycsun, Eryckson, Erycksun, Erykson, Eryksun, Ericsen, Ericksen, Eriksen, Erycsen, Erycksen, Eryksen

Erin (Gaelic) A man from Ireland
Erienne, Erine, Erinn, Erinne, Eryne, Eryn, Erynne, Erynn, Erryn, Errin, Eri, Erie, Ery, Erey, Eree, Erea

Erland (English / Norse) From the nobleman's land / a foreigner; stranger
Erlande, Erlend, Erlende, Eorland, Erlan, Earland, Earlan, Erlin, Erlyn, Earlin, Earlyn, Erlen, Earlen

Erling (English) The son of a nobleman
Erlyng

Ermin (German) A man of the army; a soldier
Ermyn, Erman, Ermano, Erminio, Ermino, Ermen, Ermon, Ermun, Ermanno

Ernest (English) One who is sincere and determined; serious
Earnest, Ernesto, Ernestus, Ernst, Erno, Ernie, Erni, Erney, Erny, Ernee, Ernea, Earnesto, Earni, Earnie, Earnee, Earnea, Earny, Earney

Eron (Spanish) Form of Aaron, meaning "one who is exalted"
Erun, Erin, Eran, Eren, Eryn

Eros (Greek) In mythology, the god of love
Erose, Eroce

Errapel (Basque) A divine healer
Errapal, Erapel, Erapal, Errapol, Erapol, Errapul, Erapul, Errapil, Erapil, Errapyl, Erapyl

Errigal (Gaelic) From the small church
Errigel, Errigol, Errigul, Errigil, Errigyl, Erigal, Erigel, Erigol, Erigul, Erigil, Erigyl

Erroll (English) A wanderer
Errol, Erryl, Erryle, Eryle, Eroll, Eryl

Erskine (Gaelic) From the high cliff
Erskin, Erskyne, Erskyn, Erskein, Erskeine, Erskien, Erskiene

Erving (English) A friend of the sea
Ervyng, Ervine, Ervyne, Erv, Erve

Erwin (English) A friend of the wild boar
Erwine, Erwinn, Erwinne, Erwen, Erwenn, Erwenne, Erwyn, Erwynn, Erwynne, Earwine, Earwin, Earwinn, Earwinne, Earwen, Earwenn, Earwenne, Earwyn, Earwynn, Earwynne

Esam (Arabic) A safeguard
Essam

Esau (Hebrew) A hairy man; in the Bible, Jacob's older twin brother
Esaw, Eesau, Eesaw, Easau, Easaw

Esben (Scandinavian) Of God
Esbin, Esbyn, Esban, Esbon, Esbun

Esbjorn (Norse) A bear of the gods
Esbern, Esborn, Esburn, Esbirn, Esbyrn, Esbjorne, Esberne, Esburne, Esbirne, Esbyrne

Escott (English) From the cottage near the stream
Escot

Eshkol (Hebrew) A cluster of grapes
Eshkoll, Eshkole, Eshckol

Esias (Hebrew) God is my salvation
Esyas, Esaias, Esiason, Esiasson

Eskel (Norse) From the cauldron of the gods
Eskell, Eskil, Eskill, Eskyl, Eskyll

Esmé (French) One who is esteemed
Esmay, Esmaye, Esmai, Esmae, Esmeling, Esmelyng

Esmond (English) One who is protected by God's grace
Esmonde, Esmund, Esmunde, Esmont, Esmonte, Esmunt, Esmunte

Esmun (American) A kind man
Esmon, Esman, Esmen, Esmin, Esmyn

Espen (Scandinavian) Form of Esbjorn, meaning "a bear of the gods"
Espan, Espin, Espyn, Espon, Espun, Espn

Esperanze (Spanish) Filled with hope
Esperance, Esperence, Esperenze, Esperanzo, Esperenzo

Essex (English) From the eastern place
Esex

Essien (African) The sixth-born son
Esien, Essyen, Esyen

Estcott (English) From the eastern cottage
Estcot

Este (Italian) A man from the east

Esteban (Spanish) One who is crowned in victory
Estebon, Estevan, Estevon, Estefan, Estefon, Estebe, Estyban, Estyvan

Estes (Latin) One who lives near the estuary
Estas, Estis, Estys

Eston (English) From the eastern town
Estun, Estown, Esten, Estin, Estan, Estyn

Etchemin (Native American) A canoe man

Etereo (Spanish) A spiritual man
Eterio, Etero, Etereyo, Eteriyo, Eteryo

Eth (Irish) Born of fire
Ethe

Ethan ✪ ♂ (Hebrew) One who is firm and steadfast
Ethen, Ethin, Ethyn, Ethon, Ethun, Eitan, Etan, Eithan, Eithen, Eithin, Eithyn, Eithon, Eithun, Eythan, Eytan

Ethanael (American) God has given me strength
Ethaniel, Ethaneal, Ethanail, Ethanale

Ethel (Hebrew) One who is noble
Ethal, Etheal

Ethelwin (Anglo-Saxon) A wellborn friend
Ethelwinn, Ethelwinne, Ethelwine, Ethelwen, Ethelwenn, Ethelwenne, Ethelwyn, Ethelwynn, Ethelwynne

Ethelwulf (Anglo-Saxon) A noble wolf
Ethelwolf

Etienne (French) One who is crowned
Estienne, Ettie, Etta

Etlelooaat (Native American) One who shouts

Ettore (Italian) One who is loyal
Etore, Ettoer, Etoer, Etor, Ettor

Etu (Native American) Of the sun
Etue, Etow, Etowe, Etou

Euan (Gaelic) The little swift one
Ewan, Euen, Ewen, Eoghan, Eoghann

Euclid (Greek) An intelligent man
Euclyd, Euclide, Euclyde, Euclides, Euclydes

Eudocio (Greek) One who is respected
Eudoceo, Eudociyo, Eudoceyo, Eudoco

Eudor (Greek) A good gift
Eudore

Eugene (Greek) A wellborn man
*Eugen, Eugenio, Eugenios, Eugenius,
Evgeny, Evgeni, Evgenie, Evgeney*

Eulogio (Greek) A reasonable man
Eulogiyo, Eulogo, Eulogeo, Eulogeyo

Euodias (Greek) Having good fortune
Euodeas, Euodyas

Euphemios (Greek) One who is well-spoken
*Eufemio, Eufemius, Euphemio, Eufemios,
Euphemius, Eufemius*

Euphrates (Turkish) From the great river
*Eufrates, Euphraites, Eufraites, Euphraytes,
Eufraytes*

Eural (American) From the mountains
Eurel, Eurol, Eurul, Euril, Euryl

Eusebius (Greek) One who is devout
*Esabio, Esavio, Esavius, Esebio, Eusabio,
Eusaio, Eusebio, Eusebios, Eusavio,
Eusevio, Eusevios*

Eustace (Greek) Having an abundance of
grapes
*Eustache, Eustachios, Eustachius, Eustachy,
Eustaquio, Eustashe, Eustasius, Eustatius,
Eustazio, Eustis, Eustiss, Eustys, Eustyss,
Eustacio, Eustasio*

Evan ○ ○ (Welsh) Form of John, meaning
"God is gracious"
*Evann, Evans, Even, Evin, Evon, Evyn,
Evian, Evien, Evion, Eviun, Evanus,
Evaristo, Evariso, Evaro*

Evander (Greek) A benevolent man
Evandor, Evandar, Evandir, Evandur, Evandyr

Evangel (Greek) A bringer of good news
*Evangelin, Evangelino, Evangelo,
Evangelio, Evangeliyo, Evangeleo,
Evangeleyo, Evagelo, Evagelos*

Evelyn (German) A birdlike man
*Evelean, Eveleen, Evaline, Evalyn, Evelin,
Eveline, Evelyne, Evelynn, Evelynne, Evie,
Evlynn*

Everest (American) From the highest
mountain peak
Evrest

Everett (English) Form of Everhard, mean-
ing "as strong as a boar; as brave as a boar"
*Everet, Everrett, Everret, Everitt, Everit,
Everritt, Everrit*

Everhard (English) As strong as a boar; as
brave as a boar
*Evarado, Everado, Everardo, Evered,
Everhart, Evrard, Evraud, Everard*

Everild (English) As battle-ready as a boar
*Evald, Evaldo, Everald, Everhild, Everildo,
Everyld, Everyldo*

Everley (English) From the boar's meadow
*Everly, Everli, Everlie, Everleigh, Everlee,
Everlea, Everleah*

Evers (English) Resembling a wild boar
Ever, Evert, Everte

Everton (English) From the boar town
Evertun

Evett (American) A bright man
Evet, Evatt, Evat, Evitt, Evit, Evytt, Evyt

Evgenii (Russian) A wellborn man; a nobleman

Evo (German) Of the yew wood
Evoh, Evoe, Evoeh, Evow, Evowe

Evzen (Czech) Of noble birth
Evzin, Evzyn, Evzan, Evzon, Evzun

Ewald (English) A powerful man
Ewalde

Ewert (English) A shepherd
*Ewart, Ewerd, Eward, Eweheorde, Eawart,
Eawert, Eaward, Eawerd*

Ewing (English) A lawyer; a friend of the law
*Ewine, Ewyng, Ewinn, Ewin, Ewinne,
Ewyn, Ewynn, Ewynne*

Excalibur (English) In Arthurian legend,
King Arthur's sword
*Escalibur, Excaliber, Escaliber, Excalibor,
Escalibor, Excalibar, Escalibar*

Excell (American) A competitive man
Excel, Exsell, Exsel

Extany (English) One who is not like others
Extaney, Extani, Extanie, Extanee, Extanea

Eyab (Arabian) One who has returned

Eyad (Arabic) A powerful man

Eyal (Hebrew) Having great strength

Eyolf (Norwegian) A lucky wolf
Eyulf

Eystein (Norse) A lucky man
Eistein, Eysteinn, Eisteinn

Eze (African) A king

Ezeji (African) The king of yams
Ezejie, Ezejy, Ezejey, Ezejee, Ezejea

Ezekiel (Hebrew) Strengthened by God
Esequiel, Ezechiel, Eziechiele, Eziequel, Ezequiel, Ezekial, Ezekyel, Esquevelle

Ezer (Hebrew) One who offers help
Eizer, Ezar, Eizar, Ezzy, Ezzey, Ezzi, Ezzie, Ezzee, Ezzea, Ezy, Ezey, Ezi, Ezie, Ezea, Ezee

Ezhno (Native American) One who walks alone
Ezno, Ezhnoe, Eznoe

Ezio (Italian) Resembling an eagle
Eziyo, Ezeo, Ezeyo

Ezra (Hebrew) A helper
Ezrah, Esdras, Esra, Ezri, Ezrie, Ezree, Ezrea, Ezry, Ezrey, Eza, Ezira, Ezyra, Ezirah, Ezyrah

Fabian (Latin) One who grows beans
Fabe, Fabek, Faber, Fabert, Fabianno, Fabiano, Fabianus, Fabien, Fabio, Fabion, Fabius, Fabiyus, Fabyan, Fabyen, Faebian, Faebien, Faybian, Faybien, Faybion, Faybionn, Faberto

Fable (American) One who tells stories
Fabel, Fabal, Fabol, Fabul, Fabyl, Fabil

Fabrice (French) One who works with his hands
Fabriano, Fabricius, Fabritius, Fabrizio, Fabrizius, Fabryce, Fabreece, Fabreace, Fabriece, Fabreice

Fabron (French) A young blacksmith
Fabre, Fabroni, Fabronie, Fabrony, Fabroney, Fabronee, Fabronea

Fabulous (American) One who is vain
Fabulus, Fab, Fabby, Fabbi, Fabbey, Fabbie, Fabbee

Fabunni (African) Whom God has given
Fabunny, Fabuni, Fabuny, Fabunney, Fabuney, Fabunnee, Fabunee, Fabunnie, Fabunie

Fachnan (Irish) The name of a saint
Fachnen, Fachnin, Fachnyn, Fachnon, Fachnun

Factor (English) A businessman
Facter, Factur, Factir, Factyr, Factar

Faddis (American) One who keeps to himself
Faddys, Fadis, Fadys, Faddiss, Faddyss, Fadiss, Fadyss, Fadice, Fadyce, Fadise, Fadyse

Fadi (Arabic / Slavic) A savior / a courageous man
Fadie, Fady, Fadey, Fadee, Fadea, Fadeyka

Fadil (Arabic) A generous man
Fadeel, Fadeal, Fadiel, Fadeil, Fadyl, Fadl

Fafnir (Norse) In mythology, a dragon
Fafner, Fafnyr, Fafnor, Fafnur

Fagan (Gaelic) The little ardent one
Fegan, Feggan, Fagin, Fagen, Fagon, Fagun, Fagyn, Faegan, Faigan, Faygan

Fahd (Arabic) Resembling a leopard or a panther
Fahad

Fahesh (Arabic) Excessive
Faheshe

Fahey (Irish) From the green field
Fahy, Fahi, Fahie, Fahee

Fahim (African) A learned man
Faheem, Faheim, Fahiem, Faheam, Fahym

Fai (Chinese) Of the beginning; a bright light

Fairbairn (Scottish) A fair-haired boy
Fayrbairn, Faerbairn, Fairbaern, Fayrbaern, Faerbaern, Fairbayrn, Fayrbayrn, Faerbayrn

Fairbanks (English) From the bank along the path
Fayrbanks, Faerbanks, Farebanks

Fairchild (English) A fair-haired child
Faerchild, Fayrchild, Farechild, Fairchyld, Faerchyld, Fayrchyld, Farechyld

Fairfax (English) A blonde-haired man
Fayrfax, Faerfax, Farefax

Faisal (Arabic) One who is decisive; resolute
Faysal, Faesal, Fasal, Feisal, Faizal, Fasel, Fayzal, Faezal, Fazel

Faiyaz (Indian) An artistic man
Fayyaz, Faeyza, Fayaz

Faizon (Arabic) An understanding man
Fayzon, Faezon, Fazon, Faizun, Fayzun, Faezun, Fazun, Faizan, Fayzan, Faezan, Fazan

Fakhir (Arabic) A proud man
Fakheer, Fakhear, Fakheir, Fakhier, Fakhyr, Faakhir, Faakhyr, Fakhr, Fakhri, Fakhrie, Fakhry, Fakhrey, Fakhree

Fakih (Arabic) A legal expert
Fakeeh, Fakeah, Fakieh, Fakeih, Fakyh

Falak (Indian) Of the sky
Falac, Falach, Falack

Falakee (Arabic) An astronomer
Falake, Falaki, Falakie, Falaky, Falakey, Falakea

Falco (Latin) Resembling a falcon; one who works with falcons
Falcon, Falconer, Falconner, Falk, Falke, Falken, Falkner, Faulconer, Faulconner, Faulkner

Falgun (Hindi) A Hindu month
Falgon, Falgen, Falgan, Falgin, Falgyn

Falguni (Hindi) Born during the month of Falgun
Falgunie, Falguny, Falguney, Falgunee, Falgunea

Faline (Hindi) A fertile man
Faleene, Faleane, Faleine, Faliene, Falyne, Falin, Faleen, Falean, Falien, Falein, Falyn

Fallon (Irish) A ruler
Fallun, Fallen, Fallan, Fallin, Fallyn, Fallamhain

Fallows (English) From the unplanted field
Fallow, Fallos, Fallo, Fallowe, Fallowes

Fam (American) A family-oriented man

Famous (American) One who is well-known
Fame

Fane (English) Filled with joy
Fain, Faine, Fayn, Fayne, Faen, Faene, Fannin, Fannon, Fannen, Fannun, Fannan, Fannyn

Fang (Scottish) From the sheep pen
Faing, Fayng, Faeng

Faolan (Gaelic) Resembling a little wolf
Felan, Faelan, Faolen, Faelen, Felen, Faolin, Faelin, Felin, Faolyn, Faelyn, Felyn

Faraj (Arabian) One who offers remedies
Farag

Faraji (African) One who provides consolation
Farajie, Farajy, Farajey, Farajee, Farajea

Faramond (English) A protected traveler
Faramund, Farrimond, Farrimund, Farimond, Farimund

Faran (Anglo-Saxon / American) One who advances / a sincere man
Faren, Faron, Farin, Faryn, Farun, Fahran, Feran, Feren

Fardoragh (Irish) Having dark features

Fares (Arabic) A knight or horseman
Farees, Fareas, Faries, Fareis, Farys

Fargo (American) One who is jaunty
Fargoh, Fargoe, Fargouh

Farha (Arabic) Filled with happiness
Farhah, Farhad, Farhan, Farhat, Farhani, Farhanie, Farhany, Farhaney, Farhanee

Farid (Arabic) One who is unequaled
Fareed, Faread, Faryd, Faried, Fareid, Faride, Farideh

Fariq (Arabic) One who holds rank as lieutenant general
Fareeq, Fareaq, Fareiq, Farieq, Faryq, Farik, Fareek, Fareak, Fariek, Fareik, Faryk

Farkas (Hungarian) Resembling a wolf
Farckas, Farcas, Farkes, Farckes, Farces, Farkus, Farckus, Farcus

Farlan (Scottish) A son of the furrows
Farlane, Farlain, Farlaine, Farlayn, Farlayne, Farlaen, Farlaene

Farley (English) From the bull pasture
Farly, Farleigh, Farlee, Farlea, Farleah, Farle,
Farli, Farlie, Fairlay, Fairlee, Fairleigh,
Farlay, Fairlea, Fairleah, Fairli, Fairlie,
Farlow, Farlowe, Farlo

Farmer (English) One who works the earth
Farmar, Farmor, Farmur, Farmir, Farmyr

Farmon (Anglo-Saxon) A traveler
Farmun, Farmen, Farman, Farmin, Farmyn

Farnell (English) From the fern hill
Farnel, Farnall, Farnal, Fernauld, Farnauld,
Fernald, Farnald

Farnham (English) From the fern field
Farnam, Farnum, Fernham, Farnam,
Fernam

Farnley (English) From the fern meadow
Farnly, Farnli, Farnlie, Farnlee, Farnleigh,
Farnlea, Farnleah

Farold (English) A mighty traveler
Farould, Farald, Farauld, Fareld

Faron (Spanish) A pharoah
Faro, Farun, Faren, Faran

Farouk (Arabic) One who knows the truth
Farouke, Faruk, Faruke, Faruq, Farouq

Farquhar (Scottish) One who is very dear
Farquar, Farquharson, Farquarson, Fearchar

Farr (English) A traveler; a voyager
Faer, Farrs, Faers, Far, Fars, Farrson, Farson

Farran (Irish / Arabic / English) Of the land
/ a baker / one who is adventurous
Fairran, Fayrran, Faerran, Farren, Farrin,
Farron, Ferrin, Ferron

Farrar (English) A blacksmith
Farar, Farrer, Farrier, Ferrar, Ferrars, Ferrer,
Ferrier, Farer, Farier, Ferar, Ferars, Ferer,
Ferier

Farrell (Irish) A courageous man
Farrel, Farel, Farell, Farryl, Faryl, Faryll

Farris (English) One who is as strong as iron
Farrys, Faris, Farys, Farice, Ferris, Ferrys,
Feris, Ferys

Farro (Italian) Of the grain
Farroe, Faro, Faroe, Farrow, Farow

Farry (Irish) One who is manly and strong
Farrey, Farri, Farrie, Farree, Farrea

Fasta (Spanish) One who makes an offering
Fastah

Faste (Norse) One who is firm
Fasti, Fastie, Fastee, Fastea, Fasty, Fastey

Fateh (Arabic) A victorious man
Fath, Fathe, Fathi, Fathie, Fathy, Fathey,
Fathee, Fathea

Fatik (Indian) Resembling a crystal
Fateek, Fateak, Fatyk, Fatiek, Fateik

Fatin (Arabic) An intelligent man
Fateen, Fatean, Fatien, Fatein, Fatyn

Faunus (Latin) In mythology, the god of
nature and the forests
Fawnus, Faunos, Fawnos

Faust (Latin) Having good luck
Fauste, Faustino, Fausto, Faustos, Faustus,
Fauston, Faustin, Fausten, Faustun, Faustan

Favian (Latin) Full of wisdom
Favien, Favyan, Favyen

Fawcett (American) An audacious man
Fawcet, Fawcette, Fawcete, Fawce, Fawci,
Fawcie, Fawcy, Fawcey, Fawcee, Fawcea

Fawwaz (Arabic) A successful man
Fawaz, Fawwad, Fawad

Fawzi (Arabic) The winner
Fawzie, Fawzy, Fawzey, Fawzee, Fawzea

Faxon (Latin) One who has thick, long
hair
Faxen, Faxan, Faxin, Faxyn, Faxun

Fay (Irish) Resembling a raven
Faye, Fai, Fae, Feich

Faysal (Arabic) A judge
Faisal, Faesal, Fasal

Fazil (Arabic) A virtuous man
Fazill, Fazyl, Fazyll, Fazeel, Fazeal, Fazeil,
Faziel

Febronio (Spanish) A bright man
Febroneo, Febrono, Febroniyo, Febroneyo

February (American) Born in the month of
February
Februari, Februarie, Februarey, Februaree,
Februarea

Februus (Latin) A pagan god

Fedde (Italian) One who is true

Fedor (Russian) A gift from God
Faydor, Feodor, Fyodor, Fedyenka, Fyodr, Fydor, Fjodor

Fedrick (American) Form of Cedric, meaning "one who is kind and loved; of the spectacular bounty"
Fedrik, Fedric, Fedryck, Fedryk, Fedryc

Feechi (African) One who worships God
Feechie, Feechy, Feechey, Feechee, Feachi, Feachie, Feachy, Feachey, Feachee

Feige (Hebrew) Resembling a bird

Feivel (Hebrew) The brilliant one
Feival, Feivol, Feivil, Feivyl, Feivul, Feiwel, Feiwal, Feiwol, Feiwul, Feiwil, Feiwyl

Fela (African) A warlike man
Felah, Fella, Fellah

Felding (English) From the field
Feldyng, Felman, Felmann

Feldon (English) From the town near the field
Feldun, Felton, Feltun

Feleti (Italian) A peaceful man
Feletie, Felety, Feletey, Feletee, Feletea

Felim (Gaelic) One who is always good
Felym, Feidhlim, Felimy, Felimey, Felimee, Felimea, Felimi, Felimie

Felipe (Spanish) Form of Phillip, meaning "one who loves horses"
Felippe, Filip, Filippo, Fillip, Flip, Fulop, Fullop, Fulip, Fullip, Filib, Fillib

Felix (Latin) One who is happy and prosperous
Felyx, Fee, Felic, Felice, Feliciano, Felicio, Felike, Feliks, Felizio

Fell (English) From the field
Fel, Felle, Fele

Felton (English) From the town near the field
Feltun, Felten, Feltan, Feltyn, Feltin

Fenn (English) From the marsh
Fen

Fenner (English) An able-bodied man
Fennar, Fennir, Fennyr, Fennor, Fennur

Fenris (Norse) In mythology, a giant wolf
Fenrys

Fenton (English) From the town near the marsh
Fentun, Fenten, Fentan, Fentyn, Fentin

Fentress (English) One who is natural
Fentres, Fentriss, Fentris, Fentryss, Fentrys

Fenwick (English) From the village near the marsh
Fenwyck, Fenwik, Fenwyk, Fenwic, Fenwyc

Feo (Native American / Spanish) A confident man / an ugly man
Feeo, Feyo

Feoras (Gaelic) Resembling a smooth rock
Feores, Feoris, Feorys, Feoros, Feorus

Ferda (Czech) A brave man
Ferdah, Firda, Firdah, Furda, Furdah

Ferdinand (German) A courageous voyager
Ferd, Ferdie, Ferdinando, Ferdo, Ferdynand, Fernand, Fernandas, Fernando, Fernande

Ferenc (Hungarian) An independent man; one who is free
Ferenck, Ferenk, Ferko

Fergall (Gaelic) A strong and brave man
Fergal, Fearghall, Ferghall, Ferghal, Forgael

Fergus (Gaelic) The first and supreme choice
Fearghas, Fearghus, Feargus, Fergie, Ferguson, Fergusson, Furgus, Fergy, Fergi, Fergee, Fergea

Ferhan (Arabic) One who rejoices
Ferhen, Ferhon, Ferhun, Ferhin, Ferhyn

Ferlin (American) A man from the country
Ferlyn, Ferlen, Ferlan, Ferlon, Ferlun

Fermin (Spanish) Having great strength
Firmin, Fermyn, Firmyn, Fermen, Firmen, Ferman, Firman, Fermon, Firmon, Fermun, Firmun

Fernley (English) From the fern meadow
Fernly, Fernli, Fernlie, Fernlee, Fernleigh, Fernlea, Fernleah, Fearnleah, Fearnlea, Fearnli, Fearnlie, Fearnlee, Fearnleigh, Fearnly, Fearnley

Ferran (Arabic) A baker
Ferren, Ferron, Ferrun, Ferrin, Ferryn

Ferrand (French) A gray-haired man
Farand, Farrand, Farrant, Ferand, Ferrant, Ferant, Farant

Ferrell (Irish) A brave man; a hero
Ferell, Ferel, Ferrel

Ferreres (Spanish) A blacksmith
Ferares, Fereres

Festus (Latin) A joyous man
Festis, Festys, Festos, Festas, Festes

Fews (Celtic) From the woods

Fiacre (Celtic) Resembling a raven
Fyacre, Fiacra, Fyacra, Fiachra, Fyachra, Fiachre, Fyachre

Fidel (Latin) A faithful man
Fadelio, Fedele, Fidele, Fedelio, Fidal, Fidalio, Fidelio, Fidelis, Fidelix, Fidello, Fidelo, Fido, Fidelity

Fielding (English) From the field
Fieldyng, Fielder, Field, Fielde, Felding, Feldyng, Fields

Fien (American) An elegant man
Fiene, Fine

Fiero (Spanish) A fiery man
Fyero

Fikri (Arabic) A strong and intelligent man
Fikrie, Fikry, Fikrey, Fikree, Fikrea, Fykri, Fykrie, Fykree, Fykrea, Fykry, Fykrey

Filbert (German) A brilliant man
Filberte, Filberto, Filbertos, Filbertus

Filmore (English) One who is famous
Filmor, Fillmor, Fillmore, Fylmore, Fylmor, Fyllmore, Fyllmor, Filmer, Fylmer, Filmar, Fylmar, Filmarr, Fylmarr

Filomelo (Spanish) A beloved friend
Fylomelo, Filo, Fylo

Finbar (Irish) A fair-haired man
Finnbar, Finnbarr, Fionn, Fionnbharr, Fionnbar, Fionnbarr, Fynbar, Fynnbar, Fynbarr, Fynnbarr, Finnobarr, Finobarr, Finnobar, Finobar

Finch (English) Resembling the small bird
Fynch, Finche, Fynche, Finchi, Finchie, Finchy, Finchey, Finchee

Fineas (Egyptian) A dark-skinned man
Fyneas, Finius, Fynius

Finian (Irish) A handsome man; fair
Finan, Finnian, Fionan, Finien, Finnien, Finghin, Finneen, Fineen, Finnean, Finean, Finnin, Finnine

Finlay (Gaelic) A fair-haired hero
Findlay, Findley, Finlea, Finlee, Finley, Finly, Finli, Finlie, Findly, Findlee, Findlea, Findli, Findlie, Finnly, Finnley, Finnlee, Finnli, Finnlie

Finn (Gaelic) A fair-haired man
Fin, Fynn, Fyn, Fingal, Fingall

Finnegan (Irish) A fair-haired man
Finegan, Finnegen, Finegen, Finnigan, Finigan

Fintan (Irish) The little fair-haired one
Finten, Finton, Fintun, Fintyn, Fintin, Fyntan, Fynten, Fynton, Fyntun, Fyntin, Fyntyn

Fiorello (Italian) Resembling a little flower
Fiorelo, Fiorelio, Fioreleo, Fiorellio, Fiorelleo

Firdus (Indian) From paradise
Fyrdus, Firdos, Fyrdos

Firman (French) A loyal man
Firmin, Firmen, Firmon, Firmun, Firmyn

Firoze (Indian) Resembling turquoise
Fyroze, Firoz, Fyroz, Feroze, Feroz

Firth (Scottish) From an inlet of the sea
Firthe, Fyrth, Fyrthe

Fishel (Hebrew) Resembling a fish
Fyshel, Fishell, Fyshell, Fishele, Fyshele, Fishelle, Fyshelle

Fisher (English) A fisherman
Fysher, Fischer, Fisscher, Fyscher, Fysscher, Fish, Fyshe, Fysh, Fishe

Fisk (English) Resembling a fish
Fiske, Fysk, Fyske

Fitch (English) Resembling an ermine
Fytch, Fich, Fych, Fitche, Fytche

Fitz (French) The son of ...
Fytz

Fitzadam (English) The son of Adam
Fytzadam

Fitzgerald (English) The son of Gerald
Fytzgerald

Fitzgibbon (English) The son of Gibson
Fytzgibbon, Fitzgibon, Fytzgibon

Fitzgilbert (English) The son of Gilbert
Fytzgilbert

Fitzhugh (English) The son of Hugh
Fytzhugh

Fitzjames (English) The son of James
Fytzjames

Fitzpatrick (English) The son of Patrick
Fytzpatrick

Fitzroy (English) The son of Roy
Fytzroy

Fitzsimon (English) The son of Simon
*Fytzsimon, Fitzsymon, Fytzsymon,
Fitzsimmons, Fytzsimmons, Fitzsimons,
Fytzsimons*

Fitzwalter (English) The son of Walter
Fytzwalter

Fitzwilliam (English) The son of William
Fytzwilliam

Fiyas (Indian) An artistic man

Flag (American) A patriotic man
Flagg

Flaminio (Spanish) A Roman priest
Flamino, Flamineo, Flaminiyo, Flamineyo

Flann (Irish) One who has a ruddy complexion
*Flan, Flainn, Flannan, Flannery, Flanneri,
Flannerie, Flannerey, Flanneree, Flannerea,
Flanagan, Flannagain, Flannagan*

Flash (American) A shining man; one who
is fast
*Flashy, Flashey, Flashee, Flashea, Flashi,
Flashie, Flashe*

Flavian (Latin) Having yellow hair
*Flavel, Flavelle, Flaviano, Flavien, Flavio,
Flavius, Flawiusz, Flaviu, Flavean, Flabio,
Flabien, Flabian*

Fleada (American) One who keeps to himself
*Flayda, Flaida, Flaeda, Fleade, Flayde,
Flaide, Flaede*

Fleetwood (English) From the forest with
the stream
Fleetwode

Fleming (English) A man from Flanders
Flemyng, Flemming, Flemmyng

Fletcher (English) One who makes arrows
Fletch, Fletche, Flecher

Flint (English) Resembling the hard quartz;
from the stream
Flynt, Flintt, Flyntt

Florent (French) Resembling a flower; one
who is flourishing
*Fiorentino, Florentin, Florentino, Florentz,
Florenz, Florinio, Florino, Floris, Florys,
Florus, Florentius, Florian, Florien,
Floryan, Florrian, Florrien*

Floyd (Welsh) A gray-haired man
Floyde, Floid, Floide

Flux (English) One who is constantly moving
Fluxx

Flynn (Irish) One who has a ruddy
complexion
Flyn, Flinn, Flin, Flen, Flenn, Floinn

Fodjour (African) The fourth-born child
Fodjur, Fodjure, Fodjoure

Fodor (Hungarian) A curly-haired man
Fodur, Fodir, Fodyr, Fodar, Foder

Fogarty (Irish) One who has been exiled
*Fogartey, Fogartee, Fogartea, Fogarti,
Fogartie, Fogerty, Fogertey, Fogerti, Fogertie,
Fogertee, Fogertea, Fogartaigh, Fogertaigh*

Foley (English) A creative man
Foly, Folee, Foleigh, Folea, Foli, Folie

Folker (German) A guardian of the people
*Folkar, Folkor, Folkur, Folkir, Folkyr, Folke,
Folko, Folkus, Folkos, Floke, Floker, Flokar,
Flokur, Flokir, Flokyr, Flokor*

Foma (Hebrew) One of twins
Fomah

Fonda (Spanish) One who is profound

Fonso (German) Form of Alfonso, mean-
ing "prepared for battle; eager and ready"
*Fonzo, Fonsie, Fonzell, Fonzie, Fonsi,
Fonsy, Fonsey, Fonsee, Fonsea, Fonzi,
Fonzey, Fonzy, Fonzee, Fonzea*

Fontaine (French) From the water source
*Fontayne, Fontaene, Fontane, Fonteyne,
Fontana, Fountain*

Forbes (Gaelic) From the field
Forbs, Forba, Forb, Forbe

Ford (English) From the river crossing
*Forde, Forden, Fordan, Fordon, Fordun,
Fordin, Fordyn, Forday, Fordaye, Fordai,
Fordae*

Forend (American) One who is bold
Foren, Forind, Forin, Forynd, Foryn

Forest (English) From the woodland
*Forester, Forrest, Forrester, Forestor,
Forrestor, Forster, Forstor*

Fortney (Latin) Having great strength
*Fortny, Fortni, Fortnie, Fortnee, Fortnea,
Fourtney, Fourtny, Fourtni, Fourtnie,
Fourtnee, Fourtnea, Fortenay, Forteney,
Forteney, Forteni, Fortenie, Fortenee,
Fortenea*

Fortune (French) A lucky man
*Fortino, Fortunato, Fortunatus, Fortunio,
Fortuny, Fortuney, Fortuni, Fortunie,
Fortunee, Fortunea*

Foster (English) A forest ranger
Fost, Foste, Fosti, Fostie, Fostee, Fostea

Fouad (Arabic) One who has heart
Fuad

Fowler (English) One who traps birds
Fowlor, Fowlar, Fowlir, Fowlyr, Fowlur

Fox (English) Resembling the animal
*Foxe, Foxx, Foxen, Foxan, Foxon, Foxun,
Foxin, Foxyn*

Foy (Celtic) An adventurous man; a journey
Foye, Foi

Fraco (Spanish) One who is weak
Fracko, Frako

Fraley (English) A friar
*Fraly, Frali, Fralie, Fralee, Fraleigh, Fralea,
Frayley, Frayly, Frayli, Fraylie, Frayleigh,
Fraylea, Fraylee, Fraeley, Fraely, Fraeli,
Fraelie, Fraelee, Fraeleigh, Frailey, Fraily,
Frailee, Frailea, Fraileigh, Fraili, Frailie*

Francis (Latin) A man from France; one
who is free
*Fran, Frances, Francesco, Franche,
Franchesco, Franchesko, Franchot,
Francisco, Franciscus, Franciskus, Francois,
Franio, Frann, Frannie, Frans, Fransisco,
Frants, Frantz, Franz, Franzel, Franzen,
Franzin, Frasco, Frascuelo, Frasquito,
Frisco, Frisko, Frascuelo, Frang*

Franciszek (Polish) Form of Francis,
meaning "a man from France; one who is
free"
Frantisek, Franciszec, Frantisec

Frank (Latin) Form of Francis, meaning
"a man from France; one who is free"
*Franc, Franco, Franck, Francke, Frankie,
Franky, Franki, Frankey, Frankee, Frankea*

Franklin (English) A free man; a landholder
*Franklinn, Franklyn, Franklynn, Francklin,
Francklyn*

Fraomar (Anglo-Saxon) The name of a king
Fraomarr, Fraomare, Fraomarre

Fraser (Scottish) Of the forest men
*Fraiser, Frayser, Fraeser, Frazer, Frayzer,
Fraezer, Fraizer, Frasier, Frazier*

Frayne (English) A foreigner
*Frayn, Frain, Fraine, Fraen, Fraene, Frane,
Freyne, Freyn, Frayme, Fraym, Fraime,
Fraim, Frame, Fraem, Fraeme, Freyme,
Freym*

Fred (German) Form of Frederick, meaning
"a peaceful ruler"
*Freddi, Freddie, Freddy, Freddey, Freddee,
Freddea, Freddis, Fredis, Freddys, Fredys*

Frederick (German) A peaceful ruler
*Federico, Federigo, Fredek, Frederic,
Frederich, Frederico, Frederik, Fredric,
Fredrick, Fredrik, Frido, Friedel, Friedrich,
Friedrick, Fridrich, Fridrick, Fryderky,
Frederyck, Fredryck, Fredryc, Fredryk,
Frederyc, Frederyk, Fryderyk, Fico*

Freeborn (English) One who was born a
free man
*Freeborne, Freebourn, Freebourne,
Freeburn, Freeburne, Free*

Freed (English) A peaceful man; one who
is free
Freid, Fried, Fread

Freedom (American) An independent man

Freeman (English) One who is free
*Freemen, Freemon, Freemin, Freemyn,
Freemun, Freman, Fremen, Fremon,
Fremun, Fremin, Fremyn*

Fremont (French) The protector of freedom
*Freemont, Fremonte, Freemonte, Fremond,
Freemond, Fremonde, Freemonde,
Frimunt, Frimont, Frimond, Frimund,
Frimunte, Frimonte, Frimunde, Frimonde*

French (English) A man from France

Fresco (Spanish) A fresh-faced man
Frescko, Fresko, Frescoe, Fresckoe, Freskoe

Frewin (English) A noble or free friend
*Frewine, Frewinn, Frewinne, Frewen,
Frewenn, Frewenne, Frewyn, Frewynn,
Frewynne, Freowine*

Frey (Scandinavian) One who is exalted; in
mythology, the god of peace, prosperity,
and good weather

Frick (English) A courageous man
Fryck, Frik, Fric, Fryc, Fryk

Fridolf (English) The peaceful wolf
*Freydolf, Freydulf, Friedolf, Fridulf,
Friedulf, Fridolph, Freydolph, Fridulph,
Freydulph, Friedolph, Friedulph,
Friduwulf, Friduwolf, Fridwolf, Fridwulf,
Friedwolf, Friedwulf, Frieduwolf,
Frieduwulf*

Fridolin (German) A free man
*Frydolin, Fridolinn, Frydolinn, Fridolyn,
Frydolyn, Fridolynn, Frydolynn*

Friedhelm (German) One who wears the
helmet of peace
Friedelm, Fridhelm, Fridelm

Frigyes (Hungarian) A mighty and peaceful
ruler

Frika (English) One who is bold
*Fryka, Fricka, Frycka, Frica, Fryca, Freca,
Frecka, Freka*

Friso (English) A curly-haired man
Fryso

Fritz (German) Form of Frederick, mean-
ing "a peaceful ruler"
*Frits, Fritzchen, Fritzi, Fritzl, Fritzie, Fritzy,
Fritzey, Fritzee, Fritzea*

Frode (Norse) A wise man
Froad, Froade

Fromel (Hebrew) An outgoing man
Fromell, Fromele, Fromelle

Frost (English) One who is cold
*Frosty, Frostey, Frosti, Frostie, Frostee,
Frostea*

Froyim (Hebrew) A kind man
Froiim

Fructuoso (Spanish) One who is fruitful
Fructo, Fructoso, Fructuso

Fry (English) A father's offspring
Frye, Fryer

Fu (Chinese) A wealthy man

Fudail (Arabic) Of high moral character
*Fudaile, Fudayl, Fudayle, Fudale, Fudael,
Fudaele*

Fugol (Anglo-Saxon) Resembling a bird
Fugul, Fugel, Fugal, Fugil, Fugyl

Fukuda (Japanese) From the field

Fulbright (English) A brilliant man
*Fullbright, Fulbrite, Fullbrite, Fulbryte,
Fullbryte, Fulbert, Fullbert*

Fulgentius (Latin) A shining man
*Fulgentios, Fulgentio, Fulgento, Fulgencio,
Fulgenteos, Fulgenteus, Fulgenteo*

Fulke (English) Of the people
*Fulk, Folke, Folk, Fawk, Fawke, Fowk,
Fowke*

Fulki (Indian) A spark
Fulkie, Fulkey, Fulky, Fulkee, Fulkea

Fuller (English) One who presses, shrinks,
and thickens cloth
*Fullar, Fullor, Fullur, Fullir, Fullyr, Fullere,
Fuler*

Fullerton (English) From Fuller's town
*Fullertun, Fullertin, Fullertyn, Fullertan,
Fullerten*

Fulton (English) From the people's town
*Fultun, Fulten, Fultan, Fultin, Fultyn,
Fulaton, Fulatun, Fulatin, Fulaten,
Fulatyn, Fulatan, Fugeltun, Fugelton,
Fugeltan, Fugeltin, Fugeltyn, Fugelten*

Furlo (American) A manly man
*Furlow, Furlowe, Furloe, Furl, Furle,
Furlio, Furleo*

Furman (German) A ferryman
*Furmen, Furmin, Furmyn, Furmon,
Furmun, Furmann, Fuhrman, Fuhrmen,
Fuhrmon, Fuhrmun, Fuhrmin, Fuhrmyn*

Fursey (Gaelic) The name of a missionary
saint
Fursy, Fursi, Fursie, Fursee, Fursea

Fyfe (Scottish) A man from Fifeshire
Fife, Fyffe, Fiffe, Fibh

Fyren (Anglo-Saxon) A wicked man
Fyrin, Fyryn, Fyran, Fyron, Fyrun

Fyrsil (Welsh) Form of Virgil, meaning
"the staff-bearer"
Fyrsyl, Fyrsill, Fyrsyll

Gaagii (Native American) Resembling a raven
Gaagi, Gagii, Gagi

Gabai (Hebrew) A delightful man

Gabal (Arabian) From the mountain
Gaball

Gabbana (Italian) A creative man
Gabbanah, Gabana, Gabanah, Gabbanna, Gabanna

Gabbar (Arabian) A proud and strong man
Gabber, Gabbor, Gabbur, Gabbir, Gabbyr

Gabbay (Hebrew) A tax collector
Gabbaye, Gabbai, Gabbae

Gabbo (English) To joke or scoff
Gabboe, Gabbow, Gabbowe

Gabor (Hebrew) God is my strength
Gabur, Gabar, Gaber, Gabir, Gabyr

Gabra (African) An offering
Gabre

Gabriel ○ ♂ (Hebrew) A hero of God
Gabrian, Gabriele, Gabrielli, Gabriello, Gaby, Gab, Gabbi, Gabbie, Gabby, Gabe, Gabi, Gabie, Gabey, Gabee, Gabbey, Gabbee, Gable, Gabrio, Gabino, Gabrielo

Gace (French) Of the pledge
Gayce, Gayse, Gaese, Gaece, Gaice, Gaise

Gad (Hebrew / Native American) Having good fortune / from the juniper tree
Gadi, Gadie, Gady, Gadey, Gadee, Gadea

Gaddis (American) A high-maintenance man
Gaddys, Gadis, Gadys, Gaddiss, Gaddyss, Gadiss, Gadyss, Gaddes

Gaderian (Anglo-Saxon) A gatherer
Gaderean, Gadrian, Gadrean, Gaderyan, Gadryan

Gadiel (Arabic) God is my fortune
Gadiell, Gadiele, Gadielle, Gaddiel, Gaddiell, Gadil, Gadeel, Gadeal, Gadeil, Gadyl

Gadish (Arabic) A shock of corn
Gadysh, Gadishe, Gadyshe

Gael (English) One who is or speaks Gaelic
Gaele, Gaell, Gaelle, Gall

Gaerwn (Welsh) From the white fort

Gaetan (Italian) A man from Gaeta
Gaeten, Gaeton, Gaetun, Gaetin, Gaetyn, Gaetano, Gaetanio, Gaetaneo, Gaetaniyo, Gaetaneyo

Gaffney (Irish) Resembling a calf
Gaffny, Gaffni, Gaffnie, Gaffnee, Gaffnea

Gagan (French) A dedicated man
Gagen, Gagon, Gagun, Gagin, Gagyn

Gage (French) Of the pledge
Gaige, Gaege, Gayge

Gahan (Scottish) Form of John, meaning
"God is gracious"
Gahen, Gahon, Gahun, Gahin, Gahyn, Gehan, Gehen, Gehon, Gehun, Gehin, Gehyn

Gahuj (African) A hunter

Gaillard (English) A brave and spirited man
Gailliard, Gaillhard, Gaillardet, Gaillhardt, Gaillart

Gaines (English) One who acquires
Gaynes, Gaenes, Ganes, Gaine, Gayne, Gaene, Gane

Gair (Gaelic) A man of short stature
Gayr, Gaer, Gaire, Gayre, Gaere, Gare

Gaius (Latin) One who rejoices
Gaeus

Gaizka (Basque) A savior
Gayzka, Gaezka

Gajendra (Indian) The king of elephants

Gal (Hebrew) From the rolling wave

Galahad (English) One who is pure and selfless

Galal (Arabic) A majestic man
Galall, Gallal, Gallall

Galanos (Greek) Having blue eyes
Galanios, Galanus, Galanius

Galav (Hindi) The name of a sage

Galbraith (Irish) A foreigner; a Scot
Galbrait, Galbreath, Gallbraith, Gallbreath, Galbraithe, Gallbraithe, Galbreathe, Gallbreathe

Gale (Irish / English) A foreigner / one who is cheerful
Gail, Gaill, Gaille, Gaile, Gayl, Gayle, Gaylle, Gayll

Galegina (Native American) Resembling a deer
Galagina, Galegyna, Galagyna, Galegena, Galagena

Galen (Greek) A healer; one who is calm
Gaelan, Gaillen, Galan, Galin, Galyn, Gaylen, Gaylin, Gaylinn, Gaylan, Gaelen, Gaelin, Gailen, Gailan, Gailin, Gaylon, Galon, Gaelon, Gailon

Galeno (Spanish) A bright child
Galenio, Galeneo, Galeniyo, Galeneyo, Galenios, Galeneos

Gali (Hebrew) From the fountain
Galie, Galy, Galey, Galee, Galea, Galeigh

Galil (Hebrew) From the hilly place
Galeel, Galeal, Galeil, Galiel, Galyl

Galileo (Italian) A man from Galilee
Galilio, Galyleo, Galylio, Galiliyo, Galileyo, Galeleo, Galelio, Galeleyo, Galeliyo

Galip (Turkish) A victorious man
Galyp, Galup, Galep, Galap, Galop

Gallagher (Gaelic) An eager helper
Gallaghor, Gallaghar, Gallaghur, Gallaghir, Gallaghyr, Gallager, Gallagar, Gallagor, Gallagur, Gallagir, Gallagyr

Gallatin (American) From the river
Gallatyn, Gallaten, Gallatan, Gallaton, Gallatun

Galloway (Latin) A man from Gaul
Galoway, Gallowaye, Galowaye, Galo, Gallo, Galway, Gallway, Gallman, Galman, Gallmann, Galmann

Galt (English) From the high wooded land
Galte, Gallt, Gallte

Galtero (Spanish) Form of Walter, meaning "the commander of the army"
Galterio, Galteriyo, Galtereo, Galtereyo, Galter, Galteros, Galterus, Gualterio, Gualtier, Gualtiero, Gutierre

Galton (English) From the town on the high wooded land
Galtun, Galten, Galtan, Galtin, Galtyn, Gallton, Galltun, Gallten, Galltin, Galltyn, Galltan

Galvin (Irish) Resembling a sparrow
Galvyn, Galven, Galvan, Galvon, Galvun, Gallvin, Gallvyn, Gallvon, Gallvun, Gallven, Gallvan

Gamal (Arabic) Resembling a camel
Gamul, Gemal, Gemali, Gemul, Gamali, Gamalie, Gamalee, Gamaleigh, Gamalea, Gamaly, Gamaley, Gemalie, Gemaly, Gemaley, Gemalea, Gemalee, Gemaleigh

Gamaliel (Hebrew) God's reward
Gamliel, Gamalyel, Gamlyel, Gamli, Gamlie, Gamly, Gamley, Gamlee, Gamlea, Gamleigh

Gamba (African) A warrior
Gambah

Gamble (Norse) An old man; of an old family
Gamblen, Gambling, Gamel, Gammel, Gamlin, Gamlen, Gamblin, Gamblyn, Gamlyn

Gameel (Arabic) A handsome man
Gameal, Gamil, Gamiel, Gameil, Gamyl

Gamon (American) One who enjoys playing games
Gamun, Gamen, Gaman, Gamin, Gamyn, Gammon, Gammun, Gamman, Gammin, Gammyn, Gammen

Gan (Chinese) A wanderer

Gandy (American) An adventurer
Gandey, Gandi, Gandie, Gandee, Gandea

Ganesh (Hindi) In Hinduism, the god of wisdom
Ganeshe, Ganesha, Ganeshah

Ganit (Hebrew) The defender
Ganyt, Ganot, Ganut

Gann (English) One who defends with a spear
Gan

Gannet (German) Resembling a goose
Gannett, Ganet, Ganett

Gannon (Gaelic) A fair-skinned man
Gannun, Gannen, Gannan, Gannin, Gannyn, Ganon, Ganun, Ganin, Ganyn, Ganen, Ganan

Ganso (Spanish) Resembling a goose
Gansio, Ganseo, Gansos, Gansios, Gansius, Ganzo, Ganzio, Ganzeo, Ganz, Gans

Ganya (Russian) Having great strength
Ganyah, Ganiya, Ganiyah

Garaden (English) From the triangle-shaped hill
Garadin, Garadan, Garadon, Garadun, Garadyn

Garafeld (English) From the triangle-shaped field
Garafield

Garai (Basque) A conqueror

Garan (Welsh / German) Resembling a stork / a guardian
Garen, Garin, Garyn, Garon, Garun

Garbhan (Irish) One who is rough
Garbhen, Garbhon, Garbhun, Garbhin, Garbhyn, Garban, Garben, Garbin, Garbyn, Garbon, Garbun

Garcia (Spanish) One who is brave in battle
Garce, Garcy, Garcey, Garci, Garcie, Garcee, Garcea

Gardner (English) The keeper of the garden
Gardener, Gardenner, Gardie, Gardiner, Gardnar, Gardnard, Gard, Gardell, Gardi, Gardy, Gardey, Gardee, Gardea, Gardenor, Gardnor, Gardenir, Gardnir, Gardenyr, Gardnyr

Gared (English) Form of Gerard, meaning "one who is mighty with a spear"
Garad, Garid, Garyd, Garod, Garud

Gareth (Welsh) One who is gentle
Garith, Garreth, Garrith, Garyth, Garryth, Garath, Garrath

Garfield (English) From the spear field
Garfeld

Garland (French / English) One who is crowned / from the spear land
Garlan, Garlen, Garlend, Garlin, Garlind, Garllan, Garlland, Garlyn, Garlynd, Garlon, Garlond, Garlun, Garlund, Gariland, Garilend

Garman (English) A spearman
Garmann, Garmen, Garmin, Garmon, Garmun, Garmyn, Gar, Garr, Garrman, Garrmen, Garrmon, Garrmun, Garrmin, Garrmyn

Garn (American) One who is prepared
Garne, Garni, Garnie, Garny, Garney, Garnee, Garnea

Garner (English) One who gathers or keeps grain
Garnar, Garnor, Garnur, Garnir, Garnyr, Garnier, Garnell, Garnel

Garnett (English / French) Resembling the dark-red gem / one who wields a spear
Garnet, Garnette, Garnete

Garnock (Welsh) From the river of alder trees
Garnoc, Garnok, Gwernach, Garnoch

Garrad (English) Form of Gerard, meaning "one who is mighty with a spear"
Garred, Garrod, Garrud, Garrid, Garryd

Garrett (English) Form of Gerard, meaning "one who is mighty with a spear"
Garett, Garret, Garretson, Garritt, Garrot, Garrott, Gerrit, Gerritt, Gerrity, Garrity, Garet

Garrick (English) One who rules by the spear
Garek, Garreck, Garrik, Garryck, Garryk, Garick, Garik, Garic, Garyck, Garyk, Garyc, Garric, Garryc

Garridan (English) One who is quiet
Garriden, Garridin, Garridyn, Garridon, Garridun

Garrison (English) From the spear-fortified town
Garrisun, Garrisen, Garison, Garisun, Garisen, Garris, Garrys, Garryson, Garrysun, Garrysen, Garrysan, Garrysin, Garrysyn

Garron (Gaelic) Resembling a gelding; workhorse
Garrion, Garran, Garren, Garrin, Garrun, Garryn

Garroway (English) One who fights with a spear
Garoway, Garrowaye, Garowaye, Garrowae, Garowae, Garrowai, Garowai, Garwig, Garwyg, Garrwig, Garrwyg

Garson (English) The son of Gar (Garrett, Garrison, Gareth, etc.)
Garrson, Garsen, Garrsen, Garsun, Garrsun, Garsone, Garrsone

Garth (Scandinavian) The keeper of the garden
Garthe, Gart, Garte

Garthay (Irish) Form of Gareth, meaning "one who is gentle"
Garthaye, Garthai, Garthae

Garton (English) From the triangle-shaped town
Gartun, Garrton, Garrtun, Garten, Garrten, Garaton, Garatun, Garatin, Garatyn, Garaten, Garatan

Garvey (Gaelic) A rough but peaceful man
Garvy, Garvee, Garvea, Garvi, Garvie, Garrvey, Garrvy, Garrvee, Garrvea, Garrvi, Garrvie, Garve

Garvin (English) A friend with a spear
Garvyn, Garven, Garvan, Garvon, Garvun

Garwin (English) Form of Garvin, meaning "a friend with a spear"
Garwine, Garwinn, Garwinne, Garwen, Garwenn, Garwenne, Garwyn, Garwynn, Garwynne, Gaarwine

Garwood (English) From the triangle-shaped forest; from the spear forest
Garrwood, Garwode, Garrwode

Gary (English) One who wields a spear
Garey, Gari, Garie, Garea, Garee, Garry, Garrey, Garree, Garrea, Garri, Garrie

Gaspar (Persian) The keeper of the treasure
Gasper, Gaspir, Gaspyr, Gaspor, Gaspur, Gaspare, Gaspard, Gasparo

Gassur (Arabic) A courageous man
Gassor, Gassir, Gassyr, Gassar, Gasser

Gaston (French) A man from Gascony
Gastun, Gastan, Gasten, Gascon, Gascone, Gasconey, Gasconi, Gasconie, Gasconee, Gasconea, Gascony

Gate (American) One who is close-minded
Gates, Gait, Gaite, Gaits, Gaites, Gayt, Gayte, Gayts, Gaytes, Gaet, Gaete, Gaets, Gaetes

Gaudy (American) One who is colorful
Gaudey, Gaudi, Gaudie, Gaudee, Gaudea, Gauden, Gaudan, Gaudin, Gaudyn, Gaudon, Gaudun

Gaurav (Hindi) A proud man

Gaute (Norse) A great man
Gauti, Gautie, Gauty, Gautey, Gautee, Gautea

Gauthier (Teutonic) A strong ruler
Gaultier, Gautier, Gualterio, Gualtiero, Gualtereo, Gaulterio, Gaultereo, Gaultiero, Gauther

Gavin ⚙ (Welsh) A little white falcon
Gavan, Gaven, Gavino, Gavyn, Gavynn, Gavon, Gavun, Gavyno, Gaveno, Gawain, Gawaine, Gawayn, Gawayne, Gawaine, Gwayne, Gwayn, Gawen, Gawath, Gawin

Gavriel (Hebrew) God is my strength
Gavriell, Gavril, Gavrilo, Gavryel, Gavryell, Gavryl, Gavrill, Gavryll, Gavrylo, Gavi, Gavie, Gavy, Gavey, Gavee, Gavea, Gavri, Gavrie, Gavry, Gavrey, Gavree, Gavrea

Gaylord (French) One who is high-spirited
Gay, Gayelord, Gayler, Gaylor, Gaylur, Gaylar, Gaylir, Gaylyr, Gaylard

Gaynor (Gaelic) The son of a fair-haired man
Gaynur, Gayner, Gaynir, Gaynar, Gaynyr, Gainor, Gainur, Gainer, Gainar, Gainir, Gainyr, Gaenor, Gaenur, Gaenar, Gaener, Gaenir, Gaenyr

Gazali (African) A mystic
Gazalie, Gazaly, Gazaley, Gazalee, Gazalea, Gazaleigh

Gazsi (Hungarian) One who protects the treasure
Gazsie, Gazsy, Gazsey, Gazsee, Gazsea

Geary (English) One who is flexible
Geari, Gearie, Gearey, Gearee, Gearea, Gery, Gerey, Geri, Gerie, Geree, Gerea

Gedaliah (Hebrew) God is great
Gedalia, Gedaliahu, Gedalio, Gedalya, Gedalyah

Geedar (Arabian) From the enclosure
Geeder, Geedor, Geedur, Geedir, Geedyr

Geert (German) One who is brave and strong
Geart, Geerte, Gearte

Gefen (Hebrew) Of the vine
Gafni, Gefania, Gefaniah, Gefanya, Gefanyah, Gefanyahu, Geffen, Gephania, Gephaniah, Gefni, Gefnie, Gefney, Gefny, Gefnea, Gefnee

Geir (Scandinavian) One who wields a spear
Geire, Geer, Geere, Gear, Geare

Geirleif (Norse) A descendant of the spear
Geirleaf, Geerleif, Geerleaf

Geirolf (Norse) The wolf spear
Geirulf, Geerolf, Geerulf

Geirstein (Norse) One who wields a rock-hard spear
Geerstein, Gerstein

Geldersman (Dutch) A man from Guelders
Geldersmann, Geldersmen, Geldersmon

Gellert (Hungarian) A mighty soldier
Gellart, Gellirt, Gellyrt, Gellort, Gellurt

Gemini (Latin) The twins; the third sign of the zodiac
Gemineye, Gemyni, Geminie, Gemynie

Genaro (Latin) A dedicated man
Genaroh, Genaroe, Genarow, Genarowe

Gene (English) Form of Eugene, meaning "a wellborn man"
Genio, Geno, Geneo, Gino, Ginio, Gineo

General (American) A military leader
Generel, Generol, Generil, Generyl, Generul

Genero (Latin) One who is generic
Generoe, Generoh, Generow, Generowe

Generoso (Spanish) One who is generous
Generosio, Generoseo, Generos

Genesis (Hebrew) Of the beginning
Genesys, Gennesis, Ginesis, Ginesys, Gennesys

Genet (African) From Eden
Genat, Genit, Genyt, Genot, Genut

Gennaro (Italian) Born of Janus
Gennarius, Gennaros, Gennarios, Gennarus, Gennareo, Gennario

Genoah (Italian) From the city of Genoa
Genoa, Genovise, Genovize

Gent (English) A gentleman
Gente, Gynt, Gynte

Gentian (Latin) Resembling the blue flower
Genshian

Gentile (Latin) A foreigner or heathen
Gentyle, Gentilo, Gentylo, Gentilio, Gentylio, Gentileo, Gentyleo, Gentil

Gentry (English) Of good breeding; holding a high social standing
Gentrey, Gentree, Gentrea, Gentri, Gentrie

Gentza (Basque) A peaceful man
Gentzah

Geoffrey (English) Form of Jeffrey, meaning "a man of peace"
Geffrey, Geoff, Geoffery, Geoffroy, Geoffry, Geofrey, Geofferi, Geofferie, Geofferee, Geoffri, Geoffrie, Geoffree, Geffry, Geffri, Geffrie, Geffree

Geol (English) Born at Christmastime
Geoll, Geole, Geolle

Geomar (German) One who is famous in battle
Geomarr, Geomare, Geomarre, Giomar, Giomarr, Giomare, Giomarre

George (Greek) One who works the earth; a farmer
Georas, Geordi, Geordie, Georg, Georges, Georgi, Georgie, Georgio, Georgios, Georgiy, Georgy, Gheorghe, Giorgi, Giorgio, Giorgios, Giorgius, Goran, Gyorgy, Gyuri, Georgii

Geraghty (Irish) From the court
Geraghtey, Geraghti, Geraghtie, Geraghtee, Geraghtea

Geraint (Latin) An old man
Gerainte, Gerant, Geraynt, Geraynte, Geraent, Geraente

Gerald (German) One who rules with the spear
Garald, Garold, Gearalt, Geralde, Geraldo, Geraud, Gere, Gerek, Gerik, Gerold, Gerolld, Gerolt, Gerollt, Gerrald, Gerrell, Gerri, Gerrild, Gerrold, Geryld, Giraldo, Giraud, Girauld, Girault, Geralt, Gerred

Gerard (English) One who is mighty with a spear
Garrard, Gearard, Gerardo, Geraud, Gerrard, Girard, Girault, Giraud, Gherardo, Gerhard, Gerard, Gerd, Gerod

Gerbold (German) One who is bold with a spear
Gerbolde

Geremia (Italian) Form of Jeremiah, meaning "one who is exalted by the Lord"
Geremiah, Geremias, Geremija, Geremiya, Geremyah, Geramiah, Geramia

Gerlach (Scandinavian) A spear thrower
Gerlaich

Germain (French / Latin) A man from Germany / one who is brotherly
Germaine, German, Germane, Germanicus, Germano, Germanus, Germayn, Germayne, Germin, Germaen, Germaene

Gerodi (Italian) A hero
Gerodie, Gerody, Gerodey, Gerodee, Gerodea

Geron (French) A guardian
Gerun, Geren, Geran, Gerin, Geryn

Geronimo (Spanish) Form of Jerome, meaning "of the sacred name"; a great Native American chief
Geronimus, Geronimos, Geronymo

Gerontius (Latin) An old man
Gerontios, Gerontio, Geronteo

Gerry (German) Short form of names beginning with Ger-, such as Gerald or Gerard
Gerrey, Gerri, Gerrie, Gerrea, Gerree

Gershom (Hebrew) One who has been exiled
Gersham, Gershon, Gershoom, Gershem, Gershim, Gershym, Gershum, Gersh, Gershe, Gerzson

Gervase (German) One who is honored; one who serves the spear
Gervais, Gervaise, Gervasio, Gervasius, Gervaso, Gervayse, Gerwazy, Gerwazey, Gerwazi, Gerwazie, Gerwazee, Gerwazea, Gervis, Gervys

Getachew (African) Their master

Geteye (African) My master

Gethin (Welsh) A dark-skinned man
Gethyn, Gethan, Gethen, Gethon, Gethun

Gevariah (Hebrew) The strength of God
Gevaria, Gevarya, Gevaryah, Gevarayahu, Gevariya, Gevariyah

Ghalib (Arabic) A victorious man
Ghaleeb, Ghaleab, Ghaleib, Ghalieb, Ghalyb

Ghassan (Arabic) One who is in the prime of his youth
Ghasan, Ghassen, Ghasen, Ghasson, Ghason, Ghassun, Ghasun, Ghassin, Ghasin, Ghassyn, Ghasyn

Ghayth (Arabic) The winner
Ghaith, Ghaeth, Ghathe, Ghaythe, Ghaithe, Ghaethe

Ghazal (Arabian) Resembling a deer
Ghazall, Ghazale

Ghazi (Arabic) An invader; a conqueror
Ghazie, Ghazy, Ghazey, Ghazee, Ghazea

Ghedi (African) A traveler
Ghedie, Ghedy, Ghedey, Ghedee, Ghedea

Ghislain (German) Of the oath
Ghislaine, Ghislayn, Ghislayne, Ghislaen, Ghislaene, Ghislane

Ghoshal (Hindi) A speaker
Ghoshil, Ghoshyl

Ghoukas (Armenian) Form of Lucas, meaning "a man from Lucania"
Ghukas

Giacomo (Italian) Form of James, meaning "he who supplants"
Gyacomo

Gian (Italian) Form of John, meaning "God is gracious"
Gyan, Gianney, Gianni, Gianny, Giannie, Giannee, Giannea, Gyanney, Gyanny, Gyanni, Gyannie, Gyannee, Gyannea, Gi, Gy, Giann, Gyann

Giancarlo (Italian) One who is gracious and mighty
Gyancarlo

Gibor (Hebrew) Having great strength
Gybor, Gibbor, Gybbor

G

Gibson (English) The son of Gilbert
Gibb, Gibbes, Gibby, Gibbons, Gibbs, Gibsen, Gibsun, Gilson, Gilsun, Gilsen, Gillson, Gillsun, Gillsen, Gibbon, Gibbens, Gibben, Gibbesone

Gideon (Hebrew) A mighty warrior; one who fells trees
Gideone, Gidi, Gidon, Gidion, Gid, Gidie, Gidy, Gidey, Gidee, Gidea, Gedeon, Gedion, Gedon

Gidney (English) Having great strength
Gidny, Gidni, Gidnie, Gidnee, Gidnea, Gydney, Gydny, Gydni, Gydnie, Gydnee, Gydnea

Giffin (English) A giving man
Giffen, Giffyn, Giffon, Giffun, Giffan, Giff, Gyf, Gyff, Giffe, Gyffe

Gifford (English) One who gives bravery
Gyfford, Gifforde, Gyfforde, Giffurd, Gyffurd, Gifferd, Gyfferd, Giffurde, Gyffurde, Gifferde, Gyfferde, Giffard, Giffarde, Gyffard, Gyffarde, Gifuhard

Gifre (Anglo-Saxon) A greedy man
Gifri, Gifrie, Gifree, Gifrea, Gifry, Gifrey

Gijs (English) An intelligent man

Gilad (Hebrew / Arabic) From the monument / a camel's hump
Gylad, Gilead, Giladi, Giladie, Gilady, Giladey, Giladee, Giladea, Gyladi, Gyladie, Gylady, Gyladey, Gyladee, Gyladea

Gilam (Hebrew) The joy of the people
Gylam, Gilem, Gylem, Gilim, Gylim, Gilym, Gylym, Gilom, Gylom, Gilum, Gylum, Gil, Gyl

Gilamu (Basque) A determined soldier
Gilamue, Gilamou, Gylamu, Gylamue, Gylamou

Gilbert (French / English) Of the bright promise / one who is trustworthy
Gib, Gibb, Gil, Gilberto, Gilburt, Giselbert, Giselberto, Giselbertus, Guilbert, Gilbirt, Gilbyrt, Gilbart, Gilibeirt, Giliburt, Gilibert, Gilibirt, Gilleabart, Guilbert, Guilbirt, Guilburt

Gilby (Norse / Gaelic) From the hostage's estate / a blonde-haired man
Gilbey, Gilbee, Gilbea, Gilbi, Gilbie, Gillbey, Gillbie, Gillby, Gillbi, Gillbee, Gillbea

Gilchrist (Irish) A servant of Christ
Gylchrist, Gillchrist, Gyllchrist, Gikhrist, Gilkhrist, Gilkrist

Gildas (Irish / English) One who serves God / the golden one
Gyldas, Gilda, Gylda, Gilde, Gylde, Gildea, Gyldea, Gildes, Gyldes

Giles (Greek) Resembling a young goat
Gyles, Gile, Gil, Gilles, Gillis, Gilliss, Gyle, Gyl, Gylles, Gylliss, Gyllis

Gilfred (Teutonic) One who has taken an oath of peace
Gilfrid, Gilfryd, Gilfried, Gilfreid, Gylfred, Gylfrid, Gylfryd, Gylfried, Gylfreid

Gill (Gaelic) A servant
Gyll, Gilly, Gilley, Gillee, Gillea, Gilli, Gillie, Ghill, Ghyll, Ghilli, Ghillie, Ghilly, Ghilley, Ghillee, Ghillea

Gillanders (Scottish) A servant of St. Andrew
Gyllanders, Gilanders, Gylanders

Gillean (Irish) A servant of St. John
Gyllean, Gillian, Gyllian, Gilean, Gilian, Gillan, Gillen, Gilleon, Gillion, Gillon

Gilleasbuig (German) One who is bold

Gillespie (Gaelic) A servant of the bishop; the son of the bishop's servant
Gillespi, Gillespy, Gillespey, Gillespee, Gillespea, Gillaspi, Gillaspie, Gillaspee, Gillaspea, Gillaspy, Gillaspey

Gillett (Spanish) A little or young Gilbert
Gilet, Gilett, Gillet, Gylet, Gylett, Gyllet, Gyllett

Gillies (Scottish) A servant of Jesus
Ghilles, Ghillies, Gillees, Ghillees

Gillivray (Scottish) A servant of God
Gillivraye, Gillivrae, Gillivrai

Gilman (Gaelic) A manservant
Gillman, Gilmann, Gillmann, Gylman, Gylmann, Gyllman, Gyllmann

Gilmat (Scottish) One who wields a sword
Gylmat, Gilmet, Gylmet

Gilmer (English) A famous hostage
Gilmar, Gilmor, Gilmur, Gilmir, Gilmyr, Gillmer, Gillmar, Gillmor, Gillmur, Gillmir, Gillmyr

Gilmore (Gaelic) A servant of the Virgin Mary
Gillmore, Gillmour, Gilmour

Gilon (Hebrew) Filled with joy
Gilun, Gilen, Gilan, Gilin, Gilyn, Gilo

Gilpin (English) A trustworthy man
Gilpen, Gilpyn, Gilpan, Gilpon, Gilpun

Gilroy (Gaelic) The son of a red-haired man
Gilderoy, Gildray, Gildroy, Gillroy, Gillray, Gilray

Gimm (Anglo-Saxon) As precious as a gem
Gim, Gymm, Gym

Ginton (Arabic) From the garden
Gintun, Gintan, Ginten, Gintin, Gintyn

Giona (Italian) Form of John, meaning "God is gracious"
Gion, Gione

Giovanni (Italian) Form of John, meaning "God is gracious"
Geovani, Geovanney, Geovanni, Geovanny, Geovany, Giannino, Giovan, Giovani, Giovanno, Giovanny, Giovel, Giovell, Giovonni

Giri (Indian) From the mountain
Girie, Giry, Girey, Giree, Girea

Girioel (Welsh) A lord

Girvan (Gaelic) The small, rough one
Gyrvan, Girven, Gyrven, Girvin, Gyrvin, Girvyn, Gyrvyn, Girvon, Gyrvon, Girvun, Gyrvun

Gitano (Italian) A gypsy
Gytano, Gitanos, Gytanos, Gitanio, Gitaneo

Gitel (Hebrew) A good man
Gitell, Gitele, Gitelle, Gytel, Gytell, Gytele, Gytelle

Giulio (Italian) One who is youthful
Giuliano, Giuleo

Giuseppe (Italian) Form of Joseph, meaning "God will add"
Giuseppi, Giuseppie, Giuseppy, Giuseppee, Giuseppea, Giuseppey, Guiseppe, Guiseppi, Guiseppie, Guiseppey, Guiseppy, Guiseppea, Guiseppee

Giustino (Italian) Form of Justin, meaning "one who is just and upright"
Giusto, Giustio, Giusteo, Giustinian, Giustiniano

Givon (Arabic) From the heights
Givun, Given, Givan, Givin, Givyn

Gizmo (American) One who is playful
Gismo, Gyzmo, Gysmo, Gizmoe, Gismoe, Gyzmoe, Gysmoe

Gjest (Norse) A stranger

Gjord (Norse) Form of Godfried, meaning "God is peace"
Gjurd, Gjorn, Gjurn

Glad (American) One who is lighthearted and happy
Gladd, Gladdi, Gladdie, Gladdy, Gladdey, Gladdee, Gladdea

Glade (English) From the clearing in the woods
Glayd, Glayde, Glaid, Glaide, Glaed, Glaede

Gladstone (English) From the kite-shaped stone
Gladston

Gladus (Welsh) One who is lame
Glados, Glades, Gladas, Gladis, Gladys

Gladwin (English) A lighthearted and happy friend
Gladwine, Gladwinn, Gladwinne, Gladwen, Gladwenn, Gladwenne, Gladwyn, Gladwynn, Gladwynne

Glaisne (Irish) One who is calm; serene
Glaisny, Glaisney, Glaisni, Glaisnie, Glaisnee, Glasny, Glasney, Glasni, Glasnie, Glasnee

Glancy (American) Form of Clancy, meaning "son of the red-haired warrior"
Glancey, Glanci, Glancie, Glancee, Glancea, Glansey, Glansy, Glansi, Glansie, Glansee, Glansea

Glanville (French) From the village of oak trees
Glanvil, Glanvill, Glanvylle, Glanvyl, Glanvyll

Glasgow (Scottish) From the city in Scotland
Glasgo

Glen (Gaelic) From the secluded narrow valley
Glenn, Glennard, Glennie, Glennon, Glenny, Glin, Glinn, Glyn, Glynn, Glean, Glendale, Glendayle, Glendail, Glendael, Glenney, Glenni, Glenard, Glennerd, Glenerd

Glenavon (English) From the valley near the river Avon
Glennavon, Glenavin, Glennavin, Glenavyn, Glennavyn, Glenaven, Glennaven, Glenavan, Glennavan, Glenavun, Glennavun

Glendon (Gaelic) From the town in the glen
Glendun, Glendan, Glenden, Glendin, Glendyn

Glendower (Welsh) From the valley near the water
Glyndwer, Glyndwr, Glendwer, Glendwr, Glyndower

Glenville (Gaelic) From the village in the glen
Glenvil, Glenvill, Glenvyll, Glenvyl, Glenvylle, Glinville, Glinvill, Glinvil, Glinvylle, Glinvyll, Glinvyl

Glenwood (English) From the forest near the glen
Glenwode

Glover (English) One who makes gloves
Glovar, Glovir, Glovyr, Glovur, Glovor

Gobha (Scottish) A smith
Gobhah

Gobind (Sanskrit) The cow finder
Gobinde, Gobinda, Govind, Govinda, Govinde

Goby (American) An audacious man
Gobi, Gobie, Gobey, Gobee, Gobea

Godana (African) A male child
Godanah, Godanna, Godannah

Goddard (German) One who is divinely firm
Godard, Godart, Goddart, Godhart, Godhardt, Gothart, Gotthard, Gotthardt, Gotthart

Godfrey (German) God is peace
Giotto, Godefroi, Godfry, Godofredo, Goffredo, Gottfrid, Gottfried, Godfried, Godfreid, Godfrid, Godfred, Godfryd, Gofraidh, Gofried, Gofreid, Gofryd, Gofred, Gofrid, Gothfraidh

Godric (English) One who rules with God
Godrick, Godrik, Godryc, Godryk, Godryck, Goderick, Goderyck, Goderic, Goderyc, Goderik, Goderyk

Godwin (English) A friend of God
Godwine, Godwinn, Godwinne, Godwen, Godwenn, Godwenne, Godwyn, Godwynn, Godwynne, Godewin, Godewen, Godewyn

Goel (Hebrew) One who has been redeemed
Goell, Goele, Goelle

Gogarty (Irish) One who has been banished
Gogartey, Gogarti, Gogartie, Gogartee, Gogartea

Gogo (African) A grandfatherly man

Gohn (American) A spirited man
Gon

Goku (Japanese) From the sky

Golding (English) The golden one
Goldyng, Golden, Goldan, Goldin, Goldyn, Goldon, Goldun, Goldman, Goldmann, Gold, Golde, Goldo

Goldsmith (English) One who works with gold
Goldschmidt, Goldshmidt

Goldwin (English) A golden friend
Goldwine, Goldwinn, Goldwinne, Goldwen, Goldwenn, Goldwenne, Goldwyn, Goldwynn, Goldwynne, Goldewin, Goldewen, Goldewyn

Goliath (Hebrew) One who has been exiled; in the Bible, the giant killed by David
Goliathe, Golliath, Golliathe, Golyath, Golyathe, Gollyath, Gollyathe

Gomda (Native American) Of the wind
Gomdah

Gomer (English) Of the good fight
Gomar, Gomor, Gomur, Gomir, Gomyr

Gong (American) A forceful man

Gonzalo (Spanish) Of the battle; resembling a wolf
Gonsalve, Gonzales, Gonsalo, Gonsales, Gonzalez, Gonze, Gonz

Goode (English) An upstanding man
Good, Goodi, Goodie, Goody, Goodey, Goodee, Goodea

Goodman (English) An upstanding man
Goodmann, Guttman, Guttmann

Goodrich (English) A good ruler
Goodriche

Goodwin (English) A beloved friend
*Goodwine, Goodwinn, Goodwinne,
Goodwen, Goodwenn, Goodwenne,
Goodwyn, Goodwynn, Goodwynne*

Gordain (Scottish) Form of Gordan,
meaning "from the great hill; a hero"
*Gordaine, Gordayn, Gordayne, Gordaen,
Gordaene, Gordane*

Gordon (Gaelic) From the great hill; a hero
*Gorden, Gordin, Gordyn, Gordun,
Gordan, Gordi, Gordie, Gordee, Gordea,
Gordy, Gordey, Gordo*

Gore (English) From the triangle-shaped land
Goring, Gor, Gorre, Gorr

Goren (Hebrew) From the granary
*Gorin, Goryn, Goran, Gorun, Goron, Gorren,
Gorrin, Gorryn, Gorran, Gorrun, Gorron*

Gorham (English) From the village in the
triangle-shaped land

Gorka (Basque) A farmer
*Gorko, Gorke, Gorki, Gorkey, Gorky,
Gorkie, Gorkee, Gorkea, Gyurka*

Gorman (Irish) Having blue eyes
*Gormain, Gormaine, Gormayn,
Gormayne, Gormaen, Gormaene*

Gormley (Irish) The blue spearman
*Gormly, Gormlee, Gormlea, Gormleah,
Gormleigh, Gormli, Gormlie, Gormaly,
Gormaley, Gormalee, Gormaleigh,
Gormalea, Gormaleah, Gormali,
Gormalie, Gormilly, Gormilley, Gormillee,
Gormilleigh, Gormillea, Gormilleah,
Gormilli, Gormillie*

Goro (Japanese) The fifth-born child

Gorrell (English) From the marsh thicket
Gorell, Gorrel

Gorry (Irish) One who achieves peace
through God
Gorrey, Gorri, Gorrie, Gorrea, Gorree

Gorton (English) From the town in the
triangle-shaped land
Gortun, Gorten, Gortan, Gortin, Gortyn

Gosheven (Native American) One who leaps
*Goshevin, Goshevyn, Goshevan,
Goshevon, Goshevun*

Gotam (Indian) The best ox
*Gotem, Gautam, Gautem, Gautom,
Gotom*

Gotzon (Basque) A heavenly messenger; an
angel

Govannon (Irish) In mythology, the god of
the forge
*Govannen, Govannan, Govannun,
Govannin, Govannyn, Govan, Govane*

Govind (Indian) The one who finds and
owns cows
*Govinde, Govynd, Govynde, Govend,
Govende*

Gow (Scottish) A smith
Gowe, Gowan

Gower (Welsh) One who is pure; chaste
*Gwyr, Gowyr, Gowir, Gowar, Gowor,
Gowur*

Gowon (African) A rainmaker
Gowun

Gowyn (English) A friend of God
*Gowynn, Gowynne, Gowen, Gowenn,
Gowenne, Gowin, Gowinn, Gowinne,
Gowine*

Gozal (Hebrew) Resembling a baby bird
Gozall, Gozel, Gozell, Gozale, Gozele

Graceland (American) From the land of
grace
*Graiceland, Grayceland, Graeceland,
Gracelan, Graycelan, Graicelan, Graecelan*

Grady (Gaelic) One who is famous; noble
*Gradey, Gradee, Gradea, Gradi, Gradie,
Graidy, Graidey, Graidee, Graidea, Graidi,
Graidie, Graydy, Graydey, Graydee,
Graydea, Graydi, Graydie, Graedy,
Graedey, Graedee, Graedea, Graedi,
Graedie, Graden, Gradan, Gradon,
Gradun, Gradin, Gradyn*

Graham (English) From the gravelled area;
from the gray home
*Grahame, Graeham, Graeme, Graehame,
Graeghamm, Graem, Grahem, Gram*

Grail (English) One who is greatly desired
Graile, Grayl, Grayle, Grael, Graele, Grale

Grand (English) A superior man
*Grande, Grandy, Grandey, Grandi,
Grandie, Grandee, Grandea, Grander*

G

Granderson (English) The son of Grand
Grandersun, Grandersen, Grandersin,
Grandersyn, Grandersan, Granders

Granger (English) A farmer
Grainger, Graynger, Graenger, Grange,
Graynge, Graenge, Grainge, Grangere

Granite (American) One who is steadfast;
unyeilding
Granit, Granyte, Granyt, Granete, Granet

Grant (English) A tall man; a great man
Grante, Graent

Grantham (English) From the large estate

Grayton (English) From the gray town
Graytun, Graiton, Graytun, Graeton,
Graetun, Graydon, Graydun, Graidon,
Graidun, Graedon, Graedun, Greytun,
Greyton, Greydon, Greydun

Graziano (Italian) One who is dearly loved
Gracian, Graciano, Grazian

Greeley (English) From the gray meadow
Greely, Greeli, Greelie, Greeleigh, Greelee,
Greelea, Greeleah

Greenley (English) From the green meadow
Greenly, Greenleigh, Greenlea, Greenleah,
Greenli, Greenlie, Greenlee

GRANT

Our quest to come up with another one-syllable name for our son (his big sisters are Kate and Brooke) eventually led to an Elite Eight list of names on the delivery-room ink board. We eliminated the names of people we knew too well—Mitch, Josh, Scott, and Ross—and a couple others—Heath, Drake—before picking Grant. —Cam, CA

Grantland (English) From the land of
large fields
Grantlande, Granteland, Grantelande

Grantley (English) From the large meadow
Grantly, Grantleah, Grantlee, Grantlea,
Grantleigh, Grantli, Grantlie

Granville (French) From the large village
Granvylle, Granvil, Granvyl, Granvill,
Granvyll, Granvile, Granvyle, Grenvill,
Grenville, Grenvyll, Grenvylle, Grenvil,
Grenvile, Grenvyl, Grenvyle

Graves (English) From the burial ground
Graives, Grayves, Graeves, Grave, Graive,
Grayve, Graeve

Gray (English) A gray-haired man
Graye, Grai, Grae, Greye, Grey, Graylon,
Graylen, Graylin, Graylyn, Graylun,
Graylan

Grayson (English) The son of a gray-
haired man
Graysen, Graysun, Graysin, Graysyn,
Graysan, Graison, Graisun, Graisen,
Graisin, Graisyn, Graisan, Graeson,
Graesun, Graesan, Graesen, Graesin,
Graesyn, Greyson, Greysun, Greysin,
Greysyn, Greysen, Greysan

Greenwood (English) From the green forest
Greenwode

Gregory (Greek) One who is vigilant;
watchful
Graig, Greer, Greg, Greger, Gregg,
Greggory, Gregoire, Gregoor, Gregor,
Gregori, Gregorio, Gregorius, Gregos,
Grygor, Grzegorz, Gregorie, Gregorey,
Gregorios, Gergo, Greguska, Griogair,
Grioghar, Griorgair

Gregson (English) The son of Greg
Gregsun, Gregsen, Gregsan, Gregsin,
Gregsyn

Gremian (Anglo-Saxon) One who enrages
others
Gremien, Gremean, Gremyan

Gresham (English) From the grazing land
Greshem, Greshim, Greshym, Greshom,
Greshum, Grisham, Grishem, Grishim,
Grishym, Grishom, Grishum

Greyley (English) From the gray meadow
Greyly, Greyli, Greylie, Greylea, Greyleah,
Greyleigh, Greylee, Grayley, Grayly, Graylee,
Grayleigh, Graylea, Grayleah, Grayli,
Graylie, Graeley, Graely, Graelee, Graelea,
Graeleah, Graeleigh, Graeli, Graelie

Gridley (English) From the flat meadow
Gridly, Gridlee, Gridlea, Gridleah, Gridleigh, Gridli, Gridlie

Griffin (Latin) Having a hooked nose
Griff, Griffen, Griffon, Gryffen, Gryffin, Gryphon, Gryphen, Gryphin, Gryphyn, Griffyn

Griffith (Welsh) A mighty chief
Griffyth, Gryffith, Gryffyth, Griphith, Gryphith, Gryphyth

Grigori (Russian) Form of Gregory, meaning "one who is vigilant; watchful"
Grigor, Grigorios, Grigory, Grigorie, Grigorey, Grigoree, Grigorea, Grig, Grigg, Grigorii, Grisha

Grimaldo (German) A mighty protector
Grymaldo, Grimaldi, Grymaldi, Grimaldie, Grymaldie, Grimaldy, Grymaldy, Grimaldey, Grymaldey, Grimaldee, Grymaldee, Grimaldea, Grymaldea

Grimbold (Anglo-Saxon) One who is fierce and bold
Grymbold, Grimbald, Grymbald

Grimm (Anglo-Saxon) One who is fierce; dark
Grimme, Grymm, Grymme

Grimshaw (English) From the dark woods
Grymshaw, Grimshawe, Grymshawe

Grimsley (English) From the dark meadow
Grimsly, Grimslee, Grimslea, Grimsleah, Grimsleigh, Grimsli, Grimslie

Grindan (Anglo-Saxon) A sharp man
Grinden, Grindon, Grindun, Grindin, Grindyn, Gryndan, Grynden, Gryndon, Gryndun, Gryndin, Gryndyn

Gris (German) A gray-haired man
Griz, Grys, Gryz

Griswold (German) From the gray forest
Griswald, Gryswold, Gryswald, Greswold, Greswald

Grosvenor (French) A great hunter
Grosveneur

Grover (English) From the grove of trees
Grovar, Grovor, Grovur, Grovir, Grovyr, Grafere

Gruffydd (Welsh) A fierce lord
Gruffyd, Gruffud, Gruffudd, Gruffen, Gruffin, Gruffyn, Gruffan

Guadalupe (Spanish) From the river of the wolf
Guadaloupe, Guadaloope

Guang (Chinese) Of the light

Guard (American) One who protects others
Guarde, Guarder, Guardor, Guardar, Guardur

Guban (African) One who has been burnt
Guben, Gubin, Gubyn, Gubon, Gubun

Guedado (African) One who is unwanted

Guerdon (English) A warring man
Guerdun, Guerdan, Guerden, Guerdin, Guerdyn

Guerrant (French) One who is at war

Guido (Italian) One who acts as a guide
Guidoh, Gwedo, Gwido, Gwydo, Gweedo

Guildford (English) From the flowered ford
Guildforde, Guildferd, Guildferde, Guildfurd, Guildfurde, Gilford, Gilferd, Gilfurd, Gilforde, Gilfurde, Gilferde, Guilford, Guilforde, Guilferd, Guilferde, Guilfurd, Guilfurde

Guillaume (French) Form of William, meaning "the determined protector"
Gillermo, Guglielmo, Guilherme, Guillermo, Gwillyn, Gwilym, Guglilmo

Gulshan (Hindi) From the gardens

Gulzar (Arabic) One who is flourishing
Gulzarr, Gulzaar

Gundy (American) A friendly man
Gundey, Gundee, Gundea, Gundi, Gundie

Gunn (Scottish) A white-skinned man; a white-haired man
Gunne, Gun

Gunnar (Scandinavian) A bold warrior
Gunner, Gunnor, Gunnur, Gunnir, Gunnyr

Gunnbjorn (Norse) A warrior bear
Gunbjorn

Gunnolf (Norse) A warrior wolf
Gunolf, Gunnulf, Gunulf

Gunther (German) A warrior
Guntur, Guenter, Guenther, Gunthir,
Gunthyr, Gunth, Gunthe, Gunterson,
Guntar, Gunter, Guntero, Gunthar,
Gunthor, Gunthur, Guntersen

Gunyon (American) A tough man
Gunyan, Gunyen, Gunyin, Gunyun

Gur (Hebrew) Resembling a lion cub
Guryon, Gurion, Guriel, Guriell, Guryel,
Guryell, Guri, Gurie, Guree, Gurea, Gury,
Gurey

Gure (African) A left-handed man

Gurpreet (Indian) A devoted follower
Gurpreat, Gurpriet, Gurpreit, Gurprit,
Gurpryt

Guru (Indian) A teacher; a religious head

Gurutz (Basque) Of the holy cross
Guruts

Gus (German) A respected man; one who is
exalted
Guss

Gustave (Scandinavian) Of the staff of
the gods
Gustaaf, Gustaf, Gustaff, Gustaof, Gustav,
Gustavo, Gustavus, Gustaw, Gustovo,
Gustus, Gusztav

Gusty (American) Of the wind; a revered
man
Gustey, Gustee, Gustea, Gusti, Gustie, Gusto

Guthrie (Gaelic) From the windy spot
Guthri, Guthry, Guthrey, Guthree,
Guthrea, Guth, Guthe

Guwayne (American) Form of Wayne,
meaning "one who builds wagons"
Guwayn, Guwain, Guwaine, Guwaen,
Guwaene, Guwane

Guy (German / Welsh / French) A warrior;
from the wood / a lively man / one who
acts as a guide
Gui, Guido, Guydo, Gye

Guyapi (Native American) One who is
frank; candid
Guyapie, Guyapy, Guyapey, Guyapee,
Guyapea

Guyon (English) A lively man
Guyen, Guyun, Guyan, Guyin

Guzet (American) One who puts on a
show of courage
Guzzet, Guzett, Guzzett, Guzzi, Guzzie,
Guzzy, Guzzey, Guzzee, Guzzea

Gwalchmai (Welsh) A battle hawk

Gwandoya (African) Suffering a miserable
fate

Gwern (Welsh) An old man
Gwerne, Gwirn, Gwirne, Gwyrn, Gwyrne

Gwill (American) Having dark eyes
Gwil, Gwyll, Gwyl, Gewill, Guwill,
Gewyll, Guwyll

Gwri (Celtic) The golden-haired boy
Gwrie, Gwree, Gwrea, Gwry, Gwrey

Gwydion (Welsh) In mythology, a magician
Gwydeon, Gwydionne, Gwydeonne

Gwynn (Welsh) A handsome man; one
who is fair
Gwynne, Gwyn, Gwen, Gwenn, Gwenne,
Gwin, Gwinn, Gwinne, Gwynedd,
Gwyned, Gwenedd, Gwened, Gwinedd,
Gwined, Gwynfor, Gwenfor, Gwinfor

Gyala (Hungarian) A youth

Gyan (Hindi) Having knowledge or wisdom
Gyandev

Gyasi (African) A superior man
Gyasie, Gyasy, Gyasey, Gyasee, Gyasea

Gylfi (Scandinavian) A king
Gylfie, Gylfee, Gylfea, Gylfi, Gylfie,
Gylphi, Gylphie, Gylphey, Gylphy,
Gylphee, Gylphea

Gypsy (English) A wanderer; a nomad
Gipsee, Gipsey, Gipsy, Gypsi, Gypsie,
Gypsey, Gypsee, Gipsi, Gipsie, Gipsea,
Gypsea

Gyth (American) An able-bodied man
Gythe, Gith, Githe

Gyula (Hungarian) One who is honored
Gyulah, Gyulla, Gyullah

Gyuszi (Hungarian) One who is youthful
Gyuszie, Gyuszy, Gyuszey, Gyuszee,
Gyuszea

Haas (Scandinavian) A good man

Habakkuk (Hebrew) One who embraces others
Habakuk, Habacuk, Habaccuk, Habacuc, Habackuc, Habacuck, Habaccuc

Haben (African) A proud man
Haban, Habin, Habyn, Habon, Habun

Habib (Arabic) One who is dearly loved
Habeeb, Habeab, Habieb, Habeib, Habyb, Habeyb

Habimama (African) One who believes in God
Habymama

Hache-Hi (Native American) Resembling a wolf

Hachiro (Japanese) The eighth-born son
Hachyro

Hackett (German) A little woodsman
Hacket, Hackitt, Hackit, Hakett, Haket

Hackman (French) A woodsman; a hewer of wood
Hackmann, Hakman, Hakmann, Hacman, Hacmann

Hadar (Hebrew) Glory and splendor; one who is respected
Hadur, Hader, Hador, Hadaram

Haddad (Arabic) A smith
Hadad

Hadden (English) From the heather-covered hill
Haddan, Haddon, Haddin, Haddyn, Haddun

Hadeon (Ukrainian) A destroyer
Hadion, Hadeyon, Hadiyon

Hades (Greek) In mythology, the god of the underworld
Hadies, Hadees, Hadiez, Hadeez

Hadi (Arabic) One who guides others along the right path
Hadie, Hady, Hadey, Hadee, Hadea

Hadley (English) From the heather meadow
Hadly, Hadleigh, Hadlee, Hadlea, Hadleah, Hadli, Hadlie, Haddy, Haddey, Haddee, Haddea, Haddi, Haddie

Hadrian (English) Form of Adrian, meaning "a man from Hadria"
Hade, Hadiran, Hadrain, Hadrean, Hadreean, Hadreyan, Hadreeyan, Hadriaan, Hadriano, Hadrien, Hadrin, Hadrino, Hadrion, Hadron, Hadryan, Hadya, Harjen, Haydrean, Haydreean, Haydrian, Haydrien, Hadrianus, Hadrianos

Hadriel (Hebrew) The splendor of God
Hadryel, Hadriell, Hadryell

Hadwin (English) A friend in war
Hadwinn, Hadwinne, Hadwen, Hadwenn, Hadwenne, Hadwyn, Hadwynn, Hadwynne, Hadwine, Hedwin, Hedwine, Hedwinn, Hedwinne, Hedwen, Hedwenn, Hedwenne, Hedwyn, Hedwynn, Hedwynne, Haethowine, Haethowin, Haethowen, Haethowyn

Hafiz (Arabic) A protector
Haafiz, Hafeez, Hafeaz, Hafiez, Hafeiz, Hafyz, Haphiz, Haaphiz, Hapheez, Hapheaz, Haphiez, Hapheiz, Haphyz

Hagar (Hebrew) A wanderer

Hagaward (English) The guardian of the hedged enclosure
Hagawerd

Hagen (Gaelic) One who is youthful
Haggen, Hagan, Haggan, Hagin, Haggin, Hagyn, Haggyn, Hagon, Haggon, Hagun, Haggun

Hagley (English) From the enclosed meadow
Hagly, Haglee, Haglea, Hagleah, Hagleigh, Hagli, Haglie, Hagaleah, Hagalea, Hagalee, Hagaleigh, Hagali, Hagalie, Hagaly, Hagaley

Hagop (Armenian) Form of James, meaning "he who supplants"
Hagup, Hagap, Hagep, Hagip, Hagyp

Hagos (African) Filled with happiness

Hahn (German) Resembling a rooster

Hahnee (Native American) A beggar
Hahnea, Hahni, Hahnie, Hahny, Hahney

Hai (Vietnamese) Of the river

Haiba (African) One who is charming
Haibah, Hayba, Haybah, Haeba, Haebah, Haba, Habah

Haidar (Arabic) Resembling a lion
Haider, Haydar, Hayder, Haedar, Haeder, Haidor, Haydor, Haedor, Haidur, Haydur, Haedur, Haidir, Haydir, Haedir, Haidyr, Haydyr, Haedyr

Haig (English) From the hedged enclosure
Haeg, Hayg

Haike (Asian) From the water

Haim (Hebrew) A giver of life
Hayim, Hayyim

Haines (English) From the vined cottage; from the hedged enclosure
Haynes, Haenes, Hanes, Haine, Hayne, Haene, Hane

Hajari (African) One who takes flight
Hajarie, Hajary, Hajarey, Hajaree, Hajarea

Haji (African) Born during the hajj
Hajie, Hajy, Hajey, Hajee, Hajea

Hajime (Japanese) Of the beginning

Hakan (Norse / Native American) One who is noble / a fiery man

Hakim (Arabic) One who is wise; intelligent
Hakeem, Hakeam, Hakeim, Hakiem, Hakym

Hako (Japanese) An honorable man

Hakon (Scandinavian) Of the chosen race; one who is exalted
Haaken, Haakin, Haakon, Hacon, Hackon, Haken, Hakin, Hakyn, Haakyn

Hal (English) Form of Henry, meaning "the ruler of the house"

Haland (English) From the island
Halande, Halland, Hallande

Halbert (English) A shining hero
Halberte, Halburt, Halburte, Halbirt, Halbirte, Halbyrt, Halbyrte, Halbart, Halbarte

Haldas (Greek) A dependable man

Halden (Scandinavian) A man who is half-Dane
Haldan, Haldane, Halfdan, Halfdane, Halvdan, Halfden, Halvden, Haldayne, Haldaene, Haldayn, Haldaen

Haldor (Scandinavian) Of the thunderous rock
Haldur, Halder, Haldar, Haldir, Haldyr

Hale (English) From the hall; a hero
Hail, Haile, Hayl, Hayle, Hael, Haele

Halen (Swedish) From the hall of light
Hallen, Hailen, Haylen, Haelen, Halan, Hailan, Haylan, Haelan, Halin, Haylin, Haelin, Hailin, Halyn, Haylyn, Hailyn, Haelyn, Halon, Haylon, Hailon, Haelon, Halun, Haylun, Hailun, Haelun

Haley (English) From the field of hay
Haly, Halee, Haleigh, Haleah, Halea, Hali, Halie, Hayley, Hayly, Haylee, Hayleigh, Hayleah, Haylea, Hayli, Haylie, Haeley, Haely, Haeleigh, Haeleah, Haelea, Haeli, Haelie, Hailey, Haily, Haileigh, Haileah, Hailea, Haili, Hailie

Halford (English) From the hall by the ford
Hallford, Halfurd, Hallfurd, Halferd, Hallferd

Halian (Native American) One who is youthful
Haliann, Halyan, Halyann, Halien, Halyen, Halienn, Halyenn

Halig (Anglo-Saxon) A holy man
Halyg

Haligwell (English) Form of Halliwell, meaning "from the holy spring"
Haygwell, Haligwel, Halygwel, Haligwiella

Halil (Turkish) A beloved friend
Haleel, Haleal, Haleil, Haliel, Halyl

Halim (Arabic) One who is gentle
Haleem, Haleam, Haleim, Haliem, Halym

Hall (English) From the manor
Heall

Halla (African) An unexpected gift
Hallah, Hala, Halah

Hallam (English) From the hills; from the rocks
Hallem, Hallim, Hallum, Hallom, Hallym

Hallberg (Norse) From the rocky mountain
Halberg, Hallburg, Halburg

Halle (Norse) As solid as a rock

Halley (English) From the hall near the meadow
Hally, Halli, Hallie, Halleigh, Hallee, Halleah, Hallea

Halliwell (English) From the holy spring
Hallewell, Hallowell, Helliwell, Halliwel, Hallewel, Hallowel, Helliwel, Hallwell, Haliwell, Haliwel, Halewell, Halewel, Halowell, Halowel, Heliwell, Heliwell, Hallwell, Halwell, Hallwel, Halwel, Holwell, Hollwell, Holwel, Hollwel

Hallward (English) The guardian of the hall
Halward, Hallwerd, Halwerd, Hallwarden, Halwarden, Hawarden, Haward, Hawerd

Halmer (English) A robust man
Halmar, Halmir, Halmyr, Halmor, Halmur

Halsey (English) From Hal's island
Halsy, Halsi, Halsie, Halsee, Halsea, Hallsey, Hallsy, Hallsi, Hallsie, Hallsee, Hallsea, Halcey, Halcy, Halcea, Halci, Halcie, Hallcey, Hallcy, Hallcee, Hallcea, Hallci, Hallcie, Halsig, Halsyg

Halstead (English) From the manor grounds
Hallstead, Hallsted, Halsted

Halton (English) From the manor on the hill
Hallton, Haltun, Halltun, Halten, Hallten, Halston, Halstun, Halsten, Hallston, Hallstun, Hallsten

Halvard (Norse) The guardian of the rock
Hallvard, Hallverd, Hallvor, Halvar, Halver, Halverd, Halvor

Halwende (Anglo-Saxon) One who is lonely
Hallwende, Halwendi, Hallwendi, Halwendie, Hallwendie, Halwendy, Hallwendy, Halwendey, Hallwendey, Halwendee, Hallwendee

Ham (Hebrew) One who produces heat
Hamaker, Hamu, Hamue, Hamou, Hamm, Hammu, Hammue, Hammou

Hamal (Arabic) Resembling a lamb
Hamahl, Hamall, Hamaal, Hamaahl

Hamar (Norse) One who wields a hammer
Hamer, Hamor, Hamur, Hamir, Hamyr

Hamden (Arabic) One who is praised
Hamdan, Hamdin, Hamdyn, Hamdon, Hamdun

Hamid (Arabic / Indian) A praiseworthy man / a beloved friend
Hameed, Hamead, Hameid, Hamied, Hamyd, Haamid

Hamidi (Swahili) One who is commendable
Hamidie, Hamidy, Hamidey, Hamidee, Hamidea, Hamydi, Hamydie, Hamydee, Hamydea, Hamydy, Hamydey, Hamedi, Hamedie, Hamedy, Hamedey, Hamedee, Hamedea, Hammad

Hamill (English) One who is scarred
Hamil, Hamel, Hamell, Hamyll, Hamyl, Hammill, Hammil

Hamilton (English) From the flat-topped hill
Hamylton, Hamiltun, Hamyltun, Hamilten, Hamylten, Hamelton, Hameltun, Hamelten, Hamilston, Hamilstun, Hamelston, Hamelstun

Hamish (Scottish) Form of James, meaning "he who supplants"
Haymish, Haemish, Haimish, Hamesh, Haymesh, Haemesh, Haimesh

Hamlet (German) From the little home
Hamlett, Hammet, Hammett, Hamnet, Hamnett, Hamlit, Hamlitt, Hamoelet

Hamlin (German) The little home-lover
Hamlyn, Hamblin, Hamelin, Hamlen, Hamlan, Hamlon, Hamlun, Hamelen, Hamelan, Hamelyn, Hamelon, Hamelun

Hammer (German) One who makes hammers; a carpenter
Hammar, Hammor, Hammur, Hammir, Hammyr

Hammond (German) The protector of the home
Hammund, Hammend, Hammand, Hammind, Hammynd, Hamond, Hamund, Hamend, Hamand, Hamind, Hamynd

Hamon (Scandinavian) A great leader
Hamun, Hamen, Haman, Hamin, Hamyn

Hampden (English) From the home in the valley
Hampdon, Hampdan, Hampdun, Hampdyn, Hampdin

Hampton (English) From the home town
Hamptun, Hampten, Hamptan, Hamptin,
Hamptyn, Hamp, Hampe

Hamza (Arabic) Having great strength
Hamzah, Hammza, Hammzah

Han (German) A gift from God
Hann, Hano, Hanno

Hanan (Hebrew) Of God's grace
Hananel, Hanenel, Hananell, Hanenell,
Hanania, Hananiah

Hanani (Arabic) One who is merciful
Hananie, Hanany, Hananey, Hananee,
Hananea

Hancock (English) One who owns a farm
Hancok, Hancoc

Hand (English) A hardworking man
Hande, Handy, Handey, Handi, Handie,
Handea, Handee

Ha-Neul (Korean) Of the sky

Hanford (English) From the high ford
Hanferd, Hanfurd, Hanforde, Hanferde,
Hanfurde

Hani (Arabic) Filled with joy
Hanie, Hany, Haney, Hanee, Hanea

Hania (Native American) A spirit warrior
Haniah, Hanya, Hanyah, Haniya, Haniyah

Hanif (Arabic) A true believer of Islam
Haneef, Haneaf, Haneif, Hanief, Hanyf

Hanisi (Swahili) Born on a Thursday
Hanisie, Hanisy, Hanisey, Hanisee,
Hanisea, Hanysi, Hanysie, Hanysy,
Hanysey, Hanysee, Hanysea

Hank (English) Form of Henry, meaning
"the ruler of the house"
Hanke, Hanks, Hanki, Hankie, Hankee,
Hankea, Hanky, Hankey

Hanley (English) From the high meadow
Hanly, Hanleigh, Hanleah, Hanlea,
Hanlie, Hanli, Handlea, Handleigh,
Handley, Handleah, Handly, Handlie,
Handli

Hanna (Arabic) Form of John, meaning
"God is gracious"
Hannah, Hana, Hanah

Hannan (Arabic) Having warm feelings
Hannen, Hannon, Hannun, Hannin,
Hannyn

Hannibal (Hebrew) Having the grace of Baal
Hanibal, Hanniball, Haniball, Hannybal,
Hanybal, Hannyball, Hanyball

Hanoch (Hebrew) One who is dedicated
Hanock, Hanok, Hanoc

Hanraoi (Irish) Form of Henry, meaning
"the ruler of the house"

Hans (Scandinavian) Form of John, mean-
ing "God is gracious"
Hanz, Hannes, Hanns, Hansel, Hanss,
Hanzel, Hons, Hansa, Hanza

Hanson (Scandinavian) The son of Hans
Hansen, Hanssen, Hansson, Hansun,
Hanssun

Hansraj (Hindi) The swan king

Hanuman (Indian) The monkey god
Hanumant, Hanumanth, Hanumane,
Hanumante, Hanumanthe

Hao (Vietnamese) A good man

Happy (American) Filled with joy
Happey, Happi, Happie, Happee, Happea

Haqq (Arabic) A truthful man
Haq

Harac (English) From the ancient oak tree
Harak, Harack

Harailt (Scottish) Form of Harold, mean-
ing "the ruler of an army"
Haraylt, Haraelt, Haralt, Haraild, Harayld,
Haraeld

Harb (Arabic) A war
Harbe

Harbin (French) A bright warrior
Harben, Harbyn, Harbon, Harbun,
Harban, Harbi, Harbie, Harbee, Harbea,
Harby, Harbey

Harcourt (French) From the fortified farm
Harcourte, Harcort, Harcorte

Harden (English) From the hare's valley
Hardan, Hardin, Hardyn, Hardon, Hardun

Hardik (Indian) One who has heart
Hardyk, Hardick, Hardyck, Hardic, Hardyc

Harding (English) The son of the courageous one
Hardyng, Hardinge, Hardynge

Hardwick (English) From the courageous
man's settlement
*Harwick, Hardwyck, Harwyck, Hardwik,
Harwik, Hardwyk, Harwyk*

Hardwin (English) A courageous friend
*Hardwinn, Hardwinne, Hardwen,
Hardwenn, Hardwenne, Hardwine,
Hardwyn, Hardwynn, Hardwynne*

Hardy (German) One who is bold and
courageous
Hardey, Hardi, Hardie, Hardee, Hardea

Hare (English) Resembling a rabbit

Harean (African) One who is aware; alert
*Hareane, Harian, Hariane, Haryan,
Haryane*

Harel (Hebrew) From the mountain of God
*Haral, Haril, Haryl, Harol, Harul, Harell,
Harrell, Harall, Harrall, Haroll, Harroll,
Harull, Harrull, Harill, Harrill, Haryll,
Harryll*

Harelache (English) From the hare's lake
*Harlache, Harelach, Harlach, Harelock,
Harlock, Harelocke, Harlocke, Harlak,
Harelak, Harlake, Harelake*

Harence (English) One who is swift
*Harince, Harense, Harinse, Harynce,
Harynse*

Harford (English) From the hare's ford
*Harforde, Harrford, Harrforde, Harfurd,
Harfurde, Harrfurd, Harrfurde, Harferd,
Harferde, Harrferd, Harrferde, Haraford,
Haraferd, Harafurd*

Hargrove (English) From the hare's grove
Hargrave, Hargreaves

Hari (Indian) Resembling a lion
Harie, Hary, Harey, Haree, Harea

Harim (Arabic) A superior man
*Hareem, Haream, Hariem, Hareim,
Harym*

Hariman (German) One who is protective
Harimann, Haryman, Harymann

Harith (African) A cultivator; a provider
*Harithe, Haryth, Harythe, Hareth,
Harethe*

Harkin (Irish) Having dark red hair
*Harkyn, Harken, Harkan, Harkon,
Harkun*

Harlan (English) From the army
*Harlen, Harlon, Harlun, Harlin, Harlyn,
Harlenn, Harlinn, Harlynn, Harlann,
Harlonn, Harlunn, Harland*

Harlemm (American) A soulful man
*Harlam, Harlom, Harlim, Harlym,
Harlem*

Harley (English) From the meadow of
the hares
*Harlea, Harlee, Harleen, Harleigh,
Harlene, Harlie, Harli, Harly, Harleah,
Harlean, Haraleigh, Haralee, Haralea,
Haraleah, Harali, Haralie, Haraly, Haraley*

Harlow (English) From the army on the hill
Harlowe, Harlo, Harloe

Harman (French) A soldier
*Harmann, Harmen, Harmon, Harmonn,
Harmenn*

Harmony (English) Unity; musically in
tune
*Harmonie, Harmoni, Harmonee,
Harmonia, Harmoney, Harmonea,
Harmonio*

Harod (Hebrew) A heroic man; in the
Bible, a king
Harrod, Herod, Herrod

Harold (Scandinavian) The ruler of an
army
*Harald, Haralds, Harolda, Haroldo,
Heraldo, Herald, Herold, Herrold*

Harper (English) One who plays or makes
harps
*Harpur, Harpar, Harpir, Harpyr, Harpor,
Hearpere*

Harpo (American) A cheerful man
Harpoe, Harpow, Harpowe, Harpoh

Harrington (English) From of Harry's
town; from the herring town
*Harringtun, Harryngton, Harryngtun,
Harington, Haringtun, Haryngton,
Haryntun*

Harrison (English) The son of Harry
Harrisson, Harris, Harriss, Harrisun,
Harryson, Harrysun, Harrys, Harryss

Harry (English) Form of Harold, meaning
"the ruler of an army"; form of Henry,
meaning "the ruler of the house"
Harri, Harrie, Harrey, Harree, Harrea

Harshad (Indian) A bringer of joy
Harsh, Harshe, Harsho, Harshil, Harshyl,
Harshit, Harshyt

Hart (English) Resembling a stag
Harte, Heort, Heorot

Hartford (English) From the stag's ford
Harteford, Hartferd, Harteferd, Hartfurd,
Hartefurd, Hartforde, Harteforde, Hartferde,
Harteferde, Hartfurde, Hartefurde

Harti (German) One who is daring
Hartie, Harty, Hartey, Hartee, Hartea

Hartley (English) From the stag's meadow
Hartly, Hartli, Hartlie, Hartleigh, Hartlea,
Hartleah, Hartlee

Hartman (German) A hard and strong man
Hartmann, Hartmen, Hartmon, Hartmun,
Hartmin, Hartmyn

Hartun (English) From the gray estate
Harton, Harten, Hartan, Hartin, Hartyn

Hartwell (English) From the stag's spring
Hartewell, Hartwel, Hartewel, Hartwill,
Hartewill, Hartwil, Hartewil, Harwell,
Harwel, Harwill, Harwil, Heortwiella,
Heortweill

Hartwig (German) One who is brave
during battle

Hartwood (English) From the stag's forest
Hartwode, Hartewood, Hartewode,
Heortwode, Heortwood

Haru (Japanese) Born during the spring

Haruki (Japanese) One who shines brightly
Harukie, Haruky, Harukey, Harukee,
Harukea

Haruko (Japanese) The firstborn child

Harun (Arabic) A superior man; one who
is exalted
Haroun, Harune, Haroune, Haroon,
Haroone

Haruni (African) A mountaineer
Harunie, Haruny, Haruney, Harunee,
Harunea

Harvard (English) The guardian of the
home
Harverd, Harvord, Harvurd, Harvird,
Harvyrd, Havard, Haverd, Havord,
Havurd, Havird, Havyrd

Harvey (English / French) One who is
ready for battle / a strong man
Harvy, Harvi, Harvie, Harvee, Harvea,
Harv, Harve, Hervey, Hervy, Hervi, Hervie,
Hervee, Hervea, Harvae, Herve

Harwin (English) A friend of the hare
Harwinn, Harwinne, Harwen, Harwenn,
Harwenne, Harwyn, Harwynn,
Harwynne

Harwood (English) From the hare's forest
Harewood, Harwode, Harewode

Hasad (Turkish) The harvester

Hasdai (Aramaic) A good man
Hasday, Hasdaye, Hasdae

Hashim (Arabic) The destroyer of evil
Hasheem, Hasheam, Hashiem, Hasheim,
Hashym

Hasim (Arabic) One who is decisive
Haseem, Haseam, Hasiem, Haseim,
Hasym

Hasin (Arabic) A handsome man
Haseen, Hasean, Hasein, Hasien, Hasyn

Haskel (Hebrew) An intelligent man
Haskle, Haskell, Haskil, Haskill, Haske,
Hask

Haslett (English) From the hazel-tree head-
land
Haslet, Haslit, Haslitt, Hazel, Hazlett,
Hazlet, Hazlitt, Hazlit, Haslyt, Haslytt,
Hazlyt, Hazlytt

Hassan (Arabic) A handsome man
Hassaun, Hassawn, Hasan, Hasani,
Hasanie, Hasany, Hasaney, Hasanee,
Hasanea, Hassain

Hasso (German) Of the sun
Hassoe, Hassow, Hassowe

Hassun (Native American) As solid as a
stone

H

Hastiin (Native American) A man

Hastin (Hindi) Resembling an elephant
Hasteen, Hastean, Hastien, Hastein, Hastyn

Hastings (English) Son of the stern and grave man
Hasting, Hastyngs, Hastyng, Hasti, Hastie, Hasty, Hastey, Hastee, Hastea

Hatim (Arabic) A judge; one who is determined
Hateem, Hateam, Hateim, Hatiem, Hatym

Hattan (American) From Manhattan; a sophisticated man
Hatten, Hattin, Hattyn, Hatton, Hattun

Hau (Vietnamese) One who is bold

Havelock (Scandinavian) One who takes part in a sea battle
Havlock, Havelocke, Havlocke

Haven (English) One who provides sanctuary; shelter
Havan, Havin, Havyn, Havon, Havun, Haeven, Haevon, Haevin, Haevyn, Haevan, Haevun, Haiven, Haivan, Haivin, Haivyn, Haivon, Haivun, Haefen, Hayven, Hayvan, Hayvon, Hayvun, Hayvin, Hayvyn

Hawaii (Hawaiian) From the homeland; from the state of Hawaii

Hawes (English) From the hedged place
Haws, Hayes, Hays, Hazin, Hazen, Hazyn, Hazon, Hazan, Hazun

Hawiovi (Native American) One who descends on a ladder
Hawiovie, Hawiovy, Hawiovey, Hawiovee, Hawiovea

Hawk (English) Resembling the bird of prey
Hawke, Hauk, Hauke

Hawkins (English) Resembling a small hawk
Haukins, Hawkyns, Haukyn

Hawley (English) From the hedged meadow
Hawly, Hawleigh, Hawlea, Hawleah, Hawli, Hawlie, Hawlee

Hawthorne (English) From the hawthorn tree
Hawthorn

Hayden ⚉ ⦿ (English) From the hedged valley
Haydan, Haydon, Haydun, Haydin, Haydyn, Haden, Hadan, Hadon, Hadun, Hadin, Hadyn, Haiden, Haidan, Haidin, Haidyn, Haidon, Haidun, Haeden, Haedan, Haedin, Haedyn, Haedon, Haedun, Haydn, Haidn, Haedn, Hadn

Haye (Scottish) From the stockade
Hay, Hae, Hai

Haytham (Arabic) Resembling a young hawk
Haythem, Haitham, Haithem, Haetham, Haethem, Hatham, Hathem

Hayward (English) The guardian of the hedged area
Haywerd, Haiward, Haiwerd, Haeward, Haewerd, Hayword, Haiword, Haeword

Haywood (English) From the hedged forest
Haywode, Haiwood, Haiwode, Haewood, Haewode

Hazaiah (Hebrew) God will decide
Hazaia, Haziah, Hazia

Hazard (French) One who takes chances; having luck
Hazzard, Hazerd, Hazzerd

Hazleton (English) From the hazel-tree town
Hazelton, Hazletun, Hazelton, Hazleten, Hazelten

Hazlewood (English) From the hazel-tree forest
Hazelwood, Hazlewode, Hazelwode

Heath (English) From the untended land of flowering shrubs
Heathe, Heeth, Heethe

Heathcliff (English) From the cliff near the heath
Heathecliff, Heathclyff, Heatheclyff, Heathclif, Heathclyf, Heatheclif, Heatheclyf, Hetheclif, Hethecliff, Hetheclyf, Hetheclyff

Heathden (English) From the heath
Heathdan, Heathdon, Heathdin, Heathdyn, Heathdun

Heathley (English) From the heath meadow
Heathly, Heathleigh, Heathlea, Heathleah, Heathli, Heathlie, Heathlee

Heaton (English) From the town on high ground
Heatun, Heeton, Heetun, Heaten, Heeten

Heber (Hebrew) A partner or companion
Heeber, Hebar, Heebar, Hebor, Heebor, Hebur, Heebur, Hebir, Heebir, Hebyr, Heebyr

Hector (Greek) One who is steadfast; in mythology, the prince of Troy
Hecter, Hectur, Hectar, Hectir, Hectyr, Hektor, Hekter, Hektar, Hektir, Hektyr, Hektur, Hecktor, Hecktar, Heckter, Hecktur, Hecktir, Hecktyr, Heitor

Heddwyn (Welsh) One who is peaceful and fair
Heddwynn, Hedwyn, Hedwynn, Heddwen, Heddwenn, Hedwen, Hedwenn, Heddwin, Heddwinn, Hedwin, Hedwinn

Hedeon (Russian) One who fells trees
Hedion, Hedyon, Hedeyon, Hediyon

Hedley (English) From the meadow of heather
Hedly, Hedlie, Hedli, Hedleigh, Hedlea, Hedleah, Hedlee, Headleigh, Headley, Headly, Headlea, Headleah, Headli, Headlie, Headlee

Heer (Indian) Resembling a diamond

Hegarty (Irish) One who is unjust
Hegartey, Hegartee, Hegartea, Hegarti, Hegartie

Hei (Korean) Of grace

Heikki (Finnish) Form of Henry, meaning "the ruler of the house"
Heiki, Heicki, Heicci, Heici

Heimdall (Norse) The white god; in mythology, one of the founders of the human race
Heimdal, Heiman, Heimann

Heinrich (German) Form of Henry, meaning "the ruler of the house"
Heinrick, Heinric, Heinrik, Heine, Heini, Heinie, Heiny, Heiney, Heinee, Heinea, Heimrich, Heimrick, Heimric, Heimrik

Heinz (German) Form of Hans, meaning "God is gracious"
Heins, Hines, Hein, Hine, Heiner, Heinlich, Hynes, Hynz

Heladio (Spanish) A man who was born in Greece
Heladeo, Heladiyo, Heladeyo, Helado

Helaku (Native American) Born on a sunny day
Helakue, Helakou

Helgi (Norse) One who is productive and happy
Helgie, Helgy, Helgey, Helgee, Helgea, Helge, Helje, Helji, Heljie, Heljy, Heljey, Heljee, Heljea

Helio (Greek) Son of the sun
Heleo, Helios, Heleos

Helki (Native American) To touch
Helkie, Helky, Helkey, Helkee, Helkea, Hekli, Heklie, Hekly, Hekley, Heklee, Heklea, Hekleigh

Heller (German) Of the sun; one who is bright or brilliant
Hellar, Hellor, Hellur, Hellir, Hellyr, Helly, Helley, Helli, Hellie, Hellee, Hellea, Helleigh

Helmer (Teutonic) A warrior's wrath
Helmar, Helmor, Helmir, Helmyr, Helmur

Helmut (French) One who is protected
Helmot, Helmet, Helmat, Helmit, Helmyt, Helmuth, Helmuthe, Helmutt, Helmett, Helmatt, Helmitt, Helmytt, Helmott, Hellmut, Hellmat, Hellmet, Hellmit, Hellmyt, Hellmot, Helmond, Hellmond, Helmund, Hellmund, Helmand, Hellmand

Hem (Indian) The golden son

Hemadri (Indian) Of the Himalaya
Hemadrie, Hemadree, Hemadrea, Hemadry, Hemadrey

Heman (Hebrew) A faithful man
Hemann, Hemen, Hemenn

Hemendra (Indian) A wealthy man
Hemindra, Hemyndra

Hemendu (Indian) Born beneath the golden moon
Hemendue, Hemendoo, Hemendou

Hemi (Maori) Form of James, meaning "he who supplants"
Hemie, Hemy, Hemee, Hemea, Hemey

Henderson (Scottish) The son of Henry
Hendrie, Hendries, Hendron, Hendri, Hendry, Hendrey, Hendree, Hendrea, Henryson, Hendersun, Henrysun, Hendrun, Henson, Hensun, Hender, Hend, Hensen

Hendrick (English) Form of Henry, meaning "the ruler of the house"
Hendryck, Hendrik, Hendryk, Hendric, Hendryc

Henley (English) From the high meadow
Henly, Henleigh, Henlea, Henleah, Henlee, Henli, Henlie

Henning (Scandinavian) Form of Henry, meaning "the ruler of the house"
Hening, Hennyng, Henyng, Hemming, Heming, Hemmyng, Hemyng

Henry ✪ (German) The ruler of the house
Henri, Henrie, Henrey, Henree, Henrea, Henrick, Henrik, Henrique, Henryk, Henryck, Henryc, Henric, Henning, Hening, Hennyng, Henyng

Heolstor (Anglo-Saxon) Of the darkness
Heolster, Heolstir, Heolstur, Heolstyr, Heolstar

Heorhiy (Ukrainian) A farmer; one who works the earth

Heraldo (Spanish) Of the divine

Herbert (German) An illustrious warrior
Herbirt, Herburt, Harbert, Harbirt, Harburt, Heribert, Heriberto, Herb, Herbi, Herbie, Herbee, Herbea, Herby, Herbey, Herbst

Hercules (Greek) In mythology, a son of Zeus who possessed superhuman strength
Herakles, Hercule, Herculi, Herculie, Herculy, Herculey, Herculee, Herculea, Herculeigh, Herkules, Herckules, Herkuel, Hercuel

Heremon (Gaelic) Form of Irving, meaning "a friend of the sea"
Hereman, Heremen, Heremun, Heremin, Heremyn

Hererinc (Anglo-Saxon) A hero
Hererink, Hererinck, Hererync, Hererynk, Hererynck

Heretoga (Anglo-Saxon) A commander or ruler

Herman (German) A soldier
Hermon, Hermen, Hermun, Hermin, Hermyn, Hermann, Hermie, Herminio, Hermi, Hermy, Hermey, Hermee, Hermea

Hermes (Greek) In mythology, the messenger of the gods
Hermus, Hermos, Hermis, Hermys, Hermilo, Hermite, Hermez

Hermod (Scandinavian) One who welcomes others

Hernando (Spanish) A bold adventurer
Hernandez, Hernan

Herndon (English) From the heron's valley
Hernden, Herndan, Herndin, Herndyn, Herndun

Herne (English) Resembling a heron
Hern, Hearn, Hearne

Hernley (English) From the heron's meadow
Hernly, Hernleigh, Hernlee, Hernlea, Hernleah, Hernli, Hernlie

Hero (Greek) The brave defender
Heroe, Herow, Herowe

Herodotus (Greek) The father of history
Herodotos, Herodotius, Herodotios

Herrick (German) A war leader or ruler
Herric, Herrik, Herryck, Herryc, Herryk

Hershel (Hebrew) Resembling a deer
Hersch, Herschel, Herschell, Hersh, Hertzel, Herzel, Herzl, Heschel, Heshel, Hirsch, Hirschel, Hirschl, Hirsh, Hirsche, Hirshe, Hershey, Hershy, Hershi, Hershie, Hershee, Hershea, Herzon, Herzun, Herzan, Herzin, Herzyn, Herzen

Hertz (German) My strife

Herwin (Teutonic) A friend of war
Herwinn, Herwinne, Herwen, Herwenn, Herwenne, Herwyn, Herwynn, Herwynne

Hesed (Hebrew) A kind man

Hesperos (Greek) Born beneath the evening star
Hesperus, Hesperios, Hespero, Hesperius

Hessel (Dutch) One who is bold
Hessle, Hess, Hes

Hesutu (Native American) A rising yellow-jacket nest
Hesutou, Hesoutou

Hevataneo (Native American)
A hairy rope
Hevatanio, Hevataneyo, Hevataniyo

Hevel (Hebrew) A life source; breath
Hevell, Hevle

Hewett (French) The small intelligent one
Hewet, Hewie, Hewitt, Hewlett, Hewit, Hewlet, Hewlitt, Hewlit, Hewi, Hewy, Hewey, Hewee, Hewea

Hewney (Irish) Refers to the color green; one who is innocent
Hewny, Hewni, Hewnie, Hewnea, Hewnee

Hewson (English) The son of Hugh
Hewsun

Heywood (English) Form of Haywood, meaning "from the hedged forest"
Heywode

Hezekiah (Hebrew) God is my strength
Hezekia, Hezekyah, Hezekya, Hezeki, Hezekie, Hezekea, Hezekee, Hezeky, Hezekey

Hiamovi (Native American) The high chief
Hiamovie, Hiamovy, Hiamovey, Hiamovee, Hiamovea

Hiawatha (Native American) He who makes rivers
Hiawathah, Hyawatha, Hiwatha, Hywatha

Hickey (Irish) One who heals others
Hicky, Hickee, Hickea, Hicki, Hickie

Hickok (American) A famous frontier marshal
Hickock, Hickoc, Hikock, Hikoc, Hikok, Hyckok, Hyckock, Hyckoc, Hykoc, Hykok, Hykock

Hidalgo (Spanish) The noble one
Hydalgo

Hideaki (Japanese) A clever man; having wisdom
Hideakie, Hideaky, Hideakey, Hideakee, Hideakea

Hideo (Japanese) A superior man
Hideyo, Hydeo

Hien (Vietnamese) A gentle and kind man

Hieremias (Hebrew) God will uplift
Hieremeas, Hyeremias, Hyeremeas

Hiero (Irish) The name of a sain
Hyero

Hieronim (Polish) Form of Jerome, meaning "of the sacred name"
Hieronym, Hieronymos, Hieronimos, Heronim, Heronym, Heronymos, Heronimos

Hietamaki (Finnish) From the sand hill
Hietamakie, Hietamaky, Hietamakey, Hietamakee, Hietamakea

Hieu (Vietnamese) A pious man

Hifz (Arabic) One who is memorable
Hyfz

Higgins (Irish) An intelligent man
Hyggins, Higins, Hygins, Higgyns, Hyggyns, Higyns, Hygyns

Higinio (Spanish) A forceful man
Higineo, Higiniyo, Higineyo

Hikmat (Islamic) Filled with wisdom
Hykmat

Hilary (Greek) A cheerful woman; bringer of joy
Hillary, Hilaree, Hilarie, Hilarey, Hilari, Hillari, Hillarie, Hillaree, Hillarey, Hillory, Hilaire, Hilorio, Hilery, Hillery, Hiliary, Hiliarie, Hylary, Hylarie, Hylari, Hylarey, Hylaree, Hyllari, Hyllary, Hilaeiro, Hiolair, Hillarea, Hylarea, Hyllarea, Hilarea, Helario, Hilaire, Hilar, Hilarid, Hilarius, Hilario, Hilarion

Hildebrand (German) One who wields a battle sword
Hyldebrand, Hildbrand, Hyldbrand, Hildehrand, Hildhrand, Hyldehrand, Hyldhrand, Hildebrant, Hyldebrant, Hildbrant, Hyldbrant

Hildefuns (German) One who is ready for battle
Hildfuns, Hyldefuns, Hyldfuns

Hilderinc (Anglo-Saxon) A warrior
Hilderink, Hilderinch, Hilderinck, Hilderync, Hilderynck, Hilderynch, Hilderynk

Hillel (Hebrew) One who is praised
Hyllel, Hillell, Hyllell, Hilel, Hylel, Hilell, Hylell

Hilliard (German) A defender or guardian during war
Hillyard, Hillierd, Hillyerd, Hillier, Hillyer, Hylliard, Hyllierd, Hyllyard, Hyllyerd, Hillard, Hillerd

Hillock (English) From the small hill
Hillok, Hilloc, Hillocke, Hilloke, Hill, Hille, Hilli, Hillie, Hilly, Hilley, Hillee, Hillea, Hilleigh

Hilton (English) From the town on the hill
Hillton, Hiltun, Hilltun, Helton, Hellton, Heltun, Helltun, Hilten, Hillten, Helten, Hellten

Himesh (Indian) The snow king
Himeshe, Hymesh, Hymeshe

Hinto (Native American) Refers to the color blue
Hintoe, Hynto, Hyntoe

Hippocrates (Greek) A great philosopher
Hyppocrates, Hipocrates, Hypocrates

Hippolyte (Greek) Of the stampeding horses
Hippolytos, Hippolit, Hippolitos, Hippolytus, Hyppolytos, Hyppolyte, Hyppolit, Hippolitus

Hiram (Hebrew) My brother has been exalted
Hirom, Hirum, Hirem, Hyram, Hyrom, Hyrum, Hyrem

Hiramatsu (Japanese) One who is exalted

Hiranmay (Indian) The golden one
Hiranmaye, Hiranmai, Hiranmae, Hyranmay, Hyranmaye, Hyranmai, Hyranmae

Hiro (Japanese) A giving man
Hyro

Hiromasa (Japanese) One who is open-minded and just
Hyromasa

Hiroshi (Japanese) A generous man
Hiroshie, Hiroshy, Hiroshey, Hiroshee, Hiroshea, Hyroshi, Hyroshie, Hyroshey, Hyroshy, Hyroshee, Hyroshea

Hirsi (African) An amulet
Hirsie, Hirsy, Hirsey, Hirsee, Hirsea

Hirza (Hebrew) Resembling a deer
Hyrza, Hirzah, Hyrzah

Hisham (Arabic) A generous man
Hysham, Hishem, Hyshem

Hisoka (Japanese) One who is secretive
Hysoka, Hisokie, Hysokie, Hisoki, Hysoki, Hisokey, Hysokey, Hisoky, Hysoky, Hisokee, Hysokee, Hisokea, Hysokea

Hitakar (Indian) One who wishes others well
Hitakarin, Hitakrit

Hitesh (Indian) A good man
Hiteshe, Hytesh, Hyteshe

Hjalmar (Norse) One who wears an army helmet
Hjalmarr, Hjalamar, Hjallmar, Hjalamarr, Hjalmer, Hjalamer, Hjalmerr, Hjalamerr, Hjallmer

Ho (Chinese) A good man

Hoai (Vietnamese) For eternity; always

Hoang (Vietnamese) The phoenix

Hoashis (Japanese) Of God
Hoashys

Hobart (American) Form of Hubert, meaning "having a shining intellect"
Hobarte, Hoebart, Hoebarte, Hobert, Hoberte, Hoburt, Hoburte, Hobirt, Hobirte, Hobyrt, Hobyrte, Hobard, Hobi, Hobie, Hoby, Hobey, Hobee, Hobea, Hobbard

Hobbes (English) Form of Robert, meaning "one who is bright with fame"
Hobbs, Hob, Hobs, Hobbi, Hobbie, Hobby, Hobbey, Hobbee, Hobbea

Hobson (English) The son of Robert
Hobsen, Hobsun, Hobsin, Hobsyn, Hobsan, Hobbson, Hobbsun, Hobbsen, Hobbsan, Hobbsin, Hobbsyn

Hoc (Vietnamese) A studious man

Hockley (English) From the high meadow
Hockly, Hocklee, Hockleigh, Hocklea, Hockleah, Hockli, Hocklie

Hockney (English) From the high island
Hockny, Hocknee, Hockneigh, Hocknea, Hockni, Hocknie

Hodge (English) Form of Roger, meaning "a famous spearman"
Hoge, Hodges, Hoges, Hodger, Hoger, Hodgi, Hodgie, Hodgey, Hodgy, Hodgee, Hodgea

Hodgson (English) The son of Roger
Hodgsen, Hodgsin, Hodgsyn, Hodgsan, Hodgsun

Hodson (English) The son of the hooded man
Hodsun, Hodsen, Hodsan, Hodsin, Hodsyn, Hodeson

Hoffman (German) A courtier
Hoffmann, Hofman, Hofmann, Hoffmen, Hofmen

Hogan (Gaelic) One who is youthful
Hogen, Hogin, Hogyn, Hogun, Hogon

Hohberht (German) One who is high and bright
Hohbert, Hohburt, Hohbirt, Hohbyrt, Hoh

Hoireabard (Irish) A soldier

Hojar (American) Having a wild spirit
Hogar, Hobar, Hodar

Hok'ee (Native American) One who has been abandoned

Holbrook (English) From the hollow near the stream
Holbrooke

Holcomb (English) From the deep valley
Holcom, Holcombe

Holden (English) From the hollow in the valley
Holdan, Holdin, Holdyn, Holdon, Holdun

Holder (English) One who is muscially talented
Holdar, Holdor, Holdur, Holdir, Holdyr

Holic (Czech) A barber
Holyc, Holick, Holyck, Holik, Holyk

Holiday (American) Born on a festive day
Holliday, Holidaye, Hollidaye, Holidai, Hollidai, Holidae, Hollidae

Holland (American) From the Netherlands
Hollend, Hollind, Hollynd, Hollande, Hollende, Hollinde, Hollynde

Holleb (Polish) Resembling a dove
Hollab, Hollob, Hollub, Hollib, Hollyb

Hollis (English) From the holly tree
Hollys, Holliss, Hollyss, Hollace, Hollice, Holli, Hollie, Holly, Holley, Hollee, Hollea, Holleigh, Hollyce, Hollister, Hollistar, Hollistir, Hollistyr, Hollistur, Hollistor

Hollywood (American) One who is cocky; one who is flashy
Holliwood, Holliewood

Holman (English) A man from the valley
Holmann, Holmen, Holmin, Holmyn, Holmon, Holmun

Holmes (English) From the river island
Holmmes, Holm, Holme, Holms, Hulmes, Hulmmes, Hulm, Hulme, Hulms

Holt (English) From the forest
Holte, Holyt, Holyte, Holter, Holtar, Holtor, Holtur, Holtir, Holtyr

Homain (American) A homebody
Homaine, Homayn, Homayne, Homaen, Homaene, Homane

Homer (Greek) Of the pledge; an epic poet
Homar, Homere, Homero, Homeros, Homerus, Hohmer, Hohmar

Honani (Native American) Resembling a badger
Honanie, Honany, Honaney, Honanee, Honanea

Honaw (Native American) Resembling a bear
Honawe, Honau

Honcho (American) A leader
Honchi, Honchey, Honchee, Honchea, Honchie, Honchy, Honche, Honch

Hondo (African) A warring man
Hondoh, Honda, Hondah

Honesto (Spanish) One who is honest
Honestio, Honestiyo, Honesteo, Honesteyo, Honestoh

Hong (Vietnamese) Refers to the color red

Honi (Hebrew) A gracious man
Honie, Honey, Hony, Honee, Honea

Honiahaka (Native American) Resembling a little wolf

Honnesh (Indian) A wealthy man
Honneshe, Honesh, Honeshe

Honon (Native American) Resembling a bear
Honun, Honen, Honan, Honin, Honyn

Honoré (Latin) One who is honored
Honord, Honorius, Honorios, Honoratus, Honoratos, Honore, Honorato, Honoray, Honoraye, Honorae, Honorai

Honovi (Native American) Having great strength
Honovie, Honovy, Honovey, Honovee, Honovea

Hont (Hungarian) One who breeds dogs
Honte

Honza (Czech) A gift from God

Hooker (English) A shepherd
Hookar, Hookor, Hookur, Hookir, Hookyr

Hooper (English) One who makes hoops for barrels
Hoopar, Hoopor, Hoopur, Hoopir, Hoopyr

Hopkins (Welsh) The son of Robert
Hopkin, Hopkinson, Hopkyns, Hopper, Hoppner, Hopkyn, Hopkynson, Hopkinsen, Hopkynsen

Horace (Latin) The keeper of time
Horacio, Horatio, Horatius, Horaz, Horase, Horice, Horise, Horate, Horaysho, Horashio, Horasheo, Horado, Horatiu

Horsley (English) From the horse meadow
Horsly, Horslea, Horsleah, Horslee, Horsleigh, Horsli, Horslie

Horst (German) From the thicket
Horste, Horsten, Horstan, Horstin, Horstyn, Horston, Horstun, Horstman, Horstmen, Horstmon, Horstmun, Horstmin, Horstmyn

Hortense (Latin) A gardener
Hortence, Hortus, Hortensius, Hortensios

Horton (English) From the gray town
Hortun, Horten, Hortan, Hortin, Hortyn

Horus (Egyptian) In mythology, the god of light

Hosaam (Arabic) A handsome man
Hosam

Hosea (Hebrew) One who reaches salvation
Hoshea, Hoseia, Hosheia, Hosi, Hosie, Hosy, Hosey, Hosee, Hosaya

Hoshi (Japanese) Resembling a star
Hoshiko, Hoshyko, Hoshie, Hoshee, Hoshea, Hoshy, Hoshey

Hosni (Arabic) A superior man
Hosnie, Hosney, Hosny, Hosnee, Hosnea

Hotah (Native American) A white-skinned man; a white-haired man

Hototo (Native American) One who whistles; a warrior spirit that sings

Houerv (English) A bitter man

Houghton (English) From the town on the headland
Houghtun, Houghtin, Houghtyn, Houghten, Houghtan, Hough

Houston (Gaelic / English) From Hugh's town / from the town on the hill
Hughston, Housten, Hughsten, Houstin, Hughstin, Houstyn, Hughstyn, Huston, Husten, Hustin, Hustyn, Houstun, Hughstun, Houstan, Hughstan, Hustan

Hovannes (Armenian) Form of John, meaning "God is gracious"
Hovennes, Hovann, Hovenn, Hovane, Hovene, Hovan, Hoven

Hovsep (Armenian) Form of Joseph, meaning "God will add"
Hovsepp

How (German) One who is lofty
Howe

Howahkan (Native American) Having a mysterious voice

Howard (English) The guardian of the home
Howerd, Howord, Howurd, Howird, Howyrd, Howi, Howie, Howy, Howey, Howee, Howea

Howell (Welsh) A distinguished or eminent man
Howel, Howill, Howil, Howyll, Howyl, Hywell, Hywel

Howi (Native American) Resembling a turtledove

H

Howland (English)From the highlands; from the hilly land
Howlande, Howlend, Howlende, Howlan, Howlen, Howlin, Howlyn, Howlon, Howlun, Howlond, Howlonde, Howlind, Howlinde, Howlynd, Howlynde, Howlund, Howlunde

Hoyte (Norse) A soulful man
Hoyt, Hoit, Hoite, Hoyce, Hoice

Hriday (Indian) Of the heart and mind
Hridaye, Hridae, Hridai, Hryday, Hrydaye, Hrydai, Hrydae

Hroc (English) Resembling a crow

Hrocby (English) From the crow's farm
Hrocbey, Hrocbee, Hrocbea, Hrocbi, Hrocbie

Hrocley (English) From the crow's meadow
Hrocly, Hroclee, Hroclea, Hrocleah, Hrocleigh, Hrocli, Hroclie

Hrocton (English) From the crow's town
Hroctun, Hrocten, Hroctin, Hroctyn, Hroctan

Hrothgar (Anglo-Saxon) A king
Hrothgarr, Hrothegar, Hrothegarr, Hrothgare, Hrothegare

Huang (Chinese) A wealthy man

Hubert (German) Having a shining intellect
Huberte, Huburt, Huburte, Hubirt, Hubirte, Hubyrt, Hubyrte, Hubie, Hubi, Hubey, Huby, Hubee, Hubea, Hube, Huberto, Humberto, Hubbard

Huckleberry (English) Resembling the fruit
Hucklebery, Hukleberry, Huklebery, Huckleberri, Hukleberri, Huckleberi, Hukleberi, Huckleberrie, Hukleberrie, Huckleberie, Hukleberie, Huck, Hucke, Hucks, Huk, Huc

Hud (English) A hooded man
Hudd, Houd, Houdd, Hudde, Hood, Hoodi, Hoodie, Hoodee, Hoodea, Hoody, Hoodey, Hod, Hodd, Hodde

Hudak (Czech) A blonde-haired man
Hudack, Hudac

Hudson (English) The son of Hugh; from the river
Hudsun, Hudsen, Hudsan, Hudsin, Hudsyn

Hudya (Arabic) One who follows the correct path
Hudyah, Hudiya, Hudiyah

Huelett (English) A young Hugh
Hughlett, Huelet, Hughlet

Hugh (German) Having a bright mind
Hew, Hewe, Huey, Hughes, Hughie, Hugues, Huw, Hugo, Hughi, Hughy, Hughey, Hughee, Hughea, Hu, Hue

Hugi (English) An intelligent man
Hugie, Hugy, Hugey, Hugee, Hugea

Hugin (Norse) A thoughtful man
Hugyn, Hugen, Hugan, Hugon, Hugun

Huland (English) A bright man
Hulande, Hulend, Hulende, Hulind, Hulinde, Hulynd, Hulynde

Hulbert (German) A bright and graceful man
Hulburt, Hulbirt, Hulbyrt, Hulbart, Hulberd, Hulburd, Hulbird, Hulbyrd, Hulbard, Huldiberaht

Hull (American) A spirited man
Hulle

Humam (Arabic) A generous and brave man

Humayd (Arabic) One who is praised
Humayde, Humaid, Humaide, Humaed, Humaede, Humade

Humbert (German) A famous warrior
Humberto, Humberte, Humbirt, Humbirte, Humbirto, Humburt, Humburte, Humburto, Humbyrt, Humbyrte, Humbyrto, Humbart, Humbarte, Humbarto

Hume (Scottish / English) From the cave / one who promotes peace
Home

Humility (English) One who is modest
Humilitey, Humiliti, Humilitie, Humilitee, Humilitea

Humphrey (German) A peaceful warrior
Humphry, Humphri, Humphrie, Humphree, Humphrea, Humfrey, Humfry, Humfri, Humfrie, Humfree, Humfrea, Humfrid, Humfryd, Humfried, Humfreid, Humph, Humphredo, Humfredo

Humvee (American) Resembling the vehicle; a macho man
Humvi, Humvie, Humvey, Humvy, Humvea, Hummer

Hunfrid (German) A peaceful Hun
Hunfryd, Hunfried, Hunfreid

Husam (Arabic) One who wields a sword

Husani (African) Form of Hussein, meaning "the small handsome one; a good man"
Husanie, Husany, Husaney, Husanee, Husanea, Hussani, Hussanie, Hussany, Hussaney, Hussanee, Hussanea

---

HUNTER

My father Henry passed away while I was pregnant with our son. We had to find a name that started with an H. We felt Hunter was the perfect name. It's both modern yet fairly uncommon. We feel it signifies strength, independence, and masculinity. —Wendy, Toronto

---

H

Hung (Vietnamese) A hero

Hungan (Haitian) A spirit master or priest
Hungen, Hungon, Hungun, Hungin, Hungyn

Hungas (Irish) A vigorous man

Hunn (German) A warring man
Hun

Hunter ○ ○ (English) A great huntsman and provider
Huntar, Huntor, Huntur, Huntir, Huntyr, Hunte, Hunt, Hunting, Huntyng, Huntler, Huntlar, Huntlor, Huntlur, Huntlir, Huntlyr

Huntington (English) From the hunter's town
Huntingtun, Huntingten, Huntingtan, Huntingtin, Huntingtyn, Huntingdon, Huntingdan, Huntingden, Huntingdun, Huntingdin, Huntingdyn

Huntley (English) From the hunter's meadow
Huntly, Huntlee, Huntlea, Huntleah, Huntleigh, Huntli, Huntlie, Huntle

Huon (Hebrew) Form of John, meaning "God is gracious"

Huritt (Native American) A handsome man
Hurit, Hurytt, Huryt, Hurett, Huret

Hurlbert (English) Of the shining army
Hurlberte, Hurlburt, Hurlburte, Hurlbirt, Hurlbirte, Hurlbyrt, Hurlbyrte, Hurlbutt, Hurlbart, Hurlbarte

Hurley (Irish) Of the sea tide
Hurly, Hurleigh, Hurlea, Hurleah, Hurlee, Hurli, Hurlie

Hurst (English) From the tree thicket
Hurste, Hearst, Hearste, Hirst, Hirste, Hyrst, Hyrste

Husky (American) A big man; a manly man
Huski, Huskie, Huskey, Huskee, Huskea, Husk, Huske

Huslu (Native American) Resembling a hairy bear
Huslue, Huslou

Hussein (Arabic) The small handsome one; a good man
Hussain, Husain, Husayn, Husein, Hussayn, Hussaen, Husaen, Husane, Hussane

Husto (Spanish) A righteous man
Hustio, Husteo, Hustiyo, Husteyo

Hutch (American) A unique man
Hutche, Hutchi, Hutchie, Hutchey, Hutchy, Hutchee, Hutchea

Hutter (English) One who lives near the bluff
Huttar, Huttor, Huttir, Huttyr, Huttur, Hutti, Huttie, Hutty, Huttee, Huttea, Huttey, Hutte, Hutt

Hutton (English) From the town on the bluff
Huttun, Hutten, Huttan, Huttin, Huttyn

Huw (Welsh) Of great intellect
Huwe

Huxford (English) From Hugh's ford
Huxeford, Huxforde, Huxeforde, Huxferd, Huxferde, Huxeferd, Huxeferde, Huxfurd, Huxfurde, Huxefurd, Huxefurde

Huxley (English) From Hugh's meadow
Huxly, Huxlea, Huxleah, Huxleigh, Huxlee, Huxli, Huxlie, Huxle

Huy (Vietnamese) A bright or glorious man

Huynh (Vietnamese) An older brother

Hwang (Japanese) Refers to the color yellow
Hwange

Hwitby (English) From the white farm
Hwitbey, Hwitbee, Hwitbea, Hwitbi, Hwitbie

Hwitcomb (English) From the white hollow
Hwitcom, Hwitcombe, Hwitcum,
Hwitcumb, Hwitcumbe

Hwitely (English) From the white meadow
Hwiteley, Hwitelee, Hwitelea, Hwiteleah,
Hwiteleigh, Hwiteli, Hwitelie

Hwitford (English) From the white ford
Hwitforde, Hwitferd, Hwitferde, Hwitfurd,
Hwitfurde

Hyacinthe (French) Resembling the
hyacinth flower
Hyacinthos, Hyacinthus, Hyakinthos,
Hyakinthus

Hyatt (English) From the high gate
Hyat, Hiatt, Hiat, Hyett, Hyet, Hyutt,
Hyut, Hiett, Hiet, Hiut, Hiutt

Hydd (Welsh) Resembling a deer
Hydde

Hyde (English) From the hide
Hyd, Hide, Hid

Hyman (Hebrew) A giver of life
Hymann, Hayim, Hayyim, Hymie, Hymi,
Hymy, Hymey, Hymee, Hymea, Hyam, Hy

Hyroniemus (Latin) A holy man
Hyroneimus, Hyronemus, Hyronimus,
Hyroniemos, Hyroneimos, Hyronemos,
Hyronimos

I

Iagan (Scottish) A fiery man
Iagen, Iagin, Iagyn, Iagon, Iagun

Iago (Spanish) Form of James, meaning
"he who supplants"
Iyago, Iagoh, Iyagoh

Iakovos (Hebrew) Form of Jacob, meaning
"he who supplants"
Iakovus, Iakoves, Iakovas, Iakovis, Iakovys

Ian ✪ (Gaelic) Form of John, meaning
"God is gracious"
Iain, Iaine, Iayn, Iayne, Iaen, Iaene, Iahn

Iassen (Bulgarian) From the ash tree
Iassan, Iassin, Iassyn, Iasson, Iassun

Iau (Welsh) Form of Zeus, meaning
"ruler of the gods"
Iaue

Iavor (Bulgarian) From the sycamore tree
Iaver, Iavur, Iavar, Iavir, Iavyr

Ib (Danish) Of the pledge
Ibb

Ibaad (Arabic) One who believes in God
Ibad

Ibrahim (Arabic) Form of Abraham, mean-
ing "father of a multitude; father of nations"
Ibraheem, Ibraheim, Ibrahiem, Ibraheam,
Ibrahym

Ibu (Japanese) One who is creative
Ibue, Iboo, Ibou

Icarus (Greek) In mythology, the man who
attached wings with wax which melted off
when he flew too close to the sun
Ikarus, Ickarus, Icaros, Ikaros, Ickaros

Ich (Hebrew) Form of Ichabod, meaning
"the glory has gone"
Iche, Ichi, Ichie, Ichy, Ichey, Ichee, Ichea

Ichabod (Hebrew) The glory has gone
Ikabod, Ickabod, Icabod, Ichavod, Ikavod,
Icavod, Ickavod, Icha

Ichiro (Japanese) The firstborn son
Ichyro, Ichirio, Ichyrio, Ichireo, Ichyreo

Ichtaca (Nahuatl) A secretive man
Ichtaka, Ichtacka

Icnoyotl (Nahuatl) A beloved friend

Ida (Anglo-Saxon) A king
Idah

Idal (English) From the yew-tree valley
Idall, Idale, Idail, Idaile, Idayl, Idayle,
Idael, Idaele

Idan (Hebrew) Of the time; of the era

Iden (English) One who is prosperous;
wealthy
Idin, Idyn, Idon, Idun

Idi (African) Born during the holiday of
Idd
Idie, Idy, Idey, Idee, Idea

Ido (Arabic / Hebrew) A mighty man / to
evaporate
Iddo, Idoh, Iddoh

Idona (Teutonic) A hardworking man
Idonah

Idowu (Welsh) A dark-haired man
Idowue, Idowoo, Idowou

Idris (Welsh) An eager lord
Idrys, Idriss, Idrisse, Idryss, Idrysse

Idwal (Welsh) A well-known man
Idwall, Idwale, Idwalle

Iefan (Welsh) Form of John, meaning
"God is gracious"
*Iefon, Iefen, Iefin, Iefyn, Iefun, Ifan, Ifon,
Ifen, Ifin, Ifyn, Ifun*

Ieuan (Welsh) Form of Ivan, meaning
"God is gracious"
Iuan, Ieuane, Iuane

Ife (African) One who is widely loved
Iffe, Ifi, Ifie, Ifee, Ifea, Ify, Ifey

Ifor (Welsh) An archer
Ifore, Ifour, Ifoure

Iftikhar (Arabic) One who brings honor
*Iftichar, Iftickhar, Iftikar, Ifticar, Iftickar,
Iftykhar, Iftykar, Iftychar, Iftycar, Iftyckhar,
Iftyckar*

Igasho (Native American) A wanderer
Igashoe, Igashow, Igashowe

Ige (African) One who is delivered breech
Igi, Igie, Igy, Igey, Igee, Igea

Iggi (African/Latin) The only son/form of
Ignatius, meaning "a fiery man; one who is
ardent"
Iggie, Iggy, Iggey, Iggee, Iggea

Ignatius (Latin) A fiery man; one who is
ardent
*Ignac, Ignace, Ignacio, Ignacius, Ignatious,
Ignatz, Ignaz, Ignazio, Inacio, Ignatia,
Ignado, Ignatios, Ignaci, Ignacy, Ignacie,
Ignacey, Ignacee, Ignacea*

Igon (Basque) The ascension
Igun

Igor (Scandinavian/Russian) A hero/Ing's
soldier
Igoryok

Ihab (Arabic) A gift

Ihaka (Maori) Form of Isaac, meaning
"full of laughter"
*Ihaca, Ihacka, Ihakah, Ihackah, Ihacah,
Ihacca, Ihakka*

Iham (Indian) One who is expected

Ihit (Indian) One who is honored
Ihyt, Ihitt, Ihytt

Ihsan (Arabic) A charitable man
Ihsann, Ihsen, Ihsin, Ihsyn, Ihson, Ihsun

Iiari (Basque) A cheerful man
Iiarie, Iiary, Iiarey, Iiaree, Iiarea

Ikaika (Hawaiian) Having great strength
*Ikaica, Ikayka, Ikayca, Ikaeka, Ikaeca,
Ikaka, Ikaca*

Ike (Hebrew) Form of Isaac, meaning
"full of laughter"
Iki, Ikie, Iky, Ikey, Ikee, Ikea

Iker (Basque) A visitor
Ikar, Ikir, Ikyr, Ikor, Ikur

Ilan (Hebrew) Of the tree
*Illan, Ilen, Illen, Ilin, Illin, Ilyn, Illyn, Ilon,
Illon, Ilun, Illun*

Ilario (Italian) A cheerful man
*Ilareo, Ilariyo, Ilareyo, Ilar, Ilarr, Ilari,
Ilarie, Ilary, Ilarey, Ilaree, Ilarea*

Ilhuitl (Nahuatl) Born during the daytime

Ilias (Hebrew) Form of Elijah, meaning
"Jehovah is my God"
*Ileas, Ili, Ilie, Ily, Iley, Ilee, Ileigh, Ilea,
Illias, Illeas, Ilyas, Illyas*

Illanipi (Native American) An amazing man
*Illanipie, Illanipy, Illanipey, Illanipee,
Illanipea*

Illinois (Native American) From the tribe
of warriors; from the state of Illinois

Illtyd (Welsh) The land of the populas
Illtud, Illtid, Illted, Illtad, Illted

Ilo (African) Of the sunshine; filled
with joy
Iloe, Ilow, Ilowe

Ilom (African / Welsh) Having many enemies / filled with happiness
Ilum, Ilem, Ilam, Ilim, Ilym

Iluminado (Spanish) One who shines brightly
Illuminado, Iluminato, Illuminato, Iluminados, Iluminatos, Illuminados, Illuminatos

Ilya (Russian) Form of Elijah, meaning "Jehovah is my God"
Ilyah, Ilia, Iliah, Iliya, Iliyah

Im (Norse) In mythology, a giant

Imad (Arabic) One who offers support

Imaran (Indian) Having great strength
Imaren, Imaron, Imarun, Imarin, Imaryn

Immanuel (German) Form of Emmanuel, meaning "God is with us"
Imanuel, Iman, Imani, Imanoel, Immannuel, Imanie, Imany, Imaney, Imanee, Imanea, Imanol, Imanole

Imran (Arabic) One who acts as a host
Imren, Imrin, Imron, Imrun, Imryn

Imre (Hungarian / German / Hebrew) One who is innocent / ruler of the home / of my words
Imray, Imri, Imrie, Imry, Imrey, Imree, Imrea, Imraye, Imrai, Imrae

Ina (African) An illuminated man
Inah, Inna, Innah

Inaki (Basque) An ardent man
Inakie, Inaky, Inakey, Inakee, Inakea, Inacki, Inackie, Inackee, Inackea, Inacky, Inackey

Inapo (Chamoru) Of the waves
Inapoe, Inapow, Inapowe

Inazin (Native American) Resembling a standing elk
Inazen, Inazyn, Inazon, Inazun, Inazan

Ince (Hungarian) One who is innocent
Inse

Incendio (Spanish) Of the fire
Incendeo, Incendiyo, Incendeyo

Independence (American) One who has freedom
Independance, Indepindence, Indipindince, Indypyndynce

Indiana (English) From the land of the Indians; from the state of Indiana
Indianna, Indyana, Indyanna

Indivar (Indian) Resembling a blue lotus
Indyvar, Indivarr, Indyvarr

Indore (Indian) From the city in India
Indor, Indoor, Indoore

Indra (Hindi) In Hinduism, the god of the sky and weather
Indrah, Inder, Inderjeet, Inderjit, Inderjyt, Indervir, Indrajit, Indrajeet, Indrajyt

Ine (Anglo-Saxon) A king

Inerney (Irish) The church's steward
Inerny, Inernee, Inernea, Inerni, Inernie

Infinity (American) A man unbounded by space or time
Infinitey, Infiniti, Infinitie, Infinitee, Infinitye, Infinitea

Ing (Norse) In mythology, god of fertility

Ingall (German) A messenger of God; an angel
Ingal, Ingalls, Ingals, Ingel, Ingell, Ingels, Ingells

Ingemar (Scandinavian) The son of Ing
Ingamar, Ingemur, Ingmar, Ingmur, Ingar, Ingemer, Ingmer

Inger (Scandinavian) One who is fertile
Inghar, Ingher

Inglebert (German) As bright as an angel
Ingbert, Ingelbert, Ingelburt, Ingburt, Ingleburt, Ingelbirt, Ingbirt, Ingelbyrt, Inglebirt, Inglebyrt, Ingbyrt

Ingo (Scandinavian / Danish) A lord / from the meadow
Ingoe, Ingow, Ingowe

Ingolf (Norse) Ing's wolf
Ingulf, Ingolfe, Ingulfe

Ingra (English) Form of Ingram, meaning "a raven of peace"
Ingrah, Ingri, Ingrie, Ingree, Ingrea

Ingram (Scandinavian) A raven of peace
Ingrem, Ingrim, Ingrym, Ingrum, Ingrom, Ingraham, Ingrahame, Ingrams, Inghram

Ingvar (Scandinavian) A soldier of Ing's army
Ingevar, Ingevur, Ingvur

Inigo (Portuguese) An ardent man
*Inygo, Inigoe, Inygo, Inigow, Inygow,
Inigowe, Inygowe*

Iniko (African) Born during troubled times
Inicko, Inico, Inyko, Inycko, Inyco

Inman (English) An innkeeper
Innman, Inmann, Innmann

Innis (Scottish) From the island
Innes, Inness, Inniss, Inis, Iniss, Ines, Iness

Innocenzio (Italian) One who is innocent
*Incencio, Innocencio, Innocenzeo,
Inocenzeo, Inocenzio, Innocent, Innocenty,
Innocente, Innocenti, Innocentie,
Innocentee, Innocentey*

Intekhab (Indian) The chosen one
Intechab, Inteckhab

Inteus (Native American) One who has no
shame
Intius, Intyus

Inver (Gaelic) From the estuary
Invar, Invir, Invyr, Invor, Invur

Ioakim (Russian) Form of Joachim, mean-
ing "one who is established by God; God
will judge"
*Ioachim, Iakim, Ioacheim, Ioaquim,
Ioaquin, Iosquin, Ioakim, Ioakeen, Iokim,
Iokin, Ioachime, Iaokim*

Ioanis (Russian) Form of John, meaning
"God is gracious"
*Ioanys, Ioaniss, Ioanyss, Ioan, Ioane, Iohanis,
Iohanys, Iohaniss, Iohanyss, Ioanes, Ioaness*

Iomhair (Gaelic) An archer
Iomhaire

Ion (Greek) In mythology, the son of Apollo
Ionn, Ione, Ionne, Ionnes

Ior (Welsh) An attractive man
Iore

Iorgos (Greek) An outgoing man
Iorgas, Iorges, Iorgis, Iorgys, Iorgus

Iorwerth (Welsh) A handsome lord
*Ioworth, Iowerthe, Iowerthe, Iowirth,
Iowirthe, Iowyrth, Iowyrthe*

Ioseph (Gaelic) Form of Joseph, meaning
"God will add"
Iosef, Iosep, Iosip, Iosyp

Iov (Hebrew) God will establish
Iove

Ira (Hebrew) One who is vigilant; watchful
Irah, Irra, Irrah

Iram (Hebrew) A shining man
*Irham, Irem, Irhem, Irim, Irhim, Irym,
Irhym, Irom, Irhom, Irum, Irhum*

Iranga (Sri Lankan) One who is special

Iravath (Scandinavian) Indra's elephant
Iravathe, Iravat, Iravate

Ireland (American) One who pays homage
to Ireland

Irenbend (Anglo-Saxon) From the iron bend
Ironbend

Irenio (Spanish) A peaceful man
*Ireniyo, Ireneo, Ireneyo, Irenaeus, Ireneus,
Irenious, Irenius, Irenios*

Irfan (Indian / Arabic) One who is knowledgeable / one who is thankful
Irfen, Irfin, Irfyn, Irfon, Irfun

Irish (American) Man from Ireland
Irysh, Irishe, Iryshe

Irshad (Indian) A sign or signal
Irshaad

Irving (English) A friend of the sea
Irv, Irven, Irvin, Irvine, Irvyn, Irvyne, Irvene

Irwin (English) A friend of the wild boar
*Irwinn, Irwinne, Irwyn, Irwynne, Irwine,
Irwen, Irwenn, Irwenne*

Isaac ○ ○ (Hebrew) Full of laughter
*Isaack, Isaak, Isac, Isacco, Isak, Issac,
Itzak, Itzhak, Izaac, Izaak, Izak, Izik,
Izsak, Isaakios*

Isaiah ○ ○ (Hebrew) God is my salvation
*Isa, Isaia, Isais, Isia, Isiah, Issiah, Izaiah,
Iziah, Isaias, Isai*

Isam (Arabic) One who is protected
Issam

Isandro (Spanish) The liberator of man
*Isander, Isandero, Isandoro, Isanderio,
Isandorio, Isandereo, Isandoreo*

Isas (Japanese) One who is worthwhile

Iseabail (Hebrew) One who is devoted to God
Iseabaile, Iseabayl, Iseabyle, Iseabael, Iseabaele

Isen (Anglo-Saxon) Of iron
Isin, Isyn, Ison, Isun, Isan

Isha (Hindi) One who is protective
Ishah

Ishaan (Hindi) Of the sun
Ishan

Isham (English) From the iron one's estate
Ishem, Ishom, Ishum, Ishim, Ishym, Isenham, Isenhem, Isenhim, Isenhym, Isenhom, Isehum

Ishaq (Arabic) A laughing child
Ishak, Ishack, Ishac

Ishi (Japanese) As solid as a rock
Ishie, Ishy, Ishey, Ishee, Ishea

Ishmael (Hebrew) God will listen
Ismail, Ismaal, Ismael, Ismal, Ismayl, Izmail, Ishmaal, Ishmal, Ishmayl, Ishmail

Isidore (Greek) A gift of Isis
Isador, Isadore, Isidor, Isidoro, Isidorus, Isidro, Issy, Izidor, Izydor, Izzy, Issey, Issi, Issie, Issee, Izzey, Izzi, Izzie, Izzee, Isidoros, Izidro, Izydro, Isydro

Iskander (Arabic) Form of Alexander, meaning "helper and defender of mankind"
Iskinder, Iskandar, Iskindar, Iskynder, Iskyndar, Iskender, Iskendar

Ismat (Arabic) One who is protective

Ismet (Turkish) One who is honored
Ismit, Ismyt

Isra (Turkish) An independent man; one who is free
Israh

Israel (Hebrew) God perseveres
Israeli, Israelie, Israely, Israeley, Israelee, Israeleigh, Israelea, Isreal, Izreal, Izrael

Israj (Hindi) The king of gods

Issa (Hebrew) A gift of God
Issah

Issachar (Hebrew) He will be rewarded
Isachar

Issay (African) One who is hairy
Issaye, Issai, Issae

Isser (Slavic) One who is creative
Issar, Issir, Issyr, Issor, Issur

Istaqa (Native American) A coyote man
Istaka, Istaca, Istacka

Istu (Native American) As sweet as sugar
Istue, Istoo, Istou

Istvan (Hungarian) One who is crowned
Istven, Istvin, Istvyn, Istvon, Istvun

Itai (Hebrew) God is beside me
Ittai, Itiel, Itiell, Ittiel

Italo (Italian) A man from Italy
Itallo, Italio, Italeo, Italiyo, Italeyo

Itamar (Hebrew) From the island of palms
Ittamar, Itamarr, Ittamarr, Ithamar, Ithamarr

Iulian (Romanian) A youthful man
Iulien, Iulio, Iuleo

Iuwine (Anglo-Saxon) A beloved friend
Iuwin, Iuwinn, Iuwinne, Iuwyn, Iuwynn, Iuwynne, Iuwen, Iuwenn, Iuwenne

Iva (Japanese) Of the yew tree
Ivah

Ivan (Slavic) Form of John, meaning "God is gracious"
Ivann, Ivanhoe, Ivano, Iwan, Iban, Ibano, Ivanti, Ivantie, Ivante, Ivant, Ivanty, Ivantey, Ivantee, Ivantea

Ives (Scandinavian) The archer's bow; of the yew wood
Ivair, Ivar, Iven, Iver, Ivo, Ivon, Ivor, Ivaire, Ivayr, Ivayre, Ivaer, Ivaere, Ivare, Ibon, Ive

Ivo (German / English) Of cut wood / an archer's bow
Ivoe, Ivow, Ivowe, Ivoh, Ivon, Ivor

Ivory (English) Having a creamy-white complexion; as precious as elephant tusks
Ivorie, Ivorine, Ivoreen, Ivorey, Ivoree, Ivori, Ivoryne, Ivorea, Ivoreah, Ivoreane

Ivrit (Hebrew) The Hebrew language
Ivryt

Ivy (English) Resembling the evergreen vining plant
Ivee, Ivey, Ivie, Ivi, Ivea, Iveah

Ixaka (Basque) Laughter
Ixaca, Ixacka

Iyar (Hebrew) Surrounded by light
Iyyar, Iyer, Iyyer

Iye (Native American) Of the smoke

Izaan (Arabic) One who is obedient
*Izan, Izane, Izain, Izaine, Izaen, Izaene,
Izayn, Izayne*

Ja (Korean / African) A handsome man /
one who is magnetic

Jabal (Indian) An attractive man
Jaball

Jabari (African) A valiant man
Jabarie, Jabary, Jabarey, Jabaree, Jabarea

Jabbar (Indian) One who consoles others
Jabar

Jabez (Hebrew) One who is delivered in
pain
Jabes, Jabesh, Jabeshe, Jabezz

Jabilo (African) A medicine man
Jabylo, Jabeilo, Jabielo, Jabeelo, Jabealo

Jabin (Hebrew) God has built; one who is
perceptive

Jabir (Arabic) One who provides comfort
Jabeer, Jabier, Jabeir, Jabear, Jabyr, Jaber

Jabon (American) A feisty man
Jabun, Jabin, Jabyn, Jaben, Jaban

Jabulani (African) Filled with happiness
*Jabulanie, Jabulany, Jabulaney, Jabulanee,
Jabulanea*

Jacan (Hebrew) A troublemaker
Jachin, Jachan, Jacen, Jachen, Jacin

Jace (Hebrew) God is my salvation
*Jacen, Jacey, Jacian, Jacy, Jaice, Jayce,
Jaece, Jaycen, Jaecen, Jaicen, Jacie, Jaci,
Jaicey, Jaicy, Jaici, Jaicie, Jaycey, Jaycy,
Jayci, Jaycie, Jaecey, Jaecy, Jaeci, Jaecie,
Jaycee*

Jacinto (Spanish) Resembling a hyacinth
*Jacynto, Jacindo, Jacyndo, Jacento, Jacendo,
Jacenty, Jacentey, Jacentee, Jacentea, Jacenti,
Jacentie, Jacek, Jacent, Jacint*

Jack ☺ (English) Form of John, meaning
"God is gracious"
*Jackie, Jackman, Jacko, Jacky, Jacq, Jacqin,
Jak, Jaq, Jacki, Jackee*

Jackal (Sanskrit) Resembling a wild dog
Jackel

Jackson ☺ (English) The son of Jack or
John
*Jacksen, Jacksun, Jacson, Jakson, Jaxen,
Jaxon, Jaxun, Jaxson, Jaxsen, Jaxsun,
Jaksen, Jacsen, Jax*

Jacob ☺ ☻ (Hebrew) He who supplants
*Jaco, Jacobo, Jacobi, Jacoby, Jacobie,
Jacobey, Jacobo, Jacobus, Jakob, Jakov,
Jakub, Jacobe, Jachym, Jacobs, Jakobs,
Jaykob, Jaycob*

Jacquard (French) A distinguished man
*Jaquard, Jaquarde, Jaqard, Jacquarde,
Jackard, Jackarde, Jakard, Jakarde*

Jacques (French) Form of Jacob, meaning
"he who supplants"
Jacot, Jacque, Jaques, Jock, Jocke, Jok, Jacue

Jadal (American) One who is punctual
Jadall, Jadel, Jadell

Jade (Spanish) Resembling the green
gemstone
Jaide, Jaid, Jayd, Jayde, Jaed, Jaede, Jada

Jaden ☺ ☻ (Hebrew / English) One who is
thankful to God; God has heard / form of
Jade, meaning "resembling the green
gemstone"
*Jadine, Jadyn, Jadon, **Jayden**, Jadyne,
Jaydyn, Jaydon, Jaydine, Jadin, Jaydin,
Jaidyn, Jaedan, Jaeden, Jaedin, Jaedon,
Jaedyn, Jaidan, Jaidin, Jaidon, Jaidyn,
Jaydan, Jader*

Jadrien (American) One who is bold
*Jadrian, Jadrienn, Jadriann, Jadrienne,
Jadrianne, Jadrion, Jadriun*

Jaegar (German) A mighty hunter
*Jaygar, Jaiger, Jagar, Jaeger, Jayger, Jaiger,
Jager, Jaecar, Jaycar, Jaicar, Jacar, Jaecer,
Jaycer, Jaicer, Jacer*

Jaegel (English) A salesman
Jaygel, Jagel, Jaigel

Jael (Hebrew) Resembling a mountain goat
Jaele

Jaequon (American) An outgoing
young man
*Jaquon, Jaiquon, Jayquon, Jaequan,
Jaquan, Jaiquan, Jayquan*

Jafar (Arabic) From the small stream
*Jaffar, Jafaar, Jaffaar, Jaafar, Jaaffar, Jafari,
Jafarie, Jafary, Jafarey, Jafaree, Jafaru,
Jafarue, Jafaroo, Jafarou*

Jagan (English) One who is self-confident
Jagen, Jagin, Jagyn, Jagon, Jagun, Jago

Jagger (English) One who carts provisions
Jaggar, Jaggor, Jaggir, Jaggur, Jaggyr

Jago (English) Form of Jacob, meaning
"he who supplants"
Jagoe, Jagow, Jagowe

Jaguar (English) Resembling the animal;
one who is fast
Jagwar, Jaghuar, Jagwhar

Jahan (Indian) Man of the world
Jehan, Jihan, Jag, Jagat, Jagath

Jahi (African) A dignified man
Jah, Jahie, Jahy, Jahey, Jahee, Jahea

Jaichand (Indian) The victory of the moon
*Jaychand, Jachand, Jaechand, Jaichande,
Jaychande, Jachande, Jaechande*

Jaidayal (Indian) The victory of kindness
Jadayal, Jaydayal, Jaedayal

Jaidev (Indian) The victory of God
Jaydev, Jadev, Jaidev, Jaedev

Jaime (Spanish) Form of James, meaning
"he who supplants"
*Jamie, Jaime, Jaimee, Jaimey, Jaimi, Jaimie,
Jaimy, Jamee, Jamei, Jamey, Jami, Jaymey,
Jayme, Jaymi, Jaymy, Jaymie, Jaymee,
Jammie*

Jaimin (French) One who is loved
*Jaimyn, Jamin, Jamyn, Jaymin, Jaymyn,
Jaemin, Jaemyn*

Jaimini (Indian) A victorious man
*Jaymini, Jaemini, Jaiminie, Jayminie,
Jaeminie, Jaiminy, Jayminy, Jaeminy*

Jairdan (American) One who enlightens
others
*Jardan, Jayrdan, Jaerdan, Jairden, Jarden,
Jayrden, Jaerden*

Jairus (Hebrew) God enlightens
Jairo, Jair, Jaire

Jaiwant (Indian) A victorious man
Jaywant, Jaewant, Jawant

Jaja (African) A gift from God

Jajuan (American) One who loves God

Jakar (English) A man from Jakarta
Jakart, Jakarte

Jake (English) Form of Jacob, meaning
"he who supplants"
Jaik, Jaike, Jayk, Jayke, Jakey, Jaky

Jakeem (Arabic) One who is exalted
Jakeim, Jakiem, Jakeam, Jakim, Jakym

Jakhi (American) Having great strength
Jakhie, Jakhy, Jakhey, Jakhee, Jakhea

Jakome (Basque) Form of James, meaning
"he who supplants"
Jackome, Jakom, Jackom, Jacome

Jal (English) A traveler; wanderer
Jall

Jaladhi (Hindi) Of the ocean
*Jaladhie, Jaladhy, Jaladhey, Jaladhee,
Jaladi, Jaladie, Jalady, Jaladey, Jaladee,
Jeladi, Jeladie, Jelady, Jeladey, Jeladee*

Jalal (Arabic) A superior man
Jalall, Jallal, Jalil, Jaliyl, Jelal, Jellal

Jaleel (Arabic) A majestic man
Jaleal, Jalil, Jalyl, Jaleil, Jaliel

Jalen ♂ (American) One who heals others;
one who is tranquil
*Jaelan, Jaelin, Jaelon, Jailin, Jaillen, Jaillin,
Jailon, Jalan, Jalin, Jalon, Jayelan, Jayelen,
Jaylan, Jaylon, Jaylonn, Jaylin, **Jaylen***

Jam (American) As sweet as the condiment

Jamaine (Arabic) An attractive man
*Jamain, Jamayn, Jamayne, Jamaen,
Jamaene, Jamane*

Jamal (Arabic) A handsome man
*Jahmal, Jamaal, Jamael, Jamahl, Jamall,
Jamaul, Jameel, Jamel, Jamell, Jamiel,
Jamil, Jamile, Jamill, Jammal, Jemaal,
Jemahl, Jemall, Jimal, Jimahl, Jomal,
Jomahl, Jomall, Jemal, Jamaal*

Jamar (American) Form of Jamal, meaning "a handsome man"
Jamarr, Jemar, Jemarr, Jimar, Jimarr, Jamaar, Jamari, Jamarie, Jamary, Jamarey, Jamaree

Jamarion (American) A strong-willed man
Jamareon, Jamarrion, Jamarreon, Jamarien, Jamarrien

James ❂ ❂ (Hebrew) Form of Jacob, meaning "he who supplants"
Jaimes, Jaymes, Jame, Jaym, Jaim, Jaem, Jaemes, Jamese, Jascha

Jameson (English) The son of James
Jaimison, Jamieson, Jaymeson, Jamison, Jaimeson, Jaymison, Jaemeson, Jaemison, Jamisen, Jaimesen, Jaymesen

Jamin (Hebrew) The right hand of favor
Jamian, Jamiel, Jamon, Jaymin, Jaemin, Jaymon, Jaemon, Jaimin, Jaimon

Jan (Slavic) Form of John, meaning "God is gracious"
Janek, Jano, Janos, Jonam, Jens, Janak

Janaan (Arabic) Having heart and soul
Janan, Janen, Janin, Janyn, Janon, Janun

Janesh (Hindi) A leader of the people
Janeshe

Jani (Finnish) Form of John, meaning "God is gracious"
Janie, Jannes, Janes, Jancsi, Jancsie, Janne, Janeth, Janneth, Janko, Janco, Jankya, Jussi, Jussie, Janksi, Janksie, Jantje

Janson (Scandinavian) The son of Jan
Janse, Jansen, Janssen, Jansson, Jantzen, Janzen, Jensen, Jenson, Jansahn, Jantz, Janzon

Jantis (German) One who wields a sharp spear
Jantys, Jantiss, Jantyss, Janyd, Janid

Janus (Latin) From the archway; in mythology, the god of gateways and beginnings
Januus, Janiusz, Januarius, Janusz, Jenaro, Jenarius, Jennaro

Japa (Indian) One who chants
Japeth, Japesh, Japendra

Japheth (Hebrew) May he expand; in the Bible, one of Noah's sons
Jaypheth, Jaepheth, Jaipheth, Jafeth, Jayfeth, Jaefeth, Jaifeth, Japhet, Jafet

Jarah (Hebrew) One who is as sweet as honey
Jarrah, Jara, Jarra

Jard (American) One who is long-lived
Jarrd, Jord, Jorrd, Jerd, Jerrd

Jardine (French) Of the gardens
Jardyne, Jardeen, Jardean, Jardeene, Jardeane

Jareb (Hebrew) He will struggle

Jared (Hebrew) Of the descent; descending
Jarad, Jarid, Jarod, Jarrad, Jarryd, Jarred, Jarrid, Jarrod, Jaryd, Jerad, Jerod, Jerrad, Jerred, Jerrod, Jerryd, Jered

Jarek (Slavic) Born during the spring
Jareck, Jarec

> **JAMES**
> We love traditional-sounding names, especially ones that run in our family. We named our son after my husband's grandfather, and still love it. When people asked about his name before he was born, I was surprised how consistently they said it was such a strong name. —Kristi, FL

Jareth (American) One who is gentle
Jarethe, Jarreth, Jarrethe, Jereth, Jerreth, Jerethe, Jerrethe

Jarlath (Irish) A tributary lord
Jarleath, Jarlaith, Jarlaeth, Jarlayth, Jarleeth, Jariath, Jaryath

Jarman (German) A man from Germany
Jarmann, Jerman, Jermann

Jaromil (Czech) Born during the spring
Jaromyl, Jaromeel, Jaromeal, Jaromiel, Jaromeil, Jarmil, Jarmyl

Jaromir (Slavic) From the famous spring
Jaromeer, Jaromear, Jaromeir, Jaromier, Jaromyr

Jaron (Israeli) A song of rejoicing
Jaran, Jaren, Jarin, Jarran, Jarren, Jarrin, Jarron, Jaryn, Jeran, Jeren, Jerren, Jerrin, Jerron

Jaroslav (Slavic) Born with the beauty of spring
Jaroslaw

Jarrell (English) One who rules with the spear
Jarel, Jarrel, Jarell, Jarrall, Jarall, Jarral, Jerall, Jeryl, Jerel, Jeriel, Jeril, Jeroll, Jerrall, Jerrel, Jerrill, Jerroll, Jerryl, Jaryl, Jerrell, Jerriel, Jerriell

Jarrett (English) One who is strong with the spear
Jarett, Jarret, Jarrot, Jarrott, Jerett, Jerrett, Jerrot, Jerrott, Jarrit, Jarritt, Jaret, Jarot, Jeret, Jerot, Jarit, Jerit

Jarvis (French) One who wields a spear
Jarvee, Jarvell, Jarvey, Jary, Jervey, Jervis, Jarvys, Jervys, Jarvi, Jarvie, Jarvy

Jasbeer (Indian) A victorious hero
Jasbir, Jasbear, Jasbier, Jasbeir, Jasbyr

Jase (American) Form of Jason, meaning "God is my salvation / a healer"
Jaise, Jayse, Jaese

Jaser (Arabic) One who is fearless
Jasir, Jasyr, Jasar, Jasor, Jasur

Jaskirit (Indian) One who praises the lord
Jaskiryt, Jaskyryt, Jaskyrit

Jason ✪ ⚧ (Hebrew / Greek) God is my salvation / a healer; in mythology, the leader of the Argonauts
Jacen, Jaisen, Jaison, Jasen, Jasin, Jasun, Jayson, Jaysen, Jaeson, Jaesen

Jaspal (Indian) One who is pure; chaste

Jasper (Persian) One who holds the treasure
Jaspar, Jaspir, Jaspyr, Jesper, Jespar, Jespir, Jespyr

Jatan (Indian) One who is nurturing

Jathan (American) An attractive young man
Jaithan, Jaethan, Jaythan, Jathen, Jaithen, Jaethen, Jaythen, Jathun, Jaithun, Jaethun, Jaythun, Jathe, Jath

Jatin (Hindi) A saintly man
Jatyn, Jateen, Jatean, Jatien, Jatein

Javan (Hebrew) Man from Greece; in the Bible, Noah's grandson
Jayvan, Jayven, Jayvern, Jayvon, Javon, Javern, Javen

Javaris (American) One who is ever-ready
Javarys, Javares, Javarez, Javariz, Javy, Javey, Javi, Javie, Javee

Javas (Indian) One who is quick; having bright eyes

Javed (Persian) One who is immortal
Javid, Javyd

Javier (Spanish) The owner of a new house
Javiero

Javonte (American) A cheerful man
Javontay, Javontaye, Javontai, Javontae, Javawnte, Javawntay, Javawntaye, Javawntai, Javawntae, Jevonte, Jevontay, Jevontaye, Jevontai, Jevontae

Jawad (Arabic) A generous man
Jawaid, Jawayd, Jawaide, Jawayde, Jawaed, Jawaede, Jawade

Jawara (African) One who loves peace
Jawarra, Jawarah, Jawarrah

Jawdat (Arabic) One who is superior
Jaudat

Jawhar (Arabic) As precious as a jewel
Jawahar

Jawon (American) One who is shy
Jawan, Jawaun, Jawawn, Jawaughn

Jay (Latin / Sanskrit) Resembling a jaybird / one who is victorious
Jae, Jai, Jaye, Jayron, Jayronn, Jey

Jayant (Indian) One who is victorious
Jayante, Jayanti, Jayantie, Jayantee, Jayantea, Jayantey, Jayanty

Jayvyn (African) Having a light spirit
Jayvin, Jaivyn, Jaivin, Javyn, Javin, Jaevyn, Jaevin

Jazon (Polish) One who heals others
Jazen, Jazin, Jazyn, Jazun

Jazz (American) Refers to the style of music
Jaz, Jaze, Jazzy, Jazzey, Jazzee, Jazzi, Jazzie

Jean (French) Form of John, meaning "God is gracious"
Jeanne, Jeane, Jene, Jeannot, Jeanot

Jebediah (Hebrew) A friend of God
Jebedia, Jebadiah, Jebadia, Jebidia, Jebidiah, Jeb, Jebb, Jebbe, Jebby, Jebbey, Jebbi, Jebbie

Jecori (American) An exuberant man
Jecorie, Jecory, Jecorey, Jecoree, Jekori, Jekorie, Jekory, Jekorey, Jekoree

Jediah (Hebrew) God knows all
Jedia, Jedaiah, Jediya, Jediyah, Jedya, Jedyah, Jedi, Jedie, Jedy, Jedey, Jedee

Jedidiah (Hebrew) One who is loved by God
Jedadiah, Jedediah, Jed, Jedd, Jedidiya, Jedidiyah, Jedadia, Jedadiya, Jedadiyah, Jededia, Jedediya, Jedediyah

Jedrek (Polish) Having great strength
Jedrec, Jedreck, Jedrik, Jedrick, Jedric, Jedrus

Jeevan (Hindi) Full of life
Jeeven, Jeevon, Jeevin, Jeevyn

Jefferson (English) The son of Jeffrey
Jeferson, Jeffersun, Jefersun, Jeffersen, Jefersen

Jeffrey (German) A man of peace
Jefery, Jeff, Jefferey, Jefferies, Jeffery, Jeffree, Jeffries, Jeffry, Jeffy, Jefry, Jeoffroi, Joffre, Joffrey

Jehoiakim (Hebrew) God will judge
Jehoioachim, Jehoiakin, Jehoiachim, Jehoiachin

Jehu (Hebrew) He is God
Jayhu, Jahu, Jehue, Jeyhu, Jeyhue, Jayhue, Jahue, Jehew, Jayhew, Jeyhew, Jahew

Jela (Swahili) During birth, the father suffered
Jelah, Jella, Jellah

Jelani (African) One who is mighty; strong
Jelanie, Jelany, Jelaney, Jelanee, Jelanea

Jem (English) Form of Jacob, meaning "he who supplants"
Jemm, Jemme, Jemmi, Jemmie, Jemmy, Jemmey, Jemmee

Jemonde (French) A man of the world
Jemond, Jemont, Jemonte

Jenci (Hungarian) A wellborn man
Jencie, Jency, Jencey, Jencee, Jencea, Jensi, Jensie, Jensy, Jensey, Jensee, Jensea

Jenda (Czech) Form of John, meaning "God is gracious"
Jendah, Jinda, Jindah, Jynda, Jyndah

Jengo (African) One who has a ruddy complexion
Jengoe, Jengow, Jengowe

Jenkin (Flemish) Little John; son of John
Jenkins, Jenkyn, Jenkyns

Jennett (Hindi) One who is heaven-sent
Jenett, Jennet, Jenet, Jennitt, Jenitt, Jennit, Jenit

Jennings (English) A descendant of John
Jenning, Jennyngs, Jennyng

Jens (Scandinavian) Form of John, meaning "God is gracious"
Jensen, Jenson, Jensin, Jennsen, Jennson, Jennsin, Jenns

Jenski (English) One who has come home
Jenskie, Jensky, Jenskey, Jenskee, Jenskea

Jep (American) An easygoing man
Jepp, Jeppe

Jephthah (Hebrew) God will judge
Jephtha, Jephtah, Jephta

Jerald (English) Form of Gerald, meaning "one who rules with the spear"
Jeraldo, Jerold, Jerrald, Jerrold

Jerard (English) Form of Gerard, meaning "one who is mighty with a spear"
Jerrard, Jerardo, Jerrardo

Jeremiah ○ ❶ (Hebrew) One who is exalted by the Lord
Jeremia, Jeremias, Jeremija, Jeremiya, Jeremyah, Jeramiah, Jeramia

Jeremy (Hebrew) Form of Jeremiah, meaning "one who is exalted by the Lord"
Jemmie, Jemmy, Jeramee, Jeramey, Jeramie, Jeramy, Jerami, Jereme, Jeremie, Jeromy, Jeremey, Jeremi, Jeremee, Jeromey, Jeromi, Jeromie, Jeromee

Jeriah (Hebrew) God has seen
Jeria, Jera, Jerah, Jerra, Jerrah

Jericho (Arabic) From the city of the moon
Jericko, Jeriko, Jerikko, Jerico, Jericco, Jerycho, Jeryko, Jeryco, Jerychko, Jerrico, Jerricho, Jerriko, Jerricko

Jermaine (French / Latin) A man from Germany / one who is brotherly
Jermain, Jermane, Jermayne, Jermin, Jermyn, Jermayn, Jermaen, Jermaene, Jerma, Jermi, Jermie, Jermy, Jermey

Jermon (American) One who is dependable
Jermonn, Jermun, Jermunn

Jerney (Slavic) A humorous man
Jerny, Jerne, Jerni, Jernie, Jernee, Jernea

Jero (American) One who is cheerful
Jeroh, Jerro, Jerroh

Jeroen (Arabic) A holy man

Jerome (Greek) Of the sacred name
Jairome, Jeroen, Jeromo, Jeronimo, Jerrome, Jerom, Jerolyn, Jerolin

Jerone (English) Filled with hope
Jerohn, Jeron, Jerrone

Jerram (Hebrew) Form of Jeremiah, meaning "one who is exalted by the Lord"
Jeram, Jerrem, Jerem, Jerrym, Jerym

Jerrick (English) A strong and gifted ruler
Jerack, Jereck, Jerek, Jeric, Jerick, Jerric, Jerrik, Jerriq

Jerry (Greek) A holy man; having great strength
Jerri, Jerrie, Jerrey, Jerree, Jerre, Jerrye, Jere

Jersey (English) From a section of England; one who is calm
Jersy, Jersi, Jersie, Jersee, Jersea

Jerzy (Polish) One who works the earth; a farmer
Jerzey, Jerzi, Jerzie, Jerzee, Jerzea

Jeshurun (Hebrew) A righteous man

Jesimiel (Hebrew) The Lord establishes
Jessimiel

Jesse (Hebrew) God exists; a gift from God; God sees all
Jess, Jessey, Jesiah, Jessie, Jessy, Jese, Jessi, Jessee, Jessamine, Jessamyne, Jesmar, Jessmar, Jesmarr, Jessmarr

Jesuan (Spanish) One who is devout

Jesus ✪ (Hebrew) God is my salvation
Jesous, Jesues, Jesús

Jethro (Hebrew) Man of abundance
Jethroe, Jethrow, Jethrowe, Jeth, Jethe

Jeton (French) A feisty man
Jetan, Jetun, Jetaun, Jetawn

Jett (English) Resembling the jet-black lustrous gemstone
Jet, Jette, Jete, Jettie, Jetty, Jetti, Jettey, Jettee, Jettea, Jettal, Jetal, Jetahl, Jettale

Jevon (American) A spirited man
Jeavan, Jeaven, Jeavin, Jevan, Jeven, Jevin, Jevvan, Jevven, Jevvin, Jevvyn

Ji (Chinese) One who is organized

Jibben (American) A lively man
Jiben, Jybben, Jyben

Jibril (Arabic) Refers to the archangel Gabriel
Jibryl, Jibri, Jibrie, Jibry, Jibrey, Jibree

Jie (Chinese) One who is pure; chaste

Jignesh (Indian) A curious man
Jigneshe, Jygnesh, Jygneshe

Jiles (American) The shield bearer
Jyles

Jilt (Dutch) One who has money
Jylt, Jilte, Jylte

Jim (English) Form of James, meaning "he who supplants"
Jimi, Jimmee, Jimmey, Jimmie, Jimmy, Jimmi, Jimbo

Jimiyu (African) One who is born during a dry period
Jimiyue, Jimiyoo, Jimiyou

Jimoh (African) Born on a Friday
Jymoh, Jimo, Jymo

Jin (Chinese / Korean) The golden one / one who is treasured
Jyn

Jinan (Arabic) From the garden of paradise
Jynan

Jindrich (Czech) A great ruler
Jindrick, Jindrik, Jindric, Jindrisek, Jindrousek, Jindra

Jing (Chinese) One who is flawless
Jyng

Jirair (Armenian) A hardworking man
Jiraire, Jirayr, Jirayre, Jiraer, Jiraere, Jirare

Jiri (African / Czech) From the fruitful forest
/ one who works the earth; a farmer
*Jirie, Jiry, Jirey, Jiree, Jirea, Jirka, Jira,
Jirisek, Jiricek*

Jiro (Japanese) The second-born son
Jyro, Jeero, Jearo

John ✡ ✝ (Hebrew) God is gracious; in the
Bible, one of the Apostles
*Jian, Jianni, Joannes, Joao, Jahn, Johan,
Johanan, Johann, Johannes, Johnn, Johon,
Johnie, Johnnie, Johnny, Jon, Jona, Jonn,
Jonnie, Jonny, Jonte, Johntay, Johnte,
Jontae, Jontell, Jontez, Jaan, Joen, Jonni*

Johnavon (American) From God's river
Jonavon, Johnaven, Jonaven

JONAH
Due to family reasons, we wanted our child to have a J name. We have a big family, so many of the J names have already been used. We decided on Jonah, as it is a traditional, but not commonly used, name. —Sarah, IA

Jivan (Hindi) A giver of life
Jivin, Jiven, Jivyn, Jivon

Joab (Hebrew) To praise God
Joabe

Joachim (Hebrew) One who is established
by God; God will judge
*Jachim, Jakim, Joacheim, Joaquim, Joaquin,
Josquin, Joakim, Joakeen, Jokim, Jokin*

Joash (Hebrew) God has given
Joashe

Job (Hebrew) One who is persecuted;
afflicted
*Johb, Jobe, Joby, Jobey, Jobi, Jobee, Jobie,
Jobson, Jobsun*

Joben (Japanese) One who enjoys being
clean
Joban, Jobin, Jobyn, Jobun, Jobon

Jocheved (Hebrew) The glory of God

Jody (English) Form of Joseph, meaning
"God will add"
Jodey, Jodi, Jodie, Jodee, Jodea

Joe (English) Form of Joseph, meaning
"God will add"
Jo, Joemar, Jomar, Joey, Joie, Joee, Joeye

Joed (Hebrew) God is witness

Joel (Hebrew) Jehovah is God; God
is willing
Joell

Johar (Hindi) As precious as a jewel
Joharr, Jahar, Jahara

Johnson (English) The son of John
*Jonson, Johnsun, Jonsun, Johston,
Johnstun, Jonstun, Jonston*

Joji (Japanese) Form of George, meaning
"one who works the earth; a farmer"
Jojie, Jojy, Jojey, Jojee

Jokull (Scandinavian) From the glacier
Jokule, Jokulle, Jokul

Jolon (Native American) From the valley of
dead oak trees
Jolun, Jolin, Jolyn, Jolen, Jolan

Jomei (Japanese) One who spreads light
Jomay, Jomaye, Jomai, Jomae

Jomo (African) One who works the earth;
a farmer
Jomoe, Jomow, Jomowe

Jonah (Hebrew) Resembling a dove; in the
Bible, the man swallowed by a whale
Joenah, Jonas, Jonasco, Joah

Jonathan ✡ ✝ (Hebrew) A gift of God
*Johnathan, Johnathon, Jonathon, Jonatan,
Jonaton, Jonathen, Johnathen, Jonaten,
Jonathyn, Johnathyn, Jonatyn*

Jonco (Slavic) Form of John, meaning
"God is gracious"
Jonko, Joncko, Joncco, Jonkko

Jones (English) From the family of John

Joo-chan (Korean) One who praises
the lord

Jorah (Hebrew) God has reproached
Jora

Joram (Hebrew) Jehovah is exalted
Jorim, Jorem, Jorom, Jorum, Jorym

Jordan ✪ ⊕ (Hebrew) Of the down-flow-ing river; in the Bible, the river where Jesus was baptized
Johrdan, Jordain, Jordaine, Jordane, Jordanke, Jordann, Jorden, Jordaen, Jordaene, Jordayn, Jordayne, Jourdayne, Jordenn, Jordie, Jordin, Jordyn, Jordynn, Jorey, Jori, Jorie, Jorrdan, Jorry, Jourdan, Jourdain, Jourdayn, Jourdaen, Jourdaene, Jordell, Jordel, Jordy, Jordey, Jordi, Jory, Jordon, Jourdano, Jourdon

Josiah ✪ (Hebrew) God will help
Josia, Josias, Joziah, Jozia, Jozias

Jotham (Hebrew) God is perfect

Journey (American) One who likes to travel
Journy, Journi, Journie, Journee, Journye, Journea

Jovan (Latin) One who is majestic; in mythology, another name for Jupiter, the supreme god
Jeovani, Jeovanni, Jeovany, Jovani, Jovann, Jovanni, Jovanny, Jovany, Jove, Jovi, Jovin, Jovito, Jovon, Jov

> **JOEY**
> My husband has always told me that Italian tradition is that the first grandson should be named after the paternal grandfather. We wanted a more American name than my husband's father, Giuseppe, so we chose Joseph. We used my dad's name, Richard, for the middle name, so Joey is named after his grandfathers. —Dana, IL

Jordison (American) The son of Jordan
Jordyson, Jordisun, Jordysun, Jordisen, Jordysen

Joren (Scandinavian) Form of George, meaning "one who works the earth; a farmer"
Joran, Jorian, Jorien, Joron, Jorun, Joryn, Jorin, Jorn, Jorne, Joergen, Joris, Jorma

Jorge (Spanish) Form of George, meaning "one who works the earth; a farmer"
Jorje

Jorn (German) A vigilant watchman
Jorne

Jorryn (American) Loved by God
Jorrin, Jorren, Jorran, Jorron, Jorrun

Joseph ✪ ⊕ (Hebrew) God will add
*Jessop, Jessup, Joop, Joos, José, **Jose**, Josef, Joseito, Joselito, Josep, Josip, Josif, Josephe, Josephus, Joss, Josslin, Joslin, Joszef, Jozef, Joseba, Joosef, Joosep, Jooseppi, Joosepe, Joosepi, Jopie, Jopi, Josu, Joza, Jozka*

Joshua ✪ ⊕ (Hebrew) God is salvation
Josh, Joshuah, Josua, Josue, Joushua, Jozua, Joshwa, Joshuwa, Joshuam, Joshyam, Joshka, Josha

Joyner (English) One who works with wood; a carpenter
Joiner

Juan ✪ ⊕ (Spanish) Form of John, meaning "God is gracious"
Juanito, Juwan, Jwan

Jubal (Hebrew) Resembling a ram
Juball, Joubal, Jouball, Joobal, Jooball

Jubilo (Spanish) One who is rejoicing
Jubylo, Jubilio, Jubylio, Jubileo, Jubyleo

Judah (Hebrew) One who praises God
Juda, Jude, Judas, Judsen, Judson, Judd, Jud, Judule

Judge (English) One who sits in judgment of others
Judg, Juge

Juha (Hebrew) A gift from God
Juhah, Juka, Jukah, Jukka, Jukkah, Juca, Jucah, Jucca, Juccah

Julian ✪ (Greek) The child of Jove; one who is youthful
Juliano, Julianus, Julien, Julyan, Julio, Jolyon, Jullien, Julen, Julean, Jilliann, Jillian, Jilian

Julius (Greek) The child of Jove; one who is youthful
Julis, Jule, Jules, Julious, Julios, 38899, Juli, Julee, Juley, Juleus, Junius

Juma (African) Born on a Friday
Jumah

Jumaane (African) Born on a Tuesday

Jumbe (African) Having great strength
Jumbi, Jumbie, Jumby, Jumbey, Jumbee

Jumoke (African) One who is dearly loved
Jumok, Jumoak

Jun (Japanese) One who is obedient

Junaid (Arabic) A warrior
*Junaide, Junayd, Junayde, Junade, Junaed,
Junaede*

June (Latin) One who is youthful; born
during the month of June
Junae, Junel, Junell, Juin

Jung (Korean) A righteous man

Junior (English) The younger one
Junyor, Junyer, Junier

Juniper (Latin) Resembling the evergreen
shrub with berries
Junyper, Junipyre, Junypyre

Jupiter (Latin) In mythology, the
supreme god
Jupyter, Juppiter, Juppyter

Jurass (American) Resembling a dinosaur
Juras, Jurassic, Jurassik, Jurasic, Jurasik

Jurgen (German) Form of George, meaning "one who works the earth; a farmer"
Jorgen, Jurgin, Jorgin, Jurgyn, Jorgyn

Juri (Slavic) Form of George, meaning
"one who works the earth; a farmer"
*Jurie, Jurey, Juree, Jurea, Jury, Jurg,
Jeirgif, Jaris*

Justice (English) One who upholds moral
rightness and fairness
*Justyce, Justiss, Justyss, Justis, Justus,
Justise*

Justin ○ ○ (Latin) One who is just and
upright
*Joost, Justain, Justan, Just, Juste, Justen,
Justino, Justo, Justyn*

Justinian (Latin) An upright ruler
*Justinien, Justinious, Justinius, Justinios,
Justinas, Justinus*

Juvenal (Latin) A young boy
*Juvinal, Juvenel, Juvinel, Juventino, Juvy,
Juvey, Juvee, Juvi, Juvie*

Kaaria (African) A wise, soft-spoken man
Karia, Kaarya, Karya, Kaariya, Kariya

Kabaka (African) A king
Kabakka, Kabaaka

Kabili (African) A possession
*Kabilie, Kabily, Kabiley, Kabilee,
Kabileigh, Kabilea*

Kabir (Indian) A spiritual leader
*Kabeer, Kabear, Kabier, Kabeir, Kabyr,
Kabar*

Kabonero (African) A sign or symbol
Kabonerio, Kabonereo

Kabonesa (African) One who is born
during difficult times

Kabos (Hebrew) A swindler
Kaboes

Kacancu (African) The firstborn child
*Kacancue, Kakancu, Kakancue, Kacanku,
Kacankue*

Kacey (Irish) A vigilant man; one who
is alert
*Kacy, Kacee, Kacea, Kaci, Kacie, Kasey,
Kasy, Kasi, Kasie, Kasee, Kasea, Kaycey,
Kaycy, Kayci, Kaycie, Kaycee, Kaicey,
Kaicy, Kaici, Kaicie, Kaicee, Kaysey, Kaysy,
Kaysi, Kaysie, Kaysee, Kaisey, Kaisy, Kaisi,
Kaisie, Kaisee*

Kachada (Native American) A white-
skinned man

Kade (Scottish) From the wetlands
*Kaid, Kaide, Kayd, Kayde, Kaed, Kaede,
Kady, Kadey, Kadee, Kadea, Kadi, Kadie*

Kaden ○ (Arabic) A beloved companion
*Kadan, Kadin, Kadon, Kaidan, Kaiden,
Kaidin, Kaidon, Kaydan, Kayden, Kaydin,
Kaydon, Kaeden, Kaedan, Kaedin, Kaedon*

Kadir (Arabic) One who is capable; one
who is competent
Kadeer, Kadear, Kadier, Kadeir, Kadyr

Kadmiel (Hebrew) One who stands before God
Kamiell

Kado (Japanese) From the gateway
Kadoe, Kadow, Kadowe

Kaelan (Gaelic) A mighty warrior
Kaelen, Kaelin, Kaelyn, Kalan, Kalen, Kalin, Kalyn, Kaylan, Kaylin, Kaylen, Kaylin, Kailan, Kailen, Kailin, Kailyn, Kaele, Kael, Kail, Kaile, Kale, Kayl, Kayle

Kaelem (American) An honest man
Kalem, Kaylem, Kailem

Kaemon (Japanese) Full of joy; one who is right-handed
Kamon, Kaymon, Kaimon

Kafele (Egyptian) A son to die for
Kafel, Kafell, Kafelle

Kafi (African) A quiet and well-behaved boy
Kafie, Kafy, Kafey, Kafee, Kafea

Kafka (Czech) Resembling a bird
Kofka

Kaga (Native American) One who chronicles
Kagah, Kagga, Kaggah

Kagen (Irish) A fiery man; a thinker
Kaigen, Kagan, Kaigan, Kaygen, Kaygan, Kaegen, Kaegan

Kahale (Hawaiian) A homebody
Kahail, Kahaile, Kahayl, Kahayle, Kahael, Kahaele

Kaherdin (English) In Arthurian legend, the brother of Isolde
Kaherden, Kaherdan, Kaherdyn

Kahlil (Arabic) A beloved friend
Kahleil, Kahlyl, Kahleel, Kalil, Kaleil, Kalyl, Kaleel, Khalil, Khaleil, Khalyl, Khaleel, Kahil, Kaheil, Kahyl, Kaheel

Kahn (Hebrew) A priest
Kan, Khan

Kahoku (Hawaiian) Resembling a star
Kahokue, Kahokoo, Kahokou

Kaholo (Hawaiian) A running boy

Kai (Hawaiian / Welsh / Greek) Of the sea / the keeper of the keys / of the earth
Kye, Keh

Kaihe (Hawaiian) One who wields a spear
Kayhe, Kaehe, Kaihi, Kayhi, Kaehi, Kaihie, Kayhie, Kaehie

Kaikara (African) God

Kaikura (African) Resembling a ground squirrel

Kaila (Hawaiian) A stylish man
Kayla, Kaela

Kailas (Hindi) The home of Lord Shiva

Kaili (Hawaiian) A god
Kailie, Kaily, Kailey, Kailee, Kaileigh, Kailea

Kaimi (Hawaiian) The seeker
Kaimie, Kaimy, Kaimey, Kaimee, Kaimea

Kain (Hebrew) The acquirer

Kaipo (Hawaiian) One who embraces others; a sweetheart
Kaypo, Kaepo, Kapo

Kairo (African) From the city of Cairo

Kaiser (German) An imperial ruler
Keyser, Kaizer, Keyzer, Kyser, Kyzer, Kiser, Kizer

Kaj (Scandinavian) Of the earth

Kajika (Native American) One who walks silently
Kajica, Kajicka, Kajyka, Kajyca, Kajycka, Kijika, Kyjika

Kala (Hawaiian) Son of the sun
Kalah, Kalla, Kallah

Kalama (Hawaiian) A source of light
Kalam, Kalame

Kalani (Hawaiian) From the heavens
Kalanie, Kalany, Kalaney, Kalanee, Kaloni, Kalonie, Kalonee, Kalony, Kaloney, Kalonea, Keilani, Kalanea

Kaleb (Hebrew) Resembling an aggressive dog
Kaileb, Kaeleb, Kayleb, Kalob, Kailob, Kaelob, Kaylob, Kalb

Kalei (Hawaiian) An attendant of the king

Kalevi (Finnish) A hero
Kalevie, Kalevy, Kalevey, Kalevea, Kalevee

Kali (Polynesian) One who provides comfort
Kalie, Kaly, Kaley, Kalee, Kaleigh, Kalea

Kalidas (Hindi) A poet or musician;
a servant of Kali
Kalydas

Kaliq (Arabic) One who is creative
*Kaleeq, Kaleaq, Kalieq, Kaleiq, Kalyq,
Kaleek, Kaleak, Kaliek, Kaleik, Kalik,
Kalyk*

Kalki (Indian) Resembling a white horse
Kalkie, Kalky, Kalkey, Kalkee, Kalkea

Kalkin (Hindi) The tenth-born child
Kalkyn, Kalken, Kalkan, Kalkon, Kalkun

Kallen (Greek) A handsome man
Kallin, Kallyn, Kallon, Kallun, Kallan

Kalman (French) Having great strength
*Kalmann, Kalle, Kalli, Kallie, Kally, Kalley,
Kallee, Kallea*

Kalogeros (Greek) One who ages well

Kaloosh (Armenian) A blessed birth
Kalooshe, Kaloush, Kaloushe

Kalunga (African) One who is alert and
watchful

Kalvin (English) The little bald one
Kalvyn, Kalvon, Kalvan, Kalven, Kalvun

Kalyan (Indian) One who is happy and
prosperous

Kamaka (Hawaiian) Having a handsome
face

Kamal (Arabic) The perfect man
*Kamall, Kamaal, Kamil, Kameel, Kameal,
Kameil, Kamiel, Kamyl*

Kamau (African) A quiet warrior

Kamden (English) From the winding valley
*Kamdun, Kamdon, Kamdan, Kamdin,
Kamdyn*

Kame (African) From a desolate land
*Kaim, Kaime, Kaym, Kayme, Kaem,
Kaeme*

Kameron (English) Having a crooked nose
*Kamerin, Kameryn, Kamrin, Kamron,
Kamryn, Kamren, Kameren, Kamran,
Kameran, Kam*

Kami (Hindi) A loving man
*Kamie, Kamy, Kamey, Kamee, Kamea,
Kamilyn, Kamilin*

Kamon (American) Resembling an
alligator
*Kaman, Kaymon, Kayman, Kaimon,
Kaiman, Kaemon, Kaeman*

Kamuzu (African) One who heals others
*Kamuzue, Kamuezue, Kamouzu,
Kamouzou*

Kamwimbile (African) One who praises
God

Kana (Hawaiian) In mythology, a demigod
who could transform into rope

Kanad (Indian) An ancient
Kaned, Kanid, Kanyd

Kanak (Indian) The golden one
Kanac, Kanack, Kanek, Kanec, Kaneck

Kanan (Indian) From the garden
Kanen, Kanin, Kanyn, Kanon, Kanun

Kanaye (Japanese) A zealous man
Kanay, Kanai, Kanae

Kance (American) An attractive man
*Kanse, Kaince, Kainse, Kaynce, Kaynse,
Kaence, Kaense*

Kane (Gaelic) The little warrior
Kayn, Kayne, Kaen, Kaene, Kahan, Kahane

Kanelo (African) Enough
Kaneloh, Kanello, Kanelloh

Kang (Korean) A healthy man

Kanga (Native American) Resembling a
raven
*Kange, Kangee, Kangea, Kangy, Kangey,
Kangi, Kangie*

Kaniel (Hebrew) Supported by the Lord
Kaniell, Kanielle, Kanyel, Kanyell, Kanyelle

Kannon (Japanese) The Buddhist deity of
mercy
Kannun, Kannen, Kannan, Kannin, Kannyn

Kano (Japanese) A powerful man
Kanoe, Kanoh

Kanoa (Hawaiian) One who is free

K

Kansas (Native American) Of the south wind people; from the state of Kansas

Kant (German) A philosopher
Kante

Kantrava (Indian) Resembling a roaring animal

Kantu (Indian) Filled with joy
Kantue, Kantou, Kantoo

Kanva (Indian) From the river; a sage

Kanvar (Indian) A young prince
Kanvarr

Kaori (Japanese) Having a pleasant scent
Kaorie, Kaory, Kaorey, Kaoree, Kaorea

Kaper (American) One who is capricious
Kahper, Kapar, Kahpar

Kapila (Hindi) A prophet
Kapyla, Kapil, Kapyl

Kaplony (Hungarian) Resembling a tiger
Kaploney, Kaploni, Kaplonie, Kaplonee, Kaplonea

Kapono (Hawaiian) A righteous man

Karan (Greek) One who is pure; chaste

Karcher (German) A handsome blonde-haired man
Karchar, Karchir, Karchyr, Karchor, Karchur

Karcsi (French) A strong manly man
Karcsie, Karcsy, Karcsey, Karcsee, Karcsea

Kardal (Arabic) Of the mustard seed
Kardall

Kardos (Hungarian) One who wields a sword

Kare (Scandinavian) An enormous man
Kair, Kaire, Kayr, Kayre, Kaer, Kaere

Kareem (Arabic) A generous man
Kaream, Karim, Karym, Kariem, Kareim, Karam, Kharim, Khareem, Khaream, Khariem, Khareim, Kharym

Kari (Norse) Of the wind/one with curly hair
Karie, Kary, Karey, Karee, Karea

Karif (Arabic) Born during autumn
Kareef, Kareaf, Karief, Kareif, Karyf

Karl (German) A free man
Karel, Karlan, Karle, Karlens, Karli, Karlin, Karlo, Karlos, Karlton, Karrel, Karol, Karoly, Karson, Kaarl, Kaarlo, Karlis, Karlys, Karlitis

Karman (Gaelic) The lord of the manor
Karmen, Karmin, Karmyn, Karmon, Karmun

Karmel (Hebrew) From the garden or vineyard
Karmeli, Karmelli, Karmelo, Karmello, Karmi, Karmie, Karmee, Karmy, Karmey, Karmelie, Karmellie, Karmely, Karmelly, Karmeley, Karmelley

Karolek (Russian) A small strong man
Karolec, Karoleck

Karr (Scandinavian) From the marshland
Kerr, Kiarr

Karsa (Hungarian) Resembling a falcon
Karsah

Karsten (Greek) The anointed one
Karstan, Karstin, Karstyn, Karston, Karstun

Kartal (Hungarian) Resembling an eagle
Kartall

Kartar (Indian) A master

Karu (Indian) One who shows compassion
Karue, Karun, Karuen, Karune, Karunal, Karunakar

Karunamay (Indian) Surrounded by light
Karunamaye, Karunamai, Karunamae

Kasar (Indian) Resembling a lion
Kasarr

Kasch (German) Resembling a blackbird
Kasche, Kass, Kas, Kasse

Kaseko (African) One who is mocked

Kasem (Asian) Filled with joy

Kasen (Basque) Protected by a helmet
Kasin, Kasyn, Kason, Kasun, Kasan

Kashka (African) A friendly man
Kashkah

Kashvi (Indian) A shining man
Kashvie, Kashvy, Kashvey, Kashvee, Kashvea

Kasib (Arabic) One who is fertile
Kaseeb, Kaseab, Kasieb, Kaseib, Kasyb

Kasim (Arabic) One who is divided
*Kassim, Kaseem, Kasseem, Kaseam,
Kasseam, Kasym, Kassym*

Kasimir (Slavic) One who demands peace
*Kasimeer, Kasimear, Kasimier, Kasimeir,
Kasimyr, Kaz, Kazimierz, Kazimir, Kazmer,
Kazmeirz, Kazimeerz, Kazimearz,
Kazimyrz*

Kaspar (Persian) The keeper of the treasure
*Kasper, Kaspir, Kaspyr, Kaspor, Kaspur,
Kasbar, Kasber, Kansbar, Kansber*

Kassa (African) One who has been
compensated

Kassidy (English) A curly-haired man
*Kassidey, Kassidi, Kassidie, Kassidee,
Kasidy, Kasidey, Kasidi, Kasidie, Kasidee,
Kassidea, Kasidea*

Kasumi (Japanese) From the mist
*Kasumie, Kasume, Kasumy, Kasumey,
Kasumee, Kasumea*

Kateb (Arabic) A writer

Kathan (American) Form of Nathan,
meaning "a gift from God"
*Kaithan, Kathun, Kathon, Kathen,
Kaithun, Kaithon, Kaithen, Kaethan,
Kaethun, Kaethon, Kaethen, Kaythan,
Kaythun, Kaython, Kaythen*

Kato (Latin / African) A man of good
judgment / the second born of twins
Kaeto, Kaito, Kayto

Katungi (African) A wealthy man
*Katungie, Katungy, Katungey, Katungee,
Katungea*

Katura (African) To ease the burden

Katzir (Hebrew) The harvester
Katzyr, Katzeer, Katzear, Katzier, Katzeir

Kauai (Hawaiian) From the garden island
Kawai

Kaufman (German) A merchant
*Kauffman, Kaufmann, Kauffmann,
Kofman, Koffman, Kofmann, Koffmann*

Kaushal (Indian) One who is skilled
Kaushall, Koshal, Koshall

Kavan (Irish) A handsome man
*Kavin, Kaven, Kavyn, Kavon, Kavun,
Kayvan, Kayven, Kayvon, Kayvun, Kayvin,
Kayvyn*

Kavanagh (Gaelic) A follower of Kevin
Kavanau, Kavanaugh, Kavana

Kavi (Hindi) A poetic man
*Kavie, Kavy, Kavey, Kavee, Kavea,
Kavindra, Kavian, Kavien, Kaviraj,
Kavyanand*

Kawaii (Hawaiian) Of the water

Kay (Welsh) Filled with happiness; rejoicing
Kaye, Kae

Kayin (African) A long-awaited child
Kayen, Kayan, Kayon, Kayun

Kayonga (African) Of the ash
Kayunga

Kazan (Greek) A creative man
Kazen, Kazin, Kazyn, Kazon, Kazun

Kazi (African) A hardworking man
Kazie, Kazy, Kazey, Kazee, Kazea

Kazim (Arabic) An even-tempered man
Kazeem, Kazeam, Kaziem, Kazeim, Kazym

Kazuo (Japanese) A peaceful man

Keahi (Hawaiian) Of the flames
Keahie, Keahy, Keahey, Keahee, Keahea

Kealoha (Hawaiian) From the bright path
Keeloha, Kieloha

Kean (Gaelic / English) A warrior / one
who is sharp
*Keane, Keen, Keene, Kein, Keine, Keyn,
Keyne, Kien, Kiene*

Keandre (American) One who is thankful
*Kiandre, Keandray, Kiandray, Keandrae,
Kiandrae, Keandrai, Kiandrai*

Keanu (Hawaiian) Of the mountain breeze
*Keanue, Kianu, Kianue, Keanoo, Kianoo,
Keanou, Kianou*

Kearn (Irish) Having dark features
Kearne, Kern, Kerne

Kearney (Irish) The victor
*Kearny, Kearni, Kearnie, Kearnee,
Kearnea, Karney, Karny, Karni, Karnie,
Karnee, Karnea*

Keaton (English) From the town of hawks
Keatun, Keeton, Keetun, Keyton, Keytun

Keawe (Hawaiian) A lovable young man

Keb (African) Of the earth
Kebb

Kecalf (American) One who is inventive
Keecalf, Keacalf, Keicalf, Kiecalf, Keycalf

Kedar (Arabic) A powerful man
Keder, Kedir, Kedyr, Kadar, Kader, Kadir, Kadyr

Kedem (Hebrew) An old soul
Kedam, Kedim, Kedym, Kedom, Kedum

Kedrick (English) A gift of splendor
Kedryck, Kedrik, Kedryk, Kedric, Kedryc, Keddrick, Keddrik, Keddric

Keefe (Gaelic) A handsome and beloved man
Keef, Keafe, Keaf, Keif, Keife, Kief, Kiefe

Keerthi (Indian) Having fame and glory
Kearthi, Keerthie, Kearthie, Keerthy, Kearthy, Keerthey, Kearthey

Kefir (Hebrew) Resembling a young lion
Kefyr, Kefeer, Kefear, Kefier, Kefeir

Keiji (Japanese) A cautious ruler
Keijie, Keijy, Keijey, Keijee, Kayji, Kayjie, Kayjee, Kayjy, Kayjey

Keir (Gaelic) Having dark features
Keer, Kear, Keire, Keere, Keare, Keirer, Kearer, Keirer, Kerer

Keita (African) A worshiper

Keitaro (Japanese) One who is blessed
Kaytaro

Keith (Scottish) Man from the forest
Keithe, Keath, Keathe, Kieth, Kiethe, Keyth, Keythe, Keithen, Keethan, Keathen, Keythen

---

KEATON

My fourth child was supposed to have been a girl, so we had no boy name picked out. The other kids all had six-letter, two-syllable names of cities, so we had to think hard to match! We all spent two days in the hospital trying to come up with a name, and Keaton was the only name that everyone liked. —Beth, IA

Keegan (Gaelic) A small and fiery man
Kegan, Keigan, Kiegan, Keagan, Keagen, Keegen, Keeghan, Keaghan

Keelan (Gaelic) A slender man
Kelan, Kealan, Keallan, Keallin, Keilan, Keillan, Keelin, Keellan, Keellin, Keeland, Kealand, Keiland

Keely (Irish) A handsome man
Keeley, Keeli, Keelie, Keelee, Keeleigh, Kealey, Kealy, Keali, Kealie, Kealee, Kealeigh

Keenan (Gaelic) Of an ancient family
Keenen, Keenon, Kennan, Kennon, Kienan, Kienen, Keanan, Keanen, Keanon, Kienon, Keandre

Keeney (American) Having a clear and sharp mind
Keeny, Keeni, Keenie, Keenee, Keaney, Keany, Keani, Keanie, Keanee

Kekipi (Hawaiian) A rebel
Kekipie, Kekipy, Kekipey, Kekipee, Kekipea

Kekoa (Hawaiian) A warrior
Kekowa

Kelby (Gaelic) From the farm near the spring
Kelbey, Kelbe, Kelbee, Kelbea, Kelbi, Kelbie

Kele (Native American) Resembling a sparrow hawk

Keleman (Hungarian) One who is kind and gentle
Kelemen, Kelemin, Kelemyn, Kelemon, Kelemun, Kellman, Kellmen, Kellmin, Kellmyn, Kellmon, Kellmun, Kelman, Kelmen, Kelmin, Kelmyn, Kelmon, Kelmun

Kelii (Hawaiian) The chief

Kelile (African) My protector
Kelyle

Kell (Norse) From the spring
Kelle, Kel

Kellach (Irish) One who suffers strife during battle
Kelach, Kellagh, Kelagh, Keallach

Kelleher (Irish) A loving husband
Keleher, Kellehar, Kelehar, Kellehir, Kelehir, Kellehyr, Kelehyr

Kellen (Gaelic / German) One who is slender / from the swamp
Kelle, Kellan, Kellon, Kellun, Kellin, Kellyn

Keller (German / Celtic) From the cellar / a beloved friend
Kellar, Kellor, Kellur, Kellir, Kellyr

Kelley (Celtic / Gaelic) A warrior / one who defends
Kelly, Kelleigh, Kellee, Kellea, Kelleah, Kelli, Kellie

Kellicka (Latin / Irish) One who is strong-willed / a charming man
Kelicka, Kellika, Kelika, Kellica, Kelica

Kelsey (English) From the island of ships; of the ship's victory
Kelsie, Kelcey, Kelcie, Kelcy, Kellsie, Kelsa, Kelsea, Kelsee, Kelsi, Kelsy, Kellsey, Kelcea, Kelcee

Kelton (English) From the town of keels
Keldon, Kelltin, Kellton, Kelten, Keltin, Keltun, Kelltun, Keltyn, Kelltyn

Kelvin (English) A friend of ships; a man of the river
Kellven, Kelvan, Kelven, Kelvon, Kelvyn, Kelwin, Kelwinn, Kelwinne, Kelwyn, Kelwynn, Kelwynne, Kelwen, Kelwine, Kelwenn, Kelwenne

Kelvis (American) One who is ambitious
Kelviss, Kelvys, Kelvyss, Kellvis, Kellvys

Kemal (Turkish) One who receives the highest honor
Kemall

Keme (Native American) A secretive man

Kemen (Spanish) Having great strength
Keman, Kemin, Kemyn, Kemon, Kemun

Kemenes (Hungarian) One who makes furnaces

Kemp (English) The champion
Kempe, Kempi, Kempie, Kempy, Kempey, Kempee

Kemper (American) One who is noble
Kempar, Kempir, Kempyr, Kempor, Kempur

Kempton (English) From the champion's town
Kemptun

Kemuel (Hebrew) God's helper

Ken (English / Japanese) Form of Kenneth, meaning "born of the fire; an attractive man" / one who is strong and healthy
Kenny, Kenney, Kenni, Kennie, Kennee

Kenan (Hebrew) One who acquires
Kenen, Kenin, Kenyn, Kenon, Kenun

Kenaz (Hebrew) A bright man
Kenez, Kenaaz

Kendall (Welsh) From the royal valley
Kendal, Kendale, Kendel, Kendell, Kendill, Kendle, Kendyl, Kendyll, Kendhal, Kendhall

Kendan (English) Having great strength
Kenden, Kendin, Kendyn, Kendon, Kendun

Kende (Hungarian) One who is honored

Kendi (African) One who is much loved
Kendie, Kendy, Kendey, Kendee, Kendea

Kendis (American) One who is pure; chaste
Kendiss, Kendys, Kendyss

Kendrew (Scottish) A warrior
Kendru, Kendrue

Kendrick (English / Gaelic) A royal ruler / the champion
Kendric, Kendricks, Kendrik, Kendrix, Kendryck, Kenrick, Kenrik, Kenricks, Kendryk, Kendryc, Kenric, Kendriek, Kendryek, Kenrich, Kendrich, Kenriek, Kenryk

Kenelm (English) Of the brave helmet
Kenhelm

Kenji (Japanese) A smart second son; one who is vigorous
Kenjie, Kenjy, Kenjey, Kenjee, Kenjiro

Kenley (English) From the king's meadow
Kenly, Kenlee, Kenleigh, Kenlea, Kenleah, Kenli, Kenlie

Kenn (Welsh) Of the bright waters

Kennard (English) Of the brave or royal guard
Kennerd, Kennaird, Kennward, Kenard, Kenerd, Kenward

Kennedy (Gaelic) A helmeted chief
Kennedi, Kennedie, Kennedey, Kennedee, Kennedea, Kenadie, Kenadi, Kenady, Kenadey, Kenadee, Kenadea, Kennady, Kennadey, Kennadee, Kennadi, Kennadie

Kenner (English) An able-bodied man
Kennar, Kennir, Kennor, Kennur, Kennyr

Kenneth (Irish) Born of the fire; an attractive man
Kennet, Kennett, Kennith, Kennit, Kennitt

Kent (English) From the edge or border
Kentt, Kennt, Kentrell

Kentaro (Japanese) One who is sharp/ a big boy

Kentigem (Celtic) A chief
Kentygem, Kentigim, Kentygim

Kentley (English) From the meadow's edge
Kentleigh, Kentlea, Kentleah, Kentlee, Kently, Kentli, Kentlie

Kenton (English) From the king's town
Kentun, Kentan, Kentin, Kenten, Kentyn

Kentucky (Native American) From the land of tomorrow; from the state of Kentucky
Kentucki, Kentuckie, Kentuckey, Kentuckee, Kentuckea

Kenway (English) A brave or royal warrior
Kennway, Kenwaye, Kennwaye

Kenyatta (African) One who is musically talented
Kenyata, Kenyatt, Kenyat

Kenyi (African) A son born after daughters
Kenyie, Kenyee, Kenyea, Kenyey

Kenyon (Gaelic) A blonde-haired man
Kenyun, Kenyan, Kenyen, Kenyin

Kenzie (Gaelic) One who is fair; light-skinned
Kenzi, Kenzy, Kenzey, Kenzee, Kenzea

Keoki (Hawaiian) Form of George, meaning "one who works the earth; a farmer"
Keokie, Keoky, Keokey, Keokee, Keokea

Keola (Hawaiian) Full of life; one who is vibrant

Keon (Irish) Form of John, meaning "God is gracious"
Keyon, Kion, Kiyon, Keoni, Keonie, Keony, Keoney, Keonee, Keonea

Keontay (American) An outrageous man
Keontaye, Keontai, Keontae, Kiontay, Kiontaye, Kiontai, Kiontae

Kepler (German) One who makes hats
Keppler, Kappler, Keppel, Keppeler

Keran (Armenian) A wooden post
Keren, Keron, Kerun, Kerin, Keryn

Kerbasi (Basque) A warrior
Kerbasie, Kerbasee, Kerbasea, Kerbasy, Kerbasey

Kerecsen (Hungarian) Resembling a falcon
Kereksen, Kerecsan, Kereksan, Kerecsin, Kereksin

Kerel (African) One who is forever young
Keral, Keril, Keryl, Kerol, Kerul

Kerem (Turkish / Hebrew) A kind and noble man / from the vineyard

Kerman (French) A man from Germany
Kermen, Kermin, Kermyn, Kermon, Kermun

Kermit (Gaelic) One who is free of envy
Kermyt, Kermot, Kermet, Kermat, Kermut, Kerme, Kerm, Kermi, Kermie, Kermy, Kermey, Kermee

Kernaghan (Gaelic) A victorious man
Kernohan, Kernahan, Kernoghan

Kerrick (English) Under the king's rule
Kerryck, Kerrik, Kerryk, Kerric, Kerryc

Kerry (Gaelic) Having black hair
Kerrey, Kerri, Kerrie, Kerree, Keary, Kearey, Kearee, Keari, Kearie, Keri, Kerie, Kery, Kerey, Keree, Kerrigan, Kerigan

Kers (Indian) Resembling the plant

Kersen (Indonesian) Resembling a cherry
Kersan, Kersin, Kersyn, Kerson, Kersun

Kershet (Hebrew) Of the rainbow

Kert (American) One who enjoys the simple pleasures of life
Kerte

Kerwin (Irish / English) Little dark one / a friend from the swamp
Kerwinn, Kerwinne, Kerwyn, Kerwynn, Kerwynne, Kerwen, Kerwenn, Kerwenne, Kervin, Kervyn, Kirwin, Kirvin, Kirwyn, Kirvyn, Kirwinn, Kirwinne, Kirwynn, Kirwynne, Kirwen, Kirwenn, Kirwenne

Kesegowaase (Native American) One who is swift

Keshawn (American) A friendly man
Keshaun, Keshon, Keyshawn, Keyshaun, Keyshon

Keshi (Indian) A long-haired man
Keshie, Keshey, Keshy, Keshee, Keshea

Kesler (American) An energetic man; one who is independent
Keslar, Keslir, Keslyr, Keslor, Keslur

Keslie (American) Form of Leslie, meaning "from the holly garden; of the gray fortress"
Keslea, Keslee, Kesleigh, Kesley, Kesli, Kesly, Kezlee, Kezley, Kezlie, Kezleigh, Kezli, Kezlea

Kesse (American) An attractive man
Kessee, Kessea, Kessi, Kessie, Kessy, Kessey

Kestejoo (Native American) A slave
Kesteju, Kestejue

Kester (Latin / Gaelic) From the Roman army's camp / a follower of Christ
Kestar, Kestir, Kestyr, Kestor, Kestur

Kestrel (English) One who soars
Kestral, Kestril, Kestryl, Kestrol, Kestrul

Kettil (Swedish) Of the cauldron
Ketil, Keld, Kjeld, Ketti, Kettie, Ketty, Kettey, Kettee, Ketill

Keung (Chinese) A universal spirit

Keval (Indian) One who is pure; chaste
Kevel, Kevil, Kevyl, Kevol, Kevul

Keve (Hungarian) Resembling a pebble

Kevin ✪ (Gaelic) A beloved and handsome man
Kevyn, Kevan, Keven, Keveon, Kevinn, Kevion, Kevis, Kevon, Kevron, Kevren, Kevran, Kevrun, Kevryn, Kevrin

Kevork (Armenian) One who works the earth; a farmer
Kevorke, Kevorc, Kevorkk, Kevorcc, Kevorck

Khadim (Arabic) A servant of God
Khadeem, Khadym, Khadiem, Khadeim, Khadeam, Kadeem, Kadim, Kadeam, Kadiem, Kadeim

Khairi (Swahili) A kingly man
Khairie, Khairy, Khairey, Khairee, Khairea

Khaldun (Arabic) An eternal soul
Khaldon, Khaldoon, Khaldoun, Khaldune

Khalid (Arabic) One who is immortal
Khaleed, Khalead, Khaleid, Khalied, Khalyd, Khaled

Khalon (American) A strong warrior
Khalun, Khalen, Khalan, Khalin, Khalyn

Khambrel (American) One who is well-spoken
Kambrel, Khambrell, Kambrell

Khamisi (Swahili) Born on a Thursday
Khamisie, Khamisy, Khamisey, Khamisee, Khamisea

Khan (Turkish) Born to royalty; a prince
Khanh

Kharouf (Arabic) Resembling a lamb
Karouf, Kharoufe, Karoufe

Khayri (Arabic) One who is charitable
Khayrie, Khayry, Khayrey, Khayree, Khayrea

Khayyat (Arabic) A tailor
Khayat, Kayyat, Kayat

Khorshed (Persian) Of the sun

Khortdad (Persian) A man of perfection
Khourtdad, Kortdad, Kourtdad

Khouri (Arabic) A spiritual man; a priest
Khourie, Khoury, Khourey, Khouree, Kouri, Kourie, Koury, Kourey, Kouree

Khushi (Indian) Filled with happiness
Khushie, Khushey, Khushy, Khushee

Khuyen (Vietnamese) One who offers advice

Kian (Irish) From an ancient family
Kiann, Kyan, Kyann, Kiyan, Keyan, Kianni, Kiannie, Kianny, Kianney, Kiannee, Kiani, Kianie, Kianey, Kiany, Kianee

Kibbe (Native American) A nocturnal bird
Kybbe

Kibo (African) From the highest moutain peak
Keybo, Keebo, Keabo, Keibo, Kiebo

Kibou (Japanese) Filled with hope
Kybou

Kidd (English) Resembling a young goat
Kid, Kydd, Kyd

Kiefer (German) One who makes barrels
Keefer, Keifer, Kieffer, Kiefner, Kieffner, Kiefert, Kuefer, Kueffner

Kieran (Gaelic) Having dark features; the little dark one
Keiran, Keiron, Kernan, Kieren, Kiernan, Kieron, Kierren, Kierrin, Kierron, Keeran, Keeron, Keernan, Keeren, Kearan, Kearen, Kearon, Kearnan

Kiet (Thai) One who is honored; respected
Kyet, Kiete, Kyete

Kifle (African) My due
Kyfle, Kifel, Kyfel

Kiho (African) Of the fog
Kihoe, Kyho, Kyhoe

Kijana (African) A youthful man
Kyjana

Kildaire (Irish) From county of Kildare
Kyldaire, Kildare, Kyldare, Kildair, Kyldair, Killdaire, Kylldaire, Kildayr, Kyldayr, Kildayre, Kyldayre, Kildaer, Kildaere, Kyldaer, Kyldaere

Killian (Gaelic) One who is small and fierce
Killean, Kilean, Kilian, Killyan, Kilyan, Kyllian, Kylian

Kim (Vietnamese) As precious as gold
Kym

Kimane (African) Resembling a large bean
Kymane, Kimain, Kimaine, Kymain, Kymaine, Kimaen, Kimaene, Kymaen, Kymaene, Kimayn, Kimayne, Kymayn, Kymayne

Kimathi (African) A determined provider
Kimathie, Kimathy, Kimathey, Kimathee, Kymathi, Kymathie, Kymathy, Kymathey, Kymathee

Kimball (English) One who leads warriors
Kimbal, Kimbel, Kimbell, Kimble

Kimberly (English) Of the royal fortress
Kimberley, Kimberli, Kimberlee, Kimberleigh, Kimberlin, Kimberlyn, Kymberlie, Kymberly, Kymberlee, Kim, Kimmy, Kimmie, Kimmi, Kym, Kimber, Kymber, Kimberlie, Kimbra, Kimbro, Kimbrough, Kinborough, Kimberlea, Kimberleah, Kymberlea, Kymberleah

Kimn (English) A great ruler

Kimo (Hawaiian) Form of James, meaning "he who supplants"
Kymo

Kimoni (African) A great man
Kimonie, Kimony, Kimoney, Kimonee, Kymoni, Kymonie, Kymony, Kymoney, Kymonee

Kin (Japanese) The golden one
Kyn

Kincaid (Celtic) The leader during battle
Kincade, Kincayd, Kincayde, Kincaide, Kincaed, Kincaede, Kinkaid, Kinkaide, Kinkayd, Kinkayde, Kinkaed, Kinkaede, Kinkade

Kindin (Basque) The fifth-born child
Kinden, Kindan, Kindyn, Kindon, Kindun

Kindle (American) To set aflame
Kindel, Kyndle, Kyndel

Kinfe (African) Having wings
Kynfe

King (English) The royal ruler
Kyng

Kingman (English) The king's man
Kingmann, Kyngman, Kyngmann

Kingsley (English) From the king's meadow
Kingsly, Kingsleigh, Kingslea, Kingsleah, Kingsli, Kingslie, Kingslee, Kinsley, Kinsly, Kinsleigh, Kinslee, Kinslea, Kinsleah, Kinsli, Kinslie

Kingston (English) From the king's town
Kingstun, Kinston, Kinstun, Kingdon, Kindon, Kingdun, Kindun

Kingswell (English) From the king's spring
Kinswell, Kyngswell, Kynswell

Kinion (English) Of the family
Kinyon

Kinnard (Irish) From the tall hill
*Kinard, Kinnaird, Kinaird, Kynnard,
Kynard, Kynnaird, Kynaird*

Kinnell (Gaelic) From the top of the cliff
*Kinel, Kinnel, Kinell, Kynnell, Kynel,
Kynnel, Kynell*

Kinnon (Scottish) One who is fair-born
Kinnun, Kinnen, Kinnan, Kinnin, Kinnyn

Kinsey (English) The victorious prince
*Kynsey, Kinsi, Kynsi, Kinsie, Kynsie,
Kinsee, Kynsee, Kinsea, Kynsea, Kensey,
Kensy, Kensi, Kensie, Kensee, Kensea*

Kintan (Hindi) One who is crowned
Kinten, Kinton, Kintun, Kintin, Kintyn

Kione (African) One who has come from
nowhere

Kioshi (Japanese) One who is quiet
*Kioshe, Kioshie, Kioshy, Kioshey, Kioshee,
Kyoshi, Kyoshe, Kyoshie, Kyoshy, Kyoshey,
Kyoshee, Kiyoshi, Kiyoshie, Kiyoshey,
Kiyoshy, Kiyoshee*

Kipp (English) From the small pointed hill
*Kip, Kipling, Kippling, Kypp, Kyp, Kiplyng,
Kipplyng, Kippi, Kippie, Kippar, Kipper,
Kippor, Kippur, Kippyr*

Kirabo (African) A gift from God
*Kiraboe, Kirabow, Kyrabo, Kyraboe,
Kyrabow*

Kiral (Turkish) The supreme chief; a lord
Kyral, Kirall, Kyrall

Kiran (Hindi) A ray of light
*Kyran, Kiren, Kyren, Kiron, Kyron, Kirun,
Kyrun, Kirin, Kyrin, Kiryn, Kyryn*

Kirby (German) From the village with the
church
*Kirbey, Kirbi, Kirbie, Kirbee, Kerby,
Kerbey, Kerbi, Kerbie, Kerbee*

Kiri (Vietnamese) Resembling the mountains
Kirie, Kiry, Kirey, Kiree, Kirea

Kiril (Greek) Of the Lord
Kirill, Kirillos, Kyril, Kyrill

Kirit (Hindi) One who is crowned
Kiryt, Kireet, Kireat, Kiriet, Kireit

Kirk (Norse) A man of the church
Kyrk, Kerk, Kirklin, Kirklyn

Kirkan (Armenian) One who is vigilant
*Kirken, Kirkin, Kirkyn, Kirkon, Kirkun,
Kirkor, Kirkur, Kirkar, Kirker, Kirkir,
Kirkyr*

Kirkland (English) From the church's land
*Kirklan, Kirklande, Kyrkland, Kyrklan,
Kyrklande*

Kirkley (English) From the church's meadow
*Kirkly, Kirkleigh, Kirklea, Kirkleah,
Kirklee, Kirkli, Kirklie*

Kirkwell (English) From the church's
spring
Kyrkwell, Kirkwel, Kyrkwel

Kirkwood (English) From the church's forest
Kirkwode, Kyrkwood, Kyrkwode

Kishi (Native American) Born at night
*Kishie, Kishy, Kishey, Kishee, Kishea,
Kyshi, Kyshie, Kyshy, Kyshey, Kyshee,
Kyshea*

Kisho (Japanese) A self-assured man
Kysho

Kit (English) Form of Christopher, meaning "one who bears Christ inside"
Kitt, Kyt, Kytt

Kitchi (Native American) A brave young
man
Kitchie, Kitchy, Kitchey, Kitchee, Kitchea

Kito (African) One who is precious
Kyto

Kitoko (African) A handsome man
Kytoko

Kivi (Finnish) As solid as stone
Kivie, Kivy, Kivey, Kivee, Kivea

Kizza (African) One who is born after twins
Kyzza, Kiza, Kyzza

Kizzy (Hebrew) Resembling cinnamon
Kizzi, Kizzey, Kizzie, Kizzee, Kizzea

Klaus (German) Of the victorious people
Klaas, Klaes

Klay (English) A reliable and trustworthy
man
Klaye, Klai, Klae, Klaie

Kleef (Dutch) From the cliff
Kleefe, Kleaf, Kleafe, Kleif, Kleife, Klief, Kliefe, Kleyf, Klyf

Klein (German) A man of small stature
Kline, Kleiner, Kleinert, Kleine

Klemens (Latin) A merciful man
Klemenis, Klement, Kliment, Klimens

Kleng (Norse) Having claws

Knight (English) A noble solidier
Knights

Knightley (English) From the knight's meadow
Knightly, Knightli, Knightlie, Knightleigh, Knightlee, Knightlea, Knightleah

Knoll (English) From the little hill
Knolles, Knollys, Knowles

Knoton (Native American) Of the wind
Knotun, Knotan, Knoten, Knotin, Knotyn

Knox (English) From the rounded hill
Knoxx, Knoks, Knocks

Knud (Danish) A kind man
Knude

Knut (Norse) A knot
Knute

Koa (Hawaiian) A fearless man
Koah

Kobi (Hungarian) Form of Jacob, meaning "he who supplants"
Kobie, Koby, Kobey, Kobee, Kobea, Kobe

Kodiak (American) Resembling a bear
Kodyak

Kody (English) One who is helpful
Kodey, Kodee, Kodea, Kodi, Kodie

Koen (German) An honest advisor
Koenz, Kunz, Kuno

Kofi (African) Born on a Friday
Kofie, Kofee, Kofea, Kofy, Kofey

Kohana (Native American/Hawaiian) One who is swift/the best

Kohler (German) One who mines coal
Koler

Koi (Hawaiian) One who implores

Kojo (African) Born on a Monday
Kojoe, Koejo, Koejoe

Koka (Hawaiian) A man from Scotland

Kokil (Indian) Resembling a nightingale
Kokyl, Kokill, Kokyll

Kolbjorn (Swedish) Resembling a black bear
Kolbjorne, Kolbjourn, Kolbjourne

Kolby (German) A dark-haired man
Kolbey, Kolbee, Kolbea, Kolbie, Kolbi

Koldobika (Basque) One who is famous in battle
Koldobyka

Kole (English) The keeper of the keys
Koal, Koale

Kolichiyaw (Native American) Resembling a skunk

Kolinkar (Danish) Of the conquering people
Kolynkar, Kolin, Kollin, Kolyn, Kollyn

Koll (Norse) Having dark features
Kolli, Kollie, Kolly, Kolley, Kollee, Kolleigh

Kolos (Hungarian) A scholar

Kolton (English) From the coal town
Koltun, Koltan, Kolten, Koltin, Koltyn, Kolt, Kolte

Kolya (Slavic) The victorious warrior
Koliya, Kolenka

Konala (Hawaiian) A world ruler
Konalla

Konane (Hawaiian) Born beneath the bright moon
Konain, Konaine, Konayn, Konayne, Konaen, Konaene

Kondo (African) A fighter
Kondoe, Kondow, Kondowe

Kong (Chinese) A bright man; from heaven

Konnor (English) A wolf-lover; one who is strong-willed
Konnur, Konner, Konnar, Konnir, Konnyr

Kono (African) An industrious man

Konrad (Polish) A bold advisor

Konstantine (English) One who is
steadfast; firm
*Konstant, Konstantio, Konstanty,
Konstanz, Kostas, Konstantinos,
Konstance, Kostantin, Kostenka, Kostya*

Kontar (Ghanese) An only child
Kontarr

Koofrey (African) Remember me
Koofry, Koofri, Koofrie, Koofree

Korbin (Latin) A raven-haired man
Korbyn, Korben, Korban, Korbon, Korbun

Kordell (English) One who makes cord
Kordel, Kord, Kordale

Koren (Hebrew) One who is gleaming
Korin, Koryn

Koresh (Hebrew) One who digs in the
earth; a farmer
Koreshe

Korneli (Basque) Resembling a horn
*Kornelie, Kornely, Korneley, Kornelee,
Korneleigh, Kornell, Kornel, Kornelisz,
Kornelius*

Korrigan (English) One who wields a spear
*Korigan, Korregan, Koregan, Korrighan,
Korighan, Korreghan, Koreghan*

Kort (Danish) One who provides counsel
Korte

Korvin (Latin) Resembling a crow
Korvyn, Korvan, Korven, Korvon, Korvun

Kory (Irish) From the hollow; of the
churning waters
*Korey, Kori, Korie, Koree, Korea, Korry,
Korrey, Korree, Korrea, Korri, Korrie*

Kosey (African) Resembling a lion
Kosy, Kosi, Kosie, Kosee, Kosea

Koshy (American) A lighthearted man
Koshey, Koshi, Koshe, Koshie, Koshee

Kosmo (Greek) A universal man
*Kozmo, Kasmo, Kazmo, Kosmos, Kozmos,
Kasmos, Kazmos*

Koster (American) A spiritual man
Kostar, Kostor, Kostur, Kostir, Kostyr

Kosumi (Native American) One who uses
a spear to fish
*Kosumie, Kosume, Kosumee, Kosumy,
Kosumey*

Kotori (Native American) A screech-owl
spirit
Kotorie, Kotory, Kotorey, Kotoree

Kourtney (American) One who is polite;
courteous
*Kourtny, Kordney, Kortney, Kortni,
Kourtenay, Kourtneigh, Kourtni, Kourtnee,
Kourtnie, Kortnie, Kortnea, Kourtnea,
Kortnee, Kourtnee*

Kovit (Scandinavian) An expert; a learned
man
Kovyt

Kozel (Czech) Resembling a goat
Kozell, Kozele, Kozelle

Kozma (Greek) One who is decorated
Kozmah

Kozue (Japanese) Of the tree branches
Kozu, Kozoo, Kozou

Kraig (Gaelic) From the rocky place;
as solid as a rock
*Kraige, Krayg, Krayge, Kraeg, Kraege,
Krage*

Kral (Czech) A king
Krall

Kramer (German) A shopkeeper
*Kramar, Kramor, Kramir, Kramur, Kramyr,
Kraymer, Kraimer, Kraemer, Kraymar,
Kraimar, Kraemar*

Kramoris (Czech) A merchant
Kramorris, Kramorys, Kramorrys

Krany (Czech) A man of short stature
Kraney, Kranee, Kranea, Krani, Kranie

Krikor (Armenian) A vigilant watchman
Krykor, Krikur, Krykur

Kripal (Indian) One who is merciful
Krypal, Kripa, Krypa

Krishna (Hindi) In Hiniduism, an avatar
of Vishnu, portrayed as a handsome man
playing the flute
*Kryshna, Krishnadeva, Krishnachandra,
Krishnakanta, Krishnakumar, Krishnala,
Krishnamurari, Krishnamurthy,
Krishnendu*

K

Krispin (English) A curly-haired man
Kryspin, Krispyn, Krispen, Kryspen, Krisoijn

Kristian (Scandinavian) An anointed Christian
Kristan, Kristien, Krist, Kriste, Krister, Kristar, Khristian, Khrist, Khriste, Khristan

Kristopher (Scandinavian) A follower of Christ
Khristopher, Kristof, Kristofer, Kristoff, Kristoffer, Kristofor, Kristophor, Krystof, Krystopher, Krzysztof, Kristophoros, Kristos, Khristos, Khristopher, Khristo, Kris, Krys, Krystos, Krysto

Kruz (Spanish) Of the cross
Kruze, Kruiz, Kruize, Kruzito

Kuba (Polish) Form of Jacob, meaning "he who supplants"
Kubas

Kuckunniwi (Native American) Resembling a little wolf
Kukuniwi

Kueng (Chinese) Of the universe

Kugonza (African) One who loves and is loved

Kulbert (German) One who is calm; a bright man
Kulberte, Kuhlbert, Kuhlberte, Kulbart, Kulbarte, Kuhlbart, Kuhlbarte

Kuleen (Indian) A highborn man
Kulin, Kulein, Kulien, Kulean, Kulyn

Kuma (Japanese) Resembling a bear

Kumar (Indian) A prince; a male child

Kumi (African) A forceful man
Kumie, Kumy, Kumey, Kumee, Kumea

Kunsgnos (Celtic) A wise man

Kupakwashe (African) A gift from God
Kupakwashi, Kupakwashie, Kupakwashy, Kupakwashey, Kupakwashee, Kupak, Kupakwash

Kuper (Hebrew) Resembling copper
Kupar, Kupir, Kupyr, Kupor, Kupur

Kuri (Japanese) Resembling a chestnut
Kurie, Kury, Kurey, Kuree, Kurea

Kuron (African) One who gives thanks
Kurun, Kuren, Kuran, Kurin, Kuryn

Kurt (German) A brave counselor
Kurte

Kurtis (French) A courtier
Kurtiss, Kurtys, Kurtyss

Kuruk (Native American) Resembling a bear
Kuruck, Kuruc

Kushal (Indian) A talented man; adroit
Kushall

Kutty (American) One who wields a knife
Kutti, Kuttey, Kuttie, Kuttee, Kuttea

Kwabena (African) Born on a Tuesday
Kwabina, Kwabyna, Kwabana

Kwahu (Native American) Resembling an eagle
Kwahue, Kwahoo, Kwaho

Kwaku (African) Born on a Wednesday
Kwakue, Kwakou, Kwako, Kwakoe

Kwame (African) Born on a Saturday
Kwam, Kwami, Kwamie, Kwamy, Kwamey, Kwamee

Kwan (Korean) Of a bold character
Kwon

Kwasi (African) Born on a Sunday
Kwasie, Kwasy, Kwasey, Kwasee, Kwase, Kwesi, Kwesie, Kwesey, Kwesy, Kwesee, Kwese

Kwatoko (Native American) Resembling a bird with a large beak

Kwesi (African) Born on a Sunday
Kwesie, Kwesy, Kwesey, Kwesee, Kwasi, Kwasie, Kwasy, Kwasey, Kwasee

Kwintyn (Polish) The fifth-born child
Kwentyn, Kwinton, Kwenton, Kwintun, Kwentun, Kwintan, Kwentan, Kwinten, Kwenten, Kwint, Kwynt

Kyan (American) The little king
Kyann

Kyle ✪ (Gaelic) From the narrow channel
Kile, Kiley, Kye, Kylan, Kyrell, Kylen, Kily, Kili, Kilie, Kileigh, Kilee, Kyley, Kyly, Kyleigh, Kylee, Kyli, Kylie

Kylemore (Gaelic) From the great wood
Kylmore, Kylemor, Kylmor

Kyler (Danish) An archer
Kylar, Kylir, Kylyr, Kylor, Kylur

Kynan (Welsh) The chief; a leader
Kynen, Kynon, Kynun, Kynin, Kynyn

Kynaston (English) From the peaceful royal town
Kynastun, Kinaston, Kinastun

Kyne (English) Of the royalty
Kine, Kyn

Kyran (Persian / Irish) A lord / having dark features
Kyren, Kyrin, Kyryn, Kyron, Kyrun, Kyri, Kyrie, Kyree, Kyrea, Kyrey, Kyry

Kyrone (English) Form of Tyrone, meaning "from Owen's land"
Kyron, Keirohn, Keiron, Keirone, Keirown, Kirone

Kyros (Greek) A leader or master
Kiros

Laban (Hebrew) A white-haired or white-skinned man
Laben, Labon, Labin, Labyn, Labun, Lavin, Lavan, Lavyn, Laven, Lavon, Lavun, Labarn, Labarne

Labaron (French) The baron
LaBaron

Label (Hebrew) Resembling a lion
Labell, Labal, Laball

Labhras (Irish) Form of Lawrence, meaning "man from Laurentum; crowned with laurel"
Lubhras, Labhrus, Lubhrus, Labhros, Lubhros, Labhrainn, Labhrain

Labib (Arabic) One who is sensible
Labeeb, Labeab, Labieb, Labeib, Labyb

Laborc (Hungarian) As brave as a panther
Labork, Laborck

Labryan (American) One who is brash
Labrian, Labrien, Labryant, Labrion

Lacey (French) Man from Normandy; as delicate as lace
Lacy, Laci, Lacie, Lacee, Lacea

Lachie (Scottish) A boy from the lake
Lachi, Lachy, Lachey, Lachee, Lachea

Lachlan (Gaelic) From the land of lakes
Lachlen, Lachlin, Lachlyn, Locklan, Locklen, Locklin, Locklyn, Loklan, Laklan, Laklin, Laklen, Lakleyn, Laochailan, Lochlan, Lochlen, Lochlin, Lochlyn, Loche, Loch, Lach, Lache, Lakeland, Lochlann, Lochlain

Lachman (Gaelic) A man from the lake
Lachmann, Lockman, Lockmann, Lokman, Lokmann, Lakman, Lakmann

Lachtna (Irish) One who ages with grace

Lacrosse (French) Of the cross; a player of the game
Lacross, Lacros, Lacrose

Ladan (Hebrew) One who is alert and aware
Laden, Ladin, Ladyn, Ladon, Ladun

Ladd (English) A servant; a young man
Lad, Laddey, Laddie, Laddy, Laddi, Laddee, Laddea, Ladde

Ladden (American) An athletic man
Laddan, Laddin, Laddyn, Laddon, Laddun

Ladisiao (Spanish) One who offers help
Ladysiao, Ladiseao, Ladyseao, Ladisio, Ladiseo

Ladislas (Slavic) A glorious ruler
Lacko, Ladislaus, Laslo, Laszlo, Lazlo, Ladislav, Ladislauv, Ladislao, Ladislaw, Laco, Lako, Lado, Lazuli, Lazulie, Lazuly, Lazuley, Lazulee

Ladomér (Hungarian) One who traps animals
Ladomir, Ladomeer, Ladomear, Ladomyr

Lae (Laos) A dark-skinned man
Lai, Lay, Laye

Lael (Hebrew) One who belongs to God
Lale, Lail, Laile, Laele, Layl, Layle

Laertes (English) One who is adventurous
Lairtes, Layrtes, Lartes

Lafay (American) A lighthearted man
Lafaye, Lafai, Lafae, Lafayye, Laphay, Laphai, Laphae, Laphaye, Lafee, Laphee

Lafayette (French) Man of the faith
Lafeyette, Lafayet, Lafeyet, Lafayett, Lafeyett

Lafe (American) One who is on time
Laif, Laife, Layf, Layfe, Laef, Laefe

Lafi (Polynesian) A shy young man
Lafie, Lafy, Lafey

Lagan (Indian) One who arrives at the appropriate time
Lagen, Lagon, Lagin, Lagyn, Lagun

Lagrand (American) A majestic man
Lagrande

Lahib (Arabic) A fiery man
Laheeb, Laheab, Lahieb, Laheib, Lahyb

Lahthan (Arabic) A thirsty man
Lahthen, Lahthin, Lahthyn, Lahthon, Lahthun

Laibrook (English) One who lives on the road near the brook
Laebrook, Laybrook, Laibroc, Laebroc, Laybroc, Laibrok, Laebrok, Laybrok

Laidley (English) From the meadow with the creek
Laidly, Laidleigh, Laidlee, Laidlea, Laidleah, Laidli, Laidlie, Laedley, Laedly, Laedleigh, Laedlea, Laedleah, Laedli, Laedlee, Laedlie, Laydley, Laydly, Laydleigh, Laydlea, Laydleah, Laydli, Laydlie, Laydlee

Laionela (Hawaiian) As bold as a lion
Laionele, Laionel, Laionell

Laird (Scottish) The lord of the manor
Layrd, Laerd, Lairde, Layrde, Laerde

Laith (Arabic) Resembling a lion
Laithe, Layth, Laythe, Laeth, Laethe, Lath, Lathe, Lais

Lajos (Hungarian) A well-known holy man
Lajus, Lajcsi, Lali, Lalie, Laly, Laley, Lalee

Laken (American) Man from the lake
Laike, Laiken, Laikin, Lakin, Lakyn, Lakan, Laikyn, Laeken, Laekin, Laekyn, Layke, Laeke, Lake, Layken, Laykin, Laykyn, Laykan, Laikan, Laekan, Laec

Lakista (American) One who is bold
Lakeista, Lakiesta, Lakeesta, Lakeasta, Lakysta

Lakota (Native American) A beloved friend
Lakoda, Lacota, Lacoda, Lackota, Lackoda

Lakshman (Hindi) A man of good fortune
Lakshmann, Lakshmana, Lakshan

Lakshya (Indian) A target; a mark
Lakshiya, Lakshyah, Lakshiyah

Lal (Sanskrit / Slavic) One who is dearly loved / resembling a tulip
Lall, Lalle

Lalam (Indian) The best
Lallam, Lalaam, Lallaam

Lalit (Indian) One who is simple and handsome
Laleet, Laleat, Laleit, Laliet, Lalyt, Lalitmohan

Lalo (Latin) One who sings a lullaby
Lallo, Laloh, Lalloh

Lalor (Irish) A leper
Lalur, Laler, Lalir, Lalyr, Lalar, Leathlobhair

Lam (Vietnamese) Having a full understanding

Laman (Arabic) A bright and happy man
Lamaan, Lamann, Lamaann

Lamar (German / French) From the renowned land / of the sea
Lamarr, Lamarre, Lemar, Lemarr

Lambert (Scandinavian) The light of the land
Lambart, Lamberto, Lambirt, Landbert, Lambirto, Lambrecht, Lambret, Lambrett, Lamber, Lambur, Lambar

Lambi (Norse) In mythology, the son of Thorbjorn
Lambie, Lamby, Lambey, Lambe, Lambee

Lamech (Hebrew) One who is strong and powerful
Lameche, Lameck, Lamecke

Lameh (Arabic) A shining man

Lamont (Norse) A man of the law
Lamonte, Lamond, Lamonde, Lammond

Lamorak (English) In Arthurian legend, the brother of Percival
Lamerak, Lamurak, Lamorac, Lamerac, Lamurac, Lamorack, Lamerack, Lamurack, Lamorat

Lancelot (French) An attendant; in Arthurian legend, a knight of the Round Table
Launcelot, Lance, Lancelin, Lancelyn, Lanse, Lancelott, Launcelott, Launci, Launcie, Launcey, Launcy, Launcee

Lander (English) One who owns land
Land, Landers, Landis, Landiss, Landor, Lande, Landry, Landri, Landrie, Landrey, Landree, Landrea, Landise, Landice, Landus

Landmari (German) From the renowned land
Landmarie, Landmaree, Landmare, Landmary, Landmarey, Landmarea

Lando (American) A manly man
Landoe, Landow, Landowe

Landon ♂ ♀ (English) From the long hill
Landyn, Landan, Landen, Landin, Lando, Langdon, Langden, Langdan, Langdyn, Langdin, Lancdon, Lancden, Lancdin

Lane (English) One who takes the narrow path
Laine, Lain, Laen, Laene, Layne, Layn

Lang (Norse) A tall man
Lange, Leng, Lenge, Longe, Long, Langer, Lenger, Langham

Langford (English) From the long ford
Langforde, Langferd, Langferde, Langfurd, Langfurde, Lanford, Lanforde, Lanferd, Lanferde, Lanfurd, Lanfurde

Langhorn (English) Of the long horn
Langhorne, Lanhorn, Lanhorne

Langilea (Polynesian) Having a booming voice, like thunder
Langileah, Langilia, Langiliah

Langiloa (Polynesian) Resembling a tempest; one who is moody
Langiloah

Langley (English) From the long meadow
Langleigh, Langly, Langlea, Langleah, Langlee, Langli, Langlie

Langston (English) From the tall man's town
Langsten, Langstun, Langstown, Langstin, Langstyn, Langstan, Langton, Langtun, Langtin, Langtyn, Langten, Langtan, Lankston, Lankstun, Lanston, Lanstun

Langundo (Native American / Polynesian) A peaceful man / one who is graceful

Langward (Native American) A tall guardian
Lanward, Langwerd, Lanwerd, Langwurd, Lanwurd

Langworth (English) One who lives near the long paddock
Langworthe, Lanworth, Lanworthe

Lanh (Vietnamese) One who is quick-witted

Lani (Hawaiian / Irish) From the sky; one who is heavenly / a servant
Lanie, Lany, Laney, Lanee, Lanea

Lanier (French) One who works with wool

Lann (Celtic) Man of the sword
Lan

Lanny (English) Form of Roland, meaning "from the renowned land"
Lanney, Lanni, Lannie, Lannee, Lannea

Lansa (Native American) Man of the spear

Lantos (Hungarian) One who plays the lute
Lantus

Lanty (Irish) Full of life
Lantey, Lantee, Lantea, Lanti, Lantie

Lanzo (German) From the homeland
Lanzio, Lanziyo, Lanzeo, Lanzeyo

Laochailan (Scottish) One who is waning

Laoidhigh (Irish) One who is poetic

Lap (Vietnamese) An independent man
Lapp

Laphonso (American) One who is centered
Lafonso, Laphonzo, Lafonzo

Lapidos (Hebrew) One who carries a torch
Lapydos, Lapidot, Lapydot, Lapidoth, Lapydoth, Lapidus, Lapydus

L

Lapu (Native American) Of the cedar's bark
Lapue, Lapoo, Lapou

Laquinton (American) Form of Quinton, meaning "from the queen's town or settlement"
Laquinntan, Laquinnten, Laquinntin, Laquinnton, Laquintain, Laquintan, Laquintyn, Laquintynn, Laquintin, Laquinten, Laquintann, Laquint, Laquinte, Laquynt, Laquynte, Laquinneton, Laquienton, Laquientin, Laquiten, Laquitin, Laquiton

Lar (Anglo-Saxon) One who teaches others

Laramie (French) One who is pensive
Larami, Laramee, Laramea, Laramy, Laramey

Larch (Latin) Resembling the evergreen tree
Larche

Larcwide (Anglo-Saxon) One who provides counsel
Larkwide, Larcwyde, Larkwyde

Lare (American) A wealthy man
Larre, Layr, Layre, Lair, Laire, Laer, Laere

Largo (Spanish) A tall man

Lariat (American) A cowboy
Lariatt, Laryat, Laryatt

Lark (English) Resembling the songbird
Larke

Larkin (Gaelic) One who is fierce
Larkyn, Larken, Larkan, Larkon, Larkun

Larmine (American) One who is boisterous
Larmyne, Larrmine, Larrmyne, Larmen, Larrmen

Larnell (American) A generous man
Larnel, Larndell, Larndel, Larndi, Larndie, Larndy, Larndey, Larne, Larn

Laron (American) An outgoing young man
Larron, Larone, Larrone

Larson (Scandinavian) The son of Lawrence
Larsan, Larsen, Larsun, Larsin, Larsyn

Lasalle (French) From the hall
Lasall, Lasal, Lasale

Lashaun (American) An enthusiastic man
Lashawn, Lasean, Lashon, Lashond

Laskey (English) A lighthearted man
Lasky, Laskie, Laski, Laskee, Laskea, Laske, Lask

Lassen (English) From the mountain's peak
Lassan, Lassin, Lassyn, Lasson, Lassun, Lasen, Lasan, Lasin, Lasyn, Lason, Lasun

Lassit (American) One who is open-minded
Lassyt, Lasset

Lassiter (American) One who is quick-witted
Lassyter, Lasseter, Lassater

Latafat (Indian) One who is elegant
Lataphat

Latham (Scandinavian) One who lives near the barn
Lathom, Lathum, Lathem, Lathim, Lathym

Lathan (American) Form of Nathan, meaning "a gift from God"
Lathen, Lathun, Lathon, Lathin, Lathyn, Latan, Laten, Latun, Laton

Lathrop (English) From the farm with the barn
Lathrup

Latif (Arabic) One who is kind and gentle
Lateef, Lateaf, Latief, Lateif, Latyf

Latimer (English) One who serves as an interpreter
Latymer, Latimor, Latymor, Latimore, Latymore, Lattemore, Lattimore

Latorris (American) A notorious man
Latoris, Latorrys, Latorys

Latravious (American) A healthy and strong man
Latraveus, Latravius, Latravios, Latraveos, Latrave

Latty (English) A generous man
Lattey, Latti, Lattie, Lattee, Lattea

Laud (Latin) One who is praised
Laude, Lawd, Lawde

Laughlin (Irish) From the land of the fjord; a servant
Loughlin, Laughlyn, Loughlyn

Launder (English) From the grassy plains
Lawnder

Launfal (English) In Arthurian legend, a knight
Lawnfal, Launfall, Lawnfall, Launphal, Lawnphal

Laurian (English) One who lives near the laurel trees
Laurien, Lauriano, Laurieno, Lawrian, Lawrien, Lawriano, Lawrieno

Lavaughn (American) A spirited man
Lavon, Lavawn, Lavan, Lavonn, Levaughn, Levon, Levone

Lave (Italian) Of the burning rock
Lava

Lavesh (Hindi) One who is calm
Laveshe

Lavi (Hebrew) Form of Levi, meaning "we are united as one"
Lavie, Lavy, Lavey, Lavee, Lavea

Law (English) From the hill
Lawe

Lawford (English) From the ford near the hill
Lawforde, Lawferd, Lawferde, Lawfurd, Lawfurde

Lawler (Gaelic) A soft-spoken man; one who mutters
Lauler, Lawlor, Loller, Lawlar, Lollar, Loller, Laular, Laulor

Lawley (English) From the meadow near the hill
Lawly, Lawli, Lawlie, Lawleigh, Lawlee, Lawlea, Lawleah

Lawrence (Latin) Man from Laurentum; crowned with laurel
Larance, Laranz, Larenz, Larrance, Larrence, Larrens, Larrey, Larry, Lars, Laurance, Lauren, Laurence, Laurens, Laurent, Laurentios, Laurentius, Laurenz, Laurie, Laurits, Lauritz, Lavrans, Lavrens, Lawrance, Lawrey, Lawrie, Lawry, Lenci, Lon, Lonny, Lorance, Lorant, Loren, Lorenc, Lorence, Lorencz, Lorens, Lorentz, Lorenz, Lorenzen, Lorenzo, Lorin, Loritz, Lorrence, Lorrenz, Lorry, Larri, Larrie, Lowrance, Laureano, Larz, Larenzo, Loron, Lorren, Lorrin, Laren, Laurin, Laurins, Laurentij, Laurenty, Laurentzi, Laurentiu, Lorand, Loran, Lırinc

Lawson (English) The son of Lawrence

Lawton (English) From the town on the hill
Lawtun, Lawtown, Laughton, Loughton, Laughtun, Loughtun, Litton, Littun, Lytton, Lyttun, Lanton, Lantun, Lifton, Liftun

Lawyer (American) An attorney; one who defends or prosecutes others
Lauyer, Lawyor, Lauyor

Layt (American) A fascinating young man
Layte, Lait, Laite, Laet, Laete, Late

Lazarus (Hebrew) Helped by God; in the Bible, the man raised from the dead by Jesus
Lazar, Lazare, Lazarillo, Lazaro, Lazear, Lazer, Lazzaro, Lazre

Laziz (Arabic) One who is pleasant
Lazeez, Lazeaz, Laziez, Lazeiz, Lazyz

Le (Chinese) Filled with joy

Leal (French) A faithful man
Leale, Leel, Leele, Liel, Liele, Lele

Leaman (American) A powerful man
Leeman, Leamon, Leemon, Leamond, Leamand

Leander (Greek) A lion of a man; in mythology, Hero's lover who swam across the Hellespont to meet her
Liander, Leandre, Liandre, Leandro, Liandro, Leandrew, Leandros, Leanther, Leiandros, Leand, Leande

Leanian (Anglo-Saxon) One who has been rewarded
Leanien, Leanion, Leaniun

Lear (Greek) Of the royalty
Leare, Leer, Leere

Learly (English) A majestic man
Learly, Learli, Learlie, Learlee, Learle, Learlea, Learleigh

Leary (Irish) A cattle herder
Learey, Learee, Learea, Leari, Learie, Laoghaire

Leathan (Scottish) Of the river
Leethan, Leathen, Leethen

Leather (American) As tough as hide
Lether

Leavery (American) A generous man
Leaverey, Leaveri, Leaverie, Leaveree, Leavry, Leavrey, Leavri, Leavrie, Leavree

Leavitt (English) A baker
Leavit, Leavytt, Leavyt, Leavett, Leavet

Leax (Anglo-Saxon) Resembling salmon

Leben (English) Filled with hope

Lebna (African) A soulful man
Lebnah, Leb

Lebrun (French) A brown-haired man
*Lebrune, Labron, Labrun, Lebron,
Lebrone, Labrone, Labrune*

Lech (Slavic) In mythology, the founder of
the Polish people
Leche

Lector (American) One who is disturbed
Lictor, Lektor, Liktor

Ledyard (Teutonic) The protector of the
nation
Ledyarde, Ledyerd, Ledyerde

Lee (English) From the meadow
Leigh, Lea, Leah, Ley

Leeto (African) One who embarks on a
journey
Leato, Leito, Lieto

Lefty (American) A left-handed man
Leftey, Lefti, Leftie, Leftee, Leftea

Legend (American) One who is memorable
Legende, Legund, Legunde

Leggett (French) A delegate
*Leget, Legget, Legett, Legate, Leggitt, Legit,
Legitt, Leggit, Liggett, Liget, Ligget, Ligett*

Lehman (German) One who rents; a tenant
Lehmann

Lei (Hawaiian / Chinese) Adorned with
flowers / resembling thunder

Leibel (Hebrew) Resembling a lion
Leib, Leibe

Leidolf (Norse) A descendant of the wolf
Leidulf, Leidolfe, Leidulfe

Leif (Scandinavian) A beloved heir
*Lief, Leef, Leaf, Leyf, Life, Layf, Laif, Laef,
Lyf, Leof*

Leighton (English) From the town near the
meadow
Leightun, Layton, Laytun, Leyton, Leytun

Leil (Arabic) Born at night
Leile, Leel, Leele, Leal, Leale

Leilani (Hawaiian) Child of heaven;
adorned with heavenly flowers
*Lalani, Leilanie, Leilanee, Leilaney,
Leilany, Lalanie, Lalaney, Lalanee, Lalany,
Leilanea, Lalanea*

Leith (Gaelic) From the broad river
*Leithe, Leath, Leathe, Leeth, Leethe, Lieth,
Liethe, Leithan, Liethan, Leathan, Leethan*

Lekhak (Hindi) An author
Lekhan

Lel (Slavic) A taker
Lél

Leland (English) From the meadow land
Leeland, Leighland, Lealand, Leyland

Leldon (American) A bookworm
Leldun, Leldan, Lelden, Leldin, Leldyn

Lema (African) One who is cultivated
Lemah, Lemma, Lemmah

Lemon (American) Resembling the fruit
*Lemun, Lemin, Lemyn, Limon, Limun,
Limin, Limyn, Limen, Lemen*

Lemuel (Hebrew) One who belongs to
God
*Lemyouel, Lemyuel, Lemuell, Lemmi,
Lemmie, Lemmy, Lemmey, Lemmee, Lem*

Len (Native American) One who plays the
flute

Lencho (African) Resembling a lion
*Lenchos, Lenchio, Lenchiyo, Lencheo,
Lencheyo*

Lennart (Scandinavian) One who is brave
Lennert

Lenno (Native American) A brave man
Lennoe, Leno, Lenoe

Lennon (English) Son of love
Lennan, Lennin, Lenon, Lenan, Lenin

Lennor (English) A courageous man

Lennox (Scottish) One who owns many
elm trees
Lenox, Lenoxe, Lennix, Lenix, Lenixe

Lenoris (American) A respected man
Leenoris, Lenorris, Leanoris

Lensar (English) One who stays with his parents
Lenser, Lensor, Lensur

Lenton (American) A pious man
Lentin, Lentyn, Lentun, Lentan, Lenten, Lent, Lente

Leo (Latin) Resembling a lion
Lio, Lyo

Leocadie (French) Having the heart of a lion
Leocadi, Leocady, Leocadey, Leocadee, Leocado, Leocadio, Leocadeo

Leod (Scottish) An ugly man
Leode

Leolin (Polynesian) One who is alert; watchful
Leolyn, Leoline, Leolyne

Leomaris (Latin) The lion of the sea
Liomaris, Leomariss, Liomariss, Leomarys, Liomarys, Leomaryss, Liomaryss

Leon (Greek) Form of Leo, meaning "resembling a lion"
Leoncio, Leone, Lioni, Lionisio, Lionni, Lionie, Lionnie, Liony, Lionny, Lioney, Lionney, Lionee, Lionnee, Leonce, Leonel, Leonell

Leonard (German) Having the strength of a lion
Len, Lenard, Lenn, Lennard, Lennart, Lennerd, Lennie, Lenny, Leonardo, Leondaus, Leonerd, Leonhard, Leonid, Leonidas, Leonides, Leonis, Lonnard, Lenni, Lonni, Lonnie, Lonny, Lenya, Lyonechka, Lennell, Lennel, Lenel, Lenell, Leovardo, Leovard

Leonidus (Latin) Having great strength
Leonydus, Leonidos, Leonydos, Leonidas, Leonydas

Leopaul (American) One who exhibits calm bravery
Leopaule

Leopold (German) A bold ruler of the people
Leopoldo, Leupold, Leupoldo, Leopolde, Leupolde, Luitpold, Luitpolde, Lepold, Lepolde, Lepoldo, Lopold, Lopolde, Lopoldi

Leor (Latin) One who listens well
Leore

Leoti (American) An outdoorsy man
Leotie, Leoty, Leotey, Leotee, Leotea

Leotis (American) One who is carefree
Leodis, Leotys, Leodys, Leeotis, Leeodis

Lepolo (Polynesian) A handsome man
Lepoloh, Lepollo, Lepolloh

Lerato (Latin) The song of my soul
Leratio, Lerateo

Leron (French / Arabic) The circle / my song
Lerun, Leran, Leren, Lerin, Leryn

Leroux (French) The red-haired man
Larue, Lerue, Laroux

Leroy (French) The king
Leroi, Leeroy, Leeroi, Learoy, Learoi

Lesharo (Native American) The chief
Leshario, Leshareo

Leshem (Hebrew) Resembling a precious stone

Leslie (Gaelic) From the holly garden; of the gray fortress
Leslea, Leslee, Lesleigh, Lesley, Lesli, Lesly, Lezlee, Lezley, Lezlie, Lezleigh, Lezli, Lioslaith, Lezlea, Les, Lez

Lesner (American) A serious-minded man
Lezner

Lester (English) A man from Leicester
Lestor, Lestir, Lestyr, Lestar, Lestur

Lev (Hebrew / Russian) Of the heart / form of Leo, meaning "resembling a lion"
Levka, Levushka

Levant (French) One who rises above
Levante, Levent, Levente

Levar (American) One who is soft-spoken
Levarr, Levare

Leverett (French) Resembling a young rabbit
Leveret, Leveritt, Leverit

Leverton (English) From the rush town
Levertun, Levertown

Levi (Hebrew) We are united as one; in the Bible, one of Jacob's sons
Levie, Levin, Levyn, Levy, Levey, Levee

Leviticus (Greek) Of the Levites
Levyticus, Levitikus, Levytikus

L

Lew (German / Slavic / English) A famous warrior / resembling a lion / one who provides shelter
Leu, Lewe

Lex (English) Form of Alexander, meaning "helper and defender of mankind"
Lexer, Lexis, Lexys, Lexus, Lexo, Lexiss, Lexyss

Leyati (Native American) Having a smooth and round head
Leyatie, Leyatee, Leyatea, Leyaty, Leyatey, Leyti, Leytie, Leytee, Leytea, Leyty, Leytey

Leyman (English) Man of the meadow
Leighman, Leman, Leaman, Leahman, Lyman

Lezane (American) One who is dearly loved
Lezain, Lezaine, Lezayn, Lezayne, Lezaen, Lezaene

Li (Chinese) Having great strength

Liam ✪ (Gaelic) Form of William, meaning "the determined protector"
Lyam

Lian (Chinese) Of the willow

Liang (Chinese) A good man
Lyang

Liberio (Latin) One who is independent; free
Liberato, Liberatus, Liberto, Libero

Liberty (English) An independent man; having freedom
Libertey, Libertee, Libertea, Liberti, Libertie, Libertas, Libyr, Liber, Libor

Lidio (Portugese) A man from Lydia
Lydio, Lidiyo, Lydiyo, Lideo, Lydeo, Lideyo, Lydeyo

Lidmann (Anglo-Saxon) A man of the sea; a sailor
Lidman, Lydmann, Lydman

Lidon (Hebrew) Judgment is mine
Lydon, Leedon, Leadon, Liedon, Leidon, Ledon

Liem (Vietnamese) An honest man

Lif (Scandinavian) An energetic man; lively

Lihau (Hawaiian) A spirited man

Like (Asian) A soft-spoken man
Lyke

Liko (Hawaiian) A flourishing young man
Lyko

Lilo (Hawaiian) One who is generous
Lylo, Leelo, Lealo, Leylo, Lielo, Leilo

Limu (Polynesian) Resembling seaweed
Lymu, Limue, Lymue

Lincoln (English) From the village near the lake
Lincon, Lyncoln, Lyncon, Linken, Lynken, Linkoln, Link, Linc, Lynk, Lync

Lindberg (German) From the linden tree hill
Lindbergh, Lindburg, Lindburgh, Lindi, Lindie, Lindee, Lindy, Lindey, Lindeberg, Lindebergh, Lindeburg, Lindeburgh

Lindell (English) From the valley of linden trees
Lendell, Lendall, Lindall, Lyndall, Lindel, Lendel, Lendal, Lindal, Lyndal, Lyndell, Lyndel, Lindael, Lindale, Lindayle, Lindayl, Lindaele

Linden (English) From the lime tree
Lindenn, Lindon, Lindynn, Lynden, Lyndon, Lyndyn, Lyndin, Lindin, Lind, Linde, Lin, Linddun, Lindun

Lindford (English) From the linden-tree ford
Linford, Lindforde, Linforde, Lyndford, Lynford, Lyndforde, Lynforde

Lindhurst (English) From the village by the linden trees
Lyndhurst, Lindenhurst, Lyndenhurst, Lindhirst, Lindherst, Lyndhirst, Lyndherst, Lindenhirst, Lyndenhirst, Lindenherst, Lyndenherst

Lindley (English) From the meadow of linden trees
Lindly, Lindleigh, Lindlea, Lindleah, Lindlee, Lindli, Lindlie, Lyndley, Lyndly, Lyndleigh, Lyndlea, Lyndleah, Lyndlee, Lyndli, Lyndlie

Lindman (English) One who lives near the linden trees
Lindmann, Lindmon, Lindmonn

Lindo (American) One who is sturdy
Lindoh, Lyndo, Lyndoh

Lindsay (English) From the island of linden trees; from Lincoln's wetland
Lind, Lindsea, Lindsee, Lindseigh, Lindsey, Lindsy, Linsay, Linsey, Linsie, Linzi, Linzee, Linzy, Lyndsay, Lyndsey, Lyndsie, Lynnsey, Lynnzey, Lynsey, Lynzey, Lynzi, Lynzy, Lynzee, Lynzie, Lindse

Line (English) From the bank

Linley (English) From the flax field
Linly, Linleigh, Linlee, Linlea, Linleah, Linli, Linlie, Lynley, Lynly, Lynleigh, Lynlea, Lynleah, Lynli, Lynlie

Linton (English) From the flax town
Lynton, Lintun, Lyntun

Linus (Greek) One who has flaxen-colored hair; in mythology, the musician son of Apollo
Lynus, Lino, Linos, Lynos, Lyno

Linwood (English) From the forest of linden trees
Linwode, Lynwood, Lynwode

Lion (English) Resembling the animal
Lyon, Lions, Lyons

Lionel (Latin) Resembling a young lion
Leonel, Leonello, Lionell, Lionelo, Lionello, Lionnel, Lionnell, Lionnello, Lonell, Lonnell, Lyonel, Lyinell, Lyonelo, Lyonnel, Lyonnell, Lyonnello

Lipot (Hungarian) A brave young man

Lirit (Hebrew) Having musical grace

Liron (Hebrew) My song
Leeron, Learon, Lieron, Leiron, Lyron

Lise (Native American) Resembling a rising salmon

Lisiate (Polynesian) A courageous man

Lisimba (African) One who has been attacked by a lion
Lisymba, Lysimba, Lysymba

List (Anglo-Saxon) One who is cunning
Liste, Lyst, Lyste, Lister, Lyster

Liu (Asian) One who is quiet; peaceful

Liuz (Polish) Surrounded by light

Livingston (English) From the town of a beloved friend
Livingstun, Livingsten, Livingstin, Livingstone

Liviu (Romanian) Of the olive tree

Liwanu (Native American) Having the growl of a bear
Lywanu, Liwanue, Lywanue, Liwanou, Lywanou

Lleu (Welsh) A shining man
Lugh, Lugus

Llewellyn (Welsh) Resembling a lion
Lewellen, Lewellyn, Llewellen, Llewelyn, Llwewellin, Llew, Llewe, Llyweilun

Lloyd (Welsh) A gray-haired man; one who is sacred
Lloid, Loyd, Loid, Llwyd

Llyr (Celtic) In mythology, a king; of the sea

Loba (African) One who talks a lot

Lobo (Spanish) Resembling a wolf
Loboe, Lobow, Lobowe

Lochan (Hindi / Irish) The eyes / one who is lively

Locke (English / German) Man of the forest / from the fortress
Lock

Lockhart (English) Resembling a deer from the forest
Lokhart, Lockharte, Lokharte

Lockwood (English) From the fortress near the forest
Lokwood, Lockwode, Lokwode

Lodewuk (Scandinavian) A famous warrior
Ladewijk, Lodovic, Lodovico, Lojza

Lodge (English) One who provides shelter

Lodur (Norse) In mythology, one who participated in animating humans
Lodor, Loder, Lodir, Lodyr

Loeb (German) Resembling a lion
Loebe, Loeber, Loew, Loewe

Loefel (English) One who is dearly loved

L

Loey (American) A daring man; one who is adventurous
Loeey, Lowee, Lowi, Lowie, Loie

Logan ♂ ♀ (Gaelic) From the little hollow
Logann, Logen, Login, Logyn, Logenn, Loginn, Logynn

Lohengrin (English) In Arthurian legend, the son of Percival
Lohengren, Lohengryn

Lokela (Hawaiian) One who is known for throwing spears
Lokelah, Lokella, Lokellah

Lokene (Hawaiian) One who is open-minded
Lokeen, Lokeene, Lokean, Lokeane, Lokein, Lokeine, Lokien, Lokiene, Lokyn, Lokyne

Loki (Norse) In mythology, a trickster god
Lokie, Loky, Lokey, Lokee, Lokea

Lokni (Hawaiian) As dashing as a red rose
Loknie, Lokny, Lokney, Loknea, Loknee

Lolonyo (African) The beauty of love
Lolonyio, Lolonyeo, Lolonio, Lolonea

Lolovivi (African) The sweetness of love
Lolovyvy, Lolovivie, Lolovievie, Lolovivee

Loman (Gaelic) One who is small and bare
Lomann, Loeman, Loemann

Lomar (English) The son of Omar
Lomarr

Lomas (Spanish) A good man

Lombard (Latin) One who has a long beard
Lombardi, Lombardo, Lombardie, Lombardy, Lombardey, Lombardee

Lonan (Native American) Resembling a cloud
Lonann

Lonato (Native American) Possessing a flint stone

London (English) From the capital of England
Lundon, Londen, Lunden

Long (Chinese) Resembling a dragon
Longe

Longfellow (English) A tall man
Longfello, Longfelow, Longfelo

Lonzo (Spanish) One who is ready for battle
Lonzio, Lonzeo

Lootah (Native American) Refers to the color red
Loota, Loutah, Louta, Lutah, Luta

Lorcan (Irish) The small, fierce one
Lorcen, Lorcin, Lorcyn, Lorcon, Lorcun, Lorkan, Lorken, Lorkin, Lorkyn, Lorkon, Lorkun

Lord (English) One who has authority and power
Lorde, Lordly, Lordley, Lordlee, Lordlea, Lordleigh, Lordli, Lordlie

Lore (Basque / English) Resembling a flower / form of Lawrence, meaning "man from Laurentum; crowned with laurel"
Lorea

Loredo (Spanish) A cowboy; one who is intelligent
Lorado, Loraydo, Loraido, Loraedo, Larado, Laredo

Lorimer (Latin) One who makes harnesses
Lorrimer, Lorimar, Lorrimar, Lorymar, Lorrymar, Lorymer, Lorrymer

Loring (German) One who is famous in battle
Loryng, Lorring, Lorryng

Lorne (English) Form of Lawrence, meaning "a man from Laurentum; crowned with laurel"
Lorn, Lornel, Lornell, Lornele, Lornelle

Lot (Hebrew) One who is veiled; hidden; in the Bible, the man who fled God's destruction of Sodom and Gomorrah

Lothar (German) A famous warrior
Lathair, Lother, Lothair, Lothario, Lothur, Lotharing

Louden (American) One who is enthusiastic
Loudon, Loudan, Lowden, Lowdon, Lowdan, Loudun, Lowdun

Louis ♂ (German) A famous warrior
*Lew, Lewes, Lewis, Lodewick, Lodovico, Lou, Louie, Lucho, Ludovic, Ludovicus, Ludvig, Ludvik, Ludwig, Luigi, **Luis**, Luiz, Lewi, Lewie, Lewy, Ludweg, Ludwik, Luduvico*

Loundis (American) A visionary
Loundys, Loundas, Loundes, Loundos, Loundus, Lowndis, Lowndys, Lowndas, Lowndes, Lowndos, Lowndus

Louvain (English) From the city in Belgium
Louvaine, Louvayn, Louvayne, Louvane, Louvaen, Louvaene

Lovett (English) One who is full of love
Lovet, Lovatt, Lovat, Lovitt, Lovit, Lovytt, Lovyt

Lowell (French) Resembling a young wolf
Lowel, Louvel, Lovel, Lovell, Lowe

Lowman (English) A dearly loved man
Loweman, Lowmann, Lowemann

Lowry (English) A great leader
Lowrey, Lowri, Lowrie, Lowree, Lowrea

Loyal (English) One who is faithful and true
Loyalty, Loyalti, Loyaltie, Loyaltee, Loyaltea, Loyaltey, Loys, Loyse, Loyce

Luba (Yugoslavian) One who loves and is loved
Lubah

Lubomir (Polish) A great love
Lubomeer, Lubomear, Lubomyr

Lucan (Latin) A man from Lucania
Lukan, Loucan, Louccan, Luckan, Louckan

Lucas ✪ ✪ (English) A man from Lucania
Lukas, Loucas, Loukas, Luckas, Louckas, Lucus, Lukus

Lucho (Spanish) Surrounded by light; a lucky man
Luchio, Luchiyo, Lucheo, Lucheyo

Lucian (Latin) Surrounded by light
Luciano, Lucianus, Lucien, Lucio, Lucjan, Lukianos, Lukyan, Luce, Lucero, Lucius, Luca, Lucca, Luka, Lukka, Lucious, Luceous, Lushus

Lucky (English) A fortunate man
Luckey, Luckee, Luckea, Lucki, Luckie

Lucretius (Latin) A successful or wealthy man
Lucretious

Ludlow (English) The ruler of the hill
Ludlowe

Ludoslaw (Polish) Of the glorious people
Ludoslav, Luboslaw, Luboslav

Lufian (Anglo-Saxon) One who is full of love
Lufyan, Lufyann, Lufiann

Lufti (Arabic) A kind man
Luftie, Luftee, Luftea, Lufty, Luftey

Luke ✪ ✪ (Greek) A man from Lucania
Luc, Luken

Luki (German) A renowned fighter
Lukie, Luky, Lukey, Lukee, Lukea

Lulani (Polynesian) Sent from heaven
Lulanie, Lulaney, Lulany, Lulanee, Lulanea

Lumumba (African) A talented or gifted man
Lumomba

Lundy (French / Gaelic) Born on a Monday / from the marshland
Lundey, Lundi, Lundie, Lundee, Lundea, Lunde, Lund

Lunn (Gaelic) Having great strength; one who is warlike
Lun, Lon, Lonn

Lunt (Scandinavian) From the grove
Lunte

Luong (Vietnamese) From the bamboo land

Lusk (American) An energetic man
Luske, Luski, Luskie, Lusky, Luskey, Luskee, Luskea

Lutalo (African) A bold warrior

Luthando (Latin) One who is dearly loved

Luther (German) A soldier of the people
Louther, Luter, Luthero, Lutero, Louthero, Luthus, Luthas, Luthos

Lutz (German) A famous warrior

Lux (Latin) A man of the light
Luxe, Luxi, Luxie, Luxee, Luxea, Luxy, Luxey

Ly (Vietnamese) A reasonable man

Lyall (Gaelic / Norse) A faithful man / resembling a wolf
Lyell, Lyal, Lyel

L

Lydell (English) From the open valley
Lydel, Ledell, Ledel

Lyle (English) From the island
Lisle, Lysle, Lile, Lyell

Lynn (English) A man of the lake
Linn, Lyn, Lynne, Linne

Lyric (French) Of the lyre; the words of
a song
Lyrik, Lyrick

Lysander (Greek) The liberator
Lesandro, Lisandro, Lizandro, Lysandros

Maahes (Egyptian) Resembling a lion

Mablevi (African) Do not deceive
*Mablevie, Mablevy, Mablevey, Mablevee,
Mablevea*

Mabon (Welsh) Our son
Mabun, Maban, Mabin, Mabyn, Maben

Mac (Gaelic) The son of ...
*Mack, Mak, Macky, Macky, Macki,
Mackie, Mackee, Mackea, Macken, Mackan,
Mackon, Mackin, Mackyn, Mackun*

Macadam (Gaelic) The son of Adam
*Macadhamh, MacAdam, McAdam,
MacAdhamh*

Macallister (Gaelic) The son of Alistair
*MacAlister, McAlister, McAllister,
Macalister*

Macalpin (Gaelic) The son of Alpine
*MacAlpin, Macalpine, MacAlpine,
McAlpine, MacAlpyn, Macalpyn,
MacAplyne, Macalpyne, MacAlpyne,
McAlpyne, McAlpin, McAlpyn*

Macandrew (Gaelic) The son of Andrew
MacAndrew, McAndrew

Macardle (Gaelic) The son of great
courage
*MacArdle, McCardle, Macardell,
MacArdell, McCardell*

Macario (Spanish) Filled with happiness
Macareo, Makario, Makareo

Macartan (Gaelic) The son of Artan
*MacArtan, McArtan, Macarten,
MacArten, McArten*

Macarthur (Gaelic) The son of Arthur
*MacArthur, McArthur, Macarther,
MacArther, McArther*

Macauley (Gaelic) The son of righteousness
*Macaulay, McCauley, McCaulay,
MacCauley, MacCaulay*

Macauliffe (Gaelic) The son of Olaf
*MacAuliffe, Macaulife, MacAulife, Macaulif,
MacAulif, McAuliffe, McAulife, McAulif*

Macauslan (Gaelic) The son of Absalon
*MacAuslan, McAuslan, Macauslen,
MacAuslen, McAuslen*

Macbain (Gaelic) The son of Beathan
*MacBaine, McBain, McBaine, MacBayn,
MacBayne, McBayne, McBayne, MacBean,
McBean, MacBeane, McBeane, MacBain*

Macbeth (Gaelic) The son of Beth
*McBeth, MacBethe, McBethe, MacBeth,
Macbethe*

Macbride (Gaelic) The son of a follower
of St. Brigid
*Macbryde, MacBride, MacBryde, McBride,
McBryde*

Maccabee (Hebrew) A hammer
*Macabee, Mackabee, Makabee, Maccabea,
Macabea, Mackabea, Makabea, Maccus*

Maccallum (Gaelic) The son of Callum
*MacCallum, MacCalum, Macalum,
McCallum, McCalum*

Macclennan (Gaelic) The son of Finnian's
servant
*Maclennan, MacClennan, McClennan,
MacClenan, McClenan, Macclenan*

Maccoll (Gaelic) The son of Coll
McColl, Maccoll, MacColl

Maccormack (Gaelic) The son of Cormac
*McCormack, MacCormack, Maccormak,
MacCormak, Maccormac, MacCormac,
McCormak, McCormak*

Maccoy (Gaelic) The son of Hugh
MacCoy, McCoy, Mccoy

Maccrea (Gaelic) The son of grace
*McCrea, Macrae, MacCrae, MacCray,
MacCrea*

Macdonald (Gaelic) The son of Donald
*McDonald, MacDonald, Macdonell,
Macdonel, MacDonell, MacDonel,
McDonell, McDonel, MacDomhnall,
McDomhnall*

Macdougal (Gaelic) The son of Dougal
*MacDougal, MacDowell, McDougal,
Macdowell, McDowell, MacDubhgall,
McDubhgall, Macdubhgall*

Macduff (Gaelic) The son of the black-
skinned man
*McDuff, MacDuff, Macduf, MacDuf,
McDuf*

Mace (English) One who wields the
medieval weapon
*Mayce, Maice, Maece, Maceo, Macio,
Maci, Macey, Macie, Macy, Macee,
Macea, Macerio, Macereo*

Macedonio (Greek) A man from
Macedonia
Macedoneo, Macedoniyo, Macedoneyo

Macegan (Gaelic) The son of Egan
*MacEgan, McEgan, Macegen, MacEgen,
McEgen*

Macelroy (Gaelic) The son of Elroy
MacElroy, McElroy

Macewen (Gaelic) The son of Ewen
McEwen, MacEwen

Macfarlane (Gaelic) The son of Farlan
*MacFarlane, McFarlane, Macfarlan,
MacFarlan, McFarlan, Macfarlin,
MacFarlin, McFarlin*

Macgill (Gaelic) The son of Gill
*MacGill, Macgyll, MacGyll, McGill,
McGyll*

Macgowan (Gaelic) The son of a
blacksmith
*MacGowan, Magowan, McGowan,
McGowen, McGown, MacCowan,
MacCowen*

Macgregor (Gaelic) The son of Gregor
McGregor, MacGregor

Machakw (Native American) Resembling
a horny toad

Machar (Scottish) Plain
*Machair, Machaire, Machare, Machayr,
Machayre, Machaer, Machaere*

Machau (Hebrew) A gift from God

Machenry (Gaelic) The son of Henry
MacHenry, McHenry

Machk (Native American) Resembling a
bear

Machupa (African) One who likes to
drink
*Machupah, Machoupa, Machoupah,
Machoopa, Machoopah*

Macintosh (Gaelic) The son of the thane
*MacIntosh, McIntosh, Macintoshe,
MacIntoshe, McIntoshe, Mackintosh,
MacKintosh*

Macintyre (Gaelic) The son of the
carpenter
*MacIntyre, McIntyre, Macintire,
MacIntire, McIntire*

Maciver (Gaelic) The son of an archer
MacIver, McIver

Mackay (Gaelic) The son of fire
*MacKay, McKay, Mackaye, MacKaye,
McKaye*

Mackendrick (Gaelic) The son of Henry
*MacKendrick, Mackendrik, MacKendrik,
Mackendric, MacKendric, Mackendryck,
Mackendryk, Mackendryc, MacKendryck,
MacKendryk, MacKendryc, McKendrick,
McKendrik, McKendric, McKendryck,
McKendryk, McKendryc*

Mackenzie (Gaelic) The son of a wise
leader; a fiery man; one who is fair
*Mackenzey, Makensie, Makenzie,
M'Kenzie, McKenzie, Meckenzie,
Mackenzee, Mackenzy, Mackenzi,
Mackenzea, MacKenzie, MacKensie,
McKensie*

Mackinley (Gaelic) The son of the white
warrior
*MacKinley, McKinley, MacKinlay,
McKinlay, Mackinlay, Mackinlie, MacKinlie*

Mackinnon (Gaelic) The son of the fair
one
*MacKinnon, Mackennon, MacKennon,
Mackinon, MacKinon, Mackenon,
MacKenon*

Macklin (Gaelic) The son of Flann
*Macklinn, Macklyn, Macklynn, Macklen,
Macklenn*

Maclachlan (Gaelic) The son of Lachlan
MacLachlan, Maclachlen, MacLachlen,
Maclachlin, MacLachlin, McLachlan,
McLachlen, McLachlin

Maclaine (Gaelic) The son of John's
servant
MacLaine, Maclain, MacLain, Maclayn,
McLaine, McLain, Maclane, MacLane,
McLane, Maclean, MacLean, McLean

Maclaren (Gaelic) The son of Laren
MacLaren, McLaren

Macleod (Gaelic) The son of the ugly one
MacLeod, McLeod, McCloud, MacCloud

Macmahon (Gaelic) The son of the bear
MacMahon, McMahon

Macmillan (Gaelic) The son of the bald
one
MacMillan, McMillan, Macmillen,
MacMillen, McMillen

Macmurray (Gaelic) The son of Murray
MacMurray, McMurray, Macmurra,
MacMurra

Macnab (Gaelic) The son of the abbot
MacNab, McNab

Macnachtan (Gaelic) The son of the
chaste or pure one
MacNachtan, McNachtan, Macnaughton,
MacNaughton, McNaughton

Macnair (Gaelic) The son of the heir
MacNair, McNair, Macnaire, MacNaire,
McNaire

Macneill (Gaelic) The son of Neil
MacNeill, Macneil, MacNeil, Macneal,
MacNeal, Macniel, MacNiel, McNeill,
McNeil, McNeal, McNiel, Macniall,
MacNiall, McNiall

Macon (English / French) To make / from
the city in France
Macun, Makon, Makun, Maken, Mackon,
Mackun

Macpherson (Gaelic) The son of the parson
MacPherson, McPherson, Macphersen,
MacPhersen, McPhersen, Macphersan,
MacPhersan, McPhersan

Macquaid (Gaelic) The son of Quaid
MacQuaid, McQuaid, Macquaide,
MacQuaide, McQuaide

Macquarrie (Gaelic) The son of the proud
one
MacQuarrie, McQuarrie, Macquarie,
MacQuarie, McQuarie, Macquarry,
MacQuarry, McQuarry, Macquarrey,
MacQuarrey, McQuarrey

Macqueen (Gaelic) The son of the good
man
MacQueen, McQueen

Macrae (Gaelic) The son of Ray
MacRae, McRae, Macray, MacRay,
McRay, Macraye, MacRaye, McRaye

Macsen (Welsh) Form of Maximilian,
meaning "the greatest"
Macsan, Macsin, Macsyn, Macson,
Macsun, Maksen, Maksan, Makson,
Maksun, Maksin, Maksyn, Macksen,
Macksan, Macksin, Macksyn, Mackson,
Macksun

Madan (Indian) The god of love

Madden (Pakistani) One who is organized;
a planner
Maddon, Maddan, Maddin, Maddyn,
Maddun, Maden, Madon, Madun, Madin,
Madyn

Maddock (Welsh) A generous and
benevolent man
Madock, Maddok, Madok, Maddoc,
Madoc, Madog

Maddox (Welsh) The son of the benefactor
Madox, Madocks, Maddocks

Madelhari (German) A battle counselor
Madelharie, Madelhary, Madelharey,
Madelharee, Madelharea

Madhav (Indian) A kind or sweet man

Madhu (Indian) As sweet as honey
Madhue, Madhou

Madhuk (Indian) Resembling a honeybee

Madhur (Indian) A sweet man

Madison (English) Son of a mighty warrior
Maddison, Madisen, Madisson, Madisyn,
Madyson, Madysen, Madisan, Maddisan,
Maddi, Maddie, Maddy, Maddey, Maddee,
Maddea

Madu (African) A manly man
Madue, Madou

Madzimoyo (African) One who is nourished with water
Madzymoyo

Maemi (Japanese) An honest child
Maemie, Maemy, Maemey, Maemee, Maemea

Maeron (Gaelic) One who is bitter
Maeren, Maerun, Maerin, Maeryn, Maeran

Magaidi (African) The last-born child
Magaidie, Magaidy, Magaidey, Magaidee, Magaydey, Magaydy, Magaydi, Magaydie, Magaydee, Magaedey, Magaedy, Magaedi, Magaedie, Magaedee, Magadey, Magady, Magadi, Magadie, Magadee

Magal (Hebrew) One who uses a scythe
Magel, Magol, Magul, Magil, Magyl

Magan (Anglo-Saxon) One who is competent
Magen, Magin, Magyn, Magon, Magun

Magar (Armenian) An attendant
Magarr, Mager, Magor, Magur, Magir, Magyr

Magee (Gaelic) The son of Hugh
MacGee, McGee, MacGhee, Maghee

Magglio (Hispanic) One who is healthy and strong; athletic
Maggleo, Maggliyo, Maggleyo

Magic (American) One who is full of wonder and surprise
Majic, Magyc, Magik, Magick, Majik, Majick

Magnar (Polish) A strong warrior
Magnarr, Magnor, Magnorr

Magne (Norse / Latin) A fierce warrior / a great man
Magni, Magnie, Magnee, Magnea, Magney, Magny

Magnus (Latin) A great man; one who is large
Magnos, Magnes, Magnusson, Magno, Mago

Maguire (Gaelic) The son of the beige one
Magwire, MacGuire, McGuire, MacGwire, McGwire

Magus (Latin) A sorcerer
Magis, Magys, Magos, Magas, Mages

Mahabala (Indian) Having great strength
Mahabahu

Mahan (American) A cowboy
Mahahn, Mahen, Mayhan, Maihan, Maehan, Mayhen, Maihen, Maehen

Mahanidhi (Indian) One who is treasured

Mahaniya (Indian) One who is worthy of honor

Mahant (Indian) Having a great soul
Mahante

Mahari (African) A forgiving man
Maharie, Mahary, Maharey, Maharee, Maharea

Mahatma (Hindi) Of great spiritual development

Mahavira (Hindi) A great hero
Mahaveera, Mahaveara, Mahaveira, Mahaviera, Mahavyra, Mahavir, Mahaveer, Mahavear, Mahaveir, Mahavier, Mahavyr

Mahdi (African) One who is expected
Mahdie, Mahdee, Mahdea, Mahdey, Mahdy

Maher (Irish) A generous man

Mahesh (Hindi) A great ruler
Maheshe

Mahfouz (Arabic) One who is protected
Mafouz, Mahfooz, Mafooz, Mahfuz, Mafuz

Mahieu (French) A gift from God

Mahin (Indian) Of the earth
Mahen, Mahyn

Mahir (Arabic) One who is skilled
Maheer, Mahear, Mahier, Maheir, Mahyr

Mahkah (Native American) Of the earth
Mahka, Makah, Maka

Mahlon (Hebrew) One who is sick
Mahlun, Mahlin, Mahlyn, Mahlan, Mahlen

Mahluli (African) A conqueror
Mahlulie, Mahluly, Mahluley, Mahlulee, Mahlulea

Mahmud (Arabic) One who is praiseworthy
Mahmood, Mahmoud, Mehmood, Mehmud, Mehmoud

Mahogany (English) Resembling the rich, dark wood
Mahogani, Mahoganey, Mahoganie, Mahogane, Mahogonee, Mahogonea

Mahomet (Arabic) One who is much praised
Mahomat, Mahomit, Mahomyt,
Mahomot, Mahomut

Mahon (Gaelic) Resembling a bear
Mahone, Mahoni, Mahonie, Mahoney,
Mahony, Mahonee, Mahonea

Mahpee (Native American) Of the sky
Mahpea, Mahpi, Mahpie, Mahpy, Mahpey

Mahuizoh (Nahuatl) A glorious man
Mahuizo

Maiele (Hawaiian) One who is well-spoken
Mayele, Maielle, Mayelle, Maiel, Mayel,
Maiell, Mayell

Mailhairer (French) An ill-fated man

Maimon (Arabic) One who is dependable;
having good fortune
Maymon, Maemon, Maimun, Maymun,
Maemun, Mamon, Mamun

Maine (French) From the mainland; from
the state of Maine

Maisel (Persian) A warrior
Maysel, Maesel, Meisel, Meysel

Maitland (English) From the meadow land
Maytland, Maetland, Maitlande,
Maytlande, Maetlande

Majdy (Arabic) A glorious man
Majdey, Majdi, Majdie, Majdee, Majdea

Majid (Arabic) Of noble glory
Majeed, Majead, Majied, Majeid, Majyd,
Majed

Major (Latin) The greater
Majur, Majer, Majar, Majir, Majyr, Majeur

Makaio (Hawaiian) A gift from God

Makani (Hawaiian) Of the wind
Makanie, Makany, Makaney, Makanee,
Makanea, Makan

Makarios (Greek) One who is blessed
Makkarios, Macaire, Macario, Macarios,
Macarius, Maccario, Maccarios,
Mackario, Mackarios, Makar, Makari,
Makario, Makary, Makarie, Makarey,
Makaree

Makena (Hawaiian) Man of abundance
Makenah

Makepeace (English) One who promotes
peace
Maekpeace, Maykpeace, Maikpeace,
Makepeece, Maikpeece, Maykpeece,
Maekpeece

Maki (Finnish) From the hill
Makie, Maky, Makey, Makee, Makea

Makin (Arabic) Having great strength
Makeen, Makean, Makein, Makien,
Makyn

Makis (Hebrew) A gift from God
Madys, Makiss, Makyss, Makisse, Madysse

Makkapitew (Native American) One who
has big teeth

Makonnen (African) A king
Makonnan, Makonnon, Makonnun,
Makonnin, Makonnyn, Makonen,
Makonan, Makonin, Makonyn,
Makonun, Makonon

Makoto (Japanese) A good and sincere
man

Makram (Arabic) A noble and generous
man
Makrem, Makrim, Makrym, Makrom,
Makrum

Makya (Native American) An eagle hunter
Makyah

Mal (Irish / Hindi / Hebrew) A chief / of
the gardens / a messenger of God

Malachi (Hebrew) A messenger of God
Malachie, Malachy, Malaki, Malakia,
Malakie, Malaquias, Malechy, Maleki,
Malequi, Malakai, Malak, Maeleachlainn

Malajit (Indian) A victorious man
Malajeet, Malajeit, Malajiet, Malajyt,
Malajeat

Malawa (African) A flourishing man

Malay (Indian) From the mountain
Malaye, Malae, Malai

Malcolm (Gaelic) Follower of St. Columbus
Malcom, Malcolum, Malkolm, Malkom,
Malkolum

Malden (English) From the valley of the
strong warrior
Maldan, Maldin, Maldyn, Maldon, Maldun

Malfred (German) A peaceful ruler
Malfried, Malfreid, Malfryd, Malfrid

Mali (Indian) A ruler; the firstborn son
Malie, Maly, Maley, Malee, Malea

Malik (Arabic) The sovereign
*Maleek, Maleak, Maleik, Maliek, Malyk,
Maleeq, Malek, Maliq, Malique, Malyq,
Maleaq, Malieq, Maleiq, Malic, Malyc,
Maleec, Maleac, Maleic, Maliec, Maalik*

Malin (English) The little warrior
*Malyn, Malen, Malon, Malun, Malan,
Mallin, Mallyn, Mallon, Mallun, Mallan,
Mallen*

Malise (French) One who is masterful
Malyse

Malki (Hebrew) My king
*Malkie, Malky, Malkey, Malkee, Malkea,
Malcam, Malkam, Malkiel, Malkior,
Malkiya, Malqui*

Mallory (French) An unlucky young man;
ill-fated
*Mallary, Mallerey, Mallery, Malloreigh,
Mallorey, Mallori, Mallorie, Malorey,
Malori, Malorie, Malory, Malloree,
Mallorea, Malorea, Maloree*

Mallow (Gaelic) From the river Allo
Mallowe, Malow, Malowe

Malo (Hawaiian) A victorious man
Maloh, Maloe, Mallo, Malloh

Malone (Irish) A follower of St. John
*Malon, Maloney, Malony, Maloni,
Malonie, Malonee, Malonea*

Malvin (Celtic / English) A leader / a
friend who offers counsel
*Malvinn, Malvinne, Malvyn, Malvynn,
Malvynne, Malven, Malvenn, Malvenne*

Mamduh (Arabic) One who is praised
Mamdouh, Mamdu, Mamdou

Mamo (African) A little boy
Mamoe, Mamow, Mamowe

Mamoru (Japanese) Of the earth
*Mamorou, Mamorue, Mamorew,
Mamoroo*

Mamun (Arabic) A trustworthy man
Ma'mun, Mamoun, Mamoon, Mamune

Manasseh (Hebrew) One who is forgetful
*Manassas, Manases, Manasio, Menashe,
Menashi, Menashi, Menashy, Menashey,
Menashee, Menashea, Manasses, Manasas*

Manchester (English) From the city in
England
*Manchestar, Manchestor, Manchestir,
Manchestyr, Manchestur*

Manchu (Chinese) One who is pure;
unflawed
Manchue, Manchew, Manchou, Manchoo

Manco (Peruvian) A king
Mancko, Manko, Mancoe, Mancoh

Mandan (Native American) A tribal name
*Manden, Mandon, Mandun, Mandin,
Mandyn*

Mandar (Indian) Of the sacred tree
Mandarr, Mandare

Mandeep (Indian) One who has a bright
mind
*Mandip, Mandeap, Mandeip, Mandiep,
Mandyp*

Mandek (Polish) A soldier
Mandeck, Mandec

Mandel (German) Resembling an almond;
having almond-shaped eyes
Mandell, Mandelle, Mandele

Mander (English) My son
Mandir, Mandyr, Mandur, Mandor

Mandhatri (Indian) A prince; born to
royalty
*Mandhatrie, Mandhatry, Mandhatrey,
Mandhatree, Mandhatrea*

Mandy (English) One who is much loved
Mandee, Mandea, Mandi, Mandie, Mandey

Manelin (Persian) The prince of all princes
*Manelen, Manelyn, Manelan, Manelon,
Manelun*

Manfred (German) A man of peace
*Manfreid, Manfried, Manfrid, Manfryd,
Mannfred, Mannfreid, Mannfried,
Mannfrid, Mannfryd, Manfredo, Manfrit,
Mannfrit, Manfryt, Mannfryt*

Mani (African) From the mountain
Manie, Many, Maney, Manee, Manea

M

Maninder (Hindi) A manly man

Manipi (Native American) An amazing man; a wonder
Manipie, Manipy, Manipey, Manipee, Manipea

Manjit (Indian) A conqueror of the mind; having great knowledge
Manjeet, Manjeat, Manjeit, Manjiet, Manjyt

Mankato (Native American) Of the blue earth

Manley (English) From the man's meadow; from the hero's meadow
Manly, Manli, Manlie, Manlea, Manleah, Manlee, Manleigh

Manmohan (Indian) A handsome and pleasing man
Manmohen, Manmohin, Manmohyn

Mann (English) A man; a hero
Man

Manneville (English) From the hero's estate; from the man's estate
Mannevylle, Mannevile, Mannevyle, Mannevill, Mannevyll, Mannevil, Mannevyl, Mannville, Mannvylle, Mannvile, Mannvyle, Mannvill, Mannvyll, Mannvil, Mannvyl, Manville, Manvylle, Manvile, Manvyle, Manvill, Manvyll, Manvil, Manvyl

Mannheim (German) From the hamlet in the swamp
Manheim

Manning (English) The son of the man; the son of the hero
Mannyng, Maning, Manyng

Mannis (Irish) A great man
Mannys, Manniss, Mannyss, Mannes, Mannus, Manis, Manys, Manes, Manus, Mannuss, Manness, Mannas, Mannass, Manas

Mannix (Irish) A little monk
Manix, Mannicks, Manicks, Manniks, Maniks, Mannyx, Manyx, Mannyks, Manyks, Mannycks, Manycks

Mannley (English) From the hero's meadow; from the man's meadow
Mannly, Mannli, Mannlie, Mannleigh, Mannlee, Mannlea, Mannleah

Mano (Hawaiian) Resembling a shark
Manoe, Manow, Manowe

Manoach (Hebrew) A restful place
Manoah, Manoa, Manoache

Manohar (Indian) A delightful and captivating man
Manoharr, Manohare

Mansa (African) A king
Mansah

Manse (English) A victorious man

Mansel (English) From the clergyman's house
Mansle, Mansell, Mansele, Manselle, Manshel, Manshele, Manshell, Manshelle

Mansfield (English) From the field near the small river
Mansfeld, Maunfield, Maunfeld

Mansur (Arabic) One who is victorious with God's help
Mansour, Mansure, Mansoor

Mantel (French) One who makes clothing
Mantell, Mantele, Mantelle, Mantle

Manton (English) From the man's town; from the hero's town
Mantun, Manten, Mannton, Manntun, Mannten

Mantotohpa (Native American) Of the four bears

Manu (African) The second-born child
Manue, Manou, Manoo

Manuel (Spanish) Form of Emmanuel, meaning "God is with us"
Manuelo, Manuello, Manolito, Manolo, Manollo, Manny, Manni, Manney, Mannie, Mannee, Mannea

Manville (French) From the great town
Manvil, Manvile, Manvylle, Manvyl, Manvyle, Mandeville, Mandevil, Mandevill, Mandevile, Mandevylle, Mandevyll, Mandevyl, Mandevyle, Manvill, Manvyll

Manya (Indian) A respected man
Manyah

Manzo (Japanese) The third son with ten-thousand-fold strength

Maolmuire (Scottish) A dark-skinned man

Maponus (Anglo-Saxon) In mythology, the god of music and youth

Mar (Spanish) Of the sea
Marr, Mare, Marre

Maram (Arabic) One who is desired

Marcel (French) The little warrior
Marceau, Marcelin, Marcellin, Marcellino, Marcell, Marcello, Marcellus, Marcelo, Marcely, Marciano, Marceley, Marceli, Marcelie, Marcelee, Marceleigh, Marcelino, Marcelus, Marcial

March (French) From the borderland; born during the month of March
Marche, Marzo, Marcio

Marconi (Italian) One who is inventive
Marconie, Marcony, Marconey, Marconee, Marconea

Marcus (Latin) Form of Mark, meaning "dedicated to Mars, the god of war"
Markus, Marcas, Marco, Markos, Marcos, Marko, Marqus, Marqos, Marcoux

Marden (Old English) From the valley with the pool
Mardin, Mardyn, Mardon, Mardun, Mardan

Mareechi (Indian) A sage
Mareechie, Mareechy, Mareechey, Mareechee, Mareechea

Marek (Polish) Form of Mark, meaning "dedicated to Mars, the god of war"
Marik, Maryk, Mareck, Maryck, Marick

Mareo (Japanese) One who is rare; unlike others
Marayo, Maraeo, Maraio

Margarito (Spanish) Resembling a pearl

Mariano (Spanish) A manly man
Marianos, Marianus, Meirion, Marion

Mariatu (African) One who is pure; chaste
Mariatue, Mariatou, Mariatoo

Marid (Arabic) A rebellious man
Maryd

Marino (Latin) Of the sea
Marinos, Marinus, Mareno, Marenos, Marenus

Mario (Latin) A manly man
Marius, Marios, Mariano, Marion, Mariun, Mareon

Marjuan (Spanish) A contentious man
Marwon, Marhjuan, Marhwon

Mark ○ (Latin) Dedicated to Mars, the god of war
Marc, Markey, Marky, Marki, Markie, Markee, Markea, Markov, Marq, Marque, Markell, Markel, Marx

Markham (English) From Mark's village
Markam

Markku (Scandinavian) A rebel
Markkue, Marku, Markue, Markkou, Markou

Marland (English) From the land near the lake
Marlond, Marlande, Marlonde, Marlando, Marlondo

Marlas (Greek) From the high tower
Marles, Marlos, Marlis, Marlys, Marlus

Marley (English) From the meadow near the lake
Marly, Marlea, Marleah, Marlee, Marleigh, Marli, Marlie, Marl, Marle

Marlon (English) Resembling a little hawk
Marlan, Marlen, Marlin, Marlyn, Marlun, Marlonn, Marlinn, Marlynn, Marlann, Marlenn, Marlunn

Marlow (English) Resembling driftwood
Marlowe, Marlo, Marloe

Marmaduke (Irish) An upper-class man; a follower of St. Maedoc
Marmeduke

Marmion (French) Our little one
Marmyon, Marmeon

Marnin (Hebrew) One who brings joy to others
Marnyn, Marnon, Marnun, Marnen, Marnan

Maro (Japanese) Myself

Marom (Hebrew) From the peak
Merom, Marum, Merum

M

Marquis (French) A lord of the borderlands; a nobleman
Markeece, Markeese, Markese, Markess, Markise, Markiss, Markize, Markwees, Markwess, Marques, Marquess, Marquez, Marqui, Marquise, Marquiz, Marquel, Marqes

Marr (German) From the marshland
Mar

Marriner (English) Of the sea; a seaman; a sailor
Mariner, Marrinor, Marinor, Marrinur, Marinur, Marrinar, Marinar, Marrinir, Marinir, Marrinyr, Marinyr, Marrinel, Marinel, Marrin, Marin, Marryn, Maryn, Maren

Mars (Latin) The god of war

Marsden (English) From the valley near the marshland
Marsdon, Marsdun, Marsdan, Marsdin, Marsdyn

Marsh (English) From the marshland
Marshe

Marshall (French / English) A caretaker of horses / a steward
Marchall, Marischal, Marischall, Marschal, Marshal, Marshell, Marshel, Marschall

Marshawn (American) An outgoing young man
Marshon, Marsean, Marshown, Mashawn, Masean, Mashon, Mashaun, Marshaun

Marston (English) From the town near the marsh
Marstun, Marsten, Marstin, Marstyn, Marstan

Martin (Latin) Dedicated to Mars, the god of war
Martyn, Mart, Martel, Martell, Marten, Martenn, Marti, Martie, Martijn, Martinien, Martino, Martinos, Martinus, Marton, Marty, Martey, Martee, Martea, Martainn, Maarten, Marcin, Martial, Martinez, Martiniano

Martinek (Czech) Form of Martin, meaning "dedicated to Mars, the god of war"
Martineck, Martinec, Martynek, Martyneck, Martynec

Marut (Indian) Of the wind
Marout, Marute, Maruti, Marutie, Marutee, Marutea, Maruty, Marutey

Marvell (Latin) An extraordinary man
Marvel, Marvele, Marvelle, Marveille

Marvin (Welsh) A friend of the sea
Marvinn, Marvinne, Marven, Marvenn, Marvenne, Marvyn, Marvynn, Marvynne, Marwen, Marwenn, Marwenne, Marwin, Marwinn, Marwinne, Marwine, Marwyn, Marwynn, Marwynne, Murvyn, Murvynn, Murvynne, Murvin, Murvinn, Murvinne, Murven, Murvenn, Murvenne, Marv, Marve

Marwood (English) From the forest near the lake
Marwode

Maryland (English) Honoring Queen Mary; from the state of Maryland
Mariland, Maralynd, Marylind, Marilind, Marylend, Marilend

Masa (African) One who is centered
Masah, Massa, Massah

Masaaki (African) An unfortunate man
Masaki, Masakie, Masakee, Masakea, Masaky, Masakey

Masajiro (Japanese) Having integrity
Masajyro, Masaji, Masajie, Masajy, Masajey, Masajee, Masajea

Masamba (African) One who leaves

Masamitsu (Japanese) A sensitive man

Masanao (Japanese) A good man

Masao (Japanese) A righteous man

Masato (Japanese) One who is just
Masatoe, Masatow, Masatowe

Masayuki (Japanese) One who causes trouble
Masayukie, Masayuky, Masayukey, Masayukee, Masayukea

Masefield (English) From the cornfield
Masefeld, Maisefield, Maisefeld

Mashaka (African) One who causes trouble

Mashiro (Japanese) One who is open-minded
Mashyro

Masichuvio (Native American) Resembling a gray deer

Maska (Native American) Having great strength

Maskini (African) A poor man
Maskinie, Maskiny, Maskiney, Maskinee, Maskinea

Maslin (French) Little Thomas
Maslyn, Maslen, Maslan, Maslon, Maslun, Masling, Masslin, Masslyn, Masslon, Masslun, Masslan, Masslen

Mason ✪ ❂ (English) One who works with stone
Masun, Masen, Masan, Masin, Masyn, Masson, Massun, Massen, Massan, Massin, Massyn

Masos (Hebrew) Filled with happiness

Massachusetts (Native American) From the big hill; from the state of Massachusetts
Massachusets, Massachusette, Massachusetta, Massa, Massachute, Massachusta

Masselin (French) A young Thomas
Masselyn, Masselen, Masselan, Masselon, Masselun, Maselin, Maselyn, Maselon, Maselun, Maselan, Maselen

Mathani (African) Of the commandments
Mathanie, Mathany, Mathaney, Mathanee, Mathanea

Mathau (American) A lively man
Mathow, Mathowe, Mathou, Mathoy

Mather (English) Of the powerful army
Matther, Maither, Mayther, Maether

Matherson (English) The son of Mather
Mathersun, Mathersin, Mathersyn, Mathersen, Mathers

Matheson (English) The son of Matthew
Mathesun, Mathesen, Mathesin, Mathesyn, Mathison, Mathisun, Mathisen, Mathisin, Mathisyn, Mathyson, Mathysen, Mathysin, Mathysyn, Mathysun, Matthews, Mathews, Matson, Matsen, Matsun, Matsin, Matsyn, Matteson, Mattesun, Mattesin, Mattesyn, Mattesen, Mattison, Mattisun, Mattisen, Mattisin, Mattisyn, Matthewson, Matthewsun, Matthewsen, Matthewsin, Matthewsyn, Mathewson, Mathewsun, Mathewsin, Mathewsyn, Mathewsen

MASON
We chose Mason because he was our first child and a boy, and because a mason is a "brick builder"; our Mason would be our foundation, the builder of our family. —Sheila, MO

Massey (English) A superior man
Massy, Massee, Massea, Massi, Massie, Masey, Masy, Masi, Masie, Masee, Masea

Masud (African) A fortunate man
Masood, Masoode, Masoud, Masoude, Masude, Mas'ud

Masura (Japanese) A good destiny
Masoura

Mataniah (Hebrew) A gift from God
Matania, Matanya, Matanyahu, Mattania, Mattaniah, Matanyah

Matata (African) One who causes trouble

Matchitehew (Native American) One who has an evil heart

Matchitisiw (Native American) One who has a bad character

Math (Scottish) Resembling a bear
Mathe

Matin (Arabic) Having great strength
Maten, Matan, Matyn, Maton, Matun

Matisse (French) One who is gifted
Matiss, Matysse, Matyss, Matise, Matyse

Matland (English) From Matthew's land
Matlande, Mattland, Mattlande

Matlock (American) A rancher
Matlok, Matloc

Matoskah (Native American) Resembling a white bear
Matoska

Matsu (Japanese) From the pine
Matsue, Matsoo, Matsou

Matsya (Indian) Resembling a fish
Matsyah

Matthew ✪ ✆ (Hebrew) A gift from God
Madteo, Madteos, Madtheos, Mat, Mata,
Mateo, Mateus, Mateusz, Mathé,
Matheu, Mathew, Mathian, Mathias,
Mathieu, Matias, Matico, Mats, Matt,
Mattaeus, Mattaus, Matteo, Matthaus,
Mattheus, Matthias, Matthieu, Matthiew,
Mattias, Mattie, Mattieu, Matty, Matvey,
Matyas, Matz, Matai, Mate, Matei,
Matfei, Matro, Matteus, Mattithyahu,
Mattox

Matunde (African) One who is fruitful
Matundi, Matundie, Matundy, Matundey,
Matundee, Matundea

Matvey (Russian) Form of Matthew,
meaning "a gift from God"
Matvy, Matvee, Matvea, Matvi, Matvie,
Motka, Matviyko

Matwau (Native American) The enemy

Mauli (Hawaiian) A black-haired man; a
giver of life
Maulie, Mauly, Mauley, Maulee,
Mauleigh, Maulea

Maurice (Latin) A dark-skinned man;
Moorish
Maurell, Maureo, Mauricio, Maurids,
Maurie, Maurin, Maurio, Maurise,
Maurits, Mauritius, Mauritz, Maurizio,
Mauro, Maurus, Maury, Maurycy, Mauri,
Maurey, Mauree, Maurea, Maurilio

Mawali (African) A lively man; one who is
vibrant
Mawalie, Mawaly, Mawaley, Mawalee,
Mawalea, Mawaleigh

Mawulol (African) One who gives thanks
to God

Max (Latin) Form of Maximilian, meaning
"the greatest"
Macks, Maxi, Maxie, Maxy, Maxey,
Maxee, Maxea, Maxx, Maxen, Maxon,
Maxan, Maxin, Maxyn, Maks

Maxfield (English) From Mack's field
Mackfield, Maxfeld, Macksfeld

Maximilian (Latin) The greatest
Maksim, Maksym, Maksymilian,
Massimiliano, Massimo, Maxemillian,
Maxemilion, Maxie, Maxim, Maxime,
Maxemilian, Maximiliano, Maximilianus,
Maximilien, Maximillien, Maximino,
Maximo, Maximos, Maxymillian,
Maxymilian, Maximous, Maximus,
Maksimilian, Maxinen, Maxanen

Maxwell (English) From Mack's spring
Maxwelle, Mackswell, Maxwel,
Mackswel, Mackwelle, Maxwill,
Maxwille, Mackswill, Maxwil, Mackswil

Mayer (Latin / German / Hebrew) A large
man / a farmer / one who is shining bright
Maier, Mayar, Mayor, Mayir, Mayur,
Meyer, Meir, Myer, Mayeer, Meier

MATTHEW

At a gathering two nights before my son was born, my family shot down every name I had picked
out. When asked his choice, my husband said "Matthew," a name he'd never mentioned before. I
said "Fine, no more discussion!" Matthew arrived two days later—five weeks early. He really is my
"gift of the Lord." —Stephanie, MI

Maverick (English) An independent man;
a nonconformist
Maveric, Maverik, Mavrick, Mavric,
Mavrik

Mavi (Turkish) Refers to the color blue
Mavie, Mavy, Mavey, Mavee, Mavea

Mavis (English) Resembling a small bird
Mavys, Maviss, Mavyss, Mavisse,
Mavysse, Mavas, Mavus, Mavasse,
Mavass, Mavuss, Mavusse

Mayes (English) From the field
Mays

Mayfield (English) From the strong one's
field
Mayfeld, Maifield, Maifeld, Maefield,
Maefeld

Mayhew (French) Form of Matthew,
meaning "a gift from God"
Maihew, Maehew, Mayhugh, Maihugh,
Maehugh, Mayhue, Maehue, Maihue

Maynard (German) One who is brave and strong
Maynhard, Maynor, Meinhard, Meinhardt, Menard, Mainard, Maenard, Maynar, Mainor, Maenor, Mainar, Maenar, Maynerd

Mayne (German) A powerful and great man
Mayn, Main, Maine, Maen, Maene, Mane

Mayo (Gaelic) From the yew-tree plain
Mayoe, Maiyo, Maeyo, Maiyoe, Maeyoe, Mayoh, Maioh

Maz (Hewbrew) One who provides aid
Maiz, Maze, Maiz, Maez, Maeze, Mazi, Mazie, Mazee, Mazea, Mazy, Mazey, Mazin, Mazyn, Mazon, Mazun, Mazen, Mazan

Mazal (Arabic) One who is calm; tranquil
Mazall

Mazor (Hebrew) One who is bandaged
Mazur, Mazar, Mazer, Mazir, Mazyr

Mccoy (Gaelic) The son of Coy
McCoy

McKenna (Gaelic) The son of Kenna; to ascend
McKennon, McKennun, McKennen, McKennan

Mckile (Gaelic) The son of Kyle
McKile, Mckyle, McKyle, Mackile, Mackyle, MacKile, MacKyle

Mead (English) From the meadow
Meade, Meed, Meede, Maed, Maede

Meallan (Irish) A kind man
Meallen, Meallon, Meallun, Meallin, Meallyn

Meara (Irish) Filled with joy
Meare, Mearie, Meari, Meary, Mearey, Mearee, Mearea, Meadhra

Medad (Hebrew) A beloved friend
Meydad

Medford (English) From the meadow near the ford
Medforde, Medfurd, Medfurde, Medferd, Medferde, Meadford, Meadforde, Meadfurd, Meadfurde, Meadferd, Meadferde

Medgar (German) Having great strength
Medgarr, Medgare, Medgard, Medard

Medwin (German) A strong friend
Medwine, Medwinn, Medwinne, Medwen, Medwenn, Medwenne, Medwyn, Medwynn, Medwynne, Medvin, Medvinn, Medvinne, Medven, Medvenn, Medvenne, Medvyn, Medvynn, Medvynne

Meged (Hebrew) One who has been blessed with goodness

Megedagik (Native American) One who has conquered many

Mehdi (Arabian) One who is guided
Mehdie, Mehdy, Mehdey, Mehdee, Mehdea

Mehetabel (Hebrew) One who is favored by God
Mehetabell, Mehitabel, Mehitabell, Mehytabel, Mehytabell

Mehrdad (Persian) Gift of the sun
Mehrded, Mehrdod, Mehrdid, Mehrdyd, Mehrdud

Meilyr (Welsh) A regal ruler

Meino (German) One who stands firm
Meinke

Meinrad (German) A strong counselor
Meinred, Meinrod, Meinrud, Meinrid, Meinryd

Meka (Hawaiian) Of the eyes
Mekah

Mekledoodum (Native American) A conceited man

Mekonnen (African) The angel
Mekonnin, Mekonnyn, Mekonnan, Mekonnon, Mekonnun

Mel (Gaelic / English) A mill worker / form of Melvin, meaning "a friend who offers counsel"
Mell

Melancton (Greek) Resembling a black flower
Melankton, Melanctun, Melanktun, Melancten, Melankten, Melanchton, Melanchten, Melanchthon, Melanchthen

Melanio (Spanish) Born into royalty
Melaniyo, Melaneo, Melaneyo

M

Melbourne (English) From the mill stream
Melborn, Melburn, Milbourn, Milbourne,
Milburn, Millburn, Millburne, Melburne,
Melborne, Milborne, Melbyrne, Millbyrne,
Milbyrne, Millborn, Millbourne, Millborne

Melchior (Polish) The king of the city
Malchior, Malkior, Melker, Melkior,
Melchoir, Melchor, Melcher

Melchisedek (Hebrew) My God is
righteousness
Melchisadak, Melchisadeck, Melchizadek

Meldon (English) From the mill on the hill
Meldun, Melden, Meldan, Meldin, Meldyn

Meldrick (English) The ruler of the mill
Meldrik, Meldric, Melderick, Melderik,
Melderic, Meldryck, Meldryc, Meldryk,
Melderyck, Melderyk, Melderyc

Mele (Hawaiian) One who is happy

Melesio (Spanish) An attentive man; one
who is careful
Melacio, Melasio, Melecio, Melicio,
Meliseo, Milesio

Melesse (African) He has returned
Melisse, Melysse

Meletius (Greek) A cautious man
Meletios, Meletious, Meletus, Meletos

Meli (Native American) One who is bitter
Melie, Mely, Meley, Melee, Melea, Meleigh

Melito (Spanish) A calm boy
Melyto

Melker (Swedish) A king
Melkar, Melkor, Melkur, Melkir, Melkyr

Mellen (Gaelic) The little pleasant one
Mellin, Mellyn, Mellan, Mellon, Mellun

Melos (Greek) The favorite
Milos, Mylos

Melroy (American) Form of Elroy, meaning "a red-haired young man / a king"
Melroye, Melroi

Melton (English) From the mill town
Meltun, Meltin, Meltyn, Melten, Meltan

Melville (English) From the mill town
Melvill, Melvil, Melvile, Melvylle, Melvyll,
Melvyl, Melvyle

Melvin (English) A friend who offers
counsel
Melvinn, Melvinne, Melven, Melvenn,
Melvenne, Melvyn, Melvynn, Melvynne,
Melwin, Melwinn, Melwinne, Melwine,
Melwen, Melwenn, Melwenne, Melwyn,
Melwynn, Melwynne, Melvon, Melvun,
Melvan, Maelwine

Melvis (American) Form of Elvis, meaning
"one who is wise"
Melviss, Melvisse, Melvys, Melvyss, Melvysse

Memphis (American) From the city in
Tennessee
Memfis, Memphys, Memfys, Memphus,
Memfus

Menachem (Hebrew) One who provides
comfort
Menaheim, Menahem, Menachim,
Menachym, Menahim, Menahym,
Machum, Machem, Mechum, Mechem

Menassah (Hebrew) A forgetful man
Menassa, Menass, Menas, Menasse,
Menasseh

Mendel (Farsi) A learned man
Mendell, Mendle, Mendeley, Mendely,
Mendeli, Mendelie, Mendelee, Mendelea,
Mendeleigh

Menefer (Egyptian) Of the beautiful city
Menefar, Menefir, Menefyr, Menefor,
Menefur

Menelik (African) The son of a wise man
Menelick, Menelic, Menelyk, Menelyck,
Menelyc

Mensah (African) The third-born child
Mensa

Mentor (Greek) A wise guide
Mentur, Menter, Mentar, Mentir, Mentyr

Menyhért (Hungarian) Of the royal light

Mercator (Latin) A merchant
Mercatur, Mercater, Mercatar, Mercatir,
Mercatyr

Mercer (English) A storekeeper
Merce, Mercar, Mercor, Mercur, Mercir,
Mercyr, Murcer, Murcar, Murcir, Murcyr,
Murcor, Murcur

Mercury (Latin) In mythology, the god of commerce and a messenger god
Mercuri, Mercurie, Mercuree, Mercurea, Mercurey, Mercure, Mercher, Mercutio, Mercurius

Mercy (English) One who shows compassion and pity
Mercey, Merci, Mercie, Mercee, Mercea, Mirci, Mircee, Mircea, Mircey, Mircy, Mircie, Mersy, Mersie, Mersi, Mersey, Mersee, Mersea

Meredith (Welsh) A great ruler; protector of the sea
Meredyth, Merideth, Meridith, Meridyth, Meredeth

Mereston (English) From the town near the lake
Merestun, Meresten, Merston, Merstun, Mersten

Merewood (English) From the forest with the lake
Merwood, Merewode, Merwode

Meris (Latin) Of the sea
Meriss, Merisse, Merys, Meryss, Merysse

Merle (French) Resembling a blackbird
Merl, Meryle, Meryl, Myrle, Myrl

Merlin (Welsh) Of the sea fortress; in Arthurian legend, the wizard and mentor of King Arthur
Merlyn, Merlan, Merlon, Merlun, Merlen, Merlinn, Merlynn, Merlonn, Merlunn, Merlann, Merlenn

Merlow (English) From the hill near the lake
Merelow, Merlowe, Merelowe

Merrick (English) Form of Maurice, meaning "a dark-skinned man; Moorish"
Merric, Merrik, Merryck, Merryc, Merryk, Merick, Meric, Merik, Meryck, Merik, Meric, Meyrick, Meyrik, Meyric, Meyryck, Meyryc, Meyryk, Myrick, Myric, Myrik, Myryck, Myryc, Myryk

Merrill (English) Of the shining sea
Meril, Merill, Merrel, Merrell, Merril, Meryl, Merryll, Meryll, Merryl, Merel, Merell

Merritt (English / Latin) From the boundary's gate / one who deserves good fortune
Merit, Meritt, Merrit, Merrett, Meret, Merett, Merret, Merrytt, Meryt, Merryt, Merytt

Merry (English) Filled with joy
Merri, Merrie, Merrey, Merree, Merrea

Mersey (English) From the river
Mersy, Mersi, Mersie, Mersee, Mersea

Merton (English) From the town near the lake
Mertun, Mertan, Merten, Mertin, Mertyn, Murton, Murtun, Murten, Murtan, Murtin, Murtyn

Mervin (Welsh) Form of Marvin, meaning "a friend of the sea"
Mervinn, Mervinne, Mervyn, Mervynn, Mervynne, Merven, Mervenn, Mervenne, Merwin, Merwinn, Merwinne, Merwine, Merwyn, Merwynn, Merwynne, Merwen, Merwenn, Merwenne, Merv, Merve

Meshach (Hebrew) An enduring man
Meshack, Meshac, Meshak, Meeshach, Meeshack, Meeshak, Meeshac

Mesquite (American) A spicy man
Meskeet, Mesqueet, Mesqeet

Methodios (Greek) A traveling companion
Methodius, Methodious

Methuselah (Hebrew) He who was sent; in the Bible, the longest-living man
Methusela, Methusella, Methusellah, Mathusela, Mathuselah, Mathusella, Mathusellah

Mhina (African) One who is delightful
Mhinah, Mheena, Mheenah, Mheina, Mheinah, Mhienah, Mhienah, Mhyna, Mhynah

Miach (Gaelic) A medic
Myach, Miack, Myack, Miak, Myak, Miac, Myac

Micah (Hebrew) Form of Michael, meaning "who is like God?"
Mica, Mycah, Myca, Micaiah, Mycaiah, Maacah, Mika, Mikah, Myka, Mykah

Michael ○ ☻ (Hebrew) Who is like God?
Makai, Micael, Mical, Micha, Michaelangelo, Michail, Michal, Micheal, Michel, Michelangelo, Michele, Michiel, Miguel, Mihail, Mihaly, Mikael, Mike, Mikel, Mikell, Mikey, Mikkel, Mikhail, Mikhalis, Mikhos, Miko, Mikol, Miky, Miquel, Mischa, Misha, Mychael, Mychal, Mykal, Mykel, Mykell, Micheil, Maichail, Mckale, McKale, Mihangel, Mikeal, Mikhael, Mikko, Miksa, Mysha, Myscha

Michigan (Native American) From the great waters; from the state of Michigan
Mishigan, Michegen, Mishegen

Michio (Japanese) One who has the strength of three thousand
Mychio

Michon (Hebrew) Form of Michael, meaning "who is like God?"
Mychon, Michonn, Mychonn, Mishon, Myshon, Mishonn, Myshonn, Micheon

Mick (English) Form of Michael, meaning "who is like God?"
Micke, Mickey, Micky, Micki, Mickie, Mickee, Mickea, Mickel

Middleton (English) From the central town
Midleton, Middletun, Midletun, Middleten, Midleten

Mieko (Japanese) A bright man

Migdal (Hebrew) From the tower
Migdall, Migdahl, Migdol, Migdoll

Mihir (Indian) Of the sun
Miheer, Mihear, Miheir, Mihier, Mihyr

Mikaili (African) Form of Michael, meaning "who is like God?"
Mikailie, Mikailee, Mikailey, Mikaily, Mikailea, Mikaley, Mikaly, Mikalee, Mikalea, Mikaleigh, Mikali, Mikalie

Mikasi (Native American) Resembling a coyote
Mikasie, Mikasy, Mikasey, Mikasee, Mikasea

Miki (Japanese) From the trees
Mikie, Miky, Mikey, Mikee, Mikea

Mikio (Japanese) From the three trees standing together
Mikeo, Mikeyo, Mikiyo

Mikolas (Basque) Form of Nicholas, meaning "of the victorious people"
Mikolaus, Miklas, Mickolas, Mickolaus, Micklas, Mikolus, Mickolus, Mikolaj, Mikolai, Milek, Mileck, Milec

Milagro (Spanish) A miracle child
Milagros, Milagrio, Milagreo, Milagrios, Mylagro, Mylagros, Mylagrio, Mylagreo, Mylagrios

Milan (Latin) An eager and hardworking man
Mylan

Miland (Indian) Resembling a bee
Myland, Milande, Mylande, Milind, Milinde, Mylinde, Mylind, Milend, Milende, Mylend, Mylende

Milap (Native American) A charitable man
Mylap

Milbank (English) From the mill on the riverbank
Millbank, Mylbank, Myllbank

Miles (German / Latin) One who is merciful / a soldier
Myles, Milo, Mylo, Miley, Mily, Mili, Milie, Milee, Milea, Milos, Mylos, Milosh, Mylosh

Milford (English) From the mill's ford
Millford, Milfurd, Millfurd, Milferd, Millferd, Milforde, Millforde, Milfurde, Millfurde, Milferde, Millferde

Millard (English) The guardian of the mill
Milard, Millerd, Milerd, Millward, Milward, Millwerd, Milwerd

Miller (English) One who works at the mill
Millar, Millor, Millur, Millir, Millyr, Myller, Millen, Millan, Millon, Millun, Millin, Millyn, Millman, Millmann, Milman, Milmann, Muller, Mueller, Melar, Mellar, Meler, Meller

Mills (English) One who lives near the mill
Mylls

Miloslav (Czech) One who is honored; one who loves glory
Myloslav, Miloslaw, Myloslaw

Milson (English) The son of Miles
Milsun, Milsen, Milsin, Milsyn, Milsan

Milton (English) From the mill town
Miltun, Milten, Millton, Milltun, Millten, Mylton, Myllton, Mylten, Myllten, Myltun, Mylltun, Milt, Mylt, Milte, Mylte, Milty, Miltee, Miltea, Milti, Miltie, Miltey

Mimir (Norse) In mythology, a giant who guarded the well of wisdom
Mymir, Mimeer, Mimyr, Mymeer, Mymyr, Meemir, Meemeer, Meemyr

Miner (Latin / English) One who works in the mines / a youth
Minor, Minar, Minur, Minir, Minyr

Mingan (Native American) Resembling a gray wolf
Mingen, Mingin, Mingon, Mingun, Mingyn

Mingo (American) A flirtatious man
Mingoe, Myngo, Myngoe

Minh (Vietnamese) A clever man

Minnesota (Native American) From the sky-tinted waters
Minesota, Minnesoda, Minesoda, Minisota, Minisoda

Minninnewah (Native American) Of the whirlwind

Minnow (American) A beachcomber
Mynnow, Minno, Mynno, Minnoe, Mynnoe

Minoru (Japanese) To bear fruit
Minorue, Minoroo, Minorou, Mynoru, Mynorue, Mynoroo, Mynorou

Minos (Greek) In mythology, the king of Crete who constructed the labyrinth
Mynos

Minster (English) Of the church
Mynster, Minstar, Mynstar, Minstor, Mynstor, Minstur, Mynstur, Minstir, Mynstir, Minstyr, Mynstyr

Minty (English) One who collects his thoughts
Mintey, Mintee, Mintea, Minti, Mintie, Minte, Mint

Mio (Spanish) He is mine
Myo

Miracle (American) An act of God's hand
Mirakle, Mirakel, Myracle, Myrakle

Mirage (French) An illusion
Myrage

Mirek (Czech) A peaceful ruler
Myrek, Mireck, Myreck, Mirec, Myrec

Mirit (Hebrew) A bitter man
Miryt, Myrit, Myryt

Miroslav (Russian) Of peaceful glory
Miroslaw, Mircea, Myroslav, Myroslaw, Myrcea

Mirsab (Arabic) One who is judicious
Myrsab

Mirumbi (African) Born during a period of rain
Mirumbie, Mirumby, Mirumbey, Mirumbee, Mirumbea

Miruts (African) The chosen one
Mirut, Myruts, Myrut

Mirza (Turkey) A well-behaved child
Myrza, Myrzah, Mirzah

Misae (Native American) Born beneath the white-hot sun
Misay, Misaye, Mysae, Mysay, Mysaye

Mishal (Arabic) One who holds the torch
Myshal, Mishall, Myshall, Mishaal, Myshaal

Mississippi (Native American) Of the great river; from the state of Mississippi
Misisipi, Missisippi, Mississipi, Misissippi, Misisippi

Missouri (Native American) From the town of large canoes; from the state of Missouri
Missourie, Mizouri, Mizourie, Missoury, Mizoury, Missuri, Mizuri, Mizury, Missury

Mistico (Italian) A mystical man
Misticko, Mystico, Mysticko, Mistiko, Mystiko

Misu (Native American) From the rippling water
Mysu, Misue, Mysue, Misou, Mysou

Mitali (Indian) A beloved friend
Mitalie, Mitaly, Mitaley, Mitalee, Mitaleigh, Mitalea

Mitchell (English) Form of Michael, meaning "who is like God?"
Mitch, Mitchel, Mitchill, Mytchell, Mytch, Mytchel, Mytchill, Mitchil, Mytchil, Mitchem, Mitcham, Mitchum, Mitchom, Mitchim, Mitchym

Mithra (Persian) In mythology, the god of light
Mitra, Mythra, Mytra

Mitsu (Japanese) Of the light
Mytsu, Mitsue, Mytsue

Mizell (English) Resembling a tiny gnat
Myzell, Mizel, Myzel, Mizele, Myzele, Mizelle, Myzelle

M

Mladen (Slavic) One who is eternally young
Mladan, Mladon, Mladun, Mladin,
Mladyn

Mochni (Native American) Resembling a
talking bird
Mochnie, Mochny, Mochney, Mochnee,
Mochnea

Modesty (Latin) One who is without conceit
Modesti, Modestie, Modestee, Modestus,
Modestey, Modesto, Modestio, Modestine,
Modestin, Modestea

Modig (Anglo-Saxon) A courageous man
Modyg, Modigg, Modygg

Moe (American) A dark-skinned man
Mo, Moey, Moeye

Mogens (Dutch) A powerful man
Mogen, Mogins, Mogin, Mogyns, Mogyn,
Mogan, Mogans

Mogue (Irish) The name of a saint

Mohajit (Indian) A charming man
Mohajeet, Mohajeat, Mohajeit, Mohajiet,
Mohajyt

Mohammed (Arabic) One who is greatly
praised; the name of the prophet and
founder of Islam
Mahomet, Mohamad, Mohamed,
Mohamet, Mohammad, Muhammad,
Muhammed, Mehmet, Mihammed,
Mihammad, Muhamed, Muhamad,
Muhamet, Mehemet, Muhameed

Mohan (Hindi) A charming and alluring
man; in Hinduism, one of the names of
Krishna
Mohann, Mohana, Mohanna

Mohandas (Hindi) A servant of Mohan
Mohandes, Mohandos, Mohandus

Mohave (Native American) A tribal name
Mohav, Mojave

Mohawk (Native American) A tribal name
Mohauk, Mohawke, Mohauke

Mohegan (Native American) A tribal name
Moheegan, Mohican, Mahican, Mohikan,
Mahikan, Moheagan

Mojag (Native American) One who is
never quiet

Moki (Native American) Resembling a deer
Mokie, Moky, Mokey, Mokee, Mokea

Molan (Irish) The servant of the storm
Molen

Molimo (Native American) Resembling a
bear seeking shade
Molymo, Moleemo, Moliemo, Moleimo,
Moleamo

Moline (American) A narrow-minded man
Moleen, Moleene, Molean, Moleane, Molyn,
Molyne, Molein, Moleine, Molien, Moliene

Molloy (Irish) A noble chief
Molloi, Malloy, Malloi, Malloye, Molloye

Momo (American) A warring man

Mona (African) A jealous man
Monah

Monahan (Gaelic) A monk; a religious man
Monahen, Monahon, Monahun, Monahin,
Monahyn, Monohan, Monohen, Monohon,
Monohun, Monohin, Monohyn

Monckton (English) From the monk's
settlement
Moncktun, Monckten, Monkton,
Monktun, Monkten

Monet (French) A solitary man; one who
advises others
Monay, Monaye, Monai, Monae

Money (American) A wealthy man
Moni, Monie, Mony, Monee, Monea,
Muney, Muny, Muni, Munie, Munee, Munea

Mongo (African) A well-known man
Mongoe, Mongow, Mongowe

Mongwau (Native American) Resembling
an owl

Monroe (Gaelic) From the mouth of the
river Roe
Monro, Monrow, Monrowe, Munro,
Munroe, Munrow, Munrowe

Montague (French) From the pointed
mountain
Montagew, Montagu, Montaigu,
Montaigue, Montaigew

Montaine (French) From the mountain
Montain, Montayn, Montayne, Montaen,
Montaene, Montane

Montana (Spanish) From the mountainous region; from the state of Montana
Montanna, Montanus

Montaro (Japanese) A big boy

Monte (English) Form of Montague, meaning "from the pointed mountain"
Montae, Montay, Montel, Montes, Montez, Montaye, Montrel, Montrell, Montrele, Montrelle

Montego (Spanish) From the mountains
Montaygo, Montayego, Montaego, Monteego, Monteigo, Montiego, Monteygo, Monteago

Montenegro (Spanish) From the black mountain

Montgomery (French) From Gomeric's mountain
Montgomerey, Montgomeri, Montgomerie, Montgomeree, Montgomerea

Montrae (American) A high-maintenance man
Montraie, Montray, Montraye, Montrey

Montrose (French) A high and mighty man
Montroce, Montros

Monty (English) Form of Montgomery, meaning "from Gomeric's mountain"
Montey, Monti, Montie, Montee, Montea, Montes, Montez

Monyyak (African) Born during a drought

Moody (American) A tempermental man
Moodi, Moodie, Moodee, Moodea, Moodey

Moon (American) Born beneath the moon; a dreamer

Mooney (Irish) A wealthy man
Moony, Mooni, Moonie, Maonaigh, Moonee, Moonea, Moone

Moore (French) A dark-skinned man; one who is noble
More, Moor, Mör, Möric, Mooring, Mooryng

Moose (American) Resembling the animal; a big, strong man
Moos, Mooze, Mooz

Moral (American) An upstanding man

Moran (Irish) A great man
Morane, Morain, Moraine, Morayn, Morayne, Moraen, Moraene

Morathi (African) A wise man
Morathie, Morathy, Morathey, Morathee, Morathea

Mordecai (Hebrew) A servant of Marduk, a Babylonian god
Mordechai, Mordekai, Mordeckai, Morducai, Morduchai, Mordukai, Morduckai

Mordred (English) A brave counselor; in Arthurian legend, Arthur's illegitimate son
Modraed, Modrad, Moordred, Moordrad, Moordraed, Modred, Mordraed, Mordread, Mordrad

Moreland (English) From the moors
Moorland, Morland

Morell (French) A dark-skinned man; Moorish
Morel, Morelle, Morele, Morrell, Morrelle, Morrel, Morrele

Morenike (African) Having good luck
Moreniky, Morenikey, Morenikie, Moreniki, Morenikee, Morenikea

Morgan (Welsh) Circling the bright sea; a sea dweller
Morgaine, Morgann, Morgance, Morgane, Morganne, Morgayne, Morgen, Morgin, Morgaen, Morgaene, Morgaena, Morgon, Morgun

Moriarty (Irish) A warrior of the sea
Moriarti, Moriartey, Moriartie, Moriartee, Moriartea

Moriel (Hebrew) God is my teacher
Moryel, Moriell, Moryell, Moriah, Moria

Morio (Japanese) A boy from the forest

Morlen (English) From the moor
Morlan, Morlin, Morlyn, Morlon, Morlun

Morley (English) From the meadow on the moor
Morly, Morleigh, Morlee, Morlea, Morleah, Morli, Morlie, Moorley, Moorly, Moorlea, Moorleah, Moorlee, Moorleigh, Moorli, Moorlie, Moreley, Morely, Morelee, Morelea, Moreleah, Moreleigh, Moreli, Morelie

Morpheus (Greek) In mythology, the god of dreams
Morfeus, Morphius, Mofius

Morris (Latin) Form of Maurice, meaning "a dark-skinned man; Moorish"
Morriss, Morey, Morice, Moricz, Morino, Moris, Moritz, Moriz, Morrel, Morrey, Morrice, Morrill, Moriss, Mori, Morie, Moree, Mory, Morri, Morrie, Morree, Morry

Morrison (English) The son of Morris
Morison, Morrisun, Morisun, Morrisen, Morisen, Morse

Morrissey (Irish) The sea's choice
Morrissy, Morrissi, Morrissie, Morrissee, Morrissea, Morrisey, Morrisy, Morrisey, Morrisi, Morrisie, Morrisee, Morisy, Morisey, Morisi, Morisie, Morisee, Morrisea, Morisea

Mortimer (French) Of the still water; of the dead sea
Mortimar, Mortimor, Mortimur, Mortimir, Mortimyr, Mortymer, Mortymar, Mortymir, Mortymyr, Mortymor, Mortymur

Morton (English) From the town near the moor
Mortun, Morten, Mortan, Mortin, Mortyn

Morty (French) Form of Mortimer, meaning "of the still water; of the dead sea"
Mortey, Morti, Mortie, Mortee, Mortea, Mort, Morte

Morven (Gaelic) From the large mountain gap
Morvin, Morvyn, Morvan, Morvun, Morfin, Morfen, Morfyn, Morfun, Morfan

Mosaed (Arabic) A samaritan; a good man

Moses (Hebrew) A savior; in the Bible, the leader of the Israelites; drawn from the water
Mioshe, Mioshye, Mohsen, Moke, Moise, Moises, Mose, Moshe, Mosheh, Mosiah, Mosie, Mosie, Mozes, Moyses, Moss, Moesen, Moeshe

Mosi (African) The firstborn child
Mosie, Mosy, Mosey, Mosee, Mosea

Mostyn (Welsh) From the mossy settlement
Mostin, Mosten, Moston, Mostun, Mostan

Moswen (African) A light-skinned man
Moswenn, Moswenne, Moswin, Moswinn, Moswinne, Moswyn, Moswynn, Moswynne

Motavato (Native American) Of the black kettle
Motavatoe, Motavatow, Motavatowe, Mokovaoto, Mokovato, Meturato, Mokatavatah, Moketavato, Moketaveto

Motega (Native American) A new arrow
Motayga, Motaega, Motaiga, Motaga

Motor (American) One who is fast
Motar, Moter, Motir, Motyr, Motur

Mottel (Hebrew) A warrior
Mottell, Mottle

Moubarak (Arabian) One who is blessed
Mubarak, Moobarak

Moukib (Arabic) The last of the prophets
Moukeeb, Moukeab, Moukeib, Moukieb, Moukyb

Moulik (Indian) A valuable man
Moulyk

Moulton (English) From the mule town
Moultun, Moulten, Moultan, Moultin, Moultyn

Mounafes (Arabic) A rival

Mountakaber (Arabic) A conceited man

Moyo (African) Of the heart

Moyolehuani (Aztec) The enamored one

Mozam (African) A man from Mozambique
Mozambi, Mozambe, Mozambie, Mozamby, Mozambey, Mozambee, Mozambea

Muata (Native American) Of the yellow-jackets' nest

Mudawar (Arabic) One who has a round head
Mudawarr, Mudewar, Mudewarr

Muenda (African) A caring man

Mufid (Arabic) One who is useful
Mufeed, Mufeid, Mufied, Mufead, Mufyd

Mufidy (Scottish) A man of the sea
Mufidey, Mufidee, Mufidea, Mufidi, Mufidie

Muhannad (Arabic) One who wields a sword
Muhanned, Muhanad, Muhaned, Muhunnad, Muhunad, Muhanned, Muhaned

Muhsin (Arabic) A charitable man
Muhsyn, Muhseen, Muhsean, Muhsein, Muhsien

Muhtadi (Arabic) One who is guided along the right path
Muhtadie, Muhtady, Muhtadey, Muhtadee, Muhtadea

Muir (Gaelic) From the moor
Muire

Mujahid (Arabic) A warrior
Mujaheed, Mujaheid, Mujahied, Mujahead, Mujahyd

Mukasa (Ugandan) An adminstrator of God

Mukhtar (Arabic) The chosen one
Muktar

Mukisa (Ugandan) Having good fortune
Mukysa

Mukki (Native American) Our child
Mukkie, Mukky, Mukkey, Mukkee, Mukkea

Mukonry (Irish) From the prosperous house
Mukonrey, Mukonree, Mukonrea, Mukonri, Mukonrie

Mukti (Sanskrit) One who is born free
Muktie, Mukty, Muktey, Muktee, Muktea

Mukul (Indian) One who is flourishing
Mukoul, Mukule, Mehul, Mehule

Mulcahy (Irish) A war chief
Mulcahey, Mulcahi, Mulcahie, Mulcahee, Mulcahea

Mulder (American) Of the darkness
Muldar, Muldor, Muldur, Muldir, Muldyr

Munachiso (African) God is with me
Munachyso

Munchin (Gaelic) A little monk
Munchyn, Munchen, Munchan, Munchon, Munchun, Mainchin, Mainchen, Mainchyn, Mainchon, Mainchun, Mainchan

Mundhir (Arabic) One who cautions others
Mundheer, Mundhear, Mundheir, Mundhier, Mundhyr

Mundo (Spanish) Form of Edmundo, meaning "a wealthy protector"
Mundoe, Mundowe, Mundow, Mondo, Mondow, Mondowe, Mondoe

Mungo (Gaelic) One who is very dear
Mungoe, Mungow, Mungowe

Munir (Arabic) A luminous man
Muneer, Munear, Muneir, Munier, Munyr, Mouneer, Mouneir, Mounir, Mounier, Mounear, Mounyr

Muraco (Native American) Born beneath the white moon
Murako, Muracko

Murali (Indian) One who plays the flute
Muralie, Muraly, Muraley, Muraleigh, Muralee, Muralea

Murdock (Scottish) From the sea
Murdok, Murdoc, Murdo, Murdoch, Murtagh, Murtaugh, Murtogh, Murtough

Mureithi (African) A shepherd
Mureithie, Mureithy, Mureithey, Mureithee, Mureithea

Murfain (American) Having a warrior spirit
Murfaine, Murfayn, Murfayne, Murfaen, Murfaene, Murfane

Muriel (Gaelic) Of the shining sea
Muryel, Muriell, Muryell, Murial, Muriall, Muryal, Muryall, Murell, Murel, Murrell, Murrel

Murphy (Gaelic) A warrior of the sea
Murphey, Murphee, Murphea, Murphi, Murphie, Murfey, Murfy, Murfee, Murfea, Murfi, Murfie, Murf, Murph

Murray (Gaelic) The lord of the sea
Murrey, Murry, Murri, Murrie, Murree, Murrea, Murry

Murron (Celtic) A bitter man
Murrun, Murren, Murran, Murrin, Murryn

Murrow (Celtic) A warrior of the sea
Murow, Murough, Murrough, Morrow, Morow, Morrowe, Murrowe, Morowe, Murowe, Morogh, Morrough

Murtadi (Arabic) One who is content
Murtadie, Murtady, Murtadey, Murtadee, Murtadea

Musa (Arabic) Form of Moses, meaning "a savior"
Musah, Mousa, Mousah, Moosa, Moosah

Musad (Arabic) One who is lucky
Musaad, Mus'ad

Musawenkosi (African) The Lord is generous

Mushin (Arabic) A charitable man
Musheen, Mushean, Mushein, Mushien, Mushyn

Muskan (Arabic) One who smiles often
Musken, Muskon, Muskun, Muskin, Muskyn

Muslim (Arabic) An adherent of Islam
Muslym, Muslem, Moslem, Moslim, Moslym

Musoke (African) Born beneath a rainbow
Musoki, Musokie, Musoky, Musokey, Musokee, Musokea

Mustapha (Arabic) The chosen one
Mustafa, Mostapha, Mostafa, Moustapha, Moustafa

Mutazz (Arabic) A powerful man
Mutaz, Mu'tazz, Mu'taz

Muti (Arabic) One who is obedient
Mutie, Muty, Mutey, Mutee, Mutea, Muta

Mutka (African) Born on New Year's Day
Mutkah

Muwaffaq (Arabic) A successful man

Mwaka (African) Born on New Year's Eve

Mwinyi (African) The lord or master
Mwinyie, Mwinyey, Mwinyee, Mwinyea

Mwita (African) One who calls
Mwitah, Mwyta, Mwytah

Mykelti (American) Form of Michael, meaning "who is like God?"
Mykeltie, Mykelty, Mykeltey, Mykeltee, Mykeltea

Myron (Greek) Refers to myrrh, a fragrant oil
Myrun, Myran, Myren, Myrin, Myryn, Miron, Mirun, Miran, Miren, Mirin, Miryn

Myrzon (American) A humorous man
Mirzon, Merzon, Myrzun, Mirzun, Merzun, Myrzen, Mirzen, Merzen, Merz, Myrz, Mirz

Mystery (American) A man of the unknown
Mysteri, Mysterie, Mysterey, Mysteree, Mistery, Misteri, Misterie, Misteree, Misterey, Mysterea, Misterea

Mystique (French) A man with an air of mystery
Mystic, Mistique, Mysteek, Misteek, Mystiek, Mistiek, Mysteeque, Misteeque, Mystik, Mystikal, Mistikal

Naal (Gaelic) A celebrated birth; the name of a saint

Naalnish (Native American) A hardworking man
Nalnish, Naalnysh, Nalnysh

Naaman (Hebrew) A pleasant man

Naaz (Indian) A proud man
Naz

Nabarun (Indian) Born beneath the morning sun
Nabaron

Nabendu (Indian) Born beneath the new moon
Nabendue, Nabendoo, Nabendou

Nabha (Indian) Of the sky
Nabhah

Nabhan (Arabic) An outstanding man; a noble man
Nabhann

Nabhi (Indian) The best
Nabhie, Nabhy, Nabhey, Nabhee, Nabhea

Nabhomani (Indian) Of the sun
Nabhomanie, Nabhomany, Nabhomaney, Nabhomanee, Nabhomanea

Nabil (Arabic) A highborn man
Nabeel, Nabeal, Nabeil, Nabiel, Nabyl

Nabu (Babylonian) In mythology, the god of writing and wisdom
Nabue, Naboo, Nabo, Nebo, Nebu, Nebue, Neboo

Nachman (Hebrew) One who comforts others
Nacham, Nachmann, Nahum, Nachmanke, Nechum, Nachum, Nehum

Nachshon (Hebrew) An adventurous man; one who is daring
Nachson

Nachton (Scottish) One who is pure; chaste
Nachtun, Nachten, Nachtin, Nachtyn, Nachtan, Naughton, Naughtun, Naughten, Naughtin, Naughtyn, Nechtan, Nechton, Nechtun, Nechtin, Nechtyn, Nechten

Nada (Arabic) Covered with the morning's dew
Nadah

Nadav (Hebrew) A generous man
Nadaav

Nadif (African) One who is born between seasons
Nadeef, Nadief, Nadeif, Nadyf, Nadeaf

Nadim (Arabic) A beloved friend
Nadeem, Nadeam, Nadiem, Nadeim, Nadym

Nadir (Arabic) One who is precious and rare
Nadeer, Nadear, Nadier, Nadeir, Nadyr, Nader

Nadish (Indian) Of the sea
Nadysh, Nadeesh, Nadeash, Nadiesh, Nadeish

Nadiv (Hebrew) One who is noble
Nadeev, Nadeav, Nadiev, Nadeiv, Nadyv

Naftali (Hebrew) A struggling man; in the Bible, one of Jacob's sons
Naphtali, Naphthali, Neftali, Nefthali, Nephtali, Nephthali, Naftalie, Naphtalie, Naphthalie, Neftalie, Nefthalie, Nephtalie, Nephthalie, Nafis, Naphis, Nafys, Naphys

Nagel (German) One who makes nails
Nagle, Nagler, Naegel, Nageler, Nagelle, Nagele, Nagell

Nagid (Hebrew) A great leader; ruler
Nageed, Naged, Nagead, Nagyd, Nageid, Nagied

Nahele (Native American) A man of the forest
Naheel, Naheal, Nahiel, Naheil, Naheyl, Nahyl

Nahiossi (Native American) Having three fingers
Nahiossie, Nahiossy, Nahiossey, Nahiossee, Nahiossea

Nahir (Hebrew) A clearheaded and bright man
Naheer, Nahear, Naheir, Nahier, Nahyr, Naher

Nahum (Hebrew) A compassionate man
Nahom, Nahoum, Nahoom, Nahuem

Naim (Arabic) One who is content
Naeem, Naeam, Naiym, Naym, Naeim, Naeym

Nairit (Indian) From the southwest
Nayrit, Nairyt, Nayryt, Naerit, Naeryt, Narit, Naryt

Nairn (Scottish) From the alder-tree river
Nairne, Nayrn, Nayrne, Naern, Naerne

Nairobi (African) From the capital of Kenya
Nairobie, Nayrobi, Nayrobie, Naerobi, Naerobie, Nairoby, Nairobey, Nairobee

Naiser (African) A founder of the clans
Nayser, Naeser, Naizer, Nayzer, Naezer

Naji (Arabic) One who is safe
Najea, Naje, Najee, Najie, Najy, Najey, Nanji, Nanjie, Nanjee, Nanjea, Nanjy, Nanjey

Najib (Arabic) Of noble descent; a highborn man
Najeeb, Najeab, Najeib, Najieb, Najyb, Nageeb, Nageab, Nagyb, Nageib, Nagieb, Nagib

Najjar (Arabic) One who works with wood; a carpenter
Najjer, Najjor, Najjur

Nakos (American) A sage
Nakus, Nakes, Nakis, Nakys, Nakas

Nalani (Hawaiian) A calmness of the skies; heaven's calm
Nalanie, Nalany, Nalaney, Nalany, Nalanee, Nalaneigh, Nalanea, Nalanya

N

Naldo (Spanish) Form of Reginald, meaning "the king's advisor"
Naldio, Naldiyo

Nalin (Hindi) Resembling the lotus flower
Naleen, Nalean, Nalein, Nalien, Nalyn

Nally (Irish) A poor man
Nalley, Nalli, Nallie, Nallee, Nallea, Nalleigh

Nalo (African) One who is lovable
Naloh, Nallo, Nalloh

Nam (Vietnamese) A man from the south

Naman (Indian) A friendly man; salutations
Namann, Namaan

Namdev (Indian) A poet or saint

Nami (Japanese) Of the waves
Namie, Namy, Namey, Namee, Namea

Namid (Native American) The star dancer
Nameed, Namead, Namied, Nameid, Namyd

Namir (Israeli) Resembling a leopard
Nameer, Namear, Namier, Nameir, Namyr

Nand (Indian) Filled with joy
Nande, Nandi, Nandie, Nandy, Nandey, Nandee, Nandea

Nandan (Indian) One who is pleasing
Nanden, Nandin, Nandyn, Nandon, Nandun

Nansen (Scandinavian) The son of Nancy
Nansan, Nansyn, Nansin, Nanson, Nansun

Nantai (Native American) The chief
Nantae, Nantay, Nantaye

Nantan (Native American) A spokesman
Nanten, Nantun, Nanton, Nantyn, Nantin

Naois (Celtic) In mythology, a great warrior
Naoys, Nayois, Nayoys, Naoise, Naoyse

Naoko (Japanese) One who is straightforward; honest

Naolin (Spanish) The Aztec sun god
Naolyn, Naolinn, Naolynn

Naotau (Indian) Our new son
Naotou

Napayshni (Native American) Having great strength; a courageous man
Napayshnie, Napayshnee, Napayshnea, Napayshny, Napayshney, Napaishni, Napaishnie, Napaishny, Napaishney, Napaishnee, Napaishnea

Napier (French / English) A mover / one who takes care of the royal linens
Neper

Napoleon (Italian / German) A man from Naples / son of the mists
Napolean, Napolion, Napoleone, Napoleane, Napolione

Narcissus (Greek) Resembling a daffodil; self-love; in mythology, a youth who fell in love with his reflection
Narciso, Narcisse, Narkissos, Narses, Narcisus, Narcis, Narciss

Nardo (Italian) A strong and hardy man
Nardio, Nardiyo, Nardoe

Naren (Hindi) The best among all men
Narin, Naryn, Naran, Naron, Narun

Naresh (Indian) A king
Nareshe, Natesh, Nateshe

Narsi (Hindi) A poet; a saint
Narsie, Narsy, Narsey, Narsee, Narsea

Narve (Dutch) Having great strength

Nasario (Spanish) One who is devoted to God
Nasareo, Nassario, Nassareo, Nazario, Nazareo, Nasaro, Nazaro

Nash (English) From the cliffs
Nashe

Nashashuk (Native American) As loud as thunder
Nashua

Nashoba (Native American) Resembling a wolf

Nasih (Arabic) One who advises others
Nasyh

Nasim (Arabic) As refreshing as a breeze
Nasym, Naseem, Naseam, Nasiem, Naseim

Nasir (Arabic) One who offers his support
Naseer, Nasear, Nasier, Naseir, Nasyr, Naser, Nasr, Naasir

Nasser (Arabic) One who is triumphant
Nassar, Nassor, Nassur, Nassyr, Nassir

Nastas (Native American) Curved like foxtail
Nastis, Nastys, Nastes, Nastus, Nastos

Natal (Spanish) Born at Christmastime
Natale, Natalino, Natalio, Natall, Natalle, Nataleo, Natica

Nathair (Scottish) Resembling a snake
Nathaer, Nathayr, Nathaire, Nathaere, Nathayre, Nathrach, Nathraichean

Nathan ♂ ♀ (Hebrew) Form of Nathaniel, meaning "a gift from God"
Nat, Natan, Nate, Nathen, Nathon, Nathin, Nathyn, Nathun, Natty, Natti, Nattie, Nattee, Nattey, Nayan

Nathaniel ♀ (Hebrew) A gift from God
Natanael, Nataniel, Nathanael, Nathaneal, Nathanial, Nathanyal, Nathanyel, Nethanel, Nethaniel, Nethanyel

Natine (African) A tribal name
Nateen, Nateene, Natean, Nateane, Natien, Natiene, Natein, Nateine, Natyn, Natyne, Natin

Navarro (Spanish) From the plains
Navaro, Navarrio, Navario, Navarre, Navare, Nabaro, Nabarro

Naveed (Persian) Our best wishes
Navead, Navid, Navied, Naveid, Navyd

Naveen (Gaelic / Indian) A pleasant, handsome man / one who is strong-willed
Naveene, Navine, Navyne, Navin, Navyn, Navean, Naveane

Navon (Hebrew) A wise man
Navun

Nawat (Native American) A left-handed man
Nawatt, Nawate, Nawatte

Nawkaw (Native American) From the woods
Nawkah, Nawka, Naukaw, Naukau, Naukah, Nauka

Nay (Arabic) His grace
Naye, Nai, Nae, Nayef, Naief

Nayati (Native American) One who wrestles
Nayatie, Nayate, Nayatee, Nayatea, Nayaty, Nayatey

NATHAN

We named our son Nathan Joseph, just because we liked it. We expected to only call him Nate, but we find ourselves using both. —Peter, IL

Nation (American) A patriotic man

Natividad (Spanish) Refers to the Nativity
Natividade, Natyvydad, Nativydad, Natyvidad

Nato (American) One who is gentle
Natoe, Natow, Natowe

Natsu (Japanese) Born during the summer
Natsue, Natsoo, Natsou

Nature (American) An outdoorsy man
Natural

Naufal (Arabic) A handsome man
Naufall, Nawfal, Nawfall

Naval (Indian) A wonder

Naylor (English) Of the sea/one who makes nails
Nayler, Nailor, Nailer, Naelor, Naeler, Nalor, Naler

Nazaire (Latin) A man from Nazareth
Nazaere, Nazayre, Nazare, Nazor, Nasareo, Nasarrio, Nazario, Nazarius, Nazaro

Nazih (Arabic) One who is pure; chaste
Nazeeh, Nazieh, Nazeih, Nazeah, Nazyh

Nazim (Arabian) Of a soft breeze
Nazeem, Nazeam, Naziem, Nazeim, Nazym

Nazir (Arabic) One who is observant
Nazeer, Nazear, Nazier, Nazeir, Nazyr

Ndulu (African) Resembling a dove
Ndooloo, Ndulou, Ndoulou

Neander (Greek) A new man
Neandar, Neandor, Neandur, Neandir, Neandyr

Neason (Irish) The name of a saint
Neeson, Nessan, Neasan

Nebraska (Native American) From the flat water land; from the state of Nebraska

Neci (Hungarian) A fiery man
Necie, Necy, Necey, Necee, Necea

Neckarios (Greek) Of the nectar; one who is immortal
Nectaire, Nectarios, Nectarius, Nektario, Nektarius, Nektarios, Nektaire

Ned (English) Form of Edward, meaning "a wealthy protector"
Nedd, Neddi, Neddie, Neddy, Neddey, Neddee, Neddea

Nedrun (American) One who is difficult
Nedron, Nedren, Nedran, Nedrin, Nedryn

Neelmani (Indian) Resembling a sapphire
Nealmani, Neelmanie, Nealmanie, Neelmany, Nealmany, Neelmaney, Nealmaney, Neelmanee, Nealmanee

Neelotpal (Indian) Resembling the blue lotus
Nealotpal, Nielotpal, Neilotpal, Nilothpal, Neelothpal

Neely (Gaelic) Form of Neil, meaning "the champion"
Neeley, Neeli, Neelie, Neeleigh, Neelea, Neelee

Neeraj (Indian) Resembling a lotus
Nearaj, Neiraj, Nieraj, Niraj

Neese (Celtic) Our choice
Nease, Neise, Niese, Neyse, Neece, Neace, Neice, Niece, Nyce, Nyse, Neyce

Nefin (German) A nephew
Nefen, Nefyn, Neffin, Neffyn, Neffen, Neff, Nef

Negasi (African) He will become the king
Negassi, Negasie, Negassie, Negasy, Negassy, Negasey, Negassey, Negasee, Negassee, Negashe, Negash

Negm (Arabian) Resembling a star

Negus (African) Of the royalty; a king; an emperor
Negos, Negous

Nehal (Indian) Born during a period of rain
Nehall, Nehale, Nehalle

Nehemiah (Hebrew) God provides comfort
Nehemia, Nechemia, Nechemiah, Nehemya, Nehemyah, Nechemya, Nechemyah

Nehru (Indian) From the canal
Nehrue, Nehroo, Nehrou

Neil (Gaelic) The champion
Neal, Neale, Neall, Nealle, Nealon, Neel, Neilan, Neile, Neill, Neille, Neils, Niel, Niles, Nyles, Neele, Niels

Neirin (Irish) Surrounded by light
Neiryn, Neiren, Neerin, Neeryn, Neeren

Neka (Native American) Resembling a wild goose
Nekah, Nekka, Nekkah

Nelek (Polish) Resembling a horn
Nelec, Neleck

Nels (Scandinavian) Of the victorious people
Nells, Nils, Nills, Nyls, Nylls

Nelson (English) The son of Neil; the son of a champion
Nealson, Neilson, Neillson, Nelsen, Nilson, Nilsson, Nelli, Nellie, Nellee, Nellea, Nelleigh, Nelly, Nelley, Nell, Nelle

Nemesio (Spanish) A man of justice and vengeance
Nemeseo, Nemeses, Nemesies, Nemesiyo

Nemo (Latin) A nobody; a no-name
Nemoe, Nemow, Nemowe

Nen (Arabic) From the ancient waters
Nenn

Neo (Greek) Brand-new
Neyo, Nio, Niyo

Neptune (Latin) In mythology, god of the sea
Neptun, Neptoon, Neptoone, Neptoun, Neptoune

Ner (Hebrew) Born during Hanukkah

Nereus (Greek) In mythology, the father of the Nereids, the sea nymphs
Nereos, Nereo, Nerius, Nerios, Nerio

Nerian (Anglo-Saxon) One who protects others
Nerien, Neriun

Nero (Latin) A powerful and unyielding man
Neroh

Neroli (Italian) Resembling an orange blossom
Nerolie, Neroly, Neroley, Neroleigh, Nerolea, Nerolee

Neron (Spanish) One who is strong and firm
Nerun, Neren, Nerin, Neryn, Neran

Nery (Spanish) One who is daring
Nerey, Neri, Nerie, Neree, Nerea, Nerry, Nerrey, Nerri, Nerrie, Nerree, Nerrea

Nesbit (English) One who lives near the bend in the road
Nezbit, Naisbit, Naisbitt, Nesbitt, Nisbet, Nisbett

Ness (Scottish) From the headland
Nesse, Nessi, Nessie, Nessy, Nessey, Nessee, Nessea

Nesto (Spanish / Greek) A serious man / one who is adventurous
Nestoh, Nestoro, Nestio, Nestorio, Neto

Nestor (Greek) A traveler; in mythology, a wise man who counseled the Greeks at Troy
Nester, Nesterio, Nestore, Nestorio, Netzer, Netzor

Netar (American) A bright man
Netardas, Netardos

Nevada (Spanish) From the place covered in snow; from the state of Nevada

Nevan (Irish) The little saint
Naomhan

Neville (French) From the new village
Nev, Nevil, Nevile, Nevill, Nevylle, Nevyl, Nevyle, Nevyll, Neuveville, Neuville, Neuvevylle, Neuvylle

Nevin (Latin) One who is sacred; little bone
Neven, Nevins, Nevon, Nevun, Niven, Nevyn, Nivon, Nivun

Newbie (American) A novice
Newbi, Newby, Newbey, Newbee, Newbea, Neubie, Neubi, Neuby, Neubey, Neubee, Neubea

Newbury (English) From the new settlement
Newbery, Newburry, Newberry, Neubury, Neubery, Neuburry, Neuberry

Newcomb (English) From the new valley
Newcom, Newcome, Newcombe, Neucomb, Neucombe, Neucom, Neucome

Newell (English) From the new manor
Newel, Newelle, Newele, Newhall, Newhal, Neuwell, Neuwel, Neuwele, Neuwelle, Niewheall, Nuell

Newland (English) From the new land
Newlande, Neuland, Neulande

Newlin (Welsh) From the new pond
Newlinn, Newlyn, Newlynn, Neulin, Neulinn, Neulyn, Neulynn

Newman (English) A newcomer
Newmann, Neuman, Neumann

Newport (English) From the new port
Neuport

Newton (English) From the new town
Newtun, Newtown, Neuton, Neutun, Neutown, Newt, Newte

Neylan (Turkish) Our wish has been granted
Neylen, Neylin, Neylyn, Neylon, Neylun

Neyman (American) A bookworm
Neymann

Nezer (Hebrew) One who is crowned
Nezar, Nezor, Nezur, Nezir, Nezyr

Nhat (Vietnamese) Having a long life
Nhatt, Nhate, Nhatte

Niabi (Native American) Resembling a fawn
Niabie, Niaby, Niabey, Niabee, Niabea, Nyabi, Nyabie, Nyaby, Nyabey, Nyabee, Nyabea

Niall (Celtic) Form of Neil, meaning "the champion"
Nial, Niallan, Nyall, Nyal, Nyallan, Niallen, Nyallen

Niamh (Gaelic) A bright man

Niaz (Persian) A gift
Nyaz

Nibal (Arabic) Man of the arrows
Nybal, Niball, Nyball

Nibaw (Native American) One who stands tall
Nybaw, Nibau, Nybau

Nicandro (Spanish) A victorious man
Nicandreo, Nicandrios, Nicandros, Nikander, Nikandreo, Nikandrios

Nicholas ⚪ ⚤ (Greek) Of the victorious people
Nicanor, Niccolo, Nichol, Nicholai, Nicholaus, Nichole, Nicholl, Nichols, Nicklas, Nickolas, Nickolaus, Nicol, Nicola, Nicolaas, Nicolai, Nicolao, Nicolas, Nicolaus, Nicolay, Nicolet, Nicoli, Nicolis, Nicoll, Nicollet, Nicolls, Nicolo, Nikita, Nikkolas, Nikkolay, Niklaas, Niklas, Niklos, Nikolai, Nikolas, Nikolaus, Nikolay, Nikolos, Nikos, Nilos, Neacal, Neakail, Nickson, Nico, Nikalus, Nikkos, Niko

Nick (English) Form of Nicholas, meaning "of the victorious people"
Nik, Nicki, Nickie, Nickey, Nicky, Nickee, Nickea, Niki, Nikki, Nikie, Nikkie, Niky, Nikky, Nikey, Nikkey, Nikee, Nikkee, Nic

Nickleby (English) From Nicholas's farm
Nicklebey, Nicklebee, Nicklebea, Nicklebi, Nicklebie, Nikelby, Nikelbey, Nikelbe, Nikelbee, Nikelbea, Nikelbi, Nikelbie, Nikleby, Niklebey, Niklebee, Niklebea, Niklebi, Niklebie

Nickler (American) One who is swift
Nikler, Nicler, Nyckler, Nykler, Nycler

Nicodemus (Greek) The victory of the people
Nicodemo, Nikodema, Nikodemus, Nikodim, Nikodemos, Nikodem, Nicodem

Nicomedes (Greek) One who thinks of victory
Nikomedes, Nicomedo, Nikomedo

Nida (Native American) Resembling an elf
Nyda, Nidah, Nydah

Nigan (Native American) One who surpasses others
Nygan, Nighan, Nyghan

Nigarvi (Indian) A humble man
Nigarvie, Nigarvy, Nigarvey, Nigarvee, Nigarvea

Nigel (English) Form of Niall, meaning "the champion"
Nigellus, Niguel, Nijel, Njal, Nygel, Nigell, Nygell

Night (American) Born during the evening
Nite

Nihal (Indian) One who is content
Neehal, Neihal, Niehal, Neahal, Neyhal, Nyhal

Nihar (Indian) Covered with the morning's dew
Neehar, Niehar, Neihar, Neahar, Nyhar

Niichaad (Native American) One who is swollen
Nichad, Niichad, Nichaad

Nikan (Persian) One who brings good things
Niken, Nikin, Nikyn, Nikon, Nikun

Nike (Greek) One who brings victory
Nyke, Nykko, Nikko

Nikeese (African) One who is greatly loved
Nikease, Nikeise, Nikiese, Nikeyse, Nikyse, Nikeece, Nikeace, Nikeice, Nikiece, Nikeyce, Nikyce

Nikhil (Indian) One who is complete
Nikhel, Nykhil, Nykhel, Nykhyl, Nikhyl

Nikiti (Native American) Having a smooth and round head
Nikitie, Nikity, Nikitey, Nikitee, Nikitea

Nikostratos (Greek) Of the victorious army
Nicostrato, Nicostratos, Nicostratus, Nikostrato, Nikostratus

Nikshep (Indian) One who is treasured
Nykshep

Nikunja (Indian) From the grove of trees

Nilalochan (Indian) Having blue eyes

Nili (Hebrew) Of the pea plant
Nilie, Nily, Niley, Nilee, Nilea, Nileigh

Nimbus (Latin) Resembling a rain cloud
Nymbus, Nimbos, Nymbos

Nimrod (Hebrew) A mighty hunter

Ninian (Armenian) A studious man
Ninien, Ninyan, Ninyen

Nino (Italian / Spanish) God is gracious / a young boy
Ninoshka

Ninyun (American) A high-spirited man
Ninion, Ninyan, Nynyn, Nynion, Nynyan

Nipun (Indian) A clever man
Nypun, Nipon, Nypon

Nirad (Indian) Of the clouds
Nyrad

Nirajit (Indian) An illuminated man
Nirajeet, Nirajyt, Nirajeat

Nissim (Hebrew) A believer; a wondrous boy
Nissym, Nyssim, Nyssym

Nitis (Native American) A beloved friend
Nitiss, Nitisse, Nitys, Nityss, Nitysse, Nytis, Nytys

Nixkamich (Native American) A grand-fatherly man

NOAH

Our second son is one of five Noahs in his year at school—four boys and one girl. (One of them has even changed his name to AJ!) There are no Noahs in our older son's year; the love of the name seems to have started seven years ago. Had I know how popular that name would be I would never have chosen it. Never! —Rachelle, FL

Niran (Thai) The eternal one
Nyran, Niren, Nirin, Niryn, Niron, Nirun, Nyren, Nyrin, Nyryn, Nyron, Nyrun

Nirav (Indian) One who is quiet
Nyrav

Nirbheet (Indian) A fearless man
Nirbhit, Nirbhyt, Nirbhay, Nirbhaye, Nirbhai, Nirbhae

Nirel (Hebrew) From God's field
Niriel, Nirle, Nirell, Nirele, Nirelle

Niremaan (Arabic) One who shines as brightly as fire
Nyremaan, Nireman, Nyreman

Nirmal (Indian) One who is peaceful; pure
Nirmall, Nyrmal, Nyrmall, Nischal, Nyschal

Nirmohi (Indian) One who is unattached
Nirmohie, Nirmohy, Nirmohey, Nirmohee, Nirmohea

Niru (Persian) Having great strength and power
Nirue, Niroo, Nirou

Nishan (Armenian) A sign or symbol

Nishant (Indian) Born with the dawn; one who is peaceful
Nyshant, Nishante, Nyshante, Nishanth, Nishanthe, Nyshanth, Nyshanthe

Nishok (Indian) Filled with happiness
Nyshok, Nishock, Nyshock

Nissan (Hebrew) A miracle child
Nisan

Nixon (English) Form of Nicholas, meaning "of the victorious people"
Nixen, Nixun, Nixin, Nixyn, Nixan, Nix, Nixs

Niyol (Native American) Of the wind

Njau (African) Resembling a young bull

Njord (Scandinavian) A man from the north
Njorde, Njorth, Njorthe

Nkrumah (African) The ninth-born child
Nkruma

Noach (Hebrew) One who provides comfort

Noadiah (Hebrew) God has assembled
Noadia, Noadya, Noadyah, Noadiya, Noadiyah

Noah ✪ ✪ (Hebrew) A peaceful wanderer
Noa

Noam (Hebrew) A beloved friend
Noame

Noble (Latin) A wellborn man
Nobel, Nobile, Nobe, Nobie, Nobie, Nobee, Nobea

Nodin (Native American) Of the wind
Nodyn, Noden, Nodan, Nodon, Nodun

Noe (Spanish) One who is peaceful; resting; quiet
Noeh

Noel (French) Born at Christmastime
Noele, Noell, Noelle, Noél

N

Noi (Laos) A man of small stature
Noy, Noye

Nolan (Gaelic) A famous and noble man;
a champion of the people
Nolen, Nolin, Nolon, Nolun, Nolyn,
Noland, Nolande

Nolden (American) One who is noble
Noldan, Noldin, Noldyn, Noldon, Noldun

Nolly (Scandinavian) Filled with hope
Nolley, Nolli, Nollie, Nollee, Nollea,
Nolleigh, Noll, Nolle

Nonnie (Latin) The ninth-born child
Nonni, Nonny, Nonney, Nonnee, Nonnea,
Noni, Nonie, Nony, Noney, Nonee, Nonea

Noor (Arabic) Surrounded by light
Nour, Nur

Nootau (Native American) A fiery man
Noutau, Nutau, Nuetau

Norbert (English) One who shines from
the north
Norberte, Norberth, Norberthe, Norberto,
Norbie, Norbi, Norby, Norbey, Norbee,
Norbea, Norb, Norbe

Norcross (English) From the northern
crossroads
Norcros, Northcross, Northcros,
Norcrosse, Northcrosse

Nordin (Norse) A handsome man
Norden, Nordyn, Nordon, Nordun, Nordan

Norice (French) One who takes care
of others
Noryce, Norise, Noryse, Noriece, Noreice,
Noreece, Noreace, Noriese, Noreise,
Noreese, Norease

Noriyuki (Japanese) Filled with happiness

Norman (English) A man from the north
Normand, Normano, Normando,
Normi, Normie, Normee, Normea,
Normy, Normey, Normun, Normon,
Normen, Normin, Normyn, Norm,
Norme

Norris (English) A man from the north
Noris, Noriss, Norriss, Norrys, Norryss,
Norys

Norshell (American) One who is brash
Norshel, Norshelle, Norshele

North (English) A man from the north
Northe

Northcliff (English) From the northern cliff
Northcliffe, Northclyf, Northclyff,
Northclyffe

Northrop (English) From the northern
farm
Northrup

Norton (English) From the northern town
Nortun, Nortown, Norten, Nortin,
Nortyn, Nortan, Northtun, Northton,
Northten, Northtin, Northtyn, Northtan

Norval (Scottish) From the northern valley
Norvall, Norvale, Norvail, Norvaile,
Norvayl, Norvayle, Norvael, Norvaele

Norvel (English) From the northern state

Norville (English) From the northern
settlement
Norvil, Norvill, Norvile, Norvylle, Norvyl,
Norvyll, Norvyle

Norward (English) A guardian of the
north
Norwarde, Norwerd, Norwerde, Norwurd,
Norwurde

Norwell (English) From the northern spring
Norwel, Norwele, Norwelle

Norwin (English) A friend from the north
Norwinn, Norwinne, Norwyn, Norwynn,
Norwynne, Norwen, Norwenn, Norwenne,
Norwine, Norvin, Norvinn, Norvinne,
Norvyn, Norvynn, Norvynne, Norven,
Norvenn, Norvenne

Norwood (English) From the northern
forest
Norwoode, Northwood, Norwode,
Northwode

Noshi (Native American) A fatherly man
Noshie, Noshy, Noshey, Noshee, Noshea,
Nosh, Noshe

Notaku (Native American) Resembling a
growling bear
Notakou, Notakue, Notakoo

Nova (Latin) New
Novah, Novva, Novvah

Novak (Czech) A newcomer
Novac, Novack

November (American) Born in the month of November
Novimber, Novymber

Now (Arabic) Born of the light
Nowe

Nowey (American) One who knows all
Nowy, Nowi, Nowie, Nowee, Nowea

Nowles (English) From the forest cove
Nowels, Nowel, Nowle

Nripa (Indian) The king
Nrypa, Nripah, Nrypah

Nripesh (Indian) The kings of all kings
Nrypesh, Nripeshe, Nrypeshe

Nuhad (Arabic) A brave young man
Nuehad, Nouhad, Neuhad

Nukpana (Native American) An evil man
Nukpanah, Nukpanna, Nukpannah, Nuckpana, Nucpana

Nulte (Irish) A man from Ulster
Nulti, Nultie, Nulty, Nultey, Nultee, Nultea

Numair (Arabic) Resembling a panther
Numaire, Numayr, Numayre, Numaer, Numaere

Nuncio (Spanish) A messenger
Nunzio

Nunri (American) A generous man
Nunrie, Nunry, Nunrey, Nunree, Nunrea

Nuri (Arabic) Surrounded by light
Nurie, Nury, Nurey, Nuree, Nurea, Nuriya, Nuriyah, Nuris

Nuriel (Hebrew) God's light
Nuriell, Nuriele, Nurielle, Nuryel, Nuryell, Nuryele, Nuryelle, Nooriel, Nooriell

Nuru (African) My light
Nurue, Nuroo, Nurou, Nourou, Nooroo

Nyack (African) One who is persistent
Niack, Nyak, Niak, Nyac, Niac

Nyasore (African) A thin man
Niasore, Nyasoar, Niasoar

Nye (English) One who lives on the island
Nyle, Nie, Nile

Nyék (Hungarian) From the borderlands

Nyoka (African) Resembling a snake
Nyokah, Nioka, Niokah

Nyoko (Japanese) Resembling a gem
Nioko

Oakes (English) From the oak-tree grove
Oaks, Oak, Oake, Ochs, Oachs, Oaki, Oaki, Oaky, Oakey, Oakee, Oakea, Okes

Oakley (English) From the meadow of oak trees
Oakly, Oakleigh, Oaklee, Oaklea, Oakleah, Oakli, Oaklie

Oba (African) A king
Obah, Obba, Obbah

Obadiah (Hebrew) A servant of God
Obadias, Obadya, Obed, Obediah, Obbi, Ovadiah, Ovadiach, Obbie, Obbee, Obbea, Obby, Obbey, Ovediah, Ovedia, Ovadya, Ovedya

Obasi (African) One who honors God
Obasie, Obasy, Obasey, Obasee, Obasea

Obayana (African) The king of fire

Obedience (American) A well-behaved man
Obediance, Obedyence, Obedeynce

Obelix (Greek) A pillar of strength
Obelex, Obelux, Obelius, Obelias

Oberon (German) A royal bear; having the heart of a bear
Oberron

Obert (German) A wealthy and bright man
Oberte, Oberth, Oberthe, Odbart, Odbarte, Odbarth, Odbarthe, Odhert, Odherte, Odherth, Odherthe, Orbart, Orbarte, Orbarth, Orbarthe, Orbert, Orberte, Orberth, Orberthe

Obi (Nigerian) Having a big heart
Obie, Oby, Obey, Obee, Obea

Obiajulu (African) One whose heart has been consoled
Obyajulu, Obiajulue, Obiajuloo, Obiajooloo

Obike (African) One who is dearly loved;
from a strong household
Obyke

Oceanus (Greek) Of the ocean; deity of
the sea; in mythology, a Titan
*Oceanos, Oceane, Ocean, Ocie, Oci, Ocee,
Ocea, Ocy, Ocey*

Ocelfa (English) From the elevated plains
*Ocelfah, Ocelpha, Ocelphah, Ocelfus,
Ocelphus, Ocelfos, Ocelphos*

Ochen (African) One of twins
*Ochein, Ochin, Ochyn, Ochan, Ochon,
Ochun*

Ochi (African) Filled with laughter
Ochie, Ochee, Ochea, Ochy, Ochey

Ociel (Latin) From the sky
*Ociell, Ociele, Ocielle, Ocyel, Ocyele,
Ocyelle, Ocyell*

Octavio (Latin) The eighth-born child
*Octave, Octavius, Octavian, Octovien,
Octavious, Octavo, Octavus, Ottavio*

October (American) Born during autumn;
born in the month of October
Oktober, Octobar, Oktobar

Ocumwhowurst (Native American)
Resembling a yellow wolf
*Ocumwhowerst, Ocumwhowirst,
Ocunnowhurst, Ocunnowherst,
Ocunnowhirst*

Ocvran (English) In Arthurian legend, the
father of Guinevere
Ocvrann, Okvran, Okvrann

Odakota (Native American) A friendly man
Odacota, Odakoda, Odacoda

Odale (English) From the valley
*Odayl, Odayle, Odail, Odaile, Odael,
Odaele*

Odam (English) A son-in-law
Odom, Odem, Odum

Odanodan (Irish) Of the red earth
*Odanoden, Odanodin, Odanodyn,
Odanodon, Odanodun*

Oddvar (Norse) The point of the spear
Oddvarr, Odvarr, Odvar

Ode (Egyptian / Greek) Traveler of the road
/ a lyric poem

Oded (Hebrew) One who is supportive and
encouraging

Odell (Greek / German) A sweet melody /
one who is wealthy
*Odall, Odelle, Odel, Odele, Odie, Ody,
Odi, Odey, Odee, Odea, Odyll, Odylle*

Oder (English) From the river
Odar, Odir, Odyr, Odur

Odhran (Gaelic) Refers to a pale-green
color
Odran, Odhrann, Odrann

Odilo (German) One who is fortunate in
battle
*Odile, Odilio, Odilon, Otildo, Ottild,
Ottildo*

Odin (Norse) In mythology, the supreme
deity
Odyn, Odon, Oden, Odun

Odinan (Hungarian) One who is wealthy
and powerful
Odynan, Odinann, Odynann

Odion (African) The firstborn of twins
Odiyon, Odiun, Odiyun

Odissan (African) A wanderer; traveler
*Odyssan, Odisan, Odysan, Odissann,
Odyssann, Odisann, Odysann*

Odolf (German) A prosperous wolf
*Odolfe, Odolff, Odolffe, Odulf, Odulff,
Odulffe, Odulfe, Odwolf, Odwolfe,
Odwulf, Odwulfe*

Odongo (African) The second-born of
twins
Odongyo, Odongio, Ondgiyo

Odysseus (Greek) One who roams; an
angry man; in mythology, a hero who
spends ten years trying to return home
from war
*Odysse, Odisoose, Odysseos, Odyseus,
Odyseos*

Oengus (Irish) A vigorous man
Oenguss

Offa (Anglo-Saxon) A king
Offah

Ofir (Hebrew) The golden son
Ofeer, Ofear, Ofyr, Ofier, Ofeir, Ofer

Og (Aramaic) A king

Ogaleesha (Native American) A man wearing a red shirt
Ogaleasha, Ogaleisha, Ogaleysha, Ogalesha, Ogaliesha, Ogalisha

Ogano (Japenese) A wise man

Ogden (English) From the valley of oak trees
Ogdin, Ogdyn, Ogdan, Ogdon, Ogdun, Oakden, Oakdin, Oakdyn, Oakdan, Oakdon, Oakdun

Ogelsvy (English) A fearsome warrior
Ogelsvey, Ogelsvi, Ogelsvie, Ogelsvee, Ogelsvea, Ogelsby, Ogelsbey, Ogelsbee, Ogelsbea, Ogelsbi, Ogelsbie

Oghe (Irish) One who rides horses
Oghi, Oghie, Oghee, Oghea, Oghy, Oghey

Ogilvy (Scottish) From the high peak
Ogilvey, Ogilvi, Ogilvie, Ogilvee, Ogilvea, Ogilhinn, Ogylvy, Ogylvey, Ogylvi, Ogylvie, Ogylvee, Ogylvea

Ogima (American) Holding the rank of chief
Ogyma, Ogimo, Ogymo

Ogun (Japanese) One who is undaunted
Ogin, Ogyn, Ogen, Ogan, Ogon

Oguz (Hungarian) An arrow
Oguze, Oguzz, Oguzze

Ohad (Hebrew) One who is dearly loved
Ohed

Ohanko (Native American) A reckless man
Ohankio, Ohankiyo

Ohanzee (Native American) A shadow
Ohanzea, Ohanzi, Ohanzie, Ohanzy, Ohanzey

Ohcumgache (Native American) Resembling a little wolf
Ohkumgache, Ohcumgachi, Ohkumgachi, Ohcumgachie, Ohkumgachie, Ohcumgachy, Ohkumgachy, Ohcumgachey, Ohkumgachey, Ohcumgachee, Ohkumgachee, Okhmhaka, Okhmhaca, Okmhaka, Okmhaca

Ohin (African) A chief
Ohine, Ohini, Ohinie, Ohiny, Ohiney, Ohinee, Ohinea, Ohene, Oheen, Oheene, Ohean, Oheane

Ohio (Native American) Of the good river; from the state of Ohio

Ohitekah (Native American) A courageous man
Ohiteka, Ohytekah, Ohyteka

Oidhche (Scottish) Born at night
Oidche, Oidhchi, Oidchi, Oidhchie, Oidchie, Oidhchy, Oidchy, Oidhchey, Oidchey, Oidhchee, Oidchee

Oisin (Irish) Resembling a little deer; in mythology, a warrior and poet
Ossian, Ossin, Oissine, Oissene, Oisseen, Oisene, Oiseen, Oisean

Ojaswit (Indian) A powerful and radiant man
Ojaswyt, Ojaswin, Ojaswen, Ojaswyn, Ojas

Ojay (American) One who is brash
Ojaye, Ojai, Ojae, O.J.

Oji (African) One who brings gifts
Ojie, Ojy, Ojey, Ojee, Ojea

Ojo (African) Of a difficult birth
Ojoe

Okal (African) To cross
Okall

Okan (Turkish) Resembling a horse
Oken, Okin, Okyn

Okapi (African) Resembling an animal with a long neck
Okapie, Okapy, Okapey, Okapee, Okapea, Okape

Oke (Hawaiian) Form of Oscar, meaning "a spear of the gods / a friend of deer"

Okechuku (African) Blessed by God

Okello (African) One who is born following twins
Okelo

Okemos (African) One who provides counsel

Oki (Japanese) From the center of the ocean
Okie, Oky, Okey, Okee, Okea

Oklahoma (Native American) Of the red people; from the state of Oklahoma

Oko (African / Japanese) One of twins / a charming man

Okon (Japanese) Born of the darkness
Okun

Okoth (African) Born during a period of rain
Okothe

Okpara (African) The firstborn son
Okparra, Okparo, Okparro

Oktawian (African) The eighth-born child
Oktawyan, Oktawean, Octawian, Octawyan, Octawean

Ola (African) A wealthy man; an honored child
Olah, Olla, Ollah

Oladele (African) One who is honored at home
Oladel, Oladell, Oladelle

Olaf (Norse) The last of the ancestors
Olaff, Olav, Olave, Olle, Olof, Olov, Olef, Oluf, Olan, Oleif

Olafemi (African) A lucky young man
Olafemie, Olafemy, Olafemey, Olafemee, Olafemea

Olajuwon (Arabic) An honorable man
Olajuwun, Olajouwun, Olajouwun, Olajuwan, Olujuwon, Olujuwun, Olujuwan

Olakeakua (Hawaiian) One who lives for God
Olakeekua, Olakeykua, Olakiekua, Olakeikua, Olakekua, Olakikua, Olakykua

Olamide (African) Our son is our prosperity
Olamyde, Olamidi, Olamydi, Olamidie, Olamydie, Olamidy, Olamydy, Olamidey, Olamydey, Olamidee, Olamydee

Olamina (African) A spirited man
Olameena, Olamine, Olameene, Olameana, Olameane, Olameina, Olameine, Olamiena, Olamiene, Olamyna, Olamyne

Olaniyan (African) Honored by all
Olaniyen, Olaniyon, Olaniyin, Olaniyun

Oldrich (Czech) A strong and wealthy leader
Oldriche, Oldrisk, Oldriske, Oldrisek, Oldra, Olda, Olecek, Olouvsek

Ole (Scandinavian) One who is alert; watchful
Olaye, Olay, Olai, Olae

Oleg (Russian) One who is holy
Olezka

Oleos (Spanish) A sacred oil

Olexei (Slavic) Form of Alexander, meaning "helper and defender of mankind"
Oleksei, Oleksey, Oleksi, Oleksiy, Olexey, Olexi, Olexiy, Oles

Olimpio (Greek) From Mount Olympus
Olimpo, Olympio, Olympios, Olympus

Olin (English) Filled with happiness
Olyn, Olen

Olindo (Latin) Having a pleasant scent
Olyndo, Olendo

Oliphant (Scottish) Having great strength
Olyphant, Oliphent, Olyphent, Oliphont, Olyphont

Olis (German) A powerful man
Olys, Oliss, Olyss, Olisse, Olysse

Oliver (Latin) From the olive tree
Oliverio, Olivero, Olivier, Oliviero, Olivio, Olivor, Olley, Ollie, Olliver, Ollivor, Oilbhries, Oliveer, Oliverios, Oliveros, Oluvor, Olghar

Oliwa (Hawaiian) Of the army of elves
Olywa, Oliwah, Olywah

Olney (English) From the loner's field
Olny, Olnee, Olnea, Olni, Olnie, Ollaneg, Olaneg

Olorun (African) One who counsels others
Oloron, Oloroun, Oloroon

Olubayo (African) Filled with happiness

Olufemi (African) Loved by God
Olufemie, Olufemy, Olufemey, Olufemee, Olufemea

Olugbala (African) The God of all
Olugbalah, Olugballa, Olugballah

Olujimi (African) One who is close to God
Olujimie, Olujimy, Olujimey, Olujimee, Olujimea

Olumide (African) God has arrived
*Olumidi, Olumidie, Olumidy, Olumidey,
Olumidee, Olumidea, Olumyde, Olumydi,
Olumydie, Olumydy, Olumydey,
Olumydee, Olumydea*

Olumoi (African) One who has been
blessed by God
Olumoy

Olushegun (African) One who walks with
God
*Olushigun, Olushygun, Olushagun,
Olushegon, Olushigon, Olushygon,
Olushygan*

Olushola (African) Blessed by God
Olusholah, Olusholla, Olushollah

Oluwa (African) One who believes in God
Oluwah

Oluwatosin (African) A servant of God
Oluwatosyn, Oluwatosen

Oluyemi (African) Full of God; a pious man
*Oluyemie, Oluyemy, Oluyemey, Oluyemee,
Oluyemea*

Olvery (English) One who draws others
Olverey, Olveri, Olverie, Olveree, Olverea

Olviemi (African) Loved by God
*Olviemie, Olviemy, Olviemey, Olviemee,
Olviemea*

Oma (Arabic) A commanding man
Omah, Omma, Ommah

Omanand (Hindi) A happy and thoughtful
man
Omamande, Omanando

Omar (Arabic) A flourishing man; one
who is well-spoken
Omarr, Omer, Omerr, Ommar, Ommer

Omari (Arabic / African) One who is full
of life / from God the highest
*Omarie, Omary, Omarey, Omaree,
Omarea*

Omeet (Hebrew) My light
*Omeete, Omeit, Omeite, Omeyt, Omeyte,
Omit, Omeat, Omeate, Omite, Omyt,
Omyte, Omet, Omete*

Omega (Greek) The last great one; the last
letter of the Greek alphabet
Omegah

Omie (Italian) A homebody
Omi, Omee, Omea, Omey, Omy, Omye

Omkar (Hindi) A sacred letter and sound

Omprakash (Indian) Surrounded by a
divine light
Omparkash, Omprakashe, Omparkashe

Omri (Hebrew) A sheaf of grain; a servant
of God
Omrie, Omry, Omrey, Omree, Omrea

On (Chinese / African) A peaceful man /
one who is desirable

Onacona (Native American) Resembling a
white owl
Onakona, Onaconah, Onakonah

Onan (Turkish) A wealthy man
Onann

Onani (Asian) A sweet man
Onanie, Onany, Onaney, Onanee, Onanea

Onaona (Hawaiian) Having a pleasant scent

Ond (Hungarian) The tenth-born child
Onde

Ondré (Greek) Form of André, meaning
"manly; a warrior"
*Onndre, Ohndrae, Ohndray, Ohndre,
Ohndrei, Ohndrey, Ondrae, Ondray,
Ondrei, Onndrae, Onndrai, Onndray*

Ondrej (Czech) A manly man
Ondrejek, Ondrejec, Ondrousek, Ondravsek

Onesimo (Spanish) The firstborn son
*Onesymo, Onesimio, Onesimiyo,
Onesymio, Onesymiyo*

Onkar (Indian) The purest one
Onckar, Oncar, Onkarr, Onckarr, Oncarr

Onofrio (Italain) A defender of peace
*Onofre, Onofrius, Onophrio, Onophre,
Onfrio, Onfroi*

Onslow (Arabic) From the hill of the
enthusiast
Onslowe, Ounslow, Ounslowe

Onur (Turkish) One who shows promise
Onurr, Onure, Onurre

Onwaochi (African) A pious man
*Onwaochie, Onwaochy, Onwaochey,
Onwaochee, Onwaochea*

Onyebuchi (African) God is in everything
Onyebuchie, Onyebuchy, Onyebuchey, Onyebuchee, Onyebuchea

Oqwapi (Native American) Resembling a red cloud
Oqwapie, Oqwapy, Oqwapey, Oqwapee, Oqwapea

Or (Hebrew) Surrounded by light

Oracle (Greek) One who provides divine messages
Orakle, Orackle, Oracel, Orakel, Orackel

Oral (Latin) An eloquent speaker

Oram (English) From the enclosure near the riverbank
Oramm, Oraham, Orahamm, Orham, Orhamm

Oran (Aramaic / Gaelic) Surrounded by light / a pale-skinned man
Orann

Orane (Greek) A flourishing man
Oraine, Orain, Orayn, Orayne, Oraen, Oraene

Orazio (Italian) One who prays to God
Oratio

Orbon (Hungarian) One who lives in the city
Orbo

Ord (Anglo-Saxon) A spear
Orde

Ordell (Latin) Of the beginning
Ordel, Ordele, Ordelle, Orde

Ordland (English) From the pointed hill
Ordlande

Ordway (Anglo-Saxon) A fighter armed with a spear
Ordwaye, Ordwai, Ordwae

Orel (Latin) The golden one
Oral, Oriel, Orrel, Orry, Orrey, Orri, Orrie, Orree, Orrea

Oren (Hebrew / Gaelic) From the pine tree / a pale-skinned man
Orenthiel, Orenthiell, Orenthiele, Orenthielle, Orenthiem, Orenthium, Orin

Orestes (Greek) From the mountain; in mythology, the son of Agamemnon who murdered his mother for being unfaithful
Oreste

Orev (Hebrew) Resembling a raven

Orford (English) From the cattle ford
Orforde

Ori (Hebrew) Surrounded by the light of truth
Orie, Ory, Orey, Oree, Orea

Oringo (African) One who enjoys hunting
Oryngo

Oriole (Latin) Resembling the gold-speckled bird
Oreolle, Oriolle, Oreole, Oriol, Orioll, Oriolle

Orion (Greek) In mythology, a great hunter; a constellation
Oryon, Orian, Oryan, Orien, Oryen, Oreon

Oris (Hebrew) Of the trees
Oriss, Orisse, Orys, Oryss, Orysse

Orji (African) Of the majestic tree
Orjie, Orjy, Orjey, Orjee, Orjea

Orkeny (Hungarian) A frightening man
Orkeney, Orkenee, Orkenea, Orkeni, Orkenie

Orlando (Spanish) From the renowned land
Orlan, Orland, Orlondo, Orlond, Orlon, Orlande, Orlonde, Olo

Orleans (Latin) The golden child
Orlean, Orleane, Orleens, Orleen, Orleene, Orlins, Olryns, Orlin, Orline, Orlyn, Orlyne

Orlege (Anglo-Saxon) Suffering strife during war

Orly (Hebrew) Surrounded by light
Orley, Orli, Orlie, Orlee, Orleigh, Orlea

Orman (English / German) One who wields a spear / a man of the sea
Ormand, Ormande, Ormeman, Ormemand, Ormemande, Ordman, Ordmand, Ordmande

Orme (English) A kind man
Orm

Ormod (Anglo-Saxon) A sorrowful man

Ormond (English) One who defends with a spear; from the mountain of bears
Ormonde, Ormund, Ormunde, Ormemund, Ormemond, Ordmund, Ordmunde, Ordmond, Ordmonde

Ormos (Hungarian) From the cliff

Orn (Scandinavian) Resembling an eagle
Orne

Ornice (Irish / Hebrew) A pale-skinned man / from the cedar tree
Ornyce, Ornise, Orynse, Orneice, Orneise, Orniece, Orniese, Orneece, Orneese, Orneace, Ornease

Oro (Spanish) The golden one

Oron (Hebrew) Having a light spirit

Orpheus (Greek) Having a beautiful voice; in mythology, a talented musician, trained by the Muses
Orphius, Orphyus, Orfeus, Orfius, Orfyus, Orphi, Orphie, Orphy, Orphey, Orphee, Orphea, Orpheo, Orfeo

Orrick (English) From the old oak tree
Orick, Orrik, Orik, Orric, Oric

Orrin (English) From the river
Orran, Orren, Orryn

Orris (Latin) One who is inventive
Orriss, Orrisse, Orrys, Orryss, Orrysse

Ors (Hungarian) A heroic man

Orson (Latin) Resembling a bear; raised by a bear
Orsen, Orsin, Orsini, Orsino, Orsis, Orsonio, Orsinie, Orsiny, Orsiney, Orsinee, Orsinea

Orth (English) An honest man
Orthe

Orton (English) From the settlement by the shore
Ortun, Oraton, Oratun

Orunjan (African) Born beneath the noon sun
Orunjun, Orunjon, Orunjen, Orunjin, Orunjyn

Orval (English) Having the strength of a spear
Orvall, Orvalle, Orvald, Orwald, Ordval, Ordwald, Ordvald

Orville (French) From the gold town
Orvell, Orvelle, Orvil, Orvill, Orvele, Orvyll, Orvylle, Orvyl, Orvyle

Orvin (English) A courageous friend; a spear friend
Orvyn, Orwen, Orwenn, Orwenne, Orwyn, Orwynn, Orwynne, Orwin, Orwinn, Orwinne, Ordwen, Ordwenn, Ordwenne, Ordwin, Ordwinn, Ordwinne, Ordwyn, Ordwynn, Ordwynne, Ordwine

Orway (American) A kind man
Orwaye, Orwai, Orwae

Orwel (Welsh) Of the horizon
Orwell, Orwele, Orwelle

Os (English) The divine

Osage (Native American) A tribal name

Osakwe (Japanese) Having a favorable destiny
Osakwi, Osakwie, Osakwy, Osakwey, Osakwee, Osakwea

Osama (Arabic) Resembling a lion
Osamah, Osamma, Osammah

Osayaba (Japanese) A great thinker

Osaze (Hebrew) One who is favored by God
Osazi, Osazie, Osazee, Osazea, Osazy, Osazey

Osbert (English) One who is divinely brilliant
Osberte, Osberth, Osberthe, Osbart, Osbarte, Osbarth, Osbarthe, Osbeorht, Osburt, Osburte, Osburth, Osburthe

Osborn (Norse) A bear of God
Osborne, Osbourn, Osbourne, Osburn, Osburne

Oscar (English / Gaelic) A spear of the gods / a friend of deer
Oskar, Osker, Oscer, Osckar, Oscker, Oszkar, Oszcar

Oscard (Greek) A warrior
Oscarde, Oskard, Oskarde, Osckard, Osckarde

Osei (African) An honorable man

Osgood (English) A Goth god
Osgoode, Ozgood, Ozgoode

Oshea (Hebrew) A kind spirit
Oshey, Oshay, Osheye, Oshaye, Oshae, Oshai

Osher (Hebrew) A man of good fortune

Osias (Greek) Salvation
Osyas

Osier (English) One who lives near the willows
Osyer, Osiar, Osyar, Osior, Osyor, Osiur, Osyur

Osileani (Polynesian) One who talks a lot
Osileanie, Osileany, Osileaney, Osileanee, Osileanea

Osip (Ukrainian) Form of Joseph, meaning "God will add"
Osyp, Osipp, Osypp

Osman (Scandinavian) Protected by God
Osment, Osmin, Osmond, Osmonde, Osmont, Osmund, Osmunde, Osmonte

Osmar (English) The glory of God
Osmarr

Osred (English) One who receives counsel from God
Osraed, Osread, Osrad, Osrade, Osrid, Osryd

Osric (English) One who follows God's rule
Osrick, Osrik, Osryc, Osryck, Osryk, Osrec, Osreck, Osrek

Ossie (English) Form of Oswald, meaning "the power of God"
Ossi, Ossy, Ossey, Ossee, Ossea

Osten (Latin) One who is worthy of respect; a magnificent man
Ostan, Ostin, Ostyn, Ostun, Oistin, Oisten, Oistan

Oswald (English) The power of God
Oswalde, Osvald, Osvaldo, Oswaldo, Oswell, Osvalde, Oswallt, Osweald, Osweld, Oswalt

Oswin (English) A friend of God
Oswinn, Oswinne, Oswen, Oswenn, Oswenne, Oswyn, Oswynn, Oswynne, Oswine

Oswiu (Anglo-Saxon) A king
Oswy, Oswey, Oswi, Oswie, Oswee, Oswea

Ota (Czech) A wealthy man

Otadan (Native American) A man of plenty

Otaktay (Native American) One who kills many
Otaktaye, Otaktai, Otaktae

Othman (German) A wealthy man
Otheman, Othmann, Othemann, Othoman, Othomann

Othniel (Hebrew) God's lion
Othniell, Othnielle, Othniele, Othnyel, Othnyell, Othnyele, Othnyelle

Otieno (African) Born at night
Othieno, Otyeno, Othyeno

Otik (German) One who is lucky
Otick, Otic, Otyk, Otyck, Otyc

Otis (German / Greek) A wealthy man / one who is acute
Otys, Otess, Ottis

Otmar (Teutonic) A famous warrior
Otmarr, Othmar, Othmarr, Otomar, Ottomar, Otomarr, Ottomarr

Otoahhastis (Native American) Resembling a tall bull

Otoahnacto (Native American) Resembling a bull bear

Otoniel (Spanish) A stylish man
Otoniell, Otoniele, Otonielle, Otonel, Otonell, Otonele, Otonelle

Otskai (Native American) One who leaves

Ottah (African) A slender boy
Otta

Ottar (Norse) A warrior

Ottfried (German) A wealthy and peaceful man
Ottfrid, Ottfryde, Ottfryd, Ottfred, Ottfrede

Otto (German) A wealthy man
Otess, Ottis, Othello, Ottone, Oto, Odo, Oddo, Otho

Ottokar (German) A spirited warrior
Otokar, Otokarr, Ottokarr, Ottokars, Otokars, Ottocar, Otocar, Ottocars, Otocars

Ottway (Teutonic) One who is fortunate in battle
Otway, Ottoway, Otoway, Ottwae, Otwae, Ottwai, Otwai

Otu (Native American) An industrious man
Otoo, Otue, Otou

Oukounaka (Asian) From the surf
Oukoonaka, Oukunaka, Okounaka, Okoonaka, Okunaka, Okonaka, Oukonaka

Ouray (Native American) The arrow
Ouraye, Ourae, Ourai

Ourson (French) Resembling a little bear
Oursun, Oursoun, Oursen, Oursan, Oursin, Oursyn

Oved (Hebrew) One who worships God
Ove

Overton (English) From the upper town
Overtun, Overtown

Ovid (Latin) A shepherd; an egg
Ovyd, Ovidio, Ovido, Ovydio, Ovydo, Ovidiu, Ovydiu, Ofydd, Ofyd, Ofid, Ofidd

Owen ♂ (Welsh / Gaelic) Form of Eugene, meaning "a wellborn man" / a youthful man
Owenn, Owenne, Owin, Owinn, Owinne, Owyn, Owynn, Owynne, Owain, Owaine, Owayn, Owayne, Owaen, Owaene, Owane, Owein, Oweine

Owney (Irish) An elderly man
Owny, Owni, Ownie, Ownee, Ownea, Oney, Ony, Oni, Onie, Onee, Onea

Ox (American) Resembling the animal; having great strength
Oxe, Oxy, Oxey, Oxee, Oxea, Oxi, Oxie

Oxford (English) From the oxen's crossing
Oxforde, Oxxford, Oxxforde, Oxferd, Oxferde, Oxfurd, Oxfurde, Oxnaford, Oxnaferd, Oxnafurd

Oxley (English) From the meadow of oxen
Oxly, Oxleigh, Oxlea, Oxleah, Oxlee, Oxli, Oxlie, Oxnaley, Oxnaly, Oxnaleigh, Oxnalea, Oxnaleah, Oxnali, Oxnalie, Oxnalee

Oxton (English) From the oxen town
Oxtun, Oxtown, Oxnaton, Oxnatun, Oxnatown

Oysten (Norse) Filled with happiness
Oystein, Oystin, Oystyn

Oz (Hebrew) Having great strength
Ozz, Ozzi, Ozzie, Ozzy, Ozzey, Ozzee, Ozzea, Ozi, Ozie, Ozy, Ozey, Ozee, Ozea

Oziel (Spanish) Having great strength
Oziell, Ozielle, Oziele, Ozell, Ozel, Ozele, Ozelle

Ozni (Hebrew) One who knows God
Oznie, Ozny, Ozney, Oznee, Oznea

Ozséb (Hungarian) A pious man

Ozturk (Turkish) One who is pure; chaste

Ozuru (Japanese) Resembling a stork
Ozurou, Ozourou, Ozuroo, Ozooroo

Paavo (Finnish) Form of Paul, meaning "a small or humble man"
Paaveli

Pablo (Spanish) Form of Paul, meaning "a small or humble man"

Pace (Hebrew / English) Refers to Passover / a peaceful man
Paice, Payce, Paece, Pacey, Pacy, Pacee, Paci, Pacie, Paicey, Paicy, Paicee, Paici, Paicie, Paycey, Paycy, Paycee, Payci, Paycie, Paecey, Paecy, Paecee, Paeci, Paecie, Pacian, Pacien

Pacho (Spanish) An independent man; one who is free

Pachu'a (Native American) Resembling a water snake

Paciano (Spanish) A man of peace
Pacyano

Pacifico (Spanish) One who is calm; tranquil
Pacificus, Pacificos, Pacificas

Packard (German) From the brook; a
peddler's pack
*Packarde, Pakard, Pakarde, Pacard, Pacarde,
Packer, Packert, Packe, Pack, Pac, Pak*

Paco (Spanish) A man from France
Pacorro, Pacoro, Paquito

Paddy (Irish) Form of Patrick, meaning
"a nobleman; patrician"
*Paddey, Paddee, Paddea, Paddi, Paddie,
Padraic, Padraig, Padhraig*

Padgett (French) One who strives to better
himself
*Padget, Padgette, Padgete, Padgeta,
Padgetta, Padge, Paget, Pagett*

Padman (Indian) Resembling the lotus
Padmann

Padre (Spanish) A father
Padray, Padraye, Padrai, Padrae

Padruig (Scottish) Of the royal family

Pagan (Latin) A man from the country
Paige

Page (English) A young assistant
Paige, Payge, Paege

Pagiel (Hebrew) God disposes
Pagiell, Pagiele, Pagielle

Pahana (Native American) A lost white
brother
Pahanah, Pahanna, Pahannah

Paine (Latin) Man from the country;
a peasant
Pain, Payn, Payne, Paen, Paene, Pane, Paien

Paisley (English) Man of the church
*Paisly, Paisli, Paislie, Paislee, Paysley, Paysly,
Paysli, Payslie, Payslee, Pasley, Pasly, Pasli,
Paslie, Paslee, Paizley, Payzley, Pazley,
Paislea, Paizlea, Paslea, Payslea*

Pajackok (Native American) Resembling
thunder
*Pajakok, Pajacok, Pajackock, Pajakock,
Pajakoc, Pajackoc, Pajacoc, Pajakoc*

Paki (African) One who sees the truth
Pakie, Paky, Pakey, Pakee, Pakea

Paladio (Spanish) A follower of the god-
dess Athena
*Palladius, Palladio, Paladius, Paladios,
Palladios*

Palamedes (English) In Arthurian legend,
a knight
*Palomydes, Palomedes, Palamydes,
Palsmedes, Palsmydes, Pslomydes*

Palani (Hawaiian) A free man; one who is
independent
Palanie, Palanee, Palanea, Palany, Palaney

Palash (Indian) Resembling a flowering
tree
Palashe

Palban (Spanish) A blonde-haired man
Palben, Palbin, Palbyn, Palbon, Palbun

Paley (English) Form of Paul, meaning
"a small or humble man"
Paly, Pali, Palie, Palee, Palea

Palila (Hawaiian) A birdlike man
Palilla, Palilah, Pallila, Pallilla, Palyla, Palylla

Palladin (Greek) Filled with wisdom
*Palladyn, Palladen, Palladan, Paladin,
Paladyn, Paladen, Paladan*

Pallaton (Native American) A tough warrior
Pallatin, Pallatyn, Pallaten, Pallatun

Palma (Latin) A successful man

Palmer (English) A pilgrim bearing a palm
branch
*Pallmer, Palmar, Pallmar, Palmerston,
Palmiro, Palmeero, Palmeer, Palmire, Palmere*

Palomo (Spanish) Resembling a dove;
a peaceful man
Palomio, Palomiyo

Paltiel (Hebrew) God is my deliverance
*Paltiell, Paltiele, Paltielle, Palti, Paltie, Palty,
Paltey, Paltee, Paltea, Platya, Platyahu*

Pan (Greek) In mythology, god of the
shepherds
Pann

Panama (Spanish) From the canal

Pananjay (Hindi) Resembling a cloud
Pananjaye, Pananjae, Pananjai

Pancho (Spanish) A man from France

Pancrazio (Italian) One who is all-powerful
Pankrazio, Pancraz, Pankraz, Pancrazie, Pancrazi, Pancrazy, Pancrazey, Pancrazee, Pankrazi, Pankrazie, Pankrazy, Pankrazey, Pankrazee

Pandu (Indian) A pale-skinned man

Panfilo (Spanish) One who loves nature
Panphilo, Panfilio, Panphilio

Pankaj (Indian) Resembling the lotus flower

Panos (Greek) As solid as a rock

Pantias (Greek) A philosophical man
Pantyas

Panya (African) Resembling a mouse
Panyah

Panyin (African) The firstborn of twins
Panyen

Parakram (Indian) A strong and brave man

Paras (Hindi) A touchstone
Parasmani, Parasmanie, Parasmany, Parasmaney, Parasmanee

Parfait (French) The perfect man

Paris (English / Greek) Man from the city in France / in mythology, the prince of Troy who abducted Helen
Pariss, Parisse, Parys, Paryss, Parysse, Peris, Perris, Perys, Perrys

Park (English / Chinese) Of the forest / from the cypress tree
Parke, Parkey, Parky, Parki, Parkie, Parkee, Parkea

Parker ♂ (English) The keeper of the park
Parkar, Parkes, Parkman, Parks

Parkins (English) As solid as a rock; son of Peter
Parkens, Parken, Parkin, Parkyns, Parkyn, Parkinson

Parley (Scottish) A reluctant man
Parly, Parli, Parlie, Parlee, Parlea, Parle

Parmenio (Spanish) A studious man; one who is intelligent
Parmenios, Parmenius

Parnell (Latin) From the country
Parnel, Parnelle, Parnele, Parrnel, Parrnell, Parrnele, Parrnelle, Pernell, Pernel, Pernele, Pernelle

Paros (Greek) From the island
Paro

Parounag (Armenian) One who is thankful

Parr (English) From the castle's park
Parre

Parrish (Latin) Man of the church
Parish, Parrishe, Parishe, Parrysh, Parysh, Paryshe, Parryshe, Parisch, Parrisch

Parry (Welsh) The son of Harry
Parrey, Parri, Parrie, Parree, Parrea

Parryth (American) An up-and-coming man
Parrythe, Parrith, Parrithe, Paryth, Parythe, Parith, Parithe, Parreth, Parrethe, Pareth, Parethe

Parsons (English) A man of the clergy
Parson, Person, Persons, Pherson, Pharson, Phersons, Pharsons

Parthenios (Greek) One who is pure; chaste
Parthenius

Parthik (Greek) One who is pure; chaste
Parthyk, Parthick, Parthyck, Parthic, Parthyc

Partholon (Irish) Man of the earth; a farmer
Partholun, Partholan, Partholen, Partholyn, Parlan, Parlon, Parlann, Parlonn

Parton (English) From the town near the castle's park; from Peter's town
Partun, Parten, Partan, Partin, Partyn

Parvaiz (Persian) A commendable man
Parvez, Parviz, Parvayz, Parvaz, Parvaez, Parwiz, Parwez, Parwaiz, Parwaez, Parwayz, Parwaz

Parvath (Indian) From the mountain
Parvathe

Parveneh (Persian) Resembling a butterfly
Parvene

Pascal (Latin) Born during Easter
Pascale, Pascalle, Paschal, Paschalis, Pascoe, Pascual, Pascuale, Pasqual, Pasquale

Pastor (English) Man of the church
Pastur, Paster, Pastar, Pastir, Pastyr

Patakin (Indian) One who holds the banner
Patakyn, Patackin, Patackyn

Patamon (Native American) Resembling a tempest
Patamun, Patamen, Pataman, Patamyn, Patamin

Patch (American) Form of Peter, meaning "as solid and strong as a rock"
Pach, Patche, Patchi, Patchie, Patchy, Patchey, Patchee

Patli (Aztec) A medicine man
Patlie, Patly, Patley, Patlee, Patleigh, Patlea

Patrick (Latin) A nobleman; patrician
Packey, Padric, Pat, Patrece, Patric, Patrice, Patreece, Patricio, Patrik, Patrizio, Patrizius, Patryk, Pats, Patsy, Patty, Padrig, Patek, Patec, Pateck, Patricius, Patrido

Patriot (American) One who is devoted to his country
Patryot, Patriotic, Patryotic, Patriotik, Patryotik

Patterson (English) The son of Peter
Paterson, Pattison, Patison

Patton (English) From the town of warriors
Paten, Patin, Paton, Patten, Pattin, Paddon, Padden, Paddin, Paddyn, Paegastun, Payden

Patwin (Native American) A manly man
Patwinn, Patwinne, Patwyn, Patwynne, Patwynn, Patwen, Patwenn, Patwenne

Paul (Latin) A small or humble man
Pal, Paolo, Pasha, Pauel, Pauli, Paulie, Paulin, Paulino, Paulinus, Paulo, Paulos, Paulsen, Paulson, Paulus, Pauly, Pavel, Pavle, Pavlik, Pavlo, Pawel, Pol, Poll, Poul, Pascha, Pashenka, Pavlushka, Paulis, Paulys, Pavlof, Pawl

Paurush (Indian) A courageous man
Paurushe, Paurushi, Paurushie, Paurushy, Paurushey, Paurushee

Pavan (Indian) Resembling a breeze
Pavann

Pavanjit (Indian) Resembling the wind
Pavanjyt, Pavanjeet, Pavanjeat, Pavanjete

Pavit (Indian) A pious man
Pavyt

Pavithra (Indian) One who is holy
Pavythra

Pawnee (Native American) A tribal name
Pawnea, Pawni, Pawnie, Pawny, Pawney

Pax (Latin) A peaceful man
Paxx, Paxi, Paxie, Paxy, Paxey, Paxee, Paxea

Paxton (English) From the peaceful town
Packston, Paxon, Paxten, Paxtun, Packstun, Packsten

Payat (Native American) He is coming
Payatt, Pay, Paye

Payod (Indian) Resembling a cloud
Paiod, Paeod, Paod

Payoj (Indian) Resembling a lotus
Paioj, Paeoj, Paoj

Paytah (Native American) A fiery man
Payta, Paetah, Paeta, Paitah, Paita, Patah, Pata

Paz (Spanish) A peaceful man
Pazz

Pazel (Hebrew) God's gold; treasured by God
Pazell, Pazele, Pazelle

Pazman (Hungarian) One who is right

Peabo (Irish) As solid as a rock
Peebo, Peybo, Peibo

Peak (English) From the mountain's top; one who surpasses others
Peake, Peek, Peeke, Peke, Pico

Peale (English) One who rings the bell
Peal, Peall, Pealle

Pearroc (English) Man of the forest
Pearoc, Pearrok, Pearok, Pearrock, Pearock

Pecos (American) From the river; a cowboy
Pekos, Peckos

Pedahel (Hebrew) One who has been redeemed by God
Pedael, Pedayel

Pedaias (Hebrew) Loved by God
Pedias

Pedro (Spanish) Form of Peter, meaning "as solid and strong as a rock"
Pedrio, Pepe, Petrolino, Piero, Pietro

P

Peel (English) From the fortified tower
Peele

Pegasus (Greek) In mythology, a winged
horse

Pekar (Czech) A baker
Pecar, Peckar

Pekelo (Hawaiian) Form of Peter, meaning
"as solid and strong as a rock"
Pekeloh, Pekello, Pekelloh

Pelagios (Greek) Man of the sea
Pelagius, Pelayo, Pelagos, Pelagus

Peleh (Hebrew) A miracle child
Pele

Pelham (English) From the house of furs;
from Peola's home
Pellham, Pelam, Pellam

Pell (English) A clerk or one who works
with skins
Pelle, Pall, Palle

Pellegrin (Hungarian) A traveler; a pilgram
*Pellegrine, Pelegrin, Pelegrine, Pellegryn,
Pelegryn*

Pelly (English) Filled with happiness
Pelley, Pelli, Pellie, Pellee, Pellea

Pelon (Spanish) Filled with joy
Pellon

Pelton (English) From the town by the lake
*Pellton, Peltun, Pelltun, Peltan, Pelltan,
Pelten, Pellten, Peltin, Pelltin, Peltyn, Pelltyn*

Pembroke (Celtic) From the headland
Pembrook, Pembrooke

Penda (African) One who is dearly loved
Pendah, Penha, Penhah

Pendragon (Anglo-Saxon) From the
enclosed land of the dragon

Penley (English) From the enclosed meadow
*Penly, Penleigh, Penli, Penlie, Penlee, Penlea,
Penleah, Pennley, Pennly, Pennleigh, Pennli,
Pennlie, Pennlee, Pennlea, Pennleah*

Penn (English) From the enclosure
Pen, Pyn, Pynn

Pennsylvania (English) The land of Penn;
from the state of Pennsylvania

Penrod (German) A respected commander

Pentele (Hungarian) A merciful man
Pentelle, Pentel, Pentell

Penton (English) From the enclosed town
Pentun, Pentin, Pentyn, Penten, Pentan

Penuel (Hebrew) The face of God
Penuell, Penuele, Penuelle

Pepin (German) A determined man;
a petitioner
*Peppin, Pepyn, Peppyn, Pepun, Peppun,
Pepen, Peppen, Peppi, Peppie, Peppey,
Peppy, Peppee, Peppea*

Pepper (American) Resembling the pepper
plant; flavorful
Peper

Percival (French) One who can pierce the
vale; in Arthurian legend, the only one
who could retrieve the Holy Grail
*Parsafal, Parsefal, Parsifal, Perce, Perceval,
Percevall, Purcell, Percivall, Percyvelle,
Percyval, Percyvel*

Percy (Latin) Form of Percival, meaning
"one who can pierce the vale"
*Percey, Perci, Percie, Percee, Percea, Persy,
Persey, Persi, Persie, Persee, Persea*

Perdido (Latin) One who is lost
Perdydo, Perdedo

Peregrine (Latin) One who travels;
a wanderer
*Peregrin, Peregrino, Peregryn, Peregreen,
Peregrein, Peregreyn, Peregrien, Peregrinus*

Perez (Hebrew) To break through
Peretz

Perfecto (Spanish) One who is flawless
Perfectio, Perfectiyo, Perfection, Perfecte

Pericles (Greek) One who is in excess of
glory
*Perricles, Perycles, Perrycles, Periclees,
Perriclees, Peryclees, Perryclees, Periclez,
Perriclez, Peryclez, Perryclez*

Peril (Latin) One who undergoes a trial
or test
*Perill, Perile, Perille, Peryl, Peryll, Perylle,
Peryle*

Perine (Latin) An adventurer
Perrin, Perrine, Perin, Peryne, Perryne

Perk (American) One who is cheerful and jaunty
Perke, Perky, Perkey, Perki, Perkie, Perkee, Perkea

Perkin (English) Form of Peter, meaning "as solid and strong as a rock"
Perkins, Perkyn, Perkyns

Perkinson (English) The son of Perkin; the son of Peter
Perkynson

Perry (Latin) Form of Peregrine, meaning "one who travels; a wanderer"
Perrey, Perree, Perrea, Perri, Perrie

Perseus (Greek) In mythology, son of Zeus who slew Medusa
Persius, Persyus, Persies, Persyes

Perth (Celtic) From the thorny thicket
Perthe, Pert, Perte

Perye (English) From the pear tree

Pesach (Hebrew) One who has been spared
Pessach, Pesache, Pessache

Peter (Greek) As solid and strong as a rock
Peder, Pekka, Per, Petar, Pete, Peterson, Petr, Petre, Petros, Petrov, Piotr, Piet, Pieter, Pyotr, Peader, Peat, Peate, Petenka, Pytor, Peterka, Peterke, Petrus, Petruso, Petur, Petter, Petya

Pethuel (Aramaic) God's vision
Pethuell, Pethuele, Pethuelle

Petuel (Hindi) The Lord's vision
Petuell, Petuele, Petuelle

Peverell (French) A piper
Peverel, Peverelle, Peverele, Peverall, Peveral, Peverale, Peveralle, Peveril, Peverill, Peverile, Peverille

Peyton (English) From the village of warriors
Payton, Peytun, Paytun, Peyten, Payten, Paiton, Paitun, Paiten, Paton, Patun, Paten, Paeton, Paetun, Paeten

Phallon (Irish) The ruler's grandson
Phallen, Phallun, Phallin, Phallyn, Phallan

Pharis (Irish) A heroic man
Pharys, Pharris, Pharrys

Phelan (Gaelic) Resembling a wolf
Phelim, Phelym, Phelam, Phelin, Phelyn

Phelipe (Spanish) Filled with hope

Phelps (English) The son of Phillip
Phelpes

Phex (American) A kind man
Phexx

Philander (Greek) One who loves mankind
Phylander

Philemon (Hebrew) A loving man
Phylemon, Philimon, Phylimon, Philomon, Phylomon, Philamon, Phylamon

Philetus (Greek) A collector
Phyletus, Philetos, Phyletos

Phillip (Greek) One who loves horses
Phil, Philipp, Philippe, Philippos, Philippus, Philips, Philip, Phillips, Philly, Phyllip, Pilipo, Pip, Pippo, Phipps, Phips, Phillipe

Philo (Greek) One who loves and is loved

Phineas (Hebrew) From the serpent's mouth; an oracle
Phinehas, Pincas, Pinchas, Pinchos, Pincus, Pinhas, Pinkus, Pyncus, Pynkus, Pinckus, Pynckus, Pinkas, Pinckas, Pinchus

Phoebus (Greek) A radiant man
Phoibos

Phoenix (Greek) A dark-red color; in mythology, an immortal bird
Phoenyx

Phomello (African) A successful man
Phomelo

Phong (Vietnamese) Of the wind

Photius (Greek) A scholarly man
Photeus, Photyus, Photias, Photyas, Photeas

Phuc (Vietnamese) One who is blessed
Phuoc

Phuong (Vietnamese) One who recognizes his destiny

Phyre (Armenian) One who burns brightly
Phyr, Phire, Phir

Picardus (Hispanic) An adventurous man
Pycardus, Picardos, Pycardos, Picardas, Pycardas, Picardis, Pycardis, Picardys, Pycardys

Pickford (English) From the woodcutter's ford
Pickforde, Picford, Picforde, Pikford, Pikforde

Pickworth (English) From the woodcutter's estate
Pikworth, Picworth, Pickworthe, Pikworthe, Picworthe

Pierce (English) Form of Peter, meaning "as solid and strong as a rock"
Pearce, Pears, Pearson, Pearsson, Peerce, Peirce, Pierson, Piersson, Piers, Pyrs, Pyrse, Pyrce

Pierpont (French) A social man
Pierrepont, Pierponte, Pierrponte

Pierre (French) Form of Peter, meaning "as solid and strong as a rock"
Pyerre, Piere, Pyere, Pierrel, Pierrell, Pierel, Pierell, Pierelle, Pierrelle, Pierele, Pierrele

Pike (English) One who wields a spear
Pyke

Pilan (Native American) Of the supreme essence
Pilann, Pylan, Pylann

Pilgrim (English) A traveler; wanderer
Pylgrim, Pilgrym, Pylgrym

Pili (African) The second-born child
Pilie, Pily, Piley, Pilee, Pilea

Pillan (Native American) The god of storms
Pyllan, Pillann, Pyllann

Pillar (American) One who provides a good foundation
Pyllar, Pilar, Pylar

Pillion (French) An excellent man
Pyllion, Pillyon, Pilion, Pylion, Pilyon, Pilot

Pim (Dutch) One who is precise
Pym

Pin (Vietnamese) Filled with joy
Pyn

Piney (American) From the pine trees
Piny, Pinee, Pinea, Pini, Pinie

Ping (Chinese) One who is peaceful
Pyng

Pinya (Hebrew) A faithful man
Pinyah, Pynya, Pynyah

Pio (Latin) A pious man
Pyo, Pios, Pius, Pyos, Pyus

Piper (English) One who plays the flute
Pipere, Pyper, Pypere, Piperel, Pyperel, Piperell, Pyperell, Piperele, Pyperele, Piperelle, Pyperelle, Pepperell

Pippin (English) One who is shy
Pippen, Pippyn, Pyppin, Pyppen, Pyppyn

Pippino (Italian) Form of Joseph, meaning "God will add"
Peppino

Pirney (Scottish) From the island
Pirny, Pirnee, Pirnea, Pirni, Pirnie, Pyrney, Pyrny, Pyrnee, Pyrnea, Pyrni, Pyrnie

Pirro (Greek) A red-haired man
Pyrro

Pisces (Latin) The twelfth sign of the zodiac; the fishes
Pysces, Piscees, Pyscees, Piscez, Pisceez

Pitney (English) From the island of the stubborn man
Pitny, Pitni, Pitnie, Pitnee, Pitnea, Pytney, Pytny, Pytni, Pytnie, Pytnee, Pytnea

Pitt (English) From the ditch
Pit, Pytt, Pyt

Pittman (English) A laborer
Pyttman, Pitman, Pytman

Pivane (Native American) Resembling a weasel
Pyvane, Pivaen, Pivaene, Pyvaen, Pyvaene, Pivain, Pivaine, Pyvain, Pyvaine, Pivayn, Pivayne, Pyvayn, Pyvayne

Placido (Spanish) One who is calm
Plasedo, Placedo, Placidus, Placijo, Placyd, Placydo, Plasido, Placid, Plasid

Plaise (Irish) Having great strength
Playse, Plase, Plaese, Plaize, Playze, Plaze, Plaeze

Plan (American) An organized man
Planner, Plannar, Plannor, Plannir, Plannyr, Plann

Plantagenet (French) Resembling the broom flower

Platinum (English) As precious as the metal
Platynum, Platnum, Platie, Plati, Platee, Platy, Platey, Platea

Plato (Greek) One who has broad shoulders
Platon, Playto, Plaito, Plaeto

Platt (French) From the flat land
Plat

Plutarco (Greek) A wicked man

Pluto (Greek) In mythology, god of the underworld

Podi (Teutonic) One who is bold
Podie, Pody, Podey, Podee, Podea

Poe (English) A mysterious man
Po

Poetry (American) A romantic man
Poetrey, Poetri, Poetrie, Poetree, Poetrea, Poet, Poete

Pollard (English) A small man
Pollerd, Pollyrd

Pollux (Greek) One who is crowned
Pollock, Pollok, Polloc, Pollack, Polloch

Polo (African) Resembling an alligator
Poloe, Poloh

Polygnotos (Greek) One who loves many
Polygnotus

Pomeroy (French) From the apple orchard
Pommeroy, Pomeroi, Pommeroi, Pomeray, Pommeray, Pommelraie

Pompeo (Italian / Greek) The fifth-born child / the one in charge
Pompey, Pompeyo, Pompi, Pompilio, Pomponio

Pomposo (Spanish) A pompous man
Pomposio, Pomposiyo

Ponce (Spanish) The fifth-born child
Ponse

Pongor (Hungarian) A mighty man
Pongorr, Pongoro, Pongorro

Poni (African) The second-born son
Ponni, Ponie, Ponnie, Pony, Ponny, Poney, Ponney, Ponee, Ponnee, Ponea, Ponnea

Ponipake (Hawaiian) One who has good luck
Ponipaki, Ponipakie, Ponipaky, Ponipakey, Ponipakee, Ponipakea

Pons (Latin) From the bridge
Pontius, Ponthos, Ponthus

Pontius (Latin) The fifth-born child
Pontias, Pontios, Pontyus, Ponteas, Ponteus, Pontus

Poogie (American) A snuggly little boy
Poogi, Poogy, Poogey, Poogee, Poogea

Pooky (American) A cute little boy
Pookey, Pooki, Pookie, Pookee, Pookea

Poorna (Indian) One who is complete
Pourna

Poornachandra (Indian) Born beneath the full moon
Pournachandra, Poornachandre, Pournachandre

Poornamruth (Indian) Full of sweetness
Pournamruth

Poornayu (Indian) Full of life; blessed with a full life
Pournayu, Poornayou, Pournayou, Poornayue, Pournayue

Pope (Greek) The father

Porat (Hebrew) A productive man

Porfirio (Greek) Refers to a purple coloring
Porphirios, Prophyrios, Porfiro, Porphyrios

Poriel (Hebrew) The fruit of God
Poriell, Poriele, Porielle

Porter (English) The gatekeeper
Porteur, Portier, Port, Porte, Poart, Portur, Portor, Portar, Portir, Portyr

Portland (English) From the land near the port

Poseidon (Greek) In mythology, the god of the waters
Posidon, Posydon, Posiydon

Potter (English) One who makes pots
Pottir, Pottor, Pottar, Pottur, Pottyr

Powa (Native American) A wealthy man
Powah

Powder (American) A lighthearted man
Powdar, Powdir, Powdur, Powdor, Powdi, Powdie, Powdy, Powdey, Powdee, Powdea

Powell (English) Form of Paul, meaning "a small or humble man"
Powel

Powhatan (Native American) From the chief's hill

Powwaw (Native American) A priest

Prabal (Indian) Resembling coral
Praball, Prabale, Praballe

Prabhakar (Hindu) Of the sun

Prabhat (Indian) Born during the morning

Pradeep (Hindi) One who is surrounded by light
Pradip, Pradyp, Pradeepe, Pradype, Pradipe, Pradeap, Pradeape

Pragun (Indian) One who is straightforward; honest

Prahlad (Indian) Filled with joy

Prairie (American) From the flatlands
Prairi, Prairy, Prairey, Prairee, Prairea, Prair, Praire

Prajit (Indian) A kind man
Prajeet, Prajeat, Prajyt, Prajin, Prajeen, Prajean, Prajyn

Prakash (Indian) Surrounded by light
Parkash, Prakashe, Parkashe

Pramod (Indian) A delightful young man

Pramsu (Indian) A scholar
Pramsue, Pramsou, Pramsoo

Pran (Indian) A giver of life
Prann

Pranav (Indian) The sacred syllable Om

Pranay (Indian) One who is dearly loved
Pranaye, Pranai, Pranae

Pranit (Indian) One who is humble; modest
Pranyt, Praneet, Praneat

Prasad (Indian) A gift from God

Prashant (Indian) One who is peaceful; calm
Prashante, Prashanth, Prashanthe

Pratap (Hindi) A majestic man

Pratik (Indian) A sign or symbol
Pratyk, Prateek, Prateak, Pratim, Pratym, Prateem, Prateam

Pravat (Thai) History

Praveen (Hindi) One who is proficient
Pravean, Pravein, Pravyn, Pravin

Prem (Indian) An affectionate man

Prembhari (Indian) One who is full of love
Prembharie, Prembhary, Prembharey, Prembharee, Prembharea

Prentice (English) A student; an apprentice
Prentyce, Prentise, Prentyse, Prentiss, Prentis

Prerak (Indian) One who encourages others

Preruet (French) A brave man

Prescott (English) From the priest's cottage
Prescot, Prestcot, Prestcott, Preostcot

Presley (English) From the priest's meadow
Presly, Presle, Presli, Preslie, Preslee, Presleigh, Preslea, Prezley, Prezly, Prezli, Prezlie, Prezlee, Prezleigh, Prezlea, Prestley, Priestley, Prestly, Priestly

Preston ♂ (English) From the priest's town
Prestin, Prestyn, Prestan, Prestun, Presten, Pfeostun

Preto (Latin) An important man
Prito, Preyto, Pryto, Preeto, Preato

Prewitt (French) A brave young one
Prewet, Prewett, Prewit, Pruitt, Pruit, Pruet, Pruett

Price (French) One who is very dear; prized
Pryce, Prise, Pryse, Prys

Primerica (American) A patriotic man
Primericus, Primerico, Primerika, Primerikus, Primeriko

Primitivo (Spanish) A primitive man

Primo (Italian) The firstborn child
Preemo, Premo, Priemo, Preimo, Preamo, Prymo, Prime, Primeiro

Prince (Latin) The royal son
Printz, Printze, Prinz, Prinze, Princeton

Prine (English) One who surpasses others
Pryne

Prisciliano (Spanish) A wise and elderly man

Priyavrat (Indian) An older brother

Probert (American) A ray of sunshine
Proberte, Proberth, Proberthe

Procopio (Spanish) One who is progressive
Procopius, Prokopios

Proctor (Latin) A steward
Procter, Procktor, Prockter

Prometheus (Greek) In mythology, he stole fire from the heavens and gave it to man
Promitheus, Promethius, Promithius

Prop (American) A fun-loving man
Propp, Proppe

Prosper (Latin) A fortunate man
Prospero, Prosperus

Proteus (Greek) In mythology, a sea deity with the gift of prophecy
Protius, Protyus, Proteas, Protyas, Protias

Proverb (English) A wise saying

Prudencio (Spanish) A cautious man
Prudentius

Pryderi (Celtic) Son of the sea
Pryderie, Prydery, Pryderey, Pryderee, Pryderea

Prydwen (Welsh) A handsome man
Prydwenn, Prydwenne, Prydwin, Prydwinne, Prydwinn, Prydwyn, Prydwynn, Prydwynne

Pryor (Latin) Head of the monastery
Prior

Publias (Greek) A great thinker
Publios, Publius, Publyas, Publyos, Publyus

Pueblo (Spanish) From the city

Pullman (English) One who works on a train
Pulman, Pullmann, Pulmann

Puma (Latin) Resembling a mountain lion
Pumah, Pouma, Pooma

Pumeet (Indian) An innocent man
Pumit, Pumyt, Pumeat

Pundarik (Indian) A white-skinned man
Pundaric, Pundarick, Pundaryk, Pundaryc, Pundaryck

Purujit (Indian) One who has defeated many
Purujyt, Purujeet, Purujeat

Purvin (English) One who helps others
Purvyn, Purvon, Purven, Purvan, Purvun, Pervin, Pervyn, Pervon, Pervun, Pervan, Perven

Purvis (English) One who provides provisions
Purviss, Purvisse, Purvys, Purvyss, Purvysse

Pusan (Hindi) A wise man; a sage
Pusann, Pousan, Pousann, Poosan, Poosann

Putnam (English) One who lives by the water
Putni, Putnie, Putny, Putney, Putnee, Putnea

Pygmalion (Greek) In mythology, a king of Cyprus and talented sculptor
Pigmalion, Pymalien, Pigmalien, Pygmalian, Pigmalian

Pyralis (Greek) Born of fire
Pyraliss, Pyralisse, Pyralys, Pyralyss, Pyralysse, Pyre

Qabil (Arabic) An able-bodied man
Qabyl, Qabeel, Qabeal, Qabeil, Qabiel

Qadim (Arabic) From an ancient family
Qadeem, Qadiem, Qadeim, Qadym, Qadeam

Qadir (Arabic) A capable man; one who is competent
Qadyr, Qadeer, Qadeir, Qadear, Qadeir, Qadar, Qadry, Quadir, Quadeer

Qaiser (Arabic) A king; a ruler
Qeyser

Qaletaqa (Native American) The people's guardian

Qamar (Arabic) Born beneath the moon
Qamarr, Quamar, Quamarr

Qasim (Arabic) One who is charitable; generous
Qasym, Qaseem, Qaseim, Qasiem, Qaseam, Quasim, Quaseem, Quasym

Qays (Arabic) One who is firm
Qais, Qayse, Qaise, Qaes, Qaese, Qase

Qiao (Chinese) A handsome man

Qimat (Hindi) A highly valued man
Qymat

Qing (Chinese) Of the deep water
Qyng

Qochata (Native American) A white-skinned man
Qochatah, Qochatta, Qochattah

Qssim (Arabic) He divides
Qssym

Quaashie (American) An ambitious man
Quashie, Quashi, Quashy, Quashey, Quashee, Quashea, Quaashi, Quaashy, Quaashey, Quaashee, Quaashea

Quacey (Scottish) Of the moonlight
Quacy, Quaci, Quacie, Quacee, Quacea

Quaddus (American) A bright man
Quadus, Quaddos, Quados

Quade (Latin) The fourth-born child
Quadrees, Quadres, Quadrys, Quadries, Quadreis, Quadreys, Quadreas, Quadrhys

Quaid (Irish) Form of Walter, meaning "the commander of the army"
Quaide, Quayd, Quayde, Quaed, Quaede

Quan (Vietnamese) A dignified man; a soldier

Quanah (Native American) One who has a pleasant scent
Quana, Quanna, Quannah

Quang (Vietnamese) A clear-headed man

Quant (Latin) Our son's worth
Quante, Quantai, Quantay, Quantaye, Quantae, Quantey, Quanty, Quanti, Quantie, Quantee, Quantea, Quantez, Quantal

Quaronne (American) One who is haughty
Quarone, Quaron, Quaronn

Quarrie (Scottish) A proud man
Quarri, Quarry, Quarrey, Quarree, Quarrea, Quany, Quaney, Quanee, Quanea, Quani, Quanie

Quashawn (American) A tenacious man
Quashaun, Quasean, Quashon, Quashi, Quashie, Quashee, Quashea, Quashy, Quashey

Quauhtli (Aztec) Resembling an eagle

Qubilah (Arabic) An agreeable man
Qubila, Qubeelah, Qubeela, Qubeilah, Qubeila, Qubielah, Qubiela, Qubealah, Qubeala, Qubylah, Qubyla

Qudamah (Arabic) A courageous man
Qudama

Qued (Native American) Wearing a decorated robe

Quelatikan (Native American) One who has a blue horn
Quelatykan, Quelatican, Quelatycan, Quelatickan, Quelatyckan

Quenby (English) From the queen's estate; a giving man
Quenbey, Quenbi, Quenbie, Quenbee, Quenbea, Quinby, Quinbey, Quinbee, Quinbea, Quinbi, Quinbie

Quennell (French) From the small oak
Quennelle, Quenell, Quennel, Quenelle, Quennele, Quenel, Quentrell, Quentrelle, Quentrel, Quentrele, Quesnel, Quesnell, Quesnele, Quesnelle

Quentin (Latin) The fifth-born child
Quent, Quenten, Quenton, Quentun, Quentan, Quentyn, Quente, Qwentin, Qwenton, Qwenten

Queran (Irish) A dark and handsome man
Queron, Queren, Querin, Queryn, Querun

Quick (American) One who is fast; a witty man
Quik, Quicke, Quic

Quico (Spanish) A beloved friend
Quiko, Quicko, Quyco, Quyko, Quycko, Quiqui

Q

Quiessence (Spanish) An essential;
the essence
Quiessince, Quiessense, Quiessinse,
Quiesence, Quiesense, Quiess, Quiesse,
Quiese, Quies

Quigley (Irish) One with messy or unruly
hair
Quigly, Quigleigh, Quiglee, Quiglea,
Quigli, Quiglie

Quillan (Gaelic) Resembling a cub
Quilan, Quillen, Quilen, Quillon, Quilon

Quiller (English) A scriber
Quillar, Quillor, Quillir, Quillyr, Quillur

Quilliam (Gaelic) Form of William,
meaning "the determined protector"
Quilhelm, Quilhelmus, Quilliams,
Quilliamson, Quilliamon, Quillem,
Quillhelmus, Quilmot, Quilmott,
Quilmod, Quilmodd

Quimby (Norse) From the woman's estate
Quimbey, Quimbee, Quimbea, Quimbi,
Quimbie

Quincy (English) The fifth-born child;
from the fifth son's estate
Quincey, Quinci, Quincie, Quincee,
Quinncy, Quinnci, Quyncy, Quyncey,
Quynci, Quyncie, Quyncee, Quynncy,
Quince, Quinnsy, Quinsey

Quinlan (Gaelic) A strong and healthy man
Quindlan, Quinlen, Quindlen, Quinian,
Quinlin, Quindlin, Quinlyn, Quindlyn,
Quinnlan

Quinn (Gaelic) One who provides counsel;
an intelligent man
Quin, Quinne, Qwinn, Quynn, Qwin,
Quiyn, Quyn, Qwinne, Quinnell

Quintavius (American) The fifth-born child
Quintavios, Quintavus, Quintavies

Quinto (Spanish) The fifth-born child
Quynto, Quintus, Quintos, Quinty, Quinti,
Quintie, Quintey, Quintee, Quintea

Quinton (English) From the queen's town
or settlement
Quinntan, Quinnten, Quinntin, Quinnton,
Quintain, Quintan, Quintyn, Quintynn,
Quintin, Quinten, Quintann, Quint, Quinte,
Quynt, Quynte, Quinneton, Quienton,
Quientin, Quiten, Quitin, Quiton

Quintrell (English) An elegant and dash-
ing man
Quintrel, Quintrelle, Quyntrell, Quyntrelle,
Quyntrel, Quyntrele, Quintrele

Quirin (American) One who is magical
Quiryn, Quiran, Quiren, Quiron, Quirun

Quirinus (Latin) One who wields a spear
Quirinos, Quirynus, Quirynos, Quirinius,
Quirynius

Quito (Spanish) A lively man
Quyto, Quitos, Quytos

Qunnoune (Native American) One who
is tall
Qunnoun, Qunnoone, Qunnoon

Quoc (Vietnamese) A patriot
Quok, Quock

Quoitrel (American) A mediator
Quoytrel, Quoitrell, Quoytrell, Quoitrele,
Quoytrele, Quoitrelle, Quoytrelle

Quon (Chinese) A luminous man
Quonn, Quone, Quonne

Qusay (Arabic) One who is distant
Qusaye, Qusai, Qusae, Qussay, Qussaye,
Qussai, Qussae

Qutaybah (Arabic) An impatient man
Qutayba, Qutaibah, Qutaiba, Qutabah,
Qutaba, Qutaebah, Qutaeba

Qutub (Indian) One who is tall

Raanan (Hebrew) A fresh-faced man

Rabbaanee (African) An easygoing man

Rabbani (Arabic) Of the divine
Rabbanie, Rabbany, Rabbaney, Rabbanee,
Rabbanea

Rabbi (Hebrew) The master

Rabbit (English) Resembling the animal
Rabbyt

Rabi (Arabic) Of the gentle wind
Rabie, Rabee, Raby, Rabea, Rabey

Rabia (African) Born during the spring
Rabiah, Rabiya, Rabiyah

Rabul (Hispanic) A wealthy man
Rabule, Rabool, Raboole, Raboul, Raboule

Race (American) One who is fast;
a competitor
*Racer, Raci, Racie, Racy, Racey, Racee,
Racea*

Rach (African) Resembling a frog

Racham (Hebrew) One who shows mercy
*Rachim, Rachem, Rachym, Rachaam,
Rachan, Rachin*

Racqueab (Arabic) A homebody

Rad (English) One who provides counsel
Radd, Raad, Raadd

Radames (Egyptian) A hero
*Radamays, Radamayes, Radamais,
Radamaise, Radamaes, Radamaese*

Radbert (English) A red-haired advisor
*Radberte, Radberth, Radberthe, Radburt,
Radburth, Radburte, Radburthe*

Radburn (English) From the red brook
*Radburne, Radbern, Radberne, Radborn,
Radborne, Radbourn, Radbourne,
Radbyrne, Raedburne, Raedburn,
Raedborn, Raedborne, Raedbourn,
Raedbourne*

Radcliff (English) From the red cliff
*Radcliffe, Radclyff, Radclyffe, Ratcliff,
Ratcliffe, Ratclyff, Ratclyffe, Radclyf,
Ratclyf, Radeliffe, Raedclif, Raedclyf,
Raedcliff, Raedclyff*

Raddy (Slavic) A cheerful person
*Raddey, Raddi, Raddie, Raddee, Raddea,
Radde, Radman, Radi, Radie, Rady,
Radey, Radee, Radea*

Radek (Slavic) A famous ruler
Radec, Radeck

Radford (English) From the red ford
*Radforde, Radferd, Radfurd, Radferde,
Radfurde, Redford, Redforde, Raedford,
Raedforde, Raedfurd, Raedfurde, Raedferd,
Raedferde*

Radimir (Slavic) A well-known joyful person
*Radimeer, Radimyr, Radymir, Radymyr,
Radymeer, Radimear, Radymear, Radomir,
Radomyr, Radomeer, Radomear*

Radley (English) From the red meadow
*Radly, Radli, Radlie, Radlee, Radleigh,
Radlea, Radleah, Redley, Redly, Redli,
Redlie, Redleigh, Redlee, Redlea, Redleah,
Raedleah, Raedlea, Raedleigh, Raedlee,
Raedli, Raedlie, Raedley, Raedly*

Radnor (English) From the red shore
*Radnur, Radner, Radnar, Radnir, Radnyr,
Raedanoran, Raedanor*

Radolf (English) Resembling a red wolf
*Radolph, Radulf, Radulph, Raedwolf,
Raedwulf*

Radoslaw (Polish) One who loves peace
Radoslav

Radwan (Arabic) A delightful man

Raedan (Anglo-Saxon) One who provides
counsel
Raydan, Raidan, Radan, Raedbora

Raekwon (American) A proud man
*Raekwonn, Raykwon, Raykwonn,
Rakwon, Rakwonn, Raikwon, Raikwonn*

Rael (African) As innocent as a lamb
Raele, Rayl, Rayle, Rail, Raile, Rale

Rafe (Irish) A tough man
*Raffe, Raff, Raf, Raif, Rayfe, Raife, Raef,
Raefe*

Rafer (Gaelic) A wealthy man
Raffer

Rafferty (Gaelic) One who wields prosperity
*Raffertey, Rafferti, Raffertie, Raffertea,
Raffertee, Raffarty, Raffartey, Raffarti,
Raffartie, Raffartea, Raffartee, Raferty,
Rafertey, Raferti, Rafertie, Rafertea,
Rafertee, Rafarty, Rafartey, Rafarti,
Rafartie, Rafartea, Rafartee*

Rafi (Arabic) One who is exalted
*Rafie, Rafy, Rafey, Rafea, Rafee, Raffi,
Raffie, Raffy, Raffey, Raffea, Raffee, Rafat*

Rafiki (African) A gentle friend
Rafikie, Rafikea, Rafikee, Rafiky, Rafikey

Rafiq (Arabic) A beloved friend
*Rafeeq, Rafeaq, Rafyq, Rafik, Rafeek,
Rafeak, Rafyk*

Rafiya (African) A dignified man
Rafeeya, Rafeaya, Rafeiya, Rafieya

R

Raghib (Arabic) One who is desired
Ragheb, Ragheeb, Ragheab, Raghyb, Ragheib, Raghieb

Raghid (Arabic) One who is carefree
Ragheed, Raghead, Raghied, Ragheid, Raghyd

Ragnar (Norse) A warrior who places judgment
Ragnor, Ragner, Ragnir, Ragnyr, Ragnur, Regnar, Regner, Regnir, Regnyr, Regnor, Regnur, Ragnal, Ragnall, Raghnal, Raghnall

Rahim (Arabic) A compassionate man
Rahym, Raheim, Rahiem, Raheem, Raheam

Rahimat (Arabic) Full of grace
Rahymat

Rahman (Arabic) One who is full of compassion
Rahmann, Rahmahn, Raman

Rai (Japanese) A trustworthy man; of lightning and thunder

Ra'id (Arabic) A great leader

Raiden (Japanese) In mythology, the god of thunder and lightning
Raidon, Rayden, Raydon, Raeden, Raedon, Raden, Radon, Raijin, Rayjin, Raejin, Rajin, Raidyn, Raydyn, Raedyn, Radyn

Raighne (Irish) A strong man

Raimi (African) A compassionate man
Raimie, Raimy, Raimey, Raimee, Raimea

Rainart (German) One who provides brave counsel
Rainhard, Rainhardt, Reinart, Reinhard, Reinhardt, Reinhart, Renke

Rainer (German) A decisive warrior
Rainier, Ranier, Rainor, Rayner, Raynor, Raner

Raines (English) A wise ruler; a lord
Rain, Raine, Rains, Rayne, Raynes, Raene, Raenes

Rainey (German) One who is helpful; generous
Rainy, Raini, Rainie, Rainee, Rainea, Rayney, Rayny, Rayni, Raynie, Raynee, Raynea

Rajab (African) A glorified man

Rajan (Indian) A king
Raj, Raja, Rajah

Rajarshi (Indian) The king's sage
Rajarshie, Rajarshy, Rajarshey, Rajarshee, Rajarshea

Rajas (Indian) A famous and proud man

Rajat (Indian) As precious as silver

Rajdeep (Indian) The light of the king
Rajdip, Rajdyp, Rajdeip, Rajdiep, Rajdeap

Rajendra (Hindi) A powerful king
Rajindra, Rajyndra

Rajesh (Hindi) The king's rule

Rajit (Indian) One who is decorated
Rajeet, Rajeit, Rajiet, Rajyt, Rajeat

Rajiv (Hindi) To be striped
Rajyv, Rajeev, Rajeav

Raka (Indian) Born beneath the full moon
Rakah, Rakka, Rakkah

Rakesh (Hindi) A king

Rakin (Arabic) A respectful young man
Rakeen, Rakean, Rakyn, Rakein, Rakien

Rakshak (Indian) One who protects others

Rald (German) A famous ruler
Ralde, Rauld, Raulde

Raleigh (English) From the clearing of roe deer
Ralee, Raley, Raly, Rali, Ralie, Rawley, Rawly, Rawleigh, Rawli, Rawlie, Rawlea, Ralea, Raleah, Rawleah, Raleich, Ralegh

Ralik (Hindi) One who has been purified
Raleek, Raleak, Ralyk, Raleik, Raliek

Ralis (Latin) A thin man
Raliss, Ralisse, Ralys, Ralyss, Ralysse, Ralus, Rallis, Rallus

Ralph (English) Wolf counsel
Ralf, Ralphe, Ralfe, Ralphi, Ralphie, Ralphee, Ralphea, Ralphy, Ralphey

Ralston (English) From Ralph's town
Ralstun, Ralsten, Ralstan, Ralstin, Ralstyn

Ram (Hebrew / Sanskrit) A superior man / one who is pleasing
Rahm, Rama, Rahma, Ramos, Rahmos, Ram, Ramm

Rambert (German) Having great strength; an intelligent man
Ramberte, Ramberth, Ramberthe, Ramburt, Ramburte, Ramburth, Ramburthe, Ramhart, Ramharte

Ramel (Hindi) A godly man
Ramell, Ramele, Ramelle, Raymel, Raymell, Raymele, Raymelle

Rami (Arabic) A loving man
Ramee, Ramea, Ramie, Ramy, Ramey

Ramin (Persian) A great warrior
Ramen, Ramyn

Ramiro (Portuguese) A famous counselor; a great judge
Ramyro, Rameero, Rameyro, Ramirez, Ramyrez, Rameerez

Ramsden (English) From the ram's valley
Ramsdin, Ramsdyn, Ramsdan, Ramsdon, Ramsdun

Ramses (Egyptian) Born of the sun god
Rameses, Ramesses, Ramzes, Ramzees, Ramsees, Ramzan, Ramsies, Ramzies

Ramsey (English) From the raven island; from the island of wild garlic
Ramsay, Ramsie, Ramsi, Ramsee, Ramsy, Ramsea, Ramzy, Ramzey, Ramzi, Ramzie, Ramzee, Ramzea, Rams, Ramz

Ranajit (Indian) A victorious man
Ranajeet, Ranajyt, Ranajeat, Ranajay, Ranajaye, Ranajae, Ranajai

Rance (French / African) A type of marble / borrowed
Rencei, Rancell, Ransel, Ransell, Rancy, Rancey, Rancye, Ranci, Rancie, Rancee, Rancea

Rand (German) One who shields others
Rande

Randall (German) The wolf shield
Randal, Randale, Randel, Randell, Randl, Randle, Randon, Rendall, Rendell

Randolph (German) The wolf shield
Randolf, Ranolf, Ranolph, Ranulfo, Randulfo, Randwulf, Ranwulf, Randwolf, Ranwolf, Ranulf

Randy (English) Form of Randall or Randolph, meaning "the wolf shield"
Randey, Randi, Randie, Randee, Randea

Ranen (Hebrew) Filled with joy
Rainen, Raynen, Raenen, Ranon, Rainon, Raynon, Raenon

Rang (English) Resembling a raven
Range

Rangarajan (Hindi) A charming man

Ranger (French) The guardian of the forest
Rainger, Raynger, Raenger

Rangey (English) From raven's island
Rangy, Rangi, Rangie, Rangee, Rangea

Rangle (American) A cowboy
Rangel

Ranit (Hebrew) One who raises his voice in song
Rani, Ranie, Rany, Raney, Ranee, Ranea, Ronit

Ranjan (Indian) A delightful boy

Ranjit (Hindi) One who is charmed
Ranjeet, Ranjeat, Ranjyt

Rankin (English) The little shield
Rankinn, Rankine, Rankyn, Rankynn, Rankyne, Randkin, Randkyn, Rank

Ransford (English) From the raven's ford
Ransforde, Ransferd, Ransferde, Ransfurd, Ransfurde, Rangford, Rangforde, Rangfurd, Rangferd

Ransley (English) From the raven's meadow
Ransly, Ransli, Ranslie, Ranslee, Ransleigh, Ranslea, Ransleah, Rangley, Rangly, Ranglee, Rangleigh, Rangli, Ranglie, Ranglea, Rangleah

Ransom (English) The warrior's shield
Ransum, Ransem, Ransam, Ransim, Ransym, Ransome

Rante (American) An amorous man
Ranti, Rantie, Ranty, Rantey, Rantea, Rantee

Raoul (French) Form of Ralph, meaning "wolf counsel"
Raoule, Raul, Roul, Rowl, Raule, Roule, Rowle

Raphael (Hebrew) One who is healed by God
Rafal, Rafael, Rafaelle, Rafaelo, Rafaello, Rafel, Rafello, Raffael, Raffaello, Raphaello, Raphello

Raqib (Arabic) A glorified man
Raqyb, Raqeeb, Raqeab, Rakib, Rakeeb, Rakeab, Rakyb

Rashad (Arabic) One who has good judgment
Rashaad, Rashod

Rashard (American) A good-hearted man
Rasherd, Rashird, Rashurd, Rashyrd

Rashaun (American) Form of Roshan, meaning "born during the daylight"
Rashae, Rashane, Rashawn, Rayshaun, Rayshawn, Raishaun, Raishawn, Raeshaun, Raeshawn

Rashid (Arabic) One who is guided along the right path
Rasheed, Rasheid, Rashied, Rashead, Rashyd, Rasheyd, Raashid, Rascheed, Raschid, Raschyd

Rashne (Persian) A judge
Rashni, Rashnie, Rashnea, Rashnee, Rashney, Rashny

Rasmus (Greek) Form of Erasmus, meaning "one who is dearly loved"
Rasmos, Rasmes, Rasmis, Rasmys, Rasmas

Rasool (Arabic) A messenger; a herald
Rasule, Rasoole, Rasul, Rasoul, Rasoule

Rasputin (Russian) A mystic
Rasputyn, Rasputen, Rasputan, Rasputon, Rasputun

Rastus (Greek) Form of Erastus, meaning "a loving man"
Rastos, Rastes, Rastis, Rastys, Rastas

Ratri (Indian) Born at night
Ratrie, Ratry, Ratrey, Ratrea, Ratree

Ratul (Indian) A sweet man
Ratule, Ratoul, Ratoule, Ratool, Ratoole

Raudel (American) One who is rowdy
Raudell, Raudele, Raudelle

Rauf (Arabic) A compassionate man
Rauff, Raufe, Rauffe

Raulo (Spanish) One who is wise
Rawlo

Raven (English) Resembling the blackbird; a dark and mysterious man
Raiven, Rayvenne, Rayven, Rayvinn, Ravyn, Raevin, Raeven, Ravenne, Ravinn, Ravin

Ravi (Hindi) From the sun
Ravie, Ravy, Ravey, Ravee, Ravea

Ravid (Hebrew) A wanderer; one who searches
Ravyd, Raveed, Ravead, Raviyd, Ravied, Raveid

Ravindra (Indian) The strength of the sun
Ravyndra

Ravinger (English) One who lives near the ravine
Ravynger

Raviv (Hebrew) Resembling a raindrop
Ravyv, Ravive, Ravyve, Raveev, Raveeve, Raveav, Raveave, Raviev, Ravieve, Raveiv, Raveive

Rawdon (Teutonic) From the hill
Rawden, Rawdun, Rawdan, Rawdin, Rawdyn

Rawlins (French) From the renowned land
Rawlin, Rawson, Rawlinson, Rawlings, Rawling, Rawls, Rawl, Rawle

Ray (English) Form of Raymond, meaning "a wise protector"
Rae, Rai, Rayce, Rayder, Rayse, Raye, Rayford, Raylen, Raynell, Reigh

Rayburn (English) From the brook of the roe deer
Raeborn, Raeborne, Raebourn, Raeburn, Rayborn, Raybourne, Raybourn, Rayborne, Rayburne, Raeburne, Raiborn, Raiborne, Raibourn, Raibourne, Raiburn, Raiburne, Reyhurn, Reyhern, Reyburn, Reyborn

Rayfield (English) From the field of roe deer
Rayfeld

Rayford (French) From the roe deer crossing
Rayforde, Rayferd, Rayferde, Rayfurd, Rayfurde

Rayhan (Arabic) One who is favored by God
Raihan, Raehan, Rahan

Rayhurn (English) From the roe deer's stream
Rayhurne, Rayhorn, Rayhorne, Rayhourn, Rayhourne

Raymond (German) A wise protector
Raemond, Raemondo, Raimond, Raimondo, Raimund, Raimundo, Rajmund, Ramon, Ramond, Ramonde, Ramone, Rayment, Raymondo, Raymund, Raymunde, Raymundo, Reymond, Reymundo, Raymon, Raemon, Rayman, Raeman, Raimon, Raiman

Raymont (American) A distinguised gentleman
Raymonte, Raimont, Raimonte, Raemont, Raemonte, Ramont, Ramonte

Raynor (German) The decisive warrior
Raynar, Rayne, Raynell, Rayner, Raynord, Reinier, Renier, Ranell, Ranieri, Raniero, Raynard, Rane

Raza (Arabic) Filled with hope
Razah, Razza, Razzah

Razak (Arabic) A devoted man
Razac, Razack, Razach

Raziel (Aramaic) The Lord is my secret
Raziell, Raziele, Razielle, Razyel, Razyell, Razyele, Razyelle, Razi, Razie, Razea, Razee, Razy, Razey

Reading (English) Son of a red-haired man
Reeding, Reyding, Redding, Reiding

Reaner (American) An even-tempered man
Reener, Riener, Rener

Rebel (American) An outlaw
Rebell, Rebele, Rebelle, Rebe, Rebbe, Rebbi, Rebbie, Rebbea, Rebbee, Rebby, Rebbey

Recene (Anglo-Saxon) One who is quick
Receen, Receene, Recean, Receane, Recein, Receine, Recien, Reciene, Recyn, Recyne, Recin, Recine

Red (American) A red-haired man
Redd, Redde, Reddi, Reddie, Reddy, Reddey, Reddea, Reddee, Reod

Reda (Arabic) One who is satisfied; content
Redah, Rida, Ridah, Ridha, Ridhah, Ridhaa

Redell (English) From the red valley
Redel, Redelle, Redele, Redale, Redayl, Redayle, Redail, Redaile, Redael, Redaele

Redman (English) A red-haired advisor
Redmann, Raedmann, Raedman, Readman, Readmann, Redaman, Redamann

Redmond (English) Form of Raymond, meaning "a wise protector"
Redmonde, Radmond, Radmund, Radmonde, Radmunde, Redmund, Redmunde, Raedmund, Raedmunde, Raedmond, Raedmonde, Redmon, Redmun

Redwald (English) Strong counsel
Redwalde, Raedwalde, Raedwald

Reece (Welsh) Having great enthusiasm for life
Rees, Reese, Reice, Reise, Reace, Rease, Riece, Riese, Rhys, Rhyss, Rhyse, Rice, Ryce

Reem (Hebrew) Resembling a horned animal
Reeme, Ream, Reame

Reeve (English) A bailiff
Reve, Reave, Reeford, Reeves, Reaves, Reves, Reaford

Refugio (Spanish) One who provides shelter
Refuge, Resugio, Resuge

Regal (American) Born into royalty
Regall

Regan (Gaelic) Born into royalty; the little ruler
Raegan, Ragan, Raygan, Reganne, Regann, Regane, Reghan, Reagan, Reaghan, Reegan, Rayghun, Raygen, Regen, Riagan

Regenfrithu (English) A peaceful raven

Regent (Latin) A regal man; born into royalty
Regant, Regint, Regynt

Regenweald (English) Having great strength

Reggie (Latin) Form of Reginald, meaning "the king's advisor"
Reggi, Reggy, Reggey, Reggea, Reggee, Reg

Reginald (Latin) The king's advisor
Raghnall, Rainault, Rainhold, Raonull, Raynald, Rayniero, Regin, Reginaldo, Reginalt, Reginauld, Reginault, Regino, Reginvald, Reginvalt, Regnauld, Regnault, Reinald, Reinaldo, Reinaldos, Reinhold, Reinold, Reinwald, Renaud, Renault, Rene, Rheinallt, Rinaldo, Reginaldus, Raynaldo, Regulo

R

Regine (French) One who is artistic
Regeen, Regeene, Regean, Regeane, Regein, Regeine, Regien, Regiene, Regyn, Regyne

Reginhard (German) Having great strength; an intelligent man
Reginhart, Regynhard, Regynhart, Reginheraht, Regynheraht, Regenhard, Regenhart, Regenheraht, Reinhard, Reinhart

Regis (Latin) A kingly or regal man
Regiss, Reegis, Reagis, Regys, Regyss, Reegys, Reagys, Riegis, Riegys

Rehman (Indian) One who is merciful
Rehmat

Rei (Japanese) One who strives to uphold the law

Reid (English) A red-haired man; one who lives near the reeds
Read, Reade, Reed, Reede, Reide, Raed

Reidar (Scandinavian) A warrior or soldier
Reider, Reidor, Reidur, Reidir, Reidyr

Reilly (Gaelic) An outgoing man
Reilley, Reilli, Reillie, Reillee, Reilleigh, Reillea

Reiner (German) One who provides counsel
Reinir, Reinar, Reinor, Reinur, Reinyr

Reith (American) One who is shy
Reyth, Reeth, Reath, Rieth

Reizo (Japanese) One who is calm and well-kept

Remedios (Spanish) One who is assisted by God
Remedy, Remedi, Remedie, Remedee, Remedey, Remedea, Remedio, Remediyo

Remington (English) From the town of the raven's family
Remyngton, Remingtun, Remyngtun

Remuda (Spanish) A herd of horses
Remooda, Remouda

Remus (Latin) One who is swift; in mythology, along with his brother Romulus, one of the founders of Rome
Reemus, Remos, Reemos, Reamus, Reamos

Remy (French) Man from the town of Rheims
Remi, Remie, Remmy, Remmi, Remmie, Remy, Remmey, Remey, Rhemy, Rhemmy, Remee, Remmee, Remo, Remmo, Remigio

Rendor (Hungarian) One who keeps the peace
Rendur, Rendir, Rendyr, Render, Rendar

René (French) One who has been reborn
Ranae, Ranay, Rané, Renae, Renat, Renay, Renaye, Renee, Rene, Renato, Renell, Renelle, Renie, Reni, Renne, Rennie, Renny, Rrenae, Rennee, Renne, Rennay, Renate, Renatus, Ren, Renn

Renferd (English) One who loves peace
Renferde, Renfurd, Renfurde, Renfred

Renfield (English) From the raven's field
Renfeld, Ranfield, Ranfeld, Rangfield, Rangfeld

Renfred (English) A powerful and peaceful man
Renfreid, Renfrid, Renfryd, Renfried

Renfrew (Welsh) From the calm waters
Rhinfrew

Renfro (Welsh) One who is calm
Renfroe, Renfrow, Renfrowe, Renphro, Renphroe, Renphrow, Renphrowe

Renjiro (Japanese) An honest and upright man
Renjyro, Renjeero, Renjeryo

Renshaw (English) From the raven's forest
Renshawe, Renishaw, Renishawe

Renton (English) From the town of the roe deer
Rentun, Rentin, Rentyn, Rentan, Renten

Renweard (Anglo-Saxon) The guardian of the house
Renward, Renwarden, Renwerd

Renwick (English) From the village of the roe deer; from the village of the ravens
Renwik, Renwic, Renwyck, Renwyk, Renwyc

Renzo (Japanese) The third-born son

Reth (African) A king
Rethe

Retta (African) He has triumphed
Rettah, Reta, Retah

Reuben (Hebrew) Behold, a son!
*Reuban, Reubin, Reuven, Rouvin, Rube,
Ruben, Rubin, Rubino, Ruby, Rubi, Rubie,
Rubey, Rubee, Rubea, Reuhen, Rueban,
Re'uven*

Reuel (Hebrew) A friend of God
*Ruel, Reuell, Ruell, Reuelle, Ruelle,
Reuele, Ruele*

Rev (American) One who is distinct
*Revv, Revin, Reven, Revan, Revyn, Revon,
Revun*

Revelin (Celtic, Gaelic) Form of Roland,
meaning "from the renowned land"
Revelyn, Revelen, Revelan, Revelon, Revelun

Rex (Latin) A king
Reks, Recks, Rexs

Rexford (English) From the king's ford
*Rexforde, Rexferd, Rexferde, Rexfurd,
Rexfurde*

Rexley (English) From the king's meadow
*Rexly, Rexleigh, Rexlee, Rexlea, Rexleah,
Rexli, Rexlie*

Rexton (English) From the king's town
Rextun, Rextown, Royalton, Royaltun

Rey (Spanish) Of the kings
*Reyes, Reyni, Reynie, Reyney, Reyny,
Reynee, Reynea*

Reynard (French / German) Resembling a
fox / a strong counselor
*Reynardo, Raynard, Reinhard, Reinhardt,
Renard, Renardo, Rennard, Reinhart,
Reynaud*

Reynold (English) Form of Reginald,
meaning "the king's advisor"
*Reynald, Reynaldo, Reynolds, Reynalde,
Reynolde*

Reza (Iranian) One who is content
Rezah, Rezza, Rezzah

Reznik (Czech) A butcher
Reznick, Reznic, Reznyk, Reznyck, Reznyc

Rhene (American) One who smiles a lot
Rheen, Rheene, Rhean, Rheane

Rhett (Latin) A well-spoken man
Rett, Rhet, Ret

Rhinebeck (German) From the stream of
the Rhine
*Rheinbeck, Rhinebek, Rheinbek,
Rinebeck, Reinbeck, Rinebek, Reinbek*

Rhodes (Greek) From the place where the
roses grow
Rhoads, Rhodas, Rodas, Rodes, Roads

Rhodree (Welsh) A strong ruler
*Rhodrea, Rhodri, Rhodrie, Rhodry,
Rhodrey, Rodree, Rodrea, Rodri, Rodrie,
Rodry, Rodrey*

Rhydderch (Welsh) Having reddish-brown
hair

Rich (English) Form of Richard, meaning
"a powerful ruler"
*Richi, Richie, Richy, Richey, Richee,
Richea, Richer, Ritch, Ritchy, Ritchey,
Ritchi, Ritchie, Ritchee, Ritchea*

Richard (English) A powerful ruler
*Ricard, Ricardo, Riccardo, Richardo,
Richart, Richerd, Rickard, Rickert, Rikard,
Riocard, Ritchard, Ritcherd, Ritchyrd,
Ritshard, Ritsherd, Ryszard, Richman*

Richmond (French / German) From the
wealthy hill / a powerful protector
Richmonde, Richmund, Richmunde

Richter (English) One who is hopeful
Rickter, Rikter, Ricter

Rick (English) Form of Richard, meaning
"a powerful ruler"
*Ric, Ricci, Ricco, Rickie, Ricki, Ricky,
Rico, Rik, Rikk, Rikke, Rikki, Rikky,
Rique, Rickman, Ricman, Rikman, Ricker*

Rickward (English) A strong protector
*Rickwerd, Rickwood, Rikward, Ricward,
Rickweard, Rikweard, Ricweard*

Riddhiman (Indian) One who possesses
good fortune

Riddock (Irish) From the smooth field
*Ridock, Riddoc, Ridoc, Ryddock, Rydock,
Ryddoc, Rydoc, Ryddok, Rydok, Riddok,
Ridok, Reidhachadh*

Ridgeley (English) One who lives at the
meadow's ridge
*Ridgely, Ridgeli, Ridgelie, Ridgeleigh,
Ridgelea, Ridgeleah, Ridgelee, Ridgley,
Ridgly, Ridgli, Ridglie, Ridglea, Ridgleah,
Ridgleigh, Ridglee, Ridgeiey*

R

Ridgeway (English) One who lives on the road near the ridge
Rydgeway, Rigeway, Rygeway

Ridley (English) From the meadow of reeds
Ridly, Ridli, Ridlie, Ridleigh, Ridlee, Ridlea, Ridleah, Riddley, Riddly, Riddli, Riddlie, Riddlea, Riddleah, Riddlee, Riddleigh

Ridpath (English) One who lives near the red path
Rydpath, Ridpathe, Rydpathe, Raedpath, Raedpathe

Ridvik (Indian) A priest
Ridvic, Ridvick, Rydvik, Rydvic, Rydvick, Ritvik, Ritvic, Ritvick, Rytvik, Rytvic, Rytvick

Ridwan (Arabic) One who is accepting
Rydwan, Ridwann, Rydwann

Rigby (English) From the valley of the ruler
Rigbey, Rigbi, Rigbie, Rigbee, Rigbea

Rigel (Arabic) One who travels on foot; a blue star in the constellation Orion

Rigg (English) One who lives near the ridge
Rig, Ridge, Rygg, Ryg, Rydge, Rige, Ryge, Riggs, Ryggs

Rigoberto (Spanish) A shining warrior
Rigoberte, Rybgobert, Rygoberte, Rigoberth, Rigoberthe, Rygoberth, Rygoberthe, Rigobert, Rygoberto

Rijul (Indian) An innocent man
Rijule, Rijool, Rijoole, Rijoul, Rijoule

Rike (American) A high-spirited man
Ryke, Rikee, Rykee, Rikea, Rykea, Ryki, Rykie

Rimon (Arabic) Resembling a pomegranate
Rymon

Rin (Japanese) From the park; a good companion

Rinan (Anglo-Saxon) Born during a period of rain
Rynan, Rinen, Rinin, Rinyn, Rinon, Rinun, Rynen, Rynin, Rynyn, Rynon, Rynun

Rinc (Anglo-Saxon) A mighty warrior
Rync, Rink, Rynk, Rinck, Rynck

Ring (English) Resembling a ring
Ryng, Ringo, Ryngo, Ringling, Ryngling

Rinji (Japanese) Of the peaceful forest
Rinjie, Rinjy, Rinjey, Rinjee, Rinjea

Rio (Spanish) From the river
Reo, Riyo, Reyo, Riao, Ryo

Riobard (Irish) A bard of the royal court
Reobard, Ryobard

Riocard (German) A powerful ruler
Ryocard, Reocard

Riordain (Irish) A bright man
Riordane, Riordayn, Riordaen, Reardain, Reardane, Reardayn, Reardaen

Riordan (Gaelic) A royal poet; a bard or minstrel
Riorden, Rearden, Reardan, Riordon, Reardon

Ripley (English) From the noisy meadow
Riply, Ripleigh, Ripli, Riplie, Riplea, Ripleah, Riplee, Rip

Ripudaman (Indian) One who defeats his enemies

Ris (English) One who loves the outdoors
Riz

Rishab (Indian) One who is musically talented
Ryshab, Rishaub, Ryshaub, Rishawb, Ryshawb

Rishley (English) From the untamed meadow
Rishly, Rishli, Rishlie, Rishlee, Rishlea, Rishleah, Rishleigh

Rishon (Hebrew) The firstborn son
Ryshon, Rishi, Rishie, Rishea, Rishee, Rishy, Rishey

Risley (English) From the brushwood meadow
Risly, Risli, Rislie, Risleigh, Rislea, Risleah, Rislee, Rizley, Rizly, Rizli, Rizlie, Rizleigh, Rizlea, Rizleah, Rizlee

Risto (Finnish) Form of Christopher, meaning "one who bears Christ inside"
Rhisto, Rysto, Rhysto

Riston (English) From the brushwood settlement
Ryston, Ristun, Rystun

Ritter (German) A knight
Rytter, Ritt, Rytt

River (American) From the river
Ryver, Rivers, Ryvers

Rives (French) One who lives by the riverbank
Ryves

Riyad (Arabic) From the gardens
Riyadh, Riyaz

Ro (Anglo-Saxon / English) A red-haired man / resembling a roe deer
Roe, Row, Rowe

Roald (Norse) A famous ruler
Roal

Roam (American) One who wanders, searches
Roami, Roamie, Roamy, Roamey, Roamea, Roamee

Roark (Gaelic) A champion
Roarke, Rorke, Rourke, Rork, Rourk, Ruark, Ruarke

Rob (English) Form of Robert, meaning "one who is bright with fame"
Robb, Robbi, Robbie, Robby, Robbey, Robbea, Robbee, Robi, Robie, Roby, Robey, Robea, Robee

Robert ♦ ♂ (German) One who is bright with fame
Riobard, Roban, Robers, Roberto, Robertson, Robartach, Rubert

Robin (English) Form of Robert, meaning "one who is bright with fame"; resembling the red-breasted songbird
Robbin, Robben, Roben, Robinson, Robbinson, Robins, Robbins, Robson, Robyn, Robbyn, Robynson, Robbynson, Roibin, Roiben

Roble (African) Born during a period of rain
Robel

Rocco (Italian) One who is calm; restful
Roch, Roche, Rochus, Rock, Rocko, Rocky, Roque, Rocki, Rockie, Rockee, Rockea, Rocke

Rochester (English) From the stone fortress

Rocio (Spanish) Covered with dew

Rocket (American) One who is fast
Roket, Rocet, Rokket, Roccet

Rockford (English) From the rocky ford
Rockforde, Rokford, Rokforde, Rockferd, Rokferd, Rockfurd, Rokfurd

Rockland (English) From the rocky land
Rocklande, Rokland, Roklande

Rockley (English) From the rocky meadow
Rockly, Rockli, Rocklie, Rocklea, Rockleah, Rocklee, Rockleigh

Rockney (American) One who is brash
Rockny, Rockni, Rocknie, Rocknee, Rocknea

Rockwell (English) From the rocky spring
Rockwel, Rokwell, Rokwel

Rod (English) Form of Roderick, meaning "a famous ruler"
Rodd, Roddi, Roddie, Roddy, Roddee, Roddea, Roddey

Rodel (French) Form of Roderick, meaning "a famous ruler"
Rodell, Rodele, Rodelle, Roedel, Roedell, Roedele, Roedelle

Rodeo (French / American) One who takes part in the roundup/a cowboy
Rodio, Rodeyo, Rodiyo

Roderick (German) A famous ruler
Rhoderick, Rhodric, Rodderick, Roddric, Roddrick, Roderic, Roderich, Roderigo, Roderik, Roderyck, Rodric, Rodrick, Rodrik, Rodrigo, Rodrigue, Rodrigues, Rodriguez, Rodrique, Rodriquez, Rodryck, Rodryk, Rurek, Rurik

Rodman (German) One who is famous
Roddman, Rodmann, Roddmann

Rodney (German / English) From the famous one's island / from the island's clearing
Rodny, Rodni, Rodnie, Rodnea, Rodnee

Rodor (Anglo-Saxon) Of the sky
Rodur, Rodir, Rodyr, Roder, Rodar

Rodwell (English) One who lives on the road near the spring
Roddwell, Rodwel, Roddwel

Roe (English) One who hunts deer
Row, Rowe

Roel (French) As solid as a rock
Roele, Roell, Roelle

R

Rogan (Gaelic) A red-haired man
Rogann, Roegan, Roegann, Ruadhagan

Rogelio (Spanish) A famous soldier
*Rogelo, Rogeliyo, Rogeleo, Rogeleyo,
Rojelio, Rojeleo*

Roger (German) A famous spearman
*Rodge, Rodger, Rog, Rogelio, Rogerio,
Rogers, Rogiero, Rojay, Rufiger, Ruggero,
Ruggiero, Rutger, Ruttger, Rudiger*

Rohan (Irish / Sanskrit) A red-haired man /
one who ascends
Rohann, Rohaan, Royan, Royann, Royaan

Rohit (Indian) Refers to the color red
Rohyt, Roheet, Roheat, Roheit, Rohiet

Roho (African) A soulful man
Roehoe, Rohoe, Roeho

Rohon (American) From the horse country
Rohun

Roland (German) From the renowned land
*Roeland, Rolando, Roldan, Roley, Rollan,
Rolland, Rollie, Rollin, Rollins, Rollo,
Rolly, Rowland*

Rolf (Scandinavian) Form of Rudolph,
meaning "a famous wolf"
Rolfe, Rolph, Rolphe, Rolt, Rolte

Roman (Latin) A citizen of Rome
*Romain, Romaine, Romanes, Romano,
Romanos, Romanus, Romayn, Romayne,
Romaen, Romaene, Rome, Romeo, Romi,
Romie, Romee, Romea, Romy, Romey*

Romney (Welsh) From the winding river
Romny, Romni, Romnie, Romnee, Romnea

Romulus (Latin) In mythology, along with
his twin brother Remus, one of the founders
of Rome
Romolo, Roemello, Romulo

Ron (English) Form of Ronald, meaning
"the king's advisor"
*Ronn, Ronnie, Ronni, Ronny, Ronney,
Ronnee, Ronnea, Roni, Ronie, Rony,
Roney, Ronea, Ronee, Rohn, Rahn*

Ronak (Scandinavian) A powerful man
Ronack, Ronac

Ronald (Norse) The king's advisor
*Ranald, Renaldo, Ronal, Ronaldo,
Rondale, Roneld, Ronell, Ronello, Ronson*

Ronan (Gaelic) Resembling a little seal

Ronel (Israeli) The song of God
Ronele, Ronen, Ronnel, Ronnen

Rong (Chinese) Having glory

Ronin (Japanese) A samurai who doesn't
have a master
Ronyn

Ronith (Hindi) A charming man
Ronithe, Ronyth, Ronythe

Rook (English) Resembling a raven
Rooke, Rouk, Rouke, Ruck, Ruk

Rooney (Gaelic) A red-haired man
*Roony, Rooni, Roonie, Roonea, Roonee,
Roon, Roone*

Roopesh (Hindi) A handsome man
*Roupesh, Rupesh, Rupad, Roopad,
Roupad*

Roosevelt (Danish) From the field of roses
Rosevelt

Roper (English) One who makes rope
Rapere

Rory (Gaelic) A red-haired man
*Rori, Rorey, Rorie, Rorea, Roree, Rorry,
Rorrey, Rorri, Rorrie, Rorrea, Rorree,
Rorik, Rorric, Rorrik, Roric*

Rosario (Spanish) Refers to the rosary
*Rasario, Rasareo, Rosareo, Rosalio,
Rosaleo, Rasalio, Rasaleo*

Roscoe (German) From the forest of deer
*Rosco, Rosscoe, Rossco, Rosko, Rossko,
Roskoe, Rosskoe*

Roser (American) A red-haired man
Rozer

Roshan (Persian) Born during the daylight
*Roshaun, Roshawn, Roeshan, Roeshaun,
Roeshawn*

Rosk (American) One who is swift
Roske, Rosck, Roscke, Rosc, Rosce

Roslin (Gaelic) A little red-haired boy
*Roslyn, Rosselin, Rosslyn, Rozlin, Rozlyn,
Rosling, Rozling*

Ross (Gaelic) From the headland
*Rosse, Rossell, Rossiter, Rosston, Ros,
Rossano*

Rossain (American) Filled with hope
Rossaine, Rossaen, Rossaene, Rossayn,
Rossayne, Rossane

Roswald (German) Of the mighty horses
Rosswald, Roswalt, Rosswalt

Roswell (English) A fascinating man
Rosswell, Rozwell, Roswel, Rozwel

Roth (German) A red-haired man
Rothe

Rothwell (Norse) From the red spring
Rothwel, Rothewell, Rothewel

Roupen (American) A quiet little boy
Roupan, Roupin, Roupyn, Roupon,
Roupun

Rousseau (French) A little red-haired boy
Roussell, Russo, Rousse, Roussel, Rousset,
Rousskin

Rover (English) A traveler; wanderer
Rovor, Rovir, Rovyr, Rovar, Rovur, Rovere

Rovonte (French) A roving man
Rovontay, Rovontaye, Rovontae, Rovontai

Rowan (Gaelic) From the tree with red
berries; a little red-haired boy
Rowen, Rowin, Rowyn, Rowon, Rowun,
Roan, Roane

Rowdon (English) From the rough hill
Rowdun, Rowden, Rowdan, Rowdin,
Rowdyn

Rowdy (English) A boisterous man
Rowdey, Rowdi, Rowdie, Rowdee,
Rowdea

Rowell (English) From the spring of the
roe deer
Rowel, Roewel, Roewell

Rowley (English) From the rough meadow
Rowly, Rowli, Rowlie, Rowlea, Rowleah,
Rowlee, Rowleigh

Rowtag (Native American) Born of fire
Roetag, Rotag

Roxbert (English) A bright raven
Roxberte, Roxberth, Roxberthe, Roxburt,
Roxburte, Roxburth, Roxburthe

Roxbury (English) From the raven's
fortress
Roxburry, Roxbery, Roxberry, Roxburghe

Roy (Gaelic / French) A red-haired man / a
king
Roye, Roi, Royer, Ruy

Royal (English) Of the king; a regal man
Royale, Royall, Royle

Royce (German / French) A famous man /
son of the king
Roice, Royse, Roise

Royd (English) A good-humored man
Roid, Royde, Roide

Royden (English) From the rye hill
Roydon, Roydan, Roydin, Roydyn, Roydun

Royston (English) From Royce's town
Roystun, Roystown

Rozen (Hebrew) A great ruler
Rozin, Rozyn, Rozon, Rozun

Ruadhan (Irish) A red-haired man; the
name of a saint
Ruadan, Ruadhagan, Ruadagan

Ruarc (Irish) A famous ruler
Ruarck, Ruarcc, Ruark, Ruarkk, Ruaidhri,
Ruaidri

Rubio (Spanish) Resembling a ruby

Rudd (English) One who has a ruddy
complexion
Ruddy, Ruddey, Ruddee, Ruddea, Ruddi,
Ruddie

Rudeger (German) A friendly man
Rudegar, Rudger, Rudgar, Rudiger, Rudigar

Rudo (African) A loving man
Rudoe, Rudow, Rudowe

Rudolph (German) A famous wolf
Rodolfo, Rodolph, Rodolphe, Rodolpho,
Rudy, Rudey, Rudi, Rudie, Rudolf,
Rudolfo, Rudolpho, Rudolphus, Rudee

Rudyard (English) From the red paddock

Rufaro (African) Filled with happiness
Ruffaro

Ruff (French) A red-haired man
Ruffe, Ruffin, Rufin, Rufio, Ruffio, Rufeo,
Ruffeo, Rufo, Ruffo

Ruford (English) From the red ford; from
the rough ford
Ruforde, Rufford, Rufforde

R

Rufus (Latin) A red-haired man
Ruffus, Rufous, Ruffous, Rufino, Ruffino

Rugby (English) From the rock fortress
Rugbey, Rugbi, Rugbie, Rugbee, Rugbea

Rui (French) A regal man

Ruiz (Spanish) A good friend

Rujul (Indian) An honest man
Rujool, Rujoole, Rujule, Rujoul, Rujoule

Rulon (Native American) A spirited man
Rullon, Rulonn, Rullonn

Rumford (English) From the broad ford
Rumforde, Rumferd, Rumferde, Rumfurd, Rumfurde

Rumford (English) From the broad river crossing
Rumforde

Rumor (American) A falsity spread by word of mouth
Rumer, Rumur, Rumir, Rumyr, Rumar

Runako (African) A handsome man
Runacko, Runaco, Runacco, Runakko

Russell (French) A little red-haired boy
Russel, Roussell, Russ, Rusel, Rusell

Russom (African) The chief; the boss
Rusom, Russome, Rusome

Ruston (English) From the red-haired man's estate
Rustun, Rustown, Rusten, Rustin, Rustyn, Rustan

Rusty (English) One who has red hair or a ruddy complexion
Rustey, Rusti, Rustie, Rustee, Rustea, Rust, Ruste, Rustice

Rutherford (English) From the cattle's ford
Rutherfurd, Rutherferd, Rutherforde, Rutherfurde, Rutherferde

Rutland (Norse) From the root land; from the red land
Rotland, Rootland, Routland

Rutledge (Norse / English) From the red ledge / from the root ledge
Routledge, Rotledge, Rootledge

Rutley (English) From the root meadow
Rutly, Rutli, Rutlie, Rutlee, Rutleigh, Rutlea, Rutleah

RYAN

When I was expecting, my husband and I couldn't decide on a name. He liked traditional names, and I wanted a more trendy one. When we came across Ryan, it was the perfect compromise—not too traditional and not too trendy. His middle name, Richard, honors my father, who passed away before my son was born. —Michelle, IN

R

Rune (Norse) A secret

Rupert (English) Form of Robert, meaning "one who is bright with fame"
Ruprecht

Rush (English) One who lives near the marsh plants
Rushe, Rusch, Rusche, Rysc

Rushford (English) From the ford with rushes
Rusheford, Rushforde, Rusheforde, Ryscford

Rushkin (French) A little red-haired boy
Ruskin

Rusk (Spanish) An innovator
Rusck, Rusc, Ruske, Ruskk, Ruscc

Ruvim (Hebrew) One who is meaningful
Roovim, Rouvim, Ruvym, Roovym, Rouvym

Ryan ○ ○ (Gaelic) The little ruler; little king
Rian, Rien, Rion, Ryen, Ryon, Ryun, Rhyan, Rhyen, Rhyon, Rhyun, Rhian, Rhien, Ryne, Ryn, Rynn

Rycroft (English) From the rye field
Ryecroft, Rygecroft

Ryder (English) An accomplished horseman
Rider, Ridder, Ryden, Rydell, Rydder

Rye (English / Irish) Resembling the grain / from the island's meadow
Ry

Ryker (Danish) Form of Richard, meaning "a powerful ruler"
Riker

Ryland (English) From the place where rye is grown
Ryeland, Rylan, Ryelan, Ryle, Rygeland

Ryley (English) From the rye clearing
Ryly, Ryli, Rylie, Rylee, Ryleigh, Rylea, Ryleah, Riley, Rily, Rili, Rilie, Rilee, Rilea, Rileah, Rileigh

Ryman (English) A rye merchant
Ryeman, Rymann, Ryemann, Rygeman, Rygemann

Rypan (Anglo-Saxon) One who plunders

Ryton (English) From the rye town
Ryeton, Rytown, Ryetown, Rytun, Ryetun

Ryu (Japanese) A dragon

Ryuichi (Japanese) First son of the dragon
Ryuichie, Ryuichy, Ryuichey, Ryuichee, Ryuichea

Ryuji (Japanese) The dragon man
Ryujie, Ryujy, Ryujey, Ryujea, Ryujee

Saad (Aramaic) One who offers help; the Lord's helper
Saada, Saadya, Saadiya, Saadyo, Saadiyo, Saahdia, Saahdya, Saahdiya, Seadya, Seadiya

Saarik (Hindi) Resembling a small songbird
Saarick, Saaric, Sarik, Sarick, Saric, Saariq, Sareek, Sareeq, Sariq

Sabah (Arabic) Born during the morning hours
Saba, Sabbah, Sabba

Saber (French) Man of the sword
Sabere, Sabr, Sabre

Sabih (Arabic) A handsome man
Sabeeh, Sabeih, Sabieh, Sabeah, Sabyh

Sabino (Latin) Of a tribe of ancient Italy
Sabeeno, Sabeino, Sabieno, Sabeano, Sabin, Savin, Savino, Saveeno, Savieno, Saveino, Saveano, Sabian, Sabien

Sabir (Arabic) One who is patient
Sabyr, Sabeer, Sabear, Sabeir, Sabier, Sabri, Sabrie, Sabree, Sabry, Sabrey

Sable (English) One who is sleek
Sabel

Saburo (Japanese) The third-born son
Saburio, Saburiyo

Sacha (Russian) Form of Alexander, meaning "helper and defender of mankind"
Sascha, Sasha, Socha, Soscha, Sosha, Sashenka, Shura, Schura, Shoura, Schoura

Sachairi (Gaelic) Form of Zachary, meaning "the Lord remembers"
Sachary, Sachari, Sacharie, Sakary, Sakari, Sakarie, Sakarey, Sachery, Sacheri, Sacherie, Sackery, Sackerey, Sackeri, Sackerie

Sachar (Hebrew) One who is rewarded
Sacar

Sachchit (Indian) One who is conscious of the truth
Sachchyt, Sachchite, Sachchyte, Sachet, Sachyt, Sachit

Sachetan (Indian) One who is animated
Sacheten, Sacheton, Sachetyn, Sachetin, Sachetun

Sacheverell (French) Resembling a leaping buck
Sacheverel, Sacheverele, Sachie, Sachy, Sachi, Sachey, Sachee, Sachea

Sachiel (Hebrew) An archangel
Sachiele, Sachiell, Sachielle

Sachio (Japanese) One who is fortunately born
Sachiyo

Sackville (English) From the Saxton's town
Sakville, Sacville

Sadaka (African) A religious offering
Sadakah, Sadakka, Sadakkah

Saddam (Arabic) A powerful ruler; the crusher
Saddum, Saddim, Saddym

Sadiki (African) One who is faithful
Sadikie, Sadiky, Sadikey, Sadikee, Sadikea, Sadyki, Sadykie, Sadyky, Sadykey, Sadykee, Sadykea

S

Sadiq (Arabic) A beloved friend
Sadeeq, Sadyq, Sadeaq, Sadeek, Sadeak, Sadyk, Sadik

Sadler (English) One who makes harnesses
Saddler, Sadlar, Saddlar, Sadlor, Saddlor

Sadwrn (Welsh) Form of Saturn, in mythology, god of agriculture

Sae (American) A talkative man
Saye, Say, Sai

Saehrimnir (Norse) In mythology, a magical boar

Safar (Arabic) A devout man

Safford (English) From the willow ford
Safforde, Saford, Saforde, Salford, Salforde, Salhford, Salhforde

Saffron (English) Resembling the yellow flower
Saffrone, Saffronn, Saffronne, Safron, Safronn, Safronne, Saffran, Saffren, Saphron, Saphran, Saphren

Saga (American) A storyteller
Sago

Sagar (Indian / English) A king / one who is wise
Saagar, Sagarr, Saagarr

Sagaz (Spanish) One who is clever
Sagazz

Sage (English) Wise one; type of spice
Saige, Sayge, Saege, Saje, Saije, Sayje, Saeje

Saghir (Arabic) One who is short in stature
Sagheer, Saghyr, Saghier, Sagheir, Saghear, Sager

Saginaw (Native American) A bold and courageous man
Sagynaw, Saginau, Sagynau

Sagiv (Hebrew) Having great strength
Sagev, Segiv, Segev

Sagramour (English) In Arthurian legend, a knight
Sagremour, Sagramor, Sagramore, Sagremor, Sagremore

Saguaro (American) Resembling the cactus
Seguaro, Saguariyo, Seguariyo

Sagwau (Chinese) A silly young man
Sagwaw

Sahadev (Hindi) The son of a king
Sahadiv, Sahadyv, Sahdev, Sahdiv, Sahdyv

Sahaj (Indian) One who is natural

Sahale (Native American) Resembling a falcon
Sahail, Sahaile, Sahayl, Sahayle, Sahan, Sahane, Sahain, Sahaine, Sahayn, Sahayne, Sahaen, Sahaene, Sahael, Sahaele, Sahen

Sahansan (African) One who travels with caution

Sahas (Indian) One who shows bravery

Sahib (Indian) Lord of the house
Sahyb, Sahibe, Sahybe, Saheeb, Saheebe, Saheab, Saheabe, Sahieb, Sahiebe, Saheib, Saheibe

Sahil (Indian) A great leader
Sahile, Saheel, Saheele, Saheal, Saheale, Sahel, Sahele, Saheil, Saheile, Sahiel, Sahiele, Sahyl, Sahyle

Sahir (Arabic) One who is alert and aware
Sahire, Saheer, Sahear, Sahyr, Saheir, Sahier, Saher, Sahran

Sahyadri (Indian) From the mountain range
Sahyadrie, Sahyadry, Sahyadrey, Sahyadree, Sahyadrea

Said (Arabic) Filled with happiness
Saeed, Saiyid, Sayeed, Sayid, Syed, Sa'id, Sa'eed, Saied

Saidi (African) One who helps others
Saidie, Saidee, Saidey, Saidy, Saedi, Saedie, Saedy, Saedey, Saedee, Saydi, Saydie, Saydy, Saydey, Saydee

Saieshwar (Hindi) A well-known saint
Saishwar

Sailor (American) Man who sails the seas
Sailer, Sailar, Saylor, Sayler, Saylar, Saelor, Saeler, Saelar, Sail, Saile, Sayle, Saele

Sainsbury (English) From the saint's settlement
Sansbury, Saynsbury, Saensbury, Sainsberry, Saynsberry, Saensberry, Sansberry

Saint (Latin) A holy man
Sainte, Saent, Saente, Saynt, Saynte

Sairam (Hindi) A well-known saint
Sayram, Saeram

Saith (English) One who is well-spoken
Saithe, Sayth, Saythe, Saeth, Saethe, Sath, Sathe

Sajal (Indian) Resembling a cloud
Sajall, Sajjal, Sajjall

Sajan (Indian) One who is dearly loved
Sajann, Sajjan, Sajjann

Sajid (Arabic) One who worships God
Sajeed, Sajyd, Sajead, Sajeid, Sajied

Sakeri (Hebrew) The Lord has remembered
Sakerie, Sakery, Sakerey, Sakeree, Sakerea

Saki (Japanese) One who is cloaked
Sakie, Saky, Sakey, Sakee, Sakea

Sakima (Native American) A king
Sakeema, Sakyma, Sakema, Sakeima, Sakiema, Sakeama

Saku (Japanese) The remembrance of the Lord
Sakue, Sakoo

Salaam (African) Resembling a peach

Saladin (Arabic) One who is righteous in his faith
Saladen

Salado (Spanish) A humorous man
Saladio, Saladiyo

Salah (Arabic) A righteous man
Sala, Salla, Sallah

Salehe (African) A good man
Saleh, Salih

Salil (Indian) Of the water
Saleel, Saleil, Saliel, Salyl, Saleal

Salim (Arabic) One who is peaceful
Saleem, Salem, Selim

Salisbury (English) From the willow settlement
Sallsbury, Salisbery, Salisberry, Saulsberry, Saulsbery, Saulsbury, Saulisbury

Salman (Arabic) One who provides security
Salmann, Saman, Samann

Saloman (Hebrew) One who is peaceful
Salomon, Salamon, Salaman

Saltiel (Hebrew) Asked of God
Shaltiel, Saltiele, Shaltiele, Saltielle, Shaltielle

Salton (English) One who lives near the willow settlement
Salten, Saltan, Saltun, Salhton, Salhtun

Salus (Greek) In mythology, goddess of health
Salas, Sales, Salos

Salute (American) A patriotic man
Saloot, Saloote, Salout, Saloute

Salvador (Latin) A savior
Sal, Salvator, Salvatore, Salvidor, Salvino, Sauveur, Salvadore, Salvatorio, Salbatore, Soterios

Salvio (Latin) One who has been saved
Salvian, Salviano, Salviatus, Salviyo

Samadarshi (Indian) One who is unbiased
Samadarshie, Samadarshy, Samadarshey, Samadarshee, Samadarshea

Samanjas (Indian) One who is proper

Samantaka (Indian) A destroyer of peace

Samarth (Indian) A powerful man; one who is efficient
Samarthe

Sambaran (Indian) An ancient king

Sambhddha (Indian) Having great wisdom

Sameen (Indian) One who is treasured
Samine, Sameene, Samean, Sameane, Samyn, Samyne

Sameh (Arabic) A forgiving man
Samih

Sami (Arabic) One who has been exalted
Samie, Samy, Samey, Samee, Samea

Samir (Arabic) A special man
Sameer, Samyr, Samier, Sameir, Samear, Samere

Samiran (Indian) As gentle as a breeze
Samyran, Sameeran, Samearan, Sameran

Samman (Arabic) One who sells groceries
Sammen, Sammon

Sammohan (Indian) An attractive man
Sammohane

Sampath (Indian) A wealthy man
Sampathe, Sampat

Sampooran (Indian) One who is blissful
Sampoornanand

Sampreet (Indian) One who is content
Sampreyt, Sampryt, Sampriet, Sampreit, Sampreat

Samrakshan (Indian) One who is protected

Sanderson (English) Son of Alexander
Sanders, Saunders, Saunderson, Sandros, Sanersone

Sandhurst (English) From the sandy thicket
Sanhurst, Sandherst, Sanherst, Sandhirst, Sanhirst

Sanditon (English) From the sandy town
Sandton, Santon

Sandon (English) From the sandy hill
Sanden, Sandan, Sandun, Sandyn, Sandin

SAM

We named our son Samuel Edward. We always loved the name Sam, and Edward is a tribute to Sam's grandfather. We're so happy we chose that name. He's really grown into it! —Elaine, IL

Samson (Hebrew) As bright as the sun; in the Bible, a man with extraordinary strength
Sampson, Sansom, Sanson, Sansone

Samudra (Indian) The lord of the ocean
Samudrasen, Samudras

Samuel ✪ ✪ (Hebrew) God has heard
Sam, Sammie, Sammy, Samuele, Samuello, Samwell, Samuelo, Sammey, Sammi, Sammee, Sammea, Samoel, Sammoel, Samuka, Schmuel

Samuru (Japanese) The name of God

Samvel (Hebrew) One who knows the name of God
Samvell, Samvele, Samvelle

Sanam (Indian) One who is dearly loved

Sanborn (English) From the sandy brook
Sanborne, Sanbourn, Sanburn, Sanburne, Sandborn, Sandbourne

Sancho (Spanish) One who is sacred
Sanche, Sanctio, Sancos, Sanzio, Sauncho

Sandaidh (Gaelic) Form of Alexander, meaning "helper and defender of mankind"

Sandburg (English) From the sandy village
Sandbergh, Sandberg, Sandburgh

Sandeepen (Indian) A wise man; a sage
Sandepen, Sandeapen, Sandypen, Sandipen

Sander (German) Form of Alexander, meaning "helper and defender of mankind"
Sandino, Sandor, Sender, Sandy, Sandi, Sandie, Sandee, Sandea, Sandro, Sandu

Sanford (English) From the sandy crossing
Sandford, Sanforde, Sandforde, Sanfurd, Sanfurde, Sandfurd, Sandfurde

Sang (Vietnamese) A bright man
Sange

Sani (Native American) The old one
Sanie, Sany, Saney, Sanee, Sanea

Sanjay (Indian) One who is victorious
Sanjaye, Sanjae, Sanjai

Sanjeet (Indian) One who is invincible
Sanjyt, Sanjit, Sanjeat, Sanjeit, Sanjiet

Sanjiro (Japanese) An admirable man
Sanjyro

Sanjiv (Indian) One who lives a long life
Sanjeev, Sanjyv, Sanjeiv, Sanjiev, Sanjeav, Sanjivan

Sanketh (Indian) A sign or symbol
Sankethe, Sanket

Sanobar (Indian) From the palm tree

Sanorelle (American) An honest man
Sanorell, Sanorel, Sanorele

Sansone (Italian) Having great strength

Santana (Spanish) A saintly man
Santanna, Santanah, Santannah, Santa

Santiago (Spanish) Refers to Saint James
Sandiago, Sandiego, Santeago, Santiaco, Santigo

S

Santo (Italian) A holy man
Sante, Santino, Santos, Santee, Santi, Santie, Santea, Santy, Santey

Santob (Hebrew) One who has a good name
Shemtob

Santosh (Indian) One who is content
Santoshe

Sanyu (Japanese) Filled with happiness
Sanyoo, Sanyue

Sapan (Indian) A dream or vision
Sapann

Sapir (Hebrew) Resembling a sapphire
Safir, Saphir, Saphiros, Safiros, Sapyr, Saphyr, Sapfyr, Sapyre, Saphyre, Safyre

Saquib (Indian) A bright man
Saquyb

Sar (Anglo-Saxon) One who inflicts pain
Sarlic, Sarlik

Sarat (Indian) A wise man; a sage
Saratt, Sarrat, Sharad

Sarbajit (Indian) The conquerer
Sarbajeet, Sarbajyt, Sarbajeat, Sarbajet, Sarvajit, Sarvajeet, Sarvajyt, Sarvajeat

Sarda (African) One who is in a hurry
Sardah

Sarday (American) A sociable man
Sardaye, Sardai, Sardae

Sarfaraz (Indian) One who walks with his head held high
Safarez

Sargent (French) Officer of the army
Sarge, Sergeant, Sergent, Serjeant, Sargeant

Sarki (African) A chief
Sarkie, Sarky, Sarkey, Sarkee, Sarkea

Sarkis (Armenian) Born to royalty
Sarkiss, Sarkisse, Sarkys, Sarkyss, Sarkysse

Sarojin (Hindu) Resembling a lotus
Saroj

Sarosh (Persian) One who prays
Saroshe

Sarsour (Arabic) Resembling a bug

Sartaj (Indian) One who is crowned

Sarthak (Indian) One who is fulfilled
Sarthac, Sarthack

Sarvagya (Indian) One who is all-knowing
Sarvagiya

Sashreek (Indian) One who is prosperous
Sashrik, Sashreak, Sashryk

Sassacus (Native American) A wild man
Sasacus, Sassakus, Sasakus

Sasson (Hebrew) Filled with joy
Sassen, Sassun, Sassin, Sassyn

Satayu (Hindi) In Hinduism, the brother of Amavasu and Vivasu
Satayoo, Satayou, Satayue

Satchel (Latin) A small bag
Satchell, Sachel, Sachell

Satordi (French) Form of Saturn, in mythology, god of agriculture
Satordie, Satordy, Satordey, Satordee, Satordea

Satoshi (Japanese) Born from the ashes
Satoshie, Satoshy, Satoshey, Satoshee, Satoshea

Satparayan (Indian) A good-natured man

Satu (Japanese) From a fairy tale
Satue, Satoo, Satou

Saturday (American) Born on a Saturday
Saterday, Saturdai, Saterdai, Saturdae, Saterdae, Saturdaye, Saterdaye

Saturn (Latin) In mythology, the god of agriculture
Saturnin, Saturno, Saturnino

Satyanand (Indian) One who has found true happiness
Satyanande

Satyankar (Indian) One who speaks the truth
Satyancar, Satyancker

Satyaprakash (Indian) Glowing with the light of truth

Satyavanth (Indian) One who is honest
Satyavanthe, Satyavant, Satyavante, Satyavan

Saud (Arabic) A fortunate man

S

Saul (Hebrew) One who was prayed for
*Saulo, Shaul, Sol, Sollie, Solli, Sollee,
Sollea, Solly, Solley*

Saunak (Indian) A child sage
Saunac, Saunack, Sawnak, Sawnac, Sawnack

Savage (American) A wild man
Savag, Savaje, Savaj

Saviero (Spanish) Form of Xavier, meaning
"owner of a new house / one who is bright"
Savyero, Saverio, Saveriyo

Saville (French) From the willow town
*Savil, Savile, Savill, Savyile, Savylle, Savyle,
Sauville, Sauvile, Sauvil*

Savir (Indian) A great leader
*Savire, Saveer, Saveere, Savear, Saveare,
Savyr, Savyre*

Savoy (French) From the kingdom in France
Savoye, Savoi

Savyon (Hebrew) Resembling the yellow weed
Savion, Savionn

Sawyer (English) One who works with
wood
Sawyere, Sayer, Sawyers, Sayers, Sayres, Saer

Saxe (Swedish) Man from Saxonny
Sachs, Sachsen

Saxon (English) A swordsman
Saxen, Saxan, Saxton, Saxten, Saxtan

Sayad (Arabic) An accomplished hunter

Sayam (Indian) Born in the evening

Sayed (Indian) A great leader

Sayyid (Arabic) The master

Scadwielle (English) From the shed near
the spring
*Scadwyelle, Scadwiell, Scadwyell,
Scadwiel, Scadwyel, Scadwiele, Scadwyele*

Scafell (English) From the mountain

Scand (Anglo-Saxon) One who is disgraced
Scande, Scandi, Scandie, Scandee, Scandea

Scandleah (English) From the noisy meadow
*Scandlea, Scandlee, Scandlie, Scandli,
Scandly, Scandley, Scandleigh, Shandley,
Shandly, Shandlee, Shandli, Shandlie,
Shandleigh, Shandlea, Shandleah*

Scanlon (Irish) A devious young man
Scanlun, Scanlin, Scanlyn, Scanlen, Scanlan

Scanlon (Irish) A little trapper
*Scanlan, Scanlen, Scanlun, Scanlin,
Scanlyn, Scannalan, Scannalon, Scannalen*

Scant (American) A man of small stature
*Scante, Scanti, Scantie, Scanty, Scantey,
Scantee, Scantea*

Scead (Anglo-Saxon) One who provides
shade
Sceadu, Sceadue, Sceadou

Sceotend (Anglo-Saxon) An archer

Schae (American) One who is cautious
Schay, Schaye, Schai

Schaeffer (German) A steward
*Schaffer, Shaeffer, Shaffer, Schaeffur,
Schaffur, Shaeffur, Shaffur*

Schelde (English) From the river
Shelde

Schmidt (German) A blacksmith
Schmit, Schmitt

Schneider (German) A tailor
Shneider, Sneider, Snider, Snyder

Schubert (German) One who makes shoes
*Shubert, Schuberte, Shuberte, Schubirt,
Shubirt, Schuburt, Shuburt*

Schultz (German) The town's magistrate

Schuyler (Danish) A scholarly man
Schuylar, Schylar, Schyler, Skuyler

Scipio (Latin) A legendary general

Scipio (Greek) A great leader
Scipiyo, Scypio, Scypyo, Scypiyo

Scirloc (English) A blonde-haired man
*Scirlok, Scirlock, Scyrloc, Scyrlok,
Scyrlock*

Scirocco (Italian) Of the warm wind
Sirocco, Scyrocco, Syrocco

Scorpio (Latin) The scorpion; the eighth
sign of the zodiac
Skorpio, Scorpios, Skorpios

Scott (English) A man from Scotland
*Scot, Scottie, Scotto, Scotty, Scotti, Scottey,
Scottee, Scottea, Scottas*

Scout (American) An explorer
Scoutt, Scoutte, Skout, Skoutt, Skoutte

Scowyrhta (Anglo-Saxon) One who makes shoes

Scribner (English) A scribe
Skribner, Scribnar, Skribnar

Scully (Irish) A herald; the town crier
Sculley, Sculli, Scullie, Scullee, Scullea, Sculleigh, Scolaighe

Scur (Anglo-Saxon) Born during a storm
Scurr

Seabert (English) Of the shining sea
Seabright, Sebert, Seibert, Seebert, Seybert, Siebert, Seaburt, Seburt, Seiburt, Seeburt, Seyburt, Sieburt, Saebeorht

Seabrook (English) From the stream by the sea
Seabrooke, Seabroc, Seabrok, Seabrock

Seabury (English) From the village by the sea
Seaburry, Sebury, Seburry, Seaberry, Seabery, Seberry, Sebery

Seadon (English) From the hill by the sea

Seafraid (Irish) One who receives peace from God
Seafrayd, Seafraed, Seafra, Seafrah

Seaghda (Irish) A majestic man

Seal (English) Resembling the animal
Seale, Seel, Seele

Seaman (English) A mariner

Seamere (Anglo-Saxon) A tailor

Seamus (Irish) Form of James, meaning "he who supplants"
Seumas, Seumus, Shamus, Shemus, Sekove, Sheamus

Sean ○ (Irish) Form of John, meaning "God is gracious"
Shaughn, Shawn, Shaun, Shon, Shohn, Shonn, Shaundre, Shawnel, Shawnell, Shawnn, Shandon, Shaunden

Seanachan (Irish) One who is wise

Seanan (Hebrew / Irish) A gift from God / an old, wise man
Sinon, Senen, Siobhan

Seanlaoch (Irish) An elderly hero

Searbhreathach (Irish) One who is judicious

Searle (English) An armored man
Serle, Searl, Serl, Searlas, Searlus, Searles, Searcy, Searci, Searcey, Searcie, Searcee, Searcea

Seaton (English) From the town by the sea
Seeton, Seton, Seatown, Seetown, Setown

Seaver (Anglo-Saxon) From the fierce stronghold
Seever, Seiver, Siever, Seyver, Sener, Sever

Sebag (Arabic) One who dyes cloth
Sabag

Sebastian ○ (Greek) The revered one
Sabastian, Seb, Sebastiano, Sebastien, Sebestyen, Sebo, Sebastyn, Sebestyen

Sebes (Hungarian) One who is swift

Secundo (Italian) The second-born son
Segundo

Sedge (English) A swordsman
Secg, Sege

Sedgley (English) From the meadow of the swordsman
Sedgly, Sedgli, Sedglie, Sedglee, Sedgleigh, Sedglea, Sedgeley, Sedgelee, Sedgeleigh, Sedgeli, Sedgelie, Sedgely, Sedgelea

Sedgwick (English) From the place of sword grass
Sedgewick, Sedgewyck, Sedgwyck, Sedgewic, Sedgewik, Sedgwic, Sedgwik, Sedgewyc, Sedgewyk, Sedgwyc, Sedgwyk, Secgwic

Seeley (French) One who is blessed
Seely, Seelee, Seelea, Seeli, Seelie, Sealey, Sealy, Seali, Sealie, Sealee, Sealea

Seerath (Indian) A great man
Seerathe, Searath, Searathe

Sef (Egyptian) Son of yesterday
Sefe

Seferino (Greek) Of the west wind
Seferio, Sepherino, Sepherio, Seferyno, Sepheryno

Seff (Hebrew) Resembling a wolf
Seffe

S

Sefton (English) From the village in the rushes

Sefu (African) One who wields a sword
Sefue, Sefoo, Sefou

Segenam (Native American) One who is lazy

Seger (English) Warrior of the sea
Seager, Segar, Seagar, Saeger

Seghen (African) Resembling an ostrich
Seghan, Seghin, Seghyn

Seif (Arabic) Wielding a sword of faith
Sayf, Saef, Saif

Seignour (French) Lord of the house

Seiji (Japanese) One who manages the affairs of the state
Seijie, Seijy, Seijey, Seijee, Seijea

Seiko (Japanese) The force of truth

Sein (Spanish) One who is innocent
Seine

Sekai (African) One who laughs often
Sekani, Sekanie, Sekany, Sekaney, Sekanee, Sekanee

Sekou (African) A learned man

Sela (Hebrew) Man from the cliff
Selah

Selas (African) Refers to the Trinity
Selassi, Selassie, Selassy, Selassey, Selassee, Selassea

Selby (English) Of the manor of the farm
Selbey, Selbi, Selbie, Selbee, Selbye, Selbea, Seleby, Selebey, Selebi, Selebie, Selebee, Selebea

Seldon (English) From the valley of willows
Selldon, Selden, Sellden, Seldan, Selldan, Seldun, Selldun, Salhdene, Saldene

Selestino (Spanish) One who is heaven-sent
Selestyno, Selesteeno, Selesteano

Selig (German) One who is blessed
Seligman, Seligmann, Selyg, Selygman, Selygmann, Selik, Selyk, Selick, Selyck, Selic, Selyc, Saelac, Saelig

Selkirk (Scottish) Man of the church
Selkyrk, Selkirck, Selkyrck

Sellers (English) One who dwells in the marshland
Sellars, Sellurs, Sellirs, Sellyrs

Selvon (American) A gregarious man
Selvonn, Selvonne, Selvawn, Selvaun, Selvaughn

Selwyn (English) A friend of the manor
Selwynn, Selwynne, Selwin, Selwinn, Selwinne, Selwen, Selwenn, Selwenn, Selwenne

Seminole (Native American) A tribal name
Semynole

Sen (Japanese) A wood sprite

Senan (Irish) The people's hero

Seneca (Native American) A tribal name
Senecka, Seneka

Senghor (African) A descendant of the gods
Sengor

Senior (French) The lord of the manor
Senor

Sennet (French) One who is elderly and wise
Sennett, Senet, Senett

Senon (Spanish) Born of Zeus; one who is lively
Sennon

Seoc (Gaelic) God is gracious
Seocan, Seok, Seokan

Seoras (Gaelic) One who works the earth; a farmer
Seorass, Seorasse

Seosaph (Hebrew) Form of Joseph, meaning "God will add"
Seosamh, Sepp

Seppanen (Finnish) A blacksmith
Sepanen, Seppenen, Sepenen, Seppanan, Sepanan

September (American) Born in the month of September
Septimber, Septymber, Septemberia, Septemberea

Septimus (Latin) The seventh-born child
Septymus

Sequoia (Native American) Of the giant redwood tree
Sequoya, Sequoiya, Sekoia, Sekoya, Sequoyah

Seraphim (Hebrew) The burning ones; heavenly winged angels
Sarafino, Saraph, Serafin, Serafino, Seraph, Seraphimus, Serafim

Sereno (Latin) One who is calm; tranquil

Serfati (Hebrew) A man from France
Sarfati, Serfatie, Sarfatie, Serfaty, Sarfaty, Serfatey, Sarfatey, Serfatee, Sarfatee

Sergio (Latin) An attendant; a servant
Seargeoh, Serge, Sergei, Sergeo, Sergey, Sergi, Sergios, Sergiu, Sergius, Sergiusz, Serguei, Serjio, Sirgio, Sirgios, Seriozha, Seriozhenka

Seriannu (Welsh) A sparkling man
Serian, Serianu

Servas (Latin) One who is redeemed
Servaas, Servacio, Servatus

Sesame (English) Resembling the flavorful seed
Sesami, Sesamie, Sesamy, Sesamey, Sesamee, Sesamea

Set (Hebrew) One who has been compensated
Sett, Shet, Shett

Seth (Hebrew) One who has been appointed
Sethe, Seath, Seathe

Seung (Korean) A victorious successor

Seven (American) Refers to the number; the seventh-born child
Sevin, Sevyn

Severin (Latin) One who is strict; stern
Severino, Severinus, Severo, Sevrin, Sevryn, Severyn, Severn, Severne, Seweryn, Severus, Severius, Severince, Severence, Severynce

Sevilin (Turkish) One who is dearly loved
Sevilen, Sevylin, Sevylen

Sevillano (Spanish) Man from Sevilla
Sevilano, Sevyllano, Sevylano, Sevillanio, Sevilanio

Sewall (English) Having the strength of the sea
Sewal, Sewald, Sewalde, Sewell, Saewald, Seawell

Seward (English) A guardian of the sea
Siward, Sewerd, Siwerd, Saeweard, Seaward

Sewati (Native American) Resembling a bear claw
Sewatie, Sewaty, Sewatey, Sewatee, Sewatea

Sexton (English) The church's custodian
Sextun, Sextan, Sextin, Sextyn

Sextus (Latin) The sixth-born child
Sesto, Sixto, Sixtus

Seymour (French) From the French town of Saint Maur
Seamore, Seamor, Seamour, Seymore

Shaan (Hebrew) A peaceful man

Shabab (Arabian) One who is youthful
Shaabab

Shabat (Hebrew) The last child
Shabbat, Shabatt, Shabbatt

Shabnam (Persian) Covered with the morning's dew

Shachar (Hebrew) Born with the morning's first light
Shachare, Shacharr

Shade (English) A secretive man
Shaid, Shaide, Shayd, Shayde, Shaed, Shaede

Shadi (Persian / Arabic) One who brings happiness and joy / a singer
Shadie, Shady, Shadey, Shadee, Shadea

Shadow (English) A mysterious man
Shadoe, Shado

Shadrach (Hebrew) Under the command of the moon god Aku
Shadrack, Shadrick, Shad, Shadd

Shadwell (English) From the shed near the spring
Shadwel

Shafiq (Arabic) One who is compassionate
Shafeeq, Shafik, Shafyq, Shafyk, Shafeek

Shafir (Hebrew) A handsome man
Shafeer, Shafier, Shafeir, Shafear, Shafyr, Shafar, Shefer

Shah (Persian) The king

S

Shahid (Indian) A patriot
Shaheed, Shahead, Shahyd, Shahide, Shaheede, Shaheade, Shahyde

Shahzad (Persian) Son of the king

Shai (Hebrew) A gift from God

Shail (Indian) A mountain rock
Shaile, Shayl, Shayle, Shael, Shaele, Shale

Shaiming (Chinese) Of the sunshine
Shaeming, Shayming, Shaimyng, Shaemyng, Shaymyng

Shaka (African) A tribal leader
Shakah

Shakib (Indian) One who is patient
Shakeeb, Shakeab, Shakyb

Shakil (Arabic) A handsome man
Shakeel, Shakhil, Shakyl, Shakill, Shakille, Shaquille, Shaq, Shaqeell, Shaque, Shaqueel, Shaquil, Shaquile

Shakir (Arabic) One who is grateful
Shakeer, Shaqueer, Shakier, Shakeir, Shakear, Shakar, Shaker, Shakyr

Shakti (Indian) A powerful man
Shaktie, Shakty, Shaktey, Shaktee, Shaktea

Shakur (Arabic) One who is thankful
Shakurr, Shaku

Shalom (Hebrew) A peaceful man
Sholom, Sholem, Shelomo, Shelomi, Shlomi, Shulamith, Shlomo

Shaman (Native American) A holy man
Shawman, Shamon, Shayman, Shaeman, Shaiman, Schamane, Shamain, Shamaen, Shamane, Shamayn

Shamir (Hebrew) A material that can cut stone
Shameer, Shamyr, Shameir, Shamier, Shamear

Shamshu (Indian) A handsome man
Shamshad, Shamshue

Shan (Chinese / Gaelic) Resembling coral / one who is wise and elderly
Shann, Shandon

Shanahan (Irish) One who is clever; wise
Seanachan, Shanahen, Seanachen, Shanihan, Shanyhan

Shance (American) Form of Chance, meaning having good fortune
Shancy, Shancey, Shanci, Shancie, Shancee, Shancea

Shandar (Indian) One who is proud
Shandarr

Shandy (English) A high-spirited man
Shandey, Shandee, Shandea, Shandi, Shandie

Shane (English) Form of John, meaning "God is gracious"
Shayn, Shayne, Shaen, Shaene, Shain, Shaine, Seaghan

Shani (Hebrew) A crimson-red color
Shanie, Shany, Shaney, Shanee, Shanea

Shanley (Gaelic) An ancient hero
Shanly, Shanle, Shanlee, Shanlea, Shanli, Shanlie, Shannly, Shannley, Shannlee, Shannle, Shannli, Shannlea, Shannlie

Shannon (Gaelic) Having ancient wisdom
Shanan, Shanen, Shannan, Shannen, Shanon

Shante (American) One who is poised
Shantae, Shantai, Shantay, Shantaye

Sharang (Indian) Resembling a deer
Sharange

Shardul (Indian) Resembling a tiger
Shardule, Shardull, Shardulle

Sharif (Arabic) One who is honored
Shareef, Sharyf, Sharief, Shareif, Shareaf, Sherif, Sheryf, Shereef, Shereaf, Sherief, Shereif

Shariq (Indian) An intelligent man
Shareeq, Shareaq, Shareq, Shareek, Sharik, Shareak, Sharyk, Sharyq

Shashi (Indian) Of the moonbeam
Shashie, Shashy, Shashey, Shashee, Shashea, Shashhi

Shashwat (Hindi) One who has a long life
Shashwatt, Shashwate, Shashwatte

Shasta (Native American) From the triple-peaked mountain
Shastah

Shatrujit (Indian) One who conquers his enemies
Shatrujeet, Shatrujyt

Shaunak (Indian) A well-known sage
Shawnak, Shanak, Shaunack, Shawnack, Shanack

Shavon (American) One who is open-minded
Shavaughn, Shavonne, Shavaun, Shovon, Shovonne, Shovaun, Shovaughn

Shaw (English) From the woodland
Shawe

Shawnee (Native American) A tribal name
Shawney, Shawny, Shawnea, Shawni, Shawnie

Shawon (American) One who is optimistic
Shawan, Shawaun, Shawaughn, Shawonne

Shayan (American) Form of Cheyenne, meaning "of the tribe of the Great Plains; of the unintelligible speakers"
Shayann, Sheyan, Sheyann, Shyane, Shyanne

Shaykeen (American) A successful man
Shaykean, Shaykein, Shakeyn, Shakine

Shea (Gaelic) An admirable man/from the fairy fortress
Shae, Shai, Shay, Shaye, Shaylon, Shays

Sheehan (Gaelic) A small and peaceful man
Sheyhan, Sheahan, Sheihan, Shiehan, Shyhan, Siodhachan

Sheen (English) A shining man
Sheene, Shean, Sheane

Sheffield (English) From the crooked field
Sheffeld

Sheiling (Scottish) From the summer pasture
Sheilyng, Sheeling, Shealing, Sheelyng, Shealyng

Shel (Hebrew) Our son

Shelby (English) From the willow farm
Shelbi, Shelbey, Shelbie, Shelbee, Shelbye, Shelbea

Sheldon (English) From the steep valley
Shelden, Sheldan, Sheldun, Sheldin, Sheldyn, Shel

Shelley (English) From the meadow's ledge
Shelly, Shelli, Shellie, Shellee, Shellea, Shelleigh, Shelleah

Shelton (English) From the farm on the ledge
Shellton, Sheltown, Sheltun, Shelten, Shelny, Shelney, Shelni, Shelnie, Shelnee, Shelnea, Skelton, Skeltun

Shem (Hebrew) Having a well-known name

Shen (Chinese) A spiritual man; one who is introspective

Sheng (Chinese) One who is victorious

Shepherd (English) One who herds sheep
Shepperd, Shep, Shepard, Shephard, Shepp, Sheppard

Shepley (English) From the meadow of sheep
Sheply, Shepli, Sheplie, Sheplea, Shepleah, Sheplee, Shepleigh, Sceapleigh

Sherborne (English) From the shining brook
Sherborn, Sherbourn, Sherburn, Sherburne, Sherbourne

Sheridan (Gaelic) A seeker
Sheredan, Sheridon, Sherridan, Seireadan, Sheriden, Sheridun, Sherard, Sherrard, Sherrerd, Shererd, Sherrod, Sherod

Sherill (English) From the bright hill
Sherrill, Sheryll, Sherryll

Sherlock (English) A fair-haired man
Sherlocke, Shurlock, Shurlocke

Sherman (English) One who cuts wool cloth
Shermon, Scherman, Schermann, Shearman, Shermann, Sherm, Sherme

Shermarke (African) One who brings good luck
Shermark

Sherrerd (English) From the open field
Shererd, Sherrard, Sherard

Sherrick (English) One who has already left
Sherryck, Sherrik, Sherick, Sherik, Sheryck

Sherwin (English) A bright friend
Sherwen, Sherwind, Sherwinn, Sherwyn, Sherwynn, Sherwynne, Sherwinne, Sherwenn, Sherwenne

S

Sherwood (English) From the bright forest
Sherwoode, Shurwood, Shurwoode

Shevon (American) A humorous man
Shevonne, Shevaun, Shevaughn

Shields (Gaelic) A faithful protector
Sheelds, Shealds

Shikha (Indian) A fiery man
Shykha

Shilah (Native American) One who is brotherly
Shylah, Shila, Shyla

Shiloh (Hebrew) He who was sent
Shilo, Shyloh, Shylo

Shing (Chinese) A victorious man
Shyng

Shino (Japanese) A bamboo stem
Shyno

Shipley (English) From the meadow of ships; from the meadow of sheep
Shiply, Shiplee, Shiplea, Shipleah, Shipli, Shiplie, Shipleigh

Shipton (English) From the ship town; from the sheep town

Shire (English) From the country
Shyre

Shiriki (Native American) Resembling a coyote
Shirikie, Shiriky, Shirikey, Shirikee, Shirikea, Shyriki, Shyryki, Shyryky

Shiro (Japanese) The fourth-born son
Shyro

Shishir (Indian) Born during the winter
Shyshir, Shyshyr, Shishyr, Shisheer, Shysheer

Shiva (Hindi) One who is good; lucky; in Hinduism, the god of destruction and restoration
Shivah, Sheeva, Sheevah, Siva, Sivah, Shiv

Shiye (Native American) Our son

Shoda (Japanese) From the level field

Shomer (Hebrew) The watchman

Shoney (Celtic) In mythology, god of the sea
Shony, Shoni, Shonie, Shonee, Shonea

Shontae (American) Filled with hope
Shontay, Shontaye, Shontai, Shauntae, Shauntay, Shauntaye, Shauntai, Shawntae, Shawntay, Shawntaye, Shawntae, Shonti, Shontie, Shonty, Shontey, Shontee, Shontea

Shoorsen (Indian) One who is brave
Shoursen, Shorsen

Shorty (American) A man who is small in stature
Shortey, Shorti, Shortie, Shortee, Shortea

Shoshone (Native American) A tribal name
Shoshoni, Shoshonie, Shoshonee, Shoshonea, Shoshony, Shoshoney

Shoval (Hebrew) One who walks the path
Shovall, Shovalle, Shovale

Shoval (Hebrew) One who is on the right path
Shovall, Shovalle

Shrenik (Indian) One who is organized
Shrenyk, Shrenick, Shrenyck, Shrenic, Shrenyc

Shreshta (Indian) The best; one who is superior

Shuang (Chinese) A bright man

Shubha (Indian) A lucky man
Shubhah, Shubham

Shubhang (Indian) A handsome man

Shunnar (Arabic) Resembling a bird; a pleasant man

Shuo (Chinese) One who achieves greatness

Shuraqui (Arabic) A man from the east

Shuu (Japanese) A responsible man

Si (Vietnamese) A gentleman
Sigh

Siamak (Persian) A bringer of joy
Syamak, Siamack, Syamack, Siamac, Syamac

Sicheii (Native American) One who is grandfatherly

Sicily (Italian) From the island
Sicilly, Sicili, Sicilie, Sicilee, Sicilea, Sicilley, Sicilli, Sicillie, Sicillee, Sicillea

S

Sidell (English) From the wide valley
Sidel, Sidelle, Sydel, Sydell, Siddel, Siddell,
Syddel, Syddell, Siddael, Sidael, Siddayl,
Sidayl

Sidney (English) From the wide meadow
Sydney, Sidni, Sidnie, Sidny, Sidnee, Sidnea,
Sydny, Sydni, Sydnie, Sydnee, Sydnea, Sid,
Syd

Sidonio (Latin) Man from Sidon
Sidono, Sidoniyo, Sydonio, Sydono,
Sydoniyo

Sidor (Russian) One who is talented
Sydor

Sidus (Latin) Resembling a star
Sydus, Sidos, Sydos

Sidwell (English) From the wide spring
Sydwell, Sidwel, Sydwel

Siegfried (German) One who enjoys the
peace of victory
Sygfried, Sigfred, Sigfrid, Sigfried, Sigfryd,
Sigvard, Sygfred, Sigfreid, Sigifrid, Sigifryd,
Sigifrith, Sigfrith, Sygfrith, Sygifrith

Sierra (Spanish) From the jagged mountain
range
Siera, Syerra, Syera, Seyera, Seeara

Sigbjorn (Norse) The victorious bear
Siegbjorn

Sigehere (English) One who is victorious
Sygehere, Sigihere, Sygihere

Sigenert (Anglo-Saxon) A king
Sygenert, Siginert, Syginert

Sigmund (German) The victorious protector
Seigmond, Segismond, Siegmund,
Sigismond, Sigismondo, Sigismund,
Sigismundo, Sigismundus, Sigmond,
Szymond, Sigurd, Sigvard

Signe (Scandinavian) A victorious man
Signy, Signey, Signi, Signie, Signee, Signea

Sigourney (Scandinavian / French) One
who conquers / a daring king
Sigourny, Sigourni, Sigournie, Sigournee,
Sigournye, Sigournea, Sigurney, Sigurny,
Sigurni, Sigurnie, Sigurnea, Sigurnee

Sigurd (Norse) The protector of victory
Sigerd, Sigurde, Sigerde, Seigurd, Seigurd

Sigwald (German) A victorious leader
Siegwald, Seigwald, Sigwalt, Siegwalt,
Seigwalt, Sigiwald, Sygwald, Sigiwalt,
Sygwalt

Sihtric (Anglo-Saxon) A king
Sihtrik, Sihtrick, Syhtric, Syhtrik, Syhtrick,
Sihtryc, Sihtryk, Sihtryck

Sike (Native American) A homebody
Syke

Sik'is (Native American) A friendly man

Sikyahonaw (Native American)
Resembling a yellow bear
Sikyahonau, Sykyahonaw, Sykyahonau

Sikyatavo (Native American) Resembling
a yellow rabbit

Silas (Latin) Form of Silvanus, meaning
"a woodland dweller"
Sylas, Siles, Silus, Syles, Sylus, Silous,
Sylous

Silko (African) A king
Sylko

Sill (English) A bright as a beam of light
Sills, Syll, Sylls

Silny (Czech) Having great strength
Silney, Silni, Silnie, Silnee, Silnea

Silsby (English) From Sill's farm
Sillsby, Silsbey, Sillsbey, Silsbi, Sillsbi,
Silsbie, Sillsbie, Silsbee, Sillsbee

Silvanus (Latin) A woodland dweller
Silvain, Silvano, Silverio, Silvino, Silvio,
Sylvanus, Sylvio, Silvaine, Silvaen, Silvaene,
Silvayn, Silvayne, Silvius, Silviu, Silvan,
Sylvan

Silver (English) A precious metal; a white-
skinned man
Sylver

Silverman (German) One who works with
silver
Sylverman, Silberman, Sylberman,
Silvermann, Sylvermann, Silbermann,
Sylbermann

Silverton (English) From the silver town
Sylverton, Silvertown, Sylvertown

Simba (African) Resembling a lion
Simbah, Symba, Symbah

S

Simbarashe (African) The power of God
*Simbarashi, Simbarashie, Simbarashy,
Simbarashey, Simbarashee*

Simcha (Hebrew) Filled with joy
Symcha, Simha, Symha

Simmons (Hebrew) The son of Simon
*Semmes, Simms, Syms, Simmonds,
Symonds, Simpson, Symms, Simson*

Simon (Hebrew) God has heard
*Shimon, Si, Sim, Samien, Semyon, Simen,
Simeon, Simone, Symon, Szymon, Siman,
Simu, Siomon, Simao, Symeon*

Sinai (Hebrew) From the clay desert

Sinbad (Arabic) A wealthy adventurer
Synbad, Sindbah, Syndbah

Sinclair (English) Man from Saint Clair
*Sinclaire, Sinclare, Synclair, Synclaire,
Synclare*

Sindile (African) The survivor
Syndile, Sindyle, Syndyle

Singer (American) A vocalist
Synger

Singh (Indian) Resembling a lion
Syngh

Sinh (Vietnamese) A flourishing boy

Sinjin (English) Refers to Saint John
Sinjon, Synjin, Synjon

Sinley (Anglo-Saxon) A friendly man
Sinly, Sinlee, Sinleigh, Sinlea, Sinli, Sinlie

Sion (Armenian) From the fortified hill
Sionne, Syon, Syonne

Siraj (Arabic) One who holds the torch
Syraj

Sirius (Greek) Resembling the brightest star
Syrius

Sisto (American) A cowboy
Systo

Sitanshu (Indian) Born beneath the moon
*Sytanshu, Sitanshue, Sytanshue, Sitanshoo,
Sytanshoo, Sitanshou, Sytanshou*

Sivan (Hebrew) Born during the ninth
month
Syvan

Sivney (Gaelic) A good and sweet boy
*Sivny, Sivni, Sivnie, Sivnee, Sivnea, Syvney,
Syvny, Syvni, Syvnie, Syvnee, Syvnea,
Sivneigh, Syvneigh*

Siwili (Native American) The fox's tail
*Siwilie, Siwile, Siwiley, Siwily, Siwilee,
Siwileigh, Siwilea*

Six (American) Refers to the number; the
sixth-born child

Siyamak (Persian) A man who has dark eyes
Siyamac, Siyamack

Siyavash (Persian) One who owns black
horses
Siyavashe

Skah (Native American) A white-skinned
man

Skeet (English / Norse) One who is swift /
one who shoots
*Skeets, Skeete, Skeat, Skeate, Skeit, Skeite,
Skete, Sketes, Skeeter, Skeetz*

Skelly (Gaelic) A storyteller; a bard
Skelli, Skellie, Skelley, Skellee, Skellea

Skerry (Norse) From the rocky island
*Skereye, Skerrey, Skerri, Skerrie, Skerree,
Skerrea*

Skilling (American) One who is masterful
Skillings, Skylling, Skyllings

Skinner (English) One who skins hides
Skinnor, Skinnar, Skinnur, Skinnir, Skinnyr

Skipper (English) The master of a ship
Skippere, Skip, Skipp

Skye (Gaelic) Man from the Isle of Skye
Sky, Skie

Skyler (English / Danish) One who is
learned; a scholar / a fugitive
*Skylare, Skylar, Skielar, Skylor, Skylir, Skylur,
Skielor, Skyelar, Skylen, Skyller, Skylarr*

Slade (English) Son of the valley
Slaid, Slaide, Slaed, Slaede, Slayd, Slayde

Sladkey (Slavic) A glorious man
Sladky, Sladki, Sladkie, Sladkee, Sladkea

Slater (English) One who installs slate
roofs
Slator, Slatar, Slatur, Slatir, Slatyr

Slavek (Polish) One who is intelligent
Slavek, Slaveck, Slavyk, Slavyc, Slavyck,
Slavik, Slavick

Slavin (Gaelic) Man from the mountains
Slavyn, Slaven, Slawin, Slawen, Slawyn,
Sleven, Slevan, Slevyn, Slevin

Slavomir (Czech) Of renowned glory
Slavomeer, Slavomyr, Slavomere, Slawomir,
Slawomeer, Slawomyr, Slawomere

Slean (Anglo-Saxon) One who strikes
Sleane, Slene, Sleen, Sleene

Slim (English) A slender man
Slym

Sloan (Gaelic) A high-ranking warrior
Sloane, Slown, Slowne, Slone

Slobodan (Croatian) Having a strong
intellect

Slocum (English) Filled with happiness
Slocom, Slocumb, Slocomb

Smedley (English) From the flat meadow
Smedly, Smedli, Smedlie, Smedlee,
Smedleigh, Smedlea, Smedleah, Smetheleah

Smith (English) A blacksmith
Smyth, Smithe, Smythe, Smedt, Smid, Smitty,
Smittee, Smittea, Smittey, Smitti, Smittie

Smithson (English) The son of a black-
smith
Smythson, Smitheson, Smytheson,
Smithesone, Smythesone

Smokey (American) One with a raspy
voice; a rebel
Smoky, Smoki, Smokie, Smokee, Smokea

Snell (Anglo-Saxon) One who is bold
Snel, Snelle, Snele

Snowden (English) From the snowy peak
Snoden, Snowdon, Snodon, Snowdun,
Snodun

So (Vietnamese) A smart man

Soberano (Spanish) A sovereign

Socorro (Spanish) One who offers help
Socorrio, Socoro, Socorio

Socrates (Greek) An ancient philosopher
Sokrates, Socratees, Sokratees

Sofian (Arabic) A devoted man

Sofronio (Greek) A self-controlled man
Sofrono, Sophronio, Sophrono

Sofus (Greek) Having great wisdom
Sophus

Sohan (Indian) A handsome man
Sohil, Sohail

Solange (French) An angel of the sun

Solaris (Greek) Of the sun
Solarise, Solariss, Solarisse, Solarys,
Solaryss, Solarysse, Solstice, Soleil

Solomon (Hebrew) A peaceful man
Salmon, Salomo, Salomon, Salomone,
Shalmon, Sol, Solaman, Sollie, Soloman

Solt (Hungarian) One who is honored
Solte

Solyom (Hungarian) Resembling a falcon

Somansh (Indian) Born beneath the half
moon
Somanshe, Somanshi, Somanshie,
Somanshy, Somanshey, Somanshee,
Somanshea

Somer (French) Born during the summer
Somers, Sommer, Sommers, Sommar, Somar

Somerby (English) From the summer village
Somersby, Sommersby, Somerbey, Somerbi,
Somerbie, Somerbee, Somerbea

Somerley (Gaelic) Of the summer sailors;
from the summer meadow
Somerly, Somerli, Somerlie, Somerlee,
Somerleigh, Somerlea, Somerleah, Somerled

Somerset (English) From the summer
settlement
Sommerset, Sumerset, Summerset

Somerton (English) From the summer town
Somertown, Somerville, Somervile,
Somervil, Sumarville, Sumarton, Sumerton,
Sumertun, Sumerville

Sondo (African) Born on a Sunday

Songaa (Native American) Having great
strength
Songan

Sonny (English) Our son
Sonney, Sonni, Sonnie, Sonnee, Sonnea

S

Sophocles (Greek) An ancient playwright
Sofocles

Soren (Scandinavian) Form of Severin, meaning "one who is strict; stern"
Soran, Soron, Sorun, Sorin, Soryn

Sorley (Irish) Of the summer vikings
Sorly, Sorlee, Sorlea, Sorli, Sorlie

Sorrell (French) Having reddish-brown hair
Sorel, Sorelle, Sorrelle, Sorrel

Soto (Spanish) From the marshland

Soumil (Indian) A beloved friend
Soumyl, Soumille, Soumylle, Soumill, Soumyll

Southern (English) Man from the south
Sothern, Suthern

Southwell (English) From the south spring
Sothwell

Sovann (Cambodian) The golden son
Sovan, Sovane

Sowi'ngwa (Native American) Resembling a black-tailed deer

Spalding (English) From the split field
Spaulding, Spelding

Spanky (American) One who is outspoken or stubborn
Spanki, Spankie, Spankey, Spankee, Spankea

Spark (English / Latin) A gallant man / to scatter
Sparke, Sparki, Sparkie, Sparky, Sparkey, Sparkee, Sparkea

Spear (English) One who wields a spear
Speare, Spears, Speer, Speers, Speir, Speirs, Spier, Spiers, Spere

Speed (English) Having good fortune
Speede, Sped, Spede, Spead, Speade

Spencer (English) One who dispenses provisions
Spenser, Spence, Spensar, Spincer, Spince

Spengler (German) One who works with tin
Spangler

Spider (English) Resembling the arachnid
Spyder

Spike (English) A large, heavy nail
Spyke, Spiker, Spyker

Spiridon (Greek) One who transports goods; a basket
Speero, Spero, Spiridion, Spiro, Spiros, Spyridon, Spyro, Spyros

Sprague (German) A lively man; full of energy

Springer (English) A fresh-faced man
Sprynger

Sproul (English) An active man
Sproule, Sprowl, Sprowle

Spud (American) A little boy; a potato
Spudd

Spunk (American) A lively man
Spunky, Spunkey, Spunkee, Spunkea, Spunki, Spunkie

Spurs (American) A cowboy
Spur, Spurr, Spurrs

Squire (English) A knight's companion; the shield-bearer
Squier, Squiers, Squires, Squyre, Squyres

Stacey (English) Form of Eustace, meaning "having an abundance of grapes"
Stacy, Staci, Stacie, Stacee, Stacea, Stace, Stayce, Staice, Staece

Stafford (English) From the landing ford
Stafforde, Staford, Staforde, Steathford

Stamos (Greek) A reasonable man
Stammos, Stamohs, Staymos, Staimos, Staemos

Stanbury (English) From the stone fortress
Stanberry, Stanbery, Stanburghe, Stansberry, Stansburghe, Stansbury, Stanburh, Stanbeny

Stancliff (English) From the stone cliff
Stancliffe, Stanclyffe, Stanscliff, Stanscliffe, Stanclyf

Standish (English) From the stony park
Standysh, Standishe, Standyshe

Stanfield (English) From the stony field
Stansfield, Stanfeld, Stansfeld

Stanford (English) From the stony ford
Standford, Standforde, Standforde, Stamford, Stamforde

Stanhope (English) From the stony hollow
Stanhop

Stanislaus (Slavic) The glory of the camp
*Stana, Stanek, Stanicek, Stanislas,
Stanislav, Stanislav, Stanislaw, Stannes,
Stanousek, Stanislov*

Stanley (English) From the stony meadow
*Stanly, Stanli, Stanlie, Stanlee, Stanleigh,
Stanlea, Stanleah, Stan*

Stanmore (English) From the stony lake
Stanmere, Stanmor

Stanton (English) From the stone town
*Stantown, Stanten, Staunton, Stantan,
Stantun*

Stanway (English) From the stone road
*Stanwaye, Stanwae, Stanwai, Stanaway,
Stannaway, Stannway, Stanweg, Stannweg*

Stanwick (English) One who lives in the
stone village
*Stanwic, Stanwik, Stanwicke, Stanwyck,
Stanwyc, Stanwyk*

Stanwood (English) From the stony forest
Stanwode, Stannwood, Stanwoode

Star (American) A celestial body; as bright
as a star
*Starr, Starre, Starry, Starrie, Starri, Starrey,
Starree*

Starbuck (American) An astronaut
*Starrbuck, Starbuk, Starrbuk, Starbuc,
Starrbuc*

Stark (German) Having great strength
Starke, Starck, Starcke

Starling (English) Resembling the bird
Starrling, Starlyng, Starrlyng, Staerling

Stash (American) Of the sun's rays
Stashe

Stavros (Greek) One who is crowned

Steadman (English) One who lives at the
farm
*Stedman, Steadmann, Stedmann,
Stedeman*

Steed (English) Resembling a stallion
Steede, Stead, Steade

Steele (English) As strong as steel
Steel

Stein (German) As solid as a stone
*Steen, Sten, Steno, Stensen, Steene,
Stenssen, Steiner, Stine*

Steinar (Norse) A rock-hard warrior
Steinard, Steinart, Steinhardt

Stennis (Scottish) From the place of the
standing stones
Stennys, Stinnis, Stinnys

Stephen (Greek) Crowned with garland
*Staffan, Steba, Steben, Stefan, Stefano,
Steffan, Steffen, Steffon, Stefon, Stephan,
Stephano, Stephanos, Stephanus, Stephens,
Stephenson, Stephon, Stevan, Steve, Steven,
Stevenson, Stevie, Stevey, Stevy, Stéphane,
Stevon, Stevyn, Stefanas, Stefanos,
Stefanus, Stephanas, Step*

Stepney (English) From Stephen's island
Stepny, Stepni, Stepnie, Stepnee, Stepnea

Sterling (English) One who is highly valued
Sterlyng, Stirling, Sterlyn

Sterne (English) A serious-minded man;
one who is strict
Stern, Stearn, Stearne, Stearns

Stetson (American) A cowboy
Stettson, Stetcyn, Stetsen, Stetsan

Stian (Norse) A voyager; one who is swift
*Stig, Styg, Stygge, Stieran, Steeran, Steeren,
Steeryn, Stieren, Stieryn*

Stillman (English) A fisherman; one who is
quiet
Stilleman, Styllman, Stylleman, Stillmann

Stilwell (Anglo-Saxon) From the quiet spring
*Stillwell, Stilwel, Stylwell, Styllwell,
Stylwel, Stillwel*

Stobart (German) A harsh man
Stobarte, Stobarth, Stobarthe

Stock (English) From the tree stump
Stok, Stoc, Stocke, Stoke

Stockard (English) From the yard of tree
stumps
Stockhard, Stockhard, Stokkard, Stocker

S

Stockley (English) From the meadow of tree stumps
Stockly, Stockli, Stocklie, Stocklee, Stockleigh, Stocklea, Stockleah, Stocleah, Stoclea

Stockton (English) From the town of tree stumps
Stocktown, Stocktun, Stocktan, Stockten

Stockwell (English) From the spring near the tree stumps
Stocwielle, Stockwiell

Stod (English) Resembling a horse
Stodd

Stoddard (English) The guardian or keeper of horses
Stodard, Stoddart, Stodart

Stonewall (English) From the stone fortress
Stonwall, Stanwall, Stannwall

Stoney (English) As solid as a stone
Stony, Stoni, Stonie, Stonee, Stonea, Stoner, Stone, Stones

Storm (American) Of the tempest; stormy weather; having an impetuous nature
Storme, Stormy, Stormi, Stormie, Stormey, Stormee, Stormea

Stowe (English) A secretive man
Stow, Stowey, Stowy, Stowee, Stowea, Stowi, Stowie

Strahan (Gaelic) A poet; a minstrel
Sruthan, Strachan

Stratford (English) From the street near the river ford
Strafford, Stratforde, Straford, Strafforde, Straforde

Stratton (Scottish) A homebody
Straton, Stratten, Straten, Strattan, Stratan, Strattun, Stratun

Straus (German) Resembling an ostrich
Strauss, Strause, Strausse

Stretch (American) An easygoing man
Stretcher, Strech, Strecher

Strickland (English) From the flax field
Stryckland, Strikland, Strykland

Strider (English) A great warrior
Stryder

Striker (American) An aggressive man
Strike, Stryker, Stryke

Strom (German) From the brook
Stromm, Strome, Stromme

Strong (English) A powerful man
Stronge, Strang

Stroud (Old English) from the thicket
Strod, Strode, Stroude

Struthers (Irish) One who lives near the brook
Struther, Sruthair, Strother, Strothers

Stuart (English) A steward; the keeper of the estate
Steward, Stewart, Stewert, Stuert, Stu, Stew

Studs (English / American) From the homestead / a cocky man
Studds, Stud, Studd

Sture (Scandinavian) A difficult man

Styles (English) From the stairway
Stiles, Stigols

Stylianos (Greek) A stylish man
Styli, Stylie, Style, Stylee, Stylea, Styleigh

Suave (American) A smooth and sophisticated man
Swave

Subhash (Indian) One who speaks well
Subhashe

Subhi (Arabic) Born during the early morning hours
Subhie, Subhy, Subhey, Subhee, Subhea

Sudbury (English) From the southern settlement
Sudbery, Sudberry, Sudborough

Sudi (African) A successful or lucky man
Sudie, Sudee, Sudea, Sudy, Sudey

Suffield (English) From the southern field
Suffeld, Suthfeld, Suthfield

Suffolk (English) Of the southern people

Suhail (Arabic) A gentle man; bright star
Suhaile, Suhayl, Suhayle, Suhael, Suhaele, Suhale

Sujay (Indian) Winning a good victory
Sujaye, Sujai, Sujae, Sujit

Sukarno (African) The chosen one

Sukumar (Indian) A tender man

Sulayman (Arabic) Form of Solomon, meaning "a peaceful man"
Sulaiman, Suleiman, Suleyman, Sulaymaan

Sule (African) An adventurous man

Surur (Arabic) Filled with joy

Sutcliff (English) From the southern cliff
Sutcliffe, Sutclyff, Sutclyf, Suthclif, Suthcliff, Suthclyf, Suthclyff, Suttecliff, Sutteclyff

Sutherland (Norse) From the southern island
Suthrland, Southerland

SULLIVAN

We chose my son's name purely because I really liked it. He's Sullivan, and not after any TV show, Irish heritage, or family names. It just came down to the fact that I thought Sully was really original. Letting my husband pick his middle name sealed the deal. —Ranae, MN

Sullivan (Gaelic) Having dark eyes
Sullavan, Sullevan, Sullyvan

Sully (English) From the southern meadow
Sulley, Sulli, Sullie, Sulleigh, Sullee, Sullea, Sulleah, Suthley, Suthly, Suthleigh, Suthlee, Suthli, Suthlie, Suthlea, Suthleah

Sultan (African / American) A ruler / one who is bold
Sultane, Sulten, Sultun, Sulton, Sultin, Sultyn

Suman (Hindi) A wise man

Sumner (English) A legal official; one who serves summons
Sumenor, Sumernor

Sunday (American) Born on a Sunday
Sundae, Sundai, Sundaye

Sundiata (African) Resembling a hungry lion
Sundyata, Soundiata, Soundyata, Sunjata

Sundown (American) Born at dusk
Sundowne

Sunil (Indian) A deep dark-blue gem
Suneel, Sunyl, Suneil, Suniel, Suneal

Sunny (American) Of the sun; one who is brilliant and cheerful
Sunni, Sunney, Sunnie, Sunnea, Sunnye, Sonnenschein

Sunukkuhkau (Native American) He who crushes

Suraj (Indian) Of the sun
Sooraj, Souraj

Sutton (English) From the southern town
Suttun, Sutter

Su'ud (Arabic) One who has good luck
Suoud

Svan (Norse) Resembling a swan
Svann

Svatomir (Slavic) Of sacred glory
Svatomeer, Svatomear, Svatomyr

Svatoslav (Slavic) One who celebrates sacredness

Sven (Norse) A youthful man; a lad
Svein, Sveinn, Svend, Swain, Swen, Swensen, Swenson

Svenbjorn (Swedish) Resembling a young bear

Swahili (Arabic) Of the coastal people
Swahily, Swahiley, Swahilee, Swahiley, Swaheeli, Swaheelie, Swaheely, Swaheeley, Swaheelee

Swain (English) A country boy; one who herds swine; a knight's attendant
Swain, Swayn, Swayne, Swane, Swaen, Swaene

Swanton (English) From the swan town
Swantun, Swantown

Sweeney (Gaelic) Little hero; a brave young boy
Sweeny, Sweeni, Sweenie, Sweenee, Sweenea, Suidhne

S

Swift (Anglo-Saxon) One who is fast
*Swifte, Swyft, Swyfte, Swifty, Swiftey,
Swifti, Swiftie, Swiftee, Swiftea*

Swinburne (English) From the swine
stream
*Swinborn, Swinbourne, Swinburn,
Swinbyrn, Swynborne, Swynburne*

Swinford (English) From the swine ford
Swynford, Swinforde, Swynforde

Swinton (English) From the swine town
Swynton, Swintun, Swyntun

Swithin (English) One who is quick and
strong
Swithinn, Swithun

Sydney (English) Of the wide meadow
*Sydny, Sydni, Sydnie, Sydnea, Sydnee,
Sidney, Sidne, Sidnee, Sidnei, Sidni, Sidnie,
Sidny, Sidnye*

Sylvester (Latin) Man from the forest
*Silvester, Silvestre, Silvestro, Sylvestre,
Sylvestro, Sly, Sevester, Seveste*

Symotris (African) A fortunate man
*Symetris, Symotrise, Symotrice, Symotrys,
Symotryce, Symotryse*

Syon (Indian) One who is followed by good
fortune

Szemere (Hungarian) A man of small
stature
Szemir, Szemeer, Szemear, Szemyr

Szervac (Hungarian) One who has
been freed

Taaveti (Hebrew) One who is dearly loved
*Taavetie, Taavety, Taavetey, Taavetee,
Taavetea, Taveti, Tavetie, Tavetee, Tavetea,
Tavety, Tavetey, Taavi, Taavetti, Tavetti*

Tab (German / English) A brilliant man / a
drummer
Tabb

Taban (Gaelic) A genius
Taben, Tabon, Tabin, Tabyn, Tabun

Tabansi (African) An enduring man
*Tabansie, Tabansy, Tabansey, Tabansee,
Tabansea*

Tabari (Arabic) A famous historian
Tabarie, Tabary, Tabarey, Tabaree, Tabarea

Tabasco (American) Resembling the spicey
pepper
Tabasko, Tabascko

Tabbai (Hebrew) A well-behaved boy
Tabbae, Tabbay, Tabbaye

Tabbart (German) A brilliant man
Tabbert, Tabart, Tabert, Tahbert, Tahberte

Tabbebo (Native American) Son of the sun
Tabebo, Tabbebio, Tabebio

Tabib (Turkish) One who heals others; a
doctor
Tabibe, Tabeeb, Tabeebe, Tabeab, Tabeabe

Tabor (Hungarian / Hebrew) From the
trenches / having bad luck
*Taber, Taibor, Tavor, Taybor, Tayber,
Taiber, Taebor, Taeber*

Tacari (African) As strong as a warrior
Tacarie, Tacary, Tacarey, Tacaree, Tacarea

Tacitus (Latin) A well-known historian
Tacitas, Tacites

Tadao (Japanese) One who is satisfied

Tadashi (Japanese) One who is accurate
*Tadashie, Tadashy, Tadashey, Tadashee,
Tadashea*

Tadelesh (African) A lucky man
Tadelesho, Tadeleshio, Tadeleshiyo

Tadeo (Spanish) Form of Thaddeus, meaning "having heart"
Taddeo, Tadzio, Tadzo

Tadeusuz (Polish) One who is worthy of
praise
Tadesuz

Tadi (Native American) Of the wind
Tadie, Tady, Tadey, Tadee, Tadea

Tadzi (American / Polish) Resembling the
loon / one who is praised
Tadzie, Tadzy, Tadzey, Tadzee, Tadzea

Taff (American) A sweet man
Taffy, Taffey, Taffi, Taffie, Taffee, Taffea

Taft (French / English) From the homestead / from the marshes
Tafte

Tage (Danish) Born during the daytime

Taggart (Gaelic) Son of a priest
Taggert, Taggort, Taggirt, Taggyrt

Taghee (Native American) A chief
Taghea, Taghy, Taghey, Taghi, Taghie

Taha (Polynesian) The firstborn child
Tahatan

Taheton (Native American) Resembling a hawk

Tahi (Polynesian) One who lives by the sea
Tahie, Tahy, Tahey, Tahee, Tahea

Tahir (Arabic) One who is pure; chaste
Tahire, Taheer, Taheere, Tahier, Tahiere, Taheir, Taheire, Tahear, Taheare, Tahyr, Tahyre, Taher, Tahu

Tahkeome (Native American) The little robe
Tahkiome, Tahkyome, Takeome, Takiome, Takyome

Tahmelapachme (Native American) Wielding a dull knife

Tahmores (Persian) Resembling a strong wild dog

Tahoe (Native American) From the big water
Taho

Tahoma (Native American) From the snowy mountain peak
Tehoma, Tacoma, Takoma, Tohoma, Tocoma, Tokoma, Tekoma, Tecoma

Tahurer (English) A drummer
Tahurar, Tahurir, Tahuryr, Tahuror, Tahurur

Tai (Vietnamese) One who is talented

Taicligh (Irish) One who is peaceful

Taima (Native American) Of the thunder
Tayma, Taema

Taine (Gaelic) Of the river
Tain, Tayn, Tayne, Taen, Taene, Tane

Taishi (Japanese) An ambitious man
Taishie, Taishy, Taishey, Taishee, Taishea

Taiwo (African) The firstborn of twins
Tawo, Taewo, Taywo

Taizeen (Indian) One who offers encouragement
Tazeen, Taezeen, Tayzeen, Taizean, Tazean, Taezean, Tayzean

Taizo (Japanese) The third-born son
Tayzo, Tazo, Taezo

Taj (Indian) One who is crowned
Tahj, Tajdar

Taji (Japanese) A yellow and silver color
Tajie, Tajy, Tajey, Tajee, Tajea

Tajo (Spanish) Born during the daytime

Takeo (Japanese) As strong as bamboo
Takio, Takyo, Takeshi, Takeshie, Takeshee, Takeshea, Takeshy, Takeshey

Taklishim (Native American) A gray-haired man
Taklishym, Taklisheem, Taklisheam, Taklyshim, Taklyshym, Taklysheem, Taklysheam

Takoda (Native American) One who is a friend to everyone
Tacoda, Tackoda

Taksa (Hindi) In Hinduism, a son of Bharata
Taksha

Takshaka (Indian) One who works with wood

Taksony (Hungarian) One who is content; well-fed
Taksoney, Taksoni, Taksonie, Taksonee, Taksonea, Tas

Tal (Hebrew) Covered with the morning's dew
Tahl

Talak (Indian) One who is superior
Talac, Talack

Talasi (Native American) Resembling a cornflower
Talasie, Talasy, Talasey, Talasee, Talasea

Talat (Indian) One who prays
Talatt, Tallat, Tallatt

Talbert (English) Born to the nobility
*Talbet, Talbot, Talbott, Tallbot, Tallbott,
Talbort, Tallbet, Talbett, Tallbett, Tolbert,
Tollbert, Tolbart, Tollbart, Tolburt,
Tollburt*

Talcot (English) One who lives in a cottage
by the lake
Talcott, Talcote, Talcotte

Talehot (French) Resembling a blood-
hound

Talford (English) From the high ford
Talforde, Tallford, Tallforde

Talfryn (Welsh) From the high hill
*Talfrynn, Talfrin, Talfrinn, Talfren,
Talfrenn, Tallfryn, Tallfrin, Tallfren*

Talib (Arabic) One who seeks knowledge
*Talibe, Taleeb, Taleebe, Taleib, Taleibe,
Talieb, Taliebe, Taleab, Taleabe, Talyb,
Talybe, Taleb, Talebe*

Taliesin (Welsh) Having a shiny forehead
*Taliesyn, Taliesen, Talieson, Talyessin,
Talessin*

Talleen (Hindi) One who is engrossed
*Tallein, Tallean, Talleyn, Tallien, Tallene,
Talline, Tallen*

Talli (Native American / Hebrew) A legendary hero / of the morning dew
Tallie, Tally, Talley, Tallee, Tallea

Tallis (English) A composer of religious
music
Talles, Tallas, Tallys, Talis, Talys, Tales, Talas

Talmadge (English) One who loves nature
Tallmadge, Talmidge, Tallmidge

Talmai (Hebrew) From the furrows
Talmae, Talmay, Talmaye

Talmon (Hebrew) One who is oppressed
Talman, Talmin, Talmyn, Talmen

Talo (Finnish) From the homestead

Talon (English) Resembling a bird's claw
Tallon, Talen, Talin, Tallan, Tallen, Tallin

Talos (Greek) In mythology, the protector
of Minos island; a giant

Tam (Vietnamese / Hebrew) Having heart /
one who is truthful

Tamal (Hindi) Of the dark tree
Tamall, Tamalle

Tamam (Arabic) One who is generous

Taman (Hindi) One who is needed

Tamar (Hebrew) From the palm tree
Tamare, Tamarr, Tamarre

Tamarack (Latin) From the tree
Tamarak, Tamarac

Tamarisk (Latin) Resembling the
shrublike tree
Tamarysk, Tamaresk

Tamarius (American) A stubborn man
*Tamarias, Tamarios, Tamerius, Tamerias,
Tamerios*

Tamerlane (English) One who is lame
*Tamarlain, Tamarlayn, Tamberlain,
Tamberlaine, Tamberlane, Tamburlaine,
Tamburlane, Tamurlaine, Tamurlayn*

Tameron (American) Form of Cameron,
meaning "having a crooked nose"
*Tameryn, Tamryn, Tamerin, Tamren,
Tamrin, Bamron*

Tamir (Arabic / Hebrew) A wealthy man /
one who stands tall
*Tamire, Tameer, Tameere, Tamear,
Tameare, Tamyr, Tamyre, Tamier, Tamiere,
Tameir, Tameire*

Tamirat (African) A miracle child
Tamyrat, Tamiratt, Tamyratt

Tammany (Native American) A friendly
chief
*Tammani, Tammanie, Tammaney,
Tammanee, Tammanea*

Tamson (English) Son of Thomas
Tamsen, Tamsin, Tamsyn, Tamsun

Tan (Japanese) A high achiever

Tanafa (Polynesian) A drumbeat

Tanaki (Polynesian) One who counts
*Tanakie, Tanaky, Tanakey, Tanakee,
Tanakea*

Tanay (Hindi) Our beloved son
Tanaye, Tanai, Tanae, Tanuj

Tancred (German) One who gives thoughtful counsel
Tancreid, Tancried, Tancrid, Tancryd, Tancredo, Tancreed, Tancread, Tancredi, Tancredie, Tancredy, Tancredey, Tancredee, Tancredea

Tandy (Scottish) Form of Andrew, meaning "a warrior"
Tandi, Tandey, Tandie, Tandee, Tandea

Tanek (Polish) One who is immortal

Taneli (Hebrew) He will be judged by God
Tanelie, Tanely, Taneley, Tanelee, Tanelea

Tangakwunu (Native American) Resembling a rainbow
Tangakwunoo, Tangakwunou

Tangaloa (Polynesian) A courageous man
Tangalo

Tanguy (Celtic) A warrior

Tanh (Vietnamese) One who gets his way

Tanish (Indian) An ambitious man
Tanishe, Taneesh, Taneeshe, Taneash, Taneashe, Tanysh, Tanyshe

Tanjiro (Japanese) The prized second-born son
Tanjyro

Tank (American) A man who is big and strong
Tankie, Tanki, Tanky, Tankey, Tankee, Tankea

Tanmay (Indian) One who is absorbed
Tanmaye, Tanmae, Tanmai

Tanner (English) One who makes leather
Tannere, Tannor, Tannar, Tannir, Tannyr, Tannur, Tannis

Tannon (German) From the fir tree
Tannan, Tannen, Tannin, Tansen, Tanson, Tannun, Tannyn

Tano (Ghanese) From the river
Tanu

Tansy (Greek / Native American) Having immortality / resembling the flower
Tansey, Tansi, Tansie, Tansee, Tansea

Tanton (English) From the town near the quiet river
Tanten, Tantan, Tantown, Tantun, Tantin, Tantyn, Tamtun, Tamton, Tamten, Tamtan, Tamtyn, Tamtin

Tanvir (Indian) An enlightened man
Tanvire, Tanveer, Tanveere, Tanvyr, Tanvyre, Tanvear, Tanveare

Tao (Chinese) One who will have a long life

Taos (Spanish) From the city in New Mexico

Tapani (Hebrew) A victorious man
Tapanie, Tapany, Tapaney, Tapanee, Tapanea

Tapko (American) Resembling an antelope

Tapomay (Indian) A virtuous man
Tapomaye, Tapomai, Tapomae

Tappen (Welsh) From the top of the cliff
Tappan, Tappon, Tappin, Tappyn, Tappun

Tarachand (Indian) Of the silver star
Tarachande

Tarafah (Arabic) From the trees
Tarafa, Taraphah, Tarapha

Tarak (Indian) One who protects others
Tarac, Tarack

Taral (Indian) Resembling the honeybee
Tarall, Taralle

Taramandal (Indian) Of the Milky Way

Taran (Gaelic) Of the thunder
Taren, Taron, Tarin, Taryn, Tarun

Taranga (Indian) Of the waves

Tarasios (Greek) Man of Tarentum
Taraseos, Tarasio, Taraseo

Tardos (Hungarian) One who is bald
Tardus, Tardis, Tardys, Tardas

Taregan (Native American) Resembling a crane
Taregen, Taregon, Taregin, Taregyn

Tarhe (Native American) Having the strength of a tree
Tarhi, Tarhie, Tarhy, Tarhey, Tarhee, Tarhea

T

Tarif (Arabic) Unlike the others; one who is unique
Tarife, Taryf, Taryfe, Tareef, Tareefe, Tareif, Tareife, Tarief, Tariefe, Tareaf, Tareafe

Tarin (Gaelic) From the rocky hill
Taren, Taron, Taran, Taryn, Tarun

Tariq (Arabic) One who demands entry; of the morning star
Tarique, Tareek, Tarek, Tareq, Tarick, Tarik, Tareak, Tareeq, Tareaq, Taryq, Taryque

Tarit (Indian) Resembling lightning
Tarite, Tareet, Tareete, Tareat, Tareate, Taryt, Taryte

Tarun (Indian) A youthful man
Taroun, Taroon, Tarune, Taroune, Taroone

Taruntapan (Indian) Born beneath the morning sun

Tashi (Tibetan) One who is prosperous
Tashie, Tashy, Tashey, Tashee, Tashea

Tashunka (Native American) One who loves horses
Tashunko, Tashunke, Tasunka, Tasunko, Tasunke

Tassilo (Scandinavian) A fearless defender
Tassillo, Tasilo, Tasillo

TATE

By the time we were expecting our fourth son, we already had three boys: Travis, Tyler, and Trevor. We couldn't find any other "T" names we liked, but my friend Brenda suggested Tate. I immediately liked it, and my due date was her late father's birthday, so it seemed right. —Mary, IA

Tarjan (Hungarian) One who is honored

Tarleton (English) From the thunder town
Tarlton, Tarletown, Tarltown

Tarmon (Gaelic) From the church's land
Tarman, Tarmen, Tarmun, Tarmin, Tarmyn

Tarn (Norse) From the mountain pool

Taro (Japanese) The firstborn son; a big boy
Taroe

Tarquin (Latin) One who is impulsive
Tarquinn, Tarquinne, Tarquen, Tarquenn, Tarquenne, Tarquyn, Tarquynn, Tarquynne

Tarquin (Latin) A king
Tarquen, Tarquinn, Tarquinne, Tarquyn, Tarquynn, Tarquynne, Tarquenn, Tarquenne, Tarquinius, Tarquino, Tarquinus

Tarrant (Welsh) Son of thunder
Tarrent, Tarrint, Tarrynt, Tarront, Tarrunt

Tarrant (American) One who upholds the law
Tarrent, Tarrint, Tarrynt, Tarront, Tarrunt

Tarso (Italian) A dashing young man
Tarsio, Tarsiyo

Tassos (Greek) A harvester
Tasso, Tassus, Tassu, Tasses

Tatankamimi (Native American) Resembling a walking buffalo

Tate (English) A cheerful man; one who brings happiness to others
Tayt, Tayte, Tait, Taite, Taet, Taete

Tatonga (Native American) Resembling a deer

Tatry (English) From the mountain in Poland
Tatrey, Tatri, Tatrie, Tatree, Tatrea

Tau (African) Resembling a lion

Taurus (Latin) The bull; the second sign of the zodiac
Taurean, Taurino, Tauro, Toro, Taurinus, Taurin

Tausiq (Indian) One who provides strong backing
Tauseeq, Tauseaq, Tausik, Tauseek, Tauseak

Tavaris (American) Of misfortune; a hermit
Tavarius, Tavaress, Tavarious, Tavariss, Tavarous, Tevarus, Tavorian, Tavarian, Tavorien, Tavarien

Tavas (Hebrew) Resembling a peacock

Taverner (English) One who keeps a tavern
Tavener, Tavenner, Tavernier, Tavernar,
Tavenar

Tavi (Aramaic) A good man
Tavie, Tavy, Tavey, Tavee, Tavea

Tavin (German) Form of Gustav, meaning
"of the staff of the gods"
Tavyn, Taven, Tavan, Tavon, Tavun, Tava,
Tave

Tavio (Spanish) Form of Octavio, meaning
"the eighth-born child"
Taviyo, Taveo, Taveyo

Tavish (Scottish / Irish) A twin / from the
hillside
Tavishe, Tavysh, Tavyshe, Tavis, Tevis,
Tavi, Tavie, Tavee, Tavea, Tavy, Tavey

Tavon (American) An outdoorsy man;
lover of nature
Tavion, Taveon

Tawa (Native American) Born beneath
the sun
Tawah

Tawagahe (Native American) One who
builds
Tawagahi, Tawagahie, Tawagahy,
Tawagahey, Tawagahee, Tawagahea

Tawanima (Native American) One who
tries to measure the sun
Tawaneema, Tawaneama, Tawanyma,
Tawanema

Taweel (Arabic) A tall man
Taweil, Taweal, Taweyl, Tawil, Tawl

Tawfiq (Arabic) One who is successful
Tawfeeq, Tawfeaq, Tawfyq

Tawno (American) A man of small stature
Tawnio, Tawniyo

Tay (Scottish) From the river
Taye, Tae, Tai

Tayib (Arabic) A good man
Tayeeb, Tayibe, Tayeebe, Tayeib, Tayeibe,
Tayieb, Tayiebe, Tayeab, Tayeabe, Tayyib

Taylor ♂ (English) One who alters garments
Tailer, Tailor, Tayler, Taelor, Taeler, Taylan,
Taylon, Tayson

Taymullah (Arabic) A servant of God
Taemullah, Taimullah, Taymulla,
Taemulla, Taimulla

Taysir (Arabic) One who helps others
Taysire, Taesir, Taesire, Taisir, Taisire,
Taysyr, Taesyr, Taisyr

Tayton (American) A bringer of happiness
Tayten, Taytin, Teytan, Teyten, Teytin, Teyton

Taz (American) Man from Tasmania
Tazz, Tazze, Tazman, Tazzman, Tasman

Teagan (Gaelic) A handsome man
Teegan, Teygan, Tegan, Teigan

Teague (Gaelic) A wise poet
Tadhg, Teagam, Tegan, Teger, Teigan, Teige,
Teigen, Teigue, Teeg, Teege, Teag, Teage,
Teaghue, Tighe, Tadleigh, Taidghin, Tag

Teal (American) Having greenish-blue eyes
Teale, Teel, Teele

Tearlach (Scottish) Having great strength
Tearloch

Techoslav (Native American) One who
provides comfort to others

Tecumseh (Native American) A traveler;
resembling a shooting star
Tekumseh, Tecumse, Tekumse

Ted (English) Form of Theodore, meaning
"a gift from God"
Tedd, Teddy, Teddi, Teddie, Teddee,
Teddea, Teddey, Tedric, Tedrick, Tedric

Tedmund (English) A protector of the land
Tedmunde, Tedmond, Tedmonde, Tedman,
Theomund, Theomond, Theomunde,
Theomonde

Teetonka (Native American) One who
talks too much
Teitonka, Tietonka, Teatonka, Teytonka

Teferi (African) A ferocious man; feared by
his enemies
Teferie, Tefery, Teferey, Teferee, Teferea

Tefo (African) One who pays his debts

Tegene (African) My protector
Tegeen, Tegeene, Tegean, Tegeane

Teiji (Japanese) One who is righteous
Teijo

Teilo (Welsh) A saintly man

Teithi (Celtic) In mythology, the son of Gwynham
Teethi, Teithie, Teethie, Teithy, Teethy, Teithey, Teethey, Teithee, Teethee

Tejano (Spanish) Man from Texas
Tejanio, Tejaniyo

Tejas (Indian) A lustrous man; brilliance; splendor
Tejus, Tejes

Tejomay (Hindi) A glorious woman
Tejomaye, Tejomae, Tejomai

Teka (African) He has replaced

Tekeshi (Japanese) Formidable and brave man
Tekeshie, Tekeshy, Tekeshey, Tekeshee, Tekeshea

Tekle (African) The fruit of my seed
Tekli, Teklie, Tekly, Tekley, Teklee, Teklea

Tekonsha (Native American) Resembling a caribou
Tekonsho

Telamon (Greek) In mythology, the father of Ajax
Telemon, Telimon, Telomon, Telumon

Telemachus (Greek) In mythology, the son of Penelope and Odysseus
Telamachus, Telemakus, Telamakus, Telemechus, Telamechus, Telemekus, Telamekus

Telford (French) One who works with iron
Telforde, Telfer, Telfor, Telfour, Tellfer, Tellfour, Tellford, Tellforde, Taillefer, Telek

Tellan (Anglo-Saxon) One who considers his decisions
Tellen, Tellun, Tellon, Tellin, Tellyn

Teller (English) One who tells stories
Tellar, Tellor, Tellir, Tellur, Tellyr

Telly (Greek) The wisest man
Telley, Tellee, Tellea, Telli, Tellie

Tem (English) A man from the country

Temani (Hebrew) Man from the south
Temanie, Temany, Temaney, Temanee, Temanea, Teman, Temeni, Temenie, Temeny, Temeney, Temenee, Temenea

Temman (Anglo-Saxon) One who has been tamed

Tempest (French) One who is stormy; turbulent
Tempesto, Tempeste, Tempestio, Tempestt, Tempist, Tempiste, Tempisto

Temple (Latin) From the sacred place
Tempel, Templar, Templer, Templo

Templeton (English) From the town near the temple
Templetown, Templeten, Tempeltun, Tempelton, Tempelten

Tempo (Italian) A keeper of time

Tenchi (Japanese) Of heaven and earth
Tenchie, Tenchy, Tenchey, Tenchee, Tenchea

Tendoy (Native American) One who climbs higher
Tendoye, Tendoi

Tene (African) One who is much loved

Teneangopte (Native American) Resembling a high-flying bird

Teneil (American) Form of Neil, meaning "the champion"
Teneile, Teneal, Teneale, Teneel, Teneele

Tenen (African) Born on a Monday

Teng (Greek) A well-known warrior
Tenge

Tennant (English) One who rents
Tennent, Tenant, Tenent

Tennessee (Native American) From the state of Tennessee
Tenese, Tenesee, Tenessee, Tennese, Tennesee, Tennesse

Tennyson (English) Son of Dennis
Tennison, Tenneson, Tenny, Tenni, Tennie, Tennee, Tennea, Tenney

Teo (Spanish) A godly man
Teyo

Teom (African) One of twins

Teon (Anglo-Saxon) One who harms others

Teoxihuitl (Aztec) As precious as turquoise

Tepiltzin (Aztec) Born to privelege

Teppo (Hebrew) A victorious man

Terach (Hebrew) Resembling a wild goat
Terah, Terrah

Terciero (Spanish) The third-born child
Terceiro, Tercyero, Terceyero

Terence (Latin) From an ancient Roman clan
Tarrants, Tarrance, Tarrence, Tarrenz, Terencio, Terrance, Terrence, Terrey, Terri, Terris, Terrious, Terrius, Terry, Terrey, Terree, Terrea, Terronce, Terenge

Teris (Irish) The son of Terence
Terys, Teriss, Teryss, Terris, Terrys, Terriss, Terryss

Tern (Latin) Resembling a marine bird
Terne

Terran (English) Man of the earth
Terrin, Terren, Terryn, Terrun

Terrell (French / German) One who is stubborn / a powerful man
Tarrall, Terell, Terrall, Terrel, Terrelle, Terrill, Terryal, Terryl, Terryll, Tirrell, Tyrell, Tyrel, Tyrelle, Tyrrel, Tyrrell

Terrian (American) One who is strong and ambitious
Terrien, Terriun, Terriyn

Terron (English) Form of Terence, meaning "from an ancient Roman clan"
Tarran, Tarren, Tarrin, Tarron, Tarryn, Teron, Teran

Terryal (American) One who harvests
Terrial, Terryall, Terriall

Tertius (Greek) The third-born child

Teryysone (English) The son of Terrell
Terryysone, Terrysone, Terysone

Tesar (Czech) One who works with wood

Tesfaye (African) Our hope
Tesfay, Tesfai, Tesfae

Tesher (Hebrew) A gift from God

Teshi (African) One who is full of laughter
Teshie, Teshy, Teshey, Teshee, Teshea

Teshombe (American) An able-bodied man
Teshomb

Tessema (African) One to whom people listen

Tet (Vietnamese) Born on New Year's

Teteny (Hungarian) A chieftain

Teva (Hebrew) A natural man
Tevah

Tevaughn (American) Resembling a tiger
Tevan, Tevaughan, Tivaughn, Tivaughan, Tevaun, Tevawn

Tevel (Hebrew) One who is dearly loved
Tevell, Tevele, Tevelle

Tevey (Hebrew) A good man
Tevy, Tevi, Tevie, Tevee, Tevea

Tevin (American) Son of Kevin
Tevyn, Tevan, Teven, Tevinn, Tevonn

Tevis (American) One who is flamboyant
Tevas, Teviss, Tevys, Tevyss

Tewodros (African) Form of Theodore, meaning "a gift from God"

Tex (American) Man from Texas
Texx, Texan, Texon, Texun, Texen

Texas (Native American) One of many friends; from the state of Texas
Texus, Texis, Texes, Texos, Texys

Teyrnon (Celtic) A regal man
Teirnon, Tayrnon, Tairnon, Taernon, Tiarchnach, Tiarnach

Thabiti (African) A real man
Thabitie, Thabity, Thabitey, Thabitee, Thabitea, Thabit, Thabyt

Thabo (African) Filled with happiness

Thackary (English) Form of Zachary, meaning "the Lord remembers"
Thackery, Thakary, Thakery, Thackari, Thackarie, Thackarey, Thackaree, Thackarea, Thackerey, Thackeree, Thackerea, Thackeri, Thackerie

T

Thaddeus (Aramaic) Having heart
Tad, Tadd, Taddeo, Taddeusz, Thad,
Thadd, Thaddaios, Thaddaos, Thaddaeus,
Thaddaus, Thaddius, Thadeus, Thady,
Thaddy, Thaddeaus

Thai (Vietnamese) Man from Thailand

Thakur (Indian) A godly leader
Thackur

Than (Vietnamese) A brilliant man
Thann

Thandiwe (African) One who is dearly
loved
Thandie, Thandi, Thandy, Thandey,
Thandee, Thandea

Thane (English) One who owns land
Thayn, Thayne, Thain, Thaine, Thaen,
Thaene, Theyn, Theyn

Thang (Vietnamese) One who is victorious

Thanh (Vietnamese) One who is
accomplished

Thanos (Greek) One who is noble and
praiseworthy
Thanasis, Thanasos

Thanus (American) One who owns land

Thao (Vietnamese) One who is courteous

Thaqib (Arabic) Resembling a shooting
star
Thaqeeb, Thaqeab, Thaqyb, Thaqieb,
Thaqeib

Thatcher (English) One who fixes roofs
Thacher, Thatch, Thatche, Thaxter,
Thacker, Thaker, Thackere, Thakere

Thaw (English) The process of melting
Thawe, Thawain, Thawayne, Thawaine,
Thawaen, Thawaene, Thawayn

Thayer (Teutonic) Of the nation's army

Thelred (English) One who receives good
counsel
Thelread, Thellred, Thellread

Themba (African) One who is trustworthy
Thembah

Thembalwethu (African) Our hope

Theobald (German) Of the courageous
and bold people
Teobaldo, Thebault, Thibaud, Thibault,
Thibaut, Tibold, Tiebold, Tiebout,
Tybald, Tybalt, Tybault, Theobold,
Thieny, Tibbot, Tibalt, Tibault, Tihalt,
Tihault, Tyhalt, Tyhault

Theodore (Greek) A gift from God
Teador, Teodoor, Teodor, Teodoro, Theo,
Theodon, Theodor, Theodorus, Theodosios,
Theodosius, Todo, Tedor, Theodis, Tudor,
Tedros, Teyo

Theodoric (German) The power of the
people
Teodorico, Thedric, Thedrick, Theodorik,
Theodric, Theodrik, Thedrik, Thierry,
Thierri, Thierrey, Thierree, Thierrea

Theon (French) An untamed man
Theone

Theophilus (Greek) One who is loved by
God
Teofil, Teofilo, Theofil, Theofilo,
Théophile, Theophil, Theophilos

Theron (Greek) A great hunter
Therron, Tharon, Theon, Tharron

Theseus (Greek) In mythology, hero who
slew the Minotaur
Thesius, Thesyus

Thialfi (Norse) In mythology, a servant of
Thor
Thialfie, Thialfy, Thialfey, Thialfee,
Thialfea

Thiassi (Scandinavian) A crafty man
Thiassie, Thiassy, Thiassey, Thiassee,
Thiassea

Thierry (French) A ruler of the people
Thierrey, Thierree, Thierrea, Thierri,
Thierrie, Thiery, Thierey, Thieri, Thierie,
Thieree, Thierea

Thimba (African) One who hunts lions
Thymba, Thimbah, Thymbah

Thinh (Vietnamese) A prosperous man

Tho (Vietnamese) Having a long life

Thomas ✪ (Aramaic) One of twins
Tam, Tamas, Tamhas, Thom, Thoma, Thomason, Thomson, Thompson, Tomas, Tomaso, Tomasso, Tomasz, Tome, Tomek, Tommie, Tommey, Tomislaw, Tommaso, Thomkins, Tom, Tommy, Tuomas, Tomik, Tomo, Tomos, Tamasine, Tamnais

Thor (Norse) In mythology, god of thunder
Thorian, Thorin, Thorsson, Thorvald, Tor, Tore, Turo, Thorrin, Thors, Thour

Thorald (Norse) Follower of Thor
Thorualdr, Torald, Thorauld, Torauld, Thorold, Torold, Thoreau, Thoraux, Thorer, Thorvald, Thorvauld, Thorvid

Thoraldtun (English) From Thor's esate
Thoraldton, Thoraldten, Thoraldtan

Thorbert (Norse) Shining with the glory of Thor
Thorbiartr, Thorberte, Thorbierte, Torbert

Thorburn (Norse) Thor's bear
Thorburne, Thorbern, Thorberne, Thorbjorn, Thorbjorne, Torbjorn, Torborg, Torben, Torbern, Torburn

Thorne (English) From the thorn bush
Thorn

Thornley (English) From the thorny meadow
Thornly, Thornlee, Thornleigh, Thornli, Thornlie, Thornlea

Thornton (English) From the town of thorn bushes
Thorntown, Thorntun, Thornten, Thorntan

Thornycroft (English) From the field of thorn bushes
Thornicroft, Thorneycroft, Thorniecroft, Thorneecroft, Thorneacroft

Thorolf (Norse) Thor's wolf
Thorulf, Thorolfe, Thorulfe, Torolf, Torulf, Torolfe, Torulfe

Thorpe (English) From the village
Thorp

Thrythwig (English) A warrior of great strength
Thrythwyg, Thrythweg

Thu (Vietnamese) Born during the autumn

THOMAS
My father-in-law gave us a family tree dating from the present back to the Puritans. When I was expecting, we pored over all the options. Thomas Nathaniel Putnam is the classic we came up with, and so far no one has mocked him about having the initials T.P. Nathaniel was my husband's grandfather's middle name, and we really like having that connection. —Laura, MO

Thorer (Scandinavian) A great warrior

Thorley (English) From Thor's meadow
Thorly, Thorlee, Thorli, Thorlie, Thorleigh, Thorlea, Thurley, Thurly, Thurleigh, Thurlee, Thurlea, Thurleah, Thurli, Thurlie, Torley, Torly, Torli, Torlie, Torlee, Torlea, Torleigh

Thormond (Norse) Protected by Thor
Thormonde, Thormund, Thormunde, Thurmond, Thurmonde, Thurmund, Thurmunde, Thormun, Thurmun, Thorman, Thurman, Thormon, Thurmon, Therman

Thorndike (English) From the thorny embankment
Thorndyke, Thorndik, Thorndyk, Thorndic, Thorndyc, Thomdic, Thomdik, Thomdike, Thomdyke

Thuan (Vietnamese) One who is tamed
Thuann

Thuc (Vietnamese) One who is alert and aware
Tinh

Thunder (English) One with a temper

Thuong (Vietnamese) One who loves tenderly

Thurgood (English) An upstanding man
Thurgoode, Thergood, Thergoode

Thurl (Irish) From the strong fortress
Thurle, Therl, Therle

Thurlow (English) From Thor's hill
Thurlowe, Thurlo, Thurloe, Thurhloew, Thurloew

Thurston (English) From Thor's town; Thor's stone
Thorston, Thorstan, Thorstein, Thorsten, Thurstain, Thurstan, Thursten, Torsten, Torston, Thurstun, Thurstin

Thuy (Vietnamese) One who is kind

Thwaite (Scandinavian) From the fenced-in pasture
Thwait, Thwayt, Thwayte, Thwate, Thwaet, Thwaete

Tiago (Spanish) A courageous man
Tyago

Tiassale (African) It has been forgotten

Tiberio (Italian) From the Tiber river
Tibero, Tyberio, Tybero, Tiberius, Tiberios, Tyberius, Tyberios

Tibor (Slavic) From the sacred place

Tiburon (Spanish) Resembling a shark

Tien (Vietnamese) The first and foremost

Tiernan (Gaelic) Lord of the manor
Tiarnan, Tiarney, Tierney, Tierny, Tiernee, Tiernea, Tierni, Tiernie, Tiarny, Tiarnee, Tiarnea, Tiarni, Tiarnie, Tyernan, Tyrnan, Tier, Tighearnach

Tiger (American) As powerful as the animal
Tyger, Tigre, Tygre, Tige, Tigris, Tigur, Tygur

Tihamér (Hungarian) A quiet boy; one who enjoys silence

Tihkoosue (Native American) A man of short stature
Tikoosue, Tihkousue, Tikousue

T'iis (Native American) Of the cottonwood
Tiis

Tilak (Hindi) A great leader
Tylak, Tilac, Tylac, Tilack, Tylack

Tilden (English) From the fertile valley
Tillden, Tildon, Tilldon, Tildan, Tilldan, Tildin, Tilldin, Tildun, Tilldun, Tiladene

Tilford (English) From the fertile ford
Tilforde, Tillford, Tillforde

Tilian (Anglo-Saxon) One who strives to better himself
Tilien, Tiliun, Tilion

Till (German) Form of Theodoric, meaning "the power of the people"
Tille, Tilly, Tilley, Tilli, Tillie, Tillee, Tillea

Tillery (German) A great leader
Tillerey, Tilleri, Tillerie, Tilleree, Tillerea

Tilman (English) One who plows the earth
Tillman, Tilmann, Tilghman

Tilon (Hebrew) A generous man
Tilen, Tilan, Tilun, Tilin, Tilyn

Tilton (English) From the fertile estate
Tillton, Tilten, Tillten, Tiltan, Tilltan, Tiltin, Tilltin, Tiltun, Tilltun

Timeus (Greek) The perfect man

Timir (Indian) Born in the darkness
Timirbaran

Timon (Greek) A respected man
Tymon

Timothy (Greek) One who honors God
Tim, Timmo, Timmy, Timmothy, Timmy, Timo, Timofei, Timofeo, Timofey, Timoteo, Timothé, Timotheo, Timothey, Timotheus, Tymmothy, Tymoteusz, Tymothy, Timin, Timotheos, Timoleon

Timur (African) One who is timid

Tin (Vietnamese) A great thinker

Tinashe (African) One who is with the Lord
Tinashi, Tinashie, Tinashee, Tinashea, Tinashy, Tinashey

Tinks (American) One who is coy
Tynks, Tincks, Tyncks, Tink, Tinke, Tinki, Tinkie, Tinkee, Tinkea, Tinkey, Tinky

Tino (Italian) A man of small stature
Teeno, Tieno, Teino, Teano, Tyno

Tinotenda (African) One who is thankful

Tinsley (English) A sociable man
Tinsly, Tinsli, Tinslie, Tinslee, Tinslea

Tintagel (English) In Arthurian legend, the birthplace of Arthur
Tentagel, Tintagil, Tentagil

Tip (American) Form of Thomas, meaning "one of twins"
Tipp, Tipper, Tippy, Tippee, Tippea, Tippey, Tippi, Tippie

Tipu (Indian) Resembling a tiger
Tipoo, Tipou, Tippu, Tippoo, Tippou

Tiru (Hindi) A pious man
Tyru, Tirue, Tyrue

Tirumala (Hindi) From the sacred hills

Tisa (African) The ninth-born child
Tisah, Tysa, Tysah

Titus (Greek / Latin) Of the giants / a great defender
Tito, Titos, Tytus, Tytos, Titan, Tytan, Tyto

Titusz (Hungarian) Resembling a dove
Tytusz

Tivadar (Hungarian) A gift from God
Tivadarr, Tyvadar, Tyvadarr

Tivon (Hebrew) One who loves nature
Tyvon

Tjasse (Norse) In mythology, a giant

Toa (Polynesian) A brave-hearted woman

Toafo (Polynesian) One who is spontaneous

Toai (Vietnamese) One who is content

Toal (Irish) One who is deeply rooted
Toale

Toan (Vietnamese) One who is safe
Toane

Tobbar (American) An active man

Tobechukwu (African) One who praises God

Tobias (Hebrew) The Lord is good
Thobey, Thobie, Thoby, Tobe, Tobee, Tobey, Tobi, Tobia, Tobiah, Tobie, Tobin, Tobit, Toby, Tobyn, Tobyas, Tohias, Tohy, Tohey, Tohee, Tohea, Tohi, Tohie, Tobes

Tobikuma (Japanese) Resembling a cloud

Tobrecan (Anglo-Saxon) A destroyer
Tolucan, Tobrucan, Tolecan

Tocho (Native American) Resembling a mountain lion
Tochio, Tochiyo

Tochtli (Aztec) Resembling a rabbit
Tochtlie, Tochtly, Tochtley, Tochtlee, Tochtlea

Todd (English) Resembling a fox
Tod

Todhunter (English) One who hunts foxes
Toddhunter

Todor (Bulgarian) A gift from God
Todos, Todros

Toft (English) From the small farm
Tofte

Togquos (Native American) One of twins

Tohon (Native American) One who loves the water

Tohopka (Native American) Resembling a wild beast

Tokala (Native American) Resembling a fox
Tokalo

Toki (Japanese) Filled with hope
Tokie, Toky, Tokey, Tokee, Tokea

Toks (American) A carefree man

Tokutaro (Japanese) A virtuous son

Tolan (Anglo-Saxon / American) From the taxed land / one who is studious
Tolen, Toland, Tolande, Tolend, Tolende, Tollan, Tolland

Tolek (Polish) A gift from God
Toleck, Tolec

Tolfe (American) An outgoing man

Toli (Spanish) One who ploughs the earth
Tolie, Toly, Toley, Tolee, Tolea

Tolman (English) One who collects taxes
Tollman, Toleman, Tolmann

Tolomey (French) One who plans
Tolomy, Tolomee, Tolomea, Tolomi, Tolomie

Toltecatl (Aztec) An artist

Tomaj (Hungarian) Of an ancient clan

Tomeo (Japanese) One who is cautious
Tomeyo

Tomer (Hebrew) A man of tall stature
Tomar, Tomur, Tomir, Tomor, Tomyr

Tomi (Japanese / African) A wealthy man / of the people
Tomie, Tomee, Tomea, Tomy, Tomey

Tomlin (English) Little Tom; son of Tom; the smaller of twins
Tomalin, Tomlinson, Tomkin, Tompkin, Tompkins, Tompkinson, Tomkinson

Tomochichi (Hawaiian) One who seeks the truth
Tomocheechee, Tomochychy

Tonauac (Aztec) One who possesses the light

Tong (Vietnamese) Having a pleasant fragrance
Tonge

Tony (English) Form of Anthony, meaning "a flourishing man; from an ancient Roman family"
Toney, Tonee, Tonea, Toni, Tonie, Tonio, Tonye, Tonion

Tooantuh (Native American) Resembling a spring frog
Tooantu, Touantuh, Touantu

Toopweets (Native American) Having great strength
Toupweets, Toopwets, Toupwets

Topher (Greek) Form of Christopher, meaning "one who bears Christ inside"
Toffer, Tofer

Topper (English) From the hill

Topwe (American) A jovial man
Topweh

Torao (Japanese) Resembling a tiger

Torcall (Norse) One who has been summoned by Thor
Thorcall, Torcalle, Thorcalle, Torcal, Thorcal

Tord (Dutch) One who is peaceful
Torde

Torger (Norse) The power of Thor's spear
Thorger, Torgar, Thorgar, Terje, Therje

Torgny (Scandinavian) The sound of weaponry
Torgnie, Torgni, Torgney, Torgnee, Torgnea

Torht (Anglo-Saxon) A bright man
Torhte

Toribio (Spanish) Having great strength
Toribo, Toribiyo

Toril (Hindi) One who has a temper
Torill, Torril, Torrill, Torile, Torille, Torrille

Torin (Celtic) One who acts as chief
Toran, Torean, Toren, Torion, Torran, Torrian, Toryn

Torio (Japanese) Resembling a bird's tail
Toriyo, Torrio, Torriyo

Tormaigh (Irish) Having the spirit of Thor
Tormey, Tormay, Tormaye, Tormai, Tormae

Tormod (Gaelic) A man from the north

Toro (Spanish) Resembling a bull

Torquil (Gaelic) Thor's helmet
Thirkell, Thorkel, Torkel, Torkill, Torquill, Thorquil, Thorquill, Thorkill

Torr (English) From the tower
Torre

Torrence (Gaelic) From the little hills
Torence, Torrance, Torrens, Torrans, Toran, Torran, Torrin, Torn, Torne

Torry (Norse / Gaelic) Refers to Thor / form of Torrence, meaning "from the little hills"
Torrey, Torree, Torrea, Torri, Torrie, Tory, Torey, Tori, Torie, Toree, Torea

Toru (Japanese) Man of the sea

Toshan (Indian) One who is satisfied
Toshann

Toshi (Japanese) One who sees his true image
Toshie, Toshy, Toshey, Toshee, Toshea

Toshiro (Japanese) One who is talented and intelligent
Toshihiro

Toshith (Indian) Filled with happiness
Toshithe, Toshyth, Toshythe

Tostig (English) A well-known earl
Tostyg

Tosya (Russian) One who exceeds expectations
Tosiya, Tusya, Tusiya

Tototl (Aztec) Resembling a bird

Toussaint (French) All saints
Toussnint, Toussaent, Toussanynt, Toussant

Toviel (Hebrew) The Lord is good
Toviell, Toviele, Tovielle, Tovi, Tovie, Tovee, Tovea, Tovy, Tovey, Tov, Tova, Tove

Towley (English) From the town near the meadow
Towly, Towleigh, Towlee, Towlea, Towleah, Towli, Towlie, Townly, Townley, Townlee, Townleigh, Townlea, Townleah, Townli, Townlie

Townsend (English) From the end of town
Townsand, Tonsend, Tonsand

Toyo (Japanese) A man of plenty

Tracy (Gaelic) One who is warlike
Tracey, Traci, Tracie, Tracee, Tracea, Treacy, Trace, Tracen, Treacey, Treaci, Treacie, Treacee, Treacea

Trahan (English) A handsome man
Trahahn, Trahain, Trahaine, Trahaen, Trahaene, Trahane, Trahen

Trahern (Welsh) As strong as iron
Trahayarn, Trahearn, Trahearne, Traherne, Trahaearn

Traigh (Irish) A strand

Trail (English) A lover of nature
Traill, Traile, Trayl, Trayle, Trael, Traele, Trale

Trailokva (Indian) Of the three worlds
Trailokvya, Traelokva, Traelokvya, Traylokva, Traylokvya

Trang (Vietnamese) One who is honored

Tranter (English) A wagoneer
Trantir, Trantar, Trantor, Trantur, Trantyr

Trapper (American) One who traps animals
Trappar, Trappor, Trappir, Trappyr, Trappur

Traugott (German) One who has faith in God
Trawgott, Traugot, Trawgot

Travis (French) To cross over
Travys, Traver, Travers, Traviss, Trevis, Trevys, Travus, Traves

Travon (American) At the crossroads; a traveler
Travaughn, Traveon, Travion, Trayvon, Travoun, Travawn

Treadway (English) Having the strength of a warrior
Treadwai, Treadwaye, Treadwae, Tredway, Tredwaye, Tredwai, Tredwae

Treasach (Irish) A mighty fighter
Treasaigh, Treasigh

Tredan (Anglo-Saxon) One who tramples others
Treden, Tredin, Tredon, Tredun, Tredyn

Treddian (Anglo-Saxon) One who leaves
Treddien, Treddion, Treddiun

Treffen (German) One who socializes
Treffan, Treffin, Treffon, Treffyn, Treffun

Tremain (Celtic) From the town built of stone
Tramain, Tramaine, Tramayne, Tremaine, Tremayne, Tremaen, Tremaene, Tramaen, Tramaene, Tremane, Tramane

Tremont (French) From the three mountains
Tremonte, Tremount, Tremounte

Trennen (German) Of the divided people
Trennon, Trennan, Trennin, Trennun, Trennyn

Trent (Latin) From the rushing waters
Trente, Trint, Trinte, Trynt, Trynte

Trenton (English) From the town near the rapids; from Trent's town
Trenten, Trentin, Trentyn

Treoweman (English) A loyal man
Treowe

Tretan (German) One who walks
Treten, Tretun, Treton, Tretyn, Tretin

Trevelian (Welsh) From the house of Elian
Trevelien, Trevelyan, Trevelyen

Trevet (Gaelic) From the three hills
Trevett, Trevete, Trevette

Trevin (English) From the fair town
Trevan, Treven, Trevian, Trevion, Trevon, Trevyn, Trevonn

Trevor (Welsh) From the large village
Trefor, Trevar, Trever, Treabhar, Treveur, Trevir, Trevur

Trevrizent (English) In Arthurian legend, Percival's uncle

Trey (English) The third-born child
Tre, Trai, Trae, Tray, Traye, Trayton, Treyton, Trayson, Treyson

Triage (French) One who handles emergencies

Trigg (Norse) One who is truthful
Trygg

Trong (Vietnamese) One who is respected

Trory (American) The red one
Trorey, Troree, Trorea, Trori, Trorie

Trowbridge (English) From the bridge near the tree
Trowbrydge, Trowhridge, Treowbrycg

Troy (Gaelic) Son of a footsoldier
Troye, Troi

Troyes (French) A man with curly hair

True (American) One who is honest
Tru, Trew, Truit, Truitt, Truitte

Truesdale (English) From the valley of the honest man
Trusdale, Truesdayle, Trusdayle, Truesdail, Trusdail, Truesdaele, Trusdaele, Truesdayl, Trusdayl, Truesdaile, Trusdaile, Truesdael, Trusdael, Truesdell, Trusdell, Truitestall, Trudell, Trudel, Trudelle

Truman (English) One who is loyal
Trueman, Trumann, Trumain, Trumaine, Trumaen, Trumaene, Trumayn, Trumayne, Trumen

Trumbald (English) A bold man
Trumbold, Trumbalde, Trumbolde

TRISTEN

Legends of the Fall: Ladies, need I say more? His middle name is Jaxx—my husband was spewing off exotic soap opera names, and I always liked the name Jacques (from *General Hospital*). My husband liked it, but decided to spell it with two x's, because "it was much cooler than one x." — Veronica, FL

Tripp (English) A traveler
Trip, Trypp, Tryp, Tripper, Trypper

Tripsy (American) One who enjoys dancing
Tripsey, Tripsee, Tripsea, Tripsi, Tripsie

Tristan ○ (Celtic) A sorrowful man; in Arthurian legend, a knight of the Round Table
Trystan, Tris, Tristam, Tristen, Tristian, Tristin, Triston, Tristram, Tristyn, Triste

Trocky (American) A manly man
Trockey, Trocki, Trockie, Trockee, Trockea

Trond (Norse) A growing man
Tronde

Trumble (English) One who is powerful
Trumball, Trumbell, Trumbo, Trumbull

Trumhall (English) Having great strength
Trumhal, Trumhale, Trumhail, Trumhaile, Trumhayl, Trumhayle, Trumhael, Trumhaele

Trung (Vietnamese) One who is centrally located

Truong (Turkish) From the field near the school

Trygg (Scandinavian) One who speaks the truth

Trygve (Norse) One who wins with bravery

Trymian (Anglo-Saxon) One who encourages others
Trymyan, Trymien, Trymyen

Trymman (Anglo-Saxon) One who strengthens others

Tsalani (African) One who leaves
Tsalanie, Tsalany, Tsalaney, Tsalanee, Tsalanea

Tsatoke (Native American) One who hunts on horseback

Tse (Native American) As solid as a rock

Tsela (Native American) Resembling a star

Tsidhqiyah (Hebrew) The Lord is just
Tsidqiyah, Tsidhqiya, Tsdqiya

Tsiishch'ili (Native American) One who has curly hair

Tsin (Native American) One who rides a horse
Tsen, Tsyn

Tsoai (Native American) As big as a tree

Tsubasa (Japanese) A winged being
Tsubasah, Tsubase, Tsubaseh

Tsvetan (Bulgarian) Refers to Palm Sunday

Tu (Vietnamese) One who is quick-minded

Tuan (Vietnamese) A gentleman

Tuari (Native American) Resembling a young eagle
Tuarie, Tuary, Tuarey, Tuaree, Tuarea

Tucker (English) One who makes garments
Tuker, Tuckerman, Tukerman, Tuck, Tuckman, Tukman, Tuckere, Toukere

Tucson (Native American) From the city in Arizona
Tooson, Touson

Tuesday (English) Born on a Tuesday
Tewsday, Tuesdai, Tewsdai, Tuesdae, Tewsdae, Tuesdaye, Tewsdaye

Tufan (Indian) Resembling a tempest
Tufann, Tuphan, Tuphann

Tuhin (Indian) Of the snow
Tuhine, Tuhyn, Tuhyne

Tuhinsurra (Indian) As white as snow
Tuhinsura, Tuhynsurra, Tuhynsura

Tuketu (Native American) Resembling a running bear
Tuketue, Tuketoo, Tuketou, Telutci, Telutcie, Telutcy, Telutcey, Telutcee, Telutki, Telutkie, Telutky, Telutkey, Telukee

Tukuli (American) Resembling a caterpillar
Tukulie, Tukuly, Tukuley, Tukulee, Tukulea

Tulasidas (Hindi) One who is devoted to Tulasi

Tulio (Spanish) A lively man
Tuliyo, Tullio, Tulliyo

Tully (Gaelic) Of the mighty people
Tulley, Tulli, Tullie, Tullee, Tullea, Tulleigh, Tullis

Tulsi (Indian) A holy man
Tulsie, Tulsy, Tulsey, Tulsee, Tulsea

Tumaini (African) An optimist
Tumainie, Tumainee, Tumainy, Tumainey, Tumayni, Tumaynie, Tumaynee, Tumayney, Tumayny, Tumaeni, Tumaenie, Tumaenee, Tumaeny, Tumaeney

Tumbura (Indian) Resembling a celestial being
Tumburra

Tumo (African) A famous man
Tummo

Tumu (American) Resembling a deer
Tummu

Tunde (African) One who returns
Tundi, Tundie, Tundee, Tundea, Tundy, Tundey

Tune (English) One who plays melodies
Toon, Toone, Toun, Toune

Tung (Vietnamese) Resembling the coniferous tree
Tunge

Tunleah (English) From the town near the meadow
Tunlea, Tunleigh, Tunly, Tunley, Tunlee, Tunli, Tunlie

Tupac (African) A messenger warrior
Tupack, Tupoc, Tupock

Tupi (Native American) To pull up
Tupie, Tupee, Tupea, Tupy, Tupey

Tupper (English) One who herds rams
Tuper, Tuppere, Tupere

Turbo (Latin) Resembling a spinning object

Turfeinar (Norse) In mythology, the son of Rognvald
Turfaynar, Turfaenar, Turfanar, Turfenar, Turfainar

Turi (Spanish) Resembling a bear
Turie, Turee, Turea, Tury, Turey, Turio

Twain (English) One who is divided in two
Twaine, Twayn, Twayne, Twaen, Twaene, Twane, Twein, Tweine

Twitchel (English) One who lives on a narrow lane
Twitchele, Twitchell, Twitchelle

Twrgadarn (Welsh) From the strong tower

Twyford (English) From the double river crossing
Twiford, Twyforde, Twiforde

Txanton (Basque) Form of Anthony, meaning "a flourishing man; from an ancient Roman family"
Txantony, Txantoney, Txantonee, Txantoni, Txantonie, Txantonea

---

TYLER

I wanted to name our son Thomas, after my husband, but he didn't want a Jr. When he suggested the name Tyler, I instantly fell in love with it. We decided to keep their middle names the same, so now they have the same initials. —Sharol, IL

Turk (English) A man from Turkey
Turck, Turc

Turner (English) One who works with wood
Turnar, Turnir, Turnyr, Turnor, Turnur, Tournour

Tushar (Indian) Of the snow
Tusharr, Tushare

Tusharsuvra (Indian) As white as snow

Tusita (Chinese) One who is heaven-sent

Tut (Egyptian) A courageous man

Tutu (African) Man from the cliffs

Tuvya (Hebrew) The Lord is good
Tuvyah, Tov, Toviach, Tovyah, Toviah, Tuviyahu, Tutyahu

Tuwa (Native American) One who loves nature
Tuwah

Tuxford (Norse) From the spearman's ford
Tuxforde

Tuyen (Vietnamese) A heavenly messenger

Txomin (Basque) A godly man

Tybalt (Latin) He who sees the truth
Tybault, Tybalte, Tybaulte

Tychon (Greek) One who is accurate
Tycho

Tye (English) From the fenced-in pasture
Tyg, Tyge, Tie, Tigh, Teyen

Tyee (Native American) A great chief
Tyea, Tyey, Tyi, Tyie

Tyeis (French) The son of a German

Tyfiell (English) Follower of the god Tyr
Tyfiel, Tyfielle, Tyfiele

Tygie (American) Full of energy
Tygi, Tygey, Tygy, Tygee, Tygea

Tyjah (African) One who is intelligent
Tyja

Tyke (Scandinavian) One who is determined
Tike

Tyler ○ ♂ (English) A tiler of roofs
Tilar, Tylar, Tylor, Tiler, Tilor, Ty, Tye, Tylere, Tylore

Tyme (English) The aromatic herb thyme
Time, Thyme, Thime

Tynan (Gaelic) One who is dark and dusty
Tienan, Tynell, Tynen, Tynin, Tynnen, Tynnin, Tynon

Tyne (English) From the river
Tyn, Tine

Typhoon (Chinese) Of the great wind
Tiphoon, Tyfoon, Tifoon, Typhoun, Tiphoun, Tyfoun, Tifoun

Tyr (Norse) In mythology, an ancient god

Tyree (American) One who is courteous
Tyry, Tyrey, Tyrea, Tyri, Tyrie, Tyrae

Tyreece (American) One who is combative
Tyreace, Tyriece, Tyreice, Tyrece, Tyreese, Tyrease, Tyriese, Tyreise, Tyrese, Tyryce, Tyryse

Tyrique (American) A defender of the people
Tyreeque, Tyreek, Tyreaque, Tyreak, Tyreeke, Tyreake, Tyriq, Tyreeq, Tyreaq, Tyreq, Tyreque

Tyrone (Gaelic) From Owen's land
Tirone, Tirohn, Tirown, Tyron, Tyronne, Turone

Tyrus (Latin) Man from the ancient city of Tyre
Tyris, Tyres, Tyros, Tyras, Tyrys

Tyson (French) One who is high-spirited; fiery
Thyssen, Tiesen, Tyce, Tycen, Tyeson, Tyssen, Tysen, Tysan, Tysun, Tysin, Tyesone

Tywysog (Welsh) Born to royalty; a prince

Tzadok (Hebrew) One who is just and fair
Tzadock, Tzadoc, Tzadoke, Tzadocke

Tzefanyahu (Hebrew) One who is treasured by God
Tzefanyahue, Tzefanyah, Tzefanya

Tzion (Hebrew) From the mountain
Tzionn, Tzionne

Tziyon (Hebrew) The son of Zion

Tzuriel (Hebrew) God is my strength
Tzuriell, Tzuriele, Tzurielle

Tzvi (Hebrew) Resembling a deer
Tzvie, Tzvy, Tzvey, Tzvee, Tzvea

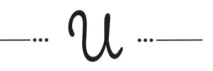

U (Korean) A kind and gentle man

Uaid (Irish) Form of Walter, meaning "the commander of the army"
Uaide, Uayd, Uayde, Uade, Uaed, Uaede

Uaithne (Gaelic) One who is innocent; green
Uaithn, Uaythne, Uaythn, Uathne, Uathn, Uaethne, Uaethn

Ualan (Scottish) Form of Valentine, meaning "one who is strong and healthy"
Ualane, Ualayn, Ualayne, Ualen, Ualon

Ualtar (Irish) A strong warrior
Ualtarr, Ualter, Ualterr

Uba (African) One who is wealthy; lord of the house
Ubah, Ubba, Ubbah

Ubadah (Arabic) One who serves God
Ubada, Ubaidah, Ubaida, Ubaydah, Ubayda, Ubaeda, Ubaedah

Ubaid (Arabic) One who is faithful
Ubaide, Ubade, Ubayde, Ubayd, Ubaed, Ubaede

Ubel (German) An evil man
Ubell, Ubele, Ubul, Ubull, Ubule

Uberto (Italian) Form of Hubert, meaning "having a shining intellect"
Ulberto, Umberto

Uchdryd (Welsh) In mythology, the son of Erim
Uchdrid, Uchdred, Uchdried, Uchdreid, Uchdread

Uchechi (African) God's will be done
Uchechie, Uchechy, Uchechey, Uchechee, Uchechea, Uchi, Uchie, Uchee, Uchea, Uchy, Uchey

U

Udadhi (Indian) Man of the sea
Udadhie, Udadhy, Udadhey, Udadhea,
Udadhee

Udank (Indian) In mythology, a sage
Udanke

Udar (Indian) A generous man
Udarr, Udarre, Udari, Udarie, Udary,
Udarey, Udaree, Udarea

Udath (Indian) One who is noble
Udathe

Uday (Indian) Our son has arrived
Udaye, Udai, Udae

Udayachal (Indian) From the eastern hill
Udayachall, Udaiachal, Udaiachall

Udayachandra (Indian) Born with the
rising moon
Udayachande

Udayan (Indian) One who is thriving
Udayen

Udayaravi (Indian) Born with the rising sun
Udayarvie, Udayarvy, Udayarvey,
Udayarvee, Udayarvea

Udbhuddah (Indian) One who is
blossoming
Udbhudda

Uddam (Indian) An exceptional man

Uddeepath (Indian) An illuminated man
Uddeepth, Uddeepthe, Udeepath,
Udeepathe, Uddepath, Uddepathe

Uddhar (Indian) One who is free; an
independent man
Uddharr, Udhar, Udharr

Uddhav (Hindi) In Hinduism, Krishna's
friend
Uddhaav, Udhav, Udhaav

Udeh (Hebrew) One who praises God
Ude

Udell (English) From the valley of yew trees
Udale, Udel, Udall, Udayle, Udayl, Udail,
Udaile, Udele, Udelle, Udael, Udaele

Udi (Hebrew) One who carries a torch
Udie, Udy, Udey, Udee, Udea

Udit (Indian) One who is thriving
Udite, Udyt, Udyte

Udo (German / African) One who is
prosperous / one who is peaceful

Udolf (English) A prosperous wolf
Udolfo, Udulf, Udulfo, Udolph, Udolpho,
Udulph, Udulpho

Udup (Indian) Born beneath the moon's
light
Udupp, Uddup, Uddupp

Udyam (Indian) One who puts forth an
effort
Udiam, Udeam

Udyan (Indian) Of the garden
Uddyan, Udyann, Uddyann

Ueli (Swedish) Form of Ulrich, meaning
"having wealth and power"
Uelie, Uely, Ueley, Uelee, Uelea

Ufuk (Turkish) Of the horizon

Ugo (Italian) A great thinker

Ugutz (Basque) Refers to John the Baptist

Uigbiorn (Norse) A warrior bear
Ugbjorn, Ugbiorn, Ugbyorn, Uigbyorn,
Uigbjorn

Uilleag (Irish) Having a playful heart
Uileag, Uilleage, Uileage, Uylleag, Uyleag,
Uylleage, Uyleage

Uilleam (Scottish) Form of William,
meaning "the determined protector"
Uileam, Uilleame, Uileame, Uylleam,
Uylleame, Uyleam, Uyleame, Uilliam,
Uylliam

Uinseann (Irish) Form of Vincent, mean-
ing "one who prevails; the conquerer"
Uinsean, Uyseann, Uysean, Uinseane,
Uynseane, Uinseanne, Uynseanne

Uisdean (Scottish) From the stone island
Uisdeann, Uysdean, Uysdeann, Uisdeane,
Uysdeane, Uysdeanne, Uisdeanne

Uistean (Teutonic) An intelligent man
Uisteane, Ustean, Usteane, Uystean, Uysteane

Ujwal (Indian) One who is bright
Ujjal, Ujal, Ujual

Ukiah (Native American) From the
deep valley
Ukia, Ukyah, Ukya

Ukko (Finnish) In mythology, god of the sky and thunder
Uko, Ucco, Ucko, Uco

Ulan (African) The firstborn of twins
Ullan, Ulann, Ullann

Uland (English) From the noble country
Ulande, Ulland, Ullande, Ulandus, Ullandus

Ulani (Hawaiian) One who is cheerful
Ulanie, Ulany, Ulaney, Ulanee, Ulana, Ulanya, Ulania, Ulane, Ulanea

Ulbrecht (German) The bright wolf
Ulbrekt, Ulbreckt, Ulbrech, Ulbrek, Ulbreck

Ulderico (Italian) A merciful ruler
Uldericco, Uldericko, Ulderiko, Ulderyco, Ulderycco, Ulderycko, Ulderyko

Ulf (German) Resembling a wolf
Ulfe, Ulff, Ulffe, Ulph, Ulphe, Ulv, Ulve

Ulfred (English) Wolf of peace
Ulfrid, Ulfryd, Ulfried, Ulfreid

Ulger (English) Rules with a wolf spear
Ulgar, Ulgerr, Ulgarr

Ulhas (Indian) Filled with happiness
Ulhass, Ullhas, Ullhass

Uli (German) A noble ruler
Ulie, Uly, Uley, Ulee, Ulea

Ulick (Gaelic) Little William; son of William
Ulik, Ulic, Ulyck, Ulyk, Ulyc

Ull (Norse) Having glory; in mythology, god of justice and patron of agriculture
Ulle, Ul, Ule

Ullok (English) The wolf sport
Ullock, Ulloc, Ulok, Ulock, Uloc, Ulvelaik, Ulvelayk, Ulvelake

Ulloriaq (Native American) Resembling a star
Uloriaq, Ulloryaq, Uloryaq

Ulmer (German) Having the fame of the wolf
Ullmer, Ullmar, Ulmarr, Ullmarr, Ulfmer, Ulfmar, Ulfmaer

Ulric (German) Having the power of the wolf; the wolf ruler
Ulryc, Ulrik, Ulryk, Ulrick, Ulryck

Ulrich (German) Having wealth and power
Ulyrich, Utz

Ultan (Gaelic) A man from Ulster
Ulltan, Ulttan, Ullttan, Ultann, Ulltann, Ullttann

Ultman (Indian) A godly man
Ultmann, Ultmane

Ulysses (Latin) Form of Odysseus, meaning "one who roams; an angry man"
Ulises, Ulisse, Ulyses, Ulysse, Ulisses

Ulz (German) A noble ruler
Ulze

Umar (Arabic) One who is thriving; prosperous
Umer, Umarr, Umare, Umerr

Umber (French) Providing shade; of an earth color
Umbar, Umbro

Umed (Hindi) Filled with desire, hope

Umi (African) A giver of life
Umee, Umy, Umey, Umea, Umie

Ummi (African) His mother's son
Ummie, Ummy, Ummey, Ummee, Ummea

Umrao (Indian) One who is noble

Umut (Turkish) Filled with hope
Umit, Umutt, Umitt, Umyt, Umytt

Unai (Basque) A shepherd
Unay, Unaye, Unae

Unathi (African) God is with us
Unathie, Unathy, Unathey, Unathee, Unathea

Uncas (Native American) Resembling a fox
Unkas, Unckas

Uner (Turkish) One who is famous
Unerr, Unar, Unarr

Ungus (Irish) A vigorous man
Unguss

Unique (American) Unlike others; the only one
Unikue, Unik, Uniqui, Uniqi, Uniqe, Unikque, Unike, Unicke, Unick

U

Unnat (Indian) An energized or elevated man
Unnatt, Unatt, Unat

Unni (Norse) One who is modest
Unnie, Unny, Unney, Unnee, Unnea

Unnikrishnan (Indian) A young Krishna
Unikrishnan, Unnikrishna, Unikrishna

Unwin (English) One who is unfriendly
Unwinn, Unwinne, Unwyn, Unwynn,
Unwynne, Unwine, Unwyne, Unwen,
Unwenn, Unwenne

Uny (Latin / Irish) United as one / one who
is pure
Uni, Unie, Uney, Unee, Unea, Uno

Uolevi (Finnish) Form of Olaf, meaning
"the last of the ancestors"
Uolevie, Uolevee, Uolevy, Uolevey,
Uolevea

Upchurch (English) From the upper church
Upchurche

Updike (English) From the upper bank
Updyk, Updyke

Upen (Hindi) In Hinduism, Indra's
younger brother
Uppen, Upenn, Uppenn

Upendo (African) One who loves and
is loved
Upendio

Upshaw (English) From the upper thicket
Upshawe

Upton (English) From the upper town
Uptun, Uptown

Upwode (English) From the upper forest
Upwood, Upwoode

Uranus (Greek) In mythology, the father of
the Titans
Urainus, Uraynus, Uranas, Uraynas,
Urainas, Uranos, Uraynos, Urainos

Urban (Latin) From the city
Urbain, Urbaine, Urbane, Urbano,
Urbanus, Urbayn, Urbayne

Urho (Finnish) A brave man

Uri (Hebrew) Form of Uriah, meaning
"the Lord is my light"
Urie, Ury, Urey, Uree, Urea

Uriah (Hebrew) The Lord is my light
Uria, Urias, Urija, Urijah, Uriyah, Urjasz,
Uriya

Urian (Greek) Sent from heaven
Urian, Uriann, Urianne, Uryan, Uryann,
Uryanne

Uriel (Hebrew) The angel of light
Uriell, Urielle, Uryel, Uryell, Uryelle

Urien (Welsh) Of a priveleged birth
Urienn, Urienne, Uryen, Uryenn, Uryenne,
Uriens

Urjavaha (Hindu) Of the Nimi dynasty

Uros (Hungarian) The little lord

Urquhart (Scottish) From the knoll with
the fountain

Ursus (Latin) Resembling a bear
Urs, Urso, Ursel, Ursino, Ursins, Ursinus

Urtzi (Basque) From the sky
Urtzie, Urtzy, Urtzey, Urtzee, Urtzea

Urvakhsha (Persian) One who is filled
with joy
Urvakhshah, Urvaksha, Urvakshah

Usamah (Arabic) Resembling a lion
Usama, Usamma, Usammah

Usbeorn (English) A divine warrior

Ushakanta (Indian) Born beneath the sun

Usher (Latin) From the mouth of the river
Ushar, Ushir, Ussher, Usshar, Usshir

Ushi (Chinese) As strong as an ox
Ushie, Ushy, Ushey, Ushee, Ushea

Usko (Finnish) Having much faith
Uskko, Uscco, Uscko

Utah (Native American) People of the
mountains; from the state of Utah

Utathya (Indian) In mythology, a sage
Utathiya, Utathyah, Utathiyah

Utgardloki (Norse) In mythology, a giant
and ruler of the city Utgard
Utgardlokie, Utgardloky, Utgardlokey,
Utgardlokee, Utgardlokea, Utgardlokki

Uther (English) In Arthurian legend, Arthur's father
Uthar, Uthir, Uthyr

Uthman (Arabic) Resembling a young bustard
Utheman, Uthmann, Usman, Useman, Usmann

Utkarsh (Indian) One who achieves advancement
Utkarshe, Utkarse, Utkars, Utckars, Utckarsh, Utckarshe, Uthkarsh, Uthkarshe

Utpal (Indian) Resembling the lotus
Utpall, Utpale, Utphal, Utphall, Utphale

Utsav (Indian) Born during a celebration
Utsavi, Utsave, Utsava, Utsavie, Utsavy, Utsavey, Utsavee, Utsavea

Utt (Arabic) One who is kind and wise
Utte

Uwe (German) Of the blade

Uxio (Galician) Form of Eugene, meaning "a wellborn man"
Uxo, Uxyo

Uzi (Hebrew) Having great power
Uzie, Uzy, Uzey, Uzee, Uzea, Uzzi, Uzzie, Uzzy, Uzzey, Uzzee, Uzzea

Uzima (African) One who is full of life
Uzimah, Uzimma, Uzimmah, Uzyma, Uzymma, Uyziema, Uzeima, Uzeema, Uzeemah, Uzeama

Uzoma (African) Born during the course of a journey
Uzomah, Uzomma, Uzommah

Uzumati (Native American) Resembling a grizzly bear
Uzumatie, Uzumatee, Uzumaty, Uzumatey, Uzumatea

Uzziah (Hebrew) The Lord is my strength
Uzzia, Uziah, Uzia, Uzzya, Uzzyah, Uzyah, Uzya, Uzziel, Uziel, Uzziell, Uziell, Uzzyel, Uzyel, Uzzyell, Uzyell

V

Vachaspati (Indian) A learned man; the lord of speech
Vachaspatie, Vachaspaty, Vachaspatey, Vachaspatee

Vachel (French) Resembling a small cow
Vachele, Vachell

Vachlan (English) One who lives near water

Vaclav (Czech) Form of Wenceslas, meaning "one who receives more glory"
Venceslav, Vaclar, Vaclovas

Vada (Hebrew) Resembling a rose
Vadah, Vadda, Vaddah, Vardis, Vardys, Vardiss, Vardyss, Vered

Vadar (Dutch) A fatherly man
Vader, Vadyr

Vaddon (Welsh) Man from Bath
Vadden, Vaddan

Vadhir (Spanish) Resembling a rose
Vadhyr, Vadheer

Vadim (Russian) A good-looking man
Vadime, Vadym, Vadyme, Vadeem, Vadeeme

Vadin (Hindi) A known speaker
Vadine, Vadeen, Vadeene, Vadyn, Vadyne, Vachan

Vagas (Spanish) From the meadow

Vagish (Hindi) In Hinduism, another name for Brahma
Vagishe, Vagysh, Vagyshe

Vahan (Armenian) One who shields others
Vahane, Vahann

Vahe (Armenian) One who is strong
Vahi, Vahee, Vahey, Vahy, Vahea, Vahie

Vahid (Persian) The only one
Vahide, Vahyd, Vahyde, Vaheed, Vaheede

Vahu (Persian) One who is well-behaved
Vahue, Vahoo

Vai (Teutonic) A mighty ruler
Vae

Vaibhav (Indian) One who is wealthy
Vabhav, Vaybhav

Vaijnath (Hindi) Refers to Lord Shiva
Vaejnath, Vaijnathe, Vaejnathe

Vail (English) From the valley
Vaile, Vayl, Vayle, Vale, Vaill, Vayll

Vainamoinen (Finnish) From the wide, slow river; in mythology, a wise magician
Vaino

Vaiveahtoish (Native American) One who lands on the cloud
Vaiveatoish, Vaive Atoish, Vaive Ahtoish

Valazquez (Spanish) Resembling a crow

Valborg (Swedish) From the powerful mountain
Valborge

Valdemar (German) A well-known ruler
Valdemarr, Valdemare, Valto, Valdmar, Valdmarr, Valdimar, Valdimarr

Valdis (Teutonic) One who is spirited in battle
Valdiss, Valdys, Valdyss

Valente (Italian) One who is valiant
Valient, Valiente

Valentine (Latin) One who is strong and healthy
Val, Valen, Valentijn, Valentin, Valentinian, Valentino, Valentinus, Valentyn, Vallen

Valerian (Latin) One who is strong and healthy
Valerien, Valerio, Valerius, Valery, Valeryan, Valere, Valeri, Valerii, Valeray, Valeriy, Valero, Valeriu, Vali, Valerik, Vallen

Valfrid (Swedish) Form of Walfried, meaning "a peaceful ruler"
Valfried, Valfred, Vallfried, Vallfrid, Vallfred, Valfryd, Vallfryd

Vali (Norse) In mythology, a son of Odin

Valin (Hindi) The monkey king

Vallabh (Indian) One who is dearly loved
Valbh, Vallab, Valab

Valle (French) From the glen
Vallejo

Vallis (French) A man from Wales
Vallois

Valo (Finnish) Man of the light
Vallo

Valri (French) One who is strong
Valrie, Valry, Valrey, Valree

Valter (Swedish) Form of Walter, meaning "the commander of the army"
Valther, Valtteri

Van (Vietnamese / Slavic) Of the clouds / form of Ivan, meaning "God is gracious"
Vann

Van Aken (Dutch) Man from Aachen

Van Eych (Dutch) From the oak tree

Van Ness (Dutch) From the headland

Vanajit (Indian) King of the forest
Vanajyt, Vanajeet

Vance (English) From the marshland
Vanse

Vandal (Latin) One who destroys

Vander (Greek) Form of Evander, meaning "a benevolent man"

Vanderbilt (Dutch) From the hill
Vanderbylt, Vanderbelt, Vanderbalt

Vanderpool (Dutch) From the pool
Vanderpol, Vanderpul, Vanderpull

Vanderveer (Dutch) From the ferry
Vandervere, Vandervir, Vandervire, Vandervyr, Vandervyre

Vandy (Dutch) One who travels; a wanderer
Vandey, Vandi, Vandie, Vandee

Vandyke (Danish) From the dike
Vandike

Vane (English) A banner; a symbol

Vanek (English) Form of John, meaning "God is gracious"
Vanko, Vanechka

Vangelo (English) Form of Evangel, meaning "a bringer of good news"
Vangelios, Vangelis

Vanig (Armenian) From a small town
Vaneg, Vanyg

Vanir (Norse) Of the ancient gods

Vannes (English) Of the grain fans
Vanness, Vannese, Vannesse

Vanya (Russian) Form of John, meaning "God is gracious"
Vanyah

Varad (Hungarian) From the fortress

Varante (Arabic) From the river

Vardon (French) From the green hill
Varden, Verdon, Verdun, Verden, Vardun, Vardan, Verddun, Varddun, Varddon, Verddon

Varen (Hindi) One who is superior
Varren, Varan, Varran, Varon, Varron, Varun, Varrun

Varfolomey (Russian) Form of Bartholomew, meaning "the son of the farmer"
Varfolomei, Varfolomew, Varfolom

Varg (Norse) Resembling a wolf

Varick (German) A protective ruler
Varrick, Varyck, Varryck, Varik, Varyk, Varek, Vareck

Varij (Indian) Resembling the lotus

Varindra (Indian) Lord of the sea
Varyndra, Varindrah, Varyndrah

Varius (Latin) A versatile man
Varian, Varinius

Variya (Hindu) The excellent one

Varlaam (Russian) Form of Barlaam, meaning "the name of a hermit"
Varlam

Varnava (Russian) Form of Barnabas, meaning "the son of the prophet; the son of encouragement"
Varnavas, Varnavus, Varnavee, Varnavey, Varnavie, Varnavus, Varnavy, Varnevas, Varnevus

Varney (Celtic) From the alder tree grove
Varny, Varni, Varnie, Varnea, Varneah, Varnee

Varten (Persian) One who gives roses
Vartan, Vartin

Varun (Hindi) The lord of the waters
Varoun, Varune, Varoune, Varoon, Varoone

Vasant (Indian) Born during the spring
Vasante, Vasanth, Vasanthe

Vasava (Hindi) Refers to Indra

Vaschel (Hebrew) From the small ash tree

Vasco (Basque) Resembling a crow

Vashon (American) The Lord is gracious
Vashan, Vashawn, Vashaun, Vashone, Vashane, Vashayn, Vashayne

Vasilis (Greek) One who is kingly; born to royalty
Vasileios, Vasilij, Vasily, Vaso, Vasos, Vassilij, Vassily, Vasya, Vasilios, Vasilii, Vasile, Vasil, Vasili, Vasilica, Vasilije, Vasek, Vaseck, Vasska, Vassil, Vassi, Vasyl, Vasylko

Vasin (Indian) A great ruler
Vasine, Vaseen, Vaseene, Vasyn, Vasyne

Vasistha (Indian) Name of a sage
Vasisstha, Vasystha, Vasysstha, Vasosta, Vasoshta

Vasu (Indian) One who is bright; an excellent man
Vasue, Vasoo

Vasudev (Indian) Refers to Lord Krishna

Vasuki (Hindi) In Hinduism, a serpent king
Vasukie, Vasuky, Vasukey, Vasukee, Vasukea

Vasuman (Indian) Son born of fire

Vatsa (Indian) Our beloved son
Vathsa

Vatsal (Indian) One who is affectionate

Vaughn (Welsh) One who is small
Vaughan

Vavrinec (Czech) Form of Lawrence, meaning "man from laurentum; crowned with laurel"
Vavrinek, Vavrynec, Vavrynek, Vavrineck, Vavryneck, Vavrin, Vavryn

V

Vayk (Hungarian) One who is wealthy

Ve (Norse) In mythology, brother of Odin

Veasna (Cambodian) One who has good fortune

Veda (Sanskrit) Refers to the sacred texts; having great knowledge
Vaada, Vaida, Vaeda, Ved, Vyda, Vedas

Vegard (Norse) One who offers protection
Vegarde, Vagard, Vagarde

Veli (Finnish) One who is brotherly
Veikko, Veiko

Velimir (Croatian) One who wishes for great peace
Velimeer, Velimyr, Velimire, Velimeere, Velimyre

Velvel (Hebrew) Resembling a wolf

Velyo (Bulgarian) A great man
Velcho, Veliko, Velin, Velko

Vencel (Hungarian) Form of Wenceslas, meaning "one who receives more glory"
Venzel, Vencele, Venzele

Venceslao (Italian) Form of Wenceslas, meaning "one who receives more glory"
Venceslas

Venedict (American) Form of Benedict, meaning "one who is blessed"
Vendick, Vendict, Venedick, Venedicto, Venedictos, Venedictus, Venedikt, Venedikte, Vennedict, Vennedikt

Venezio (Italian) Man from Venice
Venetziano, Veneziano

Venjamin (Hebrew) Form of Benjamin, meaning "son of the south; son of the right hand"
Yamin, Yamino, Venejamen, Veniamino, Venjaman, Venjamen, Venjiman, Venjimen, Veniamin, Venamin

Venkat (Indian) From the sacred hill

Venturo (Spanish) A fortunate man; one who is lucky
Venturio

Verbrugge (Dutch) From the bridge

Vercingetorix (Celtic) The king of warriors

Verdell (French) One who is flourishing
Verdel, Verdele, Vernell, Vernel, Vernele

Vere (French) From the alder tree

Verge (Anglo-Saxon) One who owns four acres

Verissimo (Portuguese) One who is very truthful

Verlyn (American) Form of Vernon, meaning "from the alder-tree grove"
Verlynn, Verlin, Verllin, Verlon, Vyrlyn, Virlyn, Vyrlin, Vyrlon, Virlon

Vermont (French) From the green mountains; from the state of Vermont

Vernados (Greek) Having the bravery of a bear
Vemados

Verner (Scandinavian) Form of Werner, meaning "of the defending army"
Verneri, Vernery, Vernerey, Verneree, Vernerie

Vernon (French) From the alder-tree grove
Vern, Vernal, Vernard, Verne, Vernee, Vernen, Verney, Vernin, Vernay, Vernus, Vernas

Verrier (French) A glassblower
Verier, Verriere, Veriere

Verrill (French) One who is faithful
Verill, Verrall, Verrell, Verroll, Veryl, Veryll, Verol, Verall, Verle, Vyrle, Verel, Verell

Vesa (Finnish) Resembling a young tree; a sprout

Vespasian (Latin) Born in the evening; resembling a wasp
Vespasiano, Vespasianus, Vespasien, Vespasieno, Vespasienus

Vester (Latin) Form of Sylvester, meaning "from the wooded place"
Vestar, Vestir, Vestor

Vesuvio (Italian) From the volcano
Vesuvo

Veto (Spanish) An intelligent man

Vibol (Cambodian) A man of plenty
Viboll, Vibole, Vybol, Vyboll, Vybole

Victor (Latin) One who is victorious; the champion
Vic, Vick, Victoriano, Victorien, Victorin, Victorino, Victorio, Vidor, Viktor, Vitorio, Vittorio, Vittoros, Victoir, Vicq, Victoro, Vico, Viko, Victorius, Viktorus, Vitor, Vittore, Vittorino

Vid (Hungarian) Form of Vito, meaning "one who gives life"
Vida, Vidas, Vidal

Vidal (Spanish) A giver of life
Videl, Videlio, Videlo, Vidalo, Vidalio, Vidas

Vidar (Norse) Warrior of the forest; in mythology, a son of Odin
Vidarr

Vidur (Indian) Having great wisdom
Vidhur, Vydur, Vydhur

Vidvan (Indian) A learned man

Vien (Vietnamese) One who is complete; satisfied

Vieno (Finnish) One who is gentle

Viet (Vietnamese) Of Vietnamese descent

Viho (Native American) One who ranks as chief

Vijay (Hindi) One who is victorious; the conquerer
Vijaye, Veejay, Veejaye, Vijun

Vikas (Indian) One who makes progress in life

Viking (Norse) Of the seafaring people
Vikyng, Vyking, Vykyng

Vikram (Hindi) One who keeps pace; in Hinduism, another name for the god Vishnu
Vicram, Vickram

Vilfred (Danish) Form of Wilfred, meaning "one who wishes for peace"
Vilfredo, Vilfrid, Vilfried, Vilfryd, Vill, Villfred, Villfredo, Villfrid, Villfried, Villfryd

Vilhelm (Danish) Form of William, meaning "the determined protector"
Villem, Vilho, Viljo, Vilchjo, Vilem, Vilhelmus, Vilhemas, Vilhelmi, Vilhelmo, Vilhelmio, Vilhelms, Vilhjalmur, Vili, Viliam, Vilis, Viljami, Viljem, Vilko, Ville, Vilmos

Villiers (French) One who lives in town

Vilmar (English) Form of Wilmer, meaning "a strong-willed and well-known man"
Vilmer, Vilmore, Villmar, Villmer, Vylmer, Vylmar, Vyllmer, Vyllmar, Villmarr, Viljalmr

Vilppu (Finnish) Form of Phillip, meaning "one who loves horses"
Vilpu, Vilppue, Vilpue

Vimal (Indian) One who is clean, pure
Vimall, Vymal, Vymall

Vinal (English) From the vine hall
Vinale, Vynal, Vynale, Vinall, Vynall, Vinay, Vinaye

Vincent (Latin) One who prevails; the conquerer
Vicente, Vicenzio, Vicenzo, Vin, Vince, Vincens, Vincente, Vincentius, Vincents, Vincenty, Vincenz, Vincenzio, Vincenzo, Vincien, Vinicent, Vinnie, Vinny, Vinzenz, Vikenti, Vincenc, Vincentas, Vinko

Vindhya (Indian) From the range of hills
Vyndhya, Vindya, Vyndya

Vineet (Indian) A modest man
Vineete, Vinyt, Vinyte, Vynyt, Vynyte

Vinh (Vietnamese) From the bay

Vinicio (Italian) Man of the vine; wine
Vinicius, Vinicios

Vinod (Indian) One who is a pleasure

Vinson (English) The son of Vincent
Vinsin, Vinsen, Vinsan, Vinsone

Vinton (English) From the vine settlement

Viorel (Romanian) Resembling the bluebell
Viorell, Vyorel, Vyorell

Vipin (Indian) From the forest
Vippin, Vypin, Vypyn, Vyppin, Vyppyn, Vipyn, Vippyn

Vipponah (Native American) Having a slender face
Vippona, Viponah, Vipona, Vypponah, Vyppona, Vyponah, Vypona

Vipul (Indian) A man of plenty
Vypul, Vipull, Vypull, Vipool, Vypool

Virag (Hungarian) Resembling a flower

Viraj (Hindi) A magnificent man;
in Hinduism, a primeval being

Viral (Indian) Our precious son

Virat (Hindi) A supreme ruler

Virendra (Hindi) One who is brave and noble
Vyrendra, Virindra, Vyrindra

Virgil (Latin) The staff-bearer
Verge, Vergil, Vergilio, Virgilio, Vergilo, Virgilo, Virgilijus

Virginius (Latin) One who is pure; chaste
Virginio, Virgino

Virgo (Latin) The virgin; the sixth sign of the zodiac

Viriato (Portuguese) One who wears the ruling bracelets

Virote (Thai) A powerful man

Vischer (German) A fisherman
Visscher, Vyscher, Vysscher

Vishal (Indian) A large man; one with broad shoulders
Vyshal, Vishall, Vyshall

Vishap (Armenian) In mythology, an evil spirit of thunder

Vishnu (Hindi) In Hinduism, the supreme god

Visvajit (Indian) Conquerer of the universe

Vitéz (Hungarian) A courageous warrior

Vito (Latin) One who gives life
Vital, Vitale, Vitalis, Vitaly, Vitas, Vitus, Vitali, Vitaliy

Vivatma (Hindu) Of a universal soul

Vivek (Hindi) One who is judicious; filled with wisdom
Vyvek, Viveck, Vyveck

Vivian (Latin) One who is full of life
Viviani, Vivien, Vivyan, Vyvian, Vyvyan, Vivianus, Vian, Viau

Vjekoslav (Croatian) Of the glorious age
Vjek, Vjeko

Vladimir (Slavic) A famous prince
Vladamir, Vladimeer, Vladimyr, Vladimyre, Vladamyr, Vladamyre, Vladameer, Vladimer, Vladamer, Vlad, Vadim, Vladalen, Vladalin, Vlatko, Vladko, Volodya, Volodymyr, Volya, Vova

Vladislav (Slavic) One who rules with glory

Vlassis (Greek) Form of Blaise, meaning "one with a lisp or a stammer"
Vlasis, Vlassys, Vlasys, Vlasi, Vlaho

Vlastimil (Czech) One who has power and favor of the people
Vlastmil, Vlastimyl, Vlastmyl

Vlastislav (Czech) One who has power and glory

Vogel (Dutch) Resembling a bird
Vogle, Vogal, Vogol, Vogil

Vohkinne (Native American) Having a Roman nose

Voistitoevitz (Native American) Resembling a white cow
Voisttitoevetz

Voitto (Finnish) One who is victorious

Vokivocummast (Native American) Resembling a white antelope

Volga (Russian) From the river

Volkan (Turkish) From the volcano

Volker (German) A defender of the people

Volney (German) The spirit of the people
Volny, Volnee, Volni, Volnie, Volnea, Vollney, Vollny, Vollni, Vollnie, Vollnee, Vollnea

Volos (Slavic) Resembling an ox; in mythology, god of cattle

Von (Norse) Filled with hope
Vonne, Vonn, Vondell, Vondel, Vondele, Vontell, Vontel, Vontele

Vortigern (English) The supreme king

Vortimer (English) A legendary king; Vortigem's son

Vromme (Dutch) Having great wisdom
Vromm, Vrom, Vrome

Vruyk (English) From the fortress

Vsevolod (Russian) The ruler of all

Vuk (Servian) Resembling a wolf
Vukasin

Vulcan (Latin) In mythology, the god of fire
Vulkan, Vulckan

Vyacheslav (Russian) Form of Wenceslas, meaning "one who receives more glory"

Waail (Arabic) One who goes back to God
Waaile, Waeil, Waeile

Waban (Native American) Of the east wind
Wabann, Wabane

Wachiru (African) The son of the lawmaker
Wachirue, Wachyru, Wachyrue

Wade (English) To cross the river ford
Wayde, Waid, Waide, Waddell, Wadell, Waydell, Waidell, Waed, Waede

Wadham (English) From the village near the ford

Wadley (English) From the meadow near the ford
Wadly, Wadlee, Wadli, Wadlie, Wadleigh

Wadron (German) A might raven; a ruling raven
Waldrone, Waldrom, Waldrome, Waldrum, Waldrume, Waldhramm, Waldhram

Wadsworth (English) From the estate near the ford
Waddsworth, Wadsworthe, Waddsworthe

Wafai (Arabic) One who is faithful
Wafae, Wafay, Wafa

Wafi (Arabic) One who is trustworthy
Wafie, Wafy, Wafey, Wafee, Wafiy, Wafiyy

Wafiq (Arabic) One who is successful
Wafiq, Wafeeq, Wafieq, Wafeiq

Wagner (German) One who builds wagons
Wagoner, Waggner, Waggoner

Wahab (Indian) A big-hearted man

Wahanassatta (Native American) One who walks pigeon-toed
Wahanasata, Wahansata, Wahanasat

Wahchinksapa (Native American) Having great wisdom
Wachinksapa, Wahchinksap, Wachinksap

W

Wacian (Anglo-Saxon) One who is watchful; aler
Wacien, Wacion

Waclaw (Polish) Form of Wenceslas, meaning "one who receives more glory"
Waclawe

Wahchintonka (Native American) One who practices often
Wachintonka

Wahib (Arabic) A giving man; one who donates
Wahibe, Waheeb, Waheebe, Wahieb, Wahiebe, Waheib, Waheibe, Wahyb, Wahybe

Wahid (Arabic) One who is unequaled; unique
Wahide, Waheed, Waheede, Wahied, Wahiede, Waheid, Waheide, Wahyd, Wahyde

Wahkan (Native American) One who is sacred
Wakan, Wahkhan, Wakhan

Wail (Arabic) One who seeks shelter
Waile, Wayl, Wayle, Wale, Wael, Waele

Wainwright (English) One who builds wagons
Wainright, Wainewright, Wayneright, Waynewright, Waynwright

Waite (English) A guardsman
Waites, Waight, Waights, Wayt, Wayte, Waytes, Wate, Wates

Waitimu (African) Born for the spear
Waytimu, Watimu

Wajih (Arabic) A noble man; one who is distinguished
Wajeeh, Wajieh, Wajyh

Wakefield (English) From the damp field
Wakfield, Wakefeld, Waikfield, Waikfeld, Waykfield, Waykfeld, Wacfeld, Waycfeld, Wacfield, Waycfield

Wakeley (English) From the damp meadow
Wakely, Wakeleigh, Wakelee, Wakeli, Wakelie, Wakelea, Wakeleah, Wacleah, Waklea, Wakleah, Wakley, Wakly, Wacly, Waclea

Wakeman (English) A watchman
Wakemann, Wake, Wacuman, Wakuman

Wakil (Arabic) A lawyer; a trustee
Wakill, Wakyl, Wakyle, Wakeel, Wakeele

Wakiza (Native American) A desperate fighter
Wakyza, Wakeza, Wakieza, Wakeiza

Wakler (English) One who thickens cloth
Wackler, Waklar, Wacklar, Waklor, Wacklor, Waklir, Wacklir

Walbridge (English) From the Welshman's bridge
Wallbridge, Walbrydge, Wallbrydge

Walby (English) From the Welshman's farm
Walbey, Walbi, Walbie, Walbee, Walbea, Wallby, Wallbey, Wallbi, Wallbie, Wallbee, Wallbea

Walcott (English) From the cottage near the wall
Wallcot, Wallcott, Wolcott, Wollcot, Wollcott, Welcott, Wellcot, Wellcott, Walcot, Welcot, Wolcot

Wald (German) Man of the forest
Walde

Waldemar (German) A famous ruler
Waldemarr, Waldemare, Waldmar, Waldmar, Weldemar, Weldemarr, Weldemar, Weldmar, Weldmarr

Walden (English) From the wooded valley
Waldan, Waldon, Waldin, Waldyn

Waldmunt (German) Mighty protector
Waldmunte, Waldmont, Waldmonte, Walmunt, Walmunte, Walmont, Walmonte, Waldmund, Waldmunde, Waldmond, Waldmonde, Walmund, Walmunde, Walmond, Walmonde

Waldo (English) A powerful ruler

Walenty (Polish) Form of Valentine, meaning "one who is strong and healthy"
Walenti, Walentie, Walentey, Walentee, Walentine, Walentyne, Walentyn

Walerian (Polish) Form of Valerian, meaning "one who is strong and healthy"
Waleran, Walerion, Waleron, Waleryan, Waleryon

Walford (English) From the Welshman's ford
Wallford, Walforde, Wallforde

Walfried (German) A peaceful ruler
Walfrid, Walfred, Wallfried, Wallfrid, Wallfred, Walfryd, Wallfryd

Walid (Arabic) Our newborn son
Walide, Waleed, Waleede, Waleid, Waleide, Walied, Waliede, Walyd, Walyde

Waljan (Welsh) The chosen one
Walljan, Waljen, Walljen, Waljon, Walljon

Walker (English) One who trods the cloth
Walkar, Walkir, Walkor

Wallace (Scottish) A Welshman; a man from the south
Wallach, Wallas, Wallie, Wallis, Wally, Walsh, Welch, Walli, Walley, Wallee, Walshe, Welche, Wallase, Wallache, Waleis

W

Walter (German) The commander of
the army
*Walther, Walt, Walte, Walder, Wat, Wouter,
Wolter, Woulter, Walthar*

Walton (English) From the walled town;
from the stream town
*Walten, Waltan, Waltin, Waltun, Waller,
Walworth, Walworthe*

Walwyn (English) A Welsh friend
*Walwynn, Walwin, Walwinn, Wallwyn,
Wallwynn, Wallwin, Wallwinn*

Wamblee (Native American) Resembling
an eagle
*Wambli, Wamblie, Wambly, Wambley,
Wambleigh, Wamblea*

Wambleeska (Native American)
Resembling the white eagle
*Wambleesha, Wambliska, Wamblisha,
Wamblieska, Wambliesha, Wambleiska,
Wambleisha, Wamblyska, Wamblysha*

Wambua (African) Born during a period
of rain
Wambooa, Wambuah, Wambooah

Wamocha (African) One who is never
satisfied
Wamocka, Wamocho, Wamocko

Wanageeska (Native American) Of the
white spirit
*Wanageska, Wanagiska, Wanagyska,
Wanagieska, Wanageiska*

Wanikiy (Native American) A savior
*Wanikiya, Wanikie, Wanikey, Waniki,
Wanikee*

Wanjala (African) Born during a famine
Wanjalla, Wanjal, Wanjall

Wapasha (Native American) Resembling
the red leaf
Wapashah, Waposha, Waposhah

Wapi (Native American) One who is
fortunate; lucky
Wapie, Wapy, Wapey, Wapee

Waquini (Native American) Having a
hooked nose
Waquinie, Waquiny, Waquiney, Waquinee

Ward (English) A guardian
Warde, Warden, Worden, Weard

Wardell (English) From the guardian's hill
*Wardel, Wardele, Weardhyll, Weardhill,
Weardell*

Wardley (English) From the guardian's
meadow
*Wardly, Wardleigh, Wardli, Wardlie,
Wardlee, Wardlea, Weardleigh, Weardlee,
Weardli, Weardlie, Weardly, Weardley,
Weardlea, Weardleah*

Warfield (English) From the field near the
weir
*Warfeld, Weirfeild, Weirfeld, Weifield,
Weifeld*

Warford (English) From the ford near
the weir
*Warforde, Weirford, Weirforde, Weiford,
Weiforde*

Warley (English) From the meadow near
the weir
*Warly, Warleigh, Warlee, Warlea, Warleah,
Warli, Warlie, Weirley, Weirly, Weirli,
Weirlie, Weirlea, Weirleah, Weirleigh,
Weirlee*

Warner (German) Of the defending army
Werner, Wernher, Warnher, Worner, Wornher

Warra (Aboriginal) Man of the water
Warrah, Wara, Warah

Warrain (Aboriginal) One who belongs to
the sea
*Warraine, Warrayne, Warrayn, Warraen,
Warraene, Warain, Waraine, Warayn,
Warayne, Waraen, Waraene*

Warren (English / German) From the
fortress; from the enclosure / a gamekeeper
*Warrane, Waran, Warane, Warrin, Warin,
Waren, Waren*

Warrick (English) Form of Varick, mean-
ing "a protective ruler"
*Warrik, Warric, Warick, Warik, Waric,
Warryck, Warryk, Warryc, Waryck, Waryk,
Waryc, Warwick, Warwik, Warwic,
Warrwick, Warrwik, Warrwic*

Warrigal (Aboriginal) One who is wild
*Warrigall, Warigall, Warigal, Warygal,
Warygall*

Warrun (Aboriginal) Of the sky
Warun

W

Warwick (English) From the farm near
the weir
Warwik, Warwyck, Warwyk

Washburn (English) From the flooding
stream
*Washbourn, Washburne, Washbourne,
Washborn, Washborne, Waescburne,
Waescburn*

Washi (Japanese) Resembling an eagle
Washie, Washy, Washey, Washee

Washington (English) From the intelligent
one's town
Washyngton, Washingtown, Washyngtown

Wasi (Arabic) An open-minded and
learned man
Wasie, Wasy, Wasey, Wasee

Wasim (Arabic) A handsome man
*Wasime, Waseem, Waseeme, Waseim,
Waseime, Wasiem, Wasieme, Wasym,
Wasyme, Wassim, Wassym, Wasseem*

Wasswa (African) The firstborn of twins
Waswa, Wasswah, Waswah

Watson (English) The son of Walter
*Watsin, Watsen, Watsan, Watkins,
Watckins, Watkin, Watckin, Wattekinson,
Wattikinson, Wattkins, Wattkin, Wattson,
Wattsen, Wattsan, Wattesone, Watts, Watt,
Watte*

Waverly (English) Of the trembling aspen
*Waverley, Waverli, Waverlie, Waverleigh,
Waverlea, Waverlee, Waefreleah, Waefrelea,
Waefreley, Wafrely, Wafrelee*

Waylon (English) From the roadside land
*Way, Waylan, Wayland, Waylen, Waylin,
Weylin, Wylan, Wyland, Wylen, Wylin,
Wegland, Weyland, Weylyn*

Wayne (English) One who builds wagons
Wayn, Wain, Waine, Wane, Waen, Waene

Wayra (Native American) Born of the
wind
Wayrah, Waira, Wairah, Waera, Waerah

Weayaya (Native American) Born with the
setting sun

Webley (English) From the weaver's meadow
*Webbley, Webly, Webbly, Webleigh,
Webbleigh, Weblea, Webblea, Webleah,
Webbleah, Webli, Webbli, Weblie, Webblie*

Webster (English) A weaver
*Weeb, Web, Webb, Webber, Weber,
Webbestre, Webestre, Webbe, Wevers, Wever*

Wednesday (American) Born on a
Wednesday
*Wensday, Winsday, Windnesday,
Wydnesday, Wynsday, Wednesdai,
Wednesdae, Wensdai, Winsdai,
Windnesdai, Wydnesdai, Wynsdai,
Wensdae, Winsdae, Windnesdae,
Wydnesdae, Wynsdae*

Wei (Chinese) A brilliant man; having great
strength

Wekesa (African) Born during the
harvest time

Welborne (English) From the spring brook
*Welborn, Welburn, Welburne, Wellborne,
Wellborn, Wellburn, Wellburne*

Welby (English) From the farm near
the spring
*Welbey, Wellby, Wellbey, Welbi, Wellbi,
Welbie, Wellbie, Welbee, Wellbee, Welbea,
Wellbea*

Welcome (English) A welcome guest
Welcom, Welcomme

Weldon (English) From the hill near a spring
*Welldon, Welden, Wellden, Wieldun,
Weildun*

Wells (English) From the springs
Welles

Welton (English) From the town near
the well
Wellton, Weltun, Welltun, Weltin, Welltin

Wematin (Native American) One who is
brotherly
*Wematen, Wematyn, Wemetin, Wemeten,
Wemetyn*

Wemilat (Native American) Born into
prosperity
Wemilatt, Wemylat, Wemylatt

Wenceslas (Slavic) One who receives
more glory
Wenzeslas, Wenceslaus, Wenzeslaus

Wendell (German) One who travels; a
wanderer
*Wendel, Wendale, Wendall, Wendele,
Wendal, Windell, Windel, Windal, Wyndell,
Wyndel, Wyndal, Windall, Wyndall*

Wenzel (German) Form of Wenceslas, meaning "one who receives more glory"
Wenzell, Wenzle, Winzel, Winzell, Winzle, Wynzel, Wynzell, Wynzle

Werther (German) A soldier worthy of the army

Wesley (English) From the western meadow
Wes, Wesly, Wessley, Westleigh, Westley, Wesli, Weslie, Wesleigh, Westli, Westlie, Wess, Weslee, Westlee, Wessel, Wessle, Wesleah, Westleah

Westbrook (English) From the western stream
Wesbrook, Westbrok, Wesbrok, Westbroc, Wesbroc, Westbrock, Wesbrock

Westby (English) From the western farm
Westbey, Wesby, Wesbey, Westbi, Wesbi, Westbie, Wesbie, Westbee, Wesbee, Westbea, Wesbea

Westcott (English) From the western cottage
Wescott, Westcot, Wescot, Westkott, Weskott, Westkot, Weskot

Weston (English) From the western town
West, Westan, Westen, Westun, Westin, Weste

Wetherby (English) From the ram farm
Wetherbey, Wetherbee, Wetherbi, Wetherbie, Whetherby, Whetherbey, Whetherbee, Whetherbi, Whetherbie, Weatherby, Weatherbey, Weatherbee, Weatherbi, Weatherbie

Wetherly (English) From the ram's meadow
Wetherley, Wetherlee, Wetherli, Wetherlie, Whetherly, Whetherley, Whetherlee, Whetherli, Whetherlie, Weatherly, Weatherley, Weatherlee, Weatherli, Weatherlie, Wetherlea, Wetherleah, Whetherlea, Whetherleah, Weatherlea, Weatherleah

Wharton (English) From the settlement near the weir
Warton, Wharten, Warten, Whartun, Wartun

Wheatley (English) From the wheat meadow
Wheatly, Wheatli, Wheatlie, Wheatleigh, Wheatlea, Wheatleah, Wheatlee, Weatley, Weatly, Weatli, Weatleigh, Weatlea, Weatleah, Weatlee, Weatlie

Wheaton (English) From the town of wheat
Wheatown, Wheeton, Wheyton, Weaton, Weeton, Weyton

Wheeler (English) A driver; one who makes wheels

Whistler (English) One who whistles

Whit (English) A white-skinned man
White, Whitey, Whitt, Whitte, Whyt, Whytt, Whytte, Whytey

Whitaker (English) From the white acre
Witaker, Whittaker, Wittaker

Whitby (English) From the white farm
Whitbey, Whitbi, Whitbie, Whitbee, Whytbey, Whytby, Whytbi, Whytbie, Whytbee, Witby, Witbey, Witbi, Witbie, Witbee, Wytby, Wytbey, Wytbi, Wytbie, Wytbee

Whitcomb (English) From the white valley
Whitcom, Whitcome, Whytcomb, Whytcome, Whytcom, Witcomb, Witcom, Witcome, Wytcomb, Wytcom, Wytcome

Whitfield (English) From the white field
Whitfeld, Whytfield, Whytfeld, Witfield, Witfeld, Wytfield, Wytfeld

Whitford (English) From the white ford
Whitforde, Whytford, Whytforde, Witford, Witforde, Wytford, Wytforde

Whitlaw (English) From the white hill
Whitelaw, Whitlawe, Whytlaw, Whytlawe, Witlaw, Witlawe, Wytlaw, Wytlawe

Whitley (English) From the white meadow
Whitly, Whitli, Whitlie, Whitlee, Whitleigh, Whytley, Whytly, Whytli, Whytlie, Whytlee, Whytleigh, Witley, Witly, Witli, Witlie, Witleigh, Witlee, Wytley, Wytly, Wytli, Wytlie, Wytleigh, Wytlee

Whitlock (English) A white-haired man
Whitlok, Whytlock, Whytlok, Witlock, Witlok, Wytlock, Wytlok

Whitman (English) A white-haired man
Whitmann, Witman, Witmann, Whitmane, Witmane, Whytman, Whytmane, Wytman, Wytmane

Whitney (English) From the white island
Whitny, Whitni, Whitnie, Whitnee, Witney, Witni, Witny, Witnie, Witnee, Whytney, Whytny, Whytni, Whytnie, Whytnee

W

Wicasa (Native American) One who is wise; a sage
Wickasa, Wikasa, Wicassa, Wickassa, Wikassa

Wickham (English) From the village paddocks
Wyckham, Wikham, Wykham, Wickam, Wyckam, Wykam, Wiccum, Wichamm

Wickley (English) From the village meadow
Wickly, Wickli, Wicklie, Wicklee, Wicklea, Wyckley, Wyckly, Wyckli, Wycklie, Wycklee, Wycklea, Wykley, Wykly, Wykli, Wyklie, Wyklea, Wikley, Wikly, Wikli, Wiklie, Wiklee, Wiklea, Wikleigh, Wickleigh, Wyckleigh, Wykleigh, Wicleah, Wicleigh, Wiclea

Wielislaw (Polish) Form of Wieslav, meaning "one who receives great glory"
Wieslaw, Wislaw

Wieslav (Slavic) One who receives great glory

Wiktor (Polish) Form of Victor, meaning "one who is victorious; the champion"
Wikter, Wiktar

Wikvaya (Native American) A bringer

Wilbert (German) One who is willful; a bright man
Wilber, Wilbur, Wilburn, Wilburt, Wilbar, Wilbart, Wilbern, Wilbarn, Wilburh, Wilperht, Wilpert

Wildon (English) From the wooded hill
Willdon, Wilden, Willden

Wilfred (English) One who wishes for peace
Wilfredo, Wilfrid, Wilfried, Wilfryd, Will, Willfred, Willfredo, Willfrid, Willfried, Willfryd

Willard (German) A resolute and brave man
Wilard, Willerd, Wilerd, Willhard, Wilhard, Willherd, Wilherd, Wilheard, Willet, Willett, Wilet, Wilett

William ✪ ⊕ (German) The determined protector
Wilek, Wileck, Wilhelm, Wilhelmus, Wilkes, Wilkie, Wilkinson, Will, Willem, Willhelmus, Willi, Williams, Williamson, Willie, Willis, Willkie, Wills, Williamon, Willy, Wilmot, Wilmott, Wim, Wilmod, Wilmodd

Willoughby (English) From the willow farm
Wiloughby, Willoughbey, Wiloughbey, Willoughbi, Wiloughbi, Willoughbee, Wiloughbee, Willoby, Wiloby, Willobey, Wilobey, Willobee, Wilobee, Wiligby, Wyligby

Willow (English) Of the willow tree
Willowe, Willo, Willoe

Wilmer (German) A strong-willed and well-known man
Wilmar, Wilmore, Willmar, Willmer, Wylmer, Wylmar, Wyllmer, Wyllmar, Willmarr

Wilson (German) The son of William
Willson, Willsn, Wilsen, Wilsin, Willsen, Willsin, Willesone, Wilesone

***

WILLIAM

William is a family name on my husband's side. My husband was the only boy in his family, and Will was supposed to be his son's name, and not one of his sisters' children. I agreed on one condition: that we would call him Will. Hopefully, he won't change it after I fought so hard to avoid Bill and Billy! —Michelle, MO

***

Wiley (English) One who is crafty; from the meadow by the water
Wily, Wileigh, Wili, Wilie, Wilee, Wylie, Wyly, Wyley, Wylee, Wyleigh, Wyli

Wilford (English) From the willow ford
Willford, Wilferd, Willferd, Wilf, Wielford, Weilford, Wilingford, Wylingford

Wilton (English) From the town on the river
Willton, Wylton, Wyllton, Wiltan, Willtan, Wilten, Willten, Wilt, Wilte, Wylton, Wyllton

Wincenty (Polish) Form of Vincent, meaning "one who prevails; the conquerer"
Wincentey, Wincenti, Wincentie, Wincentee

Winchell (English) One who draws water
Winnchell, Wynchell, Wynnchell

Windsor (English) From the river that has
a winch
*Winsor, Windser, Winser, Wyndsor, Wynsor,
Wyndser, Wynser, Wendsor, Wensor, Wenser*

Winfield (German) From a friend's field
*Winnfield, Wynfield, Wynnfield, Wynsfield,
Wynnsfield, Winefield, Winefeld*

Winford (English) From a friend's ford
*Winnford, Winforde, Winnforde, Wynford,
Wynforde, Wynnford, Wynnforde*

Winfred (English) A friend of peace
*Wynfred, Winfrid, Wynfrid, Winfryd,
Wynfryd, Winfrith, Wynfrith, Winfried,
Wynfried, Winefrith, Wynefrith, Wylfrid,
Wylfred*

Winslow (English) From a friend's hill
*Winslowe, Wynslow, Wynslowe, Winslo,
Wynslo*

Winston (English) Of the joy stone; from
the friendly town
*Win, Winn, Winsten, Winstonn, Wynstan,
Wynsten, Wynston, Winstan*

Winthrop (English) From the friendly
village
*Winthrope, Wynthrop, Wynthrope,
Winthorp, Wynthorp*

Winton (English) From the enclosed
pastureland
*Wintan, Wintin, Winten, Wynton, Wyntan,
Wyntin, Wynten*

Wirt (Anglo-Saxon) One who is worthy
Wirte, Wyrt, Wyrte, Wurt, Wurte

Wisconsin (Native American) From the
grassy place; from the state of Wisconsin
*Wisconsen, Wisconson, Wysconsin,
Wysconsen, Wysconson*

Wise (English) Filled with wisdom
Wyse, Wyze, Wize

Wissian (Anglo-Saxon) One who guides
others

Wit (Polish) Form of Vitus, meaning
"giver of life"
Witt

Witold (German) Ruler of the wide land

Wladyslaw (Polish) To rule with glory
Wladislaw, Wlodzislaw, Wlodzyslaw

Wlodzimierz (Polish) To rule with peace
Wlodzimir, Wlodzimerz

Woden (Anglo-Saxon) Form of Odin,
meaning "king of the gods"
Wodin, Wotan, Woten, Wotin, Wodan

Wohehiv (Native American) One who
wields a dull knife
*Wohehev, Wohehive, Woheheev,
Woheheeve, Wohehieve, Woheheive,
Wohehyve, Wohehiev, Woheheiv, Wohehyv*

Wokaihwokomas (Native American)
Resembling the white antelope

Wolcott (English) One who lives in Wolf's
cottage
*Wolcot, Wolfcott, Wolfcot, Woolcot,
Woolcott, Wulfcot, Wulfcott*

Wolfe (English) Resembling the wolf
Wolf, Wolff, Wolffe, Wulf, Wulfe, Wulff, Wulffe

Wolfgang (German) One who takes the
wolf's path

Wolfgar (German) Wielding a wolf spear
*Wolfgarr, Wolfgare, Wulfgar, Wulfgarr,
Wulfgare*

Wolfram (German) Resembling a black
wolf; a raven-wolf
Wolframe, Wolfrem, Wolfrim

Wolfric (German) A wolf ruler
*Wolfrick, Wolfrik, Wulfric, Wulfrick,
Wulfrik, Wolfryk, Wolfryck, Wolfryc,
Wulfryc, Wulfryck, Wulfryk*

Woodley (English) From the wooded
meadow
*Woodleigh, Woodly, Woodlee, Woodlea,
Woodleah, Woodli, Woodlie, Wodolea,
Wodoleah, Wodoleigh, Wodolee, Wodoli,
Wodolie, Wodoly, Wodoley*

Woodrow (English) From the row of
houses near the forest
Woodrowe, Woodro, Woodroe

Woody (American) A man of the forest
*Woodey, Woodi, Woodie, Woodee,
Woodward, Woods, Woodruff, Woodman,
Woudman, Woudruff, Woudward, Woudy,
Woudman, Wood, Woud*

Woorak (Aboriginal) From the plains
Woorack, Woorac

Wright (English) A wood carver; a carpenter

Wu (Chinese) Of the army; a sorcerer

Wulfhere (Anglo-Saxon) The name of a king
Wulfhear, Wulfheer, Wolfhere, Wolfhear, Wolfheer

Wuyi (Native American) Resembling a soaring turkey vulture
Wuyie, Wuyey, Wuyee, Wuyea

Wyatt ○ (English) Having the strength of a warrior
Wyat, Wyatte, Wyate, Wiatt, Wiatte, Wiat, Wiate, Wyeth, Wyath, Wyathe, Wyethe, Wye

Wybert (Anglo-Saxon) One who is smart during battle
Wyberth, Wyberte, Wyberthe, Wibert, Wiberte, Wiberth, Wiberthe

Wyborn (Norse) A warrior bear
Wybjorn

Wycliff (English) From the white cliff
Wyclif, Wyclyf, Wyclyff, Wycliffe, Wyclyffe, Wyclef, Wycleffe

Wyler (English) One who makes wheels
Wylar, Wylor, Wiler, Wilar, Wilor

Wyman (English) A fair-haired warrior
Wymann, Wymane

Wymond (English) A defender during battle
Wymonde, Wymund, Wymunde, Wimond, Wimonde, Wimund, Wimunde

Wyndam (English) From the winding path in the field
Windam

Wyndham (English) From the windy village
Windham

Wynn (Welsh / English) One who is fair-skinned/a beloved friend
Wyn, Winn, Win, Winne, Wynne, Wenn, Wen, Wenne, Wine, Wyne

Wynono (Native American) The firstborn child

Wynter (English) Born during the winter
Wynters, Winter, Winters

Wynwode (English) From the friendly forest
Wynswode, Winwode, Winswode, Wynwood, Winwood, Winward, Winwodem, Wynward, Wynwodem

Wyoming (Native American) From the large prairie; from the state of Wyoming
Wyomen, Wyom, Wyome

Wystan (English) As solid as a stone during battle
Wysten, Wistan, Wisten

Wythe (English) From the willow tree
Wyth

Xadrian (American) Form of Adrian, meaning "man from Hadria"
Xade, Xadiran, Xadrain, Xadrean, Xadreean, Xadreyan, Xadreeyan, Xadriaan, Xadriano, Xadrien, Xadrin, Xadrino, Xadrion, Xadron, Xadryan, Xadya, Xarjen, Xaydrean, Xaydreean, Xaydrian, Xaydrien

Xakery (American) Form of Zachary, meaning "the Lord remembers"
Xaccary, Xaccery, Xach, Xacharie, Xachery, Xack, Xackarey, Xackary, Xackery, Xak, Xakari, Xakary

Xalvador (Spanish) Form of Salvador, meaning "a savior"
Xalvadore, Xalvadoro, Xalvadorio, Xalbador, Xalbadore, Xalbadorio, Xalbadoro, Xabat, Xabatt, Xabate, Xabatio, Xabato

Xan (Hebrew) One who is well-fed
Xian, Xoan, Xann

Xander (Greek) Form of Alexander, meaning "helper and defender of mankind"
Xandro, Xandrio, Xandy, Xandie, Xanderlee, Xanderr, Xanderre, Xandere

Xannon (American) From an ancient family
Xanon, Xannen, Xanen, Xannun, Xanun

Xanthus (Greek) A blonde-haired man
Xanthos, Xanthe, Xanth

Xanti (Basque) Honoring St. James
Xantie, Xanty, Xantey, Xantee, Xantis, Xantys

Xanto (Greek) A blonde-haired man
Xantio, Xantow, Xantowe, Xantoe

Xarles (French) Form of Charles, meaning "one who is manly and strong / a free man"
Xarel, Xarl, Xarlo, Xarlos, Xarrol, Xarroll, Xary, Xaryl, Xhad, Xarleson, Xarley, Xarlie, Xarlot, Xarls, Xarlton, Xarly

Xavier ✪ (Basque / Arabic) Owner of a new house / one who is bright
Xaver, Xever, Xabier, Xaviere, Xabiere, Xaviar, Xaviare, Xavior, Xaviore, Xzavier, Xzabier, Xzaviar, Xzavior

Xenocrates (Greek) A foreign ruler

Xenon (Greek) From a foreign land; a stranger
Xenonn, Xenos, Xenus

Xenophon (Greek) One who speaks with a foreign voice
Xeno, Xenophone, Xenofon, Xenofone

Xerxes (Persian) A monarch; a ruler of heroes
Xerxus, Xerxos, Xerxas

Xesus (Galician) Form of Jesus, meaning "God is my salvation"

Xiang (Chinese) One who soars above others

Ximon (Hebrew) Form of Simon, meaning "God has heard"
Ximun, Ximen

Xiomar (Spanish) One who is famous in battle
Xiomarr, Xiomarre, Xiomare

Xiuhcoatl (Aztec) Wielding a weapon of destruction

Xi-wang (Chinese) One who is filled with hope

Xoan (Galician) Form of John, meaning "God is gracious"
Xoane, Xohn, Xon

Xochipilli (Aztec) In mythology, god of love and flowers

Xose (Galician) Form of Joseph, meaning "God will add"

Xuan (Vietnamese) Born during the spring

Xue (Chinese) A studious young man

Xun (Chinese) One who is swift

Xurxo (Galician) Form of George, meaning "one who works the earth; a farmer"
Xurxio

Xylon (Greek) A forest dweller
Xylun, Xylonio, Xylan, Xylanio, Xylunio, Xylono, Xyluno, Xylano

Yaakov (Hebrew) Form of Jacob, meaning "he who supplants"
Yaacob, Yachov, Yacov, Yago, Yakob, Yakov, Yaakob, Yaacov, Yaachov, Yacoub, Yakoub

Yabiss (Arabian) From the dry land
Yabyss, Yabis, Yabys

Yadid (Hebrew) One who is dearly loved
Yadide, Yadyd, Yadyde, Yadeed, Yadeede, Yadiel, Yadial

Yadon (Hebrew) The Lord will judge
Yadone, Yadun, Yadune, Yaadon

Yael (Israeli) Strength of God
Yaele

Yafeu (African) One who is bold
Yafeuh, Yafeo, Yafeoh

Yagil (Hebrew) One who rejoices, celebrates
Yagill, Yagyl, Yagylle

Yago (Hebrew) Form of Iago, meaning "he who supplants"
Yagoh, Yaggo, Yaggoh

Yaholo (Native American) One who shouts
Yaholoh, Yahollo, Yaholloh, Yaholio

Yahto (Native American) Having blue eyes; refers to the color blue
Yahtoe, Yahtow, Yahtowe

Yahweh (Hebrew) Refers to God
Yahveh, Yaweh, Yaveh, Yehowah, Yehweh,
Yehoveh

Yahya (Arabic) Form of John, meaning
"God is gracious"
Yahyah, Yahia, Yahiah, Yahea, Yaheah,
Yahyaa

Yakar (Hebrew) One who is precious
Yakarr, Yakare, Yackar, Yaccar, Yackare

Yakecan (Native American) One who
sings to the sky
Yakecann, Yakecen, Yackecan, Yakacan,
Yackacan, Yakacen

Yakim (Hebrew) Form of Joachim,
meaning "one who is established by God;
God will judge"
Yachim, Yackim, Yakeem, Yacheem, Yackeem

Yakiv (Ukranian) Form of Jacob, meaning
"he who supplants"
Yakive, Yakeev, Yakeeve, Yackiv, Yackeev,
Yakieve, Yakiev, Yakeive, Yakeiv

Yakout (Arabian) As precious as a ruby

Yale (Welsh) From the fertile upland
Yayle, Yayl, Yail, Yaile

Yamal (Hindi) One of twins
Yamall, Yamale, Yamalo, Yamalio

Yamin (English) Form of Benjamin,
meaning "son of the south; son of the
right hand"
Yemin, Yamino, Yemino, Yameen, Yemeen,
Yaman, Yamen

Yaminichandra (Hindi) Born beneath the
night moon
Yaminichandro

Yan Tao (Chinese) A handsome man

Yan (Hebrew) Form of John, meaning
"God is gracious"
Yann, Yannic, Yanni, Yanne, Yanny,
Yannick, Yannik, Yannis, Yannakis, Yanakis,
Yannig, Yanig, Yanis, Yianni, Yiannie,
Yianne, Yianny, Yianney, Yiannee, Yiannis

Yanai (Aramaic) God will answer
Yanae, Yana, Yani

Yancy (Indian) An Englishman
Yancey, Yanci, Yancie, Yancee, Yantsey,
Yance, Yank, Yankee, Yanky, Yankey

Yanisin (Native American) One who is
ashamed
Yanisen, Yanysin, Yanysen, Yanisan,
Yanysan, Yanisyn, Yanysyn

Yaniv (Hebrew) One who is prosperous
Yanive, Yaneeve, Yaneev, Yaneiv, Yaneive,
Yanieve, Yaniev

Yankel (Hebrew) Form of Jacob, meaning
"he who supplants"
Yankell, Yanckel, Yanckell, Yankle,
Yanckle

Yanko (Bulgarian) Form of Yan, meaning
"God is gracious"
Yankoh, Yancko, Yanckoh

Yaotl (Aztec) A great warrior
Yaotyl, Yaotle, Yaotel, Yaotyle

Yaphet (Hebrew) A handsome man
Yaphett, Yapheth, Yaphethe

Yaqub (Arabic) Form of Jacob, meaning
"he who supplants"
Ya'qub, Yaqob, Yaqoub

Yardan (Arabic) Form of Jordan, meaning
"of the down-flowing river"
Yarden, Yardin, Yardann, Yardane,
Yardene, Yardine

Yardley (English) From the fenced-in
meadow
Yardly, Yardleigh, Yardli, Yardlie, Yardlee,
Yardlea, Yarley, Yarly, Yeardly, Yeardley,
Yeardleigh, Yeardlee, Yeardli, Yeardlie

Yarema (Hebrew) One who has been
appointed by God
Yaryma, Yarima, Yaremo, Yarymo, Yarem,
Yaremka

Yarin (Hebrew) One who is understanding
Yaryn, Yarine, Yaryne, Yavin, Yavine,
Yavyn, Yavyne

Yaromir (Russian) Form of Jaromir, mean-
ing "from the famous spring"
Yaromire, Yaromeer, Yaromeere, Yaromyr,
Yaromyre

Yaron (Hebrew) To lift one's voice in
praise
Yarron, Yaronn, Yarone

Yaroslav (Russian) Form of Jaroslav,
meaning "born with the beauty of spring"

Y

Yarrow (English) Resembling the fragrant herb
Yarro, Yarroe, Yarrowe, Yarow, Yarowe, Yaro, Yaroe

Yas (Native American) Child of the snow

Yasahiro (Japanese) One who is peaceful and calm

Yasashiku (Japanese) One who is polite and gentle
Yasashiko

Yash (Indian) A famous man; one who is glorious
Yashe, Yashi, Yashie, Yashee, Yashy, Yashey, Yashas

Yashpal (Indian) One who is successful
Yashpall, Yashpali, Yashpalie, Yashpaley, Yashpaly, Yashpalee, Yaspal

Yashwant (Indian) A glorious man
Yaswant

Yasin (Arabic) A wealthy man
Yasine, Yaseen, Yaseene, Yasyn, Yasyne, Yasien, Yasiene, Yasein, Yaseine

Yasir (Arabic) One who is well-off financially
Yassir, Yasser, Yaseer, Yasr, Yasyr, Yassyr, Yasar, Yassar, Yaser

Yasuo (Japanese) One who is peaceful
Yasuzo

Yateem (Arabian) An orphaned boy
Yateeme, Yatim, Yatime, Yatym, Yatyme, Yatiem, Yatieme, Yateim, Yateime

Yates (English) Keeper of the gates
Yayts, Yaytes, Yaits, Yaites, Yeats

Yavuz (Turkish) A stern man

Yaw (African) Born on a Thursday
Yawo, Yao

Yazid (Arabic) One who strives to better himself
Yazide, Yazeed, Yazeede, Yazeid, Yazeide, Yazied, Yaziede, Yazyd, Yazyde

Yazid (Arabic) God will add
Yazide, Yazeed, Yazeede, Yazyd, Yazyde, Yazied, Yaziede, Yazeid, Yazeide

Yebadiah (Hebrew) A gift from God
Yebadia, Yebadiya, Yebadiyah, Yeb, Yebe, Yebediah, Yebedia, Yebediya, Yebediyah, Yebedee, Yebedi, Yebedie, Yevadiah, Yevadia, Yevadiya, Yevadiyah

Yechezkel (Hebrew) Form of Ezekiel, meaning "strengthened by God"
Yechezkiel, Yechezekiel, Yekezekiel, Yekezkel

Yedidiah (Hebrew) One who is beloved by God
Yedidia, Yedediah, Yedediah, Yedidyah, Yedidya, Yededyah, Yededya

Yefim (Russian) One who speaks well
Yeffim, Yephim, Yefem, Yephem, Yeffem

Yefrem (Russian) Form of Ephraim, meaning "one who is fertile; productive"
Yefram, Yefraim, Yefreme, Yeframe, Yefraym, Yefrayme

Yegor (Russian) Form of George, meaning "one who works the earth; a farmer"
Yegore, Yegorr, Yegeor, Yeorges, Yeorge, Yeorgis

Yehonadov (Hebrew) A gift from God
Yehonadav, Yehonedov, Yehonedav, Yehoash, Yehoashe, Yeeshai, Yeeshae, Yishai, Yishae

Yehudi (Hebrew) Form of Judah, meaning "one who praises God"
Yehudie, Yehudy, Yehudey, Yehudee, Yehuda, Yehudah, Yechudi, Yechudit, Yehudit

Yemelyan (Russian) Form of Emil, meaning "one who is eager; an industrious man"
Yemalyan, Yemalyen, Yemelyen, Yemel, Yemele, Yemil, Yemile

Yenge (African) A hardworking man
Yengi, Yengie, Yengy, Yengey, Yengee

Yentl (Hebrew) A kindhearted man
Yentle, Yentel, Yentele, Yentil, Yentile, Yentyl, Yentyle

Yeoman (English) A manservant
Youman, Yoman

Yerachmiel (Hebrew) One who loves the Lord
Yerachmiele, Yerachmiell, Yerachmyel, Yerachmial, Yerachmyal

Yered (Hebrew) Form of Jared, meaning "of the descent; descending"
Yarad, Yarid, Yarod, Yarrad, Yarrard, Yarred, Yarrid, Yarrod, Yaryd, Yerad, Yerod, Yerrad, Yerred, Yerrod

Yeriel (Hebrew) Founded by God
Yeriell, Yerial, Yeriall, Yeriele, Yeriale

Yerik (Russian) One who has been appointed by God
Yerick, Yeric, Yeryk, Yeryck, Yeryc

Yermolai (Russian) Follower of Hermes, the messenger god
Yermolah, Yermolae, Yermolay, Yermolaye, Yermolaa

Yerodin (African) One who is studious
Yerodine, Yerodyn, Yerodyne, Yerodeen, Yerodeene

Yerucham (Hebrew) One who is beloved by God
Yeruchame, Yerukam, Yerukame

Yervant (Armenian) A king; born to royalty
Yervante

Yeshaya (Hebrew) To whom God lends
Yeshayah, Yeshaia, Yeshaiah, Yeshaea, Yeshaeah

Yestin (Welsh) One who is just and fair
Yestine, Yestyn, Yestyne

Yesuto (African) This child belongs to Jesus

Yevgeny (Russian) Form of Eugene, meaning "a wellborn man"
Yevgeney, Yevgenee, Yevgeni, Yevgenie, Yevgeniy, Yevheniy, Yevheny, Yevheni, Yevhenie, Yevhenee, Yevheney

Ygor (English) Form of Igor, meaning "warrior of the bow"
Yegor, Ygorr, Ygore, Yegore, Yegorr

Yigil (Hebrew) He shall be redeemed
Yigile, Yigyl, Yigyle, Yigol, Yigole, Yigit, Yigat

Yiorgos (Greek) Form of George, meaning "one who works the earth; a farmer"
Yiorges, Yirgos, Yirges, Yorgos, Yorges

Yishachar (Hebrew) He will be rewarded
Yishacharr, Yishachare, Yissachar, Yissachare, Yisachar, Yisachare

Yiska (Native American) The night has gone

Yitro (Hebrew) A man of plenty

Yitzhak (Hebrew) Form of Isaac, meaning "full of laughter"
Yitchak, Yitzhack, Yitzchack

Ymir (Norse) In mythology, a giant from whom the earth was created
Ymire, Ymeer, Ymeere, Ymyr

Yngram (English) Form of Ingram, meaning "a raven of peace"
Yngraham, Yngrahame, Yngrams, Yngrim

Yngvar (Norse) Form of Ingvar, meaning "a soldier in Ing's army"
Yngevar, Yngvarr, Yngevarr, Yngevare, Yngevare

Yngve (Scandinavian) Refers to the god Ing

Yo (Cambodian) One who is honest

Yoan (Bulgarian) Form of John, meaning "God is gracious"
Yoane, Yohn, Yon, Yoano

Yoav (Hebrew) Form of Joab, meaning "to praise God"
Yoave, Yoavo, Yoavio

Yobachi (African) One who prays to God
Yobachie, Yobachy, Yobachee, Yobachey

Yochanan (Hebrew) Form of John, meaning "God is gracious"
Yochan, Yohannan, Yohanan, Yochannan

Yoel (Hebrew) Form of Joel, meaning "Jehovah is God; God is willing"
Yoell, Yoele

Yoelvis (English) Form of Elvis, meaning "one who is wise"
Yoelviss, Yoelvys, Yoelvyss

Yogi (Hindi) One who practices yoga
Yogie, Yogee, Yogy, Yogey, Yoganand, Yoganande

Yohan (German) Form of Johan, meaning "God is gracious"
Yohanan, Yohann, Yohannes, Yohon, Yohonn, Yohonan

Yohance (African) A gift from God

Yonah (Hebrew) Form of Jonah, meaning "resembling a dove"
Yona, Yonas

Yonatan (Hebrew) Form of Jonathan, meaning "a gift of God"
Yonaton, Yohnatan, Yohnaton, Yonathan, Yonathon, Yoni, Yonie, Yony, Yoney, Yonee

Yong (Korean) One who is courageous

Yorath (Welsh) A handsome lord
Yorathe

Yordan (Hebrew) Form of Jordan, meaning "of the down-flowing river"
Yourdan, Yorden, Yourden, Yordun, Yourdun

Yori (Japanese) One who is dependent
Yorie, Yory, Yorey, Yoree

Yorick (English) Form of George, meaning "one who works the earth; a farmer"
Yorik, Yoric, Yorrick, Yorrik, Yorric, Yurick, Yurik, Yuric, Yurrick, Yurric, Yurrik

York (English) From the yew settlement
Yorck, Yorc, Yorke

Yosemite (Native American) Resembling a grizzly bear
Yosemete, Yosemiti, Yosemity, Yosemitey, Yosemetee, Yosemitee

Yoshi (Japanese) A good-hearted man; one who is free
Yoshie, Yoshy, Yoshey, Yoshee, Yoshio

Yoshiro (Japanese) The good son; a free son
Yoshyro

Yosyp (Ukranian) Form of Joseph, meaning "God will add"
Yosip, Yosype, Yosipe

Young (Korean) One who is prosperous
Yung

Yovanny (English) Form of Giovanni, meaning "God is gracious"
Yovanni, Yovannie, Yovannee, Yovany, Yovani, Yovanie, Yovanee

Yrjo (Finnish) Form of George, meaning "one who works the earth; a farmer"
Yrjos, Yrjon, Yrjan, Yrjas

Yrre (Anglo-Saxon) An angry man

Ysandro (English) Form of Isandro, meaning "the liberator of man"
Ysander, Ysandre, Ysandrow, Ysandroe, Ysandero

Ysbaddaden (Welsh) In mythology, a giant and the father of Olwen
Ysbadaden, Ysbadda, Yspaddaden, Yspadaden, Yspadda, Ysbaddadin, Ysbadadin, Yspaddadin, Yspadadin

Ysmael (English) Form of Ishmael, meaning "God will listen"
Yshmael, Ysmaele, Ysmail, Ysmaile, Yshmaile, Yshmail, Yishmael, Yismael

Yu (Chinese) One who is honored; born during a rainfall

Yudel (Hebrew) Form of Judah, meaning "one who praises God"
Yudele, Yudell

Yue (Chinese) Born beneath the moon

Yuki (Japanese) Man of the snow; one who is lucky
Yukie, Yuky, Yukey, Yukee, Yukio, Yukiko, Yokio, Yoki, Yokiko

Yukon (English) From the settlement of gold
Youkon, Yucon, Youcon, Yuckon, Youckon

Yukta (Indian) One who is attentive and adroit
Yuktah, Yuckta, Yucktah, Yucta, Yuctah

Yule (English) Born during the winter solstice
Yuell, Yuel, Yuwell, Yuwel, Yool, Yul, Yoole

Yuliy (Russian) Form of Julius, meaning "the child of love; one who is youthful"
Yuli, Yulie, Yulee, Yuleigh, Yuly, Yuley, Yulika, Yulian, Yulien

Yuma (Native American) The son of a chief
Yumah, Yumma, Yummah, Yooma, Yoomah

Yunus (Turkish) Resembling a dolphin
Yoonus, Yunes, Yoones, Yunas, Yoonas, Yunis, Yoonis

Yuriy (Russian) Form of George, meaning "one who works the earth; a farmer"
Yuri, Yurii, Yury, Yurochka, Yurey, Yuree, Yure

Y

Yushua (Arabic) Form of Joshua, meaning "God is salvation"
Yushuah, Yoshua, Yoshuah, Yosh, Yoshe, Yusua, Yusuah, Yosua, Yosuah, Yehoshua, Yehoshuah

Yussel (Hebrew) Form of Joseph, meaning "God will add"
Yusel, Yussell, Yusell, Yusele

Yusuf (Arabic) Form of Joseph, meaning "God will add"
Yosef, Yoseff, Yusef, Yuseff, Yusuff, Yosif, Yosiff, Yusif, Yusiff, Yousef, Yousuf, Youseff, Yousuff, Youssof, Yosefu

Yuu (Japanese) A superior man
Yuuta, Yuuto

Yuudai (Japanese) A great hero
Yudai, Yuudae, Yudae, Yuuday, Yuday

Yuval (Hebrew) Form of Jubal, meaning "resembling a ram"
Yuvale, Yuvall, Yubal, Yubale, Yuball

Yves (French) A young archer
Yve, Yvo, Yvon, Yvan, Yvet, Yvete

Zabian (Arabic) One who worships celestial bodies
Zabion, Zabien, Zaabian

Zabulon (Hebrew) One who is exalted
Zabulun, Zabulen

Zacchaeus (Hebrew) Form of Zachariah, meaning "The Lord remembers"
Zachaeus, Zachaios, Zaccheus, Zackaeus, Zacheus, Zackaios, Zaccheo

Zachariah (Hebrew) The Lord remembers
Zacaria, Zacarias, Zaccaria, Zaccariah, Zachaios, Zacharia, Zacharias, Zacherish, Zackariah, Zackerias, Zakarias, Zakariyyah, Zechariah, Zecheriah, Zekariah, Zekeriah, Zackaria, Zakariyya, Zecharya, Zakhar

Zachary ✪ ✪ (Hebrew) Form of Zachariah, meaning "The Lord remembers"
Zaccary, Zaccery, Zach, Zacharie, Zachery, Zack, Zackarey, Zackary, Zackery, Zak, Zakari, Zakary, Zakarie, Zakery

Zaci (African) In mythology, the god of fatherhood

Zadeer (Arabic) Our new son
Zadir, Zadier, Zadeir, Zadyr, Zadear

Zaden (Dutch) A sower of seeds
Zadin, Zadan, Zadon, Zadun, Zede, Zeden, Zedan

Zadok (Hebrew) One who is righteous; just
Zadoc, Zaydok, Zadock, Zaydock, Zaydoc, Zaidok, Zaidock, Zaidoc, Zaedok, Zaedoc, Zaedock, Zadoq

Zador (Hungarian) An ill-tempered man
Zadoro, Zadorio

Zadornin (Basque) A follower of Saturn, god of agriculture
Zadorin, Zadornan, Zadoran, Zadornen, Zadoren

Zadrian (American) Form of Adrian, meaning "a man from Hadria"
Zade, Zadiran, Zadrain, Zadrean, Zadreean, Zadreyan, Zadreeyan, Zadriaan, Zadriano, Zadrien, Zadrin, Zadrino, Zadrion, Zadron, Zadryan, Zadya, Zarjen, Zaydrean, Zaydreean, Zaydrian, Zaydrien

Zafar (Arabic) The conquerer; a victorious man
Zafarr, Zaffar, Zhafar, Zhaffar, Zafer, Zaffer, Zaferr, Zaafar, Zaafer, Zafir, Zhafir, Zaffir, Zafirr, Zafeer, Zaffeer, Zhafeer

Zahi (Arabic) A brilliant man
Zahie, Zahey, Zahy, Zahee

Zahid (Arabic) A pious man
Zahide, Zahyd, Zahyde, Zaheed, Zaheede, Zaheide, Zahiede, Zaheid, Zahied

Zahir (Arabic) A radiant and flourishing man
Zahire, Zahireh, Zahyr, Zahyre, Zaheer, Zaheere, Zaheir, Zahier, Zaheire, Zahiere, Zhahir

Zahur (Arabic) Resembling a flower
Zahure, Zahureh, Zhahur, Zaahur

Zaim (Arabic) An intelligent leader
Zaime, Zaym, Zayme, Zame, Zaam,
Zaem, Zaeme

Zaire (African) A man from Zaire
Zair, Ziare, Ziar, Zyair, Zyaire

Zakar (Babylonian) In mythology, the god
of dreams
Zakarr, Zakarre, Zakare, Zakkar, Zaakar,
Zaakkar

Zaki (Arabic) One who is pure; innocent
Zakie, Zakee, Zakki, Zhaki, Zakae,
Zakkai, Zakkae, Zakai, Zakiy, Zakey

Zale (Greek) Having the strength of the sea
Zail, Zaile, Zayl, Zayle, Zael, Zaele

Zalman (Hebrew) Form of Solomon,
meaning "a peaceful man"
Zalaman, Zaloman, Zolomon, Zallman,
Zaleman, Zalomon, Zolemon, Zalemon,
Zulema, Zuloma

Zalmon (Hebrew) One who is shady
Zallmon, Zolmon, Zollmon

Zaman (Arabic) The keeper of time
Zamaan, Zaaman, Zamane, Zhaman

Zameel (Arabic) A beloved friend
Zameele, Zamil, Zamile, Zamyl, Zamyle,
Zameil, Zameile, Zamiel, Zamiele

Zamir (Hebrew) Resembling a songbird
Zamire, Zameer, Zameere, Zamyr, Zamyre,
Zameir, Zameire, Zamier, Zamiere

Zamor (Hungarian) One who plows
the land
Zamoro, Zamorio, Zamore, Zamorr,
Zaamor, Zamori

Zan (Hebrew) A well-fed man
Zann, Zaan

Zander (Slavic) Form of Alexander, mean-
ing "helper and defender of mankind"
Zandros, Zandro, Zandar, Zandur,
Zandre

Zane (English) Form of John, meaning
"God is gracious"
Zaan, Zayne, Zayn, Zain, Zaine, Zaen,
Zaene

Zanebono (Italian) The good son
Zanbono, Zaynebono, Zaynbono,
Zainebono, Zainbono, Zaenebono,
Zaenbono

Zani (Hebrew) A gift from God
Zanie, Zaney, Zany, Zanee, Zanipolo,
Zanipollo

Zaniel (English) Form of Daniel, meaning
"God is my judge"
Zaneal, Zanek, Zanell, Zanial, Zaniele,
Zanil, Zanilo, Zanko, Zannel, Zannie,
Zanny, Zantrell, Zanyal, Zanyel

Zapotocky (Slavic) From just beyond the
stream
Zapotocki, Zapotockey, Zapotoky,
Zapotokey, Zapotoki

Zarand (Hungarian) The golden son
Zarande

Zarathustra (Persian) The golden star
Zarathustrah, Zarathust, Zarathurst,
Zarathursta, Zoroaster, Zoroester

Zareb (African) The protector; guardian
Zarebb, Zaareb, Zarebe, Zarreb, Zareh,
Zaareh

Zared (Hebrew) One who has been trapped
Zarede, Zarad, Zarade, Zaared, Zaarad

Zarek (Greek) God protect the king
Zareke, Zareck, Zaarek

Zasha (Russian) A defender of the people
Zashah, Zosha, Zoshah, Zashiya, Zoshiya

Zavad (Hebrew) A gift from God
Zavade, Zavaad, Zaavad, Zavadi, Zawad,
Zawadi, Zaawad, Zawade

Zavier (Arabic) Form of Xavier, meaning
"owner of a new house / one who is bright"
Zaver, Zever, Zabier, Zaviere, Zabiere,
Zaviar, Zaviare, Zavior, Zaviore, Zavion,
Zavian, Zavien

Zayd (Arabic) To become greater; to grow
Zayde, Zaid, Zaide, Zade, Zaad, Zaade,
Zayden, Zaydan

Zayit (Hebrew) From the olive tree
Zayat

Zazu (Hebrew) An active man
Zazoo, Zaazu, Zaazoo

Zbigniew (Polish) One who lets go
of anger

Zdenek (Slavic) A man from Sidon
Zdeneck, Zdeneke, Zdenecke, Zdenco,
Zdenko, Zdencko

Zdravko (Croatian) One who is healthy
Zdravcko

Zdzislaw (Polish) Glorious in the moment
Zdzislav, Zdislaw, Zdeslav, Zdislav, Zdzeslaw, Zdzeslav

Ze (Portugese) Form of Joseph, meaning "God will add"

Zeal (American) A passionate man
Zeale, Zeel, Zeele, Zeyl, Zeyle

Zebadiah (Hebrew) A gift from God
Zebadia, Zebadiya, Zebadiyah, Zeb, Zebe, Zebediah, Zebedia, Zebediya, Zebediyah, Zebedee, Zebedi, Zebedie, Zevadiah, Zevadia, Zevadiya, Zevadiyah

Zebedeo (Aramaic) A servant of God
Zebedio, Zebadeo, Zebadio

Zebenjo (African) One who strives to avoid sinning
Zebinjo, Zebenjoe, Zebinjoe

Zebulon (Hebrew) One who has been exalted
Zebulone, Zebulun, Zebulune, Zevulon, Zevulone, Zevulun, Zevulune

Zedekiah (Hebrew) The Lord is just
Zedekia, Zedakiah, Zedakia, Zedekiya, Zedakiya, Zed

Zeeman (Dutch) Man of the sea; a sailor
Zeyman, Zeiman, Zieman, Zeaman

Ze'ev (Hebrew) Resembling a wolf
Ze'eve, Zeev, Zeeve, Zev, Zeve, Z'ev

Zef (Dutch) Form of Joseph, meaning "God will add"
Zefe, Zeff, Zeffe

Zefirino (Greek) Form of Zephyr, meaning "of the west wind"
Zeffirino, Zeferino, Zefferino, Zefiro, Zeffiro

Zeheb (Turkish) Covered with gold
Zehebb, Zehebe, Zeeheb, Zyheb

Zeke (English) Form of Ezekiel, meaning "strengthened by God"
Zekiel, Zeek, Zeeke, Zeeq

Zeki (Turkish) Having great intelligence
Zekie, Zekee, Zekey, Zeky

Zelen (Croatian) Green; one who is innocent
Zeleny, Zeleney, Zeleni, Zelenie, Zelenee, Zeleno, Zelenio

Zelig (German) Form of Selig, meaning "one who is blessed"
Zeligg, Zelyg, Zelygg

Zelimir (Slavic) One who advocates for peace
Zelimirr, Zelemir, Zelamir, Zelameer, Zelimeer, Zelemeer, Zelimyr, Zelamyr, Zelemyr

Zen (Japanese) One who is enlightened
Zenn

Zenas (Greek) One who is generous
Zenaas, Zenias, Zenase

Zene (African) A handsome man
Zeene, Zeen, Zein, Zeine

Zenith (English) From the highest point
Zenyth, Zenithe, Zenythe

Zeno (Greek) A gift of Zeus
Zenon, Zino, Zinon, Zenos, Zenobio, Zenobo, Zenobios, Zinoviy, Zenoviy

Zentavious (American) A thoughtful man
Zentavios, Zentavio, Zentavo

Zephaniah (Hebrew) God has hidden
Zephania, Zefaniah, Zefania, Zephan, Zephane, Zefan, Zefane, Zephaniya, Zefaniya, Zeph

Zephyr (Greek) Of the west wind
Zephirin, Zephryn, Zephiren, Zepherin, Zephren, Zephrin, Zephyrus, Zephros

Zerachiel (Hebrew) God has commanded
Zerachial, Zerecheil, Zerechial, Zerachiol, Zerechiol, Zerichiel, Zerichial, Zer, Zerr

Zereen (Arabic) The golden one
Zereene, Zeryn, Zeryne, Zerein, Zereine, Zerrin, Zerren, Zerran

Zerind (Hungarian) Man from Serbia
Zerinde, Zerynd, Zerynde, Zerend, Zerende

Zero (English) Having no value
Zeroe, Zerow, Zerowe, Zerro, Zeroh

Zeroun (Armenian) One who is respected for his wisdom
Zeroune, Zeroon, Zeroone

Zeru (Basque) Of the sky
Zeruh, Zeroo, Zerooh

Zeshawn (American) God is merciful
Zeshaun, Zeshan, Zeshane, Zeshayne, Zeshayn

Zesiro (African) The firstborn of twins
Zesirio, Zesero, Zeserio, Zesyro, Zesyrio

Zeth (English) Form of Seth, meaning "one who has been appointed"
Zethe

Zeus (Greek) In mythology, the ruler of the gods
Zeuse, Zeuc, Zeuce, Zews, Zewse, Zoos, Zoose

Zhenechka (Russian) A noble man
Zhenya, Zenechka

Zhi (Chinese) One who has good intentions

Zhivko (Bulgarian) A lively man
Zhivcko, Zhyvko, Zhyvcko, Zivko, Zivcko, Zyvko, Zyvcko

Zhorah (Russian) One who works the earth; a farmer
Zhora, Zorah, Zora, Zorya, Zhorya, Zoryah, Zhoryah

Zhou (Chinese) One who helps others

Zia (Arabic) A brilliant, glowing man
Ziah, Ziya, Ziyah

Ziemowit (Polish) Lord of the household
Ziemowitt, Ziemowitte, Ziemowite, Ziemowyt, Ziemowytt, Ziemowytte

Ziff (Hebrew) Resembling a wolf
Ziffe, Zif, Zife, Zyf, Zyff, Zyfe, Zyffe

Ziga (Sloven) Form of Sigmund, meaning "the victorious protector"
Zigah, Zigga, Ziggah, Ziggy, Ziggi, Ziggie, Ziggey

Zigor (Basque) The punished
Zigore, Zigorr, Zigar, Zigarr, Zigare

Zikomo (African) One who is thankful
Zikom, Zikome, Zykomo, Zykom, Zykome, Zikomio, Zykomio

Zimraan (Arabic) A song of praise
Zimran, Zymraan, Zymran, Zimri, Zimrie, Zimry, Zimrey, Zimree, Zimra, Zimrah, Zimre, Zimreh

Zinan (Japanese) The second-born son
Zinann, Zynan, Zynann, Zinen, Zynen

Zindel (Hebrew) Defender of mankind
Zyndel, Zindele, Zyndele, Zindell, Zyndell

Zion (Hebrew) From the citadel
Zionn, Zione, Zionne, Zionia, Zioniah, Ziona, Zionah

Ziv (Hebrew) A radiant man
Zive, Ziiv, Zivi, Zivie, Zivee, Zivy, Zivey

Ziven (Slavic) One who is vigorous; full of life
Zivon, Zivan

Ziyad (Arabic) One who betters himself; growth
Ziad

Zlatan (Croatian) The golden son
Zlattan, Zlatane, Zlatann, Zlatain, Zlatayn, Zlaten, Zlaton, Zlatin, Zlatko, Zlatcko

Zo (African) A spiritual counselor
Zoe, Zow, Zowe

Zoan (African) One who takes leave
Zoane

Zobor (Hungarian) Of the congregation
Zoborr, Zobore, Zoboro, Zoborro, Zoborio

Zody (American) Form of Cody, meaning "one who is helpful; a wealthy man / acting as a cushion"
Zodey, Zodi, Zodie, Zodee, Zodell, Zodel

Zohar (Hebrew) Surrounded by light
Zohare, Zoharr, Zohair, Zohaer, Zohayr, Zuhair, Zuhar, Zuharr, Zuhayr

Zoilo (Greek) One who is active
Zoylo, Zoiloh, Zoyloh, Zoilow, Zoylow

Zoltan (Hungarian) A kingly man; a sultan
Zoltann, Zoltane, Zoltanne, Zsolt, Zsoltan

Zoltin (Hungarian) A lively man
Zoltinn, Zoltine, Zoltyn, Zoltynn, Zoltyne

Z

Zombor (Hungarian) Resembling a buffalo
Zsombor, Zomboro, Zsomboro, Zomborio, Zsomborio

Zopyros (Greek) A glowing man

Zoraavar (Arabic) Having great courage
Zoravar, Zoraavarr, Zoravarr, Zoravare

Zoran (Slavic) Born with the morning's first light
Zorann, Zorane, Zoranne

Zorba (Greek) One who lives life to the fullest
Zorbah, Zorbiya, Zorbiyah

Zorion (Basque) Filled with happiness
Zorian, Zorien

Zorro (Slavic) Hero of the golden dawn
Zoro, Zorio, Zorrio, Zorriyo, Zoriyo

Zosimo (Greek) One who is able to survive
Zosimio, Zosimos, Zosimus

Zosio (Polish) One who is wise

Zoticus (Greek) Full of life
Zoticos, Zoticas

Zsigmond (Hungairan) Form of Sigmund, meaning "the victorious protector"
Zsigmund, Zsigmonde, Zsigmunde, Zsig, Zsiga

Zsolt (Hungarian) One who is honored
Zsolte, Zolt, Zolte

Zubair (Arabic) One who is pure
Zubaire, Zubayr, Zubayre, Zubar, Zubarr, Zubare, Zubaer

Zuberi (African) Having great strength
Zuberie, Zubery, Zuberey, Zuberee, Zubari, Zubarie, Zubary, Zubarey, Zubaree

Zubin (English) One with a toothy grin
Zubine, Zuben, Zuban, Zubun, Zubbin

Zulekha (African) Our precious son
Zuleka, Zulecka, Zulekah, Zuleckah, Zuleckha

Zulfaqar (Arabic) One who is clever; the name of Muhammad's sword
Zulphaqar, Zulfaquar, Zulphaquar, Zulfiqar, Zulphiqar, Zulfikar, Zulficar, Zulphikar, Zulphicar

Zulu (African) Man from Africa
Zuluh, Zullu, Zulluh, Zoolu, Zooluh, Zooloo

Zuriel (Hebrew) The Lord is my rock
Zurial

Zurley (English) Form of Hurley, meaning "of the sea tide"
Zurly, Zurl, Zurlee, Zurleigh, Zurli, Zurlie

Zusman (Hebrew) One with a sweet disposition
Zusmann, Zusmane, Zoosman, Zoosmann, Zhusman

Zuzen (Basque) One who is just and fair
Zuzenn, Zuzan, Zuzin

Zvi (Hebrew) Resembling a deer
Zvie, Zvee, Zvy, Zvey, Zevi, Zevie, Zevy, Zevey, Zevee

Zvonimir (Croatian) The sound of peace
Zvonimirr, Zvonimeer, Zvonimire, Zvonmeere, Zvonimer, Zvonko, Zvoncko

Zwi (Scandinavian) Resembling a gazelle
Zwie, Zwee, Zwy, Zwey

Zygfryd (Polish) Form of Siegfried, meaning "one who enjoys the peace of victory"
Zygfried, Zygfreed, Zigfryd, Zigfreed, Zigfried, Zygfrid, Zygfred, Zigfrid, Zigfred

Zygmunt (Polish) Form of Sigmund, meaning "the victorious protector"
Zygmund, Zygmont, Zygmond, Zygmunte, Zygmonde, Zygmunde, Zygmonte

Z

Notes

Tear-Out
Worksheets

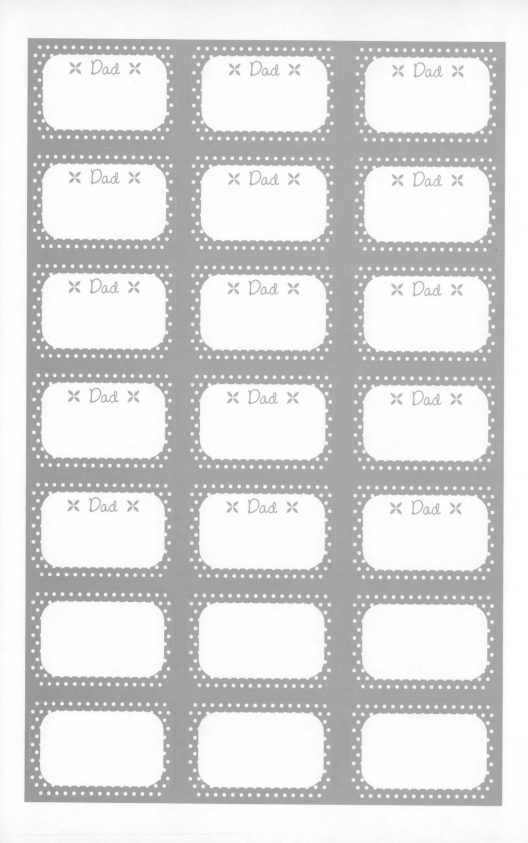

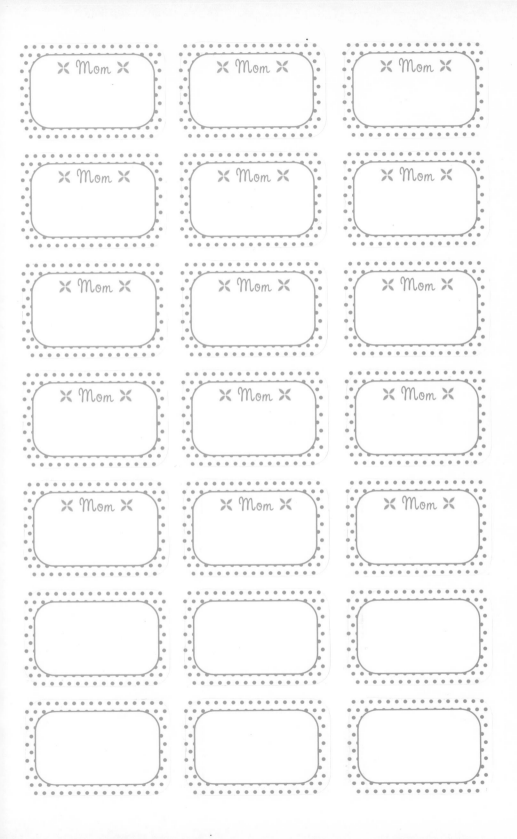

Master List of
First Names

✖　　　　　　　　　　✖

_____

_____

_____

_____

_____

_____

_____

_____

_____

_____

_____

_____

_____

_____

_____

_____

_____

_____

_____

Master List of
Middle Names

✖   ✖

_____

_____

_____

_____

_____

_____

_____

_____

_____

_____

_____

_____

_____

_____

_____

_____

_____

Mom's Girl
First Names

✖   ✖

_____

_____

_____

_____

_____

_____

_____

_____

_____

_____

_____

_____

_____

_____

_____

_____

_____

Mom's Boy
First Names

�ખ   �ખ

_____

_____

_____

_____

_____

_____

_____

_____

_____

_____

_____

_____

_____

_____

_____

_____

_____

Dad's Girl
First Names

✖   ✖

_____

_____

_____

_____

_____

_____

_____

_____

_____

_____

_____

_____

_____

_____

_____

_____

_____

_____

_____

Dad's Boy
First Names

✖   ✖

_____

_____

_____

_____

_____

_____

_____

_____

_____

_____

_____

_____

_____

_____

_____

_____

_____

✖ Things to Keep in Mind ✖

✖ Dark-Horse Ideas ✖

Other Lists, Ideas, and Thoughts